D1795420

EARLY RESPONSES TO HUME

Volume 9

Edited and Introduced by
James Fieser
University of Tennessee at Martin

THOEMMES CONTINUUM

Early Responses to Hume

Edited and Introduced by **James Fieser**
University of Tennessee at Martin, USA

Volumes 1 and 2
Early Responses to Hume's Moral, Literary and Political Writings

Volumes 3 and 4
Early Responses to Hume's Metaphysical and Epistemological
Writings

Volumes 5 and 6
Early Responses to Hume's Writings on Religion

Volumes 7 and 8
Early Responses to Hume's *History of England*

Volumes 9 and 10
Early Responses to Hume's Life and Reputation
Bibliography of Early Responses to Hume, with Indexes

EARLY RESPONSES TO HUME'S LIFE AND REPUTATION

Second Edition, Revised

I

Edited and Introduced by

James Fieser

University of Tennessee at Martin

thoemmes

First published by Thoemmes Press, 2003

Thoemmes Continuum
11 Great George Street
Bristol BS1 5RR, England

http://www.thoemmes.com

Early Responses to Hume
Second edition, revised, 2005
10 vols : ISBN 1 84371 114 1

Early Responses to Hume's Life and Reputation
Second edition, revised, 2005
2 Volumes : ISBN 1 84371 115 X

© J. Fieser, 2003, 2005

British Library Cataloguing-in-Publication Data
A CIP record of this title is available from the British Library

Printed and bound in Great Britain
by Biddles Ltd, Kings Lynn, Norfolk

CONTENTS

EARLY RESPONSES TO HUME'S LIFE AND REPUTATION

VOLUME 1

Church Censure of Hume: 1755–1756

John Home's *Douglas*: 1757

Thomas Blacklock and James Beattie

Hume's Last Days and Death: 1776

Hume's Deathbed Anguish

First Notices of Hume's Death

John Home's Discussions of Hume's Character

Reactions to Adam Smith's "Letter"

VOLUME 2

Samuel Jackson Pratt's *Apology* and Reactions

William Dodd and Hume

Hume's Posthumous Reputation: Author and Infidel

INTRODUCTION

During the latter half of his life, David Hume (1711–1776) achieved international celebrity status as a great philosopher and historian. The sceptical and anti-religious bent of his works generated hundreds of critical responses, many of which were scholarly commentaries. Other writers, though, focused less on Hume's specific publications and more on his impact as a distinguished public figure. Wittingly or unwittingly, Hume took part in several controversies. Hume's friends defended his public character, while his enemies tried to put his fame to rest. Friends and enemies alike recorded anecdotes about him, which, after his death, appeared in scattered periodicals and books. Hume biographers have drawn liberally from much of this material, but in most cases the original sources have only been summarized or briefly quoted. The final two volumes in this *Early Responses to Hume* series present nearly 150 biographically-related discussions of Hume in their most complete form. Many of these have gone unnoticed by Hume scholars, and three are transcribed from the original manuscripts for the first time. A detailed bibliography of eighteenth and nineteenth-century responses to Hume is included at the close of this collection, with indexes to that bibliography.

Hume's Early Reputation and Controversies.
The entire sequence of critical reactions to Hume's writings constitutes a record of his literary reputation. A recurring reaction among his readers is that he tried to be original in everything he wrote. As one critic states,

> The great object of Mr. Hume's ambition, as we are informed by himself, was literary fame. And in order to excite public attention, he seems to have thought it necessary to be singular. Accordingly, we find an affectation of singularity of sentiment, very predominant in his writings. [Joseph Towers, *Observations on Mr. Hume's History of England* (1778)]

In the eyes of his readers, this drive for singularity manifested itself in philosophical scepticism, religious infidelity, and political arch-conservativism. The more he wrote and critics responded, the more an aura of intrigue and even danger developed around him. This nefarious reputation became so pronounced that it often encumbered his social life and made him the target of verbal attacks and gross misrepresentation. Whatever views Hume may have voiced in his scholarly writings, in his private life he was unpretentious, charitable, witty, and, above all, sociable. As his friends tell us, he rarely engaged in serious philosophical discourse at social gatherings, and, if he did, he graciously accepted rebuttals to his sceptical and antireligious views. Critics who knew this side of Hume treated him with dignity. Others – particularly those unacquainted with him – showed no such respect.

A first group of selections in this collection offer an overview of his reputation, from the start of his writing career to his death. The first two, which appear here in print for the first time, are especially noteworthy. The anonymous author of the 1742 untitled character sketch is unimpressed with Hume's writing style, and even less with Hume's reputation as a womanizer. Moving ahead ten years, James Wodrow, a student at Glasgow University, comments on the gossip surrounding Hume's candidacy for a Chair at Glasgow and goes on to praise the novelty and sceptical drama of Hume's writings. Other early reactions are two-sided, acknowledging the brilliance and originality of his writings, yet denouncing the sceptical and irreligious components.

From the time of his first published works, Hume was engaged in various public controversies. He failed to receive teaching appointments at both Edinburgh and Glasgow largely because of his reputation as a religious infidel. His essay "Of Miracles" (1748) sparked critical reactions from clergy of different denominations. The first published volume of his *History* (1754) also struck a raw nerve because of its insinuation that Christianity was motivated by fanaticism and superstition. One of the most public of the early controversies, though, involved the efforts of some conservative clergy in the Scottish Church to excommunicate – or at least censure – Hume and his colleague Henry Home, Lord Kames, for their infidel writings. One of the instigators of this effort was retired Clergyman George Anderson (1677–1756) – although in his retired status he could not directly participate in the formal proceedings themselves. Pamphlets were published on the subject, pro and contra, and, in 1756 the case against Hume was brought before a committee of the General Assembly – the Scottish Church's highest judicial body. The conservative side argued that Hume posed a genuine threat to religion, and it was the Church's duty to take action against him. The moderate side argued that Hume's views were self-refuting and, in any event, as a non-believer, censuring him would have no impact. In a vote of 17 to 50, the decision was made to not pursue the matter further. The timeline of the controversy and related publications is this:

1748: Hume's *Philosophical Essays* appears, which attacks natural and revealed religion.

1751: Henry Home's *Essays on the Principles of Morality and Natural Religion* appears anonymously, which challenges the rational foundation of natural religion.

1752: Home is appointed Judge, becoming Lord Kames.

1753: George Anderson attacks Hume and Home in *An Estimate of the*

Profit and Loss of Religion. He is supported by the anonymous author of *A Letter to the Author of a late book, intitled, An Estimate*.

May 22, 1755: the General Assembly convenes.

May 23, 1755: John Bonar's *Analysis* appears, attacking Hume and Home for religious infidelity.

May 28, 1755: the General Assembly's Committee on Overtures unanimously passes a condemnation of recent infidel writings.

June 2, 1755: the General Assembly separates.

June 6, 1755: Hugh Blair's *Observations upon a Pamphlet* appears (four days after the General Assembly separates), which defends Home against Bonar's attack, but essentially abandons Hume.

June 1755: *Scots Magazine* issue covering the month of May reprints excerpts from *An Analysis* and *Observations*.

June 1755: Hume writes to Allan Ramsay reacting to the General Assembly's statement.

October 1755: Thomas Walker's "A Letter on Sopho's Doctrine of Necessity" appears in *Scots Magazine* issue covering the month of September, criticizing Blair's *Observations*.

May 15, 1756: Thomas Walker's *Infidelity a Proper Object of Censure* appears urging the Church to act against Hume.

May 20, 1756: General Assembly convenes.

May 27, 1756: Proposal to censure Hume is submitted to the General Assembly's Committee on Overtures, which debates the matter for two days.

May 31, 1756: General Assembly separates.

June 1756: *Scots Magazine* issue covering the month of May reprints excerpts from *Infidelity a proper object of Censure*.

July 1756: *Scots Magazine* issue covering the month of June prints a synopsis of Committee on Overtures debate regarding Hume. Robert Wallace, a moderate clergyman at the debate, pens an unpublished alternative synopsis.

July/August 1756: Anderson presents a petition and complaint to Edinburgh Presbytery against Home's printer, Kincaid and Donaldson; lawyers for Kincaid and Donaldson write a response.

December 19, 1756: Anderson dies.

December 29, 1756: Presbytery agrees to pursue the investigation.

January 29, 1757: Presbytery acknowledges that Home's phraseology had given offence, but dismisses the complaint on a majority vote, after receiving a new pamphlet, *Objections Against the Essays on Morality and Natural Religion Examined*, submitted for the author.

The previous summer's victory for Hume, though, was short-lived, as he quickly became involved in a dispute with the Church of Scotland regarding the morality of stage plays. The central figure in the controversy was Hume's close friend, clergyman John Home, who received his preaching license in 1745. For a couple years he had been refining a tragic play titled *Douglas* and, while his initial efforts of having it produced in London failed, his local friends supported him for what turned out to be a very successful Edinburgh production. This raised two concerns among conservative Scottish clergy. First, stage plays in Edinburgh were both infrequent and, so they believed, unwholesome; second, the idea of a clergyman engaged in such a production was scandalous. Hume entered the controversy by writing a dedication to Home, which was prefaced to the philosopher's *Four Dissertations* (1757). In this he extols *Douglas* as "one of the most interesting and pathetic pieces that was ever exhibited on any theatre" and says that Home possesses "the true theatric genius of *Shakespear* and *Otway*, refined from the unhappy barbarism of the one, and licentiousness of the other." Hume's public endorsement forced London critics to take notice. At the same time, though, it inexorably linked Home the clergyman with Hume the infidel. In Scotland, conservative clergy attacked Home's immoral playwriting hobby and attempted to take action against clergy who attended its production. In London, critics laughed at Hume's overblown praise of a mediocre play. One writer, John Hawkesworth, stated that Hume's "critical stocks" were thereby "reduced almost to bankruptcy." Home himself had no choice but to resign his church position. A highlight of this controversy is John MacLaurin's *Philosopher's Opera* (1757), which lampoons Hume, Home and their Edinburgh supporters. The chronology of this controversy is as follows:

Autumn 1754: John Home circulates a manuscript of *Douglas* among friends.
February 1755: David Garrick rejects London production of *Douglas*.
July 1756: Garrick rejects revised script of *Douglas* for London production.
December 1756: actors rehearse *Douglas* with Hume and other friends of Home present.
December 14, 1756: John Home's *Douglas* is performed at the Canongate Theatre in Edinburgh.
January 5, 1757: the Presbetery of Edinburgh issues "Admonition and Exhortation" against plays.
February 7, 1757: Hume's dedication to John Home appears in some copies of *Four Dissertations*.
March 14, 1757: *Douglas* is performed at the Theatre Royal in Covent Garden, London.
March 17, 1757: *Douglas* is printed in London.
March 29, 1757: *Douglas* is printed in Edinburgh.
Spring 1757: reviews and pamphlets appear criticizing Hume's praise of *Douglas*.
June 1757: Home resigns ministerial position.

The controversy surrounding Home's *Douglas* was largely a local matter. Ten years later he was embroiled in an international controversy involving his attempts at hospitality towards Jean-Jacques Rousseau. Born in Geneva and fleeing that city at age sixteen, Rousseau (1712–1778) moved to Savoy where, under the influence of his benefactress Baronne de Warens, he transformed from an uneducated apprentice to a man of letters. At age thirty he moved to Paris and, with the young Denis Diderot, formed an intellectual circle – the *philosophes*. In 1762 his two greatest theoretical works appeared, *Émile* and *The Social Contract*. The former of these sparked a religious controversy, and, fearing imprisonment, Rousseau fled Paris for Switzerland. During the next few years he wrote in defence of himself, but in 1765 was forced out of Switzerland as well. Beginning in January 1766, at Hume's invitation, he spent a year in England at a rural home that Hume arranged for him. Through political connections Hume even secured a pension for Rousseau from King George III. In the minds of many British men of letters, though, Rousseau was eccentric, arrogant, and had a martyr complex. Capitalizing on these preconceptions, British novelist Horace Walpole wrote a satirical letter in the name of Frederick, King of Prussia, inviting Rousseau to take refuge in that country. Since Rousseau thrives on misfortune, Walpole writes, "I am a king, and can make you as miserable as you can wish." The letter was printed in a London newspaper, where Rousseau first saw it. Humiliated, he was convinced that Hume was in on the joke and had even invited Rousseau to England to make him an object of ridicule. Rousseau refused his pension and, in a letter to Hume dated July 10, threatened to go public with his accusations. Hume then preemptively published *A Concise and Genuine Account of the Dispute between Mr. Hume and Mr. Rousseau: with the Letters that Passed between them during their Controversy* (1766). The pamphlet exonerated Hume, but also made Rousseau look mentally unstable. A subsequent pamphlet against Rousseau by Voltaire reinforced public perception of his mental problems. According to Hume's critics, publishing the *Concise and Genuine Account* was overkill, and violated Hume's duty as a host to treat his emotionally sensitive guest with dignity.

Four years later the tables were turned on Hume when he himself became the object of what he felt was an undignified assault. His assailant was James Beattie (1735–1803), the young professor of Moral Philosophy and Logic at Marischal College, Aberdeen, who believed that Hume's sceptical and anti-religious philosophy posed a public threat to religion and morality. His work, *An Essay on the Nature and Immutability of Truth* (1770), relentlessly attacks Hume's philosophy as it appears in his *Treatise of Human Nature*, published thirty years earlier. Beattie was soon joined by the blind poet Thomas Blacklock – Hume's former friend – who, in a series of letters in an Edinburgh newspaper, justified Beattie's attack. Hume only once refers to Beattie in his surviving letters, calling him "that bigotted silly Fellow." Outside sources, though, report that Hume's reaction was very severe:

Was there any particular BOOK [i.e., Beattie's *Essay*] ever written against him [i.e., Hume], that shook his system to pieces about his ears, and reduced it to a heap of ruins, the success and eclat of which might be supposed to have hurt his mind, and to have affected his health? Was there any AUTHOR [i,e., Beattie] whose name his friends never dared to mention before him, and warned all strangers, that were introduced to him, against doing it, because he never failed, when by any accident it was done, to fly out into a transport of passion and swearing? [George Horne, *Letter to Adam Smith* (contained in this collection)]

Beattie was aware of Hume's reaction, and was similarly aware of attempts by some of Hume's friends to tarnish his reputation in retaliation. Beattie prevailed, though, and was honoured by gaining an audience with the King and Queen, and receiving a royal pension. Hume's strong feeling about Beattie is somewhat of a puzzle in view of the mountain of critical attacks that appeared against Hume during his life. James Boswell, though, offers some explanation:

The writers who attacked David Hume before Beattie took the lash in hand, treated him with so much deference that they had no effect. He was cased in a covering of respect. But Beattie stripped him of all his assumed dignity, and having laid his back bare, scourged him till he smarted keenly, and cursed again. David was on very civil terms with his former opponents, being treated by them as Dr. Shebbeare was in the pillory, who was being allowed to wear a fine powdered flowing wig. But he was virulent against Beattie, as I have witnessed, for Beattie treated him as an enemy to morals and religion deserved. [James Boswell, *Boswelliana* (contained in this collection)]

A few months before his death, Hume composed a short autobiography titled "My Own Life." Two major events that are conspicuously missing from his account – as later critics have observed – are his disputes with Rousseau and Beattie.

Hume's Death and more Controversy.
Hume was in rapid decline during the last few months of his life from what he described as "a habitual diarrhoea of more than a year's standing;" a similar disorder led to his mother's death. He became emaciated and fatigued, and was in bed much of the time. On the advice of his physician, he took a journey during May and June 1776, hoping that the change would improve his health. Some of the events were recorded by John Home, who accompanied him much of the way. There was some improvement, but only temporary, and he returned to his Edinburgh home to prepare for death. In his final months he regularly received guests, and we have accounts of visits by James Boswell, William Cullen, and Adam Smith. We read in these accounts that he was

cheerful, fully lucid, and unflinching in his infidelity. While Cullen's and Boswell's accounts were not published until later centuries, Smith's appeared a half-year after Hume's death. It sparked instant controversy, and no fewer than thirty discussions of it in varying length appear in this collection. Two parts of Smith's account were particularly offensive. First, parodying Lucian's classic *Dialogues of the Dead*, which he was reading at the time, Hume devised several comical excuses for why Charon should not ferry him across the river Styx into Hades, one of which was so that he could see "the downfal of some of the prevailing systems of superstition." The second was Smith's concluding comment that "Upon the whole, I have always considered him, both in his lifetime and since his death, as approaching as nearly to the idea of a perfectly wise and virtuous man, as perhaps the nature of human frailty will permit." The idea of an infidel being the model of virtue was shocking. Even one hundred years after the fact, religious writers fumed over Hume's irreverent attitude towards death and Smith's eulogy, as if this was recent news.

An intriguing twist to the story of Hume's death surfaced at the turn of the nineteenth century, but was soon forgotten and has since gone unnoticed by Hume scholars. Shortly after Hume's death, it appears that Hume's housekeeper – probably Margaret Irvine – was riding in a stagecoach with three other passengers – including the father-in-law of Hume's friend James Edmonstone. The subject of Hume's death arose, and the passengers were commenting on the philosopher's peaceful state of mind. Irvine then volunteered her first-hand experience. Hume indeed appeared tranquil in the presence of visitors, Irvine related, but it was all a show. In private, he was gripped with anguish to the point that his bed shook and he did not want to be left alone; he stated that he had been in search of light all his life but was now in greater darkness than ever. Five items in this collection discuss this story from what seem to be three independent sources. The most detailed narrative of Irvine's account is "On the Death-Bed of Hume the Historian" (1831) which reprints an article that "appeared many years ago in an Edinburgh newspaper." The most convincing authentication of the story is in Alexander Haldane's *Memoirs* (1852), who traces it from Hume's housekeeper, to Mr. Abercromby of Tullibody (Edmonstone's father-in-law) who was on the coach, to Abercromby's neighbours, the Haldane family. It is beyond the scope of this introduction to analyse these five discussions. Nevertheless, as this material is newly resurrected, a brief general assessment is in order. First, it is reasonable to believe that Margaret Irvine was on a stagecoach with Abercromby and others, and that she indeed discussed Hume's dying days – though probably not in the exact words that the narrators ascribe to her. Second, it is reasonable to believe that she witnessed Hume in anguish, especially in his final weeks, and that Hume's mannerisms changed when his guests left. Third, it is not clear, however, whether the anguish she perceived was the result of Hume's reflections on an afterlife, his possible declining mental state, or his suffering from a terminal illness. In any event, we must conclude that the reports of Hume's thoroughly tranquil decline by Boswell, Cullen, and Smith are not as accurate as history has assumed.

Through Smith's account, the public perception of Hume was that, in spite of his infidelity, he was a morally virtuous person and that he died peacefully with no concern about an afterlife. This characterization inevitably led to comparisons between Hume and recently deceased believers. The first of these was William Dodd, an Anglican clergyman who was executed for forgery two months before Hume's death. The contrast here was between Hume the virtuous infidel and Dodd the immoral believer, which was explored in an anonymous work titled *A Philosophical and Religious Dialogue in the Shades* (1778). The second of these was Samuel Johnson, who died in 1784. Johnson had a well-known fear of death that threw him into fits of rage and periods of depression. The Christian faith, it was commonly presumed, offers special comfort to dying believers, and the deaths of Hume and Johnson defied this conventional wisdom from opposite ends. Using Hume and Johnson as models, William Agutter's *On the Differences Between the Deaths of the Righteous and the Wicked* (1800) explores the dying attitudes of infidels and believers.

Adam Smith was not the only one who wrote a eulogy of Hume, and others that did typically met with harsh reception. Within a few weeks of Hume's death, John Home wrote a series of anonymous letters to the *London Chronicle* in praise of Hume's character and writings. This was followed by Home's anonymous and equally flattering "Account of the Life and Writings of David Hume," which met with sharp attack. Perhaps around this time he also wrote an unpublished "Sketch of the Character of Mr. Hume." Samuel Jackson Pratt wrote a lengthy *Apology for the Life of David Hume* (1777), which, alluding to the tranquil death of the famed infidel, he opens with the extraordinary statement that "David Hume is dead! Never were the pillars of Orthodoxy so desperately shaken, as they are now, by that event." Several critics, particularly George Horne, attacked Pratt's work for its poor style and substance.

When the initial interest surrounding Hume's death subsided, works continued to appear that emphasized his reputation as an author and infidel, some of which were fictional pieces. The most notable of these is Henry Mackenzie's "Story of La Roche," which, while attempting to remain true to Hume's character, presents a completely fictional account of the young Hume's personal acquaintance with an elderly Swiss minister and his young daughter. Among the more interesting indications of Hume's posthumous reputation is a controversy surrounding the 1805 candidacy of John Leslie for Chair of Mathematics at the University of Edinburgh. A brief footnote in one of Leslie's writings endorses what purports to be Hume's view of causality. Scottish clergy from the Tory side of the moderate party opposed Leslie in favour of a candidate who was a clergyman from their own faction. Capitalizing on

Hume's controversial reputation, they brought the matter before the General Assembly of the Church of Scotland and argued that a man who supports Hume's philosophy is unfit for professorship. Ironically, the conservative clergy who supported Leslie were unaffected by such anti-Humean arguments, and, constituting a majority with the Whig moderates, they stopped the process. Leslie's candidacy ultimately succeeded. An animated account of the Leslie controversy is presented by Henry Cockburn in *Memorials of his Time* (1859).

Anecdotes, Recollections, and Editions of Hume's Letters.
The largest group of items in this collection consists of anecdotes reported of Hume and recollections about him recorded by his friends. These appear in a variety of forms and in varying degrees of reliability. The most important are by James Boswell, James Caulfeild, George Norvell, Alexander Carlyle, and William Adam. These are sustained discussions based entirely on close friendship with the philosopher, typically recorded by the authors near the end of their lives. Some detail Hume's conversations on political matters:

> He said it was all over in America: we *could* not subdue the colonists, and another gun should not be fired, were it not for decency's sake; he meant, in order to keep up an appearance of power. [James Boswell, Letters to Temple]

Others describe his physical appearance: "His face was broad and fat, his mouth wide, and without any other expression than that of imbecility" (James Caulfeild, *Memoirs*). There are accounts of his speech:

> In Common conversation, he retained the accent, expression and vulgarity of his paternal stile on the Banks of the White Water & Tweed, in such a degree that you would have imagined he had never conversed with any person but the commonest farmer. [George Norvell, "Letter to Stenhouse"]

They tell of his recreational activities: "Another thing perhaps not understood by his admirers is his fondness for whist, which he play'd well at & was successfull in the extent he practised it" (George Norvell, "Letter to Stenhouse"). There are accounts of his dinners:

> As Mr. Hume's circumstances improved he enlarged his mode of living, and instead of the roasted hen and minced collops, and a bottle of punch, he gave both elegant dinners and suppers, and the best claret, and, which was best of all, he furnished the entertainment with the most instructive and pleasing conversation, for he assembled whosoever were most knowing and agreeable among either the laity or clergy. [Alexander Carlyle, *Autobiography*]

There are stories of humour:

> When the philosopher was amusing himself in conversation with the young ladies, the chair began to give way under him, and gradually brought him to the floor. The damsels were both alarmed and amused, when Mr Hume, recovering himself, and getting upon his legs, said in his broad Scotch tone, but in English words, (for he never used Scotch,) "Young ladies, you must tell Mr Adam to keep stronger chairs for heavy philosophers." [William Adam, *Sequel*]

There are stories of heartbreak:

> Milton turned to him with great asperity, and said that he had better hold his peace on the subject, for it was owing to him, and keeping company with him, that such a clamour was raised. David made no reply, but soon after took his hat and cane, and left the room, never more to enter the house. [Carlyle, *Autobiography*]

In all, they offer a wealth of picturesque information about Hume's life that we do not find in his private correspondence.

Around thirty brief stories about Hume are included in a selection titled "Miscellaneous Hume Anecdotes." Many of these were also recorded by Hume's acquaintances. Others are of unknown origin and appeared in journals, side comments in books, and collections of anecdotes. Even these, though, have a Humean flavour and may contain a kernel of truth. I have included more than one version of the same story when they were sufficiently different. Several anecdotes appear to present Hume's utterances word for word, even within quotation marks, as was the convention of the time. These quotations, though, are embellishments by the story teller, as we see most clearly when comparing differing versions of the same story. In these cases, what is important is the gist of the conversation, and not the exact wording. This is particularly relevant when attempting to draw a subtle interpretation of Hume's views on religion based on the misleadingly precise wording of the anecdote.

The first attempt at a substantive biography of Hume and collection of his letters was Thomas Ritchie's *Account of the Life and Writings of David Hume* (1807). Although readers of the time believed it was sufficient, it has comparatively little narrative detail beyond what Hume tells us in "My Own Life," and contained only a small fraction of the total number of Hume letters that exists. Specialized collections of Hume's letters appeared in print as the originals became available. The most important of these is John Hill Burton's *Life and Correspondence of David Hume* (1846), which not only provides detailed narrative of Hume's life, but includes newly appearing letters from the 150 or so among Hume's manuscripts in possession of the Royal Society of Edinburgh.

Although these early biographies and collections of letters have since been superseded by more recent works, several contain letters that can no longer be located. The brief introductions to these works are included here, which describe the importance of their contents and the challenges that the editors faced when compiling their collections.

Editorial Conventions.
In preparing these selections, spelling and punctuation have not been modernized. Some original printers' conventions have been altered; for example, footnote references follow punctuation marks, rather than precede them. Unless noted otherwise, comments contained in square brackets are mine. The authorship of anonymous reviews in the *Monthly Review* is based on Benjamin Christie Nangle's *The Monthly Review First Series 1749–1789* (1934) and *The Monthly Review Second Series 1790–1815* (1955). Authorship of anonymous articles in nineteenth-century journals is based on *The Wellesley Index to Victorian Periodicals, 1824–1900* (1966–89), edited by Walter E. Houghton. I thank M.A. Stewart for input on this collection.

MAJOR EVENTS IN HUME'S LIFE

1711: Born in Edinburgh, April 26; divides his time between the family homes at Ninewells and Edinburgh until he leaves the area in 1734.

1721–1725: Attends Edinburgh University.

1729–1730: Becomes ill, peaking in the winter of 1730.

1731: Composes "Essay on Chivalry."

1734: Writes to physician about lingering illness. Works in merchant's office in Bristol for a few months; in Summer leaves for France, studying and writing *Treatise of Human Nature*.

1737: In Fall leaves France for London, revising and publishing *Treatise*.

1739: *Treatise*, Vols. 1 and 2 published in January; in February leaves London for his family in Ninewells and Edinburgh.

1740: *Treatise*, Vol. 3 published in Summer.

1741: *Essays Moral and Political*, Vol. 1 published.

1742: *Essays Moral and Political*, Vol. 2 published.

1744–1745: unsuccessful candidate for Chair of Moral Philosophy at Edinburgh University.

1745: Sometime in Spring Hume's mother dies; in April moves to Weld Hall near St. Albans, for one year as tutor to the Marquis of Annandale.

1746: In May recruited as secretary to General St. Clair for an expedition against Quebec; plans change in August and are instructed to attack the French coast of Brittany; set sail in September.

1747: In June is in London; returns to Ninewells in Autumn.

1748: In London in January; in February goes to Vienna and Turin as secretary to St. Clair; *Philosophical Essays Concerning Human Understanding* published in April.

1749: In Summer moves from London to his family at Ninewells and Edinburgh.

1751: In Summer permanently moves from Ninewells to his own residence in Edinburgh, for seven-year stay; unsuccessful candidate for a Chair at Glasgow; *Enquiry Concerning the Principles of Morals* published in December.

1752: *Political Discourses* is published in February; begins five-year position as Keeper of the Advocates' Library in Edinburgh at £40 a year. In September gets his apartment at Riddle's Land, Lawnmarket.

1753: In May moves to Jack's Land, Canongate.

1

1754: *The History of Great Britain* (James I and Charles I) published; disputes with Library curators and gives income from Keeper position to Thomas Blacklock.

1756: *Five Dissertations* suppressed in January; unsuccessful effort made to excommunicate Hume from the Church of Scotland. *The History of Great Britain* (Death of Charles I to the Revolution) published.

1757: *Four Dissertations* published in February; resigns Librarian position. Involved in dispute surrounding John Home's *Douglas*.

1758: Visits London.

1759: *The History of England* (Tudors) published.

1761: Visits London; *The History of England* (early periods) published.

1762: Moves to James's Court.

1763: In October moves to Paris for two and a half years working for the British Embassy under Earl of Hertford, first as personal secretary.

1765: In July is promoted to secretary of the Embassy as Hertford prepares to leave; serves as Chargé d'Affaires (senior-most official) for four months until the new Ambassador arrives; pensioned.

1766: In January leaves Paris and resides in London; disputes with Rousseau; returns to Edinburgh in September.

1767: In February moves from Edinburgh to London for one year as Under-Secretary of State for the Northern Department.

1768: In July appointment ends when his superior leaves office; pension increased.

1769: In August moves from London to Edinburgh.

1770: Attacked in Beattie's *Essay*; in Autumn engaged in building new house in St. Andrew's Square.

1771: In Spring leases James's Court apartment to Boswell; moves to St. Andrew's Square.

1775: Composes "Essay on the Authenticity of Ossian's Poems"; becomes ill.

1776: Writes "My Own Life"; in May and June visits London and Bath; on August 25 dies in Edinburgh; on August 29 buried at Calton Burial Ground.

1777: "My Own Life" published.

1779: *Dialogues Concerning Natural Religion* published.

1783: Unauthorized publication of *Essays on Suicide and the Immortality of the Soul*.

EARLY INDICATIONS OF HUME'S REPUTATION

1
UNTITLED CHARACTER SKETCH
OF DAVID HUME

Untitled character sketch of David Hume, 1742.
Complete sketch, newly transcribed by M.A. Stewart; from manuscript in
National Library of Scotland, MS 14258, fol. 30.[1]

The following thumbnail sketch of Hume, until now unpublished, is among the manuscript papers of Sir Robert Strange (1721–1792) and in his hand, but the authorship cannot be established with certainty since another copy in another hand exists in the same collection, fol. 29. Born on the Scottish island of Pomona, Orkney, Strange was an artist and a staunch Jacobite, and after the failure of the 1745 rebellion he withdrew for some years to France, eventually returning to Britain to become the foremost engraver of his age. The author of the sketch is responding to the publication of the second volume of Hume's *Essays Moral and Political* in 1742, satirizing in particular the essay "Of Essay Writing" which Hume withdrew from subsequent editions.

1742
Mr Hume Author of the Essays and Embassador Extraordinary from the Republick of Letters, to the Republick of Petticoats: Is a person of Great Abilitys, but no Genius, of some Judgement, but no Invention, of Vast reading, but no Tast; His Stile is smooth not Easy, proper not Elegant, concise not Lively, his Reflections are more uncommon than naturall, more Curious than Usefull, His Writings are larger than his fame, and his Fame less than his Vanity. He would have Merited more Praise had he never been an Author, tho it must be Confessed he would have made a good Schoolmaster: As he is a Man I Love him As he has no Witt I don't envy him, But as he affects to be a Critick I Despise him, As he would fain appear a Man of Mode I laugh at him and pity him if he be a Pedant. With many faults and few excellencies to Attone for

---

[1] The transcription, supplied by M.A. Stewart, is reproduced by kind permission of the Trustees of the National Library of Scotland.

them, he has Incurred the displeasure of the Ladies, instead of gaining their favour. I would therefore advise him to Retire from their Court to his Brothers house in the Country where he may pass the remainder of his Days in Solitude and Abstruse Speculations.

2
JAMES WODROW:
LETTER TO SAMUEL KENRICK

James Wodrow, letter from Wodrow (Glasgow) to Samuel Kenrick (Milliken, near Paisley), January 21, 1752.
Selections, newly transcribed by M.A. Stewart; from manuscript in Dr. Williams's Library, London, MS 24.157 (Wodrow-Kenrick correspondence, c. 1750–1810), item 16, in part.[1]

James Wodrow (1730–1819) was a son of the Calvinist historian Robert Wodrow. He studied at Glasgow University, graduating 1750, and was library keeper, 1750–1755. After being licensed for the ministry in 1753 and ordained in 1757, he was minister of the same parish, Stevenston, for sixty-two years (1759–1810). He published *The Measures of Divine Providence towards Men and Nations Suitable to their Behaviour* (Edinburgh, 1794) and prefixed a significant biographical account of William Leechman to his edition of Leechman's *Sermons* (2 vols, London, Strahan, 1789). Throughout his career he supported the moderate side in the Scottish Church that had been anathema to his father. His correspondent, Samuel Kenrick (1728–1812) was the son of a Welsh minister, and went into commerce at Paisley after graduating from Glasgow in 1743; he later removed to England, where he was a founder of the Bewdley Bank in Worcestershire.

In the letter that is here reproduced in part, Wodrow refers to efforts by John Anderson (1726–1796) to write a tract against Hume, probably against his religious opinions; no trace of this has so far been found. Anderson, another of Wodrow's Glasgow contemporaries, had been active in a Christian club with Wodrow. He became professor of Oriental Languages in 1756 and a famously troublesome professor of Natural Philosophy in 1760. The letter reports gossip on Hume's candidacy for a Chair following the death of Thomas Craigie, professor of Moral Philosophy in 1751, and on Adam Smith's performance as the recently appointed professor of Logic. In the event, the university's political

---

[1]   The transcription, supplied by M.A. Stewart, is reproduced by kind permission of the Trustees, Dr Williams's Trust.

managers negotiated Smith's transfer to Moral Philosophy and James Clow's appointment to Logic. It is not clear which position Hume's supporters had hoped to place Hume in. The four fellow-students referred to in the letter (Benjamin and Thomas Dawson, Daniel Noble, William Davenport) were English dissenters who had come up from Rotheram's Academy at Kendal to complete degrees and train for the ministry at Glasgow; all of them became for a time ministers of English dissenting congregations. Among others mentioned in connection with the university, Leechman was professor of Divinity; George Muirhead became professor of Humanity (Latin) in 1754; the Principal was Neil Campbell.

... I have received the 2 following sheets of the work from Anderson & am desired to show it to Professor Leechman with a Letter to myself by way of Introduction & intend to put them into the Professors hands this night. I Beleive, Kenrick, I have reason to be angry at you about this bussiness. I find it has come above board at the Colledge, that is, among the Dawson's, Noble Davenport &c, that J. Anderson intends to become Author & publish against Hume. I never gave the least hint of it to any person in the World but yourself. & this was with the strictest promises of secresy. I can scarce think you woud be so incautious, however if it be so write me to whom or how much of the matter you discoverd for if they know that you saw the sheets I shall scarce have the confidence to deny it. There would have been nothing or less in it if he had been fully determined to publish them but this is by no means the case. He writes me if I don't like them either to burn them or send them back to himself without showing them to the Professor or any body else, & if they are shown to the Professor they are to stand or fall by his oppinion of them.

You have heard something I see of the Clergy of Glasgow going in a body to the Faculty to express their desires that Hume might not be the person elected into the vacant office. The Principal received them with a hauty Air & tossing up his head asked them if they were come to Dictate to the Faculty or come as his brethren. The ministers got no answer. Every body seems to imagine he will not be the man. I have good reason to think it will go betwixt Tom Melvil & Clow altho' it is said that Hume himself has recomended Mr. George Muirhead as the fittest person in Scotland & that if Hume be out of the play, all his freinds will vote for the person recomended by him.

I have read Hume's last book His Political Essays. I am not qualifyed to give you any character of it as I have not been accustomed to think or read much upon the subjects of it. One after having read such a book finds himself pleased and Entertained (much in the same way as by a modern romance) from the Propriety of the Language Harmony of the Periods & the Novelty & oddness of some of the thoughts. He discovers more modesty or if you please Scepticism in this than in the former work indeed the subjects give more scope for it as some of them are very uncertain in their own nature others of them are of such a Kind that you may think as you please about them & the World will not think of you a bit the worse. But I don't know, how this Author affects a kind of unconcernedness & indifference with regard to the subjects he writes about be they never so important & is entirely easy & careless about the success of Arguments he uses in support of any truth. His Arguments & reasoning never or seldom produce any solid conviction, but leave the mind some way loose & more uncertain than when you began. He uses an argument to establish a point then he throws out some thing on the other side which overturns all he said & leaves you just as you were, then he sets it up; then down with it & at the end you dont know what to think. Did you ever see our children throw at their Pin-Cocks. A pin for a throw at that cock there. - you miss'd it you Dog you. - Another throw. Hollow, over he goes on his back. - Set him up again, let me have another broadside for my own cock. Hume's reasoning brings always to my mind some match of this kind. His Essay on the populousness of ancient nations (wherin he espouses the Oposite side of the question to the common oppinion namely he maintains that the World is more populous at present than it was in the flourishing ages of Greece & Rome) discovers a great acquaintance with the Ancient Historians & Orators. His Essay upon the Advantages & Disadvantages of the Hanoverian succession is very plain & popular (I mean easly understood by the people) his unconcerned manner of writing is very observable here. He talks about it fearlessly, like an event that happened 1000 years ago. There is no other copy of the book in town besides the one I had so you need not pester the Booksellers with letters.

Smiths Reputation in his Rhetorical Lectures is sinking every day. As I am not a scholar of his I don't pretend to assign the cause. He begins next week to give lectures on Jurisprudentia which I design to attend. I hear he has thrown out some contemptuos Expressions of Mr Hutchison. Let the young man take care to guard his Censures by the Lines Palisades & counterscarps of his science Rhetorick. For there are some of Mr Hutchisons scholars still about the College who perhaps will try to turn the mouths of the Cannon against himself.

3
ADMONITIONS FROM THE DEAD

Admonitions from the dead, in epistles to the living; addressed by certain spirits of both sexes, to their friends or enemies on earth, with a view either to condemn or justify their conduct while alive; and to promote the cause of religion and moral virtue. London: printed for R. Baldwin, 1754, xii, 316 p. Letters 1 and 2, complete; from first edition of 1754.

Henry St John, Viscount Bolingbroke (1678–1751) had been an English Tory politician, later turning to literature and to political and historical writing. While advocating high standards of public and private virtue, he had a reputation for fast living and religious freethinking, and his poorly edited posthumous *Works* (5 vols, London, 1754) was savaged by anti-deist critics. Several contemporaries (William Warburton, John Leland, George Anderson) grouped Hume with Bolingbroke as an infidel writer. Capitalizing on that association some decades later, a book was published titled *The Beauties of Hume and Bolingbroke* (1782), which excerpts the more controversial pieces from both authors. Upon its appearance the *Critical Review* wrote "Hume and Bolingbroke should never have been brought within reach of the world in general: we believe that Hume has hitherto done little mischief; for his works were beyond the purchase of some pretended philosophers, and above the understanding of others" (February 1783, Vol. 55 157–158).

In 1754 an anonymous work appeared titled *Admonitions from the Dead, in Epistles to the Living*, which presents fictitious letters from notable deceased figures from the afterlife. According to the book's editor, it was written by a recently deceased gentleman "well known to the learned World," who apparently intended the manuscript for eventual publication. Its purpose, as indicated in the title, is "to promote the cause of religion and moral virtue." Letters 1 and 2 are addressed to Hume from the deceased Bolingbroke, who cannot reveal whether he is in torment or paradise. In Letter 1, Bolingbroke, who respects Hume, explains how death has humbled him and that "the Eyes of Millions are upon you [i.e. Hume], and those who own you of Superior Wisdom, will, whatsoever their own Reason should prescribe, be guided by your Sentiments." In Letter 2 the Bolingbroke character argues that our two main obligations are to determine whether God exists and which religion is the best. He argues that the unbiased Aristotle concluded God's existence from natural design. But, Bolingbroke, lamenting their respective attacks on theistic proofs, asks, "what have you and I done?" He then presents a design argument and asks Hume, "Are you convinced, or is there need of more?" Turning next to the issue of determining which religion is the best, Bolingbroke argues that pagan religions are foolish and wicked: "They represent their Deities as criminal, and Crimes made up a great Part of their Worship." The author's discussion here of the historical development of religion is particularly noteworthy since, by showing how pagan religions factored into conservative defences of Christianity, it represents the general target of Hume's attack in the *Natural History of Religion* (1757). Bolingbroke concludes that the oldest and most credible religion is founded on two books, namely, the Old and New Testaments. "I have opposed the one, and you the other." "The *Jews*, then, have true Claim to Antiquity" which confirms the authority of the Old Testament. Bolingbroke repents for attacking the historical veracity of the Old Testament, and argues that Hume's critique of miracles is equally damaging to the New Testament. Hume, too, he suggests, should repent for placing "the Laws of Nature in array against the God of Nature." Hume must first agree that God *can* perform miracles, and then see that God sanctioned Christianity through "the Power of Miracles" which Jesus performed. He concludes noting that "there will be more real Merit in withdrawing your rash Opinion, than in all 'twere possible you should say to support it."

The complete review of this work in the *Monthly Review* is this: "The title sufficiently indicates the design: in the execution, this work is inferior to mrs. *Rowe's Friendship in death*" (*Monthly Review*, April 1754, Vol. 10, p. 311). A second edition of *Admonitions from the Dead* appeared later in 1754, which is only a reissue of the first edition with a cancel title page. The following is from the first edition.

ADVERTISEMENT
OF THE
EDITOR.

These Letters are a Part of what were found among the Papers of a Gentleman well known to the learned World, who died this Winter: the Editor hopes he did not judge amiss, in thinking them worthy the Notice of the Publick.

They appear to have been written at different Times; many of them not long since; a few plainly several Years ago; some of the Persons to whom they are addressed having been a considerable Time dead.

In such of them as are addressed to those yet living, the Editor, to avoid all offence, has generally either suppress'd the Names, or us'd only their initial Letters; and this not only where Censure prevail'd, but even where great and just Praise was the subject; this he has done in deference to their high Stations.

It appeared plainly from the Corrections made with the late Hand, that the Author, had he liv'd, design'd to have publishd them; and their excellent Intent, which is every where to inculcate Morality, Virtue, and a Sense of Religion, made it appear to the Person who became possess'd of them, as an Injustice to the World to suppress them.

The great Variety of their Style made him at first suppose them written by different Persons; and he was often surpriz'd with the uncommon Turn of it; but he is apt to believe, upon Re-consideration, that they are all by the same Hand; and that the Style, where it appeared singular, is designedly so: in some Places the imagin'd Language of Ghosts, in others an Imitation of the Manner of the Person from whose particular Shade they are said to come: but this he submits to the Opinion of the Publick; and only hopes, he has done no unacceptable Office, in committing them to the Press.

—

ADMONITIONS
FROM
THE DEAD

—

LETTER I.
Henry St. John *to* David Hume.

You will expect, great Metaphysician, from one, who respected you while living, Civilities and Applause; now that he writes from other Regions you will in vain expect them. Men, disrobed of their Bodies, are no longer what they were while entangled with such Incumbrances; nor does the pure Soul continue those Opinions and those Prejudices, which the Passions (Children often of the very Frame) in Part suggested. Vanity is here at an End, and there will be a Time, a Moment perhaps is all that divides you from it, when Discernment of Thought, and Propriety of Expression, will be no longer the Objects of your Pride: When, whatsoever an empty Ambition may tell you at this Time, there will be no Consolation in the Praise Men shall bestow upon your Memory: but the Recollection of one good Action shall give you more Satisfaction, and command more Applause, than a thousand Essays and Enquiries.

The pompous, proud, ambitious *Bolingbroke* nay let me speak with Freedom, for with us there is no Pride, the ostentatious *Bolingbroke* is here a thin shade, no better clothed, no more respected, than the surviving Part of some rude Peasant: But this disturbs me not. The World anticipated Death so far; and the Ingratitude of those I served too faithfully, stript me of the Ornament before, and reduced me to myself. Yet in my Period of severest Fortune I retained that Pride, which characterises those born above the Vulgar, and, like *Marcellus, Rutilus,* and *Metellus,* Heroes and Patriots who had before been driven out from devoted and ungenerous states, I found more Glory in the voluntary Sentence, than those whose more successful Counsels induced me to the Choice.

Rank, Learning, Genius, and what we call Knowledge, vanish with the World, in which we gloried in them. The first Sentence that the disrobed Being hears is this:

– stupet inscius alto
Accipiens sonitum –

he trembles at the unexpected Sound, and to his Terror quickly succeeds Conviction. He finds that Man was born not to lord it over; Man from Superiority of Talents, or Accidents of Fortune; but that to have been virtuous was his Duty. That the greater were his Accomplishments, the more opportunities he had of knowing this: and that by as much as it was in his Power more than in that of others, to have been of good to those about him, by so much he is the more inexcusable if he declined the Duty: and if he perverted the Means to Instruments of ill, he is the more to be condemned.

This is a State of Being you will enter; but I must say no more of it. No *Lazarus* is suffered to ascend from hence to warn his Friends on Earth; nor would such as you are now, and such as I once was, believe him. My thoughts alone are free: and as they rove the uncontrouling Air, if from their carrying the Marks of Reason, if from their being similar to your own, or if from the Advantage of a strong Experience, they may command your Attention; you may, while it is not yet too late, (an Opportunity which I have lost,) recover all that you have done amiss; and smile upon the Pains hereafter, which no friendly Spirit taught me to avoid.

From men like you much is expected: the Eyes of Millions are upon you, and those who own you of Superior Wisdom, will, whatsoever their own Reason should prescribe, be guided by your Sentiments. Chance commits Congregations to the Care of their Teachers; for Chance, or Interest, or Flattery appoints them; 'tis otherwise with Men like you: Heaven, in that it gave you powers of Mind, which they must distinguish, and which all, who distinguish, must also reverence, gave Half a Nation to your Conduct. You will suppose that it was Choice led you to declare your Thoughts. There was a Time when I also thought so: but here we are better informed. He who communicated Genius, communicated with it the uncontroulable Propensity of declaring itself to the general World, and if he had not, it were enough that we possessed it, and what we fancy Choice, will be on that Principle alone a Duty. All that remained with us was not the Necessity of acting, but the Choice how we wou'd act, we have made it as Men wou'd, who preferr'd Singularity to Truth; and thought more honourable to be call'd Doubters of what others received with Candour and free Faith, than to have supported that which we knew impregnable by those Talents which He who first establish'd it gave for that Purpose.

Sir, you have my general Thoughts; nor are you to wonder that you receive them from a State generally so incommunicative. I respected you when living and tho' dead, I cannot cease to think you naturally worthy of it. I shall not be ignorant with what Temper you receive this; and if you doubt it, or if you waver, I will convince you farther.

Farewell. He wishes you compleat Happiness, who must not tell you what is the State of it himself enjoys, or with what Mixture.

LETTER II.
From the Same to the Same.

Let me write freely to you, for I must. You err, and I must tell you of it. This is no Place of Compliment. Hear me: and as your own Peace, and as the Happiness of a Thousand others, which to your generous Spirit will be a superior consideration, may depend upon it, hear with Attention, and without Pride or Prejudice.

What is that Consideration, let me ask you freely, which is superior in its Nature and its Consequences to all others that can affect Beings, placed for a little Time upon one Spot, and destin'd to remain upon some other to all Eternity; Beings, to whom Freedom of Will, and Faculties for Choice have been accorded, and who must afterwards account for the Use they have made of that Freedom, and the Reasons of that Choice? You, who know Ethics to so great Perfection, cannot be ignorant that there is some such consideration: I ask you what it is. You are silent. Prejudice has ty'd your Tongue; but I will tell you what your Heart confesses. There is such an one, and it is Religion.

Men born with Talents greater than the common Rate possess, destin'd to serve their fellow Creatures, who have been less favoured in the general distribution, and accountable, for you will find it is so, for every Portion of that superior Knowledge at an unprejudiced Tribunal, owe their first Care to that Consideration: You then and I so ow'd it. Let us enquire, and let us do it freely, how you and I have fill'd this Obligation.

Two things it would require of us: first we were to determine for ourselves and to inform the World whether Religion were a Duty: whether there was a Being who expected it, and whether an Obedience to his Will were necessary. This was the first Task imposed on us, and having acknowledged, if we acknowledged this, the next was to determine which of all those Religions that had been offered to Mankind, in different Ages, and in various Countries, was the best. Whether any had the Sanction of that Power upon it, to whose Service it was ordain'd, and, if any, which: let us examine, how we have performed this Duty.

Whether there be a God, if that can be a Doubt, when you have ask'd the Question seriously of your own Mind, and find not Answers satisfactory; blush while you hearken to the Heathen. Who was that *Greek*? I think 'twas *Aristotle*; (but we have here no Libraries) who unacquainted with the Royal *Jew*, yet join'd with him in saying *the Heavens declare the Glory of God*; and rightly said to the attending World, we can be the Work of no less an Hand than what you are taught to own a Deity.

Place me, says the most inspired Philosopher, place me, some intelligent and reasoning Being, Man if you please, or something less, if less can be, a Mind capable of Reasoning, beneath the Surface of the Earth: give him an Habitation many Miles under this Plain on which we tread, and give him Creatures like himself for his Companions. Let their Apartments all be Palaces, adorn them with the Orders of most perfect Architecture, and furnish every Niche with *Grecian* Statues. Above his Head let Crystal Vases hold the burning Oil, beneath his Feet let all the Train of Marbles glow in the rich *Mosaic*; let polished Gems adorn the massy Cup from which he drinks, and let the Walls upon whatever Part he casts his Eye, live from the Pencil of *Apelles*. Ask him whence all this Pomp and Elegance? To whom he owes these Beauties, and what the Origine of these Embellishments; and ask it of him when he has had no Means of Information. He will retire into himself to know, and finding in himself the Faculties, and seeing round about him the Materials, he will at once declare that Creatures like himself had made them.

Then open him a Passage to the Surface; then let him for the first Moment see what we have always had before our Eyes, and Earth, the Ocean, and the Air; and last the Heavens; then bid him look upon the Fruits and Flowers, and tell him how they rise each Year at their appointed Season; then bid him view the Sun, too glorious to behold, diffusing Life and Motion unto every thing; let him see how after the Blaze of Day, that Luminary retires from Sight, and leaves the Firmament bespangled with a thousand Stars, and darts upon the Moon his Beams, to be returned from her with milder Radiance: Shew him all this, and then repeat the Question. He will reply that these are Works of a Superior Being; and had he been before informed there was a God, and doubted, he would be now convinced there was, and these were all his Works.

O venerable Heathen! O Glory to the human Mind! thus Man would think when he had nothing more than Reason to direct him. Void of all Prejudice, except the prejudice of honest, and free, and fair Conviction; he would proclaim what he was thus assured was Truth, and pitying those who wanted Power, or wanted the Attention to perceive what himself saw, he would have called forth all the Eloquence that rises from Conviction, to make them like himself believe it. What such a Man would have done, he, who has plan'd the imaginary Scene, has acted. The untaught *Greek* accepted that on unnatural Evidence and Reason, which has of later Time Sanctions of a superior Character.

Now what have you and I done? Are not the same Earth and Heavens spread before us; what is there in the Extent and the Oeconomy of either which he new, in which his Knowledge was not Ignorance to ours? Yet are we convinc'd like him! He who only saw that which he did not understand; convinc'd himself there was a Power that made it: We, whom superior Knowledge from ourselves has taught to comprehend, in some degree, what he admir'd; We, who are told from his own Mouth, that there is such a Being, shall, we, I say, doubt there is such? But I am silent. Had I doubted once, I should have known it now.

There is a God then: and he made all that we see about us. We owe him Gratitude; and as he who created all Things, doubtless has all Events at his Disposal, with our Thanks for the good we have received, it will be wise to deliver also our Requests for more. Thus is Religion established from the mere information which we have from Nature. We acknowledge that there is a God, and we pay him Thanks, and offer Prayers to him. This Heathens did: and how much more have you and I performed? I leave it you to answer.

If God expected we should worship him; he would inform us how: for he would not leave us ignorant in what Manner so great a Duty should be performed. It remains then to enquire in what Manner He would do that which we are convinced he would do for us. That it was necessary is evident, since, if we will believe any Records of the Times which are past, we must know that all were not of the just and rational Sentiment of the noble Heathen I have quoted, for, instead of owning a creating Power, many had paid those Honours which were his due, unto the Things created. The Sun, Stars, Animals, and Plants, the Host of Heaven, and the Inhabitants of the Earth, inferior by many Stages to ourselves, had been by Caprice and wilful Ignorance raised to the Rank of Deities. While those who established the Worship of such Beings did too much, there were in the same Times, doubtless, as there have been in ours, those who denying, or at the least doubting all, did shamefully too little: While the one Class of these had thrown themselves below the Regard of a superior Being, and the other did not merit it, having abused all his Indulgences; yet Mercy being an Attribute of the Creator, and a Love for the Things he had created, and among these most for the Principal living in the divine Nature; he would not fail to recall the wandering, though purposely wandering, and to awaken the Inattentive: He would not fail to admonish and to inform his Creatures in so necessary a Duty. Therefore as surely as there is a God, such as his Works declare him, great, wise, and benevolent, so surely he would inform Men of the Way in which he would be worshiped: not leaving the Posterity of those who had devis'd the Adoration of his Creatures instead of himself, to go on in Errors so dangerous, established by Custom.

Are you convinced; or is there need of more? Can you confess so much. He who created Man has then informed him how he shall pay his Adoration acceptably; and what are all his Duties. This has been done then; for what appeared proper to the divine Wisdom, would not be left unaccomplished. An Incident like this was of too much Importance to be passed over in Silence, at whatsoever Time it happened; neither would he, who meant it for the Information of all Mankind, leave any Age or any Nation without means of knowing of it. There is then somewhere in the World a Religion established by God himself: and we are only to determine which of the many that are received in different Places is this Religion. He who had this tender regard to his Creatures, would shew it to those of one as well as of another Period; therefore the true Religion is, beyond a doubt, that which was earliest. Then, which of all that we now know, and what we before have read of, is this true one? That is, which is most ancient?

Leave it to others to believe the vain and frivolous Pretences of the *Egyptians* of old, or of the *Chinese* of the present Time, to high Antiquity. Men, such as you are, know how to laugh at such mean Forgeries. Let them propose before the ignorant and credulous, Times in which kings of theirs have reigned, which antedate the World's Creation; and let them tell such as remain in Ignorance like their own, that the Sun twice has changed his Course within the Period of their History, journeying from West to East, as well as from the East to West; themselves, you know, affirm the one, and the Father of the *Grecian* History, I think in his *Euterpe*, names the other. You well know what to think of that Astronomy which calls the Moon a Fire, and dreads that Dragons should eat up the Sun. You will well know these men's Pretences to Antiquity are vain; That History among the Writers of Authority commences but with the Greek *Olympiads*, and that whatever they had done of older Time in their Religion, these their Successors knew not of.

Let us examine what was their Religion in the Times we know of, and what the Deities to whom they paid their Worship. These were, by their own Confession, Men, whose Virtues, or whose Successes had raised them to an imaginary Heaven; and if we examine briefly who these Men were, we find them all, except those which they confess new and additional, among the Patriarchs, the Prophets, and the Lawgivers of the early *Jews*.

The Heathen Religions were then all modern in Comparison of that which was in Use among this People. They were evident Constructions raised by Men upon some other; and except when they agreed with that other, they had no Prophecies, no Miracles to vouch for them. These Attestations, wheresoever they appeared, must come from the immediate Mouth of God; for they are more than mortal acts; and in the support of whatsoever Religion they appeared, that must be true.

But there is more than Antiquity to be produced in Favour of that, whatever it is, which shall be found, the true Religion. It is, wheresoever it is to be found, the Work of a divine Hand, and therefore it is pure and perfect. Where shall we find this pure Religion? Shall it be among the Heathens? No – their Stories of their Gods are foolish, and their Religion wicked. They represent their

Deities as criminal, and Crimes made up a great Part of their Worship. such will appear, upon a disinterested Enquiry, the Worship of the *Pagan* World; and if we cast our Eyes upon the other Faith which at this Time blinds almost half the Earth, the *Mahometan*, we shall find it of too late a Date to have any Claim to that great Testimony of Antiquity, and we shall find it unauthorised by Miracles, and in itself also criminal.

I come to one Consideration more, and do not wonder that I speak of that otherwise than I did while I was as you are: Nor doubt but you will one Time think as I do. Religion that was true must be of early Date; and there is such an one: Altho' true from the Beginning, it might not need to be from the Beginning perfect; and if not, this would be added afterwards: Such a Dispensation there might be in the Designs of Providence, and such there was, and such has been accomplished. There is a Religion earlier in its Origin than all these; supported by Prophecies; authorised by Miracles; and accomplished by a second Revelation. This rests upon two Books, themselves abounding with Conviction, and giving Testimony, in all Parts, of their Origin. Yet divine as these are, I have opposed the one, and you the other. All relied, as it ought, upon Antiquity and Miracle; and I have laboured to invalidate the Claim to that Antiquity, and you to set aside the great Support of Miracles. I feel, and you should tremble. Both acted unprovoked; both, I fear, against Conviction. Either has drawn away his multitude, and each must answer it. Now as that Admonition could come from none so well as me to you, that is one Reason of my giving it: But there is another: being voluntary, it is some Atonement for my former Fault; and coming from one who now knows more than when he wrote those Pieces, it will be credited, perhaps, by as many as they misled: I say perhaps; because Truth always comes with a worse Grace than Fiction; and for one Man who will believe what it is his Interest to find true, a Thousand will swallow Falshoods that are to their Destruction.

But let us hear this Matter fairly, for we have been accustomed so to trace all others; and instead of valuing ourselves upon a singular Opinion, let us investigate the Truth: In the Name of Justice let it appear, when found, be it against what it will: with the same impartiality let us determine that it shall also appear if it be against ourselves. We find the Gods, as they are called, of the Heathen World, were of two kinds, but both Men deify'd. Among the one Sort were those Kings and Conquerors who had been eminent in the Days of their Forefathers, who had built Cities, founded Commonwealths, or established Laws: And of the other Kind were certain Deities of elder Date, whom they had received from other Nations.

The Gods of their own constituting, then, are not [to] be regarded; and those which they received from elsewhere may well be supposed to have been also Men famous for their Exploits or Wisdom, since 'twas on such Considerations that they added of their own to the Number. We are to seek the Story of these elsewhere, since their own History, even the most fabulous Part of it, carries them up only to the Deities of their own making. Wherever we find those foreign Gods in their proper Country, and among the History of their own People, that People and that History we must conclude to have been earlier than theirs, and consequently than all other. Nowe then, where is it that we find them? It is among the *Jews*, their *Moses*, their *Noah*, and the rest were those whom these Religions deify'd. The *Jews*, then, have true claim to Antiquity, earlier by far than all the other Nations of the Earth. This, and a thousand other Things confirm it: And it is among the *Jews*, therefore, that we are, on the Principles already established, to look for the true Religion; because it is among them we are to look for the most early.

Let us enquire then fairly. Had the *Jews* any System of Religion? Certainly they had, and a divine One: What Proof have we of this? All that 'tis possible we can have of it. We have their own Testimony; and you see there are no other Nations cotemporary with them whose History is come down to us, that we might have also its Support. The Books in which it is contained, proclaim themselves divine by their very Nature and Construction. They abound with Prophecies which have been wonderfully fulfilled: Miracles are recorded in Support of the Religion they inculcate, and none amongst those who had not Opportunities of knowing whether they were true, ever doubted them. The dispersion of these People over different Countries which they conquered, or in which they were Captives, gave sufficient Means of spreading this Religion, had Men been willing to receive it: and in this Religion there was the Promise of a more perfect. Has not that Promise been fulfilled? Are not the Prophecies literally accomplished which concern it? We may speak as we please to others, but now we talk between ourselves. The Books are before you, examine them, and then declare your Answer.

From the first to the last Syllable is not all this dependent one Part on another; it is. And only Men like you and me could have led those of easier Dispositions for doubting, to have questioned it. With me the Fault is irreparable; you, Sir, have Time and Opportunity to set all right. Do it, and avoid a late Repentance.

Let us examine what we have done together. I questioned the Credit of the Old Testament in respect to its Authority as History; and you have set aside the Credibility of the New in the same manner, by denying that what is said in it, can be a Proof, or that any thing could be a Proof of Miracles having been ever wrought. If then the Authority of the Old Testament, as an History, is set aside, its Authority in all Things else falls to the Ground; for God would not countenance a Lye in any Part, and he that doubts of one Portion of it, can have no ground for crediting another. You say no Testimony whatsoever can amount to a Proof, that a Miracle was ever wrought. Nay, you go farther, you affirm no Testimony can ever amount even to a Probability that such a Miracle as is recorded, or that any the least Miracle whatever was performed. The *Christian* System is delivered in a Book where Miracles are recorded to have been performed by the divine Person, who established it. Himself appeals to these Miracles as a Proof of his divine Mission; and 'tis upon the Strength of these, and he intended that it should be so, that his Religion is established. You say we are not to believe these Stories, for you affirm that no such Stories whatsoever ought to be believed, even upon the Credit the strongest Testimony. Those who believe me, give up the one Half of the sacred Writings; those who believe you, can place but little Dependence on the other: Infidels will arise from these bold and weak Assertions; for mine are as weak as they are bold; and yours are weaker; and we, Sir, are to answer, and that before a dreadful, for 'tis a just, Tribunal; not only for the Follies and the Crimes of these, but for those of all who are, or who shall be, for Ages yet to come, misled by the Infatuation.

When I reflect upon my own Rashness, weak and absurd at once, I blush even more then I tremble, impious that I was, and daring to charge upon the People among whom the sacred Oracles of old were found, the art of *Pious Lying*, and upon their Successors and our Clergy the *extending too far their Authority*; designing, and mean 'twas in me to have said, that *Part of these old Books should be believed, and Part should not*. Nay, I have made it sure *so much should be believed*, I said, *as Christianity referr'd to*, so much, and no more. I doubted not but this would be a Reserve treated with the same Scorn by all who read, with which I treated it, who wrote. Coming from me, I knew it could not be understood otherwise than as taunting Irony, or as a forced and unallowed Compliance. If my Life had left Men in a Doubt concerning my Belief, my Death dispell'd the Mist, and they would know how much of Scripture he meant should be believed, who so having lived and so died, said so much was to be believed as served the Purposes of *Christianity*.

Impious and absurd! there was a Time when I, ignorant Being, brought to the Tribunal of my Judgment, the Works and Dispensations of my Creator; when I, in the full bent of this invalidating Argument tried the Actions of the all-wise, and all-good Creator, by what I called, and others, weak as myself established, as the Moral Fitness of Things. O glorious Undertaking! that Man should call before his Examination the Acts of his Creator! *Rejudge his Judgments*, and *be the God of God*.

I now think of what I was with more Humility; and of him whom I dared then oppose, altho' now with distant and imperfect Comprehension, yet with a Million times the Reverence. O *David*, know the Extent of human Faculties, and know 'tis nothing. Above you and below the Archangel, who in the figurative Language that adapts Things inexpressible to weak Capacities, is said to wait about his Throne. There are a thousand Beings distinct in Place and Order. The human Knowledge, compared with the Discernment of the lowest among these, is Folly; those lowest bear as mean Proportion to the higher; and all together brought in Competition with the Eternal Thought, are Ignorance. What then are you, and what have I been, single among a Crowd of weak and finite Beings, weighing Infinity. We too have tried the Oracles of God by the poor and the uncertain Test of ill established History. You, who have brought the Credibility of Miracles to the Test of (what?) of the School-boy Knowledge of Arithmetic! Know yourself, and blush: Know God, and tremble! You who have placed the Laws of Nature in array against the God of Nature: against the Power who made thee and thy Soul, that Nature and its Laws; who in Compassion for a misguided Species sent down from Heaven the Doctrines of a Religion that should reconcile that Species to his Will; and founded the certain Proof of their Original to lye in the suspending, for the Moment of Necessity, those Laws himself had established. Was this beyond his Power? I should expect from you the impiety to say so: but I should hope you would not make the Blunder. You must allow he could: and, to pursue you thro' your own Chain of reasoning, that what it is allowed a Power could at any Time effect, may at some Time have been effected. Would you know whether this which God may have done at some Time, he has yet done at any, enquire into what is said concerning this, and look to the Occasion. Ask whether that was worthy; if it were, a little Proof, ought to convince you that it has been done: but if it were not *dignus vindice*, disclaim it. You have Reason, speak. Is this, or is it not, conclusive?

You own it. O Man then speak! you and your Species doom'd to Destruction, not by an Act of arbitrary Will in your Creator, but by the Freedom of your own, and, by the Crimes you had committed; speak you, who seem to think yourself somewhat in the Scale of Beings; speak for that self, for all that are upon the Earth of the same Species; but that is little; for all that have been, or all that shall be of it in Ages past, and throughout Ages upon Ages, that shall come, speak for all these, and say when more than the Welfare of their temporal Being, when their eternal Happiness was on the Hazard, or was forfeited, was it, or was it not a worthy Cause, that he whose Power created, and whose Mercy meant to make them happy from that Creation, should interfere by some immediate Act, when no Means else could save them. You own it was. Then we are so far on the Proof. God could inspire the Prophecy, and God could stop, or suspend, or alter at his Pleasure, those Laws he had impressed on all material Things, and which we, forgetting as it were his Presence, call the Laws of Nature. He could do all this 'tis allowed; and if a worthy Cause should have offered, we have Reason to believe he would have done so: We own, you own it now, that Cause has offered, and we are told that he has so interfered. There are all the Testimonies that could be of this Event. Relations of it under different Hands; all Persons who had been Witnesses of what they relate, most of them, those who had been deeply but not to their temporal Interest concerned in it. Are these to be believed? You say not on the Testimony they deliver: Nay, to cut off all Possibility of Faith, where only Faith is of Importance, you say that no Testimony whatsoever would have been of weight, or ought to have been received as an Authority, for believing Miracles.

You set aside then the Accounts of the Evangelists and the Apostles; but you are willing to abide by the Decision of your Reason. O discerning Man! that durst prefer thine own Thought to the express Hand and Act of thy Creator. But let us bring it to this sacred Test, and see whether you so ought to doubt what is written.

God can perform Miracles, you own: You do acknowledge, that on a worthy Cause 'tis probable he will; and you allow that worthy Cause to have offered; why then do you doubt that to have been done which you acknowledge likely to have been done. Is it because of all Things that might have been performed on the Occasion, this was not the most proper. You, doubtless, are a better Judge of this than he, whom you arraign; but, according to this superior Judgment of your own, what would have been more proper, or in better Words, what is the Degree of this Appropriation?

The Creator of Mankind, perceiving his Creation in the Species lost in Error, has, as we are told, commissioned one from heaven to teach a System consonant with that which he delivered long before, and which he, in the former Work, had promised. The System is more perfect, more pure, and holy than all that Man has devised, or could devise. You will own the *Christian* Religion is such; in this it bears the Stamp of his Almighty Hand: and having commissioned one who should deliver this, he gave his Sanction to it by the Power of Miracles. What is there wonderful in all this Matter? You have allowed it possible, you must allow 'twas necessary; and had you not been told of it, I think your Reason would have led you to discover it. O! had the Books of the New Testament been lost to all the World, and fallen into your Hands by some Chance, how would your aspiring Genius have discovered their divine Original? With what Force would you have proved it, and how have shone, in the sacred Cause? And do you think it worthy of the Almighty, that to indulge a Vanity like yours, the whole Earth should have been left Two Thousand Years in Darkness and in Error? Being already received, you aim all your Artillery to overthrow that which, had it not been received, you would have employed it all and more to establish and support. Dishonourable and disingenuous Singularity.

If Miracles were proper to be wrought, what were the proper Subjects of them? Doubtless, had you been left to judge, mountains must have been removed, Seas dryed, and the whole Frame of Nature been disturbed. The Sun must have become extinguished at your Bidding, the Sky must have been filled with Meteors, and the whole Universe have been rent asunder. The fabled Exploits of fabled Giants must have been outdone before the wondering Multitude, and *Pelion, Ossa* and *Olympus* not piled on one anothers Heads alone, but thrown into the Sea. These had been Miracles of Ostentation; but he who had all Things in his Power chose only those of Use: while he instructed, he relieved; and the very Testimonies of his Power were all Acts of Goodness.

Had it been otherwise, all had been yet disputed. Some *Toland* of the subsequent Times would have pretended 'twas the Knowledge of Gunpoweder, possessed in secret, that removed the Mountains, that Sorcery deceived the Eye which fancy'd Comets in the Heavens, and natural Eclipses were called in by him who alone knew the Secret of computing their Appearance as Acts of his own Power. These would have been the Subterfuges of those Men, who with less Understanding and more Boldness than you have employed on this Occasion, have called the fiery Pillar of the Wilderness an artificial Beacon, and the drying up of the *Red Sea*, the natural Effects of Winds and Tides. but he who had the Power of doing all Things, knew better which to chuse: and you will own, at least you ought to own, that he who raised the Dead, could have removed Mountains; and that it had been less to drain a Sea, than to restore the Blind to Sight. These Things were done; and the Accounts of them are not to be invalidated. He who is said to have performed them, had the Power of doing it, and the Circumstances administered the Occasion. The System, in support of which they were wrought, is worthy the Authority of Heaven, and itself sanctifies all that was done in its Support. What then is to set aside the strongest Testimonies that ever have been given of the divine Power, and Goodness? What is to plead with us to disavow Advantages greater than all that have been offered us before, or can be offered to us again? What to extenuate the Importance; and depreciate the Authority of so great, so good, and so interesting a Relation? Were it not too serious, Men must laugh at the Reply: What God has wrought, Mr *Hume* tells us, we have no right to suppose he wrought: what he has told us, we have no Authority to believe. What has been the greatest Act of divine Power and mercy towards us (for the creating us was less) is to be disregarded and supposed of no authority, because he thinks it does not stand prov'd by the Rule of Subtraction.

Thus they talk, who being disincumbered of their Bodies, judge here of human Actions, despising what you sanctify under the Name of Wisdom. I tell you what they say who despise; and what I think, who love you. Nor are you to wonder that I see my own Faults here, as well as yours. Nor will you be surprized that a Spirit like mine, ingenuous and sincere, no sooner sees an Error, than it declares the Conviction. You will think thus some Time; but you may think it now. Employ your Reason, and despise the little Pride of singularity. Think and determine; and know, Scholar, that there will be more real Merit in withdrawing your rash Opinion, than in all 'twere possible you should say to support it. This is Candour, a Virtue rare on Earth, because with you Pride governs all Things: Here we are more wise, and it is universal.

What you have said is frivolous; all that I wrote, extended as it was, and amplified by every Circumstance which could be urged in Favour; and cloathed in all the empty Pomp of Words, was Sound instead of Meaning, and in the Place of Argument was Ostentation. I have Pride in saying this, because it calls me wiser; you aim at the same Character: Dare to pursue it by the same Means, and no Man will deny it to you. I have written to you freely, but 'tis with friendly purpose. I have written much, but 'twas my Custom, while alive, to love long Letters; and the same Things delight us here. You will receive it as a Testimony of his Regard who cannot court your Favour, and to whom your Resentment would be contemptible.

4
CARLO DENINA:
ESSAY ON THE REVOLUTIONS
OF LITERATURE

Carlo Denina, *Discorso sopra le vicende della letteratura*, Torino: Nella Stamperia Reale, 1761, [4], 242, [4] p.
Selections; from translation in *Scots Magazine*, September 1764, Vol. 26, p. 466–467.

Italian author Carlo Denina (1731–1813) was professor of Rhetoric and Literature at the Royal School of Turin. In 1761 he published his *Discorso sopra le vicende della letteratura* – *Essay on the Revolutions of Literature* – a highly successful work on the history of European literature, from the days of ancient Greece until his own time. In a chapter on modern European writers, he highlights the accomplishments of Scottish writers in particular, and praises Hume's *History* for its elegance. In 1764, Scots magazine published an excerpt from Denina's work, which they prefaced with the following statement of national pride:

Nothing can be more grateful to a lover of his country than the unbiassed decisions of foreigners in its favour. The sentiments of a native on such a subject, however just, are still liable to the suspicion of partiality. But when a gentleman of distinguished character, a professor in a foreign university, after enumerating the various revolutions of literature, and comparing its present state in the different countries of Europe, gives the palm at last to Scotland, in preference even to England, long deservedly esteemed the first nation in the world for learning and arts, such a determination must give the highest satisfaction to every Scotsman in whose breast resides the smallest spark of love for his country. We shall therefore make no apology for inserting the following extract. [*Scots Magazine*, September 1764, Vol. 26, p. 465 ff.]

In 1771 the work was translated into English[1] and reviewed in the *Critical Review*, which praised the range of Denina's knowledge and his execution of the subject:

---

[1] *An essay on the revolutions of literature*, translated by John Murdoch (1747–1824), London, Printed for T. Cadell, 1771, viii, 299 p.

His knowledge of our literature is extensive, as a foreigner, though he seems to be less acquainted with the merits of English writers, than those with whose languages we may naturally suppose him to be more conversant. Upon the whole, Signior Denina discovers a classical taste in criticism, and the Revolutions he exhibits present us with the invariable observation, that the corruption of literature is perpetually the consequence of an immoderate and affected refinement. The translator of the work seems to have discharged his part with fidelity. [*Critical Review*, 1771, Vol. 31, pp. 376–381]

After Hume's death, the *Weekly Magazine, or Edinburgh Amusement* printed an obituary notice which quoted from Denina's work, contained later in this collection.

...

The Scotch, for a long succession of ages, could scarce boast of a single author of any reputation. ... At length the spirit which had thus so successfully introduced a taste for learning into the capital and the neighbouring provinces, quickly extended itself to the most remote corners of Britain: and it is now an incontestable fact, that the principal authors who have adorned the British literature in these latter times, or do honour to it in the present days, have received their birth and education in Scotland. It were needless to enumerate the many sublime geniuses, as Simson, Maclaurin, Ferguson, Cullen, &c. who, by their happy discoveries, have illustrated the several branches of mathematics and natural philosophy. We likewise behold history, and poetry of every species, cultivated with surprising and unexpected success in Scotland. ...

England, though it abounds in almost every species of fine writing, has scarce produced one good historian. It was reserved to the Scotch to give the finishing stroke to such an essential branch of the English literature. – Amongst the learned in Europe, who does not know the celebrated works of David Hume? Who has not read, and who has not admired his History? Had not a genius so vast and sublime, too industriously, perhaps, embraced every opportunity of insinuating his peculiar opinions, he would have escaped the reproaches of the zealous professors of religion, added greater strength and efficacy to the history itself, and rendered it even more spirited and interesting. Extreme scepticism is naturally frigid and steril, and, in works of eloquence, it is better to be animated than indifferent. The faults, however, of this elevated genius are rendered almost imperceptible, by the propriety of his language, the fidelity of his relations, and the admirable sentiments with which his works are every where interspersed.

Had Mr Smollet preferred, as a great genius ought, lasting glory to present gain, and a celebrated name to the money of the bookseller, he would have had great merit as an historian.

But immortal praise is due to the ingenious Mr Robertson. That gentleman had illustrated, with great industry, the ancient history of Scotland, and the more important points of the modern. By his judgment, and exquisite discernment, he has distinguished himself amongst the best historical writers; and has excelled, by the elegance of his style, not only his compatriots, who have already acquired so much reputation, but even the most approved English authors.

Some people, infatuated with the pride and vanity of being born in the metropolis of a nation, persuade themselves that they alone are capable of writing their own language; and of course will scarcely believe that the Scotch bid fair to carry off the prize of language even from the English themselves. Let persons of this stamp, however, reflect, that the greatest masters in every branch of literature have generally been strangers in those cities that were considered as the seat of the language in which they wrote. What is still more remarkable, many of these authors came originally from small towns, which had no other pretensions to fame than their having given birth to men of such eminence. ...

5
WILLIAM RIDER:
AN HISTORICAL AND CRITICAL ACCOUNT

[William Rider], *An historical and critical account of the lives and writings of the living authors of Great-Britain. Wherein their respective merits are discussed with the utmost candour and impartiality.* London: printed for the author, 1762, [2], 34 p.
Complete introduction and entries on "Hume" and "Rider"; from 1762 edition.

Born in London, William Rider (1723–1785) was a chaplain, lecturer, and author of *A New Universal Dictionary, A New History of England,* and *The Christian Family's Bible.* Rider's brief *Historical and Critical Account* is distinguished as one of the first compilations of biographies of living British authors. The pamphlet was published anonymously by Rider himself with the closing initials "W.R." hinting at its authorship. The *Critical Review* harshly attacks the work for its inaccuracies and incompleteness:

This is such a contemptible catchpenny, that the publisher has been ashamed to set his name to the production. Who the author is we shall not pretend to discover; but we suppose he may be found up three or four pair of stairs by the Seven Dials. It is diverting enough to see with what importance this obscure balance-master weighs the merits of the different writers of the age: a circumstance that puts us in mind of the owl perched in his ivy bower, pronouncing sentence upon all the winged choristers of the forest. It is amazing, however, that any writer, even the lowest, should undertake a task for which he is so totally unqualified. Some of the best writers of the age he has left out entirely; such as Mr. Mallet, the two Wartons, Mr. Paul Whitehead, Mr. Cooper, Mr. Melmoth, Mr. Home, Dr. Robertson, Dr. Campbell, Mr. Guthrie, and many others, who have written with reputation. He appears to be as ignorant of the history as of the writings of those he has mentioned; his criticisms are equally superficial and ridiculous. He has lavished praise upon many authors, whom he seems to have raked from the profoundest depths of dullness and obscurity. He does not even know that Scotland is a part of Great Britain.... In a word, we are tired with animadverting upon this wretched hodge-podge of error, impertinence, and absurdity [*Critical Review*, May 1762, Vol. 13, pp. 441–442]

A largely negative review also appeared in the *Monthly Review* (May 1762, Vol. 26, pp. 391–392). These severe assessments are not surprising in view of Rider's attack on the abilities of book reviewers, as we read in his Introduction. Negative reactions aside, Rider's sketch of Hume is significant for being the first known printed biography of Hume. The following is from the 1762 and only edition of Rider's pamphlet.

INTRODUCTION.

As Critics by Profession are seldom entirely free from Partiality in the Judgments they pass upon the Productions of their Contemporaries, I have often thought a Work calculated to give the Public an Insight into the Merits of each modern Author; and thereby enable them to form a Judgment of what they are to expect from each new Publication, could hardly fail to prove acceptable. The Utility of such a Work appears in a still stronger Light, when we consider that the Reviewers, whose Business it is to direct the Judgment of Readers, have rather made it their Endeavour to mislead their Sense, as Nothing can be more evident than that in the Judgment which they pass upon Books, they are but too often influenced by the Name of an Author or the Publisher. In the following Treatise I have endeavoured to shew myself strictly impartial; and this I could do the more easily, as I have no Connection with any of the Authors whose Works I criticise; and must of Consequence be free from any Prejudice in their Favour, or the contrary. I intend, however, to deviate from the usual practice of Critics, who seem to have inverted the Maxim of the Civilians, and to think that if they must err in their Judgments, it should be on the Side of Severity. In the Course of this Work I have all along observed a contrary Conduct, making it a Rule to dwell more upon the Beauties of each Author, than upon his defects, as I have always observed that the ignorant and narrow-minded are most ready at finding Faults, and that Critics of real discernment shew most Indulgence in animadverting upon the Blemishes of a Composition, just as truly virtuous Men are the readiest to excuse the Frailties of human Nature. I do not, however, flatter myself that every Author who peruses the following Essay will be satisfied with the Manner in which he is treated in it, as he that adheres strictly to Truth can never expect to please every Body. I shall, however, take particular Care to avoid all personal Reflections (a Precaution which has been but too little observed by most Critics) and as I have the Good of the Public in View, not the Gratification of any particular Man, or Set of Men, I shall beg Leave to remind such as may be offended by the Liberties taken with their Writings, of the Justness of the antient Maxim, *Amicus Plato, amicus Socrates, sed magis amica veritas.*[1]

Mr. HUME.

It must be acknowledged, for the Honour of *Scotland*, that it has in the present Age produced more Men eminent for having cultivated Literature with Success, than either *Great-Britain* or *Ireland*. *David Hume*, Esq. who reflects so high an Honour upon that Country of which he is a Native, was formerly Secretary to Lord *Albemarle*, when Ambassador at the Court of *France*. As an Author, he must be allowed to possess a considerable Share of Merit. His *Essays* are equally elegant and profound; but they have been greatly censured on Account of the Vein of Scepticism, which runs through them. Those, however, who consider them as Works of Genius, cannot deny them Praise, tho' they are certainly rather superficial in some Places. In History this Author comes the nearest to Dr. *Smollet*; in one Respect he even deserves to be preferred to him; his Observations are much more sagacious and profound; but his Manner is not equally picturesque, nor his Style equally pleasing.

Mr. RIDER.

The Rev. Mr. *William Rider* is Assistant Master to St. *Paul*'s-School. He wrote an *English* Dictionary, dedicated to Mr. *W. Pitt*, which would, doubtless, have been much better received by the Public, if the great Mr. *Johnson* had not been beforehand with him in that Task. His *History of England* has been very well received by the Public, and is indeed wrote with a great Accuracy and Erudition. Mr. *Rider*, as he understands the *Saxon, Teutonic, Welsh, &c.* has given in his History many Particulars which have escaped Authors unacquainted with those Languages.

---

[1] ["I honour Plato, I honour Socrates, but I honour truth more."]

6
ESSAYS, POETICAL, MORAL AND CRITICAL

Essays, poetical, moral, and critical. Dublin: Printed by Alex. M'Culloh, 1769, xxii, 304, [4], 31 p.
Selections; from 1769 edition.

In 1769 a collection of essays appeared anonymously, the authorship of which is sometimes attributed to Brockhill Newburgh. The work contains a short poem that criticizes Hume for condescendingly maintaining that Newton was a believer. The location of such a comment in Hume's writings is not entirely clear, but it may be the following from the "Natural History of Religion":

> It is for the same reason, I maintain, that Newton, Locke, Clarke, &c. being Arians or Socinians, were very sincere in the creed they professed: And I always oppose this argument to some libertines, who will needs have it, that it was impossible but that these philosophers must have been hypocrites.

A footnote to the poem criticizes Hume further, arguing that those like Hume should "keep there Opinions to themselves" since they do more harm than good by publishing them.

On Mr. HUME's *gibing* Sir ISAAC NEWTON *for being a Christian, and for explaining the 70 Weeks mention'd by the Prophet* DANIEL.

The great, the philosophic Sage
Asserts, explains the sacred Page,
And to dark Prophecy gives Light
Long hid in Shades of darkest Night.
Hence a loose-thinking scribling Scot
With mickle Pride, small Sense I wot,
Presumes malignant, Tooth and Nail
At NEWTON's Self, to gibe and rail.

31

And what's the Crime, the heinous Deed?
NEWTON ne'er yet renounc'd his Creed.
But proves its Truth, the Prophet's Sense,
By Demonstration's Evidence.
Avaunt ye Owls and Birds of Night
The Sun ne'er shone for your dim Sight.
And you, you scribbling miscreant Loon,
Cur-like, bark on, and bay the Moon.

Whatever Credit Mr. HUME may have gain'd as an Historian, he seems to have added very little to it by his Essays; wherein he takes all Opportunities of disparaging the Christian Religion, and treating it with impious Scoffs and Ridicule. 'Tis in this Manner he has treated the great Sir ISAAC NEWTON, as an Instance of one of those Men of Sense and Learning that have suffer'd themselves to be misled by Prejudice, and an over found Religious Credulity. This Gentleman, and others in his Way of thinking, might methinks in point of Modesty, have treated the great Names of BACON, BOYLE, CLERK and NEWTON, with a little more Respect, whatever Licence they might have allowed themselves, in scoffing at a Religion that has prevail'd near 2000 Years against all Opposition, and has had at all Times such able, pious and learned Advocates to defend it. It were to be wish'd that such unhappy Persons who cannot, or will not see the Light of the Gospel, cou'd be prevail'd upon to keep their Opinions to themselves; as by the Publication of them, they may do much Mischief, but no possible Benefit to themselves or others.

CHURCH CENSURE OF HUME:
1755–1756

7
JOHN BONAR:
AN ANALYSIS

[John Bonar], *An analysis of the moral and religious sentiments contained in the writings of Sopho, and David Hume, Esq; addressed to ... the General Assembly of the Church of Scotland.* Edinburgh: printed in the year, 1755, [2], 49, [1] p.
Selections; from 1755 edition.

Born in Clackmannan, Scotland, and educated at the University of Edinburgh, John Bonar (1722–1761) was Church of Scotland minister of Cockpen, and later at Perth. Alexander Carlyle wrote of him that "John Bonar at Cockpen, though of the High party, was a man of sense – an excellent preacher; he was temperate in his opposition" (*Autobiography*, 1910, p. 247). In 1755 he joined the effort among conservative Scottish clergy to censure both Henry Home and David Hume for their infidel writings (see editor's introduction to this collection for background). To support the cause, Bonar wrote *An Analysis*, which strategically appeared on May 23, 1755, the second day of the relevant session of the Church of Scotland's General Assembly. His authorship of this pamphlet is established in "Memoir of the Rev. Archibald Bonar" (1817) written by his son James Bonar, selections from which are contained later in this collection. Early rumours, though, linked the pamphlet to George Horne. The *Analysis* consists largely of excerpts from the writings of Home and Hume which, by themselves, are supposed to expose them as infidels. Bonar opens conceding that Home's and Hume's works were published some years earlier, but insists that these two authors still publicly espouse their views, which justifies current ecclesiastical action against them. The first half of the pamphlet is devoted to Home's *Essays on the Principles of Morality and Natural Religion* (1751) and "Of the Laws of Motion" – the opening item in *Essays and Observations, Physical and Literary* (1754). Bonar lists thirteen religiously problematic contentions found in these works, and suggests that they support the view that "universal nature was God" – what we today call pantheism. The second half of the pamphlet unveils six dangerous contentions found in Hume's *Essays*, two *Enquiries* and *History*. The passages cited are among the more controversial ones in Hume's various writings. Bonar concludes that "the promoters of such impious opinions deserve the very highest censure of the church."

In their brief review, the complete text of which is as follows, the *Edinburgh Review* notes the political function of Bonar's pamphlet:

> This piece was published about the opening of the last General Assembly, with a view to engage the Church into a particular discussion of the opinions contained in the writings of two late authors. The method which the author of this Analysis follows, is, first to lay down certain propositions which he affirms them to hold, and then to verify these propositions by extracts from their books; which extracts he professes to give in their own words, and refers to the edition and the page: this method, he says, being such as these Gentlemen themselves must allow to be the most fair and candid. All that was to be required or expected of him in prosecution of this plan, was fidelity and exactness in his quotations.
>
> In this, however, he is accused of having failed; as appears from the following article [i.e., the *Observations* on *An Analysis*]. [*Edinburgh Review*, 1755, Vol. 1, p. 52]

The following is from the 1755 and only edition of the *Analysis*. I have excluded the discussion of Home's *Essays* and inserted bracketed references to the quotations from Hume.

To the REVEREND and HONOURABLE,
The Members of the ensuing General Assembly of the Church of *Scotland*.

GENTLEMEN,

As it is the great design of the Christian religion, to teach men to deny all ungodliness and worldly lusts, and to live soberly, righteously, and godly in the world; so it is the business of an established church, to employ that power with which she is invested, in promoting purity of faith, and sanctity of manners. Then, and then only, doth the act with dignity in her respective courts, when these important ends are the great objects of her attention.

For these purposes are you chosen by your respective presbyteries to represent them in this national assembly; and for these purposes our Most Gracious Sovereign countenances you with a representation of his Royal person. To you therefore, as the public guardians of religion, her friends are intitled, in confidence, to apply, with respect to whatever concerns her interests.

What particular business may come before you, I do not know. One thing of very general concern, I am sure, deserves your consideration; and that is, the public attack which in this country has of late been made on the great principles and duties of natural and revealed religion, in the works of DAVID HUME, Esq;

and in the essays of an author who has been distinguished by the name of SOPHO. It is true, one of these gentlemen have some how got the character of a fine writer, and subtle disputant; and the latter, it is said, holds a place of great importance in this country, and even bears an office in your church. But as I am well assured, that neither the art of the one, nor the power of the other, will avail to overthrow those principles they so boldly attack; so I am persuaded, that by neither will ye be diverted from doing your duty: and your duty unquestionably it is, to give warning of the poison contained in these volumes, and to testify to the whole Christian world your abhorrence of such principles.

Part of these writings have indeed been abroad for some years; and it may be asked, Why take notice of them now, when former assemblies did nothing in that matter? The answer is plain: Both these gentlemen has within these few months past renewed the attack; the one in his history of Britain, and the other in an essay published amongst the observations of the physical and literary society in Edinburgh: which plainly shews, that on their part it is a subsisting controversy; and ought therefore at last to awake the attention of all the friends of religion; and, in particular, make the clergy exert themselves with a becoming resolution, steadiness, and spirit.

It is not my design, in this paper, to enter into the confutation of these opinions. This has been done already with great success, by the smart and sensible author of the *Estimate of the profit and loss of religion*, and in the modest and elegant *Delineation of morality*. Two other authors have distinguished themselves against particular parts of the scheme, *viz.* the Reverend Mr Adams, a clergyman of the church of England, in his answer to the *Essay on miracles*; and Dr John Stewart, in his very masterly reply to the *Essay on motion*.[1]

To these authors I refer all that desire with candour to enter into the controversy. For my part, I think that the dangerous nature of these opinions is so apparent, that to them may be applied what Mr Hume says of miracles, when wrought in support of a new system of religion, "That the very positions are such as ought to be sufficient with all men of sense, not only to make them be rejected, but rejected without further examination."

My design therefore only is, to analyse the works of these celebrated authors, giving their own expressions under the different heads to which they seem to belong. This method, I imagine, will not only give the clearest view of the sentiments of these gentlemen, but is such as they themselves must allow to be the most

---

[1] [George Anderson (1677–1757) *An Estimate of the Profit and Loss of Religion* (1753); William Adams (1706–1789) *An Essay on Mr. Hume's Essay on Miracles* (1752); James Balfour (1705–1795) *A Delineation of the Nature and Obligation of Morality* (1753); John Stewart (d. 1766) "Some Remarks on the Laws of Motion, and the Inertia of Matter," in *Essays and Observations, Physical and Literary* (1754). Selections from Anderson and Adams are contained in *Early Responses to Hume's Writings on Religion* (2001). Selections from Balfour are contained in *Early Responses to Hume's Moral Philosophy* (1999).]

fair and candid; because, if in stating the proposition I should happen to mistake their meaning, their own words subjoined must immediately do them justice.

As to my fidelity in the quotations, I need say nothing further, than that I always mention the page, and quote from the following editions.

Essays and treatises on several subjects, by David Hume, Esq; 4 vols. London 1753.

Essays on the principles of morality and natural religion; Edinburgh 1751.

Essays and observations, physical and literary, read before a society in Edinburgh, and published by them; Edinburgh 1754.

The history of Great Britain, vol. 1. *by David Hume, Esq; Edinburgh* 1754.

I begin with the writings of SOPHO, whose opinions I shall sum up in the following propositions. ...

Having laid before you these extracts from the writings of this anonymous, though well-known author, I shall subjoin some passages no less remarkable from the works of his brother philosopher and friend; who has at least been more honest in this respect, that, without disguise, he has pled the cause of vice and infidelity. – I shall adduce none of my quotations from the *Treatise on human nature*, though this be the compleat system, since he has not thought fit to own it; but content myself with what I find in his *Essays* and *History*, to which he has prefixed his name, and which he seems to prophesy will be had in veneration by distant ages, to whom the very name of religion shall be unknown.

According, then, to this celebrated moralist,

PROP. I.

All distinction betwixt virtue and vice is merely imaginary.

Essays, vol. 1, *p.* 239. "Good and ill, both natural and moral, are entirely relative to human sentiment and affection." ["The Sceptic."]

Ditto, p. 235. "Were I not afraid of appearing too philosophical, I would remind my reader of that famous doctrine, supposed to be fully proved in modern times, That tastes and colours, and all other sensible qualities, lie not in the bodies, but merely in the senses. The case is the same with beauty and deformity, virtue and vice." [ibid.]

Vol. 2 *p.* 99. "The isosceles and scalenum are distinguished by boundaries more exact than vice and virtue, right and wrong." [*Enquiry Understanding*, 7.]

Vol. 4, *p.* 29. "No gratification, however sensual, can of itself be esteemed vicious. A gratification is only vicious, when it ingrosses all a man's expence, and leaves no ability for such acts of duty and generosity as are required by his situation and fortune." ["Of Refinement in the Arts."]

PROP. II.

Justice has no foundation further than it contributes to public advantage.

Essays, vol. 1. *p.* 327. "Obligation to justice is founded entirely on the interests of society, which require mutual abstinence from property, in order to preserve peace amongst mankind." ["The Sceptic."]

Vol. 3. *p.* 33. Public utility is the sole origin of justice; and reflections on the beneficial consequences of this virtue, are the sole foundation of its merit." [*Enquiry Morals*, 3.]

Ditto, p. 34. "If every external requisite for satisfaction was liberally provided without any care of man, there could be no place for the cautious, jealous virtue of justice. – It would be an idle ceremonial." [Ibid.]

Ditto, p. 41. "Reverse, in any considerable circumstance, the condition of men; produce extreme abundance or extreme necessity; implant in the human breast perfect moderation and humanity, or perfect rapaciousness and malice: by rendering justice totally useless, you thereby totally destroy its essence, and suspend its obligation upon mankind." [Ibid.]

Ditto, p. 45. "Creatures who have no power to resist or injure us, have no claim to justice." [Ibid.]

PROP. III.

Adultery is very lawful, but sometimes not expedient.

Essays, vol. 1. *p.* 256. "A man, in conjoining himself to a woman, is bound to her according to the terms of his engagement. In begetting children, he is bound, by all the laws of nature and humanity, to provide for their subsistence and education. When he has performed these two parts of duty, no being can reproach him with injustice or injury. And as the terms of his engagement, as well as the methods of subsisting his offspring, may be very various, it is mere superstition to imagine, that marriage can be entirely uniform, and will admit only of one mode or form. Did not human laws restrain the natural liberty of men, every particular marriage would be as different as contracts or bargains of any other kind or species." ["Of Polygamy and Divorces."]

He then gives instances of different modes of marriage, some for a longer, some for a shorter time; some with one wife, some with more; nay stoops so low, as to remark what passes in the brute creation; where, in some cases, one act completes the marriage, in others it subsists for the season; and then he adds,

Ditto, p. 258. "But nature having endued man with reason, has not so exactly regulated every article of his marriage-contract, but has left him to adjust them by his own prudence, according to his particular circumstances and situation. Municipal laws are a supply to the wisdom of each individual; and, at the same time, by restraining the natural liberty of men, make the private interest submit to the interest of the public. All regulations, therefore, on this head are equally lawful, and equally conformable to the principles of nature; though they are not all equally convenient, or equally useful to society. The laws may allow of polygamy, as among the eastern nations; or of voluntary divorces, as among the Greeks and Romans; or they may confine one man to one woman during the whole course of their lives, as among the modern Europeans." [Ibid.]

Vol. 3. p. 70. "The long and helpless infancy of man requires the combination of parents for the subsistence of their young; and that combination requires the virtue of chastity, or fidelity to the marriage-bed. Without such an utility it will readily be owned, that such a virtue would never have been thought of." [*Enquiry Morals*, 4.]

Having in an elaborate dialogue endeavoured to shew, that there was no fixed standard of virtue; but that what was vicious in one country, was virtuous in another; he instances in the case of adultery.

Ditto, p. 237. "Adultery was reckoned a vice among the Athenians; but in France it is in the highest vogue and esteem, and practised by every man of education, and tamely allowed by every man else." ["A Dialogue."]

Ditto, p. 70. "An infidelity of this nature is much more pernicious in women than in men. Hence the laws of chastity are much stricter over the one sex than over the other." [*Enquiry Morals*, 4.]

And in a note at the foot of the page, he intimates, that was it not for the bad example to young women, those who are past child-bearing need lay themselves under no restraints of this kind.

PROP. IV.
Religion and its ministers are prejudicial to mankind, and will always be found either to run into the heights of superstition or enthusiasm.

Essays, vol. 1. p. 163. "Chance, therefore, or secret unknown causes, must have a great influence on the rise and progress of all the refined arts." ["Of the Rise and Progress of the Arts and Sciences."]

Ditto, p. 237. "Some passions or inclinations, in the enjoyment of their object, are not so steady or constant as others, nor convey such durable pleasure and satisfaction. Philosophical devotion, for instance, like the enthusiasm of a poet, is the transitory effect of high spirits, great leisure, a fine genius, and a habit of study and contemplation. But, notwithstanding all these circumstances, an abstracted, invisible object, like that which natural religion alone presents to us, cannot long actuate the mind, or be of any moment in life. To render the passion of continuance, we must find some method of affecting the senses and imagination, and must embrace some historical, as well as philosophical accounts of the Divinity. Popular superstitions and observances are even found to be of use in this particular." ["The Sceptic."]

Having put into the mouth of a supposed friend an elaborate defence of the Epicurean opinions against providence, and a future state, from *p*. 213. to 225. *of vol*. 2. he then adds,

"You, my friend, have embraced the principles to which you know I have always expressed a particular attachment." [*Enquiry Understanding*, 11.]

Vol. 1. *p*. 279. "It is a trite, but not altogether a false maxim, That priests of all religions are the same. – They support the veneration paid them, by a continued grimace and hypocrisy." ["Of National Characters."]

Ditto, p. 280. "Those of them that are possessed of a temper more susceptible of devotion, make a zeal for religious observances compensate for many vices and enormities. The ambition of the clergy can only be satisfied, by promoting ignorance, and superstition, and implicit faith, and pious frauds. And having got what Archimedes only wanted, *viz.* another world on which he could fix his engines, no wonder they move this world at their pleasure." [Ibid.]

History, p. 27. Speaking of the church of Rome, he says, "Like all other species of superstition," (N.B. Superstition and religion are used as synonymous terms by this author), "it rouses the vain fears of unhappy mortals; but it knows also the secret of allaying these fears, and my exterior rites, ceremonies, and abasements, though sometimes at the expence of morals, it reconciles the penitent to his offended Deity." [*History* (appears only in 1754 edition).]

Ditto, p. 67. "King James had observed, in his progress through England, that a Judaical observance of the Sunday was gaining every day ground, and that the people, under pretext of religion, were, contrary to former practice, debarred from such sports and recreations as contributed both to their health and their amusement. Festivals which, in all other nations and ages, are partly dedicated to public worship, partly to mirth and society, were here totally appropriated to the offices of religion, and served to nourish those sullen and gloomy contemplations, to which the people were, of themselves, so unfortunately subject. The King falsely concluded, that it would be easy to infuse chearfulness into this dark spirit of devotion; he issued a proclamation, to allow and encourage, after divine service, all kinds of lawful games and exercises; and by his authority he endeavoured to give sanction to a practice, which his prejudiced subjects regarded as the utmost profaneness and impiety." [*History*, 47.]

Ditto, p. 330. "So congenial to the human mind are religious sentiments, that where the temper is not guarded by a philosophical scepticism, the most cool and determined, it is impossible to counterfeit long these holy fervours, without feeling some share of the assumed warmth. And, on the other hand, so precarious and temporary is the operation of these supernatural views, that the religious ecstacies, if constantly employed, must often be counterfeit, and must ever be warped by those, more familiar motives of interest and ambition, which insensibly gain upon the mind." [*History*, 55, note.]

Ditto, p. 390. "Had Charles been of a disposition to regard all theological controversy as the mere result of human folly and depravity, he yet had been obliged, in good policy, to adhere to Episcopal jurisdiction. – But Charles had never attained such enlarged principles." [*History*, 57.]

Ditto, p. 415. "Under colour of keeping the sacraments from profanation, the clergy of all Christian sects has assumed what they call the power of the keys, or the right of fulminating excommunication; and this pretext is so natural, that in most other religions, particularly that of the Druids, a like engine of priestly authority has been employed." [*History*, 58.]

Essays, vol. 1. *p.* 92. "In all ages of the world priests have been enemies to liberty." ["Of the Parties of Great Britain."]

Ditto, p. 282. "Revenge is a very natural passion to mankind; but seems to reign with the greatest force in priests and women." ["Of National Characters."]

Ditto, ibid. "Many of the vices of human nature are, by fixed moral causes, inflamed in that profession." [Ibid.]

PROP. V.
Christianity has no evidence of its being a divine revelation.

After having said that most other religions were embraced and protected by the magistrate, he adds, – *Essay, vol.*1. *p.* 87. "But the Christian religion arising, while principles directly opposite to it were firmly established in the polite part of the world, who despised the nation that first broached this novelty; no wonder, that in such circumstances it was but little countenanced by the civil magistrate, and that the priesthood were allowed to ingross all the authority in the new sect. So bad a use did they make of this power, even in those early times, that the persecutions of Christianity may, perhaps, in part be ascribed to the violence instilled by them into their followers. And the same principles of priestly government continuing after Christianity became the established religion, they have ingendered a spirit of persecution, which has ever since been the poison of human society, and the source of the most inveterate factions in every government." ["Of Parties in General."]

And in a note at the foot of the page, after having said that the conduct of the Romans towards the Christians was very different from what they had always shown towards those who differed from them in matters of religion, he adds,

"Hence we may entertain a suspicion, that these furious persecutions of Christianity were in some measure owing to the inprudent zeal and bigotry of the first propagators of that sect; and ecclesiastical history affords us many reasons to confirm this suspicion." [Ibid.]

Ditto, p. 240. "Whoever considers, without prejudice, the course of human actions, will find, that men are almost entirely guided by constitution and temper. – If a man have a lively sense of honour and virtue, with moderate passions, his conduct will always be conformable to the rules of morality; or if he depart from them, his return will be easy and expeditious. But, on the other hand, where one is born of so perverse a frame of mind, of so callous and insensible a disposition, as to have no relish for virtue and humanity, no sympathy with his fellow-creatures, no desire of esteem and applause; such a one must be allowed entirely incurable: nor is there any remedy in philosophy. – I must repeat it; my philosophy affords no remedy in such a case. – But then I ask, if any other philosophy can afford a remedy, or if it be possible, by any system, to render all mankind virtuous, however perverse may be their natural frame of mind? Experience will soon convince us of the contrary." ["The Sceptic."]

Vol. 2. p. 182. "It is a general maxim, 'That no testimony is sufficient to establish a miracle, unless the testimony be of such a kind, that its falsehood would be more miraculous, than the fact which it endeavours to establish. – But it is easy to shew, that we have been a great deal too liberal in our concessions, and that there never was a miraculous event, in any history, established on so full an evidence.'" [*Enquiry Understanding*, 10.]

Ditto, p. 184. "There are in the human mind the passions of surprise and wonder, which have in them an agreeable emotion: these being raised by miracles, give a sensible tendency towards the belief of those events. – But if the spirit of religion join itself to the love of wonder, there is an end of common sense; and human testimony, in these circumstances, loses all pretensions to authority. A religionist may be an enthusiast, and imagine he sees what has no reality: he may know his narration to be false, and yet persevere in it, with the best intentions in the world, for the sake of promoting so holy a cause." [Ibid.]

The whole intention of the *Essay on miracles*, is, to prove that miracles in their very nature are incapable of proof. And he very slily dwells on such forgeries, as bear some resemblance to the miracles in the gospel. And with this evident view, he gives a very particular account of the miracles wrought at the tomb of Abbé Paris, as collected together by the author of the *Recueil des miracles de l" Abbé Paris*. But left the thrust in the dark should not take, he adds,

Vol. 2. p. 196. "There runs however through the whole of this author's performance, a ridiculous comparison betwixt the miracles of our Saviour and those of the Abbé; wherein it is asserted, that the evidence for the latter is equal to that for the former: as if the testimony of men could ever be put in the balance with that of God himself, who conducted the pen of the inspired writers. If these writers indeed were to be considered merely as human testimony, the French author is very moderate in his comparison; since he might, with some appearance of reason, pretend, that the Jansenist miracles much surpass the others in evidence and authority." [Ibid.]

Ditto, p. 200. "What greater temptation than to appear a missionary, a prophet, an ambassador from heaven? Who would not encounter many dangers and difficulties, to attain so sublime a character? Or if, by the help of vanity and a heated imagination, a man has first made a convert of himself, and entered seriously into the delusion; who ever scruples to make use of pious frauds, in support of so holy and meritorious a cause?" [Ibid.]

Ditto, p. 202. "Upon the whole, then, it appears, that no testimony for any kind of miracle can ever possibly amount to a probability, much less to a proof." [Ibid.]

Ditto, p. 203. "We may establish it as a maxim, That no human testimony can have such force as to prove a miracle, and make it a just foundation for any system of religion." [Ibid.]

Then he instances in the case of its being affirmed that one suppose Queen Elizabeth rose from the dead, and says,

"Should all the historians who treat of England agree in affirming this; from the very nature of the thing affirmed, I should not hesitate one moment in referring it either to the knavery or folly of men. – But should this miracle be ascribed to any new system of religion; men in all ages have been so much imposed on by ridiculous stories of that kind, that this very circumstance would be a full proof of a cheat, and sufficient, with all men of sense, not only to make them reject the fact, but even reject it without farther examination. Though the being to whom the miracle is ascribed should be supposed in this case almighty, it does not on that account become a whit more probable." [Ibid.]

Ditto, p. 204. "I am the better pleased with this method of reasoning, as I think it may serve to confound those dangerous friends or disguised enemies to the Christian religion, who have undertaken to defend it by the principles of human reason. Our most holy religion is founded on faith, not on reason; and it is a sure method of exposing it, to put it to such a trial as it is by no means fitted to endure. To make this more evident, let us examine those miracles related in scripture; and not to lose ourselves in too wide a field, let us confine ourselves to such as we find in the Pentateuch, which we shall examine, as these pretended Christians would have us, not as the word and testimony of God himself, but as the production of a mere human writer and historian. Here then we are first to consider a book, presented to us by a barbarous and ignorant people, wrote in an age when they were still more barbarous, and in all probability long after the facts it relates; corroborated by no concurring testimony, and resembling those fabulous accounts which every nation gives of its origin. Upon reading this book, we find it full of prodigies and miracles. It gives an account of a state of the world, and of human nature, entirely different from the present; of our fall from that state, of the age of man extended to near a thousand years; of the destruction of the world by a deluge; of the arbitrary choice of one people, – the countrymen of the author; of their deliverance from bondage by prodigies the most astonishing imaginable: I desire any one to lay his hand upon his heart, and after serious consideration declare, whether he thinks, that the falsehood of such a book, supported by such a testimony, would be more extraordinary and miraculous than all the miracles it relates; which is, however, necessary to make it be received, according to the measure of probability above established." [Ibid.]

Ditto, p. 207. "Upon the whole we may conclude, that the Christian religion not only was at first attended with miracles, but even at this day cannot be believed by any reasonable person without one. Mere reason is insufficient to convince us of its veracity: and whoever is moved by faith to assent to it, is conscious of a continued miracle in his own person, which subverts all the principles of his understanding, and gives him a determination to believe what is most contrary to custom and experience." [Ibid.]

PROP. VI.
Of all the modes of Christianity Popery is the best, and the reformation from thence was only the work of madmen and enthusiasts.

History, p. 7. "The first reformers, who made such furious and successful attacks on the Romish superstition, and shook it to its lowest foundations, may safely be pronounced to have been universally inflamed with the highest enthusiasm. These two species of religion, the superstitious and fanatical, stand in diametrical opposition to each other; and a large portion of the latter must necessarily fall to his share, who is so courageous as to controul authority, and so assuming as to obtrude his own innovations on the world. Hence that rage of dispute, which every where seized the new religionists; that disdain of ecclesiastical subjection; that contempt of ceremonies, and of all the exterior pomp and splendour of worship. And hence, too, that inflexible intrepidity, with which they braved dangers, torments, and even death itself; while they preached the doctrine of peace, and carried the tumults of war, through every part of Christendom." [*History* (appears only in 1754 edition).]

Ditto, p. 8. "After the persecutions of Mary had chased abroad all the most obstinate reformers, who escaped her fury; they had leisure to imbibe a stronger tincture of the enthusiastic genius; and when they returned, upon the accession of Elisabeth, they imported it, in its full force and virulence, into their native country." [Ibid.]

Ditto, p. 10. "It had frequently been the practice of Puritanical clergymen, to form together certain assemblies, which they called *prophesyings*; where alternately, as moved by the spirit, they displayed their pious zeal in prayers and exhortations, and raised their own enthusiasm, as well as that of their audience, to the highest pitch, from that social contagion, which has so mighty an influence on holy fervours, and from the mutual emulation which arose in those trials of religious eloquence." [Ibid.]

Ditto, p. 21. Speaking of those engaged in the gun-powder plot, he calls them "pious devotees." – But when, in *p.* 26. he has occasion to talk of the reformers, he can find no softer term than the "enraged and fanatical reformers." [*History,* 46.]

Ditto, p. 27. "That delicious country where the Roman Pontiff resides, was the source of all modern art and refinement, and diffused on its superstition an air of politeness, which distinguishes it from the gross rusticity of the other sects."

And a little below, he calls it the mother-church, and the religion of our fathers. – In the same spirit he styles Ravillac, who murdered the good King Henry of France, a "pious madman." [*History* (appears only in 1754 edition).]

Ditto, p. 60. "As the dawn of arts appeared throughout Europe in the sixteenth century, it might have been hoped, that when they should reach Scotland, they would put an end to that feudal anarchy, which there prevailed. – But before that happy period, – the Protestant fanaticism, more rapid in its progress, soon pierced into that remote country; and being at first strongly opposed by the supreme power, civil as well as ecclesiastical, it rose to a degree of fury, and with the most destructive violence bore down all opposition." [Ibid.]

In the next page, speaking of our first reformers in Scotland, he says,

"They did not, properly speaking, lead the multitude: they only ran before them in all their fanatical extravagancies. – Determined enemies to monarchy by principle as well as inclination, the religious orators placed a vanity in affronting their prince; and would acknowledge no sovereign but Christ, whose throne, being established in heaven, imposed little restraint upon them." [Ibid.]

Ditto, p. 62. "The fire of devotion, excited by novelty, and inflamed by opposition, had so possessed the minds of the Scotch reformers, that all rites and ornaments, and even order or worship, were disdainfully rejected as useless burdens; retarding the imagination in its rapturous ecstacies, and stinting the operations of that divine Spirit, by which they supposed themselves to be animated. A mode of worship was established, the most naked and most simple imaginable; one that borrowed nothing from the senses; but reposed itself entirely on the contemplation of that divine essence, which discovers itself to the understanding only. This species of devotion, so suitable to the supreme Being, but so little suitable to human frailty, was observed to occasion the most enormous ravages in the breast, and to subvert every rational principle f conduct and behaviour. The mind, straining for these extraordinary raptures, reaching them by short glances, succumbing again under its own weakness, rejecting all exterior aid of pomp and ceremony, was so occupied in this inward life, that it fled from every intercourse of society, and from every sweet or chearful amusement, which could soften or humanize the character." [*History*, 47.]

Ditto, p. 63. "The finer arts too, though still rude in these northern kingdoms, were employed to adorn the churches; and the King's chapel, in which an organ was erected, and some pictures and statues displayed, was proposed as a model to the rest of the nation. But music was grating to the prejudiced ears of the Scotch clergy; sculpture and painting appeared instruments of idolatry; the surplice was a rag of Popery; and each motion or gesture prescribed by the liturgy, was a step towards that spiritual Babylon, so much the object of their horror and aversion. Everything was deemed impious, but their own mystical comments on the scriptures, which they idolized, and whose eastern prophetic style they employed in every common occurrence of life." [Ibid.]

Ditto, p. 81. "The genius of the church of England, so kindly to monarchy, forwarded the confederacy; its submission to Episcopal jurisdiction; its attachment to ceremonies, to order, and to a decent pomp and splendour of worship; and, in a word, its affinity to the tame superstition of the Catholics, rather than to the wild fanaticism of the Puritans." [*History*, 48, note.]

Ditto, p. 140. "If King James wrote concerning witches and apparitions; who in that age did not admit the reality of these fictitious beings? If he has composed a commentary on the *Revelations*, and proved the Pope to be Antichrist; may not a similar reproach be extended to the famous Napier; and even to Newton, at a time when learning was much more advanced?" [*History*, Appendix 4.]

Ditto, p. 303. Speaking of the design formed by the English parliament in the 1641 to reduce the Royal authority, he adds,

"But this project, it had not been in the power, scarce in the intention of the popular leaders, to execute, had it not been for the passion which seized the nation, for Presbyterian discipline, and for the wild enthusiasm which at that time accompanied it. The licence which the parliament had bestowed on this spirit, by checking ecclesiastical authority; the countenance and encouragement with which they had honoured it, had already diffused its influence to a wonderful degree; and all orders of men had drunk deep of the intoxicating poison. In each discourse or conversation this mode of religion entered; in all business it had a share; every elegant pleasure or amusement it utterly annihilated; each vice or corruption of mind it promoted; scarce any disease or bodily distemper was totally exempted from it; and it became requisite, we are told, for all physicians to be expert in the spiritual profession, and, by theological considerations, to ally those religious terrors with which their patients were so generally haunted." [*History*, 55.]

Ditto, p. 395. "Whatever ridicule, to a philosophic mind, may be thrown on pious ceremonies, it must be confessed, that, during a very religious age, no institutions can be more advantageous to the rude multitude, and tend more to mollify that fierce and gloomy spirit of devotion, to which they are so subject. Even the English church, though it had retained a share of Popish superstition, may justly be thought too naked and unadorned, and still to approach too near the abstract and spiritual religion of the Puritans. Laud and his associates, by reviving a few primitive institutions of this nature, corrected the error of the first reformers, and presented to the affrightened and astonished mind, some sensible, exterior observances, which might occupy it during its religious exercises, and abate the violence of its disappointed efforts. The thought, no longer bent on that divine and mysterious essence, so superior to the narrow capacities of mankind, was able, by means of the new model of devotion, to relax itself in the contemplation of pictures, postures, vestments, buildings; and all the fine arts which ministered to religion, thereby received additional encouragement." [*History*, 57]

Thus, Gentlemen, I have laid before you a few of the many passages which occur in the works of these two authors, and which at the very first view appear to strike at the foundations of all virtue and religion, both natural and revealed. – That the promoters of such impious opinions deserve the very highest censure of the church, is beyond dispute. What you shall think proper to do in this assembly, a short time will discover. Only I will venture to say, that if these things are overlooked, after the zeal you have lately shewn to support the authority of your own sentences, it will in some measure verify a common observation, That it is safer to revile the King than the ministry. – Nor do I know how you will pary the blow, when every one has it in his power to tell you, You deposed a minister who disowned your authority,[2] but inrol, as a member of your courts,[3] an elder who has disowned the authority of almighty God; and that some of you at least live in the greatest intimacy with one who represents the blessed Saviour as an impostor, and his religion as a cunningly-devised fable. – May your conduct be such as fully to wipe off all these reproaches; and testify to the world, that you will have no society with the workers of iniquity.

F I N I S

---

[2] [i.e., Thomas Gillespie (1708–1774). In 1752 Gillespie was removed from his ministerial position for maintaining that local congregations had the right to approve their ministers – a position contrary to the 1712 Patronage Act. In 1761, Gillespie co-founded the Relief Church.]

[3] [*Scots Magazine* inserts the following note at this spot in their excerpt of this pamphlet: "This gentleman was named a member of the commission by the assemblies 1753 and 1754; but he never sat in that court; and he is not named a member of it by the assembly 1755."]

8
HUGH BLAIR:
OBSERVATIONS UPON A PAMPHLET

[Hugh Blair], *Observations upon a pamphlet, intitled, An analysis of the moral and religious sentiments contained in the writings of Sopho, and David Hume, Esq; &c.*, Edinburgh: 1755.
Selections; from 1755 edition.

On June 6, 1755, two weeks after the publication of Bonar's *Analysis*, a pamphlet appeared titled *Observations on a Pamphlet, Intitled, An Analysis*, which defends Home and Hume against the attack in earlier work. The author opens with a general statement in support of the freedom of inquiry, contending that "The proper objects of censure and reproof are not freedom of thought, but licentiousness of action." The *Analysis*, he maintains further, quoted passages by Home and Hume out of context and ascribed views to both philosophers which they do not actually hold. In his discussion of Hume, the author concedes that many of Hume's views are inconsistent with "sound doctrine." However, Hume did not maintain that "All distinction betwixt virtue and vice is merely imaginary," and did not defend adultery. The complete review of the *Observations* in the *Edinburgh Review* is as follows:

> The design of this pamphlet is solely to examine, Whether the writer of the *Analysis* has not done injustice to the authors whom he would expose to censure, by quoting their books unfairly. This is the charge brought against him: in support of which, it is alledged, that, in several instances, he has misrepresented the meaning of these authors by mangled quotations; he has cited one part of a paragraph, and omitted another which declares or explains the meaning of the author, sometimes in direct contradiction to the proposition which the writer of the *Analysis* ascribes to him; and, in one or two instances, has cited passages as from these authors, and referred to the page, tho' neither the words nor the sense are to be found in the books which he cites. [*Edinburgh Review*, 1755, Vol. 1, p. 52]

Authorship of the *Analysis* is somewhat unclear. Initial rumour maintained that the work was penned by Henry Home himself, as we see in a 1757 pamphlet titled *An address to the Synod of Lothian and Tweedale* (selections from which are contained in this collection). As late as 1807 we find this view espoused by Thomas Edward Ritchie in his *Life and Writings of David Hume* (1807), who states that the *Observations* "was generally ascribed to the pen of Lord Kames" (pp. 57–59). In that same year, though, Alexander Fraser Tytler, Lord Woodhouselee, published *Memoirs of the Life and Writings of the Honourable Henry Home of Kames*, which attributes the *Observations* to Scottish clergyman Hugh Blair (1718–1800):

> The latter of the writings above mentioned, (and which alone seemed deserving of notice), was answered with temperate but forcible animadversion, in a pamphlet, entitled, *Observations on the Analysis*, &c., which was generally attributed to the celebrated Dr Hugh Blair, who is believed likewise to have lent his aid in the composition of a formal reply made by Mr Home himself, under the title of *Objections against the Essays on Morality and Natural Religion examined*, (Edin. 1756). [*Memoirs*, 1814 edition, p. 198]

Tytler knew Blair well, and was on very close terms with Home, which gives weight to the Blair attribution. Tytler's contention was disputed on stylistic grounds by James Boner in his "Memoir of the Reverend Archibald Bonar" (1817), selections from which are contained in this collection. The following is from the 1755 and only edition of the *Observations*; I have excluded the discussion of Home's *Essays*.

OBSERVATIONS
UPON
A Pamphlet, intitled, *An Analysis of the Moral and Religious Sentiments contained in the Writings of* SOPHO, *and* DAVID HUME, *Esq;* &c.

A pamphlet having made its appearance lately, intitled, *An Analysis of the Moral and Religious Sentiments contained in the Writings of* SOPHO, and DAVID HUME, *Esq, Addressed to the consideration of the Reverend and Honourable Members of the General Assembly of the Church of* Scotland; a few observations, which have occurred upon it, are here submitted to the public. The author's zeal for religion would deserve the highest commendation, if, in some instances, it did not seem to be misguided, in others to exceed the bounds of true piety.

The freedom of inquiry and debate, tho' it may have published some errors to the world, has undoubtedly been the source from whence many blessings have flowed upon mankind. As free inquiry alone could at first have made way for Christianity, and have borne down the opposition of synagogues, senates and schools; it is to the same noble principle we owe the Reformation, and are enabled to set at defiance the tyrannical decisions of Popes and Councils. By means of free inquiry, the church of *Scotland* was originally established. In this country, therefore, all attempts to infringe so valuable a privilege in cases where the peace of society is not concerned, must ever be regarded with concern by all reasonable men. The proper objects of censure and reproof are not freedom of thought, but licentiousness of action; not erroneous speculations, but crimes pernicious to society. Against these ought the Clergy to exert their utmost efforts; and by such a conduct they will more advance the cause of religion, than by engaging in metaphysical disputes, which may perplex the understandings, but never can impair the morals of men.

The intention of the following observations is by no means to enter into any controversy, but solely to examine, whether the Author of the *Analysis* has not, in many instances, misrepresented the meaning, and quoted unfairly the words of those books he would expose to censure. It will be admitted without dispute, that, to cite one part of a paragraph, and omit the other, which declares or explains the meaning of the author, is no less culpable than to falsify the words. ...

Were the author of the *Analysis* to meet with no greater degree of candour than he has shewn to others; it were not unnatural to conclude, from his extracts from Mr. HUME, that his zeal for religion was more affected than real. Every fair reader must admit, and regret, that there are to be found in the writings of this elegant Author some principles by no means consistent with sound doctrine. There was therefore no necessity for ascribing to him positions which he does not advance, in order to support the charge of irreligion against him. This conduct of the author of the *Analysis* can scarcely be accounted for; as it manifestly leads to do harm rather than good to the cause he pretends to support. But as it is more charitable to impute it to error than to evil intention, a very few observations upon it will suffice.

The first Proposition of the *Analysis* is, – *All distinction betwixt virtue and vice is merely imaginary.*

Every one who has the most superficial knowledge of Mr. HUME's writings must know, that he is very far from denying the reality of moral distinctions. The passages quoted by no means prove the proposition, neither are they fairly cited.

The first citation from p. 239. is the conclusion of a paragraph; the beginning of which is as follows;

"According to this short and imperfect sketch of human life, the happiest disposition of mind is the *virtuous*; or, in other words, that which leads to action and employment, renders us sensible to the social passions, steels the heart against the assaults of fortune, reduces the affections to a just moderation, makes our own thoughts an entertainment to us, and inclines us rather to the pleasures of society and conversation, than to those of the senses. This, in the mean time, must be obvious to the most careless reasoner, that all dispositions of mind are not alike favourable to happiness, and that one passion or humour may be extremely desirable, while another is equally disagreeable. And indeed, all the difference betwixt the conditions of life depends upon the mind; nor is there any one situation of affairs, in itself, preferable to another."

The second citation from p. 235. is as unfairly stated. The words which follow those quoted are;

"This doctrine, however, takes off no more from the reality of the latter qualities, than from that of the former; nor need it give any umbrage either to critics or moralists. Tho' colours were allowed to lie only in the eye, would dyers or painters ever be less regarded or esteem'd? There is a sufficient uniformity in the senses and feelings of mankind, to make all these qualities the objects of art and reasoning, and to have the greatest influence on life and manners. And as 'tis certain, that the discovery above-mention'd in natural philosophy, makes no alteration on action and conduct; why should a like discovery in moral philosophy make any alteration?"

The third citation from p. 99. v. 2. ought to have been explained by what went before it, which is,

"The great advantage of the mathematical sciences above the moral consists in this, that the ideas of the former, being sensible, are always clear and determinate; the smallest distinction betwixt them is immediately perceptible, and the same terms are still expressive of the same ideas, without ambiguity or variation. An oval is never mistaken for a circle, nor an hyperbola for an ellipsis."

It is by no means candid in the author of the *Analysis* to quote the passage from p. 29. v. 4.[1] singly; because, as it stands in the *Essay*, it makes part of a reasoning, the tendency of which is by no means immoral, as the passage going before it clearly shews. "We come now to the *second* position which we propos'd to illustrate, *viz.* that as innocent luxury, or a refinement in pleasure is advantageous to the public; so wherever luxury ceases to be innocent, it also ceases to be beneficial; and when carried a degree farther, begins to be a quality pernicious, tho' perhaps, not the most pernicious to political society."

---

[1]   P. 29. should be 32.; but that may be ascribed to an error of the press.

In p. 31. of the *Analysis*, we find the following sentence cited from the *Essays*, v. 1. p. 163. "*Chance, therefore, or secret and unknown causes, must have a great influence on the rise and progress of all the refined arts.*" This passage, which must be sought for in p. 162. is followed by

"But there is a reason, which induces me not to ascribe the matter altogether to chance, Tho' the persons, who cultivate the sciences with such astonishing success, as to attract the admiration of posterity, be always few, in all nations and all ages; 'tis impossible but a share of the same spirit and genius must be antecedently diffus'd thro' the people among whom they arise, in order to produce, form, and cultivate, from their earliest infancy, the taste and judgment of those eminent writers. The mass cannot be altogether insipid, from which such refin'd spirits are extracted."

And in p. 163. we find the conclusion in these words, "The question therefore, concerning the rise and progress of the arts and sciences, is not altogether a question concerning the taste, genius, and spirit of a few; but concerning those of a whole people, and may therefore be accounted for, in some measure, by general causes and principles."

With regard to the other propositions, it is sufficient to observe, that Mr. HUME's writings, to any candid reader, exhibit no defence of adultery; and are very far from containing any principles of licentiousness. Justice demands this acknowledgment as due to an elegant and agreeable writer, even though a Free-Thinker; and it must at the same time be observed, that it appears very like a contradiction to accuse a man in one page of scepticism and infidelity, and in the following page to tax him with an attachment to Popery and superstition.

From the whole survey of this *Analysis*, the misrepresentations and false quotations contained in it are evident. It may now, therefore, be not improper to inquire a little into the scope of it.

A number of the most horrible propositions are published in large letters, as extracted from the writings of two Gentlemen; and mangled perverted passages are produced, in order to prove so dreadful a charge. Many persons, it may be thought, will never go farther than the Propositions themselves, which are certainly sufficient to excite detestation in every sober Christian. Very few, it may be presumed, will look beyond the passages by which the Propositions seem to be supported, or consult the books from which these passages are extracted: and still fewer are capable of discernment on so delicate a subject. By arts such as these, are the characters of two Gentlemen attacked and defamed. The public will judge with how little justice, and how little candour this attack has been carried on. It is unnecessary to add any thing further. The Observations have been confined mostly to matters of fact. All reflexions upon the author of the *Analysis*, even after so full a detection, have, it is hoped, been avoided. As in common life, the habit of a clergyman ought to secure a regard to the wearer, even though it should happen to cover envy, malice, and falshood; so ought a zeal for religion, whether real or affected, to be always treated with proper respect.

FINIS

9
JAMES BONAR:
"MEMOIR OF ARCHIBALD BONAR"

James Bonar, "Memoir of the Rev. Archibald Bonar, minister of Cramond," in Archibald Bonar, *Sermons chiefly on devotional subjects*, Edinburgh: Printed for Macredie, Skelly, & Muckersy; M. Ogle, Glasgow; and T. Underwood, London, 1815–1817, 2 v.
Selections; from volume 2, 1817, pp. xxiii–xxiv.

E ducated at the University of Edinburgh, James Bonar (1757–1821) was one of eight children of John Bonar (1721–1761), the author of *An Analysis of the Moral and Religious Sentiments* (1755) contained in this collection. He worked as solicitor of the excise in Scotland, but devoted much time to scholarly projects, writing articles for encyclopaedias and editing books. Bonar's elder brother, Archibald (1753–1816), was a minister in the Scottish church and in 1815 and 1817 respectively two volumes of his sermons were published. James wrote a memoir of his brother, which is included in the second volume of sermons. In this James discusses his father's authorship of *The Analysis* and defends that work against criticisms by Lord Woodhouselee in his *Memoirs of Life and Writings of the Honourable Henry Home of Kames*. Woodhouselee writes,

Among Mr Home's opponents were some persons of so intolerant a spirit, that nothing less could satisfy their zeal, than the interference of ecclesiastical authority, to repress opinions which they conceived to be contrary to the canons of the Established Church, and subversive even of the fundamental principles of religion. Of these the most distinguished was a clergyman of the name of *Anderson*, who, in a volume entitled, *An estimate of Religion*, attempted a refutation of Mr Home's opinions, in a strain of coarse and vulgar ridicule, and with a petulance and scurrility which disgraced the cause he endeavoured to support. This publication was followed by another, from a very different pen, and in a much more liberal strain of composition, entitled, *An Analysis....* [*Memoirs*, 1814 edition, pp. 196–197]

Contrary to Woodhouselee, James Bonar argues that the *Analysis* did not constitute an attack against Home and Hume, but merely exhibited the views they contained. Neither Archibald Bonar's *Sermons* nor James Bonar's "Memoirs" were published after the 1815–1817 edition, from which the following is taken.[1]

In 1755, he published, without his name, a small pamphlet, entitled, "Analysis of the Moral and Religious Sentiments contained in the writings of Sopho, (Lord Kames), and David Hume." The object of this pamphlet was, by a fair induction from the writings of these two authors, then in great celebrity, to collect and bring into view some very obnoxious opinions, which it was pretty evident were meant to be inculcated, though not explicitly avowed. The exposure gave great offence to the friends and admirers of the two authors, and soon produced a rude and angry tract in reply, written under the title of Observations upon the Analysis, written with considerable acrimony, but no great force of argument.

{[Footnote:] Though the *Analysis* is throughout perfectly free from the least intemperance of language, and never once deviates into the path of ridicule or abuse, yet has Lord Woodhouselee, in his Life of Lord Kames, (Vol. 1. p. 142.), with equal inattention and injustice, mentioned it as "written in a similar strain" with a book just before characterised by him as "attempting a refutation of Mr Hume's opinions, in a strain of course and vulgar ridicule, and with a petulance and scurrility which disgraces the cause he endeavoured to support." The angry zeal of his Lordship in this passage, against works, sincerely *intended* at least, for the defence of Christianity, appears somewhat unaccountable, and cannot but excite surprise. His censure of the book to which it is directly applied might justly be disputed, but, as applied to the *Analysis*, nothing can be more ill founded, or remote from the real character of the work. The *Analysis* does not even profess to attempt *refutation* of any opinion; it merely proposes to *exhibit*, and in that exhibition gives in proof, the words and ideas of the authors themselves. With what pretensions to justice, then, could such a sweeping sentence of condemnation be passed upon it? Had Lord Woodhouselee never read the work, or entirely forgotten what it contained, and only concluded, that as it was written on the same side, it either must be, or at least ought to be, represented as written in a similar strain with the one so violently condemned? His Lordship asserts, that the 'Observations' were generally attributed to Dr Blair; a most improbable supposition, as must be obvious on the least attention to the spirit in which they are written; the tenderness of the author of them for the reputation of writers unfriendly to Christianity, being strikingly contrasted with his eagerness to depreciate its defenders.}

---

[1] I thank Richard B. Sher for bringing this item to my attention.

10
THOMAS WALKER:
"A LETTER ON SOPHO'S
DOCTRINE OF NECESSITY"

[Thomas Walker], "A Letter on Sopho's Doctrine of Necessity," *Scots Magazine*, September 1755, Vol. 17, pp. 417–425. Selections.

S cottish clergyman Thomas Walker (1704–1780) was minister of Dundonald and author of *A Vindication of the Discipline and Constitutions of the Church of Scotland* (1774). Alexander Carlyle wrote of him that "Walker was a rank enthusiast, with nothing but heat without light" (*Autobiography*, 1910, p. 247). Shortly after excerpts of *An Analysis* and *Observations* appeared in *Scots Magazine* (May 1755, Vol. 17, pp. 233–243), the journal published a lengthy letter pertaining to the debate in those two pamphlets. The letter itself contains no title, but the table of contents to that issue of *Scots Magazine* refers to it as "A Letter on Sopho's Doctrine of Necessity." The author is unnamed; however, in its May 1756 issue, *Scots Magazine* states that this author is also the writer of the 1756 pamphlet *Infidelity a Proper Object of Censure* – later identified as Walker (see editor's introduction to that pamphlet in this collection). While the bulk of Walker's letter indeed criticizes Home's notion of necessity, the opening specifically targets the *Observations*, and the closing relates the issue to censure of infidel writings by the General Assembly – which are excerpted below. According to Walker, the *Observations* has simply "given up" on Hume and shown the "gross inconsistencies" of Home. He states that the gloss on Home in the *Observations* is a false representation, and of the 109 passages quoted from the *Analysis* the Observator finds fault with only fifteen.

To the author of the SCOTS MAGAZINE.
SIR,
The many professions you have made of impartiality, persuade me, that it is no rule of yours to give infidelity the last word; and therefore, as there is nothing in the three last *magazines* in answer to the *Observations on the Analysis* [233.], I am apt to believe it is because nothing has been communicated to you.

Possibly the author of the *Analysis*, convinced that his quotations will be found fair by every one who with candor and judgment compares them with the *Essays*, thinks the feeble attacks of the *Observator* unworthy his notice. Or perhaps he may be of the opinion which I find entertained by many, that it is not he, but *Sopho*, or Mr *Hume*, who ought to chastise the *Observator*; who, though pretending to be their friend, has so fairly given up the *one*, and exposed the gross *inconsistencies* and *self-contradictions* of the *other*: for to this, and nothing more, do all those passages amount, which the author of the *Observations* has quoted from the *Essays* as favouring the cause of virtue and religion. For if maintaining the most atheistical opinions, be sufficiently atoned for, by sometimes asserting the truths of religion, and that perhaps ironically too, there is not one of the infidel writers, from *Spinoza* to *Lord Bolingbroke*, whose defence of our *Observator* may not with equal success undertake. But whatever may have determined the author of the *Analysis* (who is unknown to me) to be silent; yet there is in the *Observations* such a false gloss put upon things, by a misapplication of words, and confusion of ideas, as without a further examination may mislead some thoughtless readers. This therefore I shall attempt to show, in that article which I take to be of the greatest importance.

Only let me remark in the entry, that the *Observator*, who would be thought the patron of injured truth, and so freely charges falsehood upon others, has oftener than once broke his word; and instead of showing that the propositions were falsely imputed to his *authors*, has entered into the dispute anent the doctrines, though he had told us this was by no means his intention. In making this remark, I am not sensible of having done him the least injustice; though I easily see, that, according to his rules of criticism, even in the little I have said he may charge me with a false quotation; as, upon looking again into his paper, I find he does not say, *his intention*, but *the intention of the following obser-vations*.

To make every one sensible how little ground there is for the gentleman's clamour, I might observe, that of 109 passages quoted in the *Analysis*, he only pretends to find fault with 15, as doing injustice to the author either in sentiment or expression. And how fairly even this is done, will appear, if we examine that very instance of alledged injustice, which has put him into the most extraordinary ferment, and inflamed his zeal to that degree, that *uncandid, dishonest, inquisitorial, detestable, persecuting, artful, insidious, Jesuitical, false,* and *unchristian*, are the softest terms he can use on the occasion. Would any man that ever read *Sopho's Essay* imagine, that all this passion and resentment is occasioned by nothing else but imputing to him the doctrine of *man's being under an irresistible necessity in all his actions?* But the *Analyser*, it seems, in support of this indisputable fact, has, among many other quotations, (several of which, as you observe, are not controverted), in one instance taken the liberty to quote the author's words somewhat more compen-diously than they are in the *Essays*; which the *Observator* represents as the greatest villany; the reader will judge, with what foundation, when he has compared the words as they stand in the *Analysis*, and in the *Essays* themselves; which, for his ease, I here set down. ...

But the lowest and thinnest of all our author's artifices of this sort is his playing with the words *physical* and *moral*. ... How far the gentleman is conscious of the deceit there is in the use of the terms *physical* and *moral*, I will by no means take upon me to say: but as he, and his friend the *Observator*, affect a mighty surprise to find any of the ministers of the church of Scotland offended at his book, which they affirm is so conformable to the doctrine of the *Confession of Faith*; I will venture to say, that their being avowed enemies to his doctrine, is so far from being an impeachment on their understandings, that the very least suspicion of the contrary would be the highest impeachment of their characters, both as ministers of the gospel, and members of this church. – For, not to mention his other tenets, is it possible, that, with regard to our present subject, he does not advert to the consequences he admits, as well as the principles he establishes? – Let it be supposed, that, by shuffling the sense of terms, he had so far confused his own apprehension of things, as to imagine, that the Calvinist doctrine on the liberty of moral agents was the same with his own; and that he had never, either before or since his subscribing, looked into the *Confession of Faith*, where the direct contrary is taught:[1] yet, after all, he can ever persuade himself, that those whose business it is to declaim weekly upon the evil of sin, to press men to repentance and holiness of life, will ever adopt his opinion, that there is no such thing as sin in the world, and that all actions are equally good, and acceptable to God? What villains must he suppose them to be, if they were really of this opinion, and yet continued to preach the gospel?

I confess, that some of our *Shaftsburian* rather than *Calvinist* divines, seem fond of our author's principle of necessity. But it has always been reckoned unfair, to charge even the real and just consequences of a doctrine upon the maintainers of it, while they professed not to see, and expressly renounced them; and this is the case with those amongst us who seem to admit his principles: and I am persuaded, that the impious consequences which he has so fairly drawn, and so readily avowed, will open their eyes, and make them as unanimous in rejecting his principles, as the late general assembly were in passing their act against infidelity [263.], and striking off his name from the roll of their commission; decisions which plainly show, that this Venerable body was far from thinking the charge in the *Analysis* groundless, or the doctrine of an absolute necessity the doctrine of the church of Scotland. – *I am*, &c.

---

[1] "God hath endued the will of man with that natural liberty, that it is neither forced, nor by any absolute necessity of nature determined to good or evil." *Conf. of Faith, chap* 9, § 1.

11
THOMAS WALKER:
INFIDELITY A PROPER
OBJECT OF CENSURE

[Thomas Walker], *Infidelity a proper object of censure. Wherein is shewn, the indispensable obligation that lies upon church-rulers to exercise the discipline instituted by Christ, upon such avowed infidels as have been solemnly initiated members of the Christian church by baptism; and, if irreclaimable, to cast them out of the Christian society.* Glasgow: printed by John Bryce and David Paterson, 1756, 56 p.
Selections.

Thomas Walker (1704–1780) was the author of "A Letter on Sopho's Doctrine of Necessity," contained in this collection. On May 20, 1756, the General Assembly of the Church of Scotland convened, and one of the items under consideration during that session was whether Hume should be censured by the Church for his infidel writings. The issue was sparked the previous year, and two pamphlets – *An Analysis* and *Observations* (both contained in this collection) – were an important part of the dialogue. On May 15, 1756, five days before the General Assembly convened, a pamphlet by Thomas Walker appeared titled *Infidelity a Proper Object of Censure*, which argues that the Church has the right and responsibility to censure infidel writings. *Scots Magazine* printed excerpts of the pamphlet, and mentioned that its author had also penned "A Letter on Sopho's Doctrine of Necessity" which the journal previously printed:

> Our readers have seen a letter written by this author (xvii. 417); and we were favoured with a manuscript copy of the pamphlet several months ago, but we could not insert it, because of its length. [*Scots Magazine*, May 1756, Vol. 18, pp. 223–227]

Writing for the *Monthly Review*, William Rose attempts to stay neutral on the dispute, while praising the author's abilities:

> ... These principles he endeavours distinctly to consider, and advances several sensible things upon the subject: but without taking upon us to

determine any thing concerning the merits of the cause, we shall content ourselves with observing, that he is no contemptible advocate for the cause he pleads, and that he appears to have a strong regard for the interests of religion and virtue. [*Monthly Review*, January 1757, Vol. 16, pp. 95–96]

The following is from the 1756 and only edition of *Infidelity*.

INFIDELITY
THE PROPER
OBJECT OF CENSURE, *&c.*

The publication of infidel writings in *Scotland* is but of late date, and according to the reception it meets with, will certainly have no small influence, either good or bad, upon the interest of religion. The exercise of discipline upon that occasion has been expected and wished for by many who have not hitherto been able to procure it. There is still so much of the shadow at least, or remnant of christian discipline, in this church, that the neglect of it upon this occasion is more sensible, and must therefore be attended with worse consequences, than in other churches who lament the want of it altogether.

In order to excite the rulers of this church to their duty, a small pamphlet was published last year intitled, *An Analysis of the opinions of* Sopho *and* David Hume *Esq*; wherein the irreligious tenets of these two authors were represented in several propositions, and passages quoted out of their books, wherein such propositions were plainly maintained. A reply to this very soon appeared, intitled, *observations on the Analysis,* &c. wherein very grievous, but very groundless complaints, were made of the unfairness of some of the quotations. In the *Scots Magazine* for *September* last was inserted, a letter wherein the most bitter of all the observator's complaints is shown to be without the least foundation: This related to the charge against *Sopho*, of maintaining a necessity that is inconsistent with moral agency. The observator alledged, that he only maintained a moral, not a physical necessity. Altho' this was nothing to the purpose, the proposition being proved in the *Analysis*, from *Sopho*'s own words, without mentioning that distinction: Yet, *ex abundanti*, it was shown in that letter, that the necessity maintained by him is really a physical, not a moral necessity, in the just and proper meaning of these terms. And indeed, that the accountableness of moral agents was, by his principles, overthrown, that gentleman did not (with the modesty of his predecessors) leave it to his readers to infer, but expressly pointed out the inference himself, thereby doing what he could to destroy the whole foundation of religion and morality.

It is not worth while to take notice of the other particular complaints of the Observator. It is acknowledged, that he has shown by some of his extracts, what must be abundantly evident to any intelligent reader of these gentlemen's writings, that they often contradict themselves. His defence indeed amounts to this and no more, upon the propositions charg'd against them in the *Analysis*. But what calls for a more particular discussion is, that not satisfied, perhaps, with his own apology for his clients, he endeavours to screen them from censure, by insisting in the general, that erroneous speculations are not the proper objects of church censure. What he says upon this subject, is contained in the following paragraph.

"The freedom of inquiry and debate, tho' it may have published some errors to the world, has undoubtedly been the source from whence many blessings have flowed upon mankind. As free inquiry alone could at first have made way for Christianity, and have borne down the opposition of synagogues, senates and schools; it is to the same noble principle we owe the Reformation, and are enabled to set at defiance the tyrannical decisions of Popes and Councils. By means of free inquiry, the church of *Scotland* was originally established. In this country, therefore, all attempts to infringe so valuable a privilege in cases where the peace of society is not concerned, must ever be regarded with concern by all reasonable men. The proper objects of censure and reproof are, not freedom of thought, but licentiousness of action; not erroneous speculations, but crimes pernicious to society. Against these ought the Clergy to exert their utmost efforts; and by such a conduct they will more advance the cause of religion, than by engaging in metaphysical disputes, which may perplex the understandings, but never can impair the morals of men."

As it is very probable not only from the conversation one meets with every day, but from the last Assembly's taking no particular notice of these writings, that the Observator is not alone in his sentiments upon this subject; and as they appear to me of the most dangerous consequence, I have been induced to offer to the public, and particularly to the consideration of the ministers of this church, the following enquiry, how far they are founded on reason or scripture. That I may do this the more distinctly, the reader may please to observe, that this author's argument, and indeed all reasoning of the same kind, is founded on the following principles, which I shall endeavour distinctly to consider.

I. *That freedom of enquiry* has led the two gentlemen, proposed to be censured, into the infidel opinions which they have published.

II. That these infidel opinions of theirs *never can impair the morals of men, and that the peace of society is not concerned in them.*

III. That *erroneous speculations are not the proper objects of* church *censure and reproof*, and that such an application of ecclesiastic discipline would *infringe the valuable priviledge of free thinking.* ...

And now to conclude; if there are any who think Christianity indeed in so low a state, that she is past recovery, so brow-beaten and contemptible, that she has no spirit to repel an attack; or if, as at the last assembly, any effort is made, that it will serve only to betray her feeble and languishing vigour to the observation of her enemies, and expose it to the sport of triumphing infidels: if they think, that religion, which at the first, in opposition to all the powers of the world, by the splendor of its miracles, and the brighter splendor of its holiness, and heavenly spirituality, flashed like lightening from one end of the earth to the other; or rather, like an irresistible flame driven by the wind over combustible matter, fired all the countries of the world at once; is now burning with so faint and dim a light, that the least puff of infidel breath is like to blow out the almost expiring flame: if they think that, in a nation, where it has the firmest establishment that *laws* can give it, laws repeated and ratified in the most solemn manner, and made as irrevocable and unalterable as the wisdom of man could contrive, the very *lawyers* of that nation, may reward the boldest attacks upon it, by any office which they have the disposal of; while others, after a treacherous attempt to undermine it, are advanced to the highest places of dignity and authority, without the supreme church judicatory so much as appearing to know of such things; if they think the churches own printer must be allowed to purchase infidel writings at a considerable expence, and publish them to the world, without a single question being asked him on that subject: if they really take the interest of Christianity to be now reduced to so very despicable a situation, that the general assembly itself *dare not* take the least notice of such facts, but is under a necessity to pocket every affront, and dissemble the most open and bare-faced injuries done to *Christ* and his gospel: if this is the view that any of us have of the present state of religion, it will help, in some measure, to account for the dispirited conduct of the church against her open enemies; while her artillery is let fly, with its whole force upon the sincerest Christians who scruple to concur in executing the designs against her spiritual interests, which are acknowledged to have been contrived by those who were far from being her *true*, not so much has even her pretended friends.

But if, on the other hand, it be a greater crime to despair of religion, than it was among the *Romans*, even after the battle of *Cannae*, to despair of the republic: if it be certain that the *church* is *a kingdom that shall never be destroyed* (Dan. ii. 44.), and that *the gates of hell shall never prevail against her* (Mat. xvi. 18.): if the excellency and usefulness of the Christian doctrine, as well as the clearness and certainty of its evidence are such as we have no occasion to be ashamed of, and have always been approved by the *best* and *wisest* men; why may we not, even tho' we wanted that countenance and protection from the laws of men, and human establishments, which, in the goodness of divine providence, we yet have, resume some more spirit, and not *be ashamed to speak with our enemies in the gate?*

If, on the other hand, it be, indeed, a matter of no consequence for the unbelievers to continue in their infidelity, without the least attempt to *pull them out of the fire*: if it be needless, or useless, and can serve no good purpose *to deter others from the like offences*; If indeed a *little leaven* does not *leaven the whole lump*, if there be no danger of the infection spreading among the Christian society, over whom the Holy Ghost has made the rulers of this church overseers: if it is no matter what materials a Christian church is composed of: if the *honour of Christ, and the holy profession of the gospel* is not, in the least stained, by the communication of his name, and the Christian character, to those who would confound the distinction between virtue and vice, who maintain that there was no occasion for the sufferings of the Son of God to pacify his Father's wrath, who was not, and could not be at all offended for what he himself was the real author of, and that he is only deceiving mankind, when their consciences accuse them of sinful actions: if there is no hazard at all of *the wrath of God justly falling upon that church* that suffers the avowed enemies of Christ to be officers in his house, and *his covenant and the seals thereof to be profaned* by those who must think any christian sacrament an idle and ridiculous institution; then, let our present indolence be applauded, and let that lenity be applied to the enemies of Christ, which was denied to his friends.

But if, on the other hand, we have any compassion for the perishing souls of unbelievers; if it is worth the while, either on their account, or the churches, to attempt at least, *to gain our brethren;* if we have any confidence to put in the institutions of Christ for this purpose, and the promises of his countenance that are annexed to them; if the boldness of infidels is grown to such a height, that it requires the most vigorous measures *to deter others from the like offences;* if our dastardly pusillanimity has evidently encouraged the treacherous foes we hug in our bosom to trample upon us with a degree of contempt, which our own fathers could not have conceived an idea of; if *evil communications* will certainly *corrupt good manners*, and *the whole lump* is in hazard of being infected, while *the old leaven is not purged out;* if *the honour of Christ, and the holy professor of the gospel* is exposed to the scorn of the world, by a promiscuous admission to the most sacred privileges of *Christians; if the giving that which is holy unto dogs, and casting our pearls before swine,* does indeed make the persons who are represented under these characters by our Saviour himself, *trample them under their feet,* as well as *turn again, and rend us;* in a word, if such a conduct in church rulers does indeed expose them and the church *to the just wrath of God,* who will not long bear his ordinances to be so grossly profaned, and if the express commands, and institutions of Christ deserve any regard at their hand; then, let some experiment be made of the power and success of his own ordinances, in retrieving our distressed affairs, and reclaiming scandalous and important offenders; or, let his artillery be turned from his friends, and again pointed, as it ought to be, at his obstinate and irreclaimable foes.

12
"AN ACCOUNT OF THE DEBATE UPON THE MOTION FOR CENSURING INFIDEL WRITERS" (*SCOTS MAGAZINE*)

"An Account of the Debate upon the Motion for Censuring Infidel Writers," in *Scots Magazine*, June 1756, Vol. 18, pp. 280–284.
Complete; from *Scots Magazine*.

On May 28, 1755, the Committee on Overtures of the Church of Scotland's General Assembly unanimously passed the following condemnation of recent infidel writings:

> The General Assembly of the church of Scotland being filled with the deepest concern on account of the prevalence of infidelity and immorality, the principles whereof have been, to the disgrace of our age and nation, so openly avowed in several books published of late in this country, and which are but too well known amongst us; do therefore judge it proper and necessary for them, at this time, to express the utmost abhorrence of those impious and infidel principles, which are subversive of all religion, natural and revealed, and have such pernicious influence on life and morals; and they do earnestly recommend it to all the ministers of this church, to exercise the vigilance, and to exert the zeal, which becomes their character, to preserve those under their charge from the contagion of these abominable tenets, and to stir up in them a solicitous concern to guard against them, and against the influence of those who are infected with them.

A year later, after much lobbying by conservative Clergy, on May 27, 1756 the Committee of Overtures began debating whether to recommend that Hume in particular should be officially censured by Church because of his infidel writings. In a 17 to 50 vote, the decision was made not to pursue the matter further. *Scots Magazine* regularly devoted a section of its publication to reprinting some of the proceedings of the General Assembly and its committees.

In the May issue, there appeared a one-paragraph synopsis of the committee meeting regarding Hume:

> It was proposed in the committee for overtures, May 27. that the assembly should take into consideration, how far it was proper for them, to call before them, and censure, the authors of infidel books, particularly Mr David Hume. Next day an overture to the purpose was produced in the committee, and read. In opposition to this it was moved, that the committee should come to a resolution to the following purpose: That though all the members have a just abhorrence of any principles tending to infidelity, or to the prejudice of our holy religion; yet, on account of certain circumstances in this case, they drop the overture, because it would not, in their judgment, serve the purpose of edification. After debate, the question was put, Transmit the overture to the assembly, or not? and it passed in the negative, Transmit 17, Not 50: so that the resolution was agreed to. [*Scots Magazine*, May 1756, Vol. 18, pp. 248–249]

Because of strong public interest in the particulars of the debate, though, in the next month's issue *Scots Magazine* printed a more detailed account, supplied by an unnamed member of the committee. Almost a century later, this account from *Scots Magazine* was included with some alteration in the *Annals of the General Assembly of the Church of Scotland from … 1752 to … 1766* (Edinburgh, John Johnstone, 1840), pp. 86–92. The following is taken from *Scots Magazine*, and differences in the version from the *Annals* are presented in footnotes. A lengthy alternative account of the meeting was penned, though never published, by Robert Wallace (1697–1771), a member of the moderate clergy who opposed censuring Hume. The manuscript bears the title "The Necessity or Expediency of the Churches Inquiring into the Writings of David Hume Esquire" and is dated 1756. Excerpts from Wallace's account appear in Ernest Mossner's *Life of David Hume* (1980), pp. 348–352.

An account of the debate upon the motion for censuring infidel writers.

As we gave in our former *magazine* a very particular account of all the causes that came before the assembly itself, and made but slight mention of a motion made in the committee of overtures, and debated there at two successive diets, we find many of our readers are desirous of having a fuller account of that debate; as, though it came not to the assembly itself, it was of more importance than many things that did, and may possibly be resumed in some future assembly. We have therefore procured the following account from one who was a witness to the whole.[1]

---

[1] [In place of this paragraph, the *Annals of the General Assembly* opens with the following paragraph: "Some members of Assembly, not satisfied with the general

After a few general observations upon the importance of a strict and regular discipline to the purity of the Christian church, it was moved, That the assembly should be desired to take notice of some of the infidel writings published of late in this nation, and their authors; and lest it should be found difficult or improper to make it too general, it was proposed to confine the inquiry at present to one, *viz*. David Hume, Esq; because he had publicly avowed his writings, at least some of the most offensive of them, by prefixing his name. This motion was seconded, and some paragraphs of the confession of faith and form of process were read, asserting the propriety, and appointing the exercise of discipline in such cases. In a short time a written overture was given in and read; the substance of which was as follows. "The general assembly, judging it their duty, to do all in their power to check the growth and progress of infidelity; and considering, that as infidel writings have begun of late years to be published in this nation, against which they have hitherto only testified in general, so there is one person, styling himself *David Hume, Esq;* who hath arrived at such a degree of boldness, as publicly to avow himself the author of books containing the most rude and open attacks upon the glorious gospel of Christ, and principles evidently subversive even of natural religion, and the foundations of morality, if not establishing direct Atheism: therefore the assembly appoint the following persons ___ ___ ___ as a committee to inquire into the writings of this author, to call him before them, and prepare the matter for the next general assembly."

To this motion a strenuous opposition was made, and a variety of objections were raised, which we shall enumerate as far as they were recollected by our correspondent, and then shall give the answers made to them by the supporters of the overture.[2]

1. It was said, many members had not read the writings in question, and so could not judge of them.

2. It was often alledged, That it could serve no good purpose; that it was not to be imagined that prosecution or censure would convince him, or make him change his opinions, in which he seemed to be so firmly rivitted.

declaration against *infidel writings*, which had been passed the former year, (see p. 58,) proposed, in the committee of overtures, that a special censure should be directed against certain infidel *writers*. The controversy had been carried on since last Assembly; and not long before the present meeting, a pamphlet had appeared, with the title '*Infidelity a proper object of Censure*.' Though the matter did not come into debate in the Assembly itself, yet as the discussion in committee excited much interest at the time, we shall here insert an account of it, which appeared soon after: –"]

[2] [In place of this paragraph, the *Annals of the General Assembly* reads as follows: "To this motion a strenuous opposition was made, and a variety of objections were raised."]

3. It was said by some, That it would be a long and difficult inquiry, and would lead to the discussion of many philosophical opinions; the meeting was put in mind of the many long and fierce debates that had been in the Christian church about fate, free will, &c.; so that the affair, if entered upon, might last many years, and become in a manner the sole business of the assembly.

4. It was alleged, That the writings of Mr Hume contained opinions that every man of common sense detested; that they were so gross, and so evidently false, that they could not do any harm; that it would be doing them too much honour to take such public notice of them.

5. It was alleged, That however wrong his opinions were, his writings were mostly of an abstract and metaphysical kind, very little intelligible to the bulk of people; and therefore, as little danger could arise from them, so liberty of judgment ought to be allowed; and they were not proper objects of censure, which ought rather to be applied to practical errors, and things more immediately criminal.

6. It was alleged, That it would greatly please the man himself, and promote the sale of his book. Here some stories were told, how booksellers had artfully solicited the authoritative condemnation of books, in order to get them off their hands. And it was represented by some, as very dangerous thus to spread such writings, and bring them into the hands of common or country people, who would not otherwise have looked into them; and the consequences of this were painted very strongly.

7. It was insisted on by many, That Mr Hume could not be said to be a Christian at all; that he had openly and publicly thrown off the profession of it, and therefore was one of those who in scripture-language *are without*, and so not proper objects of Christian discipline.

The reader will, we hope, be sensible, that these arguments were not all used at once, nor perhaps in the same precise order as here represented; but we have chosen to enumerate them in this manner, that we might bring our account within some compass; and they are classed in the order in which they were brought forth in the debate, as nearly as could be recollected.[3]

Some of the supporters of the overture observed, in general, that several of the arguments used against their proposal, contradicted one another: that whilst some pretended to foretel, that it would lead the assembly into so long and intricate a debate, as would be almost endless; others affirm, that the writings are so gross, and evidently false, that they can do little or no harm: that some say they are so abstract and metaphysical, that they can have little connection with morals; others, that we ought to beware of exciting curiosity,

[3] [The *Annals of the General Assembly* does not include this paragraph.]

and spreading a very dangerous poison: all of which assertions could not be true, as being mutually destructive of each other.

More particularly, to the *first* objection it was answered, That it was the weakest imaginable in this case; since no sentence was immediately craved, but an inquiry proposed; for which purpose a general *fama* of the pernicious tendency of the writings, and the information of such members as had read them, was abundantly sufficient.

To the *second*, That it was a presumptuous limitation of almighty power, to affirm, that any man was incapable of being reclaimed; and that discipline, even carried to excommunication, being one mean appointed in scripture for this purpose, ought to be tried. Besides, that reclaiming offenders themselves was far from being the only, perhaps not even the chief end of the exercise of discipline; which was, to preserve others from infection, and deter them from offending.

In answer to the *third*, It was denied that there could be any difficulty or intricacy in finding the pernicious tendency of principles levelled against the very foundations of morality.

To the *fourth*, which is diametrically opposite to the former, it was answered, That the grossness of the wickedness of his assertions made it so much the greater scandal, that such a person should continue to wear the Christian name; and that as human nature is exceeding corrupt, it might tempt many to think light of the Christian character, when they saw it prostituted and left open to the possession of those who were so unworthy of it.

To the *fifth*, That whatever metaphysical turn Mr Hume might have shewn in some of his writings, the passages complained of were of the plainest, as well as the grossest kind. That liberty of judgment in doubtful matters was very necessary in the present state of human nature; but it was very strange, that men could not see the absurdity of supposing, that a good thing cannot be spoiled by excess, or wrong applied; that a man may say the most immoral things, and defend immorality, and if it be only called an opinion, it must not be considered as a crime. But why are visible crimes an object of censure or church discipline? Is it not because they are a proper evidence of a wicked heart? And is not an open profession of wickedness of heart also an evidence of it? Is an act of whoredom or of theft censurable in the professed Christian? and is it not censurable to deride chastity, and refuse its obligation; and to affirm that all justice is founded on power and conveniency? These are not metaphysical or intricate opinions, but errors having the most certain and immediate influence upon practice. Formerly it was thought sufficient to say, that forbearance is to be used in small matters, but that to overthrow the great doctrines of morality, by which society subsists, demands punishment even by the civil power; whereas now we have lived to see the grossest immorality taught and subscribed, and then defended, as freedom of inquiry. It was also observed, that if people would reflect upon the nature of church-discipline, it would appear quite absurd to consider it as any restraint upon liberty. It is not punishing men in their bodies, not even hindering them to publish their opinions; but only hindering them from injuriously possessing that to which they have no right, *viz.* the Christian name.

To the *sixth* objection it was answered, That it was not certain whether it would give the gentleman much pleasure, if it should issue in his excommunication, and this publicly intimated, and his gross assertions narrated as the cause of it; and that it would not spread his writings much among any but those who would be in least danger of infection.

But upon this, and indeed with respect to all the preceding objections, it was insisted by the friends of the overture, That as they could produce not only the confession of faith and form of process, but express passages of scripture, requiring, under strong and awful sanctions, the exercise of discipline against the maintainers of false and pernicious opinions, nothing could be more weak, than to produce human conjectures against the expediency of it. And as the meaning or application of those passages had not been debated by any who had spoke upon the point, they asked, How, as an ecclesiastical court, the assembly could excuse themselves for a direct refusal to comply with an express command of Christ?

To this there were two or three replies made. 1. It was said by one, with whom indeed it did not appear that any body concurred, That the exercise of discipline in a strict and vigorous manner might be a duty when the church was pure, and offenders few; but would any man say, that when the church was greatly corrupted, and offenders very numerous, all who deserved censure by the rules of the gospel ought to have that censure inflicted upon them? That if this were the case, it would reduce the church to a very small number. – Some of the supporters of the overture affirmed, That they had, and would follow no other rules of censure, but the rules of the gospel; and that however great a reduction this might cause in the number of the church, no greater number had any title to be in it.

2. It was said, That discipline was not of the nature of duties which were always binding independent of their consequences, but was a duty or not according to its apparent expediency. – In opposition to this, it was denied that any such licence was given in scripture; and it was affirmed, that, on the contrary, the universal and impartial application of it was its chief excellence, and did most contribute to render it successful.

But, 3. the chief reply to the requisition was that we have mentioned above, as the *last* objection against the overture, *viz.* That Mr Hume really is no Christian, has not so much as the profession of it, and therefore is to be considered as one that is *without*, and so not a subject of Christian discipline.

This was the objection most insisted upon; and with a discussion of it by mutual interrogations, the debate was closed, pretty much as follows.[4] The friends of the overture allowed, that one who was not in any sense a member of the visible church, was no subject of discipline; but they observed, That whatever gross crimes Mr Hume had committed, he had neither been formally excluded by a sentence, nor had excluded himself by any formal declaration; that he had not renounced his baptism; that he frequently in his writings ranks himself among professing Christians, saying, OUR *holy religion*, &c.; and however plainly these words are used in a way of contempt and derision, it the more shews the necessity of a visible separation; That professing Christians did ordinarily hold voluntary unnecessary communication with him, and even ministers were seen freely conversing with him, which it is presumed they would not do if he were formally excluded. It was returned, That though he had not said in express words that he was no Christian, he had said it as publicly, and as strongly by other forms of expression; that he was generally considered in this light; and that Christians were supposed to frequent his company, in order to his reformation. The supporters of the overture then said, if the court would give it as their judgment, that he was no Christian, and so no subject of discipline, and make this any way public, they were satisfied. They were then asked, whether they could in reason demand, that such a sentence should be passed, when the person had not been before them, nor any regular inquiry into his crime? They answered, That they did not demand it, and therefore had proposed in inquiry, but had spoke what is above as the consequence of the reasoning of their adversaries; and retorted the question, how they could so often use their reasoning, and apparently form their own upon, and influence the judgment of others by an argument which they refused to assign as the ground of their sentence? To this it was said by one, That he said it not as his own opinion, and perhaps had formed no opinion upon it; but that the overture itself represented Mr Hume as no Christian, and so ought not to be transmitted, as proceeding upon a supposition which rendered its own demand unnecessary; for whoever is guilty of such things as are there laid to his charge, certainly is no Christian. It was then replied, That it in no other way represented him as no Christian, than by saying, he deserved to be excluded from that character; it complains that he retains the Christian name, when he had forfeited all right to it: that, according to this way of reasoning, no person ever could be censured or excluded by a sentence; for as soon as he has been guilty of any thing that deserves it, he is no Christian, and so must be left to himself.

---

[4] [The *Annals of the General Assembly* rephrases this sentence as follows: "This was the objection most insisted upon; and, with a discussion of it by mutual interrogations, the debate was closed, pretty much as follows: – ".]

The debate ended with this. The vote was stated, and carried as we have marked. We shall only observe, that it was carried on with abundance of decency, without violent altercation or personal reflections, and was not introduced into the assembly.[5]

---

[5] [In place of this paragraph, the *Annals of the General Assembly* reads as follows: "The opposers of the overture moved, that the committee should come to the following resolution, viz., 'That though all the members have a just abhorrence of any principles tending to infidelity, or to the prejudice of our holy religion, yet, on account of certain circumstances in this case, they drop the overture, because it would not, in their judgment, serve the purpose of edification.' | The debate lasted for two days; but though characterised by Lord Woodhouselee as 'very keen,' the reporter says 'it was carried on with abundance of decency, without any violent altercation, or personal reflections.' The vote was at last put, *Transmit* the overture to the Assembly, or *Not*, and it passed in the negative; *Transmit*, 17, – *Not*, 50; and the above resolution was agreed to." The *Annals* continues describing the complaint against Henry Home's publisher that was raised before the Presbytery of Edinburgh by Reverend George Anderson.]

JOHN HOME'S *DOUGLAS*: 1757

13
REVIEW OF *DOUGLAS*
(*CRITICAL REVIEW*)

Review of John Home's *Douglas, a Tragedy*, in *Critical Review*, March 1757, Vol. 3, pp. 253–268.
Selections.

The *Critical Review* was founded in 1756 by Scottish novelist and historian Tobias Smollett (1721–1771) and printer Archibald Hamilton. Smollett previously reviewed for the *Monthly Review* – which had been in publication since 1749 – and he modelled his new journal after the successful format of the *Monthly*. For the next half-century, the two journals competed with each other for dominance, although the *Monthly Review* was always slightly in the lead in terms of sales. Like the *Monthly* and virtually all early review journals, reviews in the *Critical* appeared anonymously. Rumours circulated that Smollett himself authored the journal's review of Home's *Douglas* – a contention which Smollett denied in a letter of June 4, 1757 to J. Moore. The review notes that Hume "whose name is certainly respectable in the republic of letters, made it absolutely necessary" to expose the play's flaws because of his exaggerated dedication. *Scots Magazine* printed Hume's "Dedication," followed by the reviews of Home's *Douglas* in the *Critical Review* and the *Monthly Review* (*Scots Magazine*, June 1757, Vol. 19, pp. 293–298).

ART. VII. DOUGLAS, *a Tragedy*. 8vo. *Pr.* 1s. 6 d. Millar.

'The noble tragedy of *Douglas* (*says the celebrated Mr.* David Hume) is one of the most interesting and pathetic pieces that was ever exhibited on any theatre: should I give it the preference to the *Merope* of *Maffei*, and to that of *Voltaire*, which it resembles in its subject, should I affirm, that it contained more fire and spirit than the former, more tenderness and simplicity than the latter, *I might be accused of partiality*.'[1]

---

[1] See his dedication to the Rev. Mr. *Hume*, prefixed to the four dissertations lately published.

And so indeed, in our opinion, *he might* with great justice: for though we are ready to allow much to the bias of friendship and affection, yet would we beg leave to put this author in mind, that there is also something due to truth, taste, and judgment, which we cannot think any man hath a right to sacrifice, even to the most intimate private connections. We would gladly admit with Mr. *David Hume*, that there is a great degree of merit in his friend's performance, which we shall point out by and by; but at the same time will venture to assert in opposition to him,[2] that the author of *Douglas*, is as far from *Shakespear* and *Otway*, as *London* is from *Edinburgh*, or the banks of *Avon* from the river *Tweed*, as will sufficiently appear to any impartial reader, who shall attentively consider the intrinsic merit of this piece, unseduced by the glare of dress, the force of action, and every other ornament merely theatrical.

To form a proper judgment of the whole it is necessary to examine separately the several distinct parts of it, *viz.* the fable, characters, sentiment, and diction. ...

The lines above quoted may for ought we know be much extol'd by some critics, and Mr. *David Hume* may if he pleases call them, a close imitation of nature, and a pattern of true simplicity: We should notwithstanding rather be inclin'd to rank them in the number of vulgarisms, and much beneath the dignity of tragical expression.

Douglas, upon the whole with all its imperfections, (and what piece is without some?) is infinitely superior to *Barbarossa*, *Athelstan*, and the rest of those flimsy performances with which we have been visited for some years past: And if the author is careful to improve that genius for dramatic writing, which is visible in this essay, we have reason to expect something that may do still more honour to the *English* stage. We should not indeed have dwelt so long on the little obvious faults to be found in this tragedy, had not Mr. *David Hume*, whose name is certainly respectable in the republic of letters, made it absolutely necessary. – Every addition of praise to any work beyond its real and intrinsic merit, will always be found in the end prejudicial to it, as the same moisture which feeds and nourishes the plant, if poured on it in too great abundance may overwhelm and destroy it. ...

---

[2] 'You possess (*says Mr. D. Hume*) the true theatric genius of *Shakespear* and *Otway*, refined from the unhappy barbarism of the one, and licentiousness of the other.'

14
OLIVER GOLDSMITH:
REVIEW OF *DOUGLAS*
(*MONTHLY REVIEW*)

[Oliver Goldsmith], Review of John Home's *Douglas, a Tragedy*, in *Monthly Review*, May 1757, Vol. 16, pp. 426–429.
Selections.

According to Benjamin Christie Nangle's *Monthly Review First Series: 1749–1789* (1934), the reviewer of the article on Home's *Douglas* was Oliver Goldsmith (1730?–1774). Born in a small village in the county of Longford, Ireland, Goldsmith was the son of a minister and the sixth of nine children. An uncle funded his schooling at Trinity College, Dublin. He later studied law and medicine and, after a series of minor jobs, he established himself as an author, first writing for periodicals, and later publishing poems, novels and historical works. Goldsmith gave a mixed review of *Douglas* in the *Monthly Review*, which concludes noting that Hume's flattering Dedication built up expectations that the play could not fulfil when it was produced in London. His review was reprinted in *Scots Magazine* (June 1757, Vol. 19, pp. 293–298).

ART. VII. DOUGLAS, *a Tragedy*. 8v. Pr. 1 s. 6*d*. Millar.

When the town, by a tedious succession of indifferent performances, has been long confined to censure, it will naturally wish for an opportunity of praise; and like a losing Gamester, vainly expect every last throw must retrieve the former. In this disposition, a performance with but the slightest share of merit, is welcomed with no small share of applause; its pettiness exalt us into rapture; and the production is compared, not with our idea of excellence, but of the exploded trash it succeeds. Add to this, that the least qualified to judge, are ever foremost to obtrude their opinions; ignorance exclaims with excess of admiration; party roars in its support; and thus the trifle of the day is sure to have the loudest voices, and the most votes in its favour: nor does it cease to be *the finest piece in nature* till a newer (and consequently a finer) appears, to consign it to oblivion.

Do these men of applause, who can so easily be brought

To wonder with a foolish face of praise!

deserve our envy, or our censure? If their raptures are real, none but the ill-natured would wish to damp them; if fictitious, stupidity only can sympathize with their pretended felicity.

To direct our taste, and conduct the Poet up to perfection, has ever been the true Critic's province; and tho' it were to be wished, that all who aim at excellence would endeavour to observe the rules he prescribes, yet a failure in this respect alone, should never induce us to reject the performance. A mechanically exact adherence to all the rules of the Drama, is more the business of industry than of genius. Theatrical lawgivers rather teach the ignorant where to censure, than the Poet how to write. If sublimity, sentiment, and passion, give warmth, and life, and expression to the whole, we can the more easily dispense with the rules of the Stagyrite; but if langour, affectation, and the false sublime, are substituted for these, an observance of all the precepts of the antients, will prove but a poor compensation.

We would not willingly have applied this last observation to the performance now before us; but when a work is obtruded upon us, as the consummate picture of perfection, and the standard of taste,

Ne, quodcunque volet, poscat sibi fabula credi!

Let candour allow this Writer mediocrity now; his future productions may probably entitle him to higher applause.

With respect to his present tragedy, we could, indeed, enter on a particular examen of the beauties or faults discoverable in the diction, sentiment, plot, or characters; but, in works of this nature, general observation often characterizes more strongly than a particular criticism could do; for it were an easy task to point out those passages in any indifferent Author, where he has excelled himself, and yet these comparative beauties, if we may be allowed the expression, may have no real merit at all. Poems, like buildings, have their point of view, and too near a situation gives but a partial conception of the whole. Suffice it, then, if we only add, that this tragedy's want of moral, which should be the groundwork of every fable; his unfolding a material part of the plot in soliloquy; the preposterous distress of a married Lady for a former husband, who had been dead near twenty years; the want of incidents to raise that fluctuation of hope and fear, which interests us in the catastrophe; – are all faults we could easily pardon, did poetic fire, elegance, or the heightenings of pathetic distress, afford adequate compensation: but these are dealt to us with a sparing hand.

However, as we have perceived some dawnings of genius in this Writer, let us not dwell on his imperfections, but rather proceed to shew on what particular passages in his performance we have founded our hopes of his brightening, one day, into stronger lustre. ...

It may not be improper to observe, before we take our leave of this performance, that it was first acted with great applause in Edinburgh; but made its appearance in England under a peculiar disadvantage: the commendation a man of taste and learning had bestowed on it, previous to its representation here, perhaps raised too much expectation in some, and excited a spirit of envy and critical prejudice in others. Possibly, indeed, that Gentleman, in some degree, sacrificed his taste to his friendship. However, if this was the case, he will sustain no great loss with regard to his reputation, since he may gain as much on the one hand, as he can lose on the other: the worst that can be said, amounting only to this, that the benevolence of his disposition prevailed over the rectitude of his judgment.[1]

---

[1] In the Dedication to his *Four Dissertations*, &c. a work mentioned in the Review for February last, p. 122.

15
THE TRAGEDY OF DOUGLAS ANALYSED

The tragedy of Douglas analysed. London, Printed for J. Doughty, in Paternoster Row, 1757, 5–23 p.
Selections.

A midst the attacks on Home's *Douglas* by London critics, there appeared an anonymous pamphlet titled *The Tragedy of Douglas Analysed*, which defended the play's merits. In fact, the author argues, a close inspection of it will show that Hume's praise was justified. The title page of the work states "Amicus Plato, amicus Socrates, sed magis amica veritas. Englished, I honour Mr. David Hume; but truth more!" The complete review of the pamphlet in the *Monthly Review* is this: "An injudicious and trifling panegyric on this northern tragedy" (*Monthly Review*, May 1757, Vol. 16, p. 454). This pamphlet is discussed by John Hawkesworth in *A letter to Mr. David Hume* (1757) and in the review of *Douglas* in *Literary Magazine*, selections from which are contained in this collection.

THE
TRAGEDY
OF
Douglas ANALYSED.

While so many whispers are propagated by the emissaries of a certain dramatic personage against the *real Tragedy of Douglas*, it is the ingenuous critic's task to rise up in its defence, and put in the most glaring point of light, that not a speck therein may escape the eyes of the malevolent; wherefore it is thought not improper to indulge them with a transcript of the commendatory part of this tragedy, from the very ingenious and tastefully learned Mr. *David Hume*'s Dedication to his friend, the author Mr. *John Hume*; prefixed to his four last published essays.

"I own too, that I have the ambition to be the first who shall in public express his admiration of your noble Tragedy of *Douglas*, one of the most interesting and pathetic pieces that was ever exhibited on any theatre. Should

I give it the preference to the *Merope* of *Maffei*, and to that of *Voltaire*, which it resembles in its subject; should I affirm that it contained more fire and spirit than the former, more tenderness and simplicity than the latter, I might be accused of partiality: and how could I entirely acquit myself, after the professions of friendship which I have made you? But the unfeigned tears which flowed from every eye, in the numerous representations of it on this theatre; the unparalleled commend which you appeared to have over every affection of the human breast: These are incontestable proofs, that you possess the true theatric genius of *Shakespear* and *Otway*, refined from the unhappy barbarism of the one, and licentiousness of the other."

This virtuous glow of friendship, by whose intensity each squinting *Zoilus* affects to be offended, and turn aside from, shall be made appear not to have stretched beyond the bounds of truth; nay, receive additional lustre from a candid examination; in writing which, there is an unspeakable pleasure to herald undoubted merit, and at the same time, silence all malignant dissenters from the respectable authority of Mr. *David Hume*; whose sanction (had any modesty been left among our stage smatterers) ought to have awe-struck unlettered jabberers, and injudicious criticlings, who are ever guiltless of the praiseworthy foible,

"T'admire superior sense, and doubt their own."

But wordy declarations are vague and inconclusive; can be as easily denied, as advanced, with as much justice and vehemence: therefore let us proceed to proofs; and, that methodically. ...

16
JOHN HAWKESWORTH:
A LETTER TO MR. DAVID HUME

[John Hawkesworth], *A letter to Mr. David Hume, on the tragedy of Douglas; its analysis: and the charge against Mr. Garrick. By an English critic.* London, printed for J. Scott, 1757, 19, [1] p.
Selections; from 1757 edition.

John Hawkesworth (1715?–1773) was a poet, miscellaneous writer, and later superintendent of a women's school. In this attack on Home's *Douglas*, Hawkesworth contends that Hume's "Dedication" set expectations of the play too high, which the play could not realize, thus making Hume's "critical stocks reduced almost to bankruptcy." Hawkesworth also criticises the pamphlet *The Tragedy of Douglas Analysed* (the previous item in this collection) for being "the second part of the same tune" that Hume had begun in the "Dedication." Writing for the *Monthly Review*, Theophilus Cibber's complete review of Hawkesworth's pamphlet is this: "Unless this Critic mends his hand, and very considerably too, it will be of little consequence what country produced him" (*Monthly Review*, May 1757, Vol. 16, p. 454).

A
LETTER
TO
Mr. DAVID HUME.

Sir,
Having for a long time conceived the highest esteem for the variety of your literary merit, a recommendation from you was almost a sanction to pre-engage my implicit approbation. How high were my expectations raised by your dedicatory commendation of *the tragedy of Douglas*; but, alas! how fallen, from seeing its representation: nor has a perusal since won me over as an admirer of it.

Had the tragedy of *Douglas* been ushered into the world as the promise of a dramatic genius, as such it ought to have been received with applause; but its having been forced upon us authoritatively, in competition with all antiquity and the moderns, two obvious effects were produced in the minds of men; to wit, curiosity was excited in some, jealousy provoked in others. I am sorry to inform you, Sir, that in consequence, your *national* judgment has been greatly run upon here, and your critical stocks reduced to almost bankruptcy.

For my part, when I first read your panegyrical paragraph, I for some time hesitated as to the sincerity of it, and could not help reflecting on the passage in *The Art of Sinking in Poetry*, written by your truly ingenious countryman Dr. *Arbuthnot*.

> "Take all the best qualities you can find in the most celebrated heroes; if they will not be reduced to a consistency, lay them *all in a heap* upon him. But be sure they are qualities which your *patron* would be *thought to have*; and to prevent any mistake which the world may be subject to, select from the alphabet those capital letters that compose his name, and set them at the head of a dedication."

But, on a second reading of it, I changed opinion, and have moreover been assured, that what is written you meant, to which, in amaze, I used the famous reply of "*Est il possible*," is it possible?

The four great and revered names, *Maffie, Voltaire, Otway, Shakespear*, which you have employed as supporters of *Douglas*, put me in mind of the statue of *Lewis* XIV. in *Paris*, where the four nations, *Germany, Spain, Holland*, and *England*, are chained round him as vanquished, and lavishly accompanied with all the tokens of subjection. However this may please the national vanity of the *French*, all foreigners with reason laugh at the folly of the design, and unpardonable foppery of the execution.

I respect you too much, Sir, to make any unmannered or indelicate application: such as "All fools admire, but men of sense approve;" and shall impeach you by an evidence whom I dare say will not be objected to, yourself – and from the standard of taste.

> "Strong sense united to delicate sentiment, improved by practice, perfected by comparison, and cleared of all prejudice, can alone entitle critics to this valuable character; and the joint verdict of such, whenever they are to be found, is *the true standard of taste and beauty*.
>
> Just expressions of passion and nature are sure, after a little time, to gain public vogue, which they maintain for ever."

According to this just and admirable doctrine, what is likely to be the fate of *the tragedy of Douglas*? Neglect and oblivion: however illumined for the present by the flambeau, you (forgive the expression,) too partially, or in the mildest terms, too sanguinely, hold before it.

Not satisfied to have preluded to the assured triumph of this tragedy in your dedication, an unprovoked and congenial enforcer of the extravagance of its merit, has been artfully diffused thro' the public under the title of *The Tragedy of Douglas analysed*, a seeming attack, which the disappointed reader finds to be the second part of the same tune you had begun in your dedication, and which is there quoted, in order to be illustrated true in every article; therefore, to join issue the sooner, we shall follow the method therein observed.

...

After the discovery of *Douglas*, he is not thrown into any interesting situation, nor is there any dramatic anxiety throughout, arising from the intricacy of the plot; for from the beginning to the end, it is an uninterrupted downhill green-sword course, entirely against he revolutionary spirit of the scenic laws, which perhaps, (nay, by your miscalled dissertation, or rather dissertatiuncle on tragedy, it appears) you are not acquainted with. We had, however, a right to expect at least, unexceptionable correctness of stile, in a work by you so immoderately praised, not to say, profanely.

I now take leave of *Douglas*, this *aurora borealis* of a tragedy, that had so long corruscated over us from the North, to execute the last part of my task, to wit, to defend Mr. *Garrick*, by disculpating him from a heavy charge, disseminated every where from the drawing-room in *St. James*'s to the night-cellars; which is, that he had the impudence to refuse *The Tragedy of Douglas*, the best play ever acted, not only on the *English* stage, but on any other, ancient or modern.

The author not only absolves, but apologises for Mr. *Garrick* by his motto.

Non ego sum vates, sed prisci conscius ævi.
"I am not a poet; but well read in old ballads."

Mr. *Garrick* acquiesced to the former part of his confession; and told him that but poor materials for the stage could be derived from the latter. this is the upshot of his crime. Has he then deserved all the foul-mouthed abuse that has been lavished on him? I think not, who am not partial to him.

The pulpit and clergy of *Scotland* are irreverently treated in the *analysis*, which ends with a bullying line, that might waggishly be retorted, to wit,

The blood of *Douglas* will *defend* itself.

That is, people will keep aloof from it; because,

Nemo impune lacessit.
No body rubs to it with impunity.

The Drift of the whole being now seen thro'; with a dislike to your partiality, but esteem and veneration for your *genius* and erudition,
I am, Sir,
Your, &c.

17
REVIEW OF *DOUGLAS*
(*LITERARY MAGAZINE*)

Review of *Douglas*, in *The Literary Magazine: or Universal Review*, 1757, Vol. 2, pp. 126–141.
Selections.

The short-lived *Literary Magazine* was founded in 1756 by Samuel Johnson, and concluded publication in 1758. The January 1757 issue of the magazine printed the Presbytery of Edinburgh's "Admonition and Exhortation" against stage plays, which was prompted by Home's *Douglas*. The magazine also printed Hume's Dedication to Home from *Four Dissertations*, which it introduced with the following:

> This exhortation was occasioned, as we have already observed, by the greatness of the crouds who flocked for many successive nights to see the tragedy of *Douglas* acted. The best account of this dramatic piece with which we can at present gratify curiosity is contained in Mr. *Hume*'s dedication of his *Four Dissertations*, &c. which is in itself such a genteel composition that we insert it entire. [*Literary Magazine*, 1757, Vol. 2, pp. 87–90]

The *Literary Magazine* subsequently presented a favourable review of Home's *Douglas*, mentioning Hume's role in announcing the play to the world. The author discusses the views in two pamphlets on the subject – *The Tragedy of Douglas Analysed* and John Hawkesworth's *Letter to David Hume* (selections from which are contained in this collection). However, the author seems to confuse details about each of these pamphlets, particularly their titles.

DOUGLAS, *a Tragedy, as it is acted at the Theatre Royal in* Covent-Garden. Millar.
Non ego sum vates, sed prisci conscius ævi.

This piece bears a resemblance in some of the circumstances to the famous tragedy of *Merope* of *Maffei* in *Italian*, and *Voltaire* in *French*, and hath been pronounced by Mr. *David Hume*, author of many ingenious essays, and of the history of *great Britain*, to be greatly superior to both. We shall not take up the time of our readers with a controversy concerning this decision of that justly admired writer, but shall leave that matter to the discussion of those extraordinary pamphleteers who have drawn their quills on the occasion. One of them, in a letter to Mr. *David Hume*, is a warm partizan for the superior excellence of *Douglas*, and seems violently enraged that any man should appeal from the decree to his own judgment; he runs a muck at some other modern plays (one of them, we think, of no inconsiderable value) and he tilts at Mr. *Garrick* for having refuted it, though it is acknowledged that many alterations for the better have been made since it was in his hands. His antagonist, on the other hand, treats the play with great contempt, is studious to point out blemishes, aggravates errors, heightens faults into enormities, and *utroque pollice* condemns the piece to die. To these two zealous disputants we chuse to leave full possession of this argument, and shall proceed to give an account of the story or fable, to which we shall beg leave to annex some notes, in which we neither desire to cry out *pulchrè benè rectè*, at every word on the one hand, nor *insule, crasse, illepide*, on the other, but shall impartially speak our sentiments of the performance.

...

But not to multiply instances, we must pronounce that the author of *Douglas* seems to have a correcter taste for the Dramatic art, than any writer that has appeared of late, and from a poet who has given so good a first performance, we may expect that he will rise higher in some future composition, and give us further proofs of that excellent genius, which he seems to possess.

18
JOHN MACLAURIN:
APOLOGY FOR THE WRITERS AGAINST THE TRAGEDY OF DOUGLAS

[John MacLaurin], *Apology for the writers against the tragedy of Douglas.
With some remarks on that play.* Edinburgh, 1757, 3–15 p.
Selections; from 1757 edition.

This anonymous pamphlet is attributed to John MacLaurin (1734–1796),
who, after attending Edinburgh University was admitted advocate in 1756.
He was later appointed senator of the College of Justice. Though MacLaurin
was only twenty-three at the time, from the comments within this work we see
that he was personally acquainted with Hume and Hume's circle of friends. He
gives two anecdotes about Hume, first that Hume marked errors in his personal
copy of Addison's *Spectator*, and, second, that Hume privately said of Home's
Douglas, "he would give the *English* 200 years past, and 200 years to come,
and they would not be able to produce such another tragedy." MacLaurin
attacks not only the quality of Home's *Douglas*, but the judgment of Home's
friends as well, such as Hume, and members of the Select Society, for puffing
it far beyond its true merits.

It is at present often, and justly observed, that the tragedy of *Douglas* has given
birth to more burlesque performances, than any occurrence in *Scotland* ever
did. Most of the authors of these pieces lurk as unsuspected as they could wish;
but some of them are known. As the friends of *Douglas* have thought proper
to attack its enemies with private backbiting and calumny, and ascribed their
writings to the most ungentlemanly designs; it is hoped, the public will allow
them to explain at some length their true motives, and justify their own
conduct, by making a few observations on that play and its admirers.

It has been said, That "spite and envy induced us to ridicule this tragedy; and
that our sole aim was to damp the rising genius of its author." We must be
forgiven to say, that this insinuation is as false as it is injurious. We would have
rejoiced to see a countryman of ours excel in tragedy. We indeed are sorry that
a *Scotch* clergyman has written a play; but we would have admired the tragedy,

had it been good, though we thought it blameable in the author to write one; as *Cæsar* liked the treason, though he hated the traitor.

Some years ago, a few gentlemen in this town assumed the character of being the only judges in all points of literature; they were and still are styled the *geniuses*, and lately erected what they called a *select society*, which usurps a kind of aristocratical government over all men and matters of learning. The first and fundamental maxim of this dictatorial club is, That a punctilious correctness of style is the *summum bonum* of all compositions: though the greatest genius should shine throughout a work, yet if in it is found an unguarded expression, a slip in syntax, or a peccadillo of grammar, *ad piper et farras* with it. Hence *Shakespear* of late is so much decried, that a noted historian, the *Coryphæs* of this society, when disapproving of a wretched sentiment, adds, "What could *Shakespeare* have said worse?"[1] ADDISON, till those gentlemen appeared, was universally esteemed as the finest writer *England* produced; but they

Cast him like an useless weed away.

If you believe them, there are ten errors in every page of his *Spectators*; and the above-mentioned author has a copy of them, in which this decalogue of errors in every page is marked with his own hand. They have taken so great pains to inculcate this doctrine, that now every boy at school, if you praise Mr *Addison*, will perk it in your face, and tell you, that he is not a *correct* writer. Who can, without indignation, behold these men thus corrupting the taste of the country? A punctilious correctness, no doubt, is an accomplishment: but it is no more; nothing is more easily acquired; every blockhead who has the patience to read over dictionaries, grammars, and spelling-books, may atchieve it. But to unite fancy with judgment, the simple with the sublime, and strength of expression with delicacy of thought, is the birthright of him alone

Quem tu, Melpomene, semel
Nascentem placido lumine videris.

It would be improper to spend more time upon a proposition so plain as this. Let the reader compare *Voltaire* and *Hume*, with *Shakespear* and *Addison*, and give the preference to the former if he can.

The Reverend author of *Douglas* was a worthy member of this society; and his tragedy, long before it appeared in public, was, by this society, extolled with all the noise of declamation; and the little merit it has, exaggerated with all the amplifications of bombast. A famous author whom I have mentioned more

---

[1]   *David Hume*, Esq; in his history of *Great Britain*, vol. 1. in a note, after these words.

than once, said, in private, that "he would give the *English* 200 years past, and 200 years to come, and they would not be able to produce such another tragedy:" and the same gentleman has publicly told his namesake, that "he possesses the true theatrical genius of *Shakespear* and *Otway*, refined from the unhappy barbarism of the one, and licentiousness of the other."[2] This author must be forgiven for these rhodomontades; for he frankly owns, that "it is less my admiration of your fine genius, which has engaged me to make this address to you, than my esteem of your character, and *my affection to your person.*" Love, we all know, is blind; and it would be unpolite to blame *Corydon* for running out extravagantly in the praises of *Alexis*. Perhaps the same apology will serve for another learned gentleman, who averred, that "this was the best tragedy in *English*: but indeed, (added he) this is no great compliment; for we have no tragedies in *English*."

What mighty things have not been done by puffing?[3]

We had seen several poems by the author of *Douglas*; which, in the opinion of most people, were very poor ones; one of them particularly[4] is perhaps the worst poem ever was written in this country by a man of liberal education: and it seemed not a little paradoxical to us, that this author's muse, who had miscarreid so often, should have, for her first perfect birth, an *Herculean* boy. When we say this play acted, our expectations were fully answered. Though the friends of the author had puffed it away as a perfect tragedy, yet the very first night convinced them, and every body else, that it was *cross'd and divided with strange-coloured* absurdities; many of which were struck out of it then, and more afterwards, when it was re-reformed at *London*: so that, in one sense, this author has shone *more and more unto the perfect day*. The partisans of *Douglas* maintain, that it is the most perfect tragedy ever was written, and infinitely superior to any tragedy of *Shakespear*'s. We, on the other hand, admit it to be a tolerable modern tragedy: but we contend, that he who likens this author to *Shakespear*, might as well (to use the words of a correct writer) compare a molehill to *Teneriffe*, or a pond to the ocean.[5] The play is at length printed; and the public will judge which of the two opinions is most agreeable to truth.

One of the puffers of *Douglas* says in the newspaper, That, in the *Greek* drama,

---

[2]   See the celebrated dedication, p. 4.

[3]   See *Foot's Tea*.

[4]   The subject of it is a building near *Inverary*.

[5]   See the *Essay on taste*, p. 210. of the four late dissertations.

"no subordinate events are introduced, but what immediately tend to the completion of the principal design: That a play conducted upon this plan, must want the principal requisite to take hold of the minds of an *English* assembly of spectators; and these observations (he says) explain why *Douglas* has not been received with the same warmth with which the ingenious dedicator deservedly speaks of it."

It is not my intention to examine the plot with scrupulous severity; but I would beg to know, what brings *John of Lorn* into the tragedy of *Douglas?* "Who the devil is this *Lardella?*" Does what is said about him *tend to the completion of the principal design?* Every body must see the intention of this; and most people will readily believe, that the success this play has had, is owing, in a great measure, to this absurd and extrinsic episode. Well might the author say,

> – *Flattery direct*
> *Rarely disgusts; they little know mankind*
> *Who doubt its operation; 'tis my key,*
> *And opes the wicket of the human heart.*[6]

The beginning of the 2d Act, is, to a plain man, absolutely unintelligible. In the *dramitis personæ*, as represented at *Edinburgh*, we find

STRANGER. Mr HEYMAN.

Now, it is certain, that here Mr *Heyman* played the shepherd, who is not called the stranger, but the prisoner. In the beginning of this 2d Act, *enter servants and a stranger at one door.* Who is this stranger? The servants say,

> *This man with outcry wild has call'd us forth,*
> *So sore afraid he cannot speak his fears.*

A very odd stranger this! Like *Shirley* in the *Rehersal*, he knows not what to say, or what to do. When we turn the leaf, we find a third stranger, who turns out to be *Norval*; but who the other stranger may be, is a mystery, to explain which, we stand in need of a revelation from *David Hume*, Esq; or some other person of as uncommon sense.

... When Lady *Randolf* died, she lifted up

---

[6] See *Douglas*, p. 41.

– her head
And her white hands to heav'n, seeming to say,
Why am I forc'd to this?

How different is *Ophelia*'s death! She indeed drowns herself, but the excess of her grief had bereaved her of her judgment. *Shakespear*, poor old *Shakespear*, says, that when she fell into the water,

Her cloaths spread wide,
And, mermaid-like, a while they bore her up;
Which time she chaunted remnants of old lauds,
As one incapable of her distress.

But Lady *Randolph* dies like a virago who had carefully perused the late essay on SUICIDE.

...

19
THE USEFULNESS OF THE EDINBURGH
THEATRE SERIOUSLY CONSIDERED

*The usefulness of the Edinburgh theatre seriously considered. With a proposal
for rendering it more beneficial.* Edinburgh: 1757, [4], 12 p.
Selections; from 1757 edition.

While English critics focused on the literary merits of Home's *Douglas* –
and Hume's role as an advocate – conservative Scottish clergy attacked
it on religious grounds. To their way of thinking, the theatre was morally
corrupting and it was scandalous for a clergyman to write or even attend a play.
Public endorsement of *Douglas* by Hume the infidel only made matters worse.
In the Winter of 1757, Adam Ferguson anonymously published a short
pamphlet in defence of his friend John Home, titled *The Morality of Stage Plays
Seriously Considered*. An unusual response to this was the anonymously
published *Usefulness of the Edinburgh Theatre Seriously Considered*, which,
parodying Ferguson's pamphlet, ironically lists several absurd benefits of theatre
productions in Edinburgh. The author suggests that *Douglas* serves as an
excellent substitute for Hume's suppressed essays on suicide and immortality.

THE
USEFULNESS
OF THE
EDINBURGH THEATRE
SERIOUSLY CONSIDERED.

Of the many improvements our country has of late received, none ought to
strike the breast of a *North-British* patriot with so sensible a pleasure, as the
amazing progress we have made in cultivating a taste for amusements and
diversions.

Some years ago the puppet-show, exhibiting a lively representation of *Doctor
Faustus and the Devil*, the *Babes of the wood*, and *Robin Readbreast*, were the
fashionable entertainments of our fine ladies and gentlemen. In that happy
period, the jokes of facetious *Punch*, who had long been obliged to retail his

92

wit to the noisy rabble of a country-fair, were listened to, with the highest satisfaction, by the most polite audience. To him succeeded the seven wonders of
the world, from the wooden plates of *Henry Overton*; the dancing bear; the
wonderful rhinoceros, and arithmetical dog; who were all in their turn
honoured with crouded houses of the *beau monde*. And now, to complete our
happiness, the *tuba* of the ancients (in plain *English* a trumpet), which
proclaimed the arrival of these entertaining creatures, flourishes the entry of a
mighty monarch, or sounds the charge to a bloody battle on the stage.

That such public spectacles, and particularly stage-plays, are of the utmost
consequence to the welfare of every nation, has been allowed by most writers,
who have duly considered the subject, either in a moral or political light. After
their example, I shall endeavour to show, with brevity, and yet I hope with
perspicuity enough to convince the candid and ingenious reader, that the
encouragement given to theatrical entertainments amongst us, is the source of
numberless blessings to this once despised, but now flourishing city. ...

Another advantage peculiar to the *North-British* stage is not so well known,
but no less true. To this we owe the cure of that dark and desperate wound
given through *David*'s sides to the liberty of the press. The public need not now
lament the suppression of his celebrated essay on the *lawfulness of suicide*: This
is more beautifully represented in the character of *Lady Abarnet*, who throws
herself over a rock with more than *Roman* courage. Nor need we mourn the
loss of his incomparable treatise on the *mortality of the soul*, while viewing
Glenalven nobly *risking eternal fire*. It is hoped the next production of our
Reverend author will solace us too for the want of the 'Squire's third and last
essay, on the *advantages of adultery*, that we may have a complete triumph over
the impotent malice of the late Ch___r and B__p of L___n, who murdered
these essays in cold blood.

To this I might add, what is also of some consequence: Our players are no
mercenary hirelings; they act from the most disinterested regard to the good
of mankind, without fee or reward. The richer part of the audience pay, 'tis
true, the fiddlers; but the poorer sort, students and apprentices, &c. have the
benefit of free tickets, when their own and their masters money is exhausted.

There is another advantage that may be reaped from our stage, of greater
importance to the good town than any of the foregoing; which is in short this,
to save the whole revenue of her clergy. When the inhabitants have an opportunity, three times a-week at least, to hear, and *gratis* too, the pure gospel of
Shakespear, of *Sopho*, and *St David*, is it not ridiculous, and contrary to every
rule of good policy, to squander away some thousand pounds, in maintaining
above a score of pragmatical fellows, merely to retail the antiquated gospel of
St Matthew or *St John*, to speak evil of dignities, and bring a railing accusation
against their worthy reforming brethren?

It cannot be pretended that public worship is necessary of a *Sunday*, to pass
away a few hours in seeing and being seen, which might otherwise lie heavy

upon the hands of our fine ladies and gentlemen; for they have already agreed to divide the whole day between Mrs *J___p*'s at *P__st__n_p__ns*, the gaming-table, the tavern, and the drawing-room; and as to the manufacturers and day-labourers, &c. they are to be allowed, you know, the use of fire-arms, at the desire of the c__mm__n of the k__k, for the due sanctification of the Sabbath.
...

20
AN ADDRESS TO THE SYNOD
OF LOTHIAN AND TWEEDALE

*An address to the Synod of Lothian and Tweedale, concerning Mr Home's
Tragedy and Hume's [i.e., Henry Home's] Moral essays.* [Edinburgh, 1757],
8 p.
Selections; from 1757 edition.

The Synod of Lothian and Tweeddale was an ecclesiastical court within the
Church of Scotland. It stood in an intermediary position by considering
appeals from presbyteries beneath them and, in turn, its decisions could be
appealed to the General Assembly. The Synod convened in early May, 1757,
prior to the General Assembly, and addressed the controversy surrounding
Home's *Douglas* – specifically whether ministers should write plays or attend
their productions. An anonymously published speech delivered at the Synod
argues that the Church should censure Home. The author also discusses the
Church's actions the previous year against Henry Home and Hume for their
infidel writings.

---

*An address to the Synod of Lothian and
Tweedale, concerning Mr Home's
Tragedy and Hume's Moral essays.*

Reverend Fathers and Gentlemen,
As you are now met in a synodical way, to cognosce the conduct of your
several presbyteries, and to hear complaints, and to approve or disapprove their
conduct and management concerning what hath been before them since last
synod; you are appointed both by God and man to be watchmen over your
different flocks, and in a synodical way to watch over and inspect the conduct
of one another. ...
    That tragedy of Douglas, composed and sold, in order to be acted by Mr
John Home, hath put such an affront on the church of Scotland, as your
greatest indignation and highest censure will not be sufficient fully to
countervail. Surely such a nonsensical, profane, blasphemous, atheistical piece,

worse was never wrote by any Pagan. How contemptible must the church of Scotland now be in the eyes of other protestant churches! She once their glory, now their reproach. No doubt you have heard what noise and work was at London, what wonder and curiosity it raised to see the monstrous thing, a play wrote by a Scotch clergyman, sold by him to be acted in a public theatre; a monstrous thing indeed, such as was never heard of in the world before.

How do the numerous infidels and profane glory over you, and in you, now when they have got the Scotch clergy on their side? Those that were wont to be so strict in their doctrine and discipline, now many of them scarce differ from them in any thing; as we see an openly professed infidel dedicating his essays (some of which were prohibite printing by the influence of the English clergy, on account of their wickedness) to the now famous Mr John Home, as his dearly beloved friend; telling the world, he differs from him only in a few specu-lative points, which is a thing few, if any, doubt of; neither can the world have any better opinion of such as appear for his vindication and protection. It is well known what intimacy that infidel gentleman hath with many of our clergy, and how much they have befriended him, so as persons cannot help thinking they are no enemies to his principles.

It is owned, some of reputation among the English clergy have wrote tragedies, yet a very rare thing, and what gave offence. But were they so abominably wicked as the tragedy of Douglas? or did they several times leave their charge for many months, travelling from one nation to another, to sell them at a high price, bringing them to statesmen and play-actors to get them acted? ...

I have seen a pamphlet wrote in a smooth sophistical way, proving the morality of the stage, but it can take with none but such as are wilfully blind. It is said to be wrote by a preacher, successor to David Home [i.e., Hume] Esq; the infidel; indeed the author appears to be of the same stamp; and he pretends to prove it from scripture; but by his manner of arguing he will as soon prove the sanctity of the devil by his confessions of the most important truth. ...

The conduct of the presbytery of Haddington will come before you. Notwithstanding the letters sent them by the presbytery of Edinburgh and others, their conduct looks like an approbation of their dear brother. But the truth is, little or no better could be expected of them. It is hoped you will take notice of them, and approve or censure as you find cause.

It is also hoped the conduct of the presbytery of Edinburgh will be laid before you by those faithful ministers who entered their dissent, or by some others who have the glory of God, the interest of religion, and honour of this church, at heart. The presbytery was brought under a kind of necessity to go forward with the process which the deceast worthy Mr Anderson had begun before them concerning Home's Moral essays, because the council for the delinquent not only permitted but desired them, as he knew Mr Home had some many friends among them; yet it surprised some, that they should judicially accept of a pamphlet, said to be wrote by the author of the essays, as an answer to the objections made against them by Mr Anderson and others, and yet never require who the author was.

It is presumed the essays and objections made against them by Mr Anderson and others, learned judicious gentlemen and ministers, with Mr Anderson's verification by many fair and candid quotations from the essays, with the author's answer to them, are known to most of you; as also, what the presbytery of Edinburgh have done in the process. There was indeed some of the presbytery, who before them did read some passages of the essays, and exposed the wicked and blasphemous principles they contained; but the friends of the essays, knowing they were better able to carry their point by votes than arguments, answered nothing. You all know what just ground of offence that book hath given to Christians. It is evident, both by the essays and answers to the objections against them, the author is careful of being suspected to be a Christian: though he sometimes speaks of revealed religion, but though he writes as a philosopher, and not as a theologue, yet by his reasonings he saps the foundation of our Christian faith.

Indeed he appears to be in the dark and bewildered, and knows not how to reconcile himself, yet the most candid interpretation will not allow one to think one of his station to be so weak, as to write in such a way with a good intention. You know, it is the ordinary way of erroneous and heretical preachers and writers, to give and take, to mix and confound truth and error, that so they may stagger, jumble and perplex their hearers or readers, leaving a way to escape to themselves if questioned, and when questioned, do pick out what truth may be found as a salvo for their heresy. He speaks of a feeling, I suppose peculiar to himself, which he calls deceitful, imposed by God, as if rational creatures could not so well be governed without it, and yet makes this deceitful feeling to be the only sure test by which we know the truth of things. Whatever the author's intention might be, evident it is, the scope of those essays in their native tendency would lead the reader to scepticism and infidelity, or as I see it exprest in the introduction of the letter to the presbytery of Haddingtoun, to teach the wicked how to take a short cut with a condemning conscience.

It may be justly expected, that the reverend Synod and assembly will take the consideration of these essays in their own hand, as they are so dangerous and liable to stagger the belief of such as are not well fixed in their principles, and of strengthening the hands of the many infidels, sceptics and profane among us.

It is known, that when the consideration of David Home [i.e., Hume] Esquire's infidel and profane books was laid before, and urged by, some faithful ministers in the committee of overtures, in order to be laid before the last assembly, on the slight pretence that it was the way to make them more sought after, it was rejected; but how did infidels, and the profane, triumph in finding so many ministers befriend them.

However, it is yet hoped there will be found some faithful and zealous members of the ensuing assembly, that will yet get them brought in with the essays, in order that those books may be stigmatized, and the authors censured, especially as one of them is said to be done by an elder of this church.

...

21
JOHN MACLAURIN:
THE PHILOSOPHER'S OPERA

[John MacLaurin] *The philosopher's opera.* [Edinburgh, 1757], iv, 23, [1] p.[1] Complete; from 1757 edition.

In the midst of the sombre controversy surrounding John Home's *Douglas*, a satirical work titled *The Philosopher's Opera* appeared, which lampoons both Hume and Home. Though published anonymously, the author has been identified as John MacLaurin (1734–1796), who is also credited with writing the *Apology for the Writers Against the Tragedy of Douglas*, contained in this collection. In the "Account" of MacLaurin prefaced to the 1798 edition of his collected works, the editor provides background on this piece and explains why he excluded it from that collection:

> There is one piece, of which, since Mr MacLaurin's death, the Editor has discovered he was the Author. – It is entituled the Philosopher, an Opera, in two acts, and is a severe satire against two authors, whose works have done honour to their country, Mr David Hume, the celebrated Historian; and Mr John Home, the well-known author of the Tragedy of Douglas. It was written when that Tragedy first made its appearance. The persecution which the author of Douglas experienced in consequence of the publication of that piece, is well known. Much abuse was levelled against him; and among those who stooped to use the pen of a satirist, was Mr MacLaurin: he was at this time, it must be remarked, a very young man, under the tuition and influence of his mother, who, though possessed of no inconsiderable share of genius, could not be reconciled to the idea of a Minister of the Gospel writing a Play. By her persuasions, it seems, he was instigated to attack the author of Douglas; it is not probable he would have written this satire from any other motive. Though a man may sometimes write to indulge his fancy

---

[1] Title page: THE PHILOSOPHER's OPERA. I *E tenebris tantis tam clarum extollere lumen* I *Qui primus potuisti, illustrans commoda vitæ,* I *Te sequor, O Graiæ gentis decus, inque tuis nunc* I *Fixa pedum pono preffis vestigia signis.* Lucret. I [Price Four Pence.]

without meaning to offend, Mr MacLaurin's liberal mind could never have suffered him thus publicly to attack a man for his opinions, or stop genius in its career, whatever the profession of the author might be; besides, himself a poet, it cannot be supposed he would intentionally injure a man whose works added lustre to poetry. Mr MacLaurin, however, in maturer years, became, in many of his opinions, a disciple of the philosopher, and an admirer of the poet: conscious he had acted wrong in writing this Opera, he never mentioned or wished to see it, and has never been heard to avow it. The author of Douglas is revenged for the unmerited persecution he met with: a generous Prince rewarded his sufferings, and popular applause has sanctioned his fame. Though the publication of this Opera might now give no offence, the writer of such a Tragedy being superior to satire, yet, from respect to the feelings of the living, and the memory of the dead, it is thought more proper not to revive it; and on that account, whatever intrinsic merit it may have, the Editor is determined never to publish it. ["Account of the Life," *The Works of John MacLaurin*, Edinburgh, J. Ruthven, 1798, Vol. 1, pp. 300–302]

In spite of MacLaurin's own attitudes about his youthful composition, it is a well-crafted and humorous critique of Hume and Edinburgh society. MacLaurin even casts actors for the Opera – who were the real actors from the English acting company that performed *Douglas* in Edinburgh. Sarah Ward, who played the lead female role in *Douglas*, is here cast as a minor non-speaking character. As the Opera opens, Mr. Genius (i.e., Hume) confesses his romantic interest in Mrs. Presbytery – an older woman and widow, whose role, according to MacLaurin's fictitious cast list, is played by a man. In the recent past, Genius has been nurturing Presbytery's children, for which she thanks him since now "they swear, they drink, they whore so handsomely." Her son Jacky (i.e., John Home), a young clergyman, has written a play called *Douglas* which Genius helped promote by publishing a flattering dedication to it in one of his books. Genius and Presbytery make plans to attend the play's performance that evening. Meanwhile, Satan and two devils meet in Edinburgh and discuss Satan's recent noticeable absence in that city. Satan previously made little headway there, in spite of his great efforts, but, he says, "the tables were turned, and now almost the whole nation [of Scotland] is my most obedient humble servant." Thus, Satan no longer needs to devote time to Edinburgh, and he is there now to visit Jacky. Disguised as humans, Satan and the two devils enter a tavern where Satan converses with a patron about Genius, who the patron describes as "the best writer against Christianity in Britain." They next converse with a philosopher named "Mr. Moral Sense," who audaciously speaks and acts as he feels (probably an allusion to Henry Home and his account of moral sense in his *Essays*). Genius then enters and gives a synopsis of his philosophy; Satan, though, worries that Genius's nonsense might inadvertently convert people to Christianity. The group leaves to attend the play. After the play, Presbytery and her entourage of young women retire to a drawing room, praising Jacky's work. Genius and Jacky appear, and Presbytery proposes marriage to Genius; he accepts. As the group dances with joy, Satan and his devils arrive wanting to join in, but, no longer disguised as humans, they frighten everyone away. The following is from the 1757 and only edition of *The Philosopher's Opera*.

THE

PHILOSOPHER's

O P E R A.

E tenebris tantis tam clarum extollere lumen
Qui primus potuifti, illuftrans commoda vitæ,
Te fequor, O Graiæ gentis decus, inque tuis nunc
Fixa pedum pono preffis veftigia fignis.　　Lucret.

[Price Four Pence.]

DRAMATIS PERSONÆ
As it ought to be represented at *Edinburgh*.

[MEN.]

SATAN. – *Mr* DIGGES.
SULPHUREO (*Devil*). – *Mr* RYDER.
APOLLYO (*Devil*). – *Mr* DUNCOMB.
Mr GENIUS. – *Mr* LOVE.
Mr MORAL SENSE. – *Mr* LANCASHIRE.
The Rev. Mr MASK. – *Mr* HEYMAN.
JACKY. – *Mr* YOUNGER.

WOMEN.

Mrs SARAH PRESBYTERY, *relict of Mr* JOHN CALVIN. – *Mr* STAMPER.
ANNE, *her waiting-woman.* – *Mrs* DAVENPORT.
Miss SPRIGHTLY. – *Miss* RYDER.
Miss WEEPWELL. – *Mrs* LOVE.
Miss SOB. – *Mrs* STAMPER.
Miss PITY. – *Mrs* HOPKINS.
Miss BLUBBER. – *Mrs* SALMON.
MOLL KITCHEN. – *Mrs* WARD.

———

TO
The READER.

In the Dramatis Personæ *of this opera, there are two characters, and but two, which are not imaginary. Before you pronounce it wrong to point out two men now living, you would do well to consider the scurrilous terms in which they have pointed out two men long since dead and gone. Remember the barbarism of* Shakespear, *the licentiousness of* Otway, *and that the author of* DOUGLAS *has been preferred to both. If (as a later writer will have it) the use of ridicule is "not to investigate known truth, but to expose known falsehood," it is surely as properly employed against the man who avers, that* DOUGLAS *is a faultless play, as it was against the hair-brained knight-errant, who maintained* Dulcinea del Toboso *to be the most beautiful princess in the universe. As this tragedy was written by a* Scotch *clergyman; and as it was the first play he ever had made public, one would have expected that he and his friend would have ushered it into the world, either with a real or affected* modesty: but, on the contrary, they declared the play to be perfect, and the author to be endowed with a genius superior to that of Shakespear and Otway. *The comparison which this extravagant encomium obliged people to make, has opened the eyes of many who were at first prevailed upon to be partial to the play; and induced them to join the impartial men of sense in both kingdoms, who all agree in thinking it a very insipid performance: so that the author of this tragedy does not a little resemble the frog in the fable, who, ambitious to become big as an ox, blew and puffed himself up till he burst.*

The author of the few following pages can't agree with some, who think the little time spent on such compositions as this very ill bestowed. He can't help numbering the tragedy of DOUGLAS, *and the circumstances attending it, amongst the most remarkable occurrences that have ever happened in this country. If* Scotch *clergymen may, with impunity, not only write plays, but go to see them acted here, and absent themselves for months together from their parishes, in order to solicit their representation at* London, *the religion and manners of this country are entirely changed. If* Shakespear *and* Otway *are to be cried down, and the author of* Douglas *set up in their stead, the taste of this country is at an end. Religion will (it is hoped) be the care of those who are paid to support it. But the taste of the country seems to be in a deplorable situation, being abandoned to a club of gentlemen, who are as unable as they are willing to direct it. As some men of learning and character are amongst them, many people are misled by their authority; and more, though they detest their innovations, yet are afraid to contradict them: hence it was that* DOUGLAS *was acted here last winter thirteen times to a numerous audience; but* Othello *(which had not been played here for seven years) brought no house at all. This shews, that the run* DOUGLAS *had here, was owing to the influence of a party; or else, that the people who generally compose the audience in our theatre, are no more judges of the merit of a play, than the chairmen who carry them to see it. It is certainly the duty of every man who regards the honour of his country, to make a stand against that* unhappy barbarism *which the cabal I have already mentioned is endeavouring to establish; and as certainly every man who has felt exquisite pleasure in reading the works of* Shakespear *and* Otway, *makes them but a very ungrateful return, if he tamely looks on while they are hunted down by a set of men who owe their title of* geniuses *to the courtesy of* Scotland *alone.*

———

THE
PHILOSOPHER's
OPERA.

———

ACT I.

A drawing-room.

Curtain draws, and discovers Mrs Sarah Presbytery *sitting in an easy chair;* Anne *waiting.*

Mrs Pr. And did Mr *Genius* talk to you in that manner, *Annie?*

An. Indeed the gentleman told me, Madam, that he was desperately in love with you; that he would be miserable, nay, that he would die, if you refused to put him in possession of your fair person; and that he was to throw himself at your feet this afternoon.

Mrs Pr. Fie upon the joker; he has been diverting himself, and playing upon you, *Annie.*

An. O, not at all, Madam; what should make you think so?

Mrs. Pr. Alas! *Annie,* I am not young now.

An. Young! Madam, what then? he is not young himself. Young! why, there was Lady *Randolph;* I'm sure she was not young; and yet you see how the men teased her, poor lady!

Mrs Pr. Alas, *Annie,* I am now about 200 years of age; but Lady *Randolph* broke her neck before she had lived half a century. Go, thou flatterer, thou knowest he has captivated my heart; this, this only, makes you speak so, and give the name of love to what you know to be waggery.

An. In my conscience, Madam, I believe him to be over head and ears in love with you. Consider, Madam, that kissing goes by favour. Besides, Mr *Genius,* in his thoughts, words, and actions, has no resemblance to other men; so that you might be his flame, Madam, though you were as old as *Methusalem.*

Mrs Pr. There is something in what you say, *Annie.* O the lovely *Adonis,* his sholders, his legs, his belly! – But why should I attempt to enumerate his charms? every limb of him is bristled with the darts of love; and would to God I had never seen the too amiable porcupine.

AIR I. Can love be controul'd by advice?

The goddess who sable Night rules,
From Phœbus *purloins all her light;*
So I make opticians my tools,
And borrow from glasses my sight.

Great Genius, *for whose love this sigh,* [*sighs.*]
  Was surely created for me,
His limbs are so bulky that I
  Their beauties sans *spectacles see.*

An. Madam, there is the gentleman.

Enter Mr Genius.

Mr Gen. If Mrs *Anne,* Madam, has delivered that message which I begged her to carry from me to your Ladyship, you will not be surprised, I hope, at this piece of intrusion.

Mrs Pr. Sir, *Annie* has been telling me of a very odd conversation she had with you this forenoon; but I would have you to know, Sir, that I will not be made a jest of by you or any man.

Mr Gen. How you mistake my intentions! there is not a man in the world more sensible of the great deference and respect due to you, Madam, than I am. Jest! – be assured, Madam, [*kneeling*], that you see at your feet a man who is determined to live or die as you receive him.

Mrs Pr. Rise, Mr *Genius*; if you are serious, I am sorry for you; but I flatter myself, you will soon perceive the oddity of your passion, and the absurdity of your choice. The cheek of the town-lady may vie with the lily, that of the milkmaid with the rose; but mine, Sir, can be compared to neither. To use my son *Jacky's* words: – "In me thou dost behold – The poor remains of beauty once admir'd." Age has deadened the glance of my eye, overcast my features with a melancholy languor, and ploughed my forehead into a multiplicity of wrinkles.

Mr Gen. Pardon me, Madam; age has given to your eye a philosophical sedateness, to your features a languishing air, which girls in vain affect; and in what you call wrinkles, Madam, I see the little loves and graces sporting.

Mrs P. O Mr *Genius!*

Mr Gen. Many gentlemen have wished, Madam, for old wood to burn, old wine to drink, old friends to converse with, and old books to read; but never did I so limit my desires: I have always hoped, that sooner or later I should have an old woman to caress.

Mrs Pr. Incomparable *Genius!* I will not use you with the coquetry of a young hussy; but frankly own that I long have loved you.

Mr Gen. Is it possible? Words are inadequate to my ideas; and this is the only way my lips can express the sentiments of my heart.
[*He endeavours to kiss her; she struggles, but he prevails.*]

Mrs Pr. Lord! Sir, you are such another gentleman.

Mr Gen. These breasts, [*putting his hand in her bosom.*]

Mrs Pr. Keep off your hands, naughty gentleman that you are. – Nay now,

Mr *Genius*, you grow intolerably rude; I shall be seriously angry with you; – you must wait for the grace, Sir.

Mr Gen. Madam, I beg ten thousand pardons, if the violence of my passion has transported me beyond the bounds of decency. – Yes, Madam, I will wait, and as long as you please; for I am confident, you have more goodness than to make me repent my complaisance.

AIR II. Woe's my heart that we should sunder.

If you amuse me with vain hope,
  Till Time's unpitying fingers press us,
These my own hands shall knit me up,
  And put in practice my own essays.

Mrs Pr. *Imagine not I'll use you so:*
  Perhaps my life is everlasting;
But, lovely Genius, well I know,
  To the church-yard you fast are hasting.

Let not our interview, Mr *Genius*, end like that of two youthful lovers, without one word of common sense being spoken by either of us: Do you go to see my son's play to-night?

Mr Gen. I hope for the pleasure of seeing you there, Madam. What makes you ask the question?

Mrs Pr. Why, truly, that I may have an opportunity of expressing my gratitude. Many of my sons have been greatly obliged to you; but *Jacky* infinitely.

Mr Gen. O dear Madam!

Mrs Pr. Mr *John Calvin*, my first husband, was a very good man; but he had his oddities; and notwithstanding the affection which a woman must retain for the husband of her youth, I cannot help thinking you the better reformer of the two. Many of my sons, some time ago, before they had the honour of your acquaintance, were the most unlicked cubs ever were whelped: how stiff was their style! how starch their manner! how ridiculously grave the whole man! But since they got into your good company, they have put off the old man entirely: they have acquired a jaunty air, a military swagger, and a G__d_d__n_me look; they swear, they drink, they whore so handsomely; – in short, they are metamorphosed so very much to the better, that I scarce know them to be my own children.

Mr Gen. Your goodness, Madam, greatly magnifies my poor services.

Mrs Pr. How judicious was that fancy of yours to make *Jacky* write a play! and how inimitable the dedication with which you introduced it into the world! To it *Jacky* owes both his fame and his fortune, and ought to thank you on his knees for both.

Mr Gen. The young gentleman, Madam, is abundantly grateful; but I beg you would dwell no longer on this subject. I wish it were in my power to do more for him. I must now leave you, Madam, and join several of your sons who are to be at the playhouse tonight.

Mrs Pr. And I must away to Lady *Prelacy*, who goes along with me to the same place. Farewell till six o'clock. [Exit.]

       Mr Gen. AIR III. A free and an accepted Mason.

Unhappy are you
  If a girl you woo;
With rivals you always are fighting:
  But I am secure,
And morally sure,
  Old women alone I delight in.

Or if you shou'd wed
  A blooming young maid,
You, as at a cuckold, all stare on.
  The lewdest dragoons
Wou'd see blood and wounds,
  Ere my marriage-bed they wou'd share in.

And if ye shall shew
  Ye think my love new,
I'll do something still more worth seeing:
  For novelty's praise,
To make people gaze,
  Is the principal end of my being.

The bride I now leave,
  Has one foot in the grave;
My next shall be yet more uncommon:
  The church-yard I'll seek
The coffins I'll break,
  Till I hug some dead buried old woman. [*Exit.*]

       Arthur's Seat.

       Enter Sulphureo.

What can *Apollyo* mean? he promised to meet me here precisely at three o'clock, and now it is hard upon four. Perhaps he is wandering over this mountain in quest of me. Ho, *Apollyo!* ho! hoa! No *Apollyo* here it seems. What does he keep me waiting for? He is not *Garrick* the player, nor am I a young *Scotch* clergyman come a-beseeching him to act my tragedy; he is not a great man, nor am I an old reverend come a-begging some plurality or other, as a reward for my jobs past, present, and to come. No! we are two devils: and having said so much, I need not add, that we are honester fellows than most clergymen.

AIR IV. 'Twas when the sears were roaring.

They constantly are roaring,
  From pulpits hung with green,
'Gainst swearing, drinking, whoring,
  And ev'ry other sin.
Think not, ye simple hearers,
  When thus to you they preach,
That parsons are practisers
  Of what their sermons teach.
Their habit now is gaudy;
  Like officers they swear;
Their conversation's bawdy:
  To stage-plays they repair.
But if we by this nation
  Were paid for living well,
We wou'd have the discretion
  Or vices to conceal.

Enter Apollyo *at the other end of the stage.*

Ap. Ho, *Sulphureo!* ho! hoa!

Sulph. Here, here.

Ap. O, your servant, Mr *Sulphureo.*

Sulph. I am indeed your servant, Mr *Apollyo*; for I have waited here about an hour for your Honour.

Ap. Why, Sir, such a croud of people from this country came upon us this morning, that *Satan* could not get away from hell till a few minutes ago. So that, good Mr *Sulphureo*, I hope you'll excuse us.

Sulph. O yes, I do. But will you, *Apollyo*, who are one of our secretaries of state, be so good as to inform me why *Satan* is of late turned so negligent of his affairs in this country. I have been his *aid-de-camp* now for some time, yet I never was in this town before: there is a great change in his behaviour to this country; for I am told, about fifty years ago he used to be very often in *Scotland.*

Ap. There he comes, ask himself.

Enter Satan.

Sat. Well, my lads, how goes it? Have you, *Sulphureo*, ordered matters so that every thing be in readiness for my reception?

Sulph. I have, Sir. I saw the Reverend gentleman, and told him that you was to be in *Edinburgh* this afternoon, and would be glad of his company; he said he would meet you at five o'clock in Mrs *Kitchen*'s.

Sat. At five, very well. And how do you like the good town of *Edinburgh*, *Sulphureo?*

Sulph. Good! call you it?

AIR V. On ev'ry hill, in ev'ry grove.

In ev'ry street, in ev'ry lane,
  In ev'ry narrow slippery close,
Nothing but filth is to be seen;
  In all of them I stopt my nose.
    And ev'ry thing about it shows,
    It is a spacious little house.

'Tis not the clouds of smoke alone
  Which mount, when cookmaids dinner dress;
But 'tis the manners of the town,
  Which must oblige you to confess,
    (Forgiving your Supheureo's *Mirth),*
    Auld Reeky is a hell on earth.

Before you came up to us, I was inquiring at *Apollyo* how you came to be so indifferent about this country; you'll pardon my presumption, in begging to know the reason of this coldness, which to me at present seems to be mal-administration.

Sat. In the days of your, *Sulphureo,* I was almost constantly in Scotland, and obliged to exert all my mettle. Yet, for all that, I own the opposition here fairly got the better of me, and for a considerable time I had only a small select society that stuck by me. The ministers made conscience (as the phrase was in those days) of doing their duty; the greatest folks lived soberly; and indeed all ranks of people were in the most deplorable situation you can well imagine. I had very near have given them up altogether: however, I very luckily had the resolution to persevere; a good many years ago the tables were turned, and now almost the whole nation is my most obedient humble servant. I am the more delighted with this conquest, because, of all the countries I have subdued, this made the most obstinate resistance: but now the most of its inhabitants are more ingenious in my way than I myself can pretend to be.

AIR VI. Nansey's to the green wood gane.

So when some wild deceiving boy
  Assaults th' unspotted virgin,
At first the lass is very coy,
  And long resists his urging.
But after she is fairly won,
  And the foul deed is over,
The wanton gypsy, not half done,
  Out-paramours her lover.

Now, *Sulphureo*, I hope I have satisfied you.

Sulph. Perfectly, Sir. I see your presence here is not at all necessary.

Sat. No, it is not: and it was ceremony, not business, that brought me here just now; for I have all the reason in the world to believe that my people will be too many for their antagonists without my assistance: but as this is the third night of the first play ever was written by a *Scotch* Clergyman, I thought the least I could do was to give my countenance to such a bold attempt to serve me.

AIR VII. Susannah.

Good manners would not let me frown
  On the young tragic priest:
My company and half a crown
  Was all he did request.
Sulph. Ap. The youthful parson to refuse,
  Sure you had not done well;
And to procure him a full house
  You shou'd have empty'd hell.

Sat. There are to be nine clergymen in the playhouse to-night. Curiosity to see people of their character in such a place, would of itself secure the poet of a good third night; but my emissaries have taken care that he shall have a full house every night his play is acted.

Sulph. I am glad to hear it. Shall I show you the way to Mrs *Kitchen*'s?

Sat. Why, we must change our appearance in the first place. I think I will assume the dress of a country-gentleman just come from a journey; do you transfigure yourselves into my footmen. But stay, it is but a few minutes after four, we shall be too soon if we set out immediately for Mrs *Kitchen*'s; let us climb to the top of *Arthur's Seat*, the view from it is charming.

AIR VIII. Over the hills and far away.

Yon mountain's summit when I tread,
  The prospect will transport my sight;
Unlike to Moses, *who survey'd*
  The holy land from Pisgah's *height.*

Pensive he saw the fruitful plains,
  Plains which he never was to share:
All you shall see to me pertains,
  The possessors my vassals are.

End of the FIRST ACT.

ACT II.

A Tavern.

Enter Mask.

Who's there? Bring some bottles of claret, and a bowl of punch immediately.

Enter Satan, Sulphureo, *and* Apollyo.

Sat. My dear Mr *Mask*, I rejoice to see you. How does Mrs *Mask* do, and all your good family?
Mr Mask. Pretty well, Sir, at your service.
And pray, Sir, when you came from hell,
Our friends there did you leave them well?
Sat. All well. Pray sit down, Mr *Mask*. How my heart warms to my good old friend! Fill your glass, Mr *Mask*. Let us drink all our absent friends. [*They drink*]. Have you had any new books lately, Mr *Mask*?
Mr Mask. O, great variety, Sir.
Sat. I ask for them first; because I remember the committee of ways and means, which I had once established in this country, told me, that new books were commonly my very good friends.
Mr Mask. Commonly they are so. We have only one author of note; but his brain is a very good breeder.
Sat. What is the gentleman's name?
Mr Mask. Mr *Genius* is his name. He is the best writer against Christianity in *Britain*; nay, he gives very broad hints against the being of a God.
Sat. Come, drink his health. [*They drink*.]

AIR IX. Dear Colin, prevent my warm blushes.

The miser feels exquisite pleasure
  In touching a precious bank-note;
But I wou'd not give for his treasure,
  A leaf which an Atheist wrote.

When that's chang'd, he no doubt may bring home
  Some thousands to hide in his holes;
But this will convey to my kingdom,
  Ten thousand times ten thousand souls.

But hark ye, Mr *Mask*, does he deny my existence?

Mr Mask. O! laughs at it, Sir.

Sat. How very much surprised will he be when he goes to hell? However, I'll have his works reprinted there *typis regiis*; they well deserve it.

Mr Mask. He maintains there is no difference 'twixt right and wrong but what custom has introduced.

Sat. How much am I obliged to the gentleman! Dear Sirs, drink his health again. [*They drink.*] *Encore*, if you please. Huzza! [*They drink and huzza!*]

Mr Mask. He has broached a great number of such propositions.

Sat. I should be very glad to see him.

Mr Mask. You shall see him very soon. [*Rings.*]

Enter Moll Kitchen.

You know where Mr *Genius* is; tell him I must speak with him here. [*Exit* Moll.]

Before this philosopher arrives, I will show you another who has a great many disciples. I know he is over a bottle just now in this house. [*Rings.*]

Enter Moll.

Desire Mr *Moral Sense* to step in here for a few minutes, and do you follow him. [*Exit.*] This fellow pretends to be the most generous disinterested man alive; though, in reality, there is not a more selfish dog on the face of the earth.

Enter Moral Sense *and* Moll.

Mor. Sense. O my dear gentlemen, how I love all and every one of you! I would willingly, most willingly, lay down my life, shed my heart's blood, to serve you, my dear, dear, dear Gentlemen.

Sat. Sir, we are very much obliged to you for your kindness. Will you drink a glass of wine, Sir?

Mor. Sense. O, with all my heart. I approve of good wine. Gentlemen, your healths. [*Drinks.*] This wine is very good. I have an unbounded benevolence for it. Another glass, if you please, Sir. [*Drinks.*] O, Gentlemen, if you knew how much I love you, and your wine, you would not refuse me a third. [*Drinks.*] Yet another, Sir, to drink health and happiness to all mankind. [*Drinks.*] One more.

Mask. Sir, if you will have patience for a few minutes, you shall have your bellyfull; but I beg you would drink no more, till you have given your opinion upon a point of some consequence. What do you think of a marriage 'twixt me and *Moll* there?

Mor. Sense. Hui! Hui! Hui! [*shrieks hideously!*] it shocks me; I disapprove of it. But I will lie with her myself. [*Coming up to her.*] I will lie with you, *Moll*, [*laying hold of her.*]

Sat. Hold! hold, Sir.

Mor. Sense. I will lie with her; I approve of her. The το καλον[2] shines in her face. I will lie with you, *Moll*. [*Endeavours to throw her,* Satan *interposes.*] What do you mean, Sir? My instinct prompts me to lie with her.

Sat. You impertinent scoundrel, I'll teach your instinct better manners. [*Kicks him off.*] This is a very odd philosopher, Mr *Mask*.

Mask. Very odd, indeed, Sir. It is a rule of his, never to think a moment about what he either says or does. – There comes Mr *Genius*.

Enter Mr Genius.

Mr *Genius*, your servant: This, Sir, is Mr *Bevil*, a friend of mine, [*They salute*], who having red your books with great delight, was very curious to see you face to face.

Mr Gen. you have red my books then, Sir?

Sat. Yes, Sir, with great delight.

Mr Gen. Why, then, Sir, you are convinced, I suppose, that there is no God, no devil, no future state; – that there is no connection betwixt cause and effect; – that suicide is a duty we owe to ourselves; – adultery a duty we owe to our neighbour; – that the tragedy of DOUGLAS is the best play ever was written; and that *Shakespear* and *Otway* were a couple of dunces. – This, I think, is the sum and substance of my writings.

Sat. It is, Sir.

---

[2] [i.e., the beautiful.]

AIR X. Leaderhaughs and Yarrow.

Great Hercules, Jove's *darling son,*
    Was forc'd alone to wander;
And monsters with his club knock down,
    To glut his stepdame's anger.
Shakespear *and* Otway, *with your pen,*
    Unforc'd you have run thoro';
And therefore should be held by men,
    To be the greater hero.

Mr Gen. O, Sir, you do me too much honour. I'm sorry, Gentlemen, to leave you so soon; but I am engaged to go to the play with a party of clergymen. [Exit.]

Sat. Mr *Mask,* I protest the play had gone out of my head. You'll accompany us to the playhouse, I suppose?

Mask. Not I, indeed.

Sat. Why?

Mask, Why, because your enemies will lay hold of the proceedings that are to be this night in the playhouse, and endeavour to stir up a rebellion against you. They will soon prepare overtures and libels against the author of this play, and every other minister who saw it represented. This determines me not to go. I will seem to be rather against the author of this play, and his followers; by these means, I shall gain the good graces of the opposite party, which will enable me to quash any violent measure against him.

AIR XI. O Bessy Bell and Mary Gray.

The zealous fools will, if they can,
    With deposition end him;
But all our party to a man,
    Will vote, Rebuke, suspend him.
Such censures will not, I believe,
    His tragic genius smother;
Suspension for one play will give
    Him time to write another.

Sat. Thou reasonest well.

Mask. 'Tis our only way, Sir; but, *Satan,* what do you think of Mr *Genius?*

Sat. 'Faith, I don't know well what to think of him. Are you sure he is true blue on our side? I confess, I have some suspicion, that he is a shrewd fellow, endeavouring to convert men to Christianity, by writing nonsense against it.

Mask. You are quite mistaken, Sir: he is reckoned the ablest writer we have; so able, Sir, that all the good folks say, when he wrote his books, he had you at his elbow.

Sat. Really, Mr *Mask*, I think I may say without vanity, that had I assisted him, he would not have written so absurdly. I was very well pleased to hear him deny the existence of a God, and so forth; but his positions about suicide and adultery will certainly do our cause no good.

AIR XII. Hooly and fairly.

With hearing his nonsense in troth I am weary;
that nonsense will hurt me much, I can assure ye;
And make many people believe most sincerely.
O! gin the lad wad write hooly and fairly.
Hooly and fairly, &c.
[*Exeunt.*]

End of the SECOND ACT.

ACT III.

A drawing-room

Enter Mrs Presbytery, *Miss* Weepwell, *Miss* Pity, *Miss* Sob, *Miss* Blubber.

Mrs Pr. Ladies, now that you have seen my son *Jacky*'s play, let me have your opinions on it impartially.

Miss Weep. I believe, Madam, this company will be very unanimous in voting it to be the best play ever was written.

Mrs Pr. O, don't flatter me, Ladies.

Miss Blub. The tears, Madam, you saw shed in the playhouse, may convince you, that, without flattery, we are all of Miss *Weepwell*'s opinion.

Enter Miss Sprightly.

Miss Spr. Your servant, Ladies.

Mrs Pr. My dear Miss *Sprightly!*

Miss Weep. Bless me, child, your eyes are not at all red.

Miss Spr. What should make them so?

Miss Weep. Weeping.

Miss Spr. For what?

Miss Weep. Was you not at the play

*Miss Spr.*Yes, I was.
Miss Weep. Have you not then been crying for these three hours?
Miss Spr. Not I.
Miss Weep. Cruel creature!
Miss Spr. Why cruel, pray?
Miss Weep. Not to weep for DOUGLAS.
Miss Spr. What should make me weep for him?
Miss Weep. Not to weep for such a hero!
Miss Spr. What makes you dub him a hero, in all the world?
Miss Weep. Did not he kill the chief robber?
Miss Spr. And does that make him a hero?

AIR XIII.

Had DOUGLAS *liv'd on* English *ground,*
Where highwaymen, you know, abound;
And there, by the good-will of Fate,
Some noted robber's brains out beat;
A warrior's fame,
Or hero's name,
He in the country ne'er had found.
The sturdy lad
Wou'd just have had
A premium of neat forty pounds.

Miss Weep. You may carp as much as you will, Miss, at some particular
places of the play; but you will own, no doubt, that, upon the whole, it is the
best play ever was written.
Miss Spr. Will I so?
Miss Weep. Pray, who has written a better?
Miss Spr. Shakespear, Otway –
Miss Weep. Hold! the very naming of these two fellows is enough to make
one sick. Sure, child, you have not red Mr *Genius*'s dedication.

Miss Spr. AIR XIV. Clout the caldron.

In lapdogs, laces, hoops, stays, fans,
  And all other tackle,
Howe'er capricious you may be,
  I care not, or how fickle:
But yet, for all great Genius *says,*
  I really can't help wishing,
That Shakespear, Otway, *and their plays,*

May ne'er go out of fashion.
Fa adrie didle didle, &c.

Miss Weep. Miss *Sprightly*, I am not a little surprised to hear you talk at this rate. Sure neither you nor I can pretend to be such good judges as Mr *Jacky* and Mr *Genius*; and you know very well, what contempt they have for *Shakespear* and *Otway*.
Miss Spr. *Jacky* and *Genius*, very pretty fellows truly!

AIR XV. Gill Morris.

By the remains of Scottish *youth,*
  Who taste untainted boast,
Let all the paltry works of both
  To raging flames be tost.
This holocaust alone can sooth
  Great Shakespear's *injur'd ghost.*

Enter Mr Genius.

Miss Weep. You are come in good time, Sir. We have had a stout battle with Miss *Sprightly* about the tragedy of DOUGLAS. She has been running it down very warmly.
Mr Gen. I am sorry to hear it: for still her lips must be rubies, and her voice melody, though both be employed against the best play ever was written.
Mrs Pr. [*aside.*] So, so: this young *Jackanapes* will not only rob the son of his glory, but the mother of her gallant.

Enter Mr Jacky.

Miss Weep. O, Mr *Jacky,* your servant. I give you joy, Sir. [*They all advance, and salute him.*] I give you joy, Sir, that your tragedy has met with the success which the best play ever was written deserves. You, Sir, possess the true theatric genius of *Shakespear* –
Miss Sob. And *Otway* –
Miss Pity. Refined from the unhappy barbarism of the one –
Miss blub. And licentiousness of the other.
Jacky. O Ladies! nay, dear Ladies!

Mrs Pr. AIR XVI. Black Jock.

Dear Sir, and dear Ladies, my Jacky *is young,*
And bashfulness hinders the thanks of his tongue,

For filling his pockets with half-crowns so white.
He's sensible 'twas not the musical lasses,
Who dance, sing, and play on the top of Parnassus,
   But you who got him the half-crowns to white.
To thee, noble Genius, *the knee he shou'd bow;*
More than to Apollo *to thee does he owe:*
     Shakespear *scoffing,*
     Douglas *puffing,*
You screw'd men's opinions to such a great height,
That they filled his pockets with half-crowns so white.

Jacky. Dear mother, you have very handsomely expressed my gratitude, which a foolish bashfulness would not allow me to do. In return, I must insist on your giving to Mr *Genius* your hand; which a bashfulness still more foolish than mine, will not, I hope, make you refuse. I know you love one another; your marriage to-night will consummate my happiness.

Mrs Pr. There, Sir, is my hand; you long have had my heart.

Mr Gen. Madam, I am so very sensible of the honour you do me, that I here vow and swear never more to write essays, discourses, histories, dissertations; but to make your entertainment the sole study of my life.

AIR XVII. Logan water.

Two hundred years tho' you be old,
   And tho' your youthful bloom be fled,
Yet fear not, dearest, I'll prove cold,
   Or loiter when we are in bed.

Mrs Pr. *Two hundred years tho' I be old,*
   And tho' my youthful bloom be fled,
Yet fear not, dearest, I'll prove cold;
   I'll be but twenty when in bed.

Miss Weep. This is the only farce I could have endured to see after the tragedy of DOUGLAS. Let us have fiddles, and a dance.

[*They dance.* Satan, Sulphureo, *and* Apollyo *enter in their true shape, and offer to dance along with them; but they all run off.*]

Sat. Ay, why in such a hurry? The devil will not give himself the trouble to take the hindmost, I assure ye; for he is pretty certain to meet with all of you time and place more convenient. Well, my lads, how did you like DOUGLAS?

Sulph. It is a very moving tragedy, Sir; the tears are in my eyes yet. [*Wiping his eyes.*]

Ap. And mine too.

Sat. I agree with Mr *Genius*, in thinking it the best play ever was written. I could descant upon it all night; but we had better keep our observations for *Mask*, who will by this time be longing much for us, and more for his supper. Let us to Mrs *Kitchen*'s, and be merry.

AIR XVIII. Jolly mortals, fill your glasses.

Jolly devils, drink, I charge ye,
  Pass in sport the time away;
Bumpers swill to all the clergy,
  Who or write or see a play.

Now I wou'd not give three guilders,
  For the superstitious fry;
You shall all be ruling elders,
  And the moderator I.

FINIS.

DISPUTE WITH ROUSSEAU: 1766

22
REVIEW OF *A CONCISE AND GENUINE ACCOUNT* (*GENTLEMAN'S MAGAZINE*)

Review of Hume's *A concise and genuine account*, in *Gentleman's Magazine*, November 1766, Vol. 36, pp. 499–504.
Selections.

For background on Hume's dispute with Rousseau, see the general introduction to this collection. Shortly after Hume published his *Concise and Genuine Account* of the dispute, reviews appeared in several journals. The following excerpts are from the opening and closing of that in *Gentleman's Magazine*. The reviewer notes the origin of the English version of the work and fears that, through the publication of the account, Rousseau's ingratitude towards Hume will disincline people to show benevolence towards others in true need.

A Summary of Mr HUME's *Account of his Dispute with Mr.* ROUSSEAU.

Hume having complained, in very strong terms, of M. *Rousseau*'s ingratitude, it was doubted, even by some of his own friends, whether his sensibility had not aggravated the offence. Mr *Hume*, therefore, wrote a narrative of all that had passed between him and Mr *Rousseau*, and sent copies of it to his friends, with no other view than his own justification; and because he would not unnecessarily censure M. *Rousseau*, he refused to make his justification publick. *Rousseau*, however, having in a letter which he wrote to a bookseller at *Paris*, charged Mr *Hume* with confederating to betray and defame him, and defied him to publish the papers in his hands; and this letter having been translated and published in the *London* news papers, a publication of Mr. *Hume's* narrative became necessary: It does not, however, appear that he ever published it in *English*, but it was translated into *French*, with some liberties, to which Mr *Hume* consented, and published abroad; this foreign publication has been re-translated into *English*, and just published here, under the title of *A concise and genuine account of the dispute between Mr* Hume *and Mr* Rousseau. In the account are inserted the letters of the parties during their controversy, and the letters of the Hon. Mr *Walpole*, and Mr *d'Alembert*, relative to it, which the re-translator says in a note, will be deposited in the *Museum*. The narrative is in substance as follows....

It is much to be regretted, that the disgrace of Mr *Rousseau*, and the vexation & disappointment of Mr *Hume*, are but a small part of the mischief that such ingratitude for such friendship is likely to produce. It tends to chill benevolence, and repress liberality; many may be left to struggle with adversity unassisted, in consequence of such a return for assistance as Mr *Rousseau* has made to Mr *Hume*.

23
REVIEW OF *A CONCISE AND GENUINE ACCOUNT* *(CRITICAL REVIEW)*

Review of Hume's *A concise and genuine account*, in *Critical Review*, November 1766, Vol. 22 pp. 376–378. Complete.

The review of Hume's *Concise and Genuine Account* in the *Critical Review* comes down squarely in favour of Hume in the dispute. The reviewer finds no fault with Hume's conduct "as he appears to have acted towards Mr. Rousseau with the greatest sincerity, and the most unbounded friendship." Details of the dispute are presented, with sixteen of Rousseau's complaints listed. The reviewer argues that "It is really astonishing, that a man of Mr. Rousseau's judgment and good sense could seriously allege such trifles against Mr. Hume as crimes." The translator is criticized and several poorly translated words and phrases are cited.

---

14. *A concise and genuine Account of the Dispute between Mr.* Hume *and Mr.* Rousseau: *with the Letters that passed between them during their Controversy. As also the Letters of the Hon. Mr.* Walpole *and Mr.* D'Alembert, *relating to this extraordinary Affair. Translated from the* French. 8*vs. Pr.* I *s.* 6 *d.* Becket *and* DeHondt.

It is with concern that we find two men of such celebrated genius and approved merit at public variance, as it is much to the discredit of letters and true philosophy. We cannot, however, blame Mr. Hume for any part of his conduct, as he appears to have acted towards Mr. Rousseau with the greatest sincerity, and the most unbounded friendship: and as it was not till after Mr. Rousseau had published a very abusive letter, and boldly defied Mr. Hume to print the papers he was possessed of, that this gentleman resolved upon making the public a party concerned in judging their respective conduct.

From the most generous motives Mr. Hume conducted Mr. Rousseau into England, introduced him to his friends, and exhausted his invention to make this asylum agreeable to him; giving way to all his caprices, and winking at all his singularities. With the same view he accompanied him into various parts of England, till he was at length most agreeably settled at Mr. Davenport's, at Wooton in Derbyshire. In the mean while, Mr. Hume was using his utmost interest with his majesty's ministers to obtain for him a royal pension; and was so successful as to interest general Conway and general Græme in his favour, who gained his majesty's gracious consent. But when he was upon the point of reaping the fruit of Mr. Hume's friendly endeavours, he fancied, or chose to fancy, through the most unaccountable extravagance, that Mr. Hume was his concealed enemy, and had, in concert with M. D'Alembert and M. Voltaire, laid a plan to destroy his honour; for no other apparent reason, but because Mr. Walpole had diverted himself a little at his expence, in a supposed letter from the king of Prussia to Mr. Rousseau, which was published in the St. James's Chronicle, and which Mr. Rousseau imagined Mr. Hume had sent to the publisher of that paper; although it evidently appeared that Mr. Walpole had wrote this letter, and acknowledged himself to be the author of it.

In Mr. Rousseau's letter, or rather memorial, which he calls an Explanation, we find the following capital articles of impeachment against Mr. Hume's fidelity and friendship:

1. Not gaining him sufficient popularity.
2. Endeavouring to obtain a royal pension for him.
3. Secret kindnesses to avoid hurting his delicacy.
4. Procuring him a friendly and hospitable reception at Mr. Steward's.
5. Introducing him to the first people in England.
6. Assiduously lending him his seal.
7. Speaking four very terrible words in his sleep.
8. Not having answered a pleasantry of Mr. Walpole's, which admitted of no answer.
9. Corresponding with M. D'Alembert.
10. Lodging in the same house with the son of Dr. Tronchin.
11. Conversing along with his *gouvernante*.
12. Being desirous of serving Mr. Rousseau, after he had offended Mr. Hume.
13. Reading his *Heloise* too often.
14. Accepting of his picture as a present from Mr. Ramsay.
15. Saying he had been at the play with Mrs. Garrick.
16. And looking stern, very stern, at Mr. Rousseau, whilst he fruitlessly endeavoured to stare Mr. Hume out of countenance.

It is really astonishing, that a man of Mr. Rousseau's judgment and good sense could seriously allege such trifles against Mr. Hume as crimes. But we are afraid there is a certain characteristic turn in the philosopher of Geneva, that will not let him long enjoy any tranquillity or any friendship; and where real misfortunes are wanting, his prolific brain easily brings forth chimeras, which may be dreadful to him, but ridiculous to every body else.

Though Mr. Hume cannot in this affair be accused of any more faults than those which Mr. Rousseau has so industriously imputed to him; we must not entirely acquit his translator, who has many errors to answer for. Amongst others, we think the following should be corrected in the next edition:

Page 15, he has translated, *celui d être trop bien est un de ceux qui se tolerent le plus aisement,* "that of being *too good,* is one of those which is the most tolerable." If we may be allowed a pun, that of being *too bad* a translator) is one of those which is the most *in*tolerable:" and indeed, Mr. Translator, *trop bien* is *too well,* and not *too good.* Next comes the *models,* and *the hollow trunk of an old tree* (p. 10 and 17) instead of *busts* and *rabbit-warrens,* Page 57, he makes Mr. Hume previously acquainted with Mr. Rousseau's affairs, and yet wanting to sift his *gouvernante*; whereas, according to the original, it was the lady that was acquainted with Mr. Rousseau's affairs, which she having acknowledged to Mr. Hume, he then questioned her,[1] &c. Page 42, he renders *sourd* "absurd" – very absurd indeed!

---

[1]   This is one of Mr. Rousseau's accusations.

24
WILLIAM ROSE:
REVIEW OF *A CONCISE*
AND GENUINE ACCOUNT
(MONTHLY REVIEW)

[William Rose], review of Hume's *A Concise and Genuine Account*, in *Monthly Review*, November 1766, Vol. 35, pp. 390–402. Selections.

According to Benjamin Christie Nangle's catalogue of reviewers for the *Monthly Review*, the article on Hume's *Concise and Genuine Account* was authored by William Rose (1719–1786). A Scotsman and proprietor of a school in Chelsea, Rose regularly reviewed philosophy books for the journal and is responsible for reviewing seven of Hume's works in the *Monthly*. Like the *Critical Review*, Rose supports Hume in the dispute, but he hesitates to make pronouncements against Rousseau that would be obvious to any reader.

A concise and genuine Account of the Dispute between Mr. Hume and Mr. Rousseau: with the Letters that passed between them during their Controversy. As also, the Letters of the Hon Mr. Walpole, and Mr. D'Alembert, relative to this extraordinary Affair. Translated from the French. Octavo. 1s. 6d. Becket.

It can scarce be imagined that there are any of our Readers, to whom the names of HUME and ROUSSEAU are not familiar. Many of them too must have heard of the late quarrel between these two celebrated geniuses, and will be desirous, no doubt, to know the occasion of it. In order to gratify this curiosity, we shall give a short narrative of the whole affair, from the account now before us, without interrupting this narrative, with any reflections of our own. The reflections naturally arising from the *account* are such indeed, as cannot escape the most superficial attention. It appears with the clearest evidence that Mr. *Hume* has acted the part of a generous and disinterested friend to Mr. Rousseau: in regard to the conduct of the latter, humanity seems to dictate silence, as it can give no pleasure to a generous mind to mention what every reader must observe with concern. ...

This passage alone is sufficient to excuse us to the discerning Reader, for declining to enter into the particulars of this long letter. Those who will be at the pains of perusing it, will clearly see, that Mr. Rousseau's extreme sensibility renders him peculiarly liable to entertain suspicions even of his best friends; and that his uncommon force of imagination combines circumstances, seemingly minute and trifling, in such a manner as to impose on his own understanding. What complexion his heart is of, though appearances in regard to Mr. Hume are strongly against him, we dare not pretend to determine. The sentiments that arise in our minds, are those of compassion towards an unfortunate man, whose peculiar temper and constitution of mind must, we fear, render him unhappy in every situation. ...

25
VOLTAIRE:
A LETTER FROM
MONS. DE VOLTAIRE, TO MR. HUME

François-Marie Arouet de Voltaire, *A letter from Mons. de Voltaire, to Mr. Hume, on his dispute with M. Rousseau. Translated from the French*, London: printed for S. Bladon, 1766, [4], 16 p.
Complete; from 1766 edition.

François-Marie Arouet de Voltaire (1694–1778) was among the most notable philosophers of the eighteenth-century French Enlightenment. Hume never met Voltaire in person, but held him in high regard throughout his life. In "Of the Middle Station of Life" – first published in 1742 – Hume lists Voltaire among the greatest French writers. In a 1764 letter, Hume discusses his desire to meet Voltaire:

> When I arrived here, all M. Voltaire's friends told me of the regard he always expressed for me; that some advances on my part were due to his age, and would be well taken. I accordingly wrote him a letter, in which I expressed the esteem which are undoubtedly due to his talents; and among other things I said, that if I were not confined to Paris by public business, I should have a great ambition to pay him a visit at Geneva. This is the foundation of the report you mention; but I am absolutely confined to Paris and the Court, and cannot on any account leave them so much as for three days. [Hume to James Edmonstoune, January 9, 1764].

Between 1764 and 1769 Voltaire published his *Philosophical Dictionary* (*Dictionnaire Philosophique*). In his entry on "Religion" he discusses Hume's argument for original polytheism in "The Natural History of Religion," referring to Hume as "one of the most profound metaphysicians of the times" (selections from which are contained in *Early Responses to Hume's Writings on Religion*, 2001). In 1766 Voltaire was inadvertently dragged into the dispute between Hume and Rousseau, when Rousseau accused him of conspiring to have him exiled from Switzerland. In an open letter to Hume, translated from French, Voltaire denies involvement in any conspiracy. He describes his earlier efforts to assist Rousseau, and provides some embarrassing details about Rousseau's mental condition. Although Voltaire says nothing about Hume's role in the dispute, the letter has the effect of confirming Hume's side of the story.

The *Critical Review* suspends judgment regarding the credibility of Voltaire's charge against Rousseau; their complete review is as follows:

> This little piece appears to be genuine, tho' we meet with nothing new in it, except the copies of two billets, supposed to be written by Mr. Rousseau; the one to M. Voltaire, and the other to M. Thiel, first clerk of foreign affairs at Paris. In the first he accuses M. de Voltaire with having *asserted that he had not been secretary of embassy at Venice, which was a falsity*: and in the second it is set forth, that *he had only been a servant to the count de Montaign (ambassador at Venice) and had been shamefully turned out of his house*. We know not upon what authority Mr. de Voltaire pretends to quote these letters; but as it is reasonable to expect M. Rousseau will soon reply to these attacks, we shall suspend our judgment till we see his vindication. [*Critical Review*, November 1766, Vol. 22, p. 378]

The *Monthly Review* contends that Voltaire's assault against Rousseau was unnecessarily insensitive; the complete review is this:

> Mr. Rousseau having thought fit to rank Mr. Voltaire among the number of his enemies and calumniators, the latter, to prove the *injustice* of the charge, *abuses* and *ridicules* poor Rousseau, most unmercifully, in this letter to Mr. Hume. It is really cruel, and ungenerous, in the highest degree, thus wantonly to attack, and wound, and mangle, a man whose feelings are so extremely acute, and who is so apt to smart and agonize at every pore! It may be sport to Mr. V. but it would be no dishonour to his character if it had been a little tinctured with the *delicacy* and *sensibility* of the Swiss philosopher, whom he so much affects to despise! [*Monthly Review*, November 1766, Vol. 35, p. 406]

Voltaire's *Letter* was also attacked by Edward Burnaby Greene in *A Defence of Mr. Rousseau* (1766), contained later in this collection. Voltaire maintained a high regard for Hume long after the dispute with Rousseau subsided, as we see in a 1772 letter from John Moore to Baron Mure, sited in this collection ("Letters to William Mure of Caldwell," Letter 274).

A
LETTER
FROM
Mons. DE VOLTAIRE
TO
Mr. HUME.

I have read, Sir, the pieces in the litigation, which you have had to support before the public, against him whom you formerly protected. I acknowledge that the great soul of John James hath set forth the blackness with which you have heaped kindnesses upon him; and it hath in vain been said, that this is the suit of ingratitude against beneficence.

I find myself accused of being an accomplice in this affair. The Sieur Rousseau charges me with having written a letter to England, wherein I ridicule him. He also accuses Mr. D'Alembert with the same crime.

Were Mr. D'Alembert and myself completely guilty of this enormity, I swear to you I am not, however, guilty, of having written to him. It is seven years since I have had that honour. I am ignorant of the letter he speaks of; and I swear to you, that if I had played off some little ill-natured pleasantry against Mr. J.J. Rousseau, I would not disown it.

He has done me the honour of placing me amongst the number of his enemies, and his persecutors. Being perfectly persuaded that a statue should be erected to his memory, as he says in the polite and decent letter from *J.J. Rousseau, citizen of Geneva, to Christopher De Beaumont, archbishop of Paris*; he thinks that half the universe is engaged in raising a statue upon his pedestal, and the other half in demolishing it.

He has not only thought me an iconoclast; but he has taken it into his head, that I had conspired against him, with the council of Geneva, for the seizing of his person, and afterwards, with the council of Berne, to drive him out of Switzerland.

These things he persuaded the protectors he had at Paris to believe, and he made me be thought by them a man who, in him, persecuted wisdom and modesty. This, Sir, is the manner in which I have persecuted him.

When I was informed that he had many enemies at Paris, that he was equally fond as myself of retirement, and that I presumed he might do some service to philosophy, I proposed to him, through Mr. Marc Chapuis, citizen of Geneva, so early as the year 1759, a country house, called the *Hermitage*, which I had just purchased.

He was so touched with my offer, that he wrote to me these words:

"Sir,
I do not like you; you corrupt my republic, in giving theatrical representations in your castle of Ferney, &c."

This letter, from a man who had just given a serious opera and a comedy at Paris, was not, however, dated from bedlam. I made no answer, as you may very well believe; and I desired Mr. Tronchin, the physician, to send him a prescription for his disorder. Mr. Tronchin replied, that, as he could not cure me of the rage of still writing dramatic pieces at my age, he despaired of curing John James. We both remained much afflicted, each in our way.

In 1762 the council of Geneva undertook his cure, and issued a kind of order to make sure of him, in order to undergo a proper course of physic. John James, proscribed at Paris and at Geneva, convinced that one body cannot be in two places at the same time, flew to a third. Hew concluded, with his usual prudence, that I was his mortal enemy, as I had not answered his obliging letter. He imagined that some of the council of Geneva had dined with me, to plan his destruction; and that the minutes concerning his arrest had been penned upon my table, after the repast. He persuaded some of his fellow citizens to believe so very probable a story. This accusation became so serious, that I was at length obliged to write to the council of Geneva, a letter couched in strong terms, wherein I acquainted them, that if a single man of that body had ever given the least insinuation against the Sieur Rousseau, I consented to his being considered as a villain, as well as myself; and that I too much detested persecutors to be such.

The council answered me by a secretary of state, that I had never had, ought to have, or could have, the least share directly, or indirectly, in the sentence against the Sieur John James.

Both the letters are in the archives of the council of Geneva.

Nevertheless, Mr. R. retired in the delicious vallies of Moutier-Travers, or Motier-Travers, in the county of Neufchatel, not having, for many years, had the pleasure of communing under both forms, instantly requested of the vicar of Moutier-Travers, a man of a subtile and refined understanding, the satisfaction of being admitted to the holy-table: he told him, that his intention was, first, *to attack the Romish church:* secondly, *to rise against the infernal work of the mind, which evidently established materialism:* thirdly, *to annihilate the vain presumptuous new fangled philosophers.* He wrote and signed this declaration, which is still in the hands of M. de Montmolin, vicar of Moutier-Travers and Boveresse.

As soon as he had communed, he found his heart dilated; *he melted even into tears.* So he at least says, in his letter of the 8th of Aug. 1765.

He soon quarrelled with the vicar and preachers of Moutier-Travers and Boveresse; children pelted him with stones: he flew to the territories of Berne; and, willing no longer to be lapidated, he intreated the magistrates of Berne, *to be so kind as to shut him up the remainder of his days in some one of their castles, or such other place of their state as they should judge proper.* His letter is dated October 20, 1765.

Since the countess of Pinbèche, who was advised to get herself fettered, I believe it has entered no one's brain to make a similar request. The magistrates of Berne rather chose to drive him out of their canton, than to provide him a lodging.

The judicious J. J. failed not to conclude, that I had deprived him of the sweet consolation of perpetual imprisonment; and that I had even such influence upon the priests, as to procure his excommunication from the Christians at Moutier-Travers.

Think not, Sir, that I rally: he wrote in a letter of the 24th of June. *To be excommunicated, according to M. De V's fashion, will afford me much amusement.* And in his letter of the 23d of March, he says, *M. De V. should have wrote to Paris, that he takes great pains to drive Rousseau from his new country.*

The best of the joke is, that he has succeeded for some time to make some people believe this phrenzy; and the truth is, that if, instead of the imprisonment which he requested of the magistrates of Berne, he had taken refuge in the country house which I offered him, I would then have procured him that asylum; or I would have taken care that he should have had good broth and proper refreshments; being thoroughly persuaded that a man in his situation is more worthy to excite compassion than resentment.

It is true, that to the wisdom constantly resulting from his writings, he has added some strokes that do not testify the best of hearts. I know not whether you are acquainted with his writing *Letters from the Mountain.* In the fifth letter he declares himself my open antagonist: this is not well. A man who has communed under both forms, a sage to whom a statue should be erected, seems to degrade a little his character by such a manœuvre; he risks his salvation, and his reputation.

So the first step taken by the mediators of France, Zurich, and Berne, was to solemnly declare the letters from the mountain a libel. It is impossible for me any longer to offer J.J. a house, since he has proclaimed himself a public incendiary.

However, in pursuing the trade of a libeller, and that of a man somewhat at variance with truth, it must be acknowledged he has preserved his reputation as to modesty.

He did me the honour to write to me, before the arrival of the mediation at Geneva, these very words:

"Sir,

If you have said I was not secretary of embassy at Venice, you have lied; and if I was not secretary of embassy, and did not receive the honours as such, it is me that have lied."

I was ignorant that Mr. J.J. had been secretary of embassy. I never said a word concerning it, because I had never heard any one mention it.

I shewed this letter to a man of veracity, very intimately acquainted with foreign affairs, curious and exact; these people are very dangerous for those who quote at random. He brought to light the original letters written by J.J. of the 9th and the 13th of August 1743, to M. du Theil, first clerk for foreign affairs, then his protector. We there find these very words:

"I have been for two years servant to the count de Montaigu (embassador at Venice) – I have eaten his bread – He has shamefully driven me out of his house – He threatened to throw me out the window – And what is worse, I remained after that in Venice, &c."

Here we find a secretary of embassy very little respected, and the pride of a great soul but little curbed. I advise him to engrave upon the pedestal of his statue, the words of the embassador to the secretary of embassy.

You see, Sir, that this poor man could never behave properly under any master, or preserve any friend, because it is incompatible with the dignity of his being to have a master; and friendship is a weakness, the attacks of which should be repulsed by every sensible man.

You say that he is writing the history of his life. It has been too useful to the world, and filled with too many great events, for him to suppress the utility of its publication to posterity. His taste for truth will not allow him to disguise the smallest of his anecdotes, for the advantage of princes, who, like Emilius, chuse to be joiners.

To speak the truth, Sir, all these insignificant trifles do not deserve a moment's attention; they will soon sink into eternal oblivion. They are as little attended to as the bitter embraces of the new Heloise, with her false conception, and her gentle friend; and the letters from Vernet to a lord whom he never saw. The phrenzy of J.J. and his ridiculous pride, will do no harm to sound philosophy; and those respectable men who cultivate it in France, England, and Germany, will not be thereby the less esteemed.

There are follies and quarrels in every condition of life. Some ex-jesuits have furnished bishops with defamatory libels under the title of mandates: some parliaments have ordered them to be burnt; this was forgot at the end of a fortnight. Every thing rapidly disappears, like the grotesque figures of the magic lanthorn.

The archbishop of Novogorod, at the head of a synod, condemned the bishop of Rostou, to be degraded and shut up for the remainder of his life in a convent, for having maintained that there are two powers, the one sacerdotal, the other regal. The empress has excused him from this imprisonment. This event hath scarcely been known in Germany and the rest of Europe.

The particulars of the most bloody wars perish with the soldiers that were the victims. Even the critics of new theatrical pieces, and particularly their elogiums, are the next day buried in oblivion with them, and the periodical pamphlets that treat of them. Nothing but Keyser's sugar-plums have been able to keep their ground a little.

In the immense torrent which drives us all, and swallows us all, what is to be done? Let us stick to the advice which Mr. Horace Walpole gives John James, to be wise and happy. You are the one, Sir, and you deserve to be the other, &c.

Ferney, Oct. 24th 1766

26
EDWARD BURNABY GREENE:
A DEFENCE OF MR. ROUSSEAU

[Edward Burnaby Greene] *A defence of Mr. Rousseau, against the aspersions of Mr. Hume, Mons. Voltaire, and their associates.* London: printed for S. Bladon, 1766, [4], iv, 44 p.[1]
Complete; from 1766 edition.

Edward Burnaby Greene (d. 1788) attended Corpus Christi College, Cambridge, and, with a considerable inherited fortune, began a brewery business, which ultimately failed. Greene published several translations of Greek poetry, and had published some of his own poetic compositions. None of these, though, were well received, as was also the case for his anonymous pamphlet defending Rousseau against Hume. In this work, Greene argues that, out of jealousy for Rousseau's superior literary abilities, Hume and others sought to deflate Rousseau's fame by publicly ridiculing him. Greene presents the key letters of the dispute, giving them a much different interpretation of the matter than Hume did. Greene also attacks Voltaire's *Letter... to Mr. Hume* (1766), charging that Voltaire forged the crazed quotations from Rousseau. Greene composed his defence prior to the appearance of Hume's *Concise and Genuine Account*. As a supplement to the pamphlet, though, he includes a critique of Hume's *Account*, which came into Greene's hands after "the foregoing sheets went to press." The complete and unfavourable review of Greene's *Defence* in the *Critical Review* is as follows:

This is an attempt, and only an attempt, to vindicate Mr. Rousseau's conduct in his altercation with Mr. Hume. The bookseller's head seems to have been more at work, in producing *a well-timed eighteen-penny touch*, than the author's in compiling or writing it. [*Critical Review*, November 1766, Vol. 22, p. 378]

---

[1] Title page: A | DEFENCE | OF | MR. ROUSSEAU, | AGAINST THE | ASPERSIONS | OF | Mr. HUME, Mons. VOLTAIRE, | AND THEIR ASSOCIATES. | He that filches from me my good-name, | Robs me of that, which not enriches him, | But makes me poor indeed! | SHAKESPEAR. | LONDON, | Printed for S. BLADON, in Pater-noster-Row, | MDCLXVI.

The *Monthly Review* finds Greene's performance equally weak:

> A bare-faced catch-penny job. The Author is an impertinent intruder into a controversy, of which he appears to know nothing more than what every reader might gather from the *Concise and Genuine Account of the Dispute*, &c.. of which we gave an abstract in our last month's Review; and of which tract this officious advocate for Mr. Rousseau, has prudently availed himself, by plentifully cramming his meagre performance with extracts from it. We are sorry that Mr. R.'s cause should be scandalized by *such* a pretended *defence*. [*Monthly Review*, December 1766, Vol. 35, pp. 471–472]

The following is from the 1766 and only edition of Greene's *Defence*.

A

D E F E N C E

OF

Mr. R O U S S E A U

AGAINST THE

A S P E R S I O N S

OF

Mr. H u m e, Monf. V o l t a i r e,
AND THEIR ASSOCIATES.

He that filches from me my good name,
Robs me of that, which not enriches him,
But makes me poor indeed !
SHAKESPEAR.

LONDON,
Printed for S. Bladon, in Pater-nofter-Row,
MDCCLXVI.

TO

Mr. WALPOLE,

Sir,

The share you have taken in the dispute between Mr. Rousseau and Mr. Hume, necessarily entitles you to this address. Whatever right you might think you had to make so free with the king of Prussia's name, as it could no way affect his reputation, was scarce deserving of his consideration: but the raillery which was levelled at Mr. Rousseau, was of a very different nature – a stranger, persecuted on every side an exile in your own country, deserved at least your pity, if not your protection. Had you recollected just then the fable of the boys and frogs, you would doubtless have sacrificed this flight of genius to the dictates of humanity.

Could be the verse, how well fore'er it flow,
That tends to make but one good man your foe.

The transition is easy, and the thought equally applicable to prose. How then, Sir, could you forget it?

You say you have a hearty contempt for Rousseau, how came he then deserving of your attention? If he was so contemptible as you represent him, he was beneath ridicule.

Your friend Mr. Hume was at that time his protector, and if we may believe his own words, was fully resolved to continue so; did not this ridicule therefore partly fall upon him? It is generally believed that a professed wit, will sacrifice every thing to his joke, and, doubtless, Mr. Hume, making this allowance for your prevalent passion, joined in the laugh though it was in some measure at himself.

In the following pages, you will, perhaps, be able to discover how far this laugh was forced, or whether the historian deeply read in political lore, might not consider his whole conduct towards Rousseau, as one great system, worthy even of Machiavel; and in this case, you will find yourself to have been only an instrument to bring about the concatenation of events.

This, doubtless, would be a mortification to you, and you might ever after confine your wit and raillery to the Patagonian race, who have no historian but yourself, and cannot boast one single politician amongst them.

I am, Sir,
Your very humble
Servant,
The EDITOR.

A
DEFENCE
OF
Mr. ROUSSEAU, &c.

It behoves every citizen of the world, who pretends to have divested himself of national prejudice, to consider a foreigner, who has taken asylum in his country, as a fellow-citizen; and to treat him with the same philanthrophy and urbanity as he would expect himself to be treated under such circumstances in a foreign land. This obligation is still stronger, where a stranger of eminent merit has been invited into a country, under the most flattering promises of consideration and esteem, by men of rank and learning.

Such is the situation of M. Rousseau at present in England; and I am, therefore, induced impartially to consider, whether he has been treated with all that propriety and respect he might have expected under such circumstances; or whether he has not, in some degree, been destined for the character of the Jack-pudding, instead of that of the Quack,[2] which Mr. H. is pleased to impute to him? The impartial part of mankind will judge from facts; and all the sophistry in the world will not deceive the public eye when these are before them. We are told in the preface, to the account of the dispute between Mr. Hume and Mr. Rousseau, that "the facts are all laid before the public; and Mr. H. submits his cause to every man of sense and probity:" thus authorized, then let us candidly examine how far Mr. H. has or has not deviated from the affectionate friend, and professed patron of the unfortunate Mr. Rousseau.

This gentleman's character, in the Republic of Letters, is so well established, that no direct attacks upon it could possibly have met with any success, the shafts of envy and malevolence must have recoiled upon those who endeavoured to wound; and, like gold from the crucible, his value would have been enhanced by the assay. Mr. H. seems to have been convinced of this, and to have esteemed him as much for his merit as his virtue. He tells us –

"My connection with Mr. Rousseau began in 1762, when the parliament of Paris had issued an arrest for apprehending him, on account of his Emilius, I was then at Edinburgh. A person of great worth wrote to me from Paris, that Mr. Rousseau intended to seek an asylum in England, and desired I would do him all the good offices in my power. As I conceived Mr. Rousseau had actually put his design in execution, I wrote to several of my friends in London, recommending this celebrated exile to their favour. I wrote also to Mr. Rousseau himself, assuring him of my desire to oblige, and readiness to

---

[2]   Je sais aujoured hui avec certitude, que cette affectation de misere & de pauvreté extreme, n'est qu'une petite *charlatanerie*, que M. R. employe avec succes, &c. p. 10.

serve him. At the same time I invited him to come to Edinburgh, if the situation would be agreeable to him, and offered him a retreat in my own house so long as he should please to partake of it. There needed no other motive to excite me to this act of humanity, than the idea given me of Mr. Rousseau's personal character, by the friend who had recommended him, his well-known genius and abilities; and, above all, his misfortunes, the very cause of which was an additional reason to interest me in his favour."

Here then are the motives of Mr. H's taking Mr. Rousseau under his protection; did the latter ever give him any reason to believe that he was mistaken, or that Mr. Rousseau had practised any *quackery*, or imposed on the world at the time that he is suspected of it, which is just after Mr. H's seeing Mr. Rousseau's letter to M. Clairaut, dated March 13, 1765? If so, why did Mr. H. conduct him afterwards into England, and declare himself his protector? It is true, this reflection is qualified with – "But I was then very far from suspecting any such artifice." – Why then this ill natured remark so misplaced? It does not, indeed, appear that the letter concerning the Musical Dictionary, has any sort of connection with the present dispute, but seems introduced to lessen Mr. Rousseau's literary merit in the eyes of the world, and to accomplish this the more effectually, the English translator has thought proper to give Mr. Rousseau's words a very different, if not opposite, sense to what they have in the original. "C'est une trés mauvaise rapsodie que j'ai compileé il y a plusieurs années sous le nom de dictionnaire de Musique & je suis forcé de *donner* aujourd hui pour avoir du pain."

"It is a very paltry rhapsody, which I compiled many years ago, under the title of a Musical Dictionary, and am now obliged to *republish* it for subsistence."

This certainly implies that it has already been printed in its imperfect state, whereas, according to the original, it never had (nor hath ever yet) been printed, and he was very anxious for its being corrected by so able a hand as Mr. Clairaut before it was published. This plainly appears by the stratagem which Mr. H. proposed practising, that Mr. Rousseau might obtain a larger sum for the copy from the bookseller, than he otherwise would, and by the failure of the execution of this project at Mr. Clairaut's death, because he had not corrected the manuscript.

It is curious to observe what a deal of secresy and caution was used for Mr. S – to get lodging and board for Mr. Rousseau upon his arrival in England. "I wrote immediately to my friend Mr. John Stewart of Buckingham-street, that I had an affair to communicate to him, of so secret and delicate a nature, that I would not even venture to commit it to paper, but that he might learn the particulars of Mr. Elliot." It was paying a very bad compliment to Mr. Rousseau's judgment, to fancy he could be imposed upon so far as to believe the accommodations he met with in England for seventy or eighty pounds a year, were to be had for twenty pounds.

What could be the meaning of pursuing these stratagems and deceptions, after Mr. H. had obtained the promise of the pension, which would have enabled Mr. Rousseau to live at his ease, without such secret *friendly* machinations?

It is plain Mr. Rousseau could not be deceived in this respect, for he wrote to Mr. H. from Wooton. "The affair of the carriage is not yet adjusted, because I know I was imposed on; it is a trifling fault, however, which may be only the effect of an obliging vanity, unless it should happen to be repeated. If you were concerned in it, I would advise you to give up, once for all, these little impositions, which cannot proceed from any good motive, when converted into snares for simplicity.

I do not find that Mr. H. took any notice of this charge at that time, any more than some others, which I shall presently have occasion to mention. Could it therefore be surprising, that as Mr. H. tacitly acknowledged the imputation to be just, Mr. Rousseau should imagine he had been imposed upon in many other respects that were less excusable.

Mr. H. chuses to impute Mr. Rousseau's resentment, to his suspicion of Mr. H's being the editor of the letter which appeared in the St. James's Chronicle, supposed to be written by the king of Prussia to Mr. Rousseau, giving him an ironical invitation to his court; but if Mr. H. will recollect many parts of his conduct towards Mr. Rousseau, were suspicious, if not reprehensible, before that time.

Could it be supposed that Mr. Rousseau's vanity was inflated to that degree, as to fancy Mr. H. a person of so much acknowledged taste and extensive learning, could be continually poring over Eloise, which was always before him, whenever Mr. Rousseau called upon him – if this was a compliment, it must, by a man of discernment, have been considered like the supposed king of Prussia's, an ironical one.

The compliment he received from Mr. H. when presented to Mr. Pennick of the museum, must certainly have galled him, as it would every feeling man, especially when coming from a supposed friend. "Mr. Hume made my excuses, whilst I myself was present (says Mr. Rousseau) for not having paid him a visit. Doctor Matty, said he, invited us on Thursday to the Museum, when Mr. Rousseau should have seen you; but he chose rather to go with Mrs. Garrick to the play; he could not do both in a day."

Mr. H. does not recollect a single circumstance of this history – very possible; but it is plain that Mr. Rousseau does, and it is not reasonable to imagine that he would invent a falsity upon the occasion, as Mr. Pennick might so easily detect him in it.

Whatever grounds Mr. Rousseau might have to suspect, Mr. H's curiosity, with regard to his letters, I will not pretend to determine; but it is plain he had such a suspicion, whether well or ill grounded, as it produced that uncommon scene which Mr. H. treats as a fiction, when Mr. Rousseau cried out, *No, no,*

David Hume cannot be treacherous; if he be not the best of men, he must be the basest of mankind. It is plain however that Mr. H. took no notice of this extraordinary declaration, and required no eclaircisement upon it. If it be a groundless assertion of Mr. Rousseau, what advantage could he derive from writing such a falsity to the person who was the only actor in the scene? He certainly could not expect to persuade him of the truth of it, by asserting it; had he wrote this letter to a third person, this might have been his expectation. Be this as it may, as no body was present but Mr. H. and Mr. Rousseau, we can only have *ipse dixit* for *ipse dixit*, and they are therefore equal.

There can be no doubt however that the letter ascribed to the king of Prussia appeared, and was published in the St. James's Chronicle, with the following translation.

"My Dear John James,

You have renounced Geneva, your native soil, you have been driven from Switzerland, a country of which you have made such boast in your writings. In France you are outlawed, come then to me, I admire your talents, and amuse myself with your reveries; on which, however, by the way, you bestow too much time and attention. It is high time to grow prudent and happy, you have made yourself sufficiently talked of for singularities little becoming a truly great man. Shew your enemies that you have sometimes common sense; this will vex them without hurting you. My dominions afford you a peaceable retreat; I am desirous to do you good, and will do it, if you can but think it such. But if you are determined to refuse my assistance, you may expect I shall not say a word about it to any one. If you persist in perplexing your brains to find out new misfortunes, chuse such as you like best; I am a king, and can make you as miserable as you can wish; at the same time, I will engage to do that which your enemies never will, I will cease to persecute you, when you are no longer vain of persecution.

Your sincere friend,

FREDERIC."

We have the history of this billet in the following words. "This letter was written by Mr. Horace Walpole, about three weeks before I left Paris; but though we lodged in the same hotel, and were often together Mr. Walpole, out of regard to me, carefully concealed this piece of *pleasantry* till after my departure. He then shewed it to some friends, who took copies, and those of course presently multiplied; so that this little piece had been spread with rapidity all over Europe, and was in every bodies hands when I saw it, for the first time, in London."

Mr. H's ignorance in this respect is, indeed, not less astonishing, than Mr. W's conduct; that Mr. W. should write this letter to ridicule Mr. Rousseau, and not shew it to Mr. H. though they lived in the same hotel, and were often together, out of respect to him; and yet that Mr. W. should, upon Mr. H's departure, circulate it, and *let* it presently find its way to a public newspaper, appears somewhat incongruous. This *regard* here does not seem to have been perfectly kept up, and this ignorance, it must be owned seems rather affected. Mr. H. was more generally known to be conductor and patron of Mr. Rousseau in England, than he was in France, so that if it was believed that he intended preserving in his friendly intentions towards the exile, he was indirectly ridiculed by this satire upon Mr. Rousseau, and Mr. W's *regard* for him seems to have been entirely suppressed.

Be this as it may, Mr. H. certainly knew there was such a letter written, and published, when he read it in the St. James's Chronicle; he was sensible it was a fiction; and as the friend and patron of Rousseau, he must have been indirectly hurt by it. How came it then, that a person so capable of handling his pen as Mr. H. should omit so favourable an opportunity of convincing Mr. Rousseau and the world, that he was absolutely in earnest in the patronage he have him, and the services he endeavoured performing for him. The unfortunate exile would then have been convinced of the permanency of his friendship, and all Mr. Rousseau's apprehensions would have been removed.

But so far from this Mr. H –, if he was not instrumental in the publication of this *pleasantry*, at least approved of it, and joined in the laugh against poor Rousseau; nay, he endeavours to apologize for it with all his rhetoric, and is surprised that Mr. Rousseau can be offended at it.

I must acknowledge I have been greatly surprised to find Mr. W. adopt so ridiculous a pleasantry, since it must be a pleasantry, and the more so as the translation is wretched, and what little humour there is in the original, has entirely evaporated under the *English doer's* clumsy pen. *I will cease to persecute you, when you are no longer vain of persecution*, which is the point of the whole, but is indeed very flat, and does not convey the idea of "Je cesserai de vous persecuter, quand vous cesserez demettre votre gloire à l'etre."

The pension which Mr. Hume had seemingly so earnestly interceded for, was the capital stroke of friendship towards Mr. Rousseau, upon which he so much piques himself; for as to the flimsy stratagems of paying part of his board, and advertising for returned post-chaises, they either did not take place, or were detected by Mr. Rousseau. But now we are come to the criterion of Mr. H's protection and regard, let us observe how stedfastly he pursues the design of making Mr. Rousseau easy and happy. General Conway's illness, he tells us, had interrupted the progress of this affair; so that it lay dormant, notwithstanding his Majesty's gracious consent, from the month of February till the middle of May.

It was at this time that Mr. Rousseau, having so much reason to be displeased at the fictitious letter published under the name of the king of Prussia, and the other slights (to say no worse) that he had received from Mr. H, was induced to believe this gentleman only his *false* friend, and therefore wrote a very submissive and polite letter to general Conway, expressing the great anxiety of his mind, and the necessity he was under to suspend any resolution about an affair of such consequence, as was that of the pension. This letter Mr. H. is pleased to consider as a flat refusal of accepting the pension; but that the reader may judge how far Mr. Rousseau's words implied this, we shall give him his letter verbatim.

Mr. ROUSSEAU to General CONWAY.

May 12, 1766.

"Sir,

Affected with a most lively sense of the favour his Majesty hath honoured me with, and with that of your goodness, which procured it me; it affords me the most pleasing sensation to reflect, that the best of kings, and the minister most worthy of his confidence, are pleased to interest themselves in my fortune. This, Sir, is an advantage of which I am justly tenacious, and which I will never deserve to lose. But it is necessary I should speak to you with that frankness you admire. After the many misfortunes that have befallen me, I thought myself armed against all possible events: there have happened to me some, however, which I did not foresee; and which, indeed, an ingenuous mind ought not to have foreseen: hence it is that they affected me so much the more severely. The trouble in which they involve me, indeed, deprives me of the ease and presence of mind necessary to direct my conduct: all I can reasonably do, under so distressed a situation, is to suspend my resolutions about every affair of such importance, as that in agitation. So far from refusing the beneficence of the king from pride, as is imputed to me, I am proud of acknowledging it, and am only sorry I cannot do it more publicly. But when I actually receive it, I would be able to give up myself entirely to those sentiments which it would naturally inspire, and to have a heart replete with gratitude for his Majesty's goodness and your's. I am not at all afraid this manner of thinking will make any alteration in your's towards me. Deign, therefore, Sir, to preserve that goodness for me till a more happy opportunity; when you will be satisfied that I defer taking the advantage of it only to render myself more worthy of it. I beg of you, Sir, to accept of my most humble and respectful salutations.

J.J.R."

The well-known goodness of that truly worthy statesman, to whom this letter was addressed, no doubt prompted him to bring this affair to a conclusion; and therefore the letter, which Mr. H. wrote to Mr. Rousseau, may be entirely ascribed to that source.

It was reasonable for Mr. H. to imagine Mr. Rousseau would explain himself in his next letter, with respect to his conduct; and accordingly we find he wrote him the following, dated June 23.

Mr. ROUSSEAU to Mr. HUME.

"I imagined, Sir, that my silence truly interpreted by your own conscience, had said enough; but since you have some design in not understanding me, I shall speak. You have but ill-disguised yourself. I know you, and you are not ignorant of it. Before we had any personal connections, quarrels, or disputes, while we knew each other only by literary reputation, you affectionately made me the offer of the good offices of yourself and friends. Affected by this generosity, I threw myself into your arms; you brought me to England apparently to procure me an asylum, but in fact to bring me to dishonour. You applied to this noble work with a zeal worthy of your heart, and a success worthy of your abilities. You needed not have taken so much pains: you live and converse with the world: I with myself in solitude. The public love to be deceived, and you were formed to deceive them. I know one man, however, whom you cannot deceive; I mean yourself. You know with what horror my heart rejected the first suspicion of your designs. You know I embraced you with tears in my eyes, and told you, if you were not the best of men, you must be the blackest of mankind. In reflecting upon your private conduct, you must say to yourself sometimes, you are not the best of men: under which conviction, I doubt much if ever you will be the happiest.

"I leave your friends and you to carry on your schemes as you please, giving up to you, without regret, my reputation during life; certain that, sooner or later, justice will be done to that of both. As to your good offices in matters of interest, which you have made use of as a mask, I thank you for them, and shall dispense with profiting by them. I ought not to hold a correspondence with you any longer, or to accept of it to my advantage, in any affair, in which you are to be the mediator.

"Adieu! Sir, I wish you the truest happiness; but as we ought not to have any thing to say to each other for the future, this is the last letter you will receive from me.

J.J.R."

Thus then did Mr. Rousseau disclaim any farther connexion with Mr. H, and of course gave up all desire of the pension through his mediation; so that Mr. H's friendship to this unhappy exile, is reduced to a very small number of favours – a few dinners at Mr. Stewart's, and a few jaunts to public places.

Notwithstanding the severity of this last letter, Mr. H. persevered in writing to him, and extorted from him, whilst ill in bed, a long detail of the many grievances he had to complain of, and amongst other things, we there find this extraordinary passage.

"Strange that after I had ceased to correspond with him for three months, when I had made no answer to any of his letters, however important the subject of them, surrounded with both public and private marks of that affliction which his infidelity gave me; a man of so enlightened an understanding, of so penetrating a genius, and so dull by design, should see nothing, hear nothing, feel nothing, be moved at nothing; but, without one word of complaint, justification, or explanation, continue to give me the most pressing marks of his good will to serve me, in spite of myself! He wrote to me affectionately, that he could not stay any longer in London to do me service, as if we had agreed he should stay there for that purpose? This blindness, this insensibility, this perseverence, are not in nature, they must be accounted for therefore from other motives. Let us set this behaviour in a still clearer light; for this is the decisive point.

Mr. Hume must necessarily have acted in this affair, either as one of the first or last of mankind. There is no medium. It remains to determine which of the two it hath been.

Could Mr. Hume, after so many instances of disdain on my part, have still the astonishing generosity as to persevere sincerely to serve me? He knew it was impossible for me to accept his good offices, so long as I entertained for him such sentiments as I had conceived. He had himself avoided an explanation. So that to serve me, without justifying himself, would have been to render his services useless; this therefore was no generosity. If he supposed that in such circumstances I should have accepted his services, he must have supposed me to be an infamous scoundrel. It was then in behalf of a man whom he supposed to be a scoundrel that he so warmly solicited a pension from his Majesty. Can any thing be supposed more extravagant?

But let it be supposed that Mr. Hume, constantly pursuing his plan, should only have said to himself, This is the moment for its execution; for by pressing Rousseau to accept the pension, he will be reduced either to accept or refuse it. If he accepts it, with the proofs I have in hand against him, I shall be enabled completely to disgrace him: if he refuses, after having accepted it, he will have no pretext, but must give a reason for such refusal. This is what I expect; if he accuses me he is ruined.

If, I say, Mr. Hume reasoned with himself in this manner, he did what was consistent with his plan, and in that case very natural; indeed this is the only way in which his conduct in this affair can be explained; for upon any other supposition it is inexplicable: if this be not demonstrable, nothing ever was so. The critical situation to which he had now reduced me, recalled strongly to my mind the four words I heard him say and repeat, at a time when I did not comprehend their full force. It was the first night after our departure from Paris. We slept in the same chamber, when, during the night, I heard him several times cry out with great vehemence, in the French language, *Je tiens J.J. Rousseau* – I have you Rousseau. – I know not whether he was awake or asleep."

Mr. H's remark upon this occurrence is as remarkable as the event; He says, "I cannot answer for every thing I say in my sleep, and much less am I conscious, whether or not I dream in French. But pray, as Mr. Rousseau did not know whether I was asleep or awake, when I pronounced those terrible words, with such a terrible voice, how is he certain that he himself was well awake when he heard them?"

Shakespear, that great judge of nature and the human heart, would have reasoned very differently upon this occasion – he, who could so feeling display the terrors of Richard whilst asleep, would, perhaps, have judged like Rousseau, of Mr. H's feelings upon this occasion.

I think it clearly appears from what has been said, that Mr. Rousseau's merit and abilities were too conspicuous, and too universally acknowledged, for his cotemporaries and rivals patiently to acquiesce to them. It was necessary to level his philosophical and literary capacity to their own; nay his very misfortunes gave him a superiority over them, which they would not allow to exist, and therefore it was requisite to treat them as Chimeras, and the effect of his own quackery. Voltaire, scarcely vegitating upon the withered stalk of his exhausted faculties, was foremost in the field of Rousseau's adversaries; but his spleen and ill-nature had been too frequently manifested, when in their greatest fervor, to let their dying embers kindle a blaze of infamy against so exalted a character. The Jesuits, his implacable enemies, had exhausted every artifice to blacken his reputation, and impute to him forgeries that he had no hand in. D'Alembert had, in vain, attempted to make him ridiculous at Paris. It was left for D. H. under the mask of friendship, and by such artifices as he could the most successfully employ, at once to render him contemptible and infamous.

How far he has succeeded, the world is left to judge; but that he has not entirely accomplished such a design, may be inferred from the engines which are still set in motion both in public and private. Among the former may be reckoned those invidious paragraphs, that have lately appeared in the public papers, and more particularly a letter just published in French, said to be written from M. Voltaire to Mr. Hume. As this epistle is specious, though replete with abuse and falsehood, I shall make a few observations upon it in this place.

Mr. Rousseau is in this letter treated as a public libeller and incendiary, as a madmans vain and presumptuous beyond all bounds, an errant coward and a notorious liar. Because his letters from the mountain, were suppressed, he is a public calumniator, and Mr. Voltaire thinks himself very ill used for being taken notice of in one of these letters, though he had long before declared war against Mr. Rousseau. Because Mr. Rousseau rejected his offer of a house, which offer was dictated by Mr. Voltaire's pride and vanity, Mr. Rousseau is represented as a madman, and he writes a letter to Dr. Tronchin, to send him a prescription accordingly. In this state he is made to petition the magistrates of Berne for perpetual imprisonment, and be angry with Mr. Voltaire for his supposed intercession in his favour. But the most glaring malice of this piece is the forged letters which are imputed to Mr. Rousseau, though they are artfully drawn up to impose upon the credulous.

The first of these, which is supposed to be written by Mr. Rousseau to Mr. Voltaire, is couched in these words:

"Sir,
If you have said I was not secretary of embassy at Venice, you have lied; and if I have not been invested with that character, and received the honours that were due to it, I acknowledge myself a liar."

In order to prove Mr. Rousseau worthy of this last character, another forged letter is introduced from Mr. Rousseau, supposed to be written from him at Venice to Mr. Thiel, first clerk for foreign affairs. The words of it are, "I have been two years servant to the count de Montaign (embassador at Venice) I have eat his bread. He has shamefully turned me out of doors. He threatened to throw me out of the window, and still worse if I remained longer in Venice.

I believe no one who was ever acquainted with Mr. Rousseau, can aver that he has at any time pretended to have been secretary of embassy at Venice, and so far from this I believe he never was at Venice. But what will not implacable malice invent! Doubtless Voltaire thought to give him the *coup-de-grace* with this discovery, but it favours too much of slander and invective, to gain credit with the impartial and judicious.

If after these testimonies the public should have any doubt remaining of the injuries Mr. Rousseau has received from these various quarters; they will soon be convinced of his probity and honour, by his own authentic memoirs which will in a short time make their appearance.

The share I have taken in his defence, is not occasioned by any sort of ill will I bear to Mr. H. far from it, I always admired his talents and esteemed his merit, and could heartily have wished that he had cleared up this affair more to the satisfaction of the public, and his own glory. Neither have I any connection, personal or otherwise with Mr. Rousseau; but as Mr. Hume expresses it, *there needed no other motive to excite me to this act of humanity, than his well known genius and abilities, and, above all, his misfortunes; the very cause of which was an additional reason to interest me in his favour.*

———

ADVERTISEMENT.

———

The following general Remarks upon the Pamphlet, entitled, A concise and genuine Account of the Dispute between Mr. HUME and Mr. ROUSSEAU, *having been put into the Editors hands since the foregoing sheets went to press, he thinks they will be no improper supplement.*

———

GENERAL REMARKS, &C.

The introduction to this curious piece, which is ascribed to French editors, but which evidently bears many marks of British manufactory, is worthy of a place before so extraordinary a performance; it is replete with so much modesty and impartiality, that it must needs be the production of a Scotch writer: "The name and writings of Mr. H. have long since been well-known through Europe. At the same time his personal acquaintance have remarked, in the candour and simplicity of his manners, that impartiality and ingenuousness of disposition which distinguishes his character, and is sufficiently indicated in his writings." Doubtless the production before us is here meant, as, though he neither prefixed or subscribes his name to it, he speaks in the first person singular throughout; and he has had the modesty of placing his name first in the front page, which gives it the vague title of an Account, without supposing either of the parties to have been the writer of it. But this is not more unaccountable than its being published in French, translated from his notes and observations, and then retranslated into English by so very able an hand as his translator. This puts one in mind of an edition of Milton, that appeared some years ago, translated into English prose, from a French translation in rhyme. If Mr. H. did not think the British (I will not say the English) nation was deserving of being first complimented with the publication of this account at the very time of his own residence in England; he might, methinks, at least have vouchsafed to give his narrative and notes, as well as his letters, in their primitive dress; and then the present editor would not have had the trouble of telling us, "that they are now retranslated, for the most part, from the French."

It must be acknowledged that his love of peace is so well supported by an anecdote, that we think no one can dispute this disposition in him, or the truth of the fact by which it is maintained. "As one time, in particular, a performance of this kind (a satyr upon himself) was shewn to him; in which he had been treated in a very rude and even injurious manner; on remarking which, to the author, the latter struck out the exceptionable passage; blushing, and wondering at the force of that *polemic spirit*, which had carried him imperceptibly beyond the bounds of truth and decency."

No doubt, then, it was with great reluctance that a man, possessed of such pacific dispositions, could be brought to consent to the publication of this piece; yet we think there is something of a vindictive spirit in his letter of the 20th of June, where he says to Mr. Rousseau, "I demand you will produce me the man who will assert the contrary." – Again, "I claim the privilege of proving my innocence, and refuting any scandalous lie which may have been invented against me."

Notwithstanding he was thus warm in defence of his conduct and integrity, and though he had received and read all Mr. Rousseau's letters, even that one which he entitles *enormous*, he was still inclined to suppress his public resentment; till Mr. Rousseau wrote a letter to a bookseller at Paris, more *enormous* I suppose than the other, though by the copy I have seen of it in the papers, it was comparatively very gentle; and this letter determined Mr. H. to publish the whole affair.

Mr. H. does not think he will remain unanswered, and therefore he (I mean his French editor) prudently paves the way for it by telling us "Mr. Rousseau indeed may return to the charge; he may produce suppositions, misconstructions, inferences and new declamations, he may create and *realize* new phantoms, and envelop them in the clouds of his rhetoric; he will meet with no more contradictions" – What not if the phantoms are *realized?* Upon my word Mr. H. this idea seems to me somewhat enveloped in the clouds of your own rhetoric.

This is not, however, the only flight we meet with in this uncommon production. Mr. Rousseau is made to say in one of his letters. "I might, perhaps, be more at my ease if I were less noticed; but the solicitude of so polite an host as mine is too obliging to give offence; and as there is nothing in life without it's inconveniences, that of being too *good*, is one of those which is the most tolerable.

It's a pity that this passage had not been *re-translated*, as well as Mr. H's notes &c. as we might then perhaps have come nearer to the signification of the original author, whose words are "J'y serois peut etré plus á mon aise, si l'on y avoit pour moi moins d'attentions; mais les soins d'un si galant homme sont trop obligeans pour s'enfacher, & comme tout est melé d'inconveniens dans la vie, celui d'etre trop *bien* est un de ceux qui se tolerent le plus aisément."

I will not pay the reader so bad a compliment as to suppose such an egregious blunder can escape him; but shall only remind him, that eh modest translator had previously apologized for all the mistakes that might have happened, by a note in the French editor's preface, where he says, "In the present edition all Mr. Hume's letters are printed verbatim; and to Mr. Rousseau's the translator hath endeavoured to do justice, as well with regard to the sense as the expression. Not that he can flatter himself with having always succeeded in the *latter*." But as he appears pretty confident he has in the *former*, I shall leave him to enjoy this success, without entering into any farther critique upon his translation, which would carry me much beyond the bounds I had prescribed myself.

I know not whether Mr. d'Alembert's letter, which is subjoined, is meant as a compliment to Mr. H; but I am pretty certain it can be none to Mr. W. This gentleman, in his letter to Mr. R. upon the subject of the letter which appeared in the St. James's Evening Post, with the king of Prussia's signature, not only adopts this production for his own, but seems to derive great honour from it; but Mr. d'Alembert tells us he had some assistance in it with respect to the stile; perhaps he might, and probably the chevalier Descazeau was his assistant, as it is penned a good deal in his manner; but this is a secret which Mr. W. would certainly not have the world acquainted with, or else this *pleasantry*, which has been considered till now as the best joke he ever penned, will sink in value, in proportion as the rank of its author, or authors, is diminished; and may, perhaps, at last turn out to be a flat insipid *humbug*, that Foote would be ashamed of.

Though it is evident, that *Scotch influence* prevails in this invidious attack upon a helpless foreigner; yet an *Irish bull* has unhappily exerted his influence over the publisher, who generously promises to deposit the original letters in the British Museum, notwithstanding those from Mr. H. must necessarily be in the possession of Mr. Rousseau.

27
RALPH HEATHCOTE:
A LETTER TO THE HONORABLE
MR. HORACE WALPOLE

[Ralph Heathcote], *A letter to the Honorable Mr. Horace Walpole, concerning the dispute between Mr. Hume and Mr Rousseau*, London: printed for B. White, 1767, 23, [1] p.[1]
Complete; from 1767 edition.

Born in Leicestershire, England, son of a clergyman, Ralph Heathcote (1721–1795) was educated at Jesus College, Cambridge and was ordained in the Church of England in 1748. A miscellaneous author, Heathcote wrote religious works and was a principal author of the *Biographical Dictionary*. He was a friend of William Warburton, who wrote of Heathcote that "His matter is rational, but superficial and thin-spread. He is sensible, and has reading, but little vivacity" (*Letters from a Late Eminent Prelate*, London, Cadell, 1793). In his *Cursory Animadversions upon a late Controversy Concerning the Miraculous Powers* (1752), Heathcote attacks the sceptical tone of Hume's *Essays*. In early 1767 he anonymously published *A Letter to the Honorable Mr. Horace Walpole*, defending Hume in the dispute with Rousseau; Heathcote's authorship of this is indicated in John Nichol's *Literary Anecdotes*. He opens by arguing that Walpole's satirical letter was justified to the extent that authors "assume a kind of *public* character" and Rousseau in particular can be publicly corrected for his arrogance. Heathcote believes that Rousseau was predisposed against Hume and the British even before Walpole's letter was printed: he entered the country expecting people to fall all over him, but when he did not receive "puffs to feed his vanity" he became miserable. Rousseau was enraged, and "as sometimes happeneth among wild beasts, he fell upon [Hume] his Keeper." Weighing the respective behaviour of Hume and Rousseau, Heathcote concludes "I had rather be such a Philosopher as *Mr. Hume*, than

[1] Title page: A | LETTER | TO THE HONORABLE | Mr. Horace Walpole, | CONCERNING THE | DISPUTE | BETWEEN | Mr. HUME and Mr ROUSSEAU. | LONDON: | Printed for B. WHITE, at Horace's Head, | *Fleet*-Street. MDCCLXVII. | (Price Sixpence.)

such a Christian as *Mr. Rousseau.*" Hume's unfortunate experience with Rousseau, he suggests, helps account for why people "as they grow old, should grow less benevolent."

Writing for the *Monthly Review*, William Rose implies that the letter was written by Walpole himself to suit his own purposes:

> Who the author of this Letter is, we know not: it appears pretty evident, however, that he is well acquainted with Mr. Walpole's sentiments in regard to the quarrel between Messrs. Hume and Rousseau: and many readers will probably be inclined to think that Mr. Walpole and the Letter-writer are *extremely intimate.* ... What sentiments others may entertain of Mr. Walpole's conduct in this affair, we know not; to us, we are sorry to say, it appears neither consistent with humanity nor politeness. By an ill-judged piece of pleasantry he endeavours to expose Mr. Rousseau to public ridicule, and when he finds that this gives great uneasiness to a poor unfortunate man, who had never done him any injury, instead of expressing any concern on this account, he publishes to the world that he has a thorough contempt for him, and represents him as an object of detestation. – We are no advocates of Mr. Rousseau; but there appears to be a degree of petulance and insolence in this, altogether unworthy the character of Mr. Walpole. [*Monthly Review*, Vol. 35, December 1766, p. 469]

Hume was aware of the rumours ascribing authorship of this pamphlet to Walpole, and in the letter below he notes Walpole's denial of this, while approving of the pamphlet itself:

> I send you a Pamphlet, which was publishd near three Months ago; but I never heard of it till last Week, nor saw it till two days ago. Neither Mr Walpole nor I know any thing of the Author; tho' I am told the public ascribd it to himself, which he positively denies, and I entirely acquit him, tho the piece is not ill-wrote. [Hume to Hugh Blair, April 1, 1767]

The following is from the 1767 and only edition of Heathcote's *Letter*.

A

LETTER

TO THE HONORABLE

Mr. Horace Walpole,

CONCERNING THE

DISPUTE

BETWEEN

Mr. HUME and Mr. ROUSSEAU.

LONDON:

Printed for B. WHITE, at Horace's Head,
Fleet-Street. MDCCLXVII.

(Price Sixpence.)

A
LETTER
TO THE
HON. MR. HORACE WALPOLE.

SIR,

The simple Enthusiast is a quiet and harmless creature. He sees visions, and he dreams dreams; but he keeps these visions and dreams to himself, and enjoys the comfort of them in silent meditation. The Fanatic is ever restless and turbulent; and, though a dreamer as well as the Enthusiast, is not however content, like him, with what passes within himself, but is impatient to rage and riot abroad: ου᾽ μονον ἐνθουσιᾶν, ἀλλὰ βαυχένειν. Society must interest itself in favour of his reveries; nor is it too much for their sake, even to disturb the public peace.

Enthusiasm and Fanaticism are, both of them, compounded of Folly and Madness; and, for the latter, if dishonesty and rancor be not of its essence, they are at least consistent with it, and almost always found to tincture it very strongly.

The term *Fanatic* has usually been applied to the Religionist, when disordered, and not in his right mind: may it not, under the same circumstances, suit as well the Philosopher? The Religionist, I know, is supposed to do all for the glory of God; the Philosopher, to act only for the glory of himself. But the difference is trifling; apparent surely, not real. Self at the bottom is the principle of action; and however the one may clamour for Religion, and the other for Virtue,[2] yet the glory of *himself* is the great object of both. But I will not contend: let the Religionist, if you please, walk first. It would grieve one, that two members of Society, so useful and so amiable, should quarrel about precedency.

These reflections owe their birth to the quarrel, which hath arisen between *Mr. Hume* and *Mr. Rousseau*; and they are addressed to you, Sir, because you are supposed to have occasioned it by the flippancy of your wit. I do not believe, that you were even the innocent-occasion of this *fracas*. Dark suspicions and tormenting jealousies had plainly occupied the imagination of *Mr. Rousseau, before* your Letter was written; and a quarrel must have happened, if it had *never* been written.

The first intimation of these suspicions from *Mr. Rousseau* himself appears in his letter to *Mr. Hume* of March 22, 1766; wherein we read, as follows.

---

[2] "*Mr. Rousseau* is so passionate an admirer of *Virtue*, that his eyes always sparkle at the bare mention of that word." So at least he relates of himself. *Account of the Dispute between* Mr. Hume *and* Mr. Rousseau, p. 63.

The affair of the carriage is not yet adjusted, because I know I was imposed on: it is a trifling fault however, which may be only the effect of an obliging vanity, unless it should happen to be repeated. If you were concerned in it, I would advise you to give up, once for all, these little impositions, which cannot proceed from any good motive, when converted into snares for simplicity.[3]

Simplicity! If *Mr. Rousseau*'s be simplicity, it is such a simplicity as the devil assumed, when he tempted our first parent under the form of a serpent. *Milton* describes the beast, as soft, pleasing, undesigning, and benevolent, *without*; but *within* restless, fraudulent, treacherous, and of the most envenomed as well as the most persevering malice.

But what were these *snares* for *simplicity?* Why truly, *Mr. Rousseau* being mean enough to affect poverty, and yet too proud to be relieved, expedients were sought to serve, without disgusting him; and, among the rest, this of advertising a chaise at an under-price, contrived by *Mr. Davenport*, and assented to by *Mr. Hume*.

But was not *Mr. Hume*, however well meaning, too officious? Was there not something indelicate in these sort of services? and was it not natural for *Mr. Rousseau*, to suspect these *obliging* acts, as resulting from *vanity?* They, who ask such questions, do not consider, how extremely distressed *Mr. Rousseau* appeared to *Mr. Hume*. In his letter to *Mr. Clairaut*, of March the 3rd, 1765, he implores that gentleman to correct a work, which he is "obliged, he says, to republish for subsistence, *pour avoir du pain*; declares himself overwhelmed with a torrent of misfortunes; and assures him, that this would be doing a very great charity to the most unhappy of men."[4]

Is not this to call out, in effect, for the contributions of charitable and well-disposed persons, to preserve a poor wretch from perishing through want? Is it true, this was not the real state of *Mr. Rousseau*; for we find him speaking afterwards of his sufficiency in a strain of triumph: "I did not come over, says he, to beg my bread in England; I brought the means of subsistence with me."[5] But *Mr. Hume* at that time knew nothing of this; and had therefore just reason to say, that "this affectation of extreme poverty and distress was a mere pretence, a petty kind of imposture, which *Mr. Rousseau* successfully employed to excite the compassion of the public," and by that means if he could to engross its attention.

Soon after, Sir, your letter came forth; in which you exhibited this fantastic mortal more clearly to view, by giving the outlines of his character with much good sense and wit. That you should do this with sense and wit, I do not

[3]   Dispute, p. 14.

[4]   Dispute, p. 7.

[5]   Dispute, p. 41.

wonder; but I wonder extremely, that any man of sense and wit should disapprove of your doing this. *Mr. D'Alembert* says, that "we ought not to ridicule the unfortunate, especially when they have done us no harm."[6] You, Sir, I dare say, would be far from *ridiculing the unfortunate*. It is but justice to believe this of you; for you have given to the public many ingenious specimens of yourself, in which you appear to be a lover of Virtue, as well as of Letters: no small merit surely in a man of your rank, and especially in times, when both are despised.

But, after all, was *Mr. Rousseau* really *unfortunate?* Has he not exaggerated matters? With regard to his poverty most certainly he has; and, perhaps, with regard to his persecutions. You seem to have known this; for if I understand you, it is chiefly against this, that your ridicule is directed. You believed, that these exaggerations were the tricks of a *Charlatan*, who wanted the public to talk of nothing but him; and you justly thought, that the gentlest punishment he deserved was to be laughed at a little. It may be that *Mr. Rousseau* had never injured or offended you, *personally*, or as a *private* man: but an author assumes a kind of *public* character; and every man has a right to correct his notions and his manners too, if either the one or the other shall stand in need of correction. *Mr. D'Alembert* is a very respectable personage, but surely has not decided here with his usual accuracy.

But to what purpose dwell on your innocent letter? The grounds of discontent were laid in *Mr. Rousseau*, and the impulse to quarrel with *Mr. Hume* had doubtless begun to operate, before your letter came to his hands. He seems to have imagined, that, as soon as he arrived at Dover, the English should have been affected, as they were at the *Restoration*, or the landing of the *Prince of Orange*. "Before I arrived in England, says he, there was not a nation in Europe, in which I had a greater reputation—The public papers were full of encomiums on me—my arrival was published with triumph—England prided itself in affording me refuge."[7]

You see, Sir, that the arrival of *Mr. John James Rousseau* was in his view a national concern; so that it was natural for him to expect, and he plainly did expect, that the eyes, the ears, the thoughts of every individual, should be taken at once from their several occupations and pursuits, and fixed intirely upon him alone. The manner of his reception did by no means answer to these preconceived ideas; so far from it, that all of a sudden, as he himself relates, "without the least assignable cause, the tone was changed; and that so speedily and totally, that of all the caprices of the public never was known any thing more surprising."[8] However, while he was in London or near it, some visited him out of curiosity, as others did out of vanity; and thus, though greatly disappointed, he was not as yet in any high degree miserable.

6   Dispute, p. 94.

7   Dispute, p. 43.

8   Dispute, p. 43.

Things grew daily from bad to worse; till at length, he says, "not one of those, who had so much praised me in my absence, appeared, now I was present, to think even of my existence."[9] He flies into the country; still presuming, and most certainly desiring, that the attention of the town might fly thither after him.

Et fugit ad salices, et se cupit ante videri.

It is true, were a judgment to be formed from *Mr. Rousseau*'s declarations, we should of course conclude, that to be buried in solitude was the very thing he wishes: for he speaks of "rural walks, as the only pleasures of his life."[10] "You live and converse with the world," says he to *Mr. Hume*; "I with myself in solitude.—I live retired from the world, I am ignorant of what passes in it.—I am told nothing, and I know only what I feel."[11] The picture, you see, Sir, of a poor abject animal, who scarcely perceives by Reflection, but only knows what he feels by Sensation.

Now nothing can be more unfit to represent the original truly and as it is, than this sort of colouring. So far is *Mr. Rousseau* from desiring *not to know* what is doing in the world, that his own Letters shew him to have been constantly searching the Public Papers and Magazines for intelligence of himself; or, to speak more properly, for puffs to feed his vanity. So far is *Mr. Rousseau* from wishing to live *unknown* and unregarded, that a greater cause of misery to him, I am persuaded, does not exist.

"Arriving at this solitary, convenient, and agreeable habitation" says he, "I became tranquill, independent: and this seemed to be the wished for moment, when all my misfortunes should have an end. On the contrary, it was now they began; misfortunes more cruel than any I had yet experienced."[12] I verily believe, because I so easily conceive, it. He was never perhaps in a situation before, where he was so little liable to be molested; where he was so unnoticed, so altogether left to his own will and humor. For the good people of England, after the first stare was over, had (as their way is) entirely done with him. Far from continuing to admire, they had ceased to mention him; and, if they had not totally forgot, they cared no more about him, than if he had been in Swisserland. His misery increased: your letter appeared:[13] it became extreme. He fell into a paroxysm: he raged: and, in short, as sometimes happeneth among wild beasts, he fell upon his Keeper.[14] To speak without a figure, he quarrelled with his greatest friend and benefactor *Mr. Hume*, by all accounts

---

[9] Dispute, p. 45.

[10] Dispute, p. 60.

[11] Dispute, p. 29, 34.

[12] Dispute, p. 40.

the most quiet, the most humane, the most amiable of men; and who in the present case seems only faulty, in having condescended to humor a man, whom it is not possible to oblige: and nothing doubtless but the exceeding humanity of *Mr. Hume*, and his prejudices for *Mr. Rousseau*, could hinder one of his vast penetration from discerning somewhat earlier, than he seems to have done, that *Rousseau* was a savage, whom no offices of kindness could civilize and tame.

The dispute between these gentlemen is now before the public; which seems reasonably well convinced, that *Mr. Hume* is the first man, who was ever obliged to defend himself in form from such a train of ridiculous and groundless imputations. *Mr. Rousseau* really brings them in such a manner, as if he meant to betray his own cause, and to acquit *Mr. Hume*, while he affects to accuse him. In his letter of June 23, he says, "I thank you for the good offices in matters of interest, which you have used as a mask"[15] – for what? truly to do him ill ones. He abounds with such passages as these. In his letter of July 10, after having urged all he could invent against *Mr. Hume*, he says, that "every circumstance of the affair is equally incomprehensible. A conduct such as yours is not in nature: it is a contradiction; and yet it is demonstrable to me."[16] Thus the *credo quia impossible*, which even the Religionist is now grown ashamed of, is at length adopted by the Philosopher.

No man however but *Mr. Rousseau* will be able to perceive the least contradiction. The marks of friendship from *Mr. Hume* to him were, as the French editor observes, the least equivocal, *les moins equivoques*:[17] they did not consist of *verbiage* and professions, but of true and real services. A *Christian's* faith is generally allowed to be best determined by his works: and what better test can be contrived for the sincerity of a friend? The Methodists indeed are wont to reason otherwise; esteeming all, who contend for Works, as loose in the Faith: and *Mr. Rousseau*, who is certainly a Methodist in Philosophy, seems to have reasoned thus of *Mr. Hume*; else he would never have opposed a series of suppositions, I mean suspicions, of his own against *Mr. Hume* to a series of facts in that gentleman's favor.

---

[13] "In this letter," says *Mr. Rousseau*, "I knew the pen of *Mr. D'Alembert* as certainly, as if I had seen him write it. In a moment a ray of light discovered to me the secret cause of that touching and sudden change, which I had observed in the public respecting me; and I saw that the plot, which was put in execution at London, had been laid at Paris." Dispute, p. 58, 59. Alas! this *ray of light*, darting upon the brain, has occasioned many an unhappy mortal, before *Mr. Rousseau*, to *see*, and *hear*, and *feel* too, what never existed out of his own imagination.

[14] Je tiens J.J.R.

[15] Dispute, p. 30.

[16] Dispute, p. 82.

[17] Advertisement to Dispute, &c.

But I must not, as I have been given to understand, confine *Mr. Rousseau* altogether to Philosophy. An advocate of his declared, in my hearing, that he was indeed a very good Christian; at least a better than *Mr. Hume*, who, it was feared, is only a Philosopher. Concerning these important points I can neither affirm, nor deny any thing. *Mr. Rousseau* is evidently an heap of inconsistencies and contradictions; so that, his understanding having been undetermined to any systematical or regular way of thinking, if he was not a Christian three months ago, he may be one now. In the mean time I meddle with no man's faith. That affair lies wholly between God and himself; and can be no concern of mine. Yet, were we to judge of Christianity, as exemplified in the conduct of these two gentlemen, I should make no scruple to say, with *Averroes*, *Sit anima mea cum Philosophis*: for I had rather be such a Philosopher as *Mr. Hume*, than such a Christian as *Mr. Rousseau*.

The French editor seems afraid, Sir, lest this quarrel between Philosophers should *bring a scandal upon Philosophy*. Not much, I should think, if any at all. Sects and Professions of every kind, Philosophical as well as Religious, have long been too wise to be responsible for individuals. But whatever disgrace it may bring upon the Philosophers, he supposes, that the *blockheads* will reap from it no small comfort: which, if the numbers of each be rightly estimated, is supposing it to produce more physical good than evil by far. Let us not envy them this consolation: it seems indeed necessary, that they should sometimes have it: for who can say, what might otherwise happen? Genii of a superior order might gain too great an ascendency: they might in time pass for more than Genii: they might be reputed Gods, as *Paul* and *Barnabas* were at *Lystra*, if they did not discover by things of this kind; that they were *men of like passions* with the meanest of their species.

Other reflections more solid may be made, and lessons more useful drawn, from the dispute between these celebrated personages. We may learn from the character of *Mr. Rousseau*, and from his very strange treatment of *Mr. Hume*, to what extravagancies the human mind is capable of being carried, when the humor *atrabilaire* has once thoroughly infected it. A person thus distempered, or rather thus *possessed*, (for is he not a Demoniac?) is able to conceive any thing. The power of imagination in such a one is creative beyond measure. Existence or Non-existence are precisely to him the same: for he makes no difference at all between facts, on which alone depends the certainty of all human information; I say, between the plainest and most notorious facts, and suppositions the most wild, the most improbable, the most visionary. He overlooks or contemns the former, as non-entities: he builds demonstrations upon the latter. In short, he cannot see what actually is, while he sees intuitively what is not; and things do or do not exist with him, as they happen to suit his prejudices and passions.

We learn from the same object, that superior abilities, and even shining force of genius, are consistent with great misery in him who possesses them, if his temperament be thoroughly bad. Rigid Philosophy, I know, will not allow this temperament to be within the reach of even Alternatives; but Christianity teaches, that it may be greatly corrected and amended, if not cured. And it is surprising that *Mr. Rousseau*, who is so good a Christian, should not have labored this point more abundantly; as his whole happiness seems to have depended upon it.

From the strange and unexpected situation of *Mr. Hume* it appears, that an active benevolence may sometimes expose a man to inconveniencies and troubles. I have often wondered, why men, as they grow old, should grow less benevolent; (for I take the fact to be incontestable) but this and similar instances have helped me to account for it. And sorry am I to say it; but, alas! Human nature, thou can'st not bear to be too much obliged. It is dangerous, I have been told, with regard to the Great Ones; and if there be not an equal danger in obliging the Little Ones, it is not from the want of will, but the want of power, to hurt their benefactors. At least so it seems from the behaviour of *Mr. Rousseau*.

It appears again, that the utmost prudence and goodness are no security against the basest and most injurious usage, when a man's ill stars shall have connected him with folly and knavery; or, which is commonly the case, with these two substances united in one person. People of this make see every thing in a wrong light. They misinterpret from folly, they misrepresent from malice, every well-meant word and deed. They treat their truest friends as their most inveterate enemies; and load the best men with imputations, which can belong to none but the worst. This happens so very often, that there is hardly a man living, who has not experienced it in some degree: and, as *Calvin*, said to *Francis* I. *there would be no such thing as innocence either in words or deeds, if a simple accusation was sufficient to destroy it.*[18]

No wonder then, that the *Stoical*, not to say the Christian, principle of *doing good* should wax weak and cold with increasing years: no wonder, that so many should, like *Epicurus*, contract their sphere of action, and suffer their happiness to be dependent on none but themselves. Doubtless the great business of a wise man's life is to keep himself, as much as may be, from being teazed by fools, and over-reached by knaves: and neither can be done to any purpose, but by avoiding both the one and the other. *Vivez librement & ignoré*, says a Philosopher. *La solitude vous procurera le vrai & unique plaisir d'etre toujours content de soi. Les sots & les mechans n' exciteront que votre compassion vûs de loin; mais vûs de près il faudrait les hair ou les mepriser.*[19]

---

[18] *Perpendendum est, nullam neque in dictis, neque in factis innocentiam fore, si-accusasse sufficiat.* In Ded. Institut. &c.

[19] That is, "Live freely and unknown. Solitude will procure you the true and only pleasure of being satisfied with yourself. Fools and knaves, seen at a distance, will only move your compassion; but will force you, when near, to either hate or despise them."

I have heard it said, that more practical knowledge may be drawn by reflection from the dispute between *Messieurs Hume* and *Rousseau*, than from all that either of them hath written. This was said pleasantly. *Mr. Rousseau* is indeed of little use: he may however amuse men of mere imagination, or such as like to contemplate the caprices of the human brain. *Mr. Hume's* writings are a rich and abounding treasury of all that is either useful or entertaining; and may be read with great profit by those, who know how to read them properly. *Mr. Hume* is not without his singularities, most certainly; but they affect not a reader; and I do not find, that he requires even his friends to espouse them. The opinions of men, about which they quarrel most, concern each other least. Every man has, and ever will have, his own; and if difference of opinion is a sufficient cause of quarrelling, no two speculating men can come to an *eclaircissement*, and continue friends.

These, Sir, are a few of my thoughts upon the present dispute between *Mr. Hume* and *Mr. Rousseau*; and yours may probably run in the same train. At least I should imagine so from both your letters,[20] which are indeed very spirited, very just, and very elegant. I have the honour to be,

SIR,
    Your most humble,
        and most obedient Servant.

Westminster,
December, 1766.

FINIS.

---

[20] Two letters of *Mr. Wolpole*'s printed in the Account of the Dispute, p. 20. 88.

28
JEAN-JACQUES ROUSSEAU:
THE CONFESSIONS

Jean-Jacques Rousseau, *Les confessions de J.J. Rousseau, suivies des Reveries du promeneur solitaire*, Geneve, 1782, 2 v.
Book 11, selections; from *The confessions of Jean Jacques Rousseau*, tr. W. Conyngham Mallory, Philadelphia, G. Barrie [a. 1890], 2 v.

For background on Jean-Jacques Rousseau (1712–1778) see the general introduction to this collection. Rousseau worked on his great autobiography – the *Confessions* – on and off between 1764 and 1770. The work stands out for its vivid self-disclosure and also as a chronicle of French literary society of the time. The final chapter takes him up to events in 1765, just before he left for England. In Book 11 of this work, which covers the period of 1761, Rousseau digresses with a brief account of Hume. Written after the dispute with Hume, Rousseau looks back on his first introduction to the Scottish philosopher through their mutual friend, Madam de Verdelin. He writes of his admiration for Hume at the time, and Hume's efforts to bring him to England, with no hint as to what was to come.

BOOK 11

...

[Madam de Verdelin] frequently spoke of Mr. Hume, who was then at Paris, of his friendship for me, and the desire he had of being of service to me in his own country. It is time I should say something of Hume. He had acquired a great reputation in France amongst the Encyclopedists by his essays on commerce and politics, and in the last place by his history of the House of Stuart, the only one of his writings of which I had read a part, in the translation of the Abbe Prevot. For want of being acquainted with his other works, I was persuaded, according to what I heard of him, that Mr. Hume joined a very republican mind to the English paradoxes in favor of luxury. In this opinion I considered his whole apology of Charles I. as a prodigy of impartiality, and I had as great an idea of his virtue as of his genius. The desire of being acquainted with this great man, and of obtaining his friendship, had greatly strengthened the inclination I felt to go to England, induced by the solicitations of Madam de Boufflers, the intimate friend of Hume. After my arrival in Switzerland, I received from him, by means of this lady, a letter extremely flattering; in which, to the highest encomiums on my genius, he subjoined a pressing invitation to induce me to go to England, and the offer of all his interest, and that of his friends, to make my residence there agreeable. I found in the country to which I had retired, the lord marshal, the countryman and friend of Hume, who confirmed my good opinion of him, and from whom I learned a literary anecdote, which did him great honor in the opinion of his lordship and had the same effect in mine. Wallace, who had written against Hume upon the subject of the population of the ancients, was absent whilst his work was in the press. Hume took upon himself to examine the proofs, and to do the needful to the edition. This manner of acting was according to my own way of thinking. I had sold at six sols (three pence) a piece, the copies of a song written against myself. I was, therefore, strongly prejudiced in favor of Hume, when Madam de Verdelin came and mentioned the lively friendship he expressed for me, and his anxiety to do me the honors of England; such was her expression. She pressed me a good deal to take advantage of this zeal and to write to him. As I had not naturally an inclination to England, and did not intend to go there until the last extremity, I refused to write or make any promise; but I left her at liberty to do whatever she should think necessary to keep Mr. Hume favorably disposed towards me. When she went from Motiers, she left me in the persuasion, by everything she had said to me of that illustrious man, that he was my friend, and she herself still more his. ...

THOMAS BLACKLOCK
AND JAMES BEATTIE

29
THOMAS BLACKLOCK:
POEMS ON SEVERAL OCCASIONS

Thomas Blacklock, *Poems on several occasions. By Thomas Blacklock.*
Edinburgh: printed by Hamilton, Balfour and Neill, 1754. xvi, 181, [1] p.
"On the Refinements in Metaphysical Philosophy," complete; from 1754
edition.

B orn in Dumfriesshire, Scotland, the son of a bricklayer, Thomas Blacklock
(1721–1791) lost his eyesight in infancy from smallpox. A sympathetic
physician supported him through grammar school, after which he attended the
University of Edinburgh. Even before his schooling, Blacklock took an interest
in poetry, and manuscripts of his early works circulated among friends. In 1746
an eighty-eight page collection of his was published titled *Poems on Several
Occasions.* A much expanded edition of this appeared in 1754, and in one of
its new poems, titled "On the Refinements in Metaphysical Philosophy," he
mentions Hume's advocacy of skepticism. Blacklock had casually known
Hume for some time, but their friendship grew around 1753 and was cemented
in 1754 when Hume signed over to Blacklock his librarian salary of £40 a year
(for details on this see James Beattie's 1769 letter to Blacklock in this
collection). Hume also took it upon himself to promote Blacklock's book in
Edinburgh and London. In a glowing letter to literary critic Joseph Spence,
Hume gives a biographical sketch of Blacklock and encourages Spence in his
"scheme of publishing his poems by subscription" (Hume to Spence, October
15, 1754). Spence was indeed impressed with Blacklock and published a
pamphlet titled *An Account of the Life, Character, and Poems of Mr. Blacklock*
(1754), praising the poet and drawing liberally on the letter from Hume.
Ultimately, Spence sponsored a new edition of the *Poems* – on the condition
that references to Hume in the one poem be dropped. Blacklock was torn in
the decision, but Hume persuaded him to comply, as he relates here:

Mr Spence would not undertake to promote a London subscription, unless my
name, as well as Lord Shaftesbury's (who was mentioned in another place) were
erased: the author frankly gave up Shaftesbury, but said that he would forfeit
all the profit he might expect from a subscription, rather than relinquish the

small tribute of praise which he had paid to a man whom he was more indebted to than to all the world beside. I heard by chance of this controversy, and wrote to Mr Spence, that, without farther consulting the author, I, who was chiefly concerned, would take upon me to empower him to alter the stanza where I was mentioned. He did so, and farther, having prefixed the life of the author, he took occasion to mention some people to whom he had been obliged, but is careful not to name me; judging rightly that such good deeds were only *splendida peccata*, and that till they were sanctified by the grace of God they would be of no benefit to salvation. [Hume to John Clephane, April 20, 1756]

A review of the 1754 edition of Blacklock's *Poems* appeared in the *Monthly Review* (October 1754, Vol. 11, p. 318), which only contained a brief extract from that work.

On the REFINEMENTS in *Metaphysical Philosophy*:
AN ODE.

I. False wisdom, fly, with all thy owls;[1]
The dust and cobwebs of the schools
For me have charms no more:
The gross MINERVA of our days,
In mighty bulk my learn'd Essays[2]
Reads joyful o'er and o'er.

II. Led by her hand a length of time,
Thro' sense and nonsense, prose and rhyme,
I beat my painful way;
Long, long revolv'd the mystic page
Of many a *Dutch* and *German* Sage,
And hop'd at last for day.

III. But, as the mole, hid under ground,
Still works more dark as more profound,
So all my toils were vain:
For truth and sense indignant fly,
As far as ocean from the sky,
From all the formal train.

---

[1] Formerly the bird of MINERVA, but by the moderns ascribed to DULNESS.

[2] The Author, like others of greater name, had formerly attempted to demonstrate matters of fact *à priori*.

IV. The STAGERITE,[3] whose fruitful quill
O'er free-born nature lords it still,
Sustain'd by form and phrase
Of dire portent and solemn sound,
Where meaning seldom can be found,
From me shall gain no praise.

V. But you, who would be truly wise,
To nature's light unveil your eyes,
Her gentle call obey:
She leads by no false wand'ring glare,
No voice ambiguous strikes your ear,
To bid you vainly stray.

VI. Not in the gloomy cell recluse,
For noble deeds or gen'rous views,
She bids us watch the night;
Fair virtue shines, to all display'd,
Nor asks the tardy *Schooman's* aid,
To teach us what is right.

VII. Pleasure and pain she sets in view,
And which to shun, and which pursue,
Instructs her pupil's heart:
Then, *letter'd Pride*, says, what thy gain,
To mask, with so much fruitless pain,
Thy ignorance with art?

VIII. Thy stiff grimace and awful tone
An idiot's wonder move alone;
And, spite of all thy rules,
The wise in ev'ry age conclude,
What PYRRHO[4] taught, and HUME[5] renew'd,
"That *Dogmatists* are fools."[6]

---

[3] ARISTOTOLE, the inventor of Syllogisms, and as such only, mentioned here.

[4] Author of Scepticism.

[5] Author of a Treatise on Human Nature.

[6] [In the 1756 edition, Joseph Spence altered the previous three sentences as follows: "The wise in ev'ry age conclude | Thy fairest prospects, rightly view'd | The paradise of Fools."]

IX. The gamester's hope when doom'd to lose,
The joys of wine, the wanton's vows,
    The faithless calm at sea,
The courtier's word, the crowd's applause,
The Jesuit's faith, the sense of laws,
    Are not more false than thee.

X. Blest he! who sees, without surprize,
Thy various systems fall and rise,
    As shifts the fickle gale;
While all their utmost force exert,
To wound the foe's unguarded part,
    And all alike prevail.

XI. Thus (sacred Bards[7] of yore have sung)
High heav'n with marital clamours rung,
    And deeds of mortal wrath;
When cranes and pygmies glory sought,
And in the fields of æther fought,
    With mutual wounds and death.

XII. Let Logic's sons, mechanic throng!
Their *syllogistic war* prolong,
    And reason's empire boast:
Inshrin'd in deep congenial gloom,
Eternal wrangling be their doom,
    To truth and nature lost!

XIII. Amus'd by fancy's fleeting fire,
Let MALEBRANCHE[8] still for *Truth* inquire,
    And rack his aching sight:
While the coy goddess wings her way,
To scenes of uncreated day,
    Absorb'd in dazzling light.

---

[7]   See HOMER.

[8]   He thought the medium, by which sensible perceptions were conveyed to us, was God; in whose essence truth was seen, as in a mirror.

XIV. With firmer step and graver guise,
Whilst LOCKE[9] in conscious triumph tries,
Her dwelling to explore;
Swift she eludes his ardent chace,
A shadow courts his fond embrace,
Which HOBBES[10] caress'd before.

XV. Let DODWELL[11] with the *Fathers* join,
To strip of energy divine
The heav'n-descended soul;
The *test of sense* let BERKELEY[12] scorn,
And both on borrow'd pinions borne,
Annihilate the whole.

XVI. In Academic vales retir'd,
With PLATO'S *love* and *beauty* fir'd,
My steps let candour guide;
By tenets vain unprepossest,
Those lawless tyrants of the breast,
Offspring of zeal and pride!

XVII. Or, while thro' fields and woods I stray,
Would ASHLEY'S[13] genius dart a ray,
And all my soul inflame;
Creation,[14] and her bounteous laws,
Her order fix'd, her glorious cause,
Should be my fav'rite theme.

---

[9] His account of virtue differs not much from that of the *Leviathan*.

[10] Author of the last mentioned piece; who denied the distinction between vice and virtue, and affirmed power and right to be the same.

[11] He attempted to prove the Natural Mortality of the Soul, and quoted the fathers in favour of his opinion.

[12] Author of Dialogues on the Non-existence of Matter.

[13] Author of the *Characteristics*.

[14] The Author's intention will be ill understood, if he is thought here to recommend universal scepticism; for which reason, he may, with all decorum, declare what authors and sentiments he approves. The philosophy useful to man consists, not in abstract and uncertain propositions, but, being designed to regulate his conduct and ascertain his happiness, must not only be founded on his nature, but comprehend all the principles of an active and percipient being.

30
JAMES BEATTIE:
"THE CASTLE OF SCEPTICISM"

James Beattie, "The Castle of Scepticism: A Vision," April, 1767.
Complete; newly transcribed from manuscript at Aberdeen University Library,
MS 30/18.[1]

Born in Laurencekirk, Kincardineshire, Scotland, James Beattie (1735–1803)
was raised by his mother after his father's death when he was seven. In
1753 he received his M.A. at Marischal College, Aberdeen, and, after a job as
a schoolmaster, was appointed to the chair of moral philosophy and logic at
his *alma mater*. Throughout his life, Beattie balanced his work as both a poet
and philosopher. Along with Thomas Reid, George Campbell and other
important figures, he was a member of the Aberdeen Philosophical Society,
which between 1758 and 1773 met to read papers, frequently critiquing Hume.
Less respectful of Hume's views than others in the club, Beattie wrote a
scathing attack on the philosopher; a first draft was complete in 1767 and it
finally appeared in 1770 under the title *Essay on the Nature and Immutability
of Truth*. The work met with instant public acclaim and three years later King
George III gave Beattie a pension of £200 per year because of this work.
Hume was deeply bothered by the harsh rhetoric Beattie employed against him
in the *Essay*. Friends rallied to Hume's defence and Beattie's own supporters
hailed his victory against Hume – a battle that is reflected in several items
contained later in this collection. In 1767, when Beattie was engrossed in
writing his *Essay*, he composed a short fictional work titled "The Castle of
Scepticism," which is a satire on Hume and other sceptics. He mentions this
work in a letter to Thomas Blacklock:

> I wrote a small Essay, about twice the length of a paper in the Spectator,
> called, The Castle of Scepticism, a vision. I gave it to a Student, an excellent
> Scholar and a favourite of mine, and caused him deliver it in public as his
> Graduation-speech; and it was much applauded. If I can find time to

---

[1] The transcription is reproduced by kind permission of Aberdeen University Library.

transcribe it (for the copy I have is all blots) I shall send it in this packet: it will probably amuse you for ten or fifteen minutes. [Beattie to Thomas Blacklock, April 18, 1769, in Robinson, Letter 122]

As the story opens, Beattie falls asleep while reading Hume's *Essays*, and dreams he is caught up in a crowd of philosophers who, travelling away from the beautiful Land of Truth, are on a pilgrimage to the Castle of Scepticism, where Hume rules as Governor. Along the way Beattie listens as Henry Home incessantly praises Hume. Even Thomas Reid is on the journey for, while one of Hume's chief critics, he nevertheless admired Hume's genius and wishes to seek him out. The landscape becomes dark and ugly as they enter a region called the Paradise of Perplexity; finally they approach the Castle. Before entering, the pilgrims sacrifice in the temple of a god of their choosing. The sacrificed object is "a very small parcel neatly wrapped up, and inscribed Common Sense." The principal gods are those of Affectation, Ignorance, Self-Conceit, Fashion, Licentiousness, and Ambition. Some unsuspecting people, with large parcels of common sense, had been pulled along by the crowd and proceed to sacrifice at the temple of Hypothesis. Beattie is permitted to enter by paying a fee, without sacrificing his common sense.

Inside, he encounters a series of absurd applications of sceptical doctrines. Pyrrho is a "vegetable in human shape," only capable of eating and sleeping, and unaffected by anything else. An admirer of Pyrrho plugs his ears and attempts to suppress his other senses; he argues that sceptics must gain notoriety by contradicting commonly held beliefs. Beattie discovers two philosophers fighting over their respective – and virtually indistinguishable – sceptical contentions: one says he is certain of nothing but his own ignorance, the other that he is certain of nothing at all. A natural philosopher attempts to look for the sun through a microscope. Another tries to train chickens to abandon their "custom" of laying eggs. Moving through the Castle, Beattie debates with Voltaire about whether this is the best of all possible worlds. He then debates with Hobbes about whether people are in a state of war against each other. He finally meets Hume the Governor, who, standing on the edge of a deep pit, cordially invites people over, and then pushes them off. Lecturing Beattie on philosophy, Hume grabs hold of him, and is prepared to throw him over. Thunder roars overhead, though, and the frightened Hume lets go and falls to his knees, reciting the Apostle's Creed. Beattie slowly wakes to the sound of church bells, and heads off to prayer.

Beattie's "Castle of Scepticism" was first transcribed by Ernest Campbell Mossner in 1948 (*University of Texas Studies in English*, vol. 27, pp. 108–145). The following is newly transcribed from Beattie's manuscript, and differs from Mossner's version in several particulars of wording and punctuation.

This was written about six years ago, in the year 1767, before the Essay on Truth was finished. It was never intended for publication.

1773.

———

[THE CASTLE OF SCEPTICISM: A VISION][2]

Though I have no ambition to be thought a dreamer of dreams, nor any pretentions whatsoever to Second Sight, I find myself much disposed to lay before the world an account of a vision which lately made a strong impression upon my fancy; but of which I do not pretend to conjecture whether it issued through the gate of ivory, or through that of horn.

I am almost ashamed to mention the circumstances in which I fell asleep: but I can say with a safe conscience, that I was never so overtaken before, which I hope will plead for my pardon with the good-natured Reader. After a night of most refreshing sleep I arose last Sunday morning in perfect health. The sweetness of the air, the serenity of the sky, the fragrance and verdure of the fields, the song of birds, and the murmurs of a stream, inspired (as Milton says) "Vernal delight and joy, able to drive all sadness but despair." Every thing in nature seemed to rejoice; and for my own part I never in my life found my spirits more buoyant and chearful. After sauntering a while through the fields, (for I was then on a visit at a friend's house in the country) I [went][3] into the garden, and sat down in an arbour; where, f[inding] one of the volumes of Mr Hume's excellent Essays, I [began to] read. But, I know not how it was, I had scarce go[tten through] half a dozen pages, when I felt myself unaccountably heavy; the longer I read, the more drousy I became: at last, I fell fast asleep.

Methought I was hurried along in the midst of a multitude, who were going with great eagerness and expedition to see some curious sight. At first I imagined it might be an execution, or publick whipping, or some such delectable entertainment, that had so much roused the activity of my fellow-travellers: but on listening to the conversation of the better sort, I soon discovered that it was quite another matter. The words Ideas, Priestcraft, Sceptick, Quality, Faculty, Entity, &c. resounded on every side of me. As they were familiar enough to my ear, I suffered myself to be carried on by the croud; not doubting, but that I was got into a company of philosophers, or at least of students in philosophy; and that I should arrive at some Auditory erelong, and hear a dissertation on the nature of things.

[2] [The manuscript bears no title, although this is the name which Beattie gives it in his letter to Blacklock, April 18, 1769.]

[3] [The bottom right-hand corner of the manuscript is torn; I am following Mossner's suggestions for the missing words.]

The day, methought, was warm, and the sky remarkably pure; yet a gentle breeze prevented the heat from growing excessive, so that we travelled very comfortably. The country was beautiful, but derived its charms rather from nature than from art. My companions told me, it was called by the vulgar *The Land of Truth*, but by the learned *The Den of Prejudice*. I could not help objecting to this denomination, particularly to the word *Den*, adding that I had never seen a pleasanter region or wider prospect in all my life: but they called me a fool, and a pedant. "I am a man of fashion and a philosopher," said a gigling young fellow; "I am convinced, that till this present age the whole world was inhabited by fools: come along, and you shall see wonders; but in the meantime learn, I beseech you, as much good-breeding as not to object to what is acknowledged by all the world." I asked him, what he meant by all the world. "Why, the people of learning and fashion," he replied. "There is Tom Goblin, and the Earl of Sneer, and my lord viscount Bigwords, and honest Humphrey Hardheart, not to mention the famous German Bully and myself,[4] with three or four more, who ought to give laws to all mankind."

Not quite satisfied with this piece of information, I applied to several others. "I believe," says one, "we are going to pull down the Parsons; which I should rejoice to see, as I am told they intend to excommunicate me on Sunday next." "I hear," says another, "it has been lately discovered, that there is no God, and I want to be assured of the fact; for these superstitious notions we imbibe in our infancy are a plaguy restraint on a man of spirit." "My circumstances," said another, "are in such disorder, and my character and neck in such imminent hazard, that I have some thoughts of bilking my creditors and the publick, by shooting myself through the head: and I am now going in quest of a gentleman, who, they tell me, has written a very ingenious treatise (though he cannot publish it as yet for fear of the pillory) in which he has proved the mortality of the soul, and the lawfulness, expediency, and utility of suicide."[5] Another told me in a broad provincial dialect, that "he wanted to encourage a Countryman, and hoped I would join him in the same laudable purpose." I begged only to know, what his Countryman had done to merit encouragement. He replied, that for his part he did not understand those matters, but he was assured by the very best judges, that the gentleman was a great philosopher and author, of profound learning, and unfathomable genius.

---

[4] [We may identify "Tom Goblin" as Thomas Hobbes, "The Earl of Sneer" as Anthony Ashley Cooper, Earl of Shaftesbury, "Lord Viscount Bigwords" as Henry Saint John, Viscount Bolingbroke, "Humphrey Hardheart" as Henry Home, Lord Kames, and "the famous German Bully" as Frederick II, the Great, of Prussia.]

[5] [i.e., Hume's essays "Of Suicide" and "Of the Immortality of the Soul," which were removed from what was later published as *Four Dissertations* (1757).]

I desired him to name the persons on whose authority he had formed this judgment: and he pointed to a very well-drest man in the company,[6] who he said was a person of great rank, and consequently of great abilities. Being assured however, that he was no less eminent for his affability, I ventured to accost this personage, and asked him, with profound submission, what was his opinion of the motives and purposes of our journey. "You are going," says he, very politely, "to learn wisdom from this Great Oracle of modern times;[7] who is acknowledged by all the world to be the deepest genius and wisest philosopher ever known. It is impossible to express how much he is superior to all the sages of antiquity. The acumen of Aristotle, the eloquence of Plato, the learning of Theophrastus, the taste of Quintilian, the imagination of Lucretius, were but faint types and shadows of the great things that have now appeared in him. I have looked at some of his works, I have listened to many of his lectures; and though I pretend not to be a judge, I must say, that so far as I understand them, they seem to me unanswerable and inimitable. It is true, they are obscure, and perhaps require more thought and attention than people of fashion have to bestow; but this I take to be only a proof of their depth; for the gentleman is none of your superficial thinkers: he searches to the bottom of his subject, and brings to light those fundamental and first principles of things, which have lain hid from the beginnings of the world (if it had any beginning) to this day. And then, in his principles and way of thinking there is something so clever and genteel, something of that je-ne-sçay-quoi that every where speaks the man of fashion, something so perfectly conformable to the taste, sentiments, and manners of the Beau Monde, that it is impossible not to be convinced and delighted with them. There was a set of fellows in the last age, Addison, Steele, and one or two more, who pretended forsooth to be moral philosophers; but they were mere pedants, and, I verily believe, arrant parsons in their hearts. They found fault with their betters in every thing. Our dress, our conversation, our gaming (which however was not so considerable in those days), yea even our gallantry, and freethinking, were grievances to their righteous spirits; and they treated not only with severity, but even with contempt, all whom they suspected of such practices; for which, had they lived in our days, no gentleman would have sat in company with them. But this charming philosopher is a person of a very different stamp. His sentiments coincide with ours so exactly that they seem to be borrowed from us. How prettily he expresses himself on the subject of gallantry; that species of it, I mean, in which married people are concerned! He shows it to be not only

---

[6] [i.e., Henry Home, Lord Kames. Further on Beattie refers to this character as "his Lordship." Home was a judge, and Beattie makes reference to "good judges" in this discussion.]

[7] [i.e., Hume.]

advantageous, but necessary; which alone may satisfy you, that his principles must have received the highest polish, and that he has kept the best company in Europe. Since I have been conversant in his writings, I have often wished, that all the great world would seriously think of learning to read. Such of them I am sure, as have any taste for atheism and adultery (and which of us has not?) would find their account in the perusal of his Essays. Happy age," continued he, "and alone worthy of the name of golden! How vulgar the notions, how brutal the manners, how pedantick the learning, how shallow the philosophy, of former days! That life should have been thought worth preserving in those barbarous times, is to me perfectly amazing; and a striking proof of one of my friend's maxims, that there is nothing, how absurd, how unpleasant, how unnatural soever, to which habit will not reconcile the human mind. Mind! did I say? I ask pardon. My friend has proved, that there is no human mind; has proved it, Sir, beyond a possibility of doubt, or reply. Thank heaven (metaphysick I mean) we have nothing more to fear on that score: man has no more soul, than an oyster-shell."

This speech, though pronounced very gracefully, I did not much relish; for I really imagined his Lordship meant to banter me, and being a stranger, I thought myself entitled to better usage. I applied to many others for fuller information, but with little success. The world, I found, admired the philosopher, because good judges did so; and good judges admired him, because all the world did it.

At last I was recommended to a person of great learning,[8] whom I observed walking by himself at a distance from the croud; and whose judgment, I was told, was not liable to be biassed by any friendly partialities, as he was the declared adversary of our philosopher. Overjoyed at this intelligence, I went up to him and asked, what could induce him to undertake this journey, as he was known to be no admirer of the gentleman we were in quest of. "I go," says he, "to hear what he has to say, because every thing he says is ingenious." Not being able to reconcile this with what I had just heard, I begged him to be a little more particular, and tell me what he really thought of this wonderful man. "You stile him very properly," he replied; "he is truly a wonderful man. His abilities are astonishingly great, and justly entitled to the highest praise: though it must be confessed, that his doctrines exceed all that were ever contrived in absurdity and folly. He is a man," continued he, "of the strictest candour, and most liberal spirit: but is chargeable with the grossest misrepresentations of very plain facts, and the most obstinate partiality to his own paradoxes. In the talent of sound and subtle reasoning, he excels all mankind: but his arguments are mere sophistry founded in ambiguous expressions. He is possessed of invincible modesty and calmness of temper: but supposes all mankind, his own party

---

[8] [i.e., Thomas Reid.]

excepted, to be fools and knaves. His penetration seems to surpass the measure of human capacity: but the most glaring absurdities pass upon him, when disguised by technical words, and recommended by his favourite authors. Nothing can exceed the perspicuity and elegance of his style: though it is often almost impossible to find out his meaning. He has presented the world with a perfect model of philosophick precision: but the one half of his system destroys the other. His tenets obviously lead to the utter subversion of all truth, learning, and virtue: but he has always employed his greatest talents in promoting the cause of truth and the interests of mankind. It is equally to his honour, and to that of the age, that his philosophy, notwithstanding its subtlety and obscurity, has obtained so much credit with people of all ranks: and it is no less remarkable, that those who read it least admire it most, and none so much as they who have never read it at all." Whether it was owing to a confusion of ideas which never fails to attend us even in our liveliest dreams, or what was the matter with me, I know not: but I fancied myself so little instructed by this speech, that I determined to ask no more questions, but wait the event, and then judge for myself. This last harangue seemed somewhat ironical: only I could observe, that the speaker from time to time looked to the listening multitude with much timidity in his countenance, which tempted me to think, that it was partly for fear of giving offence, that he thus blended his censure with compliment.

Now I saw in my dream, as John Bunyan says, and behold, as we advanced, the road grew gradually more intricate and laborious; precipices appeared on either hand; and we were much annoyed by the stones, bramble, and underwood, that beset our way. The sky grew misty, and the sun of the colour of blood; screams were heard at a distance; and, if the air was quite calm, it was only to make us more sensible of a most offensive smell that on every side assaulted us. The day became darker and darker, till at last we had no more light than the full moon yields in a cloudy and stormy sky. Yet many of my fellow-travellers still went on with alacrity, because they said it was the fashion, and they did not choose to be singular. Some females declared in my hearing that it was quite charming, considering that we had so much good company. Certain grave persons among us remarked, that this twilight or rather darkness was much better for the eyes than broad day-light; that the continual screams tended to produce firmness of mind in the hearers; that the bad smell and rough road were the occasion of much wholesome exercise both to the mind and body; that to walk on the tops of precipices was an excellent preservative against vertigo and other infirmities to which persons in high elevation are subject, which they proved from what may be daily observed of sailors, masons, and house carpenters, who can sit, stand, or even walk on very high places without fear of falling; in a word, it was generally allowed, that this region, which they named The Paradise of Perplexity, was infinitely more delightful, and a much better school of discipline, than the azure skies, fresh gales, and sunny places we had left behind. Yet, notwithstanding this appearance of composure and satisfaction, it was easy to discover, that their minds were not at ease. Paleness and horror appeared in every countenance: and they often crouded together, as I have seen children do on a winter-evening, when they had terrified one another with tales of ghosts and apparitions. The old men were most to be pitied; for not being able to keep up with the rest, they were often left in the rear and alone; in which case their fears would increase upon them to such a degree, as to produce starting, shivering, and chattering of teeth. For my own part, though much fatigued and frightened, yet instigated by that curiosity which my friends have often told me is my weak side, and which it seems even sleep itself could not suppress, I still went forward, with that sort of resolution, which is more the effect of stupidity and despair, than of true fortitude. And now, we found ourselves suddenly, we knew not in what manner, hurried down a steep and almost perpendicular descent. A lofty and mishapen pile of ramparts, extending a great way on either hand, appeared at the bottom. The upper works were modern, but the foundations seemed to bear the marks of a very remote antiquity. This, they told me, was the Castle of Scepticism.

Before the great gate of the place stood a number of little temples in a very fantastick taste of architecture. It appeared by their respective inscriptions, which were in very large characters richly illuminated with the most gaudy colours, that they were dedicated to different divinities. But the names of the gods there worshiped bore no resemblance to those we commonly meet with in the systems of Pagan Theology. One temple was inscribed To Affectation, another To Ignorance, a third To Self-Conceit, a fourth To Fashion, a fifth To Licentiousness, a sixth To Ambition, and a seventh To Hypothesis. There were others, whose names I was not near enough to be able to read. My fellow-travellers told me, that it was the custom of those who wanted to be admitted into the castle, to present their offerings in some one of these temples, and asked me whether I had prepared mine. I told them, I had not; and desired to see theirs. They showed me a very small parcel neatly wrapt up, and inscribed Common Sense – at least I was told so; for most of the parcels were so exceedingly minute, as to be hardly visible to the naked eye. Every pilgrim now hastened to the shrine of his favourite divinity. The altars of Affectation, Ignorance, Fashion, and Licentiousness, were immediately crouded with ladies and fine gentlemen; certain personages, distinguished by a supercilious air, and look of great importance, took the road leading to the temples of Ambition and Self-Conceit; there were a few in shabby apparel, but well equipped with pens, inkhorns, and other implements of writing, who filed off to a dirty hovel which bore the name of Avarice: all these went forward with alacrity, and justled one another as they went. But it grieved me to the heart to observe the procedure of two or three persons of a most venerable appearance, and remarkable for the bulkiness of their offering; who, by their loitering steps, wry faces, and looking frequently behind them, seemed to be dragged against their wills, and as it were by some secret and unaccountable impulse, towards the temple of Hypothesis.

Having no particular attachment to any of the Deities here worshipped, and being much at a loss about the method of preparing my offering, as well as somewhat uneasy at the thought of parting with it, I had almost resolved to go back: when I was given to understand by a very polite gentleman, who I thought belonged to the castle, that I might get in even without making an offering, provided I agreed to pay a certain pecuniary perquisite, the property of the Governour, which would be exacted as soon as I entered the gate. "We do not object," continued he, "to the principles of any man: the sacrifice of Common Sense to the Divinities we worship is a kind of test by which we distinguish a friend from a stranger; if you choose to appear among us in the latter character, you need not expect any extraordinary civilities, but you may depend on meeting with no bad treatment." I thanked the gentleman for his information, and went up to the gate.

On one side of it stood a woman veiled, whose name I heard was Modesty; but, on peeping under her veil, I was shocked with a view of the most impudent countenance I ever beheld. On the other side stood Candour, as he was called; but by the uncommon torpor of his limbs, deadness of his eye, and thoughtlessness of his visage, which made me yawn to look at him, and still makes me yawn to think of him, I could not help being of opinion, that his true name must be Stupidity. The gate was opened by one who called himself Curiosity; a name which I heard with so much pleasure, that I believe I should have saluted him as a kinsman, if I had not got a glimpse of his face, which however he took some pains to conceal. His complexion was yellow; his nostrils distended, and elevated towards his eyes, as if he had continually smelt, or expected to smell, a disagreable odour; his brows overhung and almost covered his eyes, which by looking obliquely had contracted a most disagreeable squint; with a few yellow stumps of teeth he gnawed his skinny lips; his fists, though hid under his robe, were always clenched; rancour mingled with scorn seemed to glisten in his eye; and every part of his forehead was furrowed and twisted with habitual frowning. I had skill enough in physiognomy and genealogy, to perceive that this personage was of the family of Suspicion, and related by his mother to Captiousness, and by his grandmother to Discontent. Observing that I had no passport, he seized me rudely by the collar, and demanded in a thundering accent, whether I had any pocket-pistols, or daggers about me. I desired him to search, and satisfy his own eyes. "D–n my eyes," he replied; "I never in my life believed them, nor any of my five senses, and if I had ten, I should be equally incredulous. This is a world in which we cannot be too diffident. Nature," continued he, "is an infamous cheat; I would not take her word for a farthing: but there are some gentlemen in this castle, who have detected her impositions, and will detect yours too, let me tell you Sirrah, if you mean to put any tricks upon us." I assured him I had no such views: and as the rest of the company were now arrived from the temples, he let me go forward, and went to receive them, grumbling and swearing all the while; though methought their passports, which every one held up in his hand, entitled them to be admitted without examination.

After advancing a little way, we were overtaken by a Woman in a masque, very finely drest, who earnestly recommended to us a cordial of her own preparing, which she said was excellent, and peculiarly comfortable to the stomach of a Sceptick. Two or three grave persons refused it, and went on; but far the greater part, both males and females, pledged the lady. For my own part, being, as I thought, much fatigued with the journey, I could not resist the solicitation; but when I put my lips to the glass, I found myself in the condition of Tantalus; the liquor, of its own accord, flew off to the opposite side, and besprinkled all the lady's rich stomacher and tucker, for handkerchief she wore none: on which she threw the glass at my head, and swearing a great oath desired me to get along, for a niggardly booby. "This comes," said she, "of your not sacrificing. Had you made your offering, as the rest of the company did, and as a gentleman ought to do, I should not have met with this disaster." She accompanied this short speech with many oaths, and hard names, and other figures of speech alluding to certain parts and functions of the human body which I do not choose to name: She even seemed disposed to enforce her rhetorick by manual application; but the violence of this transaction made her masque drop off, and discovered the self-same countenance, which I had found lurking at the gate under the veil of Modesty. The effects of her beverage were soon visible in those who tasted it; but I must be excused for not mentioning particulars: Suffice it to say, that the males and females became too attentive to one another, to take any more notice for the present either of me or of the Castle. I sneaked off with great expedition, and had seen most of the rarities of the place, before they were at leisure to think of them.

It were endless to describe all that I saw in this place. In a very magnificent, though old-fashioned apartment, lay, what I at first sight took for an Egyptian mummy, but found on a closer inspection to be a living man. He was then in a profound sleep. I was informed however, that he awaked four times a day, half an hour each time, and then eat and drank voraciously, but never spoke a word; that many attempts had been made to engage his attention; that some had counterfeited convulsions, and others death, and that one man had made a show of hanging himself, in his presence; but all to no purpose: he continued to eat his victuals; and, though he looked up, and saw what was doing, never offered to stir or speak, nor seemed at all concerned. As this extraordinary indifference was judged to be the effect of scepticism and philosophy, he was regarded by all as a most respectable personage, and as one who, by attaining to Indisturbance, had improved human nature to its highest pitch of perfection. Many worshipped him as a god: and all agreed, that if Wisdom herself were to visit the earth, she would certainly assume the form and character of Pyrrho; for so, methought, they called this vegetable in human shape.

I was desired to take notice of another very accomplished Sceptick, who, they told me, denied, and hoped in a short time to bring himself to doubt, his own existence. He had tied a bandage over his eyes, and stopt his ears, which however could not entirely prevent his hearing; his nostrils also were stuffed; and his tongue and palate, and the points of his fingers were seared with a hot iron. He expected soon, he said, to get the better of his external senses, and did not despair of mastering consciousness itself (though he owned it was a very troublesome inmate) and then, says he, "I flatter myself I shall be in a fair way of reaching the true Sublime of Scepticism, and seriously call my own entity in question. By the by," added he, "it is strange, that so silly and so vulgar a prejudice, as this which all men entertain in favour of the reality of their own existence should have hitherto baffled all the attempts of our party. If I shall be so happy as to subdue it, by heavens! I shall be a greater man than even Pyrrho himself." I asked him, how he came to conceive so violent a dislike to that opinion. To which he replied, "that he suspected Nature to be an imposter in all her declarations, particularly in those which are obvious to the vulgar. We want to distinguish ourselves from the herd of mankind by our superiour wisdom; and how is this to be done, pray? By falling in with their notions we shall never be able to raise ourselves into notice: we must therefore pursue the different and opposite method of denying whatever they affirm, and doubting whatever they hold for certain. Some of us have already gone considerable lengths in the prosecution of this plan, and astonished the world with many very pretty incredibilities: but this plaguy affair, the belief of our own existence, has still been an insuperable bar to our researches, and almost given the lye to our whole system."

"And is there no other way (said I) of raising yourselves into publick notice, than by contradicting the universal voice of nature and mankind? Bacon and Newton, Archimedes & Euclid, Homer and Virgil, pursued a very different method. I apprehend (continued I) that wherever there is real genius, it may distinguish itself sufficiently without quitting the track of Common Sense." "And so (interrupted he) you would insinuate, that it is want of genius that puts us to this shift. We are much obliged to you for so polite a remark. Let me tell you, sir, our genius was never called in question before. What does it require no genius, to doubt! Does it require no genius, to frame objections! Does it require no genius, to astonish and puzzle mankind! Does it require no genius, to affirm what is incredible, and to deny what is self-evident! to disguise facts, and pervert the meaning of words!"

"I ask your pardon, Sir; but permit me (for my information) to propose one question more. What reason have you to think so hardly of nature's veracity, as to suspect all her declarations to be false?" "Because," returned he, "the rest of mankind believe them to be true: this is a sufficient answer to your question;

but I will give you another. Do you see or feel the pores in your skin?" I acknowledged I could do neither. "But your skin is all full of pores, is it not?" "It is." "Then," says he, "your senses deceive you, and nature is a cheat." "What? (said I) would you have a physician explain all the mysteries of medicine to his patient, every time he comes to see him? Is it not enough, that he remove his disease, and tell him every thing which it is good for him to know? If you consult an Architect about repairing your house, will you call him a cheat and a scoundrel, if, together with his estimate, he does not give you in writing the grand-secret of masonry?" –

Here we were interrupted by a squabble in the neighbourhood. Two philosophers, it seems, like Hudibras and the Conjurer, had fallen from dispute to fight, and were belabouring one another without mercy. After parting them with some difficulty, I begged to know the occasion of the fray; which I found to be this. One of the combatants had affirmed, that he was certain he knew nothing but his own ignorance. The other called him a traitor, and said, that his principles tended to the subversion of the state, if he held himself certain of any thing. "For my own part," says he, "I maintain that all things are equally uncertain." "Gentlemen," said I, "your principles are so nearly the same, that I cannot wonder at your mutual antipathy; and from what I know of human nature, I may venture to prophesy, that you will never agree. A Scotch Seceder, who admits the lawfulness of the burgess-oath, has some charity for a church-of-england man; but consigns to the bottomless pit without hesitation or pity such of his own brethren as deny the lawfulness of that oath. To hate those the most who differ from you the least, is in the true spirit of polemick controversy. If Servetus has been a Pagan or Mahometan, John Calvin would not have bestirred himself so vigorously in getting him burned: but for a christian and a Protestant to own his ignorance of a point which his superior maintained to be quite clear and certain, was scandalous and intolerable. A Jansenist hates a Molinist as mortally as a Scotch Presbyterian: and I have known an orthodox divine to live in the strictest amity with a professed Atheist, who would not have kept company with a poor devil of a popish priest, or Methodist teacher."

A little further on, I met with a very ingenious Experimental philosopher, who they told me denied the existence of everything but himself. I found him employed in looking for the sun through a microscope. Another was examining a piece of rotten cheese with a telescope one hundred and twenty feet long. A third held a nosegay in his left-hand, and seemed to look at it through a magnifying glass which he held in his right. I took him for a disciple of Linnæus, reconnoitring the gender of the several plants that composed his nosegay; and could not help being surprised, when they told me, that the man was blind, and only meant to improve his smell by this contrivance. I was equally surprised to see another virtuoso, who had shut both his ears, feeling the strings of an Eolus's harp, which was playing very sweetly, with the point of his great toe, to which he had fastened a couple of ear-trumpets. In a large and lofty apartment, with a vaulted roof, sat two philosophers engaged in earnest conversation. They spoke to each other through a speaking-trumpet, the sound of which was so exceedingly loud, and at the same time so indistinct by reason of a strong echo, that both were stunned with the noise, without understanding a single word of what was spoken. Another couple of grey-beards, who were engaged (as I afterwards learned) in a very profound metaphysical dispute, sat opposite to each other in two elbow chairs in an open area (for the walls of the castle were several miles in circuit) at the distance of two hundred yards; where they maintained the controversy in a whisper so soft, that I could hear nothing of it, though I held my ear within a foot of the mouth of one of the disputants.

As I wished to obtain some information concerning these uncommon modes of perception and communication, I pretended to admire every thing I saw in those general terms of applause which have obtained to many a simpleton the character of a connoisseur and critick; uttering, on all occasions, the words, admirable! excellent! prodigious fine! wonderfully ingenious! and the like. My approbation did not pass unnoticed. One of the Ciceroni's of the place seconded me with great warmth. "You have reason," said he, "to admire these contrivances; all the world admires them." It is thus that philosophers arrive at that sublime scepticism which so far transcends the conception of the generality of mankind, who, you know, have nothing to direct them but plain Common Sense. Did we examine things according to those laws of evidence, and with those faculties, which nature intended for the vehicles of truth and knowledge, we should never be able to disbelieve what is certain, nor to doubt of what is indubitable, but should be compelled, in spite of all our efforts, to deviate sometimes into the track of common sense, and to think, believe, and act, like the rest of the world. This Castle," continued he, "has, in every age since its foundation, produced several of these admirable inventions; which however are all exceeded by the ingenuity and industry of our present Governour. He has lately invented and executed one of the boldest and happiest designs that ever entered into a metaphysical head; a design which establishes universal Scepticism at once, and beyond which our most sanguine adherents have nothing to expect or desire. The hint was taken from the London News Papers. You will perhaps remember an advertisement that appeared in opposition to the scheme of the Bottle Conjurer of ridiculous memory. It was given out, that a certain harlequin was arrived in town who would exhibit a much more extraordinary performance than that of a man jumping into a quart bottle; for that he would open his mouth wide, and jump down his own throat. Something very similar to this our Governour has accomplished. To show, that all inferences of reason are false or uncertain; and that the under-standing acting alone does entirely subvert itself, and prove by argument that by argument nothing can be proved, he has contrived a puppet of mushrooms, cork, cobwebs, gossamer, and other fungous and flimsy materials, to which he gives the name of Reason. He performs with it several dextrous feats to the surprise of every spectator; and at last, by a wonderful apparatus in the machinery, he makes it to open its mouth, and with a sudden jerk throw its whole body, feet, head, trunk, legs, and arms, down its throat, where it totally disappears. He has published a full account of the whole affair in a very elaborate Treatise in three volumes,[9] which has given us all the most perfect satisfaction. The method indeed by which this operation is performed is too subtle and intricate to be understood; and he never performs it except in the dark, or behind a screen; but as he himself has assured us that it is plain to a demonstration, every body is convinced. Our adversaries indeed call the fact impossible, and the doctrine it is intended to illustrate an absurdity; but what is this, opposed to our Governour's affirmation? We Scepticks, you know, though we admit none of those tenets in which all the rest of mankind are agreed, yet believe in one another with the most implicit and most obstinate assurance, especially when our belief is required to something inconceivable. As the word of a Quaker is equivalent to another man's oath in a court of justice, so the affirmation of a Sceptick in all points of philosophy is equivalent to a demonstration from an ordinary man, or rather indeed of superior authority."

"But (said I) is not belief and assurance of every kind incompatible with the principles of Scepticism? I think I have heard so; and I always thought, that the business of a Sceptick was only, to doubt." "Right," he replied; "where matters of common sense and common opinion are concerned, we have nothing to do but to doubt, and disbelieve; but with our own systems and notions the case is otherwise. The Greek word, from which we derive our name, does not signify, to doubt; but, to deliberate, and seek for. In the opinions and notions of the rest of mankind we seek for truth without finding it; in our own we find it without seeking. We take it for granted (and Scepticks take so little for granted, that surely the world cannot grudge them this one poor axiom) that all men, ourselves only excepted, are fools and knaves. Now if we be the only wise men upon earth, it clearly follows, that our systems and opinions are the only wisdom. And if so, where is the impropriety of that implicit faith which we repose in the doctrines, reasonings, and affirmations of one another? In respect of these, our belief is not only fixed but immoveable: and in avowing and vindicating this belief, I trust we are ready to bid defiance to the pillory, to the gallows, and (if there were any such thing) to damnation itself."

This discourse beginning to grow dull, I expressed some impatience to see the other curiosities of the castle. I was then desired to take notice of an artist, who they told me was the greatest Critick of the age. I found him contemplating through a pair of spectacles a young woman's face, and with a scale and

---

[9] [i.e., Hume's three-volume *Treatise of Human Nature* (1739–1740).]

compasses taking the exact dimensions and bearings of the several features, all which he entered upon paper. He often shook his head in token of disapprobation; and when all his calculations were finished, in the course of which he employed both fluxions and logarithms, he pronounced her to be an ugly slut: a decision which surprised me, as in my humble opinion she was very handsome.

A person who called himself the Genius of Metaphysick was continually busied in turning a large engine, like that described in Gulliver's travels, which threw up an endless variety of combinations of words and letters, out of which were framed sentences and paragraphs, sections, chapters, and treatises. He told me, he was much employed, and had the custom of all the literati of the place, particularly of the Governour, who (he said) was his very good friend; adding, that if I had any job on hand in the book-making way, he would furnish me with materials in the neatest and newest fashion, and on the most reasonable terms.

Another virtuoso was watching a hencoop full of chickens, and feeding them with various kinds of food; in order (as he told me) that they might become viviparous, and lay no more eggs, which seemed to him to be a very bad custom; eggs being much more liable to rottenness and other destructive accidents than live chickens are. "However," said he, "I hope in time to get the better of this inconvenient custom, and substitute a much better one in its stead; for I am convinced there is no such thing as an innate principle or propensity, every thing that looks like it being the effect of habit and discipline. I have also," continued he, "under my care some young children, whom I am teaching to believe, that two and two are equal to six, and a whole less than one of its parts; that ingratitude is a virtue, and honesty a vice; that a rose is one of the ugliest, and a toad one of the most beautiful objects in nature; that the affections arising from a diversity of sex are as natural where the species of the animals is different, as where it is the same; that virtue deserves punishment, and vice reward; that misery is the object of hope, happiness of fear, excellence of hatred, and disagreable qualities of love; – and when I have accomplished all this, I hope the world will confess the truth of my hypothesis." And what good do you expect from all this," said I. "What," replied he, "but the discovery of truth, and the confirmation of my theory." – "But what good may society expect from such discoveries?" – "Prithee, friend," he answered, "be not impertinent; a fool may ask a question which twenty wise men cannot answer. To call in question the utility of our studies or principles, is not philosophy, but personal invective. If philosophical enquiry were to be confined to things useful, nine tenths of the literati of Europe would be left idle."

A little further, I saw an artist, who amused himself in a very extraordinary manner. He had taught a boy of four years old to crawl very stoutly on his hands and feet, and to bleat like a sheep. I found too that the child was dumb, because he had never heard any language spoken; and that by being constantly made to creep on all four, he could not walk upright without hazard of falling. He was fed with acorns, roots, and green herbs; and lay in the open air on a couch made of dung, straw, and withered leaves. His tutor had just then taken off a blistering plaister from his rump, and was applying to the wound the bloody end of a cat's tail newly cut off; not doubting, as one informed me, but it would in a short time take root, and grow there: he had likewise clapt two small plaisters to the temples of the child, from which he expected to see a couple of horns begin to sprout in due season. When I asked the meaning of all this, I was told that this philosopher was of opinion, that man was originally a beast, and would never live agreeably to nature, till he had again relapsed into that state, – that he had begun to practise in the same manner upon a young female, and hoped soon to have a promising breed of human brutes, which by their superiority of strength and sagacity would be able to exterminate the present race of two-leg'd monsters, and re-establish the golden age.

In an adjoining enclosure, I found a Sage at work upon a young child and a young monkey. He had cut off the thumbs of the one, and was endeavouring to fix them upon the paws of the other. I could not guess at the design of this operation; but the philosopher was very communicative, and explained himself as follows. "Sensation is in all animals the source not only of knowledge, but also of reason, memory, and all the other faculties. According to the opportunities which any animal by its situation enjoys of exercising more or less its powers of sensation, especially of coming in contact with other bodies, its other faculties, its memory, reason, imagination, will be more or less distinguished. Sluggish animals are never sagacious, because their want of experience makes them defective in understanding: and the same thing is true of very large ones, and nearly for the same reason; the unwieldiness of their bodies, and perhaps too a peculiar dulness in their sense of touch, disqualifies them for coming in contact with other bodies, and renders the intimations of their touch indistinct and unaffecting. If the elephant is mentioned as an exception, I would answer, that the flexibility and acute sense of his proboscis make amends for his lumpish figure, and supply him with many opportunities of information, and consequently accessions of sagacity, which other creatures do not enjoy. Dogs and foxes are very sagacious; because their size and way of life furnish them with the means of perceiving by frequent contact the nature of other things both animated and inanimated: and I have been told, that even in the new testament, a book which they say contains very little worthy of notice, the wisdom of the serpent is mentioned as extraordinary. The monkey's opportunities of observation are still better, than those of the fox, the dog, or the serpent, on account partly of his extreme agility, but especially of that circumstance in his make of having his paw or hand divided into distinct fingers; and his sagacity is proportionable. Man, by virtue of his thumb, is still better qualified for diversified sensations; and hence his superiority in point of understanding and other internal faculties. Had he wanted the thumb, he would have been to all intents and purposes a monkey; and a dull one at best, as he is by no means so nimble as that sprightly animal. So that in fact it is from his Thumb alone, that man derives his superiority; and therefore Logicians ought to have distinguished him by this organ, and called him, not the reasonable, nor the risible, nor the moral, nor the religious, but the thumb-bearing animal."

"Your theory," replied I, "is equally singular and new: and as a return for your frankness in explaining it, I shall mention a fact which perhaps you may think worth attending to. In the highlands of Scotland, where you know the gift of second sight is in great estimation, when a child happens to be born with two or more thumbs on one hand, it is always expected that he will distinguish himself by his sagacity in regard to future events, and that his prophetical abilities will be in proportion to the surplus of his thumbs above the usual number." The Sage thanked me for my intelligence, with which he seemed highly delighted, and which he immediately committed to paper; telling me, it was altogether decisive, and would establish his theory beyond the possibility of confutation. I offered to convince him of the authenticity of my narrative, by procuring letters from my friends in that country; but that, he said, was unnecessary: "its coincidence with my theory," added he, "is a sufficient proof that it is authentick; and it seems to be agreed among philosophers, that we cannot be too credulous in regard to those facts that make for our systems, nor too sceptical in regard to those of an opposite tendency."

At a little distance I found a man of a most curious aspect, all besmeared with blood, and encompassed with human carcasses which he had purchased from the hangman. These he was cutting into small parts; and he told me, he hoped soon from them to extract, by chemical operations, a species of Manure superior to all other sorts now in use: "and thus," says he, "I shall show the world, what perhaps they never dreamed of before, that private vices are really publick benefits;[10] and consequently, that those who wish to see agriculture and industry flourish, would do well to promote felony, and encourage hangmen, to the utmost of their power."

I instantly turned away from this horrid spectacle; and had not proceeded twenty paces, when a lean little old man,[11] with his face screwed into a strange sarcastick grin, that seemed to be habitual to him, laid hold of one of the buttons of my coat, and asked me in French, "whether I believed every thing to be for the best." As I wished to avoid, if possible, embroiling myself with these people, I should have endeavoured to shift the question if I had not been taken at unawares. But having no time to meditate evasions, my tongue naturally expressed the sentiments of my heart, and I answered, "Yes": upon which the querist burst out into a fit of laughter so very obstreperous, that a croud began to gather about us. "And so," continued he, "you believe, with

---

[10] [This is an allusion to Bernard Mandeville's *Fable of the Bees: or, Private Vices, Publick Benefits* (1714).]

[11] [i.e., Voltaire.]

one Pope an English poetaster, that *Whatever is is right*, and think Providence, no doubt, a mighty good sort of thing": – here he interrupted his speech with a second fit of laughing much more violent than the first, in which he was joined by the whole company. I would fain have slunk away; but, the mob still increasing, I found myself hemmed in on all sides, and the frenchman proceeded thus. "I have laughed and sneered at every thing sacred and serious, these thirty years, but this notion of those canting hypocrites is the most ridiculous piece of Christian trumpery I ever met with. Hear me, but one moment, Gentlemen, hear me, you Mr All-for-the-best, and I will satisfy you of this presently. Those cruel and hypocritical blockheads the parsons, and some philosophic pedants too, have taken for granted, that all the events of life are directed by what they call Providence, that in a future and better state of existence every thing will appear to have been ordered for the best. This you know, Gentlemen, is the same thing with saying, that the present is the best of all possible worlds."

"I presume," said I, interrupting him, "it is a very different thing. If we believe in a future world that shall be better than the present, we cannot surely believe the present to be the best world possible." "Sir," replied he, his eye glistening with inexpressible rage and disdain, my name is Voltaire – you have heard of me, I suppose; blockhead as you are, you must have heard of the greatest genius that ever appeared upon earth. I have proved Shakespear to be a madman Milton an idiot, and Homer a dreaming old-woman; rascals, whose works, for their pretending to dispute with me the sovereignty of genius, ought to be, and soon, I hope, will be, held, in universal detestation. There is not a father of the church, there is hardly a prophet, apostle, or evangelist, whom I have not rendered ridiculous: I have dressed them in sheeps skins with a vengeance; and if they were now to appear upon the earth, they would find it highly expedient to flee to dens and caves and desarts, to hide their disgrace. In my historical writings, which are models of every excellence that can take place in prose-composition, I have made the people of Europe believe my affirmations when contrary to the most authentick records, or even the testimony of their own senses. The very Booksellers I have outwitted; and there is not a great town in Europe, where my talents, as a cheat of the first magnitude, are not acknowledged and felt. I have been complimented in the name of almost all the sovereign princes of modern times; one of whom, a great hero, and an excellent writer and atheist, does me the honour to be one of my most servile imitators.[12] Sir, I am worth twelve hundred thousand livres. All the world admires me, and very justly, particularly the great world; and shall a sorry Peasant, with a threadbare coat, who I dare say will never in his life be worth ten pounds, – shall he pretend to contradict me?" The whole audience applauded this speech, and fell a hissing at me; on which I made another ineffectual effort to escape: and the orator proceeded.

[12] [i.e., Frederick the Great.]

"I say, Gentlemen, the parsons and some canting philosophers have taken it in their heads, that this is the best of all possible worlds; which may be clearly inferred from that foolish expectation, they are known to entertain, of a better. Now this, I say, is the most ridiculous of all possible notions; and I will prove it such by a very pleasant story or apologue of my own invention." Here he began a very tedious tale,[13] where it seemed hard to determine, whether obscenity or blasphemy, whether absurd fiction or bad composition, was most prevalent. The audience laughed often, and the speaker almost continually; though the whole humour of the piece consisted in these words, *The best of all possible worlds*, which he repeated every minute, with certain droll gesticulations, whether his subject admitted them or not. The audience declared themselves fully satisfied; and said he had effectually and forever overturned the notion of a good providence; tho' to me his apologue seemed as little to effect that notion, as the story of Sindbad the sailor can be supposed to affect the discovery of a north-west passage to China. "Gentlemen," resumed the Orator, "I am very happy in your approbation; and since I find you approve this sample of my abilities, I oblige myself to produce every year as long as I live half a dozen performances of the same character and tendency; and nothing shall be wanting on my part (and I think I can promise too for some of my friends) to exterminate that Scoundrel Religion from the face of the earth."

I was now left at my liberty again; and, after passing through two or three dark alleys in quest of an outlet into the fields (for by this time I was sick of the castle) I chanced to meet a croud of people, who were returning, as they told me, from seeing a very extraordinary personage.[14] One of them courteously offered to introduce me to him. We found him sitting in a narrow court, which was fortified with a ditch and rampart. He was armed cap-a-pie in the Gothick fashion, and held in each hand a cocked blunderbuss. Being somewhat disconcerted at the sight of such a figure, I happened to make a false step, at which he set up a loud laugh, which however ceased immediately on my assuring my guide, that I had received no harm. "What a pity", exclaimed the Sages in armour, "you did not break your neck! it would have been the prettiest jest I have met with these many days. Laughter," continued he, "being nothing but a sudden glory or exultation of mind arising from a sense of our own superiority to others, or to ourselves as we were formerly, it is impossible not to be greatly diverted when we see a beast, an idiot, a diseased person, a blind and lame beggar, or a dead man, who are so much and so obviously our inferiours in health, riches, understanding, sense and activity; and nothing is more mortifying, than to meet with one who is our superiour in wit or learning, which, however (added he) is not often my case."

[13] [i.e., Voltaire's *Candide*.]

[14] [i.e., Thomas Hobbes.]

I asked him in a very submissive manner (for I own I did not think myself out of danger while I was in his company) what could be his motive for putting on such a warlike appearance in a place where he seemed to be in no danger. "What?" said he, "have you not read my Leviathan and other works?" I told him, I had not as yet been so fortunate as to meet with them. "If you had," replied he, "you would not have asked so silly a question. Man's natural state is a state of war. All men have originally an equal right to all things, and an equal desire of power and superiority. Hence contention must of necessity arise, which produces violence, murder, rapine, and many other modifications of action which the vulgar reckon criminal. You, I know, would wish to possess my learning, wisdom, strength, armour, blunderbuss, and every thing else of mine which you may think it is better to have than to want; and nothing hinders you from attempting to divest me of these; but either the impossibility of success or the fear of punishment."

"Pardon me, Sir," said I, interrupting him, "however much I may admire you for those abilities and acquisitions, I assure I would not do you any harm, or divest you of any one of them even though it were in my power. My conscience, Sir, would not allow me." "Pshaw!" replied the philosopher, "what is Conscience? Nothing but the fear of inconvenience or punishment: believe me, it is nothing else. If it were not for human laws, that is, for the will of our Sovereigns, there would be no distinction between vice and virtue, and all things would be equally lawful to all. They, it seems, have in their great wisdom, declared Justice to be good, and Injustice to be evil, because of the conveniencies that result from every man's possessing his own: but, previously to such declaration, and independently on it, theft and murder are as innocent as hunger and thirst." This speech suggesting the expediency of securing my pockets, I was directing my hands that way, when I found that the Philosopher had rendered all precaution of this sort unnecessary; having already made himself master of my handkerchief and snuffbox, the only moveables which I usually carry about me. I could not help charging him with the theft, which he did not deny; "but can you prove it?" says he. I confessed I could not. "Then where is the harm?" said the sage of Malmsbury. "If it is not an object of human laws, it is neither a virtue, nor a vice: for moral distinctions, as I told you already, especially in matters of property, are nothing else than the judgments of sovereigns upon those actions that are subject to their cognisance and deliberation. I taught this doctrine to our governor," continued he, "who is very fond of it, tho' he has given it a new turn in the expression. By the by, I think he owes me several acknowledgements which he has never paid; but he is a good lad, and has been very zealous in the common cause; and I heartily forgive him. – But here, take your things (said he, throwing them at me) – I mean not to keep them; for this good reason, that I have no use for them: I mean only to show you, how easy it is for us philosophers to confute the most favourite notions of the vulgar; and to prove the innocence of those actions which in all ages and nations have been accounted intrinsically flagitious."

"You know our governour, I suppose." "I have not the honour," I replied. "Pray," says he, lowering his voice to a whisper, "are you well or ill affected to him?" – "Neither the one nor the other," I answered; "I am not his subject." "O," said he, "that is another matter; I am sorry for it. Heard you no murmurings or grumblings as you came along? No appearance of a meeting or plot going forward?" "None," I replied. "Pray (says he) if you hear of such a thing, as it is likely you may, be so good as send the malecontents to me. I would make inquiry myself; but I cannot think of leaving this fortress, where I am secure against violence of every kind. Besides I am much afraid of ghosts, though I deny their existence; and in those ugly long dark alleys, who know what might happen? G– preserve us! I shudder to think of it." "Sure (said I) if you knew of any traitors, you would deliver them up to punishment; for if I am rightly informed, none ever asserted the independent and uncontroulable rights of governours, more strenuously than you." "Perhaps (returned he) your informers may have been a little mistaken in that affair." – "How!" said I, "do you not say, that princes or governours, as they enter into no contract with the people, cannot be answerable to them for any use they may make of their power?" "Yes (he replied) that is part of my doctrine, but not the whole. The people, I say, enter into a contract, not with the sovereign, but with one another; by which they bind themselves, every man for himself, that he will obey and support the sovereign to the utmost of his power, on condition that the rest of his fellow-subjects do the same. Now you must know that, in all conditional contracts, if one party fail in the performance the other stands acquitted from the obligation: if, for instance, I promise you a sum of money on condition of your giving me a horse, your refusing or neglecting to give him must entitle me to keep my money. And if so, when any one of our fellow-subjects withdraws his allegiance, all the rest must, according to the terms of the political contract, be at liberty to withdraw theirs." "I see very well the consequences of your theory," replied I, "but permit me to ask you one question. Was this political contract entered into, previous to the existence of Sovereigns?" "Surely (he answered) for on this contract is founded the distinction of sovereign and subject." "And previous too (continued I) to the establishment of moral distinctions?" "Most certainly," said the philosopher, "for moral distinctions are established by the Sovereign." "Pray," sayd I, "could men enter into a contract or promise, who had no notion of the unlawfulness of falshood or treachery, but imagined that all sorts of human conduct were equally lawful?"

This question disconcerted the sage in armour so much, that, instead of returning any answer, he began to survey me from head to foot, with a most furious look; on which I thought it high time to be going, and accordingly took to my heels, and ran a full quarter of a mile before I ventured to take breath. Nor should I even then have ventured stop, if a new and most amazing scene had not presented itself just as I turned the corner of a long narrow alley.

I found myself at the extremities of the castle. Bloody knives, halters, daggers, and other instruments of horror, strewed the ground; ravens croaked, and adders hissed, and owls shrieked from the ramparts; and the bats flew so thick that they were flapping me in the face every moment. At a little distance appeared a postern gate, beyond which the view terminated in utter darkness: and from this darkness issued a mixture of the most terrifying sounds, which it is impossible to describe. The screams of persons in agony, the creaking of engines, the clanking of chains, the fall of torrents, and the thunder of tempestuous fire bursting, as it were, the confinement of the furnace, assailed the ear at the same instant, and seemed sufficient to drive the stoutest heart to distraction. Close by the postern, stood the Governour, in gorgeous apparel, attended by a numerous company of priests, lawyers, and fine gentlemen; and with a show of extreme politeness, yet methought very officiously, invited travellers to the threshold, and then pushed them out headlong; smiling at the same time with a mixture of contempt and self-complacency; and now and then putting his hands in his pockets, and clinking his money. Seeing me a little shy, he addressed me in a most soothing manner in the English tongue; but there seemed to be something exotick in his pronunciation, for he spoke through his teeth like a Scotchman, and through his nose like a frenchman. He spoke much about ideas, and atoms, and doubts, and impostures, and parsons, and Epicurus, and machinery; and concluded a long harangue with a few corollaries, plausible indeed and well-disguised, but of such blasphemous import that my hair stood on end with horror. From a desire to hear him the more distinctly, I gradually drew nearer to him and nearer; till at last, methought he stretched out his huge hands (for he was a man of gigantick size) to lay hold upon me; when on a sudden, a peal of thunder burst over our heads, so loud and so terrible, as if the frame of nature had been going to pieces. The orator fell on his knees, and began to repeat the Apostles creed with the utmost vehemence of voice and gesture; The crouds and castle vanished; the darkness was dissolved, and the sun shone out with the most delightful brilliance. But my attention was now wholly engrossed by a shrill and sweet voice which seemed to come from a distance, and spoke these words: "Turn, ye mortals, from the path of the destroyer, and now listen to the words of Truth." I was wonderfully affected with this address, and fixed myself in a posture of the most devout attention; when, methought, the voice gradually grew less and less articulate; and the next moment I found myself broad awake, and listening to the bell of the parish-church that now summoned me to prayers.

The End.

April. 1767.

31
JAMES BEATTIE:
LETTER TO THOMAS BLACKLOCK

James Beattie, Letter to Thomas Blacklock, October 11, 1769.
Selections; from *The Correspondence of James Beattie*, edited by Roger J.
Robinson, Thoemmes Press, Bristol, 2004, Letter 140.

James Beattie (1735–1803) was the author of "The Castle of Scepticism,"
contained in this collection. Around 1767 Beattie became close friends with
Thomas Blacklock, author of *Poems on Several Occasions* (1754), selections
from which are also contained earlier. This was a particularly discouraging
period in Blacklock's life. Earlier, at Hume's recommendation, Blacklock
studied divinity and in 1762 was appointed to the parish of Kirkcudbright. The
assignment, though, was not amicable. Not wanting a blind preacher, the
congregation felt that Blacklock was wrongly forced on them by the parish's
patrons. Blacklock endured the situation for two years, then resigned. The
humiliation from that experience, the lack of financial resources to support his
family, and an overall sense of failure all threw Blacklock into a depression.[1]
His relation with Hume soured, and he looked to Beattie as his new protector.
During 1769, Blacklock appears to have written Beattie two letters describing
his discontent with Hume. Although neither of these survive, we do have two
responses by Beattie, which enable us to reconstruct at least part of Blacklock's
concerns. Perhaps around mid April Blacklock sent the first letter; the relevant
part of Beattie's response is this:

Till the receipt of your last letter I always believed, that you was under
considerable obligations to Mr H. – and it was this supposition chiefly, that
hindered me showing you the first draught of the first Book of my Essay on
Truth, when I was in Edinbr. in the year 1767. In that first draught were

---

[1] Blacklock wrote Hume two letters during this time that reveal his discouragement.
One, dated June 24, 1766, is reprinted in John Hill Burton's *Letters of Eminent
Persons Addressed to David Hume*, Edinburgh, 1849. The manuscript of this and the
other, dated May 2, 1767, are in Hume's manuscripts in the National Library of
Scotland.

many severe expressions, most of which are now left out, as far at least as is consistent with the design of the whole. But that the Gentleman in question is a Bad philosopher, and a Bad member of Society, are points which I must certainly explain, and will explain without scruple – and let those blame me who can refute my arguments. [Beattie to Blacklock, April 18, 1769][2]

Blacklock's "obligation" to Hume, mentioned above, refers to a 1754 episode in which Hume gave Blacklock his salary of £40 from his librarian position at the Faculty of Advocates library. Beattie's letter suggests that Hume's act was not as generous as it seemed. Perhaps encouraged by Beattie's response, around September Blacklock wrote a second letter detailing his complaint with Hume. Beattie's response, given below, gives us a better – though still not complete – picture of Blacklock's troubles. Beattie states that he now sees that Hume did not act out of "disinterested benevolence." Since the publication of Burton's *Life and Correspondence of David Hume* in 1846, we know exactly what transpired. In his librarian position, Hume ordered a list of books, but, when they arrived, the library's curators removed three controversial titles. Hume was offended and for nearly a half a year thought about retiring. What kept him there, though, was his need to use the library's resources for composing his *History*. His solution was to keep the job, but, as a means of private protest, give his pay check to Blacklock. Hume explains the story in a letter to Adam Smith:

[B]eing equally unwilling to lose the Use of the Books & to bear an Indignity; I retain the Office, but have given Blacklock, our blind Poet, a Bond of Annuity for the Sallary. I have now put it out of these malicious Fellows power to offer me any Indignity; while my Motives for remaining in this Office are so apparent. I shou'd be glad that you approve of my Conduct: I own I am satisfy'd with myself. [Hume to Adam Smith, December 17, 1754]

It appears that no published discussion of Hume prior to Burton mentions the dispute with the library curators. Nevertheless, Hume's action towards Blacklock was well known, even if his motive as he described to Smith was a well kept secret. We see, for example, the view that three of Hume's good friends had about the Blacklock episode (contained later in this collection):

[S]uch was his disinterestedness and generosity, that, as I have been informed, he allotted the whole, or at least the greater part of this sum, to the support of Blacklock the blind poet, then a young student in the university of Edinburgh. [John Home, "Remarks"]

---

[2] Letter 122 in Robinson. The manuscript of this letter is in the National Library of Scotland, Acc. 4796, Box 91.

Hume, unable to bear his [i.e., Blackock's] complaints, and destitute of money to assist him, ran instantly to his desk, took out the grant, and presented it to his miserable friend, who received it with exultation, and whose name was soon after, by Hume's interest, inserted instead of his own. [James Caulfeild, *Memoirs*]

But it was not for the salary that he accepted this employment, but that he might have easy access to the books in that celebrated library; for, to my certain knowledge, he gave every farthing of the salary to families in distress. [Alexander Carlyle, *Autobiography*]

It seems that Blacklock discovered Hume's true motives and, in a word, felt used. This was no small matter for Beattie since, from his perspective, the main example of Hume's so-called charity turned out to be no more than unbridled self-interest. This new revelation to Beattie was all the justification he needed to attack Hume in full force in the *Essay* – now seeing that Hume was not only a dangerous infidel writer but a moral scoundrel as well.

The original manuscript of this letter is in the Aberdeen University Library, MS 30/1/21. The following transcription of it is from Roger Robinson's *The Correspondence of James Beattie* (2004).

I return you a thousand thanks for the very great entertainment I found in your long letter. Indeed a sense of the pleasure it yielded me in the first perusal is still so fresh and so strong in my mind, that I know not how I have so long been able to refrain from writing, to thank you for it. But whenever I was proposing to take pen in hand, it always occurred to me, that it would be better to delay till the next post-day, and then I should certainly be able to tell you the fate of my manuscript. ... Your detail respecting your connection with Mr Hume is most particular and satisfactory. I am sorry for his sake to find, that I had given him more credit for disinterested benevolence than he has any pretensions to claim. Many years ago I heard, that the whole salary arising from the office he held in the Advocates Library, was by his desire paid to you; and this I was told he did out of pure affection. I reverenced the man so much for this, that it pained to be obliged to criticize his works with so much severity, and I could not prevail with myself for a whole year to show you the Manuscript of my Essay on Truth, for fear the perusal of it should give you uneasiness. Not that I was under the least apprehension of your confounding (as many I know will do) an act of justice, whose object is the good of my fellow-creatures, with personal invective: I flattered myself you knew me too well to suspect me of any malignant dispositions towards him or any person; I knew I had every thing to hope from your candour and discernment; but I could not bear the thought of giving you any pain. Yet I freely own to you, I wish I had found Mr Hume's virtue more genuine than it seems it is. He has (I fear) many things as an author to answer for; I wish his private character at least had been as fair as his flatterers and hangers-on would have it thought. I am now convinced his heart is hard, and void of principle. I thought so at first from reading his works; his ungenerous and unmanly conduct towards Rousseau strengthened this opinion; his unequal and sneaking behaviour to you has established it. But God forbid, My Dear Sir, that ever your fame should depend on my weak efforts. Be assured it will not. I trust and believe your life will be as long as mine at least; and if Providence should see proper to disappoint me in this, your name and story are too well known, and your genius too much admired, ever to be forgotten as long as virtue taste and the English tongue remain. I will not say more on such a melancholy subject. I shall only tell you, that one of my first wishes is to see you alive and happy, or at least to hear that you are so. Many happy days are I hope yet in store for you. Banish I beseech you these melancholy and desponding views. I speak nothing but truth when I tell you, that I do not at present know any person whose character is more universally esteemed and reverenced than yours. Pray take care of your health, and write me of it, and of whatever else concerns you. [Beattie to Blacklock, October 11, 1769]

32
THOMAS BLACKLOCK, AND OTHERS: LETTERS ON HUME AND BEATTIE (*WEEKLY MAGAZINE*)

[Thomas Blacklock, Henry Grieve and Mrs. Carnegie], Letters on Hume and Beattie by "Orthdoxus," "Democritus," and "Eumenes," in *Weekly Magazine or Edinburgh Amusement*, July-Sept. 1771, Vol. 13.
Six letters to printer, complete.

In 1771, an author using the name "Orthodoxus" wrote an open letter to James Beattie, which appeared in *Weekly Magazine or Edinburgh Amusement*. Though anonymous, a letter by James Beattie identifies him as Henry Grieve, brother-in-law of John Home (Beattie to Elizabeth Montagu, March 3, 1772). Grieve states that he does not agree with Hume's philosophy, but nevertheless complains that Beattie's attack on Hume was mean-spirited and unnecessary since the abstract nature of Hume's views has no impact on society. Further, Grieve argues, Beattie himself should be reproached for advocating free will, which conflicts with traditional Calvinistic beliefs, such as original sin, the goodness of God, and prophecy. Beattie read Grieve's letter in the *Weekly Magazine*, but was unimpressed; he states to a correspondent that Grieve

> is an ill-natured man, but a contemptible author. His attack is perfectly insignificant. Perhaps he means to draw me off my own ground into a controversy about predestination and original sin. But he mistakes his man. I will never answer such writers as he, nor any writer who does not set his name and Addition to his work, as I have done. [James Dun on 14 July 1771, in Robinson's *Correspondence*, Letter 250]

In the mean time, Thomas Blacklock composed a response to Grieve. Perusing it, Beattie felt that it was far superior to its target and thus worried that its publication would both inflate Grieve's perception of his own importance and also cause some people to think that Beattie was the author (Beattie to John Gregory, July 19, 1771, Robinson, Letter 251).

Nevertheless, shortly after, Blacklock's critique appeared under the pseudonymn "Eumenes" as the opening item in that issue of *Weekly Magazine*.

Blacklock argues that Beattie's harsh attack on Hume was fully justified in view of what he feels are the devastating effects of scepticism on people's beliefs. Against Grieve's view that Hume's *Treatise* has been ignored, Blacklock writes "I was in Edinburgh soon after the original publication, and well remember how much and how frequently it was mentioned, in every literary conversation." Blacklock has two responses to Grieve's argument regarding free will. First, Calvinists are not "obliged in conscience to believe and explain every article of that system in the same manner." Second, the Westminster Confession itself espouses free will – along with the doctrine of predestination. By even offering this theological dilemma, Blacklock argues, Grieve has deviously "used the Christian religion merely as spiders do their cobwebs, to catch and torment such insects as are unguardedly intangled in the net."

A third voice, under the pseudonym "Democritus," defends Grieve against Blacklock's response; a letter from Beattie to Blacklock identifies Democritus as "Mrs. Carnegie of Pitarrow" (September 14, 1772). Writing on behalf of a large middle class of people – standing between the learned literati and the ignorant – Carnegie concedes victory to Beattie. However, she feels that the harshness of Beattie's attack was unnecessary and ungentlemanly, just as "dragging the dead body of an enemy at one's chariot-wheels, implies only vanity or meanness." As to the theological paradox of free will, Carnegie believes that Grieve was justified in raising it to show that Beattie's own system is not self-consistent, and he should have thus been more charitable towards Hume. Carnegie further accuses both Blacklock and Beattie with pedantry, "imagining the little thing about which they busy themselves, to be the most important article on earth." She concludes suggesting that "Eumenes" might really be Beattie incognito. Confessedly angered by Carnegie, Blacklock responded by ridiculing each of her points.

In a second letter, Grieve responds to Blacklock, maintaining that he possessed the "same spirit of malevolence" as Beattie, and exhibited a "spirit of candour, as could only be invocated from hell itself." He insists that he is not a sceptic and no disciple of Hume, as he met Hume on only one occasion and did not have further interaction with him. Nevertheless, he fears that Beattie's harsh attack might provoke unwarranted civil action against Hume. He insists further that the theological paradox imbedded in Beattie's view of free will involves "a sceptical doubt, equal to many that Mr Hume has proposed and published." In a final letter of response, Blacklock dismisses Grieve's worries of civil action against Hume, and states "were Mr Hume in any personal danger from such penal laws and unwarrantable exertions of power, I would be among the first to interpose for his safety, even at the hazard or expence of my own." Concerning Grieve's contention that Blacklock himself is mean-spirited, he responds, "Those who are acquainted with my life and character know, that I have suffered many unprovoked wrongs, resent few, and offered none." But, he adds, attacks on religion and a friend justify him in raising complaints. Regarding the theological paradox, Blacklock contends that, unlike Beattie who advocates free will, he himself is a necessitarian, and thus exempt from that problem. Bracketed comments identifying the anonymous authors are mine; bracketed comments in the bodies of the letters are those of *Weekly Magazine*.

"Orthodoxus" [i.e., Henry Grieve], "To Dr. James Beattie," in *Weekly Magazine or Edinburgh Amusement*, July 11, 1771, Vol. 13, pp. 51–52.

To Dr JAMES BEATTIE, *Professor of Moral Philosophy in the* Marischal College, Aberdeen, *and Author of an Essay on the Immutability of Truth*, &c.

SIR,

As you have now, in two different editions of your book on *the immutability of Truth*, addressed the public, every individual has doubtless acquired a right publicly to address you. Your book is allowed to have a considerable degree of merit; and I must own I think Mr Hume is sometimes foiled by you at his own metaphysical weapons. I am neither an admirer of his principles, nor do I approve of many of his publications; but, as he has wrapt up his speculations in a dress by which they are disguised from the vulgar eye, I can never think they can hurt society so much as some people imagine: Whoever understands them will soon be able to detect the sophistry of his arguments; and those who cannot, are obliged to you for doing this in his own manner. But where is the occasion for that acrimony of stile, and warmth of invective, so distant from the spirit of calm philosophy? Was this the temper of the antient sages? I am afraid, to put the most favourable construction upon your manner of writing, we must impute it to abstraction from the world, and to these narrow ideas and self-conceits, so readily imbibed by a college recluse.

As I was unwilling to form any bad opinions of a man whose heart appears to be good, and whose acuteness is acknowledged, I have patiently waited the second edition of your book, expecting to find many things softened; at least some hint of an apology for what had already gone abroad; but am disappointed. Mr Hume is no doubt an avowed sceptic; but you have charged him with being an avowed and dogmatical teacher of atheism: a charge which, in my opinion, is unjust. Does not Mr Hume, in his essay against miracles, build his reasoning on this foundation, That men have ideas of power, cause, and effect; and of the order, beauty and regularity of nature, which he considers as thrown into confusion by miraculous interpositions? What although, when again treating of power, cause and effect, he takes the liberty of a sceptic, and, after having formerly acknowledged a first cause, now carries the incomprehensibility of his perfections higher than can be allowed, even so far as to annihilate his former reasonings, and thus leaves full room for every miracle, prodigy, or chimera, that can disturb or distress the mind? Can this man be so formidable an enemy to religion and the good order of society as you represent him? For this must a philosopher turn knight-errant, and Don-Quixotte-like, oppose himself, with target and spear, to metaphysical windmills? If Mr Hume wrote a book upon human nature, which was never, or but by a few people read or understood, and has, as you say, republished this in his essays in more intelligible language, has he not, at the same time, confuted himself in the same essays? Should Mr Beattie bring again to light a book forgotten, and hardly to be found in any bookseller's shop in Britain; what is the consequence? This dangerous book will be again desired, and read; and perhaps another edition required, that the glory of Mr Beattie's triumph may appear more conspicuous. You maintain (and, if your publications did not contradict the assertion, I should be ready to believe it), that you are an enemy to persecution, and would wish that those who differ in opinions would assault one another with no other than with philosophical weapons. But where is the difference, whether I make the assault myself upon my adversary with wooden arguments, or do all that is in my power to stir up others, by addressing their passions, and filling my page with rant and invective? Such a person ought well to consider, whether, when he thinks proper to take a little philosophical liberty, by departing from some received principles, he does not expose himself to another group of persecuting philosophers. Mr Hume has never, so far as I have heard, signed our Confession of Faith, or sworn to the truth of Calvinistic doctrines – He then certainly escapes the charge of perjury. But what shall we say of a man, who, in consequence of his office, has signed a Formula, whereby he declares all the Calvinistic doctrines upon necessity agreeable to his own opinion, and binds himself to teach no other, that the good order of society may be preserved? Yet, suppose this man, so full of acrimony and invective against others differing from him in opinion, shall publish to the world doctrines diametrically opposite to the doctrines he has subscribed, tending to overturn government, and disturb the established church, of which he is a member; what opinion shall we form of him? Shall we allow him that goodness of heart of which he boasts? Can we consider him as a philosopher? No: we can view him in no other light than as an author adopting such opinions as will most readily promote the sale of his book among sectaries and disputers. If Mr Beattie shall answer, in a convincing manner, the following questions, which have distressed me since I read his book, I shall candidly acknowledge I am in the wrong.

1*mo*, Can we be justly punished for the sins of our first parents, if, as Mr Beattie says, we are only accountable for these actions in our own power?

2*do*, Is not the necessary goodness of the Deity a perfection which commands our approbation?

3*tio*, Must not such liberty as he allows, altogether exclude prophecy?

If these questions are not answered in a satisfying manner, what reason have

I to cry out, O enemy to the happiness of man! O murderer of souls! It vexes me to think, that any of good Mr Beattie's opinions should be imagined as destructive to the Christian faith as these of Mr Hume. I can never think that the Christian faith is to be supported in the same manner, or confirmed by evidence, in the same way as a theft of robbery, before a court of judicature. Here, though one part of the evidence may be invalidated, sufficient may remain to convince the jury, and prove the fact; but, destroy one single proof, upon which the great Author of our religion has established our faith, you destroy the veracity of the divine Founder, and thus overturn the whole fabric.

How the Arminian doctrines of liberty can be consistent with prophecy I cannot comprehend. Can prophetical events be certain while they depend on contingent actions? On the other hand, it is allowed, that the chain of causes required to bring about a prophetical event is necessary; it must follow, according to Mr Beattie's reasoning, that the persons thus acting necessarily are neither capable of merit or blame; and that Judas Iscariot, when betraying our Saviour, was guilty of no sin: a most beautiful system of opinions. – As I have no bad design in this letter, it is only intended to make persons more cautious in what manner they express themselves.

There has been a time for all things under the sun. There has been a time for burning Arminians, as well as other heretics. God forbid it should return. Let human nature groan no more! but reflect, that consistency and uniformity will be sought for in every philosopher, as well as in every honest man. It is impossible, as Arian expressed it, to be both a blockhead and a philosopher. No man can act well both the characters of Thersites and Agamamnon. I am,

SIR,

Your very humble servant,

ORTHODOXUS.

———

"Eumenes" [i.e., Thomas Blacklock], response to Orthodoxus, in *Weekly Magazine or Edinburgh Amusement*, July 25, 1771, Vol. 13, pp. 97–102.

To the PUBLISHERS *of the* WEEKLY MAGAZINE.

Qui Bavium non odit, amet tua carmina, Mævi:
Atque idem jungat vulpes, et mulgeat hircos. Virg.

"Let him whose soul for Bavius feels no hate,
O Mævius! love thy works, and share thy fate:
Such taste might try what milk he-goats would yield,
Or with yok'ed foxes plough the stubborn field."

SIR,
It is the natural privilege of mankind, and the constitutional right of Britons, to declare their sentiments upon every subject. This philosophical charter ought to be preserved scarce and inviolable; it ought not to be prostituted to licentious purposes; it ought neither to be wantonly abused nor timidly suppressed, in compliance to particular attachments or personal regards. I wish it were in my power to vindicate all authors from these imputations. I wish, from my soul, I could rank your correspondent Mr *Orthodox* among the happy number of those who are guiltless; but, in my humble opinion, far from assuming the name of *Orthodoxus,* he ought to have subscribed himself *Pseudo-prophetes,* an appellation much more expressive of his character. [51]

There are men of imaginations less extravagant than mine: I have often felt and lamented its impetuosity, when it subjected me to the ridicule of my friends and my own disapprobation; yet a phænomenon so heterogeneous, a being so incongruous as a Christian defending the principles, or patronizing the persons of sceptical philosophers, one may venture to affirm, was never either conceived by man, nor even beheld by God himself, (except in his divine prescience) before the present extraordinary period.

> – *Pictoribus atque poetis*
> *Quidlibet audendi semper fuit æqua potestas.*
> *Scimus, et hanc veniam petimusque damusque vicissim:*
> *Sed non ut placidis coeant immitia; non ut*
> *Serpentes avibus geminentur, tigribus agni.* Hor. Art. Poet.

> Painters and poets our indulgence claim,
> Their daring equal, and their art the fame.
> I own th' indulgence – such I give and take,
> But not thro' nature's sacred rules to break.
> Monstrous to mix the cruel with the kind,
> Serpents with birds, and lambs with tygers join'd! *Francis.*

These reflections may at first appear rash and malevolent; but I ask the gentleman who has incurred them, I ask every soul who has the remotest pretence to intelligence or candour, whether in heaven, earth, or hell; whether, through the whole extent of real or possible existence, two things can be found more diametrically opposite, more eternally irreconcileable, than the spirit and principles of Christianity and scepticism? If these cannot be investigated either by art or nature, from such data let those who profess Christianity and scepticism be judges. The author of our holy religion had emphatically told us, that "the tree was known by its fruit," and that "men did not gather grapes of thorns, or figs of thistles:" but his wiser disciple, Mr *Orthodox,* has, it seems, been enabled, either by experience or inspiration, to detect the fallibility of these maxims, since, if not verbally, at least virtually, he maintains their contraries. It must be acknowledged, that there are truths concerning which the spirit of God has given no decision, and therefore left us at liberty to adopt either alternative, or even to be neuter, according to the force of argument, and the lights in which things may appear; but these are not such as interest the happiness and salvation of mankind. In questions which concern the improvement of our hearts, the rectitude of our conduct, or the preservation of our souls, the decisions of the gospel are positive, as the God from whom they proceed is faithful and true. In such disquisitions, therefore, none but lunatics and traitors to God and man can be indifferent. Now, if the honor of God or the welfare of our species be the natural objects of our warmest and strongest feelings, ought an honest man to suppress them, or can he forbear to effuse them in such words as they dictate? In every practical determination of the mind, operative convictions are not produced by abstract reasoning and logical argument, except where the passions are already pre-engaged for the disputant. We may flatter ourselves as much as we please, that we are unmixed and unbiassed intelligences; but if we review our frame and conduct, we shall find, that the principles upon which we acted were not only firmly believed, but sensibly and intimately felt. Nay, where sentiment is opposed to judgment, and passion to reason, it will seldom be difficult to presage which of the two shall prove victorious. So strongly did our Saviour and his apostles feel the necessity of speaking from the heart to the heart, that perhaps there is not one instance, in which they attempted to render men virtuous and holy by syllogisms in mood and figure, or geometrical demonstration. It seems, however, that some of their followers (and amongst these the canonical Mr *Orthodox*) are of a different opinion. To them we must talk of virtue and religion as we do of news and weather.

But here again I may be deceived. The gentleman in the same breath with which he pleads the cause of scepticism, tells me, that every Christian principle is of equal authority, and that we must either admit all or none. Who therefore, but the Being that made him, can inform me in what spirit I should address him? Doubtless he will expect to be apostrophized in the spirit of meekness, with high encomiums on the merit of his Christian patience in waiting till a second edition of the Essay was published, in hopes of finding the acrimony of the first softened, or some hint of an apology for it. Does he imagine, then, that philosophers assume their sentiments and principles as their cloaths, to change them as decorum and fashion require? If so, his expectations could only be gratified by the sacrifice of ingenuity and common sense. Laudable indeed is his candour in having waited for the second edition, but miserably defective in not having persevered till he had read the postscript. In this he would have found an explicit detail of the motives which impelled, and the sentiments which animated the doctor in writing his Essay, which must be the fairest and best apology that any man can offer for his conduct.

Before he confronted Dr Beattie with the spirit and temper of antient sages, I wish he had observed in what manner the sceptics and Epicureans are handled by the stoic Epictetus, or even by the tranquil, academic Cicero. Besides, Mr *Orthodox* has certainly forgot, that none of the antient sages were ever called to defend a system of doctrines proceeding from the mouth of God himself, and marked with the indubitable signatures of its divine origin; a system of doctrines so suitable to the circumstances and interests of human nature, so salutary to our frame, so pregnant with hopes and promise of glory, honour and immortality, that he who can bear to see them attacked without resentment, could certainly bear the eternal perdition of the universe with the same serenity. In justice to Dr Beattie, he ought not to be contrasted with antient philosophers, but compared with the apologists for Christianity: and if his opponent will fairly begin this research, it may safely be affirmed, that the doctor will be found a mild antagonist. For my own part, I am not more firmly persuaded that I exist, than that he entertains no personal resentment against Mr Hume, and that all those reflections (so loudly accused of virulence and asperity) are not aimed at the man but the system: But where philosophical deductions and observations appear to be either obvious consequences, or natural indications of a personal character, is it possible that we can cease to feel those emotions of complacency or indignation, which they tend to inspire? Were it, however, easy or practicable to extinguish these feelings, it would highly become the extensive charity of Mr *Orthodox* to point out any laws, whether human or divine, from whence the obligation to suppress them results. If he wants to know how our Saviour himself treated those seducing teachers, who violated in their practice, and subverted in their doctrines, the sacred interests of religion and morality, let him consult the evangelist Matthew, chap. xxiii. verses 29, 30, 31, 32, and 33.

Had the sceptical philosophy terminated in speculation alone, I can without hesitation affirm, that it would never have been the object of Dr Beattie's animadversion: but he must indeed be a superficial observer of life and manners, who does not see the rapid progress it has made, and the dreadful innovations it has raised in both. Joy to the man who can be an unconcerned spectator of such melancholy revolutions! Certain I am, that were my constitution so pacific, I should have less reason than Judas Iscariot to hope for happiness either in this world or the next; in proportion as it is more flagitious to betray the cause, than the person of Christ.

But we are told, that such as understand the principles of that philosophy, will discern their sophistry, and such as do not, cannot be affected by them. Both these positions are so egregiously false, that I can only exculpate the gentleman's veracity who asserts them, by supposing him an absolute anchorite; between the alternatives of ignorance and falsehood, therefore, let him chuse which he thinks proper. For, in the first case, I declare upon the honour of a man, and the faith of a Christian, that I have seen and disputed with many who understand that philosophy as thoroughly as its ingenious restorer; yet, far from detecting its fallacy, were more implicitly addicted to it than their master: and, in the last, I have observed still a greater number, who, without learning or capacity to comprehend it, have imbibed its spirit, and adopted its latitudinary maxims, induced and authorized alone by the credit and reputation of those by whom it was received and propagated. Nay, others may still be found who had studied it sufficiently to fill their souls with anguish, uncertainty and gloom; and who acknowledge themselves extricated from its difficulties by the Essay on the nature and immutability of Truth. This I am properly authorised by themselves to affirm. Let Mr *Orthodox* therefore account to the world and his own conscience, if he can, for calling the sceptical philosophy a mere metaphysical windmill, and accusing those of philosophical knight-errantry, who appear in the cause of God and man. If, indeed, our natural propensities determined us to wisdom and virtue as the sovereign good of our nature, your correspondent's gratuitous affirmations might be admitted: but whilst early prepossessions, and strong passions in favour of libertinism, continually blind the understanding, and solicit the heart; whilst the force of example, and the importunities of temptation from without, concur with the intestine foes of piety and truth, how can your correspondent be so mathematically certain, that the principles of scepticism will neither be embraced by those who understand them, nor regarded by those who do not?

But his persuasion is equally sanguine, that the Dissertation on Human Nature has never been read, or but by few; that it is now forgotten, and hardly to be met with in any bookseller's shop in Great Britain. How true the last of those facts may be, I pretend not to judge; but the first and second (that the book has either been read by few, or is intirely forgotten) are absolutely false, and so grossly contradictory to universal knowledge and conviction, that he must be charitable indeed who can palliate them with the excuse of mistake. I was in Edinburgh soon after the original publication, and well remember how much and how frequently it was mentioned, in every literary conversation: and if it is now so irrecoverably involved in oblivion, how should it have happened that Dr Reid, and a number of other venerable names, have opposed the full strength of their genius to its malignity? I will, however, do Mr Hume the justice to assert, that no performance written with so much taste and genius as his own, will ever be forgotten; and whatever vicissitudes the reputation of his philosophy may suffer, the fame acquired by his spirit and elegance, will be permanent and immortal, as far as authors can hope for immortality.

But it seems this acute writer has confuted himself; and, for that reason, his philosophy is quite innoxious. We know that it is the characteristic of the sect to dispute *pro omnibus, et contra omni*: but is it therefore harmless and innocent? If a giant should take up two ordinary men, and dash them against one another till he knocked out both their brains, could he be said to have done no hurt? or would either of the persons be much consoled, when informed, that the collision was equal, and that his neighbour had suffered as much as he? Just such is the sceptical philosopher. He dashes one principle against another, till both seem annihilated; or (which has the same effect) till the intellects of his readers are so irrevocably confounded, that they cannot distinguish light from darkness, or truth from falshood. Is this situation of mind more adapted to rational life, or to Bedlam? But, whatever turn reason may take, believe me, the senses and passions are no sceptics; and, though they may be persuaded to doubt the existence of objects remotely distant either in time or place, yet have they too many in view, and even in contact, to be at a loss for present occupation: nor will they fail to chuse amongst these the nearest and most agreeable, in preference to other advantages, whose impressions may seem less poignant, and whose reality more ambiguous. It would give me pain; should it appear necessary to apply these observations more immediately to the advantages offered by religion and virtue. If sages of this sect allow us the idea of power when they would refute miracles, and deny that we possess it when another occasion requires; can the tenor of their conduct be expected more consistent than the principles by which it was inspired?

I know the sceptics generally plead, that, when any tenets are assumed as certain, conclusions equally indubitable will follow; and so there is an end of all inquiry. They tell us, that, from dogmatical opinions proceed all the implacable rage, that vindictive and persecuting spirit, which are at once the plagues and reproaches of humanity. They urge, that, however remote the principles from which our discussive faculties begin, they are led, by a necessary chain of deductions, to conclusions absolutely subversive of the data with which they set out. Yet nothing seems more plain, than that God and nature intended every active being to be moved and directed by principle. Of this, the impressions of sense, the demands of appetite, the impulses of instinct, the native and spontaneous exertions of reason, and the uniform consequences of different actions, are proofs so strongly confirmed both by intuition and experience, that he who denies or doubts them, must of consequence resign every claim to the rational character. I cannot for my soul imagine, with what propriety a sceptic complains of thirst or hunger: nor is it possible to conceive, why he should use the ordinary means of recovering health, and avoiding danger: nor, upon his own principles, can he urge the least title to our humanity, though involved in the deepest and most exquisite distress. For neither can he prove, that kind offices are due to affliction; nor that, even when administered, they will be in any degree effectual to remove or alleviate the complaint. In a word, if consistent with himself, he must neither be active nor passive, neither conscious nor insensible, neither an existence nor a non-entity, neither a medium between any, nor a compound of all these opposite extremes; for, from every one of these situations, some principle, positive or negative, must arise; and absolute negation or affirmation are both equally, and both essentially destructive of his doctrines.

But now comes the glorious and happy period of your correspondent's triumph; for now he means to confront Dr Beattie with himself: to convict him of inconsistency; nay (as he modestly insinuates), of perjury too.

Parturiunt montes et nascitur ridiculus mus.

The mountain labour'd with maternal throes,
And, lo! to birth a puny mouse arose

And now, sir, will you permit me to ask him a few questions in my turn?

1*st*, Is every Calvinist obliged in conscience to believe and explain every article of that system in the same manner? I fear, if this be the case, we shall have many more perjuries than we suspect; and give me leave to add, if *Orthodoxus* himself be a rational being, I tremble for his integrity. Thanks be to God! it was my lot to be educated, from the earliest periods of susceptibility and reason, under the tuition of parents, whose progenitors had severely and heavily felt the lash of power, both in their persons and effects, for their inflexible adherence to Presbyterian principles. To me, by all the force of expostulation, argument or example, they transmitted their principles; and I hope their spirit likewise. These were the only patrimony which they did (and, in my estimation, the most precious which they could) bequeath me. They have directed me in life; they have consoled me in misery; and I hope they will support me in the awful crisis of dissolution. Yet, dear as they are to my soul, may the true and living God, the God of benevolence and peace, the God and father of our Lord and saviour Jesus Christ, forbid, that I should exclude from christian hopes and privileges all that are not Calvinists. It has been the curse and shame of our profession, to bind the bands of union so hard, and draw them so close, that every one who differs from us in the smallest punctilio, is excluded from our communion. O Charity! Charity! thou essential constituent of the Christian character! Thou source of all that is dear and sacred upon earth! Thou favourite virtue of heaven! whither art thou fled; since thy own professed pupils disregard thy authority and influence?

With your correspondent, I am persuaded in my conscience and understanding, that predestination is taught us both by reason and revelation; but, whilst thousands of my species, whose wisdom is greatly superior, and whose sincerity is equal to mine, believe the contrary, and interpret the scriptures in a manner different from me, shall I set up my own opinions as the encounciations of the Holy Ghost? Shall I deny them the Christian name, and consequently the inestimable benefits of redemption? This, as far as human impotence can go, would be to usurp heaven, and dethrone the sovereign Judge of the universe. – But once more let me ask Mr *Orthodox*.

2*dly*, Does not the Westminster Confession of Faith [Chap. ix. Sect. 1.] assert the freedom of the human will as precisely and positively as predestination?

Has Dr Beattie then maintained any thing but the freedom of the human will? and can he be justly charged with Arminianism? Had the gentleman considered this, he would, perhaps, have spared himself and us the trouble of such ostentatious dilemmas, and insidious questions. This parade of interrogation would tempt us to think he used the Christian religion merely as spiders do their cobwebs, to catch and torment such insects as are unguardedly intangled in the net. Had it been otherwise, would he have urged prophecy as an objection against Dr Beattie's essay? We know that the predictions in question were emitted, authenticated, and published long before the days of our Saviour. We know that their corresponding events happened in such a manner, and in such circumstances, as left it beyond the power of rational inquiry to doubt their completion. How then, for heaven's sake! has contingency or prescience any thing to do in the dispute? Can the evidence of facts, which have already happened, and are supported by every testimony which is necessary to confirm the truth of history, be invalidated by any impertinent questions which may afterwards be asked, in what manner they were foreknown or produced? I will venture to affirm, that the difficulty of reconciling prophecy with contingency is not more arduous, than that of reconciling accountability with necessity. Nay, that Clarke, in his Demonstration of the Divine Attributes, and Boetius *de consolatione philosophiæ*, have offered a more plausible solution of the first, than any one that has been proposed for the last, by all the adherents of predestination, from St Augustine to Mons. Leibnitz. If this inquirer had not intended to perplex, he might have considered, that, when the author of the Essay on Truth seemed to think men accountable for such actions as are in their own power, it was possible he meant such actions alone as were personal; and therefore the doctrine of original sin had no connection with the matter.

As in philosophy I am a moral necessitarian, it is not incumbent upon me to answer all the difficulties which your correspondent proposes; nor do I believe Dr Beattie will ever undertake it. I should grieve to see the hand of Alcidea armed with a club to crush a gnat; or all the storms and lightnings of heaven collected, to quench the glow-worms's fire.

By hearing one party, you have, in some measure, become an umpire in this controversy; the other party has therefore a just title to your attention. This, as a scholar and an advocate for injured worth, I shall expect to find inserted; and insist upon it as due to my cause.

I am, SIR,
    Your constant reader,
      and obedient servant,
        EUMENES.
Glenullin, July 17.
    1771.

———

"Democritus" [i.e., Mrs. Carnegie], response to Orthodoxus and Eumenes, in *Weekly Magazine or Edinburgh Amusement*, August 15, 1771, Vol. 13, pp. 195–198.

To the PUBLISHERS of the WEEKLY MAGAZINE.

SIR,
I am not a little entertained with the two champions who have lately taken the field in your Paper for and against Mr Beattie, and beg to be allowed, as a spectator (who sometimes sees more of the game than those who are engaged), to make some remarks upon both parties. If I shall only anticipate the replies of either of them, then, without ceremony, you may lay me aside.

I shall first premise (what, perhaps, may be obvious enough, from my manner of handling the subject), that I have no pretension to be numbered amongst the literati, but hold a middle rank in that middle order of beings betwixt the learned and the ignorant, a pretty numerous class, for whose benefit, I imagine, such writers as Mr Beattie principally bestow their labours. The ignorant are already secured from all danger of infection from false philosophy, either by never hearing of it at all, or paying no attention to it when they accidentally fall in with it; and as for the learned, whose constant study and profession it is to find wisdom, let them take care of themselves; but we of the middle order, who often think too much to be indifferent, and too little to be easy, are much obliged to those geniuses who take the trouble of steering us through the depths and quicksands wherein we often intangle ourselves.

I have read the Essay on the Nature and Immuntability of Truth with tolerable attention and considerable approbation: to the best of my judgment, the author is on the right side of the question, and has the better in the arguments; but two circumstances greatly diminished both my pleasure and approbation, first, the continual attempts of the author to make the subject appear of much more consequence than any body in that middle rank above defined can be brought to believe it really is, at least as far as my acquaintance reaches: and strange it is, if it actually is of such vast importance, that, in a pretty extensive circle (not of the learned indeed, but of the intelligent and polite), not a person should treat it but as a mere *jeu d' esprit*; nay, if *Eumenes* would not doom me to associate with Judas Iscariot, or brand honest people with the appellations of traitors to religion, to God and man, I would even venture to adopt the term *metaphysical wind-mill*, as no improper expression of the sentiments of many. The other circumstance offensive to me, was what *Orthoduxus* complains of, the virulence of invective, the strength and copiousness of declamation, and the intolerable, I believe I may venture to say, insolent triumph of the author over an antagonist, who, though *possibly*, nay, perhaps *evidently mistaken*, is still respectable. Modesty, Mr Printer, is as engaging in an author as in a companion; and, for my own part, I would not argue *viva voce* with any man who would treat me in the manner that this, and some other northern philosophers treat their antagonists, but would turn from him with the silent contempt his ill manners deserved. Is it not enough, when people differ in opinion, either in conversation or upon paper, to oppose argument to argument, and let the company or the public judge who is in the right? The victory must be very dubious, if the bystanders cannot of themselves find out to whom it belongs, without a trumpet being sounded by one party to inform them. The more certain one is of the strength of their arguments, the more apparent and shining that their victory is; they ought to express themselves with the more delicacy, modesty, and reserve; far from obscuring, such a conduct gives lustre to a triumph, whilst the contrary, like dragging the dead body of an enemy at one's chariot-wheels, implies only vanity or meanness, provokes the adverse party, and even disgusts our own.

These being my sentiments, Mr Printer, it is no wonder that I, and many others (for my opinion is far from singular, but rather falls in with the multitude), was very glad to see this matter put so home to Mr Beattie himself by *Orthodoxus*. – "When a writer agrees with me (says Dr Swift), I pronounce him a clever fellow; he writes charmingly! and we are always happy when those who have incurred our censure or displeasure, are taken to task by somebody, though we did not care to meddle ourselves. The censor pays a tacit compliment to our judgment, which self-love is ever ready to lay hold of." – As to the latter part of *Orthodoxus* epistle, the charge of inconsistency, which he retorts upon Mr Beattie, and his religious queries, I was immediately of opinion with *Eumenes*, "that he makes use of the Christian religion (he had better said the Presbyterian tenets) as spiders do their cobwebs, to catch and torment those insects that are unguardedly intangled in the net." An insidious design, but justified by the end in view, which I think is very apparently neither more nor less than this, to show one writer, who so unmercifully triumphs over another for some inconsistencies in his writings, how very hard it is for any man to make all parts of his own sentiments and character consistent. – *Orthodoxus*, in spite of his name, may perhaps be a layman as well as your humble servant; and as such, being at liberty to judge for himself, independent of the Confession of Faith, may think with me, that what Mr Beattie has advanced with regard to the freedom of the human will, and man's being accountable only for his voluntary actions, is not the worst part of the Essay on the Nature and Immutability of Truth, tho' it does not become a member of the church, who has formally professed to believe its creed in all its parts, to advance things so diametrically opposite to its doctrines, and yet pretend to perfect consistency of character. This is all, I suppose, *Orthodoxus* meant by his warm attack and insnaring questions: his heat, or *virulence*, if you please to call it, is manifestly a retort, a mere transcript of the very manner which he and others find so much fault with; and Mr Beattie has only himself to blame, since it is plainly owning to his own unmerciful way of charging home his antagonists with having foreseen and admitted all the consequences which he thinks fit to deduce from their positions, that he has drawn upon himself an attack, which, though I cannot allow it to be generous or just in its own nature, as I hold it quite the opposite to beat down a churchman with some religious tenets, which, though he possibly may not agree with, yet he *dare not* contravert; yet here, I must say, I think it is but giving him his deserts: many respectable authors are guilty of yet greater inconsistencies than these objected to Mr Beattie, with a true zeal throughout their works for the cause of Christianity; yet, upon other subjects, where they had not attended to any connection with the sacred system, such observations and positions have escaped them, as, if even fairly deduced and applied, would strike at the root of revealed religion; these I could particularize, if need were; yet, so far as I know, these slips have passed unobserved, or have been admitted as mere oversights; for, not being unmerciful cavilling critics upon others, others have allowed them the indulgence of their merit and candour deserved.

I come now to the elaborate defence of *Eumenes*, in my humble opinion very little to the purpose. Mr Printer, I an a very plain dealer; I look upon perspicuity and conciseness as the best dress of argument, and would with every body to speak and write directly to the matter in hand, and not puzzle and carry people off from the subject, by long winded dissertations and useless declamation.

How, in the name of wonder, does *Eumenes* make out the extraordinary fact, which, with a rather unbecoming strength of expression, he asserts God himself never to have beheld till now? of a Christian defending the sceptical philosophy? Is it to defend a system, to allow that the head and defender of it contradicts himself? that it is evidently absurd, that there is no danger of its gaining ground? in short, that it is a metaphysical wind-mill! If this be a defence, it is certainly a most uncivil one, and what the proselytes of the sect will by no means give him thanks for. – The pompous manner of treating this defence, as *Eumenes* is pleased to call it, favours much of the first fault I found with the Essay on Truth; a pedantry which speculative men, little acquainted with the world, are very apt to run into, of imagining the little thing about which they busy themselves, to be the most important article on earth; as here, the Almighty with his adorable attributes of omniscience and prescience, is brought in about a bagatelle, nay, about nothing at all, as I absolutely deny the existence of this Christian defender of the sceptics.

Let us proceed then to the first thing, column 3d, which comes really to the business in hand, where he takes notice of *Orthodoxus* having waited for the second edition, in hopes of finding things softened, or some apology offered: to this he replies "Does he then imagine that philosophers assume their sentiments and principles as their cloaths, to change them again as decorum or fashion requires. No, Sir; but as great philosophers as your friend have thought it no disparagement to own and correct, in a second edition, the errors in expression and doctrine which they had suffered to creep into a first; I mean the candid, the modest, the ever to be reverenced Mr Locke. Nor can I see that it would have at all hurt our author's character to have corrected, in his second edition, the faults which, comparatively speaking, all the world found fault with in the first. It is not his doctrines; it is not his principles; it is his expressions and manners that are reprehended: his philosophy would remain the same, but appear in a much more amiable dress by the correction of them.

The simile [P. 100] of the giant dashing out two men's brains against each other, and making them the apology that they had only received equal hurt, is so very extravagant, that I know not how to treat it, or whether to meddle with it or not. I own I cannot see the least resemblance betwixt the simile and the thing signified; but if *Eumenes* will permit me, I shall retain his giant, giving him two clubs, instead of two men in his paws; now, if he breaks these two clubs, one against the other, our giant is disarmed, and just in the same situation as to doing mischief, as if he never had handled a club at all. Whether *Eumenes* or I have best illustrated *Orthodux's* account of the sceptical philosophy, we shall leave to the gentleman himself to determine.

The ridicule thrown out in the next column, upon the sceptics, is fighting with the wind, there being no opponent, as, by allowing them to contradict and defeat themselves, every thing was already said, but in much fewer words, by *Orthodoxus*.

As Mr Beattie has not thought proper to put his own name, nor give the sanction of his approbation to the paper signed *Eumenes*, we are not at liberty to suppose it to be his, though some *family touches*, and the assertion of his being as certain of Mr Beattie's sentiments as of his own existence, would tempt us to believe it to be himself *incog*. were not the conclusion such a rhodomontade as we cannot suppose a man of his sense either to write or approve: it were too grossly ridiculous to suppose a man comparing his *own* abilities to the club of Hercules and the thunders of heaven, and his adversaries to a gnat; nay, in my opinion, it is too far for friendship to go. The writer has, indeed, offered something in the beginning, which may be allowed to apologize for this high-flown phraseology, namely, that he is under the dominion of an extravagant imagination; but, as these circumstances, Mr Printer, leave us not at liberty to suppose this to be Mr Beattie's own defence, so the answer to *Orthodoxus'* queries signify nothing from any other hand – he must answer them *himself*, or they must remain unanswered – For my part, I agree with *Eumenes*, that it would serve no purpose to attempt it; and give it as my opinion, that *Orthodoxus* never expected it, or desired it, his end being fully answered by barely proposing them.

Let me conclude as I began, by assuring you, that I am really entertained by this contest, though I don't think it a matter to bring heaven and earth together

about; and if, by my lucubrations on the subject, I contribute my mite also to the entertainment of the public, my labour is amply rewarded. I am,
 SIR,
   Your constant reader,
     and humble servant,
       DEMOCRITUS.
August 2. 1771.

———

"Eumenes" [i.e., Thomas Blacklock], response to Democritus, in *Weekly Magazine or Edinburgh Amusement*, August 29, 1771, Vol. 13, pp. 265–269.

To *the* EDITOR *of the* WEEKLY MAGAZINE.
ANIMADVERSIONS *on* ANIMADVERSIONS.

Non tali auxilio, nec defensaribus istis,
Tempus eget. VIRG.

"The time demands not such a feeble aid;
By such defence 'tis injur'd and betray'd."

SIR,
It gives me no small pleasure, that Orthodoxus and I should have contributed so much to the entertainment of Democritus; nor has that sage and dispassionate spectator been ungrateful. I have now read his speculation twice, and shall review it a third time, not, however, with that solemnity in which he seems to have wrote it; for there are some circumstances, "when to be grave exceeds all power of face." I am far from suspecting that the gentleman intended to irritate my visible muscles so violently; but, whatever was his view, so effectually did the dose operate, that I will venture to say, *decies repetita placebit.*
   But this was not the only emotion which I felt: his sublime and important discoveries likewise filled me with the highest astonishment. He tells us, "that there are three orders of mankind, the learned, the ignorant, and a middle rank, who think too much to be indifferent, and too little to be easy;" among which number he places himself. This is one of those profound arcana, which must for ever have mocked my penetration, had he not been kind enough to reveal it. Far from guessing, either by the manner of matter of his epistle, that his talents reached mediocrity, I should have been at a loss to find out that he ever thought at all. Since, however (in his own opinion), he has so happily illustrated the sentiments of Orthodoxus, it might prove an inestimable acquisition to the learned world, if he would publish a commentary on his own illustrations; by

which we may be able to comprehend the distinction he makes between ease and indifference. There may, indeed, be cases where these words are used with propriety, to mark distinct characters and situations: indifference may signify, disengagement from prepossession; and ease, freedom from labour, fatigue and anxiety; but how they can be contrasted in this place, I have not depth enough to explore.

Another of his wonderful discoveries is, "that he, as a spectator, sees more of the game than those who are engaged." If he must be admitted in this unbiassed character, your readers may behold in him the most striking instance that nature can exhibit, how nice, how imperceptible the barriers, which divide spectators from parties. He may, perhaps, see more of the game than those who are engaged in it; but his assertion is at least a *petitio principii*, since the whole of his letter is not only a proof that he has not seen so much, but that what he has seen was beheld with a jaundiced eye.

But he has, it seems, read the Essay on the Nature and Immutability of Truth, with tolerable attention and considerable approbation. I acknowledge myself under the influence of an extravagant fancy (a circumstance which the gentleman as had the penetration to collect, and the complaisance to repeat from my own words); but however wild and excursive, it has never yet impelled me to regard any author with a degree of approbation disproportioned to the attention which I exerted in reading his work. Indeed, from the manner in which he talks of Dr Beattie's performance, it may be decently presumed, that either his understanding or attention, or both, are but merely tolerable.

Notwithstanding this considerable approbation with which *Democritus* read the work in question, he joins *Orthodoxus* in regretting two circumstances; "First, the continual attempts of the author, to make the subject appear of much more consequence than any body in that middle rank above defined can be brought to believe it really is; at least as far as his acquaintance reaches:" and we are likewise informed, that they are "a pretty extensive circle; not of the learned indeed, but of the intelligent and polite." He has, at the same time, communicated a wonderful criterion of their intelligence and politeness; for to them, it seems, the dispute between Dr Beattie and Mr Hume appears a mere *jeu d'espirit*, or a collection of metaphysical windmills. What then are the subjects of the dispute? They are the being and character of God; the existence of the material, intellectual and moral universe; the distinction between vice and virtue; the certainty of human science; the reality of every present enjoyment or future hope which the soul of man can indulge. Heaven and earth! Is this a *jeu d'esprit?* Are these metaphysical windmills? Tell me then, what can be important, sacred or dear to a conscious being? If the polite circle with which *Democritus* is acquainted, entertains the same notions of them with himself, surely their understandings must be differently modified, not only from those of the greatest number, but even of the wisest and best among their species, from the birth of time to the present period. But though the dispute should be granted a mere *jeu d'esprit*, and its subjects no ore than metaphysical windmills; yet has it ever been reckoned an instance of good manners to despise and affront the received opinions of a society, upon which the dearest hopes of its members were founded, and by which their most important actions were regulated? The polytheism of the heathens, with all the farce and mummery of their priestcraft, was sensibly perceived, and internally despised by some of their philosophers. It appears, however, that they neither thought it advantageous to the state, nor productive of private happiness, to oppose these useful prejudices. Far from endeavouring to obliterate, they cultivated these impressions, and enjoined the observation of every religious ceremony. Shall we then, among whom a much more rational and efficacious system has obtained credit and authority; shall we do our utmost to extinguish every sentiment which it inspires, and invalidate every motive which it offers? Without resuming a topic so unfashionable, as the authenticity of natural and revealed religion, I might show its utility, and what a powerful auxiliary it proves to civil government, in many cases where its powers are by no means equal to its exigencies; but this disquisition would lead me too far. Enough has been said upon them by others, to discover the absurdity and wickedness of those who wish to debilitate the authority of religious principles. They have urged, that emergencies may occur, when the secular arm is too short to reach enormities, or too weak to punish them; when the public eye is too blind, or too much prejudiced to discover crimes; in short, when the whole system is too much corrupted and degenerated to be cured by ordinary remedies. Whence then are the motives by which vices may be anticipated in their source, or checked in their progress, but from religion? But the veneration, therefore, which they pay to sacred principles and institutions, we may judge of the polished manners and profound understanding which distinguish the acquaintance of *Democritus*.

The maxim of *Orthodoxus* is still resumed, "that the ignorant cannot be affected with false philosophy, because they do not hear of it; and the learned, whose business it is to find wisdom, may take care of themselves." This was formerly answered, not from abstract theory, but plain matters of fact, from which there remains only one evasion to question their authority; but even in this, if I am properly called to account, the authors of these reiterated and unsupported assertions will find themselves egregiously mistaken; yet, before they obtain this *eclaircisement*, it will be natural to expect, from gentlemen of intelligence and politeness, that they should discover their names, otherwise they have no more right to expect such a concession, than the bravo who attacks you by night with his dark lanthorn and stiletto, to expect that you will tamely yield him your purse or your life. It seems, however, no answer will be satisfactory to these anonymous correspondents, unless given by Dr Beattie himself. Did then *Orthodoxus* wish for any solution to his questions? or did he (as *Democritus* thinks) barely propose them for the pleasure of interrogation? If so, he must rather be ranked with school-boys than philosophers. Should any person ask another, how many make two times two, will not four be the proper answer, whoever returns it? Perhaps the public may not be so fastidious as *Orthodox* and *Democritus*. The candid and impartial may possibly acquiesce in the proper solution of a question, from whatever hand it comes.

The other circumstance offensive to *Democritus*, was that *Orthodoxus* complains of; "the virulence of invective; the strength and copiousness of declamation; the intolerable, he believes he may venture to say insolent, triumph of the author over an antagonist, who, though possible, nay perhaps evidently, mistaken, is still respectable." Your correspondent proceeds upon the supposition, that the cavils of *Orthodoxus* against the Essay on Truth remain in full force, because not answered by its author in *propria persona*. In vain has it been urged, that all the feelings of the human heart impel us to maintain truth with a warmth and zeal becoming her dignity and importance. This, when it is against ourselves, or those for whom we are engaged, is immediately called bitterness of invective, and insolence of triumph. It must be acknowledged, that Dr Beattie is earnest in his cause; but, unless particular instances had been assigned, where he indecently exults in his victory, it will scarcely be taken for granted that he has used his conquest with such wanton cruelty. The only subterfuge, to which these gentlemen have recourse in their necessity, and by which they would gladly give the appearance of ill-nature and scurrility to just accusation, is by strenuously maintaining, that the object of the combat is of no moment; that Mr Hume refutes himself, and consequently leaves nothing to do for others; and that a practical sceptic is a contradiction in terms: but they do not consider, that the very design of this refutation is, not only to demolish all former systems of philosophy, but even to annihilate the foundations and materials upon which others might be erected.

Democritus is much disgusted with the simile of the giant, &c. he therefore takes the liberty of transforming the men into clubs, and thinks he has extricated his hero from the guilt of homicide, at the small expence of two innocent cudgels, after which the giant sits down in cold blood, and rejoices in the success of his atchievement. But whether we consider our athletic philosopher as a breaker of clubs, or a fabricator of metaphysical windmills, it will be easy, upon their own principles, to determine, how far he is respectable even in his mistakes. *Democritus*, however, seems to insinuate, that there is only a possibility of his being mistaken; at least when he pronounces him evidently so, it is qualified with a *perhaps*: so much has he imbibed of the spirit, which informs and characterises that philosophy to which he seems willing to reconcile us. The transition from men to clubs might perhaps have appeared violent and bold, if there were not instances how nearly modifications of flesh and blood may resemble modifications of timber, and that there may be wooden men as well as wooden clubs.

These unhappy sticks must, however, undergo another metamorphosis, and, by the virtue of *hocus pocus*, become crutches to support a cripple, who walks along the margin of a precipice. An arch wag came behind him, and, merely to show his nimbleness or dexterity, snatched them from him. The miserable suppliant, while yet he could stand, begged the aggressor, by all that was sacred or humane, to restore them; but he, in sportive mischief, broke them in pieces, and threw them at a distance, whilst the wretched man, deprived of his only resource, fell to rise no more. But a person of superior vigour, immediately passing the same way, collected the fragments, and so sensibly chastised our merry whipster, that he seemed to decline a second engagement. His friends, indeed, might bite their nails and grumble, but did not chuse, for particular reasons, to speak out, whilst echo returned the half articulated sounds in malicious mockery. This story may possibly meet with less approbation than the simile, but it is already told, and cannot be retracted.

We are now informed, that *Orthodoxus,* by retorting that inconsistency upon Dr Beattie, of which he had so clearly convicted others, kindly intended to inspire him with lenity for those errors of which he himself was not blameless. This is indeed what the logicians call *argumentum ad hominem.* Admire with me, Sir, the beauty and perspicuity of this illustration. I am sorry to say, however, there is one objection against it. Had the design of *Orthodoxus* been so mild and merciful as is pretended, he might have copied Dr Beattie's address from the title-page of his book, and sent him his thoughts in a private letter, without giving the public such a pregnant instance of his charity. I fear, therefore, that *Democritus* must still review his illustration.

Among the sublime and important discoveries which I have formerly mentioned, the supposition that Dr Beattie is a churchman must be reckoned one. I already knew, indeed, that he was a Professor and a Doctor of Laws; but to find out that he was invested with ecclesiastical orders, demanded that more enlarged acquaintance with the world, which *Orthodoxus* and his friend would be thought to monopolize, and which frees the mind from the pedantry and contracted notions of a college recluse. If, however, this extensive knowledge of mankind be only productive of such discoveries as that Dr Beattie is a churchman, unenvied and unrivalled let them possess it.

But these gentlemen are so happy and successful in every hypothesis, that, had they appeared before Sir Isaac Newton, I should not have despaired to see them publish one sufficient to solve all the phenomena of nature. Of this I cannot give a stronger proof than the inclination which *Democritus* expresses, to suppose Dr Beattie himself the author of *Eumenes's* letter. Since he wishes to entertain a conjecture so noble, and so worthy of a generous mind, I shall leave him in that agreeable suspense; but your other readers may be informed, that Dr Beattie was then on his journey, and is now at the distance of three hundred miles from the theatre of these philosophical tilts and tournaments, as ignorant of their procedure, and careless of their issue as the Grand Signior or the Cham of Tartary.

To the accusation of ill-nature, it has been replied, that there are certain subjects which cannot properly be treated with coolness, but demand and inspire a degree of emotion, which the depraved or insensible alone can suppress. To the charge of Arminianism, it was answered, that the Confession of Faith asserts the freedom of the human will, with the same decisive clearness as Dr Beattie. To the objection that prophecy appears incompatible with contingency of action, it has been returned, that the evidence of prophecy depends not on the manner in which future events are foreseen or produced, but on the authenticity of the predictions, and on the fidelity of their accomplishment; and that it seems equally difficult to accommodate our notions of moral agency with necessity, as to reconcile our ideas of prescience with freedom. To obviate the wretched quibble deduced from original sin, it has been said, that when the author of the Essay denied our being accountable for such actions as were not in our own power, he only meant such actions as were personal; But these replications they have declared unsatisfactory, unless delivered by Dr Beattie himself *viva voce*; even though he were to give them *incog.* (as *Democritus* elegantly phrases it) they could serve no purpose.

But it is not simply for exerting my logic in vain that I am culpable: no; I have likewise sinned beyond the reach of pardon, in calling *Orthodoxus* a Christian defender of scepticism. To enter into the nature of defence, it may be requisite to consider the state of the thing patronised. The sceptical philosophy (though viewed with indifference, or perhaps with partiality, by the polite and intelligent circle amongst whom *Democritus* is conversant) has not yet (and God grant it never may) become popular. It is still regarded, by the generality, with that contempt, when considered as ridiculous, or with that detestation, when viewed as a serious matter, which it richly deserves. Now, I ask, whether the advocate who obtains a tolerable composition from his creditors for an insolvent debtor, or one who mitigates the punishment of a capital offender by banishment, though he gains not a plenary pardon for either of his clients, may not be properly said to defend them?

Democritus has likewise revived, from the casuistical Jesuits, a maxim of infinite consequence, which the knavish part of mankind will never fail to adopt when it can be subservient to their interests; that the means, however insidious or ungenerous, are justified by the end. Hence it will follow, that every attempt must be applauded or condemned, not by its rectitude, but success. – A blessed precept, and worthy of all acceptation! But if the means employed by *Orthodoxus* have not accomplished their end; if, in the nature of things, they were inadequate to its accomplishment, they surely cannot claim that justification, even in the sense of *Democritus*, which he would willingly bestow upon them.

The insolence of triumph with which he upbraids Dr Beattie, the pedantry, family touches, and rhodomontade with which he reproaches me, are such illustrious specimens of his good nature and good sense, that they transcend my highest praises. But as I am born a Briton, and my actions can only be determined by the public judgment, I shall not consult his opinion, whether humble or decisive, how far I ought to proceed in the vindication of a friend; but, after having admonished him to revise the grammar of his own language,[1] leave him to that repose which seems to be most proper for people of his character and endowments.

And now, Sir, I sincerely beg your pardon for consuming so much of your time and paper in my animadversions upon a letter, which so little merits either your attention or mine. My only apology is, that I am engaged in the best of causes, and for the best of friends: yet, as my subject appears now to be exhausted, you may depend upon hearing no more of it from,

Yours, &c.

EUMENES.

Glenullin,

Aug. 23. 1771.

———

"Orthodoxus" [i.e., Henry Grieve], response to Eumenes, in *Weekly Magazine or Edinburgh Amusement*, September 5, 1771, Vol. 13, pp. 295–297.

To the PUBLISHERS *of the* WEEKLY MAGAZINE.

Let not thy weak, unknowing hand,
  Presume God's bolts to throw;
Nor deal damnation round the land,
  On each thou think'st thy foe.
      Pope's Universal Prayer.

SIR,

I have, in your Magazine of July 25. [P. 97] read the defence of *Eumenes*, for his friend Dr Beattie; and, had it not breathed the same spirit with the Essay on the Immutability of Truth, you should not have been troubled with any observations upon it. Such a spirit of candour, as could only be invocated from hell itself, seems to have filled the breast, and guided the pen of this inhabitant of Glenullin, when he charges me with being an advocate for scepticism, or sceptical writers. I detest that sceptical philosophy, which makes its adherents to dispute *pro omnibus et contra omnia,* as much as he can do; and, had not Dr Beattie mixed so much invective and declamation with his reasonings, he should have had my hearty approbation. The same spirit of malevolence makes *Eumenes* attribute my letter to connections with, or regard for Mr Hume: I never, indeed, thought the Christian religion should inspire me with such a degree of resentment against Mr

---

[1] *See* No. vii. p. 196. col. 2. l. 18, 19, &c. ["The more certain one is of the strength of their arguments, the more apparent and shining that their victory is ...."]

Hume, as to make me endeavour to bring him to the stake or the gibbet: But I assure *Eumenes* (without invoking the Deity on such frivolous occasions), that I never was in company with Mr Hume but once in my life; and, since that time, have never cultivated his acquaintance. I thought, and I dare say Mr Hume would think, that I paid no high compliment to his reasonings, when I compared them to metaphysical windmills. – I blamed not Dr Beattie for his attack, but for using weapons improper for the recounter. The figures of a popular rhetoric I have always thought unnecessary in philosophical disputes, especially when intended not to convince, but inflame. Mr Hume's reasonings are disguised from the bulk of mankind: Invectives and addresses to the passions are well understood by many, incapable of judging the propriety of their application. I shall examine the manner in which the academic Cicero, and the truly philosophical Epictetus, treat the sceptics, when I have opportunity: But *Eumenes* ought to reflect, that, in antient times, there was not so many penal laws against free inquiries as in many Christian countries: and, though the spirit of his ancestors animates *Eumenes*, their sufferings ought to have taught him the danger of inflaming the passions of men, who, in this country, are always ready enough to persecute, with unrelenting hearts, those who differ from them in opinion.

Every plea ought not to be considered a false, because it comes from the mouth of a sceptic: And sure, a spirit which animates men in violence and cruelty, can only lodge in the breasts of infernal demons, and, with them, ought to be confined to the habitations of darkness. I do not consider myself endued with the powers of such and Alcides as *Eumenes*, as to be able to throw poisoned shafts with the same violence he does; nor do I wish for them.

Integer vitæ scelerisque purus,
Non eget Mauri jaculis, neque arcu,
Nec venonatis gravida sagittis,
Fusce, pharetra
Sive per Syrtes, &c.

I have found the north of Scotland an hospitable and civilized country; but, were all its inhabitants to be animated with the same spirit with *Eumenes* and his ancestors, I should be afraid that my integrity should be less able to protect me amongst them, than amongst the most barbarous nations. *Eumenes* would have Dr Beattie compared with the antient apologists for Christianity. When Dr Beattie goes upon the same principles, and maintains the same opinions, he may claim it.

"Mr *Orthodoxus* had certainly forgot, says *Eumenes*, that none of the antient sages were called to defend a system of doctrines, proceeding from the mouth of God, and marked with the undoubted signatures of their divine origin." And has the friend of Dr Beattie so soon forgot his reasonings? Or does he change his opinions as people do their cloaths? Was the God of nature not proclaimed to philosophers? Sure the voice of nature is the voice of God.

How different the language of Holy Scripture? *He cam into the world, and the world knew him* not. Does the creation bear no signatures of the supreme Creator? Can God speak in more intelligible language, incorruptible, and to be understood by all? *Day unto day uttereth speech,* &c. *Eumenes* desires to know the laws of God, or of man, which call on him to suppress his feelings: The laws of Christianity, and the laws of universal charity, which he otherways invocated in vain, require him to suppress both his passions and his pride.

Eumenes, it seems, can cite scripture, but only on particular occasions; It were well did he always examine it before hand. – The texts, from Matth. xxiii. 29, 30, &c. can never answer his purpose, unless Dr Beattie could claim the same powers to judge the hearts of men with the Son of God: The words of the blessed Saviour he mentions, are pointed against the dogmatical Pharisees, the wickedness of whose hearts gave the lie to their strict professions. The Sadducees were the sceptics of the times; and we find not the Savour abusing them, on that account, with bad language; but teaching the world, by giving the most convincing proofs of the contrary doctrines. In the next paragraph, *Eumenes* corrects me justly. I seek not the colour of an excuse where I think I was wrong: I should have said *many,* instead of *those* who understand Mr Hume's reasoning, are likewise capable to detect the sophistry of his arguments. I believe, indeed, the sceptical philosophy has gained too many proselytes, even amongst intelligent persons; and that their authority and example may have influenced others incapable of such discernment. But sure the first class are to be convinced by argument; and, of consequence, the second class of persons will again follow their leaders; and, if Dr Beattie's manner of writing should do no hurt, I shall rejoice in the good it may do to mankind. Dr Reid's book was wrote in the spirit of true philosophy; his reasoning is just, his intention good: without too much warmth, and with no invective, he enlightens and instructs, and deserves the thanks of every lover of science, or of truth. By the questions put by *Orthoduxus* to Dr Beattie, *Eumenes* thinks the writer uses the Christian religion as a spider does her net, to catch and torment insects: The Christian religion weaves no such nets; but, if *Eumenes* weaves a net for himself, he may, perhaps, have the fate of some spiders, whom I have seen intangled and hanged in their own snares.

My design was, to shew Dr Beattie how he might be attacked by persons (though I pretend not to it) of equal rhetorical abilities with himself. The answers he gives me are not at all satisfactory. I shall, in a more plain and candid manner than he does, answer the questions he asks, in however an ostentatious and self-sufficient manner they are put.

"Is every Calvinist (says *Eumenes*) to believe and explain every article in that system in the same manner?" Certainly not.

"Does not the Westminster Confession of faith (says he) assert the freedom of the human will?" Yes – without doubt. But if *Eumenes* will take the trouble to look at chap. iii. sect. 2, he will find it maintained, that God knows whatever may or can come to pass, on all supposed conditions. does this agree with Dr Beattie's doctrines? That it may be impossible for the Deity to foresee contingent events, and yet this not derogatory from his omniscience? Whether the doctrine is Arminian, or rather Socinian and Beattian, it is a matter of little consequence, if it is contrary to truth and the word of God. Another question *Eumenes* puts, as arising from the former: "How then, for heaven's sake! (says *Eumenes*), has contingency or prescience any thing to do in the dispute?" This is about prophecy. It would appear to me they have a great deal to do, whatever *Eumenes* may think; for, if there be contingent events unforeseen by God, there can be no prophecy. If there be no foreknowledge, there can be no prophecy. A wise man may conjecture; but do we not derogate from the perfection of the Deity, when we allow God Almighty only to be the best guesser of what may happen? *Eumenes* might as well ask, what has light to do with vision? Shortly, the sum of all is this; *Eumenes* admits predestination and prophecy, but not prescience; and his conclusion is, that the difficulty of reconciling prophecy with contingency is not more arduous than to reconcile accountability with necessity. I shall not enter much further into a dispute which requires an abler pen; and in which, I am of opinion, nothing new can be advanced. It will be sufficient at present to observe, that accountability must be considered as reconcileable with necessity by every Christian who believes the account given in the scripture of a future state. For, will not the conduct of the saints in heaven, though necessarily influenced by prevailing motives and principles (without any possibility of their relapsing into sin) to what is good and right, be worthy of the approbation of the Deity, and of every reasonable Being? And may not they be said to deserve a higher degree of perfection, and more glorious rewards, upon this account? I don't know, indeed, if *Eumenes* will be satisfied with this solution, as his faith seems to be of a retrograde kind: He appears to believe what is past; but his faith does not seem to extend to that which is yet unseen and eternal. Much of the same complexion with that of the marquis of Hochincourt, who, when converted to the Popish religion, told his father confessor, that he indeed believed, though he could not say why or wherefore. But *Eumenes*, who admits of predestination and prophecy, and yet denies prescience, I am afraid will find himself greatly perplexed, and will need all the strength of the great Alcides, and of the still greater Pantagruel, to prevent his being involved in a sceptical doubt, equal to many that Mr Hume has proposed and published. May the spirit of his ancestors support him; for, as I hate controversy, and detest philosophical Billingsgate, whether in essays, appendixes, or letters, I leave, for the future, both Dr Beattie and *Eumenes*, to employ the boasted vigour of their powers against what or whom they please.

I hope you will insert this letter in your next Magazine, in justice to
 Your humble servant,
  ORTHODOXUS.
August 7. 1771

"Eumenes" [i.e., Thomas Blacklock], response to Orthodoxus, Thursday, Sept. 19, 1771, Vol. 13, pp. 358–360.

To the PUBLISHERS of the WEEKLY MAGAZINE.
More Last Words *of* EUMENES.

– – ου δε ταυτ ανεμωλια Βαζει.
Vain thy resentment, and thy words are vain.

SIR,
In the end of my last letter I told you, that, as my subject seemed then exhausted, you might depend upon hearing no more of it from me. Nothing was at that time less in my mind, than to flatter myself that the antagonists of Dr Beattie would be so profuse in their compliments: I call them compliments, for there are some men whose censure I shall ever be proud to deserve.

In my two preceding papers, I have given my reasons for thinking and pronouncing *Orthodoxus* a defender of the sceptical philosophy. Whether he has or has not been in company with Mr Hume; what degree of intercourse he may have had with him, appears a matter of the utmost indifference to the public, to me, and to the question in agitation. Dr Beattie saw the rapid progress of a philosophy, which seemed to him, and many others, subversive of every thing sacred or invaluable in human life. His soul took the alarm. He wrote like a man who felt for the most important interests of his species, but respecting this world and the next. This zeal for the order and tranquillity of life was not suited to the cool meridian of *Orthodoxus*. Men (according to him) must be cajoled and tickled into wisdom and virtue. He therefore charged his potent quill with rebuke, and brandished its vindictive point against Dr Beattie and all his adherents. If he rather chuses to call his interposition a capitulation for the Pyrrhonists, than a defence of their tenets and persons, I (who am far from being fond of Logomachies) have no inclination to contend with him. But, whoever examines the tendency of his paper, will not think any supernatural aid necessary, to believe him an advocate for scepticism; and, since he denies that imputation, it will be difficult, if not impossible, to investigate his design. He may, if he pleases, suspect me of commerce with hell, for saying what ever impartial judge must think; but the sentiments which I entertain of him are more charitable. To me there appears not, in all his writings, the least symptom of any correspondence with supernatural beings, either from above or below. His malevolence has an air too natural to be inspired, and his talents are evidently within the compass of human nature.

He tells you, "That if my letter had not breathed the same spirit with the essay on truth, you should not have been troubled with any observations upon it." I laugh to see men upbraid others with faults of which they themselves are guilty, even to a degree incompatible with common sense, humanity and good manners. Had *Orthodoxus* been animated with that philanthropy which he falsely pretends to admire and inculcate, would he not have addressed his thoughts in a private manner to Dr Beattie? Would he not have expostulated with him upon the subject as from friend to friend, without cruelly endeavouring, under the specious pretext of candour and humanity, to prejudice the public against a man, whose very errors (if he could be said to err) were intitled to universal lenity, as arising from an excess of zeal for general good. But the vizard was too translucent. *Orthodoxus's* natural was too strong for his assumed character; and he must indeed be a dupe who is deceived by such professions.

If you will believe him, his bugbear was the penal laws, which in many christian countries are cruelly exerted to refrain freedom of thought, and liberal inquiry. He was piously afraid least Dr Beattie should provoke the secular arm against Mr Hume. Is *Orthodoxus* a Briton? and does he talk in this stile? Which of these penal laws are not now in happy disuetude amongst us? What instance of oppression for the sake of conscience has our government exhibited to awaken his jealousy? For my own part, if I have the least degree of acquaintance with myself, I can honestly declare, that were Mr Hume in any personal danger from such penal laws and unwarrantable exertions of power, I would be among the first to interpose for his safety, even at the hazard or expence of my own. But in a free country, where the rights of private judgment are indulged and exercised in their utmost latitude, it is prudential, it is humane in any man who deviates into singularities of thought, to conceal such peculiar opinions as can be of no public advantage.

Orthodoxus, it seems, found the north of Scotland an hospitable and civilized country. Such to himself may he find every nation under heaven. Gratuitous violation and insult are as dishonourable to humanity in general, as injurious to the sufferer: but if he would not bear inhospitable treatment, let him be cautious of extorting it. Those who are acquainted with my life and character know, that I have suffered many unprovoked wrongs, resent few, and offered none. But when the cause of religion, and the character of a friend are attacked, it would be stupid not to feel, it would be pusillanimous not to complain and remonstrate.

I wish I could agree with him as cordially in all his sentiments, as in the panegyric he bestows on Dr Reid. That gentleman wrote with all the energy of reason, and all the tenderness of charity. But let it also be remembered, that his attack upon the sceptical philosophy was only in one point; the existence of matter, which no man can practically doubt, was what he successfully attempted to ascertain. Had he extended his plan, had he defended the existence and character of God, the reality of virtue, and such other principles as interest the strongest and noblest feelings of the human soul, he must either have assumed a different tone, or possessed a more than laudable degree of patience and serenity.

That the works of nature speak the same language with those of grace, I am far from doubting; yet the first neither so clearly nor fully as the last. Hence it cannot follow, that the antient philosophers were so intimately acquainted with the Deity and his perfections, as *Orthoduxus* seems to think them. But if he will still maintain the justice of his conclusion, let him consult the writings of Plato, the most theological philosopher known to me; or, if his authority be not sufficient, than of St Paul, it is hoped, will be allowed decisive.

Dr Beattie neither professes or claims any power to judge the human heart, beyond the indications which it gives of its own qualities. With a power to draw consequences from those, God has not only endued every man, but even enjoined and authorised its impartial exertion. Now, though the determinations of this power are not always infallible, yet are there cases, when the severity of rebuke may be deserved and inflicted, even though the minister of justice should not be omniscient.

It does not appear that the Sadducees were sceptics in morality. If, like Epicurus, they maintained pleasure to be the supreme good, it seems to have been a pleasure resulting from virtuous dispositions and actions. If they denied the existence of spirits and the resurrection of the body, they did not annihilate the sacred and eternal distinction between virtue and vice, nor the immediate sanctions of pain or pleasure connected with them. The Saviour of the world, therefore, wisely suits the poignancy of his reproofs to the character of delinquents. Nor, once more, is there any law, human or divine, by which men are prohibited to use this liberty; when the principles upon which they proceed are rational, and the ends which they propose salutary. How far Dr Beattie can be justified in this view, let any one who fairly consults the tendency of his works, and those of Mr Hume pronounce.

In a former paper I have endeavoured to shew, that the intention of *Orthodoxus*, had it been so charitable as *Democritus* and he pretend, must have operated by means more private and more congenial to its nature; nor can an *ipse dixit*, however warm and explicit, be sufficient to take off the force of that objection. If the net which he imagines I have woven for myself, be that which he mentions, I shall perhaps be able to extricate myself without the least hazard of my neck: and, though I may give him joy of his office as an executioner, he cannot blame me for taking all possible care to keep out of his hands.

It would have been esteemed an obligation, had he quoted the passage where Dr Beattie maintains, "that it may be impossible for the Deity to foresee contingent events, and yet this not derogatory from his omniscience." I can remember no such doctrine, either expressed or implied in his essay. But though it were preached by an angel from heaven, with all my soul I disclaim it. Having professed my belief in moral necessity; having (as *Orthodoxus* grants) admitted predestination and prophecy amongst the articles of my creed, it is possible that any of your readers can believe that I deny the divine prescience? Will *Orthodoxus* affirm, upon honour and conscience, that he himself believes it? If he does, I pity his invincible ignorance and perversion of spirit: if he does not, I scorn the impotent efforts of disingenuous malice. But upon recollection, this solemn appeal was unnecessary; for both he and his valiant compeer (rather than forego the luxurious opportunity of deducing a good-natured inference) have vindicated me from this accusation, and acknowledged my belief of the divine prescience. For when "he assures *Eumenes* (without invoking the Deity on such frivolous occasions) that he never was in company with Mr Hume but once in his life, &c." he alludes to a passage in the first letter, subscribed *Eumenes*, where that sacred and venerable perfection is mentioned *nominatim*. Whether, therefore, my faith be comprehensive of the past or future; whether it be retrograde or progressive, it seems, even in its lowest possible degree, more than equal to his sincerity. But perhaps this may be another exhibition of his benevolence, to fright me from the crime of detraction, by showing how severely it may be inflicted on myself. Yet however kind and well-meant such experiments may be, they are critical and dangerous; for self defence is an innate principle, and will be exerted by the injured. This, I hope, will apologize to you and the public for my violation of that silence, which, in the simplicity of my heart, I promised to preserve.

But though I acknowledge and adore that incomprehensible exertion of the divine intellect, I confess myself ignorant how it subsists and operates, or how it is connected with the volitions of subordinate beings. Upon topics so far above the human capacity as those, let such as pretend to be wise above what is written dogmatise. But whilst the evidence of prophecy is complete and clear in itself, whilst the authentic predictions are succeeded by their corresponding events, I repeat for the third time, that prescience has been wantonly and frivolously introduced into a question, where it had nothing to do. Will *Orthodoxus* then deliberately maintain, that the saints in heaven are still accountable? Surely an accountable being must be a probationary being. Shall their state of trial, therefore, be protracted to eternity? Let him beware! this may imply consequences which I have not inclination to develope, and which, because he seems not to foresee, I will not ungenerously urge against him.

And now, good Sir, though I do not presume to invocate, yet let me modestly invoke your benignity, to employ its warmest and most effectual mediation with the belligerent powers on the other side, for obtaining, if not a firm and permanent alliance, at least a temporary cessation of arms; that we may have an opportunity of burying our dead, of respiring from the wounds and fatigues of the conflict, and of recruiting our military stores; for after the imputation of personal attachment, false assertions, religious nets, mediocrity of talents, modifications of timber, disingenuity and impotence on once side, and of contracted notions, pedantry, rhodomontade, heresy, retrograde faith and philosophical Billingsgate on the other, to me the whole arsenal of scandal seems intirely exhausted, nor can my invention at present afford me a single missile weapon to annoy the enemy. But my last and most powerful motive for wishing that this negotiation may prove successful, is my fear lest some of your nicer and more delicate readers, who expect usual instruction and rational entertainment, should complain of the disappointment, and think personal altercation a prostitution of labour, time and paper.

I am, SIR,
　　Your most obedient
　　　humble servant,
　　　　EUMENES.

Glenullin,
　Sept. 7.

33
JAMES BEATTIE:
LETTER TO FRANCES MAYNE

James Beattie, Letter to Frances Mayne, January 2, 1774.
Selections; from *The Correspondence of James Beattie*, edited by Roger J.
Robinson, Bristol, Thoemmes Press, 2004, Letter 490.

James Beattie (1735–1803), was the author of "The Castle of Scepticism" and the 1769 letter to Thomas Blacklock contained in this collection. After the publication of Beattie's *Essay on the Nature and Immutability of Truth* (1770) a bitter contest erupted between Hume's and Beattie's supporters, as evident in the letters to the *Weekly Magazine* contained earlier in this collection. Unfriendly rumours circulated about Beattie, which were brought to his attention by his friend, Frances Mayne (d. 1801), wife of Irish Parlaimentarian William Mayne. Beattie met Frances Mayne in 1773 and she and her husband were instrumental in sponsoring an edition of Beattie's *Essay on the Immutability of Truth*. Mayne summarizes the accusations here:

I learnt yesterday that an Aspersion is propagated which may impose upon many well meaning People and ought to be cleard up directly ... The matter is this, some of the Friends of Hume accuse you of Ingratitude and Rancour towards him for they say he was very instrumental in procuring for him the Proffessorship he now enjoys at Aberdeen and kept up a friendly correspondence with him till at length Dr Beattie sent him a Poem of his which was never printed but Hume not liking it and being frank in his nature sent him word it was as insipid as Milk and Water upon which Dr Beattie bent on Revenge immediately set about his Essay on Truth which is full of Virulence and misquotations. I thanked the person who communicated this Intelligence to me telling them I loved Accusations when they were brought to particular facts, because then they were more easily controverted and served to mark the Characters of both the Accusers and accused and that I therefore wou'd acquaint you of it immediately. Let me interest you dear Sir to send me with the Answer an exact account of your health and Mrs Beattie's ... [Beattie to Frances Mayne, December 24, 1773][1]

Beattie responds to five specific accusations in her note, denying each contention: (1) that Beattie had ill will towards Hume; (2) that Hume assisted Beattie in obtaining his job at the University of Aberdeen; (3) that Hume and Beattie were in friendly correspondence prior to the *Essay*; (4) that Hume called one of Beattie's poems as insipid as milk and water, thereby prompting Beattie to write the *Essay*; and (5) that the *Essay* is full of misquotations and virulence. In 1780, a letter from Beattie very similar to this one was sent to the *London Review*; the journal's response is contained in this collection. The original manuscript of this letter is in the Aberdeen University Library, MS 30/1/067. The following transcription of it is from Roger Robinson's *The Correspondence of James Beattie* (2004).

...

I come now, Madam, to the heavy accusation brought against me by Mr Hume's friends; in which I do solemnly declare, that *there is not one single word of truth*. But, that I may give the fullest satisfaction on this head, I shall be somewhat more particular; and must therefore take the liberty to transcribe the whole Charge from their own account, as transmitted in Your Ladyship's letter; and then I shall make a few remarks upon it.

'Some of the friends of Hume, accuse you of ingratitude and rancour towards him: for, say they, he was very instrumental in procuring for him the professorship he now holds at Aberdeen, and kept up a friendly correspondence with him, till at length Dr Beattie sent him a poem of his which was never printed; but Hume, not liking it, and being frank in his nature, sent him word it was as insipid as milk and water; upon which, Dr Beattie bent on revenge immediately set about his Essay on Truth, which is full of virulence and misquotations.' – This is the whole charge, verbatim; and I shall answer every article of it.

1. 'I am accused of *rancour* and *ingratitude* towards Mr Hume.' – I entertain no rancour against any man whatever; nor is there one person upon earth (I do not except my bitterest enemies) to whom I would not do a service if it were in my power. Against Mr Hume I never entertained any rancour, nor any ill will: I wrote against his philosophy, but without any purpose to hurt either his soul or his body: I heartily wish him happiness both temporal and eternal; and I hope the confutation of his errors may be instrumental in promoting both; I

---

[1]   Aberdeen University Library, MS 30/2/167; summarised in Roger J. Robinson, *The Correspondence of James Beattie* (2004), Letter 488. I thank Dr. Robinson for providing me with an extract of this letter.

am sure, that, if he is what a philosopher should be, it cannot be any obstruction to either. – He himself will not, I think, charge me with *Ingratitude.* Certain it is, that I never received from him (so far as I could ever learn) one single favour in the whole course of my life: except this may considered as one (which I accidentally discovered in looking over some papers of that time) – that he purchased (at the instance I believe of Mr Arbuthnot a particular friend of mine) Two copies of the first book I published; for which two copies he paid Seven Shillings in the year 1761. This is the only obligation I ever owed him: this I acknowledge, and am ready to repay with interest, if it should not be thought that I have repaid it already by laying out more than triple the sum in purchasing some of the works of Mr Hume.

2. 'Mr Hume is said to have been very instrumental in procuring for me the office I now hold in the University of Aberdeen.' Nothing can be more false. The persons who were instrumental in getting me that office were the Earl of Erroll, Lord Adam Gordon, and Mr Arbuthnot, the gentleman formerly mentioned. They are still alive, and may be applied to by those who are unwilling to take this on my word. I have no more reason to think, that Mr Hume had any hand in that matter, than that the Emperor of China had a hand in it. And how should he? How could I think of soliciting the interest of a man, whom I did not know, whom I had never seen, and with whom I had no manner of connection! I repeat it, that I never received any favour, that I never solicited any favour, that I never thought of soliciting any favour, from Mr Hume in the whole course of my life.

3. 'Mr Hume is said to have kept up a friendly correspondence with me for some time.' It is utterly false: I never heard, till after the publication of my Book on truth, that Mr Hume was either my friend, or my enemy. I never wrote him a letter, I never wrote him a card, I never sent him a message; I never received from him message, card, or letter. I never spoke to him, I never was in company with him, either within or without doors; I am morally certain that he never saw me; I am absolutely certain, that till long after the Essay on Truth was published I never saw him, and that I then saw him at the distance of many yards in the street in Edinburgh, (for he is a man of great size and very singular appearance): – the sound of his voice I never heard; his handwriting I have indeed seen once or twice, but I never saw any thing of his writing in which I, or my affairs, or any thing relating to me, was mentioned, or alluded to, either directly or indirectly. In a word, I have not, I never in my life had, any sort of correspondence, acquaintance, or connection with Mr Hume.

4. 'It is said, that I sent him a Poem which was never printed, and which he returned to me, frankly declaring it to be insipid like milk and water; which so provoked me that I immediately set about writing the Essay on Truth.' Every word of this assertion is a falsehood. No unpublished poem of mine was ever (so far as I know) in Mr Hume's hands. I have already said, that I never sent, nor received from him, any paper, or message, or any thing whatsoever. I never

was concerned to know what he thought of my poems; for I never considered him, nor is he generally considered even in Scotland, as a judge of poetry. Some faint remembrance I have indeed, of having heard many years ago (I think about the year 1760) from my friend Mr Arbuthnot (who is Mr Hume's acquaintance) that Mr Hume had spoken *favourably* of my poetry; but to this, for the reason just now given, I paid little attention. That Mr Hume may have disliked my poems, is probable enough; there are many things in them which I myself dislike: but certain it is, that I never heard, nor knew, that he disliked them, till he was pleased to bring out the silly story of the milk and water in summer 1770, five years after the essay on truth was begun, one year after it was finished, and some weeks after it was published. What it was that induced me to write that Essay, must be evident to every person of taste sense and candour who reads it with attention; I have avowed my motive in the book itself, repeatedly, and in the most express terms, and therefore I need not repeat it here.

Lastly, it is said in the accusation above quoted, 'That my Book on truth is full of misquotations, and virulence.' – I aver, that there are no misquotations; I am conscious that I did not intend to make any; nobody has ever yet been able to specify in what part of the book the misquotations are to be found; and many persons of the greatest worth and candour, who are masters of the whole controversy, and thoroughly acquainted both with Mr Hume's writings and mine, have assured me, that I have not in one single instance misquoted or misrepresented that Author. Nay he himself, though he has abused me exceedingly on the score of virulence, never said, so far as I have reason to think, that I have misrepresented or misquoted him; – this I was assured of my by late excellent friend Dr Gregory, who often had occasion to plead my cause against my adversaries in Edinburgh, and who gave me an exact detail of all their objections. – As to the charge of *virulence*, I have fully and unanswerably confuted it in the Postscript to the Essay; and therefore shall only add, that I have had repeated assurances from the best judges of good language and good manners now upon earth, that there is no improper keenness in my stile; nothing coarse, personal or indelicate, in the whole composition; and that the zeal there displayed is such as becomes an honest man, a friend of virtue, and a son of liberty. ...

34
THOMAS HEPBURN:
A SPECIMEN OF THE SCOTS REVIEW

[Thomas Hepburn], *A specimen of the Scots Review*. [Edinburgh], [1774], 2–30 p.
Selections; from 1774 edition.

Thomas Hepburn (d. 1777), was minister of Athelstaneford from 1771 until his death. According to Thomas Carlyle, Hepburn was remarkable "for the shrewdness of his remarks and irresistible repartees" (*Autobiography*, 1910, p. 279). In 1774 Hepburn published a satirical proposal for a periodical, titled *The Scots Review*, which would critically review major publications by Scottish authors, especially in the areas of theology, literature and social policy. The proposal offers an outline of what the periodical might contain, and at the top of the editor's agenda is a critical examination of Hume's writings and those of his critics – specifically, Trail, Reid, Campbell, Gerard, Balfour, MacQueen and Beattie. He presents critical sketches of each of these, inserting some new anecdotes, and comes down especially hard on Reid, Oswald and Beattie for their common sense philosophy. The author relates the experience of a well-travelled gentleman, who has taken particular note of the number of copies of Hume's *Treatise*, *Essays*, and *History* that he has run across in Scotland. The work was reviewed in *Scots Magazine*, which notes its satirical tone:

It professes to give a prospectus, and a specimen of an intended new review; but the whole object seems to have been to laugh at some individuals obnoxious to the writer, and particularly to ridicule the virulence, and to lower the pretensions of those who had signalized themselves by their attacks upon the philosophical writings of Mr. Hume; a promise is held out, that this arch-infidel is himself to be reviewed in the first place; and next, those authors who have waged a holy war against him; of whom a list is given, with their characters, the delineation of which, in no very favourable colours, appears, as already mentioned, to have exhausted the main object of the piece, though one or two gentle hints are aimed at the historian himself. [As quoted by Burton, *Life of David Hume*, Vol. 2, p. 472]

Hepburn's authorship of the pamphlet appears to be founded on the following letter from Hume in which he speculates about the author's identity and expresses appreciation towards the pamphlet's boldness:

> You have seen, no doubt, the specimen of a Scotch review. My first conjecture was, that Carlyle was the author; but Dr Blair has convinced me that it is much more probably the production of your spiritual guide, Tom Hepburn; but, whoever be the father, the child has a great deal of salt, and spirit, and humour. I wish he would continue, tho at the hazard of my getting a rap over the knuckles from time to time: for I see in this hero the spirit of a Drawcansir, who spares neither friend nor foe. I think I can reckon about twenty people, not including the King, whom he has attacked in this short performance. I hope all his spleen is not exhausted. I should desire my compliments to him, were I not afraid that he would interpret the civility as paying blackmail to him. [Hume to John Home, June 4, 1774]

The following is from the 1774 and only edition of the *Specimen*.

THE
SCOTS REVIEW.

PREFACE by the BOOKSELLER.

The design of this Review is to calm the minds of many thousand good Christians, who have been greatly alarmed with a hue and cry of the progress of infidelity and scepticism. Beside this, the people of Scotland have been reduced of late to great poverty, by a variety of unlucky incidents: – no less than four hundred and thirty schemes have been published for the relief of the poor, who still increase in their numbers; which would not be the case, if rich people did appropriate that money to real charity which they spend in buying useless books, which is charity only to the moths and worms who feed on such stuff. The first Scots author who shall pass under our review, is that great necromancer and magician DAVID HUME, Esq; both because he has been the cause of many useless books being published, and because all the writings against him have brought some empty fame, and more solid pudding, to the authors.

The next in review will be these authors who have waged an holy war against the arch-infidel, an account of whom is subjoined.

1. Mr. ROBERT TRAIL, minister at Banff, published a synodical sermon against Mr. Hume: his reward has been a doctor's degree, and the professorship of divinity at Glasgow.[1]

2. Mr. THOMAS REID published a very ingenious book against Mr. Hume: – he is a doctor, and professor of moral philosophy at Glasgow.[2]

3. Mr. GEORGE CAMPBELL published a book against Mr. HUME's Essay on Miracles, in which he demonstrates, that if any man can prove, by two or more credible witnesses, that he carried Arthur's Seat upon his back from Edinburgh to Aberdeen, *ergo*, he did so truly and really. – As a reward of this ingenious argument, which all the lawyers hold to be unanswerable, he is both principal and professor in the Marshal college at Aberdeen.[3]

4. Mr. ALEXANDER GERARD, putting himself in place of Deity, which is no unusual thing for a professor of divinity, has proved in a book, that although infinite power, wisdom, and goodness, might have given such clear evidence of the truths of any revelation that no man could doubt of it, yet it was more agreeable to these attributes to give such weak evidence as not to convince or convert a thirtieth part of this globe. It may be said, that this ingenious argument proves the sure divineship of polemical divinity with a witness; but as this argument may be liable to some objections, the author has very wisely superadded some strictures of Mr. HUME's writings. He is a doctor and professor of divinity in the King's college at Aberdeen.[4]

5. Mr. JAMES BALFOUR wrote a book against the said Mr. HUME, which, but for us, would be forgot, although immediately after its publication he was made professor of moral philosophy, and, since that time, professor of the law of nature and nations in the university of Edinburgh. It may be doubted whether or not moral philosophy has for its end the training of youth for public life, and teaching them to act with dignity and propriety as men and citizens: we would rather adhere to the opinion of those, who think that it conflicts in teaching youth the arts of controversy, wrangling, and debate. We do not therefore hesitate, in case of any future vacancy in this class, to recommend to the

---

[1] [Robert Traill (1720–1775), *The Qualifications and Decorum of a Teacher of Christianity Considered* (1755), contained in *Early Responses to Hume's Essays, Moral, Political and Literary* (1999).]

[2] [Thomas Reid (1710–1796), *An Inquiry into the Human Mind* (1764), selections from which are contained in *Early Responses to Hume's Metaphysical and Epistemological Writings* (2000).]

[3] [George Campbell (1719–1796), *A Dissertation on Miracles* (1762), contained in *Early Responses to Hume's Writings on Religion* (2001).]

[4] [Alexander Gerard (1728–1795), *Dissertations on Subjects Relating to the Genius and the Evidences of Christianity* (1766).]

magistrates of Edinburgh the Reverend Dr. JAMES BEATTIE, as the best qualified person we know.[5]

6. Dr. DANIEL M'QUEEN has wrote a book against Mr. HUME's history, by which it appears that he has read the Roman ritual, and understands Greek; but the great ornament of this unjustly forgotten performance is an eloquent address to Mr. HUME's conscience, the same, *mutatis mutandis*, which, as minister of Stirling, he used to deliver to the unhappy convicts at the place of execution. We don't infer from this, that the author thinks Mr. Hume a combustible heretic; we would only insinuate, that the author would have been an excellent ordinary of Newgate, if he had not been better provided in being a doctor, a minister of Edinburgh, and a candidate of merit for any other ecclesiastical preferment.[6]

7. Dr. REID broached the opinion of judging of philosophical matters by common sense. In the church a champion arose, and published an appeal to common sense on behalf of religion; but of what system of religion he has not informed us. Indeed, his arguments will serve all equally well. Priests, of all denominations, are much obliged to this truly illuminated author, as his book contains a defence of all the religions that ever were, or will be in the world. His enemies say, that it pleased the late primate of Canterbury in his old age, and foolishly adduce Dr. Secker's letter on behalf of this book, as a proof of the decay of his parts.[7]

8. Mr. HUME, according to common fame, did, most unhappily for himself, express an unfavourable opinion of Mr. JAMES BEATTIE's poetical talents. This censure provoked Mr. BEATTIE to show the world that he really and truly was one of the irritable tribe, so that piety and rage produced his famous Essay on the Nature of Immutability of Truth.[8] In this precious morsel of controversy, the author advances many uncommon truths; for instance, he admits that Mr. HUME is a good historian; but, in the same breath, assures us, that he is lamentably ignorant of human nature: besides, he treats his antagonist with an asperity, some call it scurrility, which is not very decent, and surely not very necessary in an advocate for truth: But, in the last edition of this work, he has

---

[5] [James Balfour (1705–1795), *A Delineation of the Nature and Obligation of Morality* (1753), selections from which are contained in *Early Responses to Hume's Moral Philosophy* (1999).]

[6] [Daniel MacQueen (d. 1777), *Letters on Mr. Hume's History of Great Britain* (1756), contained in *Early Responses to Hume's History* (2002).]

[7] [James Oswald (1703–1793), *An Appeal to Common Sense in Behalf of Religion* (1766–1772), selections from which are contained in *Early Responses to Hume's Metaphysical and Epistemological Writings* (2000).]

[8] [James Beattie (1735–1803), *Essay on the Nature and Immutability of Truth* (1770), selections from which are contained in *Early Responses to Hume's Metaphysical and Epistemological Writings* (2000).]

given us a vindication of this scurrility; he has had many deep divines of his opinion, and his vindication is of the same kind as the Episcopalian story of the Presbyterian ministers, who excommunicated the great Montrose: They said, that they only followed the example of the Psalmist David, who was the friend of the Lord, and used to curse the enemies of the Lord, in the name of the Lord. But, without entering at present into the merits of this, or any other work, we cannot help observing, that the great rewards, conferred on the author, are an incontestible proof of the prevailing spirit of piety in our age and nation. Since the days of Leo the tenth, there has not been a more glorious spectacle than lately at Oxford, when Dr. BEATTIE was honoured with the degree of L.L.D.; chancellors, vice-chancellors, stewards, bishops, deans, doctors, proctors, fellows, students, graduates, under-graduates, men, women and children, all met on that glorious day, to do honour to the redoubted conqueror of Mr. HUME. It is true, he has not been made a bishop, or a dean, for great preferment blunts all genius; but he has got a pension of l. 200 sterl. for life, besides the honour of his degree. This pension is a sure sign of the piety of our most gracious sovereign, and his philosophical ministers, and is no bad specimen of their taste in literature. Since this time of preferment Dr. BEATTIE has returned to his favourite study of poetry, and has obliged the world with two odes, or songs, published in the Edinburgh Review, and ushered in with a panegyric, by which it appears, that these gentlemen are blessed with very long ears. In these songs there is a remarkable regard to truth, for they confirm the truth of Mr. HUME's unlucky censure of the Doctor's poetry, but they contain a very severe satire against the university of Oxford, though by no means intended by the learned author.

This gentleman is the third Scots writer in order, who appeals to common sense. Perhaps, there is no phrase in the English language whose meaning is less fixed or ascertained. If by this expression, they mean the sense of the vulgar in religion, philosophy, and truth, few people conversant in history will refuse, that the vulgar are the judges in the first of these three capital articles, and from their sentence there lies no appeal. The systems of religion, established by the common sense of these sages, differ in many articles among different nations; so that we are just where we were before those advocates for the vulgar began to write: and, after our deepest researches, we can find no philosophy or truth discovered by the vulgar, except the black art, witchcraft, and fairy-philosophy, the truth of omens, dreams, enchantments, the prejudices of education, and some prudential proverbs; of these last truths Sancho Pancho is the greatest master we know, and may be justly placed at the head of this philosophy.

A gentleman, engaged in this undertaking, who has travelled over a great part of the world, says, that in every country common sense signifies an observance of established faith and laws, and an adherence to the manners, customs, dress, and language of the country. The polite Greeks and Romans called every people who differed from them in these particulars Barbarians, which was as much as to say, they wanted common sense; so the Chinese, Tartars, Hottentots, and other nations, think and talk with contempt of all whose customs differ from their own. The vulgar people of this island thought the parliament wanted common sense, when they abrogated the acts against witchcraft, and the Scots Highlanders said the same when their dress was prohibited, and so did the Nonjurors, when their religious meetings were restrained. In the course of this gentleman's travels, many attempts were made to induce him to change his religion, but in vain; for when he told a Papist that he did not believe in transubstantiation, he replied, that he wanted common sense, and there the controversy ended. A Turk asked him whether he believed that Mohamet was the prophet of God, and being answered in the negative, Thou uncircumcised dog, said he, if thou wast not a fool, deprived of common sense, I would instantly send thee to hell – Go, and never see me more.

In short, this gentleman is of opinion, that these authors have done more harm to philosophy, religion, and truth, by this argument, than any sceptic has ever done; for philosophers of this cast leave men to reason, nature, experience, and probability, which are not bad guides so far as they go: nay, he even suspects the hostile intentions of these common-sense philosophers, against the three glorious goddesses whom they pretend to adore; but in this we beg leave to differ from him. The public will expect, and they shall not be disappointed, that the first number of the Scots Review will contain a criticism of Mr. HUME's works: We have employed for this a young zealous advocate for ecclesiastical preferment, who will not spare him, and who is too proud to desire him to correct his style. A considerable portion of the spirit of St. Dominic has descended on this divine, as well as on the Right Rev. Dr. W. and on the Rev. Dr. B., and he is confident that his reward will be deanery, or three hundred a-year for life: such pensions are wisely given, and are the most severe answers Mr. HUME has met with. But our travelling gentleman says, that sceptics are only to be pitied for their doubts and darkness; that professed infidels are bad citizens; and that those who enter into controversy with them are not much better, because, without their answers, their antagonists books would sink into oblivion; witness Lord Bolingbroke's Philosophical Works, and the Treatise of Human Nature. Our friend has travelled over all Scotland, and found only eight copies of the last book, and those in the custody of as many divines, who either had wrote, or were writing answers to it: he found many copies of Mr. HUME's essays, but not much spoiled by frequent reading; and still more of his history, all of which were the worse for the wearing. Being a political arithmetician, he took the exact number of all the freethinkers in Scotland, and they amount to sic hundred three score and six in integer numbers, besides an infinite number of small fractions, which cannot be reckoned on, as they vanish along with the pride of wealth, the boldness of youth, and the insolence of health, and are totally annihilated by sickness, marriage, poverty, and age. The rest of the people in Scotland, amounting to a million and an half, are all good believers, of various hues and denominations. He is ready to make a judicial declaration of the truth of this calculation, before the General Assembly, or the Society for propagating Christian Knowledge, on being assured of a competent reward, as he had not the honour of being employed by either of these respectable bodies in this survey. The result of his observations must be very quieting to many pious Christians, whose sleep has been so frequently disturbed by polemical authors, sounding false alarms of the growth of infidelity and scepticism.

Indeed his discoveries will be of the greatest national benefit; for it consists with our knowledge, that the late frequent failures in trade and manufacturers, and the great increase of the bills of mortality, have been in a great measure owing to these false alarms: besides, they will give our rulers a true chart of the state of religion in this country. It is therefore to be hoped, that some person of public station will mark down the name of this sage in his pocket-book with a keilavine, and recommend him to men in power to reward him. A cool hundred pounds a-year is the least they can offer him.

But not only those whose province it is to defend temples and holy things against the impotent attacks of sceptics, have drawn their pens against Mr. HUME; two learned and venerable judges have attacked him in their philosophical works.[9]

Don Quixotte accounted for every strange appearance by enchantment; the first of these sages accounts for every thing by delusion, and the last employs the categories for the same purpose: but as they are both still continuing to write for the public good, we shall defer what we have to say of their great merit till some future period. ...

---

[9] [Henry Home, Lord Kames (1696–1782), *Essays on the Principles of Morality and Natural Religion* (1751); James Burnett, Lord Monboddo (1714–1799), *Of the Origin and Progress of Language* (1773–1794); selections from these are included in *Early Responses to Hume's Metaphysical and Epistemological Writings* (2000).]

35
JOHN BRIGGS:
LETTER TO THE LONDON REVIEW

John Briggs, letter to the editors, *London Review*, March 1775, Vol. 1, pp. 244–246.
Complete.

In 1774 Joseph Priestley published *An Examination*, which attacks the common sense philosophy of Thomas Reid, James Oswald, and James Beattie. A review of Priestley's work appeared as the first item in the newly founded *London Review*. The review was not only favourable, but also pronounced complete victory to Priestley over Beattie, as the following quote indicates:

> After exploding Dr. Beattie's account of the foundation of truth and the testimony of the senses; our Author proceeds with equal success, to expose the Doctor's misconception and idle representation of the imaginary effects of Bishop Berkeley's Theory of the Ideal World. He next explodes the hackney'd objections made by Dr. Beattie to the doctrine of Necessity. [*London Review*, January 775, vol. 1, pp. 1–12, February pp. 91–96]

Shortly after, clergyman John Briggs (1728/9–1804) sent a letter to the *London Review* protesting their treatment of Beattie in the article. Briggs recently authored *The Nature of Religious Zeal* (1775), a work which criticizes religious fanaticism, recommending instead true Christian fervor. Briggs's work – which contains criticisms of Hume's religious views – was itself favourably received by the *London Review* (January 1775, Vol. 1, pp. 70–73). In his letter to the journal, Briggs contends that the review of Priestley's *Examination* implied that Beattie's ridicule of Hume was motivated by public opinion. Briggs argues that Beattie's ridicule was to expose nonsense, and that Hume's constitution was such as to take it "unmutilated, unblemished, just as if nothing had happened." Replying to Briggs's letter, the *London Review* maintained that it merely impartially quoted from Priestley's attack, and that its job is not to intervene in disputes between people as capable as Beattie and Priestley. Briggs's letter and the editorial response are presented below.

TO THE LONDON REVIEWERS.

Calverton, near Stoney Stratford, Bucks, March 18, 1775.

GENTLEMEN,

I was sorry to see your Publication commence with what I think, and I am far from being singular in my opinion, a very exceptionable character and criticism of Dr. Priestly's book. I should not, however, have troubled you, or the publick, with objections to any eulogies you might have thought proper to bestow upon it; if they had not, at the same time, conveyed a very unfavourable, and, in regard to one at least of the works under his examination, I will venture to affirm, a very injurious idea. Is it possible for any person to read, with the smallest degree of attention, the Essay on Truth, and even suspect the author of wishing to be a patron and promoter of persecution, for the sake of opinion; and of being actuated with the spirit of a Bonner or a Gardiner towards Mr. Hume, or any other of his opponents? This reproach however, Dr. Priestly is very industrious to procure him; and you yourselves, Gentlemen, have, in some degree, given the imputation your passport.

As many persons will be apt to form their opinion of Dr. Beattie, and of the spirit and tendency of his work, from what has appeared in your Review, I have so much confidence in your justice and impartiality, that you will not refuse a place in your next number to the following extracts from the Essay on Truth; which, it is charity to suppose, Dr. Priestley had, by some unaccountable inadvertency, overlooked, when he brought such a charge against the author.

If there be any obscurity in the passage censured by Dr. Priestly, which I think there is not, it is but just to explain obscure by parallel passages in the same work, that are more clear and explicit. But to pick out detached sentences, and to put the very worst constructions upon them of which they are capable, and that too in direct contradiction to the author's sentiments, plainly, expressly, and repeatedly avowed, is a practice utterly irreconcileable with candid criticism, a practice which no composition will endure, and which Dr. Priestly, for his own sake, should be one of the last authors in the world to give into.

The extracts from the Essay on Truth, which I would desire your readers to compare with your quotation from Dr. Priestly, in your first number, page 11, are these.

Essay on Truth, p. 381. "That those men act the part of good citizens, who endeavour to overturn the plainest principles of human knowledge, and to subvert the foundations of all religion, I am far from thinking. But I should be extremely sorry to see any other weapons employed against them than those of reason, and ridicule chastised by decency and truth. Other weapons this cause requires not; nay, in this cause, all other weapons would do more harm than good."

P. 563. "Liberty of speech and writing is one of those high privileges that distinguish Great Britain from all other nations. Every good subject wishes that it may be preserved to the latest posterity, and would be sorry to see the civil power interpose to check the progress of rational inquiry. Nay, even when inquiry ceases to be rational, and becomes both whimsical and pernicious, advancing as far, as some late authors have carried it, to controvert the first principles of knowledge, morality and religion, and consequently the fundamental laws of the British government, and of all well regulated society; even then, it must do more harm than good to oppose it with the arm of flesh. For persecution, and punishment for the sake of opinion, seldom fail to strengthen the party they are intended to suppress. And when opinions are combated by such weapons only, (which would probably be the case if the law were to interpose) a suspicion arises in the minds of men, that no other weapons are to be had; and therefore that the sectary, though destitute of power, is not wanting in argument. Let opinions then be combated by reason, and let ridicule be employed to expose nonsense."

That reason and *that* ridicule are the only weapons which the Essay on Truth recommends; and the only weapons which I dare say the author wishes to be employed in any literary or religious contest. Those weapons he has wielded with uncommon force and success, in beating down the arrogance of atheism and nonsense. If in a just use and application of them there be any thing of persecution, Dr. Beattie is indeed a merciless persecutor, and Mr. Hume a melancholy instance of its power and rage; for that he has been upon the rack there is no doubt, though he has had the resolution, or the wisdom, not to cry out. Less than what he has suffered would certainly have crippled the vanity of any other author for life; but such is the peculiar frame, and such the happiness of that Gentleman's literary constitution, that, at a proper time, he will come abroad again in a new edition, unmutilated, unblemished, and just as if nothing had happened. "Those great talents which he received from nature, or acquired by study, he will continue to exert, and with the same advantage, as before to truth, virtue, and society;" and the heart of Dr. Priestly will again "be rejoiced at the prospect of (what one would least expect) the great benefit that will accrue even to *religion*, both natural and revealed, from his labours."

Of the general merit of the dispute, and of the value of the objections made to the Essay on Truth, I say nothing; as I hope and believe, the author will himself be prevailed on to reconsider the subject. In the mean while, though utterly unknown to Dr. Beattie, I could not refrain from attempting to vindicate a work which I esteem, and a character which I love, from an idle calumny that would prejudice those who are unacquainted with them (for it can impose on no others) against both; from a calumny which has been circulated, with uncommon industry, by Mr. Hume's partizans, and which might seem to receive some confirmation from this fresh charge of Dr. Priestly, quoted by your Review, with seeming approbation, certainly without the reprehension it merited. And I doubt not but you will pardon the freedom of this address, which aims only at doing a common piece of justice to the reputation of an excellent writer.

Your most obedient and most humble servant,

J. BRIGGS.

[*London Review* response:] We cannot help thinking Mr. Briggs rather too severe in charging *us* with giving an *injurious idea* of Dr. Beattie's work. That our account of Dr. Priestly's Examination may to him appear exceptionable, we doubt not. *Quot homines tot sententiæ*; it is impossible for us, therefore, to be of every one's opinion: to give a reason for our own, is all that can be expected of us. In the case before us, however, we gave no opinion; setting forth only what Dr. Priestly advanced, in a fair quotation from him. If Mr. Briggs supposes we are partial to Dr. Priestly or to Mr. Hume, he is mistaken: tho' we own, we are no strangers to both. At the same time the writer of the article in question has the pleasure of personally knowing Dr. Beattie, and has an high opinion both of his moderation and benevolence; but though *amicus Plato, amicus Socrates, magis amica veritas*. As *Reviewers*, especially, it was not for us to defend a writer so well able to answer for himself as Dr. Beattie; to whom, if he has written inconsistently, we paid the proper compliment of shewing on what side he has laid himself open to his adversary. To hint that we should have censured Dr. Priestly for taking advantage of such inconsistency, is to mistake our province; there are writers, indeed, over whom we may, without much vanity, set ourselves up as arbiters; but between such as the Drs. Priestly and Beattie, we should think ourselves sufficiently honoured to be admitted amicable arbitrators.

36
"ANSWER TO AN EXTRACT
FROM A LETTER FROM DR. BEATTIE"
(*LONDON REVIEW*)

"Answer to an Extract from a Letter from Dr. Beattie," *London Review*, July 1780, Vol. 12, pp. 63–64.
Complete letter.

The *London Review* was founded in 1775 by writer William Kenrick (1725?–1779), and modelled on the format of the successful *Monthly Review* and *Critical Review*. Throughout their five-year existence, the journal showed great interest in both Hume and Beattie – most often praising Hume's philosophy and denouncing Beattie's. In their review of Hume's *Dialogues*, the reviewer alleges that Beattie wrote his *Essay* against Hume since Hume criticized his poetry:

> The *Essay on the Immutability of Truth* owed its birth to the circumstances of Mr. Hume's having called the reverend author's poetry milk and water, and of his having since that time gone under the name of the milk and water poet. May not his suggestion, that the title of the Essay was a misnomer, and that it ought to have been entitled a great lie, produce the same laudable zeal in the Doctor's breast to write a similar declamation against the Dialogues concerning Natural Religion? [Review of Hume's *Dialogues*, *London Review*, December 1779, Vol. 10, p. 365]

In reaction, Beattie apparently wrote a letter to his bookseller Charles Dilly denying the accusations. Either on his own initiative or instructed by Beattie, on around June of 1780 Dilly sent an extract of Beattie's letter to the *London Review*, most likely requesting a retraction:

> I don't know whether the late Dr Kenrick Son – who hath the conduct of the London Review – has taken notice of the extract of your letter I left with him about 2 months since – his work is much lowered in reputation so much so – that I expect every month to hear it is dropp'd – the Son has neither the industry nor the ability of his Father – and the poor materials

in every Review shew it very Plainly'. [Dilly to Beattie, London, August 31, 1780][1]

In point of fact, the final item in the final edition of the journal is an editorial response to the extract of Beattie's letter. Unfortunately, the journal failed to include the extract itself, and neither Beattie's original letter to Dilly, nor the manuscript of the extract have yet surfaced. But the editorial response, printed below, is detailed enough to infer Beattie's main concerns. Two features stand out.

First, Beattie appears to have accused Hume of some misdeed, perhaps intentionally starting the "milk and water" rumour. The *London Review* asks Beattie to produce his evidence and states that it has confidence in the source behind its original story. Second, in the only direct quote from the extract, Beattie states "I never had any personal pique at Mr. Hume." The *London Review* disagreed and produced harsh quotations from the *Essay* to show otherwise. The review concludes with an anecdote about Hume's reluctance to visit Lord Mansfield; according to Hume, "he kept very low company, being always surrounded with nothing but parsons and bishops." Beattie's two concerns, as reflected in this review, match up well with his defence in his 1774 letter to Mayne, excerpted in this collection. It seems, though, that Beattie did not send an exact copy of the Mayne letter to Dilly, since the *London Review* quotation "I never had any personal pique at Mr. Hume" does not appear there. The spirit and content, though, parallel each other.[2]

CORRESPONDENCE.
Answer to an Extract from a Letter from Dr. Beattie.

Having, we apprehend, done Dr. Beattie ample justice by publishing his defence, let us now be equally just to the memory of a man who can no longer defend himself. Dr. Beattie's defence charges Mr. Hume with the meanness of contradicting himself in a fit of disgust, and of being swayed by passion in pronouncing sentence upon his poetical works. Till he produces his evidence, this attack upon the established character of Mr. Hume will have but little weight with the public, who have been long apprised of his exemplary probity, and strict honour. Why should Dr. Beattie suppose that we should be misin-

---

[1]   The manuscript of Dilly's letter to Beattie resides in the Aberdeen University Library, MS 30/2/346. I thank Roger Robinson for bringing it to my attention and providing me with this transcription of it.

[2]   For a discussion of the *London Review*'s reception of Hume and Beattie, see James Fieser's "Beattie's Lost Letter to the *London Review*," *Hume Studies*, 1994, Vol. 20, pp. 1–12.

formed by a disinterested person, and desire us to disbelieve his testimony, when he would have us believe himself, who is not disinterested? Does he wish to prove that "we believe in all unbelief?"

The Dr. says, "I never had any personal pique at Mr. Hume." The following extracts from his essay on truth we shall present to the reader, and leave him to judge whether the rage with which they are written does not indicate something more than pique? (p. 18.) "Why should Hume's principle and talents extort at once our esteem and detestation, our applause and contempt," (p. 479.) "Why can I not devise an apology for these philosophers, to screen them from this dreadful imputation of being the plagues and enemies of mankind! Perhaps they do not themselves believe their own tenets, but publish them only as the means of getting a name and fortune. But I hope this is not the case, God forbid that it should! For then the enormity of their guilt would surpass all power of language; we could only gaze at it and tremble. Compared with such wickedness the crimes of the thief, the robber, the incendiar, would almost disappear," &c. &c. &c. (page 481.) "Yet the traitors to human kind, the murderers of the human soul, how can you answer for it to your own hearts! Surely every spark of your generosity is extinguished for ever, if this consideration do not awaken in you the keenest remorse, and make you with in bitterness of soul. – But I remonstrate in vain. All this must have often occurred to you, and been as often rejected frivolous. To plead with you on the principles of benevolence or generosity, is to address you in a language you do not understand," &c. &c. From the whole strain of the Essay on Truth, it appears that the philosopher principally aimed at in these apostrophes is Hume. Nay Dr. Beattie goes so far as to attempt to prove that Hume was destitute of common sense, by telling us, (p. 47 and 48.) "that a man defective in common sense may acquire learning, and may even possess genius to a certain degree: but the defect of nature he can never supply: a peculiar modification of scepticism, or credulity or levity will to the end of his life distinguish him from other men." – Reader be not surprised; it is Dr. Beattie who tells you this, the same man who has spent a hundred pages of his Essay on Truth, in proving that all science is founded on common sense, or on, what afterwards turns out to equivalent language, axioms or self-evident propositions! the same man who has insinuated that Mr. Hume had a cold, unfeeling heart, and no imagination, though his account of Queen Mary's death be an affecting tragedy, and much superior to the elegant Dr. Robertson's, who wrote after him, and whose business it was much more than Hume's to work upon our passions; though his Epicurean, and many other parts of his works breathe the true spirit of poetry, and shew clearly that he could never have relished the Doctor's poems, *versus inopes rerum nugæque canoræ*.

If we are not misinformed, Dr. Beattie owes more to Hume than he is aware of and ought therefore to pay more respect to his memory. Hume, whom Lord Mansfield wished to see often at his table, being asked once by a common friend, why he did not oftener favour his lordship with his company, replied that, though extremely fond of his lordship's conversation, he could not pay him frequent visits, because he kept very low company, being always surrounded with nothing but parsons and bishops. This pleasantry procured Dr. Beattie his pension.

37
JAMES HAY BEATTIE:
ESSAYS AND FRAGMENTS

James Hay Beattie (1768–1790), *Essays and fragments in prose and verse. By James Hay Beattie. To which is prefixed an account of the author's life and character.* Edinburgh, printed by J. Moir, 1794. vii, 340 p.
"The Modern Tippling Philosophers" and Dialogue between "Socrates, Mercury, and a Modern Philosopher"; from 1794 edition.

Born in Aberdeen, Scotland, James Hay Beattie (1768–1790) was the elder son of the philosopher and poet James Beattie. Shortly before his 19th birthday he was appointed assistant and successor to his ailing father. Weakened himself by an illness that lingered for a year, he died at age twenty-two. Nothing would be known of James Hay Beattie were it not for a collection of his manuscripts that were published by his father, which was prefaced with an account of his brief life – emphasizing the progress of his education. The work was printed privately in 1794, with a run of only 200 copies for friends. Two items – both satires – appear in this collection with Hume as a subject. First, a poem titled "The modern Tippling Philosophers" depicts famous thinkers of the era as drunkards, including Hume. Second, among four "Dialogues of the Dead," the third is between "Socrates, Mercury, and a Modern Philosopher" – in which Hume is intended as the modern philosopher. The dialogue opens with Socrates and Mercury discussing the dubious merits of Hume's philosophy. Hume approaches, initially unaware of Socrates' identity, and soon begins insulting the Greek sage for his lack of philosophical ability. Socrates' identity is then revealed, and Hume is quickly ensnared in a clever Socratic dialectic that forces him to concede common sense truths. Hume admits that Socrates has demolished his system, but insists that his scepticism is friendly to the fashionable life by relieving people "from all apprehensions of future existence." In the course of the dialogue, the Hume character states, "When I was in Paris, they called me (and my friends in _____ politely re-echoed the words) *Le Socrate moderne.*" This may very well have been a nickname given to the real Hume.[1] In his article on James Hay Beattie

---

[1] In a letter to the Comtesse de Boufflers Hume refers to Rousseau as "our modern Socrates" (January 12, 1766).

in the *Oxford Dictionary of National Biography*, Roger Robinson notes that some of the poems in *Essays and Fragments* were at least partly composed by James Beattie. Although there is no external evidence to suggest that this is so with the present two items, the Dialogue at least reflects the influence of James Beattie – particularly in its ridicule of Hume and scepticism, and the emphasis on common sense. Some of the satire also resembles the elder Beattie's "Castle of Scepticism."

The *Essays and Fragments* later formed Volume 2 of James Beattie's *Minstrel* in the editions of 1799, 1803, 1807 and in his 1809 *Works*. However, in these later editions the dialogue between Mercury, Socrates and Hume is removed. Several reviews of the 1799 edition of the *Minstral* appeared, which gave sympathetic approval to the pieces by James Hay Beattie. The *Critical Review* praises "The Modern Tippling Philosophers" in particular:

> The poems of so young a man, printed from uncorrected manuscripts; and perhaps not designed by himself for publication, it would be unjust to examine with minuteness. ... His ludicrous pieces discover much imagination. There are many good points in the following stanzas from 'The modern Tippling Philosophers'.... This volume may be considered as another proof that the powers as well as the diseases of intellect are sometimes hereditary. [*Critical Review*, 1800, Vol. 28, pp. 170–177]

By contrast, writing for the *Monthly Review*, Ollyett Woodhouse does not commend the "ludicrous verses" for either their wit or humour:

> Of his poetical and literary talents, the essays and fragments before us are favourable specimens; and they are also intitled to every allowance which candid criticism can afford, as they were written at an early age, and as most of them are now published without having been revised or corrected by the author. ... Of Mr. B.'s ludicrous verses, we cannot much commend either the humour or the wit; the latter is not remarkable for brilliancy, delicacy, or point; and the former is neither of the broad and palpable kind which, by its caricatured features, forces sudden and instantaneous laughter, nor of that refined and corrected species which, under the disguise of simplicity, and by means of a chaste sobriety of manners, insinuates itself into the mind, and steals the smile of approbation. [*Monthly Review*, September 1800, Vol. 33, pp. 61–66]

The *New London Review* makes allowances for the unusual length of the biographical account that James Beattie wrote about his son:

> To the second volume is prefixed an Account of the young Beattie's Life and Character, written by his father, who calls it *a short Account*. As it occupies ore than one-fourth of the whole book, some readers will, perhaps, think it

quite long enough. To the feelings of a father, however smarting under the anguish of such a sons early death, our hearts dispose us to make much allowance. [*New London Review*, 1800, Vol. 3, p. 471]

The following is from the 1794 edition of *Essays and Fragments*. Footnotes below without brackets are those of James Beattie.

THE
MODERN TIPPLING PHILOSOPHERS.

Father Hodge[2] had his pipe and his dram,
    And at night, his cloy'd thirst to awaken,
He was served with a rasher of ham,
    Which procured him the surname of *Bacon*.
He has shown, that, though logical science
    And dry theory oft prove unhandy,
Honest Truth will ne'er set at defiance
    Experiment aided by brandy.

Des Cartes bore a musquet, they tell us,
    Ere he wish'd, or was able, to write,
And was noted among the brave fellows,
    Who are bolder to tipple than fight.
Of his system the cause and design
    We no more can be posed to explain: –
The *materia subtilis* was wine,
    And the *vortices* whirl'd in his brain.

Old Hobbes, as his name plainly shows,
    At a *hob-nob* was frequently tried:
That all virtue from selfishness rose
    He believed, and all laughter from pride.[3]
The truth of this creed he would brag on,
    Smoke his pipe, murder Homer,[4] and quaff;
Then staring, as drunk as a dragon,
    In the pride of his heart he would laugh.

---

[2] Roger Bacon, the father of experimental philosophy. He flourished in the 13th century.

[3] See *The Spectator*. Numb 47.

[4] Hobbes was a great smoker, and wrote what some have been pleased to call a Translation of Homer.

Sir Isaac discover'd, it seems,
   The nature of colours and light,
In remarking the tremulous beams
   That swom on his wandering sight.
Ever sapient, sober though seldom,
   From experience *attraction* he found,
By observing, when no one upheld him,
   That his wise head fell souse on the ground.

As to Berkeley's philosophy – he has
   Left his poor pupils nought to inherit,
But a swarm of deceitful ideas
   Kept, like other monsters, in spirit.[5]
Tar-drinkers can't think what's the matter,
   That their health does not mend, but decline:
Why, they take but some wine to their water,
   He took but some water to wine.

One Mandeville once, or Man-devil,
   (Either name you many give as you please)
By a brain ever brooding on evil,
   Hatch'd a monster call'd *Fable of Bees*.
Vice, said he, aggrandizes a people;[6]
   By this light let my conduct be view'd;
I swagger, swear, guzzle, and tipple:
   And d___ ye, 'tis all for your good.

___ ___[7] ate a swinging great dinner,
   And grew every day fatter and fatter;
And yet the huge hulk of a sinner
   Said there was neither spirit nor matter.
Now there's no sober man in the nation,
   Who such nonsense could write, speak or think:
It follows, by fair demonstration,
   That he philosophized in his drink.

[5] He taught that the external universe has no existence, but an ideal one, in the mind
(or *spirit*) that perceives it: and he thought tar-water an universal remedy.

[6] Private vices public benefits.

[7] [i.e., David Hume.]

As a smuggler even P ____ [8] could sin;
  Who, in hopes the poor gauger of frightening,
While he fill'd his case-bottles with gin,
  Swore he fill'd them with thunder and lightning. [9]
In his cups, (when Locke's laid on the shelf)
  Could he speak, he would frankly confess it t'ye,
That, unable to manage himself,
  He puts his whole trust in Necessity.

If the young in rash folly engage,
  How closely continues the evil!
Old Franklin retains, as a sage,
  The thirst he acquired when a devil. [10]
That charging drives fire from a phial,
  It was natural for him to think,
After finding, from many a trial,
  That drought may be kindled by drink.

A certain high priest could explain, [11]
  How the soul is but nerve at the most;
And how Milton had glands in his brain,
  That secreted the Paradise Lost.
And sure, it is what they deserve,
  Of such theories if I aver it,
They are not even dictates of nerve,
  But mere muddy suggestions of claret.

Our Holland philosophers say, Gin
  Is the true philosophical drink,
As it made Doctor H___ imagine
  That to *shake* is the same as to *think*. [12]
For, while drunkenness throb'd in his brain,
  The sturdy materialist chose (O fye!)
To believe its vibrations not pain,
  But wisdom, and downright philosophy.

---

[8] [i.e., Joseph Priestley.]

[9] Electric batteries.

[10] Bred a printer. This was written long before Dr Franklin's death.

[11] Dr. L. Bp. of C. [i.e., Edmund Law, Bishop of Carlisle] is probably the person here alluded to. He was a zealous materialist.

[12] [i.e., David Hartley.]

Ye sages, who shine in my verse,
  On my labours with gratitude think,
Which condemn not the faults they rehearse,
  But impute all your sin to your drink.
In drink, poets, philosophers, mob, err;
  Then excuse, if my satire e'er nips ye:
When I praise, think me prudent and sober,
  If I blame, be assured I am tipsy.

DIALOGUES OF THE DEAD.

III.
MERCURY, SOCRATES,
AND A
MODERN PHILOSOPHER

MERCURY: Come hither, Socrates; I wish to introduce you to a modern British Philosopher.

s. Although I never made great pretensions to philosophy myself, I have always reckoned the acquaintance of true philosophers a most valuable acquisition; and left the world without regret, in the hope of enjoying in these regions the company and conversation of the wise men of antiquity. Where is the person, pray, with whom you mean to make me acquainted?

MERCURY: Look towards the Styx. Do you see a tall fat man, very splendidly drest, coming this way, with a little hat under his arm? He is the philosopher.

SOCRATES: That from his dress I should hardly have concluded. But I do not blame him for complying with the fashion of his age and country, as far as might be requisite to prevent the appearance of singularity. No: I shall love and esteem him as a philosopher, that is, as a friend to truth and virtue: the shape of his coat, or the twist of his periwig, do not affect my opinion. And of what science has he extended the boundaries? With what new discovery has he enriched mankind? Or has he been successful in illustrating the doctrines of morality established by others? His countrymen, I am told, have of late made considerable advances in the knowledge of, what was little known in my time, the properties of matter, and the laws of astronomy: has he employed himself in that way?

MERCURY: I know not that he has.

SOCRATES: He may, no doubt, have enquired into the nature of the human mind; strengthened by new arguments the cause of virtue; or established on a firmer foundation the liberties of his country.

MERCURY: I am afraid he has not enlarged the philosophy of the human mind by new observations, or by the advancement of truth; nay I doubt whether he believed that there is such a thing as mind in the universe.

SOCRATES: A geometrician perhaps?

MERCURY: I have not heard him spoken of as such.

SOCRATES: Many sciences may have been brought to perfection since I left my native planet, and much wonderful discovery has actually been made. Pray tell me, good Mercury, in what respect he has extended knowledge, or confirmed belief.

MERCURY: Truly, I am at a loss to say, in what he has confirmed belief; – unless you call a confirmation of belief his endeavours to make mankind doubt of every thing; of the existence of God, of spirit, of matter, and even of themselves.

SOCRATES: So – I find the gentleman is only a sceptick. That is a character, with which the world was not unacquainted in my days. But I wonder that the Britons, who have rid their country of a far less pernicious animal the wolf, would suffer a sceptick to burrow among them. And do you call such a person a philosopher, Mercury.

MERCURY: I only call him what he has been called by others. You have had occasion to prescribe, before now, for scepticism: and I should think it a favour, if you would purge this poor soul of a part at least of the corruption he has brought upon himself. He might perhaps think it a favour too; for if he be not purified in that way, he must in another less agreeable. – But he is almost come up to us. Now, my good old Grecian, arm yourself with all your philosophy, set in order your arguments, prepare your illustrations, sharpen your logical weapons; call forth the pleasantry of your wit, the fire of your imagination, the impetuosity of your eloquence, the keenness of your –

SOCRATES: Softly, softly, my friend. You know I was never distinguished as a declaimer: I have always thought it sufficient to convince a man, without either deafening or frightening him. I would rather allure than compel; for there is in human nature a strong propensity to resist violence, and not a less strong one to gentle persuasion.

MERCURY: Shall I then introduce him to you as the renown Socrates, the champion of virtue, come, not to force, but to sooth him into the truth? Do you think that an obstinate mind, which will not yield to a greater power, may be subdued by a less?

SOCRATES: Mention neither my name nor my character. I would rather on this, as on former occasions, appear a plain man than a philosopher, and seem more to favour scepticism than to oppose it: for so he will hear me without apprehension or uneasiness; and I may give my opinion of some of his tenets, without being suspected of any design either to confute or to ridicule them.

MERCURY: Well: you shall be obeyed. But he is here. – Great and learned Sir, I beg leave to introduce to you this friend of mine, a plain man, who pretends not to philosophy or literature, but has with some attention read your Essays. – Friend [turning to Socrates] this is the extraordinary person, whom you have so often expressed a desire to see: this is the philosopher, whose writings are so much admired in Europe, Asia, Africa and America; whom many read, few understand, and all are convinced by.

SOCRATES: I am happy in being presented to so great a person. That many read his writings, and that few understand them, I can readily suppose: but give me leave to doubt, whether by them any one was ever convinced.

MODERN PHILOSOPHER: 'Sdeath, Sir; – nobody convinced by my philosophical writings! – What do you mean?

SOCRATES: Far be it from me, Sir, to say that. God forbid – no, I am wrong, I ask *your* pardon, Sir. – Chance forbid – pshaw! I am wrong again. Necessity forbid – or Nothing forbid, that I should affirm any thing, or nothing, so positively. I only said, that I *doubted* whether any body was ever convinced by them. And let me tell you, Sir, that you are a particular sort of gentleman, and that your principles agree very ill with your practice, if you do not very much doubt the same thing.

MODERN PHILOSOPHER: O Sir, I thought you wished me to talk in the language of common life. Why, philosophically speaking, you are right; I doubt whether my writings ever did convince; I doubt, whether they were ever published or printed: – O yes, without doubt, Sir, I doubt very much –

SOCRATES: But surely, now, that theory of yours cannot be well founded. Is it possible, that you should, with serious confidence, doubt whether your writings ever gave conviction, or ever appeared in print?

MODERN PHILOSOPHER: But I tell you, Sir, that I doubt of it, with as great certainty, as I believe, – no, I mean as I doubt, my own existence.[13]

SOCRATES: You firmly believe that you doubt it?

MODERN PHILOSOPHER: Yes, Sir; and any one who has read my Essays will firmly, if he is a real philosopher, believe that he doubts the same thing.

SOCRATES: And pray, do you think it more favours the principle of universal scepticism to believe that you doubt, than to believe that you do not doubt?

MODERN PHILOSOPHER: I tell you, that you know nothing of the matter – And, to be sure I do doubts, whether my belief in my doubts be real or not. This I must do according to my principles: for I have said, *ipse dixi*, that a true philosopher is doubtful of his doubts, as well as of his convictions.

SOCRATES: You do not, by your principles, believe any thing, do you?

MODERN PHILOSOPHER: By no means: as a philosopher I believe nothing certainly; and have said, that he who believes any thing certainly is a fool. The phrase, you may think, has not the highest polish of Parisian civility; but of my *friends* not one ever objected to it.

---

[13] [A similar joke appears in Beattie's "Castle of Scepticism": "...and a striking proof of one of my friend's [i.e., Hume's] maxims, that there is nothing, how absurd, how unpleasant, how unnatural soever, to which habit will not reconcile the human mind. Mind! did I say? I ask pardon. My friend has proved, that there is no human mind; has proved it, Sir, beyond a possibility of doubt, or reply."]

SOCRATES: You seemed to think, that confirmed doubt implies belief; implies your believing that you are doubtful.

MODERN PHILOSOPHER: Yes; I allow that.

SOCRATES: Then you can neither believe any thing, nor doubt any thing; as the former supposes belief directly, and the latter by implication. So that your mind can never be employed on any thought at all; for, if it were, that would imply something either of belief or of doubt with respect to the thought, or with respect to the manner of your thinking of it. But you allow, that doubt implies believing that you are doubtful. Therefore you cannot think without believing: and as, according to your principles, you cannot believe, so neither, according to your principles, can you think.

MODERN PHILOSOPHER: I tell you, old gentleman, you know nothing of the matter; and that you are – no, that I doubt whether you are not, one of the most pertinacious, impertinent, ill-bred –

MERCURY: Pardon my interrupting you, good Sir. But, I must now take the liberty to inform you, that you are speaking to one nearly equal, perhaps, in philosophy, even to yourself. I must also tell you, as you are a stranger to our customs, that it will not be for your interest to maintain any doctrine *here* which you do not believe: for if such notions cannot be driven out by the conversation of Socrates, it may be tried whether they will resist –

MODERN PHILOSOPHER: Socrates, Sir, is a person for whom I must be understood to have a very great respect: it is fashionable in the best company to speak of him respectfully. When I was in Paris, they called me (and my friends in _____ politely re-echoed the words) *Le Socrate moderne.*

MERCURY: Very likely: but that is not to the present purpose. Proceed, if you please, in the argument with Socrates.

MODERN PHILOSOPHER: I deny not, that, from what he has said, it appears plain enough, that if mind did exist, and could employ itself in thinking, the first principles of investigation must be founded in belief. But as I deny the existence of mind, and consequently of thought, it is not necessary for me to allow, that his reasoning affects my theory. The mind, although it must believe if it think, yet, if it do not think, may as well doubt. Such is my doctrine: and I am proud to declare, that, while I was on earth, there were some who studied, and many who embraced it.

SOCRATES: That I am willing to believe. Even in your own house I doubt not that you must have had many disciples. Every chair in your parlour would have a smattering at least of knowledge in human nature: and the table on which you wrote your Essays might discuss a point of scepticism not much less accurately than yourself.

MODERN PHILOSOPHER: Fie, Socrates; it is beneath the dignity of a philosopher to talk so absurdly. What a jumble of inconsistencies have you thrown together! Did I ever hint, or could I ever believe, that a table or chair could reason like myself; or suppose a piece of insensible matter to be endowed with human faculties?

SOCRATES: Before I give you an answer, allow me to ask you a plain question with regard to *nothing*; that idea, or rather word, which you seem to be so fond of. Is not *nothing*, with respect to matter, for example, destitute of the qualities of magnitude and solidity, which are essential to matter? And, with regard to mind, is it not destitute of all the qualities of mind?

MODERN PHILOSOPHER: I do not well understand these questions; but I admit at once, that a non-entity cannot possess qualities.

SOCRATES: And what is your idea of *difference*? Would you call two things different, which both possess the same qualities?

MODERN PHILOSOPHER: By no means. When two things are spoken of as different, it must be meant, that one of them possesses some quality which the other does not possess.

SOCRATES: Well: if you and your table be different, must not one of the two have some quality or qualities that the other has not? And since *nothing* cannot possess any quality; and since both you and your table are (by your theory) nothing; neither of the two can possess any quality. So that when you deny the existence of matter and spirit, you in fact allow, that the same thing at the same time does possess qualities, and does not possess qualities. And you will find, that this is not the only instance of such absurdity in sceptical reasoning: you will find, that in almost all the principles of your system, as far as it is sceptical, similar contradictions are implied.

MODERN PHILOSOPHER: There does appear to be a little absurdity in supposing that spirit and matter do not exist; as they are evidently different, and therefore must possess qualities. But –

SOCRATES: And you seemed to allow, that, if the soul exist, universal scepticism is impossible, because this implies a necessary want of all thought; which is inconsistent with the nature of the soul.

MODERN PHILOSOPHER: Perhaps from what has been said, the existence of the soul, and the impossibility of universal scepticism, might appear sufficiently certain to the common herd of mankind. But you are not aware, my good Sir, that I hold one tenet, which totally destroys the force of every argument. I hold, that the senses and the memory are fallacious; and that, by consequence, one cannot be sure of the reality of what one perceives or remembers. so that we ought not by any reasoning to be convinced, as we are apt both to misunderstand and to forget it.

SOCRATES: It is strange if you do not see that, in this respect, your own arguments are liable to the same objection with those of your opponents. – But, passing this; what reason have you to think that the senses are deceitful?

MODERN PHILOSOPHER: Let me answer you by another question. Have not mankind in general agreed to call the faculty perceiving, the object perceived, and the act of perception, by one and the same name? – thereby indicating, that those three are, according to popular opinion, really the same thing. Now the *faculty perceiving* is in what we call the soul or mind; as when one says, my *sight* is weak: so likewise must the *thing perceived* be; as when one says, I see a strange *sight:* and therefore the senses give knowledge of no things external to the mind but of such things only as are contained by it, or within it.

SOCRATES: And can you really think, that men in general, when they see a river or a mountain, believe it to exist only in their own mind? Bring me one man of common sense who thinks so, and I submit to your opinion. But you will not find, that mankind never employ the same word to denote things which they believe to be totally different. – When you look at London from Highgate hill, have you not a *view* of London?

MODERN PHILOSOPHER: Yes.

SOCRATES: And when you look at a perspective representation of London, have you not a *view* of London?

MODERN PHILOSOPHER: No doubt.

SOCRATES: Does it follow, that London and the perspective representation of it are the same thing; or that, while you have the drawing in your pocket, you have the city in your pocket too?

MODERN PHILOSOPHER: No: I own there is some reason in what you say. – But though I were to admit that the senses are not deceitful, which no sceptical philosopher ever did or can admit, I must still adhere to the fallacious nature of memory; which is alone sufficient to overturn every argument: for if we are not certain that the premises are as our memory represents them, how can we be sure of our conclusion?

SOCRATES: Please to answer me a question or two. If a thousand men were to observe the same thing at the same time, and every one of the thousand, separately examined, to give the same account of it; would it be a proof of the accuracy of their observation, or of its inaccuracy?

MODERN PHILOSOPHER: Of its accuracy.

SOCRATES: If a thousand men were to remember the same thing with the same circumstances; would it be a proof of the exactness, or of the deceitfulness, of memory?

MODERN PHILOSOPHER: Of its exactness.

SOCRATES: And among the many thousands who have read and attended to history, is there, do you think, any person of a sound mind, who would differ from the rest in his remembrance of the most material and undisputed events that historians record? Would any one, for example, affirm that Julius Cesar was not stabbed by conspirators, but hanged for sheep-stealing; that William the first conquered, not England but New Zealand; that the Romans bombarded Carthage with two-and-forty-pounders; and that Scipio shot Hannibal with a rifle-barreled gun, as he was getting into an air-balloon? And if the memories of men were fallacious, and of course constantly changing, could their remembrances of the events of history so exactly coincide?

MODERN PHILOSOPHER: Socrates, I will hear you no longer: your arguments become troublesome; and if you persist in this unphilosophical way of reasoning, we must part.

MERCURY: Perhaps you will not find it so easy as you may imagine to get out of the reach of Socrates and common sense. Remember where you are: Paris and Versailles are a great way off. Believe me, it will be for your interest here, wherever it might have been in the world you have left, to listen to the truth, and to yield when you are convinced by it. Obstinacy and scepticism are of no account in these regions.

MODERN PHILOSOPHER: This matter I find begins to grow somewhat serious. If you oblige me to say what I think, I fear I must give up the deceitfulness of memory as well as of sense.

SOCRATES: Take the trouble to recollect what has been said in this conversation, and has received your assent. We have seen that neither the senses nor the memory can with any propriety be called fallacious; and that therefore every argument which reason approved, and continued to approve, may be reckoned a just one. You allowed, that spirit and matter are possessed of qualities, and consequently of existence; and that, the existence of mind being admitted, universal scepticism is impossible.

MODERN PHILOSOPHER: Your arguments seem to have something in them. And I own I was sorry to see your doctrine advanced, to the detriment both of my fame and of my bookseller, even before I left the other world.

SOCRATES: You left the other world! I will undertake to prove, according to your own mode of reasoning, that you are there still.

MODERN PHILOSOPHER: I heartily wish you could. How would you prove that, pray?

SOCRATES: I could prove it from the consideration that you are at present in the shades below.

MODERN PHILOSOPHER: You have certainly not only forgotten your philosophy, old gentleman, but lost your wits. Why, that would be proving a proposition from a principle directly contradictory to it.

SOCRATES: And is this contradiction more glaring than to deduce *universal scepticism* from any principle of *belief* whatever. Let the principle be what it will, either that Spirit and Matter do, or do not, exist; still belief is implied: and to prove, from a principle believed, that we can believe nothing, is not in my opinion less ridiculous, than to prove that you are in the other world, because you are in this. You allowed that spirit and matter have existence, and that consequently universal scepticism is impossible: you now see, that this must be thought an impossibility, even by one who could be mad enough to believe that spirit and matter do not exist.

MODERN PHILOSOPHER: I fear my system must fall to pieces. But is it not pity to overturn a scheme so friendly to the elegancies of fashionable life, and which renders the mind of man so light and easy, by relieving it from all apprehensions of future existence?

SOCRATES: You still forget where you are: you cannot, it seems, even in this world, keep clear of the licentious jargon to which you were so long accustomed in the other. As to the tendency of your doctrines, and of the inferences that may be fairly drawn from them, – no person capable of serious thought can for a moment believe them to be beneficial to mankind: you yourself will be of this opinion soon, if you are not so already. All love to God, to our neighbour, and even to ourselves, they would extinguish; for who can love that which he does not believe to exist! From no sort of wickedness, that man may wish to commit, would they deter: for they teach, that reason ought to be the servant, or rather the slave, of passion; and that the impulses of passion, being the necessary effects of necessary causes, are irresistable, and therefore need not be resisted: that there is no good reason for distinguishing moral virtue from intellectual ability; in other words, that men are under no stronger obligations to be just than to be eloquent, and that to have a weak memory is as bad a thing as to pick a pocket. But I scorn to enter into the detail of your paradoxes. I shall only say, that they are not adapted to the head or heart of any one who is not both a profligate and a fool: and that you, by endeavouring to subvert every thing that has been believed concerning *mind*, have done such a service to philosophy, as a prince would do to his people in attempting to destroy all the restraints of government, and consequently all the protection.
FEB. 18. 1787.

HUME'S LAST DAYS AND DEATH: 1776

38
"MY OWN LIFE" AND REVIEWS

David Hume, "My Own Life" (1777) and reviews.
Complete essay, selections from reviews; from *The life of David Hume, Esq. written by himself*. London: printed for W. Strahan; and T. Cadell, 1777, [4], iv, 62 p.

Anticipating his death, Hume wrote "My Own Life" in April 1776. His instructions are given in a letter to Adam Smith:

> You will find among my Papers a very inoffensive Piece, called *My own Life*, which I composed a few days before I left Edinburgh, which I thought, as did all my Friends, that my Life was despaired of. There can be no Objection, that this small piece should be sent to Messrs Strahan and Cadell and the Proprietors of my other Works to be prefixed to any future Edition of them. [Hume to Adam Smith, May 3, 1776]

In March of 1777, under the title *The Life of David Hume, Esq. Written by Himself*, Hume's "My Own Life" was published along with Smith's "Letter … to William Strahan" (contained in this collection). Although the editor of the pamphlet states in the Preface that he has not altered Hume's words, some changes were nevertheless made with spelling, punctuation and minor wording. This is evident from a comparison between the printed pamphlet and Hume's original manuscript, which now resides in the National Library of Scotland (MS 23159 item 23). Contrary to Hume's wishes, "My Own Life" was not included in the next edition of his *Essays and Treatises on Several Subjects*, published in 1777. After "My Own Life" appeared, several periodicals reprinted it in whole or part; a list of their respective treatments of the piece is as follows:

Scots Magazine (January 1777, Vol. 39, pp. 1–7): complete reprint of "My Own Life" and Smith's "Letter"; no commentary.
London Chronicle (March 11–13, 1777, Vol. 41, No 3162, pp. 244–245): reprint of first half of "My Own Life"; opening comment.
Critical Review (March 1777, Vol. 43, pp. 222–227): third person paraphrase of and extended quotations from "My Own Life"; some commentary.

Gentleman's Magazine (March 1777, Vol. 47, pp. 120–121): third person paraphrase of most of "My Own Life"; concluding editorial comment.

London Review (March 1777, Vol. 5, pp. 198–205): reprint of all of "My Own Life" except opening paragraph; much commentary.

Monthly Review (Ralph Griffiths, March 1777, Vol. 56, pp. 206–213): third person paraphrase of and extended quotations from "My Own Life"; much commentary.

Weekly Magazine or Edinburgh Amusement (March 13, 1777, Vol. 35, pp. 353–357): reprint of all of "My Own Life" except opening paragraph; no commentary.

Weekly Magazine or Edinburgh Amusement (March 20, 1777, Vol. 35, pp. 388–389): complete reprint of Smith's "Letter"; no commentary.

The Life of David Hume was published twice more in 1777, and again in 1778. "My Own Life" was included in later editions of Hume's *Essays and Treatises* and the *History*. Below is the complete text of "My Own Life" with comments from four reviews inserted at the appropriate locations.

{[*London Chronicle*:] Mr. Hume, a few months before his death, wrote this account of his own life; and, in a codicil to his will, desired that it might be prefixed to the next edition of his works.

The Following passages are selected from the life of this learned and ingenious Gentleman.}

{[*Critical Review*:] If memoirs of a celebrated person prove interesting, without any uncommon circumstance in the form of the narrative, how much more lively is the pleasure which they are calculated to afford, when he whose life and character are delineated is himself the historian? In such a case, though there be doubtless some ground for the imputation of vanity, it is so far from disgusting the reader, that it even yields him satisfaction; not only by gratifying curiosity, but by the laudable anxiety which it discovers for honest fame, and an unblemished reputation. The performance now under our notice, however, is the more particularly entitled to attention, that it was written but a few months before the decease of the author, at a time when that event was evidently very fast approaching.}

{[*London Review*:] In an advertisement, prefixed to this little performance, we are told that,}

{[*Monthly Review*:] When men of such PARTS, and such PRINCIPLES, as those which distinguished the character and writings of Mr. Hume, come to face the immediate terrors of death, the world is always curious to learn in what manner they support the trying conflict: whether the near approach of that awful change of situation which they are about to experience, (in an hour wherein one would think, the boldest mortal would not dare either to DISSEMBLE or to TRIFLE) has produced any change in their *minds*; whether they continue fixed, and steady to their past professions; or, whether *'new light'* is let into 'the soul's dark cottage,' as the poet expresses it, 'through the chinks' of its ruins, – opening wider, at the moment when the batter'd fabric is tottering to its dissolution.

The late *departure* of the celebrated philosopher just mentioned, is an event of this kind; and the public will, no doubt, be highly gratified by this unquestionable account of his LIFE, and of his DEATH.

The following advertisement is prefixed to the account of Mr. Hume's Life:}

[PRINTER'S NOTE]

Mr. Hume, a few months before his death, wrote the following short account of his own life; and, in a codicil to his will, desired that it might be prefixed to the next edition of his Works. That edition cannot be published for a considerable time. The Editor, in the mean while, in order to serve the purchasers of the former editions; and, at the same time, to gratify the impatience of the public curiosity; has thought proper to publish it separately, without altering even the title or superscription, which was written in Mr. Hume's own hand on the cover of the manuscript.

MY OWN
LIFE.

It is difficult for a man to speak long of himself without Vanity; therefore, I shall be short. It may be thought an instance of vanity that I pretend at all to write my life; but this Narrative shall contain little more than the History of my Writings; as, indeed, almost all my life has been spent in Literary pursuits and occupations. The first success of most of my writings was not such as to be an object of vanity.

I was born the 26th of April 1711, old style, at Edinburgh. I was of a good family, both by father and mother: my father's family is a branch of the Earl of Home's, or Hume's; and my ancestors had been proprietors of the estate, which my brother possesses, for several generations. My mother was daughter of Sir David Falconer, President of the College of Justice: the title of Lord Halkerton came by succession to her brother.

My family, however, was not rich, and being myself a younger brother, my patrimony, according to the mode of my country, was of course very slender.

My father, who passed for a man of parts, died when I was an infant, leaving me, with an elder brother and a sister, under the care of our mother, a woman of singular merit, who, though young and handsome, devoted herself entirely to the rearing and educating of her children. I passed through the ordinary course of education with success, and was seized very early with a passion for literature, which has been the ruling passion of my life, and the great source of my enjoyments. My studious disposition, my sobriety, and my industry, gave my family a notion that the law was a proper profession for me; but I found an unsurmountable aversion to everything but the pursuits of philosophy and general learning; and while they fancied I was poring upon Voet and Vinnius, Cicero and Virgil were the authors which I was secretly devouring.

My very slender fortune, however, being unsuitable to this plan of life, and my health being a little broken by my ardent application, I was tempted, or rather forced, to make a very feeble trial for entering into a more active scene of life. In 1734, I went to Bristol, with some recommendations to eminent merchants, but in a few months found that scene totally unsuitable to me. I went over to France, with a view of prosecuting my studies in a country retreat; and I there laid that plan of life, which I have steadily and successfully pursued. I resolved to make a very rigid frugality supply my deficiency of fortune, to maintain unimpaired my independency, and to regard every object as contemptible, except the improvement of my talents in literature.

During my retreat in France, first at Reims, but chiefly at La Fleche, in Anjou, I composed my *Treatise of Human Nature.* After passing three years very agreeably in that country, I came over to London in 1737. In the end of 1738, I published my Treatise, and immediately went down to my mother and my brother, who lived at his country-house, and was employing himself very judiciously and successfully in the improvement of his fortune.

{[*London Review*:] This narrative of Mr. Hume's life contains, as he himself observes, little more than the history of his writings; which, as it is short, we shall cite without interruption; subjoining such remarks as suggest themselves, by way of note, at the bottom of the page.}

Never literary attempt was more unfortunate than my Treatise of Human Nature. It fell *dead-born from the press*, without reaching such distinction, as even to excite a murmur among the zealots.[1] But being naturally of a cheerful

---

[1]   {[*Monthly Review*:] We remember however, that it was *distinguished* by the *Reviewers* of that time, though not in a manner suitable to the expectations or wishes of the Author. It was treated with some degree of contempt by the Writer of *the History of the Works of the Learned*, vol. ii. for the year 1739; who, nevertheless, prognosticated *better things*, from the maturer age of the [then young] author. There is a pleasant story of David's paying a visit to the Critic, and threatening to put him to the sword; but as we cannot duly authenticate the particulars, we do not chuse to repeat them.}

and sanguine temper,[2] I very soon recovered the blow, and prosecuted with great ardour my studies in the country. In 1742, I printed at Edinburgh the first part of my Essays: the work was favourably received, and soon made me entirely forget my former disappointment. I continued with my mother and brother in the country, and in that time recovered the knowledge of the Greek language, which I had too much neglected in my early youth.

In 1745, I received a letter from the Marquis of Annandale, inviting me to come and live with him in England; I found also, that the friends and family of that young noble man were desirous of putting him under my care and direction, for the state of his mind and health required it. – I lived with him a twelvemonth. My appointments during that time made a considerable accession to my small fortune. I then received an invitation from General St. Clair to attend him as a secretary to his expedition, which was at first meant against Canada, but ended in an incursion on the coast of France. Next year, to wit, 1747, I received an invitation from the General to attend him in the same station in his military embassy to the courts of Vienna and Turin. I then wore the uniform of an officer, and was introduced at these courts as aid-de-camp to the general, along with Sir Harry Erskine and Captain Grant, now General Grant. These two years were almost the only interruptions which my studies have received during the course of my life: I passed them agreeably, and in good company; and my appointments, with my frugality, had made me reach a fortune, which I called independent, though most of my friends were inclined to smile when I said so; in short, I was now master of near a thousand pounds.

I had always entertained a notion, that my want of success in publishing the Treatise of Human Nature, had proceeded more from the manner than the matter, and that I had been guilty of a very usual indiscretion, in going to the press too early. I, therefore, cast the first part of that work anew in The Enquiry concerning Human Understanding, which was published while I was at Turin. But this piece was at first little more successful than the Treatise of Human Nature. On my return from Italy, I had the mortification to find all England in a ferment, on account of Dr. Middleton's Free Enquiry, while my performance was entirely overlooked and neglected. A new edition, which had

---

[2] {[*London Review:*] So sanguine that it does not appear our author had acquired at this period of his life that command over his passions, of which he afterwards makes his boast. His disappointment at the public reception of his Essay on Human Nature had indeed a violent effect on his passions in a particular circumstance: it not having dropped so *dead-born from the press* but that it was severely handled by the *Reviewers* of those times, in a publication, entitled "The Works of the Learned." A circumstance this which so highly provoked our young philosopher, that he flew in a violent rage, to demand satisfaction of Jacob Robinson, the publisher; whom he kept, during the paroxysm of his anger, at his swords point, trembling behind the counter lest a period should be put to the life of a sober critic by a raving philosopher. *Rev.*}

been published at London of my Essays, moral and political, met not with a much better reception.

Such is the force of natural temper, that these disappointments made little or no impression on me. I went down in 1749, and lived two years with my brother at his country house, for my mother was now dead. I there composed the second part of my Essays, which I called Political Discourses, and also my Enquiry concerning the Principles of Morals, which is another part of my treatise that I cast anew. Meanwhile, my bookseller, A. Millar, informed me, that my former publications (all but the unfortunate Treatise) were beginning to be the subject of conversation; that the sale of them was gradually increasing, and that new editions were demanded. Answers by Reverends, and Right Reverends, came out two or three in a year; and I found, by Dr. Warburton's railing, that the books were beginning to be esteemed in good company. However, I had fixed a resolution, which I inflexibly maintained, never to reply to any body; and not being very irascible in my temper, I have easily kept myself clear of all literary squabbles.[3] These symptoms of a rising reputation gave me encouragement, as I was ever more disposed to see the favourable than unfavourable side of things; a turn of mind which it is more happy to possess, than to be born to an estate of ten thousand a year.[4]

{[*Monthly Review*:] We shall now proceed a little farther, in the Author's own words:}

In 1751, I removed from the country to the town, the true scene for a man of letters. In 1752, were published at Edinburgh, where I then lived, my Political Discourses, the only work of mine that was successful on the first publication. It was well received abroad and at home. In the same year was published at London, my Enquiry concerning the Principles of Morals; which, in my own opinion (who ought not to judge on that subject), is of all my writings, historical, philosophical, or literary, incomparably the best.[5] It came unnoticed and unobserved into the world.

In 1752, the Faculty of Advocates chose me their Librarian, an office from which I received little or no emolument, but which gave me the command of a

---

[3]   {[*London Review*:] Perhaps this was owing to Mr. Hume's turn of study as well as temper of mind. He ran a race in which he had few competitors. *History* and *Philosophy* are above the pursuits of *literary* squabbles. Had he been a *poet*, the *genus irritabile vatum*, the versifyers, would have tried his philosophy of temper to the utmost. Fortunately for him, he was too *wise* to be a *wit*, and thus escaped. Rev.}

[4]   {[*London Review*:] Perhaps this disposition of mind was not a little confirmed by the ridiculous figure he must be conscious he made in the before-mentioned adventure with Jacob; before he grew "callous against the impressions of public folly." Rev.}

[5]   {[*London Review*:] In this instance Mr. Hume shews himself to be a more impartial judge of his own writings than authors themselves usually are. Rev.}

large library.[6] I then formed the plan of writing the History of England; but being frightened with the notion of continuing a narrative through a period of 1700 years, I commenced with the accession of the House of Stuart, an epoch when, I thought, the misrepresentations of faction began chiefly to take place. I was, I own, sanguine in my expectations of the success of this work. I thought that I was the only historian, that had at once neglected present power, interest, and authority, and the cry of popular prejudices; and as the subject was suited to every capacity, I expected proportional applause. But miserable was my disappointment: I was assailed by one cry of reproach, disapprobation, and even detestation; English, Scotch, and Irish, Whig and Tory, churchman and sectary, freethinker and religionist, patriot and courtier, united in their rage against the man, who had presumed to shed a generous tear for the fate of Charles I. and the Earl of Strafford; and after the first ebullitions of their fury were over, what was still more mortifying, the book seemed to sink into oblivion. Mr. Millar told me, that in a twelve-month he sold only forty-five copies of it. I scarcely, indeed, heard of one man in the three kingdoms, considerable for rank or letters, that could endure the book. I must only except the primate of England, Dr. Herring, and the primate of Ireland, Dr. Stone, which seem two odd exceptions. These dignified prelates separately sent me messages not to be discouraged.

I was, however, I confess, discouraged; and had not the war been at that time breaking out between France and England, I had certainly retired to some provincial town of the former kingdom, have changed my name, and never more have returned to my native country. But as this scheme was not now practicable, and the subsequent volume was considerably advanced, I resolved to pick up courage and to persevere.

In this interval, I published at London my Natural History of Religion, along with some other small pieces: its public entry was rather obscure, except only that Dr. Hurd wrote a pamphlet[7] against it, with all the illiberal petulance,

---

[6] {[*London Review*:] About this time Mr. Hume was chosen secretary to a learned and ingenious society at Edinburgh, which published two volumes of Literary and Philosophical Essays. *Rev.*}

[7] {[*Critical Review*:] The title of the pamphlet alluded to is – *Remarks on Mr. David Hume's Essay on the Natural History of Religion. Addressed to the rev. Dr. Warburton.* - Since the appearance of Mr. Hume's Life, a new edition of this performance has been published, with the following advertisement from the bookseller to the reader.

"The following is supposed to be the pamphlet referred to by the late Mr. David Hume, in page 21, of his Life, *as being written by* Dr. Hurd. Upon my applying to the bishop of Litchfield and Coventry for his permission to republish it, he very readily gave me his consent. His lordship only added, he was sorry he could not take to himself the WHOLE infamy of the charge brought against him; but that he should hereafter, if he thought it worth his while, explain himself more particularly on that subject.

Strand, March, 1777. T. CADELL."}

arrogance, and scurrility, which distinguish the Warburtonian school.[8] This pamphlet gave me some consolation for the otherwise indifferent reception of my performance.

In 1756, two years after the fall of the first volume, was published the second volume of my History, containing the period from the death of Charles I. till the Revolution. This performance happened to give less displeasure to the Whigs, and was better received. It not only rose itself, but helped to buoy up its unfortunate brother.

But though I had been taught by experience, that the Whig party were in possession of bestowing all places, both in the state and in literature, I was so little inclined to yield to their senseless clamour, that in above a hundred alterations, which farther study, reading, or reflection engaged me to make in the reigns of the two first Stuarts, I have made all them invariably to the Tory side. It is ridiculous to consider the English constitution before that period as a regular plan of liberty.

In 1759, I published my History of the House of Tudor. The clamour against this performance was almost equal to that against the History of the two first Stuarts. The reign of Elizabeth was particularly obnoxious. But I was now callous against the impressions of public folly, and continued very peaceably and contentedly in my retreat at Edinburgh, to finish, in two volumes, the more early part of the English History, which I gave to the public in 1761, with tolerable, and but tolerable success.

But, notwithstanding this variety of winds and seasons, to which my writings had been exposed, they had still been making such advances, that the copy-money given me by the booksellers, much exceeded anything formerly known in England; I was become not only independent, but opulent. I retired to my native country of Scotland, determined never more to set my foot out of it; and retaining the satisfaction of never having preferred a request to one great man, or even making advances of friendship to any of them.[9] As I was now turned of fifty, I thought of passing all the rest of my life in this philosophical manner, when I received, in 1763, an invitation from the Earl of Hertford, with whom I was not in the least acquainted, to attend him on his embassy to Paris, with a near prospect of being appointed secretary to the embassy; and, in the

---

[8] {[*London Review*:] It is a little remarkable that the gentleman, to whose care this manuscript was entrusted, should have ever carried his hand so even between *religion* and *infidelity*, as to have been made the instrument of ushering into the world, with equal approbation, the doctrines of *divine grace*, and the dogmas of *human nature*. *Rev.*}

[9] {[*London Review*:] How few writers can say this! – The fact reflects great honour on our author's spirit of independency. Not but that his general turn of study was toward such subjects as *great men* so little understand that it could hardly recommend him to many patrons. *Rev.*}

meanwhile, of performing the functions of that office. This offer, however inviting, I at first declined, both because I was reluctant to begin connexions with the great, and because I was afraid that the civilities and gay company of Paris, would prove disagreeable to a person of my age and humour: but on his lordship's repeating the invitation, I accepted of it. I have every reason, both of pleasure and interest, to think myself happy in my connexions with that nobleman, as well as afterwards with his brother, General Conway.

Those who have not seen the strange effects of modes, will never imagine the reception I met with at Paris, from men and women of all ranks and stations. The more I resiled from their excessive civilities, the more I was loaded with them. There is, however, a real satisfaction in living at Paris, from the great number of sensible, knowing, and polite company with which that city abounds above all places in the universe. I thought once of settling there for life.

I was appointed secretary to the embassy; and, in summer 1765, Lord Hertford left me, being appointed Lord Lieutenant of Ireland. I was *chargé d' affaires* till the arrival of the Duke of Richmond, towards the end of the year. In the beginning of 1766, I left Paris, and next summer went to Edinburgh, with the same view as formerly, of burying myself in a philosophical retreat. I returned to that place, not richer, but with much more money, and a much larger income, by means of Lord Hertford's friendship, than I left it; and I was desirous of trying what superfluity could produce, as I had formerly made an experiment of a competency. But, in 1767, I received from Mr. Conway[10] an invitation to be Under-secretary; and this invitation, both the character of the person, and my connexions with Lord Hertford, prevented me from declining.[11] I returned to Edinburgh in 1769, very opulent (for I possessed a revenue of 1000 l. a year), healthy, and though somewhat stricken in years, with the prospect of enjoying long my ease, and of seeing the increase of my reputation.

In spring 1775, I was struck with a disorder in my bowels, which at first gave me no alarm, but has since, as I apprehend it, become mortal and incurable. I now reckon upon a speedy dissolution. I have suffered very little pain from my disorder; and what is more strange, have, notwithstanding the great decline of my person, never suffered a moment's abatement of my spirits; insomuch, that were I to name the period of my life, which I should most choose to pass over again, I might be tempted to point to this later period. I possess the same ardour as ever in study, and the same gaiety in company. I consider, besides, that a man

---

[10] {[*Monthly Review*:] Secretary of State for the northern department.}

[11] {[*London Review*:] It was during our author's connection with administration that he interested himself in favour of that strange and inconsistent mortal, Rousseau; whose journey to England made so much noise in the world, and whose ingratitude to his benefactor forms one among the many blemishes in that singular character. Mr. Hume, however, appears, by not deigning to mention him, to have borne no resentment against him for his extraordinary behavior. *Rev.*}

of sixty-five, by dying, cuts off only a few years of infirmities; and though I see many symptoms of my literary reputation's breaking out at last with additional lustre, I knew that I could have but few years to enjoy it. It is difficult to be more detached from life than I am at present.

To conclude historically with my own character. I am, or rather was (for that is the style I must now use in speaking of myself, which emboldens me the more to speak my sentiments); I was, I say, a man of mild dispositions, of command of temper, of an open, social, and cheerful humour, capable of attachment, but little susceptible of enmity, and of great moderation in all my passions. Even my love of literary fame, my ruling passion, never soured my temper, notwithstanding my frequent disappointments. My company was not unacceptable to the young and careless, as well as to the studious and literary; and as I took a particular pleasure in the company of modest women, I had no reason to be displeased with the reception I met with from them. In a word, though most men any wise eminent, have found reason to complain of calumny, I never was touched, or even attacked by her baleful tooth: and though I wantonly exposed myself to the rage of both civil and religious factions, they seemed to be disarmed in my behalf of their wonted fury. My friends never had occasion to vindicate any one circumstance of my character and conduct: not but that the zealots, we may well suppose, would have been glad to invent and propagate any story to my disadvantage, but they could never find any which they thought would wear the face of probability. I cannot say there is no vanity in making this funeral oration of myself, but I hope it is not a misplaced one; and this is a matter of fact which is easily cleared and ascertained.

April 18, 1776.

{*Critical Review*: The whole of this narrative breathes ingenuousness, and a noble consciousness of integrity, not without that solicitude of literary, as well as moral fame, which we may suppose to have animated a writer, so distinguished, from his earliest years, for his ardor in the pursuits of philosophy and general learning.

This performance is dated the 18th of April, 1776, from which period, to the time of Mr. Hume's death, which happened on the 25th of August, an account of his state and behaviour is delivered in a letter annexed, written by Dr. Adam Smith, to Mr. Strahan. It appears that Mr. Hume supported his illness to the last, with such patience, resignation, and composure, as perhaps may be reckoned Stoical fortitude; and that, when the discourse of his friends turned on his approaching dissolution, he was even jocular on the subject. 'Upon the whole, says Dr. Smith, I have always considered him, both in his lifetime and since his death, as approaching as nearly to the idea of a perfectly wise and virtuous man, as perhaps the nature of human frailty will permit.'}

{[*Gentleman's Magazine:*] Those who are desirous of knowing more of this celebrated author, are referred to the original, with which, as it is a small pamphlet of an easy purchase, the proprietors may think we have already made too free.}

{[*London Review*:] It is remarkable that, in the history of our author's literary career, he is totally silent on the subject of that formidable attack, on his philosophical principles, by Dr. Beattie, in the latter's Essay on the Immutability of Truth. *Formidable* we call it, on account merely of its popularity, and the very favourable reception it met with in the world; a reception very different from that of our author's Essay on Human Nature. It were difficult to speak of this work with more contempt than, we are well assured, Mr. Hume entertained of it. "Truth!" says he, "there is no truth in it; it is a horrible large lie in *Octavo*." What would he have said, had he lived to see the late splendid edition of it in Quarto? – Be the merit, however, of Dr. Beattie's work what it may, we cannot help thinking that Candour required of him to have attacked Mr. Hume's later writings, and not a work, which the author himself had abandoned, and in some measure reprobated.

To Mr. Hume's own narrative of his life, is added a letter from Dr. Adam Smith to Mr. Strahan, giving an account of the manner of his death; by which he appears to have been as much a practical as he was a theoretical philosopher. Religionists, as Mr. Hume affected to call Christians, make a mighty stir about the last moments of life, as if it were of more consequence how a man dies than how he lives: and, though they may not agree that our philosopher died the death of the righteous, it is to be wished that the latter end of all believers were like his. – We do not indeed much approve of an apparent levity here related, of his discoursing on so important a subject as his death. This is, his talking about *Charon*, and an imaginary conversation that might happen on their rencounter on the banks of the *Styx*. Granting for a moment that the Christian mythology be imaginary, surely that of the Heathen is equally fabulous! The allusion to it, therefore, on so serious an occasion seems unbecoming and frivolous. There have been men so inveterately addicted to pleasantry, as even to die jesting; but though this may be thought characteristical in a *witty* man, it is by no means becoming a *wise* man: and we should be glad to subscribe to Dr. Smith's eulogium on his friend, when he declares that "upon the whole he considers him both in his life and death, as approaching as nearly to the idea of a perfectly wise and virtuous man, as the nature of human frailty will permit." W.}

{[*Monthly Review*: By way of *continuation* of Mr. Hume's account (which carries his LIFE down to a period[12] within about four months of its final close) we have, in a letter from the celebrated Dr. Adam Smith to William Strahan,

---

[12] {[*Monthly Review*:] Mr. Hume's paper is dated April 18, 1776.}

Esq; a circumstantial detail of the manner in which he supported his last illness: the Doctor's account begins, where Mr. Hume's ends. [The review continues with a summary of Smith's Letter, inserting the following observation:] The following remarkable instance of Mr. Hume's happy serenity of mind, and even *pleasantry*, in what may, almost, be styled his dying moments, is thus related; but, first, we must attend to the particular circumstance which led to it: ....

There is a good engraving of Mr. Hume, prefixed to the Life, by way of frontispiece.}

39
JOHN HOME:
DIARY OF A JOURNEY
WITH HUME TO BATH

John Home, Diary of a Journey with Hume from Morpeth to Bath, April 23, 1776, in Henry Mackenzie, *An account of the life and writings of John Home, Esq.* Edinburgh: Printed for A. Constable and Co., Edinburgh, and Hurst, Robinson, and Co., London, 1822, vii, 184 p.
Complete Diary Entry; from 1822 edition.

Born at Leith, John Home (1722–1808) attended the University of Edinburgh and was licensed to preach in the Scottish Church in 1745. He was appointed minister in Athelstaneford, East Lothian, a position which he was compelled to resign in 1757 because of controversy surrounding the production of his play *Douglas*. He subsequently pursued a career partly literary, partly political, while retaining contacts with the Edinburgh intelligentsia. Alexander Carlyle says of Home that "He was truly irresistible, and his entry to a company was like opening a window and letting the sun into a dark room" (*Autobiography*, 1910, p. 233). Home's close friendship with Hume probably began in the early 1750s and lasted until Hume's death. Suffering from a terminal illness, on April 21, 1776, Hume left Edinburgh for London with his servant Colin, hoping that a journey would improve his health. Reaching Morpeth on the 23rd, he coincidentally met Adam Smith and Home, who were travelling from London to visit him in Edinburgh. Smith continued on to Edinburgh, but Home stayed with Hume for the remainder of the journey. Home kept a diary of the trip, which describes Hume's jovial comments about his declining condition and forthcoming death, and Hume's purchase of a plot in the Calton burial ground. Much of the recorded conversation between the two friends involved political events, both in England and France. They arrived in London on May 1, but left shortly for Bath, arriving on May 8. Home's Diary breaks off while en route to Bath. Hume stayed there over a month, sending letters to friends, updating them on his condition. At first he was encouraged by his improving health, but the situation soon reversed. He left Bath near the end of June and was in Edinburgh in early July, hosting a farewell dinner for his friends at his house.

Home intended to publish the diary, but was dissuaded by Hume's nephew, Baron David Hume. In 1822, fourteen years after Home's death, Henry Mackenzie published *An Account of the Life and Writings of John Home*, which, by permission of Baron Hume, contains the diary. It is reprinted below as it appears in that work, along with Mackenzie's prefatory comments and a letter from Adam Ferguson to Home.[1]

[Opening Comment by Henry Mackenzie.]
Among the papers [of John Home] which have been preserved, is one of a remarkable kind, – a journal of that philosopher and historian's conversation and opinions delivered during the progress of a journey, which those two friends made in company to Bath, a very short while before Mr David Hume's death. That journey was highly honourable to Mr John Home, from the cordial and disinterested attachment which it shewed him to entertain for his illustrious friend.

He was at London with his wife, when he received accounts of the dangerous situation of Mr David Hume's health, and that he proposed a journey to Bath, as one of the possible means for restoring it. Mr Home instantly set off for Scotland, with the design of attending him in that journey, and ministering to him whatever ease or comfort the society of so intimate and long-tried a friend could afford. Mr Hume felt very sensibly the kindness of this measure, and it seemed to have answered, in no inconsiderable degree, the good purpose which it was intended to serve. They travelled by easy stages, they discoursed by the road with an easy unconstrained familiarity, which a sick man, in his moments of ease, can indulge without fatigue; and, in the evening, when they came early to their resting-place for the night, they played at picquet, a game of which they were both fond enough, as well as skilful in, to find an interesting amusement. When Mr Hume went to bed, naturally from his situation, at an earlier hour than his friend, Mr John Home used to put down notes of the conversation which the preceding day had afforded.

Its value, in his estimation, was such, that he got it fairly copied out, with an intention of having it published; but the historian's nephew, our excellent colleague Mr Professor Hume, whose leave lie asked previously to carrying this design into execution, conceived, that at that time it would not have been proper for publication; and that in his own very significant words (addressed

---

[1] Mackenzie's *Account of John Home* is included in Volume 1 of *The Works of John Home*, Edinburgh, Constable, 1822, 3 vol. The manuscript of Home's diary and Mackenzie's notes for his *Account* are contained in the National Library of Scotland (Acc. 10686). Home's diary as appears in Mackenzie's *Account* was reprinted in John Hill Burton's *Life and Correspondence of David Hume* (Vol. 2, pp. 495–504) and David Fate Norton's *A Sketch of the Character of Mr. Hume*, 1976, pp. 15–25.

to Mr John Home, in answer to a letter asking his leave to make this publication), it was one which he thought his uncle, had lie been alive, would have objected to. The same reasons, however, not subsisting now, he has given me leave to insert it in this place.

The Society will perceive in those unreserved effusions, the general turn and complexion of Mr Hume's historical notions. Such familiar sketches give the bent and contour of a person's mind, perhaps more truly than his elaborate compositions, as portraits drawn in a night-gown and slippers, shew the figure more freely and more naturally, than when they are finished in the costume of rank or ceremony.

The letters from Mr Hume, which are subjoined to the journal – the notes to Dr Blair, and the Codicil to Mr Hume's Will, must interest, from the peculiar situation in which they were written. The Codicil was of his own handwriting, and dated 7th August, 1776. He died on the 25th of that month.

Copy Letter Mr ADAM FERGUSSON *to* Mr JOHN HOME, *dated at Edinburgh, the* 11*th day of April,* 1776.

I am much such a correspondent as usual; and for some little time have been in doubt where a letter might find you. But David shewed me a line from you to-day, by which you desire to have your letters sent to London, and after such a preamble, you may guess that my silence proceeded in part from want of matter here. The loss of one *friend*, and the danger of *another*, are not subjects that make people in haste to write. David, I am afraid, loses ground. He is chearful, and in good spirits as usual, but I confess that my hopes, from the effects of the turn of the season towards spring, have very much abated. A journey to the south, Particularly to Bath, has been mentioned to him; but the thoughts of being from home, hurried at inns, and exposed to irregular meals, are very disagreeable to him. Black is of opinion that he ought not to expose himself to any thing that is so; and that for his complaints, the tranquillity and usual amusement of his own fire-side, with proper diet, is his best regimen; so that I think the thoughts of any journey are at present laid aside. I hope we shall see you here soon, and that your attentions will contribute to preserve what we can so ill spare.

    I am, dear John,

        Most affectionately yours,

          Adam Fergusson.

Note by Mr JOHN HOME.

Soon after Mr Home received the letter from Dr Ferguson, he left London, and set out for Scotland with Mr Adam Smith. They came to Morpeth on the 23d of April, 1776, and would have passed Mr David Hume, if they had not seen his servant, Colin, standing at the gate of an inn. Mr Home thinks that his friend, Mr David Hume, is much better than he expected to find him. His spirits are astonishing: he talks of his illness, of his death, as matters of no moment, and gives an account of what passed between him and his physicians since his illness began, with his usual wit, or with more wit than usual.

He acquainted Mr Adam Smith and me, that Dr Black had not concealed the opinion he had of the desperateness of his condition, and was rather averse to his setting out. "Have you no reason against it," said David, "but an apprehension that it may make me die sooner? – that is no reason at all." I never saw him more cheerful, or in more perfect possession of all his faculties, His memory, his understanding, his wit. It is agreed that Smith shall go on to Scotland, and that I should proceed to Bath with David. We are to travel one stage before dinner, and one after dinner. Colin tells me that he thinks Mr Hume better than when he left Edinburgh. We had a fine evening as we went from Morpeth to Newcastle. David seeing a pair of pistols in the chaise, said, that as he had very little at stake, he would indulge me in my humour of fighting the highwaymen. Whilst supper was getting ready at the inn, Mr Hume and I played an hour at picquet. Mr David was very keen about his card playing.

Newcastle, Wednesday, 24th April.

Mr Hume not quite so well in the morning – says, that he had set out merely to please his friends; that he would go on to please them; that Ferguson and Andrew Stuart, (about whom we had been talking,) were answerable for shortening his life one week a-piece; for, says he, you will allow Xenophon to be good authority; and he lays it down, that suppose a man is dying, nobody has a right to kill him. He set out in this vein, and continued all the stage in his cheerful and talking humour. It was a fine day, and we went on to Durham – from that to Darlington, where we passed the night.

In the evening, Mr Hume thinks himself more easy and light, than he has been any time for three months. In the course of our conversation we touched upon the national affairs. He still maintains, that the national debt must be the ruin of Britain; and laments that the two most civilized nations, the English and French, should be on the decline; and the barbarians, the Goths and Vandals of Germany and Russia, should be rising in power and renown. The French king, he says, has ruined the state by recalling the parliaments. Mr Hume thinks that there is only one man in France fit to be minister, (the Archbishop of Toulouse,) of the family of Brienne.[2] He told me some curious anecdotes with regard to this prelate; that he composed and corrected without writing; that Mr Hume had heard him repeat an elegant oration of an hour and a quarter in length, which he had never written. Mr Hume, talking with the Princess Beauvais about French policy, said that he knew but one man in France capable

---

[2]   [Etienne-Charles de Lomenie de Brienne (1727–1794), became Archbishop of Toulouse in 1763; he died in prison during the French Revolution's Reign of Terror.]

of restoring its greatness; the lady said she knew one too, and wished to hear if it was the same. They accordingly named each their man, and it was this prelate.

Thursday, 25th.

Left Darlington about nine o'clock, and came to North Allerton. The same delightful weather. A shower fell that laid the dust, and made our journey to Borough-bridge more pleasant. Mr Hume continues very easy, and has a tolerable appetite; tastes nothing liquid but water, and sups upon an egg. He assured me, that he never possesed his faculties more perfectly; that he never was more sensible of the beauties of any classic author than he was at present, nor loved more to read. When I am not in the room with him he reads continually. The post-boys can scarcely be persuaded to drive only five miles an hour, and their horses are of the same way of thinking! The other travellers, as they pass, look into the chaise, and laugh at our slow pace. This evening the post-boy from North Allerton, who had required a good deal of threatening to make him drive as slow as we desired, had no sooner taken his departure to go home, than he set off at full speed. '*Pour se dedommager*,' said David.

Friday, 26th, Borough-bridge.

Mr Hume this morning not quite so well. He observes, and I see it, that he has a good day and a bad one. His illness is an internal hemorrhage, which has been wasting him for a long time. He is so thin that he chooses to have a cushion under him when he sits upon an ordinary chair. He told me to-day, that if Louis XV. had died in the time of the regency, the whole French nation were determined to bring back the King of Spain to be King of France, so zealous were they for preserving the line of succession. This evening Mr Hume not quite so well, and goes to bed at a more early hour than he used to do.

Ferry bridge, Sunday, 28th.

Mr Hume much better this morning. He told me, that the French nation had no great opinion of Cardinal Fleury; that the English had extolled him, in opposition to their own minister Sir Robert Walpole; but that Fleury was a little genius, and a cheat. Lord Marischal acquainted Mr Hume with a piece of knavery which his lordship said nobody but a Frenchman and a priest could have been guilty of. The French ambassador at Madrid came to Lord Marischal one day, and told him, that he had a letter from the French minister at Petersburgh, acquainting him that General Keith was not pleased with his situation in Russia, and wished to return to the Spanish service, (where he had formerly been;) that it would be proper for Lord Marischal to apply to the court of Spain. Lord Marischal said nothing could be more agreeable to him than to have his brother in the same country with him; but that, as he had heard nothing from himself, he could not make any application in his name. The French minister still urged him to write to the Spanish minister, but in vain. When the brothers met, several years after, they explained this matter. Keith had never any intention of coming into the Spanish service again; and if Lord Marischal had applied to the court of Spain, measures were taken to intercept the letter, and send it to the court of Russia. General Keith, who commanded the Russian army in the field against the Swedes, would have been arrested, and sent to Siberia; and the moment he had left the army, the Swedes were to attack the Russians. Mr Hume told me, talking of Fleury, that Monsieur Trudent, who was his eleve, acquainted him with an anecdote of that minister, and the late French king, which he, Mr Hume, believes Tradent had never ventured to tell to any body but him; and he (David) had never told it to any body but me. Now, since Fleury, Trudent, and Lewis, are all dead, it may be told. Trudent took the liberty of observing to Fleury, that the king should be advised to apply a little more to business, and take some charge of his own affairs. Fleury, the first time Trudent spoke to him upon this subject, made him no answer; but upon his speaking again on the same subject, he told him, that he had entreated the king to be a man of business, and assured him that the French did not like an inactive prince; that in former times, there had been a race of indolent princes who did nothing at all, and were called *Les Rois Faineants*; that one of them had been put into a convent. The king made no reply; but some time afterwards, when Fleury resumed the subject, the king asked him, whether or no the prince that was put into the convent had a good pension allowed him?

Mr Hume this day told me, that he had bought a piece of ground; and when I seemed surprised that I had never heard of it, he said it was in the New Church-yard, on the Calton Hill, for a burying-place; that he meant to have a small monument erected, not to exceed in expense one hundred pounds; that the inscription should be

DAVID HUME.

I desired him to change the discourse. He did so; but seemed surprised at my uneasiness, which he said was very nonsensical. I think he is gaining ground; but he laughs at me, and says it is impossible; that the year (76), sooner or later, he takes his departure. He is willing to go to Bath, or travel during the summer through England, and return to Scotland to die at home; but that Sir John Pringle, and the whole faculty, would find it very difficult to boat him, (formerly an usual phrase in Scotland for going abroad, that is, out of the island, for health.) This day we travelled by his desire three stages, and arrived with great ease at Grantham.

Monday, 29th.

From the treatment Mr Hume met with in France, he recurred to a subject not unfrequent with him – that is, the design to ruin him as an author, by the people that were ministers, at the first publication of his History, and called themselves Whigs, who, he said, were determined not to suffer truth to be told in Britain. Amongst many instances of this, he told me one which was new to me. The Duke of Bedford, (who afterwards conceived a great affection for Mr Hume,) by the suggestions of some of his party friends, ordered his son, Lord Tavistock, not to read Mr Hume's History of England; but the young man was prevailed upon by one of his companions (Mr Crawford of Errol) to disobey the command. He read the History, and was extremely pleased with it.

Mr Hume told me, that the Duke de Choiseul, at the time Lord Hertford was in France, expressed the greatest inclination for peace, and a good correspondence between France and Britain. He assured Lord Hertford, that if the court of Britain would relinquish Falkland Island, he would undertake to procure from the court of Spain the payment of the Manilla ransom. Lord Hertford communicated the proposal to Mr Grenville, who slighted it. Lord Hertford told Mr Hume the same day an extraordinary instance of the violence of faction. Towards the end of Queen Anne's reign, when the Whig ministers were turned out of all their places at home, and the Duke of Marlborough still continued in the command of the army abroad, the discarded ministers met and wrote a letter, which was signed by Lord Somers, Lord Townshend, Lord Sunderland, and Sir Robert Walpole, desiring the duke to bring over the troops he could depend on, and that they would seize the queen's person, and proclaim the Elector of Hanover Regent. The Duke of Marlborough answered the letter, and said it was madness to think of such a thing. Mr Horace Walpole, Sir R. Walpole's youngest son, confirmed the truth of this anecdote, which he had heard his father repeat often and often; and Mr Walpole allowed Mr Hume to quote him as his authority, and make what use he pleased of it. When George I. came to England, he hesitated whether to make a Whig or a Tory administration, but the German minister, Bernstorf, determined him to take the side of the Whigs, who had made a purse of thirty thousand guineas, and given it to this German. George I. was of a moderate and gentle temper. – He regretted all his life, that he had given way to the violence of the Whigs in the beginning of his reign. Whenever any difficulty occurred in parliament, he used to blame the impeachment of the Tories, – "Ce diable de impeachment," as he called it.

The Whigs, in the end of Queen Anne's reign, bribed the Emperor's ministers, not to consent to the peace, and to send over Prince Eugene with proposals to continue the war.

This anecdote from Lord Bath. Another anecdote Mr Hume mentioned, but distrusted the authority, for it was David Mallet who told Mr Hume, that he had evidence in his custody of a design to assassinate Lord Oxford.

Prior,[3] after the accession, was reduced to such poverty by the persecution he met with, that he was obliged to publish his works by subscription. Lord Bathurst told Mr Hume, that he was with Prior reading the pieces that were to be published, and he thought there was not enough to make two small volumes. He asked Prior if he had no more poems? He said, No more that he thought good enough. – 'What is that?' said Bathurst, pointing to a roll of paper, 'A trifle,' said Prior, 'that I wrote in three weeks, not worthy of your attention or that of the public.' Lord Bathurst desired to see it. This neglected piece was *Alma*.

Tuesday, 30th.

Last night, when Mr Hume was going to bed, he complained of cold. One part of his malady had been a continual heat, so that he could not endure a soft or warm bed, and lay in the night with a single sheet upon him; he desired to have an additional covering. Colin observed to him, that he thought it a good symptom. Mr Hume said he thought so too, for it was a good thing to be like other people. This morning he is wonderfully well, which is visible in his countenance and colour, and even the firmness of his step. Talking of the state of the nation, which he continually laments, he mentioned an anecdote of the former war. He was at Turin with General Sinclair, after the peace of Aix-la-Chapelle, and, considering the superiority which the French arms had gained, he could not conceive why France granted such good terms to Britain. He desired General Sinclair to touch upon that subject with the King of Sardinia. That prince, who was very familiar with the General, said he was at a loss to give any account of that matter; but, many years after, when Mr Hume was minister in France, and lived in great intimacy with Monsieur Puysieux, Secretary of State, who had negotiated the peace of Aix, Mr Hume asked him the reason of the conduct of France at that time? Puysieux told him, that it was the king's aversion to war; that he knew more of it than any man alive, for, the year before the peace, he was ordered by the king to propose pretty near the same terms. He remonstrated against making the offer; said that at least the proposal should come from England; and that there was always some advantage to be gained by receiving, rather than propounding terms. The king was impatient, and obliged Puysieux to write the letter, (which General Ligonier carried,) with those terms which next year were agreed to by the British court. Mr John Home said he knew that the King of France promoted the peace of Paris from the aversion he had to war; and the peace was made at a time when it seemed impossible for Britain to carry on a war of such extent, and retain her scattered conquests. Mr Hume mentioned another singular anecdote

---

[3] [Poet Matthew Prior (1664–1721); Alexander Pope said of Prior's "Alma" that he wished he had been its author.]

concerning the beginning of the last war. When a squadron of the English fleet attacked and took two French men of war, the Alcide and the Lys, Louis XV. was so averse to war, that he would have pocketed the insult; and Madame Pompadour said it was better to put up with the affront, than to go to war without any object but the point of honour. It is known, that neither the king, nor the ministers of England, wished for war. The French king abhorred the thought of war! – What then was the cause? Chiefly the fear of the popular clamour, and of the opposition in the Duke of Newcastles mind. Mr Hume thinks Lord North no great minister, but does not see a better; cannot give any reason for the incapacity and want of genius, civil and military, which marks this period. He looks upon the country as on the verge of decline. His fears seem rather too great, and things are not quite so bad as he apprehends; but certainly the first show of statesmen, generals, and admirals, is, without comparison, the worst that has been seen in this country. I said to Mr Hume, that I thought the great consideration to be acquired by speaking in Parliament, was the cause of that want of every other quality in men of rank: they do speak readily, but there are many orators who can neither judge nor act well.

Wednesday, 31st April.

Arrived in London, where we saw Sir John Pringle, who thought Mr Hume much better than he expected to see him, and in no immediate danger. We staid a few days in London, and then set out for Bath.

In travelling from London to Bath, we had occasion frequently to make our observations on the passengers whom we met, and on those who passed us, as every carriage continued to do. Nothing occurred worthy the writing down, except Mr David's plan of managing his kingdom, in case Ferguson and I had been princes of the adjacent states. He knew very well, he said, (having often disputed the point with us,) the great opinion we had of military virtues as essential to every state; that from these sentiments rooted in us, he was certain he would be attacked and interrupted in his projects of cultivating, improving, and civilizing mankind by the arts of peace; that he comforted himself with reflecting, that from our want of economy and order in our affairs, we should be continually in want of money; whilst he would have his finances in excellent condition, his magazines well filled, and naval stores in abundance; but that his final stroke of policy, upon which he depended, was to give one of us a large subsidy to fall upon the other, which would infallibly secure to him peace and quiet, and after a long war, would probably terminate in his being master of all the three kingdoms. At this sally, so like David's manner of playing with his friends, I fell into a fit of laughing, in which David joined; and the people that passed us certainly thought we were very merry travellers.

40
JAMES BOSWELL:
"AN ACCOUNT OF MY LAST
INTERVIEW WITH DAVID HUME"

James Boswell, "An Account of my Last Interview with David Hume, Esq.,"
July 7, 1776.
Complete; from *Boswell in Extremes 1776–1778*, ed. Charles McC. Weis and
Frederick A. Pottle, New York, McGraw-Hill, 1970, pp. 11–15.[1]

Born in Edinburgh, James Boswell (1740–1795) was educated at home and
later at the University of Edinburgh. In 1762 he passed his law examination
and from then on worked principally in the legal profession. It was also in 1762
that he began consistently keeping journal accounts of his daily activities and
conversations with famous people of the day, including Hume, – a task that
he continued until his death in 1795. Based largely on entries from his journal,
he published *An Account of Corsica* (1768), *The Journal of a Tour to the
Hebrides* (1785), and *The Life of Samuel Johnson* (1791) – the latter of which
is often hailed as one of the greatest biographies in English. The journals
themselves remained unpublished and cloaked in mystery until the early 20th
century when they and massive quantities of his other manuscripts were
discovered in two main caches. The first was at Malahide Castle, near Dublin,
home of one of Boswell's descendants. The second was at Fettercairn House,
near Aberdeen, home of a descendant of William Forbes – confidant to Boswell.
The journals contain accounts of two detailed visits to Hume, in 1762 and
1776.

On July 7, 1776, about eight weeks before Hume's death, Boswell paid a last
visit to Hume at his house in St Andrew's Square, eventually jotting down the
conversation in his journal. During his life Boswell dropped hints about the visit
and his record of it. In *The Journal of a Tour to the Hebrides* (1785) –
excerpted later in this collection – he states, "I have preserved some entertaining
and interesting memoirs of him, particularly when he knew himself to be
dying, which I may some time or other communicate to the world." In his *Life*

---

of Samuel Johnson (1791) – also excerpted in this collection – he writes, "I mentioned to Dr. Johnson, that David Hume's persisting in his infidelity, when he was dying, shocked me much." His most detailed revelation about the interview, though, appeared in an essay in the *London Magazine* under the pseudonym "The Hypochndriack":

> It appears to me that the fallacious prejudice which is too often entertained against Religion, is owning to its being considered only as a duty, not as a privilege, a comfort, an enjoyment; as also to dark and dismal views of it, erroneously given by men of gloomy or abjectly timorous minds. I myself visited a celebrated infidel when he was dying, and when I tried to raise the pleasing hope of a future state, he said, "You never see it but through the medium of Tartarus, or Phlegethon, or Hell." I concluded that he must in his early years have had the idea of Religion so associated with that of misery, that he was instigated to exert himself against it as an enemy, without ever having candidly examined if it might not be a friend. A friend he would have found it. But vanity, as a fascinating mistress, seized upon his fondness, and never quitted her dominion over him. [*London Magazine*, "On Religion," March 1782, No. 54]

The 1776 interview itself was finally published in 1931, based on the journal manuscript discovered at Malahide Castle.[2] A second copy of the journal – written in the hand of Boswell's clerk – was discovered at Fettercairn House, which contains some corrections by Boswell and a later addition of 300 words to the interview with Hume that is not included in the Malahide Castle copy. This was eventually published in 1970. The interview is the most candid and detailed account of Hume's personal views on atheism and life after death that we have on record. Boswell persistently questions Hume about the plausibility of an afterlife, and Hume, sticking to his guns, rejects the idea as an unreasonable fancy. Like William Cullen's and Adam Smith's accounts of Hume's final days, contained in this collection, Boswell too notes Hume's cheerful mood, sharp mind, and lack of fear about his forthcoming death.

---

[2] *Private papers of James Boswell*, ed. Geoffrey Scott and Frederick A. Pottle, Mount Vernon, N.Y., W.E. Rudge, 1931, Vol. 12, pp. 227–232.

AN ACCOUNT OF MY LAST INTERVIEW WITH DAVID HUME, ESQ.

Partly recorded in my Journal, partly enlarged from my memory, 3 March
1777

On Sunday forenoon the 7 of July 1776, being too late for church, I went to see Mr. David Hume, who was returned from London and Bath, just adying. I found him alone, in a reclining posture in his drawing-room. He was lean, ghastly, and quite of an earthy appearance. He was dressed in a suit of grey cloth with white metal buttons, and a kind of scratch wig. He was quite different from the plump figure which he used to present. He had before him Dr. Campbell's *Philosophy of Rhetoric.* He seemed to be placid and even cheerful. He said he was just approaching to his end. I think these were his words. I know not how I contrived to get the subject of immortality introduced. He said he never had entertained any belief in religion since he began to read Locke and Clarke. I asked him if he was not religious when he was young. He said he was, and he used to read *The Whole Duty of Man*; that he made an abstract from the catalogue of vices at the end of it, and examined himself by this, leaving out murder and theft and such vices as he had no chance of committing, having no inclination to commit them. This, he said, was strange work; for instance, to try if, notwithstanding his excelling his schoolfellows, he had no pride or vanity. He smiled in ridicule of this as absurd and contrary to fixed principles and necessary consequences, not adverting that religious discipline does not mean to extinguish, but to moderate, the passions; and certainly an excess of pride or vanity is dangerous and generally hurtful. He then said flatly that the morality of every religion was bad, and, I really thought, was not jocular when he said that when he heard a man was religious, he concluded he was a rascal, though he had known some instances of very good men being religious. This was just an extravagant reverse of the common remark as to infidels.

I had a strong curiosity to be satisfied if he persisted in disbelieving a future state even when he had death before his eyes. I was persuaded from what he now said, and from his manner of saying it, that he did persist. I asked him if it was not possible that there might be a future state. He answered it was possible that a piece of coal put upon the fire would not burn; and he added that it was a most unreasonable fancy that we should exist for ever. That immortality, if it were at all, must be general; that a great proportion of the human race has hardly any intellectual qualities; that a great proportion dies in infancy before being possessed of reason; yet all these must be immortal; that a porter who gets drunk by ten o'clock with gin must be immortal; that the trash of every age must be preserved, and that new universes must be created to contain such infinite numbers. This appeared to me an unphilosophical objection, and I said, 'Mr. Hume, you know spirit does not take up space."

I may illustrate what he last said by mentioning that in a former conversation with me on this subject he used pretty much the same mode of reasoning, and urged that Wilkes and his mob must be immortal. One night last May as I was coming up King Street, Westminster, I met Wilkes, who carried me into Parliament Street to see a curious procession pass: the funeral of a lamplighter attended by some hundreds of his fraternity with torches. Wilkes, who either is, or affects to be, an infidel, was rattling away, "I think there's an end of that fellow. I think he won't rise again." I very calmly said to him, "You bring into my mind the strongest argument that ever I heard against a future state"; and then told him David Hume's objection that Wilkes and his mob must be immortal. It seemed to make a proper impression, for he grinned abashment, as a Negro grows whiter when he blushes. But to return to my last interview with Mr. Hume.

I asked him if the thought of annihilation never gave him any uneasiness. He said not the least; no more than the thought that he had not been, as Lucretius observes. "Well," said I, "Mr. Hume, I hope to triumph over you when I meet you in a future state; and remember you are not to pretend that you was joking with all this infidelity." "No, no," said he. "But I shall have been so long there before you come that it will be nothing new." In this style of good humour and levity did I conduct the conversation. Perhaps it was wrong on so awful a subject. But as nobody was present, I thought it could have no bad effect. I however felt a degree of horror, mixed with a sort of wild, strange, hurrying recollection of my excellent mother's pious instructions, of Dr. Johnson's noble lessons, and of my religious sentiments and affections during the course of my life. I was like a man in sudden danger eagerly seeking his defensive arms; and I could not but be assailed by momentary doubts while I had actually before me a man of such strong abilities and extensive inquiry dying in the persuasion of being annihilated. But I maintained my faith. I told him that I believed the Christian religion as I believed history. Said he: "You do not believe it as you believe the Revolution." "Yes," said I; "but the difference is that I am not so much interested in the truth of the Revolution; otherwise I should have anxious doubts concerning it. A man who is in love has doubts of the affection of his mistress, without cause." I mentioned Soame Jenyns's little book in defence of Christianity, which was just published but which I had not yet read. Mr. Hume said, "I am told there is nothing of his usual spirit in it."

He had once said to me, on a forenoon while the sun was shining bright, that he did not wish to be immortal. This was a most wonderful thought. The reason he gave was that he was very well in this state of being, and that the chances were very much against his being so well in another state; and he would rather not be more than be worse. I answered that it was reasonable to hope he would be better; that there would be a progressive improvement. I tried him at this interview with that topic, saying that a future state was surely a pleasing idea.

He said no, for that it was always seen through a gloomy medium; there was always a Phlegethon or a hell. "But," said I, "would it not be agreeable to have hopes of seeing our friends again?" and I mentioned three men lately deceased, for whom I knew he had a high value: Ambassador Keith, Lord Alemoor, and Baron Mure. He owned it would be agreeable, but added that none of them entertained such a notion. I believe he said, such a foolish, or such an absurd, notion; for he was indecently and impolitely positive in incredulity. "Yes," said I, "Lord Alemoor was a believer." David acknowledged that *he* had *some* belief.

I somehow or other brought Dr. Johnson's name into our conversation. I had often heard him speak of that great man in a very illiberal manner. He said upon this occasion, "Johnson should be pleased with my *History*." Nettled by Hume's frequent attacks upon my revered friend in former conversations, I told him now that Dr. Johnson did not allow him much credit; for he said, "Sir, the fellow is a Tory by chance." I am sorry that I mentioned this at such a time. I was off my guard; for the truth is that Mr. Hume's pleasantry was such that there was no solemnity in the scene; and death for the time did not seem dismal. It surprised me to find him talking of different matters with a tranquillity of mind and a clearness of head which few men possess at any time. Two particulars I remember: Smith's *Wealth of Nations,* which he commended much, and Monboddo's *Origin of Language*, which he treated contemptuously. I said, "If I were you, I should regret annihilation. Had I written such an admirable history, I should be sorry to leave it." He said, "I shall leave that history, of which you are pleased to speak so favourably, as perfect as I can." He said, too, that all the great abilities with which men had ever been endowed were relative to this world. He said he became a greater friend to the Stuart family as he advanced in studying for his history; and he hoped he had vindicated the two first of them so effectually that they would never again be attacked.

Mr. Lauder, his surgeon, came in for a little, and Mr. Mure, the Baron's son, for another small interval. He was, as far as I could judge, quite easy with both. He said he had no pain, but was wasting away. I left him with impressions which disturbed me for some time.

(ADDITIONS FROM MEMORY 22 JANUARY 1778.) Speaking of his singular notion that men of religion were generally bad men, he said, "One of the men" (or "The man" – I am not sure which) "of the greatest honour that I ever knew is my Lord Marischal, who is a downright atheist. I remember I once hinted something as if I believed in the being of a God, and he would not speak to me for a week." He said this with his usual grunting pleasantry, with that thick breath which fatness had rendered habitual to him, and that smile of simplicity which his good humour constantly produced.

When he spoke against Monboddo, I told him that Monboddo said to me that he believed the abusive criticism upon his book in *The Edinburgh*

Magazine and Review was written by Mr. Hume's direction. David seemed irritated, and said, "Does the *scoundrel*" (I am sure either *that* or "*rascal*") "say so?" He then told me that he had observed to one of the Faculty of Advocates that Monboddo was wrong in his observation [blank space] and gave as a proof the line in Milton. When the review came out, he found this very remark in it, and said to that advocate, "Oho! I have discovered you" – reminding him of the circumstance.

It was amazing to find him so keen in such a state. I must add one other circumstance which is material, as it shows that he perhaps was not without some hope of a future state, and that his spirits were supported by a consciousness (or at least a notion) that his conduct had been virtuous. He said, "If there were a future state, Mr. Boswell, I think I could give as good an account of my life as most people."

41
WILLIAM CULLEN:
LETTER TO JOHN HUNTER

William Cullen, Letter to John Hunter, September 17, 1776, in John Thomson, *An account of the life, lectures and writings of William Cullen*, Vol. 1, Edinburgh: Blackwood; London: Cadell, 1832, xvi, 668 p. Complete letter; from *An Account* (1832), Vol. 1, pp. 607–609.

Born in Hamilton, Lanarkshire, William Cullen (1710–1790) studied medicine at the University of Glasgow and was later appointed professor of medicine there. He was subsequently elected professor of chemistry at Edinburgh University and authored several works in the field of medicine. Cullen and Hume were acquainted as early as 1751 when Hume was a candidate for the chair of Moral Philosophy at the University of Glasgow. Hume's supporters included Cullen, Hercules Lindesay, and Gilbert Eliot. Adam Smith wrote the following to Cullen on this occasion:

> I should prefer David Hume to any man for a colleague; but I am afraid the public would not be of my opinion; and the interest of the society will oblige us to have some regard to the opinion of the public. If the event, however, we are afraid of should happen, we can see how the public receives it. From the particular knowledge I have of Mr Elliot's sentiments, I am pretty certain Mr Lindsay must have proposed it [i.e., Hume's candidacy] to him, not he to Lindsay. I am for ever obliged to you for your concern for my interest in that affair. [Adam Smith to William Cullen, Tuesday, November, 1751; in John Thomson's *Account*, 1832, Vol. 1, p. 606]

Hume wrote a letter to Cullen thanking him for his support (January 21, 1752). During his final illness, Cullen was one of Hume's physicians and shortly before the philosopher's death Cullen wrote a detailed letter to a friend

---

[2] [Thomson deleted the words "the Christian" in his transcription of the letter; see E.C. Mossner's *Life of David Hume* (1980), p. 601.]

[3] [i.e., John Home (1722–1808).]

regarding Hume's condition. The letter was first published in *An Account of the Life, Lectures and Writings of William Cullen* (1832), from which the following is taken. Cullen repeats the story of Hume's jocular debate with Charon, probably as he heard it from Adam Smith, but providing some details that Smith omits in his version in his "Letter ... to William Strahan" (1777). Describing the contents of Hume's will, Cullen explains why Hume did not want the stones for the Chirnside bridge to come from the Ninewells quarry. The editor of the *Account*, John Thomson, took liberties with his transcription, and at one spot altered the phrase "the Christian superstition" to simply "superstition". The following is from the 1832 and only edition of Thomson's *Account* of Cullen. The manuscript of the letter is contained in the Library of the Royal College of Surgeons of England, Hunter-Baillie Collection, Letterbook, 1, 140.

EDINBURGH, 17*th September* 1776.

MY DEAR FRIEND,

I was favoured with yours, by Mr Halhed, on Sunday last, and have answered some part of it by a gentleman whom I was otherwise obliged to write by; but as I was not certain how soon that might come to your hand, I did not answer your postscript; in doing which, if I can oblige, a part of the merit must be that of the information being early, and I therefore give it you as soon as I possibly could. You desire an account of Mr. Hume's last days, and I give it you with some pleasure, for, though I could not look upon him in his illness without much concern, yet the tranquillity and pleasantry which he constantly discovered, did even then give me satisfaction, and, now that the curtain is dropped, allows me indulge the less alloyed reflection. It was truly an example "des grands hommes qui sont morts en plaisantant;"[1] and to me, who have been so often shocked with the horrors of the superstitious on such occasions, the reflection on such a death is truly agreeable. For many weeks before his death, he was very sensible of his gradual decay, and his answer to inquiries after his health, was, several times, that he was going as fast as his enemies could wish, and as easily as his friends could desire. He was not, however, without a frequent recurrence of pain and uneasiness, but he passed most part of the day in his drawing-room, admitted the visits of his friends, and, with his usual spirit, conversed with them upon literature, politics, or whatever else was accidentally started. In conversation he seemed to be perfectly at ease, and to

---

[1] [In reference to the following: André François Deslandes (1690–1757), *Reflexions sur les grands hommes qui sont morts en plaisantant. Avec des poësies diverses*, A Rochefort, Chez Jaques Le Noir, 1714, 202 p.]

the last abounded with that pleasantry, and those curious and entertaining anecdotes, which ever distinguished him. This, however, I always considered rather as an effort to be agreeable, and he at length acknowledged that it became too much for his strength. For a few days before his death he became more averse to receive visits; speaking became more and more difficult for him; and, for twelve hours before his death, his speech failed altogether. His senses and judgment did not fail till the last hour of his life. He constantly discovered a strong sensibility to the attention and care of his friends, and, amidst great uneasiness and languor, never betrayed any peevishness or impatience. This is a general account of his last days, but a particular fact or two may perhaps convey to you a still better idea of them.

Not many days before his death a friend found him reading, and, upon inquiring what was the book, Mr Hume told him it was Lucian, and that he had just been reading the dialogue entitled Kataplous, in which Megapentes, arriving on the banks of the Styx, urges many pleas for being allowed to return for some time to the world. Mr Hume said the fancy had struck him to think what pleas he himself might offer upon such an occasion. He thought he might say that he had been very busily employed in making his countrymen wiser, and particularly in delivering them from the Christian[2] superstition, but that he had not yet completed that great work. This he at first thought might be sufficiently specious; but he soon reflected that Mercury would tell him it was idle to think of remaining now for that purpose, as it would be time enough to return for it two or three hundred years hence. In short, the excuse would not be sustained, and he must pass the river.

About a fortnight before his death, he added a codicil to his will, in which he fully discovered his attention to his friends, as well as his own pleasantry. What little wine he himself drank was generally port, a wine to which his friend the poet[3] had ever declared the strongest aversion. David bequeaths to his friend John one bottle of port; and, upon condition of his drinking this, even at two downsittings, bestows upon him twelve dozen of his best claret. He pleasantly adds, that this subject of wine was the only one upon which they had ever differed. In the codicil there are several other strokes of raillery and pleasantry, highly expressive of the cheerfulness which he then enjoyed. He even turned his attention to some of the simple amusements with which he had been formerly pleased. In the neighbourhood of his brother's house in Berwickshire is a brook, by which the access is in time of floods is frequently interrupted. Mr Hume bequeaths £100 for building a bridge over this brook, but upon the express condition that none of the stones for that purpose shall be taken from a quarry in the neighbourhood, which forms part of a romantic scene in which in his earlier days Mr Hume took particular delight; otherwise the money to go to the poor of the parish.

These are a few particulars, which may perhaps appear trifling, but to me no particulars seem trifling that relate to so great a man. It is perhaps from trifles that we can best distinguish the tranquillity and cheerfulness of the philosopher, at a time when the most part of mankind are under disquiet, anxiety, and sometimes even horror. I consider the sacrifice of the Cock as a more certain evidence of the tranquillity of Socrates, than his Discourse on Immortality.[4]

I had gone so far when I was called to the country, and I have returned only so long before the post as to say that I am most affectionately yours,
WILLIAM CULLEN.

---

[4] [Upon his death, Socrates said, "Crito, I owe a cock to Asclepius; will you remember to pay the debt?" Plato, *Phaedo*.]

42
ADAM SMITH:
"LETTER TO WILLIAM STRAHAN"

Adam Smith, "Letter from Adam Smith, LL.D. to William Strahan, Esq."
Complete letter; *The life of David Hume, Esq. written by himself.* London:
printed for W. Strahan; and T. Cadell, 1777, [4], iv, 62 p.

Born in Kirkcaldy Fife, Scotland, Adam Smith (1723–1790) attended
Glasgow University, where he was a student of Francis Hutcheson, and
later Balliol College, Oxford. After briefly delivering public lectures on rhetoric
in Edinburgh, Smith was appointed professor of Logic at Glasgow in 1751, and
a year later was transferred to the chair of moral philosophy. Taking a lucrative
job as a tutor, he resigned this position in 1763, which was subsequently filled
by Thomas Reid. Smith's two principal works are his *Theory of Moral
Sentiments* (1759) and *Inquiry into the Nature and Causes of the Wealth of
Nations* (1776), both of which contain comments on Hume and are excerpted
in *Early Responses to Hume's Moral Theory* (1999) and *Early Responses to
Hume's History* (2002). Smith probably met Hume around 1749 while in
Edinburgh, and remained one of his closest friends. He shared many of Hume's
views, as is reflected in the following:

> [Smith] is a very unprejudiced and good man I see him every week at least
> once, and we are upon a very friendly footing together; he was an intimate
> friend of the late David Hume and has the same principles. [François Xavier
> Swediauer to Jeremey Bentham, September 14, 1784][1]

Smith is best known in Hume scholarship for his "Letter... to William
Strahan," which was first published along with Hume's "My Own Life" under
the title *The Life of David Hume.* The letter covers the last four months of
Hume's life, relating the progress of his illness and his cheerful state of mind
throughout his decline.

---

[1] The Correspondence of Jeremy Bentham, Volume 3 (London: University of London,
The Athlone Press, 1971).

In a letter to Hume during the last week of his life, Smith suggests the possibility of writing the "Letter ... to William Strahan" as a supplement to "My Own Life":

> If you will give me leave I will add a few lines to your account of your own life, giving some account in my own name of your behaviour in this illness, if, contrary to my own hopes, it should prove your last. Some conversations we had lately together, particularly that concerning your want of an excuse to make to Charon, the excuse you at last thought of, and the very bad reception which Charon was likely to give it, would, I imagine, make no disagreeable part of the history. You have in a declining state of health, under an exhausting disease, for more than two years together now looked at the approach of death with a steady cheerfulness such as very few men have been able to maintain for a few hours, tho' otherwise in the most perfect Health. [Smith to Hume, August 22, 1776, in *Life of Adam Smith*, John Rea, pp. 300–301.]

To this Hume replied, "You are too good in thinking any trifles that concern me are so much worth your attention, but I give you entire liberty to make what Additions you please to the account of my Life." Two days later, on August 25, Hume died. In October Smith sent a draft of his *Letter* to Hume's brother, John Home, to advise whether there should be "anything either added to it or taken from it." Smith noted further that there "is a propriety in addressing it as a letter to Mr. Strahan, to whom he has left the care of his works" (Rae, p. 304). Home replied generally approving of Smith's *Letter*, but suggested a minor change which Smith made. Shortly after, the manuscript was sent to Hume's long-time friend and printer, William Strahan. In November, Strahan wrote Smith proposing that "My Own Life" and Smith's "Letter" be published along with a series of letters that Hume wrote to Strahan over the years. At least part of Strahan's concern was to increase the size of the publication. To this Smith replied that "many of Mr. Hume's letters would do him great honour," but that Hume's dying wishes should be honoured, in particular "to burn all his Papers except the *Dialogues* and the account of his own life." Smith thus recommended publishing "My Own Life" as a short pamphlet, rather than a large book. The work finally appeared in March 1777.

Reactions to Smith's "Letter" in the review journals were on the whole favourable (see reviews of Hume's "My Own Life" in this collection). However, attitudes towards it quickly shifted, and Smith's "Letter" is harshly attacked in no less than 30 items that appear in this collection. Two comments in Smith's letter sparked this reaction. The first is the story of Hume making excuses to Charon; readers found it shocking that Hume the infidel not only had no fears about dying, but even joked about his death. It was assumed that only Christian faith and the prospect of an afterlife could provide tranquillity in the face of death. Second, Smith concludes stating that Hume approached "as nearly to the idea of a perfectly wise and virtuous man, as perhaps the nature of human frailty will permit." The idea that a religious infidel would be a model of virtue was equally unthinkable. Virtuous conduct, it was assumed, requires belief in divine judgment in the afterlife. Ten years after the appearance of Smith's *Letter* he commented that "A single, and as I thought, a very harmless Sheet of paper which I happened to write concerning the death of our late friend, Mr. Hume, brought upon me ten times more abuse than the very violent attack I had made upon the whole commercial system of Great Britain" (William Scott, *Adam Smith as Student and Professor*, p. 283). *The Life of David Hume* containing Smith's "Letter" was published twice more in 1777, and again in 1778.

LETTER

FROM

ADAM SMITH, LL.D.

TO

WILLIAM STRAHAN, Esq.

———

Kirkaldy, Fifeshire, Nov. 9. 1776

DEAR SIR,

It is with a real, though a very melancholy pleasure, that I sit down to give you some account of the behaviour of our late excellent friend, Mr. Hume, during his last illness.

Though, in his own judgment, his disease was mortal and incurable, yet he allowed himself to be prevailed upon, by the entreaty of his friends, to try what might be the effects of a long journey. A few days before he set out, he wrote that account of his own life, which, together with his other papers, he has left to your care. My account, therefore, shall begin where his ends.

He set out for London towards the end of April, and at Morpeth met with Mr. John Home and myself, who had both come down from London on purpose to see him, expecting to have found him at Edinburgh. Mr. Home returned with him, and attended him during the whole of his stay in England, with that care and attention which might be expected from a temper so perfectly friendly and affectionate. As I had written to my mother that she might expect me in Scotland, I was under the necessity of continuing my journey. His disease seemed to yield to exercise and change of air, and when he arrived in London, he was apparently in much better health than when he left Edinburgh. He was advised to go to Bath to drink the waters, which appeared for some time to have so good an effect upon him, that even he himself began to entertain, what he was not apt to do, a better opinion of his own health. His symptoms, however, soon returned with their usual violence, and from that moment he gave up all thoughts of recovery, but submitted with the utmost cheerfulness, and the most perfect complacency and resignation. Upon his return to Edinburgh, though he found himself much weaker, yet his cheerfulness never abated, and he continued to divert himself, as usual, with correcting his own works for a new edition, with reading books of amusement, with the conversation of his friends; and, sometimes in the evening, with a party at his favourite game of whist. His cheerfulness was so great, and his conversation and amusements run so much in their usual strain, that, notwithstanding all bad symptoms, many people could not believe he was dying. "I shall tell your friend, Colonel Edmondstone," said Doctor Dundas to him one day, "that I left you much better, and in a fair way of recovery." "Doctor," said he, "as I believe you would not chuse to tell any thing but the truth, you had better tell him, that I am dying as fast as my enemies, if I have any, could wish, and as easily and cheerfully as my best friends could desire." Colonel Edmondstone soon afterwards came to see him, and take leave of him; and on his way home, he could not forbear writing him a letter bidding him once more an eternal adieu, and applying to him, as to a dying man, the beautiful French verses in which the Abbé Chaulieu, in expectation of his own death, laments his approaching separation from his friend, the Marquis de la Fare. Mr. Hume's magnanimity and firmness were such, that his most affectionate friends knew, that they hazarded nothing in talking or writing to him as to a dying man, and that so far from being hurt by this frankness, he was rather pleased and flattered by it. I happened to come into his room while he was reading this letter, which he had just received, and which he immediately showed me. I told him, that though I was sensible how very much he was weakened, and that appearances were in many respects very bad, yet his cheerfulness was still so great, the spirit of life seemed still to be so very strong in him, that I could not help entertaining some faint hopes. He answered, "Your hopes are groundless. An habitual diarrhœa of more than a year's standing, would be a very bad disease at any age: at my age it is a mortal one. When I lie down in the evening, I feel myself weaker than when I rose in the morning; and when I rise in the morning, weaker than when I lay down in the evening. I am sensible, besides, that some of my vital parts are affected, so that I must soon die." "Well," said I, "if it must be so, you have at least the satisfaction of leaving all your friends, your brother's family in particular, in great prosperity." He said that he felt that satisfaction so sensibly, that when he was reading a few days before, Lucian's Dialogues of the Dead, among all the excuses which are alleged to Charon for not entering readily into his boat, he could not find one that fitted him; he had no house to finish, he had no daughter to provide for, he had no enemies upon whom he wished to revenge himself. "I could not well imagine," said he, "what excuse I could make to Charon in order to obtain a little delay. I have done every thing of consequence which I ever meant to do, and I could at no time expect to leave my relations and friends in a better situation than that in which I am now likely to leave them; I, therefore, have all reason to die contented." He then diverted himself with inventing several jocular excuses, which he supposed he might make to Charon, and with imagining the very surly answers which it might suit the character of Charon to return to them. "Upon further consideration" said he, "I thought I might say to him, 'Good Charon, I have been correcting my works for a new edition. Allow me a little time, that I may see how the Public receives the alterations.' But Charon would answer, 'When you have seen the effect of these, you will be for making other alterations. There will be no end of such excuses; so, honest friend, please step into the boat.' But I might still urge, 'Have a little patience, good Charon, I have been endeavouring to open the eyes of the public. If I live a few years longer, I may have the satisfaction of seeing the downfal of some of the prevailing systems of superstition.' But Charon would then lose all temper and decency. 'You loitering rogue, that will not happen these many hundred years. Do you fancy I will grant you a lease for so long a term? Get into the boat this instant, you lazy loitering rogue.'"

But, though Mr. Hume always talked of his approaching dissolution with great cheerfulness, he never affected to make any parade of his magnanimity. He never mentioned the subject but when the conversation naturally led to it, and never dwelt longer upon it than the course of the conversation happened to require: it was a subject indeed which occurred pretty frequently, in consequence of the inquiries which his friends, who came to see him, naturally made concerning the state of his health. The conversation which I mentioned above, and which passed on Thursday the 8th of August, was the last, except one, that I ever had with him. He had now become so very weak, that the company of his most intimate friends fatigued him; for his cheerfulness was still so great, his complaisance and social disposition were still so entire, that when any friend was with him, he could not help talking more, and with greater exertion, than suited the weakness of his body. At his own desire, therefore, I agreed to leave Edinburgh, where I was staying partly upon his account, and returned to my mother's house here, at Kirkaldy, upon condition that he would send for me whenever he wished to see me; the physician who saw him most frequently, Doctor Black, undertaking, in the mean time, to write me occasionally an account of the state of his health.

On the 22nd of August, the Doctor wrote me the following letter:

"Since my last, Mr. Hume has passed his time pretty easily, but is much weaker. He sits up, goes down stairs once a day, and amuses himself with reading, but seldom sees any body. He finds that even the conversation of his most intimate friends fatigues and oppresses him; and it is happy that he does not need it, for he is quite free from anxiety, impatience, or low spirits, and passes his time very well with the assistance of amusing books."

I received the day after a letter from Mr. Hume himself, of which the following is an extract.

Edinburgh, 23rd august, 1776.

"MY DEAREST FRIEND,

I am obliged to make use of my nephew's hand in writing to you, as I do not rise to-day....[2]

I go very fast to decline, and last night had a small fever, which I hoped might put a quicker period to this tedious illness, but unluckily it has, in a great measure, gone off. I cannot submit to your coming over here on my account, as it is possible for me to see you so small a part of the day, but Doctor Black can better inform you concerning the degree of strength which may from time to time remain with me. Adieu, &c."

Three days after I received the following letter from Doctor Black.

Edinburgh, Monday, 26th August, 1776.

"DEAR SIR,

Yesterday about four o'clock afternoon, Mr. Hume expired. The near approach of his death became evident in the night between Thursday and Friday, when his disease became excessive, and soon weakened him so much, that he could no longer rise out of his bed. He continued to the last perfectly sensible, and free from much pain or feelings of distress. He never dropped the smallest expression of impatience; but when he had occasion to speak to the people about him, always did it with affection and tenderness. I thought it improper to write to bring you over, especially as I heard that he had dictated a letter to you desiring you not to come. When he became very weak, it cost him an effort to speak, and he died in such a happy composure of mind, that nothing could exceed it."

Thus died our most excellent, and never to be forgotten friend; concerning whose philosophical opinions men will, no doubt, judge variously, every one approving, or condemning them, according as they happen to coincide or

---

[2] [Smith omits the following two paragraphs from this letter: "There is No Man in whom I have a greater Confidence than Mr Strahan, yet have I left the property of that Manuscript to my Nephew David in case by any accident it should not be published within three years after my decease. The only accident I could forsee, was one to Mr Strahans Life, and without this clause My Nephew would have had no right to publish it. Be so good as to inform Mr Strahan of this Circumstance. I You are too good in thinking any trifles that concern me are so much worth your attention, but I give you entire liberty to make what Additions you please to the account of my Life."]

disagree with his own; but concerning whose character and conduct there can scarce be a difference of opinion. His temper, indeed, seemed to be more happily balanced, if I may be allowed such an expression, than that perhaps of any other man I have ever known. Even in the lowest state of his fortune, his great and necessary frugality never hindered him from exercising, upon proper occasions, acts both of charity and generosity. It was a frugality founded, not upon avarice, but upon the love of independency. The extreme gentleness of his nature never weakened either the firmness of his mind, or the steadiness of his resolutions. His constant pleasantry was the genuine effusion of good-nature and good-humour, tempered with delicacy and modesty, and without even the slightest tincture of malignity, so frequently the disagreeable source of what is called wit in other men. It never was the meaning of his raillery to mortify; and therefore, far from offending, it seldom failed to please and delight, even those who were the objects of it. To his friends, who were frequently the objects of it, there was not perhaps any one of all his great and amiable qualities, which contributed more to endear his conversation. And that gaiety of temper, so agreeable in society, but which is so often accompanied with frivolous and superficial qualities, was in him certainly attended with the most severe application, the most extensive learning, the greatest depth of thought, and a capacity in every respect the most comprehensive. Upon the whole, I have always considered him, both in his lifetime and since his death, as approaching as nearly to the idea of a perfectly wise and virtuous man, as perhaps the nature of human frailty will permit.

I ever am, dear Sir,

Most affectionately your's,

ADAM SMITH.

43
SAMUEL JACKSON PRATT:
SUPPLEMENT TO THE
LIFE OF DAVID HUME

[Samuel Jackson Pratt], *Supplement to the life of David Hume, Esq. containing genuine anecdotes, and a circumstantial account of his death and funeral.* London: printed for J. Bew, 1777, 64 p.[1]
Complete; from 1777 edition.

Born in St Ives, Huntingdonshire, England, Samuel Jackson Pratt (1749–1814) was ordained in the Church of England and served as a cleric for a short time. Abandoning that career, he worked as an actor, bookseller, fortune teller, and ultimately as a prolific miscellaneous writer, with several of his works appearing under the pseudonym "Courtney Melmoth." In 1777, while still a young man in his twenties, he composed two works relating to Hume's recent death: *An Apology for the Life and Writings of David Hume*, and *A Supplement to the Life of David Hume*. Pratt apparently had some personal acquaintance with Hume. In the Introduction to his *Sublime and Beautiful of Scripture* (1777), he indicates that in the Winter of 1775/6 Hume attended a public reading of portions of the manuscript of that work:

These miscellaneous remarks were written in the animated moments of feeling, when their author was destined to holy orders, and while the impression, made by each passage, was yet glowing on the imagination, and the heart.

---

[1] Title page: SUPPLEMENT | TO THE | LIFE | OF | DAVID HUME, Esq. | CONTAINING | GENUINE ANECDOTES, | AND A CIRCUMSTANTIAL ACCOUNT | OF HIS | DEATH and FUNERAL. | TO WHICH IS ADDED, | A CERTIFIED COPY OF HIS | LAST WILL and TESTAMENT. | Illum aget penna metuente solvi | Fama superstes. Hor. | LONDON, | PRINTED FOR J. BEW, PATER-NOSTER-ROW. | M DCC LXXVII. [page break] Entered in Stationer's Hall, according to Act of Parliament. | It is requested of Printers of News-Papers, to be cautious of injuring the Proprietor of this little Performance.

They have now been in his possession, or in that of his literary friends, for some years; in the course of which, they have been handed about, with the most flattering attention, from one person to another, equally eminent for the justice of their criticisms, and the delicacy of their taste. In the last winter, part of them were delivered, publicly, at Edinburgh, before several of the most distinguished literary characters, not only of Scotland, but of Europe. Amongst these, might be named, a Hume, a Kames, a Robertson, a Ferguson, and a Blair. [*The Sublime and Beautiful of Scripture*, London, J. Murray, 1777, p. vii]

Also, Pratt appears to have worked as a bookseller in Bath during Hume's visit there in April of 1776; in view of the details that Pratt provides in his *Supplement* about the visit, it seems at least probable that they interacted there.

His *Supplement to the Life of David Hume*, which appeared in mid May 1777[2] – a month after the *Apology* – is a chronologically-arranged collection of stories about Hume's life and death. The principal anecdotes he relates are these: a conspiracy among booksellers that adversely affected the sale of the first published volume of Hume's *History*; his relation with Jardine; his agreement to purchase candles from a local vendor; his farewell dinner; public concern during his final days; disputes among doctors about the cause of his illness and their interest in conducting an autopsy; Hume's funeral; and public fascination with Hume's grave site. Although some of the anecdotes may have been published elsewhere, others appear to be original, based on Pratt's acquaintance with Hume or Hume's friends. In addition to biographical data, the pamphlet includes Hume's will and the lengthy footnote from the 1757 second volume of Hume's *History*, which Hume later deleted. The three leading review journals of the time dismissed Pratt's *Supplement* as insignificant, the complete reviews of these are as follows:

We observe nothing very material in this publication. [*Monthly Review*, June 1777, Vol. 56 p. 482]

The contents of the Supplement are a few anecdotes, and a copy of Mr. Hume's last will. [*Critical Review*, July 1777, Vol. 44 p. 79]

Containing a copy of Mr. Hume's will, with a few anecdotes of no material consequence. [*London Review*, December 1777, Vol. 6, p. 529]

---

[2] The Supplement was announced in the *London Chronicle* May 10–13, 1777, Vol. 41, No. 3198, p. 455.

Though more verbose, *Gentleman's Magazine* was equally dismissive; the complete review is as follows:

Whether this writer be a friend or an enemy to Mr. Hume we cannot discover so easily as that he is a foe professed to "the *mercenary* Mason", (the polite appellation which he gives Mr. Gray's executor,) going out of his way to abuse him in a long note evidently dictated by a certain Scotch bookseller, who loses no opportunity of adding scurrility to piracy. The anecdote of Mr H.s "stumbling in the dark," at Dr. Jardine's, having been frequently retailed, little new is to be found in these meagre pages, save that "his *flowery* rival in historical fame," Dr. Robertson, once "preferred the *turtle* of my Lord Advocate to the *mutton* of David Hume;" that Mr. H. "left verbally to Mr. Home the poet *one* bottle of port (knowing he disliked it) and ten dozen of claret; that Mr. H. by his own desire, was buried in the Calton church-yard, *in a rock wherein never man had been laid;* {[Footnote:] For this gloss, however, the present writer, not Mr. Hume, we suppose, is accountable. In another place our author, in the true Heathenish style, calls this "a spot for depositing his ashes," which might lead to an idea, that, as Mr. H. died, he had also been buried, like a Heathen.} and that his grave was watched and lighted eight nights for fear of insult." By his will it appears that he devised about 10,000l. all of his own acquiring, to his relations and friends; among them 200l. to M. D'Alembert, and to Dr. Adam Smith (with all his MSS. and full power over tem, the following excepted) the like sum, "to be paid immediately *after* the publication of his Dialogues on Natural Religion," which alone are expressly desired to be published. There are probably the famous tracts in defence of suicide, adultery, &c. whose publication, if we are rightly informed, authority has hitherto prevented; and if so, however free from scruples of his own, Dr. S. seems likely to lose the advantage of his bequest. Without any breach of Christian charity, and though Mr. Melmoth, no doubt, is ready to *apologize* for them, most of our readers, we fancy, will concur with us in hoping that this devise may never take place. [*Gentleman's Magazine*, July 1777, Vol. 47 p. 338]

In spite of the negative reviews, for the modern reader the *Supplement* is important since it is now the earliest known source of several anecdotes it contains. In 1788 Pratt's *Supplement* and *Apology* were republished together in a slightly altered form as *Curious Particulars and Genuine Anecdotes* (see editor's introduction to Pratt's *Apology* in this collection). A "new edition" of the *Supplement* also appeared in 1789. The following is from the 1777 edition.

S U P P L E M E N T

T O   T H E

L   I   F   E

O F

DAVID HUME, Esq.

CONTAINING

GENUINE ANECDOTES,

AND A CIRCUMSTANTIAL ACCOUNT

OF HIS

DEATH AND FUNERAL.

TO WHICH IS ADDED,

A CERTIFIED COPY OF HIS

LAST WILL AND TESTAMENT.

Illum aget penna metuente folvi
Fama fuperftes.   Hor.

L O N D O N,

PRINTED FOR J. BEW, PATER-NOSTER-ROW,

M DCC LXXVII.

—

SUPPLEMENT
TO THE
LIFE
OF
DAVID HUME, Esq.

There can be no stronger proof of the high estimation in which Mr. Hume was held, and of his being considered as an extraordinary character, than the eager, yet, perhaps, idle curiosity, which the public entertained to learn the most minute circumstances respecting his exit.

As sincere admirers of Mr. Hume, in the Historian, the Philosopher, and the Man; we felt much regret in hearing announced to the public, "The Life of David Hume Esq; written by Himself." It is an undertaking which we hesitate not to pronounce impossible to be executed with propriety: egotism is disgusting; vanity intolerable; and a just estimation of one's self, the most difficult thing in life.

Upon reading this performance, however, which has been dished out into a pamphlet, we find that it only incurs a general charge of insipidity, perhaps in some articles of injustice. Mr. Hume's natural temper disposed him to feel, with exquisite sensibility, every thing which affected his literary fame; and, notwithstanding his boasted equanimity, philosophy did not shield him from the excessive chagrin which he felt from those arrows, which envy and Prejudice darted at his reputation. Anxiety about his difference with the whimsical Rousseau extracted from him a personal, but complete justification. The illiberal criticisms which Mr. Gray[3] threw out against him, in his Epistolary

---

[3] Perhaps the mercenary Mason is more deserving of this censure than Mr. Gray. In order to swell his volume, and to fill his pockets, the former has published a loose and desultory Correspondence, which the latter never dremt would see the light, and would have reprobated could he ever have conceived the idea of his worst papers being put to the ungenerous and ungrateful use. – Nevertheless, in return to a benefactor, who conferred essential favours upon him, Mr. Mason has, as far as he was able, sacrificed his patron's reputation at the sordid alter of Plutus. The posthumous Poetical Pieces of Mr. Gray, though infinitely valuable, are few in number, and were not likely to answer the interested purposes of the hungry Editor by much emolument. This gentleman, therefore, resolving to establish a literary property or estate, by the name and writings of another, which he honestly acquaints us he was unable to perform by his own, has given to the world, with little labour, a large but meagre Quarto, containing some puerile letters, superior, however, to the Editor's notes, with which they are garnished. And by entitling these "The Poems of Mr. Gray," led the public to buy up a large impression before the deception was discovered. Thus has the ingenuous Mason bartered the high poetical and literary reputation of a worthy man who confided in him, for money.

Quid non mortalia pectora coges, Auri sacra fames?

Correspondence, gave him much concern. He saw, with mortification, the laurel wreath which Oxford weaved to cover the bald reputation of Beattie, *his antagonist, not his rival.* And such was the antipathy that subsisted between him and Mr. Tytler, the author of the Vindication of Mary Queen of Scots; that not satisfied with a most acrimonious note,[4] which he has published in the last edition of his History, he would not even sit in company with him, and the appearance of the one effected the instantaneous withdrawing of the other.

Mr. Hume, in the History of his Life, has not informed us of his having stood candidate for the Professorship of Moral Philosophy, in the University of Edinburgh; of the opposition which the Scots clergy excited to his pretensions; nor of the enquiry which was moved for in the venerable assembly of the Church of Scotland, respecting the principles inculcated in his Writings; and of the censures proposed to be inflicted on him as the author of Heretical Doctrines.

He has observed in the nineteenth page of his Life, that his History of Great Britain met at first with an indifferent reception. But with respect to this, Mr. Hume himself was mistaken. The first edition of the History of Great Britain, for the reigns of James the First and Charles the First, was printed at Edinburgh, A.D. 1754, for *Hamilton, Balfour and Neil.* Hamilton, upon his expectations from this book, took a shop, and settled in London. He applied to the London booksellers to take copies of the History from him, but none of them would deal with an *interloper.* Hamilton, sadly distressed, has recourse to *his friend,* Mr. Millar; Millar *obliges him* by taking fifty copies: but when gentlemen, in his well-frequented shop, asked for the book, "Pho (says Millar generously) it is incomplete, another volume is coming out soon. You are welcome to the use of this in the mean time." Thus did Millar circulate the fifty copies among some hundred readers, without selling one, And by this ingenious device attained his favourite purpose, of getting Hamilton to sell him his right in the copy for a trifle, as being an insignificant performance.

---

[4] This note deserves a place, as it will show that even Mr. Hume himself could occasionally be guilty of, '*the illiberal arrogance, petulance and scurrility which distinguish the Warburtonian School.*' "But there is a person, that has writ an 'Enquiry historical and critical into the evidence against Mary Queen of Scots;' and has attempted to refute the forgoing narrative. He quotes a single passage of the narrative in which Mary is said simply to refuse answering; and then a single passage from Goodall, in which she boasts simply that she will answer; and he very civilly and almost directly calls the author a liar, on account of this pretended contradiction. That whole Enquiry, from beginning to end, is composed of such scandalous artifices. And from this instance, the reader may judge of the candour, fair dealing, veracity, and good manners of the Enquirer. There are, indeed, three events in our history, which may be regarded as touchstones of partymen. An English Whig, who asserts the reality of the popish Plot, an Irish Catholic, who denies the massacre in 1641, and a Scotch Jacobite, who maintains the innocence of Queen Mary, must be considered as men beyond the reach of argument or reason, and must be left to their prejudices."

Mr. Hume, and the late Reverend Dr. Jardine, one of the ministers of Edinburgh, lived in habits of much intimacy. Religion, *natural* and *revealed*, was frequently the subject of their conversation. It happened one night, after they had entertained themselves with theological controversy, that Mr. Hume's politeness, when bidding adieu, would not permit Dr. Jardine (whose œconomy was not incumbered with many domestics) to light him down stairs. Mr. Hume stumbled in the dark, and the Doctor hearing it, ran to his assistance with a candle, and when he had recovered his guest said to him "David, I have often told you not to rely too much upon yourself, and that *natural light* is not *sufficient.*" This pleasantry Mr. Hume never relished.

As a proof of the steadiness of Mr. Hume's sceptical tenets it may be observed, that when he published the first volume of his History of Great Britain, he was advised, that the opinions he had delivered concerning matters of religion, would hurt the sale of his work; and that some apology would be proper. He accordingly in his second volume, P. 449, when speaking of the religious parties, subjoins the following note, which when his fame was established beyond the reach of party, he cancelled as unworthy of admission.

"This sophism, of arguing from the abuse of any thing against the use of it, is one of the grossest, and at the same time, the most common, to which men are subject. The history of all ages, and none more than that of the period, which is our subject, offers us examples of the abuse of religion; and we have not been sparing, in this volume more than in the former, to remark them: But whoever would thence draw an inference to the disadvantage of religion in general, would argue very rashly and erroneously. The proper office of religion is to reform mens lives, to purify their hearts, to inforce all moral duties, and to secure obedience to the laws and civil magistrate. While it pursues these salutary purposes, its operations, tho' infinitely valuable, are secret and silent, and seldom come under the cognizance of history. That adulterate species of it alone, which inflames faction, animates sedition, and prompts rebellion, distinguishes itself on the open theatre of the world, and is the great source of revolutions and public convulsions. The historian, therefore, has scarce occasion to mention any other kind of religion; and he may retain the highest regard for true piety, even while he exposes all the abuses of the false. He may even think, that he cannot better show his attachment to the former than by detecting the latter, and laying open its absurdities and pernicious tendency.

It is no proof of irreligion in an historian, that he remarks some fault or imperfection in each sect of religion, which he has occasion to mention. Every institution, however divine, which is adopted by men, must partake of the weakness and infirmities of our nature; and will be apt, unless carefully guarded, to degenerate into one extreme or the other. What species of devotion so pure, noble, and worthy the Supreme Being, as that which is most spiritual, simple, unadorned, and which partakes nothing either of the senses or imagination? Yet is it found by experience, that this mode of worship does very naturally, among the vulgar, mount up into extravagance and fanaticism. Even many of the first reformers are exposed to this reproach; and their zeal, though in the event, it proved extremely useful, partook strongly of the enthusiastic genius: Two of the judges in the reign of Charles the Second, scrupled not to advance this opinion even from the bench. Some mixture of ceremony, pomp, and ornament may seem to correct the abuse; yet will it be found very difficult to prevent such a form of religion from sinking sometimes into superstition. The church of England itself, which is perhaps the best medium among these extremes, will be allowed, at least during the age of archbishop Laud, to have been somewhat infected with a superstition, resembling the Popish; and to have payed a higher regard to some positive institutions, than the nature of the things, strictly speaking, would permit. It is the business of an historian to remark these abuses of all kinds; but it belongs also to a prudent reader to confine the representations, which he meets with, to that age alone of which the author treats. What absurdity, for instance, to suppose, that the Presbyterians, Independants, Anabaptists, and other sectaries of the present age partake of all the extravagancies, which we remark in those, who bore these appellations in the last century? The inference indeed seems juster; where sects have been noted for fanaticism during one period, to conclude, that they will be very moderate and reasonable in the subsequent. For as it is the nature of fanaticism to abolish all slavish submission to priestly power, it follows, that as soon as the first ferment is abated, men are naturally in such sects left to the free use of their reason, and shake off the fetters of custom and authority."

To say barely, that Mr. Hume in his moral character was unexceptionable, would be doing him injustice; he was truly amiable, gentle, hospitable, humane. His temper was cast in the happiest mold, if we may not except to his anxious and extreme sensibility, in every thing which affected his literary reputation. It is told, that an elderly woman in the suburbs of Edinburgh, whose excess of zeal was proportionable to her want of sense and discretion, called on Mr. Hume; declaimed violently against his sceptical principles, as she had learned them by report; represented, that he was nodding on the brink of everlasting destruction; and delivered an earnest prayer, that it would please divine grace to give him to *see* the error of his ways. Mr. Hume listened to her with attention and good humour, thanked the lady for her concern about his future welfare, and expressed a desire to know what was her line in life. She informed him, that she was a married woman, and that her husband was a tallow-chandler in the neighbourhood; upon which Mr. Hume replied, "Good woman, since you have expressed so earnest a desire that I should be inspired with *inward light*, I beg you will supply me with *outward light* also." The matron retired, not a little satisfied with the commission which he gave her, and her husband thenceforwards supplied Mr. Hume's family with candles.

Notwithstanding the ideas which zealots may have formed of Mr. Hume's principles, as latitudanarian, as atheistical, as damnable: his brother's notions of them were very different. For, speaking of the Historian one day, he expressed himself in this manner, "My brother Davie is a good enough sort of a man, *but rather narrow minded."*

As to Mr. Hume's abilities as a Philosopher, and an Historian, his Works are the basis on which posterity will rear his everlasting fame.

A few months before his death, Mr. Hume was persuaded by his friends to try the effects of a long journey, and the Bath waters: but finding his malady to increase, he resigned all hopes of life. He maintained, however, his usual chearfulness; and being resolved to make the most of the short remainder of his lease, he wrote to his friends in Edinburgh, informing them of his resolution to be in that city by a certain day, which he named; and separately requested their company to dinner on the day following. Accordingly, Lord Elibank, Professor Ferguson, Mr. Home the Dramatic Poet, Dr. Smith, Dr. Blair, Dr. Black, and others of his literary friends, obeyed the summons, and took a sort of farewel dinner with their dying friend. His *flowery* rival in historic fame was also invited. But, alas! the Lord Advocate of Scotland invites this *Reverend Doctor* on that very day to a turtle feast. What was to be done? both invitations could not be embraced; – the contest was short: For as it would seem, this Historian's taste is almost as elegant in eating, as in writing, he judiciously preferred the *turtle* of my Lord Advocate to the *mutton* of David Hume.

Never did death make more regular and visible approaches than to Mr. Hume. He met these with a chearfulness and resignation, which could only be the result of a vigorous understanding, and a well-spent life. He still went abroad, called upon his friends, but as the fatigue of a chaise was now become intolerable, he went in a sedan chair, and his ghastly looks bore the most striking appearances of speedy death. His situation was the more uncomfortable, that in his weak emaciated state, the physicians prescribed to him instead of a down bed, to lie on a rugged pallet.[5]

He had already settled his affairs, and his facetiousness still suggested to him to make some verbal legacies, which would not have been so suitable to the gravity of a solemn deed. His friend Mr. Home the Poet, affected a delicacy which abhorred even the taste of Port wine; this whimsical nicety had often been the subject of Mr. Hume's raillery, and he left verbally to his friend the poet, *one bottle* of Port, and ten dozen of Claret, but on this condition, that the poet should drink the Port at two sittings, before he tasted the Claret.

---

[5] His disease was a diarrhœa; the physicians were divided about the seat of the malady. There is a reason however to conjecture, that his disorder originated from a course of eating rather fully, without drinking in proportion.

Such was the estimation in which Mr. Hume was held, from his amiable qualities as a citizen, as well as from his literary fame, that for some weeks before his death, his situation became the universal topick of conversation and enquiry; each individual expressing an anxious solicitude about his health, as if he had been his intimate and particular friend.

On the twenty-fifth of August, Mr. Hume's character was put beyond the reach of being sullied by human frailty.[6] As soon as he conceived himself to be in a dying way, he purchased a spot for the depositing of his ashes; the south-west corner of the Calton burying ground at Edinburgh, *a rock wherein never man had been laid*. And from the particular charge he gave about his corpse, it would seem he was not altogether devoid of apprehensions of its being treated with insult.

The anxious attention with which the public viewed every circumstance respecting Mr. Hume's illness was not terminated even by his death. From the busy curiosity of the mob, one would have presumed them to entertain notions that the ashes of Mr. Hume were to have been the cause or the object of miraculous exertion. As the physicians of London and Edinburgh were divided about the seat of his disorder, those of the city where he died, proposed that his body should be opened: but this, his brother who was also his executor, agreeably to the orders of the deceased, would not permit.

It is hardly to be credited, that the grave-diggers, digging with pick-axes Mr. Hume's grave, should have attracted the gaping curiosity of the multitude. That, notwithstanding a heavy rain, which fell during the interment, multitudes of all ranks gazed at the funeral procession,[7] as if they had expected the hearse to have been consumed in livid flames, or encircled with a ray of glory; that people in a sphere much above the rabble would have sent to the sexton for the keys of the burying-ground, and paid him to have access to visit the grave. And that on a Sunday evening (the gates of the burying-ground being opened for another funeral) the company, from a public walk in the neighbourhood, flocked in such crouds to Mr. Hume's grave, that his brother actually became apprehensive upon the unusual concourse, and ordered the grave to be railed in with all expedition.

After his interment, two trusty persons, watched the grave for about eight nights. The watch was set by eight at night; at which time a pistol was fired,

---

[6] Mr. Hume, after his circumstances became affluent, lived very hospitably and genteely. Yet he left to his relations upwards of 10,000 l. of his own acquiring. He had a pension from the government of 500 l. per annum.

[7] When the mob were assembled round Mr. Hume's door to see the corpse taken out to interment, the following short dialogue passed between two of the refuse of the rabble: "Ah, (says one) he was an Atheist." "No matter, (says another) he was an *honest man*."

and so continued to be every hour till day-light. Candles in a lanthorn were placed upon the grave, where they burned all night; and the grease which dropped in renewing or snuffing the candles was to be seen upon the grave afterwards.

We cannot conclude this Supplement to the Life of Mr. Hume more properly than by applying to him and to his Works, those nervous lines, which Ovid has applied to himself.

"Quod nec Jovis ira, nec ignis,
Nec poterit ferrum, nec edax abolere vetustas.
Cum volet illa dies, quæ nil nisi corporis hujus
Jus habet, incerti spatium mihi finiat ævi:
Parte tamen meliore mei super alta perennis
Astra ferar: NOMENQUE ERIT INDELEBILE NOSTRUM.
Quaque patet domitis; Romana potentia terris;
Ore lega populi: PERQUE OMNIA SECULA FAMA
(SI QUID HABENT VERI VATUM PREÆSAGIA) VIVAM."

OVID.

———

CERTIFIED COPY
OF THE
LAST WILL AND TESTAMENT
OF
DAVID HUME, ESQ.

———

COPY

I DAVID HUME, second lawful son of Joseph Home, of Ninewells, Advocate, for the love and affection I bear to John Home, of Ninewells, my brother, and for other causes, Do, by these presents, under the reservations and burthens after mentioned, Give and Dispone to the said John Home, or, if he die before me, to David Home, his second son, his heirs and assignies whatsomever, all lands, heritages, debts and sums of money, as well heritable as moveable, which shall belong to me at the time of my decease, as also my whole effects in general, real and personal, with and under the burthen of the following legacies, *viz.* To my sister, Katherine Home, the sum of Twelve hundred pounds sterling, payable the first term of Whitsunday, or Martinmas, after my decease, together with all my English books, and the live-rent of my house in St. James's Court, or in case that house be sold at the time of my decease, Twenty pounds a year during the whole course of her life: To my friend, Adam Ferguson, Professor of Moral Philosophy in the College of Edinburgh, Two hundred pounds sterling: to my friend M. Dalembert, Member of the French Academy, and of the Academy of Sciences in Paris, Two hundred pounds: To my friend, Dr. Adam Smith, late Professor of Moral Philosophy in Glasgow, I leave all my manuscripts without exception, desiring him to publish *my Dialogues on Natural Religion*, which are comprehended in this present bequest, but to publish no other papers which he suspects not to have been written within these five years, but to destroy them all at his leisure: And I even leave him full power over all my papers, except the Dialogues above mentioned: And though I can trust to that intimate and sincere friendship, which has ever subsisted between us, for his faithful execution of this part of my Will, yet, as a small recompence of his pains in correcting and publishing this work, I leave him Two hundred pounds, to be paid immediately after the publication of it: I also leave to Mrs. Anne and Mrs. Janet Hepburn, daughters of Mr. James Hepburn, of Keith, One hundred pounds a piece: To my cousin, David Campbell, son of Mr. Campbell, Minister of Lillysleaf, One hundred pounds: To the Infirmary of Edinburgh, Fifty pounds: To all the servants who shall be in my family at the time of my decease, one year's wages; and to my housekeeper, Margaret Irvine, three years wages: And I also ordain, that my brother, or nephew, or executor, whoever he be, shall not pay up to the said Margaret Irvine, without her own consent, any sum of money which I shall owe her at the time of my decease, whether by bill, bond, or for wages, but shall retain it in his hand, and pay her the legal interest upon it, till she demand the principal: And in case my brother above mentioned shall survive me, I leave to his son, David, the sum of a Thousand pounds to assist him in his education: But in case that by my brother's death before me, the succession of my estate and effects shall devolve to the aforesaid David, I hereby burthen him, over and above the payment of the aforesaid legacies, with the payment of the sums following: To his brothers, Joseph and John, a Thousand pounds a piece: To his sisters, Catherine and Agnes, Five hundred pounds a piece: All which sums, as well as every sum contained in the present disposition (except that to Dr. Smith) to be payable the first term of Whitsunday, and Martinmas, after my decease; and all of them without exception, in sterling money. And I do hereby nominate and appoint the said John Home, my brother, and failing of him by decease, the said David Home, to be my sole executor and universal legatee, with and under the burthens above mention; Reserving always full power and liberty to me at any time in my life, even in death-bed, to alter and innovate these presents, in whole or in part, and to burthen the same with such other legacies as I shall think fit. And I do hereby declare these presents to be a good, valid, and sufficient evident, albeit found in my custody, or in the custody of any other person, at the time of my death: CONSENTING to the registration hereof in the books of council and session, or other judges books competent therein to remain for preservation, and thereto I constitute Mr. David Rae, Advocate, my procurator.

In witness whereof these presents, consisting of this and the preceding page, are written and subscribed by me on this Fourth of January, One thousand seven hundred and seventy-six, at Edinburgh, before these witnesses, the Right Honourable the Earl of Home, and Mr. John M'Gowan, clerk to the signet.

(Signed) DAVID HUME.

HOME, witness;
JO. M'GOUAN, witness.
Day and date as above.

I also Ordain, That if I shall die any where in Scotland, I shall be buried in a private manner in the Calton church-yard, the south side of it, and a monument be built over my body, at an expence not exceeding a hundred pounds, with an inscription containing only my name, with the year of my birth and death, leaving it to posterity to add the rest.

(Signed), DAVID HUME.
At Edinburgh,
15th April, 1776.

I also leave, for rebuilding the bridge of Chirnside, the sum of a hundred pounds; but on condition that the managers of the bridge shall take none of the stones for building the bridge from the quarry of Ninewells, except from that part of the quarry which has been already opened. I leave to my nephew, Joseph, the sum of Fifty pounds to enable him to make a good sufficient drain and sewer round the house of Ninewells, but on condition that if the drain and sewer be not made, from whatever cause, within a year after my death, the said Fifty pounds shall be paid to the poor of the parish of Chirnside: To my sister, instead of all my English books, I leave her a hundred volumes at her choice: To David Waite, servant to my brother, I leave the sum of Ten pounds, payable the first term after my death.

(Signed) DAVID HUME.

In this place of the original Will there are several lines deleted, after which follow these words: "This last clause was erased, and obliterated by myself."

(Signed) DAVID HUME.

FINIS.

HUME'S DEATHBED ANGUISH

44
BENJAMIN SILLIMAN:
A JOURNAL OF TRAVELS

Benjamin Silliman, *A journal of travels in England, Holland, and Scotland, in the years 1805–1806,* New York, 1810, 2 Vol.
Selections from Section 87; from 1810 edition.

Born in Connecticut, Benjamin Silliman (1779–1864) entered Yale College at age thirteen, the youngest in most of his classes. After graduation he studied law and was admitted to the bar, but set his legal vocation aside for the professorship of chemistry and natural history at Yale. Beginning in 1805 he travelled to Britain and Holland, partly to acquire supplies for the college, and partly to meet scholars in his field. He kept a journal of his visit, which was published in 1810. Around this time, stories began circulating that, contrary to Adam Smith's account of Hume's peaceful death, Hume was in fact filled with anguish. One of the first printed accounts of this is in Silliman's *Journal.* Silliman reports here that he heard the story in 1806 from an unnamed "very venerable and respectable man" who "was well acquainted" with Hume. Enough biographical information about this man is presented so that we might cautiously identify him as Isaac James – a close friend of Scottish clergyman John Witherspoon (1723–1794) and connected with the publication of Witherspoon's posthumous *Series of Letters on Education* (1798).

Silliman relates two Hume anecdotes that he heard from James, the first regarding Hume's death-bed anguish as reported by his "nurse", and the second that Hume successfully undermined his mother's faith and brushed off her request for consolation as she approached death. Silliman himself suggests that Hume's death-bed anguish may have been connected with the incident concerning his mother. Silliman's *Journal* was reviewed by the *Quarterly Review,* which excerpted the story of Hume's mother. The journal introduced the anecdote with the following: "We will quote one more anecdote from Mr. Silliman, and in his own words. It is related upon the authority of a gentleman old enough to have known the fact, and respectable enough to be entitled to full belief." Following the excerpt, the reviewer stated, "A story like this requires no comment. Thus it is that false philosophy restores the sting to Death, and gives again the victory to the grave" (July 1816, Vol. 15, p. 562).

The appearance of this sparked a critical letter to the journal from Hume's nephew, Baron David Hume. Though not printing Baron Hume's letter, the *Quarterly Review* did print a response, which is contained in this collection.

April 3, [1806]. – I have been favoured with the acquaintance of a very venerable and respectable man here, who was an early and intimate friend of Dr. Witherspoon. He informs me that those letters on the education of children, which are printed in Witherspoon's works, were written originally to himself, and that they took their rise in this way. Mr. ____ had an infant son, and his mind began of course to be directed to the subject of education; he expressed his solicitude to his friend, as they sat, one evening, conversing together, and requested his advice, which was so readily and ably given, that he was immediately urged to commit his sentiments to writing; this he did in the epistolary form, and such was the origin of some of the best observations that were ever made on this subject; I have had the pleasure of seeing the original manuscript, which is still in the hands of the gentleman to whom it was addressed.

He was intimate with Dr. Rush when he was a student of medicine in Edinburgh 30 years ago, and spoke of him to me in such terms as could not but be grateful to an American. This distinguished physician must have given early indications of the superiority which he has since exhibited, for this is not the only instance in which I have met with a person in this country who was impressed with sentiments of admiration for one who was then a youth and unknown to the world.

From the same venerable friend of Dr. Witherspoon, I have derived the following circumstances concerning Hume, with whom this gentleman was well acquainted. He alleges that this sceptical philosopher did not die in all that composure, or rather that impious levity of mind, which has been ascribed to him, by the ardent but indiscreet zeal of his friend Adam Smith; he cites the testimony of the nurse who attended the bed-side of Hume at the trying hour, and she asserted that *he died in horror*. I am sensible that the evidence of a person in so humble a station stands very little chance of being received, in opposition to the high authority of Adam Smith and Dr. Black.

The following circumstances will have to combat similar difficulties. I derived them from the same source with that which I have mentioned.

It seems that Hume received a religious education from his mother, and early in life, was the subject of strong and hopeful religious impressions; but, as he approached manhood, they were effaced, and confirmed infidelity succeeded. Maternal partiality, however alarmed at first, came, at length, to look, with less and less pain, upon this declension, and filial love and reverence seems to have been absorbed in the pride of philosophical scepticism. For, Hume now applied himself with unwearied, and, unhappily, with successful efforts, to sap the foundations of his mother's faith. Having succeeded in this dreadful work, he went abroad into foreign countries, and, as he was returning, an express met him in London, with a letter from his mother, informing him that she was in a deep decline, and could not long survive; she said she found herself without any support in her distress; that he had taken away that source of comfort, upon which, in all cases of affliction, she used to rely, and that she now found her mind sinking into despair; she did not doubt that her son would afford her some substitute for her religion, and she conjured him to hasten to her, or, at least, to send her a letter, containing such consolations as philosophy can afford to a dying mortal. Hume was overwhelmed with anguish, on receiving this letter, and hastened to Scotland in post-chaises and four, traveling night and day, but, before he arrived, his mother expired.

No permanent impression seems however to have been made on his mind by this most trying event, and whatever remorse he might have felt at the moment, he soon relapsed into his wonted scorn, and obstinacy of heart.

One would suppose that such a circumstance must have embittered his dying moments, and would of itself have produced all the horror ascribed to him by his female attendant.

...

45
EDITOR'S NOTE IN
QUARTERLY REVIEW

Editor's Note on Silliman and Baron Hume, *Quarterly Review*, October 1816, Vol. 16, p. 279.
Complete note.

The *Quarterly Review* was founded in 1809 by London publisher John Murray as a Tory answer to the Whig ideology of the newly founded *Edinburgh Review*. In 1816 the *Quarterly* reviewed Benjamin Silliman's *Journal of Travels* (1810), selections from which are contained earlier in this collection. As noted, the *Quarterly* quoted Silliman's anecdote about Hume's mother, which prompted a letter of complaint by Hume's nephew, Baron David Hume (1757–1838). The *Quarterly* did not print the letter, but it included a note of apology in their next issue. From the context of the note, it seems that Baron Hume denounced both anecdotes in Silliman's *Journal* and claimed that the *Quarterly* published the excerpt out of bigotry. Baron Hume countered the story about Hume's mother with a quotation from the as yet unpublished manuscript of Alexander Carlyle's autobiography (the work appeared forty-two years later; selections from this are contained in this collection). The *Quarterly* conceded Baron Hume's point regarding the anecdote surrounding Hume's mother. However, they suggested that they could not judge the truth or falsehood of the anecdote surrounding Hume's death-bed anguish. It is worth noting that Baron Hume may not have actually believed the story from Carlyle that he sent to the *Quarterly*. In 1812, Baron Hume heard Henry Mackenzie's oral presentation of "Account of the Life and Writings of Mr. John Home," later published in 1822, which included Carlyle's wording of the anecdote, with Carlyle cited as the authority (the original manuscript presently resides in the National Library of Scotland). In *The Anecdotes and Egotisms of Henry Mackenzie*, contained in this collection, Mackenzie states the following: "Mr. B. Hume was so delicate with regard to his uncle that he objected to my mentioning in that Life [of John Home] an anecdote told me by Mr. D. Hume's intimate friend, the Hon. Mr. Boyle, which anecdote was held by serious persons to be much to Mr. D. Hume's honour, but of which his nephew said he doubted the correctness."

Mr. David Hume, nephew to the historian of that name, has written to us respecting the anecdote of his kinsman, extracted, in our last Number, from Mr. Silliman's Travels. That anecdote he has shown to be false, by unquestionable dates, and by a circumstance related in the Manuscript Memoirs of the late Dr. Carlisle, 'an eminent clergyman of the Scottish Church,' and friend of the historian. The circumstance, interesting in itself and decisive upon the subject, we transcribe, in the words of the Manuscript, from the letter before us: 'When David and he (the Hon. Mr. Boyle, brother of the Earl of Glasgow) were both in London, *at the period when David's mother died,* Mr. Boyle hearing of it, soon after went into his apartment, for they lodged in the same house, where he found him in the deepest affliction, and in a flood of tears. After the usual topics of condolence, Mr. Boyle said to him, "My friend, you owe this uncommon grief to your having thrown off the principles of religion: for if you had not, you would have been consoled by the firm belief, that the good lady, who was not only the best of mothers, *but the most pious of Christians,* was completely happy in the realms of the just." To which David replied, "though *I throw out my speculations to entertain and employ the learned and metaphysical world,* yet, in other things, I do not think so differently from the rest of mankind as you imagine."

Mr. Silliman relates the anecdote on the authority of a very venerable and respectable man to whom he was introduced at Edinburgh, 'who was an early and intimate friend of Dr. Witherspoon,' and to whom 'those letters on the education of children which are printed in Witherspoon's Works were originally written.' This person, who may probably be easily recognized at Edinburgh, is stated to have been well acquainted with Hume. On his authority Mr. Silliman contradicts the received opinion of the composure with which the sceptical philosopher died. Mr. D. Hume expostulates with us for having lightly given credit to the anecdote which we extracted, as if we had acted from bigotry. We believed the anecdote, and in that belief quoted it, – not to detract from the character of Hume, but as showing in what manner the philosophy which he sent abroad restored the sting to death. The story concerning his own death we did not extract, knowing, whether true or false, how very little such stories are worth, how often they are feigned, and how easily delirium is interpreted according to the notions of the bystanders.

Mr. Hume requires, as he has a right to do, that we shall repair the wrong which we have done to his uncle's fame. The publicity which we gave to the anecdote, we cheerfully give to the refutation of it: this refutation will reach America; when Mr. Silliman will see that he has been misinformed, and will doubtless correct the statement which he has sent into the world.

46
"ON THE DEATH-BED OF
HUME THE HISTORIAN"

"O.B.", "On the Death-Bed of Hume the Historian," letter to the Editor, in *The Christian Observer*, November 1831, Vol. 31, No. xi, No. 359, pp. 665–666. Complete letter.

The *Christian Observer* was an Anglican monthly periodical founded in 1802 and ceased publication in 1874. In 1831 the journal published an anonymous letter from a reader who raised the question of whether Hume's death was really as peaceful as Adam Smith maintained in his "Letter ... to William Strahan." The author enclosed an article that "appeared many years ago in an Edinburgh newspaper" which counters this. In 1810 Benjamin Silliman published a story in his *Journal of Travels* involving "the testimony of the nurse who attended the bed-side of Hume at the trying hour, and she asserted that *he died in horror*." The letter provided by the anonymous correspondent is a more detailed account of this story. In brief, shortly after Hume's death, his housekeeper – presumably Margaret Irvine – was travelling in a carriage and listening to a conversation among passengers about how peacefully Hume died. Unable to stay silent, she related what she personally witnessed during Hume's final days. Hume, she states, was indeed cheerful when his friends were around, but when gone "his mental agitation was so great at times as to occasion his whole bed to shake." He would need a candle lit all night, and would not "be left alone for one minute." He also exhibited "involuntary breathings of remorse and frightful startings." After presenting the article, the anonymous author states his hope that someone familiar with Hume's housekeeper might confirm the truth of this account.

Another version of the housekeeper's story is briefly alluded to in Robert Haldane's *The Evidence and Authority of Divine Revelation* (1834) and clarified in detail by Alexander Haldane in *Memoirs* (1852), both contained in this collection.

ON THE DEATH-BED OF HUME THE HISTORIAN

To the Editor of the Christian Observer.

I inclose a passage relative to the death-bed of Hume, the historian, which appeared many years ago in an Edinburgh newspaper, and which I am not aware was ever contradicted. Adam Smith's well known narrative of Hume's last hours has been often cited, to prove how calmly a philosophical infidel can die; but, if the inclosed account be correct, very different was the picture. I copy it as I find it, thinking it possible that some of your numerous readers may be able to cast some light upon the subject. If the facts alledged in the following statement are not authentic, they ought to be disproved before tradition is too remote; if authentic, they are of considerable importance on account of the irreligious use which has been made of the popular narrative; just as was the case in regard to the death-bed of Voltaire, which to this hour, in spite of well-proved facts, infidel writers maintain was calm and philosophical. The following is the story: –

"About the end of 1776, a few months after the historian's death, a respectable looking woman dressed in black came into the Haddington stage coach while passing through Edinburgh.

The conversation among the passengers, which had been interrupted for a few minutes, was speedily resumed, which the lady soon found to be regarding the state of mind persons were in at the prospect of death. One gentleman argued that a real Christian was more likely to view the approach of death with composure, than he who had looked upon religion as unworthy his notice. Another (an English gentleman) insisted that an infidel could look forward to his end with as much complacency and peace of mind as the best Christian in the land. This being denied by his opponent, he bade him consider the death of his countrymen David Hume, who was an acknowledged infidel, and yet died not only happy and tranquil, but even spoke of his dissolution with a degree of gaiety and humor. The lady who had lately joined them, turned round to the last speaker and said, 'Sir, this is all you know about it: I could tell you another tale.' 'Madam,' replied the gentleman, 'I presume I have as good information as you can have on this subject, and I believe that what I have asserted regarding Mr. Hume has never before been called in question.' The lady continued; 'Sir, I was Mr. Hume's housekeeper for many years, and was with him in his last moments; and the mourning I now wear was a present from his relatives for my attention to him on his death-bed; and happy would I have been if I could have borne my testimony to the mistaken opinion that has gone abroad of his peaceful and composed end. I have, sir, never till this hour opened my mouth on this subject; but I think it a pity the world should be kept in the dark on so interesting a topic. It is true, sir, that when Mr. Hume's friends were with him, he was cheerful, and seemed quite unconcerned about his approaching fate; nay, frequently spoke of it to them in a jocular and playful way; but when he was alone the scene was very different; he was any thing but composed; his mental agitation was so great at times as to occasion his whole bed to shake. He would not allow the candles to be put out during the night, nor would he be left alone for a minute. I had always to ring the bell for one of the servants to be in the room, before he would allow me to leave it. He struggled hard to appear composed even before me; but to one who attended his bed-side for so many days and nights, and witnessed his disturbed sleeps and still more disturbed wakings; who frequently heard his involuntary breathings of remorse and frightful startings; it was no difficult matter to determine that all was not right within. This continued and increased until he became insensible. I hope in God I shall never witness a similar scene.'"

I leave your readers to weigh the probability of this narrative: for myself, I see nothing unlikely in it; for a man who had exerted all his talents to deprive mankind of their dearest hopes, and only consolation in the day of trial and the hour of death, might well be expected to suffer remorse in his dying hour: and the alleged narrator of the circumstance, who states herself to have been his housekeeper, is affirmed to have made the declaration on the spur of the occasion, from regard to truth, and by no means from any pique or dislike towards Mr. Hume or his family. Some of your northern readers may perhaps be able to inform me who was Mr. Hume's housekeeper at the time of his death, and whether there is any proof in writing, memory, or tradition, to the effect of her alleged statement.

O.B.

47
ROBERT HALDANE:
EVIDENCE AND AUTHORITY OF DIVINE REVELATION

Robert Haldane, *The evidence and authority of divine revelation: being a view of the testimony of the law and the prophets to the Messiah, with the subsequent testimonies*, Edinburgh: Printed by A. Balfour, Merchant Court, for Olphant, [etc], 1834, 2 v.
Selections from chapter 1; from 1839 third edition.

Born in London, and raised by his grandmother, Robert Haldane (1764–1842) was educated at the University of Edinburgh. Initially a member of the Church of Scotland, in 1799 he and his brother organized a Congregationalist church in Edinburgh. Among his most influential works is *Evidence and Authority of Divine Revelation*, which contains several discussions of Hume. In Chapter 1 of this work Haldane argues that human research is insufficient for arriving at a true understanding of religion, as we see in the failed efforts of ancient philosophers, pagan religions, and infidel modern writers on the subject, such as Hume and Gibbon. He believes that these two particular infidel writers fulfil the biblical prophecy that "there shall come in the last days scoffers." In a footnote Haldane presents a version of the story concerning Hume's death-bed anguish – see also Benjamin Silliman's *Journal of Travels* (1810) and "On the Death-Bed of Hume the Historian" (1831) contained in this collection. Haldane notes that an attendant witnessed "the gloom of his mind," which was much different than Adam Smith reported in his "Letter ... to William Strahan." Some years later, Haldane's relative provided a more detailed account of the deathbed story, indicating how it originated. See Alexander Haldane's *Memoirs* (1852), contained in this collection.

CHAPTER I.
THE NECESSITY OF A DIVINE REVELATION.

Nothing more clearly proves the darkening influence of sin in alienating man from God, than the manner in which many writers on the science of morals speak of the [lack of] necessity of a Divine Revelation. ... [T]heir systems, though not avowedly hostile to a supernatural revelation, are, with few exceptions, incompatible with the idea of its necessity, as well as with the truth of the doctrines which it has promulgated. ...

From the above account of the heathen nations, both ancient and modern, the insufficiency of what is called natural religion to enlightened mankind in their present state of apostasy may be clearly estimated, and its being totally inadequate to lead men to God fully ascertained. We see what were its effects in the most civilized nations of antiquity, on those who were most ardent in their pursuit of knowledge and most remarkable for their acquirement beyond others of their time. Amidst all their speculations and reasonings, they remained in absolute uncertainty respecting those important questions, which above every other it concerns creatures destined for immortality to resolve; – how shall man be just with God, and to what is he destined tin that future and eternal state, nearer to which each succeeding hour conducts him? And what, we may ask, are the effects at this day of the philosophical researches of the most eminent men in modern times who neglect the revelation of the gospel, which appears to them to be folly? Their studies, directed to physical or moral science, elevated and sublime as they may appear to be, leave them, when separated from the knowledge of the gospel, in ignorance of their own character and of the character of God, of their condition as sinners, and of the value and saving influences of that World which God has magnified above all his name. An unbelieving astronomer, it has been said, is mad; but the study of astronomy will never conduct men to God. So far is this from being the case, that many of the most distinguished astronomers, as well as geologists, have remained as much unacquainted with the way of salvation as the most benighted heathens, and even determinedly opposed to it. To what superior light did Mr Hume attain after all his philosophical researches? On the contrary, he involved himself in total darkness. The confession with which he shuts up his enquiries on religion should operate as a solemn warning to all who, pushing reason beyond its legitimate province, reject the abundant means of knowledge which God has vouchsafed, and are graciously adapted to the present state and nature of man. "The whole," says he, "is a riddle, an enigma, an inexplicable mystery. Doubt, uncertainty, suspense of judgment, appear the only result of our most accurate scrutiny concerning this subject." {[Footnote:] When Mr Hume's philosophical friends visited him on his death-bed, he appeared to them to be cheerful, and was even unbecomingly jocular, as is narrated in that discreditable letter which after his death was addressed by Dr Adam Smith to Mr Strahan, and which has been exposed as it deserves by Bishop Horne. But when these friends were not present, it is said to have been far otherwise with him, indeed the very reverse; and that, in the gloom of his mind, he observed on one occasion to the person who attended him, that he had been in search of light all his life, but that now he was in greater darkness than ever. This is entirely consistent with the above deliberate avowal when he was in health and at ease.} After all, the attainments of these men in their several enquiries, whether lawful and useful in themselves, like those of the astronomer, or blasphemous and pernicious, like those of the sceptical philosopher, the question that was put of old may be urged on them all, which, if they have neglected the great salvation, they must be conscious implies their condemnation; "*Who is he that overcometh the world, but he that believeth that Jesus is the Son of God?*" The comparison that may be drawn between natural religion, or the revelation of nature, and the revelation of the gospel, will exhibit in the most conspicuous manner the impossibility that the former can supply the place of the latter.

The revelation of grace in the gospel may be considered in comparison with that of nature, either as the latter came immediately from the hand of God, or in the darkness which has been occasioned to it by sin. ...

And now, in these latter times, additional testimony on this subject presents itself. We have observed the manner in which Mr Hume and Mr Gibbon, who have distinguished themselves so much among the most inveterate and insidious enemies of the gospel, have studiously misrepresented the subject of the alleged tolerating spirit of paganism. In them, therefore, is that declaration fulfilled, "*There shall come in the last days scoffers, walking after their own lusts.*" 2 Peter, iii. 3. If, then, in the early days of the church, the persecuting spirit of the world, so clearly predicted by the Lord, turned to the first Christians for a testimony, shall not this other prediction contained in his word and literally verified in our time, turn in like manner to us for a testimony? In order to falsify the prediction of Jesus Christ, and to vilify his religion, by showing it to be more destructive to every right feeling of the mind of man than all the abominations and absurdities of Pagan idolatry, Mr Gibbon and Mr Hume have laboured with all their might. But "the Lord knoweth the thoughts of the wise, that they are foolishness." ...

48
ALEXANDER HALDANE:
MEMOIRS OF ROBERT HALDANE

Alexander Haldane, *Memoirs of the lives of Robert Haldane of Airthrey, and of his brother, James Alexander Haldane*, London: Hamilton, Adams, and co., 1852 xvi, 676 p.
Selections from Chapter 24; from 1852 edition.

In his *Evidence and Authority of Divine Revelation* (1834), excerpted in this collection, Robert Haldane challenged Adam Smith's depiction of Hume's tranquil death. According to an attendant at Hume's deathbed, Haldane says, Hume was quite distressed and stated that "now he was in greater darkness than ever." In a biography of Haldane written some twenty years later, his relative Alexander Haldane illuminates the source of this anecdote. Alexander's account parallels in many respects the more detailed description given of Hume's deathbed anguish in the *Christian Observer*, contained earlier in this collection. In fact, he notes that there had indeed been alternative published accounts of the experience of Hume's housekeeper – who was probably Margaret Irvine. What is remarkable about the account here, though, is that Haldane states exactly where Robert Haldane originally heard the story: from his neighbour, Mr. Abercromby of Tullibody. Abercromby, he explains, was the father-in-law of James Edmonstoune – close friend to Hume – and Abercromby was himself present on the stagecoach when the housekeeper told her story.

CHAPTER XXIV.
[1834–1840]

... When he first sat down to write on the Evidences, he carefully re-read several of the most eminent Infidel works, particularly David Hume's "Moral Essays," and Gibbon's Infidel chapters. The self-contradictions which he brings home to these writers are striking. He singles out David Hume as an example of the folly of pushing reason beyond its legitimate province, and preferring the dubious glimmer of its darkened ray to the pure and steady light of Divine revelation. "The whole," says Hume, "is a riddle, an enigma, an inexplicable mystery. Doubt, uncertainty, suspense of judgment, appear the only result of our most accurate scrutiny concerning this subject." It is a melancholy confession, and enough to cloud the joy of any rational or thinking mind. But Hume's friends had delighted to represent their philosopher as "treading the common road into the great darkness," not only without fear, but actually with gaiety. This was the testimony of Adam Smith, the author of the "Theory of Moral Sentiments," who also considered Hume "as approaching as nearly to the idea of a perfectly wise and virtuous man as, perhaps, the nature of human frailty will permit." When Adam Smith thus wrote, he knew that Hume had in his lifetime published an essay vindicating suicide, whilst in the correspondence, published since his death, he not only justifies but even commends adultery. Had the picture drawn of the last days of the dying philosopher been a true one, it would still have been unspeakably melancholy, and it matters little to the faith of the true Christian how an unbeliever dies. Mr. Haldane has, however, stated enough to throw some doubt upon these representations. The authority for his statements is not mentioned, but it was his neighbor in the country, Mr. Abercromby, of Tullibody. The details are curious and worth preserving. It happened in the autumn of 1776, very shortly after Mr. Hume's death, that Mr. Abercromby was travelling to Haddington with two other friends, in one of those old-fashioned stage-coaches which Sir Walter Scott has so graphically described at the commencement of the "Antiquary." The conversation during the tedious journey turned on the death-bed of the great philosopher, and as Mr. Abercromby's son-in-law, Colonel Edmonstone, of Newton, was one of Hume's intimate friends, he had heard from him much of the buoyant cheerfulness which had enlivened the sick-room of the- dying man. Whilst the conversation was running on in this strain, a respectable-looking female dressed in black, who made a fourth in the coach, begged permission to offer a remark. "Gentlemen," she said, "I attended Mr. Hume on his death-bed, but I can assure you I hope never again to attend the death-bed of a philosopher." They then cross-examined her as to her meaning, and she told them, that when his friends were with him, Mr. Hume was cheerful even to frivolity, but that when alone he was often overwhelmed with unutterable gloom, and had, in his hours of depression, declared that he had been in search of light all his life, but was now in greater darkness than ever. The anecdote has been told by those who probably had it from some of the other travellers. Mrs. Haldane's version is substantially the same, and Mrs. Joass often repeated the circumstances as related by her venerable father. Other testimonies indicate that the philosopher's own friends did not themselves possess that confidence which they attributed to their hero on his death-bed. One of those anecdotes which rendered Mr. Haldane's conversation so interesting, and which generally depended on original and authentic information, related to Adam Smith. It was one fully believed by those who knew the political economist. Speculating as to "the great darkness," the philosopher, at the request of Adam Smith – a request quite in the spirit of Mr. Strachan's published letter – promised, if it were in his power, to meet his friend in the shady avenue of "the Meadows," behind George-square, and "tell the secrets of the world unknown." Probably the promise was made and received during the last days of David Hume, with the same levity as the conversation which Adam Smith has actually recorded about Charon and his boat. But such was its effect on the author of the "Theory of Moral Sentiments" and the "Wealth of Nations," that no persuasion would induce him to walk in the meadows after sunset.

FIRST NOTICES OF HUME'S DEATH

49
NOTICE OF HUME'S DEATH
(*WEEKLY MAGAZINE*)

Notice of Hume's Death, *Weekly Magazine, or Edinburgh Amusement*, August 29, 1776, Vol. 33, p. 320.
Complete.

Hume died August 25, 1776, and four days later a lengthy obituary notice appeared in the *Weekly Magazine* – several times longer than the usual death notices in that publication. The author quotes a flattering synopsis of Hume from Carlo Denina's *Essay on the Revolutions of Literature* (1771); selections from Denina's work are contained later in this collection.

DEATHS.

[August] 25. At his house in St David's street, New Town, Edinburgh, after a tedious illness, which he bore with great resignation, David Hume, Esq; author of the History of England, essays moral and political, &c. It would be altogether superfluous to give a panegyric upon an author, whose character is so well established, and whose merit as a *political* writer is universally acknowledged. Invidious also would be the task now to draw forth his frailties into public view. We shall give a character of Mr Hume, drawn by a celebrated foreigner, *Carlo Denina*, which it may be presumed is equally free from prejudice and from flattery. "That spirit of literature," says M. Denina, "which had so nobly animated London, the capital of the island, and the neighbouring provinces, has at length, it would seem, extended itself to the remotest corners of Britain. It is however an incontestible fact, that of late the principal ornaments of the British literature, have received their birth and education in Scotland. I have already observed, that though England abounds in good writers of every other kind, she has hardly produced one historian of character. [Lord Lyttleton's history was not published when Mr Denina wrote these strictures.] It was reserved for Scotland to supply so material a deficiency. Is there a man of letters in Europe unacquainted with the works of HUME? Is there a man of taste who does not read his history with particular admiration?

Endued with uncommon abilities, had he not shown so much eagerness to insinuate his pernicious opinions, he would have escaped the just censures of the religious, added greater weight to his history, and rendered it at once more interesting and spirited. Scepticism is naturally cold and barren, and in works of literature passion is generally preferable to indifference. After all, his defects, whether in point of stile, sentiment, or historical fidelity, serve but as foils to his excellencies." – Mr Hume was secretary to gen. St Clare, who commanded the expedition to Port L'Orient in the year 1746. He was afterwards secretary to lord Hertford, while ambassador at Paris, and under-secretary of state while gen. Conway held the seals.

50
NOTICES OF HUME'S DEATH
(*LONDON CHRONICLE* AND
SCOTS MAGAZINE)

Notices of Hume's Death, in *London Chronicle*, Sept. 3–5, 1776, Vol. 40, No. 3081, p. 432; *Scots Magazine*, August 1776, Vol. 38, p. 455. Complete notices.

At the close of August, the *London Chronicle* printed a one-sentence notice of Hume's death, which was followed in the next issue with one slightly longer:

> David Hume, Esq; whose death was mentioned in our last, was Secretary to General St. Clair, who commanded the expedition to Port l'Orient in the year 1746. He was afterwards Secretary to Lord Hertford, while ambassador at Paris, and under Secretary of State while General Conway held the seals. [*London Chronicle*, August 31–September 3, 1776, Vol. 40, No. 3080, p. 219.]

In their next issue they printed a flattering letter on Hume by an Aberdeen correspondent who states that "his reputation as an Historian, almost eclipses that of the Philosopher." *Scots Magazine* subsequently published the following notice of Hume's death, which includes the *London Chronicle* letter. The letter is as appears in the *London Chronicle*. Bracketed comments are those of *Scots Magazine*. The Aberdeen correspondent's letter was criticized in another letter to the *London Chronicle* (November 23–26), contained later in this collection.

DEATHS.

[August] 25. At his house in Edinburgh, after a tedious illness, David Hume, Esq; He died a bachelor. This gentleman was secretary to Gen. St Clair, when commander in chief of the troups who made a descent on the French coast in 1746 [vii. 490]; and was afterwards secretary to the Earl of Hertford while ambassador to the count of France, and undersecretary of state while Gen. Conway held the seals. – His History of England is well known, and gives him a distinguished rank in the learned world. "Very early in life he published [says one who writes a short account of him] his *Treatise on Human Nature*, to which, however, he never put his name; but he afterwards melted it down into his *Philosophical Essays*, or, *Inquiry concerning Human Understanding.* – Our readers have already seen a character of him by a learned foreigner [xxvi. 467];[1] and another has been written since his death, viz.

To the PRINTER *of the* LONDON CHRONICLE.
"Sir,
                                                                      Aberdeen, Aug. 29, 1776
No modern has been more read, or has commanded a larger share of the public approbation than the late Mr Hume.

If he was not the greatest philosopher, he possessed at least the singular merit of having put into motion more philosophical genius than any other Writer of his time: and his most violent opponents derived perhaps from the merit of their adversary, their best pretensions to literary fame. But the region of Metaphysics he soon looked through, and abandoned. The laurels he chiefly valued, were gathered in another soil. In an age and country abounding with Historians, he maintained a distinguished, and almost unrivalled pre-eminence; and his reputation as an Historian, almost eclipses that of the Philosopher.

In both lines, after ages will extol, and admire *the Author*. His contemporaries loved *the Man*. They beheld in his character, the most agreeable contradictions; The virtues of humanity, unshaken by the most absolute skepticism; The moral duties of *this life* flourishing under a total disregard of *another*; and even the graces and temper of a *Christian*, in an avowed enemy of the Christian Faith."

---

[1] [i.e., Carlo Denina *Essay on the Revolutions of Literature* (1771), which was quoted in the obituary on Hume in *Weekly Magazine.*]

51
LETTER ON HUME'S CHARACTER
(LONDON CHRONICLE)

Letter on Hume's Character to *London Chronicle*, November 23–25, 1776, Vol. 40, No. 3116, p. 509.
Complete; from *London Chronicle*.

Shortly after Hume's death, the *London Chronicle* published a flattering letter about Hume, written by an Aberdeen correspondent on August 29 (contained in this collection). An Edinburgh correspondent sent the following critical response to the *London Chronicle*, faulting the Aberdeen correspondent for glorifying scepticism. The article was reprinted in *Scots Magazine*, November 1776, Vol. 38, p. 579.

To the PRINTER *of the* LONDON CHRONICLE.

Sir,
What the late Mr. David Hume was, and what were his real principles, have long been the subject of warm dispute. I mean not here to investigate either, but leave him and them to a more unerring Judge. I cannot, however, be altogether silent, when your correspondent from Aberdeen (forgetful of the humane maxim, *de mortuis nil nisi bonum,* and no less forgetful of the interests of virtue), has attempted to mislead the young and the thoughtless, by imposing a character no where to be found but in the reveries of his own imagination.
He tells us, in the London Chronicle of the 5th Sept. last; "That Mr. Hume's contemporaries beheld in his character the most *agreeable contradictions,* the virtues of humanity unshaken by the most absolute scepticism, the moral duties of this life flourishing under a total disregard of any other, and even the graces and temper of a Christian in a speculative enemy to the Christian faith."
In what light those, who revere Mr. Hume's memory most, will view this ludicrous description of their deceased friend, to give it no worse epithet, is not mine to say; but, doubtless, contradictions more glaring, more repugnant to common sense and universal experience, and so diametrically opposite to divine revelation, cannot well be supported. The graces and temper of the

Christian, without the faith of a Christian; scepticism humanizing the heart; unbelief working by love; infidelity shewing itself by good works; the duties of a present life flourishing by denying a life to come; the spirit resigned and willing to die, from the exalted hopes of going down to the dust with the beast that perisheth. Such are the contradictions, the agreeable, the most agreeable contradictions, which your correspondent beheld in Mr. Hume.

Whether this character, equally injurious to the memory of Mr Hume and to mankind, comes from one of his mistaken friends, or from a disguised enemy, may be a question: But sure I am, the pen of a Swift, or the pencil of a Hogarth, could not have exhibited the object of satire in a more ridiculous, heterogeneous light; the *chief of Infidels*, the *best of Christians*.

In short, Sir, if this gentleman does not mean, under the mask of friendship, to insult the ashes of the dead, it seems prudent to suffer his friend to rest in the grave, crowned with the laurels which, as an historian and philosopher, his works entitle him to, without attempting a monument sacred to scepticism and infidelity, or to persuade the world upon his *ipse dixit*, that absolute scepticism has no influence in weakening the ties of humanity; that morality can flourish in its full extent, where a state of retribution and all beyond the grave is disregarded as idle dreams; and that even the graces and temper of a christian may reside in the heart, and influence the life of one to whom christianity itself is a mere fable. What a group of agreeable absurdities! how many beautiful impossibilities have we here! We have indeed heard of "the form of godliness without the power;" but your Correspondent has the honour of finding out a character entirely new, the power of godliness without the form.

It would be an unpardonable trespass on your readers patience, to dwell longer upon self evident contradictions; nor shall I further occupy your useful paper than to set before them the following beautiful lines of a celebrated poet,[1] which place the unbeliever and his principles in a light no less genuine than striking, sufficient one would imagine to stagger infidelity itself.

What then is unbelief? 'Tis an exploit;
A strenuous enterprise. To gain it, man
Must burst thro' every bar of common sense,
Of common shame, magnanimously wrong:
And what rewards the sturdy combatant?
His prize, repentance; infamy, his crown.
Faith in the future wanting, is, at least
In embryo, every weakness, every guilt;
And strong temptation ripens it to birth.
If this life's gain invites him to the deed,

---

[1]   Night thoughts, night 7. [vi. 562].

Why not his country sold, his father slain?
Has Virtue charms? – I grant her heav'nly fair;
But, if unportion'd; will all int'rest wed;
Tho' that our admiration, this our choice.
The virtues grow on immortality;
That rest destroy'd, they wither and expire.
A Deity believ'd will nought avail:
Rewards and punishments make God ador'd:
And hopes and fears give conscience all her power;
As in the dying parent dies the child,
Virtue, with immortality, expires.
Nature's first wish is endless happiness;
Annihilation is an after thought,
A monstrous wish, unborn till virtue dies.
And oh! what depth of horror lies inclos'd?
For non-existence no man ever wish'd,
But first, he wish'd the Deity destroy'd.

AN EDINBURGH CORRESPONDENT.

52
LETTER ON HUME'S BURIAL AND WILL
(*LONDON CHRONICLE* AND
SCOTS MAGAZINE)

Letter on Hume's burial and will, in *London Chronicle*, September 7–10, 1776, Vol. 40, No. 3083, p. 248, and *Scots Magazine*, September 1776, Vol. 38, p. 508.
Complete letter.

After Hume's burial on August 29, 1776, an extract of a letter from an Edinburgh correspondent was printed in the *London Chronicle*, which describes his death and the contents of his will. This was reprinted in *Scots Magazine*, with an additional paragraph relating a codicil in Hume's will regarding John Home – although it is not clear whether the added paragraph was part of the original letter. The following is as appears in *Scots Magazine*, only the first paragraph of which was printed in the *London Chronicle*. Bracketed and parenthetical comments are those of *Scots Magazine*.

"The great Mr Hume [455.] – (says a letter, dated, Edinburgh, Aug. 30. in the London Chronicle), was buried here [in the Calton burying-ground] yesterday. He had been ailing a long while, but never complained, nor was confined to his bed till a day or two before his death. He was sensible to the last, and has left an amiable character behind him for goodness and generosity. His brother is appointed heir by testament, but he has left some small legacies to several of his friends: To a servant 20l. per ann. to Dr Smith 200l. to Dr Ferguson 100 or 200l.; and 100l. to erect a monument to his memory, with an express prohibition to put any thing on it but the day of his birth and the day of his death."

Among other articles left by the celebrated Mr Hume to his friends, is the following whimsical one: He bequeathed fifteen dozen of port wine to Mr John Home, Author of Douglas, and other tragedies, upon condition of his drinking one bottle of port at what he calls a down-sitting, and signing a receipt *John Hume*. This piece of wit, if it deserves the name, proceeded from the known aversion of Mr Home to *port wine*, and his having had frequent disputes with

Mr Hume about the manner of spelling his name. It is remarkable that Mr Home, from a sincere anxiety for his friend, attended him through the whole course of his illness, and travelled with him for the benefit of his health to various parts of the kingdom, during the last summer. *Lond. Chron.*

"*Edinburgh*, Sept. 4. The late Mr Hume has left memoirs of is life and writings, with several other pieces, to Mr Strahan, of London, printer, to be published."

JOHN HOME'S DISCUSSIONS
OF HUME'S CHARACTER

53
JOHN HOME:
"A SKETCH OF THE CHARACTER
OF MR. HUME"

John Home, "A Sketch of the Character of Mr. Hume by an author of the nineteenth Century" (c. 1776).
Complete, newly transcribed; from manuscript in the National Library of Scotland (MS. 3993).[1]

John Home (1722–1808) was the author of the diary of the journey with Hume to Bath, contained earlier in this collection. At some point after Hume's death, Home wrote a short essay with the intriguing title "A Sketch of the Character of Mr. Hume by an author of the nineteenth Century." On its most elemental level, the essay surveys Hume's writings, praising them each to the highest degree and hailing Hume as the greatest author in the republic of letters since Aristotle. The work bears no date, but several features suggest that it may have been written around 1776 or 1777. First, there are indications in the handwriting. The manuscript of the sketch was penned by a skilled clerk, with several written corrections by Home. His smooth penmanship here stands in great contrast to his degenerated script near the end of his life.[2] Second, the *Sketch* makes no mention of Hume's *Dialogues* or *Essays on Suicide and Immortality*, which would have been strange if the sketch had been written after 1779 or 1783. Third, the *Sketch* in many ways parallels Home's "Remarks on the Life and Character of the late David Hume, Esq." which appeared in the *London Chronicle* during September 1776.

The attribution "by an author of the nineteenth century" reveals a polemical purpose to Home's work. It is, in essence, a fictional speculation about how someone in the future – perhaps a hundred years down the road – would

---

[1] The transcription is reproduced by kind permission of the Trustees of the National Library of Scotland.

[2] I thank M.A. Stewart for this information about Home's script, and for his help transcribing the more difficult parts of the manuscript.

perceive Hume. Several attacks on Hume's character and writings were exceptionally harsh – such as that by James Beattie – and the literary device of a nineteenth-century writer would have been an effective counterattack. This would especially be so for the following two critics who in 1777 maintained that the fame of Hume and other infidels is fleeting:

> Their elaborate theories, by which they gain the temporary fame of genius exerted, are of such manifestly evil tendency, so inimical to Christianity, and to men's best interests, that they can never go down with the wise and virtuous, but must be abjured by them; and shall therefore, it is hoped, meet with deserved contempt and neglect from our princes, our nobles, our judges, from our learned gentlemen of every order, and from all people who revere God and love mankind. ["E.M.," "Remarks on Dr Adam Smith's Letter," contained in this collection.]

> Do they boast of a *Bolingbroke*, a *Pope*, a *Hume?* We can match them with an *Addison*, a *Thompson*, a *Beattie*: whose works will be read and admired by the greater part of Mankind in all succeeding generations; while the favourers of scepticism and infidelity shall either sink into oblivion, or at best be pointed out to be shunned as dangerous and pestilential. ["Laicus," "Observations on the Address to One of the People called Christians," contained in this collection.]

Writing from the future, Home's nineteenth-century author tells us that this is not at all the case. In fact, Hume's reputation has surged in every area in which he wrote. Even Hume's essay on miracles is "the most pious of all human compositions" for putting religious "Imposters and Enthusiasts" in their place. One passage, which Home later scored out, states that Hume "left productions behind him that will last coæval with the works of the Almighty." The praises coming from the mouth of the nineteenth-century writer are far too effusive for even a close friend such as John Home to hold in earnest. The point of the piece, it seems, was to counterbalance the opposition with something almost as extreme, and not to present an impartial assessment.

Had this been published, it would have undoubtedly been controversial and generated numerous responses. We of course do not know why he held it back, but one possibility suggests itself. Without knowing beforehand that the author of the *Sketch* was a friend of Hume's, a reader might well have taken the piece to be an *attack* on the philosopher couched in irony – in the style of, for instance, *The Usefulness of the Edinburgh Theatre Seriously Considered* (1757), contained earlier in this collection. Such a consideration may have prompted Home to cross out the most extreme passages in the *Sketch*. Further consideration along these lines may have inclined him to set the whole piece aside.

The following is newly transcribed from the manuscript, which is housed in the National Library of Scotland. It was previously transcribed by David Fate Norton in *A Sketch of the Character of Mr. Hume* (Edinburgh: Tragara Press, 1976), to which I am indebted for guidance in deciphering the more illegible portions of the text. Passages scored out by Home are presented in footnotes.

A Sketch
Of the Character of Mr. Hume
by an author of the nineteenth Century.

When the reign of Queen Anne, which was reckoned the Augustan Age of England, had ceased, a man arose, who gave a new turn to the studies of the learned, and introduced a more brilliant Era of Philosophy and taste. Men of an original and creative genius, who dare to think for themselves, for the world and for posterity, are the extraordinary productions of Nature and not to be expected in every century. All Classes of mankind, the learned as well as others, seem disposed to receive thought rather than to think: What is called Enquiry, is with most men little more than taking the fashionable opinions for granted. Philosophical Errors, like vulgar Errors, are faithfully transmitted from one generation to another. Authority reigns no-where with greater violence than in the Republic of letters; the Empire of the mind, like other Empires is held by prescription, and in length of time an usurper comes to be reckoned a lawful prince. What are we to think then of this Author, who at once broke asunder the chains which had long fettered the human Understanding; threw off the yoke of the tyrants who had lorded it over the mind; and stept forth an Alexander to conquer the world and obtain an universal monarchy? Wherever he went, he went in triumph. He annihilated and created. He drew his pen and a System fell. He dispelled the darkness of many Centuries; overturned opinions which had been established upon the authority of ages, unhinged the faith of the world in all matters human and divine; gave a shock to the whole system of Literature, introduced new ideas into everything, and carried novelty and light into Religion, Metaphysics, Morality, Criticism, Politics and Commerce.

The first flight of Genius is rapid; eccentric; *extra flamniantia mœnia mundi.* It darts from earth to heaven; bursts the barriers of mortality; overleaps the boundaries of the world: Aims at Infinite; and strives to comprehend in its grasp the Immensity of the Universe.

His earliest production, the essay on human nature, will ever be regarded as a prodigy of genius. Written when the author was at the age of five and twenty, it discovers a strength, a boldness, and a comprehension of mind, an acuteness and intensity of thinking, scarcely to be met with in any other production. Composed upon a subject which had been the study of scientific men since the days of Aristotle, it is perhaps the most original work which the world ever saw. If his Course in these undiscovered regions is not a path of light, it is a track of glory; if in that *terra incognita* he did not find an inhabitable country, he shewed to future adventurers that there is none to be found.[3]

In his following productions, his various and universal talents gradually displayed themselves. His Essays are at once popular and philosophical, and contain a rare and happy union of profound Science and fine writing.

Originality, depth of thinking, happy arrangement, beautiful illustration, and elegant expressions characterise these Immortal productions. Equally qualified to invent, to illustrate and adorn, he gives novelty, order and beauty to every thing. He unites qualities and acquirements which seem to stand at the greatest distance, Originality with Erudition, Ingenuity with Profoundness, Novelty with Justness, and the most laborious Investigation with perspicuous and easy expression. He joins philosophy and taste in such happy Union, as to have made the ornamental arts a vehicle of instruction, and the abstruse Sciences an article of entertainment.

It was reserved for this Author to give us Just and temperate notions concerning classical antiquity. The Revival of letters in Europe after the dark ages was not owing to an original effort of the human mind but to the study of the ancients. These were the fountains from which our first authors drew, and the models according to which they worked. An Admiration of the ancients even to an extreme was at that time natural and proper. But when in process of time we had cultivated the arts and Sciences, produced classics of our own and had the fountains within ourselves, what was formerly a Just Admiration became a blind Enthusiasm. Perhaps it will be found too, that what is commonly called Learning, beyond a certain degree, is not friendly to Philosophy; that those who are perpetually ransacking the stores of antiquity diminish the treasures of their own mind; and being accustomed to follow a guide, and to tread in the beaten track, become so diffident of themselves as to be afraid to walk alone or venture on a new path. Mr. Hume therefore did essential service to Literature and Philosophy by showing the antients in their proper light. While he extolled their virtues, he represented their defects. While he allowed them their just applause for their progress in the Elegant arts, their public Spirit, and the benevolent genius of their religion, he exposed the defects of their government, the rudeness of their wit and the barbarity of their manners.

We are sometimes amazed at that extent of view by which he seizes a whole system as if by Intuition. In his essay concerning the association of Ideas, he traces the utmost flight and eccentricity of the mind, sets bounds to the wildest sallies

---

[3] [The following is marked out at the conclusion of this sentence: "if his flight in these regions does not resemble the Messiah in paradise lost turning a chaos into a beautiful world, it resembles the Messiah in the same poem, riding in triumph thro' the kingdom of night, and driving the princes of darkness before him to their destined abodes."]

of Imagination, and comprehends the whole world of Ideas in a few plain laws.

The essay on the Origin and progress of the Arts and Sciences contains more information and sound philosophy than all that has been written upon that subject by others. Like other works of our Author it has the merit of being at once new and complete. Other Authors have enriched their productions from this invaluable work.

Religion itself, that dark, wild, wonderful, multiform, variable, irregular fluctuating thing, which like madness or magic seemed to be without the dominion of nature and to bid defiance to Philosophy, even Religion could not escape the keenness and comprehension of his Intellect. He removed the marvellous that was spread around it, restored it to the province of nature, and reduced it to a regular System. In this Essay (on the natural history of Religion) he displays such extensive Erudition, such profound Enquiry, and writes with so much Energy and Elegance, that we do not hesitate to pronounce it his capital production.

The essay on Miracles operates both directly and indirectly against the vulgar Religion. It is a vindication of the order of Nature and a defense of divine Providence against Imposters and Enthusiasts, and in that view to be regarded as the most pious of all human compositions.

In the department of History, it is universally acknowledged, that he has attained Perfection. It was he who made the English acquainted with their own History. In that great work the Financier, the politician, the philosopher, the elegant Writer, and along with these, the personal character of the Author present themselves to view. He delineates the manners of the Age, as well as the Spirit of the Nation, and gives us the character of men and the people as well as the History of Statesmen and Things. His style varies with the Subjects; He narrates with Simplicity, as he describes with Splendor. Candid and Impartial, he makes both Parties speak. He never makes a Sacrifice. Neither the Advocate of Faction, nor the Slave of government, nor the Tool of Superstition, he always sustains the dignity of a Man, and is not only the Historian, but the Judge of Nations, It hath been fortunate for Mankind, that the two greatest Nations of the world, have had their actions recorded and celebrated by two of the most profound Geniuses who have adorned their nations, The History of the Romans, by Tacitus, and of the English, by David Hume, form a happy combination that may never again be found in the Revolution of Ages.[4]

It would be unnecessary for us to go through all his other productions. It is

---

[4] [The preceding paragraph replaces the following which is marked out: "He is one of the few Philosophical Historians, and he was the first who made the English acquainted with their own history. The Philosopher, the Politician, the Financier, and the elegant writer equally appear. He makes both parties speak. His stile does not flow in one uniform tone of declamation, it raises according to the subject. He knows to relate and to describe. In this department he is universally acknowledged to have attained perfection."]

sufficient to say that he formed an age. He thought and he set others a thinking. In the works of his Contemporaries, we trace his doctrine and we see his hand. From this fountain of Light the Planets of his System borrow their beams. He did not confine himself to the Philosophic Shade; he served his Country abroad as he had adorned it at home. By a felicity unusual to learned men he reaped the fruits of his genius and the reward of his merit.

He was no less Amiable as a man than illustrious as an Author. The Philosopher did not absorb the man and the gentleman. Ease, Naivity, Gaity, marked and beautified his manners. Tho' all men saw, no one ever felt his superiority. Celestial beings when they descend to earth are said to appear like other men. So general was the respect to his Candor and merit that even good natured believers said of him as Pope said of Garth "That he was the best Christian in the world without knowing it."

He indeed wrote freely concerning religion. He boldly published what he boldly thought. A Philosopher is of no sect nor party, he belongs to the world at large.

The Factions and Prejudices of his Countrymen prevented them for some time from knowing all his merit, but abroad he received the fulness of his fame, and was universally acknowledged to be the first writer of the age, and the Profoundest philosopher of the world.

In looking over the names that have adorned the Republic of Letters, we find none with whom we can compare our author except Aristotle, the most subtil and comprehensive genius of Antiquity, who was at once a Natural Philosopher, a Metaphysician, a Moralist, a Politician, a Critic, and a man of the world; whose philosophy was received in Asia as well as in Europe, and who reigned over the human mind for two thousand years. But even Aristotle is unequal, for he was void of elegance as a writer, and if we mistake not, wanted taste: for the taste which he discovers is that which arises from reason and reflection, not that which flows from an internal Sense.

Mr. Hume in the latter part of his life retired to his native Country, and devoted the Evening of his days to Hospitality, Elegance, Literature and Friendship.

Rewarded by his king whom he had served, applauded by his Country which he had rendered illustrious, idolized by his friends whom he passionately loved, he at last paid the debt of nature, and died as he had lived, A Philosopher, with the consolation of lying down upon the bed of Fame, and leaving behind him a name that shall never die.[5]

---

[5] [Beginning with the words "and leaving," the latter half of this sentence replaces the following which is marked out: "and with the pleasing reflection of having acquired the first name in the literary world, and of having left productions behind him that will last coæval with the works of the Almighty."]

54
JOHN HOME:
"REMARKS ON THE LIFE AND CHARACTER
OF THE LATE DAVID HUME, ESQ."
(LONDON CHRONICLE)

[John Home], "Remarks on the Life and Character of the late David Hume, Esq." in *London Chronicle*, 1776, Sept. 10–12, Vol. 40, No. 3084; p. 256, Sept. 14–17, No. 3086, pp. 271–272; Sept. 21–24, No. 3089, p. 293. Complete.

In September 1776 the *London Chronicle* printed two flattering letters about Hume from a correspondent identifying himself only as "A Friend to Merit." The letters are untitled, but in the final of three instalments of them the *London Chronicle* gives it the title "Remarks on the Life and Character of the late David Hume, Esq.," derived from the opening sentence of the first letter: "I beg you will give a place in your paper to the following short but impartial account of the life and character of the late David Hume, Esquire." Though published anonymously there are compelling reasons for ascribing the letters to Hume's close and long-time friend John Home (1722–1808), author of the diary of the journey with Hume to Bath contained in this collection. The evidence consists of parallels between these letters and Home's "Sketch of the Character of Mr. Hume by an Author of the Nineteenth Century," included in this collection. Although no passage is repeated verbatim, there are recurring turns of phrase and thought that appear in both. The most telling is this:

Remarks: "Mr. Hume retired into the shade of private life, and upon this occasion a pension was settled upon him, not as a reward for having prostituted his pen in the service of government, a thing which he never did, and which he scorned to do ..."

Sketch: "Mr. Hume in the latter part of his life retired to his native Country, and devoted the Evening of his days to Hospitality, Elegance, Literature and Friendship. Rewarded by his king whom he had served ... "

"Neither the Advocate of Faction, nor the Slave of government ..."

Other parallels are the comparisons between Hume and Tacitus, the mention of Hume's favourable reception in Continental Europe, and the descriptions of Hume's "Natural History of Religion." The closing paragraphs of the "Remarks" resemble most closely the excessive praise that characterizes the "Sketch." It is also noteworthy that, when listing Hume's friends who were "some of the most respectable members" of the Scottish clergy, Home modestly leaves off his own name, mentioning "the Drs Robertson, Blair, Jardine, Carlyle, and others."

Home's "Remarks" describes Hume's unsuccessful efforts at law and university teaching. He suggests that Hume's animosity toward religion and the Church intensified when the presbytery of Edinburgh derailed his candidacy for the Chair of Moral Philosophy at Edinburgh University in 1745. Much of the "Remarks" discusses the composition and reception of Hume's *History*. He describes a prank that Hume played on Walter Goodall – a version of which also appeared in Henry Mackenzie's *Anecdotes and Egotisms* (1927), contained in this collection.[1] Perhaps the most important new information in the "Remarks" is the account of Hume's reception in the French royal court: "Upon his arrival at Paris a mark of distinction was shewn him which perhaps had never been shown before to any but a sovereign prince. When he was first introduced into the royal presence, the king and his whole court rose up to receive him." Also of interest are anecdotes about Hume modifying two passages of the *History* and his approval of Andrew Millar's business skills.

An anonymous letter to the *London Chronicle* printed in the November 5–7 issue (contained in this collection) corrects Home's account of Hume's 1745 candidacy. Slightly modified selections from the first two instalments of Home's "Remarks" were reprinted in *The Weekly Magazine or Edinburgh Amusement* under the titles "A Short but impartial Account of the Life and Character of the late David Hume, Esq." (September 19, 1776, Vol. 33, p. 400) and "Anecdote of the late David Hume, Esq." (October 3, 1776, Vol. 34, p. 48 – regarding Hume's prank on Goodall).

Postscript.

To the PRINTER *of the* LONDON CHRONICLE.

Sir,

I beg you will give a place in your paper to the following short but impartial account of the life and character of the late David Hume, Esquire.

---

[1] [For a discussion of Hume's and Goodall's respective roles in the Queen Mary controversy, see the editor's introduction to *Early Responses to Hume's History* (2002).]

He was a younger son of a Gentleman of good family but small estate, in the Southern part of Scotland. After passing through his academical courses at the university of Edinburgh, he entered upon the study of the law, in which he made a considerable proficiency; but, as his talent lay rather for writing than speaking, he did not make so capital a figure in it as some of his contemporaries of much meaner abilities; or, to speak more properly, he saw that he had no chance of making such a figure; for, as far as I can recollect, he never took upon him the gown, or acted formally as an Advocate.

Very early in life he published his "Treatise on Human Nature," to which, however, he never put his name; and which, after remaining unanswered for thirty years, has of late furnished matter for much reasoning and more declamation to the Doctors Reid, Beatty, and Oswald. The substance, indeed, of this treatise he afterwards melted down into his "Philosophical Essays," or "Enquiry concerning Human Understanding," which was soon after published.

About the year 1746, or 1747, he stood Candidate for the professorship of moral philosophy in the university of Edinburgh, then become vacant by the resignation of Doctor (now Sir John) Pringle, who had been appointed Physician to the army in Germany. The manner of election is either this, or something very similar to it. Out of the number of Candidates, three are nominated by the town-council of Edinburgh: The Presbytery of Edinburgh have a negative upon any one of the three; and one of the remaining two is chosen professor by the Lord Provost and principal magistrates of the city. It happened unluckily upon this occasion, that the Presbytery put a negative upon Mr. Hume; and, though he had probably been before confirmed in his sceptical principles, yet it was from this period that he declared open and irreconcileable war, not only against the presbytery of Edinburgh, but against the whole body of the clergy. He continued, nevertheless, to live upon the most friendly, and even the most intimate footing with some of the most respectable members of it, such as the Doctors Robertson, Blair, Jardine, Carlyle, and others.

Finding himself, however, thus cut off from all hopes of gaining a settlement as a professor, and having no prospect of making either a figure or a fortune as a lawyer, he turned the whole force of his mind, which was certainly very great, to the study of philosophy and the belles lettres, in most of the different departments of which he made so rapid and distinguished a progress, as has placed him on an equality with the most celebrated names either in ancient or modern history.

What I have farther to say with regard to this great man, shall be sent you in my next.

A FRIEND TO MERIT.

—

To the PRINTER *of the* LONDON CHRONICLE.

Sir,

I herewith send you a few farther particulars with regard to the life and character of the late David Hume, Esq. Soon after his being disappointed in his views upon the professorship of moral philosophy, he was chosen by the dean and faculty of advocates principal keeper of the advocates' library ad Edinburgh. This indeed was in a great measure a sinecure, the chief care and management of the books being left to the under-keeper, who was at that time Mr Walter Goodall, afterwards pretty well known by the tracts which he published relative to Mary queen of Scots, and to the history and antiquities of Scotland.

A rencounter which happened between Mr. Hume and Mr. Goodall, as it is somewhat curious, or at least ludicrous, may not perhaps be unentertaining to your Readers. – While Watty, as he was familiarly called, and good-naturedly suffered himself to be called, by his acquaintance, was composing his treatise concerning Queen Mary, he one day, while sitting in the library, became drowsy, and laying down his head upon his manuscripts, in that posture fell asleep. Mr. Hume entering the library, and finding Watty in that condition, stepped up with a gentle pace, and laying his mouth to Watty's ear, roared out with the voice of a Stentor, that Queen Mary was a whore, and had murdered her husband. Watty, not knowing whether it was a dream or a real adventure, or whether the voice proceeded from a ghost or a living creature, suddenly started up, and before he was awake, or his eyes well opened, he sprung upon Mr. Hume, and seizing him by the throat, pushed him to the farther end of the library, exclaiming all the while, that he was some d____d[2] presbyterian parson, who was come to murder the character of Queen Mary, as his predecessors had contributed to murder her person. Mr. Hume used to tell this story with much glee and humour; and Watty, who in every thing but enthusiasm for Queen Mary, was really a very sensible man, was wont to acknowledge the truth of it with the greatest frankness.

The office of librarian, though sufficiently honourable, was far form being lucrative, the income I believe not amounting to above 50l. a-year; and though Mr. Hume was himself at that time in rather narrow circumstances, yet such was his disinterestedness and generosity, that, as I have been informed, he allotted the whole, or at least the greater part of this sum, to the support of Blacklock the blind poet, then a young student in the university of Edinburgh.

His appointment indeed to this office was attended with one happy consequence. It gave him a free and unlimited access to the noble collection of books contained in the advocates' library; and it is not improbable, that this

[2] [The *Weekly Magazine* prints this as "d____n'd," presumably meaning "damn'd".]

circumstance, concurring with a variety of others, might first suggest to him the idea of writing his history of Great Britain. Certain it is, that the two first volumes of that work, comprehending the reigns of the Stuarts, were ready for the press by the beginning of 1754, and were actually published in the course of that year.

They had no sooner made their appearance than all the critics and hyper-critics fell violently upon them. Some said that it was not a history, but a disser-tation upon history; others alleged, that it was merely an apology for the tyrannical house of Stuart. But though Mr. Hume, upon this and upon every other occasion, shewed the utmost contempt for the cavils of the ignorant and envious, yet he always paid a proper regard to the remarks of the candid and judicious; and hence it was, that in consequence of their remarks, he altered the language of two passages in these volumes.[3]

One was the very first sentence of the work, which originally ran thus: "The crown of England was never *transferred* from father to son with greater tranquility, than it passed from the family of Tudor to that of Stuart." Here it was said, that the transition from father to son is much more slight and gentle than that from one family to another; and yet the verb *transferred* is of much stronger import than the verb *passed*; the expression therefore does not corre-spond with the idea. Mr. Hume saw and acknowledged the force of this objection, and consequently, in all the future editions, he substituted the verb *transmitted* in place of *transferred*.

The other passage was the concluding sentence in the character of Charles II. which in the first edition was worded thus: "And the only circumstance in which it can justly be pretended he (the Emperor Tiberius) was similar to Charles is his *love of women*; a passion which is too general to form any striking resemblance, and which that detestable and detested monster possessed with *other* unnatural appetites." The critics alleged, that according to this mode of expression, the *love of women* was made to be an *unnatural* appetite, a position which Mr. Hume, who really loved the sex, was as little likely as any man living to advance. In all the subsequent editions, therefore, the latter part of the sentence was altered thus: "and which that detestable and detested monster shared also with unnatural appetites."

These remarks will not appear so trifling as at first sight they may seem, when it is considered that Mr. Hume was extremely attentive to the purity of his stile; and indeed it may be affirmed that his stile is as pure and correct, and much more vigorous, than that of any other English Writer.

---

[3] [The two criticisms that Home mentions are not contained in *Early Responses to Hume's History of England* (2002). It is possible that these criticisms came from Home himself and were verbally communicated to Hume. Perhaps Home's closeness to this event explains the two corrections to his account of it in the errata list (see note below).]

[To be concluded in another paper.]

———

Remarks on the Life and Character of the late David Hume, Esq, concluded.

The very favourable reception which the two first volumes of Mr. Hume's History of Great Britain met with, naturally encouraged him to continue the work; and to this he was still farther prompted by the liberal offers that were made him by Mr. Millar, bookseller in the Strand, who had now purchased the copy right of those two volumes from the Scotch book-sellers, who had originally bought them of Mr. Hume.

It is reported as a saying of Dr. Johnson's, that Mr. Millar had raised the price of literature fifty percent. But I believe, if Mr. Hume had been required to give his opinion on the same subject, he would have said, that he had raised not only fifty, but even a hundred percent. The fact is, that he was so well satisfied with Mr. Millar's conduct as to money-matters, that when the Earl of Bute became prime-minister, and Mr. Hume was jocularly advised by some of his acquaintances to endeavour to procure the patronage of so great a man, he bluntly replied, that he wanted no other patron than Andrew Millar.

Under the patronage, therefore, or at least by the encouragement of this very liberal bookseller (liberal, most certainly, in rewarding the labours of eminent writers, however penurious he might be in other respects) Mr. Hume went on with his historical studies, and in a short time produced the two next volumes of his History, containing the reigns of the Tudors; and, at a proper interval, he finished the two last volumes of that work, reaching from the invasion of Julius Cæsar to the accession of Henry VII. the last, I mean, in the order of publication, though the first in the order of time; for it is well known that Mr. Hume, like Tacitus, whom he resembles in many more essential respects, wrote his History backwards.

Though Mr. Hume had too much independence of spirit to cringe to the great, yet he had, at the same time, too much modesty and good sense not to embrace any honourable offer that was made him; and accordingly, when he was solicited by the Earl of Hertford to accept the office of secretary to the embassy to the court of France, he very readily complied with the proposal. Upon his arrival at Paris a mark of distinction was shewn him which perhaps had never been shown before to any but a sovereign prince. When he was first introduced into the royal presence, the king and his whole court rose up to receive him, a conduct indeed which did as much honour to them as it did to him; for if it shewed, on the one hand, the high opinion they had of his literary character, it evidently shewed, on the other, that they well knew how to treat such a character with proper respect. The truth is, there is no part of the world where literary merit is held in such high estimation as it is in France; and this surely may be allowed to atone for many of the little fopperies that distinguish the manners of the French nation in general. After discharging, for some time, the duties of his public station with equal ability and integrity, Mr. Hume retired into the shade of private life, and upon this occasion a pension was settled upon him, not as a reward for having prostituted his pen in the service of government, a thing which he never did, and which he scorned to do, but merely in compliment to his literary merit.

Most of his essays, I believe, were published before he undertook his history, though a few of them might appear during the course of that work. The last essay I think which he published was, his Natural History of Religion, a work which, like most of his other performances, discovers great reading, and is at once a proof of the depth of his thought and the solidity of his judgment. His political essays, though but few in number, and short in extent, are inestimable treasures in this branch of learning; they certainly contain more real information with regard to the science of government than many other tracts of ten times their compass. Mr. Hume, indeed, was possessed of that original genius which always goes to the bottom of a subject, and had he not been able to say something new and uncommon upon every topic which he handled, he would probably have scorned to say any thing upon it at all.

But though his merit as a philosopher and a politician be great, his merit as an historian is still greater. As penetrating and profound as Tacitus, but much more perspicuous; as pointed as Sallust; and, where occasion requires, as warm and animated as Livy; he has united in his style and manner almost all the beauties of the ancient historians, and has left all the moderns, in this species of writing, infinitely behind him. A FRIEND TO MERIT.[4]

---

4 [An errata list at the close of this article reads as follows: "In the last letter on this subject, for in a gentle pace, read *with* a gentle pace; for *in the* very first sentence, read *the* very first sentence; for *was* of much stronger import, read *is* of much stronger import." I have introduced these changes in the above.]

55
LETTER ON HUME'S 1745 CANDIDACY
(*LONDON CHRONICLE*)

Letter on Hume's 1745 candidacy, in *London Chronicle*, Nov. 5–7, 1776, Vol. 40, No. 3108, p. 444.
Complete.

In September 1776, the *London Chronicle* printed a series of letters by John Home titled "Remarks on the Life and Character of the late David Hume, Esq." In one of the instalments, Home discusses Hume's candidacy for the professorship of moral philosophy at the University of Edinburgh in 1745. A little over a month later, an anonymous comment on Hume's "Remarks" appeared in that newspaper, which politely corrected some mistakes in Home's account. The author highlights the efforts of Robert Wallace to support Hume against the majority of the clergy who opposed Hume's candidacy.

To the Printer *of the* London Chronicle.

Sir,

In an Account of the Life and Writings of the late David Hume, Esq; inserted in your and several other newspapers, I observe one particular related in the following words. "In 1746 he stood candidate for the chair of moral philosophy in the university of Edinburgh, then vacant by the resignation of the present Sir John Pringle, appointed physician to the army. Every one was convinced of Mr. Hume's abilities, and his interest was warmly supported by the nobility and gentry; but the presbytery of Edinburgh, having a right to object to one out of three candidates named by the town-council, they put their negative upon honest David, whose sentiments were too liberal for their narrow minds."

The story here told is not entirely destitute of foundation, but full of inaccuracies, and I persuade myself it will not be disagreeable either to its Author or to your Readers to be informed of its mistakes.

The lord provost, magistrates, and council of Edinburgh possess an exclusive right of choosing most of the professors of the university, but every election must be made with the advice (not of the presbytery, but only) of the ministers

360

of that city; *cum avisamento tamen ministorum meorum*, words which some people must amount to a negative, but their legal import has never, that I know, been determined, or even become the subject of judicial disquisition. A vacancy made in 1745 (not 1746) in the professorship of moral philosophy by the resignation of Dr. Pringle, who had already attended the army several years in quality of physician, occasioned all the ministers of Edinburgh to be summoned, in terms of the charter of foundation, to give their advice to the common-council about the pretensions of the different competitors who aspired to that chair. Among others proposed for the office was Mr. Hume: his interest I suspect was not warmly supported by either nobility or gentry, but depended chiefly on the influence of his friend Mr. Coutts, the late provost, a spirited man, by whom the corporation was then governed; and it is true that most of the clergy objected to the electing of honest David, grounding their objection on "A Treatise on Human Nature," published in 1739, which had been ascribed to him. All the body, however, did not concur in the measure. The late celebrated Dr. Wallace, faithful to those generous sentiments which he had early imbibed and uniformly professed, with an impartiality as well as dignity becoming them, declared to the counsellors in strong terms, that he did not think himself entitled to give his opinion, on pretext too of a juvenile as well as anonymous performance, which had been little read, and which was less understood, against chusing that ingenious gentleman, more than any of the other candidates. The Doctor's liberal mind was elevated far above, and his philosophic indignation was greatly raised at the inquisitorial zeal discovered on this occasion. I am, &c.

56
JOHN HOME:
"AN ACCOUNT OF THE LIFE AND
WRITINGS OF DAVID HUME"

[John Home], "An Account of the Life and Writings of the late David Hume, Esq."
Complete; from *Annual Register... for the year 1776*, fifth edition, pp. 27–33.

The following account of Hume's life by John Home (1722–1808) first appeared in a British periodical in 1776 (yet to be discovered) and was reprinted later in the *Annual Register... for the year 1776*. Although published anonymously, his authorship can be established on the basis of strong parallels between this and his "Remarks on the Life and Character of the late David Hume, Esq." printed in the *London Review* and contained earlier in this collection. One such parallel is this:

> Remarks: After passing through his academical courses at the university of Edinburgh, he entered upon the study of the law, in which he made a considerable proficiency; but, as his talent lay rather for writing than speaking, he did not make so capital a figure in it as some of his contemporaries of much meaner abilities; or, to speak more properly, he saw that he had no chance of making such a figure; for, as far as I can recollect, he never took upon him the gown, or acted formally as an Advocate.
>
> Account: After passing through his academical courses at the university of Edinburgh, he therefore devoted himself to the study of the Scotch laws, in which he made considerable progress; but whether from that natural modesty almost inseparably connected with great merit, a consciousness of his deficiency in elocution, the happy indolence of his temper, little fitted for the contentious bar, or any other secret cause, he never put on the gown, not even took the introductory steps necessary for that purpose.

---

[1] [The phrase "discovers all the violence of a sectary, and all the illiberality of a pedant, and rather" is absent in the *Weekly Magazine* reprint of this essay.]

Home's flattering "Account" was written some time after Hume's death, but before the close of the year 1776, and is the most detailed biography of Hume prior to his autobiography some months later. Home shows his detailed knowledge of Hume's personal life and writings, and effusively, as with his "Remarks" commends each – although making some mistakes of fact and chronology. He describes conditions under which Hume was raised and how these impacted on his choice of an occupation. He defends both the style and content of the *Treatise* and discusses Hume's discussion of female chastity as an illustration. He describes Hume's *History* as "certainly the greatest historical work of modern times." Around a year after its first appearance, Home's "Account" was reprinted with slight modifications in *The Weekly Magazine, or Edinburgh Amusement* (November 27, 1777, Vol. 38 pp. 193–197). This triggered harsh attacks from two correspondents going by the pseudonyms "The Postilion" and "Tobias Simple," which appeared in the magazine's December 1777 issue and are contained later in this collection. The following is from the *Annual Register* reprint of the "Account."

An Account of the Life and Writings of the late David Hume, *Esq. as given to the* World *in one of the periodical publications.*

The lives of literary men seldom abound with incidents. That leisure, which is necessary for the acquisition of knowledge, excludes them in some measure from the busy world, and intense study seems generally to subdue in them the spirit of enterprize. Few men, even among the learned, had ever less of that spirit than the honest, easy, indolent, but philosophic Hume. His life, consequently, affords few of those occurrences which are commonly supposed to give interest to a biographical narration. But there is a pleasure in tracing the progress of genius, and observing its various obstructions and encouragements, in the road to fame, which has made the lives of authors, though less diversified by circumstances, more universally acceptable than those perhaps of any other class of men. No apology need therefore be made for an attempt to trace the progress of a writer unequalled in his age, or in his province, one of the most eminent and extensive in the empire of science.

David Hume, so well known to the world of late, both as a philosopher and historian, was born about the year 1712, in that part of Scotland which lies between Edinburgh and Berwick. His father was a country gentleman, or laird, of good family, but small fortune, and David was unfortunately a younger son. In his early years, he was by no means distinguished as a scholar, or by any of those accomplishments which are supposed to qualify youth for the liberal professions; but as the pride of the Scottish gentry then prevented them from breeding any of their children to mechanical or mercantile employments; and as the church, in that country, can only be the object of the lower class of people, the best kirks affording no more than a decent maintenance, there was a necessity for every younger son of a genteel family being bred either a soldier, a lawyer, or a physician. – David was destined for the bar; not so much as being adapted to his genius, as the line in which his relations could most effectually serve him. After passing through his academical courses at the university of Edinburgh, he therefore devoted himself to the study of the Scotch laws, in which he made considerable progress; but whether from that natural modesty almost inseparably connected with great merit, a consciousness of his deficiency in elocution, the happy indolence of his temper, little fitted for the contentious bar, or any other secret cause, he never put on the gown, not even took the introductory steps necessary for that purpose. Other studies attracted him.

The metaphysical writings of Locke and Berkeley had turned all inquisitive men towards intellectual objects. The human mind spent its force in contemplating itself; as if man had been born for thinking, not acting; as if ideas had, in fact, only been *real*; and that material world, as conjectured by the Bishop of Cloyne, but *as a vision*. Mr. Hume had early applied himself to metaphysical inquiries: he saw, or seemed to see, the defects of the former systems, and published, in 1739, the two first volumes of his *Treatise of Human Nature*, and the third the following year.

This work, though not inferior to any thing of the moral or metaphysical kind in any language, was entirely overlooked, or decried at the time of its publication, except by a few liberal-minded men, who had courage to throw aside their popular and literary prejudices, and to follow sound reasoning without being afraid of any dangerous conclusion, or fatal discovery; of seeing errors unveiled, however sanctified by years, or supported by authorities: and the author made sensible, to the severe disappointment of his youthful hopes, that the taste for systematical writing was on the decline, divided his treatise into separate essays, and dissertations, which he published, with improvements, alterations, and additions, at different periods of his life. His enemies, however, or men desirous of raising a reputation by exposing the mistakes of a great genius, have levelled all their arguments against this juvenile production, though never dignified with the author's name; and Dr. Beattie, in particular, more than thirty years after the publication of that sceptical system, has been so successful as to obtain a pension by his *Essay on the Immutability of Truth*; in which he discovers all the violence of a sectary, and all the illiberality of a pedant, and rather abuses than confutes Mr. Hume.[1]

As the *Treatise of Human Nature* is now very scarce, some account of it may be agreeable to many readers. The author's purpose in that work, as he himself informs us, was "to introduce the experimental method of reasoning into moral subjects." The ability with which he has executed his design, can only be fully discovered by an examination of the treatise itself; which, as a composition, is admirable. The first volume treats of the understanding, the second of the passions, the third of morals. Criticism and politics were still necessary to complete his plan, and would have been added systematically, if the success had, in any degree, been answerable to the merit of the work. He thus speaks of the sciences that he meant to examine: "The sole end of logic is to explain the principles and operations of our reasoning faculty, and the nature of our ideas: morals and criticism regard our tastes and sentiments; and politics consider men as united in society, and dependent on each other. In these four sciences, logic, morals, criticism, and politics, is comprehended almost every thing, which it can any way import us to be acquainted with, or which can tend either to the improvement or ornament of the human mind." So early, and when he was thought little able to give a new direction to science, had this great man digested that ingenious system of philosophy, which had changed metaphysics from a frivolous to an useful study; and give a stability to morals, criticism, and politics, unknown in former ages! – But what is still more extraordinary, the stile and method of this first production are not less correct and happy, than those of his most admired performances, written after his taste and judgment were matured by years and experience. A single quotation will be sufficient to support this assertion, and also to exemplify his method of reasoning *experimentally* on moral subjects.

Speaking of that modesty and chastity which belongs to women, "there are some philosophers," he observes, "who attack the female virtues with great vehemence, and fancy they have gone very far in detecting popular errors, when they can shew, that there is no foundation in nature for all that exterior modesty which we require in the expressions, dress, and behaviour of the fair sex." And he proceeds to examine the origin of such notions, and their connection with the interests of society.

"Whoever considers," says he, "the length and feebleness of human infancy, with the concerns which both sexes naturally have for their offspring, will easily perceive that there must be an union of male and female for the education of the young, and that this union must be of considerable duration. But in order to induce the men to impose on themselves this restraint, and undergo cheerfully all the fatigues and expences to which it subjects them, they must believe that the children are their own, that their *natural instinct* is not directed to a wrong object, when they give a loose to love and tenderness."

"Now," adds he, with equal justice and ingenuity, "if we examine the structures of the human body, we shall find that this security is very difficult to be attained on our part; and that since in the copulation of the sexes, the principle of generation goes from the man to the woman, an error may take place on the side of the former, though it be utterly impossible on the side of the latter. In order therefore to impose a due restraint on the female sex, we must attach a peculiar degree of shame to their infidelity, above what arises merely from its injustice, and must bestow proportionable praises on their chastity. But as human creatures, especially of the female kind, are apt to overlook remote consequences, while under the influence of any present temptation, it is necessary, besides the infamy attending such licences, that there should be some preceding backwardness or dread, which may prevent their first approaches, and give the female sex a repugnance to all expressions, and postures, and liberties, that have an immediate relation to that enjoyment." So much *good sense* and *sound reasoning* was never perhaps delivered in so few words, on the subject of the female virtue, by any writer ancient or modern; yet this is an extract from the treatise, whose confutation has been impudently attempted, more than once, by mere *common sense and childish declamation*!

In the year 1742, Mr. Hume published two small volumes, consisting of essays, moral, political, and literary. These were better received than his former publication, but contributed little to his general reputation as an author, and still less to his profit; and his small patrimony being now almost spent, he was glad to accept of the office of library keeper to the faculty of advocates. The salary annexed to this place is only fifty pounds per annum; but the opportunity which it afforded him of consulting, at his leisure, all the choice authors and valuable papers in one of the best libraries in Europe, may be considered as no inconsiderable circumstance in favour of Mr. Hume's literary character.

In 1746, he stood candidate for the chair of moral philosophy in the university of Edinburgh, then vacant by the resignation of the present Sir John Pringle, appointed physician to the army. Every one was convinced of Mr. Hume's abilities, and his interest was warmly supported by the nobility and gentry; but the Presbytery of Edinburgh, having a right to object to one out of three candidates named by the town council, they put their negative upon honest David, whose sentiments were too liberal for their narrow minds.

Thus baffled in his attempt to obtain an office for which he was eminently qualified, and in which perhaps he could have been of more service to his country than in any other, Mr. Hume devoted himself entirely to study, and rested all his hopes of fame and fortune on his merit as an author. – He published in the year 1748 and 49 his Metaphysical Essays nearly as they now stand; a Dissertation on the Passions, also extracted from his Treatise of Human Nature; his System of Morals, much altered and improved: and along with these several new moral, critical, and political essays.

From politics, in which he had now made considerable progress, Mr. Hume turned his inquiries towards history, and completed in 1752, the history of Britain under the house of Stuart. The first volume of this work had been published two years before, but was little noticed, and the success of the second was by no means considerable; yet these two volumes are allowed to be equal to any part of his now justly admired History of England, or rather of Britain; for he all along connects the story of the two kingdoms.

So singular an instance of public neglect cannot be well accounted for; especially as the style is remarkably elegant, the period interesting, and the work full of new and important matter, anecdotes, and observations. The public, however, has since amply repaid Mr. Hume for its ingratitude. His History of the House of Stuart requires only to be read to be admired; and it no sooner fell into the hands of Mr. Millar, then at the head of the London booksellers, than it became a favourite performance among the higher class of people.

But Mr. Hume's reputation as an historian was not complete, till the publication of his History of the House of Tudor, in 1758. About the same time was published Dr. Robertson's History of the Reign of Mary, Queen of Scots, and her Son James, till his Accession to the Throne of England; a work which was admired, even to enthusiasm, by persons of all ranks. Many of the same subjects are treated by both writers, and at equal length. A comparison necessarily followed; and all intelligent men became sensible, after the most critical examination, that the philosophic dignity, the logical disposition, the force of diction, the just concatenation of circumstances, the lively pictures of manners, the comprehensive, yet distinct views of the interests of nations, and the intrigues of courts, independent of the many valuable disquisitions, which so eminently distinguished Mr. Hume's work, were, at least a balance for the classical purity of style, the happy selection of incidents, the keen discernment of motives, and the fine delineation of character no less conspicuous in the other, which render the History of Mary one of the most captivating in our language.

Thus encouraged by the public approbation, Mr. Hume prepared for press, with all expedition, the more early part of his History of England, from the invasion of Julius Caesar to the accession of the House of Tudor; which, with the volumes formerly published, bring down the progress of the English constitution, and the civil and military transactions of Britain, to the Revolution in 1688, an æra when the government of this country was fixed on the basis, where it continues to rest. Yet it is to be lamented that Mr. Hume did not bring down his history to the death of Q. Anne, when the manners, the literature, and the military reputation of England, and of Europe, were at an height, and when the accession of a new family gave a new direction to British policy. But such as it is, taken as a whole, it may be considered as one of the most excellent productions of the human genius, and is certainly the greatest historical work of modern times.

Mr. Hume's reputation was now complete. He was considered as the greatest writer of the age: his most significant performances were sought after with avidity; and Lord Bute, who, whatever errors he may have been guilty of as a politician, will ever be honoured as a patron of letters, procured for Mr. Hume a considerable pension. – But it was not enough that the philosophic David should be enabled, in his latter years, to eat the bread of idleness, as the reward of his many laborious researches; his political writings affording reason to believe, that he might be of use to the state, he was appointed secretary to Lord Hertford, ambassador at the court of France, and afterwards resident in the absence of that nobleman.

In France, Mr. Hume's writings had long been known and admired; so that he there found himself of still more consequence by his character than his office. He was universally caressed. Even the ladies are said to have loaded him with their favours. But of all Mr. Hume's adventures, during his residence in France, or in his own country, there is none so remarkable as that which took its rise from his acquaintance with the celebrated John James Rousseau, whom he brought over to England with him in 1766, and for whom he procured the offer of a pension from his Majesty.

The particulars of that affair have been already published, and are too numerous and complicated to enter into such a sketch as the present: it will therefore be sufficient here to observe, that Mr. Hume, understanding that M. Rousseau, persecuted every where on the continent, meant to take refuge in England, generously conducted him over, procured him a commodious retreat, and afterwards the offer of a pension; but that the jealous and peevish temper of Rousseau, led him to reject the last, abandon the first, and abuse Mr. Hume as a person who had conspired the ruin of his character, under an appearance of serving him; though every precaution, which the most refined delicacy could suggest, had been taken in order to spare the pride of that singular man, by the manner of conferring those obligations.

An anecdote or two will sufficiently shew the jealous and even suspicious temper of M. Rousseau, and the generosity and candour of Mr. Hume. On their journey to England, they happened one night to lie in the same chamber; and during the season devoted to sleep, M. Rousseau heard, or imagined he heard, Mr. Hume cry several times, with great vehemence – "Rousseau, I have you?" these words, though in themselves equivocal, and tho' M. Rousseau owns he does not know whether Mr. Hume uttered them when asleep or awake, roused his suspicions, which it appears were never afterwards entirely laid. The question which honest David asks on this occasion is equally pertinent and candid. "As M. Rousseau is not certain whether Mr. Hume was asleep or awake, is he sure that he was awake himself?"

M. Rousseau's suspicion of Mr. Hume's treachery rose in proportion to the benefits conferred upon him, and at last broke out in perfect peevishness on the slightest occasion imaginable. Mr. Davenport, a gentleman distinguished by his birth, his fortune, and his merit, had granted to M. Rousseau and his gover-nante, the use of his house called Wooton, in Derbyshire, (where he seldom resided) with all other things necessary for a livelihood; but in order to prevent Rousseau's pride from being hurt by such a benefit, he agreed to receive, in return, a trifling sum annually. He also generously pretended, as he had reason to think M. Rousseau's finances were not very high, that he had found a post-chaise, on his return to Wooton, which would carry the philosopher safely, and at small expence, to his retreat. Rousseau suspected the benevolent artifice, and accused Mr. Hume of being an accomplice in it. Mr. Hume protested his innocence, and endeavoured to shift the subject. After a sarcastical reply,

Rousseau sat for some time in seeming melancholy, then sprung up, walked two or three times across the room, and at last threw his arms about the neck of his brother philosopher, bathing the astonished David's face with tears, and crying like a child. "My dear friend," said he, as soon as he was able to speak, "will you ever forgive me this extravagance? After all the pains which you have taken to serve me, after the numberless proofs of your friendship, is it possible that I can thus repay your kindness with spleen and abuse! But in pardoning me you will give me a new mark of your regard, and I hope when you know me better, you will find that I am not unworthy of it."

This reconciliation, however, was but of short duration. Still a prey to his former suspicions, his delicacies, and his scruples, Rousseau soon broke out entirely with his benefactor, and left England.

Mr. Hume, who after his return from France, had been appointed under secretary of state, retired to Scotland on the resignation of Gen. Conway, and spent the remainder of his years at Edinburgh, among the companions of his youth, equally admired and respected; beloved as a friend, and honoured over Europe as a scholar, a gentleman, and a man of genius. He died, after a lingering illness, on the 25th of August, 1776.

57
"OBSERVATIONS ON THE CHARACTER AND WRITINGS OF MR HUME" (*WEEKLY MAGAZINE*)

"The Postilion," "Observations on the Character and Writings of Mr Hume" in *Weekly Magazine, or Edinburgh Amusement*, December 11, 1777, Vol. 38, pp. 260–261.
Complete.

This anonymous letter to *Weekly Magazine* is a critique of John Home's anonymous "Account of the Life and Writings of the late David Hume, Esq." which appeared in late 1776 and was reprinted a year later by *Weekly Magazine* (November 27, 1777, Vol. 38 pp. 193–197). The author objects to Home's attacks against Beattie and challenges his claim that Hume's view of chastity in the *Treatise* is "good sense and sound reasoning."

OBSERVATIONS *on the* CHARACTER *and* WRITINGS *of Mr* HUME.
To the PUBLISHER *of the* WEEKLY MAGAZINE.

I observe, Sir, that, sometimes, one paper in your Magazine gives birth to another. The first paper of your 9th Number is before me, and occasions what I now send to you. What now! David Hume again! said I, when I first glanced *An Account of the Life and Writings of* D.H.– But let me read this same account, said I, we shall meet with some new incidents: But I need not tell you I was disappointed; for, in Lord Chatham's phrase, we receive not one scrap of *new* intelligence, – nothing which we have not read again and again in the Weekly Magazine itself. (*Not so!*)[1]

It is a convenient trade, this of biography: What an advantage does it afford a man for shewing his superiority to all the world, who opposes the hero of the present tale! With how great ease does our biographer pour contempt on Dr

---

[1] [This parenthetical comment was inserted by the editors of *Weekly Magazine*.]

Beattie in this article: "He rather abuses, than confutes Mr Hume!" See how this panegyrist exults in his amazing and most extraordinary genius: "This great man had digested his ingenious System of Philosophy, which has changed metaphysics from a frivolous to an useful study, and given a stability to morals, criticism, and politics, unknown in former ages" in early life! But have I said *Panegyrist?* By reading on, and observing the example that proves the justness of the character aforesaid, I really suspect that this single quotation he produces will be sufficient to prove this biographer either a secret enemy of Mr Hume, or a very imprudent friend.

"So much good sense and sound reasoning was never perhaps delivered in so few words on the subject of female virtue, by any writer antient or modern." – Wonderful! I know not how others were affected with this eulogy of an indelicate sentence, and trite remark, and pernicious sentiment, – I could not refrain from laughter, which was heightened by the truly ridiculous, yet sage-like thrust against Dr Beattie for the second time, with which it concludes: "A confutation" *of this sound reasoning* "is impudently attempted by mere common sense and childish declamation."

Dear Dr Beattie, take care how you write again! Somebody is offended: To confute your work is not so easy a matter, and to reconcile absolute contradictions, to support acknowledged absurdities, and to shew the innocence of total scepticism and barefaced atheism, are tasks which every man is not fit for; but here is an easy method of putting all to rights: "Dr Beattie, and whosoever presumes to differ from Mr Hume, thou art pronounced to be *an impudent common sense childish declaimer.*"

But let us look upon this *good sense and sound reasoning*: In plain English it is this: A wife may be a w——e while the man is ignorant of it; that therefore she may not go astray, and he may have some security for the child she bears being his, and so be inclined to take care of it, it is right she be backward to grant favours to adulterers. Can I exult in the profound thinking or erudition of the man who makes this speech, and say, he is an impudent childish declaimer who ventures to write against him?

Let me just name a few consequences of this doctrine.

It would appear, if the husband is deceived effectually, she may do as she pleases; if he is careless whether the child be his or another man's, she needs make no resistance; if she feels no backwardness, or has by her parents been made to feel no backwardness in granting favours, she may grant them. Thus, I grant, *he gives a stability to merits unknown to former ages!*

I find nothing from the passage I refer to in the account to the end, either very laughable or very memorable, unless we consider the following to deserve either epithet, or both: "Even the ladies are said to have loaded Mr Hume with their favours while in France." Of the success of his History, of its progress, of his person, of his curious and amazing friendship and difference with Rousseau, we have heard over and over again.

But, pray, Mr Printer, what was the harm in writing an Essay on the Immutability of Truth thirty years after Mr Hume's book, which it often refers to, was published? Let us keep our temper, and talk calmly upon this subject: I shall suppose it enters into your head or mine, that the writings of Filmer or More, or of some high prerogative man, or some high republican, injure the happiness of individuals and of society; may not you or I write against these authors with all the zeal which, in our apprehension, the importance of our subject requires? And if Dr Beattie is persuaded that the sceptical philosophy may do, or has done harm to society, or to an individual, what blame does he incur for endeavouring to prevent this mischief for the time to come? Let us not mince matters, and speak out the half of what we think: Atheism, to me, appears a dreadful evil, and till Mr Hume's biographer gives me better evidence than his mere assertion, I must believe Mr Hume's writings are very pernicious; and I shall give you my reasons for this persuasion in very few words: I have this opinion of his writings because I believe in God, in providence, in a future state, and in the Gospel. all who think with me that atheism is so monstrous a doctrine and pernicious, that Mr Hume labours to disprove or shakes our faith in the articles I have now mentioned, must be thankful to the man who has exposed such writings, and in so effectual a manner, that the friends or proselytes of Mr Hume cannot say, and never have as yet dared to say any thing against him, but that he writes with warmth, which they pronounce impudence and declamation. I leave it to the candid to say, who deserve the characters of *impudent childish declaimers?*

It offends our biographer that Mr Beattie has received a pension. Read his Essay, and acknowledge his motives for writing it. The work he hoped might be useful, but it was not grateful. Did he seek a pension? Did he instantly receive one? Is he not acknowledged to be a man of genius as well as an able writer against the systems of irreligion? I will not speak of the King, whose favour to the doctor seems to displease the panegyrist, but I will ask any sober thinking unprejudiced man, whether that minister deserves the public approbation most who distinguishes the friend of science, religion, and virtue, of confessed genius, eloquence, and abilities, or the minister who procured three times his annuity, as I am informed, for a sceptic, an atheist, a subverter of virtue, and therefore of the present happiness, and, to us who believe in a separate existence, of the eternal happiness of mankind, whatever his genius, eloquence, or abilities may be supposed to have been.

M.M.M. Dec. 1

The POSTILION.

58
"STRICTURES ON THE 'ACCOUNT'"
(*WEEKLY MAGAZINE*)

"Tobias Simple," "Strictures on the 'Account of The Life and Writings of the Late David Hume, Esq.'" *Weekly Magazine, or Edinburgh Amusement,* December 25, 1777, Vol. 38, pp. 289–292.
Complete; from *Weekly Magazine.*

L ike the previous item in this collection, this letter to *Weekly Magazine* attacks John Home's "Account of the Life and Writings of the late David Hume, Esq.," originally published in 1776 but reprinted later in *Weekly Magazine* (November 27, 1777, Vol. 38 pp. 193–197). The author opens conceding that Hume died peacefully as an infidel, but questions Pratt's claim in the *Apology* (1777) that this fact has desperately shaken the pillars of orthodoxy. Hume is just one more freethinker in a long line of infidels who rejected God upon death. The author criticizes Hume's discussion of chastity from the *Treatise* (as appears in Home's "Account"). He lists eight Humean "dogmas" (based on Beattie's critique of Hume in his *Essay*), and shapes these into a satirical lecture that Hume might have given to his students had he obtained the chair of moral philosophy at the University of Edinburgh. Hume states in this lecture, "rejoice that, like your fellow brutes, total and eternal *annihilation* shall be your fate." Bracketed comments below are those of *Weekly Magazine.*

STRICTURES *on the Account of the Life and Writings of* DAVID HUME, *Esq.*
[P. 193]

DAVID HUME *is dead!* "Never were the pillars of orthodoxy so desperately shaken, as they are now by that event;" cries, with exultation and triumph, one of his disciples[1] – "He has proved himself, in opposition to a contrary opinion, one of these rare characters – an uniform philosopher.

---

[1] *Apology for the life and writings of David Hume.*

Pray Sir, let me ask this gentleman, What has orthodoxy, the *Christian religion* (no doubt you mean?), *or the religion of nature*, if you please, suffered by that event? Every good man, affected with religious principles, and from a humane concern for a fellow creature, must have wished, that that philosopher had, in his last moments, expressed some concern for his future existence! he did it not: that he died firm to his own tenets, they are truly sorry for: but how the *pillars of religion can be shaken* by that event, more than by the death of many a *daring atheist* that hath lived and died so, in every age, they don't see. Your philosopher, if it will please you, shall rank in the first class of that sect.

The famous *Vanini*, crying out at *the stake* the name of *God*, was careful to let it be known, that it was an involuntary exclamation.

Spinoza shut himself up with his old woman, in his last moments, giving orders, that no divine should be admitted to disturb him.

The gay *Petronius*, whose exit our hero seems to have had in his eye, having cut his veins, and bound them up again, called his friends about him – "*Audiebatque*, says the historian, *referentes, nihil de immortalitate animæ, et sapientium placitis, sed levia carmina, et faciles versus.*"

Our philosopher, as firm as any of them, in his last moments, chearfully entertained his friends with a dialogue between himself and Charon, played a game at Whist, and read Tom Jones.

Now Sir, all this is very well, and stands recorded on good evidence; and no man, I'm persuaded, will pretend to say, that our philosopher, before he made his exit, either called for the *New Testament*, was heard to invoke the Deity, or to utter the shortest ejaculation for his soul. And pray what has orthodoxy, or the Christian religion suffered from all this? have you any grounds for *insulting* the *religion of your country* upon that event?

It was the complaint of the *Free-thinkers* of the last age, that men of genius were not at liberty to canvass with freedom points of religion: that they were obliged to write in fetters, and met with great discouragement in their attempts to investigate, with freedom, these points. How far they had reason for their complaints, may be judged from the writings of *Tindal, Collins, Toland*, and the noble author of the *Characteristics*. It must be owned, indeed, that although these essays are neither remarkable for the spirit of moderation, nor for modesty, yet, simple as the appearance was, they thought themselves obliged, when writing against the religion of their country, to put on a fair outside. Thus, although they soon unmasked themselves, they carried on the show, by affecting, on every occasion, the specious words of *our holy religion, its divine Founder, the holy gospel, we Christians*, and such like phrases in their mouths. This thin disguise, it is true, imposed upon nobody, but, in some readers, it was an acknowledgement from these gentlemen, that they thought themselves, at least, under an obligation to treat with decency and respect the established religion of their country; and they were sensible too, that it would very ill have become them, while they were declaiming against the intemperate zeal of the early professors of Christianity, for insulting the religion of Paganism, then the established religion, and in extolling the mild forbearance of the *Emperor Julian*, their great hero, if they themselves had incurred the same censure. But times, it seems, are altered: the Free-thinkers of the present age seem to be insensible of the unbounded toleration, the perfect freedom which they now enjoy.

This leads me to take notice of another abuse of this liberty, in a paper which, Mr Printer, you have lately given to the public; to wit, "An account of the life and writings of the late David Hume, Esq;" than which, a more gross insult has not been offered, I wont say to religion alone (for, with the *Humean school*, religion, in every sense, is out of the question,) but to the *moral sense* and common understanding of mankind.

This piece, as it hath appeared first in the Annual Register, and lately in your Weekly Magazine, I mean to examine, and make some observes upon.

It is proper to premise, that the writer of this paper, with respect to the life and writings of the philosopher, notwithstanding his inviting title, has given us only a bald repetition of a few of the anecdotes from Mr Hume's life, written by himself. Of the observations he makes on our author's metaphysical works, I mean only to take notice.

This writer introduces his account with a high swoln panegyric on our author's first metaphysical production, *The Treatise on Human Nature* – "A work (says *this judge*) not inferior to any thing of the moral, or metaphysical kind in any language." And to justify this very decisive opinion, he is pleased to give us an abstract from our author, with respect to the *principles* of *modesty*, and *chastity of women*, and the necessary restraint they are laid under, in order to preserve their fidelity to their husbands, and to the marriage-bed. Mr Hume says, with truth, that "considering the length and feebleness of infancy, both parents must unite their care in the education of their young; therefore, *a priori*, they must believe that the children are their own." He then proceeds to tell us what is equally true and well known, that

"if we examine the structure of the human body, we shall find that this security is very difficult to be attained on our part; and that since, in the copulation of the sexes, the principles of generation goes from the man to the woman, an error may take place on the side of the former, though it be utterly impossible on the side of the latter. In order therefore, to impose a due restraint on the female sex, we must attach a peculiar degree of shame to their infidelity above what arises merely from its injustice, and must bestow proportionable praise on their chastity: But, as human creatures, especially of the female kind, are apt to overlook remote consequences while under the influence of any present temptation, it is necessary, besides the infamy attending such licences, that there should be some preceding backwardness or dread, which may prevent their first approaches, and give the female sex a repugnance to all expressions, and postures, and liberties, that have immediate relation to that enjoyment." –

"So much good sense and sound reasoning (says our observator) was never delivered in so few words on the subject of *female virtue* by any writer ancient or modern." Indeed! "Yet, (proceeds he) this is an extract from the *treatise*," (Reader mark his modesty,) "whose confutation has been *impudently* attempted, more than once, by mere *common sense*," (really!) "and childish declamation."

Equally sensible and modest is this remark! It is scarce possible, indeed, to cram more *conceit* and *nonsense* into fewer words. As for the sense and reasoning contained in the above extract from Mr Hume, it would have been truly absurd in any body to have pretended either to confute, or even to dispute; and I wish this writer had told us who had attempted to do it. As for ingenuity in the extract, or novelty, there is none. Is there an old woman that, without much knowledge of the *human structure*, does not know, that although we can, with no certainty, determine the father, yet there can be no doubt as to the mother of the child? or is it a new discovery of Mr Hume, that in order to impose due restraint on the wife, to preserve inviolate the marriage-bed, it was necessary that, besides the shame, infamy, and even punishment annexed to her breach of fidelity, the utmost caution should be exerted to inculcate the seeds of modesty into the sex from the earliest infancy? Did Dr Beattie get a pension for impudently attempting to confute this doctrine, not of Mr Hume, but established in every civilized nation so early as man could have any notion of society? No. But shall I tell this writer what detestable principles of Mr Hume, even subversive of his above doctrine, Dr. Beattie, and several others, have, with mere common sense, taken upon them to dispute, and, strange as it is, even to confute.

Mr Hume has told us, that *chastity*, considered abstractly from its *utility*, is no virtue: That the principles of chastity respect generation only; it follows, then, that, in women past child-bearing, it is no virtue at all:[2] That adultery, if frequently practised, would cease to be scandalous; and that, if secretly practised, would be thought no crime.[3] Blessed doctrine this, and tending much to reform the manners of the age! The consequences that may be drawn from these principles shall not be here stated. – Was our philosopher a man of gallantry? It is said that he affected the company of women, and the ladies, it is said, loaded him with their favours: For the honour of the *sex*, it is to be hoped that he had few pupils. To every virtuous woman such principles must have appeared shocking and detestable.

[2] *The principles of morals, page 66.*
[3] *Essays, vol. 2. page 409.*

This writer tells us,

"That, in 1746, Mr Hume stood candidate for the chair of moral philosophy in the university of Edinburgh, then vacant; every one, says he, was convinced of Mr Hume's abilities; but the *presbytery of Edinburgh*, having a right to object to one of the three candidates, they put their negative upon *honest David*, whose sentiments were *too liberal* for their *narrow minds*. As he was eminently qualified for this office, he could have been of more service to his country than in any other."

Ye illiberal and narrow-minded men of the presbytery of Edinburgh, what hurt did you not do to your country, in depriving it of David Hume for professor of morality! what a blessed system of ethicks would he have instilled into our youth!

To laugh were want of goodness, and of grace; And to be grave, exceeds all power of face.

But let us collect some of the dogmas of our philosopher.
1. "The efficacy of causes (says he) is neither placed in causes themselves, nor in the Deity, but belongs entirely to the soul."[4] The obvious conclusion is, that there is *no first cause*.
2. That we have no good reason to think that the universe proceeds from a cause.[5]
3. That matter and motion may be the cause of thought.[6]
4. That the material world does not exist. – Allow this to be called in question. What arguments have we to prove the being of God?[7]
5. That neither matter nor spirit exist. – Let us attend to our philosopher's principles of morality.
6. That justice is not a natural virtue, but artificial and arbitrary.[8]
7. That all moral virtues are of the same nature, i.e. arbitrary, and depending on the custom and institutions of men.[9]
8. That every action of man is necessary.[10]
These are some of the principles, which Dr Beattie has most impudently taken

[4] *Treatise on Human Nature, vol.* I, *p.* 291.

[5] *Hume's Essay on a particular Providence and Future State.*

[6] *Treatise of Human Nature, vol.* I. *p.* 434.

[7] *Essay on Sceptical Philosophy.*

[8] *Treatise on Human Nature, vol.* iii, *p.* 37.9Ibid.

[10] *Essays, vol.* ii. *p.* 91.

upon him to censure; and, strange to tell, has, with mere common sense, brought the whole *metaphysical system* of our philosopher in ruins about his ears.

Let us suppose, however, that our author had obtained the philosophic chair, he might, no doubt, from the above principles, have thus harangued:

> "Now, my students, having inculcated these principles, shake off the fetters of superstition, that is, religion, being convinced there is no first cause: *futurity* is a mere bugbear, as I have demonstrated in a work which I mean at my death to bequeath to you.[11] Make the most, therefore, of the advantages which my philosophy shall give you, over the weakness and superstitious prejudices of mankind. And rejoice that, like your fellow brutes, total and eternal annihilation shall be your fate.
>
> I have but one other word of comfort to give you: and that, for the universal good of mankind, I shall likewise order to be made public after my death. If, notwithstanding the liberal principles I have given you; if, in the practice of the many advantages my tenets must give you over the wives, the daughters, and fortunes of your weak fellow mortals; any of you, from the want of firmness of nerves, weakness of constitution, or from the troublesome intrusion of a certain faculty in the machine, not altogether subdued by my physics, called *conscience*, shall find yourselves disturbed and haunted, there is an easy remedy; suicide is a cure for every disease: For be assured,
> 'The worst that can befal you, measur'd right,
> Is a sound slumber, and a long good night.'"

Can it be said that this speech is not a fair induction from the above principles? I think it cannot. But it will be said, no doubt, that our philosopher was a man of virtue, and a very good member of society: abstracting from the immorality of writing and publishing such principles, I shall allow he was so: What follows? Only this, that his passions for inordinate pleasures luckily were none of the strongest; and that his constitution led him to study, entertaining his friends, and the pleasures of the table. But with all that, can any excuse be made for his attempts to take from man, (that wild beast hurried away by passions) the curbs of *justice, chastity, virtue*, and *religion*? What apology can his warmest admirers make for this?

Let me oppose to the above dogmas, only one of the precepts of another *philosopher*, I mean, the divine Instituter of our religion; for, reader, I am not ashamed to own myself one of the people called Christians. This blessed person, whose wisdom came from heaven, knew how prone poor weak mortals

---

[11] *Two pieces of our author, one on the immortality of the soul, the other on suicide, left by him in charge to his executors to publish after his death.*

were to be led astray by unguarded passions; and that the first inlet to carnal desires ought to be guarded against. Let not even your eye, says he, fix upon such objects as may, by degrees, hurry you on *to vice and criminality*; rather pull it out: For remember, that God dwells not with impurity. *Blessed*, therefore, are the *pure in heart*, for they *shall see God*.

Before I conclude, I shall make one observation, which, I dare say, daily occurs to the experience of many others, that is, That the philosophy of our author seems to be very agreeable, and often in the mouths of many of the men of fashion of the age: That he was a very subtile and acute metaphysician, his works shew; yet, amidst all his pretended admirers, it is a certain fact, that not one of a hundred of these fine gentlemen understand him, of which the writer of the account of his life, &c. stands a lamentable proof.

To conclude; may the *Freethinkers* of the present age ever rejoice in their liberty and freedom which they now enjoy; may they always thankfully cry out in the words of the historian; *Rara temporium felicitas, ubi sentire quæ velis, et quæ sentias dicere, ac scribere dicet!*[12] At the same time, let these gentlemen learn to make a better use of that liberty, than *insulting common sense and the religion of their country*.

TOBIAS SIMPLE.

[*An answer to these strictures is expected.*][13]

---

[12] *Tacitus*.

[13] [No subsequent response to this article appeared. It is unlikely that Home's unpublished "Sketch" of Hume would have served as a rebuttal to the attacks by either "The Postilion" or "Tobias Simple". Thus, Home might have been prepared to write a fourth defence of Hume.]

REACTIONS TO ADAM SMITH'S "LETTER"

59
"STRICTURES ON THE LIFE OF DAVID HUME" (*GENTLEMAN'S MAGAZINE*)

"Strictures on the Life of David Hume," in *Gentleman's Magazine*, March 1777, Vol. 46, pp. 158–159.
Complete.

Almost immediately after Hume's "My Own Life" and Smith's "Letter" appeared, critics attacked them both. Among the first of these is the following letter to the editor of *Gentleman's Magazine*, reacting to the review of those works earlier in the journal. The author quotes a letter from John Boyle, Earl of Cork, as an additional early admirer of Hume's *History*. He then criticizes Smith for including the story of Charon and claiming that Hume was "perfectly wise" – since Hume was not "wise unto salvation." This article was reprinted in abbreviated form in *Scots Magazine*, March 1777, Vol. 39, p. 153. The following is as it appears in *Gentleman's Magazine*. Bracketed comments in the text are those of *Gentleman's Magazine*; those in footnotes are mine.

Strictures on the Life of David Hume, *Esq; as written by Himself.*

Mr. URBAN,
To the extract of this performance given in your last, p. 120, I beg leave to add a few remarks.

In saying that his History of England was at first "disapproved and detested by English, Scotch, and Irish, Whig and Tory," &c. and that "the Primates of England and Ireland were the only persons considerable for rank or letters, who encouraged him to persevere," Mr Hume has surely much overcharged the piece, and has by no means done justice to himself, or to the public. Another exception, a man of rank and letters, I beg leave to mention, namely, the late Earl of Corke, who at the time [1755] thus expressed himself: "I am reading every evening Mr Hume's *History of Great Britain* [so he at first styled it]; I own myself much pleased with it in general. The style is particularly lively and excellent. Where he is obscure, I believe he is affectedly so. His materials are admirably put together; many very curious remarks; some new facts; and all old and known stories put into a new method, and perfectly entertaining."[1]

"For the otherwise indifferent reception of his Natural History of Religion, a pamphlet written against it by Dr. Hurd, with all the illiberal petulance, arrogance, and scurrility, which distinguish the Warburtonian school, (Mr. Hume is pleased to say,) gave him some consolation." The title of the pamphlet alluded to, is, *Remarks on Mr. David Hume's Essay on the Natural History of Religion. Addressed to the Rev. Dr. Warburton.* – Since the appearance of Mr. Hume's Life, a new edition of this performance has been published, with the following advertisement prefixed: – "The following is supposed to be the pamphlet referred to by the late Mr. David Hume, in p. 21 of his Life, as being written by Dr. Hurd. Upon my applying to the Bishop of Litchfield and Coventry for his permission to re-publish it, he very readily gave me his consent. His Lordship only added, he was sorry he could not take to himself the *whole* infamy of the charge brought against him; but that he should hereafter, if he thought it worth his while, explain himself more particularly on that subject. T. CADELL. *Strand, March,* 1777."

Mr. Hume concludes historically with his own character: – "I am, or rather was (for that is the style I must now use in speaking of myself,) I was, I say, a man of mild dispositions, of command of temper, of an open, social, and chearful humour, capable of attachment, but little susceptible of enmity, and of great moderation in all my passions. Even my love of literary fame, my ruling passion, never soured my temper, notwithstanding my frequent disappointments. My company was not unacceptable to the young and careless, as well as to the studious and literary; and as I took a particular pleasure in the company of modest women, I had no reason to be displeased with the reception I met with from them. In a word, though most men any wise eminent, have found reason to complain of Calumny, I never was touched, or even attacked, by her baleful tooth: and though I wantonly exposed myself to the rage of both civil and religious factions, they seemed to be disarmed in my behalf of their wonted fury. My friends never had occasion to vindicate any one circumstance of my character and conduct: not but that the zealots, we may well suppose, would have been glad to invent and propagate any story to my disadvantage; but they could never find any which they thought would wear the face of probability. I cannot say there is no vanity in making this funeral oration of myself, but I hope it is not a misplaced one; and this is a matter of fact, which is easily cleared and ascertained. – April 18, 1776."

---

[1] Hughes's Correspondence, Vol. III. p. 145. note. [*Letters by several eminent persons deceased. Including the correspondence of John Hughes*, ed. John Duncombe (1729–1786), London, J. Johnson, 1772, 2 v. The 1773 second expanded edition of this work is in three volumes and is that to which the author refers.]

In this history it is observable, that neither Rousseau, nor Dr Beattie[2] are once named. As to the manner of his death, as Mr Hume lived, so, it seems, he died, without hopes or fears of futurity. This appears by a letter annexed from Dr. Adam Smith to William Strahan,[3] Esq; containing an account of his behaviour during his last illness, and beginning where his own ends. He set out for London towards the end of April, and at Morpeth met the writer and Mr. John Home,[4] who were coming to see him. The latter went back with him to London, and accompanied him to Bath. Upon his return to Edinburgh, though his weakness still increased, his chearfulness never abated: of which we have here many instances, and, among others, one which might as well have been spared, a jocular dialogue, in the manner of Lucian, which this heathen philosopher supposed himself to hold with his friend Charon. That Mr. Hume had an amiable temper, extensive learning, and many virtues, we readily grant, but cannot, with Dr. Adam Smith, think any man "perfectly wise," who is not *wise unto salvation.*

[2] Of this writer's *Essay on Truth* Mr. Hume is reported to have said, "Truth! there is no truth in it; it is a horrible lie in octavo."

[3] To this gentleman Mr. H. left the care of all is papers.

[4] Author of Douglas.

60
GEORGE HORNE:
A LETTER TO ADAM SMITH

[George Horne], *A letter to Adam Smith LL.D. on the life, death, and philosophy of his friend David Hume Esq. By one of the people called Christians*. Oxford: at the Clarendon Press. 1777. Sold by Daniel Prince; and by J. F. and C. Rivington, G. Robinson, and T. Payne and Son, London, [1777], [4], iv, 47, [1] p.[1]
Complete; from 1799 edition.

George Horne (1730–1792) was President of Magdalen College, Oxford, Dean of Canterbury, and later Bishop of Norwich. He published two anonymous attacks against Hume, namely, *A Letter to Adam Smith* (1777) and *Letters on Infidelity* (1784); selections from the latter appear in this collection. In the first of these, Horne argues that Smith's praise of Hume's virtuous character is inconsistent with the fact that Hume's writings were atheistic. With much ridicule and drollery, Horne chides Smith for relaying Hume's nonchalant attitude about Hume's approaching death, especially in the playful dialogue between Hume and Charon. The implied point of Smith's "Letter," according to Horne, is that atheism is "the proper antidote against the fear of death." Contesting Hume's claim to be "of command of temper," Horne reports that strangers who were introduced to Hume were warned beforehand to avoid mentioning James Beattie's name since doing so would make Hume "fly out into a transport of passion and swearing." A postscript to this work contains a summary of Hume's philosophical views taken from Beattie's *Essay on the Nature and Immutability of Truth* (1770).

---

[1] Title page: A | LETTER | TO | ADAM SMITH. LL.D. | ON THE | LIFE, DEATH, AND PHILOSOPHY | OF HIS FRIEND | DAVID HUME. Esq. | BY ONE OF THE PEOPLE CALLED CHRISTIANS. | *Ibant obscuri, solâ sub nocte, per umbram,* | *Perque domos Ditis vacuas, et inania regna.* | Virg. | A NEW EDITION, | PUBLISHED BY DESIRE OF THE | SOCIETY FOR PROMOTING CHRISTIAN KNOWLEDGE. | London: | PRINTED FOR F. AND C. RIVINGTON, | BOOKSELLERS TO THE SAID SOCIETY, | NO. 62, ST. PAUL'S CHURCH-YARD | 1799.

The *Critical Review* took a neutral position on Horne's assessment of Hume (selections from this review are contained in this collection). The *London Review* felt that Horne's ridiculing tone was inappropriate:

We leave it to the advocates of Mr. Hume and his philosophy to determine whether or not this letter-writer has here stated the case as it really is, in justification of the sarcastical severity which pervades the whole of this little performance. [*London Review*, April 1777, Vol. 5, pp. 316–317]

The *Monthly Review* also criticized Horne for his needlessly harsh rhetoric:

This Author, who is said to be a dignitary of Oxford, labours by alternate and oddly mingled efforts of serious and ludicrous arguments, to convince Dr. Smith, and all the world, that David Hume as, at once, an absurd philosopher, and a pernicious writer. And this being the case, it follows, that the said Dr. Smith, the celebrated author of the *Theory of Moral Sentiments*, and the treatise on *the Wealth of Nations*, – the friend and panegyrist of the said Hume, – cannot, himself, be much wiser and better than he should be. – 'You,' says our oil and vinegar Author, 'would persuade us, by the example of David Hume, Esq; that Atheism is the only cordial for low spirits, and the proper antidote against the fear of death. But surely,' he adds, 'he who can reflect, with complacency, on a friend thus misemploying his talents in his life, and then amusing himself with *Lucian*, *Whist*, and *Charon*, at his death, may smile over BABYLON in ruins, esteem the earthquake which destroyed LISBON an agreeable occurrence, and congratulate the hardened PHARAOH on his overthrow in the Red Sea. Drollery, in such circumstances, is neither more nor less than

   – Moody madness, laughing wild,
   Amid severest woe. –'

May not this censure be, in some measure, applied to our Author himself, who affects to *sport*, as he does in some parts of his letter, with a subject the most SERIOUS! the most AWEFUL! – and of the LAST IMPORTANCE to every rational being! [*Monthly Review*, 1777, Vol. 56, p. 403]

In his *Apology for the Life and Writings of David Hume* (1777) Samuel Jackson Pratt included a reply to Horne; Horne, in turn, attacked Pratt in *Letters on Infidelity* (1784).William Jones defended Horne in *Memoirs of the Life of Dr. Horne* (1799). All three of these are contained in this collection. A remarkably successful pamphlet, the *Letter to Adam Smith* was published a second time in 1777, and again in 1784, 1786 (prefaced to *Letters on Infidelity*), 1799, 1804, 1813, and 1820. It is also included in several editions of Horne's *Works* (1795, 1809, 1818, 1830, 1831, 1846, 1848, and 1853). The following is from the 1799 edition.

A

LETTER

TO

ADAM SMITH, LL.D.

ON THE

LIFE, DEATH, AND PHILOSOPHY

OF HIS FRIEND

DAVID HUME, Esq.

BY ONE OF THE PEOPLE CALLED CHRISTIANS.

Ibant obscuri, solá sub nocte, per umbram,
Perque domos Ditis vacuas, et inania regna.

VIRG.

A NEW EDITION,

PUBLISHED BY DESIRE OF THE

SOCIETY FOR PROMOTING CHRISTIAN KNOWLEDGE.

London :

PRINTED FOR F. AND C. RIVINGTON,

BOOKSELLERS TO THE SAID SOCIETY,

NO. 62, ST. PAUL'S CHURCH-YARD.

1799.

N.B. *The Author of this Tract was GEORGE HORNE, D.D. Late Lord Bishop of Norwich.*

—

ADVERTISEMENT.

It is of no consequence, gentle Reader, to you, any more than it is to Dr. SMITH, that you should know the name of the person, who now addresseth you. Your mind cannot be biassed, either way, by that, of which you remain ignorant. The remarks in the following pages are not therefore true, or false, because I made them; but I made them, because I thought them to be true. Read, consider, and determine for yourself. If you find no satisfaction, throw the book into the fire; regret (but with moderation, as becometh a philosopher) the loss of your sixpence;[2] and take care not to lose another, in the same manner. If, on the contrary, you *should* find satisfaction (and, it is humbly hoped, you will find a great deal) neglect not to communicate to others, what has thus been communicated to you. Speak handsomely of me, wherever you go, and introduce me to your kinsfolk and acquaintance. The enemies of Religion are awake; let not her friends sleep.

I intend a much longer work; but, like the learned editor of Mr. HUME'S Life, am necessitated to "gratify," with all possible expedition, "the impatience of the public curiosity;" so eager is it to hear, what they, who believe in GOD, can possibly have to say for themselves. And if this will do the business, why should you be troubled with more? I am far from agreeing with Mr. VOLTAIRE, in all his observations. But there is one, in which it is impossible to disagree with him. "I have said, and I abide by it," cries the little hero, "that the fault of most books is, their being too large." On reviewing what I have written, I really cannot see there is occasion to add another sentence.

Had I not chosen, for reasons best known to myself, thus to make my appearance *incog.* I would certainly have sate for my picture, and have tried to cast a look at my title page, as lively and good humoured, as that of Mr. HUME himself. My bookseller, indeed, told me, it would have been a much more creditable way of doing the thing; "and then, you know, Sir," said he, "we could have charged the other sixpence."[3]

—

[2] The price of the first edition.

[3] [*The Life of David Hume* (1777) contained a portrait engraving of Hume and cost 1 shilling, 6 pence; Horne's pamphlet cost just 1 shilling.]

A
LETTER, &c.

SIR,

You have been lately employed in embalming a philosopher; his *body*, I believe I must say; for concerning the other part of him, neither you nor he seem to have entertained an idea, sleeping or waking. Else, it surely might have claimed a little of your care and attention; and one would think, the belief of the soul's existence and immortality could do no harm, if it did no good, in a *Theory of Moral Sentiments*. But every gentleman understands his own business best.

Will you do an unknown correspondent the honour, Sir, to accept a few plain remarks, in a free and easy way, upon the curious letter to Mr. STRAHAN, in which this ever memorable operation of *embalming* is performed? Our Philosopher's account of *his own life* will likewise be considered, as we go along.

Trust me, good Doctor, I am no bigot, enthusiast, or enemy to human learning – *Et ego in Arcadiâ* – I have made many a hearty meal, in private, upon CICERO and VIRGIL, as well as Mr. HUME.[4] Few persons (though, perhaps, as Mr. HUME says, upon a like occasion, "I ought not to judge on that subject"[5]) have a quicker relish for the productions of genius, and the beauties of composition. It is therefore as little in my intention, as it is in my power, to prejudice the literary character of your friend. From some of his writings I have received great pleasure, and have ever esteemed his History of England to have been a noble effort of *matter and motion*. But when a man takes it into his head to do mischief, you must be sensible, Sir, the public has always reason to lament his being a *clever fellow*.

I hope it will not be deemed vanity in me likewise to say, that I have in my composition a large proportion of that, which our inimitable SHAKESPEARE styles, *the milk of human kindness*. I never knew what envy or hatred was; and am ready, at all times, to praise, wherever I can do it, in honour and conscience. DAVID, I doubt not, was, as you affirm, a social agreeable person, of a convivial turn, told a good story, and played well at "his favourite game of whist."[6] I know not that JOHN THE PAINTER did the same. But there is no absurdity in the supposition. If he did not, he might have done it – Doctor; be not offended – I mean no harm. I would only infer thus much, that I could not, on that

---

[4] LIFE, p. 5.

[5] [In "My Own Life" Hume writes "In the same year was published at London, my Enquiry concerning the Principles of Morals; which, in my own opinion (who ought not to judge on that subject), is of all my writings, historical, philosophical, or literary, incomparably the best."]

[6] LIFE, &c. p. 43.

account, bring myself absolutely to approve his odd fancy of firing all the dockyards in the kingdom.

Concerning the *philosophical opinions* of Mr. HUME you observe,[7] that "men will, no doubt, judge variously." They are certainly at liberty so to do, because the author himself did the same. Sometimes, to be sure, he esteemed them ingenious, deep, subtile, elegant, and calculated to diffuse his literary fame to the ends of the world. But, at other times, he judged very differently; very much so, indeed. "I dine," says he, "I play a game at back-gammon, I converse, and am merry with my friends; and when, after three or four hours amusement, I would return to these speculations, they appear so *cold*, so *strained*, and so *ridiculous*, that I cannot find in my heart to enter into them any farther."[8] Now, Sir, if you will only give me leave to judge, before dinner, of Mr. HUME'S philosophy, as he judged of it after dinner, we shall have no farther dispute upon that subject. I could indeed wish, if it were possible, to have a scheme of thought, which would bear contemplating, at any time of the day; because, otherwise, a person must be at the expence of maintaining a brace of these metaphysical Hobby-Horses, one to mount in the morning, and the other in the afternoon.

After all, Sir, friend as I am to freedom of opinion (and no one living can be more so) I am rather sorry, methinks, that men should judge so *variously* of Mr. HUME's philosophical speculations. For since the design of them is to banish out of the world every idea of truth and comfort, salvation and immortality, a future state, and the providence, and even existence of GOD, it seems a pity, that we cannot be all of a mind about them, though we might have formerly liked to hear the author crack a joke, over a bottle, in his life time. And I could have been well pleased to have been informed by you, Sir, that, before his death, he had ceased to number among his happy effusions tracts of this kind and tendency.

For – (let me come a little closer to you, Doctor, if you please, upon this subject – Don't be under any apprehensions – my name does not begin with a B___[9]) Are *you* sure, and can you make *us* sure, that there really exist no such things as a GOD, and a future state of rewards and punishments? If so, all is well. Let us *then*, in our last hours, read LUCIAN, and play at WHIST, and droll upon CHARON and his boat;[10] let us die as foolish and insensible, as much like our brother philosophers, the calves of the field, and the asses of the desart, as

---

[7] LIFE, &c. p. 59.

[8] Treatise of Human Nature. I. 467. In the Postscript to this Letter, a view will be exhibited of the HUMIAN system, taken exactly as it appeared to it's author at six o'clock in the evening.

[9] [i.e., "Beattie."]

[10] LIFE, &c. p. 47, et seq.

we can, for the life of us. But – if such things BE – as they most certainly ARE – Is it right in you, Sir, to hold up to our view, as "perfectly wise and virtuous,"[11] the *character* and *conduct* of one who seems to have been possessed with an incurable antipathy to all that is called RELIGION; and who strained every nerve to explode, suppress, and extirpate the spirit of it among men, that it's very name, if he could effect it, might no more be had in remembrance? Are we, do you imagine, to be reconciled to a character of this sort, and fall in love with it, because it's owner was *good company*, and knew how to manage his *cards*? Low as the age is fallen, I will venture to hope, it has grace enough yet left, to resent such usage as this.

You endeavour to entertain us with some *pleasant conceits* that were supposed by Mr. HUME to pass between himself and old CHARON. The philosopher tells the old gentleman, that, "he had been endeavouring to open the eyes of the Public;" that he was "correcting his works for a new edition," from which great things were to be expected; in short, "if he could but live a few years longer (and that was the only reason why he would wish to do so), he might have the satisfaction of seeing the downfal of some of the prevailing systems of *superstition*."[12]

We all know, Sir, what the word SUPERSTITION denotes, in Mr. HUME'S vocabulary, and against what Religion his shafts are levelled, under that name. But, Doctor SMITH, do you believe, or would you have us to believe, that it is CHARON, who calls us out of the world, at the appointed time? Doth not HE call us out of it, who sent us into it? Let me, then, present you with a paraphrase of the Wish, as addressed to HIM, to whom it should, and to whom alone, with any sense and propriety it can be addressed. – Thus it runs –

"LORD, I have only one reason why I would wish to live. Suffer me so to do, I most humbly beseech thee, yet a little while, till mine eyes shall behold the success of my undertaking to overthrow, by my metaphysics, the faith which thy SON descended from heaven to plant, and to root out the knowledge and the love of thee from the earth."

Here are no rhetorical figures, no hyperbole's or exaggerations. The matter is even so. I appeal, in the face of the world, Sir, to yourself, and to every man, who can read and understand the writings of Mr. HUME, whether this be not, in plain, honest English, the drift of his *philosophy* as it is called; for the propagation of which alone he wished to live; and concerning which you are pleased to say cooly, "men will judge variously, every one approving or condemning these opinions, according as they happen to coincide or disagree

[11] LIFE, &c. p. 62.

[12] LIFE, &c. p. 50.

with his own."[13] Our thoughts are very naturally carried back, upon this occasion, to the author of the *first philosophy*, who likewise engaged to *open the eyes of the Public* – He did so; but the only discovery they found themselves able to make, was, – that they were NAKED.

You talk much, Sir, of our philosopher's *gentleness* of manners, *good nature, compassion, generosity, charity*. Alas, Sir, whither were they all fled, when he so often sate down calmly and deliberately to obliterate from the hearts of the human species every trace of the knowledge of GOD and his dispensations; all faith in his kind providence, and fatherly protection; all hope of enjoying his grace and favour, here, or hereafter; all love of him, and of their brethren for his sake; all the patience under tribulation, all the comforts, in time of sorrow, derived from these fruitful and perennial sources? Did a good man think himself able, by the force of metaphysic incantation, in a moment, to blot the sun out of heaven, and dry up every fountain upon earth, would he attempt to do it? – TULLY had but a faint glimpse of the country to which we are all travelling; yet, so pleasing was any the most imperfect and shadowy prospect into futurity, that TULLY declared, no man should ravish it from him.[14] And surely, TULLY was a philosopher, as well as HUME. O had he seen the light which shone upon HUME, he would not have closed his eyes against it; had the same cup been offered to him, he would not have dashed it untasted from him!

"Perhaps our modern sceptics are ignorant, that without the belief of a GOD, and the hope of immortality, the miseries of human life would often be insupportable. But can I suppose them in a state of total and invincible stupidity, utter strangers to the human heart, and to human affairs? Sure, they would not thank me for such a supposition. Yet this I must suppose, or I must believe them to be the most cruel, the most perfidious, and the most profligate of men. Caressed by those who call themselves the great, ingrossed by the formalities of life, intoxicated with vanity, pampered with adulation, dissipated in the tumult of business, or amidst the vicissitudes of folly, they perhaps have little need and little relish for the consolations of religion. But let them know, that in the solitary scenes of life, there is many an honest and tender heart pining with incurable anguish, pierced with the sharpest sting of disappointment, bereft of friends, chilled with poverty, racked with disease, scourged by the oppressor; whom nothing but trust in Providence, and the hope of a future retribution could preserve from the agonies of despair. And do they, with sacrilegious hands, attempt to violate this last

---

[13] LIFE, &c. p. 59.

[14] Quod si in hoc erro, quod animos hominum immortales esse credam, libenter erro; nec mihi hunc errorem, quo delector, dum vivo, extorqueri volo.
DE SENECTUTE, ad Fin.

refuge of the miserable, and to rob them of the only comfort that had survived the ravages of misfortune, malice, and tyranny? Did it ever happen, that the influence of their execrable tenets disturbed the tranquillity of virtuous retirement, deepened the gloom of human distress, or aggravated the horrors of the grave? Is it possible, that this may have happened in many instances? Is it probable, that this hath happened in one single instance? – Ye traitors to human kind, ye murderers of the human soul, how can you answer for it to your own hearts! Surely, every spark of your generosity is extinguished for ever, if this consideration do not awaken in you the keenest remorse, and make you wish in bitterness of soul – But I remonstrate in vain. All this must have often occurred to you, and been as often rejected, as utterly frivolous. Could I enforce the present topic by an appeal to your vanity, I might possibly make some impression. But to plead with you on the principles of BENEVOLENCE or GENEROSITY, is to address you in a language ye do not, or will not understand; and as to the shame of being convicted of absurdity, ignorance, or want of candour, ye have long ago proved yourselves superior to the sense of it. – But let not the lovers of truth be discouraged. Atheism cannot be of long continuance, nor is there much danger of it's becoming universal. The influence of some conspicuous characters hath brought it too much into fashion; which, in a thoughtless and profligate age, it is no difficult matter to accomplish. But when men have retrieved the powers of serious reflection, they will find it a frightful phantom; and the mind will return gladly and eagerly to it's old endearments. One thing we certainly know; the fashion of sceptical and metaphysical systems passeth away. Those unnatural productions, the vile effusion of a hard and stupid heart, that mistakes it's own restlessness for the activity of genius, and it's own captiousness for sagacity of understanding, may, like other monsters, please awhile by their singularity; but the charm is soon over; and the succeeding age will be astonished to hear, that their fore-fathers were deluded, or amused, with such fooleries."

You, Sir, have read the preceding paragraph before; but this Letter may come into the hands of many, who have not. It is the alarum bell to the admirers of Mr. HUME; and should be rung in their ears, till succeeded by the last trumpet.

And now, Sir, will you give me leave to ask you a few questions? Why all this hurry and bustle, this eagerness to gratify the pretended "impatience of the Public,"[15] and satisfy it, that our philosopher lived and died perfectly composed and easy? Was there, then, any suspicion, in SCOTLAND, that he might not, at times, be quite so composed and easy as he should have been? Was there any particular BOOK ever written against him, that shook his system to pieces

---

[15] Preface to LIFE, &c.

about his ears, and reduced it to a heap of ruins, the success and eclat of which might be supposed to have hurt his mind, and to have affected his health? Was there any AUTHOR,[16] whose *name* his friends never dared to mention before him, and warned all strangers, that were introduced to him, against doing it, because he never failed, when by any accident it was done, to fly out into a transport of passion and swearing?[17] Was it deemed necessary, or expedient, on this account, that he should represent himself, and that you should represent him, to have been perfectly secure of the growth and increase of his philosophic reputation, as if no book had been written, which had impaired it; it having been judged much easier to dissemble the fall of DAGON, than to *set him upon his stumps again?* I am a *South* Briton, and, consequently, not acquainted with what passes so far in the opposite quarter. You, Sir, can inform us how these things are; and likewise, when the great work of *benevolence* and *charity*, of *wisdom* and *virtue*, shall be crowned by the publication of a treatise designed to prove the SOUL'S MORTALITY, and another, to justify and recommend SELF MURDER; for which, without doubt, the present and every future age will bless the name of the *gentle* and *amiable* author.

Upon the whole, Doctor, your meaning is good; but I think you will not succeed, this time. You would persuade us, by the example of DAVID HUME, Esq; that atheism is the only cordial for low spirits, and the proper antidote against the fear of death. But, surely, he who can reflect, with complacency, on a friend thus misemploying his talents in his life, and when amusing himself with LUCIAN, WHIST, and CHARON, at his death, may smile over BABYLON in ruins; esteem the earthquake, which destroyed LISBON, an agreeable occurrence; and congratulate the hardened PHARAOH, on his overthrow in the Red sea. Drollery, in such circumstances, is neither more nor less than

> Moody Madness, laughing wild,
> Amid severest woe.

---

[16] [The "book" and "author" referred to in these two sentences is *An Essay on the Nature and Immutability of Truth* (1770) by James Beattie, which attacks Hume's philosophy.]

[17] "I was a man of mild dispositions, of command of temper, little susceptible of enmity, and of great moderation in all my passions. Even my love of literary fame, my ruling passion, never soured my temper." LIFE, p. 32. Yet even by what is said of the Reverends and Right Reverends - Bishop Warburton, Bishop Hurd, the Zealots (that is, the Christians) and of the resolution once taken to 'change his name and settle in France,' because his writings did not meet with sufficient encouragement – by these circumstances, I say, there seems to have been something of the irritable in his constitution. But these are trifles. My quarry lies not in this way, at present. I fly at nobler game. The atrocious wickedness of diffusing atheism through the land, is a subject which concerns every body.

Would we know the baneful and pestilential influences of false philosophy on the human heart? We need only contemplate them in this most deplorable instance of Mr. HUME.

These sayings, Sir, may appear harsh; but they are salutary. And if departed spirits have any knowledge of what is passing upon earth, that person will be regarded by your friend as rendering him the truest services, who, by energy of expression, and warmth of exhortation, shall most contribute to prevent his writings from producing those effects upon mankind, which he no longer wishes they should produce. Let no man deceive himself, or be deceived by others. It is the voice of eternal TRUTH, which crieth aloud, and saith to you, Sir, and to me, and to all the world – *He that believeth on the Son hath everlasting life; and he that believeth not the Son, shall not see life; but the wrath of God abideth on him.*[18]

By way of contrast to the behaviour of Mr. HUME, at the close of a life, passed *without* GOD *in the world*, permit me, Sir, to lay before yourself, and the Public, the last sentiments of the truly learned, judicious, and admirable HOOKER, who had spent *his* days in the service of his Maker and Redeemer.

After this manner, therefore, spake the author of the *Ecclesiastical Polity,* immediately before he expired –

> "I have lived to see, that this world is made up of perturbations; and I have been long preparing to leave it, and gathering comfort for the dreadful hour of making my account with GOD, which I now apprehend to be near. And though I have, by his grace, loved him in my youth, and feared him in mine age, and laboured to have a conscience void of offence, towards him, and towards all men; yet, if thou, Lord shouldest be extreme to mark what I have done amiss, who can abide it? And therefore, where I have failed, Lord, shew mercy to me; for I plead not my righteousness, but the forgiveness of my unrighteousness, through his merits, who died to purchase pardon for penitent sinners. And since I owe thee a death, Lord, let it not be terrible, and then take thine own time; I submit to it. Let not mine, O Lord, but thy will be done! – GOD hath heard my daily petitions; for I am at peace with all men, and he is at peace with me. From such blessed assurance I feel that inward joy, which this world can neither give, nor take from me. My conscience beareth me this witness; and this witness makes the thoughts of death joyful. I could wish to live, to do the church more service; but cannot hope it; for my days are past, as a shadow that returns not."

[18] JOHN iii. 36.

His worthy Biographer adds –

"More he would have spoken, but his spirits failed him; and, after a short conflict between nature and death, a quiet sigh put a period to his last breath, and so, he fell asleep – And now he seems to rest like Lazarus in Abraham's bosom. Let me here draw his curtain, till, with the most glorious company of the Patriarchs and Apostles, and the most noble army of Martyrs and Confessors, this most learned, most humble, most holy man shall also awake to receive an eternal tranquillity, and with it a greater degree of glory, than common Christians shall be made partakers of."

Doctor SMITH, when the hour of his departure hence shall arrive, will copy the example of the BELIEVER, or the INFIDEL, as it liketh him best. I must freely own, I have no opinion of that reader's *head*, or *heart*, who will not exclaim, as I find myself obliged to do –
Let ME *die the death of the Righteous, and let* MY *last end be like his!*
I am, Sir,
    Your very sincere
      Well-wisher, and
        Humble Servant,
One of the People called CHRISTIANS.

POSTSCRIPT.

AS it is possible, Sir, nay probable, that this little tract, because it is a little one, may be perused by many, who have not leisure or inclination to go through large volumes, and yet wish to know what Mr. HUME'S philosophical system is; I shall here subjoin a short, but comprehensive summary of the doctrines which compose it, drawn up, some few years ago, by a learned gentleman, for his amusement, with proper references to those parts of our philosopher's works, where such doctrines were to be found. And though I never heard, the compiler had the thanks of Mr. HUME for doing, yet neither could I ever find, that he or his friends disputed the fidelity and accuracy with which it was done.[19]

---

[19] See Dr. BEATTIE'S Essay on Truth, Part II. Ch. I. Sect. I. and Part III. Ch. II.

A SUMMARY OF MR. HUME'S DOCTRINES, METAPHYSICAL AND MORAL

OF THE SOUL.

That the soul of man is not the same this moment, that it was the last; that we know not what it is; that it is not one, but many things; and that it is nothing at all.

That in this soul is the agency of all the causes that operate throughout the sensible creation; and yet that in this soul there is neither power nor agency, nor any idea of either.

That matter and motion may often be regarded as the cause of thought.

OF THE UNIVERSE.

That the external world does not exist, or at least, that it's existence may reasonably be doubted.

That the universe exists in the mind, and that the mind does not exist.

That the universe is nothing but a heap of perceptions, without a substance.

That though a man could bring himself to believe, yea, and have reason to believe, that every thing in the universe proceeds from some cause; yet it would be unreasonable for him to believe, that the universe itself proceeds from a cause.

OF HUMAN KNOWLEDGE.

That the perfection of human knowledge is to doubt.

That we ought to doubt of every thing, yea, of our doubts themselves, and therefore, the utmost that philosophy can do, is to give us a doubtful solution of doubtful doubts.[20]

That the human understanding, acting alone, does entirely subvert itself, and prove by argument, that by argument nothing can be proved.

That man, in all his perceptions, actions, and volitions, is a mere passive machine, and has no separate existence of his own, being entirely made up of other things, of the existence of which he is by no means certain; and yet, that the nature of all things depends so much upon man, that two and two could not be equal to four, nor fire produce heat, nor the sun light, without an act of the human understanding.

OF GOD.

---

[20] The fourth section of Mr. HUME'S *Essay on the Human Understanding*, is called *Sceptical doubts concerning the operations of the human understanding*; and the fifth section bears this title, *Sceptical Solution of those doubts.*

That it is unreasonable to believe GOD to be infinitely wise and good, while there is any evil or disorder in the universe.

That we have no good reason to think the universe proceeds from a cause.

That as the existence of the external world is questionable, we are at a loss to find arguments by which we may prove the existence of the Supreme Being, or any of his attributes.

That when we speak of Power, as an attribute of any being, GOD himself not expected, we use words without meaning.

That we can form no idea of power, nor of any being endued with power, *much less* of one endued with infinite power; and that we can never have reason to believe, that any object, or quality of any object exists, of which we can form an idea.[21]

OF THE MORALITY OF HUMAN ACTION.

That every human action is necessary, and could not have been different from what it is.

That moral, intellectual, and corporeal virtues are nearly of the same kind – In other words, that to want honesty, and to want understanding, and to want a leg, are equally the objects of moral disapprobation.

That adultery must be practised, if men would obtain all the advantages of life; that, if generally practised, it would in time cease to be scandalous; and that, if practised secretly and frequently, it would by degrees come to be thought no crime at all.

Lastly, as the soul of man, according to Mr. HUME, becomes every moment a different being, the consequence must be, that the crimes committed by him at one time, cannot be imputable to him at another.[22]

I believe, Doctor Smith, the reader is now fully prepared to enter into the spirit of your concluding sentence, which therefore shall be mine.

"I have always considered Mr. HUME, both in his life-time, and since his death, as approaching as nearly to the idea of A PERFECTLY WISE AND VIRTUOUS MAN, as perhaps the nature of human frailty will permit."

THE END.

---

[21] The poor prodigal Gentile, in the parable, was hardly reduced to feed upon such HUSKS as these. How good and how joyful a thing must it be, for one, that has been so reduced, to return to the house of his heavenly Father, where there is bread enough and to spare – to *know the only true* GOD, *and* JESUS CHRIST, *whom he hath sent*!

[22] 'My Enquiry concerning the Principles of Morals, is of all my writings, historical, philosophical, or literary, incomparably the BEST.' LIFE, p. 16.

61
REVIEW OF HORNE'S *LETTER*
(*CRITICAL REVIEW*)

Review of George Horne's *Letter to Adam Smith*, in *Critical Review*, 1777, Vol. 43, pp. 306–308.
Selections.

The review of George Horne's *Letter to Adam Smith* in the *Critical Review* was especially detailed, yet at the same time strangely neutral in its judgment about Horne's pamphlet. The author graphically makes clear Horne's hostile position towards Hume – in language even stronger than Horne's own – but then hedges on the question of whether Hume's philosophy is as mischievous as Horne alleges. This review was reprinted in *Weekly Magazine, or Edinburgh Amusement*, July 3, 1777, Vol. 37, pp. 22–23.

A Letter to Adam Smith, *LL.D. on the Life, Death, and Philosophy of his Friend* David Hume, *Esq. Small 8vo. 1s. Rivington.*

A short but comprehensive summary of the doctrines which compose Mr. Hume's philosophical system, is given by Dr. Beattie in his Essay on Truth (page 160, & seq.) with proper references to those parts of the philosopher's works, where such doctrines are to be found. It is drawn up with an accuracy, and fidelity, which have never been questioned. Even Mr. Hume himself, who would not, for many reasons, have suffered any imposition on the public in this matter, did not, neither do any of his friends, deny that it contains his sense, and that it is a very faithful abridgement of the original.

This summary (from whence an extract is made in the work before us) may be sufficient for the information of those, who not having leisure, or inclination, or patience, or dexterity to decypher large volumes, draw out in all the forms of metaphysic, and written in a language hardly intelligible, but to those who are philosophers by profession, may yet wish to know the nature and value of those discoveries, with which so *famous* an author, and so *perfectly wise, virtuous, and benevolent* a man, has enriched the world.

The belief of a God, and of a future state of rewards and punishments, is, at times, apt to create, especially in *weak* minds, some little restraint upon their actions, some small interruption to their pleasures, or some slight disturbance to their repose. It will be a comfort to hem to find, 'that these things have no existence; that what a man calls his soul, especially if it should happen to belong to a philosopher, is not, he is sure, (and it is the only thing of which he can be sure) the same this moment, that it was the last; nor consequently punishable at one time, for crimes committed at another; that it is not one, but many things, and that it is nothing at all; that every human action is necessary, and could not have been different from what it is; that adultery must be practised, if men would obtain all the advantages of life; and that it is equally *immoral* to want honesty, to want understanding, and to want a leg.'

These are a few of the sublime discoveries brought to light by this great philosopher; equally to his own honour, and to the advantage of society.

There are however men, on whom these benefits are thrown away. There are men too blind to see, or too ungrateful to acknowledge, the merit and utility of the philosopher's labours. They can discover no marks of wisdom in the composition of his nostrums; nor honesty, in the endeavour to cram down their throats a pestilent drench, that will, as they contend, infallibly destroy them.

The author of this little tract before us, who subscribes himself a Christian (a sect, it seems, not yet entirely abolished in Britain) professes himself of these sentiments. He expostulates very warmly with Dr. Adam Smith, for *advertising* the world, apparently with a view of raising the reputation, or promoting the sale of these nostrums, that Mr. Hume took them himself, and particularly in his last illness; that they agreed with him remarkably well; and that "he always considered Mr. Hume, both in his life time, and since his death, as approaching as nearly to the idea of a *perfectly wise and virtuous man*, as perhaps the nature of human frailty will permit."

This, it must be acknowledged, is a very artful, though indirect method of recommending Mr. Hume's philosophy to the favour of the public. – Was that philosophy indeed replete with the absurdity and mischief imputed to it; was it really true, that it tends to subvert the foundations of human knowledge, and to poison the sources of human happiness, as our author pretends it does, we could not, altogether, blame him for the part he takes; nor could we, on that supposition, absolutely exculpate either Mr. Hume, or his panegyrist, for their endeavours to propagate it.

But be this as it may, the Letter to Dr. Smith is very well calculated to answer the ends, which the writer had in view. It abounds with strokes of humour, and with the most happy allusions to the peculiar tenets, and circumstances of the philosopher, or to the conduct of his encomiast. To give our readers an idea of the performance, and the entertainment to be expected from it, we have selected the following passage. ...

62
WILLIAM JONES:
MEMOIRS OF GEORGE HORNE

William Jones, *Memoirs of the life, studies, and writings of the Right Reverend George Horne, ... To which is added his Lordship's own collection of his thoughts on a variety of great and interesting subjects. By William Jones ...* London: printed for G. G. and J. Robinson, F. and C. Rivington, T. Cadell, jun. and W. Davies; J. Cooke, Oxford; and W. Keymer, jun. Colchester, 1795, [4], 418 p.
Selections; from *The Works of the Right Reverend George Horne*, London: Rivington, 1830.

Born in Lowick, Northamptonshire, England, William Jones (1726–1800) was educated at University College, Oxford, where he met George Horne, with whom he remained lifelong friends. In 1751 he was ordained in the Church of England, in which he held various positions. In addition to his ministerial duties, he published works in theology, natural philosophy and music. Horne – author of the *Letter to Adam Smith* (1777) and *Letters on Infidelity* (1784) contained in this collection – died of a stroke in 1792 while on a journey. Shortly after, Jones prepared a *Memoir* his friend that was included in the six-volume collected works of Horne, published 1795. In this he makes particular reference to Horne's two works against Hume. Jones contends here that it was the aim of Hume's life "to invent a sort of philosophy that should effect the overthrow of Christianity," and, like Horne, Jones attacks Adam Smith for setting Hume up as a model of perfection. He defends Horne's use of drollery and ridicule against Hume's infidelity, and argues that Hume based many of his views on ancient Greek Pyrrhonism. In a footnote Jones gives Horne's response to a supposed comment by Hume that all devout people he ever met were melancholy. Jones's *Memoirs* of Horne was favourably reviewed in several journals. Writing for the *Monthly Review*, William Enfield comments that "in religious controversy Bishop Horne chiefly excelled in the use of the powerful weapon of ridicule" which is most evident in Horne's *Letters on Infidelity* (*Monthly Review*, July 1796, Vol. 20, pp. 241–246). The *Critical Review* writes that "Mr. Jones has given no [misrepresenting] shade to the picture which he draws of his amiable friend and patron" (November 1795,

Vol. 15 pp. 241–248). The *British Critic* (which Jones helped found) praised
the work, but pointed out its stylistic flaws:

> As to his [i.e., Horne's] biographer, he has written (which the reader must
> have observed) with the warmth of friendship, with the fidelity of truth, and
> with a zeal for Christianity, all united together. Some little blemishes in style
> we have noted, as we have transcribed. But the author's mind is bent upon
> higher objects, than petty accuracies of language. [*British Critic*, 1796, Vol.
> 7, pp. 256–261]

The *Analytical Review* took issue with Jones's advocacy of abusive rhetoric
towards Hume:

> This is cavalierly said; and may pass very well with ignorant and bigotted
> people; but the learned know, and Mr. J. cannot be ignorant, that *this* Mr.
> David Hume, (as he sneeringly calls him) was a hardy combatant, not to be
> driven off the field by the light skirmishing of a little pleasant raillery...
> [*Analytical Review*, 1795, Vol. 22, pp. 466–471]

Jones's *Memoirs* of Horne was published again in 1799, and is included in
several editions of Horne's *Works* (1795, 1809, 1818, 1830, 1831, 1846,
1848, and 1853)

...

About the time when it was published [i.e., Horne's *Commentary on the
Book of Psalms* (1776)], that systematical infidel, David Hume, died. It had
been the aim of his life, to invent a sort of philosophy that should effect the
overthrow of Christianity. For this he lived; and his ambition was to die, or be
thought to die, hard and impenitent, yea, and even cheerful and happy, to show
the world the power of his own principles; which however, were weakly
founded, and so inconsistent with common sense, that Dr. Beattie attacked and
demolished them in the life-time of the author. Special pains were taken by
Hume himself, and by his friends after him, to persuade the world that his life,
at the last stage of it, was perfectly tranquil and composed; and the part is so
laboured and over-acted, that there is just cause of suspicion, even before the
detection appears. Dr. Horne, whose mind was ever in action for some good
end, could not sit still and see the public so imposed upon. He addressed an
anonymous *Letter to Dr. Adam Smith* from the Clarendon press; of which the
argument is so clear, and the humour so easy and natural, that no honest man
can keep his countenance while he reads it, and none but an infidel can be
angry. While Dr. Adam Smith affects to be very serious and solemn in the cause
of his friend Hume, the author of the Letter plays them both off with wonderful

effect. He alludes to certain anecdotes concerning Mr. Hume, which are very inconsistent with the account given in his Life; for at the very period, when he is reported not to have *suffered a moment's abatement of his spirits*, none of his friends dared to mention the name of a certain *author* in his presence, lest it should *throw him into a transport of passion and swearing*: a certain indication that his mind had been greatly hurt; and nobody will think it was without reason, if he will read the Essay on Truth, by Dr. Beattie; which is not only a confutation of Hume's philosophy: it is much more; it is an extirpation of his principles, and delivers them to scattered like stubble by the winds.

The Letter to Dr. Adam Smith, like the Essay of Dr. Beattie, has a great deal of truth, recommended by a great deal of wit; and if the reader has not seen it, he has some pleasure in store. We allow to the memory of Dr. Adam Smith, that he was a person of understanding and diligent research, in things relating merely to this world; of which, his Inquiry into the Causes of the Wealth of Nations will be a lasting monument; and it is a work of great use to those who would obtain a comprehensive view of business and commerce: but when he set up Mr. Hume as a pattern of perfection, and judged of all religion by the principles of that philosopher, he was very much out of his line.

The letter was followed in course of time by *Letters on Infidelity*; which are very instructive and entertaining, and highly proper for the preventing or lessening that respect which young people may conceive unawares for unbelieving philosophers. It has been objected by some readers of a more sever temper, that these Letters are occasionally too light:[1] and I must confess I should have been as well pleased if the story of Dr. Ratcliffe and his man had been omitted: but there is this to be said, that these are not sermons, but familiar letters; that Dr. Horne considered the profession of infidelity as a thing more ridiculous and insignificant in itself than some of his learned readers might do; that as it appeared in some persons, it was really too absurd to be treated with seriousness; and, as Voltaire had treated religion with ridicule instead of argument, and had done infinite mischief by it, justice required that he and his friends should be treated a little in their own way.[2] Besides, as infidels have nothing to support them but their vanity, let them once appear as ridiculous as they are impious, and they cannot live. They can never approve themselves,

---

[1] In his preface to these Letters, the author has endeavoured to obviate this objection; and we think he has done it very sufficiently.

[2] One of the severest reflections that ever came from the pen of Dr. Horne, was aimed, as I suppose, at this Mr. David Hume; yet it is all very fair. This philosopher had observed that all the *devout* persons he had ever met with were *melancholy*; which is thus answered: "This might very probably be; for, in the first place, it is most likely, that he saw very few, his friends and acquaintance being of another sort; and, secondly, the sight of *him* would make a devout person melancholy at any time." These Letters are a demonstration that all devout persons are not melancholy.

but so far only as they are upheld and approved by other people. To treat them with seriousness (as Watson has treated Gibbon) is to make them important; which is all they want. The opinions of Mr. Hume, as they are displayed in these Letters, are many of them ridiculous from their palpable absurdity: but, it must be owned, they are sometimes horrible and shocking; such as, that man is not an accountable but a necessary agent; consequently that there is no such thing as sin, or that god is the author of it: that the life of a man and the life of an oyster are of *equal* value: that it may be as criminal to act for the preservation of life, as for its destruction: that as life is so insignificant and vague, there can be no harm in disposing of it as we please: that there can be no more crime in turning a few ounces of blood out of their course (that is, in cutting one's throat), than in turning the waters of a river out of their channel. What is murder? It is nothing more than turning a little blood out of its way. And so the Irishman said, by the same figure of rhetoric, that perjury was nothing more than kissing a book, or, as he worded it, smacking the calve-skin. This is the sage Mr. Hume! whom Dr. Adam Smith delivers to the world, after his death, as a perfect character; while a man of plain sense, who takes things as they are, would think it impossible that any person, who is not out of his mind, should argue at this rate. Mr. Hume seems to me to have borrowed from the school of the old Pyrrhonists much of that system which he is supposed to have invented. They made all things indifferent, and doubted of every thing, that there might be nothing true or real left to disturb them. The chief good they aimed at in every thing, was what they called αταραξια, a state of undisturbance or tranquillity, in which the mind cares for nothing: and it was the ambition of Mr. Hume to be thought to have lived and died in this state; but by all the accounts his αταραξια was not quite perfect. His object was undoubtedly the same with that of the Pyrrhonists, and he pursues it by a like way of reasoning. The speculations of these men were so copious, that there is matter enough left for another Mr. Hume to set himself up with, and pass for an original. Of all the sects of antiquity this was the most unreasonable; though pretending to more wisdom than all the rest. That which was but folly under Heathenism, turns into desperation and madness under the light and truth of Christianity. Where all was blind tradition or wild conjecture, there might be some excuse for fixing to nothing: but to affect *undisturbance*, after what is now revealed, concerning death and judgment, and heaven and hell, is to try how far a man can argue himself out of his senses. What angels may think of such a person, I do not inquire; but how must evil spirits look upon that man who sleeps or laughs over the things at which they tremble, and then calls himself a *Philosopher!*
...

63
"REMARKS ON DR ADAM SMITH'S LETTER TO MR. STRAHAN" (*WEEKLY MAGAZINE*)

"E.M.," "Remarks on Dr Adam Smith's *Letter to Mr. Strahan, on the death of David Hume, Esq.*," in *Weekly Magazine, or Edinburgh Amusement*, April 24, 1777, Vol. 36, pp. 139–141.
Complete; from *Weekly Magazine*.

A dam Smith's "Letter ... to William Strahan" triggered a series of critical letters to *Weekly Magazine*. The anonymous author of the letter below – probably a Scottish minister – attacks Smith for setting up a Godless notion of virtue when praising Hume's character, and feels that Hume's "specious tranquillity must have been affected." The true model for facing death, the author argues, is found in the attitudes of Jacob, David and Paul who rise in grandeur "in hope of everlasting glory." Dark and hopeless infidelity, by contrast, "degrades man into the 'likeness of a beast that perisheth.'" Bracketed comments are those of *Weekly Magazine*.

REMARKS *on Dr* ADAM SMITH'S *Letter to Mr* STRAHAN, *on the Death of* DAVID HUME, *Esq*; [Vol. xxxv. P. 338]

To the PUBLISHERS *of the* WEEKLY MAGAZINE.

Sir,
In reading Dr Smith's account of Mr Hume's death, I could not help feeling pain, both for the dead and for his surviving friend, as being one in sentiment, unhappily blind to the "life and immortality brought to light by the gospel." – Doubtless the doctor intends a panegyric upon his friend; but in truth the publication of his frolicsome behaviour in dying, is a satire which must expose Mr H–'s memory to the pity, if not to the contempt, of the truly wise and virtuous part of mankind. It is an affecting picture the doctor exhibits to view. A man of distinguished intellectual powers acting the fool at his end – dying

indecently humorous – seemingly easy – "without Christ – without GOD – without hope" – dying in a manner that betrayed a blindness exceeding the darkest ignorance of an *Indian savage.*

From the doctor's narrative of Mr H–'s dying behaviour, a Christian cannot easily allow that the concluding eulogy of his character fairly follows. Can you admit it to be just, to be probable, to be credible, "that such a man approached nearly to the idea of a perfectly wise and virtuous man?" What is this gentleman's notion of wisdom and virtue? If the perfection of impiety, if downright atheism be perfect wisdom and virtue, then it must be granted that his hero was perfectly wise and virtuous. Whether God was at all in Mr H–'s thoughts; or what light God might be pleased to transmit into his mind in his last speechless moments, we know not; but, from the doctor's account, it appears that God was not in any of his words: And was it below the dignity of a philosopher to confess resting on any other prop than his own self-sufficient virtue? – Insolent vanity!

The doctor gives us a sketch of Mr H–'s sublime morals – morals which fitted him to be an agreeable companion to those of his own stamp. Besides his many other amiable qualities, he shone in humorous pleasantry, "without the slightest tincture of malignity." It were strange, indeed, if he should offend his few beloved friends, and spoil their good fellowship with any irritating stings of *malignity.* This kind of venom, which he possessed in good store, he reserved for the Christian religion, and its ministers: And how could a sincere friend of virtue be so implacably severe upon Christianity? Does it not carry virtue to its summit of perfection? Are not many of our clergy as virtuous? Are they not, according to their ability, at least as liberal in charity as any the most generous of our infidels? And though multitudes professing Christianity are dissolute and worthless, because they consider not its nature and importance, are there not many Christians of every rank who excel in virtue, and are virtuous from a nobler principle than infidels can be – from love, influenced by the amiable perfections of the Deity, and these shining in the height of their glory in Jesus Christ? Some, indeed, are generous from constitutional humanity; and as we Christians know, upon the most satisfactory evidence, that the gospel only is powerful to form the heart of man to true divine virtue, we may be allowed, consistently with charity, to suppose, yea, positively to assert, that the virtues of our infidel sophists are very lame and contracted; that the few of them which they seem to respect are tinged with the enormous pride and vanity which speak loftily in all their ingenious labours, especially in their painful lucubrations pointed at the overthrow of revelation; for effecting which laudable purpose, they, with great parade, bring up the auxiliary engine of zeal for virtue, with a superficial shew of it in life. Let their virtues be examined with severe scrutiny, and shall they not "be found wanting;" blazing high in words, but glimmering faintly in life? Are they not so far from perfection, that they are miserably destitute of that singleness which is essential to genuine virtue? In vain do infidel philosophers pretend that they are the only students of human nature; that, from their scientific theories, the world is to learn virtue. Indeed, none seem to mistake it more than they do: from what principle, and for what reason, we are not ignorant. One reason is, that, being self-confident, the disdain consulting the Bible, in which the truest account of virtue lies obvious before all, and which, I may say, is the only true history of human nature in the world.

Can any thing be more frivolous, more childish, more indecently wanton and presumptuous in a dying man, perceiving himself on the verge of time, than Mr H–'s sportful dialogue with *Charon*? – Is this nature? Is it sober reason? – To take leave of this world, of its various alluring comforts, and affluent fortune, a distinguished reputation, the agreeable society of friends, lively health and good chear, inchanting diversions and amusements; – to bid an eternal farewel to all these delights of the sons of men, without the prospect of better things, or of their equivalent in another state, but darkling to plunge into a dreary abyss, "a land of darkness, as darkness itself," under absolute uncertainty what his lot may be – whether a miserable eternal existence in separation from the body, or annihilation. To depart thus sceptical with a perfectly easy mind, without sad regret, without a wishful look "after what his soul delighted in," now flying from his sight! It cannot be – it contradicts the essential principles of nature. And was he really chearful without hope? Let him believe it who can! Those who allow themselves to understand human nature as it really is, cannot help suspecting that all this specious tranquillity must have been affected. True, indeed, the scripture says of some, "whom pride compasseth about as a chain, that there are no bands in their death;" that, being "given up to a reprobate (unfeeling) mind, they live and die in a profound peace," singing a *requiem*, "peace and safety, when destruction is near."

Mr H–'s singular composure in the near view of death, the doctor stiles *magnanimity*. What – to brave and jest with death! – death, so terrible to nature! with pertinacious contempt of its consequences! – Do you call this *magnanimity*? Is it not better named *foolhardiness*? – Consult nature, Dr S–h; consult common sense, and speak out what it dictates. Why should you be emulous of sharing in the reputation of a philosophy which commits an outrage at once against the sacred oracles, and the common feelings of humanity.

We are told that Mr H– was quite resigned. Resigned! to what? Not to the will of God. Of his name and will we hear not a word "in the course of his chearful conversation." He was resigned, it may be said, to the constitution of things – to the order of nature. An order of nature, exclusive of the Author of nature, are words without meaning. With such worldly obscure wisdom, vain men, who affect to be wiser than scripture, presume to put a blind upon the world; "who, professing themselves to be wise, are become fools; vain in their imaginations, and their foolish hearts hardened."

How miserable the comforter, who could minister no other consolation to his dying friend, than "that he was to leave his friends in great prosperity!" Alas! to leave his abundant wealth to others, and nothing left to himself in its place, but the mortifying prospect of death and worms soon to devour him! And is the man, the wise man now comforted? A fine flight this disinterested benevolence! It sounds pompously in speculation; but did it ever exist in any man's mind! Never: nor in Dr S–th's, nor in mine, nor in the almost perfect Mr H–'s. When this pitiful *cordial* is presented, he still needed that *balsam* of *Lucian's* droll tale about *Charon* and his boat to assuage, or rather to divert, the wounding thought of parting with the delicacies of this world, without the hope of better, or of as good in their place.

Upon the supposition Mr H– had no wealth to leave, to what resource shall he now turn for comfort? What remains to bear up his heart? "All refuge fails." The poor man must be quite inconsolable! – O how much earlier and happier is royal *David* in his exit! What other sort of dignity does he exhibit in dying? who, notwithstanding the unfavourable aspect of his family, could joyfully say, "Although my house be not so with God, yet he hath made me an everlasting covenant, &c." – Compare together a sceptical philosopher and a scripture saint in dying, and see the abject meanness into which the one sinks – the grandeur, in hope of everlasting glory, to which the other rises. – *Jacob*, in blessing and taking leave of the tribes on his death-bed, is divinely composed with the hope of "God's salvation." – *David* launches forth fearless into the dark vale, assuredly believing that God would be his guide to glory. – How *truly magnanimous* is *Paul* in facing death, greatly triumphing in hope of a never-fading crown of righteousness? Where now is the wise man? "Where the philosophic disputer of this world," who denies revelation and immortality? Can he compare, for true greatness, with the meanest Christian *dying in faith?* O heaven! what a dark, melancholy scene must this world be? how joyless the short life of man in it, had he not God to trust in, no immortal life to hope for, no principle to be guided and supported by, but "let us eat and drink, for to-morrow we die."

Suppose the proofs of revelation were doubtful, and not so satisfactory as they are, is it not more for the good of the world, more for the honour, for the comfort, and happiness of mankind, to admit, than to question its truth? The effects of true faith in scripture dignify and exalt human nature in life and in death. What so powerful to influence the practice of virtue, to support under the evils of life, and in the last conflict with death, as are the comforts of the gospel? Philosophers will tell us, that to the practice of virtue, another motive is necessary than the attraction of its own beauty. And where is its beauty displayed to such perfection as in scripture? But, besides the beauty of virtue, such degenerate creatures as we are, and in such a tempting world as this, do need further subsidiary motives of divine authority, and the lively hope of a happy immortality, to hold us to its practice with persevering fortitude. – In the death of a true Christian, divinely submissive to the will of God, and amid the pains of dissolving nature, exulting in the hope of eternal glory, you have an exalted view of human nature; whereas dark, hopeless infidelity degrades man into the "likeness of a beast that perisheth." When I reflect upon that grave saying of Jesus, "If ye believe not that I am He, ye shall die in your sins," I cannot but lament the death of an Infidel.

Good God! to what a pitch of incredulity and callousness do curious men, with fruitless labour, from a vain affectation of singularity, work themselves? What scripture says, Isa. xivii. 10. applies properly to such men; "Their wisdom and their knowledge hath perverted them, and they say in their hearts (and in words too), we are, and none else besides us." – But, however much they value themselves upon their ingenious subtleties, they shall not by them prevail, they shall not succeed in their malevolent designs against revelation; nor shall they, by their impotent attempts to overthrow it, establish what they most affect, a name of immortal renown. They are sure to be vexed with a disappointment of their hope with respect to both. Their proselytes shall be only among the vain and vicious, who, without the help of false philosophy, are of themselves disposed to get free of the restraints of religion, and for liberty to live at large, form their notion of virtue, after their own hearts. Their elaborate theories, by which they gain the temporary fame of genius exerted, are of such manifestly evil tendency, so inimical to Christianity, and to men's best interests, that they can never go down with the wise and virtuous, but must be abjured by them; and shall therefore, it is hoped, meet with deserved contempt and neglect from our princes, our nobles, our judges, from our learned gentlemen of every order, and from all people who revere God and love mankind.

I am, SIR
Yours, &c.

E.M.

B–r–h, April 17.

64
"OBSERVATIONS RELATIVE TO THE LATE DAVID HUME, ESQ."
(*WEEKLY MAGAZINE*)

"Idem," "Observations relative to the late David Hume, Esq.," in *Weekly Magazine, or Edinburgh Amusement*, Thursday, May 8, 1777, Vol. 36, pp. 193–196.
Complete; from *Weekly Magazine*.

Perhaps a friend of Hume, the anonymous author of the letter below to *Weekly Magazine* defends Hume and Smith against "E.M.", the author of the previous article in *Weekly Magazine*. Expressing ironic approval of E.M, the author attacks that writer for effectively announcing Hume's arrival in hell on no other grounds than religious speculation. The author lists twelve defences he had heard against the charges by E.M. concerning Hume's attitude toward his death. Couched in irony, the author praises Hume's critique of the clergy, pursuit of truth, generosity, modesty, and his writings – both philosophical and historical.

OBSERVATIONS *relative to the late* DAVID HUME, *Esq*;
To the PUBLISHER *of the* WEEKLY MAGAZINE.

Lord, how are they increased that trouble me! Many are they that rise up against me; many there be which say of my soul, There is no help for him in God. Selab. PSALM iii.

SIR,
When a great man comes to town, we have it in the papers next day: though there should be nothing of the marvellous in the manner of his arrival, yet it is a satisfaction to know it; but when a man of eminence is sent to hell, there are such unavoidable delays, owning to the distance – the badness of the roads, and other circumstances, that we cannot have the pleasure of hearing such great news till many months after his decease.
It was, I think, in March or April, 1773, that the late celebrated earl of Ch–f–d died, and it was not till March 1775 that his damnation was notified

in your Magazine by an elegant writer who subscribes himself *Eusebius*. It is, therefore, less surprising that we have not had an earlier account of the fate of the late David Hume, Esq; who died in August last, than that in your Magazine, P. 141. communicated by a gentleman who signs the initials E.M. Both Eusebius and Mr E.M. decline disclosing the sources of their intelligence, though every man must be sensible they would not have hazarded such assertions without something more convincing than mere speculation to warrant them. They chuse rather to treat that affair as a point of doctrine, than as an article of intelligence, and produce proofs rather than authorities; indeed, they bring such damning proof, that there is little occasion for any thing else to convince the great admirers of these eminent men of their deplorable condition. Thus the doctrine of these men's perdition resembles, in some measure, those great truths which men could never have found out of themselves, but being imparted by revelation, have afterwards been made out by reason.

With regard to Mr Hume, it is a consummation devoutly to be wished for by every good Scotsman. This man, without having the fear of poverty before his eyes, from which our whole nation are scampering away to the tune of *Devil take the hindmost*, trifled away the best part of his life in improving his mind, and had the effrontery to produce such works as no other Scotsman was ever capable of, and to display such candour, moderation, impartiality, penetration, and taste, as was never heard, or seen, or conceived, in this country before; and we hope, for the preservation of that national character which we have enjoyed ever since Fergus I. will never be imitated while sun and moon endure. It is chiefly to his preposterous exertions that we own a literary reputation, for which we had no occasion, which we have no prospect of ever being able to support, and which will soon bring us into double disgrace with the nations around us, by raising the expectations that we never can answer. Should his lukewarm sceptical humour, which has already chilled the native fire of so many of our youth, continue to spread its baleful influence, we shall soon be deprived of that characteristical fervour, which formerly impelled us to so many surprising undertakings. The only thing that can alleviate the evils that are come upon us through his means, is that good news which your correspondent's letter affords us, which may be very useful in deterring others from the like attempts for many years to come: yet many are so hardened, that they raise objections to the solid arguments upon which this salutary doctrine of Hume's perdition is grounded, nay, even some professed Christians have ventured to cavil against it.

I shall repeat some of those things I have heard advanced against your correspondent's reasoning, without attempting to answer them, though that would be no hard task, because the honour properly belongs to him of settling, beyond dispute, that great and important truth in which we all have need to be well established, in such trying and shaking times.

1. Some take upon them to deny that Mr Hume acted the fool at his end; for they say that his conversations and behaviour was so much in the usual strain,

that his argument would prove too much, as even his enemies do not pretend that he lived like a fool.

2. They likewise deny that he died indecently humorous; for they alledge that there is nothing in the humorous part of Mr Hume's conversation, recited by Dr Smith, but what is decent enough, and that conversation happened more than a fortnight before his death. They do not presume, however, to deny, that if a man should happen to laugh upon any occasion, and be so ill advised as to die within twenty-fours after, it might go hard with him.

3. They deny that he died *seemingly easy*, for they affirm that he died easy in truth and reality.

5. That he died without hope, they endeavour to disprove by the testimony of his physician, who writes that he died in such a happy composure of mind, that nothing could exceed it.[1]

6. That he was perfectly impious, and a downright Atheist, they say is a charge that should never be brought against any man without bringing some reasons to support it. When I heard them talk at this rate, I begged them to hold their peace, for they only exposed their own ignorance. Ever since the world began, all such men as Hume have been reckoned Atheists and impious wretches, and sometimes treated as such, and nobody was ever so foolish as to ask what was the reason of it. That they are such, is one of those primary truths which strike the mind at once, and are incapable of being deduced by reasoning from any of the principles of human knowledge. It is a truth, of which the most illiterate clowns are fully convinced, merely by its own evidence, without the smallest aid of reasoning: the common sense of mankind teaches it.

7. That he rested on his virtue they do not intirely deny, but that he laid more weight on it than it was able to support, requires to be proved. They assert boldly, that he had more modesty than he had occasion for.

8. That his virtues were tinged with enormous pride and vanity, is a charge, they say, that destroys itself, while the meaning of these words remains the same as at present.

9. That he disdained consulting the Bible, is what they are surprised to hear, when they consider how many strokes of his work discover greater intimacy with that book, than falls to the share of some of those who are paid for studying it.

10. They alledge further, that he did not jest death, nor brave it, but waited its approach with great composure; and though he had jested with death, he was not much to blame, as it appears from the account of his lingering illness, that death had long jested with him.

---

[1] [The text contains no fourth point.]

11. That he outraged the sacred oracles, and the common feelings of humanity, they aver, is as difficult to be proved, as all the other charges brought against them. If the scriptures represents the wicked as tortured with remorse at the approach of death, he did nothing to prevent the fulfilling of the scripture; as he had not been a wicked man, it was none of his business to die with remorse. His last letter to Dr Smith shows that he still retained some feelings of humanity, and some grains of politeness.

12. That he left nothing to himself, they say, is not strictly true, for he still retained something of a good conscience, and hopes of a better state, and a reputation for learning and genius so peculiarly his own, that none of his cotemporaries can have any share in it. They add further, with great assurance, that this charge would have been more heavily urged, if it had been thus worded, "He left nothing to Mr E.M."

Such are the pitiful cavils with which they endeavour to impugn a doctrine of the greatest importance to the consolation and upbuilding of very many respectable and serious people. No doubt, Mr E.M. your correspondent, will soon answer them so effectually, as for ever to stop the mouths of these vain babblers.

In the mean time, there are some of his arguments that, with all their malice, they have not been able to shake. It is undeniable, that God was not in any of his words, from which Mr E.M. rightly infers, that he was not resigned to the will of God. The whole argument is founded upon this great truth, that God is not named in those parts of Mr Hume's conversation recited in Dr Smith's letter. Let any intelligent person carefully examine that letter, laying his finger on every line where Mr Hume is introduced speaking (that he may be sure not to miss one of them), and if he there finds the word GOD, Mr E.M. and I are willing to allow this argument to have no weight or force; nay, if he examine the whole letter in the same manner, he will be convinced, that Dr Smith and Dr Black are as hardened and regardless of God as Mr Hume. – Such is the force of bad example!

Another thing that must for ever ascertain Mr Hume's commendation is, that he was venomous to the clergy. Other profligate persons have treated these holy men injuriously, and brought false accusations against them, which gave them no small trouble to clear themselves from; but Mr Hume has carried his malignity so far, that he has said things against them which they will never be able to answer. To lay things to men's charge that are too true to be denied, is being venomous to the highest degree.

These quibbling defenders of Mr Hume have not been able to justify his reading such profane authors as Lucian within a month of his death; it is a thing that will admit of no palliation. Indeed, I tremble when I consider the desperate wickedness of our professors and schoolmasters, who are so hardened, that I have seen some of them stand with an erect countenance, in the midst of a large room, prelecting to a croud of scholars from such profane authors as Anacreon, Xenophon, Terence, and Horace, whilst, in the mean time, they did not know but that they were standing on the brink of eternity, and, in the twinkling of an eye, the house might tumble about their ears and crush them to atoms.

How well this poor man deserved that fate, which it so evidently appears he has found, the serious reader will easily perceive if he considers the following particulars:

Though he knew he was born to a small fortune, and that knowledge and prudence are of much more value than riches, power, or pleasure, yet he was seized very early with a passion for literature, which became the ruling passion of his life.

Though he knew that God had fixed no limits to human industry, but has given us the faculty of reason to exert and improve, to the utmost, in every useful and innocent inquiry, yet he ventured to think for himself, and, what is more, to differ in opinion, not only from his predecessors, but even from his cotemporaries, and some of them younger than himself.

Though he knew that he was liable, like most other men, to fall into mistakes, and entertain false opinions, yet he insulted the common sense of mankind to such a degree, that he scarce ever advanced any thing in his writings without attempting to prove it.

So little regard had he for truth, that neglecting and despising all those methods which have been invented for its defence, and established as the laws of disputation among all civilized nations, he neither impeached the morals, abused the persons, vilified the understandings, insulted the misfortunes, nor put malicious constructions on the words and actions of those who did not immediately adopt all his new-fangled notions, but left his reasoning to stand or fall by their own merit.

Though he knew that impartiality is one of the first duties of an historian, and that the bitterness which gives such relish and poignancy to modern history is but ill calculated to improve posterity, yet he was so besotted as to neglect attaching himself to that party which was in a capacity to reward his labours, and, as if he had not been a Scotsman, but only a citizen of the world, he exposed, with great coolness, the excesses of those who contended for liberty, as well as for those who defended the prerogative.

Though he knew that death was appointed for all men, and that melancholy or anxiety could be of no avail in averting the stroke, yet he waited for it with cheerfulness and intrepidity.

And to crown all, and fill up the cup of his iniquities, though he knew that a time of sickness and languishing is improper for serious studies, yet in his last illness he amused himself with books of entertainment, and talked facetiously of his own death in Lucian's manner on the 8th of August 1776, although it was decreed that he was to depart this life on the 25th of the same month, and though he was unapprised of that decree.

What a different reputation would this man have left, had he followed a quite contrary course! How much more would he have been regretted by your ingenious correspondent, and that numerous and respectable part of the nation who think like him.

Had he spent the prime of his life in the diligent use of all feasible means of acquiring riches, without reckoning any other object deserving of his attention; had he prudently regarded human affairs no farther than to make them contribute as much as possible to the advancement of his fortune; had he left all consideration of divine things to those who are appointed by law to watch over them; or, if he must needs dabble in philosophy and reasoning, had he confined himself to the beaten track, and employed his talents in vilifying every one who ventured to depart from it one inch either to the right hand or to the left; had he abstained from corrupting the age with a dangerous scepticism, but rather asserted the most unintelligible propositions with a manly boldness, and disdained the mean artifices of reasoning and investigation, so much esteemed by the disputers of this world; had he, on the approach of death, shown that becoming contrition and tenderness of spirit which makes the last period of life so edifying to spectators; had he expressed a sincere regret for every profane and undutiful expression that he had ever in his life thrown out against the ministers of the gospel, charging them with any of the imperfections of human nature; had he spent his last days in committing to memory the choicest compositions of his namesake, the royal Psalmist, to assist him, in behaving godly, by retailing them upon his death-bed; had he conducted himself thus through life, and in death, he would have left a memory dear and venerable to the far greater part of his countrymen, and his friends would not have been shocked with the news of his damnation in public prints.

Yours, &c.

IDEM.

April 26.

65
"OBSERVATIONS ON
MR. HUME'S LIFE LATELY PUBLISHED"
(*WEEKLY MAGAZINE*)

"Agricola," "Observations on Mr. Hume's Life lately published," in *Weekly Magazine, or Edinburgh Amusement*, June 12, 1777, Vol. 36, pp. 364–365. Complete; from *Weekly Magazine*.

The author of this article states that he is in some degree an admirer of Hume's character and of his writings, but is "sorry to see that little biographical account of himself *imposed* on the public." The author believes the work will have "an obvious, although, perhaps, an undesigned tendency" to subvert a person's "future and eternal welfare." Smith's account of Hume's dying jocularity, the author argues, will give more support to Hume's anti-Christian writings than "all his metaphysical subtleties." Libertine people, he fears, who "catch at every little twig of infidelity," will wrongly feel that Hume's calmness towards death was the result of his religious notions. The author concludes noting that the *Life* is "a dry, unsatisfactory narrative; as little answering its title as the expectation of the public."

Observations on Mr. HUME'S *Life lately published.*

To the PRINTER, &c.

Sir,

Though I am in some degree an admirer of Mr Hume's character and of his writings, yet I am sorry to see that little biographical account of himself *imposed* on the public. I would not have troubled you with reasons for the disapprobation of an individual, were they not rather suggested by the spirit of humanity than of criticism. For surely, Sir, to the former may be attributed to an hearty desire to forewarn our fellow-creatures of errors which may prove subversive of their future and eternal welfare. To which dreadful purpose the little pamphlet alluded to had an obvious, although, perhaps, an undesigned tendency.

Mr Hume's writings, it is universally known, are inimical to Christianity, and they seem to me likely to receive more support from that jocularity, and unconcerned composure with which, we are told, he wound up the thread of his life, than from all his metaphysical subtleties. And why, methinks I hear some one say, should the character of a man, so eminent for his virtues and capacity, be smothered or tarnished in compliance with the opinion of a bigotted zealot? Or, is your cause so weak as to want so mean a subterfuge? – No. – But unfortunately the thinking part of the world is small. Most men judge from a partial and superficial view of things, and those whose lives and morals are libertine, are apt, like drowning men, to catch at every little twig of infidelity, to bear them up at that awful moment, when they are sinking into eternity, the approach of which Mr Hume met with such complacency. Such men will suppose this to be rather the result of his opinions than of his actions. I know it was – it must be the reverse; the memory of a well directed moral conduct, and the *cleanness* of his *hands*, if I may use the expression, in opposition to the notions of religion, which he unhappily entertained in his heart, could not only support him in that dread hour. These alone could smooth the horrors of death, and divest, if possible, the doubts of the sceptic of their sting, and will, I sincerely hope, make the balance of divine justice preponderate in his favour.

But let not, therefore, the vicious and profligate think to find an asylum from the horrors of their consciences under the cover of their infidelity; or that even the degrading hope of annihilation will be able to dispel that gloom which the poignant recollection of an ill-spent life will throw over their last moments. The highest state of moral perfection, which fallible man is capable of attaining to in this life, cannot, unless accompanied with too over-weening an opinion of his own merits, give the calm composure of secure innocence to that awful scene. – Without the Christian virtue of faith and hope to accompany the recollection of a well-spent life, on what rational foundation besides can we, who have the opportunity of cultivating them, build the expectation of an happy immortality?

I should have altered the word *imposed* in the first sentence of these remarks, were I not sure that every curious reader, as well as myself, will retire much disappointed from the perusal of the Life of Hume; a dry, unsatisfactory narrative; as little answering its title as the expectation of the public.

AGRICOLA.

66
WILLIAM WILBERFORCE:
PRACTICAL VIEW OF THE PREVAILING RELIGIOUS SYSTEMS

William Wilberforce, *A practical view of the prevailing religious system of professed Christians, in the higher and middle classes in this country, contrasted with real Christianity. By William Wilberforce.* London: printed for T. Cadell, jun. and W. Davies, (successors to Mr. Cadell), 1797, [4], 491, [19] p. Chapter 6, selections; from 1797 edition.

Born in Hull and educated in law at Cambridge, William Wilberforce (1759–1833) was elected member of Parliament in 1780. In his years there, he is most noted as a prominent voice in the effort to abolish the slave trade, a conviction that was grounded in his evangelical religious beliefs. His two principal writings are *A Practical View of the Prevailing Religious System of Professed Christians* (1797) and *An Appeal... on Behalf of the Negro Slaves* (1823). The first of these is an attempt to warn his countrymen that they are strangers to real Christianity. In the selection below he contends that many writers are unbelievers, such as Hume and Smith, and most others feel united to them through the bonds of literature. Writing for the *Monthly Review*, William Enfield comments that, contrary to Wilberforce, if the authority of religion is to be preserved, "it must not be done by addressing the passions, but by appealing to reason" (July 1797, Vol. 23, pp. 241–248). The *Analytical Review* finds problems with the dogmatic tone of the work:

Through the whole of this work, while the author expresses himself with all the warmth of genuine piety and benevolence, he speaks the strong language of confident dogmatism, and seems to entertain no suspicion, that his views of christianity may possibly be erroneous. Without entering into a discussion of the grounds of his tenets, which he himself has declined, we will hazard a conjecture, that his work will make little impression on minds not already prepossessed in favour of his system. To a pretty numerous body, who appropriate to themselves the character of *real christians*, this work, which is written *con amore*, and in a captivating style, will be highly acceptable; but by every other class of readers it will, probably, from different considerations, be rejected. [*Analytical Review*, 1797, Vol. 25, pp. 503–511]

By the turn of the century, Wilberforce's *Practical View* went through ten editions – although three appear to be reissues of the first edition with cancel title pages. The following is from the first edition.

CHAP. VI.
BRIEF INQUIRY INTO THE PRESENT STATE OF CHRISTIANITY

...

But to make an end of this discussion concerning the degree in which the peculiarities of Christianity have fallen into neglect, and concerning one of the principal of the causes which have produced it; if this be the state of things even in the case of sermons, and of the compositions of those whose sphere of information must be supposed larger than that of the bulk of mankind, it must excite less wonder, that in the world in general, though Christianity be not formally denied, people know little about it; and that in fact you find, when you come to converse with them, that admitting in terms the Divine Revelation of Scripture, they are far from believing the propositions which it contains.

It has also been a melancholy prognostic of the state to which we are progressive, that many of the most eminent of the literati of modern times have been professed unbelievers; and that others of them have discovered such lukewarmness in the cause of Christ, as to treat with especial good will, and attention, and respect, those men, who, by their avowed publications, were openly assailing, or insidiously undermining the very foundations of the Christian hope; considering themselves as more closely united to them by literature, than severed from them by the widest religious differences.[1] Can it then occasion surprise, that under all these circumstances, one of the most acute and most forward of the professed unbelievers[2] should appear to anticipate, as at no great distance, the more complete triumph of his sceptical principles; and that another author of distinguished name,[3] not so openly professing those infidel opinions, should declare of the writer above alluded to, whose great abilities had been systematically prostituted to the open attack of every principle of religion, both natural and revealed, "that he had always considered him, both in his life-time and since his death, as approaching as nearly to the idea

---

[1] It is with pain that the author finds himself compelled to place so great a writer as Dr. ROBERTSON in this class. ...

[2] Mr. HUME.

[3] Vide Dr. A. Smith's letter to W. Strahan, Esq.

of a perfectly wise and virtuous man as perhaps the nature of human frailty will permit?"

Can there then be a doubt, whither tends the path in which we are travelling, and wither at length it must conduct us? If any should hesitate, let them take a lesson from experience. In a neighbouring country, several of the same causes have been in action; and they have at length produced their full effect. Manners corrupted, morals depraved, dissipation predominant, above all, Religion discredited, and infidelity grown into repute and fashion,[4] terminated in the public disavowal of every religious principle which had been used to attract the veneration of mankind. The representatives of a whole nation publicly witnessing, not only without horror, but to say the least, without disapprobation, an open unqualified denial of the very existence of God; and at length, as a body, withdrawing their allegiance from the Majesty of Heaven. ...

[4] What is here stated must be acknowledged by all, be their political opinions concerning French events what they may; and it makes no difference in the writer's view of the subject, whether the state of morals was or was not, quite, or nearly as bad, before the French revolution.

67
CHARLES PETTIT MCILVAINE:
EVIDENCES OF CHRISTIANITY

Charles Pettit McIlvaine, *The evidences of Christianity: in their external division, exhibited in a course of lectures, delivered in Clinton hall, in the winter of 1831-2, under the appointment of the University of the city of New York.* New York, G. & C. & H. Carvill, 1832, xvi, [17] - 565 p. Selections from Lecture 11; from 1861 edition.

American clergyman Charles Pettit McIlvaine (1799–1873) was Episcopal bishop of Ohio from 1831 until his death, and during the Civil War represented Lincoln on a diplomatic mission to England. His *Evidences of Christianity*, which appeared in 1832, offers an array of arguments for the truth of the Christian faith. In Chapter 11 he argues that the effects of Christianity on believers' lives – particularly as they face death – confirms its truth. In this discussion he contests Adam Smiths claim in his "Letter ... to William Strahan" that Hume was the model of virtue. Hume's essays, McIlvaine argues, contain gratuitously unchaste comments that show Hume for what he truly was. And, Hume's cheerfulness while facing death was "evidently contrived for stage effect" and was "an affected piece of over acting." McIlvaine inserts an abridgment of the 1831 letter to the *Christian Observer* on Hume's deathbed anguish (contained earlier in this collection), and he argues that Hume's actual anxiety over death demonstrates an "internal evidence" of God's existence.

LECTURE XI.
THE FRUITS OF CHRISTIANITY

...

Hume pretended to a great diligence in search of truth and spent all his powers against the gospel, and yet, says Dr. Johnson, "confessed that he had *never read the New Testament with attention.*" His friend in scepticism, Adam Smith, considered him "as approaching as nearly to the idea of a perfectly wise and virtuous man as perhaps the nature of human frailty will permit." But since, in his estimation, female infidelity, when unknown, was nothing; one needs pretty positive evidence to believe that he was specially pure.

{[Note:] That Hume was virtuous, *without chastity*, is evident from his essays. They contain passages, by way of wit or illustration, not only gratuitously introduced, but forced in by a mere *amateur* taste of the writer, which a chaste mind would not have thought of, and a man of chaste habits and principles would have rejected, as both polluting to his pages and disgraceful to his character. I cannot believe that one who could venture on such sentences before the public eye, and show such pleasure and evident facility in grovelling indecencies of writing, was free from unclean practice where no public eye was to be encountered. And still, in Adam Smith's opinion, he may have been "as perfectly virtuous *as the nature of human frailty would permit.*" What exceptions are included under this last clause, who can say? In an infidel's creed, virtue has no more quarrel with unchasteness, than in the creed of the Spartans, it had with theft. Among the latter, nothing was required to make stealing virtuous but *concealment.* Among the virtuosi of infidelity, what more is required to establish the innocence of impurity.

The person who put out an edition of Hume's Essays in this country, dedicating it to the president of the United States, and lauding Hume and his principles to the skies, showed very plainly how he had profited by his favourite volume, at least by the Essay in defence of Suicide. – He killed himself by drunkenness!}

... No case of a dying unbeliever has been made so much of, by way of a set-off to the testimony of Christians, as that of David Hume. The evident object of Adam Smith, the narrator, is to put up his friend for a comparison with believers. Gibbon says: "He died the death of a philosopher." No thing can be more affected, more evidently contrived for stage effect; or, even on infidel principles, more disgraceful to such a mind as Hume's, than the manner of his death, according to the account given by his friend. He knew his end was near. Whether he was to be annihilated, or to be for ever happy, or for ever miserable, was a question involved on his own principles, in impenetrable darkness. It was the tremendous question to be then decided. Reason and decency demanded that it should be seriously contemplated. How does he await the approach of eternity? Said Chesterfield (an infidel also): "When one does see death near, let the best or the worst people say what they please, it is a serious consideration." Does Hume treat it as a serious consideration? He is *diverting himself*! With what? With preparing his Essay in defence of *Suicide* for a new edition; reading books of amusement; and sometimes with a game at cards! He is *diverting himself* again! With what next? With talking silly stuff about Charon and his boat, and the river Styx! Such are a philosopher's diversions, where common sense teaches other people to be, at least, grave and thoughtful. But why *divert* himself? Why turn off his mind from death? Why the need of his writings, and his cards, and his books of amusements, and his trifling conversations? Was he afraid to let his mind settle down quietly and alone to the contemplation of all that was at stake in the crisis before him'? Whatever the explanation of his levity, it was ill-timed, out of taste badly got up; an affected piece of over acting, intended for posthumous fame, to say the best of it. He died "as a fool dieth." Take his own views, as thus expressed, at the end of his Natural History of Religion: "The comfortable views exhibited by the belief of futurity are ravishing and delightful. But how quickly vanish on the appearance of its terrors, which keep a more firm and durable possession of the human mind. The whole is a riddle, an enigma, an inexplicable mystery. Doubt, uncertainty, suspense of judgment, appear the only result of our most accurate scrutiny concerning this subject." In his own estimation, then, *futurity has its terrors.* Doubt, inexplicable mystery, hung over his future destiny! Whether he was not to be a child of hell for ever, his most accurate scrutiny could only suspend his judgment! In this tremendous suspense, he plays cards, as it were, on his coffin lid! jests about ridiculous fables, as he steps down to the momentous uncertainties, but eternal realities, of the future! If a finger had been about to receive its sentence, whether to be amputated or not, he would at the least have been more grave. How far such a death-bed scene is honourable to philosophy or infidelity, or fit to be compared with that of millions of Christians, I need not say. But this is the fairest aspect of the matter on the side of infidelity.

{[Note:] There is reason to believe that, however unconcerned Hume may have seemed in the presence of his infidel friends, there were times when, being diverted neither by companions, nor cards, nor his works, nor books of amusement, but left to himself and the contemplation of eternity, he was any thing but composed and satisfied.

The following account was published many years ago in Edinburgh, where he died. It is not known to have been ever contradicted. "About the end of 1776, a few months after the historian's death, a respectable looking woman, dressed in black, came into the Haddington stage coach, while passing through Edinburgh. The conversation among the passengers, which had been inter-rupted for a few minutes, was speedily resumed, which the lady soon found to be regarding the state of mind persons were in at the prospect of death. An appeal was made, in defence of infidelity, to the death of Hume, as not only happy and tranquil, but mingled even with gayety and humour. To this the lady said: 'Sir, this is all you know about it; I could tell you another tale.' 'Madam,' replied the gentleman, 'I presume I have as good information as you can have on this subject, and I believe that what I have asserted regarding Mr. Hume has never been called in question.' The lady continued: 'Sir, I was Mr. Hume's housekeeper for many years, and was with him in his last moments; and the mourning I now wear was a present from his relatives for my attention to him on his death-bed; and happy would I have been if I could have borne my testimony to the mistaken opinion that has gone abroad of his peaceful and composed end. I have, sir, never, till this hour, opened my mouth on this subject; but I think it a pity the world should be kept in the dark on so interesting a topic. It is true, sir, that when Mr. Hume's friends were with him he was cheerful, and seemed quite unconcerned about his approaching fate; nay, frequently spoke of it to them in a jocular and playful way; but when he was alone, the scene was very different; he was any thing but composed; his mental agitation was so great at times as to occasion his whole bed to shake. He would not allow the candles to be put out during the night, nor would he be left alone for a minute. I had always to ring the bell for one of the servants to be in the room, before he would allow me to leave it. He struggled hard to appear composed, even before me. But to one who attended his bedside for so many days and nights, and witnessed his disturbed sleeps and still more disturbed wakings; who frequently heard his involuntary breathings of remorse and frightful startings; it was no difficult matter to determine that all was not right within. This continued and increased until he became insensible. I hope in God I shall never witness a similar scene.'" – *Christian Observer*, vol. xxxi. p. 665.

There is internal evidence of truth attached to the above. Hume had no opinions with regard to God, or the future, except that all was doubtful. Whether there was a God, a future state, a hell, or annihilation, he did not profess to know. The future had its terrors, he acknowledged. To him they were terrors of darkness and uncertainty. He spoke of "the calm, though obscure regions of philosophy." He called the whole question as to man's future destiny, "*a riddle, an enigma, an inexplicable mystery.*" All he could arrive at was, "*doubt, uncertainty, suspense of judgment.*" In this state of mind, nothing could have been more forced or unnatural than the levity described by Smith. That was his stage-dress. If a man lay a hundred pounds upon a game, he is anxious till the uncertainty as to its fate be removed. But Hume knew that his ALL, FOR EVER, was at stake; and that he was unconcerned, unanxious, when not *diverted*, is incredible. On the other hand, the account presented above is exactly what nature and reason would expect from the state of mind in which the philosopher described himself, as to all that awaited him. Not to be penetrated with anxiety of the most painful kind, when a few hours were to decide whether he was to be annihilated, or to be carried to the judgment seat of God, and find all that he had ridiculed in the gospel true, and be condemned to eternal misery – a destiny which, on his own principles, was as likely as any thing else – could only be accounted for on the supposition that disease or friends diverted his attention from the decision approaching.}

68
MISCELLANEOUS COMMENTS ON ADAM SMITH'S "LETTER"

In addition to the more sustained critiques of Adam Smith's "Letter... to William Strahan" regarding Hume's final days, various short reactions also appeared, often as tangential comments by ministers or theologians. Along with critical comments by John Wesley – founder of the Methodist movement – brief selections are also included below from William Julius Mickle, Thomas Dick, George Burgess, Alonzo Potter, James McFarlane Mathews, John Reid, John Marshall Lowrie, Arthur Penrhyn Stanley, and William Jackson.

Even that politician in the late reign neither knew the heart of himself or of other men, whose favourite saying was: "Do not tell me of your virtue, or religion: I tell you, every man has his price;" yes, sir R[obert Walpole], every man like you; every one that sells himself to the devil. Did that right honourable wretch, compared to whom Sir R[obert] was a saint, know the heart of man? He that so earnestly advised his own son, "never to speak the truth? To lie or dissemble as often as he speaks? To wear a mask continually?" That earnestly counselled him, "not to debauch *single women,* (because some inconveniences might follow,) but always married women." Would one imagine this grovelling animal ever had a wife or a married daughter of his own? Oh rare Lord C[hesterfield]! Did ever man so well deserve, though he was a peer of the realm, to die by the side of Newgate? Or did ever book so well deserve to be burned by the common hangman, as his letters? Did Mr. David Hume, lower, if possible, than either of the former, know the heart of man? No more than a worm or a beetle does. After "playing so idly with the darts of death," do you now find it a laughing matter? What think you now of Charon? Has he ferried you over Styx? At length he has taught you to know a little of your own heart! At length you know it is a fearful thing to fall into the hands of the living God! [John Wesley (1703–1791), "The Deceitfulness of the Human Heart" Halifax, April 21, 1790; from Wesley's *Sermons,* New York, Darlton and Lanahan, n.d.]

Silence, ye noisy wolves and bears,/ And hear the song of Russel!/ Hark! how upon the Parnassus' hill/ This bard kicks up a bustle!

426

He calls the Muses lying jades,/ A pack of venal strumpets:/ And reason good; for none of them/The death of David trumpets.

But say – shall Shakspeare's Muse bedew/ This David's leaden urn?/ Or at his tomb, O Milton! say,/ Shall thy Urania mourn?

Shall gentle Spenser's injur'd shade / For him attune the lay? / No! none of these o'er his cold grave / Shall strew one sprig of bay.

For him, the modern Midas, these / No grateful chaplets owe; / Yet shall his friends; with proper bays, / Adorn his heavy brow.

For him shall Russel rant and rave / In hobbling rumbling lays; /And Smith, in barb'rous dreary prose, / Shall grunt and croak his praise. [William Julius Mickle (1735–1788), *The poetical works of William Mickle*, London, Printed for C. Cooke, 1799.]

Dr. A. Smith, in the account he gives of the last illness of *Hume*, the historian, seems to triumph in the fortitude which he manifests in the prospect of his dissolution, and he adduces a playfulness of expression as an evidence of it, in his jocular allusion to *Charon* and his boat. But, as Dr. Cogan, in his treatise on the passions, very properly remarks, "A moment of vivacity, upon the visit of a friend, will not conduct us to the recesses of the heart, or discover its feelings in the hours of solitude." It is, indeed, altogether unnatural for a man who set so high a value upon his literary reputation, and certainly very unsuitable to the momentous occasion, to indulge in such childish pleasantries, as Hume is represented to have done, at the moment when he considered himself as just about to be launched into non-existence; and, therefore, we have some reason to suspect, that his apparent tranquillity was partly the effect of vanity and affectation. He has confessed, says Dr. Cogan, in the most explicit terms, that his principles were not calculated to administer consolation to a thinking mind. This appears from the following passage in his treatise on Human Nature. "I am affrighted and confounded with that forlorn solitude in which I am placed by my philosophy. When I look abroad, I foresee, on every side, dispute, contradiction, and distraction. When I turn my eye inward, I find nothing but doubt and ignorance. Where am I, or what? From what causes do I derive my existence, and to what condition shall I return? I am confounded with these questions, and begin to fancy myself in the most deplorable condition imaginable, environed with the deepest darkness." [Thomas Dick (1774–1857), *On the improvement of society by the diffusion of knowledge*, Glasgow & London, W. Collins, 1833, 336 p.]

Whatever be the expectations of the dying man, he feels as yet no break of his existence. The very atheist who takes what, like Hobbes, he calls "the leap in the dark," would not call it such, had he not a secret recoil from a decision which that leap is to make, and of which he is to be conscious. When Hume, in his last hours, was jesting with his friends in allusion to the Pagan fable of

Charon and his boat, the consciousness of continuous life was seen in the very choice of his jest. If Priestley expressed, almost as he died, his expectation of a sleep till the resurrection, such a sleep would be no extinction; but he looked to its close, as if to waking in the morning. [George Burgess (1809–1966), *The Last Enemy; Conquering and Conquered*, Philadelphia: H. Hooker, 1850, "The Mind in Death," p. 163.]

Philosophical Scepticism, which founds its doubts exclusively on speculative considerations, may, as we have said, be merely theoretical. In respect to many matters it must be so. In regard, for example, to the life that now is, no man is a practical sceptic, nor even in respect to the life which is to come, if his soul be suddenly confronted with its more awful realities. But we are far from intimating that speculative scepticism is therefore innocuous. In regard to the more spiritual truths that pertain to the soul's welfare, it is easy to suppress, and, by degrees, almost eradicate them. The habit of doubting and cavilling about evidence is one, too, that soon engenders either a profane levity or a profound despondency. Mr. Hume's death-bed, signalized by coarse jests about the Styx, Charon and his boatmen, seems no unnatural conclusion to a life so much of which had been devoted to unsettling the very foundations of all belief. [Alonzo Potter (1800–1865), Introduction, in *Lectures on the evidences of Christianity, delivered in Philadelphia, by clergymen of the Protestant Episcopal church*. Philadelphia, E.H. Butler & co., 1855.]

Quite and array of testimony might be here introduced from the last hours of sceptics, but we satisfy ourselves with a single reference. "I have always considered the death of Hume as described by Adam Smith, Dr. Black and others, to be a scene of the most flimsy hypocrisy to be found on record. Hume's friends, like those of Voltaire, were anxious that he should evince no sign of misgiving or fear, and should persist in his infidelity to the last. But both he and they over acted so far in the matter, as to betray themselves. They tell us of his great composure; of his utter unconcern as he sat with them at the card-table, knowing himself to be on the brink of the grave; how he could repeat the silly jests which he might have with Charon, the boatman sent according to the fables of Paganism, to carry the dead across the river which was said to divide this world from the world of spirits." Pitiful gossamer covering of what was going on in the breast of the dying man! Fallen as poor human nature is, she is not so far sunk as this; she is neither so blinded or hardened. She has sympathies that tell of something better, was it merely friend parting with friend, for a period they know not how long, and to encounter they know not what."[1] The utter unreasonableness of the whole

---

[1] [James McFarlane Mathews (1785–1870), *The Bible and men of learning; in a course of lectures*, New York, Fanshaw, 1855, 392 p., p. 176.]

scene and the art manifest in it show that the spirit of the sceptical philosopher was not easy. He needed God more than he was willing to confess. A joke on a death-bed is proof positive that the soul fears the Deity. Men only laugh at death when they would hush the tumult within. Many an unbeliever believes while he does not want to believe. And this makes the proof all the stronger for our important theme. It shows that no specious opinions can avail to cheat the soul out of its God when the great sifting moment comes. [John Reid (fl. 1865–1891), *Voices of the soul answered in God*. New York: R. Carter & brothers, 1865, Part 3, Chapter 2.]

In all the range of English literature I know no more lamentable evidence of the weakness and folly of irreligion and infidelity than the account of David Hume's dying hours, as given in a letter from one of his most intimate friends. Let any one read that account and Dr. Mason's remarks upon it, or let any one compare the last thoughts and words of the ancient David, a believer, and of the modern David, a skeptic; let him see the one rejoicing and the other whiling away the declining hours of life with a game of cards and with affected jesting upon the ancient heathen mythology, and he can easily decide upon which couch – that of the infidel or that of the believer – he would wish to stretch his dying limbs. [John Marshall Lowrie (1817–1867), *The life of David*, Philadelphia: Presbyterian Board of Publications, 1869.]

It is not too much to say that the name of Hume was, and is still, one of the chief objects of theological terror – not only in Great Britain, but in Europe. Hume was the great skeptic of a skeptical age. But if so good a judge as Adam Smith could say of him that he was the "most perfectly wise and virtuous man he had ever known," it is worthy the consideration of Christian ministers to ponder well before they treat such a character as an enemy of religion. Nor did he put himself forward as an unbeliever. "I am no Deist – I do not so style myself; neither do I desire to be known by that appellation."[2] He was constant in his attendance at the worship of the Church (Burton's *Hume*, ii, 453), and he presents a delicacy of expression on religious subjects which, even if prudential, stood in remarkable contrast with many of the contemporary scoffers both in England and on the Continent. His reward was that the graces of his character were acknowledged by the clergy even more readily than by the laity. [Arthur Penrhyn Stanley (1815–1881), *Lectures on the history of the Church of Scotland, delivered in Edinburgh in 1872*, London: J. Murray, 1872, 1872.]

---

[1] [James McFarlane Mathews (1785–1870), *The Bible and men of learning; in a course of lectures*, New York, Fanshaw, 1855, 392 p., p. 176.]

No doubt the actual course of Hume's philosophising was determined by his zeal against everything he deemed superstitious. It was this dominant motive which made him less a calm philosopher than a skilful advocate, and laid him open to the influences of the French Deism of his period. How strong the tendency was we may infer from the following anecdote, which occurs in an account of his declining days by his friend and admirer, Dr. Adam Smith. [William Jackson (1817?–1891?), *The philosophy of natural theology. As essay, in confutation of the scepticism of the present day*, New York, A.D.F. Randolph & co., 1875.]

EARLY RESPONSES TO HUME

Volume 10

Edited and Introduced by
James Fieser
University of Tennessee at Martin

THOEMMES CONTINUUM

Early Responses to Hume

Edited and Introduced by **James Fieser**
University of Tennessee at Martin, USA

Volumes 1 and 2
Early Responses to Hume's Moral, Literary and Political Writings

Volumes 3 and 4
Early Responses to Hume's Metaphysical and Epistemological
Writings

Volumes 5 and 6
Early Responses to Hume's Writings on Religion

Volumes 7 and 8
Early Responses to Hume's *History of England*

Volumes 9 and 10
Early Responses to Hume's Life and Reputation
Bibliography of Early Responses to Hume, with Indexes

EARLY RESPONSES TO HUME'S LIFE AND REPUTATION

Second Edition, Revised

II

Edited and Introduced by

James Fieser

University of Tennessee at Martin

thoemmes

First published by Thoemmes Press, 2003

Thoemmes Continuum
11 Great George Street
Bristol BS1 5RR, England

http://www.thoemmes.com

Early Responses to Hume
Second edition, revised, 2005
10 vols : ISBN 1 84371 114 1

Early Responses to Hume's Life and Reputation
Second edition, revised, 2005
2 Volumes : ISBN 1 84371 115 X

© J. Fieser, 2003, 2005

Printed and bound in Great Britain
by Biddles Ltd, Kings Lynn, Norfolk

SAMUEL JACKSON PRATT'S
APOLOGY AND REACTIONS

69
SAMUEL JACKSON PRATT:
AN APOLOGY

[Samuel Jackson Pratt], *An apology for the life and writings of David Hume, Esq. with a parallel between him and the late Lord Chesterfield: to which is added an address to one of the people called Christians. By way of reply to his letter to Adam Smith, L.L.D.* London: printed for Fielding and Walker, D. Prince, Oxford, T. and J. Merrill, Cambridge, and W. Creech, Edinburgh, 1777, [4], xv, [1], 167, [1] p.
Selections; from 1777 edition.

Samuel Jackson Pratt (1749–1814) was the author of *A Supplement to the Life of David Hume* (1777) contained in this collection. His *Apology* appears to have been published in April 1777, a month or so before the *Supplement*. The work contains no table of contents; its main divisions are these:

To William Strahan, Esq.
Preliminary Address.
Section 1. Of Hume's Philosophical Consistency.
Section 2. Of Religious Hypocrisy.
Section 3. On the Natural Dignity of the Literary Character, and the Reasons which have Brought it into Contempt.
Section 4. Of Hume's Principles, and his Motive for making them Public, with some Remarks on his Conduct in his Last Moments.
Section 5. Parallel betwixt Hume and lord Chesterfield, both with respect to Abilities, and Principles.
Section 6. Of Proper Cautions Prior to the Establishment of our Religious Credenda.
An Address to one of the People Called Christians. By way of Reply, to his Letter to Adam Smith, L.L.D. On the Life, Death, and Philosophy of his Friend David Hume, Esq.

The *Apology* aims to defend Hume's character on several grounds. He argues that Hume was philosophically consistent and died as he lived – that is, without repenting in his final hours. He was also not a religious hypocrite, did not flatter royalty with dedications, and had sound motives for his philosophy. The discussions of religious hypocrisy and book dedication only tangentially relate to Hume, and appear to have been originally composed as separate essays, tailored for this publication. To highlight Hume's virtues, Pratt draws a sharp contrast between the philosopher's character and that of the politician and courtier Philip Dormer Stanhope, Lord Chesterfield (1694–1773). Chesterfield's recently published *Letters to his Son* (1774) had revealed an unseemly side to that otherwise amiable figure, particularly as he urged his son to be deceitful. The contrast between Hume and Chesterfield was one of the more controversial parts of Pratt's *Apology*, mainly because his critics mistook his purpose and felt that he was sincerely *comparing* rather than *contrasting* the two figures. For, although Pratt suggests at the outset of the chapter that he is drawing a "parallel" between the two, it is soon clear that he is being ironic in order to magnify Hume's moral superiority. In the final Section, Pratt argues that Hume was entitled to voice a view in opposition to widely held conservative statements of philosophy and religion. It is the job of rational readers to determine which arguments are stronger, without being swayed by the names of famous writers in the dispute. He concludes his work with an attack on Horne's anonymous *Letter to Adam Smith* (1777), contained in this collection. Apparently aware of Horne's identity, Pratt harshly argues that, although his cause may be just, his malice and drollery are not.

Pratt's *Apology* was negatively reviewed in four journals. The complete article in the *Critical Review* is as follows:

> It must be acknowledged that the author of this performance is a *tight hand* at a title-page, and a complete master of those necessary implements in modern book-making, a pair of scissars and a paste-brush. – It is undoubtedly, a piece of literary patchwork, without Beginning, middle, or end, and owes its existence to the present popularity of the subject. [*Critical Review*, April 1777, Vol. 43 p. 320]

Devoting a full-length article to Pratt's *Apology*, the *London Review* opens its assessment as follows:

> The hasty production of some ingenious advocate for Mr. Hume, better qualified to imitate his ease and brilliancy of stile than to investigate the difficulty and profundity of his sentiments. ... Nothing is more common, in town, than for a book to be published, or an event to happen, one day, and a long printed treatise on it to appear the next. ... The death of David Hume afforded one of these opportunities, tho' not so sudden as not to have been for some time anticipated. Hence it appears that, hard as the present writer spurred his Pegasus, one of the people called christians whipped his Oxonian *Bidet* to town before him. Luckily the little Christian took a different side of

the question, and thence enabled our author to kill two birds with one stone, by annexing an *Answer* to his *Apology*.

Concerning the comparison between Hume and Chesterfield, the reviewer writes "What put it into the writer's head, to draw such a whimsical parallel, we cannot conceive; the very reasons, he himself assigns, should certainly have kept two such heterogeneous characters far enough asunder." Pratt's reflections in Section 6, according to the reviewer, consist "of mere trite common-place reflections." Regarding Pratt's reply to Horne, the reviewer states the following:

In the annexed *address*, in answer to the author of the Remarks on Dr. Smith's letter, the writer pertinently-enough replies to several little imperti- nencies in the Remarker's letter to Dr. Smith. We wish, however, he had more satisfactorily answered his adversary's question, respecting the umbrage, which Mr. Hume is said to have taken at Dr. Beattie's Essay on Truth; a work, the mention of which, it has been reported, he could not bear with any tolerable patience. ... As to the rest, it does not appear to us that either the *Apologist*, or the writer, who stiles himself, *One of the People called Christians*, hath the advantage in criticising on each other respecting Mr. Hume's Metaphysics, which neither of them seems clearly to comprehend. [*London Review*, May 1777, Vol. 5, pp. 332–339]

At the close of the review a footnote appears as follows: "Since this article was sent to the press, we are informed that the apology, which is the object of it, was written by the fertile young genius, Mr. Courtney Melmoth."

Gentleman's Magazine printed a lengthy anonymous letter to the editor which attacked Pratt's *Apology* and *Supplement* ("Observations on the Address," July 1777, Vol. 47, pp. 322–328, contained later in this collection). Their brief review of the *Apology* defers judgment to that letter:

Our review of the "Supplement" to this performance is happily anticipated by the judicious observations of a correspondent, page 322; to which therefore we shall only refer; and as for the "Apology" itself, shall wave discussing it for the reasons assigned by that writer in its second paragraph, with which our opinion perfectly coincides. [*Gentleman's Magazine*, July 1777, Vol. 47, pp. 338]

Writing for the *Monthly Review*, William Enfield accused Pratt of inconsistency for writing both a book on revelation – *The Sublime and Beautiful of Scripture* – and a defence of Hume.

If the Life and Writings of Mr Hume need an apology, they merit a better apologist than Mr. Courtney Melmoth. The plain facts related in Mr. Hume's

short and artless account of himself, can receive no illustration, nor the
deductions which arise from them, any support, from the comment of so
superficial a declaimer. An indiscriminate charge of hypocrisy brought
against the advocates of religion, and oblique insinuations to the discredit of
Christianity, from a writer who has so lately pleaded the cause of revelation,
may serve to expose his own inconsistency, and narrowness of spirit; and
digressive declamations, on dedications, on the character of the Great, and
on the vices of Lord Chesterfield, may swell out the volume to a convenient
size. But to stand forth as an apologist for Mr. Hume, and an advocate for
his philosophy, requires depth of penetration, strong powers of reasoning,
and a truly philosophical spirit; all of which the present work affords but
slender appearance. [*Monthly Review*, September 1777, Vol. 57, p. 242]

Enfield's review was reprinted in *Scots Magazine* (September 1777, Vol. 39. pp.
497–498).

In addition to these reviews, Pratt was attacked in an anonymous pamphlet
titled *A Letter to Courtney Melmoth* (1777). Like Enfield, the author charges
Pratt with inconsistently advocating scripture in one book while defending
Hume in another. The author says further of Pratt, that "This present work of
yours is a plain proof that you have imbibed their principles. Any person may
easily find out your ironical scoffs against christians." In their review of this
Letter, the *London Review* attempts to reconcile the inconsistency:

There is doubtless a great appearance of inconsistency in all this, if Mr. M.
be really the writer of the Apology {[footnote:] Of which, however, we have
only anonymous and unsupported information.}: but before our Country
Curate took upon him to be so severe on this gentleman on that account, he
should have remembered that the Comment on the Scriptures was written
many years ago, while the author was a candidate for holy orders. – He may
possibly have entered into very different orders since; and, tho' that denote
his apostacy, it skreens him from the charge of inconsistency. [*London
Review*, August 1777 Vol. 6, pp. 141–144]

In the same year an anonymous pamphlet titled *A Panegyrical Essay* attacked
the style and substance of Pratt's *Apology*, citing it as an example of low
culture. The author ironically makes his point here:

Forgive me, gentle reader, if in this place I cannot forbear apostrophizing in
favour of the author to whose compositions I am indebted for the above
quotation. A writer who has rendered my arguments on this head wholly
unanswerable, by the multitude of beautiful examples he has furnished, of
a style, not only unknown to the venerable authors of antiquity, but, till now,
even to ourselves. Nor does the matter of his performance less deserve my

Enconiums than the words in which it is delivered. With rapture could I dwell upon the closeness of his reasoning, the boldness of his assertions, his consummate wisdom in not making it his *chief* design to digress from his subject, and many other perfections; but that I am unwilling to forestall any remarkable topics that might grace a *separate Panegyric*, which it is not impossible so *remarkable* a work may be thought to serve. [*A Panegyrical Essay*, Oxford, Daniel Prince, 1777, pp. 21–22]

Pratt's *Apology* was more systematically attacked in "Observations on the Address" in *Gentleman's Magazine*, and George Horne's *Letters on Infidelity* (1784), both of which are contained in this collection.

In 1788, an anonymous editor compiled a book titled *Curious Particulars and Genuine Anecdotes* from parts of Pratt's *Apology* and *Supplement* – along with some other items relating to Lord Chesterfield. Apparently during the printing of this work the editor discovered Pratt's identity as the author of the two original pamphlets. Like previous respondents to Pratt, the Editor was struck by the religious inconsistency in his various publications and accordingly inserted the following remark near the close of *Curious Particulars*:

After this pamphlet had been written, the Editor – (to his surprize) found, that the author of the Apology for the life and writings of David Hume, who hath thrown out such unmerited, false accusations against the advocates for christianity is no other than Courtney Melmoth, Esq; author also of a book lately published, entitled "The *Sublime and Beautiful of Scriptures;*" – in which he says, "I shall account myself singularly fortunate, if such endeavours have in any degree, done a service to compositions which are so able to support the trial."

The inconsistency and contradictions which so strongly mark the writings of this declamatory publisher, in the two productions above-mentioned, would seem deeply to *affect* his *sincerity*, or lay him open to be *taxed* with that *hypocrisy*, of which, he would insinuate, the *friends of revealed religion*, stand chargeable.

This remark cannot be deemed uncandid, as it immediately respects a writer, who has opened a *masked battery* against his *own works!* [*Curious Particulars*, London, G. Kearsley, 1788, p. 74]

Curious Particulars was negatively reviewed by three journals. The *Critical Review* questioned the comparison between Chesterfield and Hume; the complete review is as follows:

To compare men so little alike, was an attempt which excited our attention, and led us to suspect that the ingenious author possessed some acuteness to discover what to common eyes was imperceptible. But, though neatly written, it is equally deficient in novelty and in facts; and is a meagre compilation from works already known. [*Critical Review*, October 1788, Vol. 66, p. 344]

Writing for the *Monthly Review* Andrew Becket dismisses the work; the complete review is as follows:

These 'curious particulars, and genuine anecdotes' are chiefly collected from magazines and other periodical prints. The pamphlet may, however, answer the editor's purpose, since it serves for the vehicle of abuse both general and particular. *General*, as it respects the great, the fashionable part of mankind, who, we are here informed, 'are but too commonly the least of all God's little atoms;' and *particular* as it affects Mr. M__ (a very ingenious writer and respectable character), who is represented in the present pages as 'an hungry editor; a man who has sacrificed his patron's reputation at the sordid alter of Plutus.'

A copy of David Hume's last will and testament, and Lord Chesterfield's speech against licensing the stage, are among our editor's *curiosities*. The 'parallel' amounts to nothing: and how could it be otherwise? [*Monthly Review*, December 1788, Vol. 79, p. 558]

The *Analytical Review* is baffled by the attempted comparison between Hume and Chesterfield; the complete review is this:

This is a farrago collected from a variety of publications. It contains some pieces and anecdotes entertaining and valuable, among the best of which is Lord Chesterfield's celebrated speech on the Licensing Act. It also contains some very ill-written and ill-digested fragments. The author of the Parallel between these celebrated personages, who, we understand is the author of 'An Apology for the Life and Writings of David Hume,' is deficient both in *grammar* and sense. Besides this, Lord Chesterfield and Mr. Hume appear to have had no one principle in common, nor can we possibly conceive what motives the author could have for forcing two such characters, so totally unconnected, into comparison. [*Analytical Review*, 1789, Vol. 3, p. 226]

Pratt's *Apology* was not published again after *Curious Particulars*. The following is from the 1777 edition of the *Apology*. It appears complete, except for Section 2 on religious hypocrisy and Section 3 on book dedications, which I have shortened.

TO
WILLIAM STRAHAN, Esq.

SIR,

The late Mr. David Hume hath left to your care, the publication of his posthumous papers. As there is every reason to believe they turn upon similar researches with such as have been already printed; or, as it is more likely, they may carry his philosophy still nearer to that point, which he might not think it discreet to push too vigorously in his life-time, the critical and Christian clamour, no doubt, will be raised afresh against him. It is well known, Sir, that you were considered by Mr. Hume, in a much higher light than that of a mere publisher. There was, apparently, a mixture of trust and tenderness, as well as a good opinion of you, *officially*, blended with the idea of his connection. His memory, therefore, and the honours or disgraces which shall hereafter attend it, must, in a particular manner, interest and affect you. As he was your "most *excellent friend*," his friendship, and the virtues which produced it, are, I trust, "never to be forgotten."[1]

Dr. Adam Smith hath signed his name to a letter, at the close of which, he thus concisely sums up the character of Mr. Hume.

"I have always considered him, both in his life-time and since his death, as approaching as nearly to the idea of a perfectly wise and virtuous man, as perhaps the nature of human frailty will permit."

It has been long imagined, that, persons who were tinctured in any degree with that philosophy, which Mr. Hume was supposed to favour, could not possibly have any title to such a character, as is here drawn by Dr. Smith. That gentleman, however, hath, with a commendable fortitude, asserted, the virtues of his deceased friend. – The object of the following pages, is a confirmation of that assertion, as well as a philosophical plea for the justice on which it is founded.

Three other views, however, are connected with the design of this Apology. Some personal knowledge of Mr. Hume; some expectation of the popular censure, which, will soon be revived against him, if not against his affectionate Dr. Smith, and a wish I have long entertained to have a fit opportunity of introducing such strictures on the most atrocious species of dissimulation as will be found, in the course of the work, are all arguments which have had a share in making it public.

My thoughts have, indeed, been thrown upon *paper* in haste; yet they are, by no means, hasty thoughts; but, have resulted from contemplating the death

---

[1] [Quotations in this paragraph are from Adam Smith's "Letter ... to William Strahan," included in this collection.]

of Mr. Hume, some months before it actually happened. – In short, Sir, it is conceived, these remarks, upon the Life, Death, Consistency, and Philosophy, of David Hume, may, very properly, precede any new edition of his works, – may, likewise, do some service to the writer, and some to the man; place truth and the affectation of it, like the sun and its shadow, in the water, side by side, in order to shew the splendour of one, and the mockery of the other.

As to yourself, Sir, it would be an insult upon your feelings, not to suppose every thing of this nature is acceptable.

I am,
Your most obedient Servant,
THE AUTHOR.

PRELIMINARY
ADDRESS.

Reader, be not startled, at the title of this performance. It means no ill either to you or your religion, or whatever cast that religion may be. The Apology here offered to your inspection, that truth, or Christianity itself would not, of their own accord, admit. I beseech you to peruse these detached thoughts from the beginning to the end; and indulge the impulses of the pauser, reason, before you determine upon any of the subjects here treated, with that liberality which becomes the independent spirit of scientific enquiry, in a free state. An Apology, for the philosophy of the metaphysical Mr. Hume, appears to denote in this suspicious age, to be either abstruse, or difficult, or else dangerous, and deistical. From this work, fear neither of these. It is written without profaneness or irreverence. It promotes all morality flowing from all faiths, and it corrects all hypocrisy, wherever it is detected. The prostitution of Christianity, or, in other words, the Christian religion made use of as a cloak to cover the most irreligious purposes, is more fatal to the Supreme Governor of the world, and to his subordinate creatures, than a much greater latitude of principle than was indulged by Mr. Hume. Avowed Atheism itself, is not half so bad, as concealed deception, especially when it takes refuge under the plausible and unsuspected robe of Christian professors. An extraordinary something, betwixt superstition, and Popery pleads in favour of this worst species of enormity; for which reason, it is less chastised than any other. Common minds, which are terribly trammeled by any shallow signals of authority, are afraid of yielding to the suggestions of their own understanding, and so the evil is permitted, through mere vulgar cowardice, to arise till the effects of the mischief become almost irreparable. Hence it is, also, that the truth of a whole library, were it closely analyzed, and then consolidated to the exclusion of every thing adventitious, and imaginary, – the whole amount of matter of fact, with respect to things important, would be reduced to a few scanty volumes; or, at most, supply the shelves of a small book-case.

Having a due veneration for the rights of the press, I have here, I hope, not unadvisedly, ventured to investigate subjects, or rather, to start hints, which a pusilanimity, very prejudicial to candid enquiry, hath commonly passed over. I have started matters, which it is to be wished, were more philosophically pursued by some able hand, and I am not without hope that what is here rudely sketched, will be formed into a correcter system by a masterly writer.

In the mean time, what is offered in the subsequent pages, however it may offend the zealots, will not be ill received by those who are liberal and consistent.

AN
APOLOGY, &c.

SECTION I.
OF HUME'S PHILOSOPHICAL CONSISTENCY.

David Hume is dead! Never were the pillars of Orthodoxy so desperately shaken, as they are now, by that event. It was attended by every thing that contradicts the general prophecy concerning it. He hath proved himself, in opposition to a contrary opinion, one of those rare characters, which so seldom adorn either this, or any other country; to wit, an *uniform Philosopher*. He is one of the few, who died in the practice of precepts, which he laid down in the earliest periods of a speculative life. The last scene is lately painted by himself, and every touch of it corresponds, corroborates, and confirms those which precede it. He took up the pen, to prove his consistency, at a crisis, commonly esteemed by men, the most alarming and pathetic. Air, physic, exercise, and the alleviating solicitudes of friendship, were all tried, and were all ineffectual: even adulation, which is so seldom unwelcome, either to the sick, or healthy, was not able to seduce our philosopher into the hope of an existence protracted beyond the limits of a few months. – "I happen to come into his room," said one of his most respectable friends, "when he was reading a letter, sent him by Colonel Edmonstone, who had written an eternal adieu to him, and which, Mr. Hume immediately shewed to me: I told him, that, though I was sensible how very much he was weakened, and that appearances, in many respects, were very bad, yet his chearfulness was still so great, the spirit of life seemed still to be so very strong in him, that, I could not help entertaining some faint hopes. He answered, "Your hopes are groundless. An habitual diarrhœa of more than a year's standing, would be a very bad disease at any age; at *my* age, it is a mortal one. When I lie down in the evening, I feel myself weaker, than when I rose in the morning; and when I rise in the morning, weaker than when I lay down in the evening. I am sensible, besides, that some of my vital parts are affected, so that I *must* soon die."

I have admitted this extract, because it marks, in the most vivid colours, the invariable, practical, consistency of Hume to his own theory. Those, to whom that theory is obnoxious, wished, and expected a very different deportment of its author in his last moments; the more especially, if those moments were past (which was the case) under the declinings of a disorder that should waste the body, without imparing the mind. The persons, who maintained opposite, and what is esteemed, correcter tenets, imagined, that all the subtlety of a scepticism, avowed in the vigour of gay and glowing youth; and of arguments to support them, written when the pulse was full, among the ardours of science, and for the sake of singularity, would, upon the bed of a lingering distemper, all fly off, as the prospect of dissolution became apparent, and leave their author in the agonies of terror-struck repentance, or in the horrors of overwhelming despair. I, myself, know one person, in particular, and he still living, and not unknown in the Christian world, who prognosticated the most tragical exit to David Hume. – "Take my word for it, sir," said he, one day to me, "the triumph of that man, (meaning Hume) is short-lived. He breaks apace: from an almost athletic corpulency, he is, within a few months, shrunk into the very shadow of himself. I hear he still affects his accustomed gaiety, and persists in his unchristian principles: but this conduct will wear away in proportion as he gets worse and worse. As Dean Swift stands upon record the victim of disappointment, pique, pride, ill-nature, so, I foresee, will David Hume be a mournful example of that vain, and vicious philosophy, which he hath long had the audacity to espouse. Methinks, I already see him, sir, in the extremity; tortured at once, by the lashes of his conscience and labouring to continue life, that he may publicly give the lie to his former horrible documents. Poor wretch – I pity him, I could almost wish his prayer granted, that he might do some justice to posterity; and, in that justice, propitiate the wrath, the omnipotent wrath, which must necessarily be kindled against him. Instead of which, – shocking reverse, – observe him struggling at the same time with death, and with a thorough consciousness of having misguided mankind; of having endeavoured to undermine the foundation of religion – and of meriting detestation."

In all the phrenzy of a fiery zeal, bordering, I fear, somewhat upon bigotry, did a celebrated *Christian* author, as near as I can recollect, in these words, foretell the miseries of David Hume; and in the same furor of language, hath he, doubtless, been treated, by many others. On the perusal of that pamphlet, which states the accounts of his last illness, and all the concomitant circumstances that attended it, I should like much, as a matter of curiosity only, to know the unaffected state of *their* feelings: their prophecy is, at all events, unfulfilled: and, what is worse, all the *minute* articles (which are generally the most marking) rather add to, than deduct from, the great aggregate of their consternation.

In justice to the memory of an extraordinary man, who hath, it is presumed, many secret and many public enemies, at least in a literary and scientific sense, it is worth while to take a view of some of those points, which prove him, beyond the possibility of a dispute, to be at least a *sincere believer in his own sentiments*. Many, indeed, will think, that this, however perspicuously proved, will be doing him no real honour; since, in proportion to the clearness of the evidence upon this matter, it will only shew his impiety and obstinate infidelity the plainer; thereby, in the end, incurring upon him a more general disgrace. I am of a different opinion. The terms Infidelity, Impiety, and Atheism, should not be lavishly trusted from the lip. We should not presume

"To deal damnation through the land
  On each, we deem our foe:"

But, it is less the design of these papers to *defend* Hume's principles, than to shew, upon the best authority, that he was earnest in what he wrote, and that, through every part of his life, even to the very moment of his death, he made precept and practice go, amicably, hand in hand together. First, however, be it observed, that, whatever might be the force of his *faith*, no one, it is conjectured, will charge him with having neglected *good works*. I do not pretend to say how far those *are*, or are *not* sufficient. Such enquiries are digressive from my subject. At the same time, I could wish (and sure it is but a reasonable request) that, for these, he may have a proper *degree of credit*.

Perhaps, it is one of the very worst circumstances against the cause of Christianity, that, very few of its professors were ever, either so moral, so humane, or could so philosophically govern their *passions*, as the sceptical David Hume. The simple dictates of this gentleman's own heart, unassisted by those examples, and sacred sentiments, which are supposed to inspire universal "love and good will amongst men," inspired him to practise all the duties, decencies, and charities. Thus Hume the Unbeliever, as he hath been called, led a life that might even, when scrutinized by the eye of malevolence itself, call a blush into the cheeks of those, who would fain be thought, in the imaginations of men, to be *steadfast and immoveable in the faith*. It is not a little shocking to thinking people, to perceive that the spirit of hypocrisy so generally gone forth; and it is still worse, to see *that* hypocrisy (according to the assurance of a late lord) so generally successful and carry all before it.

It demands, alas! no search into the records of antiquity, to prove that, the *Christian* world prosecutes this duplicity with a vigour, to which the sceptic Hume never had the infamy to stoop. I do not say this in an argument to destroy, or to invalidate the faith of Christians; but I *will* take upon me to say, it is a dreadful symptom of an unsoundness in its professors, and friends, when they so commonly sulk behind the holy shield of their religion, as a *hiding place* from the eyes of the world, whenever they have a mind to do any thing in direct opposition to its most obvious and elementary principles. Either the religion is somewhere defective in itself, (which I, by no means, think so likely as the alternative) or else the votaries themselves have a much worse opinion of its *real* origin than sceptics; because, were not one of these, or perhaps, a mixture of them both, the *fact* surely they could not, so much oftener than those sceptics, act in general defiance of its maxims. I, however, principally confine myself to that miserable hypocrisy, which hath so very frequently been *discovered* amongst the votaries of this amiable religion; and, in particular, such of them as have gained the greatest popularity, by an ostentatious display of it. I beg these sentiments may not be thought to have any tendency to hurt the Christian religion, of whose excellence I am not now to treat; yet, till some of its professors can, by the conjunction of *faith and good works*, back'd by the prospect of *futurity*, surpass, or at least equal, the virtues of a man who was tender, friendly, generous, and social; let these vain glorious boasters have the modesty to hold their tongues, and speak nothing; since nothing can be spoken, but to their disgrace. – It is to the honour of David Hume, then, that he was no *hypocrite* in philosophy; and that, unlike the many *detected* hypocrites in *Christianity*, he acted as he wrote, and wrote no more than, at all times, he actually felt.

This may be evidenced more accurately, when we run our eye over that posthumous paper, which he hath, very characteristically, called, *A Funeral Oration.*[2] Prior to this, I would just turn an old subject on a new side: I would make a comment or two, on that shameful species of delusion, which, arrayed in the fair and unsuspicious robes of orthodoxy, makes the most fatal depredations upon society; and, indeed, does infinitely more mischief than the most daring and declared infidelity.

SECTION II.

OF RELIGIOUS HYPOCRISY.

One of the distinguishing features, by which we mark the present age, is religious hypocrisy, or that abominable *prudery* in Sentiment, which, from the lip outwards, deceives the shallow multitude, who mistake it for the conscientious scruples of moral sanctity. A philosopher, who looks into the heart, and can trace many of its manœuvres to their source; whose acquaintances with life, and whose skill in detecting the chicane of men, sees, clearly, at a single glance, that the whole apparatus of external appearance, is only a political veil thrown over the real feelings and propensities of nature: this fallacy, to his penetrating eye, is sufficiently obvious; he detects the cheat in a moment, and, did not know how easily the major part of mankind were disposed to favour *that* which suits

---

[2]   [i.e., "My Own Life," which Hume closes by saying, "I cannot say there is no vanity in making this funeral oration of myself, but I hope it is not a misplaced one; and this is a matter of fact which is easily cleared and ascertained."]

equally their own purposes of imposing upon each other (by which means the Hypocrisy becomes general), he would wonder how those, who are supposed to stand at the top of rarefied and rationalized matter, could be so constantly the bobbles of imagination. Bubbles, however, they notoriously are, in defiance of the very feelings which contradict their puritanical pretensions. This duplicity hath *ever* existed in life, and hath now crept into *letters*. There is a set of writers, who affect a chastity of sentiment, and a kind of primitive preciseness in style, with a view of passing upon the superficial part of the public (which is infinitely the larger part) as orthodox moralists, and the most zealous promoters of Christian rectitude. Copious is the catalogue of authors, whose performances are read and relished, upon this very principle. ...

SECTION III.

ON THE NATURAL DIGNITY OF THE LITERARY CHARACTER, AND THE REASONS WHICH HAVE BROUGHT IT INTO CONTEMPT.

Let us now advert to *another* species of Hypocrisy, from which our Philosopher was totally exempt; to which, indeed, his temper was perfectly superior. Among the instances of generous independency in David Hume, must not be forgotten that manliness, which prevented him from wading through the prostituted puddle of fawning DEDICATION. To this magnanimity – to this firmness it was owning, that, his feelings were never disgraced, nor his spirit at any time weighed down by the burden of favours, ignominiously begged, and ungraciously bestowed. Alexander, when he had won his world, had less reason to sing forth the Io Pean of triumph, than had our author to gratulate himself on the satisfaction of "never having preferred a request to one great man, or ever of having made advances to any of them." To confess the truth, he wrote, generally, upon subjects of which the modern nobility are, for the most part, so contemptibly ignorant, that to have inscribed performances so scientific to such patrons, would involve the Philosopher in a similar error of judgment. Indeed, nothing is more offensive to men of true taste, and right feeling, than the *condescension* of persons of genius, to persons of rank, merely as such. This it is, more than any thing else, that hath helped to degrade the literary character; which, as it implies a superior vigour of intellect, and a more enlarged capacity, possesses, naturally, an unrivalled dignity. ...

Perhaps, this doctrine of dedications, may be little relished by those who are daily pampered into conceit by daily panegyric, but it is a justice which every man of letters owes to a character, founded on qualities, which ought to be a better passport to honorary distinctions, than any that can be conferred by royal grant, or by the pride of ancestry.

On such qualities was founded the reputation of David Hume, so that upon *this* occasion, at least, his example may be held up to persons engaged in literary pursuits, as a proper standard.

SECTION IV.

OF HUME'S PRINCIPLES, AND HIS MOTIVE FOR MAKING THEM PUBLIC, WITH
SOME REMARKS ON HIS CONDUCT IN HIS LAST MOMENTS. ˙

But to go on with the moral character of David Hume. Whoever places the
writings of this philosopher beside those of many Christian authors who have
been much celebrated for them, will be able to judge without prejudice. It is
impossible for the sentiments of the elegant Tillotson, or the orthodox Addison,
to be more the champions of every part of conduct, which tends to the welfare
of the social world, than those sentiments which are to be collected from
Hume – Nay, the most rational spirit of morality, the most likely of all others
in the world, to affect this, breathes ardently through all his philosophy:
elegance of taste, chastity of sentiment, delicacy of passion, decency of manners,
love of truth, command of passion, cultivation of friendship, and the good
order, and political prosperity of the state, are every where recommended. Very
few of our eminent writers on the opposite side of the question can say as much.
But, with respect to Mr. Hume, every effort of his pen stands in testimony of
it.

These observations cannot, nevertheless, be called sceptical. I do not, nor
shall I presume to say, how far Hume's philosophy was right or erroneous in
its *principle*. Sufficient for my purpose, if I can convince any reader (that
might hesitate before) of his *consistency with himself*: a point, which, is of the
utmost consequence to the cause of *every* system, be its purport, and its objects
what they may.

The science pursued with such vigorous curiosity by Hume was, to use his
own expressions, "to know the different operations of the mind, to separate
them from each other, to class them under their proper heads, and to correct
all that seeming disorder, in which they lie involved, when made the object of
reflection and enquiry!"

It hath, generally, been thought that, our author carried this mental
geography, as he calls it, too far into the realms of scepticism, and into the
abstruse, bewildering deserts of unchearful metaphysics. Yet, however ardent
he was in speculations of this abstract and difficult nature, no one will deny,
that he drew the form of virtue, upon all occasions, as the most lovely and
estimable of all objects. He firmly believed, that, in some very important
respects, truth was overwhelmed in error and superstition; he was, therefore,
sufficiently enterprizing to try, if, by the aids of application, care, art, and
discriminating accuracy, he could not "unite the boundaries of the different
species of philosophy, by reconciling profound enquiry with clearness, and truth
with novelty."

This, it is confessed, was the labour of a long, healthy, and contemplative life:
he persisted in the pursuit, in defiance of all opposing fatigues, clamours,
oppositions, neglects, oppressions. It could not be the love of an established

literary fame, that urged him to the prosecution of such researches, because he knew there was, in *his* species of philosophy, an abstractedness, as well as a supposed spirit of fallacy, which, could not, in the nature of things, and certain prevailing modes, become for many ages, either a popular, or a pleasing science. It was, to all intents and purposes, "*caviare* to the multitude." Nay, he was well persuaded in all this, not only by the odium which was cast upon his Treatise on Human Nature, which "fell dead born from the press," but also from the following passage, which shews how little hope he had of making the abstruse philosophy so generally relished as that which is more gay, elegant, and superficial. "Nothing can be more useful," says he, "than compositions of the easy style and manner, which draw not too much from life, require no deep application, to be comprehended: and send back the student among mankind, full of noble sentiments and wise precepts, applicable to every exigence of human life. By means of such compositions, virtue becomes amiable, science agreeable, company instructive, and refinement entertaining."

A Philosopher of Hume's close, and difficult reasoning, who was hardy enough to scrutinize subjects, imagined to puzzle more, as they are more investigated – a man, who had either patience or fortitude enough to cultivate metaphysical science, with a determined view of overturning, and eradicating, root and branch, prejudices which appeared *to him* at least, to merit an analysis which should prove their futility. – Such a man, could not expect the same eclat with the generality of mankind, as those who only played prettily on the surface of "a more easy and obvious philosophy." Hume contented himself with less general gratifications. His own remarks very fully convince us what he felt, what he expected, and what he enjoyed on this subject.

Speaking of the common dictate to which men have for speculations that require *thinking*, to comprehend them, he hath these sentiments in the first section of his Enquiry concerning Human Understanding.

"But may we not hope, that philosophy, if cultivated with care, and encouraged by the attention of the public, may carry its researches still farther, and discover, at least in some degree, the secret springs and principles, by which the human mind is actuated in its operations? Astronomers had long contented themselves with proving, from the phænomena, the true motions, order, and magnitude of the heavenly bodies: till a philosopher, at last, arose, who seems, from the happiest reasoning, to have also determined the laws and forces, by which the revolutions of the planets are governed and directed. The like has been performed with regard to other parts of nature, and there is no reason to despair of equal success in our enquiries concerning the mental powers and œconomy, if prosecuted with equal capacity and caution. It is probable, that one operation and principle of the mind depends on another; which, again, may be resolved into one more general and universal: and how far these researches may possibly be carried, it will be difficult for us, before, or even after, a careful trial, exactly to determine. This is certain, that attempts of this kind are every day made even by those who philosophize the most negligently: and nothing can be more requisite than to enter upon the enterprize with thorough care and attention; that, if it lie within the compass of human understanding, it may at last be happily achieved; if not, it may, however, be rejected with some confidence and security. This last conclusion, surely, is not desirable; nor ought it to be embraced too rashly. For how much must we diminish from the beauty and value of this species of philosophy, upon such a supposition? Moralists have hitherto been accustomed, when they considered the vast multitude and diversity of actions that excite our approbation or dislike, to search for some common principle, on which this variety of sentiments might depend. and though they have sometimes carried the matter too far, by their passion for some one general principle, it must, however, be confessed, that they are excusable in expecting to find some general principles, into which all the vices and virtues were justly to be resolved. The like has been the endeavour of critics, logicians, and even politicians: nor have their attempts been wholly unsuccessful; though perhaps longer time, greater accuracy, and more ardent application, may bring these sciences still nearer their perfection. To throw up at once all pretensions of this kind may justly be deemed more rash, precipitate, and dogmatical, than even the boldest and most affirmative philosophy, which has ever attempted to impose its crude dictates and principles on mankind.

"What though these reasonings concerning human nature seem abstract, and of difficult comprehension? this affords no presumption of their falsehood. On the contrary, it seems impossible, that what has hitherto escaped so many wise and profound philosophers can be very obvious and easy. And whatever pains these researches may cost us, we may think ourselves sufficiently rewarded, not only in point of profit but of pleasure, if, by that means, we can make any addition to our stock of knowledge, in subjects of such unspeakable importance."

But as we read Mr. Hume's life, written by his own hand, we shall have fresh opportunities to clear up any doubts that may remain of his sincerity. It seems pretty evident, that the little sketch, called MY OWN LIFE, was thought necessary, by Mr. Hume, to be before hand with his philosophic antagonists, whom, he foresaw, would raise new outcries against him, upon the ideas they might indulge concerning those closing sensations which would attack him, within sight of the grave. To prevent little triumphs of this nature, I say, it is highly probable he chose the fairer method of being his *own* historian; and never was there a biographical tract drawn up by any man in the highest health, with more coolness, more conciseness, more impartiality.

He sat down to this extraordinary employment, and took up the pen, exactly at the time that hundreds – I might, I believe, extend the number, to thousands, – were thinking he would begin the bitter groans of recantation. I certainly shall not take upon me to say how far this employment was proper, but the annals of the world cannot possibly produce any instance, whereby philosophy became so much *of a piece*. Whatever were the singularities of that philosophy, I once more insist upon it, it was a strong evidence that he disdained any of the popular hypocrisy now in vogue. He could not counterfeit the alterations which he did not feel risen in his mind; he was calm enough to give a candid account of his literary life, when he *knew* himself to be *incurable*.

After he had written it, he observes the same tranquil composure, in regard to the nearer approaches of death: Nay, such was his steadiness to the principles by which he was directed, that, in a codicil to his will, he desired the narrative of his life might be prefixed to the next edition of his works.

Having finished the account of his life, he had no farther opportunity to employ the pen, except from time to time, to send notes of information to the tender enquiries of his friends; among the most beloved and distinguished of these, appears to have been Mr. Adam Smith, to whom, two or three days before the stroke which carried him out of the world, he sent the following letter.

"MY DEAREST FRIEND.

I am obliged to make use of my Nephew's hand in writing to you; as I do not rise to day. * * * *

I go very fast to decline, and last night had a small fever, which I hoped, might put a quicker period to this tedious illness, but unluckily it has, in a great measure, gone off. I cannot submit to your coming over here on my account, as it is possible for me to see you so small a part of the day; but Doctor Black can better inform you concerning the degree of strength, which may, from time to time, remain with me. Adieu, &c."

This letter, may be brought, by every man who wishes well to Hume's Philosophy, as another instance of that invariable congruity, with which he maintained his character. *Heroism*, on these occasions approaches, for the most part, so near to *enthusiasm*, and *that* is so closely allied to absolute *frenzy*, that I shall not hazard such an appellation. I shall not say Hume died like a *hero*; I will content myself with saying, that he died like a *Philosopher*; perhaps, the word *Philosophy*,[3] hath no very precise idea, generally affixed to it; because,

---

[3]   The best and exactest definition of the *true*, as distinguishable from the *adulterate* on the one hand, and the *superficial*, Philosopher on the other, is defined by our Author, and discovers, in a very precise and affirmative manner, not only the thing itself, but his *own indefatigable character*.

"The other species of philosophers consider man in the light of a reasonable rather than an active being, and endeavour to form his understanding more than cultivate his manners. They regard human nature as a subject of speculation; and with a narrow scrutiny examine it, in order to find those principles, which regulate our understanding, excite our sentiments, and make us approve or blame any particular object, action, or behaviour. They think it a reproach to all literature, that philosophy should not yet have fixed, beyond controversy, the foundation of morals, reasoning,

it has been much confounded with the pragmatical pretensions of the ignorant, the affected, and the superficial. There is a true, and a false philosopher. Mr. Hume is to be classed amongst the noblest of the *former* kind. He founded his system upon thought, science, argument, and reasonings, which, after many assiduous years, remained, in his mind, the same. Neither could the dissipation of youth allure him from his favourite studies, nor could the threats of dissolution itself frighten him from making preparations for a *new* edition of those works, which were to destroy, what he considered, as the prevailing systems of *superstition.*

In support of these observations, we may very properly call in the letter of his[4] physician, written the day after the decease of his patient.

Edinburgh, Monday, 26th August, 1776.
   "DEAR SIR,
   Yesterday about four o'clock afternoon, Mr. Hume expired. The near approach of his death became evident in the night between Thursday and Friday, when his disease became excessive, and soon weakened him so much, that he could no longer rise out of his bed. He continued to the last perfectly sensible, and free from much pain or feelings of distress. He never dropped the smallest expression of impatience; but when he had occasion to speak to the people about him, always did it with affection and tenderness. I thought it improper to write to bring you over, especially as I heard that he had dictated a letter to you desiring you not to come. when he became very weak, it cost him an effort to speak, and he died in such a happy composure of mind, that nothing could exceed it."

Who would not wish, after reading this account, that *their* end, may be like *his?*

and criticism; and should for ever talk of truth and falsehood, vice and virtue, beauty and deformity, without being able to determine the source of these distinctions. While they attempt this arduous task, they are deterred by no difficulties; but proceeding from particular instances to general principles, they still push on their inquiries to principles more general, and rest not satisfied till they arrive at those *original* principles, by which, in every science, all human curiosity must be bounded. Though their speculations seem abstract, and even unintelligible to common readers, they aim at the approbation of the learned and the wise; and think themselves sufficiently compensated for the labours of their whole lives, if they can discover some hidden truths, which may contribute to the instruction of posterity."

[4]   Dr. Black, of Edinburgh, universally known, beloved, and admired, as a friend, a physician, his chymical skill, and as a man.

SECTION V.
PARALLEL BETWIXT HUME AND LORD CHESTERFIELD, BOTH WITH RESPECT TO ABILITIES, AND PRINCIPLES.

We have now surveyed our object in the most trying moments – We have seen him superior to all ordinary terrors, and equal to all occasions. It is taken for granted, therefore, that as a philosopher, both in precept and practice, it will be allowed he was compleat, exact, unchangeable – that, whether wrong or right, he acted, immediately, from his own bosom conviction; a conviction grounded upon intense and abstract attention, and not taken up suddenly without respect either to cause or to consequence. Thus far, then, the point is cleared before me; but I cannot persuade myself to resign Mr. Hume till I have done ampler justice to his memory, and to that social, and *honest* conduct which so much endears it.

I would draw a slight parallel betwixt this gentlemen, and another celebrated writer, who descended into the tomb a little before him. I would persuade the reader to compare with me the system of David Hume, and that of the late Earl of Chesterfield. Not with a view of proposing the former to his imitation – for that point should always be settled by a man's own mind, after a great deal of premeditation upon the matter – but, as it may serve to shew, what hath, indeed, been a principal endeavour in these pages, that it is possible even for sceptics, to be more worthy members of society, more reverend to a first cause, whatever it may be, and more essentially the friend[5] of mankind, than the most illustrious

---

[5] Thus it is more and more obvious, that, the desire of literary fame, had not the greatest share in prevailing with Mr. Hume to persist in a philosophy little understood, little liked, and much disrelished by the most powerful bodies in the world, to wit, the superstitious and hypocritical.

He was, therefore, not only a *consistent*, but an *honest* writer. After he had tried the experiment with his unfortunate Treatise and failed: after he had, in *vain*, cast anew the Enquiry concerning Human Nature: after he had published his Moral and Political Essays, with as little success: after the appearance of his Natural History of Religion had met with a very cool reception; after all these mortifications, as he himself terms them, after all these variety of "winds and seasons," to which his writings had been exposed, with only those little gales of fugitive good fortune, to console him; the railing of Doctor Warburton, and illiberality of Bishop Hurd; such "was the force of his natural temper," such his "unsurmountable aversion to every thing but the pursuits of philosophy" that, we find, by his dying confession," these disappointments made little or no impression on him." "I was ever more disposed," says he, "to see the favourable than unfavourable side of things; a turn of mind, which it is more happy to possess, than to be born to an estate of ten thousand a year."

From these several circumstances, nothing can be plainer, than that, he was a serious enquirer into the extent of the human understanding: that he submitted patiently to every impediment that arose in the progress of so arduous and unpopular a contemplation: that he was neither attracted by fame, nor deterred by censure. If he hath too fully indulged his passion, he did not err from any desire to *deceive*, because

persons who have never ventured so far into the recesses of enquiry. Lord Chesterfield was a character more distinguished for the brilliancy of his wit, than the solider powers of his understanding. – In points of philosophy, he was exceedingly superficial, in politics he did not want sagacity or experience. Assisted, however, very much, by the splendours of his title – for a little spark will make the large lustre in a Lord – he sustained his character with singular eclat, and passed in the world (which is very easily dazzled) as a compound of elegance, humour, *morality*, gaiety, and patronage. – These qualities, in a certain degree, we allow him to have possessed, except one: it certainly is not now necessary to observe that it is the word *morality* which must be scratched out of this list. For many years, however, Lord Chesterfield's *morals* were unsuspected; at length, too superficial to be consistent, or, perhaps, weary of deceiving the world into notions of his plain-dealing, he condescended, in the eve of life, to shew mankind what a bubble he had made of it; how long, and how successfully he had sported upon its weaknesses – with how much ease he had played the elegant trifler, and by what modes and manœuvres, he had, with a facility which required no effort but a smooth face, and pliable features, led, in victorious chains, a thousand fools to the altars either of ridicule, or debauchery, or destruction.

Such were the principles; such is the system of this *distinguished hypocrite*, by the adoption of whose precepts, it is utterly impossible either for youth or age, wit or wisdom, to escape every thing that is execrable, contemptible, and delusive. The atheistical Hume, as some have called him, was, in comparison

he certainly hoped to extricate truth from obscurity, and absurdity. If he was too adventrous he had the singular merit of not expecting either reputation or fortune for his mistakes. In one sentence, to concenter the whole force of his Apology, by clearing him of the most universal crime of all ages – *He was no Hypocrite.*

Violent verbal asseverations, and religious tenacity of opinion are exceedingly suspicious to the judicious, though they captivate and enthral the vulgar and simple. I must once more advert to a horrid contradiction of the zealots – the little correspondence, and, indeed, generally speaking, the constant quarrelling there is betwixt their precept, and practice! Well might Hume observe, that, if we examine the lives of these men, we should scarcely think that they reposed the smallest confidence in their pious protestations. What! cannot the delightful belief of an ever-protecting real Presence, – cannot the charming hopes of Omnipotent favour, nor the merits of a Saviour, nor the expectations of a blessed Immortality, infuse into these sluggish religionists, and emulative spirit to exceed the goodness, and common conduct of men, like David Hume, who believed all these fair prospects, to be "a riddle, an ænigma, an inexplicable mystery."

Shall the very sages of our church, the examples and representative of a Redeemer, by covetous, vain, dissolute, voluptuous, fraudulent, abandoned? while those, who professedly, sit loose to the letter of the law, are, by the settled force of mere philosophy, temperate, moderate, sober? What pretensions can men have to credit who belie *themselves?* I still dispute not the propriety of the Christian Religion, but I must be candid enough to confess, I lay no great stress upon the manner of some of its *followers*, – and yet they have modestly enough to be very angry if any one questions their sincerest pretensions.

with Chesterfield, deserving of every epithet that could be formed in language to express virtue. In his life, writing, and at his death, he seems to have abhorred *dissimulation*; and yet, his company "was not unacceptible to the young and careless, as well as to the studious, and literary;" nor had he "any reason to complain of the reception he met from *modest* women, in whose company he was particularly delighted." He did not, nevertheless, profess a fondness for the society of *modest* women, because it was *safer* to have an affair of gallantry with such, than with a prostitute professed; or because the connection was more elevated and consistent with the amours of a gentleman; nor did he mix with the gay, and careless, with any latent design to take an advantage of the chearful hour, in order to make himself master of the secrets of the heart, imparted in its fullness – and consequently master of the person to whom that entrapped heart had the misfortune to belong. By no means. – Whatever objections may lie against the philosophy of Hume; none of these are of this nature; since his most abstract researches were in favor of a behaviour perfectly irreproachable.

Whoever is acquainted with Mr. Hume's writings, will bear witness, that he was a lover of decency, order and decorum. whoever knew the man, can attest, that, the following passages are no wise exaggerated.

> "I *am*," says he, "or rather *was*, (for that is the style I must now use in speaking of myself, which emboldens me the more to speak my sentiments); I was, I say, a man of mild dispositions, of command of temper, of an open, social, and cheerful humour, capable of attachment, but little susceptible of enmity, and of great moderation in all my passions. Even my love of literary fame, my ruling passion, never soured my temper, notwithstanding my frequent disappointments. My company was not unacceptable to the young and careless, as well as to the studious and literary; and as I took a particular pleasure in the company of modest women, I had no reason to be displeased with the reception I met with from them. In a word, though most men any wise eminent, have found reason to complain of calumny, I never was touched, or even attacked by her baleful tooth: and though I wantonly exposed myself to the rage of both civil and religious factions, they seemed to be disarmed in my behalf of their wonted fury. My friends never had occasion to vindicate any one circumstance of my character and conduct: not but that the zealots, we may well suppose, would have been glad to invest and propagate any story to my disadvantage, but they could never find any which they thought would wear the face of probability. I cannot say there is no vanity in making this funeral oration of myself, but I hope it is not a misplaced one; and this is a matter of fact which is easily cleared and ascertained."

To a character so amiable, so complacent, and so little tinctured by that pedantry which always sticks to an *affected* philosopher, *who*, that hath any sense of agreeable qualities, will ever bring near him such a frivolous compound of whim, wickedness, cunning, and congee, as Lord Chesterfield; unless, indeed, he is brought forward by way of contrast. There appears likewise to me, to have been as wide a difference in the size of their abilities, as there was in the honesty of their principles: every page in those Letters, which have laid open his Lordship's hypocrisy, furnishes us with examples of his futility: it would be the drudgery of a day to detect a single light sentence in Hume. The Earl of Chesterfield's utmost stretch of penetration, amounts to little more than shrewdness, partly caught from the suggestions of a mind naturally suspicious, and partly from observations upon the weaknesses, and tender imperfections of men less capable to dissemble. This faculty, is at best, but a principal ingredient in the character of a *cunning* fellow, who, as it were, by imperceptible slight of hand, hath the art of appearing what he is not; and of cheating you, with singular dexterity, even before your face.

But all the fame, or popular etiquette that could possibly arise from such practices, Hume would have discarded with disdain. And, chiefly for two reasons: first, his genius had not a single grain of the petit maitre in it, which, by the way, was a considerable ingredient in Lord Chesterfield's; and, secondly, he had too much dignity in his nature, and too just a sense of the social compact between the individual, and the whole human race, to find any zest in gratifications, which emanated from, neither more, nor less, than flagrant treachery. Hence it appears obvious enough, that the Earl of Chesterfield's heart and head, were both unable to bear any sort of parallel, with the head and heart of David Hume. The one is the Author of a system which seems to have been pillaged from the Dancing-master,[6] the Perfumer, and the Devil: the other pursues a philosophy, which, with all its exceptions, gives countenance neither to the follies of a coxcomb, nor the meanness, and mischief of a hypocrite – a wretch, which, in the course of these pages, hath been marked with singular reprobation; and above all other hypocrites, one that, in a kind of moral masquerade dress, perpetrates every baseness, and passes upon the world as a *mighty good Christian creature.*

SECTION VI.

OF PROPER CAUTIONS PRIOR TO THE ESTABLISHMENT OF OUR RELIGIOUS
CREDENDA.

With regard to the sceptical doubts which might start into the philosophical and reasoning mind of Mr. Hume, it is, I once more repeat, no part of my office, to defend or to censure them. As a variety of men have employed their talents on *one* side of an important subject, he hath taken the liberty, as a philosopher, to offer his opinions, on the *other* side: considered in the light of speculation,

---

[6] [Samuel Johnson stated that Chesterfield's letters "teach the morals of a whore, and the manners of a dancing-master" *The Life of Samuel Johnson* (1791).]

this is certainly fair; for who can circumscribe the efforts of a mind, bent for any length of time, on one favourite point?

The systems of either party, however, ought not to sway any man against the concurrence of his own reason; for, at that rate, one might be a Christian, a Deist, a Mohemetan, or an Atheist, in obedience to the bidding of another: by which means our religion would have more colours than the camelion, and more alterations than Proteus. A sensible man, will never have servility enough for this. If he is yet unestablished in his more serious tenets, he will se what can be said both *for* and *against*: of opposite principles, it is his business to fix upon those which appear the most congruous, and probable. Reason and his feelings may generally be trusted upon the occasion.[7] But let him not be hasty, nor yet vibrate equipois'd too long, between fluctuating sentiments. *Fixing*, let him *fix*; unless, afterwards, upon, very cautious, and clear grounds, he hath weighty arguments to warrant an alteration. If his intellect is *sound* enough for science,

[7] Reason, indeed, I know not why, hath long been *unreasonably* denied a proper exercise of her power, in religious matters; while Faith is honoured with the priviledge of insisting upon implicit obedience: yet the former, is called the noblest faculty of human nature, and the latter, should, certainly, only be allowed to follow in the train. The common argument, is little more than this, – You must believe, because you must believe. It is in vain to pretend any regard to probabilities; or to urge, against things sacred, the convictions of close reasoning – Reason is out of the question. – Is it not written in *the Book?* The question, to be sure, must not be answered, but in one way. You *must* have Faith. – Now, it appears to me, that to call Reason our sovereign distinction, and yet reject its influence in points of eternal moment, while we affect to observe its dictates in matters indifferent, is just as rational as if we were to hold sacred and obligatory, those edicts of parliament which regulate our more public spectacles, – such as plays and puppet-shews; while we snap our fingers at the state, and the personage who rules it, whenever a mandate is issued for the good order, and welfare of what is most important to the policy, power, or prosperity of nations. This method of *forcing* any particular faith upon a man, though it is taking an enemy by surprise, is, yet, ridiculous enough in its nature, to admit an illustration, in the following passages from Henry Fielding's Romance of Joseph Andrews.

"Mr. Barnabas was again sent for, and with much difficulty prevailed on to make another visit. As soon as he entered the room, he told Joseph, 'he was come to pray by him, and to prepare him for another world: In the first place therefore, he hoped he had repented of all his sins?' Joseph answered, 'he hoped he had: but there was no one thing which he knew not whether he should call a sin; if it was, he feared he should die in the commission of it, and that was the regret of parting with a young woman, whom he loved as tenderly as he did his heart-strings?' Barnabas bad him be assured, that 'any repining at the Divine Will, was one of the greatest sins he could commit; that he ought to forget all carnal affections, and think of better things.' Joseph said, 'that neither in this world, nor the next, he could forget his Fanny, and that the thought, however grievous, of parting from her for ever, was not half so tormenting, as the fear of what she would suffer when she knew his misfortune.' Barnabas said, 'that such fears argued a diffidence and despondence very criminal; that he must divest himself of all human passion, and fix his heart above.' Joseph answered, 'that was what he desired to do, and should be obliged to him, if he would enable him to accomplish it.' Barnabas replied, 'that must be done by Grace.' Joseph besought him to discover

– shallowness is perilous in philosophy, as well as learning, – he can receive no injury from having heard both the pro and con. The case of a Judge upon a cause, brings the matter home to the "business and bosom" more familiarly. A magistrate is not qualified to decide of any point before him, till witnesses on *both* sides are examined: to these, very often, for conscience sake, are added cross-examinations, to see if the story told any other way, hath the same consistence and congruity. The evidence once satisfactory to the senses of the judge, and all doubt removed by several facts, each agreeing with the other, and all resolving themselves into an harmonious whole, he proceeds, without farther debate or delay, to the final sentence, which, whether it dispenses life or death, is given with the same firmness, energy, and resolution.

Similar to this, should be the procedure of any person unestablished in his religious concerns. It is too important an article to take up on mere trust. A thinking man will not be a Deist, or a Christian, only because his father before him, and all the other branches of his family were one of those. He will look with an eye of penetration into the circumstances: he will see why, wherefore, and upon what considerations, this adopts Christianity, that Deism. He will compare one system to another; examine their distinct parts, and correspondencies. – Trace out the points where they separate, where they blend: in what they are utterly different, and wherein they are obviously, or apparently analogous.

When this sober talk is diligently done, let reason assert her dignity, and having scrutinized liberally, let her liberally determine. To which ever side she

how he might attain it.' Barnabas answered, 'by Prayer and Faith.' He then questioned him concerning his forgiveness of the Thieves. Joseph answered, 'he feared, that was more than he could do: for nothing would give him more pleasure than to hear they were taken.' 'That,' cries Barnabas, 'is for the sake of justice.' 'Yes,' said Joseph, 'but if I was to meet them again, I am afraid I should attack them, and kill them too, if I could.' 'Doubtless,' answered Barnabas, 'it is lawful to kill a thief: but can you say, you forgive them as a Christian ought?' Joseph desired to know what that forgiveness was. 'That is,' answered Barnabas, 'to forgive them as – as – it is to five them as – in short, it is to forgive them as a Christian.' Joseph replied, 'he forgave them as much as he could.' 'Well, well,' said Barnabas, 'that will do.' 'He then demanded of him, if he remembered any more sins unrepented of; and if he did, he desired him to make haste and repent of them as fast as he could: that they might repeat over a few prayers together.' Joseph answered, 'he could not recollect any great crimes he had been guilty of, and that those he had committed, he was sincerely sorry for.' Barnabas said that was enough, and then proceeded to prayer with all the expedition he was master of: some company then waiting for him below in the parlour, where the ingredients for punch were all in readiness; but no one would squeeze the oranges till he came."

I am afraid the arguments of Mr. Barnabas are, for the most part, full as cogent as those which impose a system upon us, without allowing us to consult the understanding. – Are they *afraid* we should refer to so sober an authority as Reason? Is it for their *interest* to make us the mere tools of credulity? Is it political to beat us, *vi, et armis*, into adoption of their favourite tenets? such an assault upon vulgar, timid minds, may be very alarming; but, I confess, I could never be inclined, either to Deism, Mohamatism, or Christianity by *compulsion*. The Philosopher, will, so far at least, be a free agent, and, like poor Joseph, believe *as well*, and *as much as he can*.

inclines, let it be upon the result of her conviction, without paying any regard to passion, or prejudice, two mercenary counsellors, which, in the court of moral arbitration, are too apt to take bribes, and turn the issue of the cause, while they endeavour to blind the equity and discernment of the magistrate.

Above all other *fatal things*, I warn you not to give implicit credit to *great authorities*, which, in religious cases, are never to have an undue influence. Let not the force, splendour, or power of a name, seduce, or awe you into a partial choice. Religion, like matrimony, should be, if possible, settling for life. Let neither Hume, or Addison, or Bacon, or Bolingbroke, Locke, or Tillotson, sway you by any thing, but the actual weight of arguments, which strike eventually and irresistibly upon the *rational* faculty.

These hints pursued, will, I cannot but believe, serve, in some degree, every hesitating person; and, when carried into practice, I have faith enough in them to conjecture, they will enable every one who is pleased to lend them his attention, to act honestly, amiably, uprightly; and to discharge his duty according to the truth that is in him, whether he be of one religion or another.

Of David Hume, or of his philosophy, I shall say no more; but from a succinct view of the whole matter, I apprehend it may very fairly be concluded, in repetition of Mr. Smith's words, that, "though men will, no doubt, judge variously of his philosophical opinions, every one approving, or condemning them, according as they happen to coincide or disagree with his own, yet, concerning his character and conduct, there can scarce be a difference of opinion."

———

AN
ADDRESS
TO
One of the People called CHRISTIANS.
By way of REPLY,
TO HIS
LETTER
TO
ADAM SMITH, L.L.D.
ON THE
LIFE, DEATH, AND PHILOSOPHY
OF HIS FRIEND
DAVID HUME, Esq.

———

AN
ADDRESS, &c.

Sir,

Your very *Christian* epistle, wet from the Clarendon press, was brought to me by my bookseller, just as I was correcting a proof sheet of that Apology, from the first advertisement of which, in the newspapers, you seem to have caught the hint of your title: I mean so much of it as relates to the Life, Death, and Philosophy of David Hume, Esq.

Upon shewing *my* original title-page[8] to a learned acquaintance, he said he discovered therein a visible impropriety. An Apology for the Death for any man, he thought, unnecessary. Your letter convinces me, the blunder would not have amounted to an Iricism, had it been admitted agreeable to my first design; – since you have, I find, as many, and as powerful objections to Mr. Hume's manner of dying, as to his manner of living. But your letter to Dr. Smith is too singular not to command as much of my attention, as can, at this late period of my time, when THE APOLOGY is just stepping abroad, be allowed.

Your epistle, Sir, is the first of those – though I confess it came out rather sooner than I expected – which I prognosticated would be levelled both at David Hume and Dr. Smith. It is certainly right that the people called Christians, should, with all decent earnestness, espouse the cause of that religion, upon whose sacred foundations their faith is established. I blame you not, therefore – the more especially if you are of the holy order, which I take to be the case – for drawing your weapon in behalf of what appears to you, to be the only system that ought to be universally adopted. It is laudable: it is amiable: it is noble. But then it should have been done – a business so important – so delicate – should have been done, Sir, without spleen, without rancour, without uncharitableness.

Hath this been the case? – The rage of a hurried composition is now gratified, your zeal hath almost kindled the wheels in its journey to London, and you are, perhaps, – or you will be, by the time this reaches you, in your – I will not call it – *easy* chair. – Pray – reverend Sir – you see I cannot help thinking I am addressing a clergyman, though without your precaution I should have known you were not writing with the pen of a B — .

Pray, reverend Sir, let your pamphlet lie upon the table, as you and I – with the pleasantry which I perceive is so dear to you – examine some of its paragraphs.

Your *style* is, as you say, "free and easy"[9] enough; but neither in *that*, nor in your sentiment, do you appear to have "in your composition any large

---

[8] The original title-page, printed in the London Packet, runs thus: An Apology for the Life, Death, and Philosophy of David Hume, &c.

[9] Letter, p. 2.

proportion of that which our inimitable Shakespeare styles, *the milk of human kindness.*"[10] And though it must be confessed, you now and then are, as you say, ready to praise, yet it is of that sort, as if

"Your spirit mock'd itself."

or to apply another poetical expression, which seems not to be ill-suited –

"You *damn* with *faint praise.*"

The other part of this memorable couplet must, however, be parodied, to be apposite; for, your *leer* is by no means *civil,* and you *do* sneer yourself most horribly, even while you are teaching *others* to sneer –
    Proceed we to the proof.
    It is with a very considerable share of prudence, that you advise such readers as find no satisfaction in your book, to "throw it into the fire."[11] – I confess, I was, in the progress of the perusal, more than once tempted to make a sacrifice of this nature; and I more than once, also, heartily regretted the loss of my shilling,[12] and I shall, certainly, take care "not to lose another in the same manner."[13] Not, Sir, because "I am an enemy to human learning,"[14] or that I could not have made a hearty meal, upon a good, fair, and candid defence of Christianity, as yourself; but because, I cannot possibly consider, as candid or fair, or good, a pamphlet, which is written with an indecent degree of warmth, and with very little regard to liberality. What have you not, upon the present occasion, *drolled upon?* – You have chosen to write your letter to Dr. Smith in a *droll* way, upon the most serious of all human subjects, and yet you are very angry that our dying philosopher, should, in his last hours, "read Lucian – play at whist, and *droll* upon Charon and his boat."[15] – I should not – I *shall* not, Sir, – oppose Mr. Hume's philosophy, to the principles of Christianity – but I think it very hard that you should so entirely forget, the Christian temper, the Christian meekness, and the Christian charity, which so eminently distinguished its divine master. – Nay, you are deficient in the very liberality, which should mark every fair, and rational enquirer. – Is it liberal, Sir, to turn the arrows of ridicule against a long life of – *good-nature, compassion, generosity,*

---

[10] Letter, p. 4.

[11] See advertisement to Letter, p. i.

[12] Ditto, p. ii.

[13] Advertisement, p. ii.

[14] See Letter, p. 3.

[15] See Letter, p. 10.

charity; merely because his opinion happen to differ from yours? – Is that rectitude of conduct, which confessedly marked Mr. Hume, to be dwindled down to nothing, for the sake of supporting an argument on the opposite side of the question? Is it I say, Sir, to be shrunk into the idea of his being "*good company*, and knew how to manage his *cards?*"[16] – But almost every part of your letter to Dr. Smith allows sufficient scope for the severest censure. The witticism of turning Mr. Hume's History of England into a noble effort of *matter and motion*,[17] is wretched: to pay you, however, a compliment, in *kind*, I must just express my notion, that, your pamphlet neither possesses such valuable *matter*; nor do I think it will have, by any means, so noble a *motion*: it will, I trust, like one of Hume's treatises, *fall dead born from the press*, and be amongst the things which are no more remembered, although you have, boastingly, called it an *alarum*[18] bell to the admirers of Mr. Hume: yea, even though you insist upon it – with a zeal which relishes more of bigotry than Christianity – that it should be rung in their ears, till succeeded by the last trumpet.[19]

The questions you address to Dr. Smith, are, most of them, exceedingly superficial; the first is perfectly ridiculous. "Why all this hurry and bustle, to satisfy the public, that our Philosopher lived and died perfectly composed and easy? Was there, say you, any suspicion in *Scotland*, that he might not, at times, be quite so composed and easy as he should have been?"

And would you really have a serious answer to so silly a question? Pray, Sir, was there ever yet a being so uniformly tranquil, so perpetually serene, as to be always the same, and appear to his family, to his friends, and to his foes, without some little discomposure? If you speak in a *religious* sense: I desire to know, whether the firmest Christian – to pay you the compliment – Sir – whether *you*, have not, at times, had upon you those feelings which have run counter to the general tenor of a more collected conduct; and whether, now and then, you have not been, even in points of orthodoxy, less composed, and less easy than you could wish to have been? The best men upon earth, are, in proportion to their sensibility, the most susceptible of these occasional disorders; nor can all the Religion, or Fortitude, or Philosophy in the whole world prevent it.

Your second interrogatory, and the third, which is directly connected with the second, are not more aptly proposed, nor deserve they a more sober answer than the first.

---

[16] Letter, p. 11.

[17] Letter, p. 3.

[18] Ditto, p. 24.

[19] Letter, p. 25.

"Was there ever any *Book* written against Mr. Hume – which shook his system to pieces about his ears, and reduced it to a heap of ruins, the success and eclat of which might be supposed to have hurt his mind, and to have affected his health?"[20] "Was there any *Author*, whose *name*, his friends never dared to mention before him, and was not all strangers, that were introduced to him, against doing it; because he never failed, when by any accident it was done, to fly out into a transport of passion and swearing? or hath no book been written to impair the growth and increase of his philosophic reputation? – In reply to these several points I shall wave all stricture upon the scurility, and unchristian spirit which is mixed up with them, and only observe, that, no book *has* been written, that has impaired Hume's philosophical reputation; a philosophic reputation, subsists only among philosophers; and they, to a man, hold Beattie's Book in contempt; which, is a philosophy calculated only for ladies, and fine gentlemen.

Your arguments, Sir, are not much happier than your questions; as your remarks are in general, poorer than both. I shall expose the futility of these, as their absurdity occurs to my mind, upon a re-examination of your Letter.

What you have called a "summary of Mr. Hume's doctrines, metaphysical and moral,"[21] is either a *wilful* or an *ignorant*, misrepresentation of Hume's system, which never in any one part or passage, gave you first cause to say, its author, at any time "sat down calmly and deliberately to obliterate from the hearts of the human species every trace of the knowledge of God and his dispensations."[22] Much less did he endeavour to "extirpate all hope of enjoying God's grace and favour." On the contrary, I do again insist, that Mr. Hume's philosophical system, inculcated every thing praise-worthy.[23]

Secondly, Sir, you are upon a wrong ground in asserting that, to want honestly, and to want understanding, and to want a leg, are equally the objects of *moral* disapprobation.

This cannot be any part of David Hume's doctrine, neither can bear critical examination. In fact, the most pitiable of all human objects is a dishonest probate, for nothing can so truly be compassionated as a man who hath not even *policy* enough to be *honest*, yet he is certainly an object of moral disapprobation; and tho' it may be very proper to pity him, it is equally proper that, for the sake of an example, and for the service of mankind, he should be punished. A criminal pleaded upon his trial, as an extenuation of his offence, that he was *predestined* to commit it: I am heartily sorry for that friend, said the judge, but by the same rule, I am predestined to order you to be hanged.

[20] Letter, p. 25.

[21] Letter, p. 39.

[22] Letter, p. 16.

[23] See Apology, Sect. 3. p. 70. 71. 72.

Breaking a leg is assuredly a pitiable circumstance, but, in point of culpability, shall it be equally immoral with want of honesty? Nor did I ever know before that, want of *understanding*, was to be imputed to a man, as criminal, though it may sometimes be attributed to his weakness, or want of application. – Again, can a *whole* leg be called a corporeal *virtue*; or can a broken one be termed with any propriety, a corporeal *vice?* Corporeal virtues, must be personal virtues; such as charity, cleanliness, continence, &c. &c.

There is something so unaccountable in this sentence, Sir, that I should esteem myself very much obliged to you if you would intercede with your learned friend,[24] who drew up a comprehensive summary of Hume's doctrines, to refer me to that passage in our Philosopher's Works which treats of this matter.

I beg references also, by help of the same medium, to those parts of Hume, which is, you say,[25] "designed to prove the *soul's mortality*," an attempt which I cannot with the closest attention perceive, was ever made. Hints about his justification of *self-murder*, are, as some critics have already observed, "candour itself requires, we should not attack a work, which the Author himself had abandoned, and in some measure reprobated."[26]

By way of contrast to the behaviour of Mr. Hume, you lay before us, for the choice of our adoption, the behaviour of Hooker the Christian. – I am curious to know the reasons for proposing Hooker as a contrast to Hume. – Was there any thing in the conduct of their last moments which so materially distinguished them? Let us draw the curtain, and observe.

Immediately before the Author of the Ecclesiastical Polity expired, he spake thus:

> "I have lived to see, that this world is made up of perturbations; and I have been long preparing to leave it, and gathering comfort for the dreadful hour of making my account with God, which I now apprehend to be near. And though I have, by his grace, loved him in my youth, and feared him in mine age, and laboured to have a conscience void of offence, towards him, and towards all men, yet, if thou, Lord, shouldest be extreme to mark what I have done amiss, who can abide it? And therefore, where I have failed, Lord, shew mercy to me; for I plead not my righteousness, but the forgiveness of my unrighteousness, through His merits, who died to purchase pardon for penitent sinners. And since I owe thee a death, Lord, let it not be terrible, and then take thine own time; I submit to it. Let not mine, O Lord, but thy will be done! – God hath heard my daily petitions; for I am at peace with all men, and he is at peace with me. From such blessed assurance I feel that inward

[24] Postscript to Letter, p. 38.

[25] Letter, p. 28.

[26] London Review. [Review of *The Life of David Hume*, March 1777, Vol. 5, pp. 198–205, excerpted in this collection.]

joy, which this world can neither give, nor take from me. My conscience beareth me this witness; and this witness makes the thoughts of death joyful. I could wish to live, to do the Church more service; but cannot hope it; for my days are past, as a shadow that returns not."

When Hume's symptoms returned with violence upon him, he from that moment gave up all thoughts of recovery, and submitted with the utmost chearfulness, and the most perfect resignation and complacency:[27] he always talked of his approaching dissolution with great cheerfulness, but never affected to make any parade of his magnanimity.[28] When even the conversation of his friends became oppressive and fatiguing, he was quite free from anxiety, or impatience.[29] Even the last stage of his disorder, when it even cost him an effort to speak, and when he had occasion to address the people about him, he always did it with affection and tenderness.[30] – After all this he died "in such a happy composure of mind, that nothing could exceed it."

I look in vain for a *distinct difference* between the last moments of Hume and Hooker, Sir. Did Hooker "labour to be at peace with all men?" So did Hume, who had "no enemies on which he wished to revenge himself."[31] Did Hooker live to see, that, "this world is made up of perturbations?"[32] So did Hume, who – though the later period of his life was the most agreeable to him, and though he saw many symptoms of his literary reputation breaking out at last with additional lustre – considered that, "a man of sixty-five, by dying, cuts off only a few years of infirmities,"[33] insomuch that he declares, almost with his dying breath, that, "it would be difficult to be more detached from life" than he was at that crisis.

Point out to me then, I conjure you, Sir, the superiority in the manner of Hooker's dying. I own I cannot, without some peculiar assistance, find it out. And, I trust, likewise, that such readers of my APOLOGY, as are neither, "bigots, enthusiasts, nor enemies to human learning,"[34] will be fully convinced that the influences of the philosophy which are the object of our present dispute, were in no degree pestilential.[35]

[27] Life, p. 42.

[28] Dr. Smith's Letter, p. 51.

[29] Dr. Smith's Letter, p. 54.

[30] Dr. Smith's Letter, p. 58.

[31] Dr. Smith's Letter to Mr. Strahan, p. 48.

[32] Letter, p. 32.

[33] Life, p. 31.

[34] Letter, p. 2.

[35] Letter, p. 30.

From what has been already urged, you will perceive, Sir, that I by no means think that your Letter to Dr. Adam Smith is *ingenuously* written;[36] nor do I think the Doctor's deceased friend, will very cordially accept services, so maliciously offered, even IF (as you cautiously observe) departed spirits *have* any knowledge of what is passing upon earth.[37]

After all, Sir, how can you allow your pen such a licence – a licence, you would not dared to have indulged, had the philosopher been in the land of the living – as to say that his existence was passed without God in the world?[38] Though his notions of a supreme Power might not perhaps directly tally with yours, how are you able to tell that such a power did not as highly approve his arguments as your own? Would you pronounce a sentence of damnation against the Indian for his worship to the sun – against the Mahometan for his homage to the Prophet – against the Chinese for his idolatry to a sculptured image – against the Persian for his prostration to a cloud? All these people have different ideas of a Deity from you. – None of these are Christians – Millions of them believe nothing about the Son[39] – Many of them are, moral, social, pious, humane, charitable – Shall they, nevertheless, not see life, but shall the wrath of God, so furiously denounced by St. John, abide on them?

I am shocked at such a system. Yet the case is parallel. Fie upon it, Sir. It is not the part of a Christian pastor to be extreme to mark even what is done amiss, nor is it characteristic either of a follower of Jesus, or of a servant of the eternal Father, to snatch from the hand of that father,

– "the ballance or the rod."[40]

[36] It were no difficult matter, to prove also that you have not written *ingeniously*; several gross blunders, which even hurry cannot excuse, occurring in different parts of your pamphlet. Thus, in Advertisement, p. I. you "made your remarks, because you thought them true." What, Sir, "did you think them true *before* the thoughts were made." P. 4. of Letter, you use the word *proportion* for portion, by which mistake the passage is truly ridiculous. P. 4. you say you never knew what hatred was? No! What, do not you hate vice, and the villain? Good, meek, milky-minded man, the friends of virtue and honesty are much obliged to you for that truly! P. 10. you talk facetiously of *dying* as insensibly and foolishly as you can for the *life* of you: you say you are a *South Britain*. Who would not have thought you were just exported from the banks of the Shannon? P. 14. is the word *yourself* for the word *you*, and various other errors – not of the press, but, – to adopt your own language – "these are trifles; my quarry lies not this way. I fly at nobler game. The atrocious cruelty of insisting that a writer diffused *Atheism*, who never *did* diffuse any such thing, is a subject that concerns every body."

[37] Letter, p. 30.

[38] Letter, p. 32.

[39] Letter, p. 31.

[40] Essay on Man.

Although, you have taken upon you to "rejudge his justice, and be the God of God." All that part of your Letter, therefore, Sir, which would represent Mr. Hume as unworthy the mercy, or protection of a Providence, is arrogant, insolent, ignorant, and presumptuous.

But, to say the truth, and do you full justice, you seem, Sir, to profess a notable talent for misrepresenting the sentiments of those whom you are pleased to censure. I am sorry to find you do not think Dr. Smith's *good meaning* will succeed; because, – without the least mixture of your beloved irony – I really think his design was perfectly laudable. I see nothing wrong in his persuading us to follow the example of David Hume, because, I perceive, not a syllable that proposes Atheism as a cordial for low spirits, and the proper antidote against the fear of death. If *you* perceive such sentiments, I again repeat, that, it becomes you, Sir, as a fair-dealing Christian, who ought to do justice betwixt man and man, to be more particular in your references, and not to be

"laughing wild in *merry* madness."

Your simile of John the Painter is very elevated, indeed, and soars superior to all reply: I am not offended, and accept, very good humouredly, your declaration of meaning no harm.[41] The misfortune is, that I am afraid you will do no good. Your pamphlet, like what *you* take to be Mr. Hume's definition of the soul – a thing by the bye which he never mentions – is not one, but many things, and being a jumble of many things together, is, ultimately, nothing at all.[42] You more than once, subvert your own hypothesis, and prove, by your ungracious manner of arguing, that by such argument nothing can be proved.[43]

These, Sir, among many other reasons, induce me not to speak quite so handsomely of you as I could wish;[44] and these are also my motives for refusing to introduce you to my kinsfolk, and acquaintance.

Upon the whole, Sir, after accurately examining your Letter to Dr. smith, and carefully re-considering the whole subject of the preceding APOLOGY in consequence of it, I am able to conclude with an application of your *own closing expressions*, and of my motto, namely, that, "on reviewing what I have written, I really cannot see there is any occasion for me to alter, or to add another sentence."[45]

---

[41] Letter, p. 5.

[42] Letter, p. 39.

[43] Letter, p. 42.

[44] Advertisement to Letter, p. 2.

[45] See Advertisement, p. 4.

"For modes of faith, let graceless zealots fight:
His can't be wrong, whose *life* is in the right."

Consequently, David Hume's system, upon accounting of the rectitude of his life, cannot be wrong.

     I am, Sir,
        Your humble Servant,
One of the People who venerate SINCERITY.

              FINIS.

70
"OBSERVATIONS ON THE ADDRESS"
(*GENTLEMAN'S MAGAZINE*)

"Laicus," "Observations on the Address to One of the People called Christians," in *Gentleman's Magazine*, July 1777, Vol. 47, pp. 322–328. Complete; from *Gentleman's Magazine*.

The author of this anonymous article implies that he is a friend of George Horne, whose *Letter to Dr. Adam Smith* (1777) he seeks to defend against Pratt's attack in the *Apology* (1777). The author points out stylistic problems and inconsistencies with Pratt's work, accusing him of deism, and he defends Beattie against Pratt's comment that the *Essay on the Immutability of Truth* "is a philosophy calculated only for ladies, and fine gentlemen." The author notes the history of Hume's essays on suicide and immortality after they were expunged from *Five Dissertations* and eventually printed in a corrupt edition in Holland. Bracketed comments are those of the author.

Mr. URBAN,

The following Observations are intended to lay before your numerous readers the futility of the remarks in "an Address to One of the People called Christians, by way of reply to his Letter to Dr. Adam Smith," annexed to "An Apology for the Life and Writings of David Hume, Esq;" (see p. 338.)

It would be a tedious and disagreeable task to unravel the whole of this "Apology," designedly perplexed with studied obscurity, incoherent, and frequently inconsistent with itself.[1]

---

[1] I am utterly astonished to think that the same author who so severely treats *religious hypocrisy*, as he is pleased to call it, should at the same time give birth to works of such a different cast, as "the Apology" and "the Sublime and Beautiful of Scripture." See pp. 110–111. – [Our correspondent's astonishment will surely cease when he reflects that Mr. Melmoth admires the books of Scripture rather as elegant compositions, or moral lessons, in the same manner as he would admire Homer or Virgil, or any heathen author, than as inspired writings, and evidently stamped by the seal of the Almighty.] EDITOR.

I shall therefore pass on to the "Address" with a slight observation or two; as, that, in his title-page, the Apologist talks of a "parallel between David Hume, Esq; and the late Lord Chesterfield;" and, after all his labour and time spent in drawing it out, concludes, that there is no parallel at all, but a great contrast.[2] As well, says an ingenious friend, might the geometrician expect applause for informing us that he had produced two parallel lines till they met in a right angle.

He has likewise taken great pains to expose the hypocrisy of a fawning dedication; yet at the same time, forgetful of the generous example set before him in Mr. Hume, he has written himself several pages of dedication to his small pamphlet,[3] and humbly prefers a petition to have this Apology precede any new edition of Mr. Hume's works: yet I am apt to think it will "neither do service to the writer, or the man."

I wonder in what sense a philosopher could say, "the sun and its *shadow*," p. vii. I have been always taught to consider the sun as the cause of the shadow, its rays falling on the intervening body; and the representation of that body is what we call the *shadow*, as it intercepts the light. Now, his acceptation of the word is by no means compatible with the usual definition of it; – on consulting his dictionary he will find no such thing there; we may view the image, or reflection of the sun on the water, but I believe we never saw its shadow.

For these and other more weighty reasons, which will be shewn in the Observations, I would advise others, for a much smaller fee, not to be taken in, as I have been, for half a crown, through the specious title of the Apology – and must observe, unless Hume is happy enough to find a better Apologist, he must inevitably sink into disrepute; or rather, I should say, if Hume's writings do not apologize for themselves, this author will not be found of sufficient abilities to plead the cause.

This objection, it may be said, holds equally good when urged against myself, as against the Apologist. True, but even then I do but follow his example: I am conscious of my inability to apologize for the "letter:" in short, I do not see it needs any: – my design is only to vindicate it by exposing the weakness of his objections, and an humble endeavour to wipe away the stains he throws on it, which may deform, but will never deface it.

And now, kind reader, if you will favour me with a perusal, I will give you my reasons for using this language.

---

[2] See section V. p. 112.

[3] I am since informed, also, that it was without the consent, and to the great dissatisfaction, of Mr. Strahan.

OBSERVATIONS.

I should not have dared to take up the pen, if there was not great reason to suspect that no abler advocate would condescend to take notice of it; much less the author of the Letter to Dr. A. Smith, with whose pacific disposition we (as being in the secret) are not unacquainted; and whose *LIFE* and actions, as well as writings, plainly demonstrate that he does not vainly boast of "the milk of human kindness." I am afraid lest it should be deemed giving it too much honour to think even of sending a *formal* answer from the press; so have taken this means to convey it to the public. I shall not dwell on the ambiguous expressions of the motto,

> For modes of Faith let graceless zealots fight;
> His can't be wrong, whose *LIFE* is in [the right:]

as we all know the cunning of these lines, how easily they may be transformed into orthodoxy. We are not ignorant how the poet stood affected to the church of England; and, as the age is very fond of *taking affront,* the very motto, I think, is sufficient to make us arm in our own defence, and *require satisfaction.*

If, indeed, to profess scepticism and infidelity be the mark of the learned head, or the ingenious undertaking alone; however highly these excellent qualifications are esteemed, I find myself inclined to say, with an admired poet,[4] that here,

> "Where ignorance is bliss
> 'Tis folly to be wise."

I am happy to find that this Apology, especially the latter part of it, does not abound with many soars of imagination, many flights of genius; nor is it set off with many rhetorical ornaments; and will venture to say, few, in comparison of those which the brief, but poignant, Letter to Dr. S. contains. I am induced, therefore, to hope, were it for this recommendation only, as the taste of the present times seems chiefly to favour the beauties of composition, and attend particularly to hte elegance of language, that the Letter will be more read and admired than the Apology; since of the former, I am bold to say, as we read of another brief but eminent publication, "Multæ et cum Gravitate, Faccitæ: quodque *est difficile,* Idem et *peronatus* et brevis."

In my perusal of this Apology with an ingenious friend, I could hardly restrain him from offering it as a sacrifice to Vulcan: and if the Apologist

[4] Gray.

heartily regretted the loss of his shilling (p. 137), much more have I reason to lament the loss of more than double that sum; and shall take care myself, and it is the intent of this to advise all others, not to lose another in the same manner.

But stop, my reader may say, this is all invective on one hand, and adulation on the other. The passions kindled by a zeal for what is called superstition and enthusiasm, may perhaps be answerable for the first; the last I totally disclaim, and assure all persons, that I write this privately, no one perusing it, or even knowing my intentions, till it comes to Mr. Urban's hands.

To come now more to the point. – Pray what means, "An Apology for the death *for* any man?" Page 132. Is this an Iricism, Solœcism, or an error of the press?[5] I should be glad to know what idea to affix to it. – Our author complains much of the rancour, spleen, and uncharitableness of the Epistle. Were we to grant this, (which concession will hardly be made,) yet the importance of the cause demands the sharpest weapons; and no wonder, when the foe is powerful and inveterate, that the blow falls heavier, and that no quarter be given; especially should it prove, that the writer is "of the *Holy Order*," and, n the usual mode of speaking of the Reverends by their opponents, is *paid for fighting*.

Admire, reader, if you can, the following sentence (p. 134): "The rage of a hurried composition is now gratified; your zeal hath almost kindled the wheels in its journey to London, and you are, perhaps, – or you will be, by the time this reaches you, in your – I will not call it – *easy* chair." And again, p. 136: "The other part of this memorable couplet must, however, be parodied, to be apposite; for your *leer* is by no means *civil*, and you *do* sneer yourself most horribly, even while you are teaching *others* to sneer." Are you about to laugh, reader? or Do you sneer too? Do not you see the wit? Poo! you are blinded with prejudice.

It is not for one personally unacquainted with Mr. Hume to say how far he might have displayed in his actions the glorious virtues of *good-nature, compassion, generosity, charity:* I beg leave only to advise the modern deriders of those unfortunate clergymen whose lives are not suitable to their profession, that, lest they be convicted of the greatest inconsistency, they will drop the stale subject, for the sake of their favourite Hume; since, the proposition being reversed, we have the strongest similarity: the former are *said*[6] to disgrace good doctrines

---

[5]   Evidently the latter, as appears by this note annexed: "The original title-page, printed in the London Packet, run (*ran*) thus: 'An Apology for the Life, Death, and Philosophy *of* D. Hume,' &c." *Editor.*

[6]   It is far from being a hard matter to prove, that the doctrines of Christianity are by no means affected by the lives of its professors; and that the boasted religious hypocrisy of our adversaries will little avail their cause.

and precepts by their lives; the latter disgraced a good life by his pernicious tenets and doctrines. This is the most that his sanguine votaries require us to grant; and, though it must be allowed there is a great contradiction in both, yet of the two, perhaps, we may find ourselves more disposed to pity the infirmities of our nature, than pardon the voluntary productions of a sceptical imagination.

As to the witticism of *matter* and *motion*, however "*wretched*" in the eyes of the Apologist, (tho', by the bye, I see no affectation of wit in it,) it must be allowed to be just: for, if *matter* and *motion* are to be considered as the chief causes of human thoughts, of which actions are the result, and if the human mind is merely passive, it must follow as a consequence, by every rule of logic, that it could be no other than "an effort of *matter* and *motion*," however great or "noble."

The compliment in *kind* paid to the author of the Epistle, I thus am bold to transform, and with truth: that, as a *proof* of its possessing "*valuable matter*," and of its having "*a noble motion*," so far is it from "*falling dead born from the press*," and being "amongst the things which are no more remembered," as the adversary predicts (p. 141), that it has already acquired a second edition. – I doubt whether the boasted Apology will have this success.

I believe he is mistaken this time as to the person: but be that as it will, proceed we to another ingenious sentence.

It is not surprising, that, whilst the Apologist is exclaiming against the Divine for want of candour, and *manifest perversion*, he should so far forget himself as to be guilty of such a flagrant instance of it, in the very next sentence. P. 141: "Although you have, boastingly, called it an *alarum*-bell to the admirers of Mr. Hume; yea, even though you insist upon it – with a zeal which relished more of bigotry than christianity – that it should be rung in their ears, till succeeded by the last trumpet."

Does the author speak this of his own work? Would the Apologist have us rank him as so ignorant, so unacquainted with books, as not to know whence this extract is taken? I have therefore only one question to ask, and a very material one it is: Is this eulogium directly, or indirectly, bestowed by our author on himself? If not, Where is the boasting? Let him answer with truth, with impartiality; and let him deny, if he can, that what is here said, is spoken of an eminent divine (in our opinion), Dr. Beattie: from whose Essay on the *nature and Immutability* of *Truth*, in opposition to *Scepticism* and *Sophistry*, (part III. ch. iii. p. 480. 4th edit. 8vo. Lond. 1773,) this excellent quotation, which aptly introduces the offensive clause, is taken.

The effect of this admirable work, both as conducive to the overthrow of Mr. Hume's system, and perhaps to the impairing the health of his body, and the tranquillity of his mind, is a fact too commonly known to be denied, or, if denied, at least to gain credit, however it may be dissembled.

Who could think any one would have the effrontery, after the many learned treatises that have been written against Mr. Hume's tenets, (besides Dr.

Beattie's,) as Dr. Campbell *on Miracles,* of which Mr. Hume himself had a good opinion; Dr. Adams's *Essay,* and Bishop Pearce's; Leland's *View of Deistical Writers,* &c; to say, "that no book *has* been written that has impaired Hume's philosophical reputation. Let us hear his argument: "A philosophic reputation subsists only among philosophers; and they, to a man, hold Beattie's book in contempt; which is a philosophy calculated only for ladies and fine gentlemen." P. 145, 146.

Have not we great need "to wave all strictures upon the scurrility" here? Well! he does allow it to be a *philosophy* at least, though it is "calculated only for ladies and fine gentlemen;" it is a wonder he would make this concession. Now, supposing we grant, "that a philosophic reputation subsists only among philosophers," – Who are to be the arbiters fixed on? Shall one party only nominate philosophers to decide the debate? What criterion shall be mutually agreed upon? Are none but sceptics and infidels to be judges? Is deism and free-thinking, alone, to be the standard? Such "philosophers" indeed as these, "may, to a man, hold Beattie's book in contempt:" weighed in such a partial balance, "his philosophy" may be deemed so light and trivial, as to be "calcu-lated only for ladies and fine gentlemen."

But, be it known, that we Christians, however we appear to the *narrow* view of the Free-thinker and Sceptic to be injudicious and biassed; we, I say, being the greater part of mankind, do not chuse tamely to be counted fools, and men of no understanding. "We have still spirit enough left among us to resent such ill-treatment as this. 'Tis the presumptuous and proud man alone, who dares to trample on those truths which the rest of the world reverence, and can sit down quietly in the assurance, that He alone is in the right, and all mankind beside in the wrong." See the elegant discourse of Bishop Atterbury, vol. I. p. 178, on the words, "A scorner seeketh wisdom, and findeth it not:" in which the reasons of his failure are set down, in a manner evidently convincing; than which nothing can be more truly applicable to our present *scorners.* We enjoy, in common with them, the gift of reason, though we may widely differ as to the means of our obtaining it: we may superstitiously ascribe it to the mercy of a benign Creator: they may, as they please, deem chance, or the power of nature, or *no cause,* its proper origin.[7] Yet still let them not be so arrogant as to deprive us of the common use of it with themselves: let them give *us* leave, too, to put in our voice of approbation or condemnation. The brain of the sceptical philosopher, or speculative infidel, may be of a fine contexture; yet we can oppose to the votaries of deism, christians, as famous in their times, as learned, as ingenious, as the supporters of such pernicious tenets. – Do they boast of a *Bolingbroke,* a *Pope,* a *Hume?* We can match them with an *Addison,*

---

[7] Seeing, in the *Humian* system, the mind or soul is *nothing,* and it is unreasonable to believe the universe proceeds "from a cause," surely we may conclude, *Ex nihilo nihil fit.*

a *Thompson*, a *Beattie*: whose works will be read and admired by the greater part of Mankind in all succeeding generations; while the favourers of scepticism and infidelity shall either sink into oblivion, or at best be pointed out to be shunned as dangerous and pestilential.

We come next (page 146) to a vindication of Mr. H.'s doctrine, wherein the author, to preserve consistency, pretends to say, and would have us believe, that Mr H. is a favourer of religion; and insists again, that "his philosophical system inculcated every thing praise-worthy:" i.e. we may say, to give an instance or two, suicide, adultery; which even his Apologist discommends, by deeming as "corporeal or personal virtues" those of "charity, cleanliness, *continence*," &c. Page 150.

The author is very *charitable* in that part, especially p. 148. Who, before ever doubted Hume's opinion respecting the soul's *mortality?* A slight attempt of the *impartial*, much less the *prejudiced* christian, will easily discover it; and *we* may be allowed to draw an inference, surely, as well as our adversaries. – We are not ignorant that our objectors, also, have sometimes had their eyes blinded by partiality and prejudice, and we deem it so in the present case. – Credulous as we are, this will not go down with us. – I will tell you my sentiments, "*Credat Judæus Apella.*"

I want to see the sense and meaning of the next passage before I say any thing about it, and to have the connexion pointed out to me, lest I be condemned for rash censure. "Hints about his justification of self-murder, *are*, some critics[8] have already observed, "Candour itself requires that we should not attack a work which the author himself had abandoned, and in some measure repro-bated." Is not this "a gross blunder, which even hurry cannot excuse?" Note, p. 158.

If report says true, and sometimes it does, the *Essay on Suicide* has been published, and was suppressed by public authority. A great legacy was left to an eminent bookseller to publish it again, and, on his refusal, was offered to others; and when the more generous of the trade in Britain refused to give birth to such a national evil, it was dispatched into Holland, to return hither again, and scatter its pestilential influence over the fellow-subjects and fellow-citizens of the *good*, and *humane*, the *social* Mr. Hume.

It was observed in the public papers, that Mr. H. shewed great anxiety in his last moments, to "poison the air he could no longer subsist in." – Every friend to his country, independent of his being a christian, must think that we have suicides enough, without a recommendation of the crime from so able a writer; and its fatal tendency hath been already proved by example.

Perhaps, as to *external* appearances, we see no "*distinct difference* between the last moments of Hume and Hooker" – but one would think a philosopher

---

[8]   London Reviewers.

(as the Apologist seems to lay claim to that title) would not attend to outward appearances only. "*Fronti nulla fides*" is an old maxim. Let him take a view of the mind, the internal reason and sentiment, which is the noble characteristic between the brute and the man; and see if there is no difference then. – If in this view he "conjures the author of the Letter to point out" to him "the superiority in the manner of Hooker's dying," I will answer for the author of the *Ecclesiastical Polity*, that he died as becomes a rational being, having a pleasing hope that he was endued with a soul *immortal*; and thus maintaining to the last his superior rank above the brute creation. The other died in doubt and uncertainty, as he had ever lived, and at death sunk (according to his own system) into a state level with the irrational beasts of the field. Let this writer count me, if he pleases, a "bigot, an enthusiast, or an enemy to human learning" (p. 158): I will still maintain that this is a noble superiority; and am apt to believe that the more rational part of mankind will be of the same opinion.

(Page 158.) "You made your remarks because you thought them true; what, Sir, did you think them true *before* the thoughts were made?" I wonder whether the Apologist intended to expose himself here, or the author of the Epistle? What fallacy! What perversion! Let us quote the original words: "The remarks in the following pages are not, therefore, true or false, because I made them; but I made them because I thought them to be true." What, is there no difference between a thought and a remark? Is not one the result of the other? A "thought," or an idea, is an act of the simple apprehension; it is a representation of the thing perceived. – A "remark" is an act of the judgment, which, on comparison, or recollection, approves or disapproves of the thought. Is not the common definition of it *a note*, an *observation?* As such then the author might truly and elegantly say, that the nature of the remarks could not be altered, because they proceeded from him; and, as truly add, that he made these remarks, because in his judgment (in which light they will appear to every impartial person capable of an unbiassed reflection) they carry with them an evidence of truth. Let him blush for shame at such a flagrant perversion.

As to the correction of the word "*proportion*," which, he says, "makes the passage truly ridiculous," let us see if there is not some sense in it thus taken; for the truth of which, reader, I pledge you my word, "that the author of the Letter has such" a *proportion* of the "milk of human kindness," in comparison of the bulk of mankind, that one would be apt to imagine that he had engrossed too much, and had robbed the Apologist, and many more, of their due *proportion*."

His following remarks merit only a contemptuous silence.

We are now arrived at a more material passage. – Page 160: "Though his [Mr. H.'s] notions of a Supreme Power might not, perhaps, directly tally with yours, how are you able to tell that such a power did not as highly approve his arguments as your own?" – What! approve of notions that directly tend to subvert his very existence, which plainly assure us, that, "as long as there is any evil or disorder in the universe, it is unreasonable to believe *God* to be infinitely wise." Take away his attributes, you rob him of his divinity. – However, according to Hume, there is no occasion for him – "if we have no good reason to think the universe proceeds from a cause."

We do not presume to "pronounce the sentence of damnation against the Indian for his worship to the sun; nor against the Persian for his prostration to a cloud:" we set no bounds to the mercy of God. These objections have been long ago confuted.

It were only to be wished that "millions of them [alone] believed nothing about the Son."

What if I should be so uncharitable as to deem the Apologist himself a deist at least (I venture not to proceed to the higher step of atheism); Is it not immediately deducible from his own words? "Shall they, nevertheless, not see life, but shall the wrath of God, so furiously denounced by St. John, abide on them? I am shocked at such a system."

What system is this at which he is shocked? It is no other than christianity, of which St. John was the inspired propagator, and as a foundation of which this his Gospel was written. If he reckons these as *furious* expressions only, and rejects this book, universally received as canonical, can we imagine him to be a friend to christianity, or a christian?

Believe me, there is a wide difference between the unlettered Indian, or the ignorant Persian, on whom the light of the Gospel never shone, and him who wilfuly shuts his eyes against it, "who dashes the cup untasted from him." Therefore, I conclude, "the case is *not* parallel." The horrid, I had almost said, blasphemous expressions that follow next, merit no other observation, than that the whole is a rank falshood, a scandalous perversion; of which the idea will shock the pious humanity of the author of the Epistle: so that I may again reply with the Apologist's own words, p. 163: "To say the truth, and to you full justice, you seem, Sir, to profess a notable talent for misrepresenting the sentiments of those whom you are pleased to censure." He may perhaps "see nothing wrong in Dr. Smith's persuading us to follow the example of David Hume:" but let us hear again his reason; "because I perceive," says he, 'not a syllable that proposes atheism as a cordial for low spirits, and the proper antidote against the fear of death." – So from hence we may infer, whoever does not propose atheism as a cordial for low spirits," &c. may require us to follow his example, or propose another example to be followed, without there being any thing wrong in it.

He talks of "motives (p. 166) for refusing to introduce" the author "to his kinsfolk and acquaintances:" and yet he has lugged him forth into the pen world to deride him. I fear the laugh will turn against the Apologist.

Lastly, his conclusion is above all truly worthy so excellent a logician! From his elegant motto, he infers, that "David Hume's system, on account of the rectitude of his *life*, cannot be wrong."

Now, consistently with his own principles, he is certainly reduced to a dilemma.

If the author of the Letter's *LIFE* be good, "or in the right," (for which I could give more than my bare assertion, though even that may be equivalent to his for Hume,) why not his system as well as the *Humain*? The premises necessarily bring us to this conclusion. – It remains then for him to extricate himself, either by reconciling two such opposite and contradictory systems, or else joining with me (which seems the best scheme) in denying the premises, and looking out for a better test than the vague expression of a poet; lest such a criterion be found to favour every visionary enthusiast, or seeming sectarist, who grounds the truth of his doctrine on the rectitude of his life; and as it must necessarily introduce much more confusion, and a multiplicity of opinions more *irrational* and *absurd*, than even those of the Christian religion are judged to be by *some*.

LAICUS.

71
GEORGE HORNE:
LETTERS ON INFIDELITY

[George Horne], *Letters on infidelity. By the author of A letter to Doctor Adam Smith*. Oxford: at the Clarendon Press. Sold by D. Prince and J. Cooke, Oxford: G. Robinson, J.F. and C. Rivington, and T. Cadell, London, 1784, [2], III, [3], 301, [1] p.
Letters 1–3 complete; from 1784 edition.

George Horne (1730–1792) was the author of *A Letter to Adam Smith* (1777), contained in this collection, which attacks Smith's praise of Hume's character. In 1784 his *Letters on Infidelity* appeared, again anonymously, but indicating in the title that they are "By the author of a letter to Doctor Adam Smith." Horne's *Letters on Infidelity* is a series of loosely related essays written over a several year period. He notes in the introduction that he preferred to publish the essays as a collection of letters since that style "admits of matter however miscellaneous, and may be continued or broken off at pleasure." The first seven letters are on Hume, and most of the remaining 10 letters are on Biblical themes. Letters 1–3 criticize Pratt's *Apology* of Hume, maintaining that little can be said in Hume's defence in view of his commitment to spreading atheism (Letters 4–7 are Hume's *Dialogues* and two *Essays* on suicide and immortality, included in *Early Responses to Hume's Writings on Religion*).

The *English Review* opens their article condemning the extent of Horne's use of ridicule in the *Letters*:

This is one of the most extraordinary compositions of scurrility, buffoonery and intolerance, that ever passed through our hands. Its professed design is, by detecting some of the late publications in favour of deism, to prevent the growth of infidelity; and we believe the author is in earnest. But if the infidels had been desirous to bring forward a fictitious defence of Christianity, so written as most to discredit the cause it pretended to support, they could scarcely have been more successful. The performance very completely presents us with that most disgustful of all assemblages, the vindictive malice of an inquisitor with the broad humour of a jack-pudding.

Did you ever see a miserable rascal of a pedagogue cutting his abortive jokes, at the same time that he lashes his unfortunate victim? Such is the author of the Letters on Infidelity.

Regarding the opening three letters on Pratt's *Apology*, the reviewer writes that no harm is done to Christianity by acknowledging Hume's virtues:

Among the performances that come under his examination are the posthumous works, and Mr. Pratt's Apology for the Life of Hume. It has been generally allowed, that Mr. Hume was an amiable and a virtuous man, and for our parts, we see no mischief that can accrue to Christianity from the concession. Our author acknowledges indeed, that Mr. Hume was regular and friendly, and not absolutely destitute of common honesty. But he "has written Essays, containing certain doctrines, and leading to certain consequences. Weighted against a conduct like this," continues he, "the *moralities of social life* are dust upon the balance!" In fine, he is clearly of opinion, that his proceedings claimed the animadversion of the secular arm, and that to be pilloried was the mildest punishment that could in reason be inflicted upon him. [*English Review*, July 1784, Vol. 4, pp. 31–34]

In their brief review, *Gentleman's Magazine* comments that "when old objections are retailed, old answers must be given, and therefore on the above subjects little new can be expected, except in the manner." The reviewer concludes, "May every poison meet with as good an antidote!" (August 1784, Vol. 54, pp. 607–609). Writing for the *Monthly Review*, William Rose begins by praising the work as a whole:

These Letters contain strictures on the nature, tendency, principles, and reasonings, of some late productions on the side of infidelity. They are well calculated to suit the taste and turn of the present age, which is not fond of long and elaborate dissertations on religious subjects; being written in a concise, lively, and entertaining manner, and with a due mixture of serious argument, good humour, and pleasantry. The Author appears to be well acquainted with the writings of Hume, Voltaire, and other modern infidels; and often combats their opinions very successfully, in their own way, by placing their arguments in a ludicrous point of view, and turning the laugh against themselves. In our opinion, however, he succeeds better in the way of argument, than in that of ridicule, and appears, indeed, to be a very able advocate on the side of religion.

Regarding Horne's discussion of Pratt, Rose writes, "We are told by Mr. Hume's friends, that few of the professors of Christianity ever equalled him in morality, humanity, and the government of their passions. What our author

says in answer to this appears to us very sensible, and just; and we doubt not
of its appearing so to the serious part of our Readers." Although approving of
Horne's criticism of Hume, Rose reiterates a point that he made in his earlier
review of Hume's *Essays* on suicide and immortality (June 1784, Vol. 70, pp.
427–428), namely, that they do not warrant any serious discussion:

> Our Author is, no doubt, highly to be commended for combating opinions
> which he thinks prejudicial to society, and we are persuaded he was actuated
> by the most honourable motives; but what Mr. Hume has advanced on the
> subject must be treated with contempt by every man of plain common sense,
> – and was scarcely worth a serious reply. [*Monthly Review*, November
> 1785, Vol. 73, pp. 338–343]

Two works in this collection discuss Horne's *Letters*, namely Vicesimus
Knox's *Winter Evenings* (1788), and William Jones's *Memoirs ... of the Right
Reverend George Horne* (1795). Horne's *Letters on Infidelity* was reprinted in
1786, 1806 and 1831. It is also included in several editions of Horne's *Works*
(1795, 1809, 1818, 1830, 1831, 1846, 1848, and 1853). The following is from
the 1784 edition of the *Letters*.

LETTERS
ON
INFIDELITY.

—

INTRODUCTORY LETTER.
TO W.S. ESQ.

DEAR SIR,
You express your surprise, that after the favourable manner in which the
Letter to Dr. Smith was received by the public, and the service which, as you
are pleased to say, was effected by it, nothing farther should have been
attempted: especially as an *Apology for the life and writings of David Hume,
Esq.* made it's appearance soon afterwards, and some posthumous tracts of that
philosopher have been since published, to complete the good work he had so
much at heart; not to mention other productions on the side of infidelity. A few
strictures on the nature and tendency, the principles and reasonings of such
performances, thrown out from time to time, in a concise and lively way, you
observe, are better calculated to suit the taste and turn of the present age, than
long and elaborate dissertations; and you see no reason why a method practised
by Voltaire (and so much commended by D'Almbert) *against* religion, should

not be adopted by those who write *for* it. In compliance with these hints, and that you may not think me desirous of leading an idle life, when there is so much work to be done, I have formed a resolution to look over my papers, and address what I may happen to find among them to yourself, in a series of letters; a species of composition much in vogue, and which has these two advantages to recommend it, that it admits of matter however miscellaneous, and may be continued or broken off at pleasure.

LETTER I.

I Begin, Dear Sir, with a few observations on the *Apology for the Life and Writings of David Hume, Esq.* drawn up soon after that work came out, but reserved in expectation of Mr. H___'s posthumous tracts.

With difficulty I am able to persuade my friends, that this author and myself have not written in concert; for his Apology and my Letter fit each other like two tallies.[1] In his Dedication, he expresses his apprehension, that "the CHRISTIAN clamour would be raised afresh." A clamour is accordingly raised by "one of the people called CHRISTIANS." Elsewhere he intimates his expectation that Mr. H___'s "affectionate Dr. Smith" would come in for his share. A letter is accordingly written to that very Doctor.

You see, Dear Sir, how I have done my best to fulfil his predictions. Let us now enquire whether he may not have returned the favour, and been equally kind to me.

In my Advertisement I ventured to suppose, that, by a late publication, the admirers of Mr. H. imagined religion to have received it's *coup de grace*, and that the astonished public was utterly at a loss to conceive, "what they, who believed in God, could possibly have to say for themselves." To convert my supposition into matter of fact, he opens his Apology with a kind of funeral oration, most solemnly pronounced over Christianity as a breathless corpse, about to be for ever interred in the grave of Mr. H.

"David Hume is dead! Never were the pillars of Orthodoxy so desperately shaken, as they are now by the event!" And at P. 9. he speaks of "the particular circumstances of this event" as "increasing the aggregate of our *consternation!*"

Here, the distempered imagination of the Apologist sees Mr. H. like another Samson, bowing himself with all his might between the *pillars*, and saying more at his *death*, than all that he slew in his *life*. He sees the believing world

---

[1] The Apology was *written* before the publication of the Letter, though sent into the world after it.

aghast, the church tottering from it's foundations, and Christians *assembling in an upper chamber, with the doors shut, for fear of the philosophers.* What may be the state of religion upon earth, before the end shall come, we cannot tell. We have reason to think it will be very bad. But let us hope, notwithstanding all which has happened in Scotland, that the Gospel will last our time.

Thus again – I scrupled not to assert, that the end proposed in giving an account of Mr. H___'s life and death was, to recommend his sceptical and atheistical notions. Dr. Smith indeed was wary and modest. He gave us a detail of circumstances, and then only added, that, "as to his philosophy, men would entertain various opinions, but, to be sure, all must allow his conduct was unexceptionable," &c. But the Apologist has blurted it all out at once. – David Hume's life was *right*, and therefore his system cannot be *wrong*. My friend Dr. Smith will take him to task for this, as sure as he is alive.

And now for another piece of complaisance on *my* side – P. 9. He "wishes only out of curiosity, to know the unaffected state of our feelings," on perusing the account given by Dr. Smith – As if I had been privy to his thoughts, the wish was no sooner formed, than gratified by my Letter, which communicated to him and to the public the *state of our feelings*, and in a manner; I do assure him, perfectly *unaffected*. But it is a difficult matter to please him; for now *he hath seen me, he doth not like me.*

At the close of his *Address*, he tells me, that "after accurately examining my Letter, and carefully reconsidering the whole subject of the preceding Apology in consequence of it, he sees no occasion to alter a single sentence." Let us therefore take a view of the Apology, which is pronounced to be unaffected by it.

P. 11. "It is less the design of these papers to defend H___'s principles, than to shew, upon the best authority, that he *was earnest in what he wrote*; and that, through every part of his life, even to the very moment of his death, *he made precept and practice go hand in hand together.*"

But, surely, if the principles are not to be *defended*, if they are, as they have been represented, sceptical and atheistical, does the man, who propagated them during his life, and took the requisite measures that they should be propagated after his death – does such a man deserve commendation, because he was *in earnest*? an Apology of this kind may be offered in behalf of every felon executed at Tyburn, provided only that by dying hard, he *make precept and practice go hand in hand together.* And the A. very judiciously observes as much.

P. 10. "Many, indeed, will think, that this, however perspicuously proved, will be doing him no real honour; since in proportion to the clearness of the evidence upon this matter, it will only shew his impiety and obstinate infidelity the plainer; thereby, in the end, incurring upon him a more general disgrace."

Truly he has hit the mark. This is the very objection, which caused a friend of mine, on reading his book, to say, he should think it a less misfortune, to have the disgrace of hanging *incurred upon him*, than to have such an Apologist. And yet, in the case before us, he had a reason for making this Apology, namely, that there was no other to be made. The only question is, whether it might not have been better if he had said nothing, and suffered things to take their chance? However, it is now too late. The objection is fairly stated, and we all stand, *arrectis auribus*, in expectation of the answer – Lo, it comes – "I am of a different opinion. The terms Infidelity, impiety, and Atheism, should not be lavishly trusted from the lip" – Such a sentence (by the way_ should not have been *lavishly trusted from the pen* – "We should not presume

> To deal damnation round the land
> On each we deem our foe."

Sir, your very humble servant – I most heartily wish you a good night – here was the *jugulum causæ*, the precise point to be argued, over which I hoped to have had the honour of his good company for the evening; when, in the twinkling of an eye, he slips through my hands, like an eel, and is out of sight, in the mud.

We are not about to *deal damnation* on any man. But are there not such things as Infidelity, Impiety, and Atheism? And are not the writings of Mr. H. justly chargeable with them? These are the questions.

The A. knows, as well as I do, that Mr. H___'s Essays contain arguments downright Epicurean, against the being of a God. Some of them are mentioned in the *Summary*, at the end of the Letter to Dr. Smith, and no notice is taken of the matter. In the *Natural History of Religion* Dr. Hurd thought our philosopher was approaching towards the *borders* of Theism. But I never could find that he penetrated far into the *country*. These same arguments stand to this hour unretracted; the Essays which contain them are published and republished with the rest; whether, at the hour of death, he thought there was a God, or thought there was none, we have not a single hint given us; and concerning his posthumous papers,[2] the A. informs us, in his dedication, "there is every reason to believe they turn upon similar researches with such as have been already printed; or, as it is more likely, they may carry his philosophy still nearer to THAT POINT, which he might not think it DISCREET to *push too vigorously* in his life time." New discoveries in irreligion, then, it seems, still remain to be made. They who have duly considered the *vigour* displayed by Mr. H. in his life time, are rather at a loss to conceive, what THAT POINT may be, to which, by posthumous efforts, his *philosophy* is to be *carried*. It must lie somewhere

---

[2]   These have been since published.

Beyond the realms of Chaos and old Night!

Discretion is, undoubtedly, as Sir John Falstaffe says, *the better part of valour*; but really, in these days of freedom, there is scarce a possibility of it's ever being called for. Something, however, is to come, which the A. supposes will occasion more CHRISTIAN *clamour*. When we are so severely *pinched*, he imagines we shall *cry out*. – Certainly, it cannot be thought we are *lavish* of the terms Infidelity, Impiety, and Atheism, when we apply them to such proceedings as these. What other terms can we apply, or would he himself wish us to apply? And he gravely apologizes for their author, by telling us, he was *consistent*, he was *in earnest*, he *died* as he *lived*, and left blasphemies to be published after his death, which he dared not to publish while he was yet alive. Whom shall we most admire, the Philosopher or his Apologist?

LETTER II.

Our A. observes, Dear Sir, p. 11. "Whatever might be the force of Mr. H__'s *faith*, no one, it is conjectured, will charge him with having neglected *good works*. I do not pretend (adds he) to say how far those *are*, or are *not* sufficient."

Indeed I believe there will be no absolute necessity, upon this occasion, of going deep into the controversy concerning *faith and works*. The character in which Mr. H. principally appeared, and on which he chiefly valued himself, was that of an *author* . He passed his life in *writing*; the effects of his writings are visible in his worthy Apologist, and many others; they are likely to go down to posterity. An unwearied endeavour to propagate the principles contained in those writings, is what we can never consent to dignify with the appellation of a *good work*. To worship, to love, and to serve God, oneself, is the first of good works; to teach and incite others to do the same, is the second. To renounce every thing of this kind, oneself, is the first of evil works; and the second is like unto it, to tempt and seduce others, that they may fall after the same example of unbelief. This is the employment of that person, whom the A. mentions, as having joined with the *dancing master*, and the *perfumer*, in compounding a system of manners, recommended by the late Earl of Chesterfield.[3] He might possibly divert himself in that way, at his leisure hours; but when he set to business in good earnest, the issue was, AN ENQUIRY CONCERNING HUMAN UNDERSTANDING.

The A. is fond of citing two lines, which have been often cited by others, with a similar view –

---

[3] P. 112. '- A system which seems to have been pillaged from the dancing-master, the perfumer, and the devil.'

For modes of faith let graceless zealots fight,
His can't be wrong, whose life is in the right.

The Christian faith, at it's first appearance, endured the trial of ten perse-cutions, and triumphed over the wit, wisdom, and power of the whole Roman empire. Offered openly to the inspection and examination of the world, it has now stood it's ground above seventeen hundred years. The A. hardly expects it should at length fall before a couplet of Mr. Pope. Poets, he knows, are not upon oath; and *one for sense, and one for rhyme*, is often a fair composition. The verses rhyme well; but as to sense, that is another question. Their author somewhere tells us, that in reading religious controversy, he still found himself to agree with the last author he perused. One cannot therefore well take him for a guide in these matters. The bright son of the morning fell from his exalted station in the heavens; and he, who penned MESSIAH, was afterwards unfortu-nately duped by the sophistry of Bolingbroke. "Evil communications corrupt good manners."

As to the verses in hand, I know not that they were designed to extend by any means so far as, by the present application, the A. means to extend them. If they were, the proposition contained in them will be this; that provided a man discharge the relative and social offices, it matters not what deity he acknowl-edges and worships; or whether he acknowledge and worship any.

I am sorry I should be obliged to go back to a thing so vulgar and antiquated, as my CATECHISM. But so it happens – I cannot forget, that, when a boy, *I learned two things, my duty towards God, and my duty towards my neighbour.* And, from that day to this, it never entered into my head, that the performance of the *latter* would atone for the neglect of the *former*. Surely one might as well say, the performance of the *former* would atone for the breach of the *latter*. But the A. will never allow one; and we cannot submit to allow the other. What? Shall we make a conscience of discharging our duty to men like ourselves, and none of discharging that to our Maker, our Redeemer, our God? Is it reckoned praise worthy, generous, noble, great, and good, to love and celebrate an earthly parent or benefactor; and can it be deemed a point of indifference, whether we believe or deny, whether we bless or blaspheme our heavenly and eternal Father and Friend, who gives us life, and breath, and all things, in this world, and invites us to a far more happy and glorious state of existence in another? May we adore Jehovah, or Baal; the Creator of the Universe, or a Monkey, or Matter, or Chance, or Nothing, as the whim takes us, and be blameless? Tell it not to the believers; publish it not among the Christians!

The matter of fact is – that *life* cannot be *in the right*, which is spent in *doing wrong*. And if to question all the doctrines of Religion, even to the providence and existence of a God, and to put Morality on no other foot than that of UTILITY – if to do this, be not to do *wrong* – then farewell all distinction between right and wrong, for evermore. To maintain and diffuse the truth of

God, is to *do his will*; to deny, corrupt, or hinder it, is to *work iniquity*; and a life so employed is a *wicked life* – perhaps the *most* wicked, that can be imagined. For what comparison is there between one who commits a crime of which he may repent, or, at worst, it may die with him; and one who, though he do not himself commit it, teaches and encourages all the world to commit it, by removing out of the way the strongest sanctions and obligations to the contrary, in writings which may carry on the blessed work from generation to generation? Let not these errors be called errors of *speculation* only. Action flows from speculation. No man ventures upon sin, till he has, for the time at least, adopted some false principle. And

> "when men begin to look about for arguments in vindication of impiety and immorality, such speculations as those of Mr. Hume become interesting, and can hardly fail of a powerful and numerous patronage. The corrupt judge; the prostituted courtier; the statesman, who enriches himself by the plunder and blood of his country; the petty-fogger, who fattens on the spoils of the fatherless and widow; the oppressor, who, to pamper his own beastly appetite, abandons the deserving peasant to beggary and despair; the hypocrite, the debauchee, the gamester, the blasphemer – all prick up their ears, when they are told, that a celebrated author has written Essays, containing such doctrines, and leading to such consequences."[4]

Weighed against a conduct like this, the moralities of social life (a system of which, by the way, according to Mr. H. every man is left to compound for himself) are dust upon the balance; they are like the salutation of Joab, when he smote Amasa to the heart –

> "And Joab said to Amasa, Art thou in health, my brother? And Joab took Amasa by the beard with the right hand, *to kiss him*. But Amasa took no heed to the sword that was in Joab's hand; so he smote him therewith in the fifth rib, and shed out his bowels to the ground."[5] –

In short, if faith in God be not the effect of superstition and imposture, which no man has yet proved it to be, we are bound to regard it as our most valuable possession, and to esteem those who would rob the world of it as the worst of thieves, however, towards each other, they may practise what the A. styles the *duties*, the *decencies*, and the *charities*.[6]

---

[4] [James Beattie (1735–1803), *Essay on the Nature and Immutability of Truth* (1770), Chapter 1.]

[5] 2 Sam. xx. 9.

[6] P. 13.

P. 12. "Perhaps it is one of the very worst circumstances against Christianity, that very few of it's professors were ever either so moral, so humane, or could so philosophically govern their passions, as the sceptical DAVID HUME."

And yet, we do not every day hear of a *Christian* running around a counter with his drawn sword after a *Reviewer*, or quitting a room on the entrance of his antagonist.[7] It appears, from a variety of instances, that Mr. H. when his literary character was concerned, could by no means "govern his passions so philosophically" as his A. wishes to have it believed. But it is not my desire to depreciate any thing that might be really commendable in him. Thus much only I will venture to assert, that whatever it was, the merit of it is not due to his philosophical principles. These afford no motives to restrain men who have once embraced them from any vices to which their constitutions may happen to incline. It is too much for the same person to excel in every branch. It is enough, if he point the way. All evil beings are not *immoral*. Lord Chesterfield's friend, himself, mentioned above, offends not in the articles of eating, wine, or women; he is differently employed. He is employed in tempting others to offend.

The A. tells us, "Mr. H___'s most abstract researches were in favour of a behaviour perfectly irreproachable. – Whoever is acquainted with Mr. H___'s writings will bear witness, that he was a lover of decency, order, and decorum – It would be the drudgery of a day to detect a single light sentence in H."[8]

I shall transcribe two or three sentences which lie pretty near together, in a *Dialogue* subjoined to his *Enquiry into the Principles of Morals.*

"There is almost as great difficulty, I acknowledge, to justify French, as *Greek gallantry*; except only, that the former is much more natural and agreeable than the latter. But our neighbours, it seems, have resolved to sacrifice some of the *domestic* to the *sociable* pleasures; and to prefer *ease, freedom*, and an open commerce, to a strict fidelity and constancy. *These ends are both good*, and are sometimes difficult to reconcile; nor need we be surprized, if the customs of nations incline too much, sometimes to the one side, and sometimes to the other[9] – It is needless to dissemble: the consequences of a very free commerce between the sexes, and of their living much

---

[7] [In their reviews of *The Life of David Hume*, the *Monthly Review* and the *London Review* both relate a story of Hume approaching reviewer Jacob Robinson with a sword in response to an unfavourable review of the *Treatise*. Pratt himself, in the *Supplement to the life of David Hume* (1777), reports that Hume would leave a room if William Tytler was there. These three discussions are contained in this collection.]

[8] P. 106. 110.

[9] Essays Vol. ii. P. 397. edit. 1772.

together, will often terminate in intrigues and gallantry. We must sacrifice somewhat of the *useful*, if we be very anxious to obtain all the *agreeable* qualities; and cannot pretend to reach alike *every kind of advantage*. Instances of licence, daily multiplying, will weaken the scandal with the one sex, and teach the other, by degrees, to adopt the famous maxim of La Fontaine with regard to female infidelity, *that if one knows it, it is but a small matter; if one knows it not, it is nothing.*"[10]

Verily, as Lord Foppington says to his brother, in the stage play – A NICE MARALITY, TAM, STAP MY VITALS!

When we consider these sentences as proceeding from the pen of "the first philosopher of the age," in his palmary and capital work, designed to settle the principles of morality on their only proper foundation, "it would be the drudgery of a MONTH" to find any thing in the system of Chesterfield and his three associates, "the dancing-master, the perfumer, and the devil," better calculated to multiply new *connections*, and dissolve old ones; any thing, that so much deserves the profoundest acknowledgements from – the gentlemen of DOCTORS COMMONS.

LETTER III.

It may still perhaps be asked, Dear Sir, how it should happen, that when Mr. H___'s principles were so bad, his practices should be no worse? Let me offer the solution given of such a phænomenon in the intellectual world, by a very ingenious and sagacious writer, who had not only studied mankind in general, but, as it should seem, had bestowed some pains upon the very case now before us.

"This fact hath been regarded as unaccountable: that sober men, of morals apparently unblameable, should madly unhinge the great principles of religion and society, without any visible motive or advantage. But by looking a little farther into human nature, we shall easily resolve this seeming paradox. These writers are generally men of speculation and industry; and therefore, though they give themselves up to the dictates of their ruling passion, yet that ruling passion commonly leads to the tract of abstemious manners. That desire of distinction and superiority, so natural to man, breaks out into a thousand various and fantastic shapes; and in each of these, according as it is directed, becomes a virtue or a vice. In times of luxury and dissipation, therefore, when every tenet of irreligion is greedily embraced,

---

[10] Essays Vol. ii. P. 402.

what road to present applause can lie so open and secure, as that of disgracing religious belief? Especially if the writer help forward the vices of the times, by relaxing *morals*, as well as destroying *principle*. Such a writer can have little else to do, but to new model the paradoxes of ancient scepticism, in order to figure it in the world, and be regarded, by the smatterers in literature, and adepts in folly, as a prodigy of parts and learning. Thus his vanity becomes deeply criminal, and is execrated by the wise and good; because it is gratified at the expence of his country's welfare. But the consolation which degenerate manners receive from his fatal tenets, is repaid by eager praise: and vice impatiently drinks in and applauds his hoarse and boding voice, while, like a raven, he sits croaking universal death, despair, and annihilation to the human kind."

But taking the account of Mr. H___'s manners as his friends have given it, to say "that few of the professors of Christianity ever equalled him in morality, humanity, and the government of their passions," is certainly going a great deal too far. Thousands, in the first ages of the Gospel, gave all their goods to feed the poor; renounced, indeed as well as word, the world and the flesh, and joyfully met death in it's most horrid forms, for the love of their Redeemer. On the same principle, unnumbered multitudes, in every succeding age, have manfully sustained the heaviest calamities of human life, and with faith unfeigned, and hope that maketh not ashamed, yielded up their souls into the hands of their Creator. Scenes of this kind are daily and hourly passing in the chambers of the sick and dying, as they, whose office it is to visit those chambers, well know. To others they must remain unknown, for want of biographers to record them. Every Christian who lives in piety and charity, does not favour the public with – HIS OWN LIFE. Every Christian, who expires in peace and hope, has not the happiness of a Dr. Smith to pen the story of his death –

Full many a gem of purest ray serene,
The dark unfathom'd caves of ocean bear;
Full many a flower is born to blush unseen,
And waste it's sweetness in the desert air.
Far from the madding crowd's ignoble strife,
Their sober wishes never learn'd to stray;
Along the cool sequester'd vale of life
They kept the noiseless tenor of their way.

"Christianity," says a learned writer,

"has in every age produced good effects on thousands and ten thousands, whose lives are not recorded in history; which is, for the most part, a register of the vices, the follies, and the quarrels of those who made a figure and a noise in the world; insomuch that Socrates, at the close of his work, observes, that if men were honest and peaceable, historians would be undone for want of materials. "

But, whether the professors of a religion be many or few; whether they be influenced by the spirit of it, or not; whether they be sincere, or hypocrites; whether they be detected, or undetected; the religion is still the same: it does not change with the changing tempers, dispositions, and interests of mankind, in different times and places; nor is it to be charged with the guilt of practices, against which it protests in every page. No demonstration in Euclid can be clearer than this.

To account for the opposition often so visible between the lives and the opinions of Christians, one must enumerate all the various methods, by which, in matters of moral and spiritual concern, men are wont to impose upon themselves. Appetite and passion, sloth and interest, will work wonders in this way – wonders, of which he has no idea, who has not been accustomed, with this view, to contemplate the conduct of those around him, and impartially to scrutinize his own. The religion of many a person, professing Christianity, is, by these means, laid by, like a best coat, for sundays and holidays. Not a single thought occurs of the necessity there is for its being brought into the daily and hourly concerns of common life. It is a speculative belief, deposited in the understanding, to which it's owner recurs, when he has nothing else to do; he finds it where he left it, and is fully satisfied with its being there, instead of bearing it always about him, in his heart and affections, as an active principle, ready for use, to operate at all seasons, and on all occasions. He will even spend his days in discoursing and disputing upon the sublimest doctrines, and most holy precepts of religion, his own life still continuing unreformed. Nay, what is yet more strange, he will preach seriously, earnestly, affectionately, and repeatedly, against a failing, to which he himself is notoriously subject, and every one who hears him knows him to be so. It follows not necessarily, that he is designedly playing the hypocrite, and acting a part. He has some method of concealing himself from himself, or of excusing himself to himself. He does not *see* that he is the person, against whom all his own arguments are pointed. He does not *think* of it. He stands in need of a friend – or an enemy – to tell him – THOU ART THE MAN. – This may seem to be a species of madness; but this is human nature. Let me conclude with a story.

A friend of mine was much afflicted with a dangerous disorder, part hereditary, and part the fruit of his own industry. He sent for one of the best physicians in the kingdom, who, having discoursed, greatly to his satisfaction, on the excellency of medicine in general, and of a medicine proper for that disorder in particular, wrote his prescription, and took his leave. My friend, who was a scholar, had a learned gentleman with him at the time; and the doctor was hardly out of the door, before a very warm controversy began between them, concerning the *style* of the prescription, whether it were *classical*, or not. This and the virtues of the medicine were now the constant subjects of my friend's conversation, and he inveighed, with great zeal and indignation, against the folly of those, who would languish under disease, when there was such a remedy to be had. The distemper, mean while, increased upon himself, and began to seize the vitals. The doctor was again sent for; and knowing his patient to be a remarkably ABSENT man, Pray, Sir, said he, give me leave to ask you one question – Have you TAKEN the medicine? A summons to the bar of judgment could hardly have astonished my friend more than this question. He awoke as one out of a dream, and very honestly owned, he had been so occupied in talking and writing about it, and recommending it to others, that he had really quite forgotten that part of the prescription. He did indeed recollect to have once tasted the draught, but finding it rather bitter, a flavour always disagreeable to him, he had set it by again, trusting, it seems, for his cure, to the virtues which might escape the cork, as it stood upon the mantle-piece. – You see how easy it is for him who possesses the medicine to be like him who possesses it not; the medicine itself continuing all the while perfectly irreproachable.

And now, if you please, Dear Sir, we will take our leave of the Apology; for I have no design to meddle with the farrago of *extraneous* matters which it contains, respecting *gallantry, flattery, dedications, &c. &c. &c. and as to the crude and angry remarks at the end of it, on the Letter to Dr. Smith – valeant quantum valere possunt!* – I will trust any man with them, if, during the perusal, he will only hold in his hand the pamphlet to which they relate – The Apology is indeed, both for matter and manner, sentiment and language, so mean and wretched a performance, that one cannot sufficiently wonder, how any person, accustomed to write, could permit such a piece to come abroad, with all it's imperfections on its head. I have selected those parts which afforded room for enlarging on topics useful to be discussed, and have now done with it for ever.

WILLIAM DODD AND HUME

72
WILLIAM DODD:
THOUGHTS IN PRISON

William Dodd, *Thoughts in prison: in five parts. Viz. The imprisonment. The retrospect. Publick punishment. The trial. Futurity. By the Rev. William Dodd, LLD. To which are added, ... other miscellaneous pieces.* London: printed for Edward and Charles Dilly; and G. Kearsly, 1777, iii, 232 p.
Selections from Week the Fifth; from *Thoughts in Prison*, Philadelphia, Robert Johnson, 1806.

William Dodd (1729–1777) was an Anglican clergyman whose extravagant lifestyle outstripped his legitimate financial resources. He began his career by successfully raising funds for religious charities, and gradually attracted a large following. He acquired a taste for lavish feasts and was thus nicknamed "the Macaroni Parson." In spite of the scandals that surrounded his lifestyle, his congregation supported him. Dodd was finally removed from the clergy because of a mismanaged scheme of his wife to raise money. When his continuing debts became too great, he forged the name of his former student, the young Lord Chesterfield, on a bond for 4,200 pounds. The evidence incontestable, he was quickly arrested. During his trial, he gave a pious appeal expressing his good intentions. People were initially outraged that, through this immoral deed, Dodd betrayed his divine calling. Public opinion soon reversed, though, and petitions circulated supporting a pardon, one of which had 23,000 signatures. Dodd was convinced that his sentence would never be carried out. Nevertheless, King George III chose not to reverse the conviction, and on June 27, 1777 Dodd was hanged. Even as the noose was placed around his neck, he quietly asked the hangman to specially arrange it to avoid complete strangulation. He also had a surgeon on the side ready to revive him. But, when the gallows floor dropped, the heavy crowd of spectators caused a delay for the surgeon, and the plot failed. While in prison, Dodd composed his final work, which is in unrhymed verse. In a section titled "Week the Fifth: On Futurity" he attacks Hume for rejecting Christianity and the notion of a future state. According to Dodd, Hume was "Hoodwink'd by dark infatuation's veil."

Reviews of *Thoughts in Prison* were mixed. The *Critical Review* expressed compassion for Dodd, and was convinced by the sincerity of his repentance:

In almost every page of this work there is an appearance of the author's unfeigned contrition, piety, and benevolence. He speaks of his guilt with the deepest sensibility, of his prosecutors without acrimony, of his wife and friends with the warmest affection. He mentions his concern in several charitable institutions.... But we do not mean to offer an apology for the author's criminal conduct: we only express the sentiments, which have suggested themselves to us, on the perusal of these melancholy reflections, his Thoughts in Prison. [*Critical Review*, 1777, Vol. 44, pp. 218–221]

This review was reprinted in the *Weekly Magazine or Edinburgh Amusement* (October 30, 1777, Vol. 38, pp. 119–120). Writing for the *London Review*, William Kenrick felt that Dodd's condemnation of Hume was hypocritical:

Let this delinquent divine also have been as sincere a believer, as he may, it is with an ill grace that in his circumstances he casts censure on infidels of any kind, particularly on such characters as the late Mr. Hume. There appears farther something egregiously vain and self-important in his writing a long prayer the night previous to his suffering, if indeed he can be supposed at such a time to have amused himself with scribbling. [*London Review*, September 1777, Vol. 6, pp. 226–229]

The *Monthly Review* suggests that Dodd's final repentance is suspect:

God only knows what really passed in the heart of a man (arrived at the gates of death) who is, universally, said to have spent his whole life in a continual exercise of the most consummate hypocrisy. [*Monthly Review*, October 1777, Vol. 57, pp. 328–329]

Dodd became an important symbol which contradicted the long-held view that Christians were morally superior to infidels. Dodd's situation was sometimes contrasted to that of Hume's – an infidel who, unlike Dodd, was moral. The contrast between Dodd and Hume is explored in *A Philosophical and Religious Dialogue* (1778), and Dodd's execution is discussed by James Boswell in *The Life of Samuel Johnson* (1791), both contained in this collection. An exceptionally popular work, Dodd's *Thoughts in Prison* went through over 20 editions by 1850.

WEEK THE FIFTH.
FUTURITY.

...
    HUME, thou are gone!
Amidst the catalogue of those mow'd down
By Time's huge scythe, late noted; thou be sure,
Wast not forgotten! Author, thou has gain'd
Thy vast ambition's summit. Fame was thine;
Wealth too, beyond thy amplest wish's bound
Encompass'd thee; and lo, the pageant ends!
For who without compassion's generous tear
Thy mind at once capacious and humane,
Can view, to truth, to hope immortal dead?
Thy penetrating reason, subtle, strong,
Hoodwink'd by dark infatuation's veil;
And all thy fine and manly sense employ'd,
Even on eternity's thrice awful verge,
To trifle with the wonders of a state
Respectably alarming! Of a state
Whose being gives to man, had given thee,
Accepted by the humble hand of faith,
True glory, solid fame, and boundless wealth!
Treasures that wax not old.
    Oh the high blessings of humility!
Man's first and richest grace! Of virtue, truth,
Knowledge, and exaltation, certain source,
And most abundant; pregnant of all good;
And, poor in show, to treasures infinite
Infallibly conducting her sure gift!
So, when old Hyems has deform'd the year,
We view, on fam'd Burgundia's craggy cliffs,
The slow vines, scarce distinct, on the brown earth
Neglected lie and groveling; promise poor
From plant so humble, of the swelling grape
In glowing clusters purpling o'er the hills;
When all impregnating rolls forth the sun,
And from the mean stalk pours a luscious flood
Of juice nectareous thro' the laughing land!
    Nervous essayist! haply had thy pen,
Of masculine ability, this theme
Pursu'd intelligent; from lowly heart
Delineating true the features mild

Of genuine humility; mankind,
Now wilder'd by thy sophistry, had bless'd
And honour'd well thy teaching; whilst thyself
Secure had sail'd and happy; nor been cast
On pride's black rocks, or empty scorn's bleak shore!
Proud scorn, how poor and blind! How it at once
Destroys the sight, and makes us think we see;
While desperate ridicule in wit's wild hands
Implants a dangerous weapon! How it warps
From clear discernment, and conclusions just,
Even captive reason's self! How gay soe'er,
(Ah misplac'd gait, on such a theme,)
In life's last hour! on Charon's crazy bark,
On Tartarus and Elysium, and the pomp
Solemn and dreaded of dark Pagans hell;
Thy reasoning powers knew well, full well to draw
Deductions true from fables gross as these,
By poet's fancy heighten'd. Well thou knew'st
The deep intelligence, the solid truth
Conceal'd beneath the mystic tale; well knew'st
Fables like these, familiar to mankind
In every nation, every clime, through earth
Widely disseminate, through earth proclaim'd
In language strong, intelligent and clear,
"A future state retributive." Thou knew'st,
That in each age the wise embrac'd the truth,
And gloried in a hope, how dim soe'er,
Which thou amidst the blaze, the noon day blaze
Of christian information, madly scorn'dst
And diedst insulting. Hail, of ancient times
Worthies and fam'd believers! PLATO, hail!
And thou, immortal SOCRATES! Of Rome
Prime ornament and boast, my TULLY, hail!
Friend and companion of my studious life,
In eloquence and sound philosophy
Alike superlative! With minds enlarg'd,
Yet teachable and modest, how ye sought,
You and your kindred souls, how daily dug
For wisdom, as the labourer in the mines!
How grop'd, in fancy's and dark fable's night,
Your way assiduous, painful. How discern'd
By the mind's trembling, unassisted sight,
Or, haply, aided by a scatter'd ray

Or distant revelation, half extinct
The glimmer of a dawn; the twinkling star
Of day light far remote; how sigh'd sincere
For fuller information; and how long'd,
How panted for admission to that world
O're which hung veils impervious! Sages, yes,
Your search ingenuous proves it; every page
Immortal of your writings speaks this truth.
Hear, ye minute philosophers; ye herd
Of mean half thinkers, who chief glory place
In boldness to arraign and judge your GOD,
And think that singularity is sense,
Here, and be humbled. SOCRATES himself,[1]
And him you boast your master, would have fallen
In humble thankful reverence at the feet
Of JESUS, and drank wisdom from his tongue. ...

[1] Alluding to his celebrated wish of divine illumination from some superior power.

73
A PHILOSOPHICAL AND RELIGIOUS DIALOGUE

A philosophical and religious dialogue in the shades, between Mr. Hume and Dr. Dodd. With notes by the editor. London: printed for the editor, and sold by Hooper and Davis, London; Charles Elliot, Edinburgh, and T. Wilson, York, 1778, 37, [1] p.[1]
Complete; from 1778 edition.

William Dodd's arrest and execution took place around the time that Adam Smith's "Letter to Strahan" and Samuel Jackson Pratt's *Apology* were published. Since Hume's and Dodd's deaths were both sensational public events, it was inevitable that contrasts would be drawn between the two characters: Dodd was a religious believer, but a moral degenerate, whereas Hume was a religious infidel but, according to Smith, the model of a "perfectly wise and virtuous man." At the heart of both paradoxes was the longstanding assumption that religion and virtue go hand in hand: belief in an afterlife is essential to ensure proper moral conduct. In their own ways, Dodd and Hume each defied this view. In early 1778, this issue was addressed in an anonymous pamphlet titled *A Philosophical and Religious Dialogue in the Shades, Between Mr. Hume and Dr. Dodd.* Throughout the dialogue, the spirits of Hume and Dodd discuss their respective motives for religious infidelity and moral corruption. The dialogue opens with Dodd doing much of the speaking, explaining the basis of his moral corruption. He then suggests that there is a natural harmony between religion and philosophy, particularly insofar as "repentance, mediation and forgiveness" are essential ingredients of Christianity as well as other religious systems. Hume suggests that people would take advantage of that system by pursuing their favourite vices throughout life, and asking forgiveness before dying.

---

[1] Title page: A | PHILOSOPHICAL AND RELIGIOUS | DIALOGUE | IN THE SHADES, | BETWEEN | MR. HUME AND DR. DODD. | WITH NOTES BY THE EDITOR. | LONDON: | PRINTED FOR THE EDITOR, | AND SOLD BY HOOPER AND DAVIS, No. 25, LUDGATE-HILL, LONDON; CHARLES ELLIOT, EDINBURGH, AND T. WILSON, YORK, | MDCCLXXVIII. | [Price 2s.]

Dodd responds that "continued habits of depravity" are hard to break, which reduces the chances of someone engaging in a last minute act of repentance.

The dialogue shifts to Hume's views, and begins by tracing the development of his infidelity. He states that he was especially influenced by the model of ancient and venerable philosophers who threw off superstition, the chaos produced by Christian fanatics, the incommensurability of miracle accounts in different religions, the tolerant spirit of polytheism, and the reprehensible conduct of the Christian clergy. Hume adds, though, that he never went "so far as to deny the existence of a Deity, or the unalterable distinction between vice and virtue." Instead, he sought to establish "the rational principles of pure theism." Hume next explains the development of his moral character and states that laws and punishment are the most powerful sanctions of virtue in society: "society is more obliged to him who builds a prison than to him who founds a chapel." Hume feels that, on balance, his writings have done more good to society than harm. He concludes, speaking to Dodd, that "Posterity will review your character with a high degree of abhorrence on account of your vices, and the pernicious tendency of my metaphysical system will considerably lessen their admiration of my virtues and genius."

Reviews of the dialogue were largely neutral. The *Critical Review* concluded its brief review stating that "This ingenious performance is intended to furnish an antidote against the pernicious influence of the opinions of the one, and the morals of the other" (January 1778, Vol. 45, pp. 73–74). The *London Review* states that "We can say little more of this publication than is said in the advertisement prefixed to it" (January 1778, Vol. 7, p. 69). Writing for the *Monthly Review*, William Enfield found the pamphlet interesting, but not profound:

> Though the Writer of this dialogue does not enter into a profound examination of Mr. Hume's principles, nor into a minute inquiry into Dr. Dodd's real character, he suggests many pertinent observations and reflections, and expresses them in an agreeable style. His professed intention is to furnish a slight antidote against the pernicious influence of Mr. Hume's opinions, and of Dr. Dodd's morals. Whether an antidote so slight can be expected to produce any material effect, may be doubted. [*Monthly Review*, April 1778, Vol. 58, p. 312]

The following is from the 1778 and only edition of this work.

A

PHILOSOPHICAL AND RELIGIOUS

D I A L O G U E

IN THE

S H A D E S,

BETWEEN

MR. HUME AND DR. DODD,

WITH

NOTES BY THE EDITOR.

TROS TYRIUSQUE MIHI NULLO DISCRIMINE AGETUR.

LONDON:
PRINTED FOR THE EDITOR,
AND SOLD BY
HOOPER AND DAVIS, No. 25, LUDGATE-HILL, LONDON,
CHARLES ELLIOT, EDINBURGH, AND T. WILSON, YORK.
MDCCLXXVIII.
[Price 2s.]

Mr. Hume and Dr. Dodd are two singular and opposite characters. Their extensive abilities, their dissimilar opinions, morals, and fortunes form a striking contrast. Though this dialogue contains nothing so profound as the reader might perhaps naturally expect, it may furnish a slight antidote against the pernicious influence of the opinions of the one, and of the morals of the other. Mr. Hume is a splendid and interesting object to the eye. The memory of Dr. Dodd, it must be confessed, does not fill the imagination with grateful ideas, but it affords us matter of serious reflection.

—

A
DIALOGUE
IN THE
SHADES.

MR. HUME: Dr. Dodd! Your most humble servant. – I am a little surprized to see you here. When I left the upper regions, I understood that you was in perfect health, and active in preaching the gospel to the ladies. But human life is precarious.

DR. DODD: Mr. Hume, this rencounter is unexpected. You must excuse my not entering so abruptly into the particulars of my unfortunate story: but really, Sir, I am equally surprized to meet with you here. I thought you had long ago passed the irremeable gulf. But we in the other world are but very imperfectly informed of the destination of spirits, and the modes of a future state. Pray, Sir, what cause has so long detained you amid these dreary scenes?

MR. HUME: That question I would gladly evade. I amused myself somewhat inconsiderately before my death, with inventing ingenious and ludicrous reasons, why Charon ought to permit me a longer stay in the world. Now, to my no small vexation, I find a spirit of a severe countenance that is stationed here feigns several serious causes for retarding my passage into the Elysian abodes.

DR. DODD: Such as –

MR. HUME: Pardon me, Doctor, they are of no consequence to you. You must not here busy yourself with a fruitless curiosity. Your own affairs will, I presume, give you trouble enough.

DR. DODD: Alas! they have given me much trouble and exquisite anguish already. But, Mr. Hume, it is a great consolation to me to find that you still exist as a self-conscious being, and that there is some hope beyond the grave. I always shrunk at the idea of the dissolution or annihilation of the soul. But as you have had now some experience in the spiritual world, and your views of things must be enlarged, permit me to ask your present sentiments of those great principles of religion and philosophy, concerning which you raised so many doubts in your life-time.

MR. HUME: I perceive these subjects may be interesting to you, but before we enter into such serious conversation, I must insist on knowing that part of your story to which I am a stranger.

DR. DODD: Your request, however reasonable, touches my breast with poignant regret. "The name of chesterfield how can I repeat!"

MR. HUME: I suppose you mean your old friend and patron Lord Chesterfield. Had you been here sometime ago, you might have seen that celebrated personage in great distress wandering about in company with three famous French ladies, all of them soiled with stygian clay. Ah! how changed from him, the gay, the witty, the elegant Chesterfield! When I beheld that man, who was the ornament of social life, a dejected and melancholy spectre, I could not help bewailing the fate of human nature. I hope his lordship fares better now. He used much address, and urged many refined reasons for being admitted into the realms of bliss; but all his wit and political ability availed him nothing with this inexorable spirit. At last he mentioned several acts of true benevolence, which seemed to reflect much honour upon his heart. Upon this the disgraced nobleman was received into favour.

DR. DODD: Ah! Sir, I mean not him – his successor – but my crime, my shame, my punishment – Oh! agonizing thoughts! Forgery – my brain will madden –

MR. HUME: In my life-time I had no doubt but that your brain was mad with fanaticism; and I always esteemed the virtue of men of that complexion, to be of a very ambiguous and frail nature. But I feel for a man of your parts, rank and character. It would seem that you have experienced no mercy from your country.

DR. DODD: In the beginning of my misfortunes, the general voice of the people was against me. The loud call of impartial justice drowned the soft whispers of pity. The circumstances of ecclesiastical dignity, of learning and character, instead of exciting compassion, were, to a nation jealous of that great principle of liberty, the original equality of mankind, so many arguments against my being pardoned.[2] Afterwards indeed my sufferings and sorrows melted the hearts of multitudes, and produced many petitions in my behalf. For such is the peculiar progress of the feelings of my countrymen, that the very man whom they in the first emotions of resentment and odium, hurry away to punishment, they would gladly rescue, when they see him overwhelmed with misery and woe. However, their petitions, and my plea of thirty years spent in

[2]   "Hang him, exclaimed the peasant and the tradesman; were I in his case, they would hang me without any ceremony." But in the extremity of his sufferings, the general cry was, "pardon him; he has done much good to society; his intentions were not evil; he has made restitution; his repentance is sincere." the gentle feelings and the ingenious sophistry of pity reflect lustre on our nature, but it is justice alone which can secure our rights and our laws.

cultivating humanity and religion were unavailing. The guardians of the laws were inexorable. I suffered as a common malefactor. I hope that mankind have reaped some benefit and instruction from my life. My death, I am sure, may teach them a severe lesson of wisdom and virtue.

MR. HUME: Your idea,[3] Doctor, of mitigating the rigor of penal laws was worthy of a philosophical sage. Some reformation of that kind is still wanted in the polished countries of Europe: but till such a reformation is effected, I am of opinion that the established laws ought to be impartially executed. The clemency of the sovereign may perhaps with propriety temper their severity on some occasions; but I am afraid the circumstances of your case were not such as to deserve the mild interposition of royal mercy. Ah! Doctor, I know you have often reproached me for my principles; I could now in my turn reproach you for your conduct, but I should dishonour the name of a philosopher were I capable of indulging so mean a revenge. Alas! the characters of men are in general so chequered with foibles, that we seldom have much reason to be insolent and forward in upbraiding any individual. For my own part, in all my various delineations of human character, I have endeavoured to paint impartially the defects and virtues of every person.[4] This habit has inured me to moderation and candor in judging of men. Nay, I am inclined to think that they are with respect to virtue and estimation, much nearer an equality than is generally supposed.

DR. DODD: Mr. Hume, though I have tarnished the whole contexture of my better days by the last part of my life, yet I should be sorry to lay aside all distinction of character. I conceive that nature originally bestows on men different degrees of excellence, and that such original superiority of mind may be pushed much farther by culture and habit. So far I coincide with you as to think that the most elevated spirits[5] and the most celebrated geniuses (among whom I cannot class myself) have weaknesses and foibles, which sufficiently depress human pride and vanity.

---

[3] The Doctor has written a sermon professedly on this subject. Whoever would wish to see it treated at large may consult "The Essay on Crimes and Punishments," written by that profound and amiable philosopher the Marquiss Beccaria.

[4] Mr. Hume has given us many just and masterly paintings of human minds; but he seems to have carried this love of impartiality to an extreme. the tints of virtue and vice (if I may so speak) are in his pictures so insensibly blended as to reduce the originals too near an equality. The authors of the Biographia Britannica are accused of the same fault. Tacitus, Gibbons, &c. have a very different style and manner. With a decisive penetration they seize the predominant features, and boldly determine the complexion of the character either towards virtue or vice.

[5] Mr. Melmoth in his elegant translation of Cicero's Letters has the following note: "To turn from the actions of Cicero to his writings, is changing our point of view, it must be acknowledged, extremely to his advantage. It is on this side indeed, that his character can never be too warmly admired: and admired it will undoubtedly be, so

MR. HUME: I know that it is as impossible to meet with two minds, as it is with two faces exactly similar. I grant you likewise that some men are born with happier dispositions and more splendid talents than others. Neither can it be denied that education, and the occurrences of life have powerful effects on the mind. Yet when we come to determine from the combined influence of all these circumstances the comparative merit of characters, how often do we find them upon the whole reduced nearly to the same level! There have been indeed some distinguished favourites of heaven, such as Socrates, Marcus Antoninus, &c. who seem to have been uniformly inspired and governed by a moral spirit. There may be also some anomalous monsters in nature distinguished for their immorality. But the ordinary run of mankind have a more mixed character and approach nearer to each other.

DR. DODD: Whatever deference I have for your superior understanding, I cannot in this case submit to your philosophical decision. The scripture hath taught me, that between the extremes of virtue and vice there is a long gradation of characters. Besides, you seem to have attributed all to original constitution, education and fortune, and to have overlooked what part every man has in the improvement or corruption of his own mind. I once leaned to a religious opinion which ascribed as little to human liberty as those philosophers who maintain the blind power of fate and necessity.

MR. HUME: There is some hope that after we have passed the gulf these diffi- culties which appeared so inexplicable to us in the other world may be cleared

---

long as manly eloquence and genuine philosophy have any friends. Perhaps there is something in that natural mechanism of the human frame necessary to constitute a fine genius, which is not altogether favourable to the excellencies of the heart. It is certain at least (and let it abate our envy of uncommon parts) that a great superiority of intel- lectual qualifications has not often been found in conjunction with the much nobler advantages of a moral kind." Vol. i, p. 201. Before we acquiesce in this melancholy conclusion, it were to be wished that some one would attempt a solution of the question by a deeper enquiry into the constitution of the human frame, and a more accurate survey of the history of men of genius. It is presumed (and the presumption is pleasing) that such an enquiry might lead us to the contrary conclusion. Genius has no doubt been often found united with great vices, but oftener, I think, with great virtues.

Perhaps the splendor of high abilities gives a more striking and blacker appearance to the foibles of their possessor, as the motes in a room otherwise invisible are rendered conspicuous by the beams of the sun. Had the elegant translator collected all the favourable and unfavourable circumstances relative to Cicero's character into one point of view, his judgement of that great man would perhaps have been less severe. Mr. Melmoth adopts a more liberal sentiment in another place, when giving his sanction to an observation of Monsieur Dacier concerning the fair sex, he thus expresses himself: "May I add my suffrage to that of this celebrated critic, by declaring from the same domestic experience, that uncommon knowledge and a superior under- standing are perfectly consistent with those more valuable qualities of the heart, which constitute the principal grace and ornament of the female character?" Vol. i, p. 319.

up. At present I am involved in a state of greater perplexity than ever. I am embarrassed by a commixture of old and new ideas. The enlargement of my views has disturbed my former system of opinions. But after all were a person of ordinary understanding to reflect on the contrast between my character, principles, fortunes, &c. and yours, I think you must allow that he would be at a loss to determine which he would prefer.

DR. DODD: It is to me at present an ungrateful reflection, that my example may raise such doubts and prejudices among mortals. My conduct has dishonoured my principles, and your manners have affixed a specious splendor to yours. But consider, Sir, that the blameable parts of my life were in direct contradiction to my principles. Consider likewise, that by a happy singularity your practice was inconsistent with the opinions you professed. I conceive then that the source of my errors ought not to be sought for in my religious tenets, and that your virtues ought not to be ascribed to your philosophical system. To account for these appearances we must have recourse to other causes. But still I repeat it with sorrow that the vicious spots of my life, and my ignominious exit,[6] have obscured all my virtues, and in some measure frustrated my labours for the good of mankind. When the current of popular odium runs violently against a character, the bulk of mankind cannot judge with any degree of moderation or candor. They cannot conceive him to be virtuous or vicious by halves; they even refuse him any merit from the antecedent virtues of his life, not reflecting how easy it is in the present corrupt state of human nature for a man once virtuous[7] to degenerate into vice. But upon serious reflection how little do a few unhappy exceptions like me weigh against the principles of christianity when compared with the many sublime characters formed upon that elevated and pure system?

MR. HUME: I have lately been considering whether the character of a christian and philosopher might not be happily united. I confess that I once thought the elements of christianity and philosophy such discordant materials as to refuse any cemented union. I wish however that like Locke, Bacon, Grotius, Boyle, and some other great men I had attempted to reconcile these apparent differences. It is possible after all that there may be no natural inconsistence between faith

---

[6] The fame of a great man suffers only a momentary eclipse from disgrace and an ignominious death. It afterwards breaks forth with redoubled lustre. Crimes alone can leave an indelible stain on reputation.

[7] That elegant philosopher Xenophon, accounting for the corruption and degeneracy of Critias and Alcibiades after they had forsaken the society and conversation of Socrates, enlarges on the truth of this opinion (Xenoph, Memor. Lib. I. C. 2). It is a truth which ought to be ever present to our minds, and to teach us to keep a vigilant eye over the passions. There can be no greater proof of the corruption of human nature than that the descent to vice is rapid and easy, but the re-ascent to virtue slow and laborious.

and reason. Better then had it been for you, Doctor, that you had mingled a little more of rational philosophy with your theology; better for me that my inquiries had favoured a little more of religion.

DR. DODD: Probably your cool temperament inclined you to scepticism. I must confess that an extravagant fancy and irregular passions hurried me into the other extreme of enthusiasm, which bias or inclination was not a little cherished by popular applause. My mind was naturally susceptible of the warmest impressions of religion, but it sacrificed them with equal ease to the solicitations of ardent passion. However good and benevolent my intentions might be, yet this unsteady and changeful complexion has given me the appearance of a theatrical performer in religion and virtue, rather than of a real, uniform and consistent christian. Thus the natural texture of my constitution disposed me to an irregular enthusiasm rather than to philosophic speculation and saturnine habits. Yet I do not maintain that there is any necessary opposition between faith and reason, between religion and sound philosophy.[8] On the contrary they may happily co-operate in a comprehensive and elevated mind. The eminent instances you have mentioned, are sufficient to convince us how much the mixed character of a christian and philosopher engages our admiration; they have shewn us that religion prohibits no investigations useful to mankind, or adequate to the human capacity. Yet it becomes not philosophy to encroach too far on the province of theology, or to pretend to investigate its inscrutable mysteries. We learn from ecclesiastical history, what corruption was introduced into theology by an improper coalition of christianity with the heterogeneous and mystic ideas of Platonism. Perhaps also the subtle school of Aristotle has upon the whole proved unfavourable to the same divine cause.[9]

MR. HUME: The complexion of my writings might convince you that I was not of so cold a temperament as you suppose. But to wave that question, may it not be presumed that the moral conduct of a philosopher is actuated and governed by sentiments and ideas very different from those of christianity? it may even be doubted whether his principles are not of a more sublime cast. That humiliating idea of human nature which Monsieur Paschal has carried to such an extravagant length, that despondent diffidence of its powers, and

---

[8] Let us hear with what propriety that honest and amiable enthusiast Petrarch expresses himself on this subject. "I love truth, says he, and not sects. I am sometimes a Peripatetic, a Stoic or an Academician, and often none of them; but – always a Christian. To philosophize, is to love wisdom; and the true wisdom, is Jesus Christ. Let us read the historians, the poets and the philosophers; but let us have in our hearts the Gospel of Jesus Christ: in which alone is perfect wisdom and perfect happiness." Life of Petrarch, Book i, p. 27.

[9] Lord Bacon the greatest philosophical genius of modern times is remarkably cautious and even timid in referring the truths of religion to the discussion of reason. Instaurat. Magna, Lib. ix.

constant recourse to superior beings, may depress the generous sentiments of the mind. Hence an abject superstition seems so frequently to have been productive of pusillanimity, and to have checked the more elevated efforts of virtue in modern times.

DR. DODD: I cannot think, Mr. Hume, that there is any contrariety between the practical principles of religion and those of true Philosophy. Moral maxims seem to be immutable and eternal; hence the morality of the greatest philosophers of antiquity coincides as far as it goes with that of christianity. The only difference is that the moral precepts of antiquity are carried to a still higher degree of purity by the gospel, a circumstance surely in its favour. – The representation which the scripture gives of human nature is agreeable to the uniform tenor of experience and history. It describes it with that mixture of virtue and vice, of greatness and weakness, which appear so conspicuous in every page of history, in every country, in every age, and every individual. Further, by unfolding the original causes of the perfection and degeneracy of the mind, and the manner of restoring it to virtue and happiness, the scripture accounts for those phænomena of the moral world, which to the antients appeared totally inexplicable. This moderate and just account of man steers between the extremes of a vain ostentation and abject pusillanimity, and is perfectly consonant to the facts which we know relative to human nature. To charge the general spirit of the religion with the weaknesses of individuals, and the corruptions of superstition, would be extremely unfair. To observe some of the greatest men that ever Rome produced anxiously consulting the will of the Gods by the chirping of birds and the entrails of beasts furnishes as proper matter for ridicule and severe reflection, as the most superstitious appearances of degenerate christianity. Yet these rites of the Romans were, if I mistake not, the corrupt language of a noble spirit of religion. But say you, "an abject pusillanimity has prevented the more elevated efforts of virtue in modern times." The truth of the matter seems to be that the impressions which the classes make upon our minds in the agreable period of youth prepossess us with an enthusiastic admiration of the celebrated characters of antiquity. In that uncorrupted but unreflecting season the mind indulges at large in the contemplation of the virtues of favourite personages, but does not examine their foibles with that jealous and cautious judgment, which we use when we come to study modern history. The distance of the times in which those heroical Beings lived throws an additional grandeur over their memory. But upon an impartial survey of history, we shall find the characters formed upon the principles of christianity no ways inferior to the most illustrious persons which adorn the annals of human nature. We shall find such examples of magnanimity, heroism, patriotism and humanity as can hardly be parallelled by the most famous passages of antient story. We are apt to think that man has reaped his highest honours in Greece and Rome; we seem frequently to suppose that we ourselves are the descendants of a barbarous, pusillanimous or degenerate race; but nothing can be more contrary to fact. The whole history of modern Europe confutes this false hypothesis. The British and the French heroes are no ways inferior to the Roman and the Grecian.

That constant reliance on heaven which the gospel inculcates cannot have any tendency to depress the mind: it is a principle of all others the best calculated to inspire it with magnanimity and fortitude. In fact we find that the most admired characters of antiquity were supported by this very principle. I know very well that men of the world consider these religious appearances of great men as mere political stratagems or pious frauds to overawe or persuade the credulous multitude. In some cases they may naturally admit of this construction, but in general such an account of them is quite improbable. Of all the sects of antiquity that of the stoics is supposed to have ascribed most to the internal strengths and fortitude of human nature. They are commonly supposed to have held this grand principle of constant dependance on heaven in contempt. I recollect however a very singular passage relating to this very subject in that celebrated letter of Marcus Antoninus, which he wrote in answer to the applications of some heathens for leave to persecute the christians on account of prodigies and earthquakes with which the country had been terrified. "As to those earthquakes, for sometime past, which yet continue, it is proper to admonish you, to compare your conduct with theirs. They, on such occasions, confide more in their God; but you all this time, through your ignorance, neglect the Gods as well as other things, and all the worship due to that immortal Being, whose worshippers the christians you are harrassing and persecuting to death." From this passage we see what opinion that great stoic philosopher had of the principle now in question. The stoic school was the principal nursery of great men of every kind, and it is remarkable that there is a great similarity between its tenets and those of christianity. For my own part I could never discover any thing like an abject tendency in the spirit of the gospel. There is no opposition surely between that humility which it recommends and magnanimity. Humility is itself the highest proof of greatness of mind. All that elevation which is founded on pride is of a bastard kind, and inconsistent with the more refined sentiments of philosophy as well as religion.

MR. HUME: There is another plausible objection against the influence of christianity on the heart. It may be alledged that the idea of forgiveness through repentance and the intercession of another Being must by constantly operating on the mind render it less cautious in trespassing the boundaries of morality. The confession and absolution practised in the church of Rome is, you know, a very easy and agreeable institution for the consciences of mankind.

DR. DODD: Those grand ideas, Mr. Hume, of repentance, mediation and forgiveness, though unfolded in their pure and genuine colours by christianity, are not, I presume, peculiar to that system alone. Though involved in mists and obscurity, they seem to have formed a part of the essence of every species of religion of which we have any credible accounts. Hence one would be tempted to conclude, that such extraordinary principles are interwoven with the frame of human nature, or have been transmitted down and disseminated through mankind in consequence of some early celestial revelation. In what age or country do we not find the sense of guilt, the contrite supplication, the sacred ode, the altar and the sacrifice? How should these singular principles so universally prevail, if there was not an invariable consistence between them and the constitution and situation of man? – If we should attempt to banish repentance, intercession, forgiveness, and mercy from the moral system, we must change the frame of human nature. These mysterious methods of religion, however inexplicable to our limited faculties, must appear to every man who reasons from facts, necessary in the system of nature. Our condition without them is hopeless. Men of the most irreproachable virtue are obliged to confess with sorrow the imperfection of their conduct, and the necessity of repentance and a Saviour. – But you object that the hope of forgiveness encourages men to proceed in vice: and it must be confessed that nothing is more common. But such delusive presumption is not only unwarranted by christianity, but involves an absolute contradiction to its principles. The first idea of christianity is to stop the farther progress of the mind in vice. "Repent ye, for the kingdom of heaven is at hand." The gospel requires the heart not only to be filled with contrition for past errors, but to adhere firmly to the side of virtue for the future. To be thus uniformly influenced by a pious sorrow for former misconduct, and by the most sincere and steady resolutions of reformation, are essential preliminaries in the christian covenant. –

MR. HUME: But, Doctor, if no period in life can be assigned at which if a man reforms his manners and embraces the offers of the gospel, he may not hope for future happiness, the mind may naturally reason thus with itself; "why may I not yet pursue my favourite vices and pleasures, as I may afterwards, by contrition, reformation, and the mediation of an all-powerful Saviour, obliterate my faults and obtain eternal felicity? – "

DR. DODD: Notwithstanding the corruption of our nature, it still retains some portion of its original honour. Hence it is observable that a person in whose bosom there is the least tincture of generosity, is not naturally apt to persist in insulting the clemency of a noble and forgiving benefactor from the hopes of impunity. Forgiveness forms a strong chain of gratitude and obedience. At any rate a person, who still proceeds in the course of immorality from the hope of forgiveness in consequence of future repentance, acts upon principles directly opposite to those of christianity.[10] And here I ought not to forget remarking that every step a man advances in the career of corruption and vice increases the difficulty, and lessens the probability of his attaining to that

---

[10] "Shall we continue in sin that grace may abound? God forbid: how shall we that are dead to sin live any longer therein?" Romans, ch. i, ver. 1,2.

happiness which the gospel offers, so that at last the difficulty may become almost insuperable and the probability almost as nothing. We have some ground both from reason and scripture to infer that the soul may by continued habits of depravity become as incurable (according to the ordinary course of things) as the body does by a long and rooted mortification.

MR. HUME: Some have objected to christianity "that the notion of future rewards and punishments is mercenary and detracts from the generous nature of true virtue. But possibly this objection may appear somewhat too refined."

DR. DODD: Of all the arguments employed by men of your sect that which you have now mentioned seems to me the most strained and affected. I remember that even the moral, but enthusiastic Lord Shaftsbury throws a slur upon that fundamental principle of future rewards and punishments. But no one determines against it in such bold and triumphant terms as the celebrated Royal philosopher of Sans Souci[11] towards the conclusion of that famous specimen of infidelity his letter to Mareschal Keith. Yet still I cannot help treating the objection as frivolous. Every percipient Being must be determined by some motives of pleasure and pain, of happiness or misery. To suppose man not to be influenced by any such motives is to suppose him unpercipient and insensible. If a philosopher avers that he is determined by the absolute rectitude of a certain line of behaviour, that very idea of rectitude is a motive of happiness to him. The motives of happiness which christianity proposes are of the most pure and generous kind, nor can it be deemed any disadvantage to them that they extend beyond the limits of time into the invisible world.

MR. HUME: The defence you have made for the practical principles of christianity has, I own, a plausible air; but if they have necessarily so powerful and so salutary an influence on the heart as the gentlemen of your order maintain, I cannot help expressing my surprize that a man daily conversant with them like you should have so egregiously deviated from the line of moral rectitude. A great part of your life was devoted to sensual pleasure, and your last action was a crime of a deep and malignant hue.

DR. DODD: My original constitution disposed me to pleasure, and the fatal consequences of pleasure drove me to the last disgraceful measure of my life. But let me once more repeat to you that as far as I adhered to the principles of christianity, so far I found myself happy and fortunate, and in proportion as

---

[11] Allez, lâches chrêtiens, que les feux éternels
Empêchent d'assouvir vos desirs criminels,
Vos austeres vertus n'en ont que l'apparence.
    Mais nous qui renonçons à toute recompense;
Nous qui ne croyons point vos éternels tourmens,
L'intéret n'a jamais souillé nos sentimens,
Le bien du genre humain, la vertu nous anime,
L'amour seul du devoir nous a fait fuir le crime.

I deviated from them I found myself miserable. It is to the influence of these good principles that I attribute all the virtuous and honourable parts of my conduct. Did they not operate frequently on my mind, I might have exceeded Villiars and Rochester in profligacy. – A licentious passion for the other sex predominated in my frame, and I must in a great measure attribute to it that ruinous dissipation of life, which has disgraced my reputation. The passion of love, if not carefully regulated by religion and reason, proves the most artful and dangerous snare to human virtue. It insinuates itself under the alluring appearance of gentleness and tenderness, and so wins insensibly upon a soft and sympathetic temper. But if it is improperly indulged, it inevitably introduces indolence, unmanly effeminacy, and not unfrequently a total depravation of sentiment into the soul. The manners of Europe are verging apace to a total contempt of chastity. I must confess with sorrow of heart that the influence of the example of the gay, and the maxims of the world, prevailed too often over those sentiments of purity which I had imbibed in the school of christianity. – I well know that your notions of this virtue are far from being strict; indeed there is no subject which is treated with more ridicule among the fashionable part of mankind. The poison is still more pernicious as this libertine disposition is frequently found united with an insinuating sweetness of manners and a specious humanity. Yet I remember that great moralist the Emperor Marcus Antoninus does not hesitate to adopt upon this subject the opinion of Theophrastus, however contrary it may be to the polished and luxurious idea of modern Europe,[12] "that in comparing crimes those are greater which men are incited to by lust or desire of pleasure, than those which flow from anger."

Ambition, the love of pleasure, of show and popular applause, with their ordinary concomitant extravagance, I consider as the causes of my ruin. For such unreal shadows have I sacrificed the solid pleasures of religion. The genteel was the predominant idea in my mind, and to it I have fallen a victim like many other thousands who perpetually aspire to reach that unfixed imaginary standard. Tho' the love of fame when considered as a subordinate passion is laudable, yet to employ the sacred eloquence of the gospel merely as an instrument to acquire vulgar eclat, as I have often done, is a species of prostitution on which I can never reflect but with pain. –

Oh! that I had cultivated severe virtue with the same ardor with which I worshipped at the shrines of pleasure, ambition, and popularity! But, Mr. Hume, I cannot help in my turn expressing my surprise that a man of your sound judgment in other matters should adopt such absurd opinions on the subject of religion; and it is still more extraordinary how a man of such principles should retain so fair a moral character through life. One would think that you acted as much against your own conviction as I did.

[12] Mar. Ant. Medit. Book ii, sect. 10.

MR. HUME: I had all the prejudices of education in favour of religion and virtue as much as you had. To describe the progress of my sentiments and account for the change of my opinions at large would require more leisure than I now have. At my entrance into life I found myself encompassed with difficulties, and my breast inflamed with the most ardent passion for fame. I judged that if I proceeded in the common and beaten tract of opinions, I should find it extremely difficult to attract the attention of mankind. I thought it therefore necessary to usher in the dawn of my fame by some singular appearance.

The operation of this notion on my mind, and my commerce with men and books of free principles, gradually gave a different turn to my opinions. Ideas which at first occurred to me as mere paradoxes or experiments of ingenuity, being long dwelt upon gave me insensibly a habit of scepticism and suspence, and seemed to assume the appearance of serious truths. Mankind in general are apt to flatter themselves that their opinions and principles are the result of mature reasoning, and do not consider what a share the prejudices of fancy have in the formation of them. I cannot however help thinking that if the most singular and obstinate opinions of men were to be traced back to their origin, but that we should find that they owed their rise to extraordinary incidents in their lives and the prejudices of the imagination, rather than to any cool and deliberate inquiry. When an acute metaphysical genius and an inflexible temper come to the aid of notions thus originally conceived, the spell becomes almost indissoluble. Many were the prejudices which biassed my mind on this subject of religion.

DR. DODD: You will much oblige me by enumerating them. Your studied reasonings and arguments I am not at all unacquainted with, but your primary prejudices which inclined you to such opinions I can only guess.

MR. HUME: I. In the first place, the example of the venerable philosophers of antiquity was full before my eyes. I could not help entertaining the highest admiration for those enlarged minds who soared above their contemporaries, broke the fetters of superstition and asserted the rights of reason. To imitate these great men, you must allow, was no object of vulgar ambition.

II. The various and fantastic appearances of religion in the different ages and countries of the world filled my mind with disgust and perplexity. Amid such a chaos where was I to find any steady and fixed principles? what criterion could I adopt but my reason? I always allowed that there were circumstances in favour of christianity which seemed to entitle it to the first rank among the religions of the earth. But afterwards when I reflected upon that miserable distraction of sentiments, and the endless variety of hostile sects among christians; when I recollected how many rational, absurd, and pernicious tenets had been alternately maintained, refuted and revived, I was once more lost in doubt and returned to the principles of scepticism. I could not review the history of my native religion but with some degree of contempt. Those scenes of enthusiasm and rage which it presents could not but hurt a calm and philosophic eye. Though I had imbibed early prejudices in its favour, yet I found by experience that in this naked system, where they were not rivetted by the habitual enchantment of rites and ceremonies, these favourable prepossessions were easily obliterated.

III. The seeming contradiction between prophecies and miracles and the ordinary apparent course of nature in a great measure determined me against the belief of divine revelation. I confess that Dr. Campbell the most liberal and ingenious of all my adversaries has opposed me on this ground with much ability and success. However I thought it very improbable that the Deity should violate those laws of nature which he had constituted; and I was surprised to find that they who believed and defended the prophecies and miracles on which the proof of christianity hangs, denied facts of a similar kind among other nations, though they seemed to wear marks of almost equal authenticity. – After all I am inclined to think that such extraordinary phænomena must be considered not as violations of the laws of nature, but as involved in its general system, nor can I see upon what principles we can entirely reject all the divine revelations and interpositions recorded among the heathens, if we implicitly adopt those that relate to the Mosaic and Christian systems.

Of a kin to this prejudice was the following: Praise and thanksgiving always appeared to me proper and essential parts of religious worship, but I had great doubts with respect to the efficacy of prayer. I esteemed it no small presumption in mortals to think of interesting the Divinity in their little affairs, or of altering the course of his government by their supplications. It did not then occur to me that the Supreme Being might accomplish the ends of the moral, as he does those of the natural world, by the instrumentality of secondary causes and means.

IV. I could not review the religious wars and animosities of Europe but with a mixture of horror and pity. When I reflected what fatal effect these sacred quarrels entailed on mankind, I could not help admiring the tolerating spirit of antient Polytheism. Christianity, it is true, professes itself to be the religion of charity and peace, but what a fierce and implacable temper many of its propagators[13] have shewn, I need not tell you.

---

[13] To argue against a thing from the corruption of it is a common error in reasoning. Monsieur Bayle falls into it, when he talks of the evils which have resulted to society from religion. Mr. Hume, though he seems here to confess that his detestation of religious wars and controversies prejudiced him against christianity itself, highly condemns in one passage of his writings the false mode of reasoning now in question. Hume's Hist. chap. 71.

The prejudices and aversions of many however are of so infectious and diffusive a nature as to extend to every thing that has any relation to their object in spite of their reason.

V. My unfavourable impressions of religion were not a little strengthened by the aversion which I had conceived against the ecclesiastic order in general. Their ambition, their narrow cast of sentiment, and their unfeeling severity of disposition gave me a strong dislike to their character. The opposition which I met with from that quarter confirmed me in this opinion. Their severity might be naturally derived from their strict attention[14] to the interests of virtue; but I was not disposed to adopt favourable constructions.

It is wonderful what effect all these combined prejudices had on my mind, and how they engaged my reason on their side. Such was the progress of my sentiments that at length it appeared to me no inglorious enterprize to overturn the motley systems of superstition, as I deemed them, which prevailed over Europe, and to establish upon their ruins the rational principles of pure theism. The subtlety of my genius supplied me with a sufficient store of ingenious arguments; and the reception which my writings met with from the fashionable part of mankind encouraged me to proceed. This, Doctor, is a sketch of the history[15] of my speculations: I never advanced however, as some have imagined, so far as to deny the existence of a Deity, or the unalterable distinction between vice and virtue. Some of the gentler foibles of human nature, I must confess, I have treated with too much lenity. I have been too indulgent to the gallantry of the age.

DR. DODD: This account of your opinions I conceive, but your moral character remains still an inexplicable paradox. You seemed some time ago to confess that your temperament was not cold nor insensible to the solicitations of pleasure, &c.

Indeed I am inclined to think that an imagination so lively and vigorous as you possessed is seldom, if ever found[16] unconnected with warm passions. Yet it appears that you all along treated with contempt that grand principle of philosophy and religion, which is the most powerful sanction of the laws of virtue, "the immortality of the soul".

---

[14] The vulgar prejudice against the clergy is precisely of the same nature with that of Monsieur Bayle's against religion in general.

[15] If there be any probability in this theory of the origin and progress of Mr. Hume's opinions, it ought to teach the young and the ingenious how insensibly the mind may contract a dark and sceptical colouring.

[16] Whither an ardent fancy and moderate passions may not subsist in the same constitution is a question attended with some difficulty. A chaste and amiable imagination, like that of Mr. Addison, may be found united with cool and temperate passions, and this auspicious union promises the fairest view of happiness to the individual. An ardent and bold imagination on the contrary will, I presume, naturally tinge the passions, and if not tempered by an uncommon solidity of understanding, hurry away its professor into extravagant opinions and actions.

MR. HUME: In consequence of a virtuous education and early habits, the maxims[17] of virtue had taken deep root in my heart. The utmost libertinism of opinion was not able to eradicate them. The ardor of my imagination and passions was tempered by the solidity of my judgement: and though I treated the immortality of the soul with disrespect, yet there are other sanctions of virtue which did not escape my attention. To a man, who does not with puerile weakness consign himself to every transient pleasure or bound prospects by present appearances, but extends his views to the remote consequences of things, it will appear a principle of great certainty and importance "that even in the course of human life, virtue and pleasure, vice and misery are found as inseparably connected as cause and effect in the physical system." The love of reputation, the ordinary ideas, maxims and laws of society are powerful sanctions of the rules of virtue. To acquire fame and the admiration of mankind was the principal object of my ambition, and experience and history had taught me that these were not to be attained without the appearances of virtue. Besides I reckoned it extremely inconsistent with that philosophic character to which I aspired to be enslaved by my appetites, Temperance is essential to the character of a sage. – In the last place, I cultivated the principles of humanity and benevolence with peculiar attention. Happily the social disposition was strongly implanted by nature in my heart, and I have continually distinguished it with care from the principle of selfishness. Many ingenious and honest men have in their theories endeavoured to resolve both into the same origin, but such a corruption of ideas and misapplication of words has certainly a tendency to deprave and contract the more generous sentiments of the mind. I have at all times considered self-love[18] and the love of mankind as essentially distinct, and have uniformly revered the social principle.

DR. DODD: Mr. Hume, you have certainly been guilty of one great violation of the social principle in attempting to demolish the established religion of your country. History brings us information from every quarter that the decline of religion is invariably attended with the corruption of morals, the ruin of national felicity, and the downfall of the state. When that system of useful

---

[17] "Since Mr. Hume ascribes so much to education and early habits, we cannot "help reflecting how much he owed his virtues to christianity, though he seems not to have been aware of it." Indeed it were much to be wished, that deists would be more candid in acknowledging their obligations to revelation. It is remarkable that Lord Herbert of Cherbury who may be considered as the father of modern deism has gleaned and selected the best principles of his system from the Scripture.

[18] To the honour of Mr. Hume be it said that this distinction was no less apparent in his practice than his theory. It seems to have been peculiarly reserved for our age to consider the more generous sentiments of human nature as the effects of madness, and to substitute a principle of deliberate selfishness in the room of that sublime virtue denominated by the antients PRUDENCE.

truths or prejudices as you may term them, which regulated the wayward ideas of mortals, is disarranged or dissolved, their unreined minds run wild and involve the society in every species of folly, vice and misery.

MR. HUME: That charge has continually resounded in my ears for many years. My free and paradoxical thoughts were not intended for the ordinary tribe of mankind, but for men of ingenuity and reflection, who are capable of judging for themselves. I well knew that the vulgar were not to be regulated by the principles of pure theism or philosophy. I did not mean to abolish those pious arts and ideas, which are found so useful and salutary in managing that class of men, I was only desirous to reduce them nearer the standard of probability, reason and truth. Yet the most[19] candid apology for those severe strictures which I was obliged to throw out against every species of religious corruption, and the most ample encomium on true piety, have not secured me from the vehement attacks of my enemies. Undoubtedly I always attributed a great deal of good to the silent influence of religion, but still I was of opinion that the punishments of human laws were the most powerful sanctions of virtue to the populace, and that society is more obliged to him who builds a prison than to him who founds a chapel.

After all I may venture to affirm that my freedom of inquiry has been productive of more beneficial consequences to mankind, than is generally supposed. Since the religious wars and animosities of Europe have subsided, the minds of men have sunk into a kind of lethargy or listless inconcern with respect to subjects of a theological[20] nature, I may therefore fairly plead that the doubts which I have started, have awakened mankind from this extreme of languor and indifference to an attentive concern for their sacred interests.

[19] "This sophism, of arguing from the abuse of any thing against the use of it, is one of the grossest, and at the same time the most common, to which men are subject. The history of all ages, and none more than that of the period, which is our subject, offers us examples of the abuse of religion; and we have not been sparing to remark them: but whoever would thence draw an inference to the disadvantage of religion in general, would argue very rashly and erroneously. The proper office of religion is to reform men's lives, to purify their hearts, to inforce all moral duties, and to secure obedience to the laws and civil magistrate. While it pursues these salutary purposes, its operations, though infinitely valuable, are secret and silent, and seldom come under the cognizance of history. That adulterate species of it alone, which inflames faction, animates sedition, and prompts rebellion, distinguishes itself on the open theatre of the world, and is the great source of revolutions and public convulsions. The historian therefore, has scarce occasion to mention any other kind of religion; and he may retain the highest regard for true piety, even while he exposes all the abuses of the false. He may even think, that he cannot better shew his attachment to the former than by detecting the latter, and laying open its absurdities and pernicious tendency, &c. &c." Vid. Note Hume's History of England, Chap. lxxi, Vol. VIII. in 8vo.

[20] We are induced to coincide with Mr. Hume in this stricture upon the age. It is not improbable that such transient sceptics may be permitted by the Deity in the moral world, as earthquakes and tempests are allowed in the natural to purify the air.

My political and historical labours are universally acknowledged to have great merit.

DR. DODD: Whoever compares your apology for your aspersions on every religious sect that comes in your way with the strain of your essays, will not be inclined to think them very consistent. In many passages you seem to strike at the root of all religion, though you have carefully disguised your real sentiments and intentions under the mask of an aversion to superstition and enthusiasm. Your professing to address these libertine thoughts to men of reflection only is an insufficient excuse. The polite and elegant strain of your writings has rendered them familiar to a numerous part of mankind, and particularly to the young, whose reason is immature and whose principles are unfixed. Besides, you know that the inferior ranks naturally imitate the manners and adopt the sentiments of the more learned and fashionable part of society, to whom your deistical labours are peculiarly addressed. In short, Sir, I do not see how you can vindicate yourself upon this head. May I not venture to affirm that you have injured society by your speculations as much as I have by my practice?

MR. HUME: If those who embrace my principles imitate my morals, I can see no great detriment to society upon them.

DR. DODD: Ah! Sir, you know that Epicurus was himself a man of pure and uncorrupted morals, yet his principles had such a pernicious influence on the minds of his followers, that the great politician and moralist Montesquieu, does not scruple to assign the prevalence[21] of the Epicurean system as one of the causes of the decline of the Roman empire.

MR. HUME: I am desirous to put an end to this conversation. There may be a philosophical as well as a religious madness. The man who directing his labours towards the good of mankind, happily unites philosophy and religion, is one of the most illustrious and venerable objects in nature. Such a man becomes the dupe neither of fanaticism, superstition, or scepticism. He ought to be more revered by mankind than the Delphic oracle was by the antients; men of such sublime and enlarged minds are the only true guardians of the interests of the human race. Posterity will review your character with a high degree of abhorrence on account of your vices, and the pernicious tendency of my metaphysical system will considerably lessen their admiration of my virtues and genius.[22]

---

[21] Reflections on the Causes of the Rise and Fall of the Roman Empire, Cap.x.

[22] Admirable is the inscription which that great rural philosopher Mr. Evelyn ordered to be inscribed upon his tomb; that "Living in an age of extraordinary events and revolutions, he had learned from thence this truth, which he desired might be thus communicated to posterity; *That all is vanity which is not honest; and that there is no solid wisdom but in real piety!*" – Life of Mr. Evelyn.

HUME'S POSTHUMOUS REPUTATION:
AUTHOR AND INFIDEL

74
DIALOGUES IN THE SHADES

Dialogues in the shades, between General Wolfe, General Montgomery, David Hume, George Grenville, and Charles Townshend. London: printed for G. Kearsley, 1777, iv, 120 p.
Complete Dialogue 1, selections from Dialogue 3; from 1777 edition.

Following a popular format of fictitious dialogue between famous deceased figures, *Dialogues in the Shades* takes on the issue of which side is right in the American revolution, and the criteria of a just war. The key figure in favour of the revolution is American general Richard Montgomery (1738?–1775), who, born in Ireland, was captain in the British army and later settled in America. Opposing British colonial rule, Montgomery became brigadier general in the Continental army in 1775; he was killed later that year in an attack on Quebec. Staunchly opposing the revolution is General James Wolfe (1727–1759), commander of the British army during the 1759 capture of Quebec from the French – a military victory that led to British supremacy in Canada. As Dialogue 1 opens, Montgomery argues that the revolution was a question of liberty, which every English person was raised to appreciate. Wolfe insists that Montgomery needs to show precisely how liberty justifies the American Revolution. Hume then appears and the two generals ask him for guidance. Hume admits that, philosophically, he was "in the wrong" and is now free from prepossessions. He now feels that "war in general is not only unjustifiable, but also the ignominy of mankind," and thus Montgomery will have a hard time making his case. Wolfe feels that war is indeed justified to extend culture around the world. Hume, though, contends that this can be done through peaceful commerce, and that the blame for the current war rests on English leaders who in the past dried up the resources of foreign lands through "fraud, slaughter, and desolation." In Dialogue 3, George Grenville (1712–1770) and Charles Townshend (1725–1767) – English politicians whose taxation policies caused unrest in America – enter the conversation. Near the end of the Dialogue, Montgomery, Townshend, and Wolfe carve out a peace treaty involving subsidies to be paid to the English. Hume, who had been secretly listening to the discussion, emerges from behind a tree laughing, and reminds the group that they are dead and cannot affect any change on earth. Ultimately, according to Hume "nothing but empty notions, puerile prejudices, govern the generality of mankind, and decide the fate of empires."

Dialogues in the Shades was favourably, though briefly, reviewed in three journals. The complete review from each is as follows:

> The subject of these Dialogues is the dispute with America, which is treated in an argumentative manner, enlivened occasionally by the warmth and abruptness natural to colloquial controversy. The speakers are, general Wolfe, Montgomery, David Hume, George Grenville, and Charles Townshend; who, except Montgomery, a violent partizan of the colonies, are each in the interest of Great Britain. [*Critical Review*, 1777, Vol. 43, p. 471]

> A whimsical groupe of characters are here assembled to canvass the matter in dispute between Great Britain and her Colonies: Montgomery being a stout advocate for the Americans. The disputants, though in the shades, talk, nevertheless, exactly like folks of this world, and just to as little purpose. [*London Review*, June 1777, Vol. 5, p. 529]

> The principles of American resistance are sensibly debated in these Dialogues. All the speakers, except Montgomery, espouse the claims of the mother country; but the weight of argument is finally cast into the provincial scale. The known characters and quondam principles of all the disputants are well supported; and the controversy is kept up with spirit. [*Monthly Review*, September 1777, Vol. 57, p. 251]

For an account of Hume's actual views on the American Revolution, see Boswell's letters to Temple in this collection, and Hume's letter to William Strahan dated October 26, 1775. The following is from the 1777 and only edition of *Dialogues in the Shades*.

DIALOGUE I.

BETWEEN

GENERAL WOLFE,

GENERAL MONTGOMERY,

AND

DAVID HUME.

MONTGOMERY: It is an happy chance for me, brave Wolfe, to find you alone in this solitary walk, since I may, without being interrupted, expatiate with you on the unjust contempt you have shewn me from the day of my arrival in this delightful place: a treatment which ill becomes your noble and patriotic soul.

WOLFE: Do you claim in your behalf the very sentiment which excites my indignation against you?

MONTGOMERY: What can you charge me with? Have I not, with a courage as undaunted as yours, encountered an honourable death on the same spot where you gloriously fell, and which, though rendered famous by your victory, cannot be disgraced by my defeat.

WOLFE: Far be it from enlightened souls to judge of true valour according to good or ill success. no, the only difference between you and me is in the cause for which we fought.

MONTGOMERY: Was the injury you avenged by torrents of blood of so black a dye, that nothing less would have washed it off? I thought that the ground of the quarrel you deem so righteous, was only some breaches of ancient treaties, which scarcely deserved the name of trespasses.

WOLFE: Since you provoke me thus, I shall tell you in plain words, that I was the champion of my country against its natural and inveterate enemy, the French; and that you have been the leader of seditious men, who revolted against a people to whom they were bound by the most sacred tie of filial duty.

MONTGOMERY: There are so few instances recorded in the annals of mankind, to prove that parental tenderness and filial love preponderate over self-interest in private individuals, that it was not worth while to employ the absurd metaphor of the *Mother Country*, to enforce sentiments, which would not be so emphatically related, and so much admired, if they were common in the literal sense of the image. But, supposing that nature works more effectually than she generally does upon the hearts of parents and children, are not the instruments she makes use of, a familiar intercourse and a long habit?

WOLFE: I see you pretend, that the affinity between a colony and the nation whence it came, is like that which is found in the brute creation, and subsides when the weakness of early life ceases. Have you no faith either in friendship or in alliance?

MONTGOMERY: Friendship stands in the same predicament with filial duty in respect to nations, for this sentiment is raised in the human heart by the same means; except, that not possessing the mind so soon, it admits and requires the influence of reason and judgment, which, still less than a blind partiality, cannot operate on men separated at a great distance, and who hardly think upon each other's existence in the whole course of their lives. As to alliance, I acknowledge it a tie, and perhaps the only one binding among men; for it is founded on mutual advantages, and allowed to be dissolved when the balance of these advantages inclines too much on either side. On this plan has been raised the fabric of every government: the multitude have said to one or to a few, "We will obey and honour you, provided that you never misuse the power we are willing to grant you, in order to support the dignity of your stations; but observe, to conduct us and yourselves according to the constitutional laws we have unanimously approved; if ever you turn aside from that sacred standard, you are no more our leaders, but our greatest enemies."

WOLFE: Ah, ah, would you have spoken thus to an Asiatic prince, or even to some European monarchs?

MONTGOMERY: I should, undoubtedly, have had the right, though perhaps not the courage, to do it. But, as a reputed subject to the English government, I was not debased by slavery; I durst speak and even arm in defence of LIBERTY.

WOLFE: Oh, most sacred word, how much hast thou been prophaned in every age by turbulent or designing men, who claim the blessing thou expressest with deceitful sighs, while their hearts are bent upon destroying it, either by anarchy or despotism!

MONTGOMERY: I refuse not to hear your virulent apostrophes, provided you give a fair hearing to my meek arguments.

WOLFE: Forbear, if you think to impose upon me by a *Cant* which cannot serve your turn but with fools. Stand firm, if you can, on the ground of good sense; and expect not to find me ignorant of the transactions that have passed since I left the earth, for here we have daily accounts of them.

MONTGOMERY: On this is founded my hope of convincing you; since you cannot but know, that if our ancient prepossessions are left us as a punishment for them, we are, nevertheless, above uttering a voluntary falshood. Thus the facts I shall alledge in favor of my cause, being attested by the most partial shades of the opposite party, you shall have no other trouble than that of judging if my inferences are right or wrong. As to your fear of being tired with the jargon of an enthusiast, I doubt not to remove it by a simple question. Do you believe, that your soldiers would have fought as couragiously as they did, if just before the battle you had gone from rank to rank, explaining to them the true motives of your valour, and said, "Here, my friends, we are to support, at the hazard of our lives, some interest of commerce and the glory of our arms against men who have the very same reasons to fight against us, and who, upon the whole, are neither better nor worse than ourselves. Believe not the absurdities related in regard to the persons, sentiments, and design of the French, but attack them, spurred only by honour and a patriotic jealousy of fame?"

WOLFE: I confess that this harangue would have been very preposterous and imprudent.

MONTGOMERY: Such has been always the case with every general, chief, and even legislator: they knew, that common souls must be moved by springs less refined than those which put heroic ones in action, and they dealt with them accordingly. Thus the generality of the Roman warriors were urged to the conquest of the world from a prepossession that a man's head, which they found buried in the earth at the building of their Capitol, was an infallible prediction of their success. Thus your soldiers wanted their prejudices against the French, and their terror of Popery, to conquer; and thus my Americans need all the enthusiasm of a zealous sect to assert their rights.

WOLFE: Independency, I presume, is in the number of these rights or claims.

MONTGOMERY: Certainly it is, not for the Americans only, but also for all nations whatsoever; for as long as the laws to which they have consented hold the sway, as they ought to do, they are not dependent upon any other will but their own; and when these laws yield to usurpation, they are at full liberty to choose some better defence against the like encroachments, and to pursue by force what is denied to reason. Has not this been always the opinion of free-born Englishmen?

WOLFE: Yes: but wise men, in general, allow something to circumstances: they fancy no wrongs when there are none; and, above all, aim not at impossibilities. Your reasons for your rupture with England, I am willing to hear by and by; but tell me now, if in breaking your ancient connection (I will not say in shaking off your allegiance) you can reasonably expect to remain a free people amidst so many enterprizing neighbours?

MONTGOMERY: There is no choice in tyrants. Are the chains of a people lighter for being imposed upon them by a *corrupted Senate*, than they would be by an *arbitrary Monarch?* Is not, at least, the dismal prospect of future evils more bounded, when the power of inflicting them lies in the hand of a single wicked man, who may be succeeded by a righteous one, than, when many are prompted by base interest to our ruin, and leave their mischievous venality as an inheritance to their successors?

WOLFE: How dare you speak thus before me? who, well knowing that the best absolute monarchy is to our happy system of equally balanced powers, what a tree blasted from its root is to another rotten only in some of its branches, have lavished my blood to preserve you from falling into a state of slavery, not less insupportable to a noble mind for being casually softened. No, I fought not for glory only, as you are willing to insinuate I did, to rob me of the most exalted virtue. Such an empty desire had not strength enough to rouse me from the lethargy of death, when mortally wounded and just expiring at the foot of a tree, I exulted at the news of a victory bought at the price of my life, it was benevolence that raised my transport and gave me a momentary animation; a benevolence which I reluctantly denied to the brave Montcalme, then my adversary and now my intimate friend, although he deserved it better than your Americans, for whom I exerted it to the last: ungrateful men!

MONTGOMERY: Be appeased; we may deny that we were the cause of the war which has justly immortalized your name, without arraigning the private sentiments by which a generous warrior may be actuated, even in following the orders of unfeeling and artful politicians; and assure yourself, we retain a due sense of the obligation we owe you. My eagerness for being justified in your mind, is not a small proof of my veneration for your heroic and social virtues. But since you require a satisfactory answer to your last interrogation, know, that our hope of becoming a free people in the full extent of the word, seems to us not so destitute of probability as you think it. True, we cannot attain that desirable end without infinite difficulties: like the Russians, who, emerging from ignorance and rusticity, have been enabled to raise a formidable empire by many shameful defeats, we must acquire the military art with the purest of our blood; but then, our dearly-bought abilities shall be employed against any one of the nations that might attempt to enslave us, with as much fervency as we had reluctance to turn our natural, but undisciplined, valour against our ancient allies.

WOLFE: I thought no being, but animals of prey, could look upon a state of perpetual warfare without horror.

MONTGOMERY: Unhappily you are mistaken: strength will always prevail over justice among mankind, and consequently a country must now, as formerly, build its freedom upon the basis of war. These are undeniable though melancholy truths; and the Americans, in whose name I speak, have been made so sensible of them, that they are resolved never to toil for oppressors, but to substitute a martial ardour to an active industry; for the tax of blood, which war imposes, falls equally on the two adverse parties.

WOLFE: No, not always so; for, as you have justly observed, some ingredients are to be added to courage, without which the most obstinate resistance must be, at last, subdued.

MONTGOMERY: But, what can compell the heart? What can force a people to bear tamely their chains, when opportunity presents itself for shewing the abhorrence of them, and for renewing a just war?

WOLFE: Here is David Hume, who has analysed the human mind, and who comes very seasonably to answer you.

HUME: Who makes this peaceful abode resound with the odious word of war? Ah! is it you noble Wolfe and brave Montgomery, who give a fresh instance of the fatal power of prejudices, which, alas! subside not by death, but continue to alarm the soul even in its state of quiet.

MONTGOMERY: Have you not need, David, of that pity you bestow upon us?

HUME: As here the chastisement is adequate to the guilt, I must be more unhappy than both of you. You mistook passionate prepossessions for equitable sentiments; you acted accordingly, and are punished only by the continuation of your blindness. It is not the same with me. I dared to face Truth in all its splendor; and with its bright torch I traced the dark steps of men's errors from age to age: I could not consequently be seduced by shallow ambition, nor over-persuaded by insignificant interest, much less deceived by vain factions; but I suffered myself to be knowingly misled by these bad guides; and the perspicacity with which I was endued is increased to that point, now I cannot, though willingly, cover my former faults with the least shadow of excuse. You dispute with each other, and still have the consolation of thinking yourselves in the right; I arraign myself, and always conclude that I was in the wrong. In vain I seek for tranquillity in the asylums of philosophy which I have pointed out to mankind; either I miss the plain road that leads to them, by the remembrance of the crooked politics in which I imprudently wandered; or I mistake the beautiful flowers which adorn them, for the thorns every where planted in the ministerial cabinet. I no more admire the fortitude of the stoic philosopher in the midst of accidental acute pains, and voluntary austerities, when I reflect on the constancy with which the chief leader of a state suffers the mortification of disappointment, the sharpness of public reproaches, and willingly exposes himself to violent pertubations and never-ceasing trouble of mind. I am even so far disgusted with my favourite Epicurean system, for the confusion I feel at having awhile forsaken it, that, in order to be rid of myself, I often mix with the multitude, whose senseless agitations I cannot help envying.

WOLFE: After this account of your situation, we may, without encroaching on your sublime thoughts, take you for our judge in a dispute that has arisen between Montgomery and me, about our respective deaths. He pretends that he fell in a cause no less just, and honourable, than that for which I joyfully spilled the last drop of my blood. But, though he has spoken with great vehemence, and not without truth, on the topic of liberty in general, he knows, that I cannot give up the contested point, till he enters into particulars, and makes an exact application of his principles to the present rebellion of his Americans.

MONTGOMERY: This will not be a difficult task.

HUME: Not so easy, in my judgment, as you imagine.

MONTGOMERY: How! have you not told us, that you were free from all kind of prepossessions?

HUME: Be not so hasty, Montgomery: it is not my intention to give the preference over you to any warrior whatever: if I defy you to apologize for the American war, it is because in the eyes of reason, war in general is not only unjustifiable, but also the ignominy of mankind; and because a conqueror decked with the laurels of victory has no more real claim to glory, than he whose hope has been rejected by fortune, and on whose neglected corpse fall only the tears of disappointed friends.

WOLFE: What a strange paradox is this? But I will contain the indignation it raises in my soul, and hear the reasons you have to alledge in support of it.

HUME: Allow me, first, that ingratitude and infamy are taken by a generous mind for synonymous words.

MONTGOMERY: Who doubts of it?

HUME: Those doubt it, who cause benevolent nature to be accused of injustice and parsimony, by over-running the earth under the standard of envy and avarice, to spoil other countries of productions often not so valuable as those of their own, and always infinitely less adapted to their wants; for this ingratitude, being the origin of contentions among the human species, war is branded with infamy.

WOLFE: If you oblige every people to be contented with the productions of their native spot, you take from them animating variety, beneficent luxury, and at the same time all the arts and sciences, by which the social tie has been extended to the whole circumference of the world.

HUME: I should take nothing from them, if, by continuing their natural horror for blood, and by following their innate inclination for quiet, they were to substitute for reciprocal rapines and murders, the universal benefit of peaceful commerce.

MONTGOMERY: Then would no taxes be arbitrarily imposed upon industry? and the fruits of labour would be reaped by the hands that want has set to work?

HUME: Good Montgomery, no taxes at all; and it would be worthy of this enlightened age if all nations should agree on this plan of a pacific exchange. Thus the respective gifts they have received would be, as they were intended, the means of their preservation and enjoyment; instead of being, as they are, the cause of their destruction and misery.

WOLFE: But supposing mankind wise enough to agree in this design, and afterwards some people to oppose it with invincible obstinacy and determined malice; would not a war be just against these enemies of the general good?

HUME: At least this sentence should not be passed in the dark councils of ambition and interest.

WOLFE: A general, who is ordered by his prince or country to command the executioners of this sentence, is seldom called to the councils you mention, and consequently is innocent of their iniquity.

HUME: If he is a man of a generous disposition, care will be taken to keep him in that ignorance, which is not imputed as a crime by the Power who judges the heart. Thus, although the respective cause, in defence of which you lost your lives, are thought to be unjust, the one by the French, and the other by the English, you are both in these delightful fields. But, in yonder dark valley, are those who knowingly fought for injustice with all the perversity of corrupted nature. There groan these wicked men, who have forced a yielding people to abhor the English name, for which they were so favourably prepossessed, that they willingly proffered all the precious materials of a most luxuriant soil in exchange for insignificant trifles, and would have continued to enrich England, if these thirsty monsters had not, by fraud, slaughter, and desolation, almost dried up the sources of these treasures, and at the same time raised over their own heads mountains of guilt, to escape which they have vainly hastened to this place.

MONTGOMERY: Oh! let them be crushed for ever under the weight of remorse, since they are the principal cause of the American misfortune! since their depredations in that rich country have turned the eyes of avarice upon our poor land, and exposed our hard-acquired possessions to the persecuting eagerness that a spontaneous wealth inspires.

HUME: There is some foundation for this complaint: however, I advise Wolfe to beware of passionate exclamations, and to hear the arguments urged on both sides with coolness; for since he cannot be prejudiced in the American cause, this method of clearing it to satisfaction is the best I can recommend: consequently George Grenville is the properest opponent to Montgomery.

WOLFE: I would not willingly give offence to my adversary, by asking him to bear the pretence of the very man, who is deemed the first author of his wrongs.

MONTGOMERY: Would to Heaven all the enemies of the Americans were here to oppose me!

HUME: This is a truly patriotic wish! How far its accomplishment could be reconciled with justice, is more than I am willing to take the trouble to discuss. Adieu.

MONTGOMERY: this surmise favours of the Scotch policy, and this indolence comes from the selfishness breathed in the Epicurean bowers. Oh! let me exclaim with you against *the fatal power of prejudices*; since the most exalted souls, notwithstanding their just pretensions, are not, entirely, exempt from them.

END of the FIRST DIALOGUE.

———

DIALOGUE III.

BETWEEN
GENERAL WOLFE,
GENERAL MONTGOMERY,
CHARLES TOWNSHEND,
AND
DAVID HUME.

...

WOLFE: Then you accept this treaty [of peace] in the name of the Americans.

MONTGOMERY: Certainly I do; and they are very much altered in their sentiments since my death if they disown me for this assent. But I should wish that townshend were as sure to have the approbation of his party.

TOWNSHEND: It must be confessed that this may be questionable; however, by means of some secret clause –

MONTGOMERY: No clause at all, Townshend; for once, let not a treaty of peace be the foundation of a new war.

TOWNSHEND: At least we should consult about it some of the illustrious dead, and have distinguished themselves no less by a love for their country, than by their political abilities. Ah! – whence comes this insulting fit of laughter?

WOLFE: From David Hume, who, concealing himself behind this sycamore, has listened to our conversation.

MONTGOMERY: Is the important subject we have discussed so ridiculous in the eyes of philosophy?

HUME: Indeed it is so even in those of common sense. Poor souls! Miserably entranced in your former passions, you consider not, that though the access to this place is free, none of its inhabitants hath ever been allowed to return to that world which so much ingrosses your thoughts. Be not confounded at this observation; your zeal would prove equally useless, even if one of you were permitted to exert it among the living. Ask Demosthenes and Cicero concerning their former success: they will tell you how vainly they endeavoured to rescue their respective countries from the gulph of ruin. Was ever an eloquence so irresistible as theirs? So well suited for the purpose to which they employed it? They indeed ravished the minds of their hearers, but never changed their corrupted hearts; were admired for their expressions, but persecuted for their sentiments, and at last untimely sent hither to receive the reward of their virtue. It is true, a zealous patriot, a vehement orator, has now nothing to fear but the disgust and sorrow which attend ill success; happy for him, when he is convinced before his death, that nothing but empty notions, puerile prejudices, govern the generality of mankind, and decide the fate of empires. Be yourselves comforted by this truth; remember that if Julius Cæsar had returned the salutation of the senators, he might have lived to restore more freedom to his country which was effectually enslaved by his unworthy successors. Some such frivolous reasons may procure the peace you so ardently desire, better than your most solid arguments. Both the English and the Americans pretend to be in the right; to undeceive one of the parties, or both, would be only administering fuel to their fury. Let the ocean roar, we have happily reached the harbour.

MONTGOMERY: Oh! who can rejoice in his own safety, when he sees the companions of his toils tossed in the merciless waves?

WOLFE: Neither you, nor I, Montgomery, can boast of this insensibility.

TOWNSHEND: As to me, I am entirely of Hume's opinion on the subject; and think it a weakness unworthy of us to cherish useless feelings. Those men we just now inconsiderately pitied, have the same means for struggling against the evils of life as we had, and must in a short time arrive at this place of repose. Let us wait patiently for the event. I despair not to hear that both parties have acknowledged, that their fullest success against each other never can be a compensation for the reciprocal losses they must sustain in a separation of interest.

MONTGOMERY: No compensation!

TOWNSHEND: No: for a precarious absolute sovereignty on one side, and a momentary independence on the other, could not surely balance the advantages of a friendly union.

MONTGOMERY: Thus you now pretend that the Americans must – – –

TOWNSHEND: Be not angry with me, Montgomery; consider what lengths I had gone to make a treaty of peace conformable to your prepossessions, which yet were much different from my own; and confess, that the society of those who are actuated by the desire of pleasing every one, is more agreeable than that of morose men like Grenville, whose inflexible mind has not in the least been staggered by your strongest arguments.

WOLFE: This was a thing of course; for in this sort of debates the respective adversaries are too much urged by passion to listen to truth, which however finds its account in these virulent and reciprocal reproaches better than in guarded expressions, whose art may easily mislead the cool hearer. But alas! since it is in vain we have probed the wounds which discord has inflicted on the two contending countries, since we cannot pour into them the balm of a salutary advice, let us substitute the most ardent wishes to a fruitless zeal. May the eyes of our infatuated friends be open on the dangers which surround them! may they retreat in time under the wings of concord, and, by mutual tranquillity on earth, prepare themselves for eternal PEACE!

THE END.

75
HENRY MACKENZIE:
"THE STORY OF LA ROCHE"

Henry Mackenzie, "The Story of La Roche," *The Mirror*, 1779 June 19, 22, 26. Complete; from Mackenzie's *Works*, Edinburgh, Ballantyne, 1808, Vol. 4, pp. 175–207.

Born in Edinburgh to a prominent physician, Henry Mackenzie (1745–1831) was educated at the University of Edinburgh and worked in the legal profession. With the publication of *The Man of Feeling* (1771), his most successful novel, Mackenzie became a prominent literary figure. In 1779 he edited a short-lived literary magazine called *The Mirror*, to which he contributed forty-two articles. Among these is "The Story of La Roche," a fictional account of the young Hume's benevolent and unpretentious personality. Mackenzie later explained that he laboured to make Hume's character in the story as close to the real Hume's personality as possible:

[W]hen I wrote that story, being anxious there should not be a single expression in it that could give offence or uneasiness to any friend of Mr Hume's, I read it to Dr Adam Smith, and begged that he would tell me if any thing should be left out or altered. He heard it attentively, and declared he did not find a syllable to object to; but added, with his characteristic absence of mind, that he was surprised he had never heard of the anecdote before. [*An Account of the Life and Writings of John Home*, 1822, excerpted in this collection]

Set in the mid 1730s, the story opens with a young unnamed – and later famous – English philosopher retreating to a small French town where he can study in seclusion. An elderly protestant clergyman from Switzerland named La Roche, travelling with his young and beautiful daughter, takes ill while passing through the town. The English philosopher invites them both to his house, where La Roche slowly improves. The old minister and his daughter discover that their host is an infidel, but are fond and appreciative of him nonetheless. They return to Switzerland, accompanied by the young philosopher who is committed to La Roche's full recovery. The philosopher's easy and unassuming discourse endears him to his companions, and unexpressed romantic feelings take hold between him and the daughter. Arriving in their mountain village, the philosopher joins in their daily activities, including worship service. His natural conversational style fits perfectly within the rural environment. Mackenzie writes – probably as an accurate reflection of the real Hume – that "His discourse, indeed, was very remote from metaphysical disquisition, or religious controversy. Of all men I ever knew, his ordinary conversation was the least tinctured with pedantry, or liable to dissertation." In time he leaves, promising to correspond. While visiting Geneva three years later, he receives a note from the old minister announcing his daughter's engagement. Although disappointed, the philosopher journeys to their village for a visit. Upon arrival, he meets a funeral procession – that for the daughter who died of a broken heart when hearing that her betrothed was killed in a duel. The grieving father takes consolation in his religious beliefs and, after delivering a moving sermon, expresses to the philosopher "what importance religion is to calamity." Years later, when the philosopher's literary fame is established, he thinks nostalgically of La Roche, wishing "that he had never doubted."

In 1811 a pamphlet appeared titled *An Interesting Anecdote of a well known English Philosopher*, which was naively based on the plot of "La Roche." "La Roche" is included in several nineteenth-century editions of Mackenzie's works, the following of which is from the 1808 edition. Mackenzie provides background on the "Story of La Roche" in his *Account of the Life and Writings of John Home* (1822) and the *Anecdotes and Egotisms of Henry Mackenzie* (1927), excerpted later in this collection.

No. 42. SATURDAY, *June* 19, 1779.

When I first undertook this publication, it was suggested by some of my friends, and, indeed, accorded entirely with my own ideas, that there should be nothing of religion in it. There is a sacredness in the subject, that might seem profaned by its introduction into a work, which, to be extensively read, must sometimes be ludicrous, and often ironical. This consideration will apply, in the strongest manner, to any thing mystic or controversial; but it may, perhaps, admit of an exception, when religion is only introduced as a feeling, not a system, as appealing to the sentiments of the heart, not to the disquisitions of the head. The following story holds it up in that light, and is, therefore, I think, admissible into the Mirror. It was sent to my editor as a translation from the French. Of this my readers will judge. Perhaps they might be apt to suspect, without any suggestion from me, that it is an original, not a translation. Indeed, I cannot help thinking, that it contains in it much of that picturesque description, and that power of awakening the tender feelings, which so remarkably distinguish the composition of a gentleman, whose writings I have often read with pleasure. But, be that as it may, as I felt myself interested in the narrative, and believed that it would affect my readers in the like manner, I have ventured to give it entire as I received it, though it will take up the room of three successive papers.

Sir,

More than forty years ago, an English philosopher, whose works have since been read and admired by all Europe, resided at a little town in France. Some disappointments in his native country had first driven him abroad, and he was afterwards induced to remain there, from having found, in this retreat, where the connections even of nation and language were avoided, a perfect seclusion and retirement highly favourable to the development of abstract subjects, in which he excelled all the writers of his time.

Perhaps in the structure of such a mind as Mr ___'s, the finer and more delicate sensibilities are seldom known to have place; or, if originally implanted there, are in a great measure extinguished by the exertions of intense study and profound investigation. Hence the idea of philosophy and unfeelingness being united, has become proverbial, and in common language, the former word is often used to express the latter. – Our philosopher had been censured by some, as deficient in warmth and feeling: but the mildness of his manners has been allowed by all; and it is certain, that if he was not easily melted into compassion, it was, at least, not difficult to awaken his benevolence.

One morning, while he sat busied in those speculations which afterwards astonished the world, an old female domestic, who served him for a house-keeper, brought him word, that an elderly gentleman and his daughter had arrived in the village the preceding evening, on their way to some distant country, and that the father had been suddenly seized in the night with a dangerous disorder, which the people of the inn where they lodged feared would prove mortal: that she had been sent for, as having some knowledge in medicine, the village-surgeon being then absent; and that it was truly piteous to see the good old man, who seemed not so much afflicted by his own distress, as by that which it caused to his daughter. – Her master laid aside the volume in his hand, and broke off the chain of ideas it had inspired. His night-gown was exchanged for a coat, and he followed his gouvernante to the sick man's apartment.

It was the best in the little inn where they lay, but a paltry one notwith-standing. Mr ___ was obliged to stoop as he entered it. It was floored with earth, and above were the joists not plastered, and hung with cobwebs. – On a flock bed, at one end, lay the old man he came to visit; at the foot of it sat his daughter. She was dressed in a clean white bedgown; her dark locks hung loosely over it as she bent forward, watching the languid looks of her father. Mr ___ and his housekeeper had stood some moments in the room without the young lady's being sensible of their entering it. – "Mademoiselle!" said the old woman at last, in a soft tone. – She turned, and showed one of the finest faces in the world. It was touched, not spoiled, with sorrow; and when she perceived a stranger, whom the old woman now introduced to her, a blush at first, and then the gentle ceremonial of native politeness, which the affliction of the time tempered, but did not extinguish, crossed it for a moment, and changed its expression. – It was sweetness all, however, and our philosopher felt it strongly. It was not a time for words; he offered his services in a few sincere ones. "Monsieur lies miserably ill here," said the gouvernante; "if he could possibly be moved any where" – " If he could be moved to our house," said her master. – He had a spare bed for a friend, and there was a garret room unoccupied, next to the gouvernante's. It was contrived accordingly. The scruples of the stranger, who could look scruples, though he could not speak them, were overcome, and the bashful reluctance of his daughter gave way to her belief of its use to her father. The sick man was wrapt in blankets, and carried across the street to the English gentleman's. The old woman helped his daughter to nurse him there. The surgeon, who arrived soon after, prescribed a little, and nature did much for him; in a week he was able to thank his benefactor.

By that time his host had learned the name and character of his guest. He was a Protestant clergyman of Switzerland, called La Roche, a widower, who had lately buried his wife, after a long and lingering illness, for which travelling had been prescribed, and was now returning home, after an ineffectual and melancholy journey, with his only child, the daughter we have mentioned.

He was a devout man, as became his profession. He possessed devotion in all its warmth, but with none of its asperity; I mean that asperity which men, called devout, sometimes indulge in. Mr ___, though he felt no devotion, never quarrelled with it in others. His gouvernante joined the old man and his daughter in the prayers and thanksgivings which they put up on his recovery; for she, too, was a heretic, in the phrase of the village. – The philosopher walked out, with his long staff and his dog, and left them to his prayers and thanksgivings. – "My master," – said the old woman, "alas! he is not a Christian; but he is the best of unbelievers." – "Not a Christian!" – exclaimed Mademoiselle La Roche, "yet he saved my father! Heaven bless him for it; I would he were a Christian!" __ "There is a pride in human knowledge, my child," said her father, "which often blinds men to the sublime truths of revelation; hence opposers of Christianity are found among men of virtuous lives, as well as among those of dissipated and licentious characters. Nay, sometimes, I have known the latter more easily converted to the true faith than the former, because the fume of passion is more easily dissipated than the mist of false theory and delusive speculation." – "But Mr ___," said his daughter, "alas! my father, he shall be a Christian before he dies." – She was interrupted by the arrival of their landlord. – He took her hand with an air of kindness: –

she drew it away from him in silence; threw down her eyes to the ground, and left the room. – "I have been thanking God," said the good La Roche, "for my recovery." – "That is right," replied his landlord. – "I would not wish," continued the old man, hesitatingly, "to think otherwise; did I not look up with gratitude to that Being, I should barely be satisfied with my recovery, as a continuation of life, which, it may be, is not a real good. – Alas! I may live to wish I had died, that you had left me to die, Sir, instead of kindly relieving me, (he clasped Mr ___'s hand;) – but, when I look on this renovated being as the gift of the Almighty, I feel a far different sentiment – my heart dilates with gratitude and love to Him: it is prepared for doing His will, not as a duty, but as a pleasure, and regards every breach of it, not with disapprobation, but with horror." – "You say right, my dear Sir," replied the philosopher; "but you are not yet re-established enough to talk much – you must take care of your health, and neither study nor preach for some time. I have been thinking over a scheme that struck me today, when you mentioned your intended departure. I never was in Switzerland: I have a great mind to accompany your daughter and you into that country. – I will help to take care of you by the road; for, as I was your first physician, I hold myself responsible for your cure." La Roche's eyes glistened at the proposal; his daughter was called in and told of it. She was equally pleased with her father; for they really loved their landlord – not perhaps the less for his infidelity; at least that circumstance mixed a sort of pity with their regard for him – their souls were not of a mould for harsher feelings; hatred never dwelt in them.

No. 43. TUESDAY, *June* 22, 1779.
CONTINUATION OF THE STORY OF LA ROCHE.

They travelled by short stages; for the philosopher was as good as his word, in taking care that the old man should not be fatigued. The party had time to be well acquainted with on another, and their friendship was increased by acquaintance. La Roche found a degree of simplicity and gentleness in his companion, which is not always annexed to the character of a learned or a wise man. His daughter, who was prepared to be afraid of him, was equally undeceived. She found in him nothing of that self-importance, which superior parts, or great cultivation of them, is apt to confer. He talked of every thing but philosophy or religion; he seemed to enjoy every pleasure and amusement of ordinary life, and to be interested in the most common topics of discourse: when his knowledge or learning at any time appeared, it was delivered with the utmost plainness, and without the least shadow of dogmatism.

On his part, he was charmed with the society of the good clergyman and his lovely daughter. He found in them the guileness manner of the earliest times, with the culture and accomplishment of the most refined ones. Every better feeling, warm and vivid; every ungentle one, repressed or overcome. He was not addicted to love; but he felt himself happy in being the friend of Mademoiselle La Roche, and sometimes envied her father the possession of such a child.

After a journey of eleven days, they arrived at the dwelling of La Roche. It was situated in one of those valleys of the canton of Berne, where nature seems to repose, as it were, in quiet, and has enclosed her retreat with mountains inaccessible. – A stream, that spent its fury in the hills above, ran in front of the house, and a broken water-fall was seen through the wood that covered its sides; below, it circled round a tufted plain, and formed a little lake in front of a village, at the end of which appeared the spire of La Roche's church, rising above a clump of beeches.

Mr ___ enjoyed the beauty of the scene; but to his companions, it recalled the memory of a wife and parent they had lost. The old man's sorrow was silent; his daughter sobbed and wept. Her father took her hand, kissed it twice, pressed it to his bosom, threw up his eyes to heaven; and, having wiped off a tear, that was just about to drop from each, began to point out to his guest some of the most striking objects which the prospect afforded. The philosopher interrupted all this; and he could but slightly censure the creed from which it arose.

They had not been long arrived, when a number of La Roche's parishioners, who had heard of his return, came to the house to see and welcome him. The honest folks were awkward, but sincere, in their professions of regard. They made some attempts at condolence; it was too delicate for their handling; but La Roche took it in good part. "It has pleased God," said he; and they saw he had settled the matter with himself. Philosophy could not have done so much with a thousand words.

It was now evening, and the good peasants were about to depart, when a clock was heard to strike seven, and the hour was followed by a particular chime. The country folks, who had come to welcome their pastor, turned their looks towards him at the sound; he explained their meaning to the guest. That is the signal," said he, "for our evening exercises; this is one of the nights of the week in which some of my parishioners are wont to join in it: a little rustic saloon serves for the chapel of our family, and such of the good people as are with us; if you chuse rather to walk out, I will furnish you with an attendant; or here are a few old books, that may afford you some entertainment within." – "By no means," answered the philosopher; "I will attend Ma'moiselle at her devotions." – "She is our organist," said La Roche; "our neighbourhood is the country of musical mechanisms; and I have a small organ fitted up for the purpose of assisting our singing." – "'Tis an additional inducement," replied the other; and they walked into the room together. At the end stood the organ mentioned by La Roche; before it was a curtain, which his daughter drew aside, and, placing herself on a seat within, and drawing the curtain close, so as to save her the awkwardness of an exhibition, began a voluntary, solemn and beautiful in the highest degree. Mr ___ was no musician, but he was not altogether insensible to music; this fastened on his mind more strongly, from its beauty being unexpected. The solemn prelude introduced a hymn, in which such of the audience as could sing immediately joined; the words were mostly taken from holy writ; it spoke the praises of God, and his care of good men. Something was said of the death of the just, of such as die in the Lord. – The organ was touched with a hand less firm; – it paused, it ceased; and the sobbing of Ma'moiselle La Roche was heard in its stead. Her father gave a sign for stopping the psalmody, and rose to pray. He was discomposed at first, and his voice faltered as he spoke; but his heart was in his words, and his warmth overcame his embarrassment. He addressed a being whom he loved, and he spoke for those he loved. His parishioners catched the ardour of the good old man; even the philosopher felt himself moved, and forgot, for a moment, to think why he should not.

La Roche's religion was that of sentiment, not theory, and his guest was averse from disputation; their discourse, therefore, did not lead to questions concerning the belief of either; yet would the old man sometimes speak of his, from the fulness of a heart impressed with its force, and wishing to spread the pleasure he enjoyed in it. The ideas of his God, and his Saviour, were so congenial to his mind, that every emotion of it naturally awakened them. A philosopher might have called him an enthusiast; but, if he possessed the fervour of enthusiasts, he was guiltless of their bigotry. "Our Father which art in Heaven!" might the good man say – for he felt it – and all mankind were his brethren.

"You regret, my friend," said he to Mr ___, "when my daughter and I talk of the exquisite pleasure derived from music, you regret your want of musical powers and musical feelings; it is a department of soul, you say, which nature has almost denied you, which, from the effects you see it have on others, you are sure must be highly delightful. Why should not the same thing be said of religion? Trust me, I feel it in the same way, an energy, an inspiration, which I would not lose for all the blessings of sense or enjoyments of the world; yet so far from lessening my relish of the pleasures of life, methinks I feel it heighten them all. The thought of receiving it from God, adds the blessing of sentiment to that of sensation in every good thing I possess; and when calamities overtake me – and I have had my share – it confers a dignity on my affliction, so lifts me above the world! – Man, I know, is but a worm, – yet, methinks, I am then allied to God!" – It would have been inhuman in our philosopher to have clouded, even with a doubt, the sunshine of this belief.

His discourse, indeed, was very remote from metaphysical disquisition, or religious controversy. Of all men I ever knew, his ordinary conversation was the least tinctured with pedantry, or liable to dissertation. With L Roche and his daughter it was perfectly familiar. The country round them, the manners of the villagers, the comparison of both with those of England, remarks on the works of favourite authors, on the sentiments they conveyed, and the passions they excited, with many other topics in which there was an equality, or alternate advantage, among the speakers, were the subjects they talked on. Their hours too of riding and walking were many, in which Mr ___, as a stranger, was shewn the remarkable scenes and curiosities of the country. They would sometimes make little expeditions, to contemplate, in different attitudes, those astonishing mountains, the cliffs on which, covered with eternal snows, and sometimes shooting into fantastic shapes, form the termination of most of the Swiss prospects. Our philosopher asked many questions as to their natural history and productions. La Roche observed the sublimity of the ideas which the view of their stupendous summits, inaccessible to mortal foot, was calculated to inspire, which naturally, said he, leads the mind to that Being by whom their foundations were laid. – "They are not seen in Flanders!" said Ma'moiselle, with a sigh. "That's an odd remark," said Mr ___, smiling. – She blushed, and he inquired no farther.

It was with regret he left a society in which he found himself so happy; but he settled with La Roche and his daughter a plan of correspondence; and they took his promise, that, if ever he came within fifty leagues of their dwelling, he should travel those fifty leagues to visit them.

No. 44. SATURDAY, *June* 26, 1779.
CONCLUSION OF THE STORY OF LA ROCHE.

About three years after, our philosopher was on a visit at Geneva; the promise he made to La Roche and his daughter, on his former visit, was recalled to his mind, by the view of that range of mountains, on a part of which they had often looked together. There was a reproach, too, conveyed along with the recollection, for his having failed to write to either for several months past. The truth was, that indolence was the habit most natural to him, from which he was not easily roused by the claims of correspondence either of his friends or of his enemies; when the latter drew their pens in controversy, they were often unanswered as well as the former. While he was hesitating about a visit to La Roche, which he wished to make, but found the effort rather too much for him, he received a letter from the old man, which had been forwarded to him from Paris, where he had then fixed his residence. It contained a gentle complaint of Mr ___'s want of punctuality, but an assurance of continued gratitude for his former good offices; and, as a friend whom the writer considered interested in his family, it informed him of the approaching nuptials of Ma'moiselle La Roche, with a young man, a relation of her own, and formerly a pupil of her father's, of the most amiable dispositions, and respectable character. Attached from the earliest years, they had been separated by his joining one of the subsidiary regiments of the Canton, then in the service of a foreign power. In this situation, he had distinguished himself as much for courage and military skill, as for the other endowments which he had cultivated at home. The time of his service was now expired, and they expected him to return in a few weeks, when the old man hoped, as he expressed it in his letter, to join their hands, and see them happy before he died.

Our philosopher felt himself interested in this event; but he was not, perhaps, altogether so happy in the tidings of Ma'moiselle La Roche's marriage, as her father supposed him. Not that he was ever a lover of the lady's; but he thought her one of the most amiable women he had seen, and there was something in the idea of her being another's for ever, that struck him, he knew not why, like a disappointment. After some little speculation on the matter, however, he could look on it as a thing fitting, if not quite agreeable, and determined on this visit to see his old friend and his daughter happy.

On the last day of his journey, different accidents had retarded his progress: he was benighted before he reached the quarter in which La Roche resided. His guide, however, was well acquainted with the road, and he found himself at last in view of the lake, which I have before described, in the neighbourhood of La Roche's dwelling. A light gleamed on the water, that seemed to proceed from the house; it moved slowly along as he proceeded up the side of the lake, and at last he saw it glimmer through the trees, and stop at some distance from the place where he then was. He supposed it some piece of bridal merriment, and pushed on his horse that he might be a spectator of the scene; but he was a good deal shocked, on approaching the spot, to find it proceed from the torch of a person clothed in the dress of an attendant on a funeral, and accompanied by several others, who, like him, seem to have been employed in the rites of sepulture.

On Mr ___'s making inquiry who was the person they had been burying? one of them, with an accent more mournful than is common to their profession, answered, "Then you knew not Mademoiselle, Sir? – you never beheld a lovelier" – "La Roche!" exclaimed he, in reply – "Alas! it was she indeed!" – The appearance of surprise and grief which his countenance assumed, attracted the notice of the peasant with whom he talked. He came up closer to Mr ___; "I perceive, Sir, you were acquainted with Mademoiselle La Roche." "Acquainted with her! – Good God! – when – how – where did she die! Where is her father?" "She died, Sir, of heart-break, I believe; the young gentleman to whom she was soon to have been married, was killed in a duel by a French officer, his intimate companion, and to whom, before their quarrel, he had often done the greatest favours. Her worthy father bears her death, as he has often told us a Christian should; he is even so composed, as to be now in his pulpit, ready to deliver a few exhortations to his parishioners, as is the custom with us on such occasions: – Follow me, Sir, and you shall hear him." He followed the man without answering.

The church was dimly lighted, except near the pulpit, where the venerable La Roche was seated. His people were now lifting up their voices in a psalm to that Being whom their pastor had taught them ever to bless and to revere. La Roche sat, his figure bending gently forward, his eyes half-closed, lifted up in silent devotion. A lamp placed near him threw its light strong on his head, and marked the shadowy lines of age across the paleness of his brow, thinly covered with grey hairs.

The music ceased; La Roche sat for a moment, and nature wrung a few tears from him. His people were loud in their grief. Mr ___ was not less affected than they. La Roche arose. "Father of mercies!" said he, "forgive these tears; assist thy servant to lift up his soul to thee; to lift to thee the souls of they people! My friends! It is good so to do: at all seasons it is good; but, in the days of our distress, what a privilege it is! Well saith the sacred book, 'Trust in the Lord; at all times trust in the Lord.' When every other support fails us, when the fountains of worldly comfort are dried up, let us then seek those living waters which flow from the throne of God. 'Tis only from the belief of the goodness and wisdom of a Supreme Being, that our calamities can be borne in that manner which becomes a man. Human wisdom is here of little use; for, in proportion as it bestows comfort, it represses feeling, without which we may cease to be hurt by calamity, but we shall also cease to enjoy happiness. I will not bid you be insensible, my friends! I cannot, I cannot, if I would (his tears flowed afresh) – I feel too much myself, and I am not ashamed of my feelings; but therefore may I the more willingly be heard; therefore have I prayed God to give me strength to speak to you; to direct you to Him, not with empty words, but with these tears; not from speculation, but from experience, – that while you see me suffer, you may know also my consolation.

"You behold the mourner of his only child, the last earthly stay and blessing of his declining years! Such a child too! – It becomes not me to speak of her virtues; yet it is but gratitude to mention them, because they were exerted towards myself. Not many days ago you saw her young, beautiful, virtuous, and happy; ye who are parents will judge of my felicity then, – ye will judge of my affliction now. But I look towards Him who struck me; I see the hand of a father amidst the chastenings of my God. Oh! could I make you feel what it is to pour out the heart, when it is pressed down with many sorrows, to pour it out with confidence to Him, in whose hands are life and death, on whose power awaits all that the first enjoys, and in contemplation of whom disappears all that the last can inflict! For we are not as those who die without hope; we know that our Redeemer liveth, – that we shall live with him, with our friends, His servants, in that blessed land where sorrow is unknown, and happiness is endless as it is perfect. Go then, mourn not for me; I have not lost my child: but a little while, and we shall meet again never to be separated. But ye are also my children: would ye that I should not grieve without comfort? So live as she lived: that, when your death cometh, it may be the death of the righteous, and your latter end like his."

Such was the exhortation of La Roche; his audience answered it with their tears. The good old man had dried up his at the altar of the Lord; his counte-

nance had lost its sadness, and assumed the glow of faith and of hope. Mr __
followed him into his house. The inspiration of the pulpit was past; at sight of
him the scenes they had last met in, rushed again on his mind; La Roche threw
his arms round his neck, and watered it with his tears. The other was equally
affected; they went together, in silence, into the parlour, where the evening
service was wont to be performed. The curtains of the organ were open; La
Roche started back at the sight. "Oh! my friend!" said he, and his tears burst
forth again. Mr __ had now recollected himself; he stept forward, and drew
the curtains close – the old man wiped off his tears, and taking his friend's hand,
"You see my weakness," said he, "'tis the weakness of humanity; but my
comfort is not therefore lost." "I heard you," said the other, "in the pulpit; I
rejoice that such consolation is yours." "It is, my friend," said he; "and I trust
I shall ever hold it fast; if there are any who doubt our faith, let them think of
what importance religion is to calamity, and forbear to weaken its force; if they
cannot restore our happiness, let them not take away the solace of our
affliction."[1]

Mr __'s heart was smitten; and I have heard him, long after, confess, that
there were moments when the remembrance overcame him even to weakness;
when, amidst all the pleasures of philosophical discovery, and the pride of
literary fame, he recalled to his mind the venerable figure of good La Roche,
and wished that he had never doubted.

---

[1] [In *The Anecdotes and Egotisms of Henry Mackenzie* (selections from which are
contained in this collection) Mackenzie states that Hume's views expressed here are
based on Hume's true reaction to his own mother's death as witnessed by Patrick
Boyle.]

76
THOMAS TYERS:
AN HISTORICAL ESSAY ON MR. ADDISON

Thomas Tyers, *An historical essay on Mr. Addison*, London: printed by J. Nichols for the author, 1783, viii, 76 p.
Selections, from 1783 edition.

Miscellaneous writer Thomas Tyers (1726–1787) is most noted for his short biographical works on Pope, Addison, and Johnson, and his *Political Conferences Between Several Great Men, in the Last and Present Century* (1780). Tyers opens his biography of Addison with a discussion of autobiographical writing in general, and criticizes Hume's "My Own Life" for concealing important facts, particularly his dispute with Rousseau.

An intimate acquaintance of Dr. Johnson (why should not the reader know it was the author of this essay?) advised him to set about writing his own life, as soon as he concluded the biography of the English poets: for, if he totally neglected it, somebody might write it for him. A departed author and all that he leaves behind him are considered as much the property of a harpy pen, as a Cornish shipwreck or a herriot the rightful claim of the lord of the manor. To obviate this inconvenience and injury, David Hume, just before it was too late, composed an account of himself; telling the world perhaps nothing that was false, but probably concealing many things, which, if viewed through the wrong end of the perspective, he fancied might make against him. For no man is obliged to become his own accuser, or be an evidence against himself. His article in the Biographia will probably enter into more particulars of his life and opinions. On the possibility of Rousseau's outliving him (the public is reading at this time the first part of Rousseau's life written by himself with different degrees of approbation) he thought it worth his while to publish a defence of his conduct towards that great genius and unhappy man (whom he brought into England) who gave out, that the whole world was in a conspiracy against his life and his independence. Hume (who says, he was never attacked by the baleful tooth of calumny) acknowledges he was afraid of the power of his eloquence, which might make more converts than his arguments. Our passions are convinced before our reason, which is too often made a dupe of. No court but the Areopagus (annihilated by the popular Pericles) has set it's face against the seduction of oratory. Tropes and figures take the hearer and reader by storm. We must be chained to the mast, if we are determined to hear the music of the Syrens. Hume resolved to have the first word against Rousseau, which in some cases prevents the ill effects of the last, and lodged an appeal in his own favour. De Retz thinks that every statesman should be his own historian, provided he has candour enough to confess the errors of his conduct; since no one can know the truth so well as himself. Voltaire praises his ingenuousness and the dignity of his mind. Ramsay in his life of Turenne condemns the Cardinal and his memoirs. In our own times Lord Chesterfield recommends the study of them to his own Son. It is difficult, says the *melancholy* Cowley, for a man to speak of himself, though it is necessary on some occasions not to be silent. Even a little vanity, that frequent spur to splendid actions, is to be pardoned, when an illustrious servant of the public is obliged to enter into a long defensive narrative. Who is more agreeable than Cicero, Lord Herbert, Cornaro, Sir William Temple, Montangne, Clarendon, Cowley, or even Colley Cibber? ...

Addison lived not half the days of Hobbes, but to much better purpose, by his precept and example .... The fame of Hobbes is decaying very fast, while Addison, according to the observation of David Hume (no cowardly philosopher with regard to death or darkness) will be read with pleasure, when [even] Locke shall be entirely forgotten"

77
VICESIMUS KNOX:
WINTER EVENINGS

[Vicesimus Knox], *Winter evenings: or lucubrations on life and letters. In three volumes*. London: printed for Charles Dilly, 1788. 3 v. Selections from "On Dull Style" and "Of the Folly"; from 1788 edition.

B orn in Newington Green, Middlesex, Vicesimus Knox (1752–1821) was a fellow of St John's College, Oxford, and later headmaster of Tunbridge School. A miscellaneous writer and harsh critic of prevailing educational systems, Knox is best remembered for his *Essays, Moral and Literary* (1778), *Liberal Education* (1781), and *The Spirit of Despotism* (1795). In a 1788 collection of essays titled *Winter Evenings*, Knox criticizes Hume in two entries. In "Of the Dull Style" he argues that sceptics are, by nature, unsentimental, unimaginative, and sleep inducing. Hume's metaphysics, he contends, is a case in point. In "Of the Folly" Knox defends the use of wit and ridicule in religious discussions. He notes that "many parts of Hume's philosophy appear to carry with them their own refutation by inherent absurdity." However, he states that Horne's abusive attacks against Hume in *Letters on Infidelity* were justified. Reviews of Knox's work were mixed. The *Critical Review* commented that "To the proficient, it is a work of amusement rather than of novelty" (September 1788, Vol. 66, pp. 184–187). Writing for the *Monthly Review*, Andrew Becket took issue with Knox's somewhat scholastic and religiously zealous style, but acknowledged "marks of understanding" (October 1788, Vol. 79, pp. 336–342). Knox's *Winter Evenings* was published a second time in 1788, and again in 1790, 1795, 1805, 1825, and 1824 *Works* (Vols 2 and 3). The following is from the London 1788 edition.

CHAP. X.
Of the dull Style.

Writers of strong intellect are often without imagination and sentiment, and consequently dull. They syllogize admirably; but they cannot impress ideas with force, they cannot paint images with the pencil of fancy in the shape and colours of nature. They know not how to use the figure which the ancients call *Enargeia*, and which consisted in representing the actions or facts related in so lively a manner as to render the reader a spectator. Their books are therefore approved; and then laid up on the shelf, where they continue in very good condition for sale, whenever it shall be their lot to be placed in a bookseller's catalogue. The dull style is an excellent preservative of books, as far as the binding and paper are concerned.

Metaphysical writers have greatly countenanced the dull style. Their topics are of such a nature as scarcely to admit of vivacity. Yet they are voluminous. they have no pity on their readers, who, if they mean to be acquainted with the recondite authors, are obliged to toil with a pick-axe through tomes of dulness, with as much darkness around them, and labour in their progress, as if they were at work in the lead-mines. I wonder that there should be many such writers; but I wonder more that they should have any readers, except those invalids who labour under the want of sleep, and who find such pages wonderfully efficacious in promoting gentle slumbers.

There are many large works with pompous and specious titles which may be said to be written upon NOTHING, consisting of mere speculation and fanciful reasoning, which, while it pretends to argument and solidity, is more airy and visionary than the romance of Cassandra. It would be easy to enumerate many works metaphysical, theological, sceptical, philosophical, and political, which are mere cobwebs, spun from the brain of inexperienced and unlearned specialists, taking up much time in the reading, puzzling, confounding every thing they touch upon, and leading to no valuable conclusion. Then novelty, and the fame they sometimes acquire by the appearance of profound knowledge and wonderful refinement, has procured them readers, and introduced a taste for, or at least a patient attention to, dull thought in languid language.

Sceptical writers and abusers of Christianity are often men of disputatious tempers with little sentiment and fancy, and consequently their works are, with few exceptions, very soporific. Even Lord Bolingbroke, a lively writer on other occasions, displays in his philosophical writings a style and manner of writing which may be called mere lullaby. Hume's metaphysics are also worthy to be offered up at the shrine of Morpheus, unless Vulcan should make a prior claim to them.

Few, I think, would wade through the dull and dry speculations of infidels and airy metaphysicians, if they were not supported in their progress by self-flattery. They please themselves with the fancied consciousness of great depth, subtlety, and acuteness; and are also not unwilling to be considered by those who know what they read, as very profound thinkers; men above the level of the vulgar prejudice, free from the shackles of education, sitting like gods in the skies, and beholding other poor mortals blindly wandering in the regions below them. A little cloudiness, and even darkness, contributes to augment the dignity of writers and readers.

It seems probable, *a priori*, that men who write against religion should be dull; for men of great sensibility feel devotion very forcibly. Their love, their gratitude, their hopes and their fears, are all powerfully influenced by religious ideas. But the frigid philosopher allows nothing to sensations of which he is not conscious, but, at the same time, would bring every thing to the tribunal of his own reason, which he considers as infallible....

CHAP. XIV.

Of the Folly of suffering the Judgment to be seduced by Wit, in Things of Moment.

...

Dr. Horne, the present Dean of Canterbury, who has discovered a genuine spirit of piety in his writings, and displayed the beauty of holiness in all its charms, has attacked the philosophy of Hume with the arms of ridicule. Indeed many parts of Hume's philosophy appear to carry with them their own refutation by inherent absurdity; but they fall into the hands of those whose want of learning and of principles induces them to admit the arguments of sophistry in defence of libertinism. Dr. Horne justly supposed that the admirers of Hume were more likely to be disabused of their error by the fear of derision, than by any force of argumentation. He has indeed derided both Hume and the Humists, as they affect to style themselves, with singular success. I only wish that the part of his book in which they are attacked could be universally introduced to their notice. It would operate as an antidote to his poison, unless indeed its genuine effect should be prevented by the force of established prejudice.

The latter part of Dr. Horne's letters upon infidelity I should not have regretted, if it had been entirely omitted. It owes its origin to an obscure pamphlet, which would never have emerged to notice by its proper power: and the difficulties of many passages in Scripture are by no means removed by the remarks of the pious Dean, however ingenious and well-intended.

After all, it must be owned, that great caution is required in the use of wit and humour as auxiliary to the cause of religion. They induce a levity of mind, which is too apt to degenerate to a wanton disregard of every thing serious. Religion, like a chaste matron, should appear in a dress which excites sentiments of respect, and forbids familiarity. When she is introduced to mankind in a grotesque or a gay attire, she ought to be under the direction of a guide who can teach her to preserve an air of dignity in the midst of her condescension: I mean to suggest that wit and humour, like that which is applied by Dr. Horne, should never be used in religious subjects but by writers whose judgment is superior to their comic abilities, and whose comic abilities would, like Yorick's, set the table in a roar. ...

78
ISAAC DISRAELI:
MISCELLANIES

Isaac Disraeli, *Miscellanies; or, literary recreations. By I. D'Israeli.* London: printed for T. Cadell and W. Davies, 1796. xxiv, 432, [i.e., 418], [2] p. Selections; from 1796 edition.

Born in London, Isaac Disraeli (1766–1848) was from a Jewish family that migrated from Italy to England in 1748. Against the wishes of his parents, he devoted himself to literature at an early age, meeting renowned figures of his time, and at twenty-five made his mark as a narrator of literary anecdotes with the publication of his *Curiosities of Literature* (1791–1793). Following in this genre, he later published *An Essay on the Manners and Genius of the Literary Character* (1795),[1] *Calamities of Authors* (1812–1813) and *Quarrels of Authors* (1814). Disraeli's Miscellanies is a collection of twenty-one essays on writing technique, with occasional discussions of Hume. In "On Style" he discusses Hume's conception of fine writing. In "Historical Characters" he examines techniques of writing autobiography and praises Hume's as "a model of attic simplicity." In "On Erudition and Philosophy" he notes how some have criticized Hume's *History* "for intermingling with his lucid narrative, his acute reflections." In "Of Licensers of the Press" he discusses Hume's notions of the liberty of the press. In their favourable review of Disraeli's *Miscellanies*, the *English Review* applauded the uniqueness of his works, stating that "to have striking and discriminating features, of any kind, in literary composition, is no small degree of excellence" (1796, Vol. 27, pp. 334–340). Writing for the *Monthly Review*, William Taylor praises Disraeli's past writings and notes that "his progress has been marked by improvement" (December 1797, Vol. 24, pp. 374–379).

---

[1] Quotations from *Curiosities* and the *Essay* are contained in this collection under "Miscellaneous Hume Anecdotes."

ON STYLE.

...

I mean not to oppose the opinions of the warm admirers of simplicity. A beautiful simplicity itself is a species of refinement; and no writer more solicitously corrected his works than Hume, who excels in the mode of composition. But is it not an evident error in men of taste to form a predilection for any peculiar Style; since all the intermediate species of diction between simplicity and refinement are equally beautiful, when they form, the appropriate tone of the subject? We often enquire if an author's Style is beautiful or sublime; we should rather desire to know whether it was proper. ... Hume, who has all the refinement of simplicity, highly approves of Addison's definition of fine writing, who says, that it consists of sentiments which are natural, without being obvious. This is surely no definition of fine writing, but of fine thinking. The elegant author has omitted the magical graces of diction; the modulation of harmonious cadences, the art of expressing, with delicacy, delicate ideas, and painting sublime conceptions in the magnificence of language. In my opinion Shenstone has ascertained the truth; for fine writing he defines to be generally the effect of spontaneous thoughts and a laboured Style. ...

HISTORICAL CHARACTERS ARE FALSE REPRESENTATIONS *of* NATURE.

... To publish one's own life has sometimes been a poor artifice to bring obscurity into notice; it is the extravagance of vanity, and the delirium of egotism. When a great man leaves some memorial of his days, his deathbed sanctions the truth, and the grave consecrates the motive. There are certain things which relate to ourselves, which no one can know so well; a great genius obliges posterity when he records them. But they must be composed with calmness, with simplicity, and with sincerity; the Biographic Sketch of Hume, written by himself, is a model of attic simplicity. This is the only production of a man of genius, which requires no graces of style or imagination. His pencil should give dignity to the common accidents of life, by its clear and firm strokes; but he should be careful not to overshade and adorn his sketch, by a penciling too elaborate. If he is solicitous of charming and dazzling, he is not writing his life, but pourtraying the ideal adventurer of a romance. If he attempts to draw a resemblance between himself and a superior genius, let him be fearful of incurring the ridicule of those modern artists, who have painted themselves in the dress of Raphael and Rubens; this self-admiration forms a fatal contrast. Simplicity of language and thought, are sweet and natural graces, which every Self-biographer should study. ...

ON ERUDITION AND PHILOSOPHY.

...

When the elaborate labours of an Erudit, are at length published, it is discovered, that he has no skill in the art of composition. Such writers never become public favourites; their eye never dwells on an image which might enliven, or their ear on a cadence which might harmonise, a period. This numerous race of literati, have no conception of the delight in composition, without which, the writer is in vain learned. Some consider the pleasures of literature as not only superfluous, but criminal; and that a reflection, they might happen to make, would only insult their reader's understanding. An annalist is therefore preferred to an historian; Hume is censured, for intermingling with his lucid narrative, his acute reflections; and they affirm that they re capable of reflecting for themselves. But this is neither modesty nor truth. ...

OF LICENSERS OF THE PRESS.

...

With the revolution, ceased, in England, the licences for the press; but it's liberty did not commence till 1694, when every restraint was taken off, by the firm and decisive tone of the Commons. It was granted, says our philosophic Hume, "to the great displeasure of the King and his Ministers, who, seeing no where, in any government during present or past ages, any example of such unlimited freedom, doubted much of it's salutary effects, and probably thought, that no books or writings would ever so much improve the general understanding of men, as to render it safe to entrust them with an indulgence so easily abused."[2]

And the present moment verifies the prescient conjecture of the philosopher. Such, indeed, is the existing licentiousness of our press, that some, not perhaps the most hostile to the cause of freedom, would not be averse to manacle authors once more with an IMPRIMATUR. It may be honestly urged, that the worst abuse of the press, is more tolerable than would be such a violation of national liberty; but this is certain, that it is not any more in the power of a despotic Minister to annihilate this freedom; because if the great instructors of mankind could find no other redress against the capricious tyranny of the Imprimatur, they would fly to foreign presses, and it would then happen, that England, which first diffused a spirit of true freedom in Europe, would be neces-sitated to receive it from those very nations on whom she had bestowed it. The profound Hume has declared, that "THE LIBERTY OF BRITAIN IS GONE FOR EVER when such attempts shall succeed."[3] But I venture to assert, that this Liberty

---

[2]   [*History*, Chapter 71.]

[3]   [*Essays*, "Of the Liberty of the Press."]

may become a beloved exile, but never an abdicated monarch; banish her from Britain, but while there exists an open press in America, and even among our cruel rivals the French, she will be reverenced at a distance, and will, at some future day, be received again on her natal shores, as our natural sovereign.
...

79
ROBERT HALL:
MODERN INFIDELITY CONSIDERED

Robert Hall, *Modern infidelity considered with respect to its influence on society: in a sermon, preached at the Baptist meeting, Cambridge. By Robert Hall, A.M.* Cambridge: printed by M. Watson, and sold by J. Deighton, and O. Gregory; by J. James, Bristol; W. Button, and T. Conder, London, 1800, [2],viii, 81,[1] p.
Selections; from *Works*, New York, Harper, 1848, Vol. 1, pp. 21–53.

Robert Hall (1764–1831) was born in Arnesby, Leicestershire, the youngest of fourteen children of a Baptist minister. By age eleven Hall had preached at a religious meeting. He attended the Baptist Academy at Bristol, and was ordained in 1779. He received his M.A. from King's College, Aberdeen, and during his time in that city became friends with Scottish philosopher James Mackintosh (1765–1832), forming a society called the "Hall and Mackintosh Club." He worked in churches for a time in Bristol, where he gained a reputation for his powerful sermons. Beginning in 1791 he became pastor for 15 years at a Cambridge church, where he delivered his most famous sermon "Modern Infidelity Considered." Olinthus Gregory, Hall's friend and later editor of his *Works*, describes how he would prepare his sermons. Without writing them down beforehand, he would organize the material, extemporize upon it in the pulpit, and then commit it to memory. On two occasions in October 1800, Hall delivered "Modern Infidelity Considered," and after this he put it on paper at the encouragement of Gregory and others. The sermon is a harsh attack on infidels – including Hume – who not only promote atheism but have redefined the notions of morality and threaten to undermine the moral fabric of society.

Perhaps not coincidentally, Mackintosh was the author of the lengthy review of Hall's work in the *Monthly Review*. Lavishing praise on the work, Mackintosh writes, "This sermon, indeed, is in every respect entitled to rank among the first productions of the age. It is distinguished by solid and profound philosophy; the very reverse of that sorry and shallow sophistry which has of late usurped the name." However, Macintosh charges that Hall mistakenly attributed a view to Hume regarding adultery, based on a misreading of Hume's "A Dialogue":

As to some of the writers on whom Mr. Hall as animadverted in this passage, we abandon them to his just severity: but he has certainly mistaken the opinions of Mr. Hume. It is very true that, as an historian, Mr. Hume has not spoken with great harshness of the softer vices: but, as a moral philosopher, he has everywhere blamed them as injurious to society. The sentiment which Mr. Hall ascribes to him is not given as his own, but as a quotation from La Fontaine; and it is not mentioned by Mr. Hume as a maxim of morality, but as descriptive of the dissolute manners of France: – "*Quand on le sçait, c'est peu de chose; Quand on ne le sçait pas, ce n'est rien*" This is a mistake which ought to be corrected in a future edition of the sermon. [*Monthly Review*, February 1800, Vol. 31, pp. 191–197]

Later editions of Hall's sermon delete the sentence in question. The *Critical Review* took an opposite stance on the merits of Hall's sermon.

... the preacher asserts, that 'a great majority on the continent, and a considerable portion in England, of those who pursue literature as a profession, may be justly considered as the open or disguised abettors of atheism.' This assertion, as far as it relates to the writers in England, we have no scruple in contradicting. It is an idle figment of the imagination. The writer has never given himself the trouble of consulting the periodical publications, from which he may easily collect the names of the living authors in Great-Britain, so as to compare the number of persons who abet atheism with that of those who are its open and decided foes. From a much greater intercourse with the literati, we declare the assertion to be unfounded; and we see no reason for raising the spirits of atheists, whose number or talents cannot confer any distinction upon them, either in literature or in the state. This assertion of the writer is a sufficient clue to the whole of this long treatise. He is inflamed with the present mania; and the French revolution has taken from him the powers of discrimination. Atheism, scepticism, and infidelity, are terms which he uses one for the other; and being at no pains to distinguish between them, he has presented to the public a strange farrago, though he shows powers capable, under proper correction, of raising him to some degree of eminence among those 'who pursue literature as a profession.' [*Critical Review*, April 1800, Vol. 28, pp. 455–456]

Modern Infidelity Considered was republished three more times in 1800. It appeared again as a separate pamphlet in 1802, 1804, 1811, 1835, and 1853, and is included in over 30 editions of Hall's *Works*.

MODERN INFIDELITY CONSIDERED.
A SERMON.

EPHES. ii. 12.
Without God in the world.

As the Christian ministry is established for the instruction of men, throughout every age, in truth and holiness, it must adapt itself to the ever-shifting scenes of the moral world, and stand ready to repel the attacks of impiety and error, under whatever form they may appear. The church and the world form two societies so distinct, and are governed by such opposite principles and maxims, that, as well from this contrariety as from the express warnings of Scripture, true Christians must look for a state of warfare, with this consoling assurance, that the church, like the burning bush beheld by Moses in the land of Midian, may be encompassed with flames, but will never be consumed. ...

Lord HERBERT, the first and purest of our English freethinkers, who flourished in the beginning of the reign of Charles the First, did not so much impugn the doctrine or the morality of the Scriptures, as attempt to supersede their necessity, by endeavouring to show that the great principles of the unity of God, a moral government, and a future world, are taught with sufficient clearness by the light of nature. BOLINGBROKE, and some of his successors, advanced much farther, and attempted to invalidate the proofs of the moral character of the Deity, and consequently all expectations of rewards and punishments; leaving the Supreme Being no other perfections than those which belong to a first cause, or almighty contriver. After him, at a considerable distance, followed HUME, the most subtle, if not the most philosophical, of the Deists; who, by perplexing the relations of cause and effect, boldly aimed to introduce a universal skepticism, and to pour a more than Egyptian darkness into the whole region of morals. Since his time skeptical writers have sprung up in abundance, and infidelity has allured multitudes to its standard: the young and superficial by its dexterous sophistry, the vain by the literary fame of its champions, and the profligate by the licentiousness of its principles. Atheism the most undisguised has at length begun to make its appearance.

Animated by numbers, and imboldened by success, the infidels of the present day have given a new direction to their efforts, and impressed a new character on the ever-growing mass of their impious speculations.

By uniting more closely with each other, by giving a sprinkling of irreligion to all their literary productions, they aim to engross the formation of the public mind; and, amid the warmest professions of attachment to virtue, to affect an entire disruption of morality from religion. Pretending to be the teachers of virtue and the guides of life, they propose to revolutionize the morals of mankind; to regenerate the world by a process entirely new; and to rear the temple of virtue, not merely without the aid of religion, but on the renunciation of its principles, and the derision of its sanctions. Their party has derived a great accession of numbers and strength from events the most momentous and astonishing in the political world, which have divided the sentiments of Europe between hope and terror; and which, owever they may issue, have, for the present, swelled the ranks of infidelity. So rapidly, indeed, has it advanced since the crisis, that a great majority on the Continent, and in England a considerable portion[1] of those who pursue literature as a profession, may justly be considered as the open or disguised abetters of atheism....

I. The skeptical or irreligious system subverts the whole foundation of morals. It may be assumed as a maxim, that no person can be required to act contrary to his greatest good, or his highest interest, comprehensively viewed in relation to the whole duration of his being. It is often our duty to forego our own interest *partially*, to sacrifice a smaller pleasure for the sake of a greater, to incur a present evil in pursuit of a distant good of more consequence. In a word, to arbitrate among interfering claims of inclination is the moral arithmetic of human life. But to risk the happiness of the whole duration of our being in any case whatever, were it possible, would be foolish; because the sacrifice must, by the nature of it, be so great as to preclude the possibility of compensation.

As the present world, on skeptical principles, is the only place of recompense, whenever the practice of virtue fails to promise the greater sum of present good, – cases which often occur in reality, and much oftener in appearance, – every motive to virtuous conduct is superseded; a deviation from the rectitude becomes the part of wisdom; and should the path of virtue, in addition to this, be obstructed by disgrace, torment, or death, to preserve would be madness and folly, and a violation of the first and most essential law of nature. Virtue, on these principles, being in numberless instances at war with self-preservation, never can or ought to become, a fixed habit of the mind. ...

II. Hitherto we have considered the influence of skepticism on the principles of virtue; and have endeavoured to show that it despoils it of its dignity, and lays its authority in the dust. Its influence on the formation of the character remains to be examined. The actions of men are oftener determined by their character than their interest: their conduct takes its colour more from their acquired taste, inclinations, and habits, than from a deliberate regard to their greatest good. It is only on great occasions the mind awakes to take an extended survey of her whole course, and that she suffers the dictates of reason to impress a new bias upon her movements. The actions of each day are, for the most part, links which follow each other in the chain of custom. Hence the great

---

[1] By those who pursue literature as a profession, the author would be understood to mean that numerous class of literary men who draw their principal subsistence from their writings.

effort of practical wisdom is to imbue the mind with tastes, affections, and habits; the elements of character, the masters of action. ...

Modern infidelity not only tends to corrupt the moral taste, it also promotes the growth of those vices which are the most hostile to social happiness. Of all the vices incident to human nature, the most destructive to society are vanity, ferocity, and unbridled sensuality; and these are precisely the vices which infidelity is calculated to cherish. ...

The aim of all the leading champions of infidelity is to rob mankind of these benefits, and throw them back into a state of gross and brutal sensuality. [Mr. *Hume* asserts adultery to be but a slight offence *when known; when secret*, no crime at all.][2] In this spirit, Mr. HUME represents the private conduct of the profligate CHARLES, whose debaucheries polluted the age, as a just subject of panegyric. A disciple in the same school has lately had the unblushing effrontery to stigmatize marriage as the worst of all monopolies; and, in a narrative of his licentious amours, to make a formal apology for departing from his principles, by submitting to is restraints. The popular productions of the Continent which issue from the atheistical school are incessantly directed to the same purpose. ...

Before I close this discourse, I cannot omit to mention three circumstances attending the propagation of infidelity by its present abetters, equally new and alarming.

1. It is the first attempt which has been ever witnessed, on an extensive scale, to establish *the principles of atheism*; the first effort which history has recorded to disannul and extinguish the belief of all superior powers; the consequence of which, should it succeed, would be to place mankind in a situation never before experienced, not even during the ages of pagan darkness....

2. The efforts of infidels to diffuse the principles of infidelity among the common people is another alarming symptom peculiar to the present time. Hume, Bolingbroke, and Gibbon addressed themselves solely to the more polished classes of the community, and would have thought their refined speculations debased by an attempt to enlist disciples from among the populace. Infidelity has lately grown condescending; bred in the speculations of a daring philosophy, immured at first in the cloisters of the learned, and afterward nursed in the lap of voluptuousness and of courts; having at length reached its full maturity, it boldly ventures to challenge the suffrages of the people, solicits the acquaintance of peasants and mechanics, and seeks to draw whole nations to its standard....

3. The infidels of the present day are the first sophists who have presumed to innovate in the very *substance* of morals. The disputes on moral questions

---

[2]   [This sentence appears in the first edition, but is deleted in later ones, probably as a result of James Mackintosh's comment in the *Monthly Review*, noted above.]

hitherto agitated among philosophers have respected the *grounds* of duty, not the *nature of duty itself*; or they have been merely metaphysical, and related to the *history* of moral sentiments in the mind, the sources and principles from which they were most easily deduced; they never turned on the quality of those dispositions and actions which were to be denominated virtuous. In the firm persuasion that the love and fear of the Supreme Being, the sacred observation of promises and oaths, reverence to magistrates, obedience to parents, gratitude to benefactors, conjugal fidelity, and parental tenderness were primary virtues, and the chief support of every commonwealth, they were unanimous. The curse denounced upon such as remove ancient landmarks, upon those who call good evil, and evil good, put light for darkness, and darkness for light, who employ their faculties to subvert the eternal distinctions of right and wrong, and thus to poison the streams of virtue at their source, falls with accumulated weight on the advocates of modern infidelity, and on them alone. ...

80
HENRY COCKBURN:
MEMORIALS OF HIS TIME

Henry Cockburn, *Memorials of his time*, Edinburgh: Adam and Charles Black, 1856, viii, 470 p.
Selections from Chapter 3; from *Memorials of his Time*, New York, D. Appleton & Company, 1859.

In 1804 the Scottish scientist John Leslie published his *Experimental Inquiry into the Nature and Propagation of Heat*. When discussing the causal forces of gravity, he attacks previous theories that made gravity a kind of occult quality. In a note to that discussion, he defends Hume's notion of causality:

> Mr. Hume is the first, as far as I know, who has treated of causation in a truly philosophic manner. His Essay on Necessary Connexion seems a model of clear and accurate reasoning. But it was only wanted to dispel the cloud of mystery which had so long darkened that important subject. The unsophisticated sentiments of mankind are in perfect unison with the deductions of logic, and imply nothing more at bottom, in the relation of cause and effect, than a constant and invariable sequence. This will distinctly appear from a critical examination of language, that great and durable monument of human thought. [*An Experimental Enquiry*, p. 521, note 16]

Leslie soon after became a candidate for the Chair of Mathematics at Edinburgh. However, a faction within the moderate leadership of the Edinburgh clergy of the Scottish Church favoured the candidacy of their fellow-minister, Thomas Macknight. Taking advantage of Leslie's endorsement of Hume, they used this as a reason to attempt obstructing his appointment. A highly publicized controversy arose between the moderate clergy and Leslie's supporters. The issue was ultimately brought before the General Assembly of the Church of Scotland, which debated the religious implications of Hume's views. A vote was taken and Leslie's supporters prevailed.

A half-century after the fact, Scottish judge Henry Cockburn (1779–1854) presented an animated account of the controversy in *Memorials of his Time*, decisively siding with Leslie's defenders, several of whom were his friends. Born in Edinburgh, Cockburn was educated at the University of Edinburgh where he was a student of Scottish philosopher Dugald Stewart. A zealous Whig, he was a close friend of Francis Jeffery, founder of the *Edinburgh Review*. He was admitted in the Faculty of Advocates in 1800 and later appointed judge in the Courts of Session and Justiciary. Cockburn's *Memorials* was republished in 1859, 1909, 1946, and 1974. The following is from the 1859 edition.

The Case of Professor Leslie

The memorable case of Professor Leslie began early in 1805, and though settled in the General Assembly in May of that year, the public discussion was prolonged till far on in 1806. It made a deep and universal impression. The substance of the case is this: –

The promotion of John Playfair to the chair of Natural Philosophy in the University of Edinburgh, made a vacancy in Playfair's chair of Mathematics. John Leslie, whose recent treatise on heat had placed him high in science, was the only well-qualified candidate. He was patronized by Stewart, Playfair, and all good judges who had only superiority of fitness in view; and his subsequent eminence justified their recommendation. But the Moderate clergy, who had long encouraged pluralities, and wished to multiply clerical professorships, allotted the place to one of themselves. They probably cared little who the individual should be, but it was understood, and indeed never denied, that their favorite upon this occasion was the Reverend Dr. Thomas Macknight, the son of the Harmonist; a most excellent man, by no means devoid of science, but unheard of in the scientific world, and not capable of being named seriously as a worthy competitor of Leslie. However, any clergyman would have done: but the first thing was to exclude the layman. The reverend faction therefore began by proposing to put the College Test to Leslie; but this was defeated by his at once agreeing to take it. Not one of the Presbytery of Edinburgh except Macknight had read, or could understand, the work on heat; but somebody told them that that treatise contained a note with these words – "Mr. Hume is the first, as far as I know, who has treated of Causation in a truly philosophical manner. His *Essay on Necessary Connexon* seems a model of clear and accurate reasoning," &c. This supplied them with the very thing they wanted – a personal exception to the candidate whose science was unassailable. The cry of atheism was raised; a cry seldom raised in vain in this country, and to which the very name of David Hume gave particular force. It was proclaimed that these words, though only applied to physical science, involved the adoption by Mr. Leslie of the whole of Hume's doctrine of Cause and Effect, and of all the moral consequences which that cunning skeptic deduced from it. The course therefore was now clear. The Presbytery of Edinburgh announced first that, by the foundation of the University, the Town Council could only elect "*cum avisamento eorum ministrorum,*" which the clergy held to imply a veto in their favor; and then, that the note, being heretical, tainted the whole book, and the book the man; and lastly, that schools and colleges being subject to the presbytery of the bounds, it was both their right and their duty to have this philosopher excluded. The real value of this pretension was, that it would apply to every case in which the clergy could detect what they might think unsound doctrine; and therefore all the machinery, and all the rancor, of the ecclesiastical courts was put into activity to aid it. No wonder that dispassionate men were alarmed by a conspiracy of which the object was to entitle the Church to control every patron in the election of every professor, and indeed to subject learning once more to priestcraft.

The weight of metaphysical authority was on the side of the note, and Thomas Brown's fine metaphysical spear shivered all the argumentative weapons by which, as applied to this point, it was assailed. Still the assailants may possibly have had truth on their side, though they fought their battle ill. But metaphysics had nothing to do with the matter. They were the pretence; while a claim of clerical domination over seats of learning was the real subject.

The Town Council, jealous of the attempt to supersede them, and encouraged by the support of liberal and pious men, stood firm, and elected Leslie. The Presbytery, relying on ecclesiastical sympathy, stood firm also; but, after much manœuvring, it resolved to show its candor by only *Referring* the matter to the Synod for advice. It is honorable to the Presbytery that this course was only carried by fourteen against thirteen. The thirteen were for quashing the whole affair. The inquisitors formed a majority of the Synod; but this body also thought it safest to preserve the outward appearance of impartiality by *Referring* to the General Assembly. Sir Harry Moncreiff instantly entered a Complaint against this Reference – a sagacious move; for it made the Synod a party at the bar of the Assembly, and consequently excluded the votes of its members, and thus ultimately saved the case.

The prevailing public feeling was strongly against the persecution, and its horrid principle. Toryism was rather in favor of the Church: Whiggism decidedly against it. The two proper Church parties were reversed. The Moderate clergy, more indifferent about skepticism than their opponents, yet liking power above all things, were nearly unanimous against Leslie. The Wild, cordial in their horror of heresy, almost all supported the supposed disciple of Hume. This singular position for them was not produced, as their enemies absurdly said, by their hating their ecclesiastical antagonists more than they hated infidelity, but by their honest incapacity, notwithstanding their jealousy of it, to discover any infidelity in the matter. There could not have been a stronger fact against the persecutors than that, on such a question, they were opposed by the whole evangelical clergy.

The debate in the Assembly wore out two long days. The result, in point of form, was that the Complaint against the Reference was sustained; the meaning of which was, that the conduct of the Presbytery and the Synod was condemned, and the opposition stopped. The respective votes were ninety-six to eighty-four. It is frightful to think that such a result as was implied in the Reference was within twelve of receiving all the support that the ecclesiastical tribunal could give it. The Church could not settle the civil rights of the patrons or the presentee; but if the ecclesiastical decision had been that the presentee was a heretic, he would have been a bold man who would have answered for the Civil Court not giving effect to this decision in those days, when to oppose the Church was to oppose good order and the Government. It was a small House for such a question; but many of the Moderate stayed away from not liking the job, and some of the Wilds from the words David Hume.

Some of the speeches, in this the most important Scotch debate I have ever known, were excellent. Sir Harry Moncreiff's, for practical effect, was the best. Avoiding the metaphysical slough into which it was the great object of the persecutors to lead their opponents, he was concise, vigorous, and contemptuous upon the common sense and truth of the case. It must have given the Lord President Campbell, who was a liberal man, some pain to quibble, and with little of his usual acuteness, in defence of a prosecution for which he could have no taste. He suffered severely for his imprudence from Lauderdale, whose appetite was evidently whetted by catching a judge rash enough to expose himself on equal terms in public debate. Adam Gillies and Henry Erskine were strong and useful on the just side; but neither of them equal to James Moncreiff, who on this occasion displayed, for the first time, the vigorous argumentative powers which made him afterwards the most habitually useful layman in the Assembly. Dr. John Inglis, one of the deepest in the plot, was as good as ingenious metaphysics can ever be in a popular assembly. Principal Hill, the successor of Principal Robertson as the leader of the Church, was, as usual, plausible and elegant; and laid out his most dexterous and persuasive lures to fix every waverer, and to recall those who were inclined to forget their fidelity to the Moderate standard. Dugald Stewart closed the discussion by a speech which he meant to have been longer, but inexperience of such rough scenes made him too plain in his indignation, and he was called to order, and sat down; not, however, till he had delivered a few long-remembered sentences in a very fine spirit of scorn and eloquence.

A curious error was committed by the Reverend Dr. Andrew Hunter, Professor of Divinity, a deeply religious gentleman, by whom the debate was opened in favor of the Complaint; an error very innocently fallen into, and very handsomely avowed, and which shows how much inaccuracy may sometimes pass undetected not merely in history, but in the discussions of living and intelligent men. Dr. Henry Hunter, of London, a Presbyterian minister of undoubted learning and piety, translated Euler's Letters, and this translation contains a note on Hume's doctrine of Causation the same in substance as the note objected to in Leslie's book. Dr. Andrew Hunter quoted this note by his namesake; and no authority that was produced had greater effect on the Assembly. But just after closing his speech, the worthy Professor, with his usual candor and simplicity, explained that he had been informed that the note in Euler was not by Henry Hunter, but by Condorcet. Of course the detection that Leslie's doctrine was approved of, not by the Presbyterian divine, but by the French atheist, raised a hearty laugh on one side of the House against honest Andrew, and produced many a sneer at Leslie for his ally. This was so important, that James Moncreiff was at the pains to take it up next day, and to demonstrate, as he thought, that after all the first statement was correct, and that the note was by Henry Hunter himself. But the truth, then only known to Mr. Macvey Napier, was, that both statements were inaccurate, and that the note in Euler was written neither by Henry Hunter nor by Condorcet, but by John Leslie! He had assisted anonymously in a translation of one of Condorcet's works, and in doing so, composed and inserted this note, which Henry Hunter, finding it in the English Condorcet, and never doubting that it formed part of the original work, quoted as Condorcet's in his translation of Euler. All this used to be explained by Leslie afterwards. What an escape for him, and for his reverend champion in the Assembly, that no one there knew that he himself had been quoted as the strongest authority in his own support!

Hermand was in a glorious phrensy. Spurning all unfairness, a religious doubt, entangled with mystical metaphysics, and countenanced by his party, had great attractions for his excitable head and Presbyterian taste. What a figure! as he stood on the floor, declaiming and screaming, amidst the divines – the tall man, with his thin powdered locks and long pigtail, the long Court of Session cravat flaccid and streaming with the heat, and the obtrusive linen! The published report makes him declare that "the belief of the being and perfections of the Deity is the solace and delight of my life. It is a feeling which I sucked in with my mother's milk." But this would not have been half intense for Hermand; and accordingly his words were — *"Sir! I sucked in the being and attributes of God with my mother's milk!"* His constant and affectionate reverence for his mother exceeded the devotion of any Indian for his idol; and under this feeling he amazed the House by maintaining (which was his real opinion) that there was no apology for infidelity, or even for religious doubt, because no good or sensible man had any thing to do except to be of the religion of his mother; which, be it what it might, was always the best. "A skeptic, sir, I hate! With my whole heart I detest him! *But, moderator, I love a Turk!"*[1]

---

[1]   The report, which was published about five months after the debate, is as bad as possible. It omits all that was striking, and smooths everything over with a dull surface of composed proprieties and generalities. No idea or feeling of this most interesting debate can be got from its validity.

It was not without reason that the liberal, all over the country, rejoiced. Those in Edinburgh celebrated their victory by a dinner, at which Sir Harry presided admirably. The defeated leaders of the clergy never entirely recovered their reputation. Many of them were excellent, and some of them able, men; but their accession to this plot could never be forgotten. The defeat undoubtedly helped to kill Dr. Finlayson, who died in January, 1808, without ever having resumed his habitual look of hard, calm confidence. Though never exposing himself by a speech or a pamphlet, he was the underground soul of the dark confederacy. When sitting at the bar, pale with vexation, while they were taking the vote by calling the roll, and the issue became visible, Jeffrey, who was just behind, consoled him by saying, in his sharp, sarcastic style —" Take a little gingerbread, Doctor." The laugh did not relieve him. Giving the critic a slap in the face would. Finlayson's Ecclesiastical life reminds one of Pascal's saying of the Jesuits – "Les plus habiles d'entre eux sont ceux qui intriguent beaucoup, qui parlent peu, et qui n'écrivent point."

The controversy was distinguished by some publications of permanent value. Stewart contributed an "Explanation of Facts," marked by his usual taste and judgment. Brown put forth the first draught of his inquiry into the nature of our idea of Causation; a work declared by Mackintosh to "entitle him to a place very, very near the first among the living metaphysicians of Great Britain."[2] Playfair published "A Letter to one of the Ministers of Edinburgh" – one of the best controversial pamphlets in the English language. Francis Horner gave an admirable exposition of the whole contest in an article in the Edinburgh Review.[3] Dr. Inglis Was the great writer and speaker on the other side. And he wrote and spoke well. So well, that, until Brown appeared, he was thought to have the best of the metaphysical argument – the favorite bush into which he and his friends always pushed their heads. Chalmers came forward in his first publication, being "Observations on a Passage in Mr. Playfair's Letter to the Lord Provost of Edinburgh, relative to the mathematical pretensions of the Scottish Clergy." This was the famous pamphlet in which he stated, on the authority of his own experience, that, "after the satisfactory discharge of his parish duties, a minister may enjoy five days in the week of uninterrupted leisure for the prosecution of any science in which his taste may dispose him to engage." This was said before he became religious; and a noble explanation did he give, when it was quoted against him in the Assembly many years after the acquisition of his new nature.[4]

---

[2] Memoirs of Sir James Mackintosh, vol. i. p. 396.

[3] Edinburgh Review, No. 13, Art. 7. ["Professor Stewart's *Statement of Fact*," October 1805, Vol. 7, pp. 113–134.]

[4] Memoirs of Dr. Chalmers, by Dr. Hanna, vol. iii. p. 77. – ED.

JAMES BOSWELL AND SAMUEL JOHNSON

81
JAMES BOSWELL:
LETTERS TO WILLIAM TEMPLE

James Boswell, Letters to William Temple, 1758–1775.
Selections; from *Letters of James Boswell to the Rev. W.J. Temple*, London:
Sidgwick, 1908.

J ames Boswell (1740–1795) is the author of several items in this collection; for
background on him and his journals see the editor's introduction to his 1776
interview with Hume. Among Boswell's surviving correspondence of over 6,000
letters, those to the reverend William Johnson Temple (1739–1796) are particularly noteworthy for Hume scholarship. Boswell had a long and intimate
friendship with Temple, and the two corresponded regularly for almost forty
years. The letters first came to light in extraordinary circumstances. In the late
1830s, Major William Stone of the East India Company's service was in
Boulogne, France. After shopping at a grocery store, he saw that an item he had
purchased there was wrapped in old manuscript paper containing James
Boswell's signature. The document had come from a bundle of waste paper sold
to the grocer by a paper vendor who visited Boulogne a few times a year. Stone
purchased the remainder of the bundle from the grocer, which included ninety-
seven letters from Boswell to Temple, additional letters from other correspondents to Temple, and some drafts of Temple's sermons. Apparently, after
Temple's death, his manuscripts were passed to his daughter, who, with her
husband Charles Powlett, moved to France just outside Boulogne. The papers
were relinquished from their estate after the death of her husband. The letters
were first published in 1857 under the title *Letters of James Boswell, Addressed
to the Rev. W.J. Temple* and appeared in other editions in 1908, 1924 and 1997.
Temple, according to Boswell, had a particular interest in anecdotes about
Hume, which Boswell accommodated. The selections below are from letters
written between 1758 and 1775, and describe several meetings and conversations that Boswell had with Hume. He writes about his first introduction to
Hume, the quarrel with Rousseau, Hume's advice about studying modern
history, his plans for continuing the *History*, and his view's about American
independence. The 1908 edition of the letters has been used here as the copy text.

... Some days ago I was introduced to your friend Mr. Hume; he is a most discreet, affable man as ever I met with, and has really a great deal of learning, and a choice collection of books. He is indeed an extra ordinary man, – few such people are to be met with nowadays. We talk a great deal of genius, fine language, improving our style, &c., but I am afraid solid learning is much wore out. Mr. Hume, I think, is a very proper person for a young man to cultivate and acquaintance with. Though he has not perhaps the most delicate taste, yet he has applied himself with great attention to the study of the ancients, and is likewise a great historian, so that you are not only entertained in his company, but may reap a great deal of useful instruction. I own myself much obliged to you, dear Sir, for procuring me the pleasure of his acquaintance. ... [Edinburgh, July 29, 1758.]

... *4th March*. – Here I am still, and let me go on. ... Dr. Robertson will soon give the world his "Charles the Fifth." smith, I suppose, is in London; but I do not hear that his book on jurisprudence is in any forwardness. David Hume, you know, is gone back to be a Minister of State, being appointed secretary to Mr. Conway. I fancy he will hardly write any more. I was very hearty with him here this winter. Whenever you go to London, I will give you a letter of introduction to him. His quarrel with Rousseau is a literary tragi-comedy. I wrote verses in the character of each of them; I also designed a ludicrous print. They have altered my idea, and made a clyster be applied to David; but you may have the substance of it from one of the London printshops, under the title of "The Savage." Now you must know Rousseau quarrelled with me too, and wrote me last summer a peevish letter, with strong marks of frenzy in it, for he has never yet told me the cause of his offence. As you will observe, how different is our friendship! ... The session will be up this day se'nnight. I shall then set myself down to my account of Corsica, and finish it in the vacation; I have got more materials for it. I had some time ago a letter of sixteen pages from General Paoli; and lately a letter of three pages from my Lord Chatham. David Hume told me sincerely he imagined my account of Corsica would be a book that will stand, and he is obliging enough to transact the publication of it for me with Andrew Millar. ... [Edinburgh, February 1, 1767 (additions of March 4)]

... I am really the *great man* now. I have had David Hume, in the forenoon, and Mr. Johnson, in the afternoon, of the same day, visiting me. Sir John Pringle, Dr. Franklin, and some more company, dined with me to-day; and Mr. Johnson and General Oglethorpe one day, Mr. Garrick alone another, and David Hume and some more *literati* another, dine with me next week. I give admirable dinners and good claret; and the moment I go abroad again, which will be in a day or two, I set up my chariot. This is enjoying the fruit of my labours, and appearing like the friend of Paoli. By the bye, the Earl of Pembroke and Captain Meadows are just setting out for Corsica, and I have the honour of introducing them by a letter to the General. David Hume came on purpose, the other day, to tell me that the Duke of Bedford was very fond of my book, and had recommended it to the Duchess. David is really amiable: I always regret to him his unlucky principles, and he smiles at my faith; but I have a hope which he has not, or pretends not to have. So who has the best of it, my reverend friend? David is going to give us two more volumes of History, down to George II. I wish he may not mire himself in the Brunswick sands. Pactolus is there. ... [London, May 14, 1768]

... Mr. Hume is not to go to Paris: he is busy with the continuation of his History. You admire our Scottish authors too much; but you know, my worthy friend, we differ just enough to enliven us, and afford some exercise of our talents. ... [Edinburgh, December 9, 1768]

My dear Friend, – Your letter, dated April 26th, has given me both pleasure and pain; pleasure to hear from you; and pain to think, or at least doubt, that you have not received a long letter, which I wrote to you the 3rd of April,[1] containing a full account of Mr. Hume's opinion as to the study of modern history, and also, as I flattered myself, a satisfactory answer to your strange scheme of changing your profession. My letter was directed to Lord Lisburne, Mamhead, near Chudleigh, Devon. I would fain hope that my letter has before now come to your hands; but lest it should not, I now sit down to collect, as well as I can, what Mr. Hume said as to the study of modern history. He seemed to be of opinion that no fixed, exact system need be observed. You must, he said, "read the best modern history. I would begin with England, and (here he smiled) read Mrs. Macaulay. (You may guess what History of England he really thinks the best.) You may then read the history of France. I am told the new history by Velly and Villaret is the best, better than Père Dariée." He then said I might read the histories of the Low Countries, by Bentivoglio, and those of the other parts of Europe in what order I chose, as Machiavel, Father Paul, Guicciardini, etc. I would fain hope my letter has reached you; if it has not, you have here the substance of what Mr. Hume said. I told you a great deal more of him, which I shall tell you on being assured my letter has miscarried. ... [Edinburgh, May 7, 1770]

... A long letter which I lately wrote to you has, I hope, come safe to hand. I told you in it that the Rev. Mr. Henry was soon to publish the preface to his History as a prospectus or plan of the work. ... Mr. Hume, when I spoke to him of it, before I saw the plan, seemed to think it would be much of the nature

---

[1] [Boswell's letter to Temple of April 3, 1770 has not yet surfaced.]

of a book published a few years ago, Anderson's "History of Commerce." ...
[Edinburgh, June 19, 1770]

... Mr. Hume is just now at Sir Gilbert Elliot's country-seat; he will be here
again in ten days. ... [Edinburgh, September 6, 1770]

... Since I came down I have seen Mr. David Hume several times. I know you
love to hear little anecdotes of him, so I shall endeavour to cull as many as I
can. I first saw him one forenoon that I called on him; he had Macpherson's
History before him, and he said it was the worst style he had ever read, and
that Macpherson had written his two volumes in quarto in six weeks; he said
he himself did not like to continue the History of England further down,
because we have not yet had access to papers sufficient to let us know, with
authenticity, the state of affairs; and it was disagreeable to write history which
afterwards might be proved not to be true. He spoke highly of the "Histoire
Philosophique et Politique," and I wondered to find him excuse very easily the
author of that book, for translating long passages from English writers without
quoting them, but just ingrafting the passages into his text. He said there are
about fifteen pages translated from his History, but he complained of one
mistake. He has mentioned that the clergy carried their claim of tithes to so
strange an excess that they insisted to have a tenth of the gain of courtesans;
the Frenchman, mistaking courtesans for *courtisans* (courtiers) in his own
language, makes a tenth to be of the gains *de ceux qui avaient des emplois à
la Cour*. This, said David very justly, takes the salt from the observation. He
says Abbé Raynal cannot have written that book himself; the eloquence must
have been borrowed. He is, said he, a dull man in conversation; that, however,
is not a certain rule for judging that a man cannot write well. But he has written
ill; his "Histoire du Parlement d'Angleterre" is very ill written. He says, when
he was at Paris, Abbé Raynal was making collections for a work on America,
and he supposed the materials have been supplied by him.

On Wednesday last I dined at Sir Alexander Dick's, where we had the Wyvill
family, a M. de Septchênes, a very young Parisian, introduced to me in
London by Mr. Burke, and who brought letters to me and some others here
from Sir John Pringle, and was also commended by M. Buffon. Mr. Hume was
there too. Wyvill was glad to meet with him, as he had never seen him before.
He said Mr. Pitt was an instance that in this country eloquence alone, without
any other talents or fortune, will raise a man to the highest office. On Thursday
I supped at Mr. Hume's, where we had the Young Parisian, Lord Kames, and
Dr. Robertson, an elegant supper, three sorts of ice-creams. What think you
of the northern Epicurus style? I can recollect no conversation. Our writers here
are really not prompt on all occasions, as those of London.

On Saturday, the Parisian and Mr. Hume and some gentlemen supped with
me, – no fruit that night either. But the word fruit makes me recollect that

Hume said Burke's speech on Reconciliation with the Colonies, which I lent to him, had a great deal of flower, a great deal of leaf, and a little fruit.

Yesterday I met Mr. Hume at Lord Kames', in the forenoon. He said it was all over in America:[2] we *could* not subdue the colonists, and another gun should not be fired, were it not for decency's sake; he meant, in order to keep up an appearance of power. But I think the lives of our fellow-subjects should not be thrown away for such *decency*. He said we may do very well without America, and he was for withdrawing our troops altogether and letting the Canadians fall upon our colonists. I do not think he makes our *right* to tax at all clear. He says there will in all probability be a change of the Ministry soon, which he regrets. Oh, Temple, while they change so often, how does one feel an ambition to have a share in the great department! but I fear my wish to be a man of consequence in the State is much like some of your ambitious sallies.

Mr. Hume and Lord Kames joined in attacking Dr. Johnson to an absurd pitch. Mr. Hume said he would give me half-a-crown for every page of his Dictionary in which he could not find an absurdity, if I would give him half-a-crown for every page in which he did not find one: he talked so insolently, really, that I calmly determined to be at him; so I repeated, by way of telling that Dr. Johnson *could* be touched, the admirable passage in your letter, how the Ministry had set him to write in a way that they "could not ask even their infidel pensioner Hume to write."[3] Upon honour, I did not give the least hint from whom I had the letter. When Hume asked if it was from an American, I said, No, it was from an English gentleman. "Would a *gentleman* write so?" said he. In short, Davy was finely punished for his treatment of my reverend friend; and he deserved it richly, both for his petulance to so great a character and for his talking so before me(!).

I dined yesterday with Lord Kames and his Lady *en famille*, and got from my Lord a good deal of his life. He says he will put down particulars of himself if I will put them together and publish them. I think he has eminence enough to merit this. This forenoon Mr. Hume came in awhile to my brother lawyer Mr. Crosbie's, where I was sitting. He did not say much: I only remember his remark, that characters depend more on original formation than on the way we are educated; "for," said he, "princes are educated uniformly, and yet how different are they! how different was James the Second from Charles the Second!" ... [Edinburgh, June 19, 1775]

---

[2] [Hume also expresses his views on American independence in a letter to William Strahan dated October 26, 1775.]

[3] [The relevant portion of Temple's letter appears in the *Life of Johnson*, March 21, 1778: "How can your great, I will not say your *pious*, but your *moral* friend, support the barbarous measures of Administration, which they have not the face to ask even their infidel pensioner Hume to defend?"]

82
JAMES BOSWELL:
"JOURNAL OF MY JAUNT"

James Boswell, "Journal of my Jaunt," November 4, 1762.
Selections; from in *Private papers of James Boswell*, Mount Vernon, N.Y., W.E.
Rudge, 1928–1934, Vol. 1, pp. 126–131.[1]

James Boswell (1740–1795) is the author of several items in this collection;
for background on him and his journals see the editor's introduction to his
1776 interview with Hume. First introduced to Hume in 1758, Boswell had
continuous interaction with the famed philosopher right up to his death. In
his first sustained journal, titled "Journal of my Jaunt, Harvest 1762,"
Boswell details one such visit at Hume's recently acquired apartment in
James's Court. Coincidentally, Hume would lease that same apartment to
Boswell in 1771 (the large building complex was eventually destroyed by fire
in 1858). Boswell's entry is surprisingly detailed, and he states that he
"remembered the heads and the very words of a great part of Mr. Hume's
conversation." At the same time, though, his prose is sketchy, and the reader
must keep in mind that the terse sentences are distillations of Hume's words,
even though transitional phrases such as "Mr. Hume said…" are absent.
What stands out in the conversation is the breadth of literary topics and
recent publications that Hume authoritatively discusses, from politics, to
history, to literature. Hume also hints at reasons for his estrangement at this
time from Henry Home – "a man very apt to change his favourites." The
following is from the first published volume of Ralph Heyward Isham's
Private papers of James Boswell (1928). It is transcribed from the manuscripts
at Malahide Castle – which contained the only surviving copy of Boswell's
"Journal of my Jaunt."[2]

---

[1] This text is reproduced by kind permission of Yale University.

[2] It has also been published in *London journal, 1762–1763*, together with *Journal of my jaunt, harvest, 1762*, ed. Frederick Albert Pottle, London, Heineman, 1951.

Thursday 4 *November*

This was the fast day before the Sacrament. Erskine and I went and waited on David Hume. We found him in his house in James's Court, in a good room newly fitted up hung round with Strange's Prints. He was sitting at his ease reading Homer. He told us that Mr. Mallet was just going to publish his life of the Duke of Marlborough, a pretty large work in two Quarto Volumes, which would throw great light on the transactions of that period; That Mr. Mallet had the best opportunities of intelligence. He had all the Marlborough papers. Lord Chesterfield carried him to the hague, where he learnt all that they know there, and he went to Paris where he learnt what were, at the period in which Marlborough lived, the great court secrets; but might now be known to every body. Mr. Hume hoped he would be free without respect to parties; "And indeed," said he, "this is an advantageous time, as the distinction between Whig and Tory is allmost abolished. Altho' Mr. Mallett's writings possess only mediocrity, yet they discover taste and the art of Composition. Therefore," said he, "I imagine this will be a good Work." Mr. Mallet has written bad Tragedies because he is deficient in the pathetic, and hence it is doubted if he is the Author of *William and Margaret*. Mr. Hume said he knew people who had seen it before Mallet was born. Erskine gave another proof, viz that he has written *Edwin and Emma*, a Ballad in the same stile, not near so good. Smollet is continuing his history, is treading hard on the heels of time and of the *London gazette*. What a pity it is that he must write for Bread. His Magazine is the worst. He writes now very little in the *Critical Review*. Mr. Franklin, Greek Professor at Cambridge, and Mr. Campbell, Son to the Principal Campbell of St Andrews, write in it. It is an invidious task. Every month there are about 70 Authors and during the year not above 2 good ones. The Reviewers are obliged to stab these and so get a legion of ennemies. Doctor Armstrong is a man of great genius. His Poem on *health* is truly classical; the most Augustan thing that we have in English. His *Œconomy of love* is very poetical. His *Scetches by Launcelot Temple* ingenious and his Spleen in them admirable. His Essay on Criticism and his *Benevolence*, tho' written in rugged verse, have strong good sense. *Tristam Shandy* may perhaps go on a little longer; but we will not follow him. With all his drollery there is a sameness of extravagance which tires us. We have just a succession of Surprise, surprise, surprise. *Fingal* is not much heard of at present. The English were exceedingly fond of it at first but hearing that it was Scotch, they became jealous and silent. Doctor Blair's *Dissertation* will awaken attention to it. It is a fine piece of criticism; but it were to be wished that he had kept it a little lower than Homer. For it might be a very excellent Poem and yet fall short of *the Iliad*. Macpherson, the Translator, is a most curious fellow. He is full of highland Prejudices. He hates a Republic and he does not like Kings. He would have all the Nation divided into Clans, and these clans to be allways fighting. He has got a dislike to study and cannot settle to read a quarter of an hour. Lord Bute does not know what to do with him. He was offered a Professorship but that he refused, alledging that a studious life was the dullest of any. He would not go into the Church, altho' he was sure of being a Bishop tomorrow; and, except he could be brought in upon a particular good footing, he would not accept a commission in the Army. As he is a Scotchman, Lord Bute does not chuse to put him upon the list of Pensioners, and therefore generously gives him two hundred a year out of his own pocket. Mr. Samuel Johnson has got a Pension of £300 a year. Indeed his Dictionary was a kind of a national Work so he has a kind of claim to the Patronage of the state. His stile is particular and pedantic. He is a man of enthusiasm and antiquated notions, a keen Jacobite yet hates the Scotch. Holds the Episcopal Hierarchy in supreme veneration and said he would stand before a battery of cannon to have the Convocation restored to it's full powers. He holds Mr. Hume in abhorrence and left a company one night upon his coming in. Garrick told Mr. Hume that Johnson past one Evening behind the Scenes in the Green room. He said he had been well entertained. Mr. Garrick therefore hoped to see him often. "No, David," said he, "I will never come back. For the white bubbies and the silk stockings of your Actresses excite my Genitals." Lord Kames's *Elements* has genius but is abstrues. It is surprising how he should think his book adapted to female capacity. For he will probably find few Ladies who can follow him thro' all his nicities. He is a man very apt to change his favourites. He is positive in opinion. He is fond of young people, of instructing them and dictating to them; but whenever they come up and have a mind of their own, he quarrels with them. Mr. Sheridan's Lectures are vastly too enthusiastic. He is to do every thing by Oratory. It is like the verse in the Song extolling Drunkeness.

Alexander hated thinking,
Drank about at Council-board,
He subdued the world by drinking
More than by his conq'ring sword.

I asked Mr. Hume to write more. He said he had done enough and was allmost ashamed to see his own bulk on a Shelf. We payed him a few compliments in pleasant mirth. Thus did an hour and a half of our Existence move along. We were very happy. I showed away, started subjects and now and then spoke tollerably, much better than my knowledge entitles me to do. I have remembered the heads and the very words of a great part of Mr. Hume's conversation with us. We left him and went to Mrs. Love's and saw the picture of Falstaff, then walked in the Piazzas of Holyroodhouse. Erskine said he thought me in great danger of getting in with Blackguard Geniuses in London; Bucks and Choice Spirits, under players and fellows who write droll songs, Who would admire my humour, make me King of the Company and allow me to pay the bill. I owned it; and determined to be upon my guard. At two we went to Thom's and had a good dinner and a moderate glass. We reflected that we had past our forenoon well with the greatest Writer in Brittain, a comic Actress and A Royal Palace. ...

83
JAMES BOSWELL:
"BOSWELLIANA"

James Boswell, "Boswelliana" (c. 1772–1785) in *Boswelliana: the common place book of James Boswell*, ed. Charles Rogers (1825–1890), London, Grampian Club, 1874, xxiii, 343 p.
Selections; from 1876 edition.

James Boswell (1740–1795) is the author of several items in this collection; for background on him and his journals see the editor's introduction to his 1776 interview with Hume. Between 1772 and 1785, he compiled a short collection of anecdotes based on his conversations with his famous friends, perhaps with an eye towards publication. Although Boswell was also keeping a much longer and detailed record of his activities in his journal, the anecdote collection was composed independently of that, with minimal overlap in content. The manuscript remained unpublished and was passed around by several book collectors until it finally appeared in print in 1874. The editor of the volume provides this description of the original manuscript:

> ... Boswell kept in a portfolio a quantity of loose quarto sheets, inscribed on each page BOSWELLIANA. In certain of these sheets the pages are denoted by numerals in the ordinary fashion; another portion is numbered by the folios; while a further portion consists of loose leaves and letter-backs. The greater part of the entries are made so carefully as to justify the belief that the author intended to embody the while in a volume of literary anecdotes. [Preface, pp. xi–xii]

Most of the brief entries are independent of each other and in no apparent order, either chronologically or topically. Some of the entries bear a date, and some indicate the source of the story. Several anecdotes about Hume appear in the collection – the most famous of which is King George III's reflection on Allan Ramsay's portrait of Hume. *Boswelliana* was published once more in 1876, from which the following is taken.

BOSWELLIANA

Hall [i.e., John Hall-Stevenson], the author of 'Crazy Tales,' said he could not bear David Hume for being such a monarchical dog. 'Is it not shocking,' said he, 'that a fellow who does not (fear) believe in God, should (fear) believe in a king?' [p. 210]

When Mr. David Hume began first to be known in the world as a philosopher, Mr. Thomas White, a decent rich merchant of London, said to him, 'I am surprised, Mr. Hume, that a man of your good sense should think of being a philosopher. Why, I now took it into my head to be a philosopher for some time, but tired of it most confoundedly, and very soon gave it up.' 'Pray, sir,' said Mr. Hume, 'in what branch of philosophy did you employ your researches? What books did you read? 'Books?' said Mr. White; 'nay, sir, I read no books, but I used to sit you whole forenoons a-yawning and poking the fire.' SIR DAVID DALRYMPLE. [p. 221]

Allan Ramsay painted a portrait of David Hume, dressed in scarlet with rich gold lace. 'George III.,' said he, 'thought the picture very like, but thought the dress rather too fine. I wished,' said Ramsay, 'posterity should see that one philosopher during your Majesty's reign had a good coat upon his back.' [p. 255]

David Hume used to say that he did not find it an irksome task to him to go through a great many dull books when writing his history. 'I then read,' said he, 'not for pleasure, but in order to find out facts.' He compared it to a sportsman seeking hares, who does not mind what sort of ground it is that he goes over farther than as he may find hares in it. From himself. [p. 263]

[Alexander] Pope told Lord Marchmont of his intention to have Warburton write notes upon his works. 'Well said, my lord; it will be a very good trial of the strength of your genius to see how much nonsense you can carry down to posterity when you have Warburton on your back.' DAVID HUME, Esq., who had it from LORD MARCHMONT.
Warburton was a prodigious flatter of Lord Mansfield, and consequently a favourite. David Hume was one day speaking violently against him to his lordship, who said, 'Upon my word, Mr. Hume, he is quite a different man in conversation from what he is in his books.' 'Then, my Lord,' said Hume, 'he must be the most agreeable man in the world.' MR. DAVID HUME.
David Hume was one day observing to me that he could not conceive what satisfaction envious people could have by saying that a work of genius such as the 'Gentle shepherd' was not written by its reputed author, but by some other person, as one should imagine that they must be equally hurt by one

person's being admired as by another. I accounted for it in this way: that by ascribing it to another person than its reputed author, they raise doubts whether the praise is due to the one or the other, and so the admiration, instead of being fixed to one, is kept *in equilibrio*, like Mahomet's coffin between the two loadstones. [pp. 268–269]

On Monday, the 2nd November, 1772, I dined at Fortune's in company with Mr. Banks, Dr. Solander, and several more, at an entertainment given by Mr. Hamilton, of Bangour, when the following good things passed:
    Lord Kelly said of a Mr. Wright who was present, 'He has been in several parts of the world, and I expect to see him in Otaheite [i.e., Tahiti] before he dies.' 'So then, my lord,' said David Hume, ESQ. 'you expect to be there yourself.' My lord, in order to retort upon Hume for this catching at his word, set himself in a steady posture, and said, 'My dear David, if you were to go there you would be obliged to retract all your essays on miracles.' 'Oh no, my lord,' said Hume, 'everything there is in nature.' 'Aye,' said the Earl, '(but) there are different natures.'
    Mr. Hamilton of Bangour's lady, was that morning delivered of a son, who was not yet baptized. Lord Kelly proposed his health; but addressing himself to Principal Robertson, said, 'Doctor, this is not a safe toast for you, for he's not a Christian.' My lord,' said the Principal, 'there are good hopes.' Hume laughed. Said the Earl, 'David, if there are hopes, I am afraid it will be worse for you.' [pp. 270–271]

The writers who attacked David Hume before Beattie took the lash in hand, treated him with so much deference that they had no effect. He was cased in a covering of respect. But Beattie stripped him of all his assumed dignity, and having laid his back bare, scourged him till he smarted keenly, and cursed again. David was on very civil terms with his former opponents, being treated by them as Dr. Shebbeare was in the pillory, who was being allowed to wear a fine powdered flowing wig. But he was virulent against Beattie, as I have witnessed, for Beattie treated him as an enemy to morals and religion deserved. [p. 282]

84
JAMES BOSWELL:
JOURNAL OF A TOUR TO THE HEBRIDES

James Boswell, *The journal of a tour to the Hebrides, with Samuel Johnson, LL.D. By James Boswell....* London: printed by Henry Baldwin, for Charles Dilly, 1785, vii, [1], 524, [2] p.
Selections from August 14, 1773 entry; from *The life of Samuel Johnson, LL.D., including a journal of his tour to the Hebrides*, ed. John Wilson Croker, New York: Derby & Jackson, 4 vol.

James Boswell (1740–1795) is the author of several items in this collection; for background on him and his journals see the editor's introduction to his 1776 interview with Hume. In 1773 Samuel Johnson journeyed to the Scottish Hebrides with Boswell by his side. Johnson published a record of his travels shortly after in *A Journey to the Western Islands of Scotland* (1775). In 1785, one year after Johnson's death, Boswell published a revision of his journal entries surrounding the trip. During a conversation one Sunday afternoon at Boswell's house, Johnson defended the forcefulness with which Beattie attacked Hume. Digressing from the 1773 conversation, Boswell then reflected on his companionship with Hume over the years, adding that he had some memoirs of Hume that he might some day publish. He would not, though, praise Hume in the manner that Adam Smith did in the "Letter... to William Strahan." In its favourable review of Boswell's *Journal of a Tour*, the *European Magazine* criticized Johnson for supporting Humean empiricism. The specific context is a conversation in which, according to Boswell, "Johnson denied that any child was better than another, but by difference of instruction." Of this the *European Magazine* writes:

It is a well known fact, that Hume's system of scepticism is founded on that part of Locke's Essay on the Human Understanding, where innate ideas a re denied; where it is asserted that the mind is a mere *rasa tabula*, and that every impression arises from outward accident. And here, with all his zeal against Hume's philosophy, we find Dr. Johnson most cordially supporting it, though certainly without attending to the consequences drawn by Hume, that Truth[1]

---

[1] The reviewer states the following here in a note: "To combat these notions is the design of Dr. Beattie's Essay on the Immutability of Truth; a good and *easy* subject, had it been handled with more logic and less declamation."

and Virtue, Falsehood and Vice are merely artificial, and not the same in different ages and countries. [*European Magazine*, May 1786, Vol. 9, p. 342]

In his *Essay on the Life, Character, and Writings, of Dr. Samuel Johnson* (1786), excerpted in this collection, Joseph Towers discusses Boswell's view of Hume in the *Journal of a Tour.*

Sunday, 15th August.

...

Of Dr. Beattie, Mr. Johnson said, "Sir, he has written like a man conscious of the truth, and feeling his own strength. Treating your adversary with respect, is giving him an advantage to which he is not entitled. The greatest part of men cannot judge of reasoning, and are impressed by character; so that, if you allow your adversary a respectable character, they will think, that though you differ from him, you may be in the wrong. Sir, treating your adversary with respect, is striking soft in a battle. And as to Hume, – a man who has so much conceit as to tell all mankind that they have been bubbled for ages, and he is the wise man who sees better than they, – a man who has so little scrupulosity as to venture to oppose those principles which have been thought necessary to human happiness, – is he to be surprised if another man comes and laughs at him? If he is the great man he thinks himself, all this cannot hurt him: it is like throwing peas against a rock." He added "*something much too rough*," both as to Mr. Hume's head and heart, which I suppress.[2] Violence is, in my opinion, not suitable to the Christian cause. Besides, I always lived on good terms with Mr. Hume, though I have frankly told him, I was not clear that it was right in me to keep company with him. "But (said I) how much better are you than your books!" He was cheerful, obliging, and instructive; he was charitable to the poor; and many an agreeable hour have I passed with him: I have preserved some entertaining and interesting memoirs of him, particularly when he knew himself to be dying, which I may some time or other communicate to the world. I shall not, however, extol him so very highly as Dr. Adam Smith does, who says, in a letter to Mr. Strahan the printer (not a confidential letter to his friend, but a letter which is published with all formality): "Upon the whole, I have always considered him, both in his life-time, and since his death, as approaching as nearly to the idea of a perfectly wise and virtuous man as perhaps the nature of human frailty will permit." Let Dr. Smith consider: Was not Mr. Hume blest with good health, good spirits, good friends, a competent and

[2] [The manuscript edition of Boswell's *Tour* recovers this passage: "B. 'But why attack his heart?' J. 'Why, Sir, because his head has corrupted it. Or perhaps it has perverted his head. I know not indeed whether he has first been a blockhead and that has made him a rogue, or first been a rogue and that has made him a blockhead.'"]

increasing fortune? And had he not also a perpetual feast of fame? But, as a learned friend has observed to me, "What trials did he undergo, to prove the perfection of his virtue? Did he ever experience any great instance of adversity?" – When I read this sentence delivered by my old *Professor of Moral Philosophy*, I could not help exclaiming with the *Psalmist*, "Surely I have now more understanding than my teachers!"

{[Note:] This letter, though shattered by the sharp shot of Dr. *Horne* of *Oxford's* wit, in the character of "One of the People called Christians", is still prefixed to Mr. Hume's excellent History of England, like a poor invalid on the piquet guard, or like a list of quack medicines sold by the same bookseller, by whom a work of whatever nature is published; for it has no connection with his *History*, let it have what it may with what are called his *Philosophical* Works. A worthy friend of mine in London was lately consulted by a lady of quality, of most distinguished merit, what was the best History of England for her son to read. My friend recommended Hume's. But, upon recollecting that its usher was a superlative panegyrick on one, who endeavoured to sap the credit of our holy religion, he revoked his recommendation. I am really sorry for this ostentatious *alliance*; because I admire "The Theory of Moral Sentiments", and value the greatest part of "An Inquiry into the Nature and Causes of the Wealth of Nations". Why should such a writer be so forgetful of human comfort, as to give any countenance to that dreary infidelity which would "make us poor indeed!"[3]}

...

---

[3] [Shakespeare, Othello, *iii*. 3]

85
THOMAS TYERS:
A BIOGRAPHICAL SKETCH OF
DR. SAMUEL JOHNSON

Thomas Tyers, *A biographical sketch of Dr. Samuel Johnson. By Thomas Tyers, Esq.* [London, 1785], 27, [1] p.Selections; from 1785 edition.

Thomas Tyers (1726–1787) is the author of *An Historical Essay on Mr. Addison* (1783), excerpted earlier in this collection. Samuel Johnson died in December 1784, and that same month Tyers composed a sketch of Johnson which appeared in *Gentleman's Magazine* – thus making it the first biography of Johnson after his death. Tyers revised the sketch which then appeared in 1785 in *The Annual Register* and *The New Annual Register*, and then as a pamphlet. The sketch contains two anecdotes of Johnson's critical view of Hume, conveyed to Tyers by James Dunbar. These two anecdotes did not appear in the original *Gentleman's Magazine* article. The following is taken from the pamphlet of the *Biographical Sketch*.

...

"At last" he said, "If I am worse, I cannot go; if I am better, I need not go; but if I continue, neither better nor worse, I am as well where I am." The writer of this Sketch could wish to have committed to memory or paper all the wise and sensible things that dropped from his lips. If the one could have been Xenophon, the other was a Socrates. His benevolence to mankind was known to all who knew him. Though so declared a friend to the church of England, and even a friend to the Convocation, it assuredly was not in his wish to persecute for speculative notions. He used to say, he had no quarrel with any order of men, unless they disbelieved in revelation and a future state. This writer has permission, from Dr. Dunbar, to publish this specimen of his pertinacious opinion: for which Mr. Hume would have put him into his chapter of bigots. "That prominent feature in Johnson's character was strongly marked in a conversation one morning with me *tête à tête*. He reproached me in a very serious, though amicable strain, for commending Mr. Hume as I had done in my Essays on the History of Mankind. I vindicated myself from the imputation as well as I was able – But he remained dissatisfied; still condemned my praise of Hume; and added: "for my part, sir, I should as soon have praised a *mad dog.*"

Another morning when he expostulated with me on the same offence, I answered, that I had, indeed, commended Mr. Hume for talents which really belonged to him; but, by no means for his Scepticism, his Infidelity, or irreligion. "I could not, sir," said Johnson, "on any account, have been the instrument of his praise. When I published my Dictionary, I might have quoted *Hobbes* as an authority in language, as well as many other writers of his time: but I scorned, sir, to quote him at all; because I did not like his principles." He would indeed have sided with Sacheverell against Daniel Burgess, if he thought the church was in danger. His hand and his heart were always open to charity. The objects under his own roof were only a few of the subjects for relief. He was at the head of subscription in cases of distress. His guinea, as he said of another man of bountiful disposition, was always ready. He wrote an exhortation to public bounty. He drew up a paper to recommend the French prisoners, in the last war but one, to the English benevolence; which was of service. He implored the hand of benevolence for others, even when he almost seemed a proper object of it himself. ...

86
JOSEPH TOWERS:
ESSAY ON THE LIFE OF SAMUEL JOHNSON

Joseph Towers, *An essay on the life, character, and writings, of Dr. Samuel Johnson.* London: printed for Charles Dilly, 1786, [4], 124 p.
Selections; from *Tracts on Political and Other Subjects, Published at Various Times* (1796), Vol. 3.
Selections; from *Tracts on Political and Other Subjects*, London: Cadell, 1796, Vol. 1, pp. 415–419.

Born in the London borough of Southwark, Joseph Towers (1737–1799) was son to a second-hand bookseller. He briefly worked as a printer, was later a dissenting clergyman, and throughout his adult life a prolific political pamphleteer. He is best known in Hume scholarship for his *Observations on Mr. Hume's History of England* (1788), contained in *Early Responses to Hume's History*. In 1775, Towers published a polite attack against Johnson in *A letter to Dr. Samuel Johnson: occasioned by his Late Political Publications*. Two years after Johnson's death, Towers published the first substantial biographical work on Johnson. In this he criticizes Adam Smith's characterization of Hume as a model of virtue and contends that, in contrast with many illustrious Christians, Hume did not display fortitude in adversity, great generosity or uncommon benevolence. In his *Life of Samuel Johnson*, James Boswell states that Towers's *Essay* on Johnson "is very well written, making a proper allowance for the democratical bigotry of its authour; whom I cannot however but admire for his liberality in speaking thus of my illustrious friend." He also says of Towers "I esteem him as an ingenious, knowing, and very convivial man." Soon dwarfed by Boswell's work, Towers's *Essay* on Johnson was not published again as a separate volume, although it is included in his 1796 *Tracts*, from which the following is taken.

...
It is related by Mr. Boswell, that Dr. Johnson once said, that "he believed hardly any man died without affectation."[1] When he made this declaration, he

[1] Tour to the Hebrides, p. 500.

seems to have been influenced by his own habitual dread of death, which was certainly beyond what men ordinarily experience. There can be no reasonable doubt, but that men of great and noble minds have often died, even on public scaffolds, and especially in causes of the justice of which they were fully persuaded, with firmness, and even with chearfulness, without affectation. It is dishonorable to human nature, and injurious to some of the most illustrious characters that ever existed, to suppose otherwise.

In recording Dr. Johnson's sentiments concerning Mr. HUME, of whom he had formed a very ill opinion, Mr. Boswell has made some just animadversions on the character given of that celebrated writer by Dr. Adam Smith.[2] It is surely extraordinary that Mr. Hume should be represented "as approaching as nearly to the idea of a perfectly wise and virtuous man as perhaps the nature of human frailty will permit." In support of this high encomium, no proper evidence has ever been produced by Dr. Smith, nor by any other of Mr. Hume's friends and admirers. He might be a man of polite manners, a chearful and agreeable companion, be equitable in his dealings with others, and occasionally charitable to the poor; he might view the approach of death with composure and tranquility; he might be possessed of all the virtues that his friends attribute to him; and yet be very far inferior to many characters, which have appeared among the professors of Christianity. Nor is there the least reasonable doubt but that this was really the case. Many men have been found among Christians, as much superior to Mr. Hume in virtue, as in rectitude of sentiment. Of Mr. Hume's fortitude in adversity, of great generosity displayed by him, or of any uncommon benevolence, no instances are recorded: but these virtues have been eminently and illustriously conspicuous in many Christian characters. If the character of DAVID HUME be compared with that of BERNARD GILPIN, a country clergyman, or with that of THOMAS FIRMIN, a tradesman of London, but both acting under the influence of the great truths of Christianity, the striking inferiority of this celebrated sceptic will be apparent to every impartial man. These men were not merely of gentle and inoffensive manners, and of a mild and placid deportment; but they were distinguished by active and exemplary virtue, their minds were ardently engaged in the promotion of the happiness of their fellow creatures, and in their labours for this purpose they were indefatigable. But these men were formed by the sublime views of Christianity; and such men were never produced by scepticism or infidelity.

[2] Tour, p. 21, 22, 23.

87
JAMES BOSWELL:
LIFE OF SAMUEL JOHNSON

James Boswell, *The life of Samuel Johnson, LL.D. comprehending an account of his studies and numerous works, ... In two volumes. By James Boswell, Esq.*
London: printed by Henry Baldwin, for Charles Dilly, 1791, 2 v.
From 1799 edition.
Selections; from *Boswell's life of Johnson*, New York: Oxford University Press, 1922, 2 v., based on 1799 third edition.

James Boswell (1740–1795) is the author of several items in this collection; for background on him and his journals see the editor's introduction to his 1776 interview with Hume. The twenty-two-year-old Boswell first met Samuel Johnson in 1763 and the two remained in close contact for the next twenty-one years. Ninety per cent of this time, though, they were in different locations, and sometimes did not see each other for a year or two, maintaining contact through correspondence. Nevertheless, Boswell's obsessive interest in chronicling his visits with Johnson created an unparalleled wealth of material for a biography of the great English writer that he planned to someday compose. When Johnson died in 1784, as a kind of first instalment, Boswell published the *Tour to the Hebrides* the following year, which was an instant success. On and off for the next few years he prepared his *Life of Samuel Johnson*, which was published in two volumes in 1791. Although it was as successful as the *Tour*,[1] public opinion of Boswell himself was less than favourable because of his candid depiction of his own shortcomings in the narrative. Throughout the *Life*, Boswell has no less than twenty discussions of Hume – either anecdotes about the philosopher or critical reactions to him by Johnson and others. Highlights of the excerpts below are discussions of Hume's critique of miracles;

---

[1] Boswell's *Life of Samuel Johnson* was favourably reviewed in the following journals: *Analytical Review*, 1791, Vol. 10, pp. 241–250, 481–489, Vol. 11, pp. 361–357; *European Magazine*, 1791, Vol. 20, pp. 107–110, 189–193, 371–384, 1792, Vol. 21, pp. 29–33, 195–198, 287–290, 357–359; *English Review*, 1791, Vol. 18, pp. 1–8, 137–140. *Monthly Review*, January 1792, Vol. 7, pp. 1–9, February pp. 189–198, May, Vol. 8, pp. 71–82.

the dangers of Hume's infidelity; Hume's view in "The Sceptic" that those who are happy are equally happy; Johnson's fear of death compared with Hume's complacency; the propriety of associating with infidels like Hume; and Adam Smith's praise of Hume's virtues. Boswell revised the *Life* for a second edition in 1793, but died while preparing a third edition, which eventually appeared in 1799 under the supervision of Edmond Malone. The work was subsequently printed dozens of times by various publishers throughout the nineteenth and twentieth centuries. The following is from a 1922 edition, which follows Malone's 1799 edition.

THE LIFE OF SAMUEL JOHNSON, L.L.D.

[1747] These verses are somewhat too severe on the extraordinary person [i.e., Lovat] who is the chief figure in them; for he was undoubtedly brave. His pleasantry during his solemn trial (in which, by the way, I have heard Mr. David Hume observe, that we have one of the very few speeches of Mr. Murray, now Earl of Mansfield, authentically given) was very remarkable. When asked if he had any questions to put to Sir Everard Fawkener, who was one of the strongest witnesses against him, he answered 'I only wish him joy of his young wife.'

[1749] He [i.e., Johnson] for a considerable time used to frequent the *Green Room*, and seemed to take delight in dissipating his gloom, by mixing in the sprightly chit-chat of the motley circle then to be found there. Mr. David Hume related to me from Mr. Garrick, that Johnson at last denied himself this amusement, from considerations of rigid virtue; saying, 'I'll come no more behind your scenes, David; for the silk stockings and white bosoms of your actresses excite my amorous propensities.'[2]

[1763] The conversation now turned upon Mr. David Hume's style. JOHNSON. 'Why, Sir, his style is not English; the structure of his sentences is French. Now the French structure and the English structure may, in the nature of things, be equally good. But if you allow that the English language is established, he is wrong. My name might originally have been Nicholson, as well as Johnson; but were you to call me Nicholson now, you would call me very absurdly.'

---

[2] [Boswell relates this story more vulgarly in his November 4, 1762 interview with Hume: "I will never come back. For the white bubbies and the silk stockings of your Actresses excite my Genitals" *Private papers of James Boswell*, 1928–1934, Vol. 1, pp. 126–131.]

[1763] Next morning I found him alone, and have preserved the following fragments of his conversation. Of a gentleman who was mentioned, he said, 'I have not met with any man for a long time who has given me such general displeasure. He is totally unfixed in his principles, and wants to puzzle other people.' I said his principles had been poisoned by a noted infidel writer, but that he was, nevertheless, a benevolent good man. JOHNSON. 'We can have no dependance upon that instinctive, that constitutional goodness which is not founded upon principle. I grant you that such a man may be a very amiable member of society. I can conceive him placed in such a situation that he is not much tempted to deviate from what is right; and as every man prefers virtue, when there is not some strong incitement to transgress its precepts, I can conceive him doing nothing wrong. But if such a man stood in need of money, I should not like to trust him; and I should certainly not trust him with young ladies, for *there* there is always temptation. Hume, and other sceptical innovators, are vain men, and will gratify themselves at any expence. Truth will not afford sufficient food to their vanity; so they have betaken themselves to errour. Truth, Sir, is a cow which will yield such people no more milk, and so they are gone to milk the bull. If I could have allowed myself to gratify my vanity at the expence of truth, what fame might I have acquired. Every thing which Hume has advanced against Christianity had passed through my mind long before he wrote. Always remember this, that after a system is well settled upon positive evidence, a few partial objections ought not to shake it. The human mind is so limited, that it cannot take in all the parts of a subject, so that there may be objections raised against any thing. There are objections against a *plenum*, and objections against a *vacuum*; yet one of them must certainly be true.'

I mentioned Hume's argument against the belief of miracles, that it is more probable that the witnesses to the truth of them are mistaken, or speak falsely, than that the miracles should be true. JOHNSON. 'Why, Sir, the great difficulty of proving miracles should make us very cautious in believing them. But let us consider; although GOD has made Nature to operate by certain fixed laws, yet it is not unreasonable to think that he may suspend those laws, in order to establish a system highly advantageous to mankind. Now the Christian Religion is a most beneficial system, as it gives us light and certainty where we were before in darkness and doubt. The miracles which prove it are attested by men who had no interest in deceiving us; but who, on the contrary, were told that they should suffer persecution, and did actually lay down their lives in confirmation of the truth of the facts which they asserted. Indeed, for some centuries the heathens did not pretend to deny the miracles; but said they were performed by the aid of evil spirits, This is a circumstance of great weight. Then, Sir, when we take the proofs derived from prophecies which have been so exactly fulfilled, we have most satisfactory evidence. Supposing a miracle possible, as to which, in my opinion, there can be no doubt, we have as strong evidence for the miracles in support of Christianity, as the nature of the thing admits.'

[1763] On Wednesday, August 3, we had our last social evening at the Turk's Head coffee-house, before my setting out for foreign parts. I had the misfortune, before we parted, to irritate him unintentionally. I mentioned to him how common it was in the world to tell absurd stories of him, and to ascribe to him very strange sayings. JOHNSON. 'What do they make me say, Sir?' BOSWELL. 'Why, Sir, as an instance very strange indeed, (laughing heartily as I spoke,) David Hume told me, you said that you would stand before a battery of cannon to restore the Convocation to its full powers.' Little did I apprehend that he had actually said this: but I was soon convinced of my errour; for, with a determined look, he thundered out, 'And would I not, Sir? Shall the Presbyterian *Kirk* of Scotland have its General Assembly, and the Church of England be denied its Convocation?' He was walking up and down the room while I told him the anecdote; but when he uttered this explosion of high-church zeal, he had come close to my chair, and his eyes flashed with indignation. I bowed to the storm, and diverted the force of it, by leading him to expatiate on the influence which religion derived from maintaining the church with great external respectability.

[1766] I told him that a foreign friend of his, whom I had met with abroad, was so wretchedly perverted to infidelity, that he treated the hopes of immortality with brutal levity; and said, 'As man dies like a dog, let him lie like a dog.' JOHNSON. '*If* he dies like a dog, *let* him lie like a dog.' I added, that this man said to me, 'I hate mankind, for I think myself one of the best of them, and I know how bad I am.' JOHNSON. 'Sir, he must be very singular in his opinion, if he thinks himself one of the best of men; for none of his friends think him so.' – He said, 'No honest man could be a Deist; for no man could be so after a fair examination of the proofs of Christianity.' I named Hume. JOHNSON. 'No, Sir; Hume owned to a clergyman in the bishoprick of Durham, that he had never read the New Testament with attention.' I mentioned Hume's notion, that all who are happy are equally happy; a little Miss with a new gown at a dancing-school ball, a General at the head of a victorious army, and an orator, after having made an eloquent speech in a great assembly.[3] JOHNSON. 'Sir, that all who are happy, are equally happy, is not true. A peasant and a philosopher may be equally *satisfied*, but not equally *happy*. Happiness consists in the multiplicity of agreeable consciousness. A peasant has not capacity for having equal happiness with a philosopher.' I remember this very question very happily illustrated in opposition to Hume, by the Reverend Mr. Robert Brown, at Utrecht.

---

[3] ["It cannot reasonably be doubted, but a little miss, dressed in a new gown for a dancing-school ball, receives as compleat enjoyment as the greatest orator, who triumphs in the splendour of his eloquence, while he governs the passions and resolutions of a numerous assembly." – "The Sceptic". Boswell discusses this issue again in a 1778 entry quoted below.]

'A small drinking-glass and a large one, (said he,) may be equally full; but the large one holds more than the small.'

[1768] His prejudice against Scotland appeared remarkably strong at this time. When I talked of our advancement in literature, 'Sir, (said he,) you have learnt a little from us, and you think yourselves very great men. Hume would never have written History, had not Voltaire written it before him. He is an echo of Voltaire.' BOSWELL. 'But, Sir, we have Lord Kames.' JOHNSON. 'You *have* Lord Kames. Keep him; ha, ha, ha! We don't envy you him. Do you ever see Dr. Robertson?' BOSWELL. 'Yes, Sir.' JOHNSON. 'Does the dog talk of me?' BOSWELL. 'Indeed, Sir, he does, and loves you.' Thinking that I now had him in a corner, and being solicitous for the literary fame of my country, I pressed him for his opinion on the merit of Dr. Robertson's *History of Scotland*. But, to my surprize, he escaped. – 'Sir, I love Robertson, and I won't talk of his book.'

[1769] I told him that David Hume had made a short collection of Scotticisms. 'I wonder, (said Johnson,) that *he* should find them.'

[1769] The General [Paoli] asked him what he thought of the spirit of infidelity which was so prevalent. JOHNSON. 'Sir, this gloom of infidelity, I hope, is only a transient cloud passing through the hemisphere, which will soon be dissipated, and the sun will break forth with his usual splendour.' 'You think then, (said the General,) that they will change their principles like their clothes.' JOHNSON. 'Why, Sir, if they bestow no more thought on principles than on dress, it must be so.' The General said, that 'a great part of the fashionable infidelity was owing to a desire of showing courage. Men who have no opportunities of shewing it as to things in this life, take death and futurity as objects on which to display it.' JOHNSON. 'That is mighty foolish affectation. Fear is one of the passions of human nature, of which it is impossible to divest it. You remember that the Emperour Charles V. when he read upon the tomb-stone of a Spanish nobleman, "Here lies one who never knew fear," wittily said, "Then he never snuffed a candle with his fingers."'

[1769] When we were alone, I introduced the subject of death, and endeavoured to maintain that the fear of it might be got over. I told him that David Hume said to me, he was no more uneasy to think he should *not be* after this life, than that he *had not been* before he began to exist.[4] JOHNSON. 'Sir, if he

---

[4] [Boswell relates this story in his 1776 interview with Hume. Its inclusion here in the 1769 narrative is likely a literary device.]

really thinks so, his perceptions are disturbed; he is mad; if he does not think so, he lies. He may tell you, he holds his finger in the flame of a candle, without feeling pain; would you believe him? When he dies, he at least gives up all he has.' BOSWELL. 'Foote, Sir, told me, that when he was very ill he was not afraid to die.' JOHNSON. 'It is not true, Sir. Hold a pistol to Foote's breast, or to Hume's breast, and threaten to kill them, and you'll see how they behave.' BOSWELL. 'But may we not fortify our minds for the approach of death?' Here I am sensible I was in the wrong, to bring before his view what he ever looked upon with horrour; for although when in a celestial frame, in his '*Vanity of human wishes*, he has supposed death to be 'kind Nature's signal for retreat,' from this state of being to 'a happier seat,' his thoughts upon this awful change were in general full of dismal apprehensions. His mind resembled the vast amphitheatre, the Colisæum at Rome. In the centre stood his judgement, which like a mighty gladiator, combated those apprehensions that, like the wild beasts of the *Arena*, were all around in cells, ready to be let out upon him. After a conflict, he drives them back into their dens; but not killing them, they were still assailing him. To my question, whether we might not fortify our minds for the approach of death, he answered, in a passion, 'No, Sir, let it alone. It matters not how a man dies, but how he lives. The act of dying is not of importance, it lasts so short a time.' He added, (with an earnest look,) 'A man knows it must be so, and submits. It will do him no good to whine.'

I attempted to continue the conversation. He was so provoked, that he said, 'Give us no more of this;' and was thrown into such a state of agitation, that he expressed himself in a way that alarmed and distressed me; shewed an impatience that I should leave him, and when I was going away, called to me sternly, 'Don't let us meet tomorrow.'

[1773] JOHNSON. '... Whether, indeed, we take him [i.e., Goldsmith] as a poet, – comick writer, – or as an historian, he stands in the first class.' BOSWELL. 'An historian! My dear Sir, you surely will not rank his [i.e. Goldsmith's] compilation of the Roman History with the works of other historians of this age?' JOHNSON. 'Why, who are before him?' BOSWELL. 'Hume, – Robertson, – Lord Lyttelton.' JOHNSON. (His antipathy to the Scotch beginning to rise). 'I have not read Hume; but, doubtless, Goldsmith's *History* is better than the *verbiage* of Robertson, or the foppery of Dalrymple.'

[1775] The other instance [of attack on Johnson's 1775 political pamphlets] was a paragraph of a letter to me, from my old and most intimate friend, the Reverend Mr. Temple, who wrote the character of Gray, which has had the honour to be adopted both by Mr. Mason and Dr. Johnson in their accounts of that poet. The words were, 'How can your great, I will not say your *pious*, but your *moral* friend, support the barbarous measures of administration, which they have not the face to ask even their infidel pensioner Hume to defend?'[5]

[1775] Dr. Johnson proceeded: 'Sir, there is a great cry about infidelity: but there are, in reality, very few infidels. I have heard a person, originally a Quaker, but now, I am afraid, a Deist, say, that he did not believe there were, in all England, above two hundred infidels.'

[1776] Dr. Adams had distinguished himself by an able answer to David Hume's *Essay on Miracles*. He told me he had once dined in company with Hume in London: that Hume shook hands with him, and said, 'You have treated me much better than I deserve;' and that they exchanged visits. I took the liberty to object to treating an infidel writer with smooth civility. Where there is a controversy concerning a passage in a classick authour, or concerning a question in antiquities, or any other subject in which human happiness is not deeply interested, a man may treat his antagonist with politeness and even respect. But where the controversy is concerning the truth of religion, it is of such vast importance to him who maintains it, to obtain the victory, that the person of an opponent ought not to be spared. If a man firmly believes that religion is an invaluable treasure, he will consider a writer who endeavours to deprive mankind of it as a *robber*; he will look upon him as *odious*, though the infidel might think himself in the right. A robber who reasons as the gang do in the *Beggar's Opera*, who call themselves *practical* philosophers, and may have as much sincerity as pernicious *speculative* philosophers, is not the less an object of just indignation. An abandoned profligate may think that it is not wrong to debauch my wife; but shall I, therefore, not detest him? And if I catch him in making an attempt, shall I treat him with politeness? No, I will kick him down stairs, or run him through the body; that is, if I really love my wife, or have a true rational notion of honour. An Infidel then shall not be treated handsomely by a Christian, merely because he endeavours to rob with ingenuity. I do declare, however, that I am exceedingly unwilling to be provoked to anger, and could I be persuaded that truth would not suffer from a cool moderation in its defenders, I should wish to preserve good humour, at least, in every controversy; nor, indeed, do I see why a man should lose his temper while he does all he can to refute an opponent. I think ridicule may be fairly used against an infidel; for instance, if he be an ugly fellow, and yet absurdly vain of his person, we may contrast his appearance with Cicero's beautiful image of Virtue, could she be seen. Johnson coincided with me and said, 'when a man voluntarily engages in an important controversy, he is to do

---

[5]   [Boswell mentioned Temple's comment to Hume as well, as Boswell relates in a letter to Temple, contained in this collection.]

all he can to lessen his antagonist, because authority from personal respect has much weight with most people, and often more than reasoning. If my antagonist writes bad language, though that may not be essential to the question, I will attack him for his bad language.' ADAMS. 'You will not jostle a chimney-sweeper.' JOHNSON. 'Yes, Sir, if it were necessary to jostle him *down*.'

[1776] A gentleman, whom I found sitting with him one morning, said, that in his opinion the character of an infidel was more detestable than that of a man notoriously guilty of an atrocious crime. I differed from him, because we are surer of the odiousness of the one, than of the errour of the other. JOHNSON. 'Sir, I agree with him; for the infidel would be guilty of any crime if he were inclined to it.'

[1777, letter of Boswell to Johnson, July 9] Without doubt you have read what is called *The Life* of David Hume, written by himself, with the letter from Dr. Adam Smith subjoined to it. Is not this an age of daring effrontery? My friend Mr. Anderson, Professor of Natural Philosophy at Glasgow, at whose house you and I supped, and to whose care Mr. Windham, of Norfolk, was entrusted at that University, paid me a visit lately; and after we had talked with indignation and contempt of the poisonous productions with which this age is infested, he said there was now an excellent opportunity for Dr. Johnson to step forth. I agreed with him that you might knock Hume's and Smith's heads together, and make vain and ostentatious infidelity exceedingly ridiculous. Would it not be worth your while to crush such noxious weeds in the moral garden?

You have said nothing to me of Dr. Dodd. I know not how you think on that subject; though the news-papers give us a saying of your's in favour of mercy to him. But I own I am very desirous that the royal prerogative of remission of punishment should be employed to exhibit an illustrious instance of the regard which GOD'S VICEGERENT will ever shew to piety and virtue. If for ten righteous men the ALMIGHTY would have spared Sodom, shall not a thousand acts of goodness done by Dr. Dodd counterbalance one crime? Such an instance would do more to encourage goodness, than his execution would do to deter from vice. I am not afraid of any bad consequence to society; for who will persevere for a long course of years in a distinguished discharge of religious duties, with a view to commit a forgery with impunity?

[1777] I mentioned to Dr. Johnson, that David Hume's persisting in his infidelity, when he was dying, shocked me much. JOHNSON. 'Why should it shock you, Sir? Hume owned he had never read the New Testament with attention. Here then was a man, who had been at no pains to enquire into the truth of religion, and had continually turned his mind the other way. It was not to be expected that the prospect of death would alter his way of thinking, unless

GOD should send an angel to set him right.' I said, I had reason to believe that the thought of annihilation gave Hume no pain. JOHNSON. 'It was not so, Sir. He had a vanity in being thought easy. It is more probable that he should assume an appearance of ease, than so very improbable a thing should be, as a man not afraid of going (as, in spite of his delusive theory, he cannot be sure but he may go,) into an unknown state, and not being uneasy at leaving all he knew. And you are to consider, that upon his own principle of annihilation he had no motive to speak the truth.' The horrour of death, which I had always observed in Dr. Johnson, appeared strong to-night. I ventured to tell him, that I had been, for moments in my life, not afraid of death; therefore I could suppose another man in that state of mind for a considerable space of time. He said, 'he never had a moment in which death was not terrible to him.' He added, that it had been observed, that scarce any man dies in publick, but with apparent resolution; from that desire of praise which never quits us. I said, Dr. Dodd seemed to be willing to die, and full of hopes of happiness. 'Sir, (said he,) Dr. Dodd would have given both his hands and both his legs to have lived. The better a man is, the more afraid is he of death, having a clearer view of infinite purity.' He owned, that our being in an unhappy uncertainty as to our salvation, was mysterious; and said, 'Ah! we must wait till we are in another state of being, to have many things explained to us.' Even the powerful mind of Johnson seemed foiled by futurity. But I thought, that the gloom of uncertainty in solemn religious speculation, being mingled with hope, was yet more consolatory than the emptiness of infidelity. A man can live in thick air, but perishes in an exhausted receiver.

[1777] Talking of Dr. Johnson's unwillingness to believe extraordinary things, I ventured to say, 'Sir, you come near Hume's argument against miracles, "That it is more probable witnesses should lie, or be mistaken, than that they should happen."' JOHNSON. 'Why, Sir, Hume, taking the proposition simply, is right. But the Christian revelation is not proved by the miracles alone, but as connected with prophecies, and with the doctrines in confirmation of which the miracles were wrought.'

He repeated his observation, that the differences among Christians are really of no consequence. 'For instance (said he,) if a Protestant objects to a Papist, "You worship images;" the Papist can answer, "I do not insist on *your* doing it; you may be a very good Papist without it: I do it only as a help to my devotion."' I said, the great article of Christianity is the revelation of immortality. Johnson admitted it was.

[1778] On Saturday, April 4, I drank tea with Johnson at Dr. Taylor's, where he had dined. He entertained us with an account of a tragedy written by a Dr. Kennedy, (not the Lisbon physician.) 'The catastrophe of it (said he,) was, that a King, who was jealous of his Queen with his prime-minister, castrated himself. ...' [Note:] The reverse of the story of *Combabus*, on which Mr. David Hume told Lord Macartney, that a friend of his had written a tragedy. It is, however, possible, that I may have been inaccurate in my perception of what Dr. Johnson related, and that he may have been talking of the same ludicrous tragical subject that Mr. Hume had mentioned.

[1778] Upon this subject I had once before sounded him, by mentioning the late Reverend Mr. Brown, of Utrecht's, image; that a great and small glass, though equally full, did not hold an equal quantity; which he threw out to refute David Hume's saying, that a little miss, going to dance at a ball, in a fine new dress, was as happy as a great oratour, after having made an eloquent and applauded speech.[6] After some thought, Johnson said, 'I come over to the parson.' As an instance of coincidence of thinking, Mr. Dilly told me, that Dr. King, a late dissenting minister in London, said to him, upon the happiness in a future state of good men of different capacities, 'A pail does not hold so much as a tub; but, if it be equally full, it has no reason to complain. Every Saint in heaven will have as much happiness as he can hold.' Mr. Dilly thought this a clear, though a familiar illustration of the phrase, 'One star differeth from another in brightness.'

[1779] I told him [i.e., Johnson] that when I objected to keeping company with a notorious infidel, a celebrated friend of ours said to me, 'I do not think that men who live laxly in the world, as you and I do, can with propriety assume such an authority. Dr. Johnson may, who is uniformly exemplary in his conduct. But it is not very consistent to shun an infidel to-day, and get drunk to-morrow.' JOHNSON. 'Nay, Sir, this is sad reasoning. Because a man cannot be right in all things, is he to be right in nothing? Because a man sometimes gets drunk, is he therefore to steal? This doctrine would very soon bring a man to the gallows.'

[1783] He [i.e., Johnson] would not allow Mr. David Hume any credit for his political principles, though similar to his own; saying of him, 'Sir, he was a Tory by chance.'[7]

[1784] Mrs. Kennicot, in confirmation of Dr. Johnson's opinion, that the present was not worse than former ages, mentioned that her brother assured her, there was now less infidelity on the Continent than there had been; Voltaire and Rousseau were less read. I asserted, from good authority, that

---

[6] [Boswell discusses this passage from Hume's "The Sceptic" in a 1766 entry, quoted above.]

[7] [Boswell related Johnson's comment to Hume in his 1776 interview.]

Hume's infidelity was certainly less read. JOHNSON. 'All infidel writers drop into oblivion, when personal connections and the floridness of novelty are gone; though now and then a foolish fellow, who thinks he can be witty upon them, may bring them again into notice. There will sometimes start up a College joker, who does not consider that what is a joke in a College will not do in the world. To such defenders of Religion I would apply a stanza of a poem which I remember to have seen in some old collection: –

"Henceforth be quiet and agree,
   Each kiss his empty brother;
Religion scorns a foe like thee,
   But dreads a friend like t'other."'

[1784] As Johnson had abundant homage paid to him during his life, so no writer in this nation ever had such an accumulation of literary honours after his death. A sermon upon that event was preached in St. Mary's church, Oxford, before the University, by the Reverend Mr. Agutter, of Magdalen College. [Note:] It is not yet published.[8] – In a letter to me, Mr. Agutter says, 'My sermon before the University was more engaged with Dr. Johnson's *moral* than his *intellectual* character. It particularly examined his fear of death, and suggested several reasons for the apprehensions of the good, and the indifference of the infidel in their last hours; this was illustrated by contrasting the death of Dr. Johnson and Mr. Hume: the text was Job xxi. 22–26.'

---

[8] [William Agutter (1758–1835), *On the Differences Between the Deaths of the Righteous and the Wicked* (1800), selections from which are contained in this collection.]

88
WILLIAM AGUTTER:
ON THE DIFFERENCE BETWEEN
THE DEATHS OF THE RIGHTEOUS
AND THE WICKED

William Agutter, *On the difference between the deaths of the righteous and the wicked, illustrated in the instance of Dr. Samuel Johnson, and David Hume, Esq. A sermon, preached before the University of Oxford, … On Sunday, July 23, 1786. By the Rev. William Agutter.* London: printed at the Philanthropic Reform, by J. Richardson, 1800, 18, [2] p.
Selections; from 1800 edition.

Educated at Lincoln College, Oxford, William Agutter (1758–1835) was an independent preacher, theologically sympathetic to the views of Emanuel Swedenborg, and for some time was Chaplain to the Asylum for Female Orphans. A year and a half after Samuel Johnson died, Agutter delivered a sermon on the subject of the fear of death, which he describes in a letter to James Boswell,

> My sermon before the University was more engaged with Dr. Johnson's *moral* than his *intellectual* character. It particularly examined his fear of death, and suggested several reasons for the apprehensions of the good, and the indifference of the infidel in their last hours; this was illustrated by contrasting the death of Dr. Johnson and Mr. Hume: the text was Job xxi. 22–26. [*Life of Samuel Johnson*, 1791]

Fourteen years later it appeared in print as a single pamphlet, and is the most important of his published sermons. In this work Agutter discusses the commonly held view that religion gives people special triumph over death, which the unbeliever cannot experience. He feels that this generalization has been pushed too far, and he concedes that Hume's death was tranquil, and that Johnson had a well-known fear of dying. Thus, he writes, "Religion does not always triumph over the fears of death" and infidels "may enjoy an apparent peace" at the close of life. He believes, though, that careful look at such

167

counter instances will show that the general principle still holds true. Infidels may have some "recourse to the subterfuge of doubts," but this should not be seen as true courage when their calmness results from "voluntary blindness." Further, some infidels, from "obstinacy of pride," feel that they must "affix the dignifying stamp of their death to the avowed principles of their lives." The believer, by contrast, may be weighted with temptation, which in time produces "peaceable fruits of righteousness," but will be grievous for the moment.

When the sermon appeared in print, Christopher Lake Moody gave the following synopsis in the *Monthly Review*:

> The terrors of death which embittered the last moments of Johnson, and the calmness of Hume under the sensations of approaching dissolution, have been deemed unfavourable to the doctrine concerning the blessedness or superior advantages of religion. Mr. Agutter therefore endeavours to remove the misapprehensions which have arisen on this subject. The arguments deduced from the manner of our dissolution, he observes, have been forced too far. Physical causes will have their effect; and in this life they are not overruled by the Gospel, which points to a future state as its theatre of reward – Why was this discourse so long unpublished? [*Monthly Review*, 1801, Vol. 34, p. 335]

The following is from the 1800 and only edition of Agutter's work.

A

SERMON

JOB xxi.

Ver. 23. *One dieth in his full strength, being wholly at his ease and quiet;*
24. *His breasts are full of milk, and his bones are moistened with marrow:*
25. *And another dieth in the bitterness of his soul, and never eateth with pleasure.*
26. *They shall lie down alike in the dust, and the worms shall cover them.*

[§ 1.] In a few fleeting years the scenes of this mortal life must close, and the hand of death will be upon us. We all must eat that bitter fruit of sin, and encounter that last enemy, who will assault us on this side the eternal world. Now as nature shrinks at the prospect of pain, and desires an exemption from doubt and darkness; so highly reasonable is it to wish, that the conflict may not be long, nor the pangs severe, when our *strength faileth us,* and we are entering the gate of death. Such surely is the ardent desire of man: a desire which results from the constitution of his frame, of which the most active principle is self-preservation. But Divine Wisdom will teach him a higher lesson, and enable him to say, from the unshaken sincerity of a filial confidence, "Though his excellency make me afraid, and his dread fall upon me, though he slay me, yet will I trust in him."

It must be obvious to every reflecting mind, that Religion does not always triumph over the fears of death; and, likewise, that the man who is depraved in principle, or profligate in practice, may enjoy an apparent peace, or display a real indifference, at the close of life.

Let us then consider the DIFFERENCE *between the deaths of him who feareth God, and of him who feareth him not;*[1] and, more fully to investigate the subject, let us examine the CAUSES whence the difference proceeds, the EXAMPLES by which it is illustrated, and some of the various REASONS for the divine permission of it. The result of the above considerations will afford the infidel no grounds for triumph, and the sceptic no confirmation of his doubts. Let us then duly estimate the just conclusion which may be drawn from the manner of our dissolution; and not, through a sincere but erroneous zeal, force the argument too far; for I cannot but apprehend that the common assertion on this subject (that the righteous has joyful hope in his death, and peace at the close of his life) has been weakened because overstrained. It has been exposed to contradiction, because it has been advanced without limitation; but, by taking the reverse of the subject, we may more accurately ascertain the truth of the fact in particular cases, be better able to vindicate and illustrate the ways of Providence, and expose the slight pretences on which scepticism and irreligion affect to triumph.

I shall state the objection of our adversaries in its fullest force, and combat it on the fairest grounds: "You appeal," say they, "to the testimony of the dying, and recommend the truths of the gospel as the only effectual support in the hour of death; it is thus you work on the timorous, and impose on the vulgar: but, as the appeal is made to facts, have we not seen the philosophical deist and avowed sceptic depart this life in calm tranquillity and manly fortitude, cheerfully bidding his friends adieu, and smiling in the face of death? 'he died in his full strength, being wholly at ease and quiet:' while, on the other hand, a Christian philosopher has had his mind oppressed with fears, agitated with doubts, and alarmed with terrors: 'he died in the bitterness of his soul, and while he remembered death could never eat with pleasure.'"

To return a satisfactory answer to this objection. Let it be considered, that the infidel either professes his total ignorance on the subject of futurity; or, if his fears be alarmed, or his opinions shaken, he has recourse to the subterfuge of doubts. Irregular passions will make it the interest of reason to question or to deny the reality of another world; and nothing is more easy than to continue ignorant, where we are unwilling to learn; but that conduct which results from voluntary ignorance may be condemned as blind rashness, or despised as

---

[1] For instance, Dr. Johnson and David Hume.

perverse infatuation, but never can be valued as true courage. He who has rushed forward in the dark may stand on the brink of a precipice without feeling emotions of terror, and without meriting any tribute of applause. Considering the common depravity of our nature, and the awful scene of probation closed, our adversaries ought to allow that the Christian trembling, and the deist laughing, at the awful separation of soul and body, may be illustrated by the case of two criminals who are going to make satisfaction to the laws which they have violated: the one, from an habitual course of guilt, has attained that total want of reflection which induces him to deride the decision of justice, and to undergo his sentence with that stupid indifference, which superficial observers may mistake for fortitude; while the other, a novice in the practice of sin, is overwhelmed with ingenuous shame, views his violations of the law in the most glaring light, and approaches with undissembled dread to the presence of his God and his judge. The first of these characters may be applauded by those who are equally hardened in guilt, or equally blinded by infidelity; but we cannot be such strangers to the nature of man, as, from the language of confident boasting, to argue for the rectitude of his judgment, or the integrity of his cause.

Rational fear must always be proportionate to the greatness of the object which excites it, and to the interest we ourselves feel in that object. We smile at the child who trembles because it is in the dark; but we are impressed with feelings of a more serious nature, when we see any one wantonly trifling with death: for surely no wise man can esteem it a small matter to feel the last pangs of expiring humanity, to stand on the confines of the world of spirits, and to meet the king of terrors face to face. The ostentatious bravery then so unseasonably displayed may justly be imputed to the delusions of vanity, or the obstinacy of pride. Men have the character of philosophers to support, and are anxious to affix the dignifying stamp of their death to the avowed principles of their lives. Here indeed it is very difficult to discriminate the exact features of truth; for the end of the infidel is sometimes concealed with industrious secresy, and sometimes misrepresented by officious friendship.[2]

But allowing those who maintain the excellency of such examples all that they contend for, what will they gain by our concession? the history of past ages informs us, that the patrons of idolatry and superstition, of enthusiasm and heresy, of rebellion, ambition, and assassination, have encountered death with undaunted spirits, and triumphed in the agonies of expiring nature, as if supported by conscious rectitude, and animated with a hope full of immortality. Many have died martyrs to those causes which are repugnant to reason, and disgraceful to humanity; whence it must be plainly inferred, that the mere act of martyrdom cannot prove either the sincerity of faith, or the purity of morals.

---

[2]   Particularly the case with Voltaire.

Another important consideration presents itself to our view, and claims our attention, in the union between the body and the soul; the immortal spirit dwelling in an habitation of clay. The effects naturally resulting from the one are falsely ascribed to the other; which must render our reasoning confused, and our conclusions erroneous. Thus the robust constitution, the uninterrupted health, and the regular spirits of one man produce those tranquil appearances which are ascribed to a superior philosophy rising above the superstitions of the vulgar. On the other hand, a constitution enfeebled by frequent diseases, tainted by morbid melancholy, and bowed down by the pressure of age, causes those sad effects which are unjustly and invidiously attributed to the fears of superstition, the disappointments of religious hope, or the weakness of dying faith. Supposing then that the enemy of the gospel, the champion of infidelity, descended to his grave in peace, felt no remorse of conscience on the review of life, and expressed no apprehensions on the verge of the eternal world, what will this prove? Not that the religion which he so strenuously opposed was false, but that the placid appearances resulted from the strength of his constitution, or the nature of his disease. On the same principle, the sincere Christian may have his fear multiplied, his anxiety sharpened, and his conscience harrassed with distressing doubts; yet, exclusive of the ravages of sickness, and the gradations of decay, it never can be said that the humble penitent "feared where no fear was."

"The heart knoweth its own bitterness;" particularly the heart which is awakened to a sense of its danger, and is exercised with many temptations: while others are walking on in a thick mist, and therefore see no surrounding dangers; or are swimming with the rapid stream, and therefore feel no opposition: but it is not so with him. Temptation, like affliction, for the present, is not joyous, but grievous; nevertheless, it produces the peaceable fruits of righteousness to them who are exercised thereby: for temptation separates between good and evil; the corn and the chaff; wickedness is discovered and rejected; and virtue is cultivated and perfected. The pious mind may be in heaviness through manifold temptation; yet even then it is in a blessed estate, and has cause for great joy, that the trial of his faith may be found unto praise, and honour, and glory, at the appearing "of Jesus Christ. If we follow Him in the regeneration, if we suffer with Him, we shall also reign with Him. They that sow in tears shall reap in joy. He that goeth forth and weepeth, bearing precious seed, shall doubtless come again with rejoicing, bringing his sheaves with him."

It cannot excite any surprize that they should be ignorant of these spiritual temptations, these purifying trials, "who live after the flesh, and are dead in trespasses and sins;" or that they should profanely ridicule what they understood not, "who love darkness rather than light, and who come not to the light, lest their deeds should be reproved."

By sufferings, and those in the mind as well as in the body, we are conformed to the image and the example of the great Captain of our salvation, who was made perfect by sufferings, and teaches us the same sublime lesson; to be exalted by submission, and to conquer by resignation.

May we not conceive, that, in the infinite diversity of the human mind, the reality of faith may dwell in the heart, and yet no clear knowledge of the royal law of liberty, no assurance of future bliss, be given? In this painful state men impose burdens on themselves too heavy to be borne: the mind is distracted, and the peace lost, amidst needless scruples: scruples which are highly to be respected, because they are sincere; and tenderly to be opposed, because they are the source of real distress. The imperfection of all present attainments, and the boundless desire of excellence, induce men to review the scenes which are past, or to anticipate the endless ages of futurity;[3] But either of these views may distress such a mind with useless lamentations over years that are past and unimproved, and with timorous scruples concerning the scenes which are in view. Such a conduct does not altogether accord with the noble simplicity, and filial confidence, of the gospel: yet every form of sincerity must be pleasing to Him "Who searcheth the heart;" and the weakness of sincerity can easily find his tenderest pardon, "Who knows whereof we are made, Who remembers that we are but dust."

The greatness and importance of the objects placed before the Christian's view, suppress presumption, although they may not exceed belief. The deist may presume on he knows not what; but the nearer approach to the divine nature, the awful means of reconciliation, and the opening prospect of eternal glory, are calculated to inspire the believer with sacred reverence and holy peace, rather than with rapturous joy or bold confidence.

From the above remarks we may justly conclude, that the confidence or the tranquillity of the infidel are no arguments in his favour; or that the humility, fears, or sorrows of the dying Christian can form no argument against his religion, but may easily consist with the favour of his heavenly Father, and an abundant entrance into the everlasting kingdom.

§ 2. For the EXAMPLES of the best of men [i.e., David, Hezekiah] will justify his conduct, and prove how well it may accord with the sincerity of his faith, and the power of his religion. ...

§ 3. The Reasons for the Divine permission of this partial difference. The principle of this may be collected from (1) the order of Providence, and (2) the nature of the Gospel....

---

[3] "Dr. Johnson had the highest notions of the hard task of Christianity; whose daily terror, lest he had not done enough, originated in piety, but ended in little less than disease. Reasonable with regard to others, he had formed vain hopes of performing impossibilities himself; and finding his good works ever below his desires and intent, filled his imagination with fear that he should never obtain forgiveness for omissions of duty and criminal waste of time. These ideas kept him in constant anxiety about his salvation." Mrs. Piozzi's Anecdotes, p. 112–3.

It has been observed, on this subject, that the difference between the deaths of the righteous and the wicked may proceed from *total ignorance* on the part of the latter; or may be the effects of *ostentatious vanity*, or the composure of the *animal frame*. From the *examples* which authorize the fears of the best of men, and from the *reasons* alledged for the divine permission of such a conduct, I humbly conceive that the objection which introduced these observations is not only fully obviated, but, by a closer investigation of the subject, has led us to discover the wisdom and propriety in permitting no greater difference between the deaths of the righteous and the wicked.

Hence we may learn, not to "call the proud happy,"[4] either in the arrogance of his life, or the insensibility of his death; – not to envy the infidel or the sceptic the gloomy satisfaction of doubting, where truth only can afford comfort;[5] or of supposing, that they shall sink through death into dark annihilation, whence we trust that we shall rise to the life immortal: – not to make the heart of the righteous sad, whom GOD hath not made sad, by falsely interpreting the pains of death, or attempting to circumscribe the procedures of Divine Mercy within the narrow limits of our comprehension.

Rather than judging of others, and drawing doubtful conclusions from their latter ends, our only business is with ourselves. It is natural to wish for peace at the last; and this wish of Reason will be improved by Religion, if we now "die unto Sin, and live unto GOD." This divine life may exist, and yet in some cases peace and joy be withheld for a season: yet peace and joy can never animate the soul on rational principles, unless the foundation be "Faith working by Love," and producing universal holiness in heart and life. Without these, a tranquility of mind is nothing more than brutal stupidity, and the expectation of eternal happiness but a strong delusion; even the hope of the hypocrite, which shall perish. Let us then "look unto the Author and the Finisher of our Faith," whose death was the purchase of our life, and whose resurrection was the pledge of our victory; who can convert the last punishment of sin into the instrument of more exalted virtue: let us live in his faith and fear, daily perfecting holiness in his sight, and preparing for the nearer approach of

---

[4] Mal. iii. 15.

[5] "His morbid melancholy gathered such strength as to afflict him in a dreadful manner: he was overwhelmed with an horrible hypochondria: with perpetual irritation, fretfulness, and impatience; and with a dejection, gloom, and despair, that made existence misery." Anderson's Life of Johnson, p. 24.

"The serenity, the independence, and the exultation of religion were sentiments to which he was a stranger. He saw the Almighty in a different light from what He is represented in the purer page of the Gospel; and he trembled in the presence of infinite Goodness. Those tenets of the church of England which were most nearly allied to Calvinism were congenial to his general feelings, and they made an easy impression, which habits confirmed, and which reason, if ever exerted, could not efface." – Ibid. p. 29, 30.

death: "For who is among you that feareth the LORD, that walketh in darkness, and hath no light, let him trust in the name of the LORD, and stay upon his GOD." Thus we use the appointed means to secure the marks of his approbation at the last hour, that we may then confess his truth, and rejoice in the hope which is set before us: this surely is well: but if He refuse this, if He add sorrow to sickness, it is far better that we resign ourselves to the will of the Father of Mercies: for the cup, whether in life or in death, which He giveth us to drink, shall we not drink it? "Although my strength and my heart fail me, yet GOD is my portion for ever."

FINIS.

89
THOMAS CARLYLE:
"CHARACTERISTICS"

[Thomas Carlyle], "Characteristics," *Edinburgh Review*, December 1831, Vol. 108, pp. 351–383.
Selections; from *Critical and Miscellaneous*, Boston, Phillips, 1855.

Born in Ecclefechan in Dumfriesshire, Scotland, and son of a farmer, Thomas Carlyle (1795–1881) was educated at the University of Edinburgh. After considering various occupations, including the ministry and the law, he turned to essay writing, especially for the *Edinburgh Review*, and later became a prominent historian. In an article in the *Edinburgh Review* on Scottish poet Robert Burns, Carlyle expresses mixed feelings about the great Scottish writers of the previous century. They were brilliant and widely read, but were at the same time more French than Scottish. Of Hume in particular he writes,

> It is curious to remark that Scotland, so full of writers, had no Scottish culture, nor indeed any English; our culture was almost exclusively French. … Hume was too rich a man to borrow; and perhaps he reached on the French more than he was acted on by them: but neither had he aught to do with Scotland; Edinburgh, equally with La Flèche, was but the lodging and laboratory, in which he not so much morally *lived*, as metaphysically *investigated*. Never, perhaps, was there a class of writers, so clear and well-ordered, yet so totally destitute, to all appearance, of any patriotic affection, nay, of any human affection whatever. ["Burns," *Edinburgh Review*, December 1828, Vol. 48, pp. 267–312]

Shortly after this article, Carlyle published another in the same journal, reiterating his views about Hume's cosmopolitan nature. Discussing differences between Johnson and Hume, Carlyle states that Hume was "the father of all succeeding Whigs," had broad appeal overseas, had a "comprehensive eye" in his writings, and died believing that the afterlife was a lie. Johnson, by contrast, was the father of succeeding Tories, was influential only in England, had a gift for "minute detail," and died with hopes of an afterlife. They were, Carlyle states, "the two half-men of their time," whose spirits may some day be united here on earth.

CHARACTERISTICS.

...

It is worthy of note that, in our little British Isle, the two grand Antagonisms of Europe should have stood imbodied, under their very highest concentration, in two men produced simultaneously among ourselves. Samuel Johnson and David Hume, as was observed, were children of the same year: through life they were spectators of the same Life-movement; often inhabitants of the same city. Greater contrast, in all things, between two great men, could not be. Hume, well-born, competently provided for, whole in body and mind, of his own determination forces a way into Literature: Johnson, poor, moonstruck, diseased, forlorn, is forced into it "with the bayonet of necessity at his back." And what a part did they severally play there! As Johnson became the father of all succeeding Tories; so was Hume the father of all succeeding Whigs, for his own Jacobitism was but an accident, as worthy to be named Prejudice as any of Johnson's. Again, if Johnson's culture was exclusively English; Hume's, in Scotland, became European; – for which reason too we find his influence spread deeply over all quarters of Europe, traceable deeply in all speculation, French, German, as well as domestic; while Johnson's name, out of England, is hardly anywhere to be met with. In spiritual stature they are almost equal; both great, among the greatest: yet how unlike in likeness! Hume has the widest methodizing, comprehensive eye; Johnson the keenest for perspicacity and minute detail: so had, perhaps chiefly, their education ordered it. Neither of the two rose into Poetry; yet both to some approximation thereof: Hume to something of an Epic clearness and method, as in his delineation of the Commonwealth Wars; Johnson to many a deep Lyric tone of plaintiveness, and impetuous graceful power, scattered over his fugitive compositions. Both, rather to the general surprise, had a certain rugged Humour shining through their earnestness: the indication, indeed, that they *were* earnest men, and had *subdued* their wild world into a kind of temporary home, and safe dwelling. Both were, by principle and habit, Stoics: yet Johnson with the greater merit, for he alone had very much to triumph over; farther, he alone ennobled his Stoicism into Devotion. To Johnson Life was as a Prison, to be endured with heroic faith: to Hume it was little more than a foolish Bartholomew-Fair Show-booth, with the foolish crowdings and elbowings of which it was not worth while to quarrel; the whole would break up, and be at liberty, so *soon*. Both realized the highest task of Manhood, that of living like men; each died not unfitly, in his way: Hume as one, with factitious, half-false gayety, taking leave of what was itself wholly but a Lie: Johnson as one, with awe-struck, yet resolute and piously expectant heart, taking leave of a Reality, to enter a Reality still higher. Johnson had the harder problem of it, from first to last: whether with some hesitation, we can admit that he was intrinsically the better-gifted, – may remain undecided.

These two men now rest; the one in Westminster Abbey here; the other in the Calton Hill Churchyard of Edinburgh. Through Life they did not meet: as contrasts, "like in unlike," love each other; so might they two have loved, and communed kindly, – had not the terrestrial dross and darkness, that was in them, withstood! One day their spirits, what truth was in each, will be found working, living in harmony and free union, even here below. They were the two half-men of their time: whoso should combine the intrepid Candour, and decisive scientific Clearness of Hume, with the Reverence, the Love, and devout Humility of Johnson, were the whole man of a new time. Till such whole man arrive for us, and the distracted time admit of such, might the heavens but bless poor England with half-men worthy to tie the shoe-latches of these, resembling these even from afar! be both attentively regarded, let the true Effort of both prosper; – and for the present, both take our affectionate farewell!

HANNAH MORE

90
PRACTICAL PIETY

Hannah More, *Practical Piety, or the influence of the religion of the heart on the conduct of the life*. London: Printed for T. Cadell and W. Davies, 1811, 2 v. Selections from Chapter 19, "Happy Deaths"; from *Practical Piety*, Burlington, N.J., Allinson, 1811.

Hannah More (1745–1833) was born in Stapleton, Gloucestershire, England. When a young girl she knew Hume's friend John Peach, a linen draper from Bristol, and from that acquaintance conveyed an anecdote about Hume's stay in that city (see "Miscellaneous Hume Anecdotes" in this collection). Around thirty she became close friends of David Garrick, Samuel Johnson, and, as a noted poet and playwright herself, she was included in London's famed literary circles. Her religious convictions intensified with age and, no longer attending theatrical productions, many of her writings focused on religious themes. In her 1805 *Hints towards Forming the Character of a Young Princess* she criticizes the political and religious bias in Hume's otherwise elegant *History*. She was aware of the impact of Adam Smith's account of Hume's final days and cheerful death. In a letter to her sister, she conveys a story comparing Hume's and Johnson's attitudes about death:

A friend desired he [i.e., Johnson] would make his will, and as Hume in his last moments had made an impious declaration of his opinions, he thought it might tend to counteract the poison, if Johnson would make a public confession of his faith in his will. He said he would; seized the pen with great earnestness, and asked what was the usual form of beginning a will? His friend told him. After the usual forms he wrote, 'I offer up my soul to the great and merciful God; I offer it full of pollution, but in full assurance that it will be cleansed in the blood of my Redeemer.' And for some time he wrote on with the same vigour and spirit as if he had been in perfect health. When he expressed some of his former dread of dying, Sir John said, If you, doctor, have these fears, what is to become of me and others? [Hannah More to her sister, 1785, in *Memoirs of Hanna More*, London, Seeley, 1835, Vol. 1, p. 393]

Around twenty-five years later she published a book titled *Practical Piety* which contains a chapter exploring why infidels reportedly die in a state of tranquillity – or experience "happy deaths" as they are sometimes called. Most notably infidels may attempt to alleviate any "suspicion that their disbelief was not so sturdy as they would have it thought." A case in point, she says, is Hume whose courage in facing death is "almost deified" by Adam Smith in his "Letter to ... William Strahan." Contrary to Smith's eulogy extolling Hume's humanity, More feels that Hume's "Essay on Suicide" shows the philosopher to be of a much less noble character. She also discusses Rousseau's and Voltaire's deaths, noting how unpeaceful they were. More's "Happy Deaths" is discussed by two articles in the *Monthly Repository*, excerpted later in this collection.

CHAPTER XIX.

HAPPY DEATHS.

Few circumstances contribute more fatally to confirm in worldly men that insensibility to eternal things which was considered in the preceding chapter, than the boastful accounts we sometimes hear of the firm and heroick death-beds of popular but irreligious characters. Many causes contribute to these *happy deaths* as they are called. The blind are bold, they do not see the precipice they despise. – Or perhaps there is less unwillingness to quit a world which has so often disappointed them, or which they have sucked to the last dregs. They leave life with less reluctance, feeling that they have exhausted all its gratifications. – Or it is a disbelief of the reality of the state on which they are about to enter. – Or it is a desire to be released from excessive pain, a desire naturally felt by those who calculate their gain, rather by what they are escaping from, than by what they are to receive. – Or it is equability of temper, or firmness of nerve, or hardness of mind. – Or it is the arrogant wish to make the last act of life confirm its preceding professions. – Or it is the vanity of perpetuating their philosophick character. – Or if some faint ray of light break in, it is the pride of not retracting the sentiments which from pride they have maintained: – The desire of posthumous renown among their own party; the hope to make their disciples stand firm by their example; the ambition to give their last possible blow to revelation – or perhaps the fear of expressing doubts which might beget a suspicion that their disbelief was not so sturdy as they would have it thought. Above all, may they not, as a punishment for their long neglect of the warning voice of truth, be given up to a strong delusion to believe the lie they have so often propagated, and really to expect to find in death that eternal sleep, with which they have affected to quiet their own consciences, and have really weakened the faith of others?

Every new instance is an additional buttress on which the sceptical school lean for support, and which they produce as a fresh triumph. With equal satisfaction they collect stories of infirmity, depression and want of courage in the dying hour of religious men, whom the nature of the disease, timorousness of spirit, profound humility, the sad remembrance of sin, though long repented of and forgiven, a deep sense of the awfulness of meeting God in judgment; – whom some or all of these causes may occasion to depart in trembling fear; in whom, though heaviness may endure through the night of death, yet joy cometh in the morning of the resurrection.

It is a maxim of the civil law that definitions are hazardous. And it cannot be denied that various descriptions of persons have hazarded much in their definitions of a *happy death*. A very able and justly admired writer,[1] who has distinguished himself by the most valuable works on political economy, has recorded, as proofs of the happy death of a no less celebrated contemporary, that he cheerfully amused himself in his last hours with Lucian, A Game of whist, and some good humoured drollery upon Charon and his boat.

But may we not venture to say, with "one of the people called christians,"[2] himself a wit and philosopher, though of the school of Christ, that the man who could meet death in such a frame of mind "might smile over Babylon in ruins, esteem the earthquake which destroyed Lisbon an agreeable occurrence, and congratulate the hardened Pharoah on his overthrow in the Red Sea."

This eminent historian and philosopher, whose great intellectual powers it is as impossible not to admire, as not to lament their unhappy misapplication, has been eulogized by his friend, as coming nearer than almost any other man, to the perfection of human nature in his life; and has been almost deified for the cool courage and heroick firmness with which he met death. His eloquent panegyrist, with as insidious an inuendo as has ever been thrown out against revealed religion, goes on to observe, that "perhaps it is one of the very worst circumstances against christianity, that very few of its professors were ever either so moral, so humane, or could so philosophically govern their passions, as the sceptical David Hume."

Yet notwithstanding this rich embalming of so noble a compound of "matter and motion," we must be permitted to doubt one of the two things presented for our admiration; we must either doubt the so much boasted happiness of his death, or the so much extolled humanity of his heart. We must be permitted to suspect the soundness of that benevolence, which led him to devote his latest hours to prepare, under the label of *an Essay on Suicide*, a potion for posterity,

---

[1] [i.e., Adam Smith in his "Letter to ... William Strahan" (1777), contained in this collection.]

[2] The late excellent bishop Horne, See his letters to Dr. Adam Smith. [George Horne, *A Letter to Adam Smith* (1777), contained in this collection.]

of so deleterious a quality, that if taken by the patient, under all the circumstances in which he undertakes to prove it innocent, might have gone near to effect the extinction of the whole human race. For if all rational beings, according to this posthumous prescription, are at liberty to procure their own release from life "under pain or sickness, shame or poverty," how large a portion of the world would be authorized to quit it uncalled! For how many are subject to the two latter grievances; from the two former how few are altogether exempt!³

The energy of that ambition which could concentrate the last efforts of a powerful mind, the last exertions of a spirit greedy of fame, into a project, not only for destroying the souls, but for abridging the lives of his fellow creatures, leaves at a disgraceful distance the inverted thirst of glory of the man, who to immortalize his own name, set fire to the Temple at Ephesus. Such a burning zeal to annihilate the eternal hope of his fellow creatures might be philosophy; but surely to authorize them to curtail their mortal existence, which to the infidel who looks for no other, must be invaluable, but not philanthropy.

But if this death was thought worthy of being blazoned to the publick eye in all the warm and glowing colours with which affection decorates panegyrick, the disciples of the same school have been in general, anxiously solicitous to produce only the more creditable instances of invincible hardness of heart, while they have laboured to cast an impenetrable veil over the closing scene of those among the less inflexible of the fraternity, who have exhibited in their departing moments, any symptoms of doubt, any indications of distrust, respecting the validity of their principles: – Principles which they had long maintained with so much zeal, and disseminated with so much industry.

In spite of the sedulous anxiety of his satellites to conceal the clouded setting of the great luminary of modern infidelity, from which so many minor stars have filled their little urns, and then set up for original lights themselves; in spite of the pains taken – for we must drop metaphor – to shroud from all eyes, except those of the initiated, the terrour and dismay with which the Philosopher of Geneva⁴ met death, met his summons to appear before that God whose providence he had ridiculed, that Saviour whose character and offices he had vilified, – the secret was betrayed. In spite of the precautions taken by his associates to bury in congenial darkness the agonies which in his last hours

---

³ Another part of the *Essay on Suicide* has this passage – "Whenever pain or sorrow so far overcome my patience, as to make me tired of life, I may conclude that I am recalled from my station in the plainest and most express terms." – And again – "When I fall upon my own sword, I receive my death equally from the hands of the Deity, as it had proceeded from a lion, a precipice, or a fever." – And again – "Where is the crime of turning a few ounces of blood from their natural channel!"

⁴ [i.e., Jean-Jacques Rousseau (1712–1778).]

contradicted the audatious blasphemies of a laborious life spent in their propagation, at last, like his great instigator, he *believed and trembled.*

Whatever the sage of Ferney[5] might be in the eyes of Journalists, of Academicans, of Encyclopædists, of the Royal Author of Berlin, of Revolutionists in the egg of his own hatching, of full grown infidels of his own spawning, of a world into which he had been for more than half a century industriously infusing a venom, the effects of which will be long felt, the expiring philosopher was no object of veneration to his nurse. – She could have recorded "a tale to harrow up the soul," the horrours of which were sedulously attempted to be consigned to oblivion. But for this woman and a few other unbrided witnesses, his friends would probably have endeavoured to edify the world with this addition to the brilliant catalogue of *happy deaths.*[6]

---

[5] [i.e., Voltaire (1694–1778).]

[6] It is a well attested fact that this woman, after his decease, being sent for to attend another person in dying circumstances, anxiously inquired if the patient was a gentleman; for that she had recently been do dreadfully terrified in witnessing the dying horrours of Mons. de Voltaire, which surpassed all description, that she had resolved never to attend any other person of that sex unless she could be assured that he was not a philosopher. – Voltaire indeed, as he was deficient in the moral honesty and the other good qualities, which obtained for Mr. Hume the affection of his friends, wanted his sincerity. Of all his other vices, hypocrisy was the consummation. While he daily dishonoured the Redeemer by the invention of unheard of blasphemies; after he had bound himself by a solemn pledge never to rest till he had exterminated his very name from the face of the earth, he was not ashamed to assist regularly at the awful commemoration of his death at the Altar!

91
DEATH-BEDS OF UNBELIEVERS

Anonymous (pseud. "A Constant Reader"). "Death-beds of Unbelievers," in *Monthly Repository*, 1813, Vol. 8, pp. 32–33. Complete.

In her book *Practical Piety* (1811) – excerpted earlier in this collection – Hannah More speculated about whether atheists have tranquil deaths and she suggested that Hume's might not have been as peaceful as Adam Smith reported. Shortly after, an anonymous letter appeared in the *Monthly Repository* criticizing Christians who feel that unbelievers die in mental anguish. The author, using the pseudonym "A Constant Reader," also takes More to task for having "laboured in all her power to convince us that Hume's was a miserable death-bed." An anonymous response to this letter, titled "Hume and Mrs. Hannah More," appeared in the *Monthly Repository*, contained later in this collection.

DEATH-BEDS OF UNBELIEVERS.

Birmingham, Nov. 17, 1812.

SIR,

I chanced the other day to meet with a Sermon, preached and published some time ago by the Rev. John Evans, of Islington, upon the death of Mr. Stephen Lowdell (one of his congregation), in the preface to which is the following passage: "A celebrated atheist, distinguished for his parts and learning, was known through life to be afraid of *being left alone*, and when his physician assured him (at the age of *ninety-two*) that his disease was mortal, his only remark was, 'I shall be glad to find a hole to creep out of the world at.'" In order to apply this anecdote as a proof of the greater strength of mind, and consequent increase of happiness, to be derived from a belief of the existence of a Deity and of a divine revelation (for which purpose it is here introduced), I conceive it would be necessary to shew that it was in consequence of his disbelief upon these points, that the Atheist here alluded to, was affected with this weakness, and that the fear of being left alone could not be attributed to the silly tales of nurses, or the errors of early education; at all events, it would

186

be necessary to prove that all who happily have no doubts of the existence of a Deity, or the truths of Christianity, are never affected by such fears as that of being left alone. Now I much doubt whether there are not many instances upon record, and within the knowledge of most persons, of the firmest believers being subject to foolish fears of the same kind, attributable to disease or the defects of education. If I am not much mistaken, the late Dr. Priestley always felt some degree of fear from being alone in the dark. The Rev. Gentleman has therefore I think been rather unhappy in the application of this part of his anecdote.

With regard to the second part of the story, which relates the manner in which he received the report of his physician that "his disease was mortal," so far from its being a *proof* that he would have looked upon death with greater firmness, or that his mind would have been in a happier frame had he been a believer, I really think that had this part of the story been related of a Christian, it might have been brought as a proof of the excellence of a belief which would enable a man to contemplate death so firmly – I shall be glad to find a hole to creep out of the world at." I would therefore wish to impress upon the mind of the Rev. Gentleman by whom this is related to seek for other proofs of the excellent effects of a belief in Christianity, than in the weakness or unhappiness of those whose minds are unfortunately closed to its evidences; unless he is prepared to prove that this weak or unhappy frame of mind is solely attributable to their disbelief. But it is too much the fashion of many zealots of the present day to hold forth with a degree of apparent satisfaction (not betraying much Christian charity) the misery of that part of their fellow creatures who die unbelievers. A celebrated female writer in a recent work, has laboured all in her power to convince us that Hume's was a miserable death-bed. Her best friends, I am of opinion, could not wish her a greater happiness than that her mind at that solemn period may be as free from torment, and her heart from self-reproach, as Hume's was.

By inserting the above in your valuable publication, you will oblige

A CONSTANT READER

92
HUME AND MRS. HANNAH MORE

Anonymous (pseud. "N."). "Hume and Mrs. Hannah More," in *Monthly Repository*, 1813, Vol. 8, pp. 107–108. Complete.

In response to a previous letter in the *Monthly Repository* titled "Death-beds of Unbelievers" (contained earlier in this collection), this anonymous article under the pseudonym "N" appeared shortly after in the same journal. The author agrees that Christians should not conclude anything about the mental state in which unbelievers die. However, the author criticizes the correspondent for exaggerating More's discussion of Hume's death. The author believes, though, that More should be censured for her treatment of Adam Smith's account of Hume's death, since she quotes and attacks the controversial passage which (according to the author) Smith dropped from later editions of his *Letter*.

HUME AND MRS. HANNA MORE.

February 3, 1813.

SIR,

I agree with *a Constant Reader* (pp. 32, 33) that the fear of being left in solitude and darkness may happen to possess the minds even of the firmest believers in revelation: I further admit, that examples, such as those alleged by the writers on whom he animadverts, should be very cautiously adduced and very temperately applied; and, lastly, I join him in condemning the style and tone in which "many zealots of the present day" speak of the deaths of those of "their fellow creatures" who have not subscribed to the evidences of Christianity. Christianity, doubtless, is ill defended by the reasonings which these men employ and by the spirit which they exercise in its vindication.

Coinciding thus far with your correspondent, I beg permission to point out what I take to be an inaccuracy in the following sentence of his letter:

"A celebrated female writer, in a recent work, has laboured all in her power to convince us, that Hume's was a miserable death-bed."

This *celebrated female writer*, I presume, is the author of *Practical Piety*, the nineteenth chapter of which work has for its title "Happy Deaths," and, after examining as much of it as relates to the subject at issue, I can affirm, that the statement of your "Constant Reader" is inadvertently exaggerated. Mrs. M. does not "labour all in her power to convince us, that Hume's was a *miserable* death-bed." She does indeed endeavour to shew (with what success let others judge) that the closing scene of "this eminent historian and philosopher" might not be in truth so happy as is represented by his friend Dr. Adam Smith. But she is far from asserting that it was *wretched*. They are *the dying horrors* of "the sage of Ferney" on which she expatiates: in the case of Mr. Hume, she was unable to discover any thing which resembled them.

A *Constant Reader* might, with greater justice, have complained of Mrs. M. for her treatment of the author of "The Wealth of Nations." – After strongly censuring what she regards as his *extravagant* eulogium on Hume, she says of this "eloquent panegyrist,"

"With as insidious an innuendo as has ever been thrown out against revealed religion, he goes on to observe, that *perhaps it is one of the very worst circumstances against Christianity, that very few of its professors were ever either so moral, so humane, or could so philosophically govern their passions, as the sceptical David Hume.*"

Now, Sir, although these words may, I suppose, be found in the earlier editions of Dr. Smith's Letter to the late Mr. Strahan, *they are wanting in the recent impressions of it* (even in the edition of 1782, eight years *before* Dr. Smith's death); from which circumstance we may fairly infer, that the writer had judged proper to suppress them, and, consequently, that they should not be used as the materials of a charge against his memory.

There was much to be admired in the *virtues* of Mr. Hume as a man, and in his *talents* as a writer. However, let me not be accused of bigotry, if I venture to suggest, that his character might have been yet more exemplary, his last moments yet happier and more instructive, had he taken the Christianity of the New Testament for the rule of his life and the charter of his hope.

Yours, &c.

N.

RECOLLECTIONS AND ANECDOTES

93
LETTERS TO WILLIAM MURE
OF CALDWELL

Letters to William Mure of Caldwell from 1764–1775, in *Selections from the Family papers preserved at Caldwell*, ed., William Mure (1799–1860), Glasgow, [Maitland Club Publications], 1854, 2 pt. in 3 v.
Selections from Part 2, Volumes 1 and 2; from 1854 edition.

Born in Cadlwell, Ayrshire, William Mure (1618–1776) studied law at the universities of Edinburgh and Leyden, and was a member of Parliament from 1742 until 1761. Mure maintained a long and close friendship with Hume, corresponding regularly between 1742 and his death shortly before Hume's in 1776. In 1854, Mure's grandson and namesake edited a massive collection of documents pertaining to his family. Among these are numerous correspondence between Hume to Mure, and others to Mure that discuss events in Hume's life. The topics of the letters about Hume include Hume's amiable character, his reputation among the French, the quarrel with Rousseau, and his interest in whist. William Mure the grandson includes some anecdotes about Hume in footnotes to some of these letters. Writing for the *Quarterly Review*, Richard Ford praises the work for providing readers with an intimate look at an important family:

These three substantial quartos are among the very valuable of the many contributions to that excellent Society, the Maitland Club, to which our historians and archæologists have been so much indebted. By this lifting up another corner of the curtain hung over the private scenes of auld lang syne, glimpses of the manners of our Scottish forefathers are offered, and an insight is given of the hopes and fears, the joys and sorrows, by which their days were rounded off: thus introduced to their homes and hearts, we become familiar with details too much neglected by grave historians, whose stilty pen seldom condescended to deal with trifles below their dignity. ... No apology was needed from Mr. Mure on the ground of the little claim which the private memoirs of a private family might have to public attraction. It is from such untampered materials that history in the aggregate is best constructed.... [*Quarterly Review*, September 1855, Vol. 97, pp. 378–407]

A second edition of this work appeared in 1883 with a print run of only eighty-six copies. The following is from the 1854 edition.

Letter 127: Andrew Stuart to Baron Mure [Paris].[1] I wrote a note to our friend Mr. Hume, to know if the ambassadour was soon to dispatch a courier to London, mentioning that I had several papers to send to you. His answer is enclosed. I send it to you, not so much for the contents, as to shew you the blunder which the multitude of his cards has led him into. He has writ his answer upon the first piece of paper that presented itself; and this happens to be a very polite invitation from the Duchesse d' Aiguillon, a lady who is in very high style here. This is but a small circumstance, if you knew the immense court that is paid to him from all quarters of this country. All ranks of people – courtiers, ladys old and young, wits, and sçavans, vie with one another in the incense they offer up to the célébre Monsr. Hume. Amidst all this intoxicating worship, he preserves his own natural style and simplicity of manners; and deigns to be cheerful and jolly, as if no such things had happened to him. His manner, though differing in some respects from the French, does not faill, however, to succeed with them. It must be owned that some of his admirers were at first a good deal surprised with the largeness of his figure. They had generally, in idea, clothed him with a person very little encumbered with matter. Diderot, amongst others, was in this mistake, and told Mr. Hume, at their first interview, that in place of taking him for the author of his works, he would have taken him for *"un gros Bernardin bien nourri."*

Letter 173: The Rev. Dr. Hugh Blair to Baron Mure, Edinburgh, Oct. 5, 1765. ... With respect to our friend David Hume, I had a letter from him, dated 23d August, wherein he informs me that Lord Hertford had intended to carry him over as his Secretary to Ireland, in conjunct commission with his sons. But that, on his arrival at London, he found the cry so loud against the promotion of a Scotsman, that he was obliged to give it up; which he did the more easily, knowing David's reluctance to that office and line of life: that he had obtained a pension of 400£ a year to be settled on him; upon which he retires from business, and is to pass the winter with Lord Hertford at Dublin. He adds, that he has not yet determined where to pass his latter days, and speaks of his attachment to Edinburgh reviving: which, I suppose, you will join with me in wishing may increase. He says that Lord Hertford's intentions in his favour made some noise in London, upon which the Princess Amelia said, she thought

---

[1] [The editor notes the following: "The part of this Letter containing the date has been torn away, but it must have been written about the same time with the foregoing Letter of Hume," i.e., Hume to Mure, June 22, 1764.]

the matter might be accomodated easily, by making him an Irish Bishop, as the Lord Lieutenant has many good Bishopricks to dispose off. On the whole, our friend seems to have made an excellent and honourable retreat, and a happy escape, in my opinion, from the turbulent and boisterous climate of Irish politicks, for which he was but indifferently cut out. ...

Letter 181: Mr. Rouet to Baron Mure. London, Jan. 10, 1766. ... David Hume is expected every day with Rousseau, who is to lodge some where in the country; as he is obliged to wear American dress, or long robes without breeches, for some diabetes, or such like disorder. Tronchin lodges with me, and David Hume will occupy the only remaining apartment; so we shall be very happy at home. ...

Letter 210: Mr. Rouet to Baron Mure, London, Feb. 21, [1767]. ... The *philosopher* arrived last night, and is gone this day to Lord Hertford's, but lodges next door to me, as he had wrote me before he sett out. The King of France has prohibited the sale of several pieces published against him, and in favour of Rousseau, at Paris, which will be nutts to Rousseau. ...

Letter 260: Mr. David Hume to Baron Mure, Edin. Oct. 2, 1770. ... I am sorry that I should correspond so ill to your very obliging letter, by telling you that I cannot propose to see you till you come to town next winter. I am engaged in the building a house, which is the second great operation of human life ...

{[Editor's footnote:] This house, in which he afterwards died, is the one forming the south-west corner of St. Andrew's Square, with the door opening into St. David's Street.

Lord Brougham, in his Life of the Philosopher, speaks of him as "taking a house in St. David Street," and "of a monument having been erected to his memory." Pp. 232, 234. It is certain that Hume himself built, during his own life, the house in which he was to die; and although the mausoleum in which his bones were to repose was not (according to the popular tradition) actually completed by himself, the ground was bought, instructions were left, and money was bequeathed by himself for the purpose.

While engaged in this undertaking he resided in his former lodging on the northern slope of the Old Town. On his daily visits to inspect the work, he was in the habit of taking the short cut across what was then a swamp, called the North Lock, now the east end of Prince's Street gardens. On one occasion, while picking his steps along the terra firma, he made a slip, fell over, and stuck fast in the bog. Observing some Newhaven fishwomen passing with their "creels," he called aloud to them for help; but, when they came up, and recognised the wicked unbeliever David Hume, they refused any assistance, unless he first repeated, in a solemn tone, the Lord's Prayer. This he did, without pause or blunder, and was extricated accordingly. He used to tell this story himself with great glee, declaring that the Edinburgh fishwives were the most acute theologians he had ever encountered.}

... for the taking of a wife is the first, which I hope will come in time ...

{[Editor's footnote:] Hume had not always been so determined a bachelor as he was in his latter days. Early in life, he paid his addresses to a young lady of good family and great personal attractions in Edinburgh. His suit was unfavourably received; but several years afterwards, when he had obtained celebrity, it was hinted to him by a common friend that the lady had changed her mind. "So have I," replied the Philosopher.}

Letter 261: Mr. Robert Adam, Architect, to Baron Mure, Edin. Nov. 5., 1770. ... I saw John Home yesterday; he is obliged to add to his cottage, and I have schemed two wings for him, to give the conveniencys necessary for a married man.

{[Editor's Note:] The lady he married not being very remarkable for her personal attractions, David Hume, it is said, asked him "how he could ever think of such a woman?" Home, who was a man of great goodness and simplicity of character, replied, "Ah, David! if I had not, who else would have taken her?"}

Letter 273: Robert Barclay, Esq.[2] to Baron Mure, Glasgow, April 18, 1772. ... You expressed a wish to see the controversy with J.M.[3] upon whist; here it is entire, with its prologue and epilogue.

If you do take the trouble to read and consider this idle contest, calculations, &c. I shall be glad to have your sentiments whether I have established the points undertaken.

If that proves the case, or if you find a little amusement from them, or even at our expense, from the idea that you must annex to the two champions as men of business, I shall not think the labour quite lost.

I confess I have a wish that your friend the *historian* saw these papers; not merely that he may detect any latent heresy (tho' I wish that, and he ought to understand the walk,) but that it may entitle me some day or other to a party or two with him. For he too deals deep in the history of Kings, if I am rightly

---

[2] [The editor adds the following in a footnote: "The writer of this Letter (without signature,) was considered the best whist player in Glasgow. He was indebted for a valuable Revenue office in that city to the friendship of Mr. Mure. He afterwards purchased of his patron an old property of the Caldwell family, called Capelrig, which he settled by destination upon the heirs of the previous proprietor. He had also other opportunities of showing his gratitude, which he did not allow to escape. The enclosure has not been preserved."]

[3] [The editor adds the following in a footnote: "Dr. John Moore, probably."]

informed. He passes this way sometimes, and were he to favor me with a summonds, perhaps I could produce a friend to convince him, that, for all his high vogue, he is not quite the head of the Literati in this branch of history; tho' that is allowed to be his forte.

Letter 274: Dr. John Moore to Baron Mure, Geneva, Monday, Aug. 3, 1772. ... The Duke has been translating Hume's History into French; when it is finished I shall send it to your friend. We were visiting Voltaire, a privilege granted to very few. He was particularly attentive to the Duke, and, speaking of Mr. Hume, he said to me in English, "you mos write him that I am hees great admeerer; he is a very great onor to Ingland, and abofe all to Ecosse." ...

Letter 300: Baron Mure to Mr. David Hume, Caldwell, Monday, Sept. 4 [1775]. What new change is this? Mrs. Mure says you should have been a girl, for you are never two minutes of one mind; and I say you are as credulous as any girl, and believe every report you hear. I wish you had but half the faith for what you ought, and are bound, to believe. ...

94
ANNE LINDSAY BARNARD:
LETTER TO MARGARET LINDSAY

Anne Lindsay Barnard, Letter to Margaret Lindsay, c. 1770, in Alexander
Crawford Lindsay, *Lives of the Lindsays; or, A memoir of the houses of
Crawford and Balcarres*, Wigan [England], Printed by C. S. Simms, 1840, 4 v.
Complete letter fragment; from Lives of The Lindsays, London, Murray, 1858,
Vol. 2, pp. 321–322.

Born in Balcarres House, Fifeshire, Scotland, Anne Lindsay (1750–1825) was
the oldest of eleven children to James Lindsay, fifth Earl of Balcarres
(1691–1768) and Anne Dalrymple. In 1771, putting words to a traditional
song, she composed the ballad "Auld Robin Gray." In 1823 she finally revealed
the secret of her authorship of the work to Walter Scott, who prepared an
edition of it in 1825. In 1793 she married a man twelve years her junior,
Andrew Bernard, whom she accompanied to the Cape of Good Hope in 1797.
Hume was on close terms with the Lindsay and Dalrymple family. In fact, Anne
Lindsay's grandmother, Lady Dalrymple, knew Hume when he was a child.
Anne conveys the following story about the 16 year old Hume as she heard it
from her grandmother:

> You know the Truthfulness of his Honest Nature ... as a Boy he was a fat,
> stupid, lumbering clown, but full of sensibility and justice, – one day at my
> house, when he was about 16 a most unpleasant odour offended the
> Company before dinner ... "O the Dog ... the Dog," cried out everyone "put
> out he Dog; 'tis that vile Beast Pod, kick him down stairs ... pray." – Hume
> stood abashed, his heart smote him ... "Oh do not hurt the Beast" he said
> ... "it is not Pod, it is Me!" I think this is capable of being made a very good
> proverb of, "It is not Pod, it is me." How very few people would take the
> evil odour of a stinking Conduct from a guiltless Pod to wear it on their own
> rightful Shoulders.[1]

---

[1] "Memoirs of Lady Anne Lindsay," in John Rylands Library, Manchester, Crawford
Nuniments, II, 107 (1773); as quoted by Mossner, p. 65.

When older, Hume frequently visited the Balcarres House, which he relates in a 1754 letter to Anne's father:

> I wish it were in my power to pass this Christmas at Balcarres. I should be glad to accompany your Lordship in your rural improvements, and return thence to relish with pleasure the comforts of your fireside. [Hume to James Lindsay, December 12, 1754]

In 1849, Alexander Crawford Lindsay, Earl of Crawford (1812–1880), prepared a collection of manuscripts of the Lindsay family, titled *Lives of the Lindsays*, which includes a letter fragment by Anne Lindsay concerning Hume. The letter is not dated, but the placement of it in the collection and clues from the letter itself suggest a date of around 1770. The editor prefaces the letter with the following: "The following anecdote of David Hume, the historian, whom Lady Dalrymple had known from a child, occurs in a letter of Lady Anne to her sister Margaret, from her grandmother's house in Edinburgh." The letter involves two timeframes. First, during the time that the letter was composed, Anne reports to her sister that dinners at her house were frequented by Hume, Robertson, and other renowned guests. Second, she conveys a conversation at one such recent dinner between Hume and her mother Anne Dalrymple. The two were recollecting a parlor game that they played one Christmas several years ago – probably the Christmas of 1755 to which Hume refers in his letter above. The game involved writing anonymous sketches of their own character and Hume's involved a surprising confession of his vanity. The story continues that when others read the sketch, Hume took it back and tossed it into the fire. Among Hume's manuscripts is a document titled "Character of ___ ___ written by himself," which is as follows:

Character of ___ ___ written by himself.
1. A very good man the constant purpose of whose life is to do mischief.
2. Fancies he is disinterested because he substitutes vanity in place of all other passions.
3. Very industrious, without serving [either] himself or others.
4. Licentious in his pen, cautious in his words, still more so in his actions.
5. Would have had no enemies, had he not courted them, seems desirous of being hated by the public, but has only attained the being railed at.
6. Has never been hurt by his enemies, because he never hated any one of them.
7. Exempt from vulgar prejudices, full of his own.
8. Very bashful, somewhat modest, no way humble.
9. A fool, capable of performances which few wise men can execute.
10. A wise man, guilty of indiscretions which the greatest simpletons can perceive.

11. Sociable, though he lives in solitude.
12. Mirthful though he possess little wit and still less humour.
13. An enthusiast without religion, a philosopher, who despairs to attain truth.
14. A moralist who prefers instinct to reason.
15. A gallant, who gives no offence to husbands and mothers.
16. A scholar without [the] ostentation [of learning].

The document is in someone else's handwriting, with alterations in Hume's hand given in brackets. The second item on the list mentions Hume's vanity. It is thus plausible that this was a reconstruction of Hume's list by someone at the Balcarres gathering, which was then given to Hume. If it is instead the product of another such event, the content of Hume's sketch at the Balcarres House likely parallels this one.

The 1849 edition of *Lives of the Lindsays* was printed for private circulation among family and friends. In his favourable review of *Lives of the Lindsays* in the *Quarterly Review*, J.G. Lockhart writes that, although initially not intended for the public, "the extracts which we are about to present will have all the attractions of novelty for most of our readers" (March 1846, Vol. 77, pp. 465–496). The work was printed again in 1749 and 1758. The following is from the 1758 edition. I have broken the conversational exchanges into separate paragraphs and made quotation marks uniform.

Dinners go on as usual, which, being monopolised by the divines, wits, and writers of the present day, are not unjustly called the Dinners of the Eaterati by Lord Kellie,[2] who laughs at his own pun till his face is purple.

Our friend David Hume, along with his friend Principal Robertson, continue to maintain their ground at these convivial meetings. To see the lion and the lamb lying down together, the deist and the doctor, is extraordinary; it makes one hope that some day Hume will say to him, "Thou almost persuadest me to be a Christian." He is a constant morning visitor of ours. My mother jested him lately on a circumstance which had a good deal of character in it.

When we were very young girls, too young to remember the scene, there happened to be a good many clever people at Balcarres at Christmas, and as a gambol of the season they agreed to write each his own character, to give them to Hume, and make him shew them to my father, as extracts he had taken from the Pope's library at Rome.

He did: – my father said, "I don't know who the rest of your fine fellows and charming princesses are, Hume; but if you had not told me where you got this character, I should have said it was that of my wife."

[2]   Thomas Alexander Erskine, the sixth and musical Earl of Kellie.

"I was pleased," said my mother, "with my Lord's answer; it shewed that at least I had been an honest woman."

"Hume's character of himself," said she, "was well drawn and full of candour; he spoke of himself as he ought, but added what surprised us all, that, plain as his manners were, and apparently careless of attention, vanity was his predominant weakness. That vanity led him to publish his essays, which he grieved over, not that he had changed his opinions, but that he thought he had injured society by disseminating them." –

"Do you remember the sequel of that affair?" said Hume.

"Yes, I do," replied my mother, laughing: "you told me that, although I thought your character a sincere one, it was not so, – there was a particular feature emitted, that we were still ignorant of, and that you would add it; like a fool I gave you the MS., and you thrust it into the fire, adding, 'Oh! what an idiot I had nearly proved myself to be, to leave such a document in the hands of a parcel of women!'"

"Villain!" said my mother, laughing and shaking her head at him.

"Do you remember all this, my little woman?" said Hume to me.

"I was too young" said I, "to think of it at the time." –

"How's this? Have not you and I grown up together?" – I looked surprised;

"Yes," added he, "you have grown tall, and I have grown broad."

95
GEORGE NORVELL:
LETTER TO ALEXANDER STENHOUSE

George Norvell to Alexander Stenhouse, March 1, 1788.
Complete letter, newly transcribed; from manuscript at King's College Cambridge, JMK/PP/87/53.[1]

Scottish born George Norvell appears to have been a close cousin of Hume and spent some time with the philosopher. He published no books, and our current knowledge of him is limited to a letter he wrote in 1788 and his 1802 sketch of Hume in *Edinburgh Magazine*, contained in this collection. Though the letter does not indicate the addressee, another correspondence makes clear that it was sent to Alexander Stenhouse.[2] In this letter Norvell describes Hume's coarse Scottish accent and attempts to explain why he was unable to refine it. He discusses Hume's expertise at whist, his intellectual vanity and receiving of extreme unction. Norvell examines these issues with different details in his *Edinburgh Magazine* article.

Dear Sir

Reflecting on what passed with regard to David Hume, it occurred to me to mention some peculiar anecdotes with regard to him. Notwithstanding his opportunitys, his conversations in Britain, and his mastery of several languages; being so much abroad and in the best of Company, nay his propriety in penning the English language and idiom, Yet in Common conversation, he retained the accent, expression and vulgarity of his paternal stile on the Banks of the White Water & Tweed, in such a degree that you would have imagined he had never conversed with any person but the commonest farmer in the merse or ever set foot out of the parish of Chirnside, had not the matter contain'd in

---

[1] The transcription is reproduced by kind permission of King's College Library, Cambridge.

[2] [Alexander Stenhouse to George Chalmers, March 22, 1788, University of Edinburgh Library, Laing MSS, II, 451–452.]

his Discourse discovered the man of Letters. This I have heard attributed to his having no Ear, and his voice being Unmusical, it gave him no disgust, and was incapable of acquiring a proper modification; for you know a nice Ear must catch and acquire the articulation of whatever country they reside in any time & have a wondrous facility in being able to rival even a native in the pronunciation & local expression.

Another thing perhaps not understood by his admirers is his fondness for whist, which he play'd well at & was successfull in the extent he practised it – nay so fond was he of a good party at that game, that he was even anxious and uneasy to procure it, and seemed to have more joy, in two three hours spent in that manner than one hour in the abstruse investigations of the most sublime Philosophical problems. One fact I can assure you of That the famous General Scott (being so superior a master of all games, that nobody could venture to play with him & of consequence was reduced to Bate-ing we [who] none understood better the Chances of) was so Convinced of David Hume's superiority in knowledge of whist and his usual good fortune, that he made him an offer of his purse and credit to play for the most extensive sums, providing he would communicate all his winnings to the general and offered David 1000£ a year. This he rejected with a disdain, Uncommon to him possessed of such a liberality of sentiment, saying he played for his amusement but would never act as a pickpocket or for hire, what he won or risk'd on should be his own property & emolument. –

A third thing I beg leave to mention, as a distinguished mark of his Character. Pride *the predominant passion*, was surely the foundation of every Circumstance of his conduct, whatever species of Philosophical Coolness might be alledged – He despised surely every mortal as inferior to him; Therefore disdained to reply to any person attacked him, he would not involve himself in Cavils or Contorversie, an *Ipse Dixit* was sufficient on his part; nay the whole of that performance his friend the Comissioner (who did him the disservice to publish *my own life*) runs in that strain thus from the beginning proves what I assert (That pride & Egotism actuated all his conduct thro' life) and what a Chagrine does he display, on his laborious metaphysicall positions, being unattempted to answer & seemingly neglected, nay allowed to sink in oblivion, till he was received by the attack of a Right Revd. Then he Exults in triumph that he was of so much consequence as to be deemed worthy of notice. Otherways he was – determined to have retired to France and deprived the world of all his glorious discoverys, and the happiness of having, so exact and Elegant an historian's labours – happly perhaps, it had been for him; in that retreat he might been admitted into the bosom of that Church and got a worthy Absolution from the priests from whose Communion he received Extreme Unction in a dangerous illness in Italy, some years before –

What I have here expressed are but my own sentiments, as I said to day I was sorry to see a monument erected on so conspicuous a place – he would not be buried in Consecrated ground; perhaps he would now be glad to mix with these bigots he so much ridiculed.

I own him a man of superior genius, of great parts but missaplied, of sincere friendship, of benevolence, in Charity to the greatest degree, of Strict faith and kindness in friendship, of a most agreeable, facetious and entertaining conversation, of an Elegant writer and abilitys beyond any I ever knew. But I detest his principles, & abhour his partialitys and I pity his Selfishness (as to his vanity not as to money matters) – often when I have been walking &ca with him – he fell into reveries was silent for a time, was I suppose forming of a Syllogism, turning a period, or investigating a problem – then would fall a talking loud to himself. – If I askd what he was saying "Lord canna ye let a Body amuse them selves without always clattering, I did nae ken ye was there and nae matter ye had nae bus'ness to meddle wi me"

For all I have said I liked the man well & we were aye good friends and I wished him very well & should be sorry when I take my travells to another hemisphere not to find him out of purgatory (of which he had much need) and happy. I shall make inquiry for the Pamphlet & hope shall find it for you and if I can be any service to you in any shape you will do me a pleaser to command Dear sir

Your most obedient and very humble Geo Norvell

March 1st 1788

96
GEORGE NORVELL:
"ANECDOTES OF DAVID HUME"

"Anecdotes of David Hume, Esq. By one who personally knew him," *Edinburgh Magazine, or Literary Miscellany*, April 1802, Vol. 19, pp. 429–431.
Complete; from *European Magazine and London Review*, April, 1802, Vol. 41, pp. 263–264.

George Norvell was the author of the 1788 letter to Alexander Stenhouse, contained in this collection. In his sketch of Hume, appearing in 1802, he only identifies himself as "one who personally knew him" and with the initials "G.N." at the close. The article covers some of the material in the letter, which makes his authorship of the article as certain as we could have it. The article describes Hume's various jobs – probably derived from Hume's "My Own Life." He then gives a detailed account of Hume's technique at playing whist, and an equally vivid account of Hume's speech, describing it as "a creeping voice, rather effeminate than manly." Norvell closes with an account of Hume receiving extreme unction and how Hume reacted when Norvell confronted him with the story. In his *Life and Correspondence of David Hume* (1846) John Hill Burton condemned the extreme unction tale as a fabrication: "The reader will remember that, almost from the moment of his setting foot on foreign soil, he censures the Roman Catholics, in his letters to his friends; and nothing could be mentioned, more at variance with a known character, than this writer's assertion, which seems to rest on some imaginative parallel between the personal history of Hume and that of Gibbon." The episode, though, cannot be dismissed so easily in view of Norvell's letter, which, unlike the article, was not sent to his reader under the guise of anonymity. Norvell's "Anecdotes" was reprinted in *European Magazine and London Review*, from which the following is taken.

ANECDOTES OF DAVID HUME, ESQ.
BY ONE WHO PERSONALLY KNEW HIM.

David Hume was a man of parts, natural and acquired, far superior to most of mankind, of a benevolent heart, a friendly kind disposition, and a real affection for all his connections. No man is without his failings; and his great views of being singular, and a vanity to show himself superior to most people, led him to advance many axioms that were dissonant to the opinions of others, and led him into sceptical doctrines only to show how minute and puzzling they were to other folk; in so far, that I have often seen him (in various companies, according as he saw some enthusiastic person there) combat either their religious or political principles; nay, after he had struck them dumb, take up the argument on their side, with equal good humour, wit, and jocoseness, all to show his pre-eminence. For the justness of these observations, I appeal to his life, wrote by himself, and published by his friend and admirer Adam Smith, where you see he was so chagrined at no notice of, or answer being made to his Essays, and was so disappointed, that he proposed to retire to Sanmure, or some other part of France, to be lost to the unheeding world, and, in short, be a perfect hermit. But, on being answered by a bishop on some of his dogmas, and other favourable circumstances flattering him that he would at last be conspicuous, he gave up the project, and was first a companion for some time to the Marquis of Annandale; then librarian to the Advocates here; after that secretary to General Sinclair at Turin (who was, under pretence of an ambassador to his Sardinian Majesty, a spy, as his conduct was dubious to the Allies, against Louis XV.); afterwards, by General Conways interest, Secretary to Lord Hertford at Paris; left there Charge d' Affairs; and finally one of the Under Secretaries of State for about half a year. After which he settled in Edinburgh for life, and made all his friends and connections happy by the possession of so worthy a man. – Thus far I have given my real sentiments of the man, and can only now regret that he was so weak as to write his life in the style he did.

I must add, that he was a cheerful and most agreeable companion, well-informed, and who accommodated himself to the company; and, for all his abstruse learning, was never happier than in a select company of ladies and friends, and fond to engage in a party at whist, of which game he was a complete adept, and of consequence successful. He never played deep, never above a shilling, one, two, or three; and I have known him come into Edinburgh for some weeks, pay his residence there, and get a recruit of clothes and necessaries out of his gains; nay sometimes to have a pound or two to give in assistance to a necessitous relation; and carry back to his brother's house at Ninewells the cash he brought with him from that place, in order to defray the expenses of his visit to the metropolis. General Scott, of Balcomie, who was a good judge in these matters, was so convinced of his superior skill at whist, that

I was assured he offered David his purse to gamble at London, and that he would give him 1000l. a-year, if he would communicate his winnings. This be refused with disdain, saying, he played for his amusement; and though General Scott would give him ten times more per annum, he would be accessary to no such fraudulent doings.

It was very remarkable, that, though from study and reading the purest authors in the English language, he learnt to write in a correct and elegant stile, yet, in conversing, he spoke with the tone, idiom, and vulgar voice of the commonalty in the Merse or Berwickshire. This I presume arose from his having been greatly, in his early years, about his brother's house, conversing with servants, &c. and having no ear (though a foreign or even a dead language, which he acquired by grammar and rules, he wrote pointedly), it was impossible for him to attain, in speaking, any other dialect of the Scots than that he caught in his childhood: besides, he had but a creeping voice, rather effeminate than manly.

I could give you several anecdotes with regard to him; I shall content myself with one. – One day when he was advancing some irreligious maxims in a sarcastical stile, I said to him, "L____, David, ye are much altered in your sentiments since you professed yourself a sincere Roman Catholic, confessed yourself to the priests, declared yourself a sincere penitent, got absolution, and even extreme unction." He was much offended at this, as he believed none knew, in this country, that all this had happened to him at Nice. He answered, in a huff, "I was in a high fever then, and did not know what I said, or they did with me." I replied, "You put me in mind of Patie Birnie's answer to the Minister of Kinghorn, who, stumbling o'er him in a passage dead drunk, said, "Ah! Patie, is this your promise that you would never be fu again, if the Lord spared you?' – 'Wow,' quo' Pate, 'I wonder to hear ane of your honor's sense mind what ony body says in a red raving fever; I kent naithing of what was gaen.'" – David and I, for years after, were tolerable good friends, but never so cordial as before.

G.N.

97
JAMES CAULFEILD:
MEMOIRS

James Caulfeild, recollections of Hume (c. 1795), in Francis Hardy, *Memoirs of the political and private life of James Caulfeild, earl of Charlemont, knight of St. Patrick*, London, T. Cadell and W. Davies, 1810, xiv, 443 p. Selections; from the 1812 edition (London: T Cadell), Vol. 1, pp. 12–19, 230–239.

James Caulfeild, first Earl of Charlemont (1728–1799), was born in Dublin, educated at home, and throughout his adult life acted as an independent intermediary in various political disputes involving Ireland. In 1746, the eighteen-year-old Caulfeild travelled to countries around the Mediterranean Sea, and, while in Turin for a year, met Hume. He returned to Ireland in 1754 and from 1764–1773 lived in London, where again he frequently met with Hume. Caulfeild's *Memoirs* are a compilation of his letters and notes, organized with connective narrative by Francis Hardy (1751–1812). Hardy presents two biographical discussions of Hume written by Caulfeild, based on years of personal acquaintance. Both were almost certainly written after Hume's death – and probably well after the event. One indication is that Caulfeild refers to Hume's dispositional traits in the past tense. Another is that Caulfeild seems to have recorded at least some of these recollections with the intention of publishing them. For example, he opens his discussion of the Quarrel with Rousseau stating "That story is too well known to be repeated." The candid and sometimes unflattering depictions of Hume's physical characteristics suggest a date sufficiently far from that of Hume's death. As Caulfeild died in 1795, a date of 1790 is plausible.

The first narrative is a unified essay describing Hume's personal appearance, dress, and speech. Caulfeild praises Hume's philanthropy and examines his sceptical motives. The second narrative begins with events from about 1766, and is a compilation of several manuscripts relating to Hume. Caulfeild here discusses the controversy with Rousseau, Hume's views about immortality, his reception in France, denial of deism, defence of the Stuarts, and inclination to proselytize. The *Quarterly Review* praises Caulfeild's *Memoirs* as a contribution to the history of Ireland: "Not that these 'Memoirs of Lord Charlemont' form a complete history of Ireland during the life of that nobleman… but they afford a very liberal and entertaining contribution towards it; they supply a great deal of important matter which is not to be obtained from any other source." Regarding the discussions of Hume, the reviewer says "we could, with pleasure, insert the whole of two papers by Lord Charlemont, which Mr. Hardy has given us, relating entirely to Hume, but we must content ourselves with an extract or two"(October 1811, Vol. 6, pp. 124–147). Caulfeild's original manuscripts, which make up the *Memoirs*, currently reside in the Royal Irish Academy (MS 12/R/7, f. 523). The *Memoirs* was published in a two-volume second edition in 1812, from which the following selections are taken. Comments by Hardy are included in curly brackets.

{[Comment by Francis Hardy:] He [i.e., Caulfeild] went abroad in the autumn of 1746, and first visited Holland, where, as he used often to relate, he attended the whole revolution, or tumult, which terminated in the establishment of the Prince of Orange as Stadtholder. From Holland he proceeded to the English camp, in Germany, and passed some time with William, Duke of Cumberland, who was not only extremely kind to him, whilst there, but through life. He had good sense, and firmness enough of mind to go at once from the English camp, and the agreeable military society which he met there, to Turin, where he directly entered the academy, and resided at it for one year, sometimes making excursions into other parts of Italy. The Prince Royal, who was also of the academy, was very cordial and friendly to his lordship; and from the king, and all the Sardinian family, he experienced every gracious attention. Whilst he continued at Turin, he read not only books, but men, with sedulous attention. The court, at that time, abounded with political, and many eminent literary characters. Among others, whom he met there, was David Hume, the historian, whose society he was much attached to, though without the slightest deviation from those just and religious principles, which he had the good fortune to imbibe early at home. Indeed, that philosopher appears to have had as little influence over his young, and noble friend, in matters of religious faith, as at a subsequent period he had in politics; and to touch further on either subject is useless, as Lord Charlemont was ever a sincere Christian, and, from reading and experience, as unalterable a Whig as Hume was an inflexible Tory. Of this eminent man he has given an account so particular and exact, that I should be unpardonable if I did not present it to the reader.}

The celebrated David Hume, whose character is so deservedly high in the literary world, and whose works, both as a Philosopher and as an Historian, are so wonderfully replete with genius and entertainment, was, when I was at Turin, Secretary to Sir John Sinclair, plenipotentiary from the court of Great Britain to his Sardinian majesty. He had then lately published those philo-

sophical essays which have done so much mischief to mankind, by contributing
to loosen the sacred bonds by which alone man can be restrained from rushing
to his own destruction, and which are so intimately necessary to our nature,
that a propensity to be bound by them was apparently instilled into the human
mind, by the all-wise Creator, as a balance against those passions which,
though perhaps necessary as incitements to activity, must, without such
controul, inevitably have hurried us to our ruin. The world, however, uncon-
scious of its danger, had greedily swallowed the bait; the essays were received
with applause, read with delight, and their admired author was already, by
public opinion, placed at the head of the dangerous school of sceptic
philosophy.

With this extraordinary man I was intimately acquainted. He had kindly
distinguished me from among a number of young men, who were then at the
academy, and appeared so warmly attached to me, that it was apparent he not
only intended to honour me with his friendship, but to bestow on me what was,
in his opinion, the first of all favours and benefits, by making me his convert
and disciple.

Nature, I believe, never formed any man more unlike his real character than
David Hume. The powers of phisiognomy were baffled by his countenance;
neither could the most skilful, in that science, pretend to discover the smallest
trace of the faculties of his mind, in the unmeaning features of his visage. His
face was broad and fat, his mouth wide, and without any other expression than
that of imbecility. His eyes vacant and spiritless, and the corpulence of his
whole person was far better fitted to communicate the idea of a turtle-eating
Alderman, than of a refined philosopher. His speech, in English, was rendered
ridiculous by the broadest Scotch accent, and his French was, if possible, still
more laughable; so that wisdom, most certainly, never disguised herself before
in so uncouth a garb. Though now near fifty years old,[1] he was healthy and
strong; but his health and strength, far from being advantageous to his figure,
instead of manly comeliness, had only the appearance of rusticity. His wearing
an uniform added greatly to his natural awkwardness, for he wore it like a
grocer of the trained bands. Sinclair was a Lieutenant-general, and was sent to
the courts of Vienna and Turin, as a military envoy, to see that their quota of
troops was furnished by the Austrians and Piedmontese. It was, therefore,
thought necessary that his secretary should appear to be an officer, and Hume
was accordingly disguised in scarlet.

Having thus given an account of his exterior, it is but fair that I should state
my good opinion of his character. Of all the philosophers of his sect, none, I
believe, ever joined more real benevolence to its mischievous principles than my
friend Hume. His love of mankind was universal and vehement; and there was

---

[1] [Hume was in Turin in 1748 and was 37 years old at the time.]

no service he would not cheerfully have done to his fellow creatures, excepting only that of suffering them to save their souls in their own way. He was tender-hearted, friendly, and charitable in the extreme, as will appear from a fact, which I have from good authority. When a member of the university of Edinburgh, and in great want of money, having little or no paternal fortune, and the collegiate stipend being very inconsiderable, he had procured, through the interest of some friend, an office in the university, which was worth about forty pounds a year. On the day when he had received this good news, and just when he had got into his possessions the patent, or grant entitling him to his office, he was visited by his friend Blacklock, the poet, who is much better known by his poverty and blindness, than by his genius. This poor man began a long descant on the misery, bewailing his want of sight, his large family of children, and his utter inability to provide for them, or even to procure them the necessaries of life. Hume, unable to bear his complaints, and destitute of money to assist him, ran instantly to his desk, took out the grant, and presented it to his miserable friend, who received it with exultation, and whose name was soon after, by Hume's interest, inserted instead of his own. After such a relation it is needless that I should say any more of his genuine philanthropy, and generous benefi-cence; but the difficulty will now occur, how a man, endowed with such qualities, could possibly consent to become the agent of so much mischief, as undoubtedly has been done to mankind by his writings; and this difficulty can only be solved by having recourse to that universal passion, which has, I fear, a much more general influence over all our actions than we are willing to confess. Pride, or vanity, joined to a sceptical turn of mind, and to an education which, though learned, rather sipped knowledge than drank it, was, probably, the ultimate cause of this singular phaenomenon; and the desire of being placed at the head of a sect, whose tenets controverted and contradicted all received opinions, was too strong to be resisted by a man, whose genius enabled him to find plausible arguments, sufficient to persuade both himself and many others, that his own opinions were true. A philosophical knight-errant was the dragon he had vowed to vanquish, and he was careless, or thoughtless, of the conse-quences which might ensue from the achievement of the adventure to which he had pledged himself. – He once professed himself the admirer of a young, most beautiful, and accomplished lady, at Turin, who only laughed at his passion. One day he addressed her in the usual common-place strain, that he was *abimè*, *anéanti*. – '*Oh! pour* anéanti,' replied the lady, '*ce n'est en effet qu' une operation très naturelle de vôtre Systême.*'

{[Comment by Francis Hardy:] Hume will be mentioned afterwards in the course of these memoirs, as Lord Charlemont often met him in England, and always preserved an intimacy with him.]

———

{[Comment by Francis Hardy:] About this time, 1766, or somewhat before this, Lord Charlemont once more met his friend David Hume. His Lordship mentions him in some detached papers, which I shall here collect and give to the reader.}

Nothing ever shewed a mind more truly beneficient than Hume's whole conduct with regard to Rousseau. That story is too well known to be repeated, and exhibits a striking picture of Hume's heart, whilst it displays the strange and unaccountable vanity, and madness, of the French, or rather Swiss moralist. When first they arrived together from France, happening to meet with Hume in the Park, I wished him joy of his pleasing connection, and particularly hinted, that I was convinced he must be perfectly happy in his new friend, as their sentiments were, I believed, nearly similar. 'Why no, man,' said he, 'in that you are mistaken; Rousseau is not what you think him; he has a hankering after the Bible, and, indeed, is little better than a Christian, in a way of his own.' Excess of vanity was the madness of Rousseau. When he first arrived in London, he and his Armenian dress were followed by crowds, and as long as this species of admiration lasted, he was contented and happy. But in London, such sights are only the wonder of the day, and in a very short time he was suffered to walk where he pleased, unattended, unobserved. From that instant, his discontent may be dated. But to dwell no longer on matters of public notoriety, I shall only mention one fact, which I can vouch for truth, and which would, of itself be amply sufficient to convey an adequate idea of the amazing eccentricity of this singular man. When, after having quarrelled with Hume, and all his English friends, Rousseau was bent on making his escape, as he termed it, into France, he stopped at a village between London and Dover, and from thence wrote to General Conway, then Secretary of State, informing him, that, although he had got so far with safety, he was well apprized, that the remainder of his rout was so beset by his inexorable enemies, that, unprotected, he could not escape. He therefore solemnly claimed the protection of the King, and desired that a party of cavalry might be immediately ordered to escort him to Dover. This letter General Conway shewed to me, together with his answer, in which he assured him that the postillions were, altogether, a very sufficient guard throughout every part of the King's dominions. To return to Hume. In London, where he often did me the honour to communicate the manuscripts of his additional essays, before their publication, I have sometimes, in the course of our intimacy, asked him whether he thought that, if his opinions were universally to take place, mankind would not be rendered more unhappy than they now were; and whether he did not suppose that the curb of religion was necessary to human nature? 'The objections,' answered he, 'are not without weight; but error never can produce good, and truth ought to take place of all consideration. ' He never failed, in the midst of any controversy, to give its due praise to every thing tolerable what was either said, or written against him. One day that he visited me in London, he came into my room laughing, and apparently well pleased. 'What has put you into this good humour, Hume?' said I. 'Why, man,' replied he, 'I have just now had the best thing said to me I ever heard. I was complaining in a company, where I spent the morning, that I was very ill treated by the world, and that the censures past upon me were hard and unreasonable. That I had written many volumes, throughout the whole of which there were but few pages that contained any reprehensible matter, and yet, for those few pages, I was abused and torn to pieces.'[2] 'You put me in mind,' said an honest fellow in the company, whose name I did not know, 'of an acquaintance of mine, a notary public, who, having been condemned to be hanged for forgery, lamented the hardship of his case; that after having written many thousand inoffensive sheets, he should be hanged for one line.'

But an unfortunate disposition to doubt of every thing seemed interwoven with the nature of Hume, and never was there, I am convinced, a more thorough and sincere sceptic. He seemed not to be certain even of his own present existence, and could not therefore be expected to entertain any settled opinion respecting his future state. Once I asked him what he thought of the immortality of the soul? 'Why troth, man,' said he, 'it is so pretty and so comfortable a theory, that I wish I could be convinced of its truth, but I canna help doubting.'

Hume's fashion at Paris, when he was there as Secretary to Lord Hertford, was truly ridiculous; and nothing ever marked, in a more striking manner, the whimsical genius of the French. No man, from his manners, was surely less formed for their society, or less likely to meet with their approbation; but that flimsy philosophy which pervades, and deadens even their most licentious novels, was then the folly of the day. Free thinking and English frocks were the fashion, and the Anglomanie was the *ton du pais*. Lord Holland, though far better calculated than Hume to please in France, was also an instance of this singular predilection. Being about this time on a visit to Paris, the French concluded, that an Englishman of his reputation must be a philosopher, and must be admired. It was customary with him to doze after dinner, and one day, at a great entertainment, he happened to fall asleep; 'Le voilà!' says a Marquis, pulling his neighbour by the sleeve; 'Le voilà, qui pense!' But the madness for Hume was far more singular and extravagant. From what has been already said of him, it is apparent that his conversation to strangers, and particularly to Frenchmen, could be little delightful, and still more particularly, one would

---

[2] [Hume makes a similar argument in a 1761 letter to Hugh Blair regarding George Campbell: "I could wish your friend had not denominated me an infidel writer, on account of ten or twelve pages which seem to him to have that tendency; while I have wrote so many volumes on history, literature, politics, trade, morals, which, in that particular at least, are entirely inoffensive. Is a man to be called a drunkard because he has been seen fuddled once in his lifetime?]

suppose, to French women. And yet no lady's toilette was complete without Hume's attendance. At the opera, his broad, unmeaning face was usually seen *entre deux jolis minois*. The ladies in France give the ton, and the ton was deism; a species of philosophy ill suited to the softer sex, in whose delicate frame weakness is interesting, and timidity a charm. But the women in France were deists, as with us they were charioteers. The tenets of the new philosophy were à *porteè de tout, le monde*, and the perusal of a wanton novel, such, for example, as Therese Philosophe, was amply sufficient to render any fine gentleman, or any fine lady, an accomplished, nay, a learned deist. How my friend Hume was able to endure the encounter of these French female Titans I know not. In England, either his philosophic pride, or his conviction that infidelity was ill suited to women, made him perfectly averse from the initiation of ladies into the mysteries of his doctrine. I never saw him so much displeased, or so much disconcerted, as by the petulance of Mrs. Mallet, the conceited wife of Bolingbroke's editor. This lady, who was not acquainted with Hume, meeting him one night at an assembly, boldly accosted him in these words: 'Mr. Hume, give me leave to introduce myself to you; we deists ought to know each other.' – 'Madame,' replied he, 'I am no deist. I do not style myself so, neither do I desire to be known by that appellation.'[3]

Nothing ever gave Hume more real vexation, than the strictures made upon his history in the House of Lords, buy the great Lord Chatham. Soon after that speech I met Hume, and ironically wished him joy of the high honour that had been done him. 'Zounds, man,' said he, with more peevishness than I had ever seen him express, 'he's a Goth! he's a Vandal!' Indeed, his history is as dangerous in politics, as his essays are in religion; and it is somewhat extra-ordinary, that the tame man who labours to free the mind from what he supposes religious prejudices, should as zealously endeavour to shackle it with the servile ideas of despotism. But he loved the Stuart family, and his history is, of course, their apology. All his prepossessions, however, could never induce him absolutely to falsify history; and though he endeavours to soften the failings of his favourites, even in their actions, yet it is on the characters which he gives to them, that he principally depends for their vindication; and from hence frequently proceeds, in the course of his history, this singular incongruity, that it is morally impossible that a man, possessed of the character which the historian delineates, should in certain circumstances have acted the part which the same historian narrates and assigns to him. But now to return to his philo-sophical principles, which certainly constitute the discriminating feature of his

---

[3]   [In an article in the *London Magazine*, James Boswell presents this anecdote as follows: "I remember hearing a late celebrated infidel tell that he was not at all pleased when the infidel wife of his friend, a poet of some eminence, addressed him in a company in London, "we Deists," – Speak for yourself, Madam, said he abruptly" ("On Hypochondria, February 1778, No. 5).]

character. The practice of combating received opinions, had one unhappy, though not unusual, effect on his mind. He grew fond of paradoxes, which his abilities enabled him successfully to support; and his understanding was so far warped and bent by this unfortunate predilection, that he had well nigh lost that best faculty of the mind, the almost intuitive perception of truth. His sceptical turn made him doubt, and consequently dispute every thing; yet was he a fair and pleasant disputant. He heard with patience, and answered without acrimony. Neither was his conversation at any time offensive, even to his more scrupulous companions: his good sense, and good nature, prevented his saying any thing that was likely to shock, and it was not till he was provoked to argument, that, in mixed companies, he entered into his favourite topics. Where indeed, as was the case with me, his regard for any individual rendered him desirous of making a proselyte, his efforts were great and anxiously incessant.

Respecting this new, or rather revived system of philosophy, *soi disante telle*, it may perhaps be confessed, that it may possibly have done some good; but then it has certainly done much more mischief to mankind. On the one hand, it may perhaps be allowed, that to its prevalence we owe that general system of toleration which seems to prevail, and which is, I fear, the only speck of white that marks the present age.[4] Yet even this solitary virtue, if infidelity be its basis, is founded on a false principle. Christian Charity, which includes the idea of universal philanthropy, and which, when *really Christian*, is the true foundation on which this virtue should be erected, and not the opinion that all religions should be tolerated, because all are alike erroneous. But even allowing this boasted benefit its full weight, to the same cause we are, I doubt, on the other hand, indebted for that profligacy of manners, or, to call it by the most gentle name, that frivolity which every where prevails. To this cause we owe that total disregard, that fastidious dislike to all serious thought; for every man can be a deist without thinking; he is made so at his toilette, and, whilst his hair is dressing, reads himself into an adept; that shameful and degrading apathy to all that is great and noble; in a word, that perfect indifference to right or wrong, which enervates and characterizes this unmeaning and frivolous age. Neither have we reason to hope a favourable change. The present manners are the fashion of the day, and will not last. But infidelity will never subside into true piety. It will produce its contrary. The present is an age of irreligion; the next will, probably, be an age of bigotry.

> "Ætas parentum, pejor avis, tulit
> Nos nequiores, mox daturos
> Progeniem vitiosiorem."

---

[4] [Hardy inserts the following note here: "When this was written I know not."]

98
ALEXANDER CARLYLE:
AUTOBIOGRAPHY

Alexander Carlyle, recollections about Hume (c. 1800) in John Hill Burton, *The autobiography of Alexander Carlyle of Inveresk; containing memorials of the men, and events of his times*, Edinburgh, London, W. Blackwood, 1860, x, 576 p. Selections; from 1910 edition, pp. 55, 285–293, 297–298, 345–346, 426–427.

Born in Haddingtonshire, Scotland, the son of a Scottish minister, Alexander Carlyle (1722–1805) was educated at the Universities of Edinburgh, Glasgow and Leyden. He became himself a minister in the Church of Scotland, receiving his license in 1746, and two years later was appointed to the parish of Inveresk, outside Edinburgh, which he held until his death. A strong moderate within the Church, he was subjected to ecclesiastical censure for attending performances of John Home's *Douglas*. He published pamphlets on religious and political controversies, but his true claim to fame is his memoirs, which he began writing at the close of his life. The work covers the period from 1722 until 1770, which is as far as Carlyle had reached in the project before his death. The work is a vivid and candid description of Edinburgh of the time, and the lives of his famous friends, including John Home, William Robertson, Adam Smith, and Hume. Although Carlyle left instructions for the posthumous publication of his memoirs, the trustees of the manuscript hesitated for fear of offending those mentioned in it or their relatives. It finally appeared in 1860, edited by John Hill Burton (1809–1881). Carlyle's recollections of Hume are exceptionally vivid, and his most notable discussions are these: Hume's positive reception at the Adam house; Patrick Boyle's story of how Hume reacted to the news of his mother's death; Carlyle's contention that Hume was not an atheist; Hume's dinners with the literati; the naming of St David's Street; the rehearsal of John Home's *Douglas*; Hume's quarrel with Andrew Fletcher, the story surrounding *Sister Peg*; and a satirical dream in which he sees Hume in the afterlife.

Writing for the *Edinburgh Review*, James Lorimer opens his discussion of the *Autobiography* with the following general appraisal:

> This book contains by far the most vivid picture of Scottish life and manners that has been given to the public since the days of Sir Walter Scott… The term

216

autobiography scarcely describes if correctly. A far more accurate notion of its contents would have been conveyed, had the editor adhered to that which Dr. Carlyle himself seems from the opening sentence to have contemplated – viz., 'Anecdotes and Characters of the Times.

Regarding Carlyle's account of Hume, Lorimer notes,

> But one of the greater lights of Edinburgh in those days, was unquestionably David Hume. In many respects Carlyle presents Hume in a new and a more pleasing light than that in which the world has hitherto seen him. His sketches of him are of special importance, proceeding, as they do, not only from an intimate friend, but from one whose own sincerity as a Christian believer was never called in question. [*Edinburgh Review*, vol. 113, January 1861, pp. 144–181]

Burton's edition of Carlyle's *Autobiography* was republished in 1861 and in a revised edition of 1910. A new edition of Carlyle's memoirs, edited by James Kinsley, appeared in 1972 based on Carlyle's original manuscript. The following is from the 1910 edition.

[1737] The celebrated Dr. Hutchison of Glasgow, who was the first that distinguished himself in that important branch of literature [i.e., Moral Philosophy], was now beginning his career, and had drawn ample stores from the ancients, which he improved into system, and embellished by the exertions of an ardent and virtuous mind. He was soon followed by Smith, who had been his scholar, and sat for some years in his chair; by Ferguson at Edinburgh; by Reid and Beattie, which last was more an orator than a philosopher; together with David Hume, whose works, though dangerous and heretical, illustrated the science, and called forth the exertions of men of equal genius and sounder principles.

[1753] Mr. Cardonnel, whom I have mentioned, was another who excelled, like Smollett, in a great variety of pleasant stories. Sir Hew Dalrymple, North Berwick, had as much conversation and wit as any man of his time, having been long an M. P. David Hume and Dr. John Jardine were likewise both admirable, and had the peculiar talent of rallying their companions on their good qualities.

...

At this time David Hume was living in Edinburgh and composing his *History of Great Britain*. He was a man of great knowledge, and of a social and benevolent temper, and truly the best-natured man in the world. He was branded with the title of Atheist, on account of the many attacks on revealed religion that are to be found in his philosophical works, and in many places of his History – the last of which are still more objectionable than the first, which a friendly critic might call only sceptical. Apropos of this, when Mr. Robert Adam, the celebrated architect, and his brother, lived in Edinburgh with their mother, an aunt of Dr. Robertson's, and a very respectable woman, she said to her son, "I shall be glad to see any of your companions to dinner, but I hope you will never bring the Atheist here to disturb my peace." But Robert soon fell on a method to reconcile her to him, for he introduced him under another name, or concealed it carefully from her. When the company parted she said to her son, "I must confess that you bring very agreeable companions about you, but the large jolly man who sat next me is the most agreeable of them all." "This was the very Atheist," said he, "mother, that you was so much afraid of." "Well," says she, "you may bring him here as much as you please, for he's the most innocent, agreeable, facetious man I ever met with."[1] This was truly the case with him; for though he had much learning and a fine taste, and was professedly a sceptic, though by no means an atheist, he had the greatest simplicity of mind and manners with the utmost facility and benevolence of temper of any man I ever knew. His conversation was truly irresistible, for while it was enlightened, it was näive almost to puerility.

I was one of those who never believed that David Hume's sceptical principles had laid fast hold on his mind, but thought that his books proceeded rather from affectation of superiority and pride of understanding and love of vainglory. I was confirmed in this opinion, after his death, by what the Honourable Patrick Boyle, one of his most intimate friends, told me many years ago at my house in Musselburgh, where he used to come and dine the first Sunday of every General Assembly, after his brother, Lord Glasgow, ceased to be Lord High Commissioner. When we were talking of David, Mrs. Carlyle asked Mr. Boyle if he thought David Hume was as great an unbeliever as the world took him to be? He answered, that the world judged from his books, as they had a right to; but he thought otherwise, who had known him all his life, and mentioned the following incident: When David and he were both in London, at the period when David's mother died, Mr. Boyle, hearing of it, soon after went into his apartment – for they lodged in the same house – when he found him in the deepest affliction and in a flood of tears. After the usual topics of condolence. Mr. Boyle said to him, "My friend, you owe this uncommon grief to your having thrown off the principles of religion; for if you had not, you would have been consoled by the firm belief that the good lady, who was not only the best of mothers, but the most pious of Christians, was now completely happy in the realms of the just." To which David replied, "Though I threw out my speculations to entertain and employ the learned and

---

[1] [William Adam describes Hume's relationship with the Adam family in his *Sequel to the Gift of a Grandfather* (1739), selections from which are contained in this collection.]

metaphysical world, yet in other things I do not think so differently from the rest of mankind as you may imagine." To this my wife was a witness. This conversation took place the year after David died, when Dr. Hill, who was to preach, had gone to a room to look over his notes.[2]

At this period, when he first lived in Edinburgh, and was writing his *History of England*, his circumstances were narrow, and he accepted the office of Librarian to the Faculty of Advocates, worth £40 per annum. But it was not for the salary that he accepted this employment, but that he might have easy access to the books in that celebrated library; for, to my certain knowledge, he gave every farthing of the salary to families in distress. Of a piece with this temper was his curiosity and credulity, which were without bounds, a specimen of which shall be afterwards given when I come down to Militia and the Poker. His economy was strict, as he loved independency; and yet he was able at that time to give suppers to his friends in his small lodging in the Canongate. He took much to the company of the younger clergy, not from a wish to bring them over to his opinions, for he never attempted to overturn any man's principles, but they best understood his notions, and could furnish him with literary conversation. Robertson and John Home and Bannatine and I lived all in the country, and came only periodically to the town. Blair and Jardine both lived in it, and suppers being the only fashionable meal at that time, we dined where we best could, and by cadies assembled our friends to meet us in a tavern by nine o'clock; and a fine time it was when we could collect David Hume, Adam Smith, Adam Ferguson, Lord Elibank, and Drs. Blair and Jardine, on an hour's warning. I remember one night that David Hume, who, having dined abroad, came rather late to us, and directly pulled a large key from his pocket, which he laid on the table. This he said was given him by his maid Peggy (much more like a man than a woman) that she might not sit up for him, for she said when the honest fellows came in from the country, he never returned home till after one o'clock. This intimacy of the young clergy with David Hume enraged the zealots on the opposite side, who little know how impossible it was for him, had he been willing, to shake their principles.

As Mr. Hume's circumstances improved he enlarged his mode of living, and instead of the roasted hen and minced collops, and a bottle of punch, he gave both elegant dinners and suppers, and the best claret, and, which was best of all, he furnished the entertainment with the most instructive and pleasing

---

[2] [In his original 1812 oral presentation of *An Account of the Life and Writings of John Home* (1822), Henry Mackenzie presents Carlyle's account of this story. In *The Anecdotes and Egotisms of Henry Mackenzie* (1927), selections from which are contained in this collection, Mackenzie states that Baron Hume did believe Carlyle's account. Nevertheless, in 1816, Baron David Hume sent a letter to the *Quarterly Review* citing Carlyle's rendition of Boyle's story; see Editor's Note in the *Quarterly Review*, contained in this collection.]

conversation, for he assembled whosoever were most knowing and agreeable among either the laity or clergy. This he always did, but still more unsparingly when he became what he called rich. For innocent mirth and agreeable raillery I never knew his match. Jardine, who sometimes bore hard upon him – for he had much drollery and wit, though but little learning – never could overturn his temper. Lord Elibank resembled David in his talent for collecting agreeable companions together, and had a house in town for several winters chiefly for that purpose.

David, who delighted in what the French call *plaisanterie*, with the aid of Miss Nancy Ord, one of the Chief Baron's daughters, contrived and executed one that gave him very great delight. As the New Town was making its progress westward, he built a house in the south-west corner of St. Andrew Square. The street leading south to Princes Street had not yet got its name affixed, but they got a workman early one morning to paint on the corner stone of David's house "St. David's Street," where it remains to this day.[3]

He was at first quite delighted with Ossian's poems, and gloried in them; but on going to London he went over to the other side, and loudly affirmed them to be inventions of Macpherson. I happened to say one day, when he was declaiming against Macpherson, that I had met with nobody of his opinion but William Caddel of Cockenzie, and President Dundas, which he took ill, and was some time of forgetting. This is one instance of what Smellie says of him, that though of the best temper in the world, yet he could be touched by opposition or rudeness.[4] This was the only time I had ever observed David's temper change. I can call to mind an instance or two of his good-natured pleasantry. Being at Gilmerton, where David Hume was on a visit, Sir David Kinloch made him go to Athlestaneford Church, where I preached for John Home. When we met before dinner, "What did you mean," says he to me, "by treating John's congregation to-day with one of Cicero's academics? I did not think that such heathen morality would have passed in East Lothian." On Monday, when we were assembling to breakfast, David retired to the end of the dining-room, when Sir David entered: "What are you doing there, Davy? come to your breakfast." "Take away the enemy first," says David. The baronet, thinking it was the warm fire that kept David in the lower end of the room, rung the bell for a servant to carry some of it off. It was not the fire that scared David,

---

[3]   [For alternative versions of the story about Saint David's Street, see Burton's *Life* (1846), Chambers's, *Scottish Jests* (1832), and Miscellaneous Hume Anecdotes, contained in this collection.]

[4]   ["His works met with so many and often so rude attacks from a variety of authors, that, though he did not deign to answer them in writing; yet, in conversation, he frequently discovered the resentments which he felt from the indelicate and often ignorant insults of inferior scholars." William Smellie, *Literary and Characteristical Lives* (1800), selections from which are contained in this collection.]

but a large Bible that was left on a stand at the upper end of the room, a chapter of which had been read at the family prayers the night before, that good custom not being then out of use when clergymen were in the house. Add to this John Home saying to him at the Poker Club, when everybody wondered what could have made a clerk of Sir William Forbes run away with £900 – "I know that very well," says John Home to David; "for when he was taken, there was found in his pocked your *Philosophical Works* and Boston's *Fourfold State of Man.*"

David Hume, during all his life, had written the most pleasing and agreeable letters to his friends. I have preserved two of these. But I lately saw two of more early date in the hands of Mr. Sandiland Dysart, W.S., to his mother, who was a friend of David's and a very accomplished woman, one of them dated in 1751, on occasion of his brother Hume of Ninewell's marriage; and the other in 1754,[5] with a present of the first volume of the History, both of which are written in a vein of pleasantry and playfulness which nothing can exceed, and which makes me think that a collection of his letters would be a valuable present to the world, and present throughout a very pleasing picture of his mind.

I have heard him say that Baron Montesquieu, when he asked him if he did not think that there would soon be a revolution in France favourable to liberty, answered, "No, for their noblesse had all become poltroons." He said that the club in Paris (Baron Holbach's) to which he belonged, were of opinion that Christianity would be abolished in Europe by the end of the eighteenth century; and that they laughed at Andrew Stuart for making a battle in favour of a future state, and called him "L'ame Immortelle."

David Hume, like Smith, had no discernment at all of characters. The only two clergymen whose interests he espoused, and for one of whom he provided, were the two silliest fellows in the Church. With every opportunity, he was ridiculously shy of asking favours, on account of preserving his independence, which always appeared to me to be a very foolish kind of pride. His friend John Home, with not more benevolence, but with no scruples from a wish of independence, for which he was not born, availed himself of his influence and provided for hundreds, and yet he never asked anything for himself.

Adam Smith, though perhaps only second to David in learning and ingenuity, was far inferior to him in conversational talents. In that of public speaking they were equal – David never tried it, and I never heard Adam but once, which was at the first meeting of the Select Society, when he opened up the design of the meeting. His voice was harsh and enunciation thick, approaching to stammering. ...

---

[5] [Two letters from Hume to Mrs. Dysart are included in Hume's *Letters* (Greig): March 19, 1751; October 9, 1754. Two letters from Hume to Carlyle are also included: February 3, 1761, September 15, 1763.]

... [Adam Ferguson] was apt to be jealous of his rivals, and indignant against assumed superiority. His wife used to say that it was very fortunate that I was so much in Edinburgh, as I was a great peacemaker among them. She did not perceive that her own husband was the most difficult of them all. But as they were all honourable men in the highest degree, John Home and I together kept them on very good terms: I mean by them, Smith and Ferguson and David Hume; for Robertson was very good-natured, and soon disarmed the failing of Ferguson, of whom he was afraid. With respect to taste, we held David Hume and Adam Smith inferior to the rest, for they were both prejudiced in favour of the French tragedies, and did not sufficiently appreciate Shakespeare and Milton. Their taste was a rational act, rather than the instantaneous effect of fine feeling. David Hume said Ferguson had more genius than any of them, as he had made himself so much master of a difficult science – viz., Natural Philosophy, which he had never studied but when at college – in three months, so as to be able to teach it. ...

[1755] In the month of February, 1755, John Home's tragedy of *Douglas* was completely prepared for the stage, and had received all the corrections and improvements that it needed by many excellent critics, who were Mr. Home's friends, whom I have mentioned before, and with whom he daily lived. [He accordingly set out for London, and] were I to relate all the circumstances, serious and ludicrous, which attended the outset of this journey, I am persuaded they would not be exceeded by any novelist who has wrote since the days of the inimitable *Don Quixote*. Six or seven Merse ministers – the half of whom had slept at the manse of Polwarth, bad as it was, the night before – set out for Woolerhaughhead in a snowy morning in February. Before we had gone far we discovered that our bard had no mode of carrying his precious treasure, which we thought enough of, but hardly foresaw that it was to be pronounced a perfect tragedy by the best judges; for when David Hume gave it that praise, he spoke only the sentiment of the whole republic of belles lettres.

[1756] It was in the end of this year, 1756, that *Douglas* was first acted in Edinburgh. Mr. Home had been unsuccessful in London the year before, but he was well with Sir Gilbert Elliot, Mr. Oswald of Dunnikier, and had the favor and friendship of Lord Milton and all his family; and it was at last agreed among them that, since Garrick could not yet be prevailed on to get Douglas acted, it should be brought on here; for if it succeeded in the Edinburgh theatre, then Garrick could resist no longer.

There happened to be a pretty good set of players; for Digges, whose relations had got him debarred from the London theatres, had come down here, and performed many principal parts with success. He was a very handsome young man at that time, with a genteel address. He had drunk tea at Mally Campbell's, in Glasgow College, when he was an ensign in the year 1745. I was there, and thought him very agreeable. He was, however, a great profligate and spendthrift; and poltroon, I'm afraid, into the bargain. He had been on the stage for some time, having been obliged to leave the army. Mrs. Ward turned out an exceeding good Lady Randolph; Lowe performed Glenalvon well; Mr. Haymen the Old Shepherd, and Digges himself young Douglas. I attended two rehearsals with our author, and Lord Elibank, and Dr. Ferguson, and David Hume, and was truly astonished at the readiness with which Mrs. Ward conceived the Lady's character, and how happily she delivered it. To be near Digges's lodgings in the Canongate, where the first rehearsals were performed, the gentlemen mentioned, with two or three more, dined together at a tavern in the Abbey two or three times, where pork griskins being a favorite dish, this was called the Griskin Club, and excited much curiosity, as everything did in which certain people were concerned.

The play had unbounded success for a great many nights in Edinburgh, and was attended by all the literati and most of the judges, who, except one or two, had not been in use to attend the theatre. The town in general was in an uproar of exultation that a Scotchman had written a tragedy of the first-rate, and that its merit was first submitted to their judgment. There were a few opposers, however, among those who pretended to taste and literature, who endeavored to cry down the performance in libellous pamphlets and ballads (for they durst not attempt to oppose it in the theatre itself), and were openly countenanced by Robert Dundas of Arniston, at that time Lord Advocate, and all his minions and expectants. The high-flying set were unanimous against it, as they thought it a sin for a clergyman to write any play, let it be ever so moral in its tendency. Several ballads and pamphlets were published on our side in answer to the scurrilities against us, one of which was written by Adam Ferguson, and another by myself. Ferguson's was mild and temperate; and, besides other arguments, supported the lawfulness and use of dramatic writing from the example of Scripture, which he exhibited in the story of Joseph and his brethren, as having truly the effect of a dramatic composition. This was much read among the grave and sober-minded, and converted some, and confirmed many in their belief of the usefulness of the stage. Mine was of such a different nature that many people read it at first as intended to *ridicule* the performance, and bring it into contempt, for it was entitled "An Argument to prove that the Tragedy of *Douglas* ought to be publicly burned by the Hands of the Hangman." The zeal and violence of the Presbytery of Edinburgh, who had made enactments and declarations to be read in the pulpit, provoked me to write this pamphlet, which, in the ironical manner of Swift, contained a severe satire on all our opponents. This was so well concealed, however, that the pamphlet being published when I was at Dumfries, about the end of January, visiting Provost Bell, who was on his death-bed, some copies arrived there by the carriers, which being opened and read by my sister and aunt when I was abroad, they conceived it to be serious, and that the tragedy would be quite undone, till Mr. Stewart, the Comptroller of the Customs, who was a man of sense and reading, came in, and who soon undeceived them and convinced them that *Douglas* was triumphant. This pamphlet had a great effect by elating our friends, and perhaps more in exasperating our enemies; which was by no means softened by Lord Elibank and David Hume, &c., running about and crying it up as the first performance the world had seen for half a century.

[1757] Milton[6] had a mind sufficiently acute to comprehend Ferguson's profound speculations, though his own forte did not lie in any kind of philosophy, but the knowledge of men, and the management of them, while Ferguson was his admiring scholar in those articles. He had been much teased about the tragedy of Douglas, for [Peter] Cuming had still access to him at certain hours by the political back-door from Gray's Close, and had alarmed him much, especially immediately after the publication of my pamphlet, *An Argument, etc.*, which had irritated the wild brethren so much, said Peter, that he could not answer for what mischief might follow. When he had been by such means kept in a very frightful humour, he came up into the drawing-room, where David Hume was, with John and Ferguson and myself; on David's saying something, with his usual good-humour, to smooth his wrinkly brow, Milton turned to him with great asperity, and said that he had better hold his peace on the subject, for it was owing to him, and keeping company with him, that such a clamour was raised. David made no reply, but soon after took his hat and cane, and left the room, never more to enter the house, which he never did, though much pains was taken afterwards, for Milton soon repented, and David would have returned, but Betty Fletcher opposed it, rather foregoing his company at their house than suffer him to degrade himself – such was the generous spirit of that young lady. Had it not been for Ferguson and her, John Home and I would have been expelled also.

[1760] While I was busy with this important change in my domestic state [i.e., marriage], I was applied to by a friend to write a satirical pamphlet in my ironical style against the opposers of the Scotch Militia Bill, which had been rejected in the preceding session. Being too much engaged to attempt anything of that kind at the time, I proposed that it should be intrusted to Adam Ferguson, then living at Inveresk, preparing his academical lectures. My friend answered that he was excellent at serious works, but could turn nothing into ridicule, as he had no humour: I answered, that he did not know him sufficiently, but advised him to go and try him, as he would undertake nothing that he was not able to execute. This happened about the month of August, and Ferguson having undertaken it, executed that little work called Sister Peg, in the style of Dr. Arbuthnot's John Bull, which excited both admiration and animosity. The real author was carefully concealed, though it was generally ascribed to me, as I had written two small pieces in the same ironical style. The public had no doubt but that it was the work of one out of four of us, if not

[6] [Andrew Fletcher (1692–1766), Lord Milton.]

the joint work of us all. The secret was well kept by at least ten or a dozen males and females. This pamphlet occasioned a very ludicrous scene between David Hume and Dr. Jardine, who was in the secret. David was a great blab, and could conceal nothing that he thought for the honour of his friends, and therefore it had been agreed to tell him of none of our productions, except such as might have been published at the Cross. He sent for Jardine, whom he first suspected of being the author, who denying his capacity for such a work, he fixed on me (never dreaming of Ferguson); and when Jardine pretended ignorance, or refused to gratify him, he told him he had written it himself in an idle hour, and desired Jardine to mention him as the author everywhere, that it might not fall on some of us, who were not so able to bear it. This I could not have believed, had not David himself written me a letter to that purpose, which I shall transcribe in the margin.[7]

[1762] In the beginning of 1762 was instituted the famous club called "The Poker," which lasted in great vigor down to the year 1784. About the third or fourth meeting, we thought of giving it a name that would be of uncertain meaning, and not be so directly offensive as that of Militia Club to the enemies of that institution. Adam Ferguson fell luckily on the name of "Poker," which we perfectly understood, and was at the same time an enigma to the public.[8] This club consisted of all the literati of Edinburgh and its neighborhood, most of whom had been members of the Select Society, except very few indeed who adhered to the enemies of militia, together with a great many country gentlemen, who, though not always resident in town, yet were zealous friends to a Scotch militia, and warm in their resentment on its being refused to us, and an invidious line drawn between Scotland and England. The establishment was frugal and moderate, as that of all clubs for a public purpose ought to be. We met at our old landlord's of the Diversorium, now near the Cross, the dinner on the table soon after two o'clock, at one shilling a head, the wine to be confined to sherry and claret, and the reckoning to be called at six o'clock. After the first fifteen, who were chosen by nomination, the members were to be chosen by ballot, two black balls to exclude the candidate. There was to be a new preses chosen at every meeting. William Johnstone, Esq., now Sir William Pulteney, was chosen secretary of the club, with a charge of all publications that might be thought necessary by him, and two other members with whom he was to consult. In a laughing humor, Andrew Crosbie was chosen Assassin, in case any officer of that sort should be needed; but David Hume was added as his Assessor, without whose assent nothing should be done, so that between *plus* and *minus* there was likely to be no bloodshed.

---

[7] [The letter in question is dated February 3, 1761 and contained in Hume's *Letters* (Greig).]

[8] [i.e., a fire "poker" which, metaphorically, would ignite the militia issue.]

[1763] [Colonel Roberts] was truly a man of sense, and of much reading, and a great master of conversation: he was the first whom I met with who struck out an idea that has been followed since; for, talking much of Hume's and Robertson's Histories, he said that Hume appeared to him to be the Homer and Robertson the Virgil of British historians, – a criticism that has of late – been confirmed by Dugald Stewart's quotation.

[1764] I got Gregory elected into the Poker, but though very desirous at first, yet he did not avail himself of it, but desisted after twice attending, afraid, I suppose, of disgusting some of the ladies he paid court to by falling in sometimes there with David Hume, whom they did not know for the innocent good soul which he really was.

[1766] This death of Jardine was not only a breach in our society which we long felt, as John Jardine was one of the pleasantest of the whole, who played delightfully on the unbounded curiosity and dupish simplicity of David Hume.

[1769] My good aunt Paterson's husband, a cousin of Sir Hew Paterson, took care to have us visit his son's widow, Mrs. Seton, the heiress of Touch, whose first husband was Sir Hew's son, who had died without issue. There we dined one day with a large company, mostly Scots, among whom were Mrs. Walkinshaw – who had a place at court, though she was sister of the lady who was said to be mistress to Prince Charles, the Pretender's son – and David Hume, by that time Under-Secretary of State. The conversation was lively and agreeable, but we were much amused with observing how much the thoughts and conversation of all those in the least connected were taken up with every trifling circumstance that related to the Court. This kind of tittle-tattle suited Dr. John Blair of all men, who had been a tutor to the King's brother, the Duke of York, and now occasionally assisted Dr. Barton as Clerk of the Closet to the Princess Dowager of Wales. It was truly amusing to observe how much David Hume's strong and capacious mind was filled with infantine anecdotes of nurses and children.

"Scroll of a Letter [from Alexander Carlyle] to Sir JOHN MACPHERSON, Bart. 1797." Although one's correspondence with one's friend should be never so much interrupted by business or idleness, there are certain occasions when they must not be neglected, such as marriages and births, and even death itself. As the last has lately befallen me, though I am happily restored to life, I think it is proper to announce to you, my very good friend, my return to this world, and to give you some account of the slight peep I had into the other. About a month ago I was suddenly seized, after a hearty dinner, with a dreadful colic, which lasted for fifty hours, which threatened immediate dissolution, and actually sent me out of the body for a few minutes. During that short period (like Mahomet in his dream) I had a view of Elysium, hanging, as I thought, on the brink of a cloud, and every moment ready to descend. But, as I saw clearly before me, the first group I perceived was David Hume, and Adam Smith, and James Macpherson, lounging on a little hillock, with Col. James

Edmonstone standing before them, brandishing a cudgel, and William Robertson at David's feet in a listening posture. Edmonstone was rallying David and Smith, not without a mixture of anger, for having contributed their share to the present state of the world; the one, by doing everything in his power to undermine Christianity, and the other by introducing that unrestrained and universal commerce, which propagates opinions as well as commodities. The two philosophers, conscious of their follies, were shrunk into a nutshell, when James the bard, in the act of raising himself to insult them, perceiving my gray hairs hanging over them in the cloud, exclaimed, 'Damn your nonsensical palaver; there is Carlyle just coming down, and John Home and Ferguson cannot be far behind, when I shall have irresistible evidence for the authenticity of Ossian. Blair, I dare say, is likewise on the road, and I hope he'll bring his dissertation on my works along with him, which is worth a thousand of his mawkish sermons, which are only calculated to catch milk-sops and silly women.' Upon this Robertson rose to his feet, and seemed to be in act to speak one of his decisive sentences in favor of the winning side, when Joseph Black, and Charley Congalton, and Sandy Wood, who had hold of the skirts of my coat, fearing I should leap down at the sight of so many of my friends, and carry them after me, made a sudden and strong pull altogether, and jerked me back into life again, not without regret at being disappointed in meeting with so choice a company.

99
WILLIAM SMELLIE:
LITERARY AND CHARACTERISTICAL LIVES

William Smellie, *Literary and characteristical lives of John Gregory, M.D.*
Henry Home, Lord Kames. David Hume, Esq. and Adam Smith, L.L.D. To
which are added A dissertation on public spirit; and three essays. By the late
William Smellie, ... Edinburgh: printed and sold by Alex. Smellie, Bell &
Bradfute, J. Dickson, W. Creech, E. Balfour [10 others in Edinburgh, and 4 in
London], 1800, ix, [1], 450 p.
Selections from chapter on Hume; from 1800 edition.

Born in Edinburgh, William Smellie (1740–1795) began working as a
printer's apprentice at the age of twelve, attending university classes on the
side. He excelled in this trade and, from 1765 until his death, he owned a
printing business with various partners. He was instrumental in publishing the
first edition of the *Encyclopaedia Britannica* and from 1773 through 1776 co-
edited *The Edinburgh Magazine and Review*. Near the close of his life, Smellie
planned to write a biographical dictionary of famous Scottish authors with
whom he was personally acquainted. Unfortunately, he was only able to
complete the sketches of John Gregory, Henry Home, David Hume, and Adam
Smith. These were published posthumously by his son Alexander Smellie in
1800 under the title *Literary and Characteristical Lives*. The lengthy essay on
Hume is in two parts. The first consists of paraphrases and extended quotations from Hume's "My Own Life" and Adam Smith's "Letter ... to William
Strahan." However, Smellie includes interesting digressions regarding his
personal experience reading the difficult *Treatise* and the lending policy of the
Faculty of Advocates library. He also comments on the unusually high concentration of literary figures in Edinburgh so that a person could "in a few
minutes, take fifty men of genius and learning by the hand." The second part
of the sketch reprints Smellie's article on "Abridgment" in the 1771
Encyclopaedia Britannica (which discusses Hume) and three of Hume's letters
– two to George Campbell and the other to James Balfour. Again Smellie
includes interesting observations. He describes Hume's physical appearance
when discussing his critics. He gives a synopsis of the controversy with
Rousseau, and the story behind Hume's ill-fated review of Henry's *History* in

the *Edinburgh Magazine and Review*. He states that Hume's antipathy towards the Scottish clergy owes to them blocking his candidacy for professorship at the University of Edinburgh. Smellie describes a dinner at Lord Kames's at which Hume made a religious joke, prompting clergyman John Warden to walk out.

Smellie's *Literary and Characteristical Lives* met with mixed reviews. Writing for the *Monthly Review*, Alexander Hamilton felt that Smellie should have drawn more on his personal acquaintance with the authors:

> The biographical portion of this posthumous work, which was written by a person who was in intimate habits with the eminent characters mentioned in the title-page, would have communicated greater interest, had the author imparted particulars calculated to afford a more accurate view of their private conduct, opinions, and tempers, than can be collected from a perusal of their writings, or the public events of their lives, which are already sufficiently known. Such, however, was not the design of Mr. Smellie. [*Monthly Review*, 1800, Vol. 33, pp. 422–423].

The *New London Review* concurs in the *Monthly*'s general assessment:

> The life of Hume contains no new fact, nor any important anecdote beyond what we are already in possession of from his own account of it. ... The book, viewed as a biographical work, is formed upon scanty materials; but, considered as a review of the writings and opinions of a Gregory, a Kames, a Hume, and a Smith, it is ably executed. [*New London Review*, June 1800, Vol. 3, pp. 162–163]

The *European Magazine* writes that "if the present lives were intended as specimens of the intention and execution [of Smellie's planned biographical dictionary], the public will not much regret that the design is left to other hands." The review continues, however, noting that the account of Hume "is the most entertaining in the volume, but the greater part of it has appeared before, which is indeed acknowledged" (1800, Vol. 37, pp. 448–449). The following is from the 1800 and only edition of *Literary and Characteristical Lives*. The complete chapter is presented, with the exception of three widely accessible letters from Hume which have been omitted at the places indicated below.

THE
LIFE
OF
DAVID HUME, Esq.

It is an arduous task to give an impartial account of an author who has been the object of so much praise and of so much obloquy as Mr Hume: Yet the attempt must be made.

Mr Hume was born at Edinburgh on the 26th of April 1711, old style. He was descended of respectable families both on the father and mother's side. His father's family was a branch of the earl of Hume's and his mother was a daughter of sir David Falconer, president of the College of Justice. His family, however, was not opulent; and he being a younger brother, his patrimony was, of course, very trifling. His father died when Mr Hume was an infant; and he, along with a sister an elder brother, were left to the care of their mother, who devoted her whole attention to the rearing and educating of her children. Mr Hume passed through the ordinary courses of education with great success, and very early discovered an uncommon passion for literature. This last circumstance suggested to his friends the idea that the profession of the law would be a proper employment for him; but young Hume had an insuperable aversion to everything but the pursuits of philosophy and of general learning; and he tells us, that, when he was supposed to be studying Voet and Vinnius, Cicero and Virgil were the authors he was secretly devouring.

This plan, however, his narrow fortune was unable to support. He, therefore, made an attempt to enter upon a more active scene of life. With this view, in the year 1734, he went to Bristol, and had recommendations to some of the most eminent merchants in that city. In a few months, he discovered that this species of business was irksome and disagreeable to him. In order to prosecute his studies with the greater success, as well as to enable him to live upon his small fortune, he went to a country retreat. His chief residence was at La Fleche, in Anjou, where he composed his *Treatise of Human Nature*, which, after returning to London, he published in the year 1738. "Never literary attempt," Mr Hume remarks, "was more unfortunate than my Treatise of Human Nature. It fell *dead-born from the press*, without reaching such distinction as even to excite a murmur among the *zealots*."[1]

This complaint is curious, and confirms the adage, that an author is the worst judge of the merit or demerit of his own works. Mr Hume's *Treatise of Human Nature*, as he himself informs us, excited no attention, either of praise or of censure, from the public. No wonder! When much younger, I read that book with great ardour, and with great application. Some parts of it I perceived to

[1]   Vide his own Life, p. 8.

be both ingenious and brilliant, and others so involved in obscurity, that I found it impossible to comprehend the meaning. At that period of life, I naturally attributed this seeming obscurity to my own inability, and was often ashamed, for that reason, to acknowledge that I had read it, because I could not give any distinct account of the book. When older, I perused it a second time, and then perceived an ingenious literary *trick*, if I may use such an expression. Mr Hume, when he begins an essay, or turns the *corner* of any argument, most artfully lays down a seemingly simple position, to which almost every reader gives a ready assent. From that moment, however, the reader is most completely bewildered: For, whenever these plausible positions are admitted, or inadvertently passed over, such is the force of Mr Hume's reasonings, and such the beauty and energy of his eloquence, that no reader can resist the torrent. Dean Swift says, that the best way to conquer a woman, is to catch her by the *tail*. But the only successful mode of conquering Mr Hume is to catch him by the *nose*.

In the year 1742, Mr Hume published at Edinburgh the first part of his Essays. This work met with a more favourable reception from the public, and gave him some consolation for his former disappointment. In 1745, he was invited by the Marquis of Annandale, who was then indisposed both in mind and in body, to come and live with him in England, where Mr Hume continued during twelve months; and, by his appointments in that station, was enabled to make a considerable addition to his small fortune. He then received an invitation from General St Clair to attend him as secretary to an expedition against Canada, but which ended in an incursion on the coast of France. In 1747, Mr Hume was again invited by General St Clair to attend him in the same station in his embassy to the courts of Vienna and Turin. He then wore the uniform of an officer; and, in the character of aid-de-camp to the General, was introduced into these courts. These two years, he tells us, were almost the only interruptions he met with to his studies during the course of his life. But he passed them agreeably; and his appointments, joined to his own frugality, soon enabled him to amass near a thousand pounds.

Mr Hume imagined that his *Treatise of Human Nature* had failed of success more from the manner of writing than from the matter. He, therefore, to use his own expression, *cast* the first part of that work anew in his *Inquiry concerning Human Understanding*, which was published while he was at Turin. But, at first, this piece was not much more successful than the former. Mr Hume, however, though he must have felt those disappointments, was not altogether discouraged. In the 1749, he came down from London to Scotland, and lived at his brother's country-house, where he composed the second part of his Essay, which he called *Political Discourses*, and likewise his *Inquiry concerning the Principles of Morals*, which, he tells us, in another part of his *Treatise*, that he *cast* anew. Soon afterwards, he was informed by Mr A. Millar, his London bookseller, that his former publications, except his unfortunate Treatise, were beginning to be the subject of conversation; that the sale of them was gradually increasing; and that new editions were become necessary to answer the demands of the public. "Answers," he archly remarks, "by Reverands and Right Reverands, came out two or three in a year; and I found, by *Dr. Warburton's railing*, that the books were beginning to be esteemed in *good company.*"[2]

Mr Hume, in the year 1751, removed from the country, and came to Edinburgh, which he emphatically terms the *true scene for a man of letters.*[3] In 1752, he published his *Political Discourses*, the first work of his which was successful at the outset. In the same year appeared his *Inquiry concerning the Principles of Morals*, "which is," says he, "of all my writings, historical, philosophical, or literary, incomparably the best."[4] But the public were of a contrary opinion; for the book was either totally neglected, or treated with contempt.

In the same year, he was appointed by the Faculty of Advocates their Librarian, from which office he received only a trifling emolument; but it gave him the command of a great collection of books and manuscripts. When this Library falls naturally to be mentioned, it would be unpardonable not to tell a truth of which every man of letters in Edinburgh has daily experience. The collection, especially of printed books, exceeds greatly that of any library in Britain; and free access to the perusal of them is cheerfully and politely allowed. On this subject, I must go farther. The occasional use of books or manuscripts in a public library is a most valuable privilege. The Faculty of Advocates, however, not only grant this privilege, but any member of that Faculty can, by his signature, oblige his friends with such books as he chuses out of doors for a reasonable time; and such requests, on all proper occasions, are most liberally granted. The Faculty do more. Literary gentlemen, by giving bond for a certain sum, often acquire the privilege of taking out books upon their own receipts. To this noble collection, joined to the generosity of its proprietors, Scotland, for these hundred years past, has been indebted for the many productions of genius and of learning which have enabled her sons, within that period, to make such a distinguished figure in almost every department of science. I must not, however, omit her powerful auxiliaries. The libraries of the University of Edinburgh, and of the College of Physicians, are very great, and particularly enriched with books of Medicine, of Anatomy, and of Natural History. The access to these libraries is equally easy as to that of the Faculty of Advocates. But, to return. – In this most favourable situation, where he had an opportunity of consulting almost every authentic resource, Mr Hume formed the plan of

---

[2]   Mr Hume's own Life, p. 10.

[3]   Ibid. p. 11.

[4]   Mr Hume's own Life, p. 11.

writing the *History of England*. He commenced with the accession of the House of Stuart, and afterwards observed a kind of retrograde motion. Of the success of this work, he acknowledges his expectations were sanguine. "But," says he,

> "miserable was my disappointment: I was assailed by one cry of reproach, disapprobation, and even detestation; English, Scotch, and Irish, Whig and Tory, Churchman and Sectary, Freethinker and Religionist, Patriot and Courtier, united in their rage against the man who had presumed to shed a generous tear for the fate of Charles I. and the Earl of Strafford; and, after the ebullitions of their fury were over, what was still more mortifying, the book seemed to sink into oblivion."[5]

Some time afterwards, he published at London his *Natural History of Religion*. "Its public entry," he remarks, "was rather obscure, except only that Dr. Hurd wrote a pamphlet against it, with all the illiberal petulance, arrogance, and scurrility, which distinguish the Warburtonian school. This pamphlet gave me some consolation for the otherwise indifferent reception of my performance."[6]

Two years after the miscarriage of the first volume, viz. in 1756, he published the second volume of his History of England, which included the period from the death of Charles I. to the Revolution. This performance gave less umbrage to the Whigs, and was more favourably received by the public. "It not only rose itself," says he, "but helped to buoy up its unfortunate brother."[7] In the year 1759, Mr Hume published his *History of the House of Tudor*. The clamour excited by this work was nearly equal to that against the History of the two first Stuarts. The reign of Elizabeth was particularly offensive. "But," he tells us, "I was now callous against the impressions of public folly, and continued very peaceably and contentedly in my retreat at Edinburgh, to finish, in two volumes, the more early period of the English History, which I gave to the public in 1761, with tolerable, and but tolerable, success."[8]

Notwithstanding, however, a very general clamour and many rude attacks, Mr Hume's writings gradually acquired more and more reputation; and he received from the booksellers higher copy-money than had been given to any other author in Britain before that period. He now found himself not only independent, but opulent; and, therefore, he retired to his native country of

---

[5] His own Life, p. 11, and 12.

[6] His own Life, p. 11, and 12.

[7] Ibid.

[8] His own Life, p. 13.

Scotland, with a design never to leave it again. At that time, he was turned of fifty years, when, in the year 1763, he received an invitation from the Earl of Hertford to attend him on his embassy to Paris, with a near prospect of being his secretary. This offer, however, Mr Hume at first declined, on account of his age, and the reluctance he felt against mingling again with the gay company of the French metropolis. But, upon his Lordship's repeating the invitation, Mr Hume at last consented. He was afterwards appointed secretary to the embassy. In summer 1765, Lord Hertford was called home to be Lord Lieutenant of Ireland, and Mr Hume was left *chargé d' affaires* till the arrival of the Duke of Richmond about the end of the same year. In the beginning of the year 1766, Mr Hume left Paris, and next summer went to Edinburgh with the view of enjoying an agreeable retreat among philosophical friends, with which that city, though not large, peculiarly abounds. Mr Amyat, King's Chymist, a most sensible and agreeable English gentleman, resided in Edinburgh for a year or two. He one day surprised me with a curious remark. There is not a city in Europe, said he, that enjoys such a singular and such a noble privilege. I asked, What is that privilege? He replied, here I stand at what is called the *cross of Edinburgh*, and can, in a few minutes, take fifty men of genius and learning by the hand. The fact is well known; but to a native of that city, who has all his days been familiarized with it, and who has not travelled into other countries, that circumstance, though very remarkable, passes unnoticed: Upon strangers, however, it makes a deep impression. In London, in Paris, and other large cities of Europe, though they contain many literary men, the access to them is difficult; and, even after that is obtained, the conversation is, for some time, shy and constrained. In Edinburgh, the access to men of parts is not only easy, but their conversation and the communication of their knowledge are at once imparted to intelligent strangers with the utmost liberality. The philosophers of Scotland have no nostrums. They tell what they know, and deliver their sentiments without disguise or reserve. This generous feature was conspicuous in the character of Mr Hume. He insulted no man; but, when the conversation turned upon particular subjects, whether moral or religious, he expressed his genuine sentiments with freedom, with force, and with a dignity which did honour to human nature.

In the year 1767, Mr Hume was invited by Mr Conway to be under Secretary, which both the character of the person, and his connections with Lord Hertford, prevented him from declining. He returned to Edinburgh in 1769 very opulent; for he then possessed a revenue of 1000L. a year; and, though pretty far advanced in life, he was in good health, and had the prospect of long enjoying ease, and seeing the increase of his reputation.

In spring 1775, he began to be afflicted with a disorder in his bowels, which at first did not alarm him; but he soon afterwards apprehended that a mortification, and of course, a speedy dissolution, were to ensue. Still, however, his cheerfulness and usual alacrity, notwithstanding the great decline of his body, did not desert him. He considered, that a man of sixty-five, by dying, cuts off only a few years of infirmities, and perhaps of peevishness and anxiety. Mr Hume concludes his life with a short sketch of what he apprehended to be his own character and dispositions: "I am, or rather was," says he,

"a man of mild disposition, of command of temper, of an open, social, and cheerful humour, capable of attachment, but little susceptible of enmity, and of great moderation in all my passions. Even my love of literary fame, my ruling passion, never soured my temper, notwithstanding my frequent disappointments. My company was not unacceptable to the young and careless, as well as to the studious and literary; and, as I took a particular pleasure in the company of modest women, I had no reason to be displeased with the reception I met with from them."[9]

Though Mr Hume believed the disease which afflicted him was to carry him off the stage of life, as we are informed by a letter from the late most ingenious and excellent Dr Adam Smith to William Strahan, Esq; (of the latter of whom he had such a favourable opinion, that he left him the charge, with discretionary powers, of all his manuscripts, some of which, and particularly that of his own life, were afterwards published;) yet he was prevailed upon, by the entreaties of his friends, to try what might be the effects of a long journey. He, accordingly, about the end of April 1776, set out for London; and when he came the length of Morpeth, he met with Dr Adam Smith, and Mr John Home,[10] a gentleman well known for his poetical genius, and particularly for his theatrical writings. These two gentlemen were on their road from London expecting to find Mr Hume at Edinburgh. Mr Home returned with him, and "attended him," Mr Smith tells us, "during the whole of his stay in England, with that care and attention which might be expected from a temper so perfectly friendly and affectionate."[11]

Mr Hume's disease seemed to yield a little to exercise and change of air; for, when he arrived in London, he was apparently in much better health than when he left Edinburgh. He was advised to go to Bath and drink the waters, which, for some time, had so good an effect upon him, that he began to have some hopes of recovering his health. His former symptoms, however, returned with their usual violence. From that moment, he relinquished all hopes of the

---

[9] His own Life, p. 15.

[10] The AUTHOR often mentioned as a curious circumstance, that he had the honour of being acquainted with all the literary men, of his time, in Scotland, except the ingenious Mr JOHN HOME. [This note appears to have been written by Alexander Smellie about his father.]

[11] Dr Smith's Letter to Mr Strahan.

continuation of life, and of ease. But he submitted to his fate with the utmost cheerfulness and complacency. When he returned to Edinburgh, though he found himself much weaker, his spirits never failed him. His cheerfulness was so great, and his conversation and amusements continued so much in their accustomed strain, that, notwithstanding many bad symptoms, few of his friends could believe his dissolution to be so fast approaching. Doctor Dundas, when taking leave of Mr Hume one day, said to him, "I shall tell your friend Colonel Edmonstone, that I left you much better, and in a fair way of recovery." – "Doctor," Mr Hume replied, "as I believe you would not chuse to tell any thing but the truth, you had better tell him, that I am dying as fast as my enemies, if I have any, could wish, and as easily and cheerfully as my best friends could desire."[12]

Soon afterwards, Colonel Edmonstone went to see Mr Hume, and to take a last farewell of him. But, on his way home, he could not refrain from writing a letter, bidding him once more an eternal adieu. Such were Mr Hume's magnanimity and fortitude of mind, that his most intimate and affectionate friends knew they hazarded no offence in taking or writing to him as a-dying man. Mr Adam Smith happened to call upon Mr Hume when he was reading Colonel Edmonstone's letter, which he immediately showed to Mr Smith. After perusing this letter, Mr Smith remarked, that appearances were against Mr Hume; still, however, he said, your cheerfulness is so great, and your spirit of life so strong, that I must entertain some faint hopes of your recovery. Mr Hume answered, "Your hopes are groundless. An habitual *diarheoa*, of more than a year's standing, would be a very bad disease at any age. At my age, it is a mortal one. When I lie down in the evening, I feel myself weaker than when I rose in the morning; and, when I rise in the morning, weaker than when I lay down in the evening. I am sensible, besides, that some of my vital parts are affected, so that I must soon die."[13] Mr Smith replied, "If it must be so, you have at least the satisfaction of leaving all your friends, your brother's family in particular, in great prosperity."[14] Mr Hume said, he felt that satisfaction so sensibly, that, a few days before, when reading Lucian's Dialogues of the Dead, among all the excuses which are usually made to Charon by souls who are backward to be ferried in his boat over the river Styx, he could not find one that suited him. He had no house to furnish, no children to provide for, nor any enemies upon whom he wished to be revenged. "I could not well imagine," said he, "what excuse I could make to Charon, in order to obtain a little delay. I have done every thing of consequence which I ever meant to do, and I could

---

[12] Dr Smith's Letter to Mr Strahan.

[13] Ibid.

[14] Ibid.

at no time expect to leave my relations and friends in a better situation than that in which I am now likely to leave them: I, therefore, have all reason to die contented."

He then amused himself with inventing some whimsical excuses, which he supposed he might make to Charon, and with imagining the surly answers which it might suit the character of Charon to return to them. "Upon further consideration," said he, "I thought I might say to him, Good Charon, I have been correcting my works for a new edition. Allow me a little time that I may see how the public receives the alterations." But charon would answer, "When you have seen the effect of these, you will be for making other alterations. there will be no end of such excuses; so, honest friend, please step into the boat." But Mr Hume said, I might still urge, "Have a little patience, good Charon, I have been endeavouring to open the eyes of the public. If I live a few years longer, I may have the satisfaction of seeing the downfal of some of the prevailing systems of superstition." But Charon would then lose all temper and decency. – "You loitering rogue, that will not happen these many hundred years. Do you fancy I will grant you a lease for so long a term? Get into the boat this instant, you lazy loitering rogue."[15]

Though Mr Hume frequently talked of his approaching dissolution with great ease, he never affected to make a parade of his magnanimity. He never mentioned the subject but when the conversation naturally suggested it. Mr Hume had now become so weak, that the company of his most intimate companions fatigued him; for his cheerfulness was still so great, his complaisance and social disposition were still so entire, that, when any friend was with him, he could not refrain from talking more, and with greater exertion, than the weakness of his body could easily sustain. Mr Smith, therefore, agreed, at Mr Hume's desire, to leave Edinburgh, and go to live in Kirkcaldy with his mother, who then resided in that town. The ingenious and well known Dr Black, professor of chymistry in the university of Edinburgh, undertook occasionally to write Mr Smith an account of the state of his friend's health. Accordingly, on the 22d day of August, Dr Black wrote Mr Smith the following letter: "Since my last, Mr Hume has passed his time pretty easily, but is much weaker. He sits up, goes down stairs once a-day, and amuses himself with reading, but seldom sees any body. He finds, that even the conversation of his most intimate friends fatigues and oppresses him; and it is happy that he does not need it, for he is quite free from anxiety, impatience, or low spirits, and passes his time very well with the assistance of amusing books."

The next day, Mr Smith received a letter from Mr Hume himself, of which what follows is an extract.

[15] Ibid.

Edin. Aug. 23. 1776.
   "*My dearest friend,*
   I am obliged to make use of my nephew's hand in writing to you, as I do
not rise to-day. I go very fast to decline, and last night had a small fever,
which I *hoped* might put a *quicker period* to this tedious illness, but unluckily
it has, in a great measure, gone off.*"*

Three days after, Mr Smith received the following letter from Dr Black.

Edin. Aug. 26. 1776.
   "Dear sir,
   Yesterday, about four o'clock afternoon, Mr Hume expired. the near
approach of his death became evident in the night between Thursday and
Friday, when his disease became excessive, and soon weakened him so
much, that he could no longer rise out of his bed. He continued to the last
perfectly sensible, and free from much pain or feeling of distress. He never
dropped the smallest expression of impatience; but, when he had occasion
to speak to the people about him, always did it with affection and tenderness.
I thought it improper to write to bring you over, especially as I heard that
he had dictated a letter to you, desiring you not to come. – When he became
very weak, it cost him an effort to speak, and he died in such a happy
composure of mind, that nothing could exceed it."

"Thus died," says Mr Smith, in his letter to Mr Strahan,

   "our most excellent and never to be forgotten friend, concerning whose
   philosophical opinions men will no doubt judge variously, every one
   approving, or condemning them, according as they happen to coincide or
   disagree with his own; but concerning whose character and conduct there can
   scarce be a difference of opinion. His temper, indeed, seemed to be more
   happily balanced, if I may be allowed such an expression, than that, perhaps,
   of any other man I have ever known. Even in the lowest state of his fortune,
   his great and necessary frugality never hindered him, on proper occasions,
   from exercising acts both of charity and generosity. It was a frugality founded
   not upon avarice, but upon the love of independency. The extreme gentleness
   of his nature never weakened either the firmness of his mind, or the steadiness
   of his resolutions. His constant pleasantry was the genuine effusion of good
   nature and good humour, tempered with delicacy and modesty; and without
   even the slightest tincture of malignity, so frequently the disagreeable source
   of what is called wit in other men. It never was the meaning of his raillery
   to mortify; and, therefore, far from offending, it seldom failed to please and
   delight even those who were the objects of it. To his friends, who were
   frequently the objects of it, there was not, perhaps, any one of all his great

and amiable qualities, which contributed more to endear his conversation. And that gaiety of temper, so agreeable in society, but which is so often accompanied with frivolous and superficial qualities, was in him certainly attended with the most severe application, the most extensive learning, the greatest depth of thought, and a capacity in every respect the most comprehensive. Upon the whole, I have always considered him, both in his lifetime and since his death, as approaching as nearly to the idea of a perfectly wise and virtuous man, as perhaps the nature of human frailty will permit. I am, &c.

    Adam Smith."

———

Thus far have I proceeded in giving a biographical account of this great literary and worthy man. Hitherto this account has been chiefly derived from printed authorities. I shall now conclude with adding a few anecdotes from my own personal knowledge, joined to some other well known facts, which Mr Hume, in *his Own Life*, has not recorded.

His own Life, as well as Mr Adam Smith's *letter* to *Mr Strahan*, are written with great candour and truth. Mr Hume, like perhaps every man of genius, had a *keeness* of temper, which he happily balanced by a strong and decisive mode of reasoning. His works met with so many and often so rude attacks from a variety of authors, that, though he did not deign to answer them in writing; yet, in conversation, he frequently discovered the resentments which he felt from the indelicate and often ignorant insults of inferior scholars. In all cases of this kind, his forcible mode of expression, the brilliant quick movements of his eyes, and the gestures of his body, discovered the acuteness of his feelings, and the highest marks of contempt as well as of aversion.

One author, however, Dr Campbell, Professor of Morals in the University of Aberdeen, a learned, a worthy, and an ingenious man, wrote a pretty large book against Mr Hume's *Essay on Miracles*, in such a style and manner, and so much like a gentleman, that Mr Hume never spoke of him but with the utmost respect; and often said, that, of all his opponents, Doctor Campbell was not only the most acute, but wrote with the best temper, and in the mildest, though forcible and elegant terms. In the first edition of the *Encyclopædia Britannica*, which was published at Edinburgh in the year 1771, under the word *Abridgment*, as an example of what I then thought to be the best and most useful mode of abridging books, I gave a short view of Mr Hume's *Essay on Miracles*, and of Dr Campbell's *answer* to it. I still think, that, as the article is short, a transcript of it may be of some value, especially to young readers.

"*Abridgment*, in literature, a term signifying the reduction of a book into a smaller compass. The art of conveying much sentiment in a few words, is the happiest talent an author can be possessed of. This talent is peculiarly necessary in the present state of literature; for many writers have acquired the dexterity of spreading a few tritical thoughts over several hundred pages. When an author hits upon a thought that pleases him, he is apt to dwell upon it, to view it in different lights, to force it in improperly, or upon the slightest relations. Though this may be pleasant to the writer, it tires and vexes the reader. There is another great source of diffusion in composition. It is a capital object with an author, whatever be the subject, to give vent to all his best thoughts. When he finds a proper place for them, he is peculiarly happy. But, rather than sacrifice a thought he is fond of, he forces it in by way of digression, or superfluous illustration. If none of these expedients answer his purpose, he has recourse to the margin, a very convenient apartment for all manner of pedantry and impertinence. There is not an author, however correct, but is more or less faulty in this respect. An abridger, however, is not subject to these temptations. The thoughts are not his own; he views them in a cooler and less affectionate manner; he discovers an impropriety in some, a vanity in others, and a want of utility in many. His business, therefore, is to retrench superfluities, digressions, quotations, pedantry, &c. and to lay before the public only what is really useful. This is by no means an easy employment: To abridge some books requires talents equal, if not superior, to those of the author. The facts, spirit, manner, and reasoning, must be preserved; nothing essential, either in argument or illustration, ought to be omitted. The difficulty of the task is the principal reason why we have so few good abridgments. Wynne's abridgement of Locke's Essay on the Human Understanding is, perhaps, the only unexceptionable one in our language. These observations relate solely to such abridgments as are designated for the public. But, when a person wants to set down the substance of any book, a shorter and less laborious method may be followed. It would be foreign to our plan to give examples of abridgments for the public: But as it may be useful, especially to young people, to know how to abridge books for their own use, after giving a few directions, we shall exhibit an example or two, to shew with what ease it may be done.

Read the book carefully; endeavour to learn the principal view of the author; attend to the arguments employed: When you have done so, you will generally find, that what the author uses as new or additional arguments, are, in reality, only collateral ones, or extensions of the principal argument. Take a piece of paper, or a common-place book, put down what the author wants to prove, subjoin the argument or arguments, and you have the substance of the book in a few lines. For example, in his Essay on Miracles, Mr Hume's design is to prove, That miracles, which have not been the immediate objects of our senses, cannot reasonably be believed upon the testimony of others. Now, his argument (for there happens to be but one) is,

'That experience, which in some things is variable, in others uniform, is our *only* guide in reasoning concerning matters of fact. A variable experience gives rise to probability only; an uniform experience amounts to a proof. Our belief of any fact from the testimony of the eye-witnesses is derived from no other principle than our experience in the veracity of human testimony. If the fact attested be miraculous, here arises a contest of two opposite experiences, or proof against proof. Now, a miracle is a violation of the laws of nature; and, as a firm and unalterable experience has established these laws, the proof against a miracle, from the very nature of the fact, is as complete as any argument from experience can possibly be imagined; and, if so, it is an undeniable consequence, that it cannot be surmounted by any proof whatever derived from human testimony.'

In Dr Campbell's Dissertation on Miracles, the author's principal aim is to shew the fallacy of Mr Hume's argument; which he has done most success-fully by another single argument, as follows:

'The evidence arising from human testimony *is not solely* derived from experience; on the contrary, testimony hath a natural influence on belief antecedent to experience. the early and unlimited assent given to testimony by children gradually contracts as they advance in life: It is, therefore, more consonant to truth, to say, that our *diffidence* in testimony is the result of experience, than that our *faith* in it has this foundation. Besides, the uniformity of experience, in favour of any fact, is not a proof against its being reversed in a particular instance. The evidence arising from the single testimony of a man of known veracity will go far to establish a belief in its being actually reversed: If his testimony be confirmed by a few others of the same character, we cannot with-hold our assent to the truth of it. Now, though the operations of nature are governed by uniform laws, and though we have not the testimony of our senses in favour of any *violation* of them, still if, in particular instances, we have the testimony of *thousands* of our fellow-creatures, and those too men of strict integrity, swayed by no motives of ambition or interest, and governed by the principles of common sense, That they were actually eye-witnesses of these violations, the constitution of our nature obliges us to believe them.'

These two examples contain the substance of about 400 pages. – Making private abridgments of this kind has many advantages; it engages us to read with accuracy and attention; it fixes the subject in our minds; and, if we should happen to forget, instead of reading the books again, by glancing a few lines, we are not only in possession of the chief arguments, but recall, in a good measure, the author's manner and method."

Dr Campbell having sent the manuscript of his book against Mr Hume's *Essays on Miracles* to Dr Hugh Blair of Edinburgh, for his opinion of the work, Dr Blair proposed to send the manuscript to Mr Hume himself, which was accordingly done; and Mr Hume returned it to the Doctor accompanied with the following letter. [Letter from Hume to Hugh Blair, c. 1761, inserted here.][16]

In the year 1762, Mr Hume wrote the following letter to Dr Campbell, which does much honour to the writer. [Letter from Hume to George Campbell, January 7, 1762, inserted here.]

In the year 1762, Mr Hume attached himself to the celebrated Rousseau, when the latter was about to be imprisoned, by an *arrêt* of the Parliament of Paris, for publishing his famous romance called *Emile*. Mr Hume was then in Edinburgh. A person, as he says, of merit, but whose name he does not mention, wrote him from Paris, that M. Rousseau intended to come to Britain to procure an asylum from persecution in a land where freedom reigns, and genius and literature of every species are eminently encouraged. M. Rousseau, at the same time, asked Mr Hume's patronage and recommendation when he should arrive in London. Mr Hume, accordingly, wrote to several of his friends in London, in favour of this famous exile; and likewise wrote to himself, assuring him of his zeal and strong desire of doing every thing in his power to serve him. Mr Hume, at the same time, solicited Rousseau to come to Edinburgh, and offered him a secure retreat in his own house as long as he should chuse. Mr Hume's principal motives for making this offer were the celebrity of Rousseau's genius and talents, and particularly the persecution he suffered from the bigots of his own country, joined to the weak and diseased state of his body, occasioned by the passing of blood through his urethra. This disorder, like most chronical distempers, rendered his mind peevish, and, of course, made his temper and his actions frequently bizarre and disagreeable, especially to strangers. Mr Hume seems, in some parts of the controversy, not to have made sufficient allowances for the weak and painful condition of his antagonist's body. Pain, when long continued, not only induces general debility, but frets and disturbs the mind, and makes it suspicious and impatient. This circumstance, it is probable, was the principal cause of the rupture that happened between these two learned and most ingenious men. Mr Hume, however, through the whole controversy, treats M. Rousseau with humanity and respect. He, indeed, defends himself strenuously against the calumnies and insinuations of his illustrious opponent; and he was fully entitled to do so.

At the instigation of Mr Hume, Rousseau arrived in England in Spring 1766; and Mr Hume procured a pleasant residence for him in a country house

---

[16] *The following letter was sent by MR HUME to the Author of the Delineation of the Nature and Obligation of Morality.* [Letter from Hume to James Balfour, March 15, 1753, inserted here.]

belonging to Mr Davenport, a gentleman distinguished by his birth, by his fortune, and by his merit. This villa is situated in the country of Derby, and is called *Wooton*. As soon as Rousseau arrived at Wooton, he was charmed with the situation of the place, as well as with the adjacent country; and wrote Mr Hume, in the most polite and grateful terms, how much he esteemed his friendship and patronage.

When on their route to Britain, one evening at Calais, Mr Hume asked Rousseau, if he would accept a pension from the king of Britain, provided it should be obtained? Rousseau replied, that he found some difficulty in answering the question; but that he would refer the affair to Lord Marshall, who was a great friend to Rousseau. Encouraged by this response, Mr Hume, as soon as he arrived in London, applied to General Conway, then Secretary of State, and likewise to General Graeme, Secretary and Chamberlain to the Queen, asking a pension to Rousseau, which was readily granted, on the sole condition that the affair should be kept secret. This condition was highly agreeable to Rousseau, who loved to conceal such favours as he occasionally received, and particularly in what related to money-matters, because he thought they degraded the spirit of independency which he always, at least, pretended to possess. But Mr Hume had, for some time, anxiously attended to the ease and interest of M. Rousseau, who continually complained both of bodily pain and of poverty, discovered with astonishment, that the last complaint of extreme poverty was false. He employed this last artifice (for the first was no artifice), Mr Hume remarks, to render himself, as a man of genius, more interesting, and to excite the compassion of the public.

The time which Mr Hume spent with M. Rousseau gradually enabled him to unfold his real character. I at last perceived, says he, with infinite pain, that this ingenious man was born for tumult and storms; but, as Mr Hume had done every thing to accommodate Rousseau, and to render his situation comfortable, he never dreamed that he himself was to become a victim of his rage and peevishness. The origin of the rupture between these two great men took its rise from a ridiculous circumstance. Mr Horace Walpole, who, it would appear, was no great friend to Rousseau, wrote a letter, under the fictitious designation of *Frederic King of Prussia*, inviting him to come and reside in his Court at Berlin. Of this affair Mr Hume had no knowledge. But Rousseau, from what circumstances it is difficult to conjecture, imagined that Mr Hume had written and circulated that letter with a view to perplex and burlesque him. Mr Hume, in this more than foolish affair, excuses Mr Walpole by calling it an innocent *plaisanterie*. But, when the genius, the temper, and the diseased state of Rousseau's body are considered, instead of a *plaisanterie*, it was a direct *cruelty*, and had, by a natural mistake, the unhappy effect of converting two cordial and celebrated friends into mortal enemies.

M. Rousseau, though Mr Hume procured him a grant of a pension from his Majesty, actuated by some whimsical ideas of independency, and a notion that his best friend meant to betray him, refused to accept of it. Mr Hume, by friendly letters, pressed Rousseau to accept of the pension; but the latter obstinately persisted in his denial, and even reproached Mr Hume, in terms the most indecent, for so successfully endeavouring to serve him, and to render his circumstances easy for life.

The supposititious letter, written in the name of the King of Prussia, after copies of it had been circulated over Europe, was at last published in the *St James's Chronicle*. It was in that News-paper which Rousseau first saw this imprudent and ill-judged production. M. Rousseau immediately wrote to the Editors of the St James's Chronicle complaining bitterly of the imposture, and indirectly insinuating that the pretended letter was composed by Mr Hume. When Mr Hume learnt that he was suspected by M. Rousseau to be the author and publisher of this letter, it gave him much uneasiness. Mr Hume remarks, that, after the great attention and beneficent services he had, with unremitting perseverance, bestowed on M. Rousseau, he was suddenly become the object of his resentment and obloquy, upon no other foundation than a foolish and even absurd suspicion. Mr Hume, notwithstanding this unhappy affair, continued to protect and cherish Rousseau by friendly letters as well as by good offices. But, soon afterwards, Rousseau threw off every mask, and accused Mr Hume openly as a traitorous enemy, without assigning any reasons but what were evidently capricious, frivolous, and contemptible. I shall mention one example only. The first night after these two remarkable men left Paris, in their way to Britain, they both slept in the same chamber. M. Rousseau, in the last letter he ever wrote to Mr Hume, which is of an enormous length, says, that during the night, Mr Hume several times, called out, with unusual vehemence, *Je tiens J.J. Rousseau*. He, however, acknowledges, that he knew not whether Mr Hume was sleeping or waking. The expression, in the French language, is strong; but, like many verbs, *tenir* is frequently used in very different and even opposite senses. Rousseau interpreted the expression thus: *I have Rousseau in my possession*, or, *I hold him fast*. Every time these words were repeated, Rousseau tells us that he trembled with terror. This and some similar insignificant circumstances gave rise to a complete rupture between those two great men.

When the periodical paper called the *Edinburgh Magazine and Review* was publishing in the year 1773, the late Rev. Dr Henry, then one of the ministers of this city, a most laborious clergyman, as well as a facetious and good-humoured companion, brought forth the second volume of his *History of Great Britain*. Dr Henry, it was said, applied, in the most earnest manner, to Mr Hume to give an account of that volume in the Review, to which Mr Hume gave his assent. When the manuscript appeared, after reading it, the praises appeared to be so high-strained, that the Reviewers, in my presence, agreed that Mr Hume's account was meant as a burlesque upon the author. It was, therefore, committed to the farther consideration of one of their number, who still continued to be of the same opinion, and, accordingly, raised the encomiums so high, that no person could mistake the supposed meaning of the writer. The types of the Manuscript, in this last form, were composed, and proof-sheets sent to Mr Hume for his perusal and corrections. To the astonishment of the Reviewers, Mr Hume wrote them an angry letter, complaining, in the highest terms, of the freedoms they had used with his manuscript, and declaring that in the account he had given of Dr Henry's History, he was perfectly sincere. Upon which, Mr Hume's review was cancelled, and another was written by a member of the Society, condemning the book in terms perhaps too severe; so that Mr Hume's intention of serving Dr Henry was not only abortive, but produced an opposite effect.

Another circumstance in the life of Mr Hume must not be omitted. When a young man, he applied to be made *Professor of Moral Philosophy* in the University of Edinburgh. The Scottish clergy took an alarm. They represented that Mr Hume, in his principles, was an *Athiest*, or at least a *Deist*; and, consequently, that he was very ill-qualified to teach morals to youth in a Christian country. Their remonstrances were effectual; and Mr Hume's application was rejected. From that moment, as was natural, he conceived a rooted antipathy to the generality of Scottish clergymen. This antipathy was not, however, indiscriminate; for he was in intimate habits of friendship and sociality with several of the ministers of the Church of Scotland; as the celebrated Dr Robertson, Dr Blair, Dr Wallace, Mr Jardine, Dr Wishart, Dr Drysdale, Mr Home, the author of the ingenious and popular tragedy of *Douglas*, and many others. These reverend and learned gentlemen, however much they differed from Mr Hume in religious or philosophical opinions, were fully sensible of his Genius as an Author, and of his Worth as a Man.

I shall mention another anecdote. – On summer evening, I went to sup with *Lord Kames*. Soon after, Dr John Warden, a worthy, a respectable, and an useful clergyman of this City, came to Lord Kames's house with the same intention. Lord Kames was then dictating to his clerk. When his Lordship had finished, he led us to a drawing room, which was situated to the north, because the night was remarkably warm. Here we had conversed for some time, when Mr Hume joined the party. The conversation went on in the most agreeable manner. A sermon had just been published by a Mr Edwards with the strange title of *Usefulness of Sin*. Dr Warden told us, that he had read this sermon. Mr Hume repeated the words: The *Usefulness of Sin!* I suppose, says he, Mr Edwards adopts the system of Leibnitz, that *all is for the best, but*, added he, with his usual keenness of eye and forcible manner of expression, *What the Devil does the fellow make of hell and damnation?* Upon Mr Hume's pronouncing these words, for what reason I could never conjecture, Dr Warden took his hat and left the room. Lord Kames followed him, and pressed him with anxiety to return, but he obstinately refused.

After a very tedious illness, Mr Hume expired at Edinburgh on the 25th day of August 1776, in the 65th year of his age. – Some particulars relating to his death I have already given to my Readers in the letters of Dr Black to Dr Smith on that occasion.

Some time after Mr Hume's death, two Essays, ascribed to him, were published at London; the one on *Suicide*, and the other on the *Immortality of the Soul*. These essays, from the mode of writing and of reasoning, appeared evidently to be genuine productions of Mr Hume. I once intended, in this life of Mr Hume, to give an abridged view of these arguments in these two ingenious and plausible Essays. But, after more mature reflection, as I considered the sophistry of the reasoning, and the injurious effects it might have on society; and as an abridgment of them would only be another mode of administering the poison they contain, I shall now relinquish that part of my subject, and conclude with a few general remarks.

Upon the whole, Mr Hume was one of those extraordinary characters which sometimes, but rarely, appear, like luminous meteors, in almost every civilized country in Europe. For elegance of composition, for dexterous and forcible reasoning, for good humour and pleasantry in conversation, and for uniformity of temper and conduct, he was not to be excelled. Before his death, Mr Hume had written his last will, in which, beside other appointments, he allotted a certain sum for building his tomb, which he ordered to be erected in the Calton burying-ground, which is situated on a pretty high hill almost within the City of Edinburgh. Like himself, his tomb is build of massy but unadorned stones, with this simple inscription, DAVID HUME, ESQ. After the tomb was finished, one summer day I was sauntering on the Caltonhill, in company with the late well-known Dr Gilbert Stuart, and Dr John Brown, author of what is called the *Brownian System of Physic*. Dr Brown, who was a man of rough and course manners, observed to a mason, who was hewing a pavement stone, "Friend," said he, "this is a strong and massy building; but how do you think the honest gentleman can get out at the resurrection?" The mason archly replied, "Sir, I have secured that point; for I have put the *key under the door*."

100
WILLIAM MORGAN:
MEMOIRS OF RICHARD PRICE

William Morgan, *Memoirs of the life of the Rev. Richard Price*, London, Printed for R. Hunter [etc.], 1815, viii, 189 p.
Selections; pp. 15–17, 23–25.

Dissenting minister Richard Price (1723–1791) was a friendly critic of Hume. Price's nephew – son of his sister – was William Morgan (1750–1833), who was born in Bridgend, Glamorganshire, Wales, son of a surgeon. Morgan briefly worked for a London apothecary, but later, through Price's help, secured a prominent position in an insurance company. In addition to his publications on economic matters, Morgan edited Price's works and wrote *Memoirs* of his uncle which appeared in 1815. In the *Memoirs*, Morgan describes the cordial relationship between Hume and Price. He notes that on one occasion during a visit at Price's house, Hume acknowledged that Price "had succeeded in convincing him that his arguments were inconclusive."

[Richard Price] moved to Newington Green in the year 1758, in order to be near his congregation, and in that retired situation to pursue his studies with more tranquility than he could have done in a narrow street and noisy thoroughfare at Hackney. It was, however, during his residence in this latter place that he published his treatise on the foundations of morals – a work, which was the fruit of his studies from his earliest years, and which first introduced him to an acquaintance with the late excellent Dr. Adams; and as this acquaintance arose, not only from the similarity of their sentiments on this, but on many other important points in morals and religion, it produced a friendship between them which terminated only with their lives. The modesty, candor, and benevolence displayed in this work, conciliated the minds even of those who differed most widely in their sentiments from the author. In this number Mr. Hume should be particularly mentioned, who, admiring the liberal manner in which his doctrines had been controverted, conceived so favourable an opinion of the writer, that it gave rise to an acquaintance, which was continued on both sides with uninterrupted esteem and friendship. Mr. Hume had been so little accustomed to civility from his theological adversaries, that his admiration was naturally excited by the least appearance of it in any of their publications. Dr. Douglas (the late bishop of Salisbury), Dr. Adams, and Mr. Price, were splendid exceptions to this rudeness and bigotry. Having been opposed by these divines with the candor and respect which were due to his abilities, and which it is shameful should ever be wanting in any controversy, he was desirous of meeting them all together, in order to spend a few hours in familiar conversation with them. – Accordingly, they all dined by invitation at Mr. Cadell's in the Strand; and, as might be expected, passed their time in the utmost harmony and good humour. In a subsequent interview with Mr. Price, when Mr. Hume visited him at his house at Newington Green, he candidly acknowledged that on one point Mr. Price had succeeded in convincing him that his arguments were inconclusive; but it does not appear that Mr. Hume, in consequence of this conviction, made any alteration in the subsequent edition of his Essays. ...

Regarding himself as incapable of giving effect to his moral instructions by delivering them from the pulpit, he consoled himself with the hope of rendering them useful to the world by conveying them in another manner. With this view he formed the sermons which he had preached on *private prayer* into a dissertation on that subject, and in the year 1767 published it with three other dissertations, on Providence – on the Junction of Virtuous Men in the heavenly State – and on Historical Evidence and Miracles. – This work had engaged is attention and occupied his time at intervals for more than seven years; and it was not without great diffidence and hesitation, that he was at last induced to publish it. – The Dissertation on Miracles had been written as early as the year 1760, and read to Mr. Canton, Mr. Rose, and some other friends, who all concurred in recommending the publication of it. In this dissertation, which was intended as an answer to Mr. Hume's arguments against the credibility of miracles, Mr. Price had, as he thought, expressed himself improperly, by speaking of the *poor sophistry* of those arguments, and using other language of the same kind. – When he sent a copy of his book to Mr. Hume, who was then one of the under-secretaries of state, he made an apology to him, and promised that nothing of the kind should appear in another edition. He received in consequence a very flattering letter from Mr. Hume, which he regarded more as a matter of civility, than as a proof of its having wrought any change in the sentiments of that philosopher. When the work, however, appeared in a second edition he fulfilled his promise, and sent him a correct copy; for which he immediately received an acknowledgment, expressive of Mr. Hume's *wonder at such scrupulosity in one of Mr. Price's profession.*

101
ISAAC DISRAELI:
CALAMITIES OF AUTHORS

Isaac Disraeli, *Calamities of authors; including some inquiries respecting their moral and literary characters*, London, J. Murray, 1812, 2 v.
"Literary Hatred," complete; from *Calamites and Quarrels of Authors*, London, Frederick Warne, 1869, pp. 130–138.

Isaac Disraeli (1766–1848) was the author of *Miscellanies; or Literary Recreations* (1796), contained in this collection. Among Disraeli's most popular works is *Calamities of Authors*, which describes tragedies in the lives of noted writers. In a section titled "Miseries of Successful Authors," he presents a short discussion of Hume's disappointments, based on what Hume himself reveals in "My Own Life." Disraeli states,

> Hume is an author so celebrated, a philosopher so serene, and a man so extremely amiable, if not fortunate, that we may be surprised to meet his name inscribed in a catalogue of literary calamities. Look into his literary life, and you will discover that the greater portion was mortified and angried; and that the stoic so lost his temper, that had not circumstances intervened which did not depend on himself, Hume had abandoned his country and changed his name!

Elsewhere in the work, he presents a detailed account of Gilbert Stuart's efforts to ruin the literary reputation of historian Robert Henry. In 1773 Hume wrote a flattering review of Robert Henry's *History of Great Britain* Volume 2, which he submitted to Stuart's newly created journal. Stuart, however, was bent on not only attacking Henry's performance but destroying his literary career and altered Hume's review to give it a more sarcastic tone. At the outset of the review, Hume wrote "And the reader will scarcely find in our language, except in the work of the celebrated Dr. Robertson, any performance that unite together so perfectly the great points of entertainment and instruction!" However, in the proof sheets, Stuart replaced Robertson's name with that of Daniel McQueen – the author of the highly critical *Letters on Mr. Hume's History of Great Britain* (1756), contained earlier in this collection. Stuart also added a concluding paragraph of mock adulation. These sarcastic shifts in meaning prompted the following from Hume:

> I wish you woud check your Printer with some Severity for the Freedoms he uses; I suppose to divert himself. He has substituted the Name of Dr MacQueen, whom certainly I did not think of, instead of Dr Robertson, to whose Merit I meant to do some Justice. The last Paragraph which seems to be entirely his own, is also too high a Praise for a new Author like Dr Henry. But, if you want a few Sentences to fill up the Page, I have added them, and beg that you woud take care, that the Printer throw them off faithfully. [Hume to Stuart, December 23, 1773]

Stuart ultimately rejected Hume's submission, and supplied his own harsh review of Henry. He closes his review quoting from Hume:

> It is an observation made by father Paul, and it has been repeated by Mr Hume, that every performance should be as complete as possible within itself, and should never refer, for any thing material, to other works [Hume, *History*, Appendix 2]. This maxim, so judicious, is totally disregarded in the publication before us. ...
>
> ... Diffuse, vulgar, and ungrammatical, he strips history of all her ornaments. As an antiquary, he wants accuracy and knowledge; and as an historian, he is destitute of fire, taste, and sentiment. His work is a gazette, in which we find actions and events without their causes; and in which we meet with the names, not the characters, of personages. The mind of his reader is affected with no agreeable emotions: it is awakened only to disgust and fatigue. [*Edinburgh Magazine and Review*, 1774, Vol. 1, February, pp. 199–207, March, pp. 264–270]

Offended at Hume's letter, Stuart later wrote that Hume "behaved ill in the affair, and I am preparing to chastise him." The June 1774 and April 1775 reviews of Whitaker's *History of Manchester* in the *Edinburgh Magazine and Review* – authored by Stuart – include comments especially critical of Hume (for quotations see the entry on Whitaker in *Early Responses to Hume's History*).

However, the journal as a whole was not inflexibly negative towards Hume. In their reviews of Charles Crawford's *Dissertation on the Phaedon of Plato* and Alexander Gerard's *Essay on Genius*, at least one of which was authored by Stuart, Hume is praised for his theory of the association of ideas (see *Early Responses to Hume's Metaphysics and Epistemology*). We also find a not unfavourable comment about Hume in their review of de Chastellux's *Essay on Public Happiness* (1772); the reviewer writes the following:

On the subject of population, we have an account of the arguments employed on both sides, by Mr Hume and Dr Wallace, on the populousness of ancient nations. In this question, the author, consistently with his principles, embraces the opinion of Mr Hume, a writer, of whom he seldom speaks without testifying his admiration. [*Edinburgh Magazine and Review*, November 1774, Vol. 2, pp. 760–770]

From the topics and nature of these discussions of Hume, it appears that Stuart's attack was narrowly focused on Hume's *History*, and not Hume's writings as a whole.

Disraeli, gaining access to Stuart's private correspondence, reveals the deep contempt that Stuart had for Henry and other Scottish writers, and how he reacted to Hume's support for Henry. Disraeli's *Calamities* was favourably received in the *Quarterly Review*, which noted the work's ability to captivate the reader:

[T]he middle of the book is much better than the two ends: it is one of those works which are designed for the breakfast table and the sofa, and is so well adapted for its purpose, that he who takes it up will not readily lay it down. The matter is as amusing as any lover of light reading can desire, and of such a desultory kind that a comment might easily be made as extensive as the text. [*Quarterly Review*, September 1812, Vol. 8, p. 93 ff.]

William Smellie, who co-edited the *Edinburgh Magazine and Review* with Stuart, gives his own account of the story in *Literary and Characteristical Lives* (1800), contained in this collection. For more on Stuart's opinion of Hume see the editor's introduction to Stuart's *View of Society in Europe* (1778) in *Early Responses to Hume's History of England* (2002).

LITERARY HATRED.
EXHIBITING A CONSPIRACY AGAINST AN AUTHOR.

In the peaceful walks of literature we are startled at discovering genius with the mind, and, if we conceive the instrument it guides to be a stiletto, with the hand of an assassin – irascible, vindictive, armed with indiscriminate satire, never pardoning the merit of rival genius, but fastening on it throughout life, till, in the moral Retribution of human nature, these very passions, by their ungratified cravings, have tended to annihilate the being who fostered them. These passions among literary men are with none more inextinguishable than among *provincial writers*. – Their bad feelings are concentrated by their local contraction. The proximity of men of genius seems to produce a familiarity which excites hatred or contempt; while he who is afflicted with disordered passions imagines that he is urging his own claims to genius by denying them to their possessor. A whole life passed in harassing the industry or the genius which he has not equalled; and instead of running the open career as a competitor, only skulking as an assassin by their side, is presented in the object now before us.

Dr. GILBERT STUART seems early in life to have devoted himself to literature; but his habits were irregular, and his passions fierce. The celebrity of Robertson, Blair, and Henry, with other Scottish brothers, diseased his mind with a most envious rancour. He confined all his literary efforts to the pitiable motive of destroying theirs; he was prompted to every one of his historical works by the mere desire of discrediting some work of Robertson; and his numerous critical labours were all directed to annihilate the genius of his country. How he converted his life into its own scourge, how wasted talents he might have cultivated into perfection, lost every trace of humanity, and finally perished, devoured by his own fiend-like passions, – shall be illustrated by the following narrative, collected from a correspondence now lying before me, which the author carried on with his publisher in London. I shall copy out at some length the hopes and disappointments of the literary adventurer – the colours are not mine; I am dipping my pencil in the palette of the artist himself.

In June, 1773, was projected in the Scottish capital "The Edinburgh Magazine and Review." Stuart's letters breathe the spirit of rapturous confidence. He had combined the sedulous attention of the intelligent Smellie, who was to be the printer, with some very honourable critics; Professor Baron, Dr. Blacklock, and Professor Richardson; and the first numbers were executed with more talent than periodical publications had then exhibited. But the hardiness of Stuart's opinions, his personal attacks, and the acrimony of his literary libels, presented a new feature in Scottish literature, of such ugliness and horror, that every honourable man soon averted his face from this *boutefeu*.

He designed to ornament his first number with –

"A print of my Lord Mouboddo in his quadruped form. I must, therefore, most earnestly beg that you will purchase for me a copy of it in some of the Macaroni print shops. It is not to be procured at Edinburgh. They are afraid to vend it here. We are to take it on the footing of a figure of an animal, not yet described; and are to give a grave, yet satirical account of it, in the manner of Buffon. It would not be proper to allude to his lordship but in a very distant manner."

It was not, however, ventured on; and the nondescript animal was still confined to the windows of "the Macaroni print shops." It was, however, the bloom of the author's fancy, and promised all the mellow fruits it afterwards produced.

In September this ardour did not abate: –

"The proposals are issued; the subscriptions in the booksellers' shops astonish; correspondents flock in; and, what will surprise you, the timid proprietors of the 'Scots' Magazine' have come to the resolution of dropping their work. You stare at all this, and so do I too."

Thus he flatters himself he is to annihilate his rival, without even striking the first blow. The appearance of his first number is to be the moment when their last is to come forth. Authors, like the discoverers of mines, are the most sanguine creatures in the world: Gilbert Stuart afterwards flattered himself Dr. Henry was lying at the point of death from the scalping of his tomahawk pen; but of this anon.

On the publication of the first number, in November, 1773, all is exultation; and an account is facetiously expected that "a thousand copies had emigrated from the Row and Fleet-street."

There is a serious composure in the letter of December, which seems to be occasioned by the tempered answer of his London correspondent. The work was more suited to the meridian of Edinburgh; and from causes sufficiently obvious, its personality and causticity. Stuart, however, assures his friend that "the second number you will find better than the first, and the third better than the second."

The next letter is dated March 4, 1774, in which I find our author still in good spirits: –

"The Magazine rises, and promises much, in this quarter. Our artillery has silenced all opposition. The rogues of the uplifted hands decline the combat." These rogues are the clergy, and some others, who had "uplifted hands" from the vituperative nature of their adversary; for he tells us that "now the clergy are silent, the town-council, have had the presumption to oppose us; and have threatened Creech (the publisher in Edinburgh) with the terror of making him a constable for his insolence. A pamphlet on the abuses of Heriot's Hospital, including a direct proof of perjury in the provost, was the punishment inflicted in return. And new papers are forging to chastise them, in regard to the poors' rate, which is again started; the improper choice of professors; and violent stretches of the impost. The *liberty of the press*, in its fullest extent, is to be employed against them."

Such is the language of reform, and the spirit of a reformist! A little private malignity thus ferments a good deal of public spirit; but patriotism must be independent to be pure. If the "Edinburgh Review" continues to succeed in its sale, as Stuart fancies, Edinburgh itself may be in some danger. His perfect contempt of his contemporaries is amusing: –

"Monboddo's second volume is published, and, with Kaimes, will appear in our next; the former is a childish performance; the latter rather better. We are to treat them with a good deal of freedom. I observe an amazing falling off in the English Reviews. We beat them hollow. I fancy they have no assistance but from the Dissenters, – a dull body of men. The Monthly will not easily recover the death of Hawkesworth; and I suspect that Langhorne has forsaken them; for I see no longer his pen."

We are now hastening to the sudden and the moral catastrophe of our tale. The thousand copies which had emigrated to London remained there, little disturbed by public inquiry; and in Scotland, the personal animosity against almost every literary character there, which had inflamed the sale, became naturally the latent cause of its extinction; for its life was but a feverish existence, and its florid complexion carried with it the seeds of its dissolution. Stuart at length quarrelled with his coadjutor, Smellie, for altering his reviews. Smellie's prudential dexterity was such, that, in an article designed to level Lord Kaimes with Lord Monboddo, the whole libel was completely metamorphosed into a panegyric. They were involved in a lawsuit about "a blasphemous paper." And now the enraged Zoilus complains of "his hours of peevishness and dissatisfaction." He acknowledges that "a circumstance had happened which had broke his peace and ease altogether for some weeks." And now he resolves that this great work shall quietly sink into a mere compilation from the London periodical works. Such, then, is the progress of malignant genius! The author, like him who invented the brazen bull of Phalaris, is writhing in that machine of tortures he had contrived for others.

We now come to a very remarkable passage: it is the frenzied language of disappointed wickedness.

17 June, 1774.

"It is an infinite disappointment to me that the Magazine does not grow in London; I thought the soil had been richer. But it is my constant fate to be disappointed in everything I attempt; I do not think I ever had a wish that was gratified; and never dreaded an event that did not come. With this felicity of fate, I wonder how the devil I could turn projector. I am now sorry that I left London; and the moment that I have money enough to carry me back to it, I shall set off. *I mortally detest and abhor this place, and everybody in it*. Never was there a city where there was so much pretension to knowledge, and that had so little of it. The solemn foppery, and the gross stupidity of the Scottish literati, are perfectly insupportable. I shall drop my idea of a Scots newspaper. Nothing will do in this country that has common sense in it; only cant, hypocrisy, and superstition will flourish here. *A curse on the country, and all the men, women, and children of it!*"

Again. –

"The publication is too good for the country. There are very few men of taste or erudition on this side of the Tweed. Yet every idiot one meets with lays claim to both. Yet the success of the Magazine is in reality greater than we could expect, considering that we have every clergyman in the kingdom to oppose it, and that the magistracy of the place are every moment threatening its destruction."

And, therefore, this recreant Scot anathematizes the Scottish people for not applauding blasphemy, calumny, and every species of literary criminality! Such are the monstrous passions that swell out the poisonous breast of genius, deprived of every moral restraint; and such was the demoniac irritability which prompted a wish in Collot d'Herbois to set fire to the four quarters of the city of Lyons; while, in his "tender mercies," the kennels of the streets were running with the blood of its inhabitants – remembering still that the Lyonese had, when he was a miserable actor, hissed him off the stage!

Stuart curses his country, and retreats to London. Fallen, but not abject; repulsed, but not altered; degraded, but still haughty. No change of place could operate any in his heart. He was born in literary crime, and he perished in it. It was now "The English Review" was instituted, with his idol Whitaker, the historian of Manchester, and others. He says, "To Whitaker he assigns the palm of history in preference to Hume and Robertson." I have heard that he considered himself higher than Whitaker, and ranked himself with Montesquieu. He negotiated for Whitaker and himself a Doctor of Laws' degree; and they were now in the titular possession of all the fame which a dozen pieces could bestow! In "The English Review" broke forth all the genius of Stuart in an unnatural warfare of Scotchmen in London against Scotchmen at Edinburgh. "The bitter herbs," which seasoned it against Blair, Robertson, Gibbon, and the ablest authors of the age, at first provoked the public appetite, which afterwards indignantly rejected the palatable garbage.

But to proceed with our *Literary Conspiracy*, which was a pity of invention perhaps not to be paralleled in literary history. That the peace of mind of such an industrious author as Dr. HENRY was for a considerable time destroyed; that the sale of a work on which Henry had expended much of his fortune and his life was stopped; and that, when covered with obloquy and ridicule, in despair he left Edinburgh for London, still encountering the same hostility; that all this was the work of the same hand perhaps was never even known to its victim. The multiplied forms of this Proteus of the Malevoli were still but one devil; fire or water, or a bull or a lion; still it was the same Proteus, the same Stuart.

From the correspondence before me I am enabled to correct the commencement and the end of this literary conspiracy, with all its intermediate links. It thus commences: –

25 Nov. 1773.
"We have been attacked from different quarters, and Dr. Henry in particular has given a long and a dull defence of his sermon. I have replied to it with a degree of spirit altogether unknown in this country. The reverend historian was perfectly astonished, and has actually invited the Society for Propagating Christian Knowledge to arm in his cause! I am about to be persecuted by the whole clergy, and I am about to persecute them in my turn. They are hot and zealous; I am cool and dispassionate, like a determined sceptic; since I have entered the lists I must fight; I must gain the victory, or perish like a man."

13 Dec. 1773.
"David Hume wants to review Henry; but that task is so precious that I will undertake it myself. Moses, were he to ask it as a favour, should not have it; yea, not even the man after God's own heart."

4 March, 1774.
"This month Henry is utterly demolished; his sale is stopped, many of his copies are returned; and his old friends have forsaken him; pray, in what state is he in London? Henry has delayed his London journey; you cannot easily conceive how exceedingly he is humbled.[1]

I wish I could transport myself to London to review him for the Monthly. A fire there, and in the Critical, would perfectly annihilate him. Could you do nothing in the latter? To the former I suppose David Hume has transcribed the criticism he intended for us. It is precious, and would divert you. I keep a proof of it in my cabinet for the amusement of friends. This great philosopher begins to dote."[2]

Stuart prepares to assail Henry, on his arrival in London, from various quarters – to lower the value of his history in the estimation of the purchasers.

---

[1] It may be curious to present Stuart's idea of the literary talents of Henry. Henry's unhappy turn for humour, and a style little accordant with historical dignity, lie fairly open to the critic's animadversion. But the reach and application of the writer, for that day, were considerable, and are still appreciated. But we are told that "he neither furnishes entertainment nor instruction. Diffuse, vulgar, and ungrammatical, he strips history of all her ornaments. As an antiquary, he wants accuracy and knowledge; and, as an historian, be is destitute of fire, taste, and sentiment. His work is a gazette, in which we find actions and events, without their causes; and in which we meet with the names, without the characters of personages. He has amassed all the refuse and lumber of the times he would record." Stuart never imagined that the time would arrive when the name of Henry would be familiar to English readers, and by many that of Stuart would not be recollected.

[2] The critique on Henry, in the *Monthly Review*, was written by Hume – and, because the philosopher was candid, he is here said to have doted.

21 March, 1774.

"To-morrow morning Henry sets off for London, with immense hopes of selling his history. I wish he had delayed till our last review of him had reached your city. But I really suppose that he has little probability of getting any gratuity. The trade are too sharp to give precious gold for perfect nonsense. I wish sincerely that I could enter Holborn the same hour with him. He should have a repeated fire to combat with. I entreat that you may be so kind as to let him feel some of your thunder. I shall never forget the favour. If Whitaker is in London, he could give a blow. Paterson will give him a knock. Strike by all means. The wretch will tremble, grow pale, and return with a consciousness of his debility. I entreat I may bear from you a day or two after you have seen him. He will complain grievously of me to Strahan and Rose. I shall send you a paper about him – an advertisement from Parnassus, in the manner of him Boccalini."

March, 1774.

"Dr. Henry has by this time reached you. I think you ought to pay your respects to him in the Morning Chronicle. If you would only transcribe his jests, it would make him perfectly ridiculous. See, for example, what he says of St. Dunstan. A word to the wise."

March 27, 1774.

"I have a thousand thanks to give you for your insertion of the paper in the London *Chronicle*, and for the part you propose to act in regard to Henry. I could wish that you knew for certain his being in London before you strike the first blow. An inquiry at Cadell's will give this. When you have an enemy to attack, I shall in return give my best assistance, and aim at him a mortal blow, and rush forward to his overthrow, though the flames of hell should start up to oppose me.

It pleases me, beyond what I can express, that Whitaker has an equal contempt for Henry. The idiot threatened, when he left Edinburgh, that he would find a method to manage the Reviews, and that he would oppose their panegyric to our censure. Hume has behaved ill in the affair, and I am preparing to chastise him. You may expect a series of papers in the Magazine, pointing out a multitude of his errors, and ascertaining his ignorance of English history. It was too much for my temper to be assailed both by infidels and believers. My pride could not submit to it. I shall act in my defence with a spirit which it seems they have not expected."

11 April, 1774.

"I received with infinite pleasure the annunciation of the great man into the capital. It is forcible and excellent; and you have my best thanks for it. You improve amazingly. The poor creature will be stupified with amazement.

Inclosed is a paper for him. Boccalini will follow. I shall fall upon a method to let David know Henry's transaction about his review. It is mean to the last degree. But what could one expect from the most ignorant and the most contemptible man alive? Do you ever see Macfarlane? He owes me a favour for his history of George III., and would give a fire for the packet. The idiot is to be Moderator for the ensuing Assembly. It shall not, however, be without opposition.

Would the paragraph about him from the inclosed leaf of the 'Edinburgh Review' be any disgrace to the *Morning Chronicle?*"

20th May, 1774.

"Boccalini I thought of transmitting, when the reverend historian, for whose use it was intended, made his appearance at Edinburgh. But it will not be lost. He shall most certainly see it. David's critique was most acceptable. It is a curious specimen in one view of insolent vanity, and in another of contemptible meanness. The old historian begins to dote, and the new one was never out of dotage."

3 *April,* 1775.

"I see every day that what is written to a man's disparagement is never forgot nor forgiven. Poor Henry is on the point of death, and his friends declare that I have killed him. I received the information as a compliment, and begged they would not do me so much honour."

But Henry and his history long survived Stuart and his *critiques*; and Robertson, Blair, and Kaimes, with others he assailed, have all taken their due ranks in public esteem. What niche does Stuart occupy? His historical works possess the show, without the solidity, of research; hardy paradoxes, and an artificial style of momentary brilliancy, are none of the lasting materials of history. This shadow of "Montesquieu," for he conceived him only to be his fit rival, derived the last consolations of life from an obscure corner of a Burton ale-house – there, in rival potations, with two or three other disappointed authors, they regaled themselves on ale they could not always pay for, and recorded their own literary celebrity, which had never taken place. Some time before his death, his asperity was almost softened by melancholy; with a broken spirit, he reviewed himself; a victim to that unrighteous ambition which sought to build up its greatness with the ruins of his fellow-countrymen; prematurely wasting talents which might have been directed to literary eminence. And Gilbert Stuart died as he had lived, a victim to intemperance, physical and moral!

102
HENRY MACKENZIE:
AN ACCOUNT OF THE LIFE
AND WRITINGS OF JOHN HOME

Henry Mackenzie, *An account of the life and writings of John Home, esq.*,
Edinburgh, Printed for A. Constable, 1822, vii, 184 p.
Selections; from 1822 edition, pp. 20–28.

Henry Mackenzie (1745–1831) was the author of "The Story of La Roche,"
contained in this collection. On June 22, 1812, Mackenzie read an
"Account of the Life of John Home" before the *Royal Society of Edinburgh.*
Having no initial intention of publishing the piece, he was prevailed upon by
friends who believed it would be of more than local Scottish interest, and appeal
to readers in England as well. In 1822 the work appeared in print, both as a
single book and as part of an 1822 three-volume collection of Home's *Works.*
Mackenzie notes in the preface that he indulged in reflections on his literary
friends whom he had survived. One of these is Hume, to whom he devotes
several pages. Mackenzie describes Hume as having "two minds," one for
metaphysical scepticism, and another "natural, and playful, which made his
conversation delightful to his friends." He discusses Adam Smith's reaction to
Mackenzie's "La Roche," the Select Society to which Hume belonged, Hume's
exclusion from the *Edinburgh Review*, how Ferguson's authorship of *Sister Peg*
was kept from him, and Hume's membership in the Poker club. Mackenzie's
manuscript of this work is contained in the National Library of Scotland,
Acc. 10686.

But the most illustrious of that circle [of John Home's friends] was David
Hume, who had a sincere affection for his poetical namesake, - an affection
which was never abated during the life of that celebrated man. The unfortunate
nature of his opinions with regard to the theoretical principles of moral and
religious truth, never influenced his regard for men who held very opposite sentiments on those subjects – subjects which he never, like some vain and shallow
sceptics, introduced into social discourse; on the contrary, when at any time the
conversation tended that way, he was desirous rather of avoiding any serious

discussion on matters which he wished to confine to the graver and less dangerous consideration of cool philosophy. He had, it might be said, in the language which the Grecian historian applies to an illustrious Roman, two minds; one which indulged in the metaphysical scepticism which his genius could invent, but which it could not always disentangle; another, simple, natural, and playful, which made his conversation delightful to his friends, and even frequently conciliated men whose principles of belief his philosophical doubts, if they had not power to shake, had grieved and offended. During the latter period of his life I was frequently in his company amidst persons of genuine piety, and I never heard him venture a remark at which such men, or ladies – still more susceptible than men – could take offence. His good nature and benevolence prevented such an injury to his hearers; it was unfortunate that he often forgot what injury some of his writings might do to his readers. The sentiments which such good nature and benevolence might suggest, I ventured to embody, in a sort of dramatic form, in the story of La Roche in the Mirror, in which Mr Hume is made to say, "That there were times when, recollecting that venerable pastor and his lovely daughter, he forgot the pride of literary fame, and wished that he had never doubted." It will not, I hope, be an offensive egotism, if I inform the Society, that, when I wrote that story, being anxious there should not be a single expression in it that could give offence or uneasiness to any friend of Mr Hume's, I read it to Dr Adam Smith, and begged that he would tell me if any thing should be left out or altered. He heard it attentively, and declared he did not find a syllable to object to; but added, with his characteristic absence of mind, that he was surprised he had never heard of the anecdote before.

In the same *bonhommie*, Mr Hume bore with perfect good nature the pleas-antries which humorous deductions from his theoretical scepticism sometimes produced. Once, I have been told, he was in a small degree ruffled by a witticism of Mr John Home's, who, though always pleasant, and often lively, seldom produced what might be termed or repeated as wit. The clerk of an eminent banker in Edinburgh, a young man of irreproachable conduct, and much in the confidence of his master, eloped with a considerable sum with which he had been entrusted. The circumstance was mentioned at a dinner where the two Humes, the historian and the poet, and several of their usual friendly circle, were present. David Hume spoke of it as a kind of moral problem, and wondered what could induce a man of such character and habits as this clerk was said to possess, thus to incur, for an inconsiderable sum, the guilt and the infamy of such a transaction. "I can easily account for it," said his friend John Home, "from the nature of his studies, and the kind of books which he was in the habit of reading." "What were they?" said the philosopher. "Boston's Fourfold State" rejoined the poet, "and Hume's Essays." David was more hurt by the joke than was usual with him, probably from the singular conjunction of the two works, which formed, according to his friend's account, the library of the unfortunate young man.

Such was the free and cordial communication of sentiments, the natural play of fancy and good humour, which prevailed among the circle of [Scottish] men whom I have described. It was very different from that display of learning – that prize-fighting of wit, which distinguished a literary circle of our sister country, of which we have some authentic and curious records. There all ease of inter-course was changed for the pride of victory; and the victors, like some savage combatants, gave no quarter to the vanquished. This may, perhaps, be accounted for more from the situation than the dispositions of the principal members of that society. The literary circle of London was a sort of sect, a *caste* separate from the ordinary professions and habits of common life. They were traders in talent and learning, and brought, like other traders, samples of their goods into company, with a jealousy of competition which prevented their enjoying, as much as otherwise they might, any excellence in their competitors.

The learned and ingenious men whom I have just mentioned, were the principal founders of the society established in Edinburgh under the denomi-nation of the *Select Society*, of which Mr Stewart has given a list in his Life of Dr Robertson. That list, according to the information of a member, is not quite complete. Among other names omitted, may be mentioned those of the Duke of Hamilton, a man, not only of elegant manners, but of classical acquirements; but careless and dissipated in the highest degree; Lord Dalmeny, cut off, like the duke, in the prime of life, though very different in the temperance of its habits. Mr Robert Alexander was also a zealous member of that society; a very worthy, intelligent, and accomplished man, but plain and awkward in his person, and devoid of that readiness of thought and command of expression which might qualify him for a speaker. "But his suppers," says my authority, "were delightful, formed on the model of Paris, where Mr A. had occasion frequently to be; they were elegant and enjoués, frequented by all the literary, and most of the fashionable, persons of the time. By those meetings (continued he) some of the most distinguished members of the Select Society were more improved than by the debates at its sittings. Those meetings of easy but improving sociality rubbed off the corners of mere learning and science, and thus made the literati of Edinburgh less captious and less pedantic than those of any other place."

About this time (1755) was produced a periodical publication, which attracted less notice at the time than it has since excited, when its principal authors had attained such celebrity as to make the world anxious to know the smallest of their productions, – I mean the Original *Edinburgh Review*, of which only two numbers were published; the article by Adam Smith, a Criticism on Johnson's Dictionary, was very conspicuous.

David Hume was not among the number of the writers of the Review, though we should have thought he would have been the first person whose co-operation they would have sought. But I think I have heard that they were afraid both of his extreme good nature, and his extreme artlessness; that, from the one, their criticisms would have been weakened, or suppressed, and, from the other, their secret discovered. The merits of the work strongly attracted his attention, and he expressed his surprise, to some of the gentlemen concerned in it, with whom he was daily in the habit of meeting, at the excellence of a performance written, as he presumed, from his ignorance on the subject, by some persons out of their own literary circle. It was agreed to communicate the secret to him at a dinner, which was shortly after given by one of their number. At that dinner he repeated his wonder on the subject of the Edinburgh Review. One of the company said he knew the authors, and would tell them to Mr Hume upon his giving an oath of secrecy. "How is the oath to be taken," said David, with his usual pleasantry, "of a man accused of so much scepticism as I am? You would not trust my Bible Oath; but I will swear by the το καλον and the το πρεπον[1] never to reveal your secret." He was then told the names of the authors and the plan of the work, but it was not continued long enough to allow of his contributing any articles. Of another work, and one of much humour, written by Adam Ferguson, in ridicule of the opposers of the Scots militia, "The History of Sister Peg," David Hume was also kept in ignorance, from similar motives, by his literary friends. By way of a pleasant revenge for their want of confidence, David Hume wrote a letter to the publisher, assuming the work to himself, and accounting for his having till that time declined avowing it. I have seen this letter, and it is written in such a style, as, to a man not informed of the real circumstances of the case, would leave no doubt of Mr Hume's being the author of the book. I could not read this letter without being confirmed in an observation which I have often ventured to make, on the uncertainty of the evidence arising from *letters*, when the writers are dead, and the motives of their correspondence cannot be known.

The mention of *Sister Peg* leads me to take notice of another literary association, considerably later than the *Select Society*, established under the auspices of some of Mr Home's above-mentioned companions, and in conformity to his own sanguine ideas of national pride and heroism; this was the *Poker Club*, instituted in 1762, at a time when Scotland was refused a militia, and thought herself affronted by the refusal; a refusal which many sensible and moderate men thought for her advantage, as she was just then beginning that course of improvement in industry, and particularly in agriculture, which she has since so successfully prosecuted; but, perhaps, chiefly caused by that jealousy, which fifteen years had not yet extinguished, of a disaffected spirit of Jacobitism, which made it unsafe to trust the people of Scotland, or at least a great part of them, with arms. The name of this club, the *Poker*, was chosen from a quaint sort of allusion to the principles it was originally meant to excite, as a club to stir up the fire and spirit of the country. It was afterwards extended as to

---

[1] [i.e., the beautiful and the becoming.]

members, though less definite in its objects, by the admission of a number of gentlemen of this country, and chiefly resident in Edinburgh, considerable either in rank and station, or eminent for talents. At its first institution, Mr Johnston, afterwards Sir William Pulteney, was chosen Secretary, with two assistants, for the revisal of any publications that might be thought necessary; and, in a playful moment, Mr Andrew Crosbie, the celebrated barrister, (one of the most zealous advocates for the people, and one of the warmest asserters of their freedom, but the best-natured and gentlest man possible in private life,) was chosen *Assassin*, in case that office should be found necessary, with another more celebrated man, equally remarkable for the mildness of his disposition, Mr David Hume, for his assistant. I see among these careless scraps of his earlier writings, which Mr Hume had preserved, the beginning of a warm paper addressed to the landed gentlemen of Scotland, on the subject of the militia, ascribing to the want of it the early misfortunes of the Seven Years' War, to which the subsequent successes, unparalleled in British history, afforded a sufficient answer. The club flourished till 1784, when its members, according to a list I have seen, were in number sixty-six....

103
HENRY MACKENZIE:
ANECDOTES OF DAVID HUME

Henry Mackenzie, anecdotes of David Hume (c. 1830), in *The anecdotes and egotisms of Henry Mackenzie, 1745–1831, now first published, edited with an introduction by Harold William Thompson*. London: Oxford University Press, 1927, xxxiv, 303 p.
Selections; from 1927 edition.[1]

Henry Mackenzie (1745–1831) was the author of "The Story of La Roche" and the *Account of the Life and Writings of John Home* (1822), contained in this collection. Near the end of his life, Mackenzie rather unsystematically jotted down recollections from his long life, hoping to have these published in one or more books of "anecdotes" and "egotisims" as he called them. Included among the manuscript pages were several biographical sketches of famous figures with whom he was personally acquainted, including Hume. The work, though, went unpublished for nearly 100 years until Harold William Thomson tracked down the manuscripts and edited them into a collection that he titled *The Anecdotes and Egotisms of Henry Mackenzie*. The section on Hume in particular is of late date as evidenced by its reference to Mackenzie's own *Account* of Home. In his sketch of Hume, he presents several short and interesting stories about the philosopher. Among these are Hume's impartial approach to writing the *History*; the negative reception of Hume's *Concise and Genuine Account* concerning Rousseau; his enjoyment of whist; his pride in his French; his conversation with Franklin regarding American population increase; Baron Hume's hesitation in publishing Hume's letters; Hume's discussion with Boyle about his mother's death and how Mackenzie incorporated this into "La Roche"; Hume's prank on Goodall; his housekeeper's French cooking; and his defence of Archibald Stewart.

---

[1] The selection is reproduced by kind permission of Oxford University Press.

DAVID HUME

David Hume was not at all the Jacobite or Tory which he was sometimes accused of being, and as his History was supposed to evince. He had an indolent gentleness in his nature which was averse to enthusiasm and perhaps unfriendly to bold ideas and bold expression. He loved the moderate, the temperate in everything, and from that disposition as well as his propensity to disbelief he had an aversion to the fanatics and *Cromwellian* partisans of the Commonwealth. From this inclination to mildness and moderation he was perhaps not so much an admirer of Shakespeare as he ought to have been, and rather cautioned his friend John Home against an over-admiration of that great dramatist, and desired him to read constantly Corneille and Racine.

He said (certainly a great defect in an elaborate historian) that he never could compose history from manuscript, always preferring exclusively printed authority and books, to which he could attribute impartiality or an approach to it; but certainly, after all that has been said by republicans against him, he weighed without prejudice, or it may be safely said without the consciousness of it, the authorities which he consulted on both sides, and the probable conclusion which the nature of man, the experience of ages, and the conduct of political men during those ages warranted his drawing. He was much blamed and ridiculed for his letter giving an account of his quarrel with Rousseau; and in truth the absurdity of Jean Jacques was so notorious that the publication of Mr. Hume was perhaps unnecessary; but he was strong with anger and indignation at the ingratitude of Rousseau, who had his apology in that sort of madness to which he was subject, but a madness of a hateful kind, envious, malignant, and regardless of truth, engendered by an inordinate vanity (which physicians say is by much the most common cause of derangement), a vanity the most provoking of any, which walks abroad under the mask of humility.

Hume liked a party at whist and picquet and valued himself on playing whist well. I was frequently of his party at Chief Baron Ord's, whose family were great favourites of his, and he certainly at one time meant to pay his addresses to Miss Nancy Ord, at that time one of the most agreeable and accomplished women I ever knew. One of the last times I played whist with him there, he triumphed over me (who was reckoned a good player at that game) from my not *calling* with two honours in my hand; but I insisted that I did right according to the rule of the game, the adversary being only seven and, my being sure of four tricks, fearing *to beplayed through*, as the phrase of the game is; but the philosopher, contrary to all philosophical principles, disapproved of my play, and insisted that I ought to have called. His liking for a game at picquet I have particularly mentioned in my *Life of John Home*; it served to amuse him and so alleviate the pains of his disorder on their journey to Bath.

On another qualification he valued himself without so just pretensions as his play at whist, which was speaking French like a native, and was much mortified by a link-boy at the *Comédie Française,* hearing him speak, addressing him by the title of *Milor.*

When Dr. Franklin was in Scotland, he often met with D. Hume. One day, when the Doctor was detailing the natural advantages of America, and proph-esying what a country it would become, 'You have forgotten one little article,' Doctor, said David, 'among your projected manufactures, the manufacture of men'; the increase of population in America has verified this prophesy.

D. Hume was the author of that admirable illustration of the advantage of paper representing the precious metals in circulation: that it left those metals for other purposes, resembling roads of communication, which, if they could be made in the air, would save the land for the production of corn.

He was fond of letter-writing, and had an uncommon talent for it. His nephew, my friend Mr. Baron Hume, has been often importuned to publish such letters and copies of letters of his uncle's writing as are in his possession; but his extreme delicacy (I think an overstrained one) with regard to his uncle's memory has hitherto prevented him from publishing them. One admirably pleasant letter, written to Mrs. Dysert, her son, who had it, and Mr. Baron Hume, allowed me to read at the Royal Society, and to publish in the *Life of John Home.*

Mr. B. Hume was so delicate with regard to his uncle that he objected to my mentioning in that Life an anecdote told me by Mr. D. Hume's intimate friend, the Hon. Mr. Boyle, which anecdote was held by serious persons to be much to Mr. D. Hume's honour, but of which his nephew said he doubted the correctness.[2] Mr. Boyle, however, was such respectable authority, that I thought it would not have been fair to suppress it, and therefore gave it with reference to that authority. In truth his speech to Mr. Boyle in the moment of his grief for a mother whom he loved, was no more than the sentiment which I put into his mouth at the conclusion of the story of *La Roche* which his friend Adam Smith saw, and thought so natural that in his usual absence of mind he told me he wondered he had never heard the anecdote before.

He wanted a book out of the Advocates Library, of which the learned antiquarian Goodall, author of the first Vindication of Queen Mary, was then acting Librarian. He was sitting in his elbow-chair so fast asleep, that neither

---

[2]   [Mackenzie's 1822 published version of his *Account* of Home does not contain the Boyle anecdote that he mentions here. In his original 1812 oral presentation of that work, the manuscript of which is in the National Library of Scotland, he relates Alexander Carlyle's account of the story, citing Carlyle as the authority (Carlyle's account appears in his 1860 *Autobiography,* excerpted in this collection). Baron Hume quoted from Carlyle's account in a letter to the *Quarterly Review,* contained in this collection.]

David nor a friend who accompanied him could wake Goodall by any of the usual means. At last David said, 'I think I have a method of waking him,' and bawled into his ear, 'Queen Mary was a strumpet and a murtherer.' – 'It's a damned lie,' said Goodall, starting out of his sleep, and David obtained the book he sought.[3]

The Marian Controversy, as it has been called, has stirred more zeal and bile than any question of however much greater importance that I know. Dr. Robertson, talking one day to me on that subject, said: 'Mary's friends have violently censured me for my sentiments on her conduct; they do not consider that but for the sake of historical truth it would have been a principal object with me to have made her innocent as she was beautiful and accomplished; she was the natural heroine of my book had not my historical impartiality forbidden it.'

D. Hume's account of her has also been censured by her friends; while another set of critics set him down as a Jacobite; and her cause was confessedly the cause of Jacobitism.

He liked to eat, and still more to give his friends, a good dinner, and took a very sensible way of securing one. He had an old cook or *gouvernante* who had been with him ever since he took up house; when in France under the Diplomacy of his friend Lord Hertford (in whose absence he was left *Chargé d' Affaires*) he got most particular recipes for a few dishes which he liked, as the best articles of French cookery; one I particularly remember was *bouillé*, for the excellence of which I could testify. Those few dishes he made the old woman completely mistress of, and satisfied himself with this knowledge in her, following his friend A. Smith's principle of the division of labour, limiting her excellence to those few articles.

When Provost Stewart, who was a distinguished wine-merchant at that time (1746) and Provost of Edinburgh, was called to account for an alleged breach of duty in delivering the City to the rebels, D. Hume wrote a volunteer pamphlet in his defence shewing most convincingly that the City could not have been defended, and that standing a siege would have been attended with most disastrous consequences; the Provost on finding out his anonymous advocate, made him a present of a batch of uncommonly good Burgundy. 'The gift,' said David, in his good-humoured way, 'ruined me; I was obliged to give so many dinners in honour of the wine.'[4]

---

[3]   [John Home gives an alternative version of this anecdote in his "Remarks on the Life and Character of the late David Hume, Esq." (*London Review*, 1776), contained in this collection.]

[4]   [David Hume, *A true account of the behaviour and conduct of Archibald Stewart, Esq; late Lord Provost of Edinburgh*. In a letter to a friend. London: printed for M. Cooper, 1748.]

SMITH AND HUME IN LOVE

Adam Smith seriously in love with Miss Campbell of ____ (the name is so numerous that to use it cannot be thought personal), a woman of as different dispositions and habits from him as possible.

His friend, David Hume, was deeply smitten with a very amiable young lady, a great friend of mine, Miss Nancy Ord, but the disparity of age prevented his proposing to her, which he once intended. She was a great admirer of his, and he was a frequent guest at her father's, where I met him, and made one of his whist party with the young lady and some other person. I played well at the time and so did she. D. Hume was vain of his playing whist. That game has much of observation in it, and such games best suit a thinking man.

104
ROBERT CHAMBERS:
TRADITIONS OF EDINBURGH

Robert Chambers, *Traditions of Edinburgh*, Edinburgh, W. & C. Tait, 1825, 2 v.
Complete section on Hume; from London: W. & R. Chambers; Philadelphia, J.B. Lippincott, 1912, pp. 55–60.

Scottish biographer and publisher Robert Chambers (1802–1871) was born in Peebles, Scotland, and at sixteen began work as a bookseller. He soon wrote several works on Scottish culture and history. He is most remembered for the editorial and supervisory work he and his brother William did on *Chambers's Edinburgh Journal*, established in 1832, and the ten-volume *Chambers's Encyclopædia* (1859). One of Chambers's first works was *Traditions of Edinburgh* (1825), which he thoroughly revised in 1846. In 1868, near the close of his life, he revised it yet again. The selections below, which reflect both revisions, describe Hume's various dwellings in Edinburgh. Chambers includes a story about a dinner that Hume attended at the home of Alison Cockburn, which Hume left wearing some borrowed and poorly fitting outer garments. The following is from the 1912 edition of this work, which includes annotations by C.E.S. Chambers.

JAMES'S COURT.
David Hume – James Boswell – Lord Fountainhall.

James's Court, a well-known pile of building of great altitude at the head of the Earthen Mound, was erected about 1725–27 by James Brownhill,[1] a joiner, as a speculation, and was for some years regarded as the *quartier* of greatest dignity and importance in Edinburgh. The inhabitants, who were all persons of consequence in society, although each had but a single floor of four or five rooms and a kitchen, kept a clerk to record their names and proceedings, had a scavenger of their own, clubbed in many public measures, and had balls and

[1] From whom it got its name – James Court.

parties among themselves exclusively. In those days it must have been quite a step in life when a man was able to fix his family in one of the *flats* of James's Court.

Amongst the many notables who have harboured here, only two or three can be said to have preserved their notability till our day, the chief being David Hume and James Boswell.

DAVID HUME.

The first fixed residence of David Hume in Edinburgh appears to have been in Riddel's Land, Lawnmarket, near the head of the West Bow. He commenced housekeeping there in 1751, when, according to his own account, he 'removed from the country to the town, the true scene for a man of letters.' It was while in Riddel's Land that he published his *Political Discourses*, and obtained the situation of librarian to the Faculty of Advocates. In this place also he commenced the writing of his *History of England*. He dates from Riddel's Land in January 1753, but in June we find him removed to Jack's Land,[2] a somewhat airier situation in the Canongate, where he remained for nine years. Excepting only the small portion composed in the Lawnmarket mansion, the whole of the History of England was written in Jack's Land; a fact which will probably raise some interest respecting that locality. It is, in reality, a plain, middle-aged fabric, of no particular appearance, and without a single circumstance of a curious nature connected with it, besides the somewhat odd one that the continuator of the *History*, Smollett, lived, some time after, in his sister's house precisely opposite.

Hume removed at Whit-sunday 1762 to a house which he purchased in James's Court – the eastern portion of the third floor in the west stair (counting from the level of the court). This was such a step as a man would take in those days as a consequence of improvement in his circumstances. The philosopher had lived in James's Court but a short time, when he was taken to France as secretary to the embassy. In his absence, which lasted several years, his house was occupied by Dr Blair, who here had a son of the Duke of Northumberland as a pupil. It is interesting to find Hume, some time after, writing to his friend Dr Ferguson from the midst of the gaieties of Paris: 'I am sensible that I am misplaced, and I wish twice or thrice a day for *my easy-chair and my retreat in James's Court.*' Then he adds a beautiful sentiment: 'Never think, dear Ferguson, that as long as you are master of your own fireside and your own time, you can be unhappy, or that any other circumstance can add to your

---

[2]   A 'land' still standing (1912) as it was when Hume lived there. It was also the residence of the Countess of Eglinton when she left the Stamp Office Close in the High Street.

enjoyment.'[3] In one of his letters to Blair he speaks minutely of his house: 'Never put a fire in the south room with the red paper. It was so warm of itself that all last winter, which was a very severe one, I lay with a single blanket; and frequently, upon coming in at midnight starving with cold, have sat down and read for an hour, as if I had had a stove in the room.' From 1763 till 1766 he lived in high diplomatic situations at Paris; and thinking to settle there for life, for the sake of the agreeable society, gave orders to sell his house in Edinburgh. He informs us, in a letter to the Countess de Bouffiers (*General Correspondence*, 4to, 1820, p. 231), that he was prevented by a singular accident from carrying his intention into effect. After writing a letter to Edinburgh for the purpose of disposing of his house, and leaving it with his Parisian landlord, he set out to pass his Christmas with the Countess de Bouffiers at rIsle Adam; but being driven back by a snowstorm, which blocked up the roads, he found on his return that the letter had not been sent to the post-house. More deliberate thoughts then determined him to keep up his Edinburgh mansion, thinking that, if any affairs should call him to his native country, 'it would be very inconvenient not to have a house to retire to.' On his return, therefore, in 1766, he re-entered into possession of his *flat* in James's Court, but was soon again called from it by an invitation from Mr Conway to be an under-secretary of state. At length, in 1769, he returned permanently to his native city, in possession of what he thought opulence-a thousand a year. We find him immediately writing from his retreat in James's Court to his friend Adam Smith, then commencing his great work *On the Wealth of Nations* in the quiet of his mother's house at Kirkealdy: 'I am glad to have come within sight of you, and to have a view of Kirkealdy from my windows; but I wish also to be within speaking terms of you,' &c. To another person he writes: 'I live still, and must for a twelvemonth, in my old house in James's Court, which is very cheerful, and even elegant, but too small to display my great talent for cookery, the science to which I intend to addict the remaining years of my life!'

Hume now built a superior house for himself in the New Town, which was then little beyond its commencement, selecting a site adjoining to St Andrew Square. The superintendence of this work was an amusement to him. A story is related in more than one way regarding the manner in which a denomination was conferred upon the street in which this house is situated. Perhaps, if it be premised that a corresponding street at the other angle of St Andrew Square is called *St Andrew Street* – a natural enough circumstance with reference to the square, whose title was determined on in the plan – it will appear likely that the choosing of 'St David Street' for that in which Hume's house stood was not originally designed as a jest at his expense, though a second thought, and the whim of his friends, might quickly give it that application. The story, as told

---

[3] Burton's *Life of Hume*, ii. 173.

by Mr Burton, is as follows: 'When the house was built and inhabited by Hume, but while yet the street of which it was the commencement had no name, a witty young lady, daughter of Baron Ord, chalked on the wall the words, ST DAVID STREET. The allusion was very obvious. Hume's "lass," judging that it was not meant in honour or reverence, ran into the house much excited, to tell her master how he was made game of. "Never mind, lassie," he said, "many a better man has been made a saint of before."'

That Hume was a native of Edinburgh is well known. One could wish to know the spot of his birth; but it is not now perhaps possible to ascertain it. The nearest approach made to the fact is from intelligence conveyed by a memorandum in his fathers handwriting among the family papers, where he speaks of 'my son David, born in the *Tron Church parish*' – a district comprehending a large square clump of town between the High Street and Cowgate, east of the site of the church itself.

One of Hume's most intimate friends amongst the other sex was Mrs Cockburn, author of one of the beautiful songs called *The Flowers of the Forest*. While he was in France in 1764, she writes to him from *Baird's Close*,[4] *Castle-hill*: 'The cloven foot for which thou art worshipped I despise; yet I remember *thee* with affection. I remember that, in spite of vain philosophy, of dark doubts, of toilsome learning, God has stamped his image of benignity so strong upon thy heart, that not all the labours of thy head could efface it.' After Hume's return to Edinburgh, he kept up his acquaintance with this spirited and amiable woman. The late Mr Alexander Young, W.S., had some reminiscences of parties which he attended when a boy at her house, and at which the philosopher was present. Hume came in one evening behind time for her *petit souper*, when, seeing her bustling to get something for him to eat, he called out: 'Now, no trouble, if you please, about quality; for you know I'm only a glutton, not an epicure.' Mr Young attended at a dinner where, besides Hume, there were present Lord Monboddo and some other learned personages. Mrs Cockburn was then living in the neat first floor of a house at the end of Crighton Street, with windows looking along the Potterrow. She had a son of eccentric habits, in middle life, or rather elderly, who came in during the dinner tipsy, and going into a bedroom, locked himself in, went to bed, and fell asleep. The company in time made a move for departure, when it was discovered that their hats, cloaks, and greatcoats were all locked up in Mr Cockburn's room. The door was knocked at and shaken, but no answer. What was to be done? At length Mrs Cockburn had no alternative from sending out to her neighbours to borrow a supply of similar integuments, which was soon procured. There was then such fun in fitting the various

---

[4] Formerly called Blair's Close (p. 19). The name was altered to Baird's Close when the Gordon property passed into the possession of Baird of Newbyth.

savants with suitable substitutes for their own proper gear! Hume, for instance, with a dreadnought riding-coat; Monboddo with a shabby old hat, as unlike his own neat chapeau as possible! In the highest exaltation of spirits did these two men of genius at length proceed homeward along the Potterrow, Horse Wynd, Assembly Close, &c., making the old echoes merry with their peals of laughter at the strange appearance which they respectively made.[5]

I lately inspected Hume's *cheerful and elegant* mansion in James's Court, and found it divided amongst three or four tenants in humble life, *each* possessing little more than a single room. It was amusing to observe that what had been the dining-room and drawing-room towards the north were each provided with one of those little side oratories which have been described elsewhere as peculiar to a period in Edinburgh house-building, being designed for private devotion. Hume living in a house with two private chapels!

---

[5] Mrs Cockburn, writing to Miss Cumming at Balcarres, describes 'a ball' she gave in this house. 'On Wednesday I gave a ball. How do ye think I contrived to stretch out this house to hold twenty-two people, and had nine couples always dancing? Yet this is true; it is also true that we had a table covered with divers eatables all the time, and that everybody ate when they were hungry and drank when they were dry, but nobody ever sat down.... Our fiddler sat where the cupboard is, and they danced in both rooms. The table was stuffed into the window and we had plenty of room. It made the bairns all very happy.' - Mrs. Cockburn's Letters, edited by T. Craig Brown [Edinburgh: Printed for David Douglas, 1900].

105
ROBERT CHAMBERS:
SCOTTISH JESTS AND ANECDOTES

[Robert Chambers], *Scottish jests and anecdotes*, Edinburgh: W. Paterson, c.1832, 252 p.
Selections; from second edition, Edinburgh: William Tait, 1838.

R obert Chambers (1802–1871) is the author of *Traditions of Edinburgh*, contained in this collection. Among Chambers's many shorter works is *Scottish Jests*, which collects humorous anecdotes about Scottish people, particularly the literati. In the Preface, dated 1831, Chambers states that he collected most of the stories from the witnesses themselves. He presents several anecdotes relating to Hume, particularly surrounding his eating habits and religious infidelity. John Hill Burton relied upon this work in his *Life and Correspondence of David Hume* (1846), excerpted in this collection.

PREFACE.

CALEDONIA –

A land renown'd for worth and beauty's charms,
Inflexible in faith, invincible in arms, –

has never yet been allowed any credit on the score of wit or humour; but is rather understood to be a country full of very grave people, who would not penetrate a joke for the world. No mistake could be greater; as, we hope, the reader will soon find. This compilation, indeed, is designed to vindicate, for the first time, the pretensions of the Scottish nation to the character of a witty and jocular, as they are already allowed to be a painstaking and enlightened, race. The reader will here find a prodigious array of good things and humorous jests, which have been collected from all imaginable sources, but mostly from the mouths of the people themselves, so as to convince all unprejudiced fellow-Britons, that life in the north is by no means less replete with drollery and good humour than in the south, and that, in reality, we are a very mirthful nation. ...

EDINBURGH, *November*, 1831.

SCOTTISH JESTS

Dr John Brown, author of the Brownonian System of Physic, a man of somewhat coarse manners, on passing the monument of David Hume, in the Calton burying ground, observed to a mason who was laying a pavement stone for it, "Friend," said he, "this is a strong and massy building; but how do you think the honest gentleman can get out at the resurrection?" The mason archly replied, "Sir, I have secured that point, for I have put the *key under the door!*"[1]

Hume, Smith, and other literati of the last century, used to frequent a tavern in a low street in Edinburgh called the Potterrow; where, if thee accommodations were not of the first order, they had at least no cause to complain of the scantiness of their victuals. One day, as the landlady was bringing in a *third* supply of some particularly good dish, she thus addressed them: – "They ca' ye the *literawti*, I believe; od, if they were to ca' ye the *eaterawti*, they would be nearer the mark."

This distinguished philosopher was one day passing along a narrow footpath which formerly winded through a boggy piece of ground at the back of Edinburgh Castle, when he had the misfortune to tumble in, and stick fast in the mud. Observing a woman approaching, he civilly requested her to lend him a helping hand out of his disagreeable situation; but she, casting one hurried glance at his abbreviated figure, passed on, without regarding his request. He then shouted lustily after her; and she was at last prevailed upon by his cries to approach. "Are na ye Hume the Deist?" inquired she, in a tone which implied that an answer in the affirmative would decide her against lending him her assistance. "Well, well, said Mr Hume, "no matter: you know, good woman, Christian charity commands you to do good, even to your enemies." "Christian charity here, Christian charity there," replied the woman, "I'll do naething for ye till ye turn a Christian yoursell: ye maun first repeat baith the Lord's Prayer and the Creed, or faith I'll let ye groffle there as I faund ye." The sceptic was actually obliged to accede to the woman's terms, ere she would give him her help. He himself used to tell the story with great relish.

Hume one night came too late to one of the little supper parties given by his friend Mrs Cockburn, (authoress of a fine song to the tune of the Flowers of the Forest") and it so happened that the good lady's slender pantry had been almost completely desolated before he arrived. Mrs Cockburn informed him of this fact; but, at the same time, told him she would do her best. "Oh, trouble yourself very little," said the metaphysician, "about what you have, or how it appears; you know I am no *epicure*, but only a *glutton*."[2]

---

[1] [This anecdote appears in William Smellie's *Literary and Characteristical Lives* (1800), contained in this collection.]

"Pray, sir," said Lady [Elizabeth] Wallace to David Hume, "I am often asked of what age I am – what answer should I make?" Mr Hume, immediately guessing her ladyship's meaning, said, "Madam, when you are asked that question again, answer, that you are not yet come to years of discretion."

David Hume and Lady Wallace once passed the Firth from Kinghorn to Leith together, when a violent storm rendered the passengers apprehensive of a salt-water death; and her ladyship's terrors induced her to seek consolation from her friend, who, with infinite *sand froid*, assured her he thought there was great probability of their becoming food for fishes. "And pray, my dear friend," said Lady Wallace, which do you think they will eat first?" "Those that are gluttons," replied Hume, "will undoubtedly fall foul of me, but the epicures will attack your ladyship."

During Hume's last illness, he was waited on by a female member of the Berean Congregation, who supposed she had a message from Heaven to deliver to him, regarding the state of his soul. On learning her object, the good-natured philosopher ordered a bottle of wine and some other refreshments to be brought in, observing, that they could not well proceed to discuss a matter of such importance "dry-lippit." The woman was prevailed upon to take two glasses of wine; and, as she was sipping it, Mr Hume questioned her about her situation and business in life. Understanding that her husband was a candle-maker at Leith, he desired her to send him two stone weight of his best moulded candles, for which the money would be paid on delivery. The lady thought no more of the high commission she had been intrusted with, but hastened home to inform her husband of the order she had received, and quite forgot the conversion of Mr Hume.

When the New Town had reached that street which since bears the name of the tutelar saint of Wales, the house at the south-west corner of St Andrew Square, but entering from the street, was occupied by the celebrated David Hume. One day in passing, the Rev. Dr W____ waggishly chalked on the corner, *Saint David* Street. The housekeeper having noticed this mark, with eyes like saucers, ran into her master's study, and told him how he had been quized. – "Never mind, Jenny," quoth David, "a better man than I am, hath been made a saint of before me." [3]

A certain person, to shew his detestation of Hume's infidel opinions, always left any company where he happened to be, if Hume joined it. The latter, observing this, took occasion one day to reprehend it as follows: – "Friend,"

---

[2] This anecdote was taken down in 1829, from the mouth of a gentleman who was present. [i.e., Alexander Young, W.S.; see Chambers's *Traditions of Edinburgh* (1825) in this collection.]

[3] [For alternative accounts of the story behind the naming of St. David Street, see Carlyle's *Autobiography* (1860), Burton's Life (1846), and "Miscellaneous Hume Anecdotes," contained in this collection.]

said he, "I am surprised to find you display such a pointed aversion to me; I would wish to be upon good terms with you here, as, upon your own system, it seems very probable we shall be doomed to the same place hereafter. You hope I shall be damned for want of faith, and I fear you will have the same fate for want of charity."

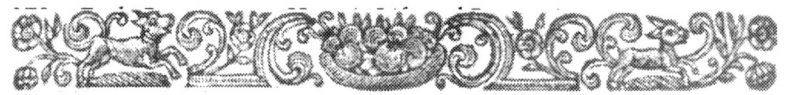

106
WILLIAM ADAM:
TWO SHORT ESSAYS (1836)

[William Adam], *Two short essays, on the study of history, and on general reading. With a preface, and concluding note. The gift of a grandfather.* [Edinburgh:] Blair Adam Press, August 1836, [1] iii-xi, 27 p. Selections; from 1836 edition.

Edinburgh native William Adam (1751–1839) was lord chief commissioner of the Scottish jury court. His father, John Adam, and uncle, Robert Adam, were architects, the latter of whom designed Hume's mausoleum in the Calton burial ground.[1] Hume was on close terms with the Adam family, and Alexander Carlyle preserves a story of one dinner that Hume had at Robert's house (contained in this collection). William Adam himself was a companion of Hume's nephew. Near the end of his life, Adam published two short works that discuss Hume based on his personal acquaintance. In the first of these, *Two Short Essays*, Adam begins by recollecting how Hume's *Essays, Moral and Political* had influenced him in his youth. Two essays in particular, "Of the Study of History" and "Of Essay Writing," he believed had special merit, but were unfortunately removed from later editions of Hume's works. In this pamphlet Adam reprints the first and part of the second of these for the benefit of his grandchildren. He describes the advice that noted Scottish writers had on the development of his mother's library, including Hume. Adam concludes the pamphlet listing the names of distinguished Scottish figures, and states "I shall, on some future occasion, attach remarks and annotations to their names." He kept his promise with a short book of anecdotes titled *Sequel to the Gift of a Grandfather* (1839), selections from which are contained in this collection. The following is from the 1836 and only edition of Adam's *Two Short Essays*. An insert in the book's opening states "There are several errors in this short work, naturally to be expected in the first attempt of a private press. They are all accurately corrected with a pen, instead of annexing, as is usual, a list of errata in a separate printed paper." I have incorporated the indicated changes.

---

[1] [See Iain Brown, "David Hume's Tomb: a Roman mausoleum by Robert Adam," *Proceedings of the Society of Antiquaries of Scotland*, 1991, Vol. 121, pp. 391–422.]

PREFACE.

In searching among, and putting in order, some old books, partly half-bound, partly in nearly worn-out binding, I found two little volumes bound in the fashion of the days of Tonson, (the great London Bookseller in the time of Addison and Pope,) but printed at Edinburgh. One appears, by its title-page, to have been printed in 1741, but not numbered as a volume either on the binding or on the title-page. The other volume appears to have been printed in 1742; it has the figure 2 on the binding, and Volume II. on the title-page. The name of the author does not appear on the title-page of either, or any where throughout the volumes. On looking into them, I discovered that they were of my very early acquaintance; and that I had known some of the Essays familiarly, more than three-score and ten years ago; two of them particularly had attracted my attention then, and had given very important direction to my reading.

The two volumes which attracted my attention, and which I have described, formed part of my Mother's collection of books, which had been chosen with great care, and under good advice. It consisted of English and French classics, with a few translations from ancient classic authors, and some select historical works. Some of them were got on the recommendation of Dr Robertson, a very near relation and intimate friend of the family, then about to distinguish himself as the elegant and interesting Historian of the extraordinary and eventful reign of Mary Queen of Scots.

Mr William Cleghorn, a man of superior genius and of great learning, recommended some of the books for the collection. He was Professor of Moral Philosophy in the University of Edinburgh; and it was always said in my family, but I think erroneously, that he was the successful competitor for that chair against David Hume. {[Footonte:] Doctor, afterwards Sir John Pringle, and physician to George III. appears to have been professor of Moral Philosophy in 1744; in that year he had occasion to be absent, and Mr Cleghorn lectured for him. In 1745 Pringle resigned, and Cleghorn had so distinguished himself that he was appointed to the vacant chair, having hardly attained his twenty-first year. That he was most eminent as a Professor is established not only on tradition, but from notes of his Plan of Lectures, which have been preserved. He died in 1754, before he could prepare any work as a memorial of his literary talents and genius. That David Hume was at one time a candidate for the Professorship of Moral Philosophy is certain, but it appears, from what is here stated, that he could not have been the competitor of Mr Cleghorn.[2]} ...

I might perhaps add to the advisers of this little collection of books, the name of David Hume. He was an intimate friend and acquaintance; and in all the

---

[2]   [Hume sought the position in 1745, but his candidacy was rejected by the Edinburgh Presbytery, and Cleghorn was appointed.]

intercourse of life, and in all he said, and wrote, and did, when not employed in his unnecessary metaphysical scepticism, (well named by a friend of mine, *intellectual rope-dancing*,) was innocent, playful, and moral, and most natural in his conversation; equally pleasing and instructive to the young and old of both sexes.

The two following Essays, of which I believe Mr Hume to be the author, are not to be found in the edition of his Essays which was published in 1767, which edition is known to have received Mr Hume's corrections. This might create a doubt as to their authorship. There is one mark however found on an old adage, *noscitur ex sociis* – a person is known by his companions. In the same little volumes in which these two treatise are found, there are many of the well known Essays of David Hume.

From the value which I set upon these productions, I am surprised that they should not have been continued in Mr Hume's permanent and established Works. One of the Essays is upon the Study of History; the other is upon General Reading.[3] Their merit does not consist in being deep or abstruse discussions, but being full of that good sense and just observation which make them worthy of the perusal of those who are advanced beyond the period of education; while their lively character will entice young learners to a right course of reading, and the moral views which they contain will confirm them in principles of virtue. It is my recollection of the impression which they made on my own mind, which is still vivid, and my conviction, that they will give the most favourable turn to the studies of the young persons to whom I address them, that I rescue these Essays from oblivion. Let me recommend them, therefore, to the careful and repeated perusal of my Grand-children of both sexes ...

CONCLUDING NOTE.

That part of this short Essay [i.e., "Of Essay Writing,"] which is matter of pure instruction, ends here. The Author next assumes the character of an ambassador between the learned and the conversable part of the world, and then concludes with some remarks on French *belles lettres*, mixing them with observations on French manners.

It is impossible to separate, in this part of the Essay, what is instructive from what is playful allegory; I therefore finish my extract from the Essay here, which, though of small compass, cannot fail, if attentively and repeatedly perused, to direct reading in a right course, and obtain much pleasant and useful information, well calculated to improve the intercourse of society.

---

[3]   This is the subject of the Essay, its Title in the Book is on "*Essay Writing*."

What I have denominated fanciful allegory, bears a strong similitude to a passage in Mr Henry Mackenzie's Life of John Home, where he gives an account of a conversation between John Home and David Hume on a journey to Bath, after David Hume had been visited with the illness of which he died. What is in the Essay was written thirty-four years before that which the Journal mentions to have been said; yet the latter is more fanciful, lively, and entertaining.[4] ...

[4] [In "Of Essay Writing" Hume develops the fictional idea that he is "Resident or Ambassador from the Dominions of Learning to those of Conversation." In John Home's Diary of a Journey with Hume to Bath, contained in this collection, Hume and Home speculate about how Europe would be ruled if each were in control of a particular country.]

107
WILLIAM ADAM:
SEQUEL TO THE GIFT OF A GRANDFATHER

[William Adam], *Sequel to the Gift of a Grandfather*, [Edinburgh], 1839, 64 p. Selections; from 1839 edition.

William Adam (1751–1839) was the author of *Two Short Essays* (1836) excerpted in this collection. Fulfilling his promise in that work, three years later he published his *Sequel* – also intended for his grandchildren – which presents anecdotes of Edinburgh's literati, based on Adam's personal acquaintance with them. In his entry on Hume, he describes the famous philosopher's visits to his parents' home, which on one occasion resulted in a chair collapsing under Hume's weight. He mentions that, contrary to Hume's rule of not giving letters of introduction, he nevertheless received one from him for a planned visit to Baron d'Holbach. In his entry on Alexander Wedderburn, he notes that authorship of the articles in the *Edinburgh Review* was kept secret from Hume. The following is from the 1739 and only edition of Adam's *Sequel*.

I have classed the following List of those distinguished persons who formed what I call the Augustan age of the ancient Metropolis of Scotland. First, those who had no particular vocation: Second, those who had regular established professional pursuits.

———

The following sketches were the amusement of irregular intervals during the winter of 1836–7. They were proceeded with when other occupation was wanting, or as a relaxation from other pursuits. They were dictated off-hand, were put aside when done, and underwent no correction or consideration afterwards.

December 1839.

———

DAVID HUME.

It would be idle to attempt to add any thing to what is known universally of this most distinguished historian and philosopher. His simple unaffected nature and kindly disposition, exalted him as much as the singular powers of his mind, and his talents for expressing in writing what he contemplated, so well described by Gibbon, as careless inimitable beauties of style, which, when he read, he laid down the book in despair that he should never be able to imitate them.

I have before shewn that he never introduced in conversation his abstruse or sceptical speculations; that all his sentiments were moral and natural and pleasing, and even playful in the extreme.[1] This is evinced by his letters, which are perfect in their kind. He could bring himself down without effort to the most familiar playfulness with young persons, and particularly delighted in the conversation of youthful females.

Mr Hume was one of our constant visitors – making, as was the custom of those days, tea-time the hour of calling. In the summer he would often stroll to my father's beautiful villa of North Merchiston. On one occasion – I was then a boy of thirteen – he, missing my mother, made his tea-drinking good with two or three young ladies of eighteen or nineteen (his acquaintances,) who were my mother's guests. I recollect perfectly how agreeably he talked to them; and my recollection has been rendered permanent by another occurrence which caused some mirth and no mischief.

When the philosopher was amusing himself in conversation with the young ladies, the chair began to give way under him, and gradually brought him to the floor.

The damsels were both alarmed and amused, when Mr Hume, recovering himself, and getting upon his legs, said in his broad Scotch tone, but in English words, (for he never used Scotch,) "Young ladies, you must tell Mr Adam to keep stronger chairs for heavy philosophers."

This simple story is a good specimen of the man. He was above all affectation. I was a companion of his eldest nephew,[2] and saw much of him when I was very young. As I grew up he used to invite me to dinner, and I took great delight in his conversation. I continued in and about Edinburgh long enough to be able to relish it, and perhaps to join in it. On one particular occasion I met him at tea at Professor Ferguson's; it was at the period of my attending Dr Blair's class on rhetoric and belles lettres; their conversation became very interesting to me, as it bore upon subjects which had an affinity to what I was

---

[1] [See William Adam's *Two Short Essays* (1736) excerpted in this collection.]

[2] [Joseph Home (1752–1832), son of Hume's elder brother John Home of Ninewells (1709–1785).]

in the habit of hearing prelected upon. They discussed particularly the Henriade of Voltaire; they were not displeased with any want of brilliancy in the versification, but they condemned the choice of the subject. Mr Hume said, "He should never choose for an epic poem, history, the truth of which is well known; for no fiction can come up to the interest of the actual story and incidents of the singular life of Henry the IV." and Professor Ferguson added, "What epic poet could improve upon the chivalrous life of Chevalier Bayard, or on the event of his extraordinary romantic death?"

After I had left Edinburgh for some years, Mr Hume, who was not willing to trouble his friends in Paris with letters of introduction, gave me a letter to Baron D. Holback. I found myself so defective in the French language, that I avoided delivering it at first; and when I had conquered that difficulty, and had determined to avail myself of the letter, I was, by the early meeting of Parliament, (in Oct. 1775) unexpectedly called to leave Paris. I mention this circumstance, because I am rather vain of having been made an exception to Mr Hume's general rule as to introductions.

The works of this great man, what he has written of himself, and what has been said of him by many others, would have made it idle to have gone into that line of observation; while the familiar domestic occurrences to which I have alluded, illustrate the character of simplicity which belonged to his superior genius.

MR WEDDERBURN.

Afterwards Solicitor General and Attorney General of England, Chief Justice of the Common Pleas, and finally, Lord High Chancellor of Great Britain. Lord Loughborough, and Earl of Rosslyn, was in the early part of his life an advocate at the Scottish Bar, a member of the Select Society, and a friend and companion of all the literary men of his day in Edinburgh. There was at that period carried in with great privacy, though David Hume was never admitted to the secret, a critical review;[3] to this Mr Wedderburn was a frequent contributor. ...

THE REV. DR WALLACE.

Was a person who stood far aloof in social intercourse from those I have mentioned. he was more advanced in years than most of them, except perhaps David Hume, who born in 1711, was about ten years older than the generality of those whom I have mentioned. Dr Wallace was the antagonist of David Hume upon the subject of the populousness of ancient nations. Wallace's is a

---

[3] [i.e., the *Edinburgh Review* (1755–1756).]

well conceived and well conducted piece of controversial reasoning; but the erudition, and the profound philosophy contained in David Hume's essay, stands superior to most of the productions of that age. In their controversy, the utmost urbanity and good humour prevailed, equally to the credit of both.

108
JOHN HILL BURTON:
LIFE AND CORRESPONDENCES
OF DAVID HUME

John Hill Burton, *Life and correspondence of David Hume: from the papers bequeathed by his nephew to the Royal Society of Edinburgh, and other original sources.* Edinburgh: W. Tait, 1846, 2 v.
Selected anecdotes from Chapters 16 and 17; from 1846 edition.

Born in Aberdeen, son of an army lieutenant, John Hill Burton (1809–1881) was educated at the University of Aberdeen and later entered the legal profession. He supplemented his income as a writer, contributing to the *Westminster Review* and *Edinburgh Review*, and assisting in the editing of Jeremy Bentham's writings. In 1846 he achieved some fame through the publication of the *Life and Correspondence of David Hume*, the first such work to draw on Hume's letters and manuscripts – bequeathed by his nephew, Baron David Hume, to the Royal Society of Edinburgh. The items are now in possession of the National Library of Scotland (MS 23151–23163). In the final chapter of the *Life*, Burton departs from Hume's letters, discussing Hume's character and relating a variety of anecdotes. Some of these he reprints or adapts from earlier works. It is apparent, though, that Burton gathered several of the anecdotes directly from relatives of Hume's friends, which had not appeared in print before. The selections below include new anecdotes and some previously appearing ones that differ enough in wording to be noteworthy. Other anecdotes that Burton cites are contained elsewhere in this collection as appear in the original sources. The following is from the 1846 and only edition of Burton's *Life*.

... Hume seems to have now commenced the building of the house, in the New Town of Edinburgh, in which he died. It was the commencement of the street leading southward from St. Andrew's Square, now called St. David Street. {[Footnote:] When the house was built, and inhabited by Hume, but while yet the street, of which it was the commencement, had no name, a witty young lady, daughter of Baron Ord, chalked on the wall, the words "St. David

286

Street." The allusion was very obvious. Hume's "lass," judging that it was not meant in honour or reverence, ran into the house much excited, to tell her master how he was made game of. "Never mind, lassie," he said; "many a better man has been made a saint of before."}[1]

... {[Footnote:] It has been said that, having once given a guinea by mistake to a beggar, the man, who was a respectable member of his trade, returned and explained the mistake. He was permitted to keep the coin, the philosopher observing, "Oh, Honesty-how poor a dwelling-place hast thou found!"} ...

... {[Footnote:] These literary parties at Mrs. Cockburn's, appear to have been frequent and agreeable. A gentleman still living, was present at many of them when a youth, and particularly recollects one occasion when a tipsy relative of that lady chose to lock the door of the room where the walking habiliments of the guests were preserved. A general borrowing of articles of clothing from surrounding neighhours took place, and those which fell to Hume's lot, happened to produce a peculiarly ludicrous effect.}

... One occasionally meets with venerable persons who remember having been dandled on Hume's knee, and the number of these reminiscences indicates that he was fond of children. {[footnote:] In one instance, a vivid recollection was preserved of the difficulty, from his fatness, of getting sufficient room on his knee, and the necessity of keeping fast hold of the corner of his laced waistcoat.}

... The broad Scottish pronunciation, in which, by all accounts, he indulged, was a rather singular habit in one who desired to throw off all marks of provincialism. Yet we are told that in this rude Doric garb he clothed a very pure English colloquial style. We must take this statement with allowances. He never probably in his most finished writings completely divested his style of Scotticisms; and the English he spoke must have been pure only in comparison with the language of his fellow countrymen. But it may be remarked, that provincial broadness of pronunciation in Scotland is far from being incompatible with a very pure and unprovincial style of language. It has often been observed, that in those parts of the country where the speech of the uneducated is most peculiar, English, when spoken at all, is found in greatest purity. Thus, an inhabitant of the border districts makes his southern tones, though hardly distinguishable from those of his English neighbours, the vehicle of intense Scotticisms; while beyond the Grampians, the deep broad Teutonic pronunciation sometimes gives voice to uncontaminated English, as established by literary and colloquial rules.

Hume had very clearly two kinds of conversation, one for strangers and the world at large, the other for his chosen friends with whom he was at ease, and

---

[1] [For alternative accounts of the story behind the naming of St. David Street, see Carlyle's *Autobiography* (1860), Chambers's, *Scottish Jests* (1832), and "Miscellaneous Hume Anecdotes," contained in this collection.]

who could understand the good humour of that jocularity which a contemporary pronounced to have something in it perfectly infantine. His friend John Home was somewhat renowned for a warlike and romantic pomp in his ideas, like those which pervade his own tragic personations. In Hume's conversation we may believe that there was nothing either heroic or enthusiastic. A good humoured sly application of the fugitive subjects of discussion, to the peculiarities of the guests; an occasional vigorous and apt remark; a fantastic wit sometimes let loose to wander where it pleased, and choose whatever it thought fit for its object, – seem to have constituted the charm of his society. Yet the tone of his thoughts sometimes rose to enthusiasm. Thus the son of his valued friend Ferguson, remembers his father saying, that, one clear and beautiful night, when they were walking home together, Hume suddenly stopped, looked up to the starry sky, and said, more after the manner of "Hervey's Meditations" than the "Treatise of Human Nature," "Oh, Adam, can any one contemplate the wonders of that firmament, and not believe that there is a God!"

... {[Footnote:] He seems, from this and other notices, to have been occasionally absent in his habits; but there is no such collection of practical illustrations of this failing, as we possess in the case of Smith and others. I only remember having heard of one trifling instance, of which I had an account from an eyewitness. Hume had been dining with Dr. Jardine, and there had been much conversation about "internal light." In descending the stair leading from the Doctor's "flat," when he left the party, Hume failed to observe that after so many flights which reached the street door, there was, according to a not uncommon practice, another flight of stairs leading to the cellars. He continued his descent, accordingly, till the very end, where some time afterwards he was found in extreme darkness and perplexity, wondering how it was that he could find no outlet. The circumstance bore rather curiously on some opinions he had been maintaining, and Jardine said, shaking his head, "Oh David! Where is your internal light?"}

Those who know him solely by his philosophical reputation, will perhaps believe him to have been "Parous deorum cultor et infrequens." But this does not seem to have been the case, at least in his outward conduct. We find him, in writing home from France, casually mentioning his not having seen Elliot's sons "in church;" and on another occasion making a like allusion, indicative of his having been a pretty regular attendant at the ambassador's chapel. He is said to have been fond of Dr. Robertson's preaching, and not averse to that of his colleague and opponent, John Erskine. A lady, distinguished in literature, remembers that in a conversation with a respectable tradesman's wife, who had been a servant to Hume, she said that her master one day asked her very seriously, why she was never seen in church, where he had provided seats for all his household. At that time there were very few of the humbler classes in Edinburgh, who did not belong to the Church of Scotland. The woman's defence was, that she belonged to a dissenting congregation; and it was admitted to be quite satisfactory.

... The Poker Club, occasionally mentioned in these pages, seems to have had no other direct and Specific object but the consumption of claret. The duty laid on that national wine, by "the English stateman," so pathetically commemorated by John Home, was a heavy blow and great discouragement to the club; but it rallied, and returned to its old esteemed beverage; and, indeed, it is a somewhat curious circumstance, that the national taste, created by the early intercourse with France and the consequent cheapness of French wines, still lingers in Scotland, where claret is much more generally consumed than in England. The club met in Fortune's tavern every Friday. It was the practice, at each meeting, to name two to be, what were called, "attendant members;" an arrangement, probably, designed to form a nucleus round which those whose attendance was uncertain, but who might drop in occasionally in the course of the evening, could form themselves; and to prevent any general desertion of the club, or, what might be, perhaps, more calamitous, the accident of any individual finding himself, for the night, its sole and solitary representative. We find Hume duly taking his turn in these attendances, and keeping the minutes according to rotation. On the 20th January, 1775, there is this emphatic entry, in his handwriting, "As Mr. Nairiie was one of the attendant members, and neglected his duty, the club sent him the bill." The last meeting of the club, attended by Hume, appears to have been that of 8th December, 1775. {[Footnote:] Minute-book of The Poker Club, in possession of Sir Adam Ferguson.}

It does not appear to be necessary that traditional anecdotes, such as the few we possess of Hume, must either be authenticated, or excluded from such a work as the present. It seems to entitle them to a place, that they were current among those who knew his character and habits. They thus afford all that is expected from such sources – passing fancy sketches, recognised as likenesses. Like several others that have appeared in these pages, as mere traditions, the following anecdote, which is eminently natural and curious, has no farther authentication than the general belief, in Edinburgh, that it "was like the man."

About the commencement of his last illness, a female member of the respectable Berean congregation, in Leith, presented herself at his door, with the information that she had been intrusted with a message to him from on High; and, becoming very urgent, succeeded in obtaining admission. "This is a very important matter, madam," said the philosopher, "we must take it with deliberation; – perhaps you had better get a little temporal refreshment before you begin. 'Lassie, bring this good lady a glass of wine.'" While she was preparing for the attack, Hume entered, good-humouredly, into conversation with her; and, discovering that her husband was a chandler, announced that he stood very much in want, at that time, of some temporal lights, and intrusted his guest with a very large order. This unexpected stroke of business at once absorbed all the good woman's thoughts; and, forgetting her important mission, she immediately trotted home to acquaint her husband with the good news.[2]

There is an anecdote, which has appeared in numerous collections of such literary scraps, which represents him as having slipped into the boggy ground at the base of the castle rock, and called to a woman to help him out. In his unwieldy and infirm state, during his latter years, the accident is not improbable. The anecdote proceeds to say, that the female called on had great doubts of the propriety of helping "Hume, the Deist," out of that slough of despond into which it had pleased Providence to cast him. "But, my good woman, does not your religion as a Christian, teach you to do good, even to your enemies?" "That may be," said she, "but ye shallna get out o' that, till ye become a Christian yersell: and repeat the Lord's Prayer and the Belief," a feat which is said to have been very rapidly performed, much to the worthy catechist's astonishment.

Some of his witticisms have a tone of sarcastic severity, which he does not appear to have been disposed to suppress, even when women were the victims, if it was called forth by affectation or folly. To a celebrated "fine woman" of his day, who said she was often pestered to tell her age, and desired his opinion what answer she should give: he is reported to have said, "Madam, say you are not yet come to years of discretion." To the same lady, who, when crossing one of the ferries of the Firth of Forth, during a fresh breeze, was making a loud outcry about danger, he remarked, with much coolness, that they would probably soon be food for fishes;" and who," said the frightened belle, probably a little confused by the horrors of their position, "who will they begin with?" The answer she received was, "Why, madam, those of them that are gluttons will begin with me; those that are epicures with your ladyship."

---

[2] [This, and some of the stories in the following paragraphs, appear to be adapted from *Scottish Jests*, excerpted in this collection.]

109
SAMUEL ROGERS:
RECOLLECTIONS OF THE TABLE-TALK

Samuel Rogers, in Alexander Dyce, *Recollections of the table-talk of Samuel Rogers*. London, E. Moxon, 1856, [v]-viii, 355 p.
Selections; from *Recollections*, New York: D. Appleton, 1856.

Born in Stoke Newington, near London, Samuel Rogers (1763–1855) was an essayist and poet, and is today best remembered for his witty conversations recorded by Alexander Dyce (1798–1869) in *Recollections of the table-talk of Samuel Rogers*. Rogers appears to have had no first hand acquaintance with Hume, being only a boy when the philosopher died. The anecdotes he relates are based on his association with Hume's surviving acquaintances, including John Fitzpatrick (1745–1818), Richard Price (1723–1791), and John Horne Tooke (1736–1812). Dyce's *Recollections* was published twice more in 1856 and again in 1887.

While Rousseau was lodging in Chiswick Terrace, Fitzpatrick called upon him one day, and had not been long in the room when David Hume entered. Rousseau had lost a favourite dog; and Hume, having exerted himself to recover it, now brought it back to its master, who thanked him with expressions of the most fervent gratitude, and shed tears of joy over the animal.

Fitzpatrick, who had been much in the company of David Hume, used always to speak of him as "a delicious creature." ...

Hume told Cadell the bookseller that he had a great desire to be introduced to as many of the persons who had written against him as could be collected; and requested Cadell to bring him and them together. Accordingly, Dr. Douglas, Dr. Adams, &c. &c., were invited by Cadell to dine at his house in order to meet Hume. They came; and Dr. Price, who was of the party, assured me that they were all delighted with David. ...

... He [Horne Tooke] said that Hume wrote his History as witches say their prayers – backwards. ...

Tooke told me that in his early days a friend gave him a letter of introduction to D'Almbert at Paris. Dressed *à-la-mode*, he presented the letter, and was very courteously received by D'Almbert, who talked to him about operas, comedies, and suppers, &c. Tooke had expected conversation on very different topics, and was greatly disappointed. When he took leave, he was followed by a gentleman in a plain suit, who had been in the room during his interview with D'Alembert, and who had perceived his chagrin. "D'Alembert," said the gentleman, "supposed from your gay apparel that you were merely a *petit maître*." The gentleman was David Hume. On his next visit to D'Alembert, Tooke's dress was altogether different; and so was the conversation. ...

I knew Jane Duchess of Gordon intimately, and many pleasant hours have I passed in her society. She used to say, "I have been acquainted with David Hume and William Pitt, and therefore I am not afraid to converse with any body." ...

... A very old gentleman, who had known Johnson intimately, assured me that the bent of his mind was decidedly towards scepticism; that he was literally afraid to examine his own thoughts on religious matters; and that hence partly arose his hatred of Hume and other such writers.

110
MISCELLANEOUS HUME ANECDOTES

As with many famous people, interesting stories about Hume circulated among his friends and townsfolk. Some of these were published as biographical sketches of the great philosopher. Shorter entries appeared in periodicals, anecdote collections, or published diaries and letters. Brief anecdotes from around thirty such sources are presented below, and categorized around common themes.

THE YOUNG HUME

[Hannah More] was much indebted for her critical knowledge to a linen-draper of Bristol, of the name of [John] Peach. He had been the friend of Hume, who had sown his confidence in his judgment, by entrusting to him the correction of his history, in which he used to say, he had discovered more than two hundred Scotticisms. But for this man, it appears, two years of the life of the historian might have passed into oblivion, which were spent in a merchant's counting-house in Bristol, whence he was dismissed on account of the promptitude of his pen in the correction of the letters entrusted to him to copy. More than twenty years after the death of Mr. Peach, the subject of these Memoirs [i.e., Hannah More], being in the company with Dr. Percy, then Bishop of Dromore, Mr. Gibbon, Sir Joshua Reynolds, and others, who were conjecturing what might have been the cause of this chasm of two years in the life of Hume (of which the Bishop was then proposing to give a sketch) she was enabled to clear up the mystery, by relating the above anecdote. As the intended life did not appear, she never knew what use the bishop made of her communication. [William Roberts, *Memoirs of the Life and Correspondence of Mrs. Hannah More*, London, 1834, Vol. 1, p. 16.]

–

HUME IN PARIS

The celebrated David Hume, the great English historian, known and esteemed by his works, was not so well gifted for that kind of amusement to which all our Ladies had decided him to be suitable. He made his *debut* at the house of Madame de T***; they had given him the part of a Sultan seated between two slaves, on which he should employ his eloquence to fix their love; when finding them

293

inexorable, he was to seek out the cause of their pains and their resistance: They place him upon a sofa between two of the prettiest women in Paris; – he looks at them attentively. He strikes his paunch and his knees repeatedly, and found nothing to say to them but – Well, young ladies – Well, there you are, then – Well, there you are – There you are, then? – This phrase was continued for a quarter of an hour, and he could not get beyond or out of it. At length one of them rose up with impatience. Ah, said she, I doubt very much if that man is good for anything but to eat his veal! From that time he exiled himself for a spectator, but is not the less feasted or cajoled. It is indeed a very comical part that he plays here; but luckily for him, or rather for his philosophical dignity, because he appears to accommodate himself very well to this sort of life – there has not been any ruling mania in this country since his arrival – and thus circumstanced they have regarded him as a lucky thing, and the effervescence of our young heads is altogether turned in his favour. All the beautiful women are taken with him; he is invited to all the fine suppers; and there is no good feast without him; in a word he is for our coquettes what the Genevan is for me. [*Memoires et Correspondance de Madame D'Epinay*, Paris, 1818, Vol. 3, p. 284 (translated).]

[Edmund Burke said of Hume that] in manners he was an easy unaffected man, previous to going to Paris as secretary to Lord Hertford; but that the adulation and caresses of the female wits of that capital had been too powerful even for a philosopher, and the result was, he returned a literary coxcomb. [James Prior (1790?–1869), *Memoir of the life and character of the Right Hon. Edmund Burke*, London, Baldwin, Cradock and Joy, 1824.]

ST. DAVID'S STREET[1]

The extreme western house upon the south side of St. Andrew's Square, entering from St. David's Street, though at present occupied by only a fashionable *schneider*, is worthy of notice, as having been, fifty years ago, the residence of the celebrated philosopher and historian, DAVID HUME. – He died here; and we have conversed with a kinswoman of the sceptic, who, when a child, was sent to attend him here upon his death-bed. What will appear strange, he, every morning and evening, caused this juvenile attendant to kneel by his side, and say her prayers aloud; and often, when very ill in bed, desired her to repeat to him the beautifully simple sentences of the Lord's Prayer. – The following more amusing, though not more valuable, anecdote, we have seen in print. Previous to the painting of the names of the streets of the New Town upon the corners, and when the philosopher's house was almost the only one built in that street, his friend, Dr. Webster, one of the

---

[1] [For alternative accounts of the story behind the naming of St. David Street, see Carlyle's *Autobiography* (1860), Chambers's, *Scottish Jests* (1832), and Burton's *Life* (1846), contained in this collection.]

ministers of the city, and a professed wit, came past one day, and, in ironical allusion to the known infidelity of its tenant, wrote with chalk upon the front, "*Saint David's Street.*" Not long after, Mr. Hume's aged female servant happened to observe the inscription, and immediately ran in to inform her master of the joke which had been payed off upon him. The philosopher, not at all disturbed, only said, in his usual quiet way, "Weel, weel, Janet, never mind. – I am not the first man of sense that has been made a saint of." [Robert Chambers, *Walks in Edinburgh*, Edinburgh, Hunter, 1825 (pp. 182–183 of 1888 edition).]

With the modern revival of mediævalism the long-forgotten virtues of St. Margaret have been recalled to mind. But this is a work of very recent date. When the New Town of Edinburgh was planned and laid out in 1768, while St. Andrew had all due honour as Scotland's patron saint, the sainted queen who is so intimately associated with its early history appears to have passed wholly out of remembrance. St. George and St. David received due recognition; St. Patrick got a niche in the southern extension; but when the name of the patron saint of England was appropriated by the rival projectors of another square, laid out on the slope of the southern meadows, no fitter substitute was thought of than that of Queen Charlotte. ... It chanced that, when David Hume deserted his old lodging in St. James's Court, for more fashionable quarters in the New Town, his house occupied the south-west corner of the street dedicated to the Welsh saint. Here he established his household, at a time when a few detached buildings alone represented the modern city. But ere long its avenues began to assume form; and one morning, as his old housekeeper passed down the street, she was startled to see the name of St. David painted on the corner of her master's house. This she interpreted as a premeditated insult on the sceptical philosopher, and bursting into his room in high indignation, she exclaimed: "What do you think the ne'er-do-weels hae gane and painted on our housefront?" When at length Mr. Hume comprehended the nature of the provocation which so excited the wrath of the good dame, he comforted her with the philosophical reply: "Tut, Jenny! is that all? many a better man than me has been called a saint!" [Daniel Wilson, *Reminiscences of Old Edinburgh*, Edinburgh: David Douglas, 1878, Vol. 2, pp. 261–262.]

HUME'S PERSONAL CHARACTER

[Hume was] a gentleman of the most amiable private Character, and much beloved by every Body that knows him. He is remarkably charitable to the poor, and has provided handsomely for several poor Families that were related to him. He never swears, nor has any one ever accused him of any immoralities of any kind. [Benjamin Rush, *Autobiography of Benjamin Rush*, Princeton: Princeton University Press, 1948, p. 49.][2]

---

[2] [Rush was in Edinburgh from 1766–1768.]

I am no admirer of Hume. In conversation he was very thick; and I do believe hardly understood a subject till he had written upon it. [*The Philadelphia Repository*, March 9, 1805, vol. 5, p. 76 (as appears in Mark Spencer's *Hume's Reception in Early America*).]

David Hume. – I do not remember to have heard, nor do his portraits show, that Hume squinted; but I find it stated as a fact in the French *Esprit des Journeaux* for June, 1789, and as the points of a sarcastic query of Rousseau, when he had most absurdly and ungratefully quarrelled with Hume: "*With which eye* does Mr. Hume look on his friends?" C. [*Notes and Queries*, January 26, 1856, Vol. 1, second series, Page 72.]

Dr. Robertson used frequently to say, that in Mr. Hume's gaiety there was something which approached to *infantine*, and that he had found the same thing so often exemplified in the circle of his other friends, that he was almost disposed to consider it as characteristical of genius.

Among the most distinguished speakers in the Select Society were Sir Gilbert Elliot, Mr. Wedderburn, Mr .Andrew Pringle, Lord Kames, Mr. Walter Stewart, Lord Elibank, and Dr. Robertson. The Right Honourable Charles Townshend spoke once. David Hume and Adam Smith never opened their lips. [Dugald Stewart, *Account of the Life and Writings of William Robertson*, Edinburgh, 1801, Sect. 2; Note A.]

Major M____, with whom I dined yesterday, said that he had frequently met David Hume at their military mess in Scotland, and in other parties; that he was very polite and pleasant, though thoughtful in company, generally reclining his head upon his hand, as if in study; from which he would suddenly recover, however, with some indifferent question; extremely inquisitive, but quite easy to himself and all around him. One is glad to catch personal notices, however slight, of memorable men and of speculative philosophers. I know no one so memorable as Hume. He seems to have so far outstripped the spirit of the times in his original and profound researches, that the world is in no condition at present to do justice to his merits. ["Diary of a Lover of Literature," in *Gentleman's Magazine*, 1834 (?), N.S. Vol. 1. p. 142 – as appears in Burton's *Life* (1846), p. 452.]

John Home was very strenuous in support of the *o* in preference to the *u*, in the spelling of his name, and held the point to be so clear in his own favour, as to admit of no debate. David Hume, at one time, jocularly proposed that they should determine the controversy by casting lots. "Nay," says John, "that is a most extraordinary proposal indeed, Mr Philosopher – for if you lose, you take your own name, and if I lose, I take another man's name." This he often told me with great glee, and nearly in these words. [Baron David Hume

(1757–1838), in Henry Mackenzie's *An Account of the Life and Writings of John Home*, Edinburgh, Printed for A. Constable, 1822, p. 164.]

Mon. Dec. 14. [1772.] [Thomas] Baker and I went with Lord Home to the house of the Celebrated David Hume, to whom his lordship was desirous of introducing us; but Mr Hume was not home, at which (on account of the badness of many of his principles and other reasons) I was not displeased. It must however be confessed that he is a man of great taste & ingenuity, tho' unhappily ill-aplied.

Mon May 17. [1773.] Mr Baker and I were introduced to the celebrated philosopher, David Hume. His manner is easy & agreeable as might be expected in a man who has seen so much of life & is so well acquainted with the world. But at first one would not take him for that first-rate genius which he really is. He often talks very vulgar Scotch.

Sat. May 22. [1773.] Baker and I supped with Dr Home by invitation. The Dr told us a remarkable anecdote of David Hume. When the Dr returned home in 1758 David was so poor that he said he would give up all expectations in life for £ 30 a year. What a change of times!

Sun. Aug. 25. [1776.] David Hume, the celebrated philosopher, is given over by his physicians, & it is supposed will die before morning. Dr Cullen gave him for a toast, saying 'I wont give him up yet. Here is to his easy passage.' [*The Diary of Sylas Neville 1767–1788*, ed. Basil Conzens-Hardy, London: Oxford University Press, 1950, pp. 192, 202, 247.]

You may judge if I am in possession by a scene that passed after supper. Sir James Macdonald had been mimicking Hume: I told the women, who, besides the mistress, were the Duchess de la Valière, Madame de Forcalquier, a demoiselle, that to be sure they would be glad to have a specimen of Mr. Pitt's manner of speaking; and that nobody mimicked him so well as Elliot. (Walpole to H. S. Conway, October 6, 1765.)

For Lord Lyttelton, if he would come hither, and turn freethinker once more, he would be reckoned the most agreeable man in France - next to Mr. Hume, who is the only thing in the world that they believe implicitly; which they must do, for I defy them to understand any language that he speaks. (Walpole Thomas Brand, Esq., October 19, 1765.) [Horace Walpole, *Letters of Horace Walpole*, Philadelphia: Lea And Blanchard, 1842, 4 v.]

---

[3] [For other accounts of Hume at dinners, see Boswell's Letters to William Temple (1758) and *Boswelliana* (1874), and Carlyle's *Autobiography* (1860) in this collection.]

HUME AT DINNERS[3]

Mr. Hume, as I have been assured by those who knew him, could immediately after dinner engage in profound speculation, without being the worse for it. [James Beattie, *Dissertations Moral and Critical,* London, Strahan, 1783, p. 37]

David Hume met Madame ——, a Dutch lady of rank and literary talents, at the house of the Earl of Fife, at Whitehall. They were exceedingly pleased with each other, and the native of Batavia observed, that where Mr. H. was, no one ought to think of eating. The justice of this remark was in some respects verified; for, although the dinner was excellent, some chickens, which had been reserved for a *bonne bouche*, were ordered to be removed, and placed at the fire; and the dissertation of Mr. H. was so long, that a cat actually ran away with them! [*Atheneum; or, Spirit of the English Magazines*, 1824, vol. 1 pp. 365 (as appears in Mark Spencer's *Hume's Reception in Early America*)]

HUME'S WEIGHT[4]

Lady [Elizabeth] Wallace and David Hume were partial to each other. They once crossed the Firth from Kinghon to Leith together, when a violent storm rendered the passengers apprehensive of a salt water death; and her ladyship's terror induced her to seek consolation from her friend, who, with infinite *sang froid*, assured her, "he thought there was great probability of their becoming food for fishes." – "And pray, my dear friend," said Lady Wallace, "which do you think they will eat first?" – "Those who are gluttons," replied the historian, "will undoubtedly fall foul of me; but the epicures will attack your ladyship." [John Adams, *Elegant anecdotes,* London, G. Kearsley, 1789.][5]

Have you heard of the *Congress* at *Inverary*. So fine a Duke, and so fine a Duchess, there, opening house after so long an *interregnum*, drew all the country – and though fifty beds were made, they were so crowded that even *David Hume*, for all his great figure as a Philosopher, and Historian, or his greater as a fat man, was obliged by the *adamantine*[6] *peg-maker* to make one of the three in a bed. [Daniel Wray, letter of October 15, 1771, in John Nichols, *Literary History,* London, Nichols, 1817, Vol. 1. pp. 141–142]

---

[4] [For other anecdotes regarding Hume's weight, see Adam's *Sequel* (1839) and Anne Lindsay's letter (1770) in this collection.]

[5] [This story also appears in Chambers's *Scottish Jests* (1832) and Burton's *Life* (1846) in this collection. Adams's version is the earliest of these.]

[6] *Si figit adamantinos* – dura *Necessitas Clavos* – Horace, Od. iii. 24.

HUME'S HISTORY

David Hume knew so little of the Law and the Constitution of England, that he one day, in company with a celebrated Lawyer of the kingdom of Ireland, was praising the system of the old Crown Law of England, as a mild and liberal one. His friend reminded him of several instances of its severity and injustice, which have within these two last centuries been done away. 'Alas!' cries David, 'I knew nothing of them – I must own, then, that the old Crown Law was a very cruel and a very arbitrary system. [*European Magazine and London Review*, 1794, Vol. 25, p. 431.]

Mr. Smith observed to me, not long before his death, that after all his practice in writing, he composed as slowly, and with as great difficulty, as at first. He added, at the same time, that Mr. Hume had acquired so great a facility in this respect, that the last volumes of his *History* was printed from the original copy, with a few marginal corrections. It may gratify the curiosity of some readers to know, that when Mr. Smith was employed in composition, he generally walked up and down his apartment, dictating to a secretary. All Mr. Hume's works (I have been assured) were written with his own hand. A critical reader may, I think, perceive in the different styles of these two classical writers, the effects of their different modes of study. [Dugald Stewart, "Account of the life and writings of Adam Smith, LL.D." in *Transactions of the Royal Society of Edinburgh*, 1794, vol. 3, pp. 55–137, Sect. 5]

One single original document has sometimes shaken into dust their palladian edifice of history. At the moment Hume was sending some sheets of his History to press, Murdin's State Papers appeared. And we are highly amused and instructed by a letter of our historian to his rival, Robertson, who probably found himself often in the same forlorn situation. Our historian discovered in that collection what compelled him to retract his pre-conceived system – he hurries to stop the press, and paints his confusion and his anxiety with all the ingenuous simplicity of his nature. 'We are all in the wrong!' he exclaims. Of Hume I have heard, that certain manuscripts at the state paper office had been prepared for his inspection during a fortnight, but he never could muster courage to pay his promised visit. Satisfied with the common accounts, and the most obvious sources of history, when librarian at the Advocates' Library, where yet may be examined the books he used, marked by his hand; he spread the volumes about the sofa, from which he rarely rose to pursue obscure inquiries, or delay by fresh difficulties the page which every day was growing under his charming pen. A striking proof of his careless happiness I discovered in his never referring to the perfect edition of Whitelock's Memorials of 1732, but to the old truncated and faithless one of 1682. [Isaac Disraeli, *Curiosities of Literature*, London, J. Murray, 1791–1793, Part 2, "True Sources of Secret History"]

The only glimpse we gain [of Hume's study method for his *History*] is through a story told by a late venerable Scottish crony. Some one having hinted that David had neglected an authority he ought to have consulted, the old gentleman replied, – 'Why, mon, David read a vast deal before he set about a piece of his book; but his usual seat was the sofa, and he often wrote with his legs up; and it would have been unco fashious to have moved across the room when any little doubt occurred.' [Francis Palgrave, "Hume and his Influence upon History," *Quarterly Review*, March 1844, Vol. 73, pp. 536–592.]

It is not generally known how much Hume revised his History. When living in Edinburgh, busy with that classical composition, he was intimate with an old Jesuit, who, like most of the order, was a scholar, and a man of taste; to his opinion, as the parts were finished, the manuscript work was submitted. Soon after the publication of Elizabeth's reign, the priest happened to turn over the pages, and was astonished to find on the printed page sins of the Scottish queen that never sullied the written one; Mary's character was directly the reverse of what he had read before. He sought the author, and asked the cause: "Why, (answered Hume,) the printer said he should lose 500*l*. by that story; indeed be [sic] almost refused to print it: so I was obliged to revise it as you saw." It is needless to add, the Jesuit reviewed no more manuscripts. ["Hume's History of England," in *The Atheneum*, 1824, Vol. 1, second series, p. 85 (as appears in Mark Spencer's *Hume's Reception in Early America*).]

HUME'S PHILOSOPHY AND RELIGION

Mr Hume was boasting to the doctor, that among his disciples in Edinburgh he had the honour to reckon many of the fair sex. "Now, tell me," said the doctor, "whether, if you had a wife or a daughter, you would *wish* them to be your disciples? Think well before you answer me; for I assure you, that, whatever your answer is, I will not conceal it." Mr Hume, with a smile, and some hesitation, made this reply: "No; I believe scepticism may be too sturdy a virtue for a woman." Miss Gregory will certainly remember, that she has heard her father tell this story. [James Beattie to Mrs. Montagu, June 25, 1779, in *The Life and Writings of James Beattie*, ed. William Forbes, Edinburgh, Constable, 1806, Vol. 2, p. 54]

I found it [i.e., Berkeley's book "against the existence of matter"] in London, and have read it, and I cannot help saying that it is as poor a piece of sophistry as ever I saw composed by a man who seems to be in earnest; though I remember to have heard David Hume say that his arguments are absolutely unanswerable. [Lord Monboddo to James Harris, June 18, 1769, in William Knight, *Lord Monboddo*, London, Murray, 1900]

In his conversations he seldom alluded to the subject [or religion], but occasionally his opinions were perceivable. Thus, when one of the University, the late Mr. John Bruce, professor of logic, asked him to revise the syllabus of his lectures, he went over the proof-sheets with him; and on coming to the section entitled 'Proofs of the Existence of the Deity,' Mr. Hume said, "Right; very well." But the next section was entitled 'Proof of the Unity of the Deity,' and then he cried out, "Stop, John, stop; who told you whether there were *ane* or *mair*?" The same professor met him one day on the staircase of the College Library, where the inscription "*Christo et Musis has ædes sacrarunt cives Edinenses*" drew from the unbeliever an irreverent observation on the junction which the piety rather than the classical purity of the good town had made between the worship of the heathen and our own. [Henry Brougham (1778–1868), *Lives of men of letters & science, who flourished in the time of George III.* London, Knight, 1845, "Hume."]

The first time that M. Hume found himself at the table of the Baron [D'Holbach], he was seated beside him. I don't know for what purpose the English philosopher took it into his head to remark to the Baron that he did not believe in atheists, that he had never seen any. The Baron said to him: "Count how many we are here." We are eighteen. The Baron added: "It isn't too bad a showing to be able to point out to you fifteen at once: the three others haven't made up their minds." [Denis Diderot, *Lettres à Sophie Volland*, Paris, 1938, Vol. 2, p. 77; translated in Mossner's *Life*, p. 483.]

I have somewhere read that Mr. Hume, being in France, passed a day in the society of certain French atheistical philosophers, with whom he had much conversation, but to whose confident denial of the existence of a supreme intelligence he hesitated to accede. On his quitting their company, the discourse turned on the character of the British sage, who, in his own land, as your readers know, was esteemed to be at the very head of the sceptics and unbelievers. One French atheist observed (and some of the others agreed in the sentiment) that their visitor was unquestionably a considerable philosopher, but that it was greatly to be regretted that he was so much of a FANATIC. [*Christian Observer and Advocate*, October 1802, Vol. 1, pp. 650–651 (as appears in Mark Spencer's *Hume's Reception in Early America*).]

This tergiversation and complete abandonment of principle we shall clearly discern in examining his [i.e., Hume's] celebrated Essay on Miracles; an essay which he valued above all others, and to which he told me twenty-two answers had been made, hinting, that if any of them had been satisfactory any other would have been judged superfluous. [Richard Kirwan, "Remarks on Some sceptical positions in Hume's Enquiry," Sect. 5, in *Transactions of the Royal Irish Academy*, 1801, Vol. 8.]

A like story is told of his speech to Peter[7] Boyle, who called on him after his mother's death, and found him sitting over to the fire. "Do you really think, that there is nothing more left of her than in those ashes." "Peter," said Hume, laying his hand on his friend's knee, "you very much mistake my opinions if you ascribe to me anything of the kind." I venture to repeat this story as it was once repeated to me from an authentic source, in a form a somewhat more lively and likely than that in which it is usually given from Dr. Carlyle.[8] [Arthur Penrhyn Stanley (1815–1881), *Lectures on the history of the Church of Scotland, delivered in Edinburgh in 1872*, London: J. Murray, 1872.]

HUME'S FRIENDS AND CRITICS[9]

Hume's philosophical indifference could often suppress that irritability which Pope and Smollet fully indulged. But were the feelings of Hume more obtuse, or did his temper, gentle as it was constitutionally, bear, with a saintly patience, the mortifications of literary life so longendured? After recomposing two of his works which incurred the same neglect in their altered form, he raised the most sanguine hopes of his history, – but he tells us, 'miserable was my disappointment!' The reasoning Hume once proposed changing his name and his country and although he never deigned to reply to his opponents, yet they haunted him; and an eye-witness has thus described the irritated author discovering in conversation his suppressed resentment – 'His forcible mode of expression, the brilliant quick movements of his eyes, and the gestures of his body,' – these betrayed the pangs of contempt, or of aversion! [Isaac Disraeli, *An Essay on the Manners and Genius of the Literary Character*, London, T. Cadell, 1795, Ch. 4.]

Upon Mr. Skelton's arrival in London, he brought his manuscript to Andrew Millar the Bookseller, to know if he would purchase it, and have it printed at his own expense. The Bookseller desired him, as is usual, to leave it with him for a day or two, until he would get a certain gentleman of great abilities to examine it, who could judge, if the sale would quit the cost of printing. These gentlemen who examine manuscripts, in the Bookseller's cant, are called "triers." "Can you guess (he [i.e., Skelton]) said to me) who this gentleman was, that tried my Deism Revealed." "No, I cannot." "Hume the infidel." He came it seems to

---

[7] [i.e., Patrick Boyle.]

[8] [Carlyle's account of Boyle's story appears in his *Autobiography* (1860) in this collection.]

[9] [For other accounts of Hume's response to his critics, see Horne, *Letter to Adam Smith* (1777) for Hume's reaction to Beattie and Morgan's *Memoirs of the Life of the Rev. Richard Price* (1815) for his acknowledgement of Price's arguments.]

Andrew Millar's, took the manuscript to a room adjoining the shop, examined it here and there for about an hour, and then said to Andrew, print." [Samuel Burdy (1760–1820), *The life of the late Rev. Philip Skelton*, Dublin: W. Jones, 1792.]

"An Essay on Taste, by Alexander Gerard...." This Essay was corrected through the press by the celebrated David Hume; who at that time [i.e., 1759] had a temporary residence in Lisle-street, Leicester-fields, where I frequently visited him. [John Nichols, *Literary Anecdotes of the Eighteenth Century*, London, Nichols, 1812, Vol. 2, p. 326.]

[B]ut the fifteenth and sixteenth chapters [of the Decline and Fall] have been reduced by three successive revisals, from a large volume to their present size; and they might still be compressed, without any loss of facts or sentiments. An opposite fault may be imputed to the concise and superficial narrative of the first reigns from Commodus to Alexander; a fault of which I have never heard, except from Mr. Hume in his last journey to London. ...
Some weeks afterwards I had the melancholy pleasure of seeing Mr. Hume in his passage through London; his body feeble, his mind firm. On Aug. 25 of the same year (1776) he died, at Edinburgh, the death of a philosopher. [Edward Gibbon, *Memoirs of my Life and Writings*, London: Strahan, 1796, 2 v.].

Mr. Hume told me that he had from Rousseau himself the secret of his principles of composition. That acute though eccentric observer had perceived that to strike and interest the public the marvelous must be produced; that the marvelous of the heathen mythology had long since lost its effect; that the giants, magicians, fairies, and heroes of romance which succeeded had exhausted the portion of credulity which belonged to their age; that now nothing was left to the writer but that species of the marvelous which might still be produced, and with as great an effect as ever, though in another way; that is, the marvelous in life, in manners, in characters, and in extraordinary situations, giving rise to new and unlooked-for strokes in politics and morals. I believe that were Rousseau alive and in one of his lucid intervals, he would be shocked at the practical frenzy of his scholars, who in their paradoxes are servile imitators, and even in their incredulity discover an implicit faith. [Edmund Burke (1729–1797) *Reflections on the revolution in France*, London: J. Dodsley, 1790.]

The celebrated Mr. Hume used to call Dr. Franklin "the first fruits of America." The American revolution has given elasticity and energy to the minds of the inhabitants, has called forth talents and abilities of every kind, and produced a more copious harvest than the solitary "first fruits" observed by Mr. Hume seemed to indicate. [*English Review*, November 1787, Vol. 10, p. 329, review of John Adams's *Defense of the Constitutions of Government* (1787).]

EARLY BIOGRAPHIES AND COLLECTIONS OF LETTERS

111
THOMAS EDWARD RITCHIE:
AN ACCOUNT OF THE LIFE AND
WRITINGS OF DAVID HUME

Thomas Edward Ritchie, *An account of the life and writings of David Hume, Esq.*, London, Printed for T. Cadell and W. Davies, 1807, 1, [v]-vi, 1, 520 p. Selections; from 1807 edition.

Thomas Edward Ritchie (fl. 1800) was the author of *The Campaign of General Bonaparte in Italy* (1799) and *Political and Military Memoirs of Europe* (1800–1802). In 1807 he published the first detailed biography of Hume. Of its 520 pages, only around 100 are Ritchie's own words, the rest being excerpted material – including Hume's letters, eight essays that Hume removed from *Essays Moral, Political and Literary*, Hume's letter to the *Critical Review* on Wilkie's *Epigoniad*, and the complete French text of Hume's *Concise Account*. The most sustained part of Ritchie's narrative is a fifty-page critical survey of Hume's writings. Three short selections from the *Account* are included here. First is Ritchie's Prefatory note about his method of assembling the material, and his reasons for detailing Hume's 1756 conflict with the Church of Scotland and 1766 dispute with Rousseau. Second is a brief footnote in which Ritchie indicates the reception he received from Hume's relatives upon requesting information from them about Hume's early years. Regrettably, Ritchie did not comply with their wishes and was thus not provided with those details. Third, Ritchie's concluding comments on Hume's character are included.

Reviews of Ritchie's *Account* indicate how low the expectations were at that time for a detailed biography of Hume. Writing for the *Eclectic Review*, John Foster states that *Account* "is by no means so ample a memoir as the number of pages would seem to indicate." Foster approves of Ritchie's matter of fact writing style, and appreciates his independence by not attempting to flatter Hume's living relations:

… In so much of the volume as we owe to the pen of Mr. Ritchie, we do not find occasion for any great measure of either praise or blame. It is written with perspicuity, in a style not clumsy, but not remarkable for elegance. The detail of the few events of Hume's life would be sufficiently orderly, if there appeared less eagerness to seize and dilate every circumstance that can be introduced as an episode. A character of sense and independence is visible throughout; and the present is one of the very few biographers who are free from the weakness of enthusiastically admiring, or the hypocrisy of affecting so to admire, the mixed and imperfect subject of their pages. If he could have brought himself to the obsequiousness of promising to laud his subject up to the pitch of eulogy which would have gratified the delicate ears of Hume's living relations, he might have been enabled to supply a great deficiency of information respecting the early years and habits of the philosophy; but we are compelled to approve the independent conduct described in the note at page 4.

Foster also notes that Hume's life events are not particularly interesting:

> It is not the biographer's fault that Hume's life furnishes but a singularly meagre and uninteresting detail. It is curious to think how many thousands of his contemporaries whose names are forgotten, would have supplied each a far more animated and entertaining narrative. The story of many a common soldier or sailor, many a highwayman, many a gipsy, many a deserted child, and many a beggar, would have kept awake the attention which is much inclined to slumber over an account of this celebrated philosopher. [*Eclectic Review* January, 1808]

Writing for the *Monthly Review*, Stephen Jones criticizes Ritchie for claiming authorship of a work that he merely compiled:

> This volume contains most if not all of the papers and documents which are worthy of notice, relative to the life and writings of the philosopher to whom it is devoted. Of original composition, the portion is small; and had it been still less, the writer's fame and the value of the work would not have suffered. To collect together, from the various sources in which they lie, the materials which form this piece of history, is an useful if a humble service: but it gives the compiler no right to announce himself as the author of 'An Account of the Life and Writings of Mr. Hume,' to which distinction he has scarcely a better claim than the printer or the publisher. The insertion of a few puerile cavils, and of a few shreds of narrative, does not change the nature of the production.

Jones argues further that Ritchie's critical comments on Hume's writings are incompetent:

> If the satisfaction which we have received from seeing the materials before us collected together, and the pleasure which we have derived from casting

our eye over them, were not sufficient to induce us to suppress our objections to an improper and too ostentatious title-page, much less will they avail to lessen the disgust which the cavils of the compiler against the statements of his original, and the pitiful criticisms on his works, have excited in our minds. More glaring proofs of ignorance and presumption are no where to be found. ... The censure which we thus pass on incompetence, in a pretended critic, will not be ascribed to any predilection for the erroneous principles and theories which have been maintained or countenanced by a great genius. [*Monthly Review*, May 1810, Vol. 62, pp. 57–65]

The following is from the 1807 and only edition of Ritchie's *Account*.

In the following work I have introduced Mr. Hume's epistolary correspondence into the narrative, instead of relegating it to the appendix. The *letters* of a man, eminent for his learning and talents, form an interesting part of his biography; yet, when a collection of them is given without any connecting detail, every one must feel, that their value is considerably diminished: few indeed have perseverance to peruse them. By the plan I have adopted, the volume still remains the same in point of size; but the reader becomes progressively acquainted with the literary connections of Mr. Hume, the habits of him and his friends, and numberless traits in their characters, which could not be easily or advantageously compressed into history.

In the biographical sketch, drawn up by Mr. Hume previous to his death, and intitled My own Life, he has passed over unnoticed two very important incidents. The first of these is the complain presented to the General Assembly of the Church of Scotland, against the metaphysical writings of our author and Lord Kames; an occurrence which derives additional importance from the late discussion of a like nature[1] before that venerable body. The other is the dispute between him and Rousseau, which it was the more necessary to relate at considerable length, as an opinion, unfavourable to Mr. Hume, prevailed very generally, and even still prevails, among the literati in foreign countries. A sentiment of delicacy seems to have restrained him from alluding to these transactions, but such a motive cannot influence a stranger; and a similar omission in a Life of Mr. Hume, written by another person, would certainly render the work very imperfect.

...

After the preparatory rudiments of a school education, Hume was removed to the college of Edinburgh; but our gleanings respecting his earlier years are

---

[1] [i.e., the John Leslie controversy, discussed in Henry Cockburn. *Memorials of his Time* (1859).]

particularly scanty. {[Note:] In the hope of being enabled to fill up any chasm in this narrative, I applied to a near relation of Mr. Hume, and was told, that if the work was to advance his fame, and a copy of the manuscript furnished to the family, the information wanted would, perhaps, be supplied. With such conditions I refused compliance, chusing rather to remain satisfied with the little I had otherwise obtained, than to fetter my sentiments, and subject myself to so laborious a task, in return for what was probably of little importance.}
...

After Mr. Hume's death, his *dialogues concerning Natural Religion* were, according to the directions he had left, published under the superintendence of Dr. Adam Smith, and now form part of his collected Essays. Two tracts, ascribed to him, were afterwards published at London; the one *On Suicide,* and the other *On the Immortality of the Soul.* These essays, though the mode of writing and of reasoning might induce one to suppose them genuine, have never been acknowledged by his friends, and are believed to be spurious.

The private character of Mr. Hume is universally acknowledged to have been unexceptionable: but notwithstanding the eulogium he sometimes bestows on the equanimity of his own temper, it is known, that he felt the attacks on his literary reputation with exquisite sensibility; and although he persevered in the resolution of writing no answers to his antagonists, except in the single case of the quarrel with Rousseau, he did not always receive the criticisms of others with the apathy he professes. The severe animadversions of Mr. Gray, in his Letters published by Mason, are said to have given him much concern; and his behaviour to Mr. Tytler, the vindicator of Queen Mary, had something like illiberality in it. Such, indeed, was the antipathy which subsisted between him and the last named gentleman, that they would not sit in company together, and the appearance of the one caused the immediate departure of the other.[2]

There is a vein of sportive humour and a playfulness of fancy in the epistolary correspondence of our author. Dr. Robertson used frequently to say, that in Mr. Hume's gaiety there was something which approached to infantine, and that he had found the same thing so often exemplified in the circle of his other friends, that he was almost disposed to consider it as characteristical of genius.[3] But the best and justest account of Mr. Hume is that given by himself in the conclusion of his biographical narrative, so often alluded to in the course of this work. ...

---

[2]   [Ritchie's apparent source for the anecdotes about Gray and Tytler is Samuel Jackson Pratt's *Supplement* (1777), contained in this collection.]

[3]   Professor Stewart's Life of Dr. Robertson; a work to which I am indebted for several letters by Mr. Hume.

112
PRIVATE CORRESPONDENCES
OF DAVID HUME

Private correspondence of David Hume with several distinguished persons,
between the years 1761 and 1776. Now first published from the originals.
London, Henry Colburn, 1820, [i-xx] [1]-285 [1] p.
Selections from Introduction; from 1820 edition.

After Hume's death, stray parts of his correspondence were printed in periodicals, pamphlets and books – many of which were reprinted in Thomas Ritchie's *Account of the Life and Writings of David Hume* (1807), excerpted in this collection. As bundles of Hume's letters were discovered, they were subsequently transcribed and printed. The first of these is an anonymously edited collection of letters from Hume to French correspondents – including Madame de Boufflers, Madame de Barbentane, Rousseau, Malesherbes, and Turgot. The editor provides English translations of the French originals. This collection is still of historical value since most of the original manuscripts have not since surfaced. In the Introduction to this work, excerpted below, the editor discusses Hume's relationship with the various correspondents. The following is from the 1820 and only edition of that work.

INTRODUCTION.

The History of England, by David Hume, has been aptly styled the "History of English Passions, by Human Reason." It, displays alike the learning, the judgment and the impartiality of its celebrated author: but it conveys little idea of his private character, of his equanimity, of the cheerfulness, and even playfulness of his disposition, and of the habits of his life. These are to be learnt only from his Private Correspondence, which, not being intended for the public eye, reveals the man, and betrays his individuality.

The following Correspondence, which the Editor feels himself particularly fortunate in having obtained, comprehends a period of sixteen years, that is, from 1761 to 1776. It consists principally of letters Written by David Hume to the Countess de Boufflers, and the Marchioness of Barbantane, at Paris; of various others, by the celebrated J. J. Rousseau, the Countess de Boufflers, the Earl Marshal of Scotland, &c.

The Letters, written by Hume to the Countess de Boufflers, are forty in number; and, independent of coming from the pen of the celebrated Historian, and referring to one of the most interesting periods of the last century, viz. the end of the reign of Louis XV. in France, and the beginning of the long and eventful reign of George III. in England, they derive an increased interest from the person to whom they are addressed.

The Countess de Boufflers-Rouvrel was not less celebrated for the beauty of her person, than for the uncommon powers of her mind, the sprightliness of her wit, and the extent of her information. On her entrance into public life, after her marriage, she became the companion of the Duchess of Orleans, the grand-mother of the present Duke. But having had some differences with Her Royal Highness, she left the Princess, and formed a very intimate connexion with the Prince de Conti. Though her accomplishments and the gracefulness of her manners rendered her a principal object of attraction at his Court, she yet found time to write a French tragedy in prose, which, indeed, was neither acted nor printed, but which was highly spoken of by the most distinguished literary characters of the age. To patronize *literature* and the arts was her delight. She was an enthusiastic admirer of *J. J.* Rousseau; and zealously attached to Hume, with whom she entered into an epistolary correspondence. The death of the Count de Boufflers, her husband, which happened in the month of October 1764, led her to aspire to the exalted rank of a Princess. On this occasion Hume gave her the most delicate advice; and afterwards, by his cheering philosophy, supported her under her disappointment. She twice visited England. Her son was educated in Holland, at the Protestant University of Leyden. He gave very great hopes, but must not be confounded with his relation the witty Chevalier de Boufflers, who was the youngest son of the Marquis de Boufflers-Rémiencourt, and whose mother enjoyed the tender regard of Stanislaus, King of Poland, and Duke of Lorraine.

The letters to the Marchioness de Barbantane, as well as those to the Countess de Boufflers, confirm the circumstance which caused so much surprise to the Baron de Grimm, that all the pretty women of France were fond of Hume, and that the stout Scotch philosopher appeared highly delighted with their society. The flattering reception which Hume met with in France from all ranks and persons, and the bitter feuds which prevailed at that period in England between the Whigs and Tories, rendered him so partial to French manners, that he thought them synonimous with politeness itself. It is not, indeed, surprising that a temper, serene and tranquil like his, should have preferred the witty conversation of accomplished Parisian ladies, in their elegant saloons, to the boisterous political discussions of English gentlemen, over their bottles at taverns and coffee-houses, which, in his time, were their places of fashionable resort.

The Editor thinks himself peculiarly fortunate, in having recovered these letters, at a period when the manners of the French before the Revolution are not yet forgotten. Every free and impartial delineation of them, as it is confirmed by witnesses, whose evidence gains respect from their years, is a valuable accession, which will enable some future *Hume* to throw a philosophical light upon the violent agitations that succeeded such gentle and refined manners.

The letters written by David Hume to a French gentleman refer to his celebrated quarrel with J. J. Rousseau; but are not among those which Hume published in his *Exposé succinct de la Contestation qui s'est élevée entre. M. Hume et M. Rousseau.*

But there is besides, among the original papers, a copy of the letter which Hume wrote to Rousseau, to invite him to England. It is no doubt authentic yet the Editor did not think himself warranted to insert it in Hume's Private Correspondence, because it is not in his hand-writing. However, as it has never been published, it may perhaps prove acceptable to some readers. It runs thus: ...

The letters of the Countess de Boufflers justify all that we before stated, respecting the accomplishments of that Lady. The ease, elegance, and vivacity of their style, and the force of their reasoning, place them almost on the same line with the celebrated letters of Madame de Sévigné.

In her letter to David Hume, the Countess is justly offended at Hume having made the Baron D'Holbach at Paris his first confidant, respecting his quarrel with J. J. Rousseau; and at his not having recommended a strict silence on the subject. His letter to the Baron had been publicly read at a brilliant supper, given by M. Necker; it began with these remarkable words: *"Mon cher Baron, Jean Jacques est un Scélérat."* The expression was, no doubt, intemperate, and too strong for the occasion; but Hume had been irritated by Rousseau's letter to him, which began with equally offensive words, viz.: *Vous êtes un traitre; vous ne m'avez mené ici que pour me perdre, apres m'avoir déshonoré.* The tone of the two epistles, gives a high degree of interest to her Ladyship's sensible letter, and palliates the bitterness of her reproaches.

The letters of the Earl Marshal of Scotland to the Countess de Boufflers, are equally remarkable. His Lordship was the eldest brother of the celebrated Prussian Field Marshal *James Keith,* who was killed in 1758, at the unfortunate affair of *Hockkirchen,* in Saxony. The Earl Marshal was, for several years, Governor of the Principality of Neufchatell, in Switzerland, which belonged to Prussia. The great Frederick was particularly fond of his Lordship's company. His Majesty often invited him to Potsdam; and it was at Potsdam, or in its neighbourhood that the Earl Marshal died in the year 1778 at a very advanced age. Frederick himself, though His Majesty was then engaged in a war with Austria, on account of the Bavarian succession, wrote in his camp the *Eloge de Milord Maréchal,* which was read at a public sitting of the Berlin Academy of Sciences by the Prussian Privy Counsellor *Formey*, its perpetual Secretary. The great Earl of Chatham had visited the Earl Marshal some months before the death of the latter, on which occasion the Earl Marshal jocosely observed, how strange it was *qu'un Ministre du Roi George vienne recevoir les derniers soupirs d'un vieux Jacobite.* Lord Chatham, however, died in England, a few days before the Earl Marshal breathed his last in Germany.

Of the sixteen original letters of J. J. Rousseau, twelve are addressed to the Countess de Boufflers, in 1762, 1763, 1764, and 1766; one, to the Earl Marshal of Scotland; one, to David Hume; one, to a Mr. Meuron; and one, to General Conway. They all relate, more or less, to Rousseau's stay in England. They bear the characteristic stamp of his genius; and establish, beyond contradiction, the unfortunate suspicious temper of that eccentric and vain, but truly eloquent writer; who, in spite of his philosophy and genius, was completely misled by his worthless housekeeper. His letters are, however, of a peculiar interest. Men who have acquired great celebrity should be thoroughly known, that their doctrines, and the parts which they have acted in public, may be compared with their individual character and private conduct. Their statues, indeed, deserve little respect, if the honors that have been paid to them were not sanctioned by truth.[1]

---

[1] [The introduction concludes with the following note: "The Originals may be inspected at the Publishers'."]

113
THOMAS MURRAY:
LETTERS OF DAVID HUME

Thomas Murray, *Letters of David Hume and extracts from letters referring to him*. Edinburgh, Adam and Charles Black, 1841, 80 p.
Complete Preface; from 1841 edition.

Born in Girthon, Kirkcudbrightshire, Thomas Murray (1792–1872) was educated at the University of Edinburgh, where he became friends with Thomas Carlyle. Ordained in the Scottish Church, Murray left this for a career in writing. In 1745 Hume became tutor to the twenty-five-year-old and mentally deranged George Annandale, third Marquess of Annandale, staying at a country manor outside St Albans, north of London. The arrangement, though lucrative, was wrought with conflict and Hume was ultimately driven away. In his final salary payment, Hume was denied a sum of £75, which prompted him to sue the Annandale estate around 1750. As late as 1761, the issue was still in negotiation, and apparently settled privately. In response to the suit, trustees of the Annandale estate gathered letters from Hume on the issue. These remained in the office of an Edinburgh attorney for some years, and, passed on to other owners, they eventually were made available to Murray who transcribed and published them in 1841. The letters are to James Johnstone, Philip Vincent, Lady Annandale (the Marquess's mother) and Lord Elibank. In his brief Preface, Murray explains the context of the correspondence. The *Letters* was reprinted in 1842; the following is from the 1841 edition.

PREFACE.

Of the various Letters contained in this volume, the originals are supposed to have been deposited, about eighty years ago, in the hands of a legal gentleman in Edinburgh, as documents for a law-suit, to which the latter portion of them refers. Since his death, they have, we believe, passed through several hands without having attracted any particular attention, or, perhaps, without having ever been read. They ultimately came into the possession of a gentleman who appreciated their value, and who, several years ago, did me the honour of

315

presenting them unconditionally to me. Since that time, they have been perused by many literary friends, to whom they were communicated; and they all, without a single exception, regarded this correspondence as calculated not merely to throw light on Mr Hume's character, but to illustrate a period of his history, which had they been destroyed, must have remained very obscure. In his well-known autobiography, the only mention of his residence with the Marquis of Annandale, – to which part of his life these Letters belong, – is sufficiently meagre, and contains no allusions to the interesting circumstances, which, while they could not but be painful to his feelings, elicited, in an eminent degree, the peculiarities of his character. 'In 1745,' says he, 'I received a letter from the Marquis of Annandale, inviting me to come and live with him in England: I found, also, that the friends and family of that young nobleman were desirous of putting him under my care and direction, for the state of his mind and health required it. I lived with him a twelvemonth. My appointment during that time made a considerable accession to my small fortune.'

Under these circumstances, I have thought it expedient to present this correspondence to the public. I have contributed a few brief notes explanatory of the occasional allusions which the Letters contain; but have not ventured to make any comment, or give any sketch of Mr. Hume's character as developed by them. On the contrary, I have left the reader to draw his own inferences, and to form his own conclusions. I flatter myself that, on the whole, this publication will be regarded as supplying no mean addition to the knowledge which we already possess respecting the life and character of an illustrious Philosopher, – and consequently, to the stock of our biographical literature.

EDINBURGH, *November* 1841.

114
JOHN HILL BURTON:
LIFE AND CORRESPONDENCE
OF DAVID HUME

John Hill Burton, *Life and correspondence of David Hume: from the papers bequeathed by his nephew to the Royal Society of Edinburgh, and other original sources.* Edinburgh: W. Tait, 1846, 2 v.
Complete Advertisement; from 1846.

For background on John Hill Burton (1809–1881) and his *Life* of Hume, see the selections from that work contained earlier in this collection. In the Advertisement to the *Life*, printed below, Burton discusses his access to Hume's manuscripts and the use he made of them.

ADVERTISEMENT.

In this work, an attempt has been made to connect together a series of original documents, by a narrative of events in the life of him to whom they relate; an account of his literary labours; and a picture of his character, according to the representations of it preserved by his contemporaries. The scantiness of the resources at the command of previous biographers, and the extent and variety of the new materials now presented to the world, render unnecessary any other apology for the present publication. How far these materials have been rightly used, readers and critics must judge; but I may be perhaps excused for offering a brief explanation of the spirit in which I desired to undertake the task; and the responsibility I felt attached to the duty, of ushering before the public, documents of so much importance to literature.

The critic or biographer, who writes from materials already before the public, may be excused if he gave way to his prepossessions and partialities, and limit his task to the representation of all that justifies and supports them. If he have any misgivings, that, in following the direction of his prepossessions, he may not have taken the straight line of truth, he may be assured, that if the cause be one of any interest, an advocate, having the same resources at his command, will speedily appear on the other side. But when original manuscripts are for the first time to be used, it is due to truth, and to the desire of mankind to satisfy themselves about the real characters of great men, that they should be so presented as to afford the means of impartially estimating those to whom they relate. We possess many brilliant Eulogiums of the leaders of our race – many vivid pictures of their virtues and their vices – their greatness or their weakness. But if a humbler, it is perhaps a no less useful task, to represent these men – their character, their conduct, and the circumstances of their life, precisely as they were; rejecting nothing that truly exemplifies them, because it is beneath the dignity of biography, or at variance with received notions of their character and the tendency of their public conduct. The desire to have a closer view of the fountain head whence the outward manifestations of a great intellect have sprung, is but one of the many examples of man's spirit of inquiry from effects to their causes; and the desire will not be gratified by reproducing the object of inquiry in all the pomp and state of his public inter-course with the world, and keeping the veil still closed upon his inner nature. It is difficult to write with mere descriptive impartiality, and without exhibiting any bias of opinion, on matters which are, at the same time, the most deeply interesting to mankind, and the objects of their strongest partialities. Though the task that was before me was simply to describe, and never to controvert, I do not profess to have avoided all indications of opinion in the departments of the work which have the character of original authorship. I have the satis-faction, however, of reflecting, that the documents, which are the real elements of value in this work, are impartially presented to the reader, and that nothing is omitted which seemed to bear distinctly on the character and conduct of David Hume.

I now offer a few words in explanation of the nature of these original documents. The late Baron Hume had collected together his uncle's papers, consisting of the letters addressed to him, the few drafts or copies he had left of letters written by himself, the letters addressed *by* him to his immediate relations, and apparently all the papers in his handwriting, which had been left in the possession of the members of his family. To these the Baron seems to have been enabled to add the originals of many of the letters addressed by him to his intimate friends, Adam Smith, Blair, Mure, and others. The design with which this interesting collection was made, appears to have been that of preparing a work of a similar description to the present; and it is a misfortune to literature that this design was not accomplished. On the death of Baron Hume, it was found that he had left this mass of papers at the uncontrolled disposal of the Council of the Royal Society of Edinburgh. This learned body, after having fully considered the coarse proper to be adopted in these circum-stances, determined that they would permit the papers to be made use of by any person desirous to apply them to a legitimate literary purpose, who might enjoy their confidence. Having for some time indulged in a project of writing a life of Hume, postponed from time to time, on account of the imperfect character of the materials at my disposal, I applied to the Council of the Royal Society for access to the Hume papers; and after having considered my application with that deliberation which their duty to the public as custodiers of these documents seemed to require, they acceded to my request. The ordinary form of returning thanks for the privilege of using papers in the possession of private parties, appears not to be applicable to this occasion; and I look on the concession of the Council as conferring on me an honour, which is felt to be all the greater, that it was bestowed in the conscientious discharge of a public duty.

The Hume papers, besides a manuscript of the "Dialogues on Natural Religion," and of a portion of the History, fill seven quarto volumes of various thickness, and two thin folios. In having so large a mass of private and confidential correspondence committed to their charge, the Council naturally felt that they would be neglecting their duty, if they did not keep in view the possibility that there might be in the collection, allusions to the domestic conduct or private affairs of persons whose relations are still living; and that good taste, and a kind consideration for private feelings should prevent the accidental publication of such passages. On inspection, less of this description of matter was found than so large a mass of private documents might be supposed to contain. There is no passage which I have felt any inclination to print, as being likely to afford interest to the reader, of which the use has been denied me; and I can therefore say that I have had in all respects full and unlimited access to this valuable collection. Before leaving this matter, I take the opportunity of returning my thanks for the kind and polite attention I have received from those gentlemen of the Council, on whom the arrangements for my getting access to these papers, imposed no little labour and sacrifice of valuable time.

A rumour has obtained currency regarding the contents of these papers, which seems to demand notice on the presentation.

It is stated in *The Quarterly Review*,[1] that "those who have examined the Hume papers-which we know only by report -speak highly of their interest, but add, that they furnish painful disclosures concerning the opinions then prevailing amongst the clergy of the northern metropolis: distinguished ministers of the gospel encouraging the scoffs of their familiar friend, the author of 'the Essay upon Miracles,' and echoing the blasphemies of their associate, the author of the 'Essay upon Suicide!'" I have the pleasing task of removing the painful feelings which, as this writer justly observes, must attend the belief in such a rumour, by saying that I could not find it justified by a single sentence in the letters of the Scottish clergy contained in these papers, or in any other documents that have passed under my eye. I make this statement as an act of simple justice to the memory of men to whose character, being a member

---

[1] No. LXXIII. p. 555.

of a different church, I have no partisan attachment: and I may add that, in the whole course of my pretty extensive researches, in connexion with Hume and his friends, I found no reason for believing that letters containing evidence of any such frightful duplicity ever existed.

Among these papers, a variety of letters, chiefly from eminent foreigners, though interesting in themselves, were entitled to no place in the body of this work, as illustrative of the life and character of Hume. These I had intended to print in an appendix, believing that, though not directly connected with my own project, the lovers of literature would not readily excuse me for neglecting the opportunity afforded by my access to these papers, for adding to the stock of the letters of celebrated men. But the work, according to its original scope and design, continuing to increase under my hands, I found that if it contained the documents specially referred to in the text, its bulk would be sufficiently extended, and I have determined to let the other papers here alluded to follow in a separate volume, which will contain letters to Hume from D'Alembert, Turgot, Diderot, Helvétius, Franklin, Walpole, and other distinguished persons.

The reader will find that many original documents printed in this collection have been obtained from other sources than the Hume papers. My acknowledgments are particularly due to the Earl of Minto, for the liberality with which he allowed me the uncontrolled use of the large and valuable collection of correspondence between Hume and Sir Gilbert Elliot. For the letters in the Kilravock collection i am indebted to Cosmo Innes, Esq., sheriff of Morayshire; and I obtained access to those addressed to Colonel Edmondstoune, through the polite intervention of George Dundas, Esq., sheriff of Selkirkshire. I am obliged to the kindness of Lord Murray for much assistance in obtaining materials and information for this work; and to Robert Chambers, Esq., who has been accustomed from time to time, to preserve such letters and other documents connected with Scottish biography, as came under his notice, I have to offer my thanks for the whole of his collections regarding Hume, which he generously transferred to me.

In the use of printed books, where the Advocates' Library, to which I have professional access, has failed me, I have found the facilities for consulting the select and well arranged collection of the Writers to the Signet of great service.

I owe acknowledgments to many friends for useful advice in the conduct of the work. To one especially, who, after having long occupied a distinguished place in the literature of his country, permits his friends still to enjoy the social exercise of those intellectual qualities that have delighted the world, I am indebted for such critical counsel as no other could have given, and few would have had the considerate kindness to bestow, were they able.

Of the two portraits engraved for this work, that which will, probably, most strikingly attract attention, is taken from a bust, of coarse and unartistic workmanship, but bearing all the marks of a genuine likeness. It was moulded by a country artist, at the desire of Hume's esteemed friend, Professor Ferguson;

and I am under obligations to his son, Sir Adam, for the privilege of using it on this occasion, and to Sir George Mackenzie, for having kindly mentioned its existence, and exerted himself in its recovery, after it had been long lost sight of. The medallion, from which the other portrait is taken, is in the possession of Charles Kirkpatrick Sharpe, Esq., by whom I was presented with the engraved plate, from which the facsimile of a letter, addressed by Hume to his collateral ancestor, is printed.

Edinburgh, February, 1846.

115
JOHN HILL BURTON:
LETTERS OF EMINENT PERSONS
ADDRESSED TO DAVID HUME

John Hill Burton, *Letters of eminent persons addressed to David Hume. From the papers bequeathed by his nephew to the Royal Society of Edinburgh,* Edinburgh, 1849, xxxi, 334 p.
Introductory Notice; from 1849 and only edition.

John Hill Burton (1809–1881) was the author of *The Life and Correspondence of David Hume* (1746), contained earlier in this collection. In preparing the *Life,* Burton drew on the extensive collection of Hume manuscripts, which was then in possession of the Royal Society of Edinburgh. The collection contained not only letters by him, but around 525 letters to him as well, many of which were from famous literary figures of the time. Realizing the value of these letters, he transcribed 147 for a collection titled *Letters of Eminent Persons Addressed to David Hume* (1749). In the Introductory Notice to the volume, presented below, he explains the value of the letters and the challenges in transcribing them.

<hr />

INTRODUCTORY NOTICE.

Having selected, from the large mass of papers placed at my disposal by the Council of the Royal Society of Edinburgh, the portions which suited my immediate object – the preparation of a Life of Hume, a quantity of documents still remained, which, though they had no reference to my own, might be serviceable to the literary pursuits of others, and would afford pleasurable reading to those who are curious in biography, and the familiar correspondence of great men. Being allowed to retain the privilege of selecting from these papers whatever might seem worthy of publication, I felt that I might be considered guilty of culpable neglect to the interests of literature, if I failed to render accessible, to those likely to appreciate them, the intellectual treasures of so curious and valuable a collection. The lover of literary history will require only to glance over the list of names, under which the several letters are

322

grouped, to estimate the character of their contents. A very few additions would make the catalogue embrace all that was intellectually great, in our own country and in France, during the twenty years which begin with the middle of the eighteenth century. The letters from eminent Englishmen, besides their literary interest, throw valuable light on some political movements, and make us better acquainted with some features of the history of the time well worthy of being known. If late events leave any portion of attention and interest to be bestowed on matters which they have driven so far back into the realm of the past and the forgotten, the glimpses into the social life of the French people anterior to the first political storm, afforded by the letters of their great authors and statesmen, may give curious and pleasant occupation to meditative minds. Much as the actual events of sixty years have done to obliterate the recollection of the faint tremours by which it was preceded, it is not without some exciting curiosity that, through the bitter little feuds and jealousies of the coteries, their magnified trifles, and their selfish devotion to the personal and the present, there is found to lurk a feeling of insecurity and uneasiness, as if the approach of some mysterious future were felt, though not seen – a consciousness to which only the manly and far-seeing mind of Turgot could give complete utterance, by predicting, as we find him doing, that society was then hurrying on to some frightful convulsion.

The letters are presented to the reader just as they have been found. An explanatory note is appended here and there, where it could be supplied with little trouble or inquiry; but I desire it to be understood that I do not profess to have fully annotated the collection, or to have worked up the letters with such information and illustrative comment as they might be capable of receiving from one who desired to make them the materials of a literary memoir. The sole merit I claim is that of having performed the drudgery necessarily incident to the publication of such a collection, for the purpose of putting others in possession of materials which appear applicable to valuable literary services. The humble duty of the copyist, especially when it relates to a foreign tongue, and grapples with handwriting not always the most legible, is far from a pleasing one; and I have to throw upon the nature of the task my excuse for having delayed this volume two years beyond the time when I expected to have published it.

I have to state that, for the purpose of securing, as far as I practically could, the French department of the Letters from inaccuracies, I was enabled to obtain, in the examination of the proofs, the valuable assistance of M. Gabriel Surenne, (F.A.S. Scot., and M.G.S. Paris,) whose reputation as the Author of the French Dictionary, and of other educational and critical works, affords a sanction for accuracy, and attention to the nicer peculiarities of idiom. All doubtful questions in this department were submitted to his absolute and unquestioned decision, and, by the favour of the Council of the Society, he was permitted to consult the originals whenever a difficulty occurred. If the English reader, very critical in French composition, should observe expressions that might be amended, he is desired to remember that in French, as well as in English, slovenly or careless composition will occur in the familiar letters of the ablest writers, and to extend, at least, the same latitude towards the productions of a foreign tongue, which may be fairly allowed to the published correspondence of our own countrymen.

J.H. BURTON.

EDINBURGH, *December* 1848.

116
GEORGE BIRKBECK NORMAN HILL:
LETTERS OF DAVID HUME
TO WILLIAM STRAHAN

George Birkbeck Norman Hill, *Letters of David Hume to William Strahan, now first edited, with notes, index, etc. by G. Birkbeck Hill, D.C.L. Pembrook College*; Oxford, Clarendon Press, 1888, xlvi p., 1 l., 386 p. Selections from Preface; from 1888 edition.

Born in Tottenham, Middlesex in England, George Birkbeck Norman Hill (1835–1903) was educated at Pembroke College, Oxford, and succeeded his father as headmaster of a school in Tottenham. He is best known for his copiously annotated edition of James Boswell's *Life of Samuel Johnson* (1887), which he worked on for twelve years; it remained the definitive edition of that text for over a century. The following year he published a collection of letters from Hume to William Strahan, with perhaps three-quarters of the volume consisting of his extensive annotations. In his Preface to the work, the key portions of which are presented below, he describes how he came upon the letters and indicates their value in giving us a more complete picture of Hume. The following is from the 1888 and only edition of Hill's *Letters*.

PREFACE.

In the summer of last year I was allowed to examine this series of Letters. The interest with which I read them made me long to save them from dispersion. Were they once scattered by auction, their fate would be the fate of the leaves of the Sibyl –

Numquam deinde cavo volitantia prendere saxo,
Nec revocare situs, aut jungere carmina curat.

The price that was asked for them, though large in itself, was moderate when the importance of the collection was considered. Yet for some weeks I almost despaired of finding a purchaser. The funds at the disposal of the Bodleian

Library were altogether inadequate. At the British Museum I should probably have met with success, had not its grant been lately curtailed. By the happy suggestion of the Master of Balliol College I applied to the Earl of Rosebery. His lordship at once consented to buy the whole collection. The obligation under which he has thereby laid men of letters will, I feel sure, be by them gratefully acknowledged. Unfortunately the series is not quite perfect, for a few of the letters had been sold separately by a previous owner. My efforts to get copies of these have been so far fruitless.

In preparing my notes I have made use of the collection of Hume Papers in the possession of the Royal Society of Edinburgh. I had hoped to find among them the other side of the correspondence, but in this I was disappointed. Only a few of Strahan's letters have been preserved. Of one letter that was missing he happily had kept a copy. Hume, with a levity which is only found in a man who is indifferent to strict truthfulness, had charged him with deception. The answer which was sent must have startled that ease-loving philosopher from his complacency, and taught him a lesson which it was a disgrace to him not to have learnt long before.

In my notes my aim has been not only to make every letter clear, but also to bring before my readers the thoughts and the feelings of Hume's contemporaries in regard to the subjects which he discusses. 'Every book,' he says, 'should be as complete as possible within itself, and should never refer for anything material to other books.' If this rule is just, I could not but let my notes swell under my hand, so varied and so interesting are the matters touched on in his letters. On his quarrel with Rousseau I dwell at considerable length. The rank which the two men held in the republic of letters was so high, the interest which their strife excited was so great, and the spectators of the contest were so eminent, that even at the distance of time it deserves to be carefully studied. My endeavour has been not only to examine the conduct of the two men, but also to exhibit the opinions which were entertained by all who were in any way concerned. The violence of Hume's feelings towards the English which is shown in many of his letters is curious enough to justify a long note. It was due it is clear partly to a deep sense of slighted merit, and partly to anger at what he describes as 'the mad and wicked rage against the Scots.' Violent as he was towards Englishmen in general, still more violent was he towards the most famous Englishman of his time. Why Lord Chatham roused his anger I have attempted to explain. The confidence of Hume's belief that the country was on the eve of bankruptcy, is one more proof how fallible may be the judgment of even the first historian and the first economist of his age. His no less confident expectations about the war with our American colonies were however speedily justified by the event. From the outset he saw that conquest was impossible. It will be seen that a few months after his death some of these letters were shown to George III. We may wonder whether the king's obstinacy was for a moment shaken, when he read the lines in which his highly-pensioned Tory historian proved that only 'the oppressive arm of arbitrary power' could crush the rebels. How much it were to be wished that he had seen also that other letter where Hume tells how he had found the First Lord of the Admiralty, with some loose associates, fishing for trout "with incredible satisfaction, at a time when the fate of the British Empire was in dependence, and in dependence on him.'

If these Letters exhibit, as they too often do, Hume's 'distempered, discontented thoughts,' his moral cowardice, his vanity, and his unmanly complaints of the neglect of the world, they show at the same time the noble industry of the scholar. If from a love of 'ignoble ease' he suppressed Essays and Dialogues, yet it was not into 'peaceful sloth' that he sank. He more than once quotes 'a saying of Rousseau's, that one half of a man's life is too little to write a book and the other half too correct it.' In truth, he never wearied of the attempt to bring his works as near to perfection as possible, and it was from his death-bed that his last corrections were sent.

Hume's spelling I have retained, for it is interesting both in its peculiarities and its blunders. That he had his own views about orthography is shown hereafter.

His brief *Autobiography*, which I have reprinted, will be a convenient introduction to the study of his Letters.

In the letters from Adam Smith, one of which is new, and from Hume's brother and nephew, some account is given of the publication of the manuscripts which he left behind him. ...

A BIBLIOGRAPHY OF
EARLY RESPONSES TO HUME

During the eighteenth and nineteenth centuries, the writings of David Hume had a major impact in the areas of metaphysics, moral philosophy, religious thought, history, economics, political theory, and aesthetics. His influence extended beyond Great Britain into Europe and North America. The first effort at a systematic list of early responses to Hume was T.E. Jessop's *A Bibliography of David Hume and of Scottish Philosophy* (1938). Prior to this, scattered citations of works on Hume appeared in different sources. Robert Watt's *Bibliotheca Britannica* (1824) listed about fifty British books discussing Hume. Biographical works on Hume put on record many more items, particularly relating to Hume's life; the most important of these are by John Hill Burton (1846), George Birkbeck Norman Hill (1888), Henry Grey Graham (1901), and J.Y.T. Greig (1932). Jessop's bibliography followed these, and is remarkable in several ways. First, he included detailed listings of Hume's publications, works on Hume, and works by dozens of other Scottish philosophers. Also, he physically examined many of the works he listed, which enhances the accuracy of his citations. His bibliography of eighteenth and nineteenth-century works on Hume contains about 150 English language items and about 100 others in foreign languages. Jessop intended to produce a revised second edition of his *Bibliography*, but unfortunately died before he could complete it. The next major advance in Hume bibliography was Ernest Campbell Mossner's *Life of David Hume* (1954), which cites dozens of previously undocumented discussions of Hume – most biographically related and written during Hume's life or shortly after.

The present bibliography aims to extend the early literature on Hume a little further. It contains over 500 main entries, around 200 of which are of items written before Hume's death. Many of these are new to Hume scholarship. In addition to these, there are around 500 citations of reviews to the early books and pamphlets on Hume – most of which also discuss Hume. Approximately 100 of the entries related to early American discussions of Hume derive from the recent work of Mark G. Spencer as appears in his *Hume's Reception in Early America* (Bristol: Thoemmes Press, 2002). Although this bibliography aims to be wide-ranging, it is limited in several ways. First, it is principally a bibliography of English-language responses to Hume; some foreign-language items are included, though, when they have been made available in English translation. Studies of Hume's reception in non-English-speaking countries require their own special efforts; some works of this sort have already appeared and others are underway. Second, greater emphasis is placed on eighteenth-century responses than the nineteenth-century ones. Third, the responses listed here are ones that are either lengthy or of intrinsic interest. Dozens – if not hundreds – of sketches of Hume appeared in encyclopaedias and biographical dictionaries, most of which recycle a core of information, largely derived from Hume's "My Own Life." These have been omitted. Also, literally thousands of single-sentence references to Hume appear in eighteenth and nineteenth-century literature, such as these:

> "Berkeley banished matter out of the world: H—e has sent the soul after it."
> "He writes not with the pen of a Smollett, nor dips his quill in the stand of a Hume."
> "Hume and Robertson are historians of the first rank. I esteem them both."
> "Neither is he equal to his countrymen, Robertson or Hume."
> "That great *light* of the world, David Hume, was the first person who ventured to remove the bandage from the eyes of his devoted countrymen."
> "It is observed by Hume, that Harvey's discovery of the circulation of the blood was not received by any physician in Europe who was past forty years of age."
> "If this theory of Mr. Hume be true, we cannot augur well of the fortunes of literature in America."
> "Among the moderns, the notion of the primary savage state of man has been held by Hume, Kaims, Smith, Monboddo, Condillac, and many others."

Even these are of some interest since they reflect common perceptions of Hume; nevertheless, compiling a full list would be unfeasible.

The entries in this bibliography record a range of information. A typical entry is this:

- [Skelton, Philip (1707–1787)]. *Ophiomaches: or, Deism revealed*. London: printed for A. Millar, 1749, 2 v.
  Notes: dialogues on philosophical theology includes a criticism of Hume's "Of Miracles" in Dialogue 5.
  In *Religion Responses*: selections from Dialogue 5, from *The Complete Works of the Late Rev. Philip Skelton*, ed. Robert Lynam (1824), Vol. 4.
  Editions: 1751 (titled *Deism revealed*), in *Works* 1770 and 1824; no further editions.
  Facsimiles: 1990 (Thoemmes Press of 1749).
  Microform: Eighteenth-century sources for the study of English literature and culture, reel no. 979 (of 1749); The Eighteenth Century, reel 2242 no. 1 (of 1751).
  Reviews: *Literary Journal*, 1749, Vol. 5, pp. 92–127 (positive).
  Discussions: Samuel Burdy *Life* (1792).

The primary citation is of the first edition of the work in question, and the citation is worded as appears in a standard bibliographical source, such as the English Short Title Catalogue, the Library of Congress Union Catalogue, OCLC and RLIN. The author's name appears in brackets if the work first appeared anonymously. The "Notes" entry describes how the work relates to Hume. If the work appears in one of several recent anthologies of responses to Hume, the details of that are next listed (abbreviations of these are given below). For example, selections from Skelton's *Ophiomaches* appear in *Religion Responses* (i.e., *Early Responses to Hume's Writings on Religion*), and the selection itself was taken from the 1824 edition of Skelton's *Works*. The "Editions" entry lists different editions of the work in question. I include the statement "no further editions" for items whose editions I have researched – although this is no guarantee that I have not erred. I leave this statement out when I was unable to assess the history of the editions. To facilitate accessing these items through interlibrary loan, I next include information about facsimile reprints or micro-forms of these works, indicating which editions they are copied from. Most of the books in this bibliography were reviewed in one or more journals and, in the "Reviews" entry I cite the ones that I have found. For many of these I have indicated whether the overall evaluation in the review is positive, negative, mixed or neutral. Authorship of reviews in the *Monthly Review* is based on Benjamin Christie Nangle's *The Monthly Review First Series 1749-1789* (1934) and *The Monthly Review Second Series* 1790–1815 (1955). Authorship of reviews in *Edinburgh Magazine and Review* is based on Robert Kerr's *Memoirs ... of William Smellie* (1811). Authorship of nineteenth-century reviews is based on the *Wellesley Index to Victorian Periodicals* (CD ROM, Routledge, 1999). Finally, under "Discussions" I list items elsewhere in this bibliography that discuss the work in question.

As noted, this bibliography contains references to recent anthologies on Hume's early reception. In addition to the ten-volume collection of *Early Responses to Hume*, of which the present collection is a part, other similar works have appeared. Abbreviations of these, as cited in this bibliography, are as follows:

Moral Responses: *Early Responses to Hume's Moral, Literary and Political Writings,* ed. James Fieser, (Bristol: Thoemmes Press, 2004), Volume 1 — Responses to Hume's Moral Philosophy.

Essays Responses: *Early Responses to Hume's Moral, Literary and Political Writings,* ed., James Fieser, (Bristol: Thoemmes Press, 2004), Volume 2 — Responses to Hume's *Essays, Moral, Political and Literary.*

Metaphysical Responses: *Early Responses to Hume's Metaphysical and Epistemological Writings,* ed. James Fieser, (Bristol: Thoemmes Press, 2004), 2 vols.

Religion Responses: *Early Responses to Hume's Writings on Religion,* ed. James Fieser, (Bristol: Thoemmes Press, 2004), 2 vols.

History Responses: *Early Responses to Hume's History of England,* ed. James Fieser, (Bristol: Thoemmes Press, 2004), 2 vols.

Life Responses: *Early Responses to Hume's Life and Reputation,* ed. James Fieser, (Bristol: Thoemmes Press, 2004), 2 vols.

Common Sense Responses: *Scottish Common Sense Philosophy,* ed. James Fieser, (Bristol: Thoemmes Press, 2000), Volumes 3 and 4 — Early Responses to Reid, Oswald, Beattie and Stewart.

Common Sense Bibliography: *Scottish Common Sense Philosophy,* ed. James Fieser,

(Bristol: Thoemmes Press, 2000), Volume 5 — A Bibliography of Scottish Common Sense Philosophy.
American Reception: *Hume's Reception in Early America*, ed., Mark G. Spencer, (Bristol: Thoemmes Press, 2002), 2 vols.
Hume on Natural Religion: *Hume on Natural Religion*, ed. Stanley Tweyman, (Bristol: Thoemmes Press, 1996).
Hume on Miracles: *Hume on Miracles*, ed. Stanley Tweyman, (Bristol: Thoemmes Press, 1996).

Some of the more interesting early responses to Hume remained unpublished for many years, such as James Boswell's now famous 1776 deathbed interview with Hume, which first appeared in print in 1931. For items with a publishing gap of more than fifty years I have listed them twice, first, when initially written and, second, when first published. This preserves the chronological contexts of the original compositions as well as their first public appearances.

1739

● Anonymous. Notice of *Treatise*, in *Bibliothèque raisonnée*, 1739, April–June, Vol. 22–2, pp. 481–482.
    Notes: short paragraph summarizing contents of Books 1 and 2, noting Hume's originality.
    In *Metaphysical Responses*: included in introduction to *Bibliothèque raisonnée* (1740).
● Anonymous. Notice of *Treatise*, in *Nuer Zeitungen von gelehrten Sachen*, May 1739, p. 318.
    Notes: the complete notice reads, "A new free-thinker has published an exhaustive *Treatise of Human Nature*, 2 volumes, octavo. In it he attempts to introduce the correct method of philosophy into moral matters, examining and explaining, first of all, the characteristics of the human understanding and then the effects. The author's intentions are sufficiently betrayed in the sub-title of the work, taken from Tacitus: *Rara temporum felicitas, ubi sentire, quae velis. & guae sentias, dicere, licet.*" (Tr. Ernest Mossner "Continental Reception of Hume's *Treatise*, 1739–1741" *Mind*, 1947, Vol. 56, pp. 31–43.)
● Anonymous. Notice of *Treatise*, in *Nouvelle bibliotheque, ou histoire litteraire des principaux ecrits gui se publient*, October 1739, Vol. 4, pp. 302.
    Notes: one sentence noting Hume's similarities with Hutcheson.
    In *Metaphysical Responses*: included in editor's introduction to *Nouvelle bibliothèque* (1740).
● Anonymous. Notice of *Treatise*, in *Bibliotheque britannigue, ou histoire des ouvrages des scavans de la Grande-Bretagne*, October–December 1739, Vol. 40–1, p. 216.
    Notes: the complete notice reads, "This is a system of logic, or rather of metaphysics, as original as can be, in which the author claims to rectify the most ingenious philosophers, particularly the famous Mr. Locke, and in which he advances the most unheard-of paradoxes, even to maintaining that operations of the mind are not free." (Tr. Mossner, "Continental Reception.").
● Anonymous. Review of *Treatise*, Book 1, in *The history of the works of the learned*, November and December 1739, Vol. 2, pp. 353–404.
    Notes: harsh critique of Book 1, containing summaries and excerpts.
    In *Metaphysical Responses*: complete review.

Discussions: 1777 reviews of "My Own Life" in *London Review* and *Monthly Review*.

● Anonymous. Notice of *Treatise*, Book 1, in *Göttingische Zeitungen*, December 21, 1739, Nr. 102, p. 904.

Notes: brief paragraph noting similarities with Hutcheson.

In *Metaphysical Responses*: included in editor's introduction to *Göttingische Zeitungen* (1740).

1740

● Anonymous. Review of *Treatise*, Book 1, in *Göttingische Zeitungen von gelehrten Sachen*, January 7, 1740, Nr. 2, pp. 9–12.

Notes: summarizes and criticizes Book 1.

In *Metaphysical Responses*: English translation of complete review by Manfred Kuehn.

● Anonymous. Notice of *Abstract*, in *Bibliothèque raisonnée*, April–June, 1740, Vol. 24–2, pp. 481–482.

Notes: the complete notice reads, "Because some have found Mr. Hume's *Treatise of Human Nature* a little too abstruse, a pamphlet has been published to help them understand it."

● Anonymous. Review of *Treatise*, Books 1 and 2, *Bibliothèque raisonnée des ouvrages des savans de l'Europe*, April–June, 1740, Vol. 24–2, pp. 324–355.

Notes: summarizes Book 1 as derived from Hume's *Abstract*.

In *Metaphysical Responses*: English translation of complete review by David Fate Norton and Mary J. Norton.

● Anonymous. Review of *Treatise*, Book 1, in *Nouvelle bibliothèque, ou histoire litteraire des principaux écrits qui se publient*, July, 1740, Vol. 6, pp. 291–316, September, 1740, Vol. 7, pp. 44–63.

Notes: summarizes Book 1.

In *Metaphysical Responses*: English translation of complete review by David Fate Norton and Rebecca Pates.

● Anonymous. Letter to the editor in *Common Sense: or the Englishman's Journal*, Saturday, July 5, 1740, pp. 1–2.

Notes: criticizes Hume's view of necessity in *Treatises* 2.3.1, and Hume's view of the indivisibility of matter in *Treatise* 1.2.

In *Metaphysical Responses*: complete article.

1741

● Anonymous. Review of *Treatise*, Book III, *Bibliothèque raisonnée des ouvrages des savans de l'Europe*. April–June, 1741, Vol. 26–2, pp. 411–427.

Notes: presents summaries, excerpts, and critical comments on the first four sections of Book 3 of the *Treatise*.

In *Moral Responses*: complete review, translated from French into English.

● Anonymous. Manuscript of comments on *Essays, Moral and Political*, (1741 or 1742).

Manuscript location: National Library of Scotland, MS 23163, Item 39.

Notes: 29 anonymous remarks on various passages in Hume's *Essays*, many of which Hume incorporated into later revisions.

In *Essays Responses*: complete; newly transcribed.

1742

● Anonymous. Queries regarding Hume's "A Character of Sir Robert Walpole" in *Newcastle Journal*, February 13, 1742.

Notes: series of critical questions on Hume's essay on Walpole, which Hume responded to in *Scots Magazine*.

Editions: *Gentleman's Magazine* February 1742, Vol. 12, p. 82, and *Scots Magazine*, March 1742, Vol. 4, pp. 119–120 (includes Hume's response).

In *Essays Responses*: complete article with Hume's replies; from reprints in *Gentleman's Magazine* and *Scots Magazine*.

- Anonymous. Untitled Character Sketch of David Hume, 1742.

  Manuscript location: National Library of Scotland, MS 14258, fol. 30.

  Notes: brief unpublished sketch of Hume that criticizes his womanizing and *Essays*. This anonymous sketch is among the papers of Robert Strange, and may have been authored by him.

  In *Life Responses*: complete sketch, newly transcribed by M.A. Stewart.

❧1745❧

- [Wishart, William (1692–1753)]. "A specimen of the principles concerning religion and morality, said to be maintain'd in a book lately publish'd, intitled, A treatise of human nature," in *A letter from a gentleman to his friend in Edinburgh*. Edinburgh, 1745, 34 p.

  Notes: Wishart presents incriminating excerpts from the *Treatise*, to which Hume responded. This is related to Hume's unsuccessful candidacy for the Chair of Moral Philosophy at Edinburgh University.

  In *Metaphysical Responses*: complete pamphlet, including Hume's response, from 1745 edition.

  Editions: no further early editions; reprinted in some recent editions of Hume's writings. Facsimiles: 1967 (Edinburgh University Press of 1745).

- Wishart, William (1692–1753), "Copy of Letter, or Speech, Intended: and Letter to John Forrest. June 5, 1745."

  See M.A. Stewart, *The Kirk and the Infidel* (1995).

  Notes: manuscript document in shorthand detailing Wishart's motives in blocking Hume's chances of academic appointment in 1745; newly transcribed by M.A. Stewart.

❧1749❧

- Anonymous. Review of *Philosophical Essays*, in *Göttingische Zeitungen von gelehrten Sachen*, June 1749, Nr. 54, pp. 431–432.

  Notes: favourable assessment of Hume's work, summarizing its contents.

  In *Metaphysical Responses*: English translation of complete review, translated by Curtis Bowman.

- [Annet, Peter (1693–1769)]. *Social bliss considered: in marriage and divorce; cohabiting unmarried, and public whoring. Containing things necessary to be known by all that seek mutual felicity, and are ripe for the enjoyment of it.* London: Printed for and sold by R. Rose, 1749, viii, 108 p.

  Notes: critiques "Of Polygamy and Divorces."

  In *Essays Responses*: selections, from *Collection of Tracts* (c 1750)

  Editions: included in *A Collection of the Tracts of a Certain Free Enquirer* (c. 1750).

- [Skelton, Philip (1707–1787)]. *Ophiomaches: or, Deism revealed*. London: printed for A. Millar, 1749, 2 vol.

  Notes: dialogues on philosophical theology includes a criticism of Hume's "Of Miracles" in Dialogue 5.

  In *Religion Responses*: relevant selections from Dialogue 5, from *The Complete Works of the Late Rev. Philip Skelton*, ed. Robert Lynam (1824), Vol. 4.

  Editions: 1751 (titled *Deism revealed*), in *Works* 1770 and 1824; no further editions.

Facsimiles: 1990 (Thoemmes Press of 1749).
Microform: Eighteenth-century sources for the study of English literature and culture, reel no. 979 (of 1749); The Eighteenth Century, reel 2242 no. 1 (of 1751).
Reviews: *Literary Journal*, March–June 1749, Vol. 5, pp. 92–127 (positive).
Discussions: Samuel Burdy *Life* (1792).
• Warburton, William (1698–1779). Paper on "Of Miracles" (1749?).
   See Francis Kilvert, *A Selection from Unpublished Papers* (1841).
   Notes: criticizes Hume's "Of Miracles."
   In *Religion Responses*: complete paper.
   In *Hume on Miracles*: complete paper with 1757 letter from Warburton to Andrew Millar.
   Discussions: Richard Hurd, *Discourse* (1794); William Warburton, *Letters* (1808).

❧1750❧

• Oswald, James, of Dunnikier (1715–1769). Letter to Hume October 10, 1750.
   See William Mure (1799–1860), ed., *Selections from the Family papers preserved at Caldwell* (1854).
   Notes: criticizes Hume's economic essay "Of the Balance of Trade" prior to its publication in *Political Discourses*.
   In *Essays Responses*: complete letter; from 1854 edition, Part 2, Vol. 1, pp. 93–107.
• Warburton, William (1698–1779). *Julian. Or a discourse concerning the earthquake and fiery eruption, which defeated that Emperor's attempt to rebuild the temple at Jerusalem. ... By the Rev. Mr. Warburton.* London: printed for J. and P. Knapton, 1750, [2], xlii, 23, 22–286 p.
   Notes: includes critical comment on Hume's *Philosophical Essays*.
   In *Religion Responses*: relevant comment included in editor's introduction to William Warburton's "Of Miracles" (1749?).
   Discussions: Richard Hurd, *Discourse* (1794); William Warburton, *Letters* (1808).

❧1751❧

• Brown, John (1715–1766). *Essays on the Characteristics*. London: Printed for C. Davis, 1751, viii, 406 p.
   Notes: criticism of Shaftesbury's *Characteristics* in three essays; Essay 2 includes a critique of Hume's view of disinterested pleasure in "Of the Dignity or Meanness of Human Nature".
   In *Essays Responses*: Essay 2, pp. 162–165; from 1751 edition.
   Editions: 1751b, 1752a–b, 1755, 1764.
   Facsimiles: 1969 (G. Olms of 1751), 1970 (Garland of 1751).
   Reviews: [William Rose], *Monthly Review*, June 1751, Vol. 5, pp. 44–65 (positive).
• Elliot of Minto, Gilbert (1722–1777). Letter to Hume (c. March 1751).
   See Dugald Stewart, *Dissertation on the Progress of Philosophy* (1821).
   Notes: criticizes a draft of Hume's *Dialogues*, at Hume's request.
   In *Religion Responses*: complete letter fragment, from Dugald Stewart, *Works* (1854–1858), Vol. 1, pp. 606–609.
• [Home, Henry, Lord Kames (1696–1782)]. *Essays on the principles of morality and natural religion in two parts.* Edinburgh: Printed by R. Fleming, for A. Kincaid and A. Donaldson, 1751, 3 p. l., 394 p.
   Notes: Home comments on Hume throughout the volume, mostly regarding Hume's view of belief, personal identity, causality, morality and "Of a Particular Providence."

In *Moral Responses*: selections from Part 1.2, chapters 6 and 9, from 1779 edition; critiques Hume's views of justice and utility.

In *Metaphysical Responses*: Part 2, Essays 1, 2, and 4, complete; from 1751 edition.

In *Religion Responses*: selections from Essay 8; from 1751 edition.

Editions: 1758, 1779; see *Common Sense Bibliography* for details on these editions.

Facsimiles: 1976 (G. Olms of 1758), 1983 (Garland of 1751), 1993 (Thoemmes Press of 1779).

Microform: The Eighteenth Century, reel 362, no. 5 (of 1751); British culture series, Group V, no. 45 (of 1751); The Eighteenth Century, reel 3996, no. 01 (of 1758).

Reviews of 1751 edition: [William Rose], *Monthly Review*, July 1751, Vol. 5, pp. 129–155 (positive).

Reviews of 1758 edition: [Benjamin Dawson], *Monthly Review*, June 1758, Vol. 18, pp. 599–601 (mixed).

Discussions: George Anderson, *Estimate* (1753); John Bonar, *Analysis* (1755); Hugh Blair *Observations* (1755); Thomas Walker, "Letter" (1755); Thomas Walker *Infidelity* (1756); *Address* (1757); John MacLaurin, *Philosopher's Opera* (1757); James Beattie, "Castle of Scepticism" (1767); Alexander Fraser Tytler, *Memoirs* (1807).

- Rutherforth, Thomas (1712–1771). *The credibility of miracles defended against the author of Philosophical essays in a discourse delivered at the primary visitation of the Right Reverend ... Thomas Lord Bishop of Ely in St. Michaels Church Cambridge Avg. XXIX. MDCCLI. By T. Rutherforth.* Cambridge: printed by J. Bentham; for W. Thurlbourn; and sold by W. Innys and J. Beecroft, London, 1751, [viii], 22 p.

Notes: criticizes Hume's "Of Miracles."

In *Religion Responses*: complete pamphlet; from 1751 edition.

In *Hume on Miracles*: complete pamphlet; from 1751 edition.

Editions: no further editions.

Microform: The Eighteenth Century, reel 3680, no. 28.

Reviews: [William Rose], *Monthly Review*, October 1751, Vol. 5, pp. 358–361 (neutral; complete review in *Hume on Miracles*).

- Wallace, Robert (1697–1771). "A Letter from a Moderate Freethinker to David Hume Esquire concerning the Profession of the Clergy. In which it is shewed that their Vices whatever they are are owing to their Disposition and not to the Bad Influence of their Profession" (1751?).

Manuscript location: University of Edinburgh Library, Laing MSS, II, 96.

Notes: as yet unpublished manuscript that criticizes Hume's attack on the clergy in "Of National Characters." A short excerpt from this appears in Mossner's *Life of David Hume* (1980), p. 260.

- Warburton, William (1698–1779). *The Works of Alexander Pope.... Together with the commentaries and notes of Mr. Warburton*, London, Knapton, Lintot, Tonson, 1751, 9 Vol.

Notes: contains a note with a critical reference to Hume's *Philosophical Essays.*

In *Religion Responses*: footnote included in editor's introduction to Warbuton's *Remarks* (1757).

Reviews: [Ralph Griffiths], *Monthly Review*, January 1751, Vol. 5, pp. 97–102 (mixed).

In *Hume on Miracles*: complete paper with 1757 letter from Warburton to Andrew Millar.

Discussions: Richard Hurd, *Discourse* (1794); William Warburton, *Letters* (1808).

❧1752❧

- Adams, William (1706–1789). *An essay on Mr. Hume's Essay on miracles. By William Adams.* London: printed by E. Say; and sold by R. Dodsley, M. Cooper, and J.

Cotton in Shrewsbury, 1752, [4], 134 p.

Notes: two-part book criticizes Parts 1 and 2 of "Of Miracles" respectively.

In *Religion Responses*: complete pamphlet, from 1752 edition.

In *Hume on Miracles*: Part 1 only.

Editions: 1754 (second edition), 1767 (third edition), 1776 (fourth edition); no further editions.

Microform: The Eighteenth Century, reel 4491, no. 03 (of 1752 edition); reel 5410, no. 5 (of 1776 edition).

Reviews: [William Rose], *Monthly Review*, January 1752, Vol. 6, pp. 71–74 (positive; complete review in *Hume on Religion*).

- Ellys, Anthony (1690–1761). *Remarks on An essay concerning miracles, published by David Hume, Esq; amongst his philosophical essays*. London: printed for G. Woodfall; and C. Corbett, [1752], [2], 5–26 p.

  Notes: criticizes Hume's "Of Miracles."

  In *Religion Responses*: complete pamphlet; from 1752 edition.

  In *Hume on Natural Religion*: complete pamphlet; from 1752 edition.

  Editions: no further editions.

  Microform: The Eighteenth Century, reel 3332, no. 3.

  Reviews: [William Rose], *Monthly Review*, April 1752, Vol. 6, p. 313 (positive).

- [Heathcote, Ralph (1721–1795)]. *Cursory animadversions upon a late controversy concerning the miraculous powers &c. ... With a prefatory discourse upon religious controversy in general*. London: printed for Thomas Payne, 1752, 62, [2] p.

  Notes: discusses Hume's "The Sceptic" in footnote "h" on page xiii.

  Editions: no further editions.

  Reviews: [William Rose], February 1752, Vol. 6, p. 107 ff.

- [Rose, William (1719–1786)]. Review of *Enquiry Concerning the Principles of Morals*, in *Monthly Review*, January 1752, Vol. 6, pp. 1–19.

  Notes: positive review, presents summaries and excerpts from Hume's moral *Enquiry*.

  In *Moral Responses*: complete review.

- [Rose, William (1719–1786)]. Review of *Political discourses*, *Monthly Review*, Vol. 6, January pp. 19–43, February, 1752, pp. 81–90.

  Notes: positive review, presents summaries of and excerpts from Hume's *Political Discourses*.

  In *Essays Responses*: complete review.

- Wodrow, James (1730–1819). Letter to Samuel Kenrick, January 21, 1752.

  Manuscript location: Dr Williams's Library, London, MS 24.157 (Wodrow-Kerrick correspondence, c. 1750–1810), item 16.

  Notes: discusses Hume's 1752 candidacy and *Political Discourses*.

  In *Life Responses*: selections; newly transcribed by M.A. Stewart.

⁐1753⁐

- Anonymous. *A Letter to the author of a late book entitled An estimate of the profit and loss of religion*. [1753?], 28 p.

  Notes: discusses George Anderson's *Estimate* (1753).

  Editions: no further editions.

- Anonymous. Review of *Philosophical Essays*, third edition, in *Göttingische Anzeigen von gelehrten Sachen*, May 14, 1753, Nr. 60, pp. 540–544.

  Notes: summarizes contents and criticizes "Of Miracles."

  In *Metaphysical Responses*: English translation of complete review, by Curtis Bowman.

- Anonymous. *Some late opinions concerning the foundations of morality examined. In a letter to a friend*. London: R. Dodsley, 1753, iv, 5–46 p.

Notes: criticizes Kames's *Essays* and Hume's moral *Enquiry*.

In *Moral Responses*: complete pamphlet; from 1753 edition.

Editions: no further editions.

Microform: The Eighteenth Century, reel 7110, no. 13.

Reviews: [William Rose], *Monthly Review*, April 1753, Vol. 8, p. 400 (positive; complete review in *Moral Responses* introduction).

• [Anderson, George (1676–1756)]. *An estimate of the profit and loss of religion personally and publicly stated: illustrated with references to Essays on morality and natural religion*. Edinburgh: 1753, iv, 392 p.

Notes: criticizes Kames's and Hume's moral theories; also discusses Hume's "Of a Particular Providence," and "Of the Protestant Succession".

In *Religion Responses*: selections from Section 6; from 1753 edition.

In *Moral Responses*: Section 1, complete; 1753 edition.

In *Essays Responses*: Section 10, selections; 1753 edition, pp. 302–310.

Editions: no further editions.

Microform: The Eighteenth Century, reel 6337, no. 23.

Reviews: [William Rose], *Monthly Review*, March 1754, Vol. 10, pp. 193–196 (mixed).

Discussions: *Address to the Synod* (1757).

• [Balfour, James (1705–1795)]. *A delineation of the nature and obligation of morality with reflexions upon Mr. Hume's book, intitled, An inquiry concerning the principles of morals*. Edinburgh: Hamilton, Balfour, and Neill, 1753, 175 p.

Notes: criticizes Hume's theories of justice, charity, virtue and religion.

In *Moral Responses*: complete Section 4; from 1753 edition.

Editions: 1763 (includes new appendix); no further editions.

Facsimiles: 1989 (Thoemmes Press of 1753).

Microform: The Eighteenth Century, reel 3332, no. 3 (of 1753); reel 317, no. 8 (of 1763).

Reviews: *Monthly Review*, May 1753, Vol. 8, pp. 364–372 (positive).

Discussions: Thomas Hepburn, *Specimen* (1774).

• [Clayton, Robert (1695–1758)]. *Some thoughts on self-love, innate-ideas, free-will, taste, sentiment, liberty and necessity, &c. occasioned by reading Mr. Hume's works, and the short treatise written in French by Lord Bolingbroke, on compassion. Together with a few remarks on the genuine sequel, … In a letter to a friend. By the author of the Essay on spirit*. Dublin: printed by George Faulkner, 1753, 63, [1] p.

Notes: pamphlet defends Clayton's earlier *Essay on Spirit*. Pages 1–19 (1763 edition) briefly quote and criticize Hume's views of self-interest and free will.

In *Moral Responses*: selections; from 1763 edition.

Editions: 1753 (Dublin and London, 66 p.), 1763 (second edition); no further editions.

Microform: The Eighteenth Century, reel 2776, no. 5 (of Dublin 1753 63 p.); reel 3043, no. 16 (of 1763).

Reviews: *Monthly Review*, September 1753, Vol. 9, pp. 216–222 (mixed).

• [Psalmanazar, George (1679?–1763)]. *Essays on the following subjects: I. On the reality and evidence of miracles, … Written some years since, … By an obscure layman in town*. London: printed for A. Millar, 1753, xxxi, [1], 360 p.

Notes: Essay 1, Letter 1 criticizes "Of Miracles" and "Of a Particular Providence".

In *Religion Responses*: Essay 1, Letter 1, complete; from 1753 edition.

Editions: no further editions.

Microform: The Eighteenth Century, reel 1777, no. 04 (of 1753).

Reviews: [William Rose], *Monthly Review*, November 1753, Vol. 9, pp. 321–330 (positive).

- [Wallace, Robert (1697–1771)]. *A dissertation on the numbers of mankind, in antient and modern times: in which the superior populousness of antiquity is maintained: with an appendix, containing additional observations on the same subject, and some remarks on Mr. Hume's Political discourse, Of the populousness of antient nations.* Edinburgh: Printed for G. Hamilton and J. Balfour, 1753, iv, 331 p.

  Notes: Appendix contains a lengthy and systematic critique of "Of the Populousness of Ancient Nations."

  In *Essays Responses*: complete Appendix; from 1809 edition.

  Editions: 1809 (second edition revised); no further editions.

  Translations: 1754 (Londres, i.e., Paris?).

  Facsimiles: 1969 (A.M. Kelley of 1809); 1992 (Thoemmes Press, of 1753).

  Microform: The Eighteenth Century, reel 11010, no. 03 (of 1753); Goldsmiths'-Kress library of economic literature, no. 8782 (of 1753), no. 19820 (of 1809).

  Reviews: [William Rose], *Monthly Review*, March 1753, Vol. 8, pp. 191–199 (mixed).

  Discussions: Dugald Stewart, *Lectures on Political Economy* (1855); François Jean, Marquis de Chastellux, *An Essay on Public Happiness* (1722).

- Witherspoon, John (1723–1794). *Ecclesiastical characteristics: or, the arcana of church policy. Being an humble attempt to open up the mystery of moderation.* Glasgow: printed in the year, 1753, 51, [1] p.

  Notes: discusses Hume's scepticism in a note.

  Editions: several editions and in *Works*.

  Reviews: [William Rose], 1754, Vol. 11, pp. 288 ff.

∽1754∽

- Anonymous. *Admonitions from the dead, in epistles to the living; addressed by certain spirits of both sexes, to their friends or enemies on earth, with a view either to condemn or justify their conduct while alive; and to promote the cause of religion and moral virtue.* London: printed for R. Baldwin, 1754, xii, 316 p.

  Notes: fictitious letter from Bolingbroke in the afterlife exhorting Hume to abandon infidelity.

  In *Life Responses*: Letters 1 and 2, complete; from first edition of 1754.

  Editions: 1754 second edition; no further editions.

  Microform: The Eighteenth Century; reel 978, no. 7 (of 1754 first edition).

  Reviews: *Monthly Review*, April 1754, Vol. 10, p. 311 (negative).

- Blacklock, Thomas (1721–1791). *Poems on several occasions. By Thomas Blacklock.* Edinburgh: printed by Hamilton, Balfour and Neill, 1754. xvi, 181,[1] p.

  Notes: 1754 edition contains a poem titled "On the Refinements in Metaphysical Philosophy" that mentions Hume as a sceptic.

  In *Life Responses*: "On the Refinements," complete; from 1754 edition.

  Editions: earlier and later editions exclude reference to Hume.

  Microform: The Eighteenth Century, reel 5600, no. 11 (of 1754 edition).

  Reviews: *Monthly Review*, October 1754, Vol. 11, p. 318 (extract only).

- [Douglas, John (1721–1807)]. *The criterion: or, miracles examined with a view to expose the pretensions of pagans and Papists.* London: printed for A. Millar, 1754, [4], 402, [2] p.

  Notes: criticizes Hume's "Of Miracles."

  In *Religion Responses*: selections; from 1807 edition (pp. 1–37, 94–131).

  Editions: 1757, 1807, 1824 (abridged), 1832; no further editions.

  Microform: The Eighteenth Century, reel 4490, no. 12.

  Reviews: [William Rose], *Monthly Review*, June 1754, Vol. 10, pp. 463–471 (mixed).

  Discussions: John Leland, *View* (1755).

• [Flexman, Roger (1708–1795)]. Review of *The History of Great Britain. Vol. 1. Containing the Reigns of James I and Charles I*, in *Monthly Review*, March 1754, Vol. 12, pp. 206–229.
  Notes: negative review charges Hume with partiality and inconsistency.
  In *History Responses*: complete review.

• [Manning, Owen (1721–1801)]. *An inquiry into the grounds and nature of the several species of ratiocination. In which the argument made use of in the philosophical essays of D. Hume, Esq; is occasionally taken notice of.* By A. G. O. T. V. O. C. London: printed for C. and W. Marsh, [1754], [2], 9–66 p.
  Notes: analysis of different kinds of human reasoning, criticizing "Of Miracles." The title page has no date; 1754 is based on the appearance of the review in *Monthly Review*.
  In *Religion Responses*: selections from Sections 2 and 7; from 1754 edition.
  Editions: no further editions.
  Facsimiles: 1989 (Thoemmes Press of 1754).
  Microform: The Eighteenth Century, reel 3333, no. 25.
  Reviews: [William Rose], *Monthly Review*, December 1754, Vol. 11, pp. 469–470 (negative).

• Spence, Joseph (1699–1768). *An account of the life, character, and poems of Mr. Blacklock; student of philosophy, in the University of Edinburgh. By the Rev. Mr. Spence*. London: printed for R. and J. Dodsley, 1754, 61, [3] p.
  Notes: Praises Thomas Blacklock's *Poems* (1754), citing Hume's letter to Spence of October 15, 1754.
  Editions: included in 1756 edition of Blacklock's *Poems*.
  Microform: The Eighteenth Century, reel 4842, no. 05.
  Reviews: [James Kirkpatrick], 1754, Vol. 11, p. 481 ff.

෨1755෨

• Anonymous. Review of *The History of Great Britain*, Vol. 1, in *Göttingische Anzeigen von gelehrten Sachen*, December 8, 1755, Nr. 147, pp. 1350–1354.
  Notes: mixed review, praising Hume's writing style but criticizing his religious views.
  In *History Responses*: Complete review.

• [Blair, Hugh (1718–1800)]. *Observations upon a pamphlet, intitled, An analysis of the moral and religious sentiments contained in the writings of Sopho, and David Hume, Esq; &c.*, Edinburgh: 1755.
  Notes: defends Home and Hume against John Bonar's *Analysis* (1755).
  In *Life Responses*: selections from 1755 edition.
  Editions: excerpts in *Scots Magazine*, May 1755, Vol. 17, pp. 233–243; no further editions.
  Microform: The Eighteenth Century, reel 3228, no. 15.
  Reviews: *Edinburgh Review*, 1755, Vol. 1, p. 52 (neutral).
  Discussions: Thomas Walker, "Letter on Sopho's Doctrine" (1755); Thomas Walker, *Infidelity* (1756); *Address to the Synod* (1757); James Bonar, "Memoir" (1815–1817);

• [Bonar, John (1722–1761)]. *An analysis of the moral and religious sentiments contained in the writings of Sopho, and David Hume, Esq; addressed to … the General Assembly of the Church of Scotland*. Edinburgh: printed in the year, 1755, [2], 49, [1] p.
  Notes: arranged excerpts from Home's and Hume's theories exposing them as infidels.
  In *Life Responses*: selections from 1755 edition.
  Editions: excerpts in *Scots Magazine*, May 1755, Vol. 17, pp. 233–243; no further editions.

Microform: The Eighteenth Century, reel 3228, no. 15.

Reviews: *Edinburgh Review*, 1755, Vol. 1, p. 52 (neutral).

Discussions: Hugh Blair, *Observations* (1755); *Address to the Synod* (1757); Alexander Fraser Tytler, *Memoirs* (1808); James Bonar, "Memoir" (1815–1817).

- Leland, John (1691–1766). *A view of the principal deistical writers of the last and present century*. London: B. Dod, 1755–1756, 2 v. and Supplement.

   Notes: a critique of 18th century deists with extensive excerpts and summaries of the works in question, connected by Leland's own critical comments. Leland criticizes Hume's view of causality, virtue, "Of a Particular Providence" and "Of Miracles."

   In *Metaphysical Responses*: complete Letter 16; from 1757 edition.

   In *Religion Responses*: Letters 17–21; from 1757 edition.

   In *Moral Responses*: Letter 4 of 1756 *Supplement*; from Letter 21 of combined 1757 third edition.

   In *Hume on Natural Religion*: Letter 2 from 1755 edition.

   Editions: 1754–1755, 1756 (supplement), 1758 (conclusion), 1757a–b, 1764, 1765, 1766, several later editions.

   Facsimiles: 1978 (Garland of 1757).

   Microform: The Eighteenth Century, reel 2535, no. 7–8 (of 1754–1755), reel 2585, no. 1 (supplement).

   Review of 1755 volume: [Roger Flexman, William Rose], *Monthly Review*, February 1754, Vol. 10, p. 161 ff (positive); [William Rose], *Monthly Review*, March 1755, Vol. 12, pp. 171–180 (neutral);

   Review of 1756 *Supplement*: *Critical Review*, April 1756, Vol. 1 pp. 193–208 (positive); [William Rose] *Monthly Review*, June 1756, Vol. 14 pp. 465–477 (positive).

   Review of 1758 *Conclusion*: *Monthly Review*, March 1758, Vol. 18, pp. 280–282 (positive).

- Riqueti, Marquis de Mirabeau, Victor (1715–1789) *L'ami des Hommes, ou Trait de la Population*, 1755, 5 vol.

   Notes: Criticises Hume's "Of the Populousness of Ancient Nations."

- Stewart, John (d. 1766). "Some Remarks on the Laws of Motion, and the Inertia of Matter."

   in *Essays and observations, physical and literary. Read before a society in Edinburgh, and published by them*. Edinburgh, Printed by G. Hamilton and J. Balfour, Printers to the University. 1754, viii, iv, 466 p.

   Notes: Stewart's essay appears in Pages 70–140 and he includes a one-paragraph critique of Hume's views of causality and personal identity.

   In *Metaphysical Responses*: relevant paragraph included in general introduction to the volume.

   Editions: no further editions of this volume.

   Facsimiles: 2002 (Thoemmes Press, of three volumes, 1754, 1756, 1771).

   Microform: The Eighteenth Century, reel 1795, no. 6.

   Reviews: [William Bewley], *Monthly Review*, 1754, Vol. 11, pp. 169 ff.

- [Traill, Robert (1720–1775)]. *The qualifications and decorum of a teacher of Christianity considered, with a view to the temper of the present age, respecting religion, and to some late attacks which have been made upon it. A sermon preached before the Synod of Aberdeen; at Aberdeen, April 8, 1755. By Robert Traill*. Aberdeen: printed by J. Chalmers; and sold by A. Thomson, 1755, 46 p.

   Notes: criticizes Hume's attack on the clergy in "Of National Characters."

   Editions: no further editions.

Microform: The Eighteenth Century; reel 4936, no. 8.

Reviews: [John Jardine], *Edinburgh Review*, Vol. 2, pp. 23–26 (positive); *Monthly Review*, March 1756, Vol. 14, p. 270 (announcement only).

Discussions: Thomas Hepburn, *Specimen* (1774).

• [Walker, Thomas (1704–1780)]. "A Letter on Sopho's Doctrine of Necessity," *Scots Magazine*, September 1755, Vol. 17, pp. 417–425.

Notes: criticizes Hugh Blair's *Observations* (1755).

In *Life Responses*: selections.

❧1756❧

• Anonymous. "An Account of the Debate upon the Motion for Censuring Infidel Writers," in *Scots Magazine*, June 1756, Vol. 18, p. 280–284.

Notes: account of General Assembly Committee of Overtures debate on May 27, 1756, regarding possible Church censuring of Hume.

In *Life Responses*: complete article.

Editions: reprinted with some alterations in *Annals of the General Assembly of the Church of Scotland from ... 1752 to ... 1766* (Edinburgh, John Johnstone, 1840), pp. 86–92.

Discussions: Robert Wallace, "The Necessity" (1756).

• Anonymous. Summary of Committee of Overtures Debate, *Scots Magazine*, May 1756, Vol. 18, pp. 248–249.

Notes: one paragraph explaining the issues and the vote tally regarding Church censuring of Hume.

In *Life Responses*: included in introduction to "An Account of the Debate" (1756).

• Birch, Thomas (1705–1766). *An inquiry into the share, which King Charles I. had in the transactions of the Earl of Glamorgan, ... for bringing over a body of Irish rebels to assist that King, in the years 1645 and 1646. ... The second edition; to which is added an appendix, containing several letters of the King to the Earl of Glamorgan, ...* London: printed for A. Millar, 1756, viii, 376 p.

Notes: originally published in 1747, second edition of 1756 contains an Appendix criticizing Hume's account of the Irish Rebellion in the *History*.

In *History Responses*: selections from Appendix; from 1756 edition.

Microform: The Eighteenth Century, reel 2992, no. 7 (of 1756 edition).

Discussions: Francis Jeffrey, review of Brodie in *Edinburgh Review* (1824).

• Erskine, John (1721–1803). *The influence of religion on national happiness. A sermon preached before the Society for propagating Christian Knowledge, ... on ... January 5. 1756. By John Erskine, ... To which is annex'd, The present state of the said Society.* Edinburgh: printed in the year, 1756, [2], 46 p.

Notes: criticizes Hume's religious infidelity.

Editions: included in Erskine's *Discourses Preached on Several Occasions* (1798, other editions in 1801 and 1818).

Reviews of *Discourses* 1798: *New London Review*, 1799, Vol. 1, pp. 467–479 (positive).

• [MacQueen, Daniel (d. 1777)]. *Letters on Mr. Hume's History of Great Britain.* Edinburgh: printed by Sands, Donaldson, Murray, and Cochran. For A. Kincaid and A. Donaldson, 1756, [4], 328 p.

Notes: criticizes Hume's account of the Protestant Reformation and religious fanaticism.

In *History Responses*: complete; from 1756 edition.

Editions: no further editions.

Facsimiles: 1990 (Thoemmes Press of 1756).

Microform: The Eighteenth Century, reel 1568, no. 10.

Reviews: [William Rose], *Monthly Review*, April 1756, Vol. 14, pp. 309–322 (positive); [Tobias Smollett], *Critical Review*, 1756, Vol. 1, pp. 248–253 (positive).

Discussions: Thomas Hepburn, *Specimen* (1774); Gilbert Stuart, review of Whitaker's *History* (1771–1775) in *Edinburgh Magazine and Review* (1774); Joseph Towers, *Observations* (1778).

● Melville, Thomas (1726–1753). "Observations on Light and Colours", pp. 12–90, in *Essays and Observations, Physical and Literary. Read before a Society in Edinburgh, and Published by them.* Volume II. Edinburgh: Printed by G. Hamilton and J. Balfour, Printers to the University, 1756.

Notes: a footnote in Melville's essay (pp. 71–72) criticizes Hume's view of indivisible space in *Treatise* 1.2.

In *Metaphysical Responses*: relevant parts of discussion included, from 1756 edition.

Editions: no further editions of this volume.

Facsimiles: 2002 (Thoemmes Press, of three volumes, 1754, 1756, 1771).

Reviews: *Monthly Review*, 1756, vol. 15, p. 381 ff.

● [Smollett, Tobias (1721–1771)]. Review of *The History of Great Britain. Vol. 2. Containing the Commonwealth and the Reigns of Charles II and James II*, in *Critical Review*, December 1756, Vol. 2, pp. 385–404.

Notes: positive review stating it is "one of the best histories which modern times have produced."

In *History Responses*: complete review.

● [Walker, Thomas (1704–1780)]. *Infidelity a proper object of censure. Wherein is shewn, the indispensable obligation that lies upon church-rulers to exercise the discipline instituted by Christ, upon such avowed infidels as have been solemnly initiated members of the Christian church by baptism; and, if irreclaimable, to cast them out of the Christian society.* Glasgow: printed by John Bryce and David Paterson, 1756, 56 p.

Notes: defends efforts of Scottish Clergy in censuring Home and Hume.

In *Life Responses*: selections; from 1756 edition.

Editions: no further editions.

Microform: The Eighteenth Century, reel 2410, no. 10.

Reviews: *Scots Magazine*, May 1756, Vol. 18, pp. 223–227 (excerpts only); [William Rose], *Monthly Review*, January 1757, Vol. 16, pp. 95–96 (positive).

● Wallace, Robert (1697–1771). "The necessity or expediency of the churches inquiring into the writings of David Hume Esquire and calling the Author to answer before the spiritual Courts" (1756).

Manuscript location: University of Edinburgh Library, Laing MSS, II, 97.

Notes: as yet unpublished manuscript that opposes the *Scots Magazine* account of the debate regarding censuring Hume. The manuscript is over 60 pages in length and heavily revised. Wallace initially intended this for publication in *Scots Magazine* in response to "An Account of the Debate" published in the journal in June 1756, but shaped it into a format as a pamphlet. Short excerpts from this appear in Mossner's *Life of David Hume* (1980), pp. 348–352.

● Witherspoon, John (1723–1794). *Essay on the connection between the doctrine of justification by the imputed righteousness of Christ, and holiness of life; ... By John Witherspoon.* Glasgow: printed by John Bryce and David Paterson, 1756, vi, 3–72 p.

Notes: criticizes Hume's broad account of the virtues.

Editions: 1756 (second edition).

&1757&

- Anonymous. Review of *Four Dissertations*, in *Critical Review*, February and March 1757, Vol. 3, pp. 97–107, pp. 209–216.
  Notes: negative review, maintaining that the essays lack originality.
  In *Religion Responses*: complete review.
- Anonymous. Review of *Four Dissertations*, in *The Literary Magazine: or Universal Review*, 1757, Vol. 2, pp. 32–36.
  Notes: negative review, maintaining that the essays lack originality.
  In *Religion Responses*: complete review.
- Anonymous. Review of John Home's *Douglas, a Tragedy*, in *Critical Review*, March 1757, Vol. 3, pp. 253–268.
  Notes: criticizes Hume's assessment of Home's *Douglas*.
  In *Life Responses*: selections.
  Editions: reprinted in *Scots Magazine*, June 1757, Vol. 19, pp. 293–298.
- Anonymous. Review of John Home's *Douglas*, in *The Literary Magazine: or Universal Review*, 1757, Vol. 2, pp. 126–141.
  Notes: discusses Hume's assessment of Home's *Douglas* and pamphlets on the subject.
  In *Life Responses*: selections.
- Anonymous. *An address to the Synod of Lothian and Tweedale, concerning Mr Home's Tragedy and Hume's [i.e., Henry Home's] Moral essays.* [Edinburgh, 1757], 8 p.
  Notes: attacks stage plays and Hume's infidel writings.
  In *Life Responses*: selections; from 1757 edition.
  Editions: no further editions.
- Anonymous. *The tragedy of Douglas analysed.* London, Printed for J. Doughty, in Paternoster Row, 1757, 5–23 p.
  Notes: defends Hume's assessment of Home's *Douglas*.
  In *Life Responses*: selections; from 1757 edition.
  Editions: no further editions.
  Reviews: *Monthly Review*, May 1757, Vol. 16, p. 454 (negative).
  Discussions: John Hawkesworth's *A Letter to Mr. David Hume* (1757); review of *Douglas* in *Literary Magazine* (1757).
- Anonymous. *A letter to the Reverend the Moderator, and members of the presbytery of Haddingtoun.* Edinburgh: 1757, 8 p.
  Notes: criticizes John Home's *Douglas* and Hume's religious infidelity.
  Microform: The Eighteenth Century, reel 7114, no. 03.
- Anonymous. *The usefulness of the Edinburgh theatre seriously considered. With a proposal for rendering it more beneficial.* Edinburgh: 1757, [4], 12 p.
  Notes: satirical criticism of Hume's assessment of Home's *Douglas*.
  In *Life Responses*: selections; from 1757 edition.
  Editions: no further editions.
  Microform: The Eighteenth Century, reel 1475, no. 58.
- Brown, John (1715–1766). *An estimate of the manners and principles of the times.* London: Printed for L. Davis, and C. Reymers, 1757–1758, 2 v., 221 p., 265 p.
  Notes: criticizes Hume's view of the clergy in "Whether the British Government inclines more to Absolute Monarchy, or to a Republic".
  In *Essays Responses*: Vol. 1, Part 2, Section 2, selections; from 1757 edition, pp. 82–85.
  Editions: several editions in 1757 and 1758, which are reissues with cancel title pages.
  Microform: The Eighteenth Century, reel 2421, no. 4 (of 1757, Vol. 1).

Reviews of 1757 volume: [William Rose], *Monthly Review*, May 1757, Vol. 16, pp. 430–443 (positive).

Reviews of 1758 volume: [Owen Ruffhead], *Monthly Review*, April 1758, Vol. 18, pp. 354–374 (negative); *Critical Review*, April 1758, Vol. 5, pp. 308–320; *Gentleman's Magazine*, June 1758, Vol. 28, 249 ff.

Discussions: Josiah Tucker, Letter to Henry Home (July 6, 1758).

● [Fleming, Caleb (1689–1779)]. *Three questions resolved. viz. what is religion? what is the Christian religion? what is the Christian catholic church? wherein popery is proved to have no claim, either as a religion, as the Christian religion, or as the Christian catholic-church. in three letters to — Esq. with a postscript on Mr. Hume's natural history of religion.* London, A Henderson, 1757, 3–56 p.

Notes: Postscript criticizes "The Natural History of Religion".

In *Religion Responses*: complete Postscript from 1757 edition.

In *Hume on Natural Religion*: complete Postscript from 1757 edition.

Editions: no further editions.

Microform: The Eighteenth Century, reel 2082, no. 7.

Reviews: [William Rose], *Monthly Review*, May 1757, Vol. 16, pp. 470–472 (positive).

● [Goldsmith, Oliver (1730?–1774)]. Review of John Home's *Douglas, a Tragedy*, in *Monthly Review*, May 1757, Vol. 16, pp. 426–429.

Notes: criticizes Hume's assessment of Home's *Douglas*.

In *Life Responses*: selections.

Editions: reprinted in *Scots Magazine*, June 1757, Vol. 19, pp. 293–298.

● [Hawkesworth, John (1715?–1773)]. *A letter to Mr. David Hume, on the tragedy of Douglas; its analysis: and the charge against Mr. Garrick. By an English critic.* London, printed for J. Scott, 1757, 19, [1] p.

Notes: criticizes Hume's assessment of Home's *Douglas*.

In *Life Responses*: selections; from 1757 edition.

Editions: 1757 (same as above with different title page), 1757 (London: Scott, 24 p.); no further editions.

Microform: The Eighteenth Century, reel 1277, no. 12 (of London: Scott, 24 p.), reel 4528, no. 11 (of London: Scott, 19 p.).

Reviews: [Theophilus Cibber], *Monthly Review*, May 1757, Vol. 16, p. 454 (negative).

Discussions: review of *Douglas* in *Literary Magazine* (1757).

● [MacLaurin, John (1734–1796)]. *Apology for the writers against the tragedy of Douglas. With some remarks on that play.* Edinburgh, 1757, 3–15, [1] p.

Notes: criticizes Hume and his friends for puffing Home's *Douglas*.

In *Life Responses*: selections; from 1757 edition.

Editions: no further editions.

Microform: The Eighteenth Century, reel 1009, no. 22.

● [MacLaurin, John (1734–1796)]. *The philosopher's opera.* [Edinburgh, 1757], iv, 23, [1] p.

Notes: satirical opera with Hume as a character.

In *Life Responses*: complete; from 1757 edition.

Editions: editor of MacLaurin's 1798 Works intentionally excludes this piece; no further editions.

Microform: The Eighteenth Century, reel 1285, no. 14.

Discussions: "Account" in *The works of the late John MacLaurin* (1798).

● [Rose, William (1719–1786)]. Review of *Four Dissertations*, in *Monthly Review*, February 1757, Vol. 16, pp. 122–139.

Notes: positive review.

In *Religion Responses*: complete review.

In *Hume on Natural Religion*: complete review.

- Hurd, Richard (1720–1808). *Q. Horatii Flacci Epistolae ad Pisones, et Augustum: with an English commentary and notes. To which are added, two dissertations; the one, on the provinces of the drama: the other, on poetical imitation: and a letter to Mr. Mason.The third edition, corrected and enlarged.* Cambridge: printed [by J. Bentham] for W. Thurlbourn & J. Woodyer; and sold by R. Dodsley in Pall-Mall, J. Beecroft and M. Cooper, London, 1757, 2 v.

  Notes: Note to line 103 of *Ars Poetica* criticizes Hume's "Of Tragedy".

  In *Essays Responses*: complete Note, from 1811 edition of *Works*.

  Editions: 1766 (fourth edition), 1768, *Works* 1811.

  Microform: The Eighteenth Century, reel 3920, no. 09 (of 1776).

  Reviews: [William Rose], *Monthly Review*, 1749, Vol. 1, p. 277 ff.; [William Rose], July 1753, Vol. 9, p. 11 ff. (positive); *Edinburgh Review*, 1755, Vol. 2, pp. 25–32.

  Discussions: George Campbell, *The Philosophy of Rhetoric* (1776).

- [Rose, William (1719–1786)]. Review of *The History of Great Britain. Vol. 2. Containing the Commonwealth and the Reigns of Charles II and James II*, in *Monthly Review*, January 1757, Vol. 16, pp. 36–50.

  Notes: positive review.

  In *History Responses*: complete review.

- [Smith, William (1727–1803)?]. "Dispute about the Tragedy of Douglas," from *The American Magazine and Monthly Chronicle for the British Colonies*, (February 1758), Vol. 1, pp. 203–209.

  Notes: probably authored by Smith, the magazine's editor. Reprint of Hume's Dedication to Home and reviews of Home's *Douglas* in Critical Review and *Monthly Review*. Smith comments on these.

  In *American Responses*: complete article.

- Wallace, Robert (1697–1771). "An Address to the Reverend the Clergy of the Church of Scotland by a Layman of their Communion on occasion of composing acting and publishing the Tragedy called Douglass" (1757).

  Manuscript location: University of Edinburgh Library, Laing MSS, II, 620, Item 2.

  Notes: as yet unpublished manuscript regarding the controversy surrounding John Home's *Douglas*. A short excerpt from this appears in Mossner's *Life of David Hume* (1980), p. 363.

- [Warburton, William (1698–1779); Hurd, Richard (1720–1808)]. *Remarks on Mr. David Hume's Essay on the natural history of religion: addressed to the Rev. Dr. Warburton.* London: printed for M. Cooper, 1757, [4], 76 p.

  Notes: criticizes Hume's "Natural History of Religion."

  In *Religion Responses*: complete pamphlet; from 1757 edition.

  In *Hume on Natural Religion*: Remarks 1, 3, and 21; from Warburton's *Works* (1788).

  Editions: 1777, in *Works* 1788, 1811, 1841 (reprints in *Works* are altered by Hurd); no further editions.

  Microform: The Eighteenth Century, reel 5431, no. 26 (of 1757); reel 7463, no. 01 (of 1777).

  Reviews: [William Rose], *Monthly Review*, August 1757, Vol. 17, pp. 189–191 (neutral; complete review in *Hume on Natural Religion*); *Critical Review*, May 1757, Vol. 3, pp. 398–401 (neutral); *London Chronicle*, April 17–19, 1777, Vol. 41, No. 3178, pp. 369–370 (reprint of Remarks 1–3 only).

  Discussions: Richard Hurd, *Discourse* (1794).

ॐ1758ॐ

- Anonymous. *The capital. A satyrical admonition. Addressed to every true lover of his country, but more particularly to the British clergy.* Staples, 1758.

    Notes: Attack in verse on politics and other subjects, with a stanza on Hume.

    Reviews: *Critical Review*, 1758, Vol. 6, p. 438 (negative); *Monthly Review*, December 1758, Vol. 19, pp. 587–588 (mixed).

- Anonymous. Review of *Four Dissertations*, in *Göttingische Anzeigen von gelehrten Sachen*, April 8, 1758 No. 42, pp. 401–403.

    Notes: positive review.

    In *Religion Responses*: English translation of complete review, translated by Curtis Bowman.

- Boswell, James (1740–1795). Letters to William Temple, 1758–1775.

    See James Boswell, *Letters of James Boswell* (1857).

    Notes: letters to temple relate Boswell's conversations with Hume.

    In *Life Responses*: selections from 1908 edition.

- Comber, Thomas (d. 1778). *A vindication of the great Revolution in England in A.D. MDCLXXXVIII. And of the characters of King William and Queen Mary; together with a confutation of the character of King James the Second; as misrepresented by the author of the complete history of England; ... By Thomas Comber, A.B.* London: printed for J. Robinson, 1758, viii, 149, [1] p.

    Notes: note to page 131 praises Hume's *History*.

    In *History Responses*: selections included in "Miscellaneous Comments on Hume's *History*"; from 1758 edition.

    Editions: 1759, no further editions.

    Microform: The Eighteenth Century, reel 6737, no. 08.

- Harris, William (1720–1770). *An historical and critical account of the life and writings of Charles I. King of Great Britain. After the manner of Mr. Bayle. Drawn from original writers and state-papers. By William Harris.* London: printed for R. Griffiths; T. Field; and C. Henderson, 1758, [8], 428, [4] p.

    Notes: Several footnotes attack Hume's *History* and his defence of Charles I.

    Editions: 1772 (second edition).

    Microform: The Eighteenth Century, reel 8061, no. 03 (of 1758); reel 10062, no. 02 (of 1772).

    Reviews: *Critical Review*, April 1758, Vol. 5, pp. 320–326 (negative); [Owen Ruffhead], *Monthly Review*, May 1758, Vol. 18, pp. 452–461 (positive).

    Discussions: mentioned by Roger Flexman in his 1754 review of Hume's *History* and in Sylvester O'Halloran's *Introduction to the Study of the History and Antiquities of Ireland* (1772).

- [Mecom, Benjamin (1732–1776)]. "The famous Oliver Cromwel's private Life" in *New-England Magazine of Knowledge and Pleasure*, October 1758, no. 2 , pp. 3–12.

    Notes: Mecom, the journal's editor, reprints Hume's account of Cromwell in the *History*, and comments on this.

    In *American Responses*: complete selections.

- Price, Richard (1723–1791). *Review of the principal questions and difficulties in morals.* London, A. Miller, 1758, viii, 485 p.

    Notes: Price criticizes empirically-oriented moral theories and argues that morality is grounded in rational intuitions. In Chapter 5 and Appendix, Note C, he criticizes Hume's analysis of induction and notion of perception.

    In *Metaphysical Responses*: relevant sections from Note C; from 1787 edition.

    Editions: 1769, 1787, *Works* 1816, 1948.

Facsimiles: 1948 (Garland facsimile of 1758), 1974 (Franklin of 1787).

Microform: The Eighteenth Century, reel 7633, no. 11 (of 1758), reel 7598, no. 01 (of 1769), reel 7634, no. 04 (of 1787).

Reviews: [William Rose], *Monthly Review*, June 1758, Vol. 18, pp. 513–527 (positive); *Critical Review*, 1758 May, Vol. 5, pp. 361–368, June, 461–467 (positive).

• [Stona, Thomas (1727/8–1792)]. *Remarks upon The natural history of religion by Mr. Hume. With dialogues on heathen idolatry, and the Christian religion. By S.T.* London: printed for R. and J. Dodsley, 1758, [2], 159, [1] p.

Notes: criticizes Hume's "Of Miracles" and his theory of original polytheism in "The Natural History of Religion".

In *Religion Responses*: pages 1–30, 119–127; from 1758 edition.

In *Hume on Natural Religion*: pages 1–27; from 1758 edition.

Editions: no further editions.

Microform: The Eighteenth Century, reel 5431, no. 4.

Reviews: [William Rose], *Monthly Review*, December 1758, Vol. 19, pp. 532–533 (negative; complete review in *Hume on Natural Religion*); *Critical Review*, November 1758, Vol. 6, pp. 411–418 (mixed).

• Tucker, Josiah (1713–1799). Letter to Henry Home, July 6, 1758.

See Alexander Fraser Tytler, *Memoirs of ... Henry Home* (1807).

Notes: critiques "Of the Balance of Trade," and Hume's letter to Henry Home (March 4, 1758); adapted into Tucker's *Four Tracts* (1774).

In *Essay Responses*: selections; from 1814 edition of Tytler's *Memoirs*.

• [Wallace, Robert (1697–1771)]. *Characteristics of the present political state of Great Britain*. London: Printed for A. Millar, 1758, [4], 256 p.

Notes: Part I criticizes Hume's view of paper credit in "Of the Balance of Trade" and "Of Money".

In *Essays Responses*: Part I, complete; from second edition of 1758, pp. 15–40.

Editions: 1758 (Dublin); 1758 (London: Millar, second edition); no further editions.

Facsimiles: 1969 (A.M. Kelley of London 1758 second edition).

Microform: The Eighteenth Century, reel 3165, no. 01 (of 1758 London second edition); reel 3396, no. 16 (of 1758 London); reel 11041, no. 14 (of 1758 Dublin); Goldsmiths'-Kress library of economic literature, no. 9326 (of 1758).

Reviews: *Critical Review*, April 1758, Vol. 5, pp. 283–292 (mixed).

Discussions: Dugald Stewart, *Lectures on Political Economy* (1854).

• Witherspoon, John (1723–1794). *The absolute necessity of salvation through Christ. A sermon, preached before the Society in Scotland for Propagating Christian Knowledge, in the High Church of Edinburgh, on Monday, January 2. 1758. By John Witherspoon*. Edinburgh: printed for W. Miller, 1758, [2], 90 p.

Notes: criticizes Hume's moral theory.

≈1759≈

• Gerard, Alexander (1728–1795). *An essay on taste. By Alexander Gerard, ... With three dissertations on the same subject. By Mr. de Voltaire. Mr. d'Alembert, F.R.S. Mr. de Montesquieu*. London: printed for A. Millar. A. Kincaid and J. Bell, in Edinburgh, 1759, [2], iii, [1], 222, [3], 224–253, [2], 258–314 p.

Notes: discusses Hume's theory of superior admiration in the *Treatise*; The third edition of 1780 adds a fourth part titled "Of the Standard of Taste" which discusses Hume's theory.

In *Essays Responses*: Part 4, Sections 2 and 3, selections; from 1780 edition.

Editions: 1764 (second edition), 1780 (third edition), 1804; for details on these editions see *Common Sense Bibliography.*

Facsimiles: 1971 (Scolar Press of 1759), 1970 (Garland Publishing of 1764), 1978 (Scholars' Facsimiles & Reprints of 1780).

Microform: The Eighteenth Century, reel 2248, no. 5 (of 1759), reel 3000, no. 6 (of 1780); Library of English literature, LEL 12248 (of 1764); Eighteenth-century sources for the study of English literature and culture, reel no. 747 (of 1780).

Reviews: [William Rose], *Monthly Review*, June 1759, Vol. 20, pp. 533–545 (positive).

Discussions: Dugald Stewart, *Philosophical Essays* (1810).

• [Hurd, Richard (1720–1808)]. *Moral and political dialogues, being the substance of several conversations between divers eminent persons of the past and present age: digested by the parties themselves, and now first published from the original mss with critical and explanatory notes.* London: printed for A. Millar; and W. Thurlborne and J. Woodyer at Cambridge, 1759, [2], xii, 304, 283–289, [1] p.

Notes: Postscript in 1759 edition criticizes Hume's Tory view of royal prerogative; this was rewritten and included in a note to Dialogue six in the 1760 edition.

In *History Responses*: Postscript from 1759 edition and selections from Dialogue 6 from *The Works of Richard Hurd*, 1811, Vol. 4.

Editions: 1760 (second edition, London), 1760 (Dublin), 1765 (third edition), 1771 (fourth edition), 1776 (fifth edition), 1778 (sixth edition) *Works* 1811.

Microform: The Eighteenth Century, reel 7247, no.04 (of 1759), reel 4280, no. 03 (of London 1760), reel 1299, no. 04 (of London 1764), reel 10628, no. 02 (of 1771), reel 5641, no. 19 (of 1776), reel 5324, no. 5 (of 1778).

Reviews: *Critical Review*, June 1759, Vol. 7. pp. 471–483 (mixed); [Owen Ruffhead], *Monthly Review*, July 1759, Vol. 21, pp. 35–46 (mixed).

Discussions: Joseph Towers, *Observations* (1778); James Boswell, *The Life of Samuel Johnson* (1791); "On Mr. Hume's Political Inconsistency" (1821); Francis Jeffrey, review of Brodie in *Edinburgh Review* (1824).

• [Ruffhead, Owen (1723–1769)]. Review of *The History of England, under the House of Tudor*, in *Monthly Review*, April and May 1759, Vol. 20, pp. 344–364, 400–417.

Notes: positive review with detailed criticism; Hume made many of the suggested changes in later editions.

In *History Responses*: complete review.

• Smith, Adam (1723–1790). *The theory of moral sentiments.* London: A. Miller, A. Kincaid, and J. Bell, 1759, 551 p.

Notes: Part 4, Sections 1 and 2 critique Hume's view of pleasure and utility.

In *Moral Responses*: complete Part 4, Sections 1 and 2; from the 1759 edition.

Editions: 1761, 1767, 1774, 1781, 1790 1793, and later editions (see 1976 critical edition of Smith's *Theory* for details of the early editions).

Facsimiles: 1971 (Garland of 1759).

Microform: The Eighteenth Century, reel 4733, no. 01 (of 1759), reel 7114, no. 02 (of 1767), reel 353, no 3 (of 1793).

Reviews: [William Rose] *Monthly Review*, July 1759, Vol. 21, pp. 1–18 (positive); *Critical Review*, May 1759, Vol. 7 pp. 383–399 (positive).

Discussions: John Bruce, *Elements* (1786); Thomas Brown, *Lectures* (1820); Dugald Stewart, *Philosophy of the Active and Moral Powers* (1828); Henry Sidgwick, *Methods of Ethics* (1874); Henry Sidgwick, *Outlines* (1886).

• [Smollett, Tobias (1721–1771)]. Review of *The History of England, under the House of Tudor*, in *Critical Review*, April 1759, Vol. 7, pp. 289–303.

Notes: positive review with some criticism; Hume made several of the suggested changes in later editions.

In *History Responses*: complete review.

❧1760❦

• Anonymous. Review of Hume's *Two Additional Essays*, in *Critical Review*, June 1760
, Vol. 9, p. 493.

Notes: one paragraph announcement of "Of the Jealousy of Trade" and "Of the Coalition of Parties".

In *Essays Responses*: complete review.

• Gerard, Alexander (1728–1795). *The influence of the pastoral office on the character examined with a view, especially, to Mr. Hume's representation of the spirit of that office: a sermon preached before the Synod of Aberdeen, at Aberdeen, April 8, 1760.*
Publisher: Aberdeen: Printed by J. Chalmers and sold by And. Millar. ... A. Kincaid and J. Bell ... and A. Thomson ..., 1760, [2], 75, [1] p.

Notes: criticizes Hume's attack on the clergy in "Of National Characters".

In *Essays Responses*: complete pamphlet; from 1760 edition.

Editions: 1761, 1762 (reissue of 1761 with cancel title page); no further editions. For details see *Common Sense Bibliography*.

Microform: The Eighteenth Century, reel 1262, no. 21 (of 1760).

Reviews: [William Rose], *Monthly Review*, January 1761, Vol. 24, pp. 22–33 (positive).

Discussions: Thomas Hepburn, *Specimen* (1774).

• [Tytler, William (1711–1792)]. *An historical and critical enquiry into the evidence produced by the Earls of Murray and Morton, against Mary Queen of Scots. With an examination of the Rev. Dr. Robertson's Dissertation, and Mr. Hume's History, with respect to that evidence.* Edinburgh: printed by. W. Gordon, and sold by him and the other booksellers; and at London by W. Owen, T. Longman, J. Scott, Davie and Law, 1760, [2], viii, 262, 31, [1] p.

Notes: detailed defence of Mary's innocence drawing on Walter Goodall's *Examination* (1754); throughout the work Tytler criticizes Hume's view of Mary Queen of Scots' guilt. Successive editions contain major revisions. Hume responded to Tytler in his *History*, Chapter 39, Note M.

In *History Responses*: selections from Preface, Chapters 1, 2, 3, 4, 6 (1760 edition) and complete Postscript (1772 edition).

Editions: 1767 (second edition), 1772 (third edition), 1790 (fourth edition); no further editions.

Microform: The Eighteenth Century, reel 1632, no. 6 (of 1760), reel 1700, no. 4 (of 1772).

Reviews: [Owen Ruffhead], *Monthly Review*, July 1760, Vol. 23, pp. 30–40 (positive); *Critical Review*, June 1760, Vol. 9, pp. 421 (positive); [Samuel Johnson] *Gentleman's Magazine*, October 1760, Vol. 30, pp. 453–456 (positive); *Annual Register* December 1761, Vol. 4, pp. 305–316 (positive).

Discussions: John Whitaker, *Mary Queen of Scots Vindicated* (1760); David Dalrymple, *Miscellaneous Remarks on "The Enquiry"* (1784); Francis Garden's *Miscellanies in Prose and Verse* (1791); *Concise State* (1795).

&1761&

- Anonymous. *Christianity older than the religion of nature, and preferable thereto: to which are added five letters, ... Likewise a rhapsody, containing a few strictures on Hobbs's and Hume's philosophy*. London: printed for J. Wilkie, 1761, [1761], [4], 83, [1] p.

  Notes: criticism of Hume's religious views.

  Editions: no further editions.

- Anonymous. Review of Hume's *History of England* in *Annual Register for the year 1761*, December 1761, Vol. 4, pp. 301–304.

  Notes: possibly reviewed by Edmund Burke, the journal's editor.

  In *History Responses*: selections.

- Denina, Carlo (1731–1813). *Discorso sopra le vicende della letteratura*, Torino: Nella Stamperia Reale, 1761, [4], 242, [4] p.

  Notes: praises the abilities of Hume and other Scottish writers.

  In *Life Responses*: selections; from translation in *Scots Magazine*, September 1764, Vol. 26, p. 466–467.

  Editions: several Italian editions.

  Translation: *An essay on the revolutions of literature*, translated by John Murdoch (1747–1824), London, Printed for T. Cadell, 1771, viii, 299 p.

  Reviews: *Scots Magazine*, September 1764, Vol. 26, p. 465 ff. (positive); *Critical Review*, 1771, Vol. 31, pp. 376–381 (positive).

  Discussions: Notice of Hume's Death, *Weekly Magazine, or Edinburgh Amusement* (1776).

- [Ruffhead, Owen (1723–1769)]. Review of *The History of England, from the Invasion of Julius Caesar to the Accession of Henry VII*, in *Monthly Review*, December 1761, Vol. 25, pp. 401–414, and February 1762, Vol. 26, pp. 81–95.

  Notes: positive review with specific criticisms; Hume made several of the recommended changes in later editions of the *History*.

  In *History Responses*: complete review.

  Discussion: Owen Ruffhead, Letter to Hume (March 1, 1763).

&1762&

- Anonymous. Review of *The History of England, from the Invasion of Julius Caesar to the Accession of Henry VII*, in *Critical Review*, January and February 1762, Vol. 13, pp. 58–65, 81–93.

  Notes: positive review.

  In *History Responses*: complete review.

- Boswell, James (1740–1795). "Journal of my Jaunt," November 4, 1762.

  See James Boswell, *The Private papers of James Boswell* (1928–1934).

  Notes: relates detailed conversation at Hume's apartment in 1762.

  In *Life Responses*: selections; from *Private papers* (1928–1934).

- Campbell, George (1719–1796). *A dissertation on miracles: containing an examination of the principles advanced by David Hume, Esq; in an Essay on miracles. By George Campbell*. Edinburgh, printed for A. Kincaid & J. Bell. Sold by A. Millar, R. & J. Dodsley, W. Johnston, R. Baldwin, and J. Richardson, London, 1762, [2], xii, 288 p.

  Notes: criticizes Hume's "Of Miracles."

  In *Religion Responses*: complete; from third edition of 1797.

  Editions: 1766, 1790, 1796, 1797, several later editions; included in 1st American edition of Hume's *Philosophical Essays* (1817). For details of these editions see *Common Sense Bibliography*.

Facsimiles: 1983 (Garland of 1762).

Microform: The Eighteenth Century, reel 6278, no. 08 (of 1762); Eighteenth-century sources for the study of English literature, reel 25; British culture series, Group VII; no. 3. (of 1797).

Reviews of 1762 edition: *Critical Review,* August 1762, Vol. 14, pp. 81–90 (mixed); [William Rose], *Monthly Review,* December 1762, Vol. 26, pp. 499–502 (positive; review included in *Hume on Miracles*).

Reviews of 1797 edition: *Analytical Review,* 1797, Vol. 26, pp. 570–572 (positive).

Discussions: Thomas Hepburn, *Specimen* (1774); William Smellie, *Encyclopaedia Britannica* (1768–1771).

- [Rider, William (1723–1785)]. *An historical and critical account of the lives and writings of the living authors of Great-Britain. Wherein their respective merits are discussed with the utmost candour and impartiality.* London: printed for the author, 1762, [2], 34 p.

  Notes: short biographical sketch of Hume.

  In *Life Responses*: complete introduction and entries on "Hume" and "Rider"; from 1762 edition.

  Editions: no further editions.

  Facsimiles: 1974 (Augustan Reprint of 1762).

  Microform: The Eighteenth Century, reel 1824, no. 3.

  Reviews: *Critical Review,* May 1762, Vol. 13, pp. 441–442 (negative); *Monthly Review,* May 1762, Vol. 26, pp. 391–392 (negative).

❧1763❧

- Doddridge, Philip (1702–1751). *A course of lectures on the principal subjects in pneumatology, ethics, and divinity; with references to the most considerable authors on each subject.* London, J. Buckland, 1763, x, 595 p.

  Notes: posthumously published handbook for students on theological controversies of the day, written in the style of a geometrical proof. The text mentions Hume in a note on justice (lecture 89), which may have been inserted by the book's editor and not Doddridge himself.

  Editions: 1776, 1794, 1799, 1822.

  Microform: The Eighteenth Century, reel 7049, no. 02 (of 1776), reel 4382, no. 01 (of 1794), reel 3336, no. 9 (of 1799).

  Reviews of 1763 edition: [William Kenrick], *Monthly Review,* July 1763, Vol. 29, 13–17 (negative).

  Reviews of 1794 edition: *Critical Review,* November 1794, Vol. 12, pp. 303–312 (positive).

- Macaulay, Catharine (1731–1791). *The history of England from the accession of James I. to that of the Brunswick line.* London: printed for J. Nourse; R. and J. Dodsley; and W. Johnston, 1763–1783, 8 v.

  Notes: contains various criticisms of Hume's *History.*

  Microform: Eighteenth Century, reel 1441, no. 02 (5 vol., 1769–1772); reel 1446, no. 01 and reel 1447, no. 01 (8 Vol. 1763–1783); reel 1565, no. 02 (1 Vol. 1778).

- Reid, Thomas (1710–1796). Critique of Hume's *Enquiry* (1763)

  See M.A. Stewart "Rational Religion and Common Sense" (2003).

  Notes: transcription by Stewart of a segment of a student's copy of Reid's Logic lectures at King's College, Aberdeen in 1763, as these bear on "Of Miracles" and "Of a Particular Providence" in Hume's first Enquiry.

- Ruffhead, Owen (1723–1769). Letter to Hume, March 1, 1763.

See John Hill Burton, *Letters of Eminent Persons* (1849).
Notes: opposes Hume's view of the powerlessness of the Saxon Commons.
In *History Responses*: complete letter, from Burton (1849).

❧1764❧

● Reid, Thomas (1710–1796). *An inquiry into the human mind, on the principles of common sense. By Thomas Reid.* Edinburgh: printed for A. Millar, London, and A. Kincaid & J. Bell, Edinburgh, 1764, xvi, 541, [1] p.
Notes: criticizes Hume's views of perception and the self.
In *Metaphysical Responses*: Chapter 1, Section 5–8, Chapter 2, Section 6, complete selections; from 1785 edition.
Editions: 1764 (Dublin), 1765, 1769, 1779, 1785, 1801, and later editions; see *Common Sense Bibliography* for details on the editions.
Facsimiles: 1990 (Thoemmes Press of 1785).
Microform: The Eighteenth Century, reel 258, no. 3 (of 1764), reel 2309, no. 8 (of 1765), The Eighteenth Century, reel 8577, no. 05 (of 1779); British culture series, Group VI, no. 65 (of 1779).
Reviews: *Critical Review*, May 1764, Vol. 17, pp. 321–329 (mixed); [William Rose], *Monthly Review*, May 1764, Vol. 30, pp. 358–379; July 1764, Vol. 31, pp. 1–21 (positive). Complete reviews included in *Common Sense Responses*.
Discussions: James Oswald, *Appeal* (1766–1772); James Beattie, "Castle of Scepticism" (1767); James Beattie, *Essay* (1770); Joseph Priestley, *Institutes* (1772–1774); Joseph Priestley *Examination* (1774); Thomas Hepburn, *Specimen* (1774); Thomas Ludlam, *Logical Tracts* (1805?); Dugald Stewart, Letter to William Forbes (c. 1806).

● Reid, Thomas (1710–1796). "Mr Humes notion of Causes." (c. 1764).
Manuscript location: Aberdeen University Library, MS.2131/6/III/3, fols. 1r–1v.
See M.A. Stewart "Rational Religion and Common Sense" (2003).
Notes: undated manuscript, relating to Reid's logic lectures at Aberdeen in the early 1760s, probably written after the *Inquiry*. Reid criticizes Hume's view of causality and necessity.
In *Metaphysical Responses*: newly transcribed by M.A. Stewart.

● Various authors. Letters to William Mure of Caldwell from 1764–1775.
See William Mure (1799–1860), ed., *Selections from the Family papers preserved at Caldwell* (1824).
Notes: stories about Hume in correspondence from acquaintances, and letter from James Oswald of Dunikier discussing Hume's essay "Of the Balance of Trade" prior to its publication in *Political Discourses*.
In *Essays Responses*: Oswald's complete letter; from 1854 edition, Part 2, Vol. 1, pp. 93-107.
In *Life Responses*: selections from Part 2, Volumes 1 and 2; from 1854 edition.

● Voltaire, François-Marie Arouet de (1694–1778). *Dictionnaire philosophique, portatif.* Londres, [i.e. Geneva: Cramer], 1764, viii, 344 p.
Notes: article on "Religion" criticizes Hume's theory of original polytheism in "The Natural History of Religion".
In *Religion Responses*: Questions 1 and 2 from "Religion"; English translation from *The philosophical dictionary, for the pocket … translated from the French edition; corrected by the author.* Catskill [N.Y.]: Printed by T. & M. Croswel, 1796, [8], 336 p.

≈1765≈

- [Blackburne, Francis (1705–1787)]. *A short historical view of the controversy concerning an intermediate state and the separate existence of the soul between death and the general resurrection.* London: printed for T. Field; and sold by Mr. Walter; Mr. Henderson; and Messrs. Todd and Southeran, at York, 1765, [2], lvii, [1], 125, [1] p.Notes: supports Hume's view in the *History* regarding superstition in the age of Thomas Becket.

  Editions: 1772 (second edition).

  Microform: The Eighteenth Century, reel 9499, no. 04.

  Reviews: *Critical Review*, 1765, Vol. 20, p. 9 ff.; [William Rose], *Monthly Review*, May 1765, Vol. 32, pp. 345–360 (positive).

- Maclaine, Archibald (1722–1804). *An ecclesiastical history, antient and modern, from the birth of Christ, to the beginning of the present century: ... By the late learned John Lawrence Mosheim, ... Translated from the original, ... by Archibald Maclaine, ... In two volumes.* London: printed for A. Millar, 1765, 2 v.

  Notes: in notes and Appendix 2, translator Maclaine criticizes Hume's view of the Protestant Reformation and fanaticism.

  In *History Responses*: Note and Appendix 2; from 1826 edition, Vol. 4 and 6.

  Editions: 1767, 1768, 1774, 1781, 1782, 1787, 1790, 1792 1797, 1800; later editions.

  Microform: The Eighteenth Century, reel 7601, no. 01 (of 1767); reel 177, no. 1 (of 1781), reel 6725, no. 01 (of 1787), reel 2987, no. 3 (of 1790).

  Reviews: [William Rose], *Monthly Review*, 1765, Vol. 33, August pp. 89–107, November pp. 329–342, December pp. 430–444 (positive); *Critical Review*, 1765, Vol. 19, pp. 401–410, Vol. 20, pp. 1–8, 81–93 (positive).

  Discussions: Joseph Towers, *Observations* (1778).

≈1766≈

- Anonymous. Review of Hume's *A concise and genuine account*, in *Critical Review*, November 1766, Vol. 22 pp. 376–378.

  Notes: defends Hume in the dispute with Rousseau.

  In *Life Responses*: complete.

- Anonymous. Review of Hume's *A concise and genuine account*, in *Gentleman's Magazine*, November 1766, Vol. 36, pp. 499–504.

  Notes: defends Hume in the dispute with Rousseau.

  In *Life Responses*: selections.

- Gerard, Alexander (1728–1795). *Dissertations on subjects relating to the genius and the evidences of Christianity. By Alexander Gerard, D.D.* Edinburgh: printed for A. Millar, London; and A. Kincaid and J. Bell, Edinburgh, 1766, xli, [1], 499, [1] p.

  Notes: discusses Hume's "Of Miracles," especially on pages 346–398.

  Editions: no further editions.

  Reviews: [William Rose], *Monthly Review*, 1766, Vol. 35, p. 176 ff., 257 ff.

- [Greene, Edward Burnaby (d. 1788)]. *A defence of Mr. Rousseau, against the aspersions of Mr. Hume, Mons. Voltaire, and their associates.* London: printed for S. Bladon, 1766, [4], iv, 44 p.

  Notes: defends Rousseau in the dispute with Hume.

  In *Life Responses*: complete; from 1766 edition.

  Editions: no further editions.

  Microform: The Eighteenth Century, reel 916, no. 14.

  Reviews: *Critical Review*, November 1766, Vol. 22, p. 378 (negative); *Monthly Review*, December 1766, Vol. 35, pp. 471–472 (negative).

- Griffet, Henri (1698–1771). *Nouveaux éclaircissements sur l'histoire de Marie, reine d'Angleterre* (1766).
  English translation: *New lights thrown upon the history of Mary Queen of England, eldest daughter of Henry VIII. Addressed to David Hume, Esq; author of The history of the Plantagenets, the Tudors, and the Stuarts. Translated from the French.* London: printed for J. Wilkie, 1771, vii, [1], 111, [1] p.
  Notes: criticizes Hume's view of Mary Queen of Scots' guilt.
  In *History Responses*: selections; from 1771 English translation.
  Microform: The Eighteenth Century, reel 1268, no. 25.
  Reviews: *Critical Review* 1771, Vol. 31, pp. 151–153 (positive); [Gilbert Stuart], *Monthly Review*, April 1771, Vol. 44, pp. 277–279 (negative).
- [Highmore, Joseph (1692–1780)]. *Essays, moral, religious, and miscellaneous. To which is added, a prose translation of Mr. Browne's Latin poem, De animi immortalitate.* London, B. White, 1766, 2 Vol.
  Notes: collection of miscellaneous essays includes "On Mr. Hume's Idea of Liberty and Necessity" (Vol. 2, pp. 40–43), which criticizes Hume's view.
  In *Metaphysical Responses*: complete essay; from 1766 edition.
  Editions: no further editions.
  Facsimiles: 1971 (Garland of 1766).
  Microform: The Eighteenth Century, reel 390, no. 2.
  Reviews: [John Langhorne], *Monthly Review,* July 1766, Vol. 35, pp. 7–10 (mixed); *Critical Review*, 1766, Vol. 21, pp. 346–350 (mixed).
- [Oswald, James (1703–1793)]. *An appeal to common sense in behalf of religion.* Edinburgh: A. Kincaid and J. Bell, 1766–1772, 2 v. viii, 390, xii, 388 p.
  Notes: work published in two volumes in 1766 and 1772 respectively argues that common sense is the authority by which we perceive the primary truths of metaphysics, morality, and religion. Oswald attacks Hume's view of causality and Hume's discussion of analogical reasoning in "Of a Particular Providence".
  In *Metaphysical Responses*: 2.3 complete, and selections from 3.2; from 1766 edition.
  In *Religion Responses*: selections from 2.2.3 and 2.8.2; from 1772 edition.
  Editions: 1768 (second edition of volume 1); 2002 (Thoemmes Press, 1766 and 1772 volumes reset).
  Microform: The Eighteenth Century; reel 351, no. 6 (of 1766 and 1772 volumes).
  Reviews of 1766 volume: *Critical Review*, February 1767, Vol. 23, pp. 100–112 (positive); [William Rose], *Monthly Review,* February 1767, Vol. 36, pp. 115–129 (positive).
  Reviews of 1772 volume: *Critical Review*, April 1772, Vol. 33, pp. 280–288 (positive); [William Rose], *Monthly Review,* July 1772, Vol. 47, pp. 47–57 (positive). Complete reviews of 1766 and 1772 volumes included in *Common Sense Responses.*
  Discussions: Joseph Priestley, *Institutes* (1772–1774); Joseph Priestley, *Examination* (1774); Translator's Preface, to Buffier's *First Truths* (1780); Philip Skelton "Some Thoughts" (1784); Dugald Stewart, Letter to William Forbes (c. 1806).
- [Rose, William (1719–1786)]. Review of Hume's *A Concise and Genuine Account*, in *Monthly Review*, November 1766, Vol. 35, pp. 390–402.
  Notes: defends Hume in the dispute with Rousseau.
  In *Life Responses*: selections.
- Voltaire, François-Marie Arouet de (1694–1778). *A letter from Mons. de Voltaire, to Mr. Hume, on his dispute with M. Rousseau. Translated from the French*, London: printed for S. Bladon, 1766, [4], 16 p.
  Notes: attacks Rousseau.

In *Life Responses*: complete; from 1766 edition.

Microform: The Eighteenth Century, reel 956, no. 4.

Reviews: *Critical Review*, November 1766, Vol. 22, p. 378 (neutral); *Monthly Review*, November 1766, Vol. 35, p. 406 (negative).

Discussions: Edward Burnaby Greene, *A Defence of Mr. Rousseau* (1766).

❧1767❧

● [Adams, John (1735–1826)]. "Remainder of Governor Winthrop's Second Letter to Governor Bradford, begun in our last," in *Boston Gazette*, February, 16 1767.

Notes: Adams discusses election practices and relies on a related discussion by Hume in the *History*.

In *American Responses*: selection.

● Beattie, James (1735–1803). "The Castle of Scepticism: A Vision," April, 1767.

Manuscript location: Aberdeen University Library, MS 30/18.

Notes: fictitious dream that satirically criticizes Hume and other sceptics.

In *Life Responses*: complete; newly transcribed from manuscript.

Editions: E.C. Mossner, *University of Texas Studies in English*, 1948, Vol. 27, pp. 108–145.

Facsimiles: 1996 (Routledge/Thoemmes Press of Mossner, 1948, in James Beattie *Miscellaneous Essays*, ed. Roger Robinson).

● Ferguson, Adam (1723–1816). *An essay on the history of civil society.* Edinburgh: A. Millar & T. Cadell, 1767, vii, [1], 430 p.

Notes: Part 3, Section 3 discusses Hume's views of population in small societies in "Of the Populousness of Ancient Nations."

In *Essays Responses*: relevant selections from Part 3.

Editions: 1767 (Dublin), 1768 (London, 430 p.), 1768 (London, 464 p.), 1773, 1782, 1789, 1793.

Microform: The Eighteenth Century, reel 3800, no. 02 (of 1767 Dublin), reel 3698, no. 07 (of London 1768, 430 p.), reel 3795, no. 05 (of London 1768 464 p.), reel 3902, no. 02 (of 1773), reel 3013, no. 3 (of 1782).

● [Heathcote, Ralph (1721–1795)]. *A letter to the Honorable Mr. Horace Walpole, concerning the dispute between Mr. Hume and Mr Rousseau*, London: printed for B. White, 1767, 23, [1] p.

Notes: defends Hume in the dispute with Rousseau.

In *Life Responses*: complete; from 1767 edition.

Editions: no further editions.

Microform: The Eighteenth Century, reel 8031, no. 10.

Reviews: [William Rose], *Monthly Review*, December 1766, Vol. 35, p. 469 (negative).

● Price, Richard (1723–1791). *Four dissertations. I. On providence. II. On prayer. III. On the reasons for expecting that virtuous men shall meet after death in a state of happiness. IV. On the importance of Christianity, the nature of historical evidence, and miracles. By Richard Price.* London: printed for A. Millar and T. Cadell, 1767, vii, [1], 439, [1] p.

Notes: Dissertation 4 criticizes "Of Miracles."

In *Religion Responses*: Dissertation 4 complete; from 1767 edition.

Editions: 1768 (second edition), 1772 (third edition), 1777 (fourth edition), 1811; no further editions.

Facsimiles: 1990 (Thoemmes Press of 1768).

Microform: The Eighteenth Century, reel 5571, no. 1 (of 1767), reel 3036, no. 1 (of

1772), reel 8150, no. 01 (of 1777).

Reviews: [William Rose], *Monthly Review*, January 1767, Vol. 36, pp. 51 ff., 81–93 (positive; second instalment of review contained in *Hume on Miracles*); *Critical Review*, January 1767, Vol. 23, pp. 9–17 (neutral).

Discussions: William Morgan, *Memoirs* (1815).

- Steuart, James (1712–1780). *An inquiry into the principles of political economy: being an essay on the science of domestic policy in free nations in which are particularly considered population, agriculture, trade, industry, money, coin, interest, circulation, banks, exchange, public credit, and taxes.* London: A. Millar and T. Cadell, 1767, 2 v.

  Notes: Book 2, Chapters 28 and 29 criticize Hume's theories of price increase in "Of Money" and trade in "Of the Balance of Trade".

  In *Essays Responses*: Chapters 28 and 29, complete; from 1805 edition of *Works*.

  Editions: 1770, 1772, 1796, in *Works* 1805; no further editions.

  Microform: The Eighteenth Century, reel 7330, no. 02. (of 1767), reel 1909, no. 02 (of 1770), reel 7504, no. 08 (of 1772); Goldsmiths'-Kress Library of Economic Literature; reel 1578, no. 16560 (of 1796).

  Reviews: [William Bewley], *Monthly Review*, April 1767, Vol. 36, p. 279 ff.; May, p. 365 ff; June, p. 464 ff.; August, Vol. 37, pp. 116–125; *Critical Review*, May 1767, Vol. 23, pp. 321–329; June, pp. 411–416; Vol. 24, July, pp. 24–32 (positive).

  Discussions: John Wheatley, *An Essay* (1807); Dugald Stewart, *Lectures on Political Economy* (1855).

ಎ1768ೕ

- [Balfour, James (1705–1795)]. *Philosophical essays....*, Edinburgh, J. Balfour, 1768, 187 p.

  Notes: Essays 1 and 2 criticize "Of the Academical or Sceptical Philosophy" and "Of the Idea of Necessary Connection."

  In *Metaphysical Responses*: selections from Essay 1 (pp. 36–62) and Essay 2 (pp. 63–81); from 1768 edition.

  Editions: no further editions.

  Microform: The Eighteenth Century, reel 258, no. 5.

  Reviews: *Critical Review*, 1768, Vol. 26 pp. 178–182 (positive).

- Priestley, Joseph (1733–1804). *The rudiments of English grammar, adapted to the use of schools; with notes and observations, for the use of those who have made some proficiency in the language. By Joseph Priestley, LL.D. F.R.S.* London: printed for T. Becket and P.A. De Hondt, and J. Johnson, 1768, xxiii, [1], 200, [4] p.

  Notes: first published in 1761, the greatly expanded 1768 edition lists stylistic errors throughout Hume's *History*. Hume made many of the suggested changes in later editions of his *History*.

  In *History Responses*: selections from "Notes and Observations"; from *Theological and Miscellaneous Works* (1817–1832), Vol. 23, pp. 87–102.

  Editions: 1769, 1771, 1772, 1784, 1786, 1789, 1798, 1826, and *Works* 1832.

  Facsimiles: 1969 (Scolar, of 1761), 1971 (Garland, of 1761).

  Microform: The Eighteenth Century, reel 2589, no. 5 (of 1768), reel 2125, no. 1 (of 1798).

  Reviews: [Andrew Kippis], *Monthly Review*, September 1768, Vol. 39, pp. 184–186 (positive); *Critical Review*, 1768, Vol. 26, pp. 101–106 (positive).

  Discussions: Joseph Towers, *Observations* (1778); Francis Palgrave, "Hume and his Influence upon History" (1826).

- [Smellie, William (1740–1795)]. *Encyclopaedia Britannica; or a dictionary of arts and sciences, compiled upon a new plan....* Edinburgh, A. Bell and C. MacFarquhar, 1768–1771, 3 Vol.

Notes: The entry on "Abridgement," written by William Smellie, abridges Hume's essay on miracles and Campbell's reply as examples of abridgment. The entry on "Academics" discusses Berkeley and Hume as modern skeptics.

In *Life Responses*: in selection from William Smellie's *Literary and Character*.

Editions: entries reprinted in the 1793 edition of *Encyclopaedia Britannica*; entry on abridgment included in Smellie's *Literary and Characteristical Lives* (1800).

Facsimiles: 1968 (Encyclopaedia Britannica of 1768–1771 edition).

Microform: Library of English literature, LEL 22049–51.

- Walpole, Horace (1717-1797). *Historic doubts on the life and reign of King Richard the Third. By Mr. Horace Walpole.* London : Printed for J. Dodsley, 1768, xv, [1], 134, [2] p.

  Notes: criticizes Hume's account of Richard III in the *History*.

  In *History Responses*: selections from Part 3; from 1768 London edition.

  Editions: 1768 (Dublin), included in *Works* (1798, Vol. 2), 1822, 1965, 1987.

  Facsimiles: 1974 (EP Publishing of London 1768).

  Microform: The eighteenth century: reel 1021, no. 5 (of London 1768); reel 7465, no. 07 (of Dublin 1768).

- Witherspoon, John (1723–1794). *An inquiry into the scripture-meaning of charity. By John Witherspoon.* Edinburgh: printed for A. Kincaid & J. Bell, and W. Gray, 1768, 28 p.

  Notes: criticizes Hume's views of female infidelity.

❧1769❧

- Anonymous. *Essays, poetical, moral, and critical.* Dublin: Printed by Alex. M'Culloh, 1769, xxii, 304, [4], 31 p.

  Notes: collection of essays, sometimes attributed to Brockhill Newburgh, contains a poem criticising Hume's religious infidelity.

  In *Life Responses*: selections; from 1769 edition.

  Facsimiles: 1972 (Garland of 1769).

- Beattie, James (1735–1803). Letter to Thomas Blacklock, October 11, 1769.

  See James Beattie, *Correspondence of James Beattie* (2004).

  Manuscript location: Aberdeen University Library, MS 30/1/21.

  Notes: discusses Blacklock's resentment of Hume.

  In *Life Responses*: selections from Letter 140 in *Correspondence* (2004).

- Burnett, James, Lord Monboddo (1714–1799). Letter to James Harris, June 18, 1769.

  See William Knight, *Lord Monboddo* (1900).

  Notes: letter to James Harris, June 18, 1769 contains a brief anecdote regarding of Hume's view of Berkeley.

  In *Life Responses*: story included in "Miscellaneous Hume Anecdotes."

- Millot, Claude Francois Xavier (1726–1785). *Élémens de l'histoire d'Angleterre, depuis son origine sous les Romains, jusqu'au regne de Georges II.* A Paris, Chez P.E.G. Durand, 1769, 3 v.

  Translation: *Elements of the history of England; from the invasion of the Romans to the reign of George II. Translated from the French of Abbe Millot, ... By Mr. Kenrick.* In two volumes. London: printed for J. Johnson, and W. Nicoll; and J. Murray, 1771, 2 v.

  Notes: First published in 1769 as *Élémens de l'histoire d'Angleterre*; praises Hume's *History* as a "treasure of philosophical and political knowledge."

  English Editions: 1771 (Dublin, 2 vol.), 1771 (London, 4 vol.) 1772 (second edition 4 vol.).

Microform: The Eighteenth Century, reel 10166, no. 02 (of 1771 London 4 vol.).
Reviews: *Critical Review*, 1771, Vol. 31, pp. 361–367, Vol. 32 pp. 56–61, pp.
337–340 (positive); *Monthly Review*, December 1769, Vol. 41, pp. 533–335
(positive).

- Priestley, Joseph (1733–1804). *Remarks on some paragraphs in the fourth volume of
Dr. Blackstone's Commentaries on the laws of England, relating to the Dissenters.
By Joseph Priestley*. London: printed for J. Johnson and J. Payne, 1769, [2], 60 p.
Notes: praises Hume's account of religious dissenters in the *History*.
In *History Responses*: selections; from *Theological and Miscellaneous Works*
(1817–1832), Vol. 22.
Editions: 1770, *Works* (1817–1832).
Reviews: *Critical Review*, 1769, Vol. 28, p. 290 (mixed).

- Walpole, Horace (1717–1797). *Supplement to the Historic doubts on the life and reign
of King Richard III. With remarks on some answers that have been made to that
Work* (1769).
See Horace Walpole, *The works of Horatio Walpole* (1798).
Notes: posthumously published in *Works* (1798), responds to Hume's "Sixteen
notes on Walpole's *Historic Doubts*" (1769, later incorporated into Hume's
History, Ch. 26).
In *History Responses*: selections; from *Works* (1798).
Editions: 1987 (included in edition of *Historic Doubts*).

☙1770❧

- Anonymous. Review of Cristof Hermann Manstein's *Memoirs of Russia* (1770), in:
Critical Review, July 1770, Vol. 13, p. 1 ff.
Notes: favourable review, reviewer comments on Hume's "Advertisement" to the
Memoirs.
- Beattie, James (1735–1803). *Essay on the nature and immutability of truth in opposition
to sophistry and scepticism*. Edinburgh: A. Kincaid and J. Bell, 1770, viii, 503 p.
Notes: among the more important early criticisms of Hume's philosophy, particularly
as appears in the *Treatise*. Beattie criticizes Hume's views of personal identity,
causality, scepticism, necessity, theistic proofs, the virtues, and Black inferiority.
In *Metaphysical Responses*: Introduction, 1.2.3, 1.2.5, 2.1.1, 2.2.1, 2.2.3, selections;
from 1770 edition.
In *Religion Responses*: selections from 1.2.5; from 1770 edition.
In *Moral Responses*: Part 3, Chapter 2, selections; from 1770 edition, pp. 421–448.
In *Essays Responses*: Part 3, Chapter 2, selections; from 1770 edition, pp. 479–484.
Editions: Beattie's *Essay* was reprinted over 20 times in the 18th and early 19th
centuries, either as an individual book or in a collection of other writings titled
Essays. For a complete bibliography of these editions see *Common Sense
Bibliography*. For a new edition of Beattie's *Essay* see James Fieser, Bristol,
Thoemmes Press, based on 1770 edition with noted changes to the 1771 and
1776 editions.
Facsimiles: 1983 (Garland Publishing, of 1770); 1973 (F. Frommann of 1770), 1996
(Routledge/Thoemmes Press of 1771), 1971 (Garland Publishing, of 1776 *Essays*);
1975 (G. Olms of 1776 *Essays*).
Microform: Eighteenth century sources for the study of English literature and culture,
reel no. 35 (sources also note reel no. 655 and reel no. 746); The Eighteenth
Century, reel 1069, no. 6 (of 1778 *Essays*); Early American imprints, second
series, no. 16964 (of 1809 edition).
Reviews of 1770 edition: [Thomas Blacklock], *Edinburgh Evening Courant*, June 2,

1770 (positive); [William Rose], *Monthly Review*, June 1770, Vol. 42, pp. 450–457;
October 1770, Vol. 43, pp. 268–283 (positive); [Thomas Blacklock], *Scots
Magazine*, August 1770, Vol. 32, pp. 428–435 (positive); [Thomas Blacklock],
Weekly Magazine or Edinburgh Amusement, June 1770, Vol. 8, pp. 303–305
(positive). All of these reviews are included in *Common Sense Responses*.

Reviews of 1771 edition: *Annual Register for the year 1771*, pp. 252–260 (positive);
Critical Review, 1771, Vol. 32, pp. 453–459; 1772, Vol. 33, pp. 34–44 (positive);
Scots Magazine, April 1771, Vol. 33, pp. 199–201 (positive). All of these reviews
are included in *Common Sense Responses*.

Discussions: John Bethune, *Essays* (1771); letters by "Orthodoxus," "Democritus,"
and "Eumenes" (i.e., Thomas Blacklock) in *Weekly Magazine*, (1771); James
Boswell, *Boswelliana* (1772); Joseph Priestley, *Institutes* (1772–1774); *The Essay
... Shewn to be Sophistical* (1773); Joseph Priestley *Examination* (1774); Thomas
Hepburn, *Specimen* (1774); John Briggs, letter to *London Review* (1777); Thomas
Gray, *Poems* (1775); John Home, "Account" (1777); Postilion, "Observations"
(1777); Tobias Simple, "Strictures" (1777); Samuel Jackson Pratt, *Supplement*
(1777); George Horne, *Letter* (1777); Laicus, "Observations" (1777); James
Boswell, *Journal of a Tour* (1785); William Jones, *Memoirs* (1795); Daniel Thomas,
An Answer (1791); James Steuart, "Observations" (1805); Dugald Stewart, Letter
to William Forbes (c. 1806); Thomas Cogan, *Ethical Questions*, (1817).

- Dana, James (1735–1812). *An Examination of the late Reverend President Edwards's
'Enquiry on Freedom of the Will;' More especially the Foundation Principle of his
Book, with the Tendency and Consequences of the Reasoning therein contained.*
Boston: Printed by Daniel Kneeland, 1770, xi, [3], 3–140 p.
Notes: contends that Jonathan Edwards espoused a Humean notion of causality.
Editions: no further editions.
In *American Responses*: selection from pp. vi, 69–71, 126, 131–6, 139.
- Lindsay-Barnard, Anne (1750–1825). Letter to Margaret Lindsay, c. 1770.
See Alexander Crawford Lindsay, *Lives of the Lindsays* (1840).
Notes: letter from Anne Lindsay-Barnard describing Hume at her family's house.
In *Life Responses*: complete letter fragment; from *Lives of The Lindsays*, London,
Murray, 1858, Vol. 2, pp. 321–322.
- Mickle, William Julius (1734–1788). *Voltaire in the shades; or, Dialogues on the deistical
controversy.* London, G. Pearch, T. and J. Merril, and D. Prince, 1770, xvi, 214 p.
Notes: fictitious dialogues on natural and revealed religion in which Hume is a speaker.
- [Stuart, Gilbert (1742–1786)]. Review of Cristof Hermann Manstein's *Memoirs of
Russia* (1770), in *Monthly Review*, July 1770, Vol. 43, p. 37–40.
Notes: favourable review, Stuart comments on Hume's "Advertisement" to the *Memoirs*.

❧1771❧

- Bethune, John (1725–1774). *Essays and dissertations on various subjects, relating to
human life and happiness.* Edinburgh printed for A.Kincaid and J.Bell, 1771, 2 v.
Notes: a footnote in Essay 15 (Volume 1 p. 131) criticizes Hume's skepticism and
praises Beattie.
Reviews: *Monthly Review*, 1771, Vol. 45, p 47 ff.
- [Blacklock, Thomas (1721–1791)] and others. Six letters in *Weekly Magazine or
Edinburgh Amusement*, July–September 1771.
Notes: six letter exchange regarding the propriety of the harsh attack on Hume by
James Beattie in his *Essay* (1770).
In *Life Responses*: six letters complete.

Letter 1: by "Orthodoxus" (i.e., Henry Grieve), (July 11, 1771, Vol. 13, pp. 51–52); open letter to James Beattie criticizing his abuse of Hume.

Letter 2: by "Eumenes" (i.e., Thomas Blacklock), (July 25, 1771, Vol. 13, pp. 97–102); criticizes Letter 1 by Orthodoxus and defends Beattie's right to abuse Hume.

Letter 3: by "Democritus" (i.e., Mrs. Carnegie of Pitarrow), (August 15, 1771, Vol. 13, pp. 195–198); criticizes Letter 2 by Eumenes and defends Orthodoxus.

Letter 4: by "Eumenes" (i.e., Thomas Blacklock), (August 29, 1771, Vol. 13, pp. 265–269); criticizes Letter 3 by Democritus.

Letter 5: by "Orthodoxus" (i.e., Henry Grieve), (September 5, 1771, Vol. 13, pp. 295–297); defends himself against Letter 2 by Eumenes.

Letter 6: by "Eumenes" (i.e., Thomas Blacklock), (September 19, 1771, Vol. 13, pp. 358–360); defends himself against Letter 5 by Orthodoxus.

- Curry, John (d. 1780). *Observations on the popery laws.* Dublin: printed by T. Ewing, 1771, 53, [1] p.

  Notes: Curry cites "the profound historian Mr. *Hume*" regarding Catholic loyalty to the Monarchy.

  Editions: 1774 (Dublin, second edition), 1774 (London); no further editions.

  Microform: The Eighteenth Century, reel 1335, no. 14 (of 1771).

- Goldsmith, Oliver (1730?–1774). *History of England, from the earliest times to the death of George II.* London, printed for T. Davies, 1771, 4 v.

  Notes: criticises Hume's views of religion and politics.

  In *History Responses*: selections from Preface; from 1789 Dublin edition.

  Editions: several editions.

  Reviews: [Gilbert Stuart], *Monthly Review*, December 1771, Vol. 45, pp. 436–444 (mixed).

- Millar, John (1735–1801). *Observations concerning the distinction of ranks in Society. By John Millar.* London: printed by W. and J. Richardson, for John Murray, 1771, [4],xv, [3], 242, [2] p.

  Notes: Chapter 6, Section 4 criticizes Hume's "Of the Populousness of Ancient Nations."

  Editions: 1779, 1781, 1793, 1806.

  Microform: Goldsmiths'-Kress library of economic literature, no. 10712 (of 1771); The Eighteenth Century, reel 3169, no. 06 (1779), reel 3166, no. 06. (of 1781), reel 5299, no. 3 (of 1793); 19th-century legal treatises; no. 8414–8418 (of 1806); Goldsmiths'-Kress library of economic literature; no. 19303.5 (of 1806).

  Facsimiles: 1986 (Scientia Verlag of 1806); 1990 (Thoemmes Press of 1806).

  Reviews: [Gilbert Stuart], *Monthly Review*, 1771, Vol. 45, p. 188 ff.

- Pinto, Isaac de (1715–1787). *Traité de la circulation et du crédit contenant une analyse raisonnée des fonds d'Angleterre ... avec un tableau de ce qu'on appelle commerce, ou plutôt jeu d'actions, en Hollande.* Amsterdam: Chez Marc Michel Rey, 1771, 368 p.

  English Translation: *An essay on circulation and credit, in four parts; and a letter on the jealousy of commerce. From the French of Monsieur de Pinto.* Translated, with annotations, by the Rev. S. Baggs. London: printed for J. Ridley, 1774, [4], xix, [1], 247, [1] p.

  Notes: Part II criticizes Hume's view of national debt in "Of Public Credit".

  In *Essays Responses*: Part II, selections; from 1774 edition, pp. 103–108.

  Editions: 1787 (French).

  Facsimiles: 1969 (Gregg of 1774).

  Microform: Goldsmiths'-Kress library of economic literature, no. 10791 (of 1771 French); The Eighteenth Century, reel 7448, no. 13 (of 1774 English).

Reviews: *Critical Review*, December 1774, Vol. 38, pp. 433–438 (mixed).

Discussions: Dugald Stewart, *Lectures on Political Economy* (1855).

- Whitaker, John (1735–1808). *The history of Manchester. In four books.* By John Whitaker. [London]: Sold by Mess. Dodsley in Pall-Mall [et al.], 1771–1775, 2 v.

  Notes: the opening chapter of Hume's *History* is criticized in a new Appendix to the 1773 revision of Volume 1, and is continued in an Appendix to Volume 2 which appeared in 1775.

  In *History Responses*: Appendices; from 1773 and 1775 editions.

  Editions of Volume 1: 1773 revision of 1771; no further editions.

  Editions of Volume 2: no further editions.

  Microform: The Eighteenth Century, reel 857, no. 3 (of 1773).

  Reviews of 1771 volume: *Monthly Review*, January 1772, Vol. 46, pp. 28–36, February, pp. 104–112 (positive); *Critical Review*, 1771, Vol. 31, 245 ff.

  Reviews of 1773 volume: [Gilbert Stuart], *Edinburgh Magazine and Review*, June 1774, Vol. 2, pp. 489–490 (positive).

  Reviews of 1775 volume: *Critical Review*, February 1775, Vol. 39, pp. 81–91 (mixed); [John Langhorne], *Monthly Review*, 1775, Vol. 52, June pp. 496–505, Vol. 53, August pp. 128–139, September pp. 231–240 (mixed); *Edinburgh Magazine and Review*, April 1775, Vol. 3, pp. 257–260 (positive); *London Review*, 1775, Vol. 1, pp. 431–439, 490–496; 1776, Vol. 2, 225–228 (positive).

  Discussions: Joseph Towers, *Observations* (1778); Samuel Rose, in his review of John Millar's *Historical View* (1787) in *Monthly Review* (1787).

- Wray, Daniel (1701–1783). Letter of October 15, 1771.

  See John Nichols, *Illustrations of the Literary History of the Eighteenth Century* (1817–1858).

  Notes: brief anecdote about Hume's weight.

  In *Life Responses*: story included in "Miscellaneous Hume Anecdotes"; from 1817 edition, Vol. 1. pp. 141–142.

❧1772❧

- Anonymous. "Quakerism defended against false representations," in *Gentleman's Magazine*, December 1772, Vol. 42, pp. 566–570.

  Notes: contains a one-paragraph attack on Hume's account of the Quakers in his *History*.

  In *History Responses*: selections.

  Discussions: "Scritator" in *Gentleman's Magazine* (February 1773, Vol. 43, pp. 122–123).

- Boswell, James (1740–1795). "Boswelliana" (c. 1772–1785).

  See James Boswell, *Boswelliana* (1884).

  Notes: posthumously published manuscript of anecdotes includes several about Hume.

  In *Life Responses*: selections; from 1876 edition.

- Chastellux, François Jean, Marquis de (1734–1788). *De la félicité publique, ou, Considérations sur le sort des hommes dans les différentes epoques de l'histoire.* A Amsterdam: Chez Marc-Michel Rey, 1772, 2 v.

  First English Translation: *An essay on public happiness: investigating the state of human nature, under each of its particular appearances, through the several periods of history, to the present times.* London: Printed for T. Cadell, 1774.

  Notes: Section 3, Chapter 5, defends Hume's "Of the Populousness of Ancient Nations".

In *Essays Responses*: Chapter 5, selections; from 1774 English translation.

English Editions 1774 (English translation), 1780, 1792.

English Facsimiles: 1969 (A.M. Kelley, of 1774).

Microform: The Eighteenth Century, reel 6311, no. 01 (of 1774).

Reviews: *Edinburgh Magazine and Review*, November 1774, Vol. 2, pp. 760–770.

● Neville, Sylas (1741–1840). 1772–1776 diary entries on Hume.

See Sylas Neville, *The Diary of Sylas Neville* (1950).

Notes: posthumously published diary includes a brief account of Neville's visit to Hume.

In *Life Responses*: story included in "Miscellaneous Hume Anecdotes"; from 1950 edition.

● O'Halloran, Sylvester (1728–1807). *An introduction to the study of the history and antiquities of Ireland: in which the assertions of Mr. Hume and other writers are occasionally considered... By Sylvester O Halloran*. Dublin: printed by Thomas Ewing, 1772, [10], xx, 96, [1], 102–384 p.

Notes: criticizes Hume's view of the 1641 Irish Rebellion.

In *History Responses*: selections from 3.3 and 3.5; from 1772 Dublin edition.

Editions: 1772 (London); no further editions.

Microform: The Eighteenth Century; reel 7852, no. 06 (of 1772 Dublin).

Reviews: *Critical Review*, 1773, Vol. 35, pp. 198–202 (negative); [William Rose: Ralph Griffiths], *Monthly Review*, September 1773, Vol. 49 pp. 193–202 (mixed).

● Priestley, Joseph (1733–1804). *Institutes of natural and revealed religion*. London, J. Johnson, 1772–1774, 3 vol.

Notes: criticizes Hume's "Of Miracles"; also criticizes Reid, Oswald and Beattie.

In *Religion Responses*: 2.2.3 and 2.6 complete; from *Theological and Miscellaneous Works* (1817–1832), Vol. 2.

In *Common Sense Responses*: Selections from Part 3, Introduction; from *Theological and Miscellaneous Works* (1817–1832), Vol. 3.

Editions: 1782 (second edition), 1794 (third edition), 1808, *Works* 1817–1832 Vol. 2.

Microform: The Eighteenth Century, reel 9600, no. 08 (of 1782).

Reviews of 1772 volume: *Critical Review*, 1772, Vol. 34, pp. 283–288 (positive); [Jabez Hirons], *Monthly Review*, May 1772, Vol. 46, pp. 498–503 (positive).

Reviews of 1774 volume: *Critical Review*, 1774, Vol. 37, pp. 153–154, 390–391 (positive); [Thomas Blacklock], *Edinburgh Magazine and Review*, October 1774, Vol. 2, pp. 701–721 (negative).

❧1773❧

● Anonymous (pseud., "Scritator"). "Hume's account of Quakerism defended," in *Gentleman's Magazine*, February 1773, Vol. 43, pp. 122–123.

Notes: includes a paragraph defending Hume's account of Quakerism; the article is a response to an earlier letter in *Gentleman's Magazine* (December 1772, Vol. 42, pp. 566–570).

In *History Responses*: complete.

● Anonymous. "Character of the Works of David Hume Esq," in *The Weekly Magazine or Edinburgh Amusement*, Friday, October 1, 1773, Vol. 22, pp. 233–234.

Notes: critical appraisal of Hume's *History* and moral theory.

In *Moral Responses*: complete.

● Anonymous (pseud. "Philoaletheias"). Letter to the editors, *Weekly Magazine or Edinburgh Amusement*, 1773, vol. 22, pp. 265–268.

Notes: defends zeal of protestant reformers and applauds the severity of Beattie's attack on Hume.

- Anonymous. *Personal slavery established, by the suffrages of custom and right reason being a full answer to the gloomy and visionary reveries of all the fanatical and enthusiastical writers on that subject.* Philadelphia: John Dunlap, 1773, 26 p.

  Notes: satirical attack on Hume's account of Blacks in "Of National Characters."

  In *American Responses*: selection from pp. 18–19.

  Microform: Selected Americana from Sabin's Dictionary, no. 25945.

- Anonymous. *The essay on the nature and immutability of truth, in opposition to sophistry and scepticism, by James Beattie... shewn to be sophistical, and promotive of scepticism and infidelity. With some remarks on priestcraft, subscriptions, and establishments. In a letter to a friend. By a professor of Moral Philosophy in the College of Common-Sense.* London, Baker & Galabin, 1773, 74 pp.

  Notes: perhaps written by Thomas Cogan (1736–1818). The pamphlet attacks Beattie's *Essay* for leading to consequences as dangerous as those resulting from Hume's scepticism.

  Editions: no further editions.

  In *Common Sense Responses*: complete pamphlet from 1773 edition.

  Reviews: *Critical Review*, June 1773, Vol. 35, pp. 480 (mixed); [Abraham Rees], *Monthly Review*, July 1773, Vol. 49, pp. 49–56 (mixed).

- [Burnett, James, Lord Monboddo (1714–1799)]. *Of the origin and progress of language.* Edinburgh, [different publishers for different volumes] 1773–1794, 6 Vol.

  Notes: criticizes Hume's view of ideas and impressions.

  In *Metaphysical Responses*: Selection from 1.1.9; from 1774 second edition, pp. 119–120.

  Editions: Vol. 1 (1773), Vol. 1 second edition (1774), Vol. 2 (1774), Vol. 3 (1776), Vol. 3 second edition (1786), Vol. 4 (1787), Vol. 5 (1789), Vol. 6 (1792); no further editions.

  Facsimiles: 1967 (Scolar Press), 1970 (Garland).

  Microform: The Eighteenth Century, reel 4603, no. 01 (of six volumes, first editions of each).

  Reviews of 1773 volume: [William Rose], *Monthly Review*, September 1773, Vol. 49, pp. 166–173, November, pp. 321–332 (positive); *Critical Review*, May 1773, Vol. 35, pp. 366–369 (positive).

- [Carroll, Charles (1737–1832); Dulany, Daniel (1722–1797)]. Letters in the *Maryland Gazette*, March 11, 1773; April 8, 1773; May 6, 1773; June 3, 1773; July 1, 1773.

  Notes: eight pseudonymous letters between "Antilon" and "First Citizen" (Dulany and Carroll respectively) debate the constitutional rights of Maryland's governor; several letters rely on related discussions in Hume's *History*.

  In *American Responses*: selections.

- Chapone, Hester (1727–1801). *Letters on the improvement of the mind, addressed to a young lady. In two volumes.* London: printed by H. Hughs, for J. Walter, 1773, 2 v.

  Notes: ten letters on various subjects; letter 10 on *History* includes a positive comment on Hume.

  Editions: over 30 18th century editions.

  Microform: The Eighteenth Century, reel 8364, no. 01. (of 1773 London), reel 3250, no. 13 (of 1773 Dublin), reel 3150, no. 06 (of 1774 London), reel 3269, no. 09 (of 1775 London).

  Reviews: *Monthly Review*, July 1773, Vol. 49 (positive).

- Lindsay-Barnard, Anne (1750–1825). "Memoirs of Lady Anne Lindsay," 1773.

  Manuscript location: National Library of Scotland, Crawford Muniments, II, 107.

  Notes: anecdote of 16 year old Hume, reported by Anne Lindsay's grandmother.

In *Life Responses*: excerpt from Mossner included in introduction to Anne Lindsay
Barnard, letter to Margaret Lindsay (*c*.1770).
Editions: partially quoted by Mossner, *Life*, p. 65.
• Mason, William (1725–1797). *An heroic epistle to Sir William Chambers, Knight, …
Enriched with explanatory notes*. London: printed for J. Almon, 1773, 19, [1] p.
Notes: satirical poem ridicules Hume.
Editions: several editions.
Microform: The Eighteenth Century, reel 1186, no. 05 (of 1773).
Reviews: *Critical Review*, June 1773, Vol. 35, p. 469 ff. (positive); *Monthly Review*,
April 1773, Vol. 48, pp. 314–315 (mixed).

&~1774~&

• Beattie, James (1735–1803). Letter to Frances Mayne, January 2, 1774.
See James Beattie, *Correspondence of James Beattie* (2004)
Manuscript Location: Aberdeen University Library, MS 30/1/067.
Notes: discusses attacks on Beattie by Hume's friends.
In *Life Responses*: selections; from *Correspondence of James Beattie* (2004), Letter 490.
• [Blacklock, Thomas (1721–1791)], review of Priestley's *Examination* (1774) in
Edinburgh Magazine and Review, November 1774, Vol. 2, pp. 771–779, December,
Vol. 3, pp. 33–37, January 1775, pp. 86–102, February, pp. 146–154, March, pp.
199–209, April, pp. 260–275.
Notes: critiques Hume's scepticism and view of impressions.
In *Metaphysical Responses*: selections from December 1774, Vol. 3, pp. 33-37.
• [Hepburn, Thomas (d. 1777)]. *A specimen of the Scots Review*. [Edinburgh], [1774],
2–30 p.
Notes: satirical attack on Hume's critics.
In *Life Responses*: selections; from 1774 edition.
Editions: no further editions.
Microform: The Eighteenth Century, reel 3055, no. 6.
Reviews: *Scots Magazine* (positive; reprinted in Burton, *Life of David Hume*, Vol. 2,
p. 472).
Discussions: letter from Hume to John Home, June 4, 1774.
• Ogilvie, John (1733–1814). *Philosophical and critical observations on the nature,
characters and various species of composition. By John Ogilvie, D.D. In two volumes*.
London: printed for G. Robinson, 1774, 2 v.
Notes: Work on rhetoric which discusses several methods of composition. A note to
Volume 1, Section 4 (pp. 206–208) contrasts Rapin's and Hume's history writing
techniques.
In *History Responses*: complete note; from 1774 edition.
Editions: 1779 (Dublin, reissue with cancel title page of 1774); no further editions.
Facsimiles: 1970 (Garland of 1774).
Microform: The Eighteenth Century, reel 1994, no. 7 (of 1774).
Reviews: *Critical Review*, August 1774, Vol. 38, pp. 81–89, September, pp. 187–194
(positive); [John Langhorne], *Monthly Review*, October 1774, Vol. 51, pp.
249–254 (neutral); [William Baron], *Edinburgh Magazine and Review*, May 1774,
Vol. 2, pp. 484–489 (negative).
• Priestley, Joseph (1733–1804). *An examination of Dr. Reid's Inquiry into the human
mind on the principles of common sense: Dr. Beattie's Essay on the nature and
immutability of truth, and Dr. Oswald's Appeal to common sense in behalf of
religion*. London, Printed for J. Johnson .., 1774, lxi, [3], 371, [3] p.

Notes: criticism of Reid, Beattie and Oswald; Priestley discusses their respective treatments of Hume.

In *Common Sense Responses*: complete book; from 1774 first edition.

Editions: 1774 (London second edition), 1775 (London second edition), in *Works* 1817–1832.

Facsimiles: 1978 (Garland facsimile of 1774 first edition).

Reviews: *London Review*, Vol. 1, January 1775, pp. 1–12, February, pp. 91–96 (positive); [William Rose], *Monthly Review*, Vol. 52, April, 1775, pp. 289–296 (mixed); [Thomas Blacklock], *Edinburgh Magazine and Review*, November 1774, Vol. 2, pp. 771–779, December, Vol. 3, pp. 33–37, January 1775, pp. 86–102, February, pp. 146–154, March, pp. 199–209, April, pp. 260–275 (negative; selections included in *Metaphysical Responses*).

Discussions: John Briggs, in *London Review* (1775).

• [Stuart, Gilbert (1742–1786)], reviews in *Edinburgh Magazine and Review*, January 1774, Vol. 1, pp. 141–150, August, Vol. 2, pp. 588–597.

Notes: reviews of Alexander Gerard's *Essay on Genius* and Charles Crawford's *Dissertation on the Phaedon of Plato* defends Hume's principles of association.

In *Metaphysical Responses*: selections from two reviews.

• Tucker, Josiah (1712–1799). *Four tracts, together with two sermons, on political and commercial subjects. By Josiah Tucker.* Glocester: printed by R. Raikes. And sold by J. Rivington, London, 1774, [2], xv, [1], 9–216, 35, [1] p.

Notes: discusses "Of the Balance of Trade."

In *Essays Responses*: selections from Tract 1; from 1774 second edition.

Editions: 1774 (second edition), 1776 (third edition).

Microform: The Eighteenth Century, reel 6128, no. 03 (of 1774) reel 1473, no. 40 (of 1774 second edition).

☙1775☜

• Briggs, John (1728/9–1804). *The nature of religious zeal, in two discourses, the substance of which was delivered at the visitation of … Pulter Forester, D.D. Arch-deacon of Bucks, at Newport Pagnell, April 27, 1774. By J. Briggs.* London: printed: and sold by T. Payne, 1775, 64 p.

Notes: attack on infidels, with a criticism of "Of Miracles."

Editions: no further editions.

Reviews: *Critical Review*, 1775, Vol. 39, p. 254 (positive); *London Review*, January 1775, Vol. 1, pp. 70–73 (positive); *Monthly Review*, April 1775, Vol. 52, pp. 365–366 (positive).

• Briggs, John (1728/9–1804). letter to the editor, *London Review*, March 1775, Vol. 1, pp. 244–246.

Notes: criticizes review of Priestley's *Examination* and defends Beattie's right to ridicule Hume.

In *Life Responses*: complete.

• Craven, William (1731–1815). *Sermons on the evidence of a future state of rewards and punishments arising from a view of our nature and condition; preached before the University of Cambridge, in the year M.DCC.LXXIV. By William Craven.* Cambridge: printed by J. Archdeacon; for T. & J. Merrill; B. White, T. Cadell, J. Wilkie, and Richardson & Urquhart, in London; and J. Fletcher, and D. Prince, at Oxford, 1775, [2], iv, 96 p.

Notes: criticizes "Of a Particular Providence."

Editions: 1783.Microform: The Eighteenth Century, reel 6096, no. 30 (of 1775), reel 1051, no. 7 (of 1783).

Reviews: *Monthly Review*, September 1776, Vol. 55, pp. 246–247 (positive).
- Curry, John (d. 1780). *An historical and Critical Review of the civil wars in Ireland, from the reign of Queen Elizabeth, to the settlement under King William. Extracted from Parliamentary records, state acts, and other authentic materials. By J. C. M.D.* Dublin: printed and sold by J. Hoey, and T. T. Faulkner; G. Burnet; and J. Morris, 1775, [4], xxi, [3], 447, [7] p.
  Notes: criticizes Hume's account of the 1641 Irish rebellion.
  In *History Responses*: selections from Introduction and 5.7; from 1775 edition.
  Editions: 1786 (Dublin), 1786 (London), 1793, 1810; no further editions.
  Microform: The Eighteenth Century; reel 76, no. 11 (of 1775), reel 7465, no. 04 (of Dublin 1786), reel 6058, no. 08 (of London 1786).
  Reviews: [Ralph Griffiths], *Monthly Review*, December 1776, Vol. 55, pp. 444–453 (positive).
- Gray, Thomas (1716–1771). *The poems of Mr. Gray. To which are prefixed Memoirs of his life and writings by W. Mason, M.A.* York: printed by A. Ward; and sold by J. Dodsley, London; and J. Todd, York, 1775, [4], 416, 111, [3] p.
  Notes: Gray's "Memoirs" includes a letter from Gray to James Beattie, July 2, 1770 criticizing Hume's shallowness.
  In *History Responses*: relevant portion of letter included in editor's introduction to John Pinkerton's *Letters* (1785).
  Editions: 1775 (Dublin), 1775 (London second edition), 1776, 1778.
  Microform: The Eighteenth Century, reel 2216, no. 4 (of 1775 York), reel 4234, no. 03 (of 1775 Dublin), reel 888, no. 5 (of 1775 London second edition), reel 11011, no. 03 (of 1776).
  Reviews: *Critical Review*, Vol. 39, pp. 378–389, 460–468; *London Review*, June 1775, Vol. 1, pp. 406–414, 477–490 (mixed); *Monthly Review*, May 1775, Vol. 52, pp. 377–387, July, Vol. 53, pp. 1–11, August, pp. 97–104 (positive); *Edinburgh Magazine and Review*, July 1775, Vol. 3, pp. 337–334.
  Discussions: Samuel Jackson Pratt, *Supplement* (1777); John Pinkerton, *Letters* (1785).
- [Hamilton, Alexander (1757–1804)]. *The Farmer Refuted: or, A more impartial and comprehensive View of the Dispute between Great-Britain and the Colonies, Intended as a Further Vindication of the Congress: In Answer to a Letter From A. W. Farmer, Intitled A View of the Controversy Between Great-Britain and her Colonies: Including A Mode of determining the present Disputes Finally and Effectually, &c.* New York, Printed by James Rivington, 1775, iv, 78 p.
  Notes: Hamilton denounces political oppression by the British and supports his view citing Hume's "Of the Independency of Parliament" and "That Politics may be Reduced to a Science."
  In *American Responses*: selection from pp. 1, 11–13, 18.
  Microform: Hazard pamphlets, v. 44, no. 13.

☙1776❧

- Anonymous. Notice of Hume's Death, *Weekly Magazine, or Edinburgh Amusement*, August 29, 1776, Vol. 33, p. 320.
  Notes: brief complimentary obituary notice.
  In *Life Responses*: complete.
- Anonymous. Notice of Hume's Death, in *Scots Magazine*, August 1776, Vol. 38, p. 455.
  Notes: brief complimentary obituary notice; includes notice from *London Chronicle*, Sept. 3–5, 1776 (Aberdeen correspondent).
  In *Life Responses*: complete notice.

- Anonymous. Notice of Hume's Death, in *London Chronicle*, Sept. 3–5, 1776, Vol. 40, No. 3081, p. 432;
  Notes: brief complimentary obituary notice from an Aberdeen correspondent.
  In *Life Responses*: complete notice.
  Editions: contained in longer article in *Scots Magazine*, August 1776, Vol. 38, p. 455.
  Discussions: letter on Hume's character to *London Chronicle*, November 23–25, 1776.
- Anonymous. Letter on Hume's burial and will, in *London Chronicle*, September 7–10, 1776, Vol. 40, No. 3083, p. 248, and *Scots Magazine*, September 1776, Vol. 38, p. 508.
  Notes: brief complimentary letter, reprinted in *Scots Magazine* with additional material.
  In *Life Responses*: complete letter.
- Anonymous. Letter on Hume's 1745 candidacy, in *London Chronicle*, Nov. 5–7, 1776, Vol. 40, No. 3108, p. 444.
  Notes: corrects mistakes in John Home's "Remarks".
  In *Life Responses*: complete.
- Anonymous. Letter on Hume's Character to *London Chronicle*, November 23–25, 1776, Vol. 40, No. 3116, p. 509.
  Notes: criticism of earlier *London Chronicle* letter (September 3–5, 1776, Vol. 40, No. 3081, p. 432).
  In *Life Responses*: complete; from *London Chronicle*.
  Editions: reprinted in *Scots Magazine*, November 1776, Vol. 38, p. 579.
- Bentham, Jeremy (1748–1832). *A fragment on government*. London: T. Payne, 1776, lvii, 208 p.
  Notes: discusses Hume's view of utility.
  In *Moral Responses*: Chapter 1, Section 36, selections; from *The Works of Jeremy Bentham*, edited by John Bowring (London: 1838–1843).
  Editions: various editions; included in *The Works of Jeremy Bentham*, edited by John Bowring (London: 1838–1843).
  Reviews: [William Enfield], *Monthly Review*, 1776, Vol. 55, p. 329 ff.
- Boswell, James (1740–1795). "An Account of my Last Interview with David Hume, Esq.," July 7, 1776.
  See James Boswell, *Private papers of James Boswell* (1928–1934).
  Notes: conversation between Boswell and Hume about life after death.
  In *Life Responses*: complete journal entry; from *Boswell in Extremes* (1970).
- Campbell, George (1719–1796). *The philosophy of rhetoric*, London: printed for W. Strahan; and T. Cadell, ... and W. Creech at Edinburgh, 1776, 2 vol.
  Notes: 1.11 criticizes of Hume's "Of Tragedy"; 1.5 discusses the notion of common sense.
  In *Essays Responses*: 1.11 complete; from 1838 edition.
  In *Common Sense Responses*: 1.5.1.3; from 1850, edition.
  Editions: 1801, 1808 (includes Campbell's final revisions); for a list of the various 19th century editions see *Common Sense Bibliography*.
  Facsimiles: 1992 (Scholar of 1841), 1963 (Southern Illinois University Press of 1850).
  Microform: Eighteenth-century sources for the study of English literature, reel 6; Library of English literature, LEL21880–81 (of 1776); Early American imprints, second series, no. 17140 (of 1809); Early American imprints, second series, no. 22467 (of 1811).
  Reviews: *Critical Review*, July 1776, Vol. 42, pp. 1–11 (positive); [William Enfield], *Monthly Review*, October 1776, Vol. 55, pp. 286–295 (positive); *London Review*, May 1776, Vol. 3, pp. 396–404, June 426–434, Appendix, 502–508; [William

Baron], *Edinburgh Magazine and Review*, July 1776, Vol. 5, pp. 325–334, August 367–373.

● Chelsum, James (ca. 1740–1801). *Remarks on the two last chapters of Mr. Gibbon's History, of the decline and fall of the Roman Empire, in a letter to a friend*,.London: printed for T. Payne and Son; and J. Robson and Co., 1776, [4], 94 p.

Notes: critiques Hume's view of polytheism in the "Natural History of Religion."

In *Religion Responses*: selections; from 1778 edition.

Editions: 1778; no further editions.

Facsimiles: 1974 (Garland, of 1778).

Microform: The Eighteenth Century, reel 1624, no. 03 (of 1776); reel 6867, no. 04 (of 1778).

Discussions: Henry Edwards Davis, *A reply to Mr. Gibbon's Vindication* (1779); Edward Gibbon, *A Vindication of some Passages* (1779).

● Cullen, William (1710–1790). Letter to John Hunter, September 17, 1776.

See William Cullen, *An account of the life, lectures and writings of William Cullen* (1832).

Manuscript location: Library of the Royal College of Surgeons of England, Hunter-Baillie Collection, Letter-book, 1, 140.

Notes: letter describing Hume's final days.

In *Life Responses*: complete letter as appears in *An Account* (1859), Vol. 1, pp. 607–609.

● Home, John (1722–1808). Diary of a Journey with Hume from Morpeth to Bath, April 23, 1776.

See Henry Mackenzie, *An account of the life and writings of John Home* (1822).

Manuscript location: National Library of Scotland, Acc. 10686.

Notes: presents conversations between Home and Hume during a trip near the end of Hume's life.

In *Life Responses*: complete Diary Entry; from Mackenzie's *Account* (1822).

● [Home, John (1722–1808)]. "An Account of the Life and Writings of the late David Hume, Esq." [1776].

Notes: Complimentary biographical sketch of Hume; the original publication in which this first appeared has not yet been identified.

In *Life Responses*: complete; from *Annual Register* reprint.

Editions: reprinted in *Annual Register... for the year 1776*, fifth edition, pp. 27–33; *The Weekly Magazine, or Edinburgh Amusement*, November 27, 1777, Vol. 38 pp. 193–197.

Discussions: "Observations on the Character and Writings of Mr Hume" in *Weekly Magazine* (1777); "Strictures on the 'Account of The Life and Writings of the Late David Hume'" in *Weekly Magazine* (1777).

● [Home, John (1722–1808)]. "Remarks on the Life and Character of the late David Hume, Esq." in *London Chronicle*, 1776, Sept. 10–12, Vol. 40, No. 3084; p. 256, Sept. 14–17, No. 3086, pp. 271–272; Sept. 21–24, No. 3089, p. 293.

Notes: complimentary account of Hume's various careers and writings.

In *Life Responses*: complete.

Editions: selections reprinted in *The Weekly Magazine or Edinburgh Amusement*, "A Short but impartial Account of the Life and Character of the late David Hume, Esq." (September 19, 1776, Vol. 33, p. 400); "Anecdote of the late David Hume, Esq." (October 3, 1776, Vol. 34, p. 48).

Discussions: Letter on Hume's 1745 candidacy, in *London Chronicle*, Nov. 5–7, 1776.

● Home, John (1722–1808). "A Sketch of the Character of Mr. Hume by an author of the nineteenth Century" (c. 1776).

Manuscript location: National Library of Scotland, MS. 3993.

Notes: unpublished essay praises Hume's character and writings.

In *Life Responses*: complete, newly transcribed.

Editions: David Fate Norton, *A Sketch of the Character of Mr. Hume* (Edinburgh: Tragara Press, 1976).

• Powell, William Samuel (1717–1775). *Discourses on various subjects. By William Samuel Powell, ... Published by Thomas Balguy, D.D.* London: printed for Lockyer Davis, 1776, xvi, 370, [4] p.

Notes: Discourse 6 criticizes "Of Miracles."

In *Religion Responses*: Discourse 6 complete; from 1776 edition.

Editions: 1794; no further editions.

Reviews: *London Review*, October 1776, Vol. 4, pp. 297–298 (neutral); *Critical Review*, 1776, Vol. 42, pp. 131–136 (mixed); [Abraham Rees], *Monthly Review*, September 1776, Vol. 55, pp. 173–176 (neutral).

• Smith, Adam (1723–1790). *An inquiry into the nature and causes of the wealth of nations.* London, W. Strahan and T. Cadell, 1776, 2 Vol.

Notes: criticizes Hume's view of credit and prices in "Of the Balance of Trade" and Hume's endorsement of state-sponsored religion.

In *Essays Responses*: Book 2, Chapter 2, selections; from 1784 edition.

In *History Responses*: selections from 5.i.g.; from 1784 edition.

Editions: 1778, 1784, 1786, 1789, 1791, and later editions (see 1976 critical edition).

Facsimiles: 1976 (Yushodo Booksellers, of 1776), 1994 (New York, Classics of Liberty Library, of 1776).

Microform: The Eighteenth Century, reel 262, no. 30 (of 1776), reel 8035, no. 07 (of 1776); Goldsmiths'-Kress Library *of* Economic Literature, reel 1319, no. 13148 (of 1786), reel 1399, no. 13794 (of 1789), reel 1465, no. 14612 (of 1791).

Reviews: *Critical Review*, 1776, Vol. 41 pp. 193–200, 258–264, 361–369, 425–433 (positive); *Edinburgh Magazine and Review*, 1776, Vol. 5, pp. 411–419 (positive); *London Review*, March 1776, Vol. 3, pp. 177–187, 271–277 (positive); [William Enfield], *Monthly Review*, April 1776, Vol. 54, pp. 299–308, Vol. 55, July, pp. 15–25, August, 81–92 (positive); *Annual Register*, 1776, Vol. 19, p. 341.

• Shaw, Duncan (1725–1795). *A comparative view of the several methods of promoting religious instruction, from the earliest down to the present time; from which the superior excellence of that recommended in the Christian institutes, ... is evinced and demonstrated. By Duncan Shaw, ... In two volumes.* London: printed for Richardson and Urquhart, 1776, 2 v.

Notes: Appendix criticizes Hume's attack on priests in "Of Superstition and Enthusiasm"; Appendix 2 criticizes "The Natural History of Religion."

In *Religion Responses*: Appendix 2 complete; from 1776 edition.

In *Essays Responses*: Appendix 1, complete; from 1776 edition, pp. 247–267.

Editions: no further editions.

Microform: The Eighteenth Century, reel 2676, no. 2.

Reviews: [John Langhorn], *Monthly Review*, July 1776, Vol. 55, p. 76 (positive); *Critical Review*, August 1776, Vol. 42, pp. 139–145 (positive); *London Review*, February 1776, Vol. 3, pp. 111–118; March, pp. 219–223 (mixed).

❧1777❧

• Anonymous. Review of *The Life of David Hume* (1777), in *Scots Magazine*, January 1777, Vol. 39, pp. 1–7.

Notes: complete reprint of "My Own Life" and Smith's "Letter" with no commentary.

- Anonymous. Review of *The Life of David Hume* (1777), in *London Chronicle*, March 11–13, 1777, Vol. 41, No 3162, pp. 244–245.

  Notes: reprint of first half of "My Own Life" with an opening comment.

  In *Life Responses*: commentary from this review is inserted into the text of "My Own Life" at the appropriate spot.

- Anonymous. Review of *The Life of David Hume* (1777), in *Critical Review*, March 1777, Vol. 43, pp. 222–227.

  Notes: third person paraphrase of and extended quotations from "My Own Life" with some commentary.

  In *Life Responses*: commentary from this review is inserted into the text of "My Own Life" at the appropriate spot.

- Anonymous. Review of *The Life of David Hume* (1777), in *Gentleman's Magazine*, March 1777, Vol. 47, pp. 120–121.

  Notes: third person paraphrase of most of "My Own Life" with a concluding editorial comment.

  In *Life Responses*: commentary from this review is inserted into the text of "My Own Life" at the appropriate spot.

- Anonymous. Review of *The Life of David Hume* (1777), in *London Review*, March 1777, Vol. 5, pp. 198–205.

  Notes: reprint of all of "My Own Life" except opening paragraph; includes much commentary.

  In *Life Responses*: commentary from this review is inserted into the text of "My Own Life" at the appropriate spot.

- Anonymous. Review of *The Life of David Hume* (1777), in *Weekly Magazine or Edinburgh Amusement*, March 13, 1777, Vol. 35, pp. 353–357.

  Notes: reprint of all of "My Own Life" except opening paragraph; no commentary.

- Anonymous. Review of *The Life of David Hume* (1777), in *Weekly Magazine or Edinburgh Amusement*, March 20, 1777, Vol. 35, pp. 388–389.

  Notes: complete reprint of Smith's "Letter"; no commentary.

- Anonymous. "Strictures on the Life of David Hume," in *Gentleman's Magazine*, March 1777, Vol. 46, pp. 158–159.

  Notes: criticizes Smith's account of Hume's death.

  In *Life Responses*: complete.

  Editions: reprinted in abbreviated form in *Scots Magazine*, March 1777, Vol. 39, p. 153.

- Anonymous. Review of George Horne's *Letter to Adam Smith*, in *Critical Review*, 1777, Vol. 43, pp. 306–308.

  Notes: criticizes Smith's account of Hume's death.

  In *Life Responses*: selections.

- Anonymous. *A letter to Courtney Melmoth, Esquire; occasioned by his Apology for the life and writings of David Hume, Esq. &. By a country curate.* Exeter: printed and sold by B. Thorn; and Mess. Richardson and Urquhart, London, [1777], [4], iv, 52p.

  Notes: criticism of Pratt's *Apology* (1777).

  In *Life Responses*: selections in editor's introduction to Pratt's *Apology* (1777).

  Editions: no further editions.

  Reviews: *Critical Review*, 1777, Vol. 43, p. 238 (positive); *London Review*, August 1777 Vol. 6, pp. 141–144 (negative); *Monthly Review*, September 1777, Vol. 57, p. 242 (negative; reprinted in *Scots Magazine*, September 1777, Vol. 39, p. 498).

- Anonymous. *A panegyrical essay, or a few serious arguments, irrefragably proving that the present times are, of all times that ever were, the most heroic, wise, and virtuous.* Oxford: printed for Daniel Prince, and sold by J. Bew, and Messrs. Payne,

London, 1777, [4], 27, [1] p.

Notes: criticism of Pratt's *Apology* (1777).

In *Life Responses*: selections in editor's introduction to Pratt's *Apology* (1777).

Editions: no further editions.

Reviews: *Critical Review*, 1777, Vol. 43, pp. 388–389 (neutral); *London Review*, August 1777, Vol. 6, pp. 141–144 (neutral); *Monthly Review*, December 1777, Vol. 57, p. 490 (negative).

- Anonymous. *Dialogues in the shades, between General Wolfe, General Montgomery, David Hume, George Grenville, and Charles Townshend.* London: printed for G. Kearsley, 1777, iv, 120 p.

  Notes: fictitious dialogue on American Revolution with Hume as a character.

  In *Life Responses*: complete Dialogues 1, selections from Dialogue 3; from 1777 edition.

  Editions: no other editions.

  Reviews: *Critical Review*, 1777, Vol. 43, p. 471 (positive); *London Review*, June 1777, Vol. 5, p. 529 (positive); *Monthly Review*, September 1777, Vol. 57, p. 251 (positive).

- Anonymous (pseud., "Academicus"). "Observations on Antient and Modern History" in n *Weekly Magazine, or Edinburgh Amusement*, November 13, 1777, Vol. 38, pp. 146–148.

  Notes: criticizes Hume's *History* for its religious infidelity.

- Anonymous (pseud., "Agricola"). "Observations on Mr. Hume's Life lately published," in *Weekly Magazine, or Edinburgh Amusement*, June 12, 1777, Vol. 36, pp. 364–365.

  Notes: criticizes Hume's "My Own Life" and Smith's account of Hume's death.

  In *Life Responses*: complete; from *Weekly Magazine*.

- Anonymous (pseud., "Criticus"). "Remarks on a Political Assertion of Mr. David Hume," in *Weekly Magazine, or Edinburgh Amusement*, August 28, 1777, Vol. 37, pp. 198–199.

  Notes: criticizes Hume's "Of Public Credit."

  In *Essays Responses*: complete.

- Anonymous (pseud., "E.M."). "Remarks on Dr Adam Smith's Letter to Mr. Strahan, on the death of David Hume, Esq.," in *Weekly Magazine, or Edinburgh Amusement*, April 24, 1777, Vol. 36, pp. 139–141.

  Notes: criticizes Smith's account of Hume's death.

  In *Life Responses*: complete; from *Weekly Magazine*.

  Discussions: "Observations relative to the late David Hume, Esq.," in *Weekly Magazine* (1777).

- Anonymous (pseud., "Tobias Simple"). "Strictures on the 'Account of The Life and Writings of the Late David Hume, Esq.'" *Weekly Magazine, or Edinburgh Amusement*, December 25, 1777, Vol. 38, pp. 289–292.

  Notes: criticizes Pratt's *Apology* (1777) and John Home's "Account of the Life" (1776), and defends Beattie.

  In *Life Responses*: complete; from *Weekly Magazine*.

- Dodd, William (1729–1777). *Thoughts in prison: in five parts. Viz. The imprisonment. The retrospect. Publick punishment. The trial. Futurity. By the Rev. William Dodd, LLD. To which are added, ... other miscellaneous pieces.* London: printed for Edward and Charles Dilly; and G. Kearsly, 1777, iii, 232 p.

  Notes: unrhymed verses written after Dodd's arrest and while awaiting execution. A section in "Week the Fifth" attacks Hume's religious infidelity.

  In *Life Responses*: relevant section from "Week the Fifth"; from *Thoughts in Prison*, Philadelphia, Robert Johnson, 1806.

Editions: over 20 editions by 1850.

Microform: The Eighteenth Century, reel 7833, no. 08 (of 1781), reel 9116, no. 02 (of 1783), reel 9482, no. 04 (of 1789), reel 2108, no. 3 (of 1793), reel 9093, no. 01 (of 1796), reel 1344, no. 08 (of 1796).

Reviews: *Critical Review*, 1777, Vol. 44, pp. 218–221 (positive, reprinted in the *Weekly Magazine*, October 30, 1777, Vol. 38, pp. 119–120); [William Kenrick], *London Review*, September 1777, Vol. 6, pp. 226–229 (negative); *Monthly Review*, October 1777, Vol. 57, pp. 328–329 (negative).

● [Griffiths, Ralph (1720–1803)]. Review of *The Life of David Hume* (1777), in *Monthly Review*, March 1777, Vol. 56, pp. 206–213.

Notes: third person paraphrase of and extended quotations from "My Own Life"; includes much commentary.

In *Life Responses*: commentary from this review is inserted into the text of "My Own Life" at the appropriate spot.

● [Horne, George (1730–1792)]. *A letter to Adam Smith LL.D. on the life, death, and philosophy of his friend David Hume Esq. By one of the people called Christians.* Oxford: at the Clarendon Press. 1777. Sold by Daniel Prince; and by J. F. and C. Rivington, G. Robinson, and T. Payne and Son, London, [1777], [4], iv, 47, [1] p.

Notes: criticizes Smith's account of Hume's death.

In *Life Responses*: complete; from 1799 edition.

Editions: 1777 (second edition), 1777 (third edition), 1784, 1786 (prefaced to *Letters on Infidelity*), 1799, 1804, 1813, 1820; included Horne's *Works*, 1795, 1809, 1818, 1830, 1831, 1846, 1848, 1853.

Facsimiles: 1994 (Thoemmes Press, of 1777).

Microform: Goldsmiths'-Kress Library of Economic Literature, reel 1109, no. 11535 (of 1777 second edition), The Eighteenth Century, reel 9144, no. 11).

Reviews: *Critical Review*, 1777, Vol. 43, pp. 306–308, (neutral); *London Review*, April 1777, Vol. 5, pp. 316–317 (negative); *Monthly Review*, May 1777, Vol. 56, p. 403 (negative).

Discussions: Samuel Jackson Pratt, *Apology* (1777); William Jones *Memoirs of the Life of Dr. Horne* (1799).

● Anonymous (pseud., "Idem"). "Observations relative to the late David Hume, Esq.," in *Weekly Magazine, or Edinburgh Amusement*, Thursday, May 8, 1777, Vol. 36, pp. 193–196.

Notes: defends Hume and Smith against "Remarks" by "E.M." in *Weekly Magazine* (April 24, 1777, Vol. 36, pp. 139–141).

In *Life Responses*: complete; from *Weekly Magazine*.

● Anonymous (pseud., "Laicus"). "Observations on the Address to One of the People called Christians," in *Gentleman's Magazine*, July 1777, Vol. 47, pp. 322–328.

Notes: criticises Pratt's *Apology* and *Supplement*.

In *Life Responses*: complete; from *Gentleman's Magazine*.

● Anonymous (pseud., "Postilion"). "Observations on the Character and Writings of Mr Hume" in *Weekly Magazine, or Edinburgh Amusement*, December 11, 1777, Vol. 38, pp. 260–261.

Notes: criticizes John Home's "Account of the Life" (1776) and defends Beattie.

In *Life Responses*: complete; from *Weekly Magazine*.

● [Pratt, Samuel Jackson (1749–1814)]. *An apology for the life and writings of David Hume, Esq. with a parallel between him and the late Lord Chesterfield: to which is added an address to one of the people called Christians. By way of reply to his letter to Adam Smith, L.L.D.* London: printed for Fielding and Walker, D. Prince, Oxford, T. and J. Merrill, Cambridge, and W. Creech, Edinburgh, 1777, [4], xv, [1], 167, [1] p.

Notes: defence of Hume's moral character and critique of Horne's *Letter*.

In *Life Responses*: complete; from 1777 edition.

Editions: 1777 (second edition, reissue of first edition with cancel title page), selections reprinted in Pratt's *Curious Particulars* (1788).

Facsimiles: 1994 (Thoemmes Press, of 1777).

Microform: The Eighteenth Century, reel 6732, no. 32.

Reviews: *Critical Review*, April 1777, Vol. 43 p. 320 (negative); *London Review*, May 1777, Vol. 5, pp. 332–339 (negative); *Gentleman's Magazine*, July 1777, Vol. 47, pp. 338 (negative); [William Enfield], *Monthly Review*, September 1777, Vol. 57, p. 242 (negative, reprinted in *Scots Magazine*, September 1777, Vol. 39, pp. 497–498).

Discussions: *A Letter to Courtney Melmoth* (1777); *A Panegyrical Essay* (1777); "Strictures on the 'Account'" in *Weekly Magazine* (1777); "Observations on the Address" in *Gentleman's Magazine* (1777), George Horne's *Letters on Infidelity* (1784).

- [Pratt, Samuel Jackson (1749–1814)]. *The sublime and beautiful of scripture, being essays on select passages of sacred composition*, London, J. Murray, 1777, 2 Vol.

Notes: Collection of 28 essays on biblical passages written by Pratt years earlier while a candidate for holy orders. The pieces were circulated privately with much praise. Preface, p. vii, mentions Hume attending a reading of this work.

In *Life Responses*: quotation from Preface included in editor's introduction to Pratt's *Apology*.

Editions: 1778, 1782, 1783, 1795,

Microform: The Eighteenth Century, reel 2403, no. 1 (of 1777), reel 470, no. 9 (of 1783).

Reviews: *Critical Review*, 1777, Vol. 43, pp. 252–256 (positive); *London Review*, February 1777 Vol. 5, pp. 91–98 (positive); *Monthly Review*, October 1777, Vol. 57, pp. 320–321 (positive); *Weekly Magazine*, March 13, 1777, Vol. 35, pp. 371–372, March 20, pp. 403–404 (positive).

- [Pratt, Samuel Jackson (1749–1814)]. *Supplement to the life of David Hume, Esq. containing genuine anecdotes, and a circumstantial account of his death and funeral*. London: printed for J. Bew, 1777, 64 p.

Notes: anecdotes about Hume; includes Hume's will.

In *Life Responses*: complete; from 1777 edition.

In *Hume on Natural Religion*: complete, without Hume's will; from 1777 edition.

Editions: 1789 ("a new edition"); selections reprinted in Pratt's *Curious Particulars* (1788).

Microform: The Eighteenth Century, reel 6843, no. 06 (of 1789).

Reviews: *Monthly Review*, June 1777, Vol. 56, p. 482 (negative); *Critical Review*, July 1777, Vol. 44, p. 79 (negative); *London Review*, December 1777, Vol. 6, p. 529 (negative); *Gentleman's Magazine*, July 1777, Vol. 47, p. 338 (negative).

- Priestley, Joseph (1733–1804). *A course of lectures on oratory and criticism. By Joseph Priestley*. London: printed for J. Johnson, 1777, [10], vi, [2], 313, [3] p.

Notes: Lecture 10 discusses Hume's method of argumentation in the moral *Enquiry*.

In *Moral Responses*: relevant selections from lecture 10; from 1777 edition, pp. 60–62.

Editions: 1781, in *Works* 1817–1832.

Facsimiles: 1971 (Garland 1777).

Microform: The Eighteenth Century, reel 8017, no. 05.

Reviews: [William Enfield], *Monthly Review*, August 1777, Vol. 57, pp. 89–99 (mixed); *Critical Review*, 1777, Vol. 44, p. 9 ff. (positive); *London Review*, September 1777, Vol. 6, pp. 207–208.

● Priestley, Joseph (1733–1804). *The doctrine of philosophical necessity illustrated; being an appendix to the Disquisitions relating to matter and spirit. To which is added an answer to the Letters on materialism, and on Hartley's Theory of the mind. By Joseph Priestley.* London: printed for J. Johnson, 1777, xxxiv, [2], 206, [2] p.

Notes: approves of Hume's defence of determinism, but criticises Hume's discussion of evil tracing back to God.

In *Metaphysical Responses*: selections from Section 10; from 1777 edition.

Editions: 1782, in *Works* 1817–1832.

Facsimiles: 1976 (Garland of 1777).

Microform: The Eighteenth Century, reel 7776, no. 05 (of 1777).

Reviews: *London Review*, February 1778, Vol. 7, pp. 120–131; [William Bewley], *Monthly Review*, May 1778, Vol. 58, pp. 354–362 (neutral).

● Priestley, Joseph (1733–1804). *Disquisitions relating to matter and spirit. To which is added, the history of the philosophical doctrine concerning the origin of the soul, and the nature of matter; with its influence on Christianity, especially with respect to the doctrine of the pre-existence of Christ. By Joseph Priestley.* London: printed for J. Johnson, 1777, xxxix, [3], 356, [4] p.

Notes: criticizes Hume's refusal to respond to antagonists.

Editions: 1782, in *Works* 1817–1832.

Facsimiles: 1976 (Garland of 1777).

Microform: The Eighteenth Century, reel 3790, no. 01. (of 1777).

Reviews: *Critical Review*, 1777, Vol. 45, p. 178 ff., p. 273 ff.; *London Review*, January 1778, Vol. 7, 1–13, February 1778, Vol. 7, pp. 113–120; [William Bewley], *Monthly Review*, May 1778, Vol. 58, pp. 347–353 (neutral).

Discussions: *An essay* (1778).

● Smith, Adam (1723–1790). "Letter from Adam Smith, LL.D. to William Strahan, Esq." in *The life of David Hume, Esq. written by himself.* London: printed for W. Strahan; and T. Cadell, 1777, [4], iv, 62 p.

Notes: describes Hume's final days and death.

In *Life Responses*: complete letter; from 1777 edition.

In *Hume on Natural Religion*: complete letter; from 1777 edition.

Editions, facsimiles, microform, reviews: see "My Own Life" in "Bibliography of Hume's Writings."

Discussions: see index to this volume for lengthy list.

∂∾1778∾∋

● Anonymous. *A philosophical and religious dialogue in the shades, between Mr. Hume and Dr. Dodd. With notes by the editor.* London: printed for the editor, and sold by Hooper and Davis, London; Charles Elliot, Edinburgh, and T. Wilson, York, 1778, 37, [1] p.

Notes: fictitious dialogue between Hume and William Dodd contrasting their faults.

In *Life Responses*: complete; from 1778 edition.

Editions: no further editions.

Microform: The Eighteenth Century, reel 1276, no. 21.

Reviews: *Critical Review*, January 1778, Vol. 45, pp. 73–74 (neutral); *London Review*, January 1778, Vol. 7, p. 69 (neutral); [William Enfield] *Monthly Review*, April 1778, Vol. 58, p. 312 (mixed).

● Burgh, William (1741–1808). *An inquiry into the belief of the Christians of the first three centuries, respecting the one Godhead of the Father, Son, and Holy Ghost. Being a sequel to a Scriptural confutation of the Rev. Mr. Lindsey's late apology. By William Burgh, Esq.* York: printed by A. Ward, for the author, and sold by W. Nicoll, London, 1778, xi, [1], 472 p.

Notes: page 70 criticizes Hume's *History* as a defence of the Stuart monarchy.

In *History Responses*: selections included in "Miscellaneous Comments on Hume's *History*"; selections from 1778 edition.

Editions: no further editions.

Reviews: *Monthly Review*, November 1779, Vol. 62, pp. 366–369 (negative); *Critical Review*, 1778, Vol. 45, p. 371 ff.

Discussions: Henry Edwards Davis, *A reply to Mr. Gibbon's vindication* (1779).

• [Caulfield (fl. 1778)]. *An essay on the immateriality and immortality of the soul, and its instinctive sense of good and evil; in opposition to the opinions advanced in the essays introductory to Dr. Priestley's abridgment of Dr. Hartley's Observations on man.* London: printed for J. Dodsley, 1778, iv, 466, [2] p.

Notes: attack on Priestley contains a defense of Beattie's critique of Hume.

Microform: The Eighteenth Century, reel 5821, no. 03.

Reviews: *Critical Review*, September 1778, Vol. 46, pp. 222–225 (mixed); *London Review*, April 1778, Vol. 7, pp. 270–279 (negative); [William Bewley], *Monthly Review*, April 1779, Vol. 60, pp. 289–291 (negative).

• Stuart, Gilbert (1742–1786). *A view of society in Europe, in its progress from rudeness to refinement: or, Inquiries concerning the history of law, government, and manners. By Gilbert Stuart, LL.D.* Edinburgh: printed for John Bell; and J. Murray, London, 1778, xx, 433, [3] p.

Notes: criticizes Hume's Tory view of royal prerogative, especially in early British history.

In *History Responses*: selections from 2.1.1; from 1778 edition.

Editions: 1778 (London second edition), 1778 (Dublin), 1782, 1783, 1792, 1797, 1813.

Microform: The Eighteenth Century, reel 4880, no. 7 (of 1777 Edinburgh), reel 8105, no. 08 (of 1777 Dublin), reel 8285, no. 04 (of 1777 London second edition), reel 7935, no. 11 (of 1782), reel 4992, no. 18 (of 1792); Goldsmiths'-Kress Library of Economic Literature; reel 1132, no. 11668.7 (of 1777 Dublin).

Reviews: *London Review*, March 1778, Vol. 7, pp. 194–201, April, pp. 254–258, May, pp. 329–339 (positive); [John Gillies], *Monthly Review*, March 1778, Vol. 58, pp. 198–207 (mixed); *Critical Review*, 1778, Vol. 45, p. 161 ff.

• Towers, Joseph (1737–1799). *Observations on Mr. Hume's History of England. By Joseph Towers.* London: printed by H. Goldney, for G. Robinson, 1778, vii, [1], 151, [1] p.

Notes: criticizes Hume's Tory view of royal prerogative.

In *History Responses*: complete book; from 1778 edition.

Editions: in *Tracts* 1796 Vol. 1.

Microform: The Eighteenth Century, reel 8096, no. 02.

Reviews of *Observations*: *Critical Review*, April 1778, Vol. 45, pp. 289–292 (mixed); [Andrew Kippis], *Monthly Review*, July 1778, Vol. 59, pp. 19–25 (positive); *London Review*, May 1778, Vol. 7, pp. 347–355 (positive).

Reviews of *Tracts*: *Critical Review*, 1796, Vol. 18, pp. 306–311; *Analytical Review*, 1796, Vol. 24, pp. 206–207.

Discussions: James Lindsay's *Sermon* (1799); Francis Jeffrey, review of Brodie in *Edinburgh Review* (1824); Francis Palgrave, "Hume and his Influence upon History" (1826).

৯১779৩

- Anonymous. Review of *Dialogues*, in *Critical Review*, September 1779, Vol. 48, pp. 161–172.

  Notes: negative review.

  In *Religion Responses*: complete review.
- Anonymous. Review of *Dialogues*, in *The London Magazine; or, Gentleman's Monthly Intelligencer*, September 1779, Vol. 48, pp. 418–419.

  Notes: negative review.

  In *Religion Responses*: complete review.
- Anonymous. Review of *Dialogues*, in *Gentleman's Magazine*, October 1779, Vol. 49, pp. 507–508.

  Notes: negative review.

  In *Religion Responses*: complete review.

  In *Hume on Natural Religion*: complete review.
- Anonymous. Review of *Dialogues*, in *The London Review*, December 1779, Vol. 10, pp. 365–373.

  Notes: positive review.

  In *Religion Responses*: complete review.

  Discussions: "Answer to an Extract" *London Review* (1780).
- Beattie, James (1735–1803). Letter to Elizabeth Montagu, June 25, 1779.

  See William Forbes, *The Life and Writings of James Beattie* (1806).

  Notes: brief anecdote about Hume's views of scepticism.

  In *Life Responses*: story included in "Miscellaneous Hume Anecdotes."
- [Burnett, James, Lord Monboddo (1714–1799)]. *Ancient metaphysics, or the science of universals*. Edinburgh, J. Balfour, 1779–1799, 6 Vol.

  Notes: criticizes Hume's views of necessity, induction, the external world, causality, and ideas.

  In *Metaphysical Responses*: selections from 1.3.21, 1.5.6, 1.5.9, 2.2.2; from Volume 1 of 1776 and Volume 2 of 1782.

  Volumes: 1 (1779), 2 (1782), 3 (1783), 4 (1795), 5 (1797), 6 (1799).

  Facsimiles: 1978 (Garland, six volumes).

  Microform: The Eighteenth Century, reel 2825, no. 2 (of Vol. 1), reel 2832, no. 8 (of Vol. 2), reel 2825, no. 4 (of Vol. 3), reel 2826, no. 2 (of Vol. 4), reel 2825, no. 5 (of Vol. 5), reel 2831, no. 4 (of Vol. 6).

  Reviews of volume 1: [John Gillies], *Monthly Review*, September 1779, Vol. 61, pp. 191–200 (negative); *Critical Review*, 1779, Vol. 48, pp. 293–301 (neutral).

  Reviews of volume 2: [Gilbert Stuart], *Monthly Review*, November 1782, Vol. 67, pp. 340–345 (negative); *Critical Review*, 1782, Vol. 54, pp. 339–348, 421–430 (mixed).

  Reviews of volume 3: *European Magazine and London Review*, 1784, Vol. 5 pp. 217–219, 365–370, 441–444 (mixed); *Critical Review*, 1784, Vol. 58, pp. 250–258.

  Reviews of volume 6: *New London Review*, 1799, Vol. 1 pp. 389–600 (mixed).
- Davis, Henry Edwards (1756–1784). *A reply to Mr. Gibbon's vindication of some passages in the fifteenth and sixteenth chapters of The History of the decline and fall of the Roman Empire. ... By Henry Edwards Davis*. London: printed for J. Dodsley, 1779, [4], 178 p.

  Notes: compares Gibbon's view of polytheism with Hume's in the "Natural History of Religion."

  Editions: no further editions.

  Facsimiles: 1974 (Garland, of 1779).

Microform: The Eighteenth Century, reel 1624, no. 07.

Reviews: *Critical Review*, 1779, Vol. 48, p. 395 ff.; *Monthly Review*, September 1780, Vol. 63, pp. 235–236.

● Gibbon, Edward (1737–1794). *A vindication of some passages in the fifteenth and sixteenth chapters of the History of the decline and fall of the Roman Empire. By the author.* London: printed for W. Strahan and T. Cadell, 1779, [4], 158 p.

Notes: Chapter 8 praises Hume's discussion of religion.

In *History Responses*: selections included in "Miscellaneous Comments on Hume's History"; selections from 1779 London edition.

Editions: 1779 (Dublin).

Microform: The Eighteenth Century, reel 36, no. 10 (of 1779 Dublin); Eighteenth Century, reel 1624, no. 06 (of 1779 London).

● [Mackenzie, Henry (1745–1831)]. "The Story of La Roche," *The Mirror*, 1779 June 19, 22, 26,

Notes: fictitious story of Hume's good natured relation with a French man and his daughter.

In *Life Responses*: complete; from Mackenzie's *Works*, Edinburgh, Ballantyne, 1808, Vol. 4, pp. 175–207.

Editions: in several 19th century editions of Mackenzie's *Works*.

Discussions: *An Interesting Anecdote of a well known English Philosopher* (1811); Henry Mackenzie, *An Account of the Life and Writings of John Home* (1822); Henry Mackenzie, *Anecdotes and Egotisims* (1927).

● [Meiners, Christoph (1740–1810)]. Review of *Dialogues*, in *Zugabe zu den Göttingischen gelehrten Anzeigen*, November 27, 1779, No. 48, pp. 753–763.

Notes: negative review.

In *Religion Responses*: English translation of complete review, translated by Curtis Bowman.

● [Parsons, Philip (1729–1812)]. *Dialogues of the dead with the living.* London: printed for N. Conant; and H. Payne, 1779, [4], ii, [2], 227, [1] p.

Notes: first two dialogues are between Hume and Lord Herbert and discuss Hume's "Of Miracles" and "The Rise of Arts and Sciences."

Editions: 1781; no further editions.

Microform: The Eighteenth Century, reel 3573, no. 15.

Reviews: *Critical Review*, 1779, pp. 444–450 (positive); *London Review*, June 1779, Vol. 9, pp. 413–417 (positive); *Monthly Review*, August 1770, Vol. 61, p. 159 (negative).

● [Rose, William (1719–1786)]. Review of *Dialogues*, in *Monthly Review*, November 1779, Vol. 61, pp. 343–355.

Notes: mixed review, applauding the style but contending that Hume previously expressed these views elsewhere.

In *Religion Responses*: complete review.

In *Hume on Natural Religion*: complete review.

● [Rush, Benjamin (1745–1813)]. "Contrast between the Death of a Deist and a Christian, David Hume and Samuel Finley," in *The United States Magazine, A Repository of History, Politics, and Literature*, 1779, Vol. 1, pp. 65–72.

Notes: reprint of Adam Smith's "Letter ... to William Strahan" followed by a reprint of an account of Samuel Finley's death.

In *American Responses*: complete article.

● Stuart, Gilbert (1742–1786). *Observations concerning the public law, and the constitutional history of Scotland: with occasional remarks concerning English antiquity. By Gilbert Stuart, LL.D.* Edinburgh: printed for William Creech; and J. Murray, London, 1779, xxii, [2], 395, [1] p.

Notes: Stuart argues against Hume that the burgesses originally had no representation in English or Scottish national councils.

Editions: no further editions.

Microform: The Eighteenth Century, reel 6392, no. 06.

Reviews: *Critical Review*, 1779, Vol. 47 p. 275 ff.; *London Review*, March 1779, Vol. 9, pp. 152–158 (positive); *Monthly Review*, April 1779, Vol. 60, pp. 269–281 (mixed).

&1780&

- Anonymous. "Answer to an Extract from a Letter from Dr. Beattie," *London Review*, July 1780, Vol. 12, pp. 63–64.

  Notes: criticizes Beattie's attack on Hume.

  In *Life Responses*: complete letter.

- Anonymous. Translator's Preface, to Claude Buffier (1661–1737), *First truths and the origin of our opinions, explained: with an enquiry into the sentiments of modern philosophers, relative to our primary ideas of things. Translated from the French of Pere Buffier. To which is prefixed a detection of the plagiarism, concealment, and ingratitude of the Doctors Reid, Beattie, and Oswald*. London, Printed for J. Johnson, 1780, lxxi, 438 p.

  Notes: translator criticizes Hume for the bad effects of his writings.

  In *Common Sense Responses*: complete Preface.

  Editions: no further editions.

  Microform: Eighteenth-century sources for the study of English literature and culture, roll 283.

  Reviews: [Samuel Badcock], *Monthly Review*, 1780, Vol. 63, p. 526 ff.

- Dunbar, James (1742–1798). *Essays on the history of mankind in rude and cultivated ages. By James Dunbar*. London, printed for W. Strahan; T. Cadell; and J. Balfour, Edinburgh, 1780, [12], 436 p.

  Notes: Note D to "On the primeval form of society" discusses Hume's view in *Treatise* Book 2 about the effects of a second marriage on parental love.

  Editions: 1781 (second edition), 1782.

  Facsimiles: 1995 (Thoemmes Press of 1781).

  Microform: Eighteenth-century sources for the study of English literature and culture, reel no. 466.

  Reviews: *Critical Review*, August 1780, Vol. 50, pp. 103–109; *London Review*, June 1780, Vol. 12, pp. 406–413 (mixed); [William Rose], *Monthly Review*, December 1780, Vol. 63, pp. 443–448; *Monthly Review*, May 1782, Vol. 66, p. 398 (positive).

- Priestley, Joseph (1733–1804). *Letters to a philosophical unbeliever. Part I. Containing an examination of the principal objections to the doctrines of natural religion, and especially those contained in the writings of Mr. Hume*. Bath, Printed by R. Cruttwell, and sold by J. Johnson, 1780, 212 p.

  Notes: criticizes Hume's view of causality, 12 sections of the *Enquiry*, the *Dialogues* and "Of a Particular Providence".

  In *Metaphysical Responses*: Letters 13 and 14 complete; from *The Theological and Miscellaneous Works* (1817–1832), Vol. 4.

  In *Religion Responses*: Letters 9 and 10; from 1787 second edition.

  In *Hume on Natural Religion*: Letters 9 and 10; from 1780 edition.

  Editions: 1787, *Works* 1817–1832 Vol. 4.

  Facsimiles: 1983 (Garland of 1817).

  Microform: The Eighteenth Century, reel 2403, no. 10 (of 1787).

Reviews: *Critical Review*, October 1780, Vol. 50, pp. 241–247 (positive); [William Bewley], *Monthly Review*, June 1781, Vol. 64, 409–412 (positive).

Discussions: Matthew Turner *Answer* (1782).

• Hayley, William (1745–1820). *An essay on history; in three epistles to Edward Gibbon, Esq. with notes*. By William Hayley, Esq., London: printed for J. Dodsley, 1780, [4], 159, [1] p.

Notes: poetic verse critique of Hume's sophistry in the *History*.

In *History Responses*: selections from Epistle 2; from 1780 edition.

Editions: 1781 (Dublin), 1781 (London), 1782 (Dublin), in Volume 1 of *Poems* 1782 (Dublin); no further editions.

Facsimiles: 1978 (Garland, of 1780 London first edition).

Microform: The Eighteenth Century, reel 4021, no. 04 (of London 1780), reel 8976, no. 05 (of Dublin 1781), reel 3409, no. 08 (of London 1781), reel 3318, no. 05 (of Dublin 1782), reel 8747, no. 01 (of 1782 *Poems*).

Reviews: *Critical Review*, July 1780, Vol. 50, pp. 10–13 (positive); [Edmund Cartwright], *Monthly Review*, July 1780, Vol. 63, pp. 30–38 (positive).

• Hayter, Thomas (1747–1799). *Remarks on Mr. Hume's dialogues, concerning natural religion*. By T. Hayter. Cambridge: printed by J. Archdeacon; for T. Cadel, 1780, [2], 65, [1] p.

Notes: discusses the problem of evil in Parts 10–12 of the *Dialogues*.

In *Religion Responses*: complete pamphlet; from 1780 edition.

In *Hume on Natural Religion*: complete pamphlet; from 1780 edition.

Editions: no further editions.

Facsimiles: 1992 (Thoemmes Press of 1780).

Reviews: *Critical Review*, April 1780, Vol. 49, pp. 315–316 (positive); *London Review*, April 1780, Vol. 11, p. 282–283 (mixed); [William Rose], *Monthly Review*, February 1781, Vol. 64, p. 159 (mixed; contained in *Hume on Natural Religion*).

❧1781❧

• Anonymous. *The beauties of Hume and Bolingbroke*. London: printed for G. Kearsly, 1782, [2], xxxii, 262, [2].

Notes: editor's introduction discusses similarities between Hume and Bolingbroke.

Editions: 1782 (second edition); no further editions.

Microform: The Eighteenth Century, reel 8782, no. 03 (of first edition).

Reviews: *Monthly Review*, December 1782, Vol. 67, p. 477 (mixed); *Critical Review*, February 1783, Vol. 55, pp. 157–158 (negative).

• Milner, Joseph (1744–1797). *Gibbon's account of Christianity considered: together with some strictures on Hume's dialogues concerning natural religion*. By Joseph Milner. York: printed by A. Ward; and sold by G. Robinson, and T. Cadell, 1781, xiii, [1]–82, 83–108, 83–262 p.

Notes: criticizes Hume's *Dialogues*.

In *Religion Responses*: Part 3.3 and 3.12 complete; from 1781 edition.

Editions: 1808; no further editions.

Facsimiles: 1989 (Thoemmes Press of 1781).

Microform: The Eighteenth Century, reel 3649, no. 01.

Reviews: *Critical Review*, September 1781, Vol. 52, p. 240 (negative); [William Rose], *Monthly Review*, February 1783, Vol. 68, pp. 112–114 (negative).

❧1782❧

- Anonymous. *Critical observations concerning the Scottish historians Hume, Stuart and Robertson: including an idea of the reign of Mary Queen of Scots, as a portion of history.* London: printed for T. Evans, 1782, [2], 53, [1] p.
  Notes: contrasts Hume's and Robertson's histories.
  In *History Responses*: Part 2, complete; from 1782 edition.
  Editions: no further editions.
  Microform: The Eighteenth Century, reel 6242, no. 10.
  Reviews: *European Magazine and London Review*, August 1782, Vol. 2, pp. 131–132 (mixed); [William Enfield], *Monthly Review*, November 1782, Vol. 67, pp. 390–391 (negative).
- Balfour, James (1705–1795). *Philosophical dissertations*, Edinburgh: printed for T. Cadell, London; and J. and E. Balfour, Edinburgh, 1782, viii, 232 p.
  Notes: criticizes Hume's broad catalogue of the virtues.
  In *Moral Responses*: Dissertation 3, Appendix 2, complete; from 1782 edition.
  Editions: no further editions.
  Facsimiles: 1994 (Thoemmes Press of 1782).
  Microform: The Eighteenth Century, reel 520, no. 15.
  Reviews: [Samuel Badcock], *Monthly Review*, January 1783, Vol. 68, p. 8 ff.; *European Magazine and London Review*, January 1783, Vol. 3, pp. 36–39 (negative).
- Hallifax, Samuel (1733–1790). *A sermon preached before the Lords spiritual and temporal, in the Abby Church of Westminster, on Friday, February 8, 1782. Being the day appointed by His Majesty's proclamation for a general fast. By Samuel, Lord Bishop of Gloucester.* London: printed for T. Cadell, 1782, 20 p.
  Notes: sermon against violence and corruption criticizes Hume's religious infidelity.
  Editions: no further editions.
  Reviews: *Critical Review*, March 1782, Vol. 53, p. 236 (neutral); *Monthly Review*, April 1782, Vol. 66, p. 318 (positive).
- Rousseau, Jean-Jacques (1712–1778). *Les confessions de J.J. Rousseau, suivies des Reveries du promeneur solitaire*, Geneve, 1782, 2 v.
  Notes: biography of Rousseau up to the year 1765; Book 11 contains a short discussion of his first acquaintance with Hume.
  In *Life Responses*: Book 11, selections; from *The confessions of Jean Jacques Rousseau*, tr. W. Conyngham Mallory, Philadelphia, G. Barrie [a. 1890], 2 v.
  Editions: several editions in French and English.
- [Turner, Matthew (d. ca. 1788) under the pseudonym of Wm. Hammon], *Answer to Dr. Priestley's Letters to a philosophical unbeliever. Part I.* London, 1782, xxxiv, 61, [1] p.
  Notes: Turner was an apparent atheist; he criticizes Priestley and defends Hume.
  In *Religion Responses*: quotation from 1782 edition (pp. 52–53) included in editor's introduction to Priestley's *Letters*.
  Editions: 1826; no further editions.
  Microfilm: The Eighteenth Century, reel 345, no. 17.
  Reviews: [Samuel Badcock], *Monthly Review*, 1783, Vol. 68, p. 129 ff.
- Warton, Joseph (1722–1800). *An essay on the genius and writings of Pope. In two volumes ... The fourth edition, corrected.* London: printed for J. Dodsley, 1782, 2 v.
  Notes: page 70 of Volume 2 (Volume 1 in 1756) quotes Hume's "The Skeptic" in regard to Pope's *Essay on Man*.
  In *Essays Responses*: selections included in "Miscellaneous Comments on Hume's *Essays*," from 1782 edition.
  Editions: 1806.

Facsimiles: 1970 (Garland, of 1772–1782).

Microform: The Eighteenth Century, reel 2899, no. 6.

Reviews: *Critical Review*, February 1782, pp. 97–108 (positive); *European Magazine and London Review*, Vol. 1, p. 129; *Monthly Review*, April 1782, Vol. 66, pp. 265–273 (positive).

᪥1783᪥

- Anonymous. Remarks in *Essays on suicide, and the immortality of the soul, ascribed to the late David Hume, Esq. Never before published. With remarks, intended as an antidote to the poison contained in these performances, by the editor. To which is added, two letters on suicide, from Rosseau's Eloisa.* London: printed for M. Smith; and sold by the booksellers in Piccadilly, Fleet-street, and Paternoster-row, 1783, iv, 107, [1] p.

  Notes: 10 notes criticizing "Of Suicide" and "Of the Immortality of the Soul."

  In *Religion Responses*: 10 Notes complete; from 1783 edition.

  Editions: 1789, 1799.

  Facsimiles: 1992 (Thoemmes Press of 1783).

  Microform: The Eighteenth Century, reel 981, no. 27 (of 1783).

  Reviews: see reviews of Hume's *Essays on Suicide and Immortality* listed separately.

- Anonymous. Anecdotes about James Balfour, *European Magazine and London Review*, Vol. 3, January, 1783, pp. 39–40.

  Notes: anecdotes includes an erroneous story that Balfour competed with Hume for the chair of moral philosophy Edinburgh.

  In *Moral Responses*: relevant quotation included in introduction to Balfour's *Delineation* (1753).

- Anonymous. Review of *Essays on Suicide and Immortality*, in *Critical Review*, December 1783, Vol. 56, p. 475.

  Notes: negative review.

  In *Religion Responses*: complete review.

- Anonymous. Review of *Essays on Suicide and Immortality*, in *The English Review*, December 1783, Vol. 2, pp. 418–426.

  Notes: negative review.

  In *Religion Responses*: complete review.

- Beattie, James (1735–1803). *Dissertations moral and critical. On memory and imagination. On dreaming. The theory of language. On fable and romance. On the attachments of kindred. Illustrations on sublimity. By James Beattie.* London, printed for W. Strahan; and T. Cadell; and W. Creech at Edinburgh, 1783, x, [6], 655, [1] p.

  Notes: brief comment on Hume at dinners.

  In *Life Responses*: comment included in "Miscellaneous Hume Anecdotes"; from 1783 edition, p. 37.

  Editions: 1783 (Dublin edition); no further editions.

  Facsimiles: 1970 (F. Frommann), 1971 (Garland Publishing), 1974 (G. Olms), 1996 (Routledge/Thoemmes Press).

  Microform: The Eighteenth Century, reel 2971, no. 01; Eighteenth-century sources for the study of English literature, reel 1; Library of English literature, LEL11549.

  Reviews: *Annual Register*, 1783, Vol. 26, pp. 125–136, 207–223; *Critical Review*, November 1783, Vol. 56, pp. 352–363; [Gilbert Stuart], *English Review*, June 1783, Vol. 1, pp. 449–460, Vol. 2, July, pp. 50–59; *Edinburgh Weekly Magazine*, August and September 1783, Vol. 57, pp. 211–214, 240–241, 307–310, 339–342. *European Magazine*, July 1783, Vol. 2, pp. 49–52; *London Magazine*, July 1783, Vol. 1, part 2, pp. 49–53; [William Rose], *Monthly Review*, July 1783, Vol. 69, pp. 30–43; *New Annual Register*, 1783, pp. 271–272; *New Review*, 1783, Vol. 3, pp. 378–385; *Scots Magazine*, June–August 1783, Vol. 45, 286–288, 372–376, 425–428.

- Blair, Hugh (1718–1800). *Lectures on rhetoric and belles lettres.* London, 2. Strahan, T. Cadell, 1783, 2 vol.

  Notes: criticizes Hume's "Of Eloquence".

  In *Essays Responses*: Lecture 26; from 1785 edition.

  Editions: several 18th and 19th century editions.

  Facsimiles: 1965 (Southern Illinois Press of 1783), 1970 (Garland of 1785).

  Microform: Microform: Eighteenth-century sources for the study of English literature, reel 6 (of 1783); Library of English literature, LEL 22114–15; British culture series Group VI; no. 23 (of 1783); The Eighteenth Century, reel 4175, no. 01 (of 1796), reel 3004, no. 10 (of 1798).

  Reviews: *Critical Review*, July 1783, Vol. 56, pp. 45–60, August, pp. 109–117 (mixed); *European Magazine and London Review*, Vol. 3, p. 435, Vol. 4, p. 35 (positive); *English Review*, Vol. 2, pp. 19–25, 81–94; [William Rose], *Monthly Review*, June 1783, Vol. 68, pp. 489–505; Vol. 69, July, p. 186 ff.; February 1784, Vol. 70, p. 173 ff.

- Mably, Abbé de (1709–1785). *De la maniere d'écrire l'histoire*, Paris: Chez Alexandre Jombert, jeune, 1783, [4], 342 p.

  Notes: criticizes Hume's writing style in the *History*.

  In *History Responses*: selections from Dialogue 2; from *Two dialogues, concerning the manner of writing history. From the French of Abbé de Mably.* London: printed for G. Kearsley, 1783, [8], 298, [6] p.

  Microform: The Eighteenth Century, reel 112, no. 2.

  Reviews of French edition: *Monthly Review*, July 1783, Vol. 69, pp. 69–70 (positive).

  Reviews of English translation: *English Review*, August 1783, Vol. 2, pp. 124–130 (positive); [William Enfield], *Monthly Review*, January 1784, Vol. 70, pp. 32–38 (negative).

- Macaulay, Catharine (1731–1791). *A treatise on the immutability of moral truth. By Catharine Macaulay Graham.* London: printed by A. Hamilton, jun. and sold by C. Dilly; G. Robinson, 1783, xvi, 325, [3] p.

  Notes: defense of Clarkean view that morality is founded on the eternal fitness of things, discusses Hume's view of conscience in "The Sceptic."

  Editions: revised portions included in *Letters on Education with Observations on Religious and Metaphysical Subjects* (1790).

  Facsimiles: 1974 (Garland of 1790 *Letters*).

  Microform: The Eighteenth Century, reel 6130, no. 04 (of 1783); Gerritsen women's history,; no. 1079.4 (of 1790 *Letters*); History of education; fiches 19,695–19,700 (of 1790 *Letters*).

  Reviews: *Critical Review*, November 1783, Vol. 56, pp. 348–352 (positive); *European Magazine and London Review*, July 1783, Vol. 4, pp. 37–39 (negative); *English Review*, 1783, Vol. 2, pp. 185–190 (negative); [Samuel Badcock], *Monthly Review*, February 1784, Vol. 70, pp. 89–100 (mixed).

- Ogilvie, John (1733–1814). *An inquiry into the causes of the infidelity and scepticism of the times: with observations on the writings of Herbert, Shaftesbury, Bolingbroke, Hume, Gibbon, Toulmin, &c. &c.* London: Richardson and Urquahart, 1783, xvi, 462 p.

  Notes: criticizes Hume's *Dialogues*, his identification of love and esteem, and his attack on the clergy in "Of National Characters".

  In *Religion Responses*: selections from Section 2; from 1783 edition, pp. 63–65, 68–70.

In *Moral Responses*: Sect. 9, selections; from 1783 edition, pp. 346–349.
Essay responses: Sect. 8, selections; from 1783 edition, pp. 309–327.
Editions: no further editions.
Microform: The Eighteenth Century, reel 2558, no. 4.
Reviews: *Critical Review* April 783, Vol. 55, pp. 305–308 (mixed); *English Review*, 1783, Vol. 1, pp. 386-389 (mixed); [Samuel Badcock], *Monthly Review*, May 1783, Vol. 68, pp. 460–461 (mixed).
• Tyers, Thomas (1726–1787). *An historical essay on Mr. Addison*, London: printed by J. Nichols for the author, 1783, viii, 76 p.
Notes: criticizes "My Own Life."
In *Life Responses*: selections; from 1783 edition.
Facsimiles: 1971 (Garland of 1783).
Microform: The Eighteenth Century, reel 2424, no. 6.

❧1784☙

• Anonymous. *An essay on the immortality of the soul; shewing the fallacy and malignity of a sceptical one, lately published, together with such another on suicide; and both ascribed, by the editor, to the late David Hume, esq.* London: printed for the author, by T. Spilsbury, 1784, [2], xiii, [1], 45, [1] p.
Notes: criticizes conclusion of "Of the Immortality of the Soul."
In *Religion Responses*: complete pamphlet from 1784 edition.
In *Hume on Natural Religion*: complete pamphlet from 1784 edition.
Editions: no further editions.
Microform: The Eighteenth Century, reel 9706, no. 07.
Reviews: *English Review*, October 1784, Vol. 4, pp. 304–305 (negative).
• Anonymous. Review of *Essays on Suicide and Immortality*, in *Gentleman's Magazine*, August 1784, Volume 54, p. 35.
Notes: negative review.
In *Religion Responses*: complete review.
In *Hume on Natural Religion*: complete review.
• Cowper, William (1731–1800), letter to William Unwin, July 12, 1784.
See William Cowper, *Memoir of the early life of William Cowper* (1816).
Notes: letter to Unwin comments on William Rose's review of Hume's essay on suicide (*Monthly Review*, June 1784, Volume 70, pages 427–428), and Cowper offers his own criticism.
In *Religion Responses*: selections; from *Memoir* (1816).
• [Dalrymple, David, Lord Hailes (1726–1792)]. *Miscellaneous remarks on "The enquiry into the evidence against Mary Queen of Scots."* London: printed for J. Robson; and G. Robinson, 1784, [2], 41, [1] p.
Notes: criticism of Tytler's *Historical and Critical Enquiry* (1760) discusses Hume's views of Mary Queen of Scots.
In *History Responses*: Sections 2 and 5, complete; from 1784 edition.
Editions: no further editions.
Microform: The Eighteenth Century, reel 1152, no. 01.
Reviews: *Critical Review*, August 1784, Vol. 53, pp. 129–132 (mixed).
Discussions: John Whitaker, *Mary Queen of Scots Vindicated* (1787).
• Feder, Johann Georg Heinrich (1740–1821). *Göttingische Anzeigen von gelehrten Sachen*, December 31, 1784, No. 210, pp. 2100–2103.
Notes: negative review.
In *Religion Responses*: English translation of complete review, translated by Curtis Bowman.

- Hamilton, Hugh (1729–1805). *An attempt to prove the existence and absolute perfection of the supreme unoriginated being, in a demonstrative manner.* Dublin, Printed by John Exshaw, 1784, 202 p.

  Notes: criticizes Hume's *Dialogues.*

  In *Religion Responses*: selections from the Introduction; from *The Works of the Right Rev. Hugh Hamilton*, 1809, Vol. 2, pp. 11–27.

  Editions: 1785, in *Works* 1809; no further editions.

  Reviews: [William Rose], *Monthly Review*, November 1785, Vol. 73, pp. 333–338 (positive); *Critical Review*, January 1786, Vol. 61, pp. 37–44 (mixed); *English Review*, 1786, Vol. 5, pp. 437–440 (positive).

- [Horne, George (1730–1792)]. *Letters on infidelity. By the author of A letter to Doctor Adam Smith.* Oxford: at the Clarendon Press. Sold by D. Prince and J. Cooke, Oxford: G. Robinson, J.F. and C. Rivington, and T. Cadell, London, 1784, [2], III, [3], 301, [1] p.

  Notes: criticizes Pratt's *Apology*, and Hume's *Dialogues* and "Of Suicide."

  In *Life Responses*: Letters 1–3 complete; from 1784 edition.

  In *Religion Responses*: Letters 4–7 complete; from 1784 edition.

  Editions: 1786, 1806, 1831; included in Horne's *Works*, 1795, 1809, 1818, 1830, 1831, 1846, 1848, 1853.

  Microform: The Eighteenth Century, reel 3960, no. 03 (of 1786).

  Reviews: *English Review*, July 1784, Vol. 4, pp. 31–34 (mixed); *Gentleman's Magazine*, August 1784, Vol. 54, pp. 607–609 (mixed); [William Rose], *Monthly Review*, November 1785, Vol. 73, pp. 338–343 (mixed).

  Discussions: Vicesimus Knox, *Winter Evenings* (1788), and William Jones, *Memoirs.*

- [Rose, William (1719–1786)]. Review of *Essays on Suicide and Immortality*, in *Monthly Review*, June 1784, Volume 70, pages 427–428.

  Notes: negative review.

  In *Religion Responses*: complete review.

  In *Hume on Natural Religion*: complete review.

  Discussions: William Cowper, *Memoir* (1816).

- Skelton, Philip (1707–1787). *An appeal to common sense on the subject of Christianity; to which are added, some thoughts on common sense thus appealed to.* Dublin, Printed for the Author, 1784, viii, 389, [7] p.

  Notes: section titled "Some Thoughts on Common Sense" argues that Hume's scepticism is its own refutation.

  In *Common Sense Responses*: complete, from *Works* 1824.

  Editions: in *Works* 1824.

  Microform: The Eighteenth Century, reel 6338, no. 09.

☙1785❧

- Anonymous. *An answer to David Hume, and others, on the subject of liberty and necessity, providence, and a future state.* London: printed for T. Hookham, 1785, pp. [3]–66.

  Notes: criticism of Hume's determinism.

  In *Metaphysical Responses*: complete pamphlet; from 1785 edition.

  Reviews: *Monthly Review*, May 1785, Vol. 72, pp. 394–395 (positive); *English Review*, 1785, Vol. 6, pp. 284–286 (mixed).

- Anonymous. *Two letters to David Hume, by one of the people called Quakers: containing a few cursory remarks on his Philosophical essays.* Chichester: printed by D. Jaques. And sold by S. Crowder, and R. Baldwin, London; and by C. Jaques, Chichester, [1785], 20 p.

Notes: attacks the sceptical implications of Hume's philosophy. The work appeared without a date; a date of 1785 is based on the appearance of reviews.

Editions: no further editions.

Reviews: *Critical Review*, January 1786, Vol. 61, p. 80 (negative); *English Review*, 1785, Vol. 5 pp. 429–430 (negative).

• Boswell, James (1740–1795). *The journal of a tour to the Hebrides, with Samuel Johnson, LL.D. By James Boswell.* London: printed by Henry Baldwin, for Charles Dilly, 1785, vii, [1], 524, [2] p.

Notes: criticizes Smith's account of Hume's death.

In *Life Responses*: selections from August 14, 1773 entry; from from *The life of Samuel Johnson, LL.D., including a journal of his tour to the Hebrides*, ed. John Wilson Croker, New York: Derby & Jackson, 4 vol.

Editions: several editions.

Reviews: [Samuel Badcock], *Monthly Review*, 1786, Vol. 74, p. 277 ff.; *European Magazine*, May 1786, Vol. 9, p. 342 (positive).

Discussions: Joseph Towers, *Essay on the Life, Character, and Writings, of Dr. Samuel Johnson* (1786).

• Paley, William (1743–1805). *The principles of moral and political philosophy*, London: printed for R. Faulder, 1785, vii, xxi, vi, 657 p.

Notes: discusses God's will and utility.

In *Moral Responses*: selections from Book 2, chapters 4–8, Book 6, chap. 12; from 1839 edition.

Editions: several editions separately and in *Works*.

Microform: The Eighteenth Century, reel 4314, no. 02 (of 1790), reel 4135, no. 02 (of 1793) reel 10330, no. 01 (of 1794), reel 5325, no. 2 (of 1794).

Reviews: *Critical Review*, July 1785, Vol. 60, pp. 29–37, September, pp. 202–210 (positive); [William Rose], *Monthly Review*, Vol. 73, 1785, August pp. 132–135, December pp. 401–414 (mixed); *English Review*, April 1785, Vol. 5, pp. 254–258 (negative).

Discussions: Daniel Dewar, *Elements of Moral Philosophy* (1826); William Belsham, *Essays* (1789–1891); Dugald Stewart, *Philosophy of the Active and Moral Powers* (1828).

• [Pinkerton, John (1758–1826)]. *Letters of literature. By Robert Heron, Esq.* London: printed for G. G. J. and J. Robinson, 1785, [8], 515, [1] p.

Notes: criticizes Hume's Tory view of royal prerogative.

In *History Responses*: Letter 42, complete; from 1785 edition.

Editions: no further editions.

Facsimiles: The Eighteenth Century, reel 1277, no. 16.

Microform: 1970 (Garland of 1785).

Reviews: *Critical Review*, December 1785, Vol. 60, pp. 405–413, January 1786, Vol. 61, pp. 18–26 (mixed); [Samuel Badcock], *Monthly Review*, March 1786, Vol. 74, pp. 175–182 (mixed); *European Magazine and London Review*, 1785, Vol. 8, pp. 106–110, 195–200, 290–293, 376–379.

• Reid, Thomas (1710–1796). *Essays on the intellectual powers of man.* Edinburgh, J. Bell, 1785, xii, 766 p.

Notes: criticizes Hume's sceptical views of ideas, external perception, induction, memory, the principles of association, contingent truths, necessary truths, and reason.

In *Metaphysical Responses*: selections from 1.1, 2.12, 2.14, 3.7, 4.4, 5.6, 6.5, 6.6, 7.4; from 1785 edition.

Editions: several edition; see *Common Sense Bibliography* for complete listing.

Facsimiles: 1971 (Garland Publishing of 1785 edition), 1971 (Scolar Press of 1785 edition).

Microform: The Eighteenth Century, reel 2825, no. 3 (of 1785 edition); The Eighteenth Century, reel 2520, no. 3 (of 1790 edition).

Reviews: *Critical Review*, October 1785, Vol. 60, pp. 241–248 (positive); *English Review*, Vol. 6, pp. 192–201, 241–245, 329–338, 448–457 (mixed); ["Arr," i.e., Arthur] *Monthly Review*, September 1786, Vol. 75, pp. 195–203; October 1786, pp. 241–252; November 1786, pp. 331–342 (positive). All of these reviews are contained in *Common Sense Responses*.

- "Republicus." "Observations on the Liberty of the press," *The American Monitor, or the Republican Magazine*, October 1785, Vol. 1, pp. 3–7.

  Notes: defense of liberty of the press, adapting parts of Hume's essay to reflect the American situation, without mentioning Hume himself.

  In *American Responses*: complete article.

- Tyers, Thomas, 1726–1787. *A biographical sketch of Dr. Samuel Johnson. By Thomas Tyers, Esq.* [London, 1785], 27, [1] p.

  Notes: anecdotes of Johnson's critical comments about Hume.

  In *Life Responses*: selections; from 1785 edition.

  Editions: early version appeared in *Gentleman's Magazine*, December 1784.

  Facsimiles: 1952 (Augustan Facsimile of 1785).

  Microform: The Eighteenth Century, reel 2424, no. 7.

෨1786෬

- Bruce, John (1745–1826). *Elements of the science of ethics, on the principles of natural philosophy.* London: A Strahan and T. Cadell, 1786, xxiii, 324 p.

  Notes: summarises Hume's moral theory.

  In *Essays Responses*: Chapter 2.2.1; from 1786 edition.

  Editions: 1796.

  Microform: The Eighteenth Century, reel 5206, no. 3.

  Reviews: [William Rose, John Rotherman], *Monthly Review*, June 1787, Vol. 76, pp. 497–500 (mixed); *English Review*, 1787, Vol. 9, pp. 356–361 (mixed).

- [Swediaur, François Xavier (1748–1824)]. *Philosophical dictionary: or the opinions of modern philosophers on metaphysical, moral, and political subjects.* London, G.G. J. and J. Robinson, 1786, 4 Vol.

  Notes: criticizes Hume's view of Black inferiority in "Of National Characters".

  In *Essays Responses*: "Men, No Original Distinction in their Intellectual Abilities," complete article; from 1822 edition.

  Editions: 1822 (revised).

  Microform: The Eighteenth Century, reel 2112, no. 4 (of 1786).

  Reviews: *Critical Review*, March 1786, Vol. 61, pp. 213–214 (mixed); *Monthly Review*, January 1787, Vol. 76, p. 85 (negative); *English Review*, 1786, Vol. 7, pp. 259–260 (negative).

- Towers, Joseph (1737–1799). *An essay on the life, character, and writings, of Dr. Samuel Johnson.* London: printed for Charles Dilly, 1786, [4], 124 p.

  Notes: criticizes Smith's account of Hume's death.

  In *Life Responses*: selections; from *Tracts* (1796), Vol. 1, pp. 415–419.

  Editions: included in *Tracts on Political and Other Subjects*, London: Cadell, 1796, Vol. 1.

✑1787✑

- Anonymous. Review of John Adams's *Defense of the Constitutions of Government* (1787), *English Review*, November 1787, Vol. 10, pp. 300–329.
  Notes: p. 329 contains a brief anecdote regarding Hume's favourable opinion of Benjamin Franklin.
  In *Life Responses*: included in "Miscellaneous Hume Anecdotes."
- Adams, John (1735–1826). *A Defence of the Constitutions of Government of the United States of America, against the attack of M. Turgot in his letter to Dr. Price, dated the twenty-second day of March, 1778*. London: Printed for C. Dilly, 1787–1788, 3 v.
  Notes: Letter 54 titled "Locke, Milton, and Hume" criticizes Hume's "Idea of a Perfect Commonwealth."
  In *American Responses*: selection from Vol. 1, pp. 369–71.
  Facsimiles: 1971 (Da Capo Press of 1787); 1979 (Scientia Verlag of 1797).
  Reviews: *English Review*, November 1787, Vol. 10, pp. 300–329.
- Millar, John (1735–1801). *An historical view of the English government: from the settlement of the Saxons in Britain to the accession of the House of Stewart*, London: Printed for A. Strahan, and T. Cadell, and J. Murray, 1787, vii, [9], 565, [19] p.
  Notes: criticizes Hume's Tory view of the Witenagemot and Elizabeth's tyranny.
  In *History Responses*: selections from 2.11; from 1803 edition.
  Editions: 1789, 1790, 1803.
  Microform: The Eighteenth Century, reel 3095, no. 03 (of 1789), reel 2945, no. 01 (of 1790).
  Reviews: *Critical Review*, May 1787, Vol. 63, pp. 369–377, July, Vol. 64, pp. 49–57 (positive); *English Review*, 1787, Vol. 10, pp. 211–223; [Samuel Rose], *Monthly Review*, Vol. 77, August 1787, pp. 106–116 (positive).
  Discussions: Francis Jeffrey, review of Brodie in *Edinburgh Review* (1824).
- Pinkerton, John (1758–1826). *A dissertation on the origin and progress of the Scythians or Goths. Being an introduction to the ancient and modern history of Europe. By John Pinkerton*. London: printed by John Nichols, for George Nicol, 1787, xxii, 207, [3] p.
  Notes: criticizes Hume's view of the Goths in the *History*.
  Editions: in Pinkerton's *Enquiry into the History of Scotland* (1789 and 1794).
  Microform: The Eighteenth Century, reel 152, no. 3 (of 1789), reel 10294, no. 01 (of 1794).
  Reviews: *Critical Review*, September 1787, Vol. 64, pp. 167–175 (mixed); *English Review*, 1787, Vol. 10, pp. 131–137 (negative); *Monthly Review*, October 1787, Vol. 77, pp. 318–319 (positive).
- Shaw, Duncan (1725–1795). *The history and philosophy of Judaism: or, a critical and philosophical analysis of the Jewish religion. From which is offered a vindication of its genius, origin, and authority, and of the connection with the Christian, against the objections and misrepresentations of modern infidels. By Duncan Shaw*. Edinburgh: printed for C. Elliot, 1787, 388 p.
  Notes: criticizes Hume's "Natural History of Religion."
  Microform: The Eighteenth Century, reel 6162, no. 02.
  Reviews: [Jabez Hirons], *Monthly Review*, 1789, Vol. 80, pp. 106 ff.
- Whitaker, John (1735–1808). *Mary Queen of Scots vindicated. By John Whitaker, ...* London: printed for J. Murray, 1787, 3 v.
  Notes: criticizes Hume's view of Mary Queen of Scots' guilt.
  In *History Responses*: selections from Preface, 1.5.4, 1.6.3, 1.7.7, 2.6.7; from 1790 edition.
  Editions: 1789, 1790, 1803; no further editions.

Microform: The Eighteenth Century, reel 2358, no. 3 (of 1789), reel 1700, no. 5 (of 1790).

Reviews: [James Anderson], *Monthly Review*, December 1787, Vol. 77 pp. 472–478, January 1788, Vol. 78, pp. 1–15 (positive); *English Review*, 1787, Vol. 10, pp. 100–111; *European Magazine and London Review*, 1787, Vol. 12 pp. 373–378, 457–460; *Critical Review*, February 1788, Vol. 65, pp. 81–87 (negative).

໑1788໑

- Anonymous (pseud., "Acosto"). Reprint of letter to a London newspaper, *Scots Magazine*, 1788, Vol. 50, pp. 211–212.

  Notes: Negative response to recent printing of Hume's February 10, 1773 letter to John Pringle regarding the Young Pretender, Charles Edward. Acosto argues that the letter unfairly attacks the Pretender's character.

- Anonymous. *An address to the deists: or an inquiry into the character of the author of the Book of Revelation. With an appendix, in which the argument of Mr. Hume against the credibility of miracles is considered and refuted. By one who thinks with that eminent judge, Sir Matthew Hale, that religion is the first concern of man.* London: printed for J. F. and C. Rivington, 1788, iv, 123, [1] p.

  Notes: criticizes Hume's "Of Miracles."

  Editions: 1792; no further editions.

  Microform: The Eighteenth Century, reel 2979, no. 2 (of 1792).

  Reviews: *Critical Review*, June 1788, Vol. 65, pp. 534–536 (positive); *Monthly Review*, September 1788, Vol. 79, p. 285 (mixed); *Monthly Review*, August 1789, Vol. 81, p. 185 (positive).

- [Hamilton, Alexander (1757–1804) and others]. *The federalist: a collection of essays, written in favour of the new Constitution, as agreed upon by the Federal convention, September 17, 1787, in two volumes.* New-York: Printed and sold by J. and A. M'Lean, 1788, 2 v.

  Notes: 85 essays published under the pseudonym "Publius" supporting the newly proposed U.S. Constitution. Most of the essays first appeared in newspapers in 1787–1788, and were then published in a single collection. Current scholarship ascribes authorship as follows: Alexander Hamilton numbers 1, 6–9, 11–13, 15–17, 21–36, 59–61, and 65–85; James Madison numbers 10, 14, 18–20, 37–58, and 62–63; and John Jay numbers 2–5 and 64. Hume's *Essays Moral, Political and Literary* are drawn on and silently quoted in many of these essays.

  Editions: several editions, many recent ones under the title *Federalist Papers*.

  Microform: 19th-century legal treatises, no. 51659–51665 (of 1826); Library of American civilization, LAC 10035 (of 1857).

- [Knox, Vicesimus (1752–1821)]. *Winter evenings: or lucubrations on life and letters. In three volumes.* London: printed for Charles Dilly, 1788, 3 v.

  Notes: attacks Hume's dull writing style and defends Horne's use of ridicule.

  In *Life Responses*: selections from "On Dull Style" and "Of the Folly"; from 1788 edition.

  Editions: 1788 (second edition), 1790, 1795, 1805, 1825; also in *Works*, 1824 (Vol. 2 and 3); no further editions.

  Facsimiles: 1972 (Garland of 1779).

  Microform: The Eighteenth Century, reel 2393, no. 3 (of 1788).

  Reviews: *Critical Review*, September 1788, Vol. 66, pp. 184–187 (positive); [Andrew Becket], *Monthly Review*, October 1788, Vol. 79, pp. 336–342 (positive); *Analytical Review*, 1788, Vol. 1, pp. 92–96, Vol. 2, pp. 88–92 (negative).

- Norvell, George (fl. 1800). Letter to Alexander Stenhouse, March 1, 1788.

Manuscript location: King's College Cambidge, JMK/PP/87/53.

Notes: stories about Hume based on personal acquaintance; similar to his "Anecdotes of David Hume" in *Edinburgh Magazine* (1802).

In *Life Responses*: complete letter, newly transcribed.

- [Pratt, Samuel Jackson (1749–1814)]. *Curious particulars and genuine anecdotes respecting the late Lord Chesterfield and David Hume, Esq. With a parallel between these celebrated personages.* ... *To which is added, a short vindication of the Christian cause and character, occasioned by a recent reflection thrown upon them, by the author of the Apology for the life and writings of David Hume. By a friend to religious and civil liberty.* London: printed for G. Kearsley, 1788, vii, [1], 107, [1] p.

  Notes: includes selections from Pratt's *Apology* (1777) and *Supplement* (1777).

  In *Life Responses*: complete; from 1777 edition.

  Editions: no further editions.

  Microform: The Eighteenth Century, reel 5500, no. 4.

  Reviews: *Critical Review*, October 1788, Vol. 66, p. 344 (negative); [Andrew Becket], *Monthly Review*, December 1788, Vol. 79, p. 558 (negative); *Analytical Review*, 1789, Vol. 3, p. 226 (negative).

- Priestley, Joseph (1733–1804). *Lectures on history, and general policy; to which is prefixed, An essay on a course of liberal education for civil and active life.* Birmingham, J. Johnson, 1788, xxxii, 548 p.

  Notes: lectures on the study of history discusses Hume's view of modern historians.

  In *History Responses*: relevant quotation included in editor's introduction to Priestley's *Rudiments* (1768).

  Editions: 1788 (Dublin), 1791, 1793, 1803, 1826, 1840, 1817–32 *Works* Vol. 24.

  Microform: The Eighteenth Century, reel 23, no. 12 (of 1788 Dublin) reel 1305, no. 05 (of 1793).

  Reviews: *English Review*, April 1790, Vol. 15, pp. 241–253 (positive); *Analytical Review*, 1788, Vol. 1, pp. 24–37, 294–299, Vol. 2, pp. 311–316 (positive); *Monthly Review*, January 1789, Vol. 80, pp. 1–8 (positive).

- Reid, Thomas (1710–1796). *Essays on the active powers of man.* Edinburgh: J. Bell, 1788, vii, 493 p.

  Notes: criticizes Hume's view of causality, determinism, artificial justice and moral sentiment.

  In *Metaphysical Responses*: selectios from Essays 1.4 and 4.9; from 1788 edition.

  In *Moral Responses*: Essay 5, Chapters 4–7, complete chapters; from 1788 edition.

  Editions: 1789, 1818, also included several collections of Reid's *Works*; for a complete listing see *Common Sense Bibliography*.

  Facsimiles: 1977 (Garland Publishing, of 1788), 1986 (Lincoln-Rembrandt, of 1788).

  Microform: British culture series, Group VIII; no. 52; Eighteenth-century sources for the study of English literature, reel 40 (of 1788 edition); Early American imprints, Second series, no. 45487 (of 1818 edition).

  Reviews: *Analytical Review*, Vol. 1, 1778, pp. 145–153, 521–529; Vol. 2, pp. 265–270, 549–558 (positive); *Critical Review*, Vol. 66, October 1788 pp. 267–274; December pp. 433–439 (positive); *English Review*, Vol. 11, pp. 401–409 (mixed); *Monthly Review*, Vol. 1, January 1790, pp. 67–76, [Lockhart Muirhead], February pp. 168–175 (positive). All of these reviews are contained in *Common Sense* responses.

  Discussions: Alexander Crombie, *An essay on philosophical necessity* (1793).

❧1789❧

- Adams, John (1750?–1814). *Elegant anecdotes, and bons-mots, of the greatest princes, politicians, philosophers, orators, and wits of modern times; ... calculated to inspire the minds of youth with noble, virtuous, generous, and liberal sentiments. By the Rev. John Adams, A.M.*, London, G. Kearsley, 1789, 359 p.

  Notes: includes a brief anecdote about Hume's weight.

  In *Life Responses*: story included in "Miscellaneous Hume Anecdotes"; from 1794 edition, p. 393.

  Editions: 1790, 1794; no further editions.

  Microform: The Eighteenth Century, reel 766, no. 3 (of 1794 edition).

  Reviews: *Critical Review*, June 1789, Vol. 67, p. 559 (mixed); *Monthly Review*, November 1789, Vol. 81, p. 466.

- [Belsham, William (1752–1827)]. *Essays, philosophical, historical, and literary.* London: Printed for C. Dilly, 1789–1791, 2 v.

  Notes: Essays 10 and 11 critique Hume's view that virtue is easy and discuss Hume's view of utility; Essay 3 criticizes Hume's Tory view of royal prerogative and Elizabeth's tyrannical reign. Short discussions of Hume appear in other Essays.

  In *Moral Responses*: Essays 10 and 11 from Volume 1 of 1799, complete essays (originally essay 7 of Vol. 1, 1789; and essays 34 and 35 of Vol. 2, 1791).

  In *History Responses*: In *History Responses*: selections from Essay 3; from 1799 edition (Essay 18 in that edition).

  Editions: 1799; no further editions.

  Facsimiles: 1971 (Garland 1799),

  Microform: The Eighteenth Century, reel 2584, no. 2 (of 1789); reel 3821, no. 01 (of 1799).

  Reviews of 1789 volume: *Analytical Review*, 1789, Vol. 6, pp. 169–175 (positive); *Critical Review*, December 1789, Vol. 68, pp. 459–469 (positive); *English Review*, November 1789, Vol. 14, pp. 365–377 (positive); *European Magazine and London Review*, November 1789, Vol. 16, p. 336 (negative); [Gilbert Stuart], *Monthly Review*, May 1790, Vol. 2, pp. 1–7 (mixed).

  Reviews of 1791 volume: *Analytical Review*, August 1791, Vol. 11, pp. 18–26 (positive); *Critical Review*, December 1791, Vol. 3, pp. 361–392 (positive); *European Magazine and London Review*, January 1792, Vol. 21, pp. 25–28, March, pp. 201–203, April, 281–283; Vol. 22, July, pp. 33–35 (mixed); [William Enfield], *Monthly Review*, April 1792, Vol. 7, pp. 428–435 (mixed).

- Bentham, Jeremy (1748–1832). *An introduction to the principles of morals and legislation. Printed in the year 1780, and now first published. By Jeremy Bentham.* London: printed for T. Payne, and Son, 1789, [4], 9, [1], cccxxxv, [33] p.

  Notes: theory of utility influenced by Book 3 of Hume's *Treatise*. Bentham's comments on moral sense theories in Chapter 2.17 may refer to Hume, although Hume is not mentioned by name.

  Editions: in *Works* 1838, Vol. 1; several recent editions.

  Microform: The Eighteenth Century, reel 4883, no. 10; Goldsmiths'-Kress Library of Economic Literature, reel 1394, no. 13759.

  Reviews: *Analytical Review*, 1789, Vol. 5, pp. 306–310 (mixed); *Critical Review*, November 1789, Vol. 68, pp. 333–340 (mixed).

- Cooper, Thomas (1759–1839). *Tracts, ethical, theological, and political,* London: W. Eyres for J. Johnson, 1789, 526 p.

  Notes: collection of five essays; the first on moral obligation criticizes Hume's view of utility.

In *Moral Responses*: Essay 1, Section 9; from 1789 edition.

Editions: no further editions.

Facsimiles: 2000 (Thoemmes Press of 1789).

Microform: The Eighteenth Century, reel 565, no. 6.

Reviews: [Christopher Lake Moody], *Monthly Review*, July 1791, Vol. 5, pp. 294–300, August pp. 361–365 (mixed); *Analytical Review*, 1790, Vol. 6, pp. 61–66 (negative).

- Gisborne, Thomas (1758–1846). *The principles of moral philosophy investigated, and briefly applied to the Constitution of civil society; together with remarks on the principle assumed by Mr. Paley as the basis of all moral conclusions, and on other positions of the same author.* London, Printed by T. Bensley, for B. White, 1789, xii, 182 p.

Notes: criticizes Hume's and Paley's views of utility.

In *Moral Responses*: Chapter 2, selections; from 1798 edition.

Editions: 1790 (second edition), 1795 (third edition), 1798 (fourth edition), no further editions.

Microform: Goldsmiths'-Kress library of economic literature, no. 16205 (of 1795); Goldsmiths'-Kress library of economic literature, no. 17228 (of 1798).

Reviews: *Analytical Review*, 1789, Vol. 4, p. 313 ff.; [William Enfield], *Monthly Review*, Vol. 2, p. 85 ff.

Discussions: Daniel Dewar, *Elements of Moral Philosophy* (1826); William Blakey, *The History of Moral Science* (1833).

❧1790❧

- Burke, Edmund (1729–1797). *Reflections on the revolution in France*, London: J. Dodsley, 1790, iv, 356 p.

Notes: includes brief anecdote of Hume reporting Rousseau's view of composition.

In *Life Responses*: story included in "Miscellaneous Hume Anecdotes."

Editions: several editions.

Reviews: *Analytical Review*, Vol. 8, 295–307, 408–414; *Critical Review*, November 1790, Vol. 70, pp. 517–530 (mixed); *European Magazine and London Review*, Vol. 19, pp. 117–120 (positive); [Thomas Pearne], *Monthly Review*, November 1790, Vol. 3, pp. 313–326, December, pp. 438–465 (mixed).

- Graham, Catharine Macaulay (1731–1791). *Letters on education. With observations on religious and metaphysical subjects. By Catharine Macaulay Graham.* London: printed for C. Dilly, 1790, [4], xv, [1], 507.

Notes: material adapted from Macaulay's *A treatise on the immutability of moral truth* (1783); critiques Hume's view of utility.

In *Moral Responses*: Part 1, Letter 20, selections; from 1790 edition.

Editions: no further editions.

Facsimiles: 1974 (Garland, of 1790).

- Moore, Charles (1743–1811). *A full inquiry into the subject of suicide. To which are added … two treatises on duelling and gaming. In two volumes. By Charles Moore.* London: printed for J. F. and C. Rivington, 1790, 2 v.

Notes: includes criticisms of Hume's essay on suicide, primarily in Volume 2.6.

Editions: no further editions.

Facsimiles: 1998 (Thoemmes Press, of 1790).

Microform: The Eighteenth Century, reel 3997, no. 03; Library of English literature, LEL 20857.

Reviews: *Analytical Review*, 1789, Vol. 4, pp. 558–559 (review of 1788 proposal); 1790, Vol. 6, pp. 402–413, Vol. 8, pp. 517–524 (positive); *Monthly Review*, April 1791, Vol. 4, pp. 394–403, May, pp. 18–32 (positive).

- Priestley, Joseph (1733–1804). *Familiar letters, addressed to the inhabitants of*

Birmingham, in refutation of several charges, advanced against the Dissenters.
Birmingham: printed by J. Thompson, London, [1790].
Notes: praises Hume's account of religious dissenters in the *History*.
In *History Responses*: selections; from *Theological and Miscellaneous Works*
(1817–1832), Vol. 19.
Editions: 1770, *Works* (1817–1832).

• Wesley, John (1703–1791). "The Deceitfulness of the Human Heart" Halifax, April 21,
1790.
Notes: includes a brief criticism of Smith's account of Hume's death.
In *Life Responses*: selections; from Wesley's *Sermons*, New York, Carlton and
Lanahan, n.d., Vol. 2; in "Miscellaneous Comments on Adam Smith's 'Letter'".
Editions: in several editions of Wesley's *Sermons*.

❧1791❧

• Anderson, Walter (1723–1800). *The philosophy of ancient Greece investigated, in its
origin and progress, to the æras of its greatest celebrity, in the Ionian, Italic, and
Athenian schools: ... By Walter Anderson.* Edinburgh: printed by Smellie. Sold in
London, by C. Dilly, 1791, [2], xiv, 588 p.
Notes: Part 8.3 criticizes Hume's view of the design argument.
Editions: no further editions.
Microform: The Eighteenth Century, reel 7352, no. 02.
Reviews: *Analytical Review*, 1792, Vol. 12, pp. 492–497 (mixed); *Monthly Review*,
December 1791, Vol. 6, pp. 361–372 (mixed).

• Boswell, James (1740–1795). *The life of Samuel Johnson, LL.D. comprehending an
account of his studies and numerous works, ... In two volumes. By James Boswell,
Esq.* London: printed by Henry Baldwin, for Charles Dilly, 1791, 2 v.
Notes: famous biography of Johnson includes stories about Hume based on Boswell's
personal acquaintance with him.
In *Life Responses*: selections; from *Boswell's life of Johnson*, New York: Oxford
University Press, 1922, 2 v., based on 1799 third edition.
Editions: several editions.
Microform: The Eighteenth Century, reel 1030, no. 1 (of 1792), reel 1027, no. 1 (of
1799).
Reviews: *Analytical Review*, 1791, Vol. 10, pp. 241–250, 481–489, Vol. 11, pp.
361–357 (positive); *European Magazine and London Review*, 1791, Vol. 20, pp.
107–110, 189–193, 371–384; Vol. 21, pp. 29–33, 195–198, 287–290, 357–359;
English Review, 1791, Vol. 18, pp. 1–8, 137–140; *Monthly Review*, January
1792, Vol. 7, pp. 1–9, February, pp. 189–198, May, Vol. 8, pp. 71–82 (positive).

• Disraeli, Isaac (1766–1848). *Curiosities of Literature*, London, J. Murray, 1791–1793, 2 vol.
Notes: collection of anecdotes of historical figures from Socrates to the 17th century;
includes a brief story about Hume's composition of the *History*.
In *Life Responses*: story included in "Miscellaneous Hume Anecdotes"; from Part 2,
"True Sources of Secret History" in *Curiosities of Literature*, New York, World
Publishing House, 1875, p. 367.
Editions: several editions.
Reviews: *Monthly Review*, March 1792, Vol. 7, pp. 270–279; 1793 Vol. 12, October,
pp. 177–183, November, pp. 276–285 (positive).

• Garden, Francis, Lord Gardenstone (1721–1793). *Miscellanies in Prose and Verse*,
Edinburgh: [Printed by J. Robertson], 1791, [3]–7, 240 p.
Notes: criticizes Hume's limited historical research and Tory ideology.
In *History Responses*: selections; from *The New-York Magazine, or Literary*

Repository, New Series, Vol. II (1797), pp. 295–299.
Editions: 1792 (second edition); no further editions.
Microform: The Eighteenth Century, reel 2878, no. 8. (1792 edition).

● Pistorius, Hermann Andreas (1730–1798). *David Hartleys Betrachtungen über den Menschen.* Rostock: J.C. Koppe, 1772–1773, 2 v.
Translation: *Observations on man ... translated from the German of the Rev. Herman Andrew Pistorius.* London: printed for J. Johnson, 1791, 2 vol.
Notes: 1791 English translation from Pistorius's 1772 German translation of Hartley's *Observations* (1748). In a discussion on page 465, Pistorius defends Hume's critique of the theistic proofs.
Editions: no further editions.
Microform: Bibliothek der deutschen Literatur, fiche 9271–9273 (of 1772 German); The Eighteenth Century, reel 257, no. 1 (of 1791 English).
Reviews: *Analytical Review*, 1791, Vol. 9, pp. 361–376 (positive).

● [Thomas, Daniel (b. 1748)]. *An answer, on their own principles to direct and consequential atheists.* London: printed for J. Ridgway, 1791, xvi, 123 p.
Notes: includes a response to Hume's scepticism and harshly attacks Beattie.
Editions: 1792; no further editions.
Reviews: *Analytical Review*, 1792, Vol. 14, p. 194.

☙1792❧

● Anonymous. "Objection Against Miracles Answered," *European Magazine and London Review*, 1792, Vol. 21, pp. 360–362.
Notes: criticism of "Of Miracles" without mentioning Hume by name.

● Anonymous. *Select parts of the introduction to Doctor Gregory's Philosophical and literary essays, methodically arranged, and illustrated with remarks, by an annotator.* London: printed for J. Johnson, 1792, xii, 119, [1] p.
Notes: attacks Gregory's criticism of Hume's determinism.
Reviews: *Analytical Review*, February 1793, Vol. 15, pp. 129–132 (positive); *Critical Review*, 1797, Vol. 19, p. 223 (negative).

● Burdy, Samuel (1760–1820). *The life of the late Rev. Philip Skelton: with some curious anecdotes*, Dublin: Printed for the author and sold by W. Jones, 1792 [14], iii, 240 p.
Notes: includes brief anecdote of Hume proofing Skelton's book.
In *Life Responses*: story included in "Miscellaneous Hume Anecdotes"; from 1824 edition, Vol. 2, p. 351.
Editions: 1824 in Skelton's *Works*; no further editions.

● Carr, William Windle. *Poems on various subjects. By the Rev. William Windle Carr.* London: printed for the author, and sold by Messrs. Edwards, 1791, [8], ii, [6], 208 p.
Notes: collection of odes, elegies, and epistles. Epistle two titled *Infidelity* attacks Voltaire, Rousseau, and Hume in verse.
Editions: no further editions.
Microform: The Eighteenth Century, reel 3250, no. 07.
Reviews: *Analytical Review*, 1792, Vol. 14, pp. 182–184 (mixed); *English Review*, 1792, Vol. 20, p. 204 ff. (negative); *Monthly Review*, April 1792, Vol. 7, pp. 449–451 (mixed).

● Ferguson, Adam (1723–1816). *Principles of moral and political science; being chiefly a retrospect of lectures delivered in the college of Edinburgh. By Adam Ferguson.* Edinburgh: printed for A. Strahan and T. Cadell, London; and W. Creech, Edinburgh, 1792, 2 v.
Notes: brief discussion of Hume's views of external objects (Vol. 1, p. 76) and utility

(Vol. 2, p. 122).

Facsimiles: 1978 (Garland of 1792).

Microform: the Eighteenth Century, reel 3825, no. 03.

Reviews: *English Review*, 1793, Vol. 21, pp. 327–332, 441–456 (positive); *Monthly Review*, June 1793, Vol. 9, pp. 164–169, August, pp. 366–375 (positive).

- Gregory, James (1753–1821). *Philosophical and literary essays. By Dr Gregory, of Edinburgh*. Edinburgh: sold by T. Cadell, London, and W. Creech, Edinburgh, 1792, 2 v. (cccxxxi, 704 p.).

Notes: major critique of Hume's view of determinism.

In *Metaphysical Responses*: selections from sections 1-4, 6, 9; from 1792 edition.

Editions: no further editions.

Facsimiles: 2001 (Thoemmes Press of 1792).

Microform: The Eighteenth Century, reel 4394, no. 03.

Reviews: *Analytical Review*, July 1792, Vol. 13, pp. 241–248, August, 489–497 (neutral); *Critical Review*, August 1793, Vol. 8, pp. 377–386, February 1794, Vol. 10, pp. 199–212 (mixed); [William Enfield], *Monthly Review*, December 1792, Vol. 9, pp. 361–373 (mixed).

Discussions: *Select Parts* (1792); Alexander Crombie, *Essay* (1793); John Allen, *Illustrations* (1795); George Gleig, *Encyclopædia Britannica* (1797); Alexander Crombie, *Letters* (1819).

- Lee, Charles, (1731–1782). *Memoirs of the life of the late Charles Lee, Esq. ... to which are added his political and military essays also, letters to, and from many distinguished characters, both in Europe and America*. London: printed for J. S. Jordan, 1792, xii, 439, [5] p.

Notes: Includes "An epistle to David Hume Esq."

Editions: 1792 (Dublin), 1792 (New York), 1797 (London second edition, under title *Anecdotes*).

Microform: The Eighteenth Century, reel 1303, no. 16 (of Dublin 1792); reel 4012, no. 05 (of London 1792).

Reviews: *Monthly Review*, August 1792, Vol. 8, pp. 469–471 (positive).

- Pye, Henry James (1745–1813). *A commentary illustrating the Poetic of Aristotle, by examples taken chiefly from the modern poets. To which is prefixed, a new and corrected edition of the translation of the Poetic. By Henry James Pye, Esq*. London: printed for John Stockdale, 1792, xvi, 564, [10] p.

Notes: Chapter six, Note 1 criticizes Hume's account of pleasurable terror in "Of Tragedy."

Editions: no further editions.

Facsimiles: 1971 (Garland of 1792).

Microform: The Eighteenth Century, reel 4294, no. 01.

Reviews: *European Magazine and London Review*, 1795, Vol. 27 pp. 97–98 (positive); *English Review*, 1793, Vol. 21, pp. 285–296 (positive); *Monthly Review*, October 1795, Vol. 18, pp. 121–133 (positive).

- Stewart, Dugald (1753–1828). *Elements of the philosophy of the human mind. By Dugald Stewart*. London: printed for A. Strahan, and T. Cadell; and W. Creech, Edinburgh, 1792, 569 p.

Notes: criticizes Hume's account of the association of ideas.

Editions: several editions and in *Works*; see *Common Sense Bibliography* for a complete list.

Facsimiles: 1971 (Garland Publishing of 1792).

Reviews: *Analytical Review*, January 1793, Vol. 15, pp. 17–26, February 131–140 (positive); *Critical Review*, November 1793, Vol. 9, p. 314–319, January 1794, Vol.

10, pp. 12–19; *English Review*, 1792, Vol. 20, pp. 285–293, 328–335 (positive); *European Magazine and London Review*, November 1992, Vol. 22, pp. 361–365, December, pp. 441–445; *Monthly Review*, January 1793, Vol. 10, pp. 59–64, February 1793, pp. 203–210, April pp. 366–373 (mixed); *Annual Register for 1793*, pp. 153–170 (all reviews included in *Common Sense Responses*).

❧1793❧

- Anonymous. "David Hume," *Encyclopædia; or, a Dictionary of Arts, Sciences, and Miscellaneous Literature*. Philadelphia, 1793, Vol. 8, pp. 708–710.
  Notes: short biography of Hume based on "My Own Life."
  In *American Responses*: complete article.
- Beddoes, Thomas (1760–1808). *Observations on the nature of demonstrative evidence, with an explanation of certain difficulties occurring in the elements of geometry, and reflections on language*. London, J. Johnson, 1793, xi, 172 p.
  Notes: passing discussions of Hume's philosophy.
  Editions: no further editions.
  Facsimiles: 1990 (Thoemmes Press of 1793).
- Crombie, Alexander (1762–1840). *An essay on philosophical necessity. By Alexander Crombie, A.M.* London, printed for J. Johnson, 1793, [2], viii, 508 p.
  Notes: detailed critique of theories of free will by Richard Price, Thomas Reid (*Essays on the Active Powers*, 1788), and James Gregory (*Philosophical and Literary Essays*, 1792). Crombie defends Hume's position, particularly against Gregory's criticism of Hume.
  In *Metaphysical Responses*: selections from 2.13, and 3.1; from 1793 edition.
  Editions: no further editions.
  Facsimiles: 1989 (Thoemmes Press).
  Microform: The Eighteenth Century, reel 259, no. 10; Eighteenth century sources for the study of English literature and culture, reel no. 978.
  Reviews: *Analytical Review*, 1794, Vol. 18 pp. 20–30 (positive); *Critical Review*, September 1795, Vol. 15, pp. 95–99 (mixed); [William Enfield], *Monthly Review*, October 1794, Vol. 15 pp. 128–136 (positive).
  Discussions: Alexander Crombie *Letters* (1819).
- [Currie, James (pseud. Jasper Wilson) (1756–1805)]. *A letter, commercial and political, addressed to the Right Hon. William Pitt....* Robinson, 1793, 86 p.
  Notes: critiques "Of Public Credit."
  In *Essays Responses*: selections included in "Miscellaneous Comments on Hume's Essays," from 1793 third edition, pp. 6, 30.
  Editions: several 1793 editions.
  Microform: The Eighteenth Century, reel 834, no. 19 (of 1793 third edition); Goldsmiths'-Kress Library of Economic Literature, reel 1518, no. 15522 (of 1793 third edition).
  Reviews: *Analytical Review*, 1793, Vol. 26, pp. 321–324 (positive); *Monthly Review*, October 1793, Vol. 12, pp. 187–194 (positive).
- Godwin, William (1756–1836). *Enquiry concerning political justice, and its influence on general virtue and happiness*. London, Printed for G.G.J. and J. Robinson, 1793, 2 Vol., 895 p.
  Notes: discusses "Of National Characters" and criticizes Hume's view of luxury in "Of Refinement in the Arts".
  In *Essays Responses*: Book 1 Chapter 6, Book 8 Chapter 7, complete chapters; from 1842 edition.
  Editions: several editions.

Microform: The Eighteenth Century, reel 3863, no. 04 (1796 of London), reel 4807, no. 01 (of Philadelphia 1796).

Reviews: *Analytical Review*, 1793, Vol. 26, pp. 121–130, 388–404 (positive); *Critical Review*, April 1793, Vol. 7, pp. 361–372; *English Review*, 1793, Vol. 28, pp. 315–319, 437–443, 501–509 (mixed); *British Critic*, July 1793, Vol. 1, pp. 307–318; [Thomas Holcroft], *Monthly Review*, March 1793, Vol. 10, pp. 311–320, April, pp. 435–445, June, pp. 187–196 (neutral).

● [Reid, Thomas (1710–1796)]. "An Examination of Hume's Essay on Justice," in *European Magazine and London Review*, 1793, Vol. 24, pp. 422–424.

Notes: perhaps an unauthorized publication of a transcript of Reid's lectures taken by a student, which parallels material in *Essays on the Active Powers* (1788); the article criticizes Hume's view of justice as an artificial virtue.

In *Moral Responses*: complete essay.

● Scott, Thomas (1747–1821). *The rights of God. By Thomas Scott*. London: printed by D. Jaques, [1793], vi, 90 p.

Notes: critique of Paine's *Rights of Man* includes an attack on "Of Miracles."

Editions: in *Works* 1823; no further editions.

Microform: The Eighteenth Century, reel 1056, no. 18.

Reviews: *Analytical Review*, 1793, Vol. 15, p. 434 (mixed); *Critical Review*, July, 1793, Vol. 8, pp. 351–352 (mixed).

● Stewart, Dugald (1753–1828). *Outlines of moral philosophy. For the use of students in the University of Edinburgh*. Edinburgh: printed for William Creech. And T. Cadell. London, 1793. xiv, 302 p.

Notes: various brief discussions of Hume in connection with religion and ethics, such as Hume's account of artificial justice.

Editions: several editions and in *Works*; see *Common Sense Bibliography* for a complete list.

Facsimiles: 1976 (Garland Publishing of 1793).

Microform: The Eighteenth Century, reel 3435, no. 02 (of 1793).

Reviews: *Analytical Review*, 1796, Vol. 23, pp. 36–39 (positive); *Critical Review*, December 1795, Vol. 15, pp. 377–384; *English Review*, August 1795, Vol. 26, pp. 125–127, September, 209–212 (positive); (all reviews included in *Common Sense Responses*).

❧1794❧

● Anonymous. "Anecdote of David Hume," *European Magazine and London Review*, 1794, Vol. 25, p. 431.

Notes: brief anecdote about Hume's knowledge of British history.

In *Life Responses*: story included in "Miscellaneous Hume Anecdotes."

● Anonymous (pseud. "J.C."). "Observations concerning the philosophy of the human mind," in *European Magazine and London Review*, 1794, Vol. 26, 23–24, 117–120.

Notes: sketch of modern British epistemology from Locke to Reid discusses Hume.

● Beattie, James Hay (1768–1790). *Essays and fragments in prose and verse. By James Hay Beattie. To which is prefixed an account of the author's life and character*. Edinburgh, printed by J. Moir, 1794. vii, 340 p.

Notes: "The Modern Tippling Philosophers" and Dialogue between "Socrates, Mercury, and a Modern Philosopher" satirize Hume's philosophy.

In *Life Responses*: above two items complete; from 1794 edition.

Editions (all of the following exclude the Dialogue): in Vol. 2 of Beattie's *Minstrel* 1799, 1803, 1807, Beattie's *Works* 1809.

Microform: The Eighteenth Century, reel 1122, no. 3;

Reviews: *Critical Review*, 1800, Vol. 28, pp. 170–177 (positive); [Ollyett Woodhouse], *Monthly Review*, September 1800, Vol. 33, pp. 61–66 (mixed); *New London Review*, 1800, Vol. 3, p. 471 (positive).

● Hurd, Richard (1720–1808). *A discourse, by way of general preface to the quarto edition of Bishop Warburton's works, containing some account of the life, writings and character of the author.* London, J. Nichols, 1794, vii, 150.

Notes: biography of Warburton intended to be part of the 1788 edition of Warburton's *Works.* The biography discusses the authorship of Warburton's *Remarks* on Hume's "Natural History of Religion."

In *Religion Responses*: relevant quotations in editor's introduction to Warburton's *Remarks* (1757).

Editions: Warburton's *Works* 1811.

Microform: The Eighteenth Century, reel 1359, no. 21.

Reviews: *Analytical Review*, 1795, Vol. 21, pp. 408–414, 597–606; *Critical Review*, 1795, Vol. 14, 204–210, 403–408, *Critical Review*, Vol. 15, 39–47 (mixed); *Monthly Review*, March 1795, Vol. 16, pp. 322–329 (mixed).

● Hutton, James (1726–1797). *An investigation of the principles of knowledge and of the progress of reason, from sense to science and philosophy.* Edinburgh: A. Strahan, and T. Cadell, 1794, 3 v.

Notes: discusses Hume's account of causality.

Editions: no further editions.

Facsimiles: 1999 (Thoemmes Press of 1794).

● Paley, William (1743–1805). *A view of the evidences of Christianity in three parts. ... By William Paley.* London: printed for R. Faulder, 1794, 3 v.

Notes: criticizes Hume's "Of Miracles."

In *Religion Responses*: "Preparatory Considerations" and 1.2.2; from fifth edition, London: R Faulder, 1796, Vol. 1, pp. 1–15, 369–383.

Editions: various editions and in *Works.*

Microform: The Eighteenth Century, reel 2708, no. 3 (of second edition of 1794), reel 2713, no. 10 (of 1795), reel 2407, no. 2 (of 1794 Dublin).

Reviews: *Analytical Review*, 1795, Vol. 20, pp. 185–196; *European Magazine and London Review*, May 1795, Vol. 27, pp. 313–318, June 384–390; *Critical Review*, August 1795, Vol. 14, pp. 371–380; [William Enfield], *Monthly Review*, August 1795, Vol. 17, pp. 404–411.

● Stewart, Dugald (1753–1828). "Account of the life and writings of Adam Smith, LL.D." in *Transactions of the Royal Society of Edinburgh*, 1794, Vol. 3, pp. 55–137.

Notes: includes a brief anecdote about Hume's composition of the *History.*

In *Life Responses*: story included in "Miscellaneous Hume Anecdotes"; from *Works of Dugald Stewart*, Edinburgh: T. Constable, 1854–1860, Vol. 10, Sect. 5.

Editions: in Stewart's *Biographical Memoirs* (1811), *Works* (1829, 1854–1860, 1877), and various editions of Smith's writings.

Microform: Goldsmiths'-Kress library of economic literature; no. 15934.

Reviews: *Edinburgh Magazine and London Review*, January 1796, Vol. 29, pp. 13–17; *English Review*, 1795, Vol. 26, pp. 91–94, ?–105, 262 ff; *Monthly Review*, January 1797, Vol. 22, p. 57.

● Sulivan, Richard Joseph (1752–1806). *A view of nature, in letters to a traveller among the Alps. With reflections on Atheistical philosophy, now exemplified in France. By Richard Joseph Sulivan.* London: printed for T. Becket, 1794, 6 v.

Notes: collection of education letters attacks "Of Miracles" in Vol. 6, p. 41 ff.

Microform: The Eighteenth Century, reel 2603, no. 3 (of 1794).

Reviews: *Analytical Review*, Vol. 19, pp. 18–35, 478–493 (positive); *Monthly*

Review, June 1794, Vol. 14, pp. 121–129, July, pp. 257–261, September, Vol. 15, pp. 43–52 (positive).

- Anonymous. *A concise state of the controversy respecting Queen Mary*. [London?, 1795?], pp. [197]–260.
  Notes: detached chapter in the British Library, London; from volume 2 of an as yet unidentified octavo work, which may be a history of Scotland. Discusses dispute between Hume and Tytler.
  Microform: The Eighteenth Century, reel 1700, no. 06.
- Anonymous. Review of 1795 edition of Hume's *History*, in *The American Monthly Review; or, Literary Journal*, Vol. 3 (1795), pp. 29–43.
  Notes: favourable review.
  In *American Responses*: complete article.
- Anonymous. Review of *The History of England, Abridged from Hume* (1795), in *Critical Review*, January 1795, Vol. 13, pp. 76–79.
  Notes: mixed, criticizing Hume but complimenting the abridgment.
  In *History Responses*: complete review.
- Allen, John (1771–1843). *Illustrations of Mr. Hume's essay concerning liberty and necessity; in answer to Dr. Gregory of Edinburgh. By a necessitarian*. London, Printed for J. Johnson, 1795, [2], 44 p.
  Notes: defends Hume's view of necessity against James Gregory's *Philosophical and Literary Essays* (1792).
  In *Metaphysical Responses*: complete pamphlet; from 1795 edition.
  Editions: no further editions.
  Reviews: *Analytical Review*, 1796, Vol. 23, pp. 35–36 (positive); [William Enfield], *Monthly Review*, May 1797, Vol. 23, pp. 10–12 (positive); *Critical Review*, 1797, Vol. 19, pp. 223–234 (negative).
  Discussions: Hamilton notes that Reid critiqued this in an unpublished letter (*Works of Thomas Reid*, p. 88).
- Bentham, Jeremy (1748–1832). *Supply without burthen; or escheat vice taxation: being a proposal for a saving in taxes by an extension of the law of escheat: ... To which is prefixed, (printed in 1793, and now first published,) A protest against law taxes: ... By Jeremy Bentham*. London: printed for J. Debrett, 1795, viii, 64, 94p.
  Notes: Section 9 criticizes Hume's account of moveable property in the *History*.
  In *History Responses*: selections included in "Miscellaneous Comments on Hume's *History*"; selections from in *The Works of Jeremy Bentham*, edited by John Bowring (London: 1838–1843), Vol. 4, Vol. 2.
  Editions: in *Works* (1838–1843), Vol. 2.
- Disraeli, Isaac (1766–1848). *An Essay on the Manners and Genius of the Literary Character*, London, T. Cadell, 1795, xxiii, 226 p., Ch. 4.
  Notes: brief anecdote of Hume's reaction to his critics.
  In *Life Responses*: story included in "Miscellaneous Hume Anecdotes."
- Jones, William (1726–1800). *Memoirs of the life, studies, and writings of the Right Reverend George Horne, ... To which is added his Lordship's own collection of his thoughts on a variety of great and interesting subjects. By William Jones*. London: printed for G. G. and J. Robinson, F. and C. Rivington, T. Cadell, jun. and W. Davies; J. Cooke, Oxford; and W. Keymer, jun. Colchester, 1795, [4], 418 p.
  Notes: discusses Horne's critique of Smith and Hume.
  In *Life Responses*: selections; from *The Works of the Right Reverend George Horne*, London: Rivington, 1830.
  In *American Responses*: includes a brief anecdote from Williams's *Memoirs* as

reprinted in *The Connecticut Evangelical Magazine*, July 1800, Vol. 1, pp. 38–39.

Editions: 1799, included in Horne's *Works*, 1795, 1809, 1818, 1830, 1831, 1846, 1848, and 1853.

Microform: The Eighteenth Century, reel 1347, no. 13 (of 1795).

Reviews: [William Enfield], *Monthly Review*, July 1796, Vol. 20, pp. 241–246 (positive); *Critical Review*, November 1795, Vol. 15 pp. 241–248 (positive); *British Critic*, 1796, Vol. 7, pp. 256–261 (positive); *Analytical Review*, 1795, Vol. 22, pp. 466–471 (mixed).

● Malkin, Benjamin Heath (1769–1842). *Essays on subjects connected with civilization. By Benjamin Heath Malkin*. London: printed by E. Hodson, for C. Dilly, 1795, [4], ii, [2], 293, [1] p.

Notes: criticizes Hume's "Of Miracles."

Microform: The Eighteenth Century, reel 363, no. 14.

Reviews: *Analytical Review*, 1795, Vol. 22, pp. 545–552 (positive); *English Review*, 1795, Vol. 26, pp. 39–42 (negative); *Monthly Review*, February 1796, Vol. 19, pp. 166–175, April, pp. 379–390, June, Vol. 20, pp. 172–178 (mixed).

ᥬ1796ᥭ

● Anonymous (pseud. "H."). "Remarks upon Hume's Essay on Miracles; more especially upon the Arguments Advanced in the first Part of this Essay," *The Theological Magazine*, 1796, Vol. 2, pp. 42–54.

Notes: criticism of Hume's "Of Miracles."

In *American Responses*: complete article.

● Disraeli, Isaac (1766–1848). *Miscellanies; or, literary recreations. By I. D'Israeli*. London: printed for T. Cadell and W. Davies, 1796, xxiv, 432, [i.e., 418], [2] p.

Notes: Collection of 21 essays on writing technique with brief references to Hume in four. Disraeli praises the simplicity of Hume's "My Own Life."

In *Life Responses*: selections; from 1796 edition.

Facsimiles: 1970 Garland (of 1796).

Microform: The Eighteenth Century, reel 10204, no. 02.

Reviews: *English Review*, 1796, Vol. 27, pp. 334–340 (positive); [William Taylor], *Monthly Review*, December 1797, Vol. 24, pp. 374–379 (positive).

● [Enfield, William (1741–1797)]. Review of *The History of England, Abridged from Hume* (1795), in *Monthly Review*, January 1796, Vol. 19, pp. 73–74.

Notes: mixed review, praising Hume but criticizing the abridgment.

In *History Responses*: complete review.

● [Enfield, William (1741–1797)]. Review of *The History of England, from the Revolution to the Commencement of the present Administration* (1795), in *Monthly Review*, January 1796, Vol. 19, pp. 74–76.

Notes: mixed review, praising Hume but criticizing the continuation.

In *History Responses*: complete review.

● Gibbon, Edward (1737–1794). *Miscellaneous works of Edward Gibbon, Esquire. With memoirs of his life and writings, composed by himself: illustrated from his letters, with occasional notes and narrative, by John Lord Sheffield. In two volumes*. London: printed for A. Strahan, and T. Cadell Jun. and W. Davies, (successors to Mr. Cadell,), 1796, 2 v.

Notes: occasional references to Hume, including his often quoted comment about "the careless inimitable beauties" in Hume's *History* and a comment in a letter stating "I hope you will not fail to visit the Stye of that fattest of Epicurus's Hogs."

Editions: 1796 (Dublin), 1796–1797 (Basil, 7 Vol.), 1814 (London, Murray, 5 vol), 1837 (London, 1 vol.).

Facsimiles: 1971 (AMS of 5 volume 1814 edition).

Microform: The Eighteenth Century, reel 1122, no. 07.

● Michell, Charles (1756–1841). *Principles of legislation.* London, printed for T. Cadell Jun. and W. Davies (successors to Mr. Cadell), 1796, 515 p.

Notes: discussion of political philosophy in two parts; criticizes Hume's view of recruiting soldiers from industry in "Of Commerce".

In *Essays Responses*: pages 113–119 from 1796 edition.

Microform: The Eighteenth Century, reel 1209, no. 05.

Reviews: [Richard Brinsley Butler Sheridan], *Monthly Review*, October 1796, Vol. 21, pp. 121–131, December, pp. 381–393 (positive); *Analytical Review*, 1796, Vol. 23, pp. 531–535 (mixed).

≈1797≈

● Gillies, John (1747–1836). *Aristotle's Ethics and Politics, comprising his practical philosophy, translated from the Greek. Illustrated by introductions and notes; the critical history of his life; and a new analysis of his speculative works; by John Gillies.* London: printed for A. Strahan; and T. Cadell jun. and W. Davies, 1797, 2 v.

Notes: Translation of Aristotle which includes notes commenting on several modern philosophers. Gillies attacks Hume's principles of association, and points out how Aristotle's notion of money differs from Hume's.

Editions: 1804.

Reviews: *Monthly Review*, April 1798, Vol. 25, pp. 383–386, May, Vol. 26, pp. 35–44, July 1798, pp. 297–306 (positive).

● [Gleig, George (1753–1840)]. *Encyclopædia Britannica; or, A dictionary of arts, sciences, and miscellaneous literature.* 3d. ed. Edinburgh, A. Bell and C. Macfarquhar, 1797, 18 v.

Notes: article on "Metaphysics" summarises and criticizes Hume's view of causal power; article on "Moral Philosophy" summarises and criticizes Hume's moral theory; article on "Miracles" criticizes "Of Miracles."

In *Metaphysical Responses*: "Metaphysics", Chap. 6, selections; from 3rd edition, Vol. 11, pp. 520–524.

In *Moral Responses*: "Moral Philosophy", selections; from 5th edition of 1817, Vol. 14, pp. 361–363.

● Hey, John, (1734–1815). *Lectures in divinity, delivered in the University of Cambridge, by John Hey.* Cambridge: printed by John Burges; and sold by W.H. Lunn, and J. Deighton, 1796–1798, 4 v.

Notes: contains a critique of "Of Miracles."

Microform: The Eighteenth Century, reel 7427, no. 04.

Reviews: *Analytical Review*, 1797, Vol. 26, pp. 268–275, Vol. 27, p. 150–155 (positive).

● Richter, Henry James (1772–1857). "On Mr. Hume's Account of the Origin of the Idea of Necessary Connection," in *Monthly Magazine, and British Register*, 1797, Vol. 4, pp. 533–536.

Notes: criticizes Hume's view of the idea of causal power.

In *Metaphysical Responses*: complete article.

● Wakefield, Gilbert, (1756–1801) and anonymous critic. Five letters in *Monthly Magazine*, 1797–1799.

Notes: five letters regarding criticisms of Hume's grammar and literary style in the *History*.

Letter 1: by Gilbert Wakefield, (June 1797, Vol. 3); criticizes the grammar and style of Hume's account of Queen Elizabeth.

Letter 2: by Gilbert Wakefield, (July 1797, Vol. 4, pp. 1–2); continues criticisms.

Letter 3: by "Atticus" (August 1797, Vol. 4, pp. 90–91); responds to Letter 1, criticizing Wakefield for "hasty and dogmatical censures" and appealing to Johnson's *Grammar* and *Dictionary*.

Letter 4: by "Atticus" (November 1797, Vol. 4. pp. 335–337); responds to Letter 2, criticizing Wakefield's comments there.

Letter 5: by Gilbert Wakefield, (May 1799, Vol. 7, pp. 265–267); criticizes the grammar and style of Hume's account of Charles II.

- Wilberforce, William (1759–1833). *A practical view of the prevailing religious system of professed Christians, in the higher and middle classes in this country, contrasted with real Christianity. By William Wilberforce.* London: printed for T. Cadell, jun. and W. Davies, (successors to Mr. Cadell), 1797, [4], 491, [19] p.

  Notes: attacks Hume and Smith for infidelity.

  In *Life Responses*: Chapter 6, selections; from 1797 edition.

  Editions: several editions.

  Microform: The Eighteenth Century, reel 10018, no. 02 (of 1797), reel 8929, no. 15 (of Dublin 1797), reel 4452, no. 06 (of 1798).

  Reviews: [William Enfield], *Monthly Review*, July 1797, Vol. 23, pp. 241–248 (negative); *Analytical Review*, 1797, Vol. 25, pp. 503–511 (negative).

❧1798❦

- Anonymous. "Account of the Life and Writings of the Author," in *The works of the late John MacLaurin*. Edinburgh, Printed for the editor, by J. Ruthven and Sons, sold by Bell & Bradfute [etc.], 1798, 2 vol.

  Notes: "Account" of MacLaurin by the anonymous editor includes a discussion of MacLaurin's *Philosopher's Opera* (Vol. 1, pp. 300–302), and the editor gives his reasons for not including it in MacLaurin's *Works*.

  Editions: no further editions.

- Bisset, Robert (1759–1805). *The life of Edmund Burke. Comprehending an impartial account of his literary and political efforts, and a sketch of the conduct and character of his most eminent associates, coadjutors, and opponents. By Robert Bisset.* London: printed and published by George Cawthorn; and sold also by Messrs. Richardson; J. Hatchard, and J. Wright, 1798, xvi, 592 p.

  Notes: biography of Burke occasionally discussing his connection with Hume, particularly their respective views of the Irish Massacre of 1641.

  In *History Responses*: selections from 1800 edition.

  Editions: Editions: 1800, 1809.

  Microform: The Eighteenth Century, reel 3595, no. 03 (of 1798).

  Reviews: *Analytical Review*, July 1798, Vol. 28, pp. 9–16 (mixed); [Thomas Wallace], *Monthly Review*, August 1798, Vol. 26, pp. 361–378, September, Vol. 27, pp. 23–38 (mixed); *Critical Review*, 1799, Vol. 25, pp. 291–298 (mixed).

- Dwight, Timothy (1752–1817). *The Nature, and Danger, of Infidel Philosophy, exhibited in Two Discourses, addressed to the candidates for the Baccalaureate, in Yale College.* New-Haven: Printed by George Bunce, 1798, 95 p.

  Notes: lists controversial philosophical views of Hume.

  Editions: 1799, 1804 (third edition).

  In *American Responses*: selection from pp. 29–32.

  Microform: Literature of theology and church history in the United States and Canada, Unit 1–12 (of 1798).

- [Malthus, Thomas (1766–1834)]. *An Essay on the principle of population, as it affects the future improvement of society, with remarks on the speculations of Mr. Godwin, M.*

Condorcet, and other writers. London: Printed for J. Johnson, 1798, v, ix, [1], 396 p.

Notes: influential work on population criticizes Hume's assessment of population increase in "Of the Populousness of Ancient Nations." The 1803 edition is retitled and expanded, and the discussion of Hume different.

In *Essays Responses*: Chapter 4 of first edition of 1798, selections; Book 1, Chapter 14 of third edition of 1806, complete chapter.

Editions: 1803, several later editions.

Facsimiles: 1986 (Verlag of 1798).

Microform: The Eighteenth Century, reel 5410, no. 6 (of 1798).

Reviews: *Analytical Review*, 1798, Vol. 28, pp. 119–125 (positive); [Thomas Wallace], *Monthly Review*, September 1798, Vol. 27, pp. 1–9; [Stephen Jones], December 1803, Vol. 42, pp. 337–357; January 1804, Vol. 43, pp. 56–70 (positive).

- Rush, Benjamin (1745–1813). *Essays, literary, moral and philosophical.* Philadelphia, Bradford, 1798, 378 p.

  Notes: "Thoughts on Common Sense" rejects the notion of common sense espoused by Hume and others and adopts Reid's view.

  In *Common Sense Responses:* complete section; from 1798 edition.

  Editions: 1806, 1988.

  Microform: The Eighteenth Century, reel 1070, no. 2 (of 1798); Early American Imprints, second series, no. 11306 (of 1798).

- Tytler, Alexander Fraser, Lord Woodhouselee (1747–1813). "Dissertation on Final Causes," in William Derham's *Physico-theology: or, a demonstration of the being and attributes of God, from His works of creation.* London: Printed for A. Strahan, Edinburgh, 1798, 2 v.

  Notes: Selections; critiques Hume's view of the design argument.

  In *Religion Responses*: Selections from *Memoirs of ... Henry Home of Kames,* Edinburgh, W. Creech, 1814, Vol. 3, Appendix 3.

  Editions: revised version included in *Memoirs of ... Henry Home* (1814).

- Vince, Samuel (1749–1821). *The credibility of Christianity vindicated, in answer to Mr. Hume's objections; in two discourses preached before the University of Cambridge. By the Rev. S. Vince.* Cambridge: printed by J. Burges; and sold by J. Deighton, and J. Nicholson; W. Wingrave, P. Emsley; W.H. Lunn; F. & C. Rivington, London, 1798, [4], 29, [1] p.

  Notes: defends New Testament account of miracles against Hume's "Of Miracles."

  Editions: 1807 (expanded); no further editions.

  In *Hume on Miracles*: selections from 1807 edition.

  Reviews: *Monthly Review,* March 1800, Vol. 31 251–254 (mixed).

- Walpole, Horace (1717–1797). *The works of Horatio Walpole.* London, G.G. and J. Robinson, 1798, 5 Vol.

  Notes: volume 2, pp. 185–220 contains the first appearance of Walpole's posthumous *Supplement* (1769), replying to Hume's "Sixteen notes on Walpole's *Historic doubts.*" Volume 4 contains a narrative and letters on the Hume-Rousseau dispute. Volume 5 contains a letter to Governor Pownall of October 23, 1783 which criticizes Hume's account of the English constitution in the *History.*

  In *History Responses*: selections from *Supplement* (1769).

  Microform: Eighteenth Century, reel 5594, no. 1.

  Reviews: *Analytical Review,* 1798, Vol. 28, pp. 622–630; *Critical Review,* 1798, Vol. 23, pp. 121–132, 248–256, Vol. 24, pp. 130–141 (positive); *New London Review,* 1799, Vol. 1, p. 113–120, 220–227, 319–326, 454–460 (positive); [Charles Burney], *Monthly Review,* July 1798, Vol. 26, pp. 323–327, September, Vol. 27, pp. 51–66, October, pp. 171–189, November, pp. 271–289.

• Willich, Anthony Florian Madinger (d. 1804). *Elements of the critical philosophy: containing a concise account of its origin and tendency*, London, printed for T.N. Longman, 1798, 3 p. l., vi, [2], 183 p., 1 l., [6], [v]–cxxxii, [2] p.

Notes: summary of Kant's philosophy with a description of Hume's impact on German philosophy; Willich translates a passage from Kant's *Prolegomena* that discusses Hume.

In *Metaphysical Responses*: selections from "Historical Introduction"; from 1798 edition.

Editions: no further editions.

Facsimiles: 1977 (Garland of 1789)

Microform: The Eighteenth Century, reel 2083, no. 2 (of 1798), reel 6721, no. 09 (of 1798 variant).

Reviews: [William Taylor], *Monthly Review*, January 1799, Vol. 28, pp. 62–69 (mixed); *Analytical Review*, 1798, Vol. 27, pp. 498–506 (mixed); *Critical Review*, 1798, Vol. 23, pp. 445–448 (positive).

❧1799❧

• Anonymous (pseud. "O."). "Parallel between Hume, Robertson and Gibbon," *The Monthly Magazine, and American Review*, Vol. 1 (May 1799), pp. 90–94.

Notes: attempts an impartial comparison.

In *American Responses*: complete article.

• Hunter, Christopher, (ca. 1746–1814). *Scepticism not separable from immorality; illustrated in the instances of Hume and Gibbon. A sermon preached in the Church of All-Saints, Northampton, ... on the 8th of May, 1799. By Christopher Hunter*. London: printed for G. Nicol; J. Sewell; Birdsall, Northampton; and Smart and Cowslade, Reading, 1799, 19, [1] p.

Notes: criticizes Hume's scepticism and religious infidelity.

Reviews: *Monthly Review*, March 1800, Vol. 31, p. 333 (mixed).

• Kett, Henry (1761–1825). *History the interpreter of prophecy, or, A view of scriptural prophecies and their accomplishment in the past and present occurrences of the world; with conjectures respecting their future completion*. Oxford, Printed for Hanwell and Parker; and J. Cooke; and sold by C. and J. Rivington [etc.] 1799, 3 v.

Notes: criticizes Hume's philosophy as it arises out of Locke.

Editions: 1799 (second edition), 1800 (third edition).

Microform: The Eighteenth Century, reel 2402, no. 2 (of 1799).

Discussions: Thomas Ludlam, *Logical Tracts* (1805?).

• Lindsay, James. *A sermon, occasioned by the death of the Rev. Joseph Towers, LL.D. delivered at Newington-Green, June 2d, 1799, by the Rev. James Lindsay, to which is added the oration, delivered at his interment, by the Rev. Thomas Jervis*. London: printed for J. Johnson, 1799, 64 p.

Notes: "Biographical Memoirs" included with this pamphlet discusses Towers's composition of the *Observations* (1778).

Reviews: *New London Review*, 1799, Vol. 2, pp. 277–278 (positive); *Monthly Review*, November 1799, Vol. 30, pp. 354–355 (positive).

• Mickle, William Julius (1735–1788). *The poetical works of William Mickle . With the life of the author*. London, Printed for C. Cooke, 1799, xxix, [30]-135 p.

Notes: contains a poem on the death of Hume.

In *Life Responses*: included in "Miscellaneous Comments on Adam Smith's Letter"; from 1806 edition.

Editions: 1806 (ed. Revend John Sim, 1764–1824).

ঌ1800ক্ষ

- Agutter, William (1758–1835). *On the difference between the deaths of the righteous and the wicked, illustrated in the instance of Dr. Samuel Johnson, and David Hume, Esq. A sermon, preached before the University of Oxford, ... On Sunday, July 23, 1786. By the Rev. William Agutter.* London: printed at the Philanthropic Reform, by J. Richardson, 1800, 18, [2] p.

  Notes: compares Hume's and Johnson's deaths.

  In *Life Responses*: selections; from 1800 edition.

  Editions: no further editions.

  Microform: The Eighteenth Century, reel 10221, no. 09.

  Reviews: [Christopher Lake Moody], *Monthly Review*, 1801, Vol. 34, p. 335 (neutral).

  Discussions: James Boswell, *Life of Samuel Johnson* (1791).

- Carlyle, Alexander (1722–1805). Recollections about Hume (c. 1800).

  See Alexander Carlyle *The autobiography of Alexander Carlyle* (1860).

  Notes: stories about Hume based on personal acquaintance.

  In *Life Responses*: selections from 1910 edition.

- Cogan, Thomas (1736–1818). *A treatise on the passions and affections of the mind, philosophical, ethical and theological. In a series of disquisitions.* London: Cadell & Davies, 1800–1813, 5 v.

  Notes: criticizes Hume's view of good and evil, pride, humility, and grief.

  In *Metaphysical Responses*: Notes F, I, N, and Q from Volume 1; from third edition, corrected, 1813.

  Facsimiles: 2004 (Thoemmes of 1800-1813).

- Hall, Robert (1764–1831). *Modern infidelity considered with respect to its influence on society: in a sermon, preached at the Baptist meeting, Cambridge. By Robert Hall, A.M.* Cambridge: printed by M. Watson, and sold by J. Deighton, and O. Gregory; by J. James, Bristol; W. Button, and T. Conder, London, 1800, [2],viii, 81,[1] p.

  Notes: criticizes Hume for undermining morality.

  In *Life Responses*: selections; from *Works*, New York, Harper, 1848, Vol. 1, pp. 21–53.

  Editions: 1800 (five additional editions), 1802, 1804, 1811, 1835, 1853; in over 30 editions of Hall's *Works*.

  Microform: The Eighteenth Century, reel 2714, no. 7 (of first edition), reel 10686, no. 06 (of 1800 third edition), reel 9350, no. 11 (of 1800 fourth edition).

  Reviews: James Mackintosh, *Monthly Review*, February 1800, Vol. 31, pp. 191–197 (positive); *Critical Review*, April 1800, Vol. 28, pp. 455–456 (negative).

- Smellie, William (1740–1795). *Literary and characteristical lives of John Gregory, M.D. Henry Home, Lord Kames. David Hume, Esq. and Adam Smith, L.L.D. To which are added A dissertation on public spirit; and three essays. By the late William Smellie, ...* Edinburgh: printed and sold by Alex. Smellie, Bell & Bradfute, J. Dickson, W. Creech, E. Balfour [10 others in Edinburgh, and 4 in London], 1800, ix, [1], 450 p.

  Notes: chapter on Hume contains biographical sketch and anecdotes.

  In *Life Responses*: selections from chapter on Hume; from 1800 edition.

  Editions: no further editions.

  Facsimiles: 1997 (Thoemmes Press of 1800).

  Microform: Eighteenth-century sources for the study of English literature, reel 18; Goldsmiths'-Kress library of economic literature, no. 17862.

  Reviews: [Alexander Hamilton], *Monthly Review*, 1800, Vol. 33, pp. 422–423 (mixed); *New London Review*, June 1800, Vol. 3, pp. 162–163 (mixed); *European Magazine*, 1800, Vol. 37, pp. 448–449 (mixed).

- Witherspoon, John (1723–1794). *The works of the Rev. John Witherspoon.* Philadelphia: Printed and Published by William W. Woodward, 1800–1801, 4 v.
  Notes: posthumously published "Lectures on Moral Philosophy," first appearing in *Works*, criticize Hume's broad account of the virtues.

&⤲1801⤳&

- Anonymous. Letter on Hume, *The Port Folio*, 1801,Vol. 1 (series 1), p. 66.
  Notes: short paragraph praising Hume's cheerful attitude.
  In *American Responses*: complete article.
- Belsham, Thomas (1750–1829). *Elements of the philosophy of the mind, and of moral philosophy.* London: Printed for J. Johnson by Taylor and Wilks, 1801, xvii, xciii, 447 p.
  Notes: Section 14 "Hume's Theory of Morals" defends Hume's view of utility.
  In *Moral Responses*: Section 14 complete, from 1801 edition, pp. 429–433.
  Reviews: *Critical Review*, February 1802, Vol. 34, pp. 143–150; [Christopher Lake Moody], *Monthly Review*, 1803, Vol. 40, p. 166 ff.
- Clarke, Thomas Brooke. *A survey of the strength and opulence of Great Britain.* London, T. Cadell, 1801, vii, 240 p.
  Notes: discusses Hume's comment in a letter to Kames that the rapid growth of the British mercantile economy will result in it being crushed by its own weight.
  Reviews: *Monthly Review*, 1801, Vol. 36, pp. 190–194 (negative).
  Microform: Goldsmiths'-Kress library of economic literature; no. 18125.
- Kirwan, Richard (1733–1812). "Remarks on some Sceptical Positions in Hume's Enquiry Concerning the Human Understanding and his Treatise of Human Nature," in *Transactions of the Royal Irish Academy*, 1801, Vol. 8, pp. 157–201.
  Notes: criticizes Hume's view of causality and "Of Miracles"; the selections contained in *Metaphysical Responses* and *Religion Responses* together comprise the complete work.
  In *Metaphysical Responses*: Sections 1–4, complete; from 1801 issue of *Transactions*.
  In *Religion Responses*: Sections 5 complete; from 1801 issue of *Transactions*.
  In *Life Responses*: brief story of Hume's view of religion included in "Miscellaneous Hume Anecdotes"
  Editions: 1801 (separate pamphlet); no further editions.
  Reviews: [Robert Woodhouse], *Monthly Review*, 1803, Vol. 41, pp. 184–188.
- Stewart, Dugald (1753–1828). *Account of the life and writings of William Robertson.* London, Printed by A. Strahan for T. Cadell, jun., and W. Davies and E. Balfour, Edinburgh, 1801, iv, 202 p.
  Notes: Sect. 2, Note A, contains a brief comment on Hume's personal character.
  In *Life Responses*: comment included in "Miscellaneous Hume Anecdotes."
  Editions: 1802 and in Stewart's *Works*; see *Common Sense Bibliography* for a complete list.
  Facsimiles: 1997 (Thoemmes Press of 1802).
  Reviews: [Henry Brougham], *Edinburgh Review*, Vol. 2, April 1803, pp. 229–249.

&⤲1802⤳&

- Anonymous (pesud "S.P."). "Letter to the Editor," *Christian Observer and Advocate*, October 1802, Vol. 1, pp. 650–651.
  Notes: discusses an anecdote that in France some atheists believed that Hume as a religious fanatic.
  In *American Responses*: complete article.
- Paley, William (1743–1805). *Natural theology or, Evidences of the existence and*

attributes of the Deity, collected from the appearances of nature. London: Printed for R. Faulder, 1802, xii, 586 p.

Notes: defense of design argument, written largely as a criticism of Hume's *Dialogues*, although Hume is mentioned by name and quoted only sporadically.

Editions: several editions.

Microform: Library of English literature, LEL 12592.

• [Norvell, George (f. 1800)]. "Anecdotes of David Hume, Esq. By one who personally knew him," *Edinburgh Magazine, or Literary Miscellany*, April 1802, Vol. 19, pp. 429–431.

Notes: stories about Hume based on personal acquaintance; similar to his letter to his letter to Alexander Stenhouse, March 1, 1788.

In *Life Responses*: complete; from reprint in *European Magazine and London Review*.

Editions: reprinted in *European Magazine and London Review*, April, 1802, Vol. 41, pp. 263–264; Burton's *Life* (1846), Vol. 2, pp. 7–9.

ॐ1803ॐ

• Anonymous (pseud., "The Philanthropist"). "A Tear to Hume," *Medley; or Monthly Miscellany*, 1803, Vol. 1, p. 249.

Notes: short poem honouring Hume.

In *American Responses*: complete article.

• Arthur, Archibald (1744–1797). *Discourses on theological and literary subjects, by Archibald Arthur, with an account of some particulars in his life and character, by William Richardson.* Glasgow, University Press; Printed by J. & J. Scrymgeour, 1803, 523 p.

Notes: posthumously published essays edited from Arthur's papers; criticizes Hume's view of causality, the *Dialogues* and "Of a Particular Providence."

In *Metaphysical Responses*: complete Discourse 1.2; from 1803 edition.

In *Religion Responses*: selections from Discourse 1.3.2; from 1803 edition.

Editions: 1812, 1817 (both under the title *Discourses on Theological and Literary Subjects*); no further editions.

Reviews: [Stephen Jones], *Monthly Review*, Vol. 48, 389 ff.; *Edinburgh Review*, April 1804, Vol. 4, p. 168 ff.

• Bentham, Jeremy (1748–1832). *A plea for the Constitution shewing the enormities committed to the oppression of British subjects, innocent as well as guilty; in breach of magna charta, the petition of right, the habeas corpus act, and the bill of rights.* London: Mawman, Poultry, 1803, ix, 68 p.

Notes: discusses Hume's view of the British Constitution in the *History*.

In *History Responses*: from *Works* (1838), Vol. 4.

Editions: included in *The Works of Jeremy Bentham*, edited by John Bowring (London: 1838–1843), Vol. 4.

Microform: 19th-century legal treatises, no. 33689 (of 1803).

• Wheatley, John (1772–1830). *Remarks on currency and commerce.* London: printed by T. Burton ... for Messrs. Cadell and Davies, 1803, vi, [2], 262 p.

Notes: discusses Steuart's critique of Hume's "Of the Balance of Trade."

In *Essays Responses*: Chapter 1, selections; from 1803 edition.

Facsimiles: 1993 (Thoemmes Press of 1803).

Reviews: [Henry Brougham], *Edinburgh Review*, October 1803, Vol. 3, pp. 231–252 (negative); [Christopher Lake Moody], *Monthly Review*, 1803, Vol. 41, p. 157 ff.

ॐ1804ॐ

• Leslie, John (1766–1832). *An experimental inquiry into the nature and propagation of heat.* London: Printed for J. Mawman, 1804, xv, 562 p.

Notes: page 521, note 16 defends Hume's notion of causality. Leslie's comment on Hume resulted in efforts among some Scottish clergy to oppose his candidacy for the Chair of Mathematics at Edinburgh.

In *Life Responses*: relevant part of note included in editor's introduction to Henry Cockburn's *Memorials* (1856).

In *Metaphysical Responses*: relevant part of note included in editor's introduction to Thomas Brown's *Observations* (1806).

Discussions: Thomas Brown, *Observations* (1805); Dugald Stewart, *Short Statement* (1805); Henry Cockburn, *Memorials* (1856).

෴1805෴

- Anonymous. "Hume and Burnet," *The Philadelphia Repository*, March 9, 1805, Vol. 5, p. 76.

  Notes: brief anecdote and criticism of Hume, contrasting him with Gilbert Burnet; the original source of this anecdote is unknown.

  In *American Responses*: complete article.

  In *Life Responses*: comment included in "Miscellaneous Hume Anecdotes" as appears in *American Responses*.

- Brown, Thomas (1778–1820). *Observations on the nature and tendency of the doctrine of Mr. Hume, concerning the relation of cause and effect*. Edinburgh, Mundell, [1805], ii, 48 p.

  Notes: defends Hume's view of cause as invariable sequence, and criticizes Hume's view of cause as founded on lively belief. First published as a 48 page pamphlet in 1805; it was expanded in 1806, and retitled in the further expanded 1818 *Inquiry into the Relation of Cause and Effect*.

  In *Metaphysical Responses*: complete book; from 1806 edition.

  Editions: 1806 (second edition, 220 p.), 1818 (third edition, 569 p.), 1822, 1835; see *Common Sense Bibliography* for a complete list.

  Facsimiles: 1977 (Scholar of 1835), 1983 (Garland of 1806).

  Microform: Eighteenth century sources for the study of English literature, reel 306, item 10 (of 1835).

  Reviews of 1806 edition: [Robert L. Woodhouse], *Monthly Review*, Vol. 50, p. 34–45.

  Reviews of 1818 edition: *Christian Spectator*, 1821, Vol. 3, pp. 583–595; [Samuel Foster Gilman], *North American Review*, 1821, Vol. 12, pp. 395–432 (positive; in *American Responses*, listed separately in this bibliography).

  Discussions: Mary Shepherd, *Essay upon the Relation of Cause and Effect* (1824); George Tucker, *Essay on Cause and Effect* (1850).

- Ludlam, Thomas (1727–1811). *Logical tracts, comprising observations and essays illustrative of Mr. Locke's treatise upon the human understanding: with occasional remarks on the writings of the two Scottish professors, Reid and Stewart, upon the same subject: and a preface in vindication of Mr. Locke, against the mistakes and misrepresentations of Mr. Milner, ... Dr. Horne, ... Mr. Kett, and Dr. Napleton.*Cambridge: Printed by M. Watson for J. Nicholson, [1805?], 31, 77 p.

  Notes: criticizes Reid and Stewart's views of knowledge and states that Hume was confused or intelligible on the subject. The title page contains no date; the dating is based on Ludlam's reference in the work to the 1802 second edition of Stewart's *Elements of the Philosophy of the Human Mind*.

  In *Common Sense Responses*: selections from "Observations", pp. 1–26; from 1805 edition.

Editions: no further editions.

Facsimiles: 1991 (Thoemmes Press).

Microform: The Eighteenth Century, reel 317, no. 11.

● More, Hannah (1745–1833). *Hints towards forming the character of a young princess: in two volumes.* London: Printed for T. Cadell and W. Davies, 1805, 2 v.

Notes: Chapter 10, "Reflections on History," contains a subsection titled "David Hume," warning that Hume should be read with caution on political and religious issues.

In *History Responses*: selections from Chapter 10; from *The Works of Hannah More*, Philadelphia, Edward Earle, 1817, Vol. 7.

Editions: several editions and in *Works*.

● [Smith, Samuel Stanhope (1751–1819), (pseud. "S.")]. "The Celebrated Objection of Mr. Hume to the Miracles of the Gospel," *The Assembly's Missionary Magazine*, April 1805, Vol. 1 pp. 182–186.

Notes: criticism of Hume's "Of Miracles." Adapted in Smith's *Comprehensive View* (1815).

In *American Responses*: complete article.

● Stewart, Dugald (1753–1828). *A short statement of some important facts, relative to the late election of a mathematical professor in the University of Edinburgh accompanied with original papers, and critical remarks.* Edinburgh, printed by Murray & Cochrane, and sold by William Creech, and Arch. Constable & Co., 1805, ii, 127 p.

Notes: discusses John Leslie controversy and lists writers who have adopted Hume's view of causality.

Microform: History of education, fiche 11,626–11,627.

Reviews: [Francis Horner], *Edinburgh Review*, October 1805, Vol. 7, pp. 113–134.

ॐ1806ॐ

● Anonymous (pseud. "G."). "On the Death of David Hume," *The Assembly's Missionary Magazine, or Evangelical Intelligencer*, 1806, Vol. 2, pp. 32–34.

Notes: criticizes Adam Smith's "Letter ... to William Strahan."

In *American Responses*: complete article.

● Anonymous (pseud. "T."). Letter on Hume, *The Port Folio*, 1806, Vol. 1 (series 2), pp. 113–114.

Notes: praises Hume's character.

In *American Responses*: complete article.

● Anonymous. "Comparison between Hume and Robertson," *The Port Folio*, 1806, Vol. 1 (series 2), pp. 44–45.

Notes: discusses respective strengths and weaknesses of Hume and Robertson as historians.

In *American Responses*: complete article.

● Forbes, William (1739–1806). *An account of the life and writings of James Beattie.* Edinburgh, Printed for A. Constable and Co. and W. Creech, 1806, 2 v.

Notes: biography and letters of Beattie, many of which discuss his opposition to Hume and the composition of the *Essay* (1770).

Facsimiles: 1996 (Routledge/Thoemmes Press), 1997 (Thoemmes Press).

Editions: 1806 (New York), 1807 (London second edition), 1807 (Edinburgh), 1807 (New York), 1824 (London).

Reviews: *Anti-Jacobin Review and* Magazine, 1806, Vol. 24, August, pp. 353–366, Vol. 25, September, pp. 36–50; *British Critic*, 1806, Vol. 28, August, pp. 105–120, September, 298–312; *Eclectic Review*, 1807, Vol. 3, pp. 1–10, 112–131; [Francis Jeffrey], *Edinburgh Review,* 1807, Vol. 10, pp. 171–199; *Monthly Magazine,* 1806, Vol. 22, part 2, pp. 633–635; [Lockhart Muirhead], *Monthly Review* 1806,

Vol. 51, September, pp. 1–14; *Scots Magazine*, 1806, Vol. 68, pp. 760–767, 844–850.

- Mason, John Mitchell (1770–1829). "Remarks on the accounts of the death of David Hume, Esqr. and Samuel Finley, D.D.," *Christian's Magazine,* 1806, Vol. 1, pp. 419–436.

  Notes: criticizes Adam Smith's "Letter … to William Strahan."

  In *American Responses*: complete article.

  Reprints in Journals: Editions: reprinted in *Panoplist*, November 1808, Vol. 1, new series, pp. 241–257; *Adviser*, May 1809, Vol. 1, no. 5 , pp. 101–108; *Adviser*, June 1809, Vol. 1, no. 6, pp. 130–133; *Religious Monitor*, November 1824, Vol. 1, pp. 294–302.

  Other Editions: *Hume and Finley, a Contrast* (1822), *Death of Hume and Finley Compared* (1827), in *Works* 1854 (Vol. 4).

  Discussions: "The Contrast" in *The Ordeal* (1809); "Considerations" in *The Ordeal* (1809); "More of the 'Contrast'" (1809).

- Stewart, Dugald (1753–1828). Letter to William Forbes on Beattie (c. 1806).

  Manuscript location: in National Library of Scotland, MS, Fettercairn collection, Box 93.

  Notes: cancelled proof from Forbes's *Account* (1806), Vol. 2, pages 387–404; defends Reid and Beattie's notions of common sense, making mention of Hume. Stewart published a revised version of this in *Elements of the Philosophy of the Human Mind* (1814), Vol. 2, chap. 1, sect. 3.

  In *Common Sense Responses*: complete section of cancelled proof.

☙1807❧

- Anonymous. Discussion of Hume on tyranny, in *The Port Folio*, 1807, Vol. 3 (series 2), p. 27.

  Notes: discusses Hume's account of tyranny in Tudor and Stuart monarchies.

  In *American Responses*: complete article.

- Fulton, Robert (1765–1815). "Mr. Fulton's Communication," in Albert Gallatin, *Report of the Secretary of the Treasury, on the Subject of Public Roads and Canals; Made in Pursuance of a Resoltuion of Senate, of March 2, 1807*, Washington: The Senate, R.C. Weightman, 1808, 123 p.

  Notes: draws on Hume's political and economic views.

  In *American Responses*: selection from pp. 108–109, 120–23.

  Editions: several 19th century editions.

  Facsimiles: 1968 (A.M. Kelley of 1808).

  Microform: Goldsmiths'-Kress library of economic literature, no. 19710 (of 1808).

- Gillies, John (1747–1836). *The history of the world, from the reign of Alexander to that of Augustus*. London, Cadell and Davies, 1807, 2 Vol.

  Notes: critiques "Of the Populousness of Ancient Nations."

  In *Essays Responses*: selections included in "Miscellaneous Comments on Hume's Essays."

  Reviews: [Henry Hallam], *Edinburgh Review*, October 1807, Vol. 11, p. 40–61.

- Jefferson, Thomas (1743–1826). Letters from Thomas Jefferson, 1807–1825.

  Notes: later correspondence from Jefferson comment negatively on Hume, particularly letters to John Norvell (June 11, 1807), William Duane (August 12, 1810), Horatio G. Spafford (March 17, 1814), and George Washington Lewis (October, 25 1825).

  In *American Responses*: selections from above noted letters.

- Kirwan, Richard (1733–1812). *Logick; or, An essay on the elements, principles, and different modes of reasoning*. London, Payne & Mackinlay, 1807, 2 v.

Notes: contains an attack on Hume's account of chance.

Reviews: [Stephen Jones], *Monthly Review*, 1809, Vol. 60, p. 417.

● Ritchie, Thomas Edward (fl. 1800). *An account of the life and writings of David Hume, esq.*, London, Printed for T. Cadell and W. Davies, 1807, 1, [v]–vi, 1, 520 p.

Notes: discusses Ritchie's methodology and Hume's character.

In *Life Responses*: selections.

Editions: no further editions.

Facsimiles: 1990 (Thoemmes Press, of 1807).

Reviews: [John Foster], *Eclectic Review*, January 1808; *Christian Observer*, Vol. 7 p. 646 ff.; [Stephen Jones], *Monthly Review*, May 1810, Vol. 62, pp. 57–65 (negative; complete review contained in *Hume on Natural Religion*).

● [Tytler, Alexander Fraser, Lord Woodhouselee (1747–1813)]. *Memoirs of the life and writings of the honourable Henry Home of Kames.* Edinburgh, W. Creech; London, T. Cadell and W. Davis, 1807, 2 Vol.

Notes: lengthy account of Henry Home, comprised largely of letters connected with Woodhouselee's narrative, including several letters from Hume. Woodhouselee discusses Hume's theories of morality and causality. Also of interest is a letter from Oswald of Dunikeir on the *Treatise*, a letter from Tucker on Hume's political economy, Carlyle's membership list of the poker club, and Woodhouselee's "Dissertation on Final Causes" which critiques Hume's view of the design argument (first included in William Derham's *Physico-theology*, 1798).

In *Essays Responses*: selections from Tucker's letter, from 1814 edition, Vol. 3, pp. 157-161.

In *Religion Responses*: selections from "Dissertation on Final Causes"; from 1814 edition, Vol. 3, Appendix 3.

Editions: 1809 (Supplement), 1814.

Facsimiles: 1993 (Thoemmes Press of 1807).

Microform: 19th-century legal treatises, no. 68315–68329.

Reviews: *Monthly Review*, January 1810, Vol. 61 pp. 84–96 (mixed); *Scots Magazine*, 1807, Vol. 69, June, pp. 432–438, July 516–522 (mixed).

Discussions: James Bonar, "Memoir" (1815–1817).

● Wheatley, John (1772–1830). *An essay on the theory of money and principles of commerce.* London: Printed for T. Cadell and W. Davies, (London: W. Bulmer), 1807, Vol.1, 379 p.

Notes: criticizes Hume's key economic principles and discusses Steuart's critique of Hume's "Of the Balance of Trade".

In *Essays Responses*: Chapter 1, selections; from 1807 edition.

Facsimiles: 1983 (Garland of 1807)

Microform: Goldsmiths'-Kress library of economic literature, no. 19448.

Reviews: [Stephen Jones], *Monthly Review*, April 1810, Vol. 61, p. 417 ff.; *Edinburgh Review*, July 1807, Vol. 10, pp. 284–299.

☙1808❧

● Anonymous. "Striking Evidences of the Divinity of the Scriptures. I. Examples of dying infidels," in *The Moral and Religious Cabinet*, March 26, 1808, Vol. 1, pp. 193–198.

Notes: short paragraph criticizing Adam Smith's "Letter ... to William Strahan."

In *American Responses*: selection pp. 196–197.

● Anonymous (pseud. "Mentor"). *The dangers of the Edinburgh review: or a brief exposure of its principles in religion, morals and politics. In three letters, addressed to its readers.* London: Printed for F.C. and J. Rivington, Law and Gilbert, 1808, 39 p.

Notes: attack on the *Edinburgh Review* for taking liberal stands on religion and politics; the author faults the journal for elevating Hume's views above those of bishops.

Editions: no further editions.

- [Foster, John (1770–1843)]. Review of Ritchie's *Account of the Life and Writings of David Hume*, in *Eclectic Review*, January 1808.

    Notes: contains attack on Smith's "Letter ... to William Strahan."

    Discussions: "Death of Hume," *Panoplist* (1810).

- Warburton, William (1698–1779); Hurd, Richard (1720–1808). *Letters from a late eminent prelate to one of his friends*. Kidderminster: Printed by George Gower, for T. Cadell and W. Davies, 1808, 380 p.

    Notes: letters from William Warburton to Richard Hurd, edited by Hurd; discusses Warburton's early contempt for Hume.

    In *Religion Responses*: quotation from relevant letter in introduction to Warburton's paper on "Of Miracles" (1779?).

    Editions: 1809 (London, second), 1809 (New York).

    Microform: Early American imprints, Second series, no. 19132 (of New York 1809).

❧1809❧

- Anonymous. Discussion of Hume's *History*, in *The Port Folio*, 1809, Vol. 1 (series 3), pp. 98–100.

    Notes: praises Hume's history.

    In *American Responses*: relevant section.

- Anonymous. "The Contrast 'Between the Death of a Deist and the Death of a Christian',￼" *The Ordeal*, January 21, 1809, pp. 42–45.

    Notes: criticizes the attack on Smith's "Letter ... to William Strahan" by John Mitchell Mason in "Remarks" (1806).

    In *American Responses*: complete article.

- Anonymous. "Considerations on the Contrast '*Between the Death of a Deist and of a Christian,*' contained in the Panoplist of November last," *The Ordeal*, January 28, 1809, pp. 63–64.

    Notes: criticizes the attack on Smith's "Letter ... to William Strahan" by John Mitchell Mason in "Remarks" (1806).

    In *American Responses*: complete article.

- Anonymous (pseud. "B."). "More of the 'Contrast.'," *The Ordeal*, February 4, 1809, pp. 72–73.

    Notes: criticizes the attack on Smith's "Letter ... to William Strahan" by John Mitchell Mason in "Remarks" (1806).

    In *American Responses*: complete article.

- Anonymous. "Hume and Finley" *The Ordeal*, February 11, 1809, p. 94.

    Notes: defends the attack on Smith's "Letter ... to William Strahan" by John Mitchell Mason in "Remarks" (1806).

    In *American Responses*: complete article.

- Anonymous (pseud. "A Believer in Miracles"). "Mr. Hume's Objection to Miracles Considered," *Monthly Repository*, 1809, Vol. 4, pp. 145–148.

    Notes: criticizes "Of Miracles"; a revised version of this article appeared in *Monthly Repository*, 1817, Vol. 12, pp. 17–20.

- Anonymous (pseud. "E.N."). "Objections to the Doctrine of Necessity," *Monthly Repository*, 1809, Vol. 4, pp. 548–551.

    Notes: criticizes Hume's argument that determinism traces evil back to God.

❧1810❧

- Anonymous. "Of the Peculiarities Attached to the Correct Reading," in *The Port Folio*, 1810, Vol. 3 (series 3), pp. 488–499.
  Notes: contains a section arguing that Hume's prose is tame and uninteresting.
  In *American Responses*: selection from pp. 488–90.
- Anonymous. "Hume and Robertson Compared," *The Port Folio*, 1810, Vol. 4 (series 3), pp. 330–333.
  Notes: prefers Hume's account of the sack of Rome by Bourbon to that of Robertson.
  In *American Responses*:
- Anonymous. "Death of Hume," *The Panoplist, and Missionary Magazine United*, March 1810, Vol. 2 pp. 462–464.
  Notes: quotes approvingly from John Foster's review of Ritchie's *Account* in the *Eclectic Review* (1808), which attacks Smith's "Letter ... to William Strahan."
  In *American Responses*: complete article.
- Caulfeild, James (1728–1799). *Memoirs of the political and private life of James Caulfeild, earl of Charlemont, knight of St. Patrick*, Francis Hardy, ed., London, T. Cadell and W. Davies, 1810, xiv, 443 p.
  Manuscript location: Royal Irish Academy, MS 12/R/7, f. 523.
  Notes: contains stories about Hume based on personal acquaintance.
  In *Life Responses*: selections; from the 1812 edition (London: T Cadell), Vol. 1, pp. 12–19, 230–239.
  Editions: 1812.
  Microform: Humanities Preservation Project 95–0253.
  Reviews: *Quarterly Review*, October 1811, Vol. 6, pp. 124–147 (positive); [Francis Jeffrey] *Edinburgh Review*, November 1811, Vol. 19, pp. 95–128.
- Ricardo, David (1772–1823). *The High Price of Bullion, a Proof of the Depreciation of Bank Notes*. London: Printed for John Murray, 1810, iv, 48 p.
  Notes: discusses Hume's theory of money circulation.
  In *Essays Responses*: selections included in "Miscellaneous Comments on Hume's Essays."
- Silliman, Benjamin (1779–1864). *A journal of travels in England, Holland, and Scotland, in the years 1805-1806,* New York, 1810, 2 Vol.
  Notes: contains an anecdote about Hume's reaction to his mother's death and another regarding Hume's deathbed anguish.
  In *Life Responses*: selections from Section 87; from 1810 edition.
  Editions: 1812, 1820.
  Facsimiles: 1980 (Arno Press of 1812).
  Microform: Library of American civilization, LAC 22521.
  Reviews: *Quarterly Review* July 1816, Vol. 15, p. 562 (positive).
  Discussions: Editor's Note on Silliman and Baron Hume, *Quarterly Review* (1816).
- Stewart, Dugald (1753–1828). *Philosophical essays*. Edinburgh: printed by George Ramsay and Company, for William Creech, and Archibald Constable and Company, etc., 1810, xii, lxxvi, 590, [2] p.
  Notes: Note X discusses Hume's "Of Tragedy"; Note EE criticizes Hume's view of venerating the past.
  In *Metaphysical Responses*: Note EE, selections; from *Collected Works* (1855), Vol. 5, pp. 445–447.
  In *Essays Responses*: Note X, selections; from *Collected Works* (1855), Vol. 5, pp. 439–441.
  Editions: see *Common Sense Bibliography* for a complete list.
  Facsimiles: 1811, 1816, 1818, and in *Works* 1854; see *Common Sense Bibliography*

for a complete list.

Reviews: [Francis Jeffrey], *Edinburgh Review*, November 1810, Vol. 17, pp. 167–211; *Quarterly Review*, October 1811, Vol. 6, p. 1–37.

ᔡ1811ᔥ

● Anonymous. *Interesting anecdote of a well known English philosopher.* Wolverhampton, 1811, 16 p.

Notes: anecdote based on Mackenzie's fictional "Story of La Roche" (1779).

● More, Hannah (1745–1833). *Practical Piety, or the influence of the religion of the heart on the conduct of the life.* London: Printed for T. Cadell and W. Davies, 1811, 2 v.

Notes: Chapter 19 "Happy Deaths" criticizes Hume's attitude about death.

In *Life Responses*: relevant selections from Chapter 19, from *Practical Piety*, Burlington, N.J., Allinson, 1811.

Editions: several editions.

Discussions: "Death-beds of Unbelievers" in *Monthly Repository* (1813); "Hume and Mrs. Hannah More" in *Monthly Repository* (1813).

ᔡ1812ᔥ

● Disraeli, Isaac (1766–1848). *Calamities of authors; including some inquiries respecting their moral and literary characters*, London, J. Murray, 1812, 2 v.

Notes: section titled "Miseries of Successful Authors" discusses Hume's literary disappointments (derived from Hume's letters and "My Own Life"); "Literary Hatred" discusses Stuart's attack on Robert Henry's *History*, and Hume's ill-fated review of it.

In *Life Responses*: "Literary Hatred," complete; from *Calamites and Quarrels of Authors*, London, Frederick Warne, 1869, pp. 130–138.

Editions: several editions.

Reviews: *Quarterly Review*, September 1812, Vol. 8, p. 93 ff.

● Nichols, John (1745–1826). *Literary anecdotes of the eighteenth century comprizing biographical memoirs of William Bowyer, printer, F.S.A. and many of his learned friends, an incidental view of the progress and advancement of literature in this kingdom during the last century and biographical anecdotes of a considerable number of eminent writers and ingenious artists with a very copious index*, London: Printed for the author, by Nichols, son, and Bentley, 1812–1816, 9 v.

Notes: brief anecdote of Hume proofing Gerard's book.

In *Life Responses*: brief story of Hume proofing Gerard's book is included in "Miscellaneous Hume Anecdotes," from 1812 edition, Vol. 2, p. 326.

● Tennemann, Wilhelm Gottlieb (1761–1819). *Grundriss der Geschichte der Philosophie: für den akademischen Unterricht.* Leipzig: Johann Ambrosius Barth, 1812, iv, 368 p.

English Translation: *A manual of the history of philosophy, translated from the German of Tennemann; by Rev. Arthur Johnson.* Oxford: D.A. Talboys, 1832, xi, 494 p.

Notes: discusses how Hume's philosophy grew from Locke, and led to skepticism.

Editions: 1852 (English); several German editions.

ᔡ1813ᔥ

● Anonymous (pseud. "A Constant Reader"). "Death-beds of Unbelievers," in *Monthly Repository*, 1813, Vol. 8, pp. 32–33.

Notes: criticism of Hannah More's attack on Hume's deathbed tranquility in *Practical Piety* (1811).

In *Life Responses*: complete.

Discussions: "Hume and Mrs. Hannah More" in *Monthly Repository* (1813).
● Anonymous (pseud. "N."). "Hume and Mrs. Hannah More," in *Monthly Repository*, 1813, Vol. 8, pp. 107–108.

Notes: defends Hannah More's attack on Hume's deathbed tranquility against "Death-beds of Unbelievers" in *Monthly Repository* (1813).

In *Life Responses*: complete.
● Hollis, John. *Free thoughts: consisting of Remarks occasioned by Paley's reply to Hume; Hypercritical strictures on certain passages in the Critical review, A letter to a friend, The reflections of a solitary; and, Thoughts on a future state.* London, R. Taylor & Co., 1812, 168 p.

Notes: discusses Hume's views on religion.

ஃ1814ஃ

● [Playfair, John (1748–1819)]. Review of La Place's *Essai Philosophique sur les Probabilités*, in *Edinburgh Review*, September 1814, Vol. 23, pp. 320–340.

Notes: praises Hume's "Of Miracles."

Editions: Playfair's *Works*, Vol. 3.

Discussions: James Somerville, *Remarks* (1815).

ஃ1815ஃ

● Bonar, James (1757–1821). "Memoir of the Rev. Archibald Bonar, minister of Cramond," in Archibald Bonar, *Sermons chiefly on devotional subjects*, Edinburgh: Printed for Macredie, Skelly, & Muckersy; M. Ogle, Glasgow; and T. Underwood, London, 1815–1817, 2 v.

Notes: discusses John Bonar's *Analysis* (1755) and Hugh Blair's *Observations* (1755).

In *Life Responses*: selections; from volume 2, 1817, pp. xxiii–xxiv.

Editions: no further editions.
● Malthus, Thomas (1766–1834). *The grounds of an opinion on the policy of restricting the importation of foreign corn : intended as an appendix to "Observations on the corn laws" by the Rev. T.R. Malthus.* London: John Murray, 1815, [2], 48 p.

Notes: discusses Hume's "Of the Balance of Trade."

In *Essays Responses*: selections included in "Miscellaneous Comments on Hume's *Essays*."

Discussions: David Ricardo *An Essay on the influence* (1815).
● Morgan, William (1750–1833). *Memoirs of the life of the Rev. Richard Price*, London, Printed for R. Hunter [etc.], 1815, viii, 189 p.

Notes: discusses Price's friendly relationship with Hume.

In *Life Responses*: selections; pp. 15–17, 23–25; from 1815 edition.

Reviews: *Monthly Repository*, 1815, Vol. 10, p. 570.
● Smith, Samuel Stanhope (1751–1819). *A Comprehensive View of the Leading and Most Important Principles of Natural and Revealed Religion.* New-Brunswick [N.J.]: Printed and published by Deare & Myer, 1815, vii, [1], 543, [1] p.

Notes: based on Smith's earlier article "The Celebrated Objection" in *Assembly's Missionary Magazine* (1805), criticizes Hume's "Of Miracles."

Editions: 1816 (second edition).

In *American Responses*: selection from pp. 81–89.

Microform: Early American imprints.; Second series, no. 38957 (of 1816); Early American imprints, Second series, no. 38957 (of 1816).
● Ricardo, David (1772–1823). *An Essay on the influence of a low price of corn on the profits of stock.* London: Printed for John Murray, 1815, 50 p.

Notes: criticizes Hume's theory regarding the effects of increased prices on industry.

Microform: Goldsmiths'-Kress library of economic literature, no. 21184.

• Somerville, James. *Remarks on an article in the Edinburgh Review: in which the doctrines of Hume on Miracles is maintained.* Edinburgh, Printed by A. Balfour, 1815, 34 p.
  Notes: based on Sommerville's previously appearing article in *Edinburgh Christian Instructor*, December 1814. Criticizes Playfair's praise of Hume's "Of Miracles" in his review of La Place in *Edinburgh Review* (1814).
  In *Hume on Miracles*: complete pamphlet.
• [West, Edward (1782–1828)]. *Essay on the application of capital to land, with observations shewing the impolicy of any great restriction of the importation of corn and that the bounty of 1688 did not lower the price of it, by a Fellow of University College.* Oxford. London: Printed for T. Underwood ... by C. Rosworth, 1815, [2], 69 p.
  Notes: discusses Hume's "Of the Balance of Trade."
  In *Essays Responses*: selections included in "Miscellaneous Comments on Hume's Essays."

ৡ১816ৡ

• Anonymous. Editor's Note on Silliman and Baron Hume, *Quarterly Review*, October 1816, Vol. 16, p. 279.
  Notes: discusses Baron Hume's reaction to anecdotes about Hume in Silliman's *Journal* (1810).
  In *Life Responses*: complete note.
• Anonymous. "Hume and Dryden," *The Port Folio*, 1816, Vol. 2 (series 5), p. 126.
  Notes: compares Hume's and Dryden's attacks on the clergy.
  In *American Responses*: complete article.
• Bentham, Jeremy (1748–1832). *Chrestomathia: being a collection of papers ...* London: Printed for Payne and Foss, and R. Hunter, by J. M'Creery, 1816. 2 v.
  Notes: Note to Appendix 4, Section 20 discusses Hume's is/ought distinction and Hume's impact on Bentham.
  In *Moral Responses*: complete note, from *The Works of Jeremy Bentham*, edited by John Bowring (London: 1838–1843).
  Editions: various editions.
• Cogan, Eliezer (1762–1855), and three anonymous critics. Five letters in *Monthly Repository* , 1816–1817.
  Notes: five letters debate Hume's "Of Miracles."
  In *Religion Responses*: five letters, complete.
  Letter 1: by Eliezer Cogan, "Mr. Hume's Argument against Miracles," (1816, Vol. 11, pp. 644–647); criticizes "Of Miracles."
  Letter 2: by respondent 1 (pseud. "A.B.C."), (1816, Vol. 11, pp. 703–704); discusses Cogan attack, agreeing with parts of it.
  Letter 3: by respondent 2 (also with editorial assigned pseud. "A.B.C."), (1817, Vol. 12, pp. 95–96); discusses Cogan attack, agreeing with parts of it.
  Letter 4: by respondent 3 (also with editorial assigned pseud. "A.B.C."), (1817, Vol. 12, pp. 96–97); discusses Cogan attack, agreeing with parts of it.
  Letter 5: Eliezer Cogan (Vol. 12 pp. 31–32); reacts to respondent 1.
• Cowper, William (1731–1800). *Memoir of the early life of William Cowper, Esq., written by himself, and never before published. With an appendix, containing some of Cowper's religious letters, and other interesting documents, illustrative of the memoir.* London: Printed for R. Edwards, 1816, xviii, 126 p.
  Notes: A letter in the Appendix to William Unwin (July 12, 1784) comments on William Rose's review of Hume's essay on suicide, and Cowper offers his own criticism.
  In *Religion Responses*: selections; from *Memoir* (1816).
  Microform: Library of English literature, LEL 12408.

Reviews: *Quarterly Review*, October 1816, Vol. 16, pp. 116–129 (positive).
- Ogilvie, James (1760–1820). *Philosophical essays to which are subjoined copious notes, critical and explanatory, and a supplementary narrative; with an appendix.* Philadelphia: John Conrad, J. Maxwell); United States; Pennsylvania; Philadelphia, 1816, xxiii, 279, cxxxi.
    Notes: discusses Hume's account of causality.
    Microform: Early American imprints, Second series, no. 38500.
    Reviews: *The Analectic Magazine*, January 1817, Vol. 9, pp. 1–32 (mixed); [Edward Tyrrel Channing], *North American Review*, 1817, Vol. 4, pp. 378–408 (mixed); both in *American Responses*, listed separately in this bibliography.

☙1817❧

- Anonymous (pseud. "A Believer in Miracles"). "An Examination of Mr. Hume's Objection to Miracles," *Monthly Repository*, 1817, Vol. 12, pp. 17–20.
    Notes: criticizes "Of Miracles"; revision of article in *Monthly Repository*, 1809, Vol. 4, pp. 145–148.
    In *Religion Responses*: complete article.
- Anonymous. Four letters between two anonymous writers in *The Portico*, 1817.
    Notes: letters debate whether genius is dependent upon passion, and draw on Hume's "Of the Delicacy of Taste and Passion."
    In *American Responses*: complete articles.
    Letter 1: by "S.N." (pseudonym), "Genius and Passion" (February 1817, Vol. 3, pp. 121–126); argues that genius is dependent upon passion.
    Letter 2: by "R." (pseudonym), "Remarks addressed to the author of the Essay on Genius and Passion, in the last number of the Portico" (March 1817, Vol. 3, pp. 229–232); replies that genius is not connected with passion.
    Letter 3: by "S." (i.e., "S.N." pseudonymn), "Passion the Soul of Genius (in Reply to 'R.')" (April 1817, Vol. 3, pp. 297–303).
    Letter 4: by "R.", "Reply to the Essay, entitled 'Genius, the soul of Passion.' Addressed to 'S.'," (May 1817, Vol. 3, pp. 373–376).
- Anonymous. "Memorandums for an Essay against Luxury" in *The National Register*, 1817 Vol. 4, pp. 66–67.
    Notes: defense of Hume's "Of Refinement in the Arts" written ironically as an attack. The article also includes an excerpt from Hume's essay.
    In *American Responses*: complete article.
- Anonymous. Review of James Ogilvie's *Philosophical Essays*, in *The Analectic Magazine*, January 1817, Vol. 9 , pp. 1–32.
    Notes: discusses Ogilvie's Humean account of causality.
    In *American Responses*: selection from pp. 6–29.
- [Channing, Edward Tyrrel (1790–1856)]. Review of James Ogilvie's "*Philosophical Essays*," in *The North American Review*, 1817, Vol. 4, pp. 378–408.
    Notes: discusses Ogilvie's Humean account of causality.
    In *American Responses*: selection from pp. 401–402.
- Cogan, Thomas (1736–1818). *Ethical questions; or Speculations on the principal subjects of controversy in moral philosophy.* London, Printed for T. Cadell and W. Davies, 1817, 439 p.
    Notes: collection of essays by Cogan written earlier in his life. Speculation 5 criticizes Beattie; Speculation 6 criticizes Hume's *Enquiry*, section by section.
    In *Metaphysical Responses*: Speculation 6, Sections 1–8; from 1817 edition.
    In *Religion Responses*: Speculation 6, Section 10; from 1817 edition.
    In *Common Sense Responses*: "Speculation Five," complete; from 1817 edition.

Editions: no further editions.

Facsimiles: 2004 (Thoemmes of 1817).

Reviews: *Monthly Repository*, 1817, Vol. 12, p. 226–236.

● Coleridge, Samuel Taylor (1772–1834). *Biographia literaria, or, Biographical sketches of my literary life and opinions*, London: Rest Fenner, 1817, 2 v.

Notes: in Chapter 5 Coleridge accuses Hume of plagiarising his principles of association from Aquinas.

Editions: several editions.

Discussions: "David Hume Charged by Mr Coleridge" (1818); James Mackintosh, *A General View* (1834).

● Ewell, Thomas (1785–1826). *Philosophical Essays on Morals, Literature, and Politics, By David Hume, Esq. To which is added the answer to his objections to Christianity, By the Ingenious Divine Dr. Campbell. Also, An account of Mr. Hume's Life, an original Essay, and a few Notes.* Georgetown, D.C.: Printed by W. Duffy, 1817, 2 vol.

Notes: includes a Preface and annotations by Ewell in which he discusses attitudes about Hume's writings in the early 19th century.

In *American Responses*: selection from Vol. 1, pp. vii–xvii, 80, 231–2, 521–3; Vol. 2, pp. 124–7, 475.

Microform: Early American Imprints, second series, no. 41099.

● Nichols, John (1745–1826). *Illustrations of the literary history of the eighteenth century*, London: Printed for the author, by Nichols, son, and Bentley, 1817–1858, 8 v.

Notes: includes a letter by Daniel Wray (1701–1783) of October 15, 1771, which contains a brief anecdote about Hume's weight.

In *Life Responses*: story included in "Miscellaneous Hume Anecdotes"; from 1817 edition, Vol. 1. pp. 141–142.

Facsimiles: 1966 (Krauss of 1817–1858).

Microform: Library of English literature; LEL 22035–42.

❧1818❧

● Anonymous. "David Hume Charged by Mr Coleridge with Plagiarism from St Thomas Aquinas," in *Blackwood's Magazine*, Sept. 1818, Vol. 3, pp. 653–657.

Notes: defends Hume against Coleridge.

In *Metaphysical Responses*: selections from article.

Discussions: James Mackintosh, *A General View* (1834).

● Austen, Jane (1775–1817). *Northanger abbey: and persuasion.* London: John Murray, 1818, 4 v.

Notes: character in novel praises Hume's *History*.

In *History Responses*: selections included in "Miscellaneous Comments on Hume's *History*."

Editions: several editions.

Facsimiles: 1994 (Routledge/Thoemmes Press, of 1818).

● Bruce, William (1757–1841). *A treatise on the being and attributes of God: with an appendix on the immateriality of the soul.* Belfast: Printed by Francis D. Finlay, 1818, xiv, 224 p.

Notes: discusses Hume's *Dialogues* in the preface and criticizes Hume's religious scepticism more generally elsewhere.

● Epinay, Louise Florence, marquise d' (1726–1783). *Memoires et Correspondance de Madame D'Epinay*, Paris, 1818,

Notes: Volume 3 page 284 contains a brief anecdote about Hume in France.

In *Life Responses*: English translation of anecdote included in "Miscellaneous Hume Anecdotes."

In *American Responses*: English translation of anecdote as appears in "Anecdote of David "Hume," *The New-England Galaxy and Masonic Magazine*, June 18, 1819, p. 144.

Reviews: [Walter Coulson], *Edinburgh Review*, December 1818, Vol. 31, pp. 1–44.

ᔒ1819ᔐ

- Crombie, Alexander (1762–1840). *Letters from Dr. James Gregory of Edinburgh, in defence of his Essay on the difference of the relation between motive and action and that of cause and effect in physics, with replies, by Alex. Crombie*. London, R. Hunter, 1819, ix, 427 p.

  Notes: contains Gregory's response to Crombie's criticisms in *An Essay on Philosophical Necessity* (1793); also contains Crombie's rebuttal. Discussions relate to Hume's view of determinism.

  Editions: no further editions.

  Facsimiles: 2001 (Thoemmes Press of 1819).

- Ely, Ezra Stiles (1786–1861). *Conversations on the Science of the Human Mind*. Philadelphia: Printed for the author, Sold by A. Finley, corner of Chestnut and Fourth streets, 1819, 228 p.

  Notes: endorses Hume's view in the *Treatise* that mental science is the only solid foundation for other sciences.

  In *American Responses*: selection pp. 17–19.

  Microform: Library of American civilization, LAC 13994 (of 1819); Early American Imprints, Second series, no. 47898 (of 1819).

- [Shepherd, Mary (1777–1847)]. *Enquiry respecting the relation of cause and effect*. Edinburgh: Printed by James Ballantyne, 1819, vii, 98 p.

  Notes: criticism of Hume's view of causality.

  Editions: revised and expanded as *Essay upon the Relation of Cause and Effect* (1824).

  Facsimiles: 2000 (Thoemmes Press of 1819).

- [Watkins, John (fl. 1792–1831)]. "Anecdotes of Infidel Morality," *Robinson's Magazine*, 1819, Vol. 2, pp. 164–168.

  Notes: criticizes Hume for immodestly puffing his *Treatise* by writing the *Abstract*.

  In *American Responses*: selection from pp. 164–165, 167–168.

ᔒ1820ᔐ

- Anonymous. Comment on Hume, *The Port Folio*, Vol. 9 (series 5), 1820, p. 135.

  Notes: brief paragraph contends that Hume was not always inclined to look on the bright side of things, as he claims in "My Own Life."

  In *American Responses*: relevant selection.

- Anonymous. *Private correspondence of David Hume with several distinguished persons, between the years 1761 and 1776. Now first published from the originals*. London, Henry Colburn, 1820, [i–xx], [1]–285 [1] p.

  Notes: discusses background of letters from Hume to Boufflers and Barbantane.

  In *Life Responses*: selections from Introduction; from 1820 edition.

  Editions: no further editions.

  Reviews: *Edinburgh Monthly Review*, Vol. 5, p. 127 ff.; *Monthly Review*, 1822, Vol. 97, p. 347 ff.

- Anonymous. Review of Kenney's *Principles and Practices of Pretended Reformers*, in *Christian Observer and Advocate*, 1820, Vol. 19, pp. 666–93.

  Notes: Discusses Hume's view that religion was the cause of the English civil war.

  In *American Responses*: selections from pp. 669–82.

- Brown, Thomas (1778–1820). *Lectures on the philosophy of the human mind.* Edinburgh: 1820, 4 vol., viii, 578; viii, 607; vii 638; vii 615.
  Notes: Lectures 34 and 35 critique Hume's principles of association; Lectures 77 and 78 critique Hume's view of utility.
  In *Metaphysical Responses*: selections from Lect. 34 and 35; from 1824 edition.
  In *Moral Responses*: From Lect. 77 and 78 from 1824 edition.
  Editions: Brown's *Lectures* was published several times throughout the 19th century; for a complete bibliography see *Common Sense Bibliography*.
  Facsimiles: 2002 (Thoemmes Press).
  Microform: Eighteenth century sources for the study of English literature, reel 335; Library of English literature, LEL 22402–05.
  Reviews: *Blackwood's Edinburgh Magazine*, 1820, Vol. 7, pp. 62–71; *Monthly Review*, 1823, Vol. 101, pp. 402–420; [S. Gilman], *North American Review*, 1825, Vol. 21, pp. 19–51; [N. Porter], *Christian Spectator*, 1826, Vol. 8, pp. 141–155; *Literary Gazette*, 1827, Vol. 6, p. 161 ff.; *Southern Review*, 1828, Vol. 3, p. 125 ff.; *Eclectic Review*, 1846, Vol. 20, pp. 674–688; *Tait's Edinburgh Magazine*, 1846, Vol. 13, pp. 699–715.

❧1821❧

- Anonymous. "Hume," *Saturday Magazine: National Recorder*, March 17, 1821, Vol. 5, p. 174.
  Notes: brief quotation from "My Own Life" is placed in the context of a discussion on the merits of reading history.
  In *American Responses*: complete paragraph.
- Anonymous. Review of William Ellery Channing's *Discourse on the Evidences of Revealed Religion*, in *The Unitarian Miscellany and Christian Monitor*, April 1821, Vol. 1, pp. 213–222.
  Notes: presents Channing's critique of Hume's "Of Miracles."
  In *American Responses*: selection from pp. 214–217.
- Anonymous (pseud. "N."). "On Mr. Hume's Political Inconsistencies as an Historian," in *Monthly Repository*, 1821, Vol. 16, pp. 472–473.
  Notes: criticizes Hume's inconsistent statements regarding individual liberty.
  In *History Responses*: complete article.
- Channing, William Ellery (1780–1842). *A discourse on the evidences of revealed religion: delivered before the University in Cambridge at the Dudleian lecture, March 14, 1821.* Boston, 1821, 36 p.
  Notes: criticizes "Of Miracles."
  In *American Responses*: relevant portions as excerpted in book review from *Unitarian Miscellany*.
  Editions: in several editions of Ellery's *Works*.
  Reviews: *Unitarian Miscellany*, April 1821, Vol. 1, pp. 213–222 (positive; contained in *American Responses*, listed separately in this bibliography).
- [Gilman, Samuel Foster (1791–1858)]. Review of Thomas Brown's *Inquiry into the Relation of Cause and Effect*, in *The North American Review*, 1821, Vol. 12, pp. 395–432.
  Notes: defends Hume's and Brown's view of causality.
  In *American Responses*: selections from pp. 395–396, 419–430.
- Hill, George (1750–1819). *Lectures in divinity*. Edinburgh: Waugh & Innes, 1821, 3 v.
  Notes: posthumously published lectures edited from his manuscript by his son, Alexander Hill. 1.4.2 criticizes "Of Miracles" (Vol. 1, pp. 72–91 in the 1821 edition).

Editions: 1825, 1833, 1842, 1847, 1850, 1854, 1858, 1860.

- Mill, James (1773–1836). *Elements of political economy*, London: Printed for Baldwin, Cradock, and Joy, 1821, viii, 240 p.

  Notes: criticizes Hume's argument in "Of Money" that an increase in money vitalises an economy.

  In *Essays Responses*: Chapter 3, Section 12, selections; from 3rd Edition, 1844.

  Editions: several editions.

- Stewart, Dugald (1753–1828). *Dissertation on the Progress of Philosophy*, Part 2, supplemental volumes to the *Encyclopædia Britannica*, 1821.

  Notes: contains a letter from Gilbert Elliot of Minto to Hume (c. March 1751), criticizing a draft of Hume's *Dialogues*. The original letter has not surfaced and Stewart's transcription is the only surviving source.

  In *Religion Responses*: complete letter fragment; from Vol. 1 of Stewart's *Works* (1854–1858), pp. 606–609.

  Editions of *Dissertations* published separately: 1822, 1835, 1842, and in *Works* (1854–1858); see *Common Sense Bibliography* for a list of the editions.

  Reviews: *Quarterly Review*, April 1817, Vol. 17, p. 39–71; [James Macintosh], *Edinburgh Review*, September 1816, Vol. 27, pp. 180–244.

- Stewart, Dugald (1753–1828). *Dissertation on the Progress of Philosophy* Parts 1 and 2, supplemental volumes to the *Encyclopædia Britannica*, 1821.

  Notes: discusses Hume's scepticism and place in philosophy.

  In *Metaphysical Responses*: Part 2, Section 8, selections; from Vol. 1 of *Works* (1854–1858), pp. 431–456.

  Editions: various editions; see *Common Sense Bibliography* for a complete list.

  Reviews of Part 1: *Quarterly Review*, April 1817, Vol. 17, p. 39–71; [James Macintosh], *Edinburgh Review*, September 1816, Vol. 27, pp. 180–244.

  Reviews of Part 2: *Quarterly Review*, January 1922, Vol. 26, pp. 474–514; [James Macintosh], *Edinburgh Review*, October 1821, Vol. 36, pp. 220–267.

❧1822❧

- Brodie, George (1786?–1867). *A history of the British Empire, from the accession of Charles I. to the Restoration; with an introduction, tracing the progress of society, and of the constitution, from the feudal times to the opening of the history; and including a particular examination of Mr. Hume's statements relative to the character of the English government.* Edinburgh, Printed for Bell & Bradfute, 1822, 4 v.

  Notes: criticizes Hume's Tory view of royal prerogative, especially during Elizabeth's reign.

  In *History Responses*: Preface, selections from Chapter 2; from 1866 edition.

  Editions: 1866 (retitled *A Constitutional History of the British Empire*); no further editions.

  Microform: 19th-century legal treatises, no. 43338–43356.

  Reviews: [Francis Jeffrey] *Edinburgh Review*, March 1824, Vol. 40, pp. 92–146; [John Stuart Mill], *Westminster Review*, October 1824, Vol. 2, pp. 346–402. See entries on Jeffrey (1824) and Mill (1824).

  Discussions: William Smyth, *Lectures on Modern History* (1840).

- Cogan, Eliezer (1762–1855). "Examination of Mr. Hume's Objection to the Argument for the Being of God," in *Monthly Repository*, 1822, Vol. 17, pp. 65–68, 209–210.

  Notes: criticism of Hume's argument in the *Dialogues* that we have no experience in the origin of worlds, hence can't make conclusions about the origins of this one.

  In *Religion Responses*: complete article.

- Mackenzie, Henry (1745–1831). *An account of the life and writings of John Home, esq.,*

Edinburgh, Printed for A. Constable, 1822, vii, 184 p.

Manuscript location: National Library of Scotland, Acc. 10686.

Notes: stories about Hume based on personal acquaintance; similar to Mackenzie's discussion in *Anecdotes and Egotisms* (1927). Includes a comment by Baron David Hume (1757–1838) on the spelling of Hume's name. Also includes Home's diary of a Journey with Hume in April 1776.

In *Life Responses*: Home's diary and selections from Mackenzie's narrative included in separate entries. Baron Hume comment is included in "Miscellaneous Hume Anecdotes." These are all taken from the 1822 edition.

Editions: included in John Home's *Works* (1822); Home's diary reprinted in Burton, *Life* (1746), Vol. 2 Vol. 2, pp. 495–504; David Fate Norton, Edinburgh: Tragara Press, 1976, pp. 15–25.

Facsimiles: 1997 (Thoemmes Press of 1822).

Microform: Goldsmiths'-Kress library of economic literature, no. 23707.4 (of 1822).

- Tucker, George (1775–1861). *Essays on various subjects of taste, morals, and national policy*, Georgetown, D.C.: J. Milligan, 1822, xi, 350 p.

  Notes: 15 essays on economic, aesthetic and historical topics; Hume's views on aesthetics and economics are discussed.

  Editions: no further editions.

∂∙1823∙∂

- Anonymous (pseud. "N.Y. Amer."). "Gibbon, Voltaire, Hume," *The Gospel Trumpet*, 1823, Vol. 2, p. 63.

  Notes: brief paragraph states "the first provisional meeting for the formation of the Auxiliary Bible society, at Edinburgh, was held in the very room in which Hume died."

  In *American Responses*: complete article.

∂∙1824∙∂

- Anonymous. "Hume's History of England," in *The Atheneum; or, Spirit of the English Magazines*, 1824, Vol. 1, second series, p. 85.

  Notes: brief anecdote about Hume revising a portion of his *History* to make it more appealing and thus increasing its sales.

  In *American Responses*: complete article.

- Anonymous. Anecdote of Hume, in *Atheneum; or, Spirit of the English Magazines*, 1824, Vol. 1 (series 2), pp. 365.

  Notes: brief anecdote about Hume at dinners (original source of this anecdote is unknown).

  In *Life Responses*: comment included in "Miscellaneous Hume Anecdotes" as appears in *American Responses*.

  In *American Responses*: complete selection.

- Anonymous. "Skepticism," *The Christian Examiner and Theological Review*, 1824, Vol. 1, p. 35.

  Notes: quotes the conclusion of *Treatise* Book 1 maintaining the mournful consequences of Hume's philosophy.

  In *American Responses*: complete article.

- Beasley, Frederick (1777–1845). *A Search of Truth in the Science of the Human Mind*, Part First (Philadelphia, 1822); Philadelphia: S. Potter, 1822, viii, 561 p.

  Notes: detailed discussion of mental philosophy discusses Hume in several locations.

  In *American Responses*: Book 1.4, "The opinions of Mr. Hume on Cause and Effect," pp. 31–45; Book 1.5, "The opinions of other authors upon Cause and Effect," pp. 47–54, 58–82; Book 1.6, "The Opinions of Professor Stewart," pp. 83–112; Book 2.6, "Mr. Hume's Principles," pp. 227–32; Book 3.8 "Upon Miracles," pp. 363–90; Book 4, pp. 559–61 (on Hume's death).

Microform: Library of American Civilization, 3787 (of 1822); American culture series, 495.2. (of 1822).

- [Carter, James G. (1795–1849)]. Review of *Hume and Smollet Abridged*, in *The United States Literary Gazette*, 1824, Vol. 1, p. 196.

  Notes: argues that Hume's account of the Commonwealth was prejudicial.

  In *American Responses*: complete article.

- [Jeffrey, Francis (1773–1850)]. Review of Brodie's *History of the British Empire* (1822), in *Edinburgh Review*, March 1824, Vol. 40, pp. 92–146.

  Notes: criticizes Hume's "speculative" Toryism.

  In *History Responses*: selections from pages 92–112.

- [Mill, John Stuart (1806–1873)]. Review of George Brodie's *History of the British Empire* (1822) in *Westminster Review*, October 1824, Vol. 2, pp. 346–402.

  Notes: discusses Hume's dishonest artifices in creating a Tory history.

  In *History Responses*: selections.

- Prior, James (1790?–1869). *Memoir of the life and character of the Right Hon. Edmund Burke*, London, Baldwin, Cradock and Joy, 1824, xxiv, 584 p.

  Notes: brief anecdote about Hume in France.

  In *Life Responses*: story included in "Miscellaneous Hume Anecdotes."

  Editions: several editions.

  Reviews: [Richard Wellesley], *Quarterly Review*, September 1826, Vol. 34, pp. 457–487.

- [Shepherd, Mary (1777–1847)]. *An essay upon the relation of cause and effect: controverting the doctrine of Mr. Hume, concerning the nature of that relation, with observations upon the opinions of Dr. Brown and Mr. Lawrence connected with the same subject.* London: Printed for T. Hookham, 1824, vii, 194 p.

  Notes: criticism of Hume's view of causality.

  In *Metaphysical Responses*: complete book, from 1824 edition.

  Editions: no further editions.

  Facsimiles: 2000 (Thoemmes Press of 1824).

- Starkie, Thomas (1782–1849). *A practical treatise of the law of evidence and digest of proofs, in civil and criminal proceedings.* London: J. & W.T. Clarke, 1824, 3 v.

  Notes: discusses Hume's notion of experience in "Of Miracles."

  Editions: several 19th century editions.

  Microform: 19th-century legal treatises, no. 64300–64329 (of 1824).

  Discussions: Alexander Hamilton Lawrence, *Examination* (1845).

❧1825❧

- [Allen, John (1771–1843)]. Review of John Lingard's *A history of England*, in *Edinburgh Review*, April 1825, Vol. 42, pp. 3–7.

  Notes: analyses Hume views of civil liberty and partiality for kings.

  In *History Responses*: selections.

  Discussions: Francis Palgrave, "Hume and his Influence upon History" (1826).

- Chambers, Robert (1802–1871). *Traditions of Edinburgh*, Edinburgh, W. & C. Tait, 1825, 2 v.

  Notes: includes section on Hume describing Hume's Edinburgh dwellings and a dinner at Alison Cockburn's house.

  In *Life Responses*: complete section on Hume; from London: W. & R. Chambers; Philadelphia, J.B. Lippincott, 1912, pp. 55–60.

Editions: several editions.

- Chambers, Robert (1802–1871). *Walks in Edinburgh*, Edinburgh, Hunter, 1825 (pp. 182–183 of 1888 edition).

  Notes: includes a brief anecdote about Hume at St. David's Street.

  In *Life Responses*: story included in "Miscellaneous Hume Anecdotes."

  Editions: several editions.

- [Sparks, Jared (1789–1866)]. Review of Edward Everett's *Oration pronounced at Cambridge* and *Oration delivered at Plymouth*, in *The North American Review*, 1825, Vol. 20, pp. 417–40.

  Notes: includes discussion of Hume's "Of the Rise and Progress of the Arts and Sciences."

  In *American Responses*: selection from pp. 418–419.

๑►1826◄๑

- Dewar, Daniel (1787?–1867). *Elements of moral philosophy and of Christian ethics.* London: J. Duncan, 1826, 2 Vol., vii, 502; vii, 598.

  Notes: criticizes Paley's and Hume's views of utility.

  In *Moral Responses*: Book 3, Ch. 5, 7, 8 and 11; from 1826 edition.

  Editions: no further editions.

- [Palgrave, Francis (1788–1861)]. "Anglo-Saxon History," in *Quarterly Review*, London, June 1826, Vol. 34, 248–298.

  Notes: attacks Hume's uncritical reliance on historical sources.

  In *History Responses*: selections; from *Quarterly Review*.

  Editions: *Palgrave's Collected Historical Works* (Cambridge, 1922, Vol. 9, pp. 375–428).

  Discussions: H.E. Maldin, editor's introduction to Palgrave's *Works*, 1922 (relevant quotations included in editors introduction to Palgrave's "Anglo-Saxon History" in *History Responses*).

๑►1827◄๑

- Jevons, William (1794–1873). *Systematic morality: or, A treatise on the theory and practice of human duty on the grounds of natural religion.* London: Printed for R. Hunter, 1827, 2 v.

  Notes: Volume 2, pages 160 ff. address Hume's account of causality and his application of it to the design argument.

  Reviews: *Monthly Repository*, January 1927, Vol. 1 (new series), p. 890 ff.

- [Shepherd, Mary (1777–1847)]. *Essays on the perception of an external universe, and other subjects connected with the doctrine of causation.* London: John Hatchard, 1827, xvi, 416 p.

  Notes: criticism of Berkeley's denial of an external physical world with criticisms of Hume's view.

  Editions: no further editions.

  Facsimiles: 2000 (Thoemmes Press of 1827)

๑►1828◄๑

- Ballantyne, John (1778–1830). *An examination of the human mind.* Edinburgh, Blackwood, 1828, vi, 502 p.

  Notes: criticizes much of the science of mind developed by Scottish philosophers from Hume to Thomas Brown, but commends Hume for seeing the importance of the associative principle.

- [Brooks, Edward (1784–1850)]. Review of Clarendon's *History of the Rebellion and Civil*

Wars in England, in *North American Review*, October 1828, Vol. 27, pp. 300–317.
Notes: criticizes Hume's *History* for sophistry and misrepresentation.
In *American Responses*: complete article.
- [Carlyle, Thomas (1795–1881)]. "Burns," *Edinburgh Review*, December 1828, Vol. 48, pp. 267–312.
  Notes: brief comment on Hume's cosmopolitan writings.
  In *Life Responses*: quotation in introduction to Carlyle's "Characteristics" (1831); from *Critical and Miscellaneous*, Boston, Phillips, 1855.
  Editions: in several editions of Carlyle's *Works*.
- Stewart, Dugald (1753–1828). *The philosophy of the active and moral powers of man*. Edinburgh: A. Black; London: Longman, Rees, Orme, Brown, and Green, 1828, 2 Vol., xv, 416; vii. 544.
  Notes: discusses reality of moral distinctions, criticizes Hume's views of utility and artificial justice.
  In Moral responses: selections from Book 2.5.1, Book 4.1.1, and Book 4.1.2; from *Works* (1854–1858).
  In *Essays Responses*: Book 2.5.1, pp. 291–295, Book 4.1.1, pp. 233–239, Book 4.1.2, pp. 254–256; from Vol. 6 and 7 of *Works* (1854–1858).
  Editions: several editions; see *Common Sense Bibliography* for a complete list.

❧1829❧

- Anonymous (pseud. "Juverna"). "A Parallel Between Hume and Robertson, as Historians," in *The Irish Shield and Monthly Milesian*, 1829, Vol. 1, pp. 403–407.
  Notes: discusses the merits of both Hume and Robertson.
  In *American Responses*: complete article.
- Anonymous. Review of Lord Mahon's *The Life of Belisarius*, in *Christian Examiner*, 1829, Vol. 7, pp. 202–212.
  Notes: states that Hume displays the power of the historian to remove "venerable errors."
  In *American Responses*: selection from pp. 204–205, 208–211.
- [Brooks, Edward (1784–1850)]. Review of John Lingard's *Constitutional History*, and three others works, in *North American Review*, July 1829, Vol. 29, pp. 265–281.
  Notes: criticizes Hume's *History*.
  In *American Responses*: complete article.
- Crombie, Alexander (1762–1840). *Natural theology; or, Essays on the existence of Deity and of Providence, on the immateriality of the soul, and a future state*. London, printed for R. Hunter [etc.], 1829, 2 v.
  Notes: criticizes Hume's *Dialogues*.
  In *Religion Responses*: 1.1.7 complete, 1.1.16, selections; from 1829 edition.
  Editions: no further editions.
  Facsimiles: 2001 (Thoemmes Press of 1829).
  Reviews: *Edinburgh Review*, September 1831, Vol. 54, pp. 147–159, [Robert Ferguson], *Quarterly Review*, March 1834, Vol. 51, pp. 213–228.

❧1830❧

- Anonymous. "Belief and Unbelief," *Christian Examiner*, January 1830, Vol. 7, pp. 358–365.
  Notes: argues that Hume was an honourable sceptic, and not a promoter of scornful, contemptuous, sneering unbelief.
  In *American Responses*: selection from pp. 363–364.
- Alexander, Archibald (1772–1851). *Evidences of the Authenticity, Inspiration and Canonical Authority of the Holy Scriptures*, Philadelphia, Presbyterian board of

publication, 1830, 308 p.

Notes: expanded from *A Brief Outline of the Evidences of the Christian Religion* (1825); criticizes "Of Miracles."

In *American Responses*: Chapter 6. "Miracles are Capable of Proof from Testimony," pp. 65–88.

Facsimiles: 1972 (Arno Press of 1836).

Editions: several later editions.

Microform: Library of American civilization, LAC 10921 (of 1836).

• Douglas, James (1790–1861). *Errors regarding Religion*. Edinburgh: Adam Black, 1830, 331 p.

Notes: Section 6 titled "Infidelity" criticizes Hume's views on religion, and also, to a lesser extent, the views of Spinoza, Bayle, Rousseau, Voltaire and Gibbon.

Editions: 1831, 1834, 1962.

• Mackenzie, Henry (1745–1831). Anecdotes of David Hume (c. 1830).

See Henry Mackenzie, *The anecdotes and egotisms of Henry Mackenzie* (1927).

Notes: contains a section of anecdotes about Hume, similar to Mackenzie's discussion of Hume in his *Account* (1822). This previous unpublished manuscript was written by Mackenzie around 1830.

In *Life Responses*: selections; from 1927 edition.

• Morehead, Robert (1777–1842). *Dialogues on natural and revealed religion*. Edinburgh, Oliver & Boyd, 1830, 468 p.

Notes: critique of Hume's philosophy in a series of dialogues involving Philo, Cleanthes and Pamphilus. Morehead argues that Philo's restless quest must lead him on his own principles to revelation. The work is prefaced with a lengthy "Preliminary Inquiry" consisting in a critique of Hume's philosophy.

Discussions: Robert Morehead, *Philosophical Dialogues* (1845).

❧1831❧

• Anonymous (pseud. "O.B."). "On the Death-Bed of Hume the Historian," letter to the Editor, in *The Christian Observer*, November 1831, Vol. 31, No. xi, No. 359, pp. 665–666.

Notes: anecdote of Hume's deathbed anguish as first appeared in an unnamed British periodical.

In *Life Responses*: complete letter, from *The Christian Observer*.

In *American Responses*: complete letter as reprinted in *The Spirit of the Pilgrims*, 1832, Vol. 5, pp. 172–173.

Discussions: Charles Pettit McIlvaine, *Evidences* (1832).

• [Carlyle, Thomas (1795–1881)]. "Characteristics," *Edinburgh Review*, December 1831, Vol. 108, pp. 351–383.

Notes: compares Hume's and Johnson's lives and deaths.

In *Life Responses*: selections; from *Critical and Miscellaneous*, Boston, Phillips, 1855.

Editions: in several editions of Carlyle's *Works*.

• D'Arblay, Alexander Charles Lewis. *The apostolic gift of tongues, contrasted with some modern claims to inspiration: a sermon, preached in Camden Chapel, St. Pancras, on January 8, 1832, preceded by an introductory discourse on the prevailing spirit of the times, and its effects on national religion*. London: J. G. & F. Rivington, 1832, pp. 60.

Notes: includes an appendix criticizing Hume's "Of Miracles."

• [Everett, Edward (1794–1865)]. Review of de Sismondi's *The Prospect of Reform in Europe*, in *The North American Review*, 1831, Vol. 33, pp. 154–190.

Notes: briefly discusses Hume's view that absolute monarchy is the true euthanasia of the British constitution (from "Whether the British Government....").

In *American Responses*: selection from p. 189.

● [Hallam, Henry (1777–1859)]. Review of John Lingard's *A history of England*, in *Edinburgh Review*, March 1831, Vol. 53, p. 1.

Notes: shows Hume's heavy reliance on Thomas Carte's *History*.

In *History Responses*: selections.

≈1832≈

● Adams, John Quincy (1767–1848). *Dermot MacMorrogh, or, The conquest of Ireland an historical tale of the twelfth century: in four cantos*. Boston: Carter, Hendee and Co., 1832, xiv, 108 p.

Notes: criticizes Hume's account of Henry II in the *History*.

Editions: 1832 (second edition), 1834, 1849, 1850.

Microform: American Poetry, 1609–1900, Segment II, no. 15 (of 1832 first edition); Segment II, no. 16 (of 1832 second edition).

Reviews: [Richard Hildreth], *New-England Magazine*, 1832, Vol. 3, pp. 503–507 (listed separately in this bibliography).

● Cullen, William (1710–1790). *An account of the life, lectures and writings of William Cullen*, John Thomson, ed., Edinburgh: Blackwood; London: Cadell, 1832, xvi, 668 p. [Vol. 1].

Notes: biography of Cullen contains a letter describing Hume's final days.

Editions: 1859 (Vol. 1 and a new Vol. 2); letter reprinted in part in Burton's *Life* (1846).

Facsimiles: 1997 (Thoemmes Press of 1859).

● [Chambers, Robert (1802–1871)]. *Scottish jests and anecdotes*, Edinburgh: W. Paterson, c.1832, 252 p.

Notes: relates anecdotes about Hume.

In *Life Responses*: relevant selections; from second edition, Edinburgh: William Tait, 1838.

In *American Responses*: contains one of these anecdotes as reprinted in "Anecdote of Hume," *Ladies' Literary Cabinet*, 1821, Vol. 4, p.

Editions: several editions.

● [Hildreth, Richard (1807–1865)]. Notice of John Quincy Adams's *Dermot MacMorrogh*, in *The New-England Magazine*, 1832, Vol. 3, pp. 503–507.

Notes: harsh review which denounces Adams's critique of Hume's *History*.

In *American Responses*: selections from pp. 504–506.

● Mackintosh, James (1765–1832). *A general view of the progress of ethical philosophy, chiefly during the seventeenth and eighteenth centuries*. Philadelphia, Carey, Lea, and Blanchard, 1832, 304 p.

Notes: opposes Samuel Taylor Coleridge's claim in *Biographia Literaria* (1817) that Hume plagiarized his principles of association from Aquinas.

Editions: 1834, 1842.

● McIlvaine, Charles Pettit (1799–1873). *The evidences of Christianity: in their external division, exhibited in a course of lectures, delivered in Clinton hall, in the winter of 1831-2, under the appointment of the University of the city of New York*. New York, G. & C. & H. Carvill, 1832, xvi, [17]–565 p.

Notes: criticizes Smith's account of Hume's death.

In *Life Responses*: selections from Lecture 11; from 1861 edition.

Editions: several editions.

≈1833≈

● Abercrombie, John (1780–1844). *The philosophy of the moral feelings*. London: J. Murray, 1833, xv, 244 p.

Notes: criticizes Hume's view of utility.

In *Moral Responses*: Part 3, Sect. 1, selections; from 1855 edition.

Editions: several editions; see *Common Sense Bibliography* for a complete list.

- [Adams, Charles Francis (1807–1886)]. Review of Robert Vaughan's *Memorials of the Stuart Dynasty*, in *The North American Review*, 1833, Vol. 37, pp. 164–189.

Notes: criticism of Hume on the Puritans and Charles I.

In *American Responses*: selection from pp. 165, 173–177.

- Blakey, Robert (1795–1878). *The history of moral science*. London: J. Duncan, 1833, 2 v.

Notes: Vol. 2, Chapter 18 defends Hume's view of utility.

In *Moral Responses*: Chapter 18 selections, from 1833 edition.

Editions: 1836, 1837.

Microform: Library of American civilization, LAC 21378; 19th-century legal treatises, no. 14122–14130.

Reviews: [Henry Rogers], *Eclectic Review*, February 1834, Vol. 59, pp 136–149.

- Dick, Thomas (1774–1857). *On the improvement of society by the diffusion of knowledge*, Glasgow & London, W. Collins, 1833, 336 p.

Notes: criticizes Adam Smith's praise of Hume in "Letter … to William Strahan."

In *Life Responses*: short quote only; from *On the Improvement*, St. Louis, Edwards, 1857, p. 163.

Editions: several editions and in differing editions of *Works*.

- Gillespie, William Honyman (1808–1875). *An argument, a priori, for the being and attributes of God*. Edinburgh: Printed for Waugh & Innes, 1833, iv, 67 p.

Notes: criticizes Hume's *Dialogues*; later editions incorporate Gillespie's response to Simpson's Refutation (1838).

Editions: 1865, 1871, 1875, 1906, 1910.

Microform: ATLA fiche 1985–1288 (of 1906).

Discussions: George Simpson, *Refutation of the Argument* (1838).

- Withington, Leonard (1789–1885). "Hume, as a Historian," *The American Quarterly Observer*, 1833, Vol. 1, pp. 189–205.

Notes: critical appraisal of Hume's *History*, noting that its contradictory character is its own refutation.

In *American Responses*: complete article.

ᕖ1834ᕗ

- Haldane, Robert (1764–1842). *The evidence and authority of divine revelation: being a view of the testimony of the law and the prophets to the Messiah, with the subsequent testimonies*, Edinburgh: Printed by A. Balfour, Merchant Court, for Olphant, [etc], 1834, 2 v.

Notes: anecdote of Hume's deathbed anguish.

In *Life Responses*: selections from chapter 1; from 1839 third edition.

Editions: several editions.

Discussions: Alexander Haldane, *Memoirs* (1852).

- More, Hannah (1745–1833); Roberts, William (1767–1849). *Memoirs of the life and correspondence of Mrs. Hannah More*, London, R.B. Seeley, 1834, 4 v.

Notes: Volume 1, page 16 Roberts includes a brief anecdote about Hume's stay in Bristol as reported by More. Volume 2, page 393 includes a letter from More to her sister that discusses Hume's attitude about death.

In *Life Responses*: Bristol story included in "Miscellaneous Hume Anecdotes," short quotation about Hume's death included in introduction to More's *Practical Piety* (1811).

Editions: 1834 (New York), 1835, 1836, 1838.

Microform: Library of English literature, LEL 22440–41 (of London 1834); History of women, reel 179, no. 1170 (of 1835).

❧1835❧

- Brougham, Henry (1778–1868). *A discourse of natural theology: showing the nature of the evidence and the advantages of the study.* London: Charles Knight, 1835, vii, 296 p.
  Notes: discusses "Of Miracles" and Hume's critique of the design argument.
  Editions: several editions.
- [Croker, John Wilson (1780–1857)]. Review of Alexander Keith's *Evidence of the truth of the Christian Religion* (1833), in *Quarterly Review*, February 1835, Vol. 53, pp. 142–174.
  Notes: contains a 10 page attack on Hume's argument against miracles.
- Whewell, William (1794–1866). *Thoughts on the study of mathematics as a part of a liberal education.* Cambridge: J. & J.J. Deighton, 1835, 46 p.
  Notes: criticizes Hume for contending that mathematical truths are learned by experience.
  Editions: 1835 (expanded).
- Withington, Leonard (1789–1885). "Hume, as a Historian," in *American Quarterly*, October 1835, Vol. 1, pp. 191–205.

❧1836❧

- [Adam, William (1751–1839)]. *Two short essays, on the study of history, and on general reading. With a preface, and concluding note. The gift of a grandfather.* [Edinburgh:] Blair Adam Press, August 1836, [1] iii–xi, 27 p.
  Notes: stories about Hume based on personal acquaintance.
  In *Life Responses*: selections; from 1836 edition.
  Editions: no further editions.
- Chalmers, Thomas (1780–1847). *On Natural Theology.* New York, Leavitt, 1836, 2 v.
  Notes: discusses Hume's criticisms of theistic proofs.
  Editions: 1840, 1844, 1845, 1851, 1852, 1853, 1855, 1857.
  Reviews: *Quarterly Christian Spectator*, May 1838, Vol. 10, Number 2, pp. 319–337 (mixed; in *American Responses*, listed separately in this bibliography).

❧1837❧

- O'Connor, Henry. *Connected essays and tracts, being a series of inferences, deduced chiefly from … the most celebrated sceptics…, And an appendix containing a brief review of Hume's Natural History of Religion.* Dublin, Hodges and Smith, 1837, xxiv, 344 p.
  Notes: Appendix 2, pages 207–228, criticizes Hume's "Natural History of Religion."
  In *Hume on Natural Religion*: complete Appendix.

❧1838❧

- Anonymous. Review of Thomas Chalmers's *Natural Theology*, in *Quarterly Christian Spectator*, May 1838, Vol. 10, Number 2, pp. 319–337.
  Notes: criticizes Chalmers's account of the design argument which he thinks concedes too much to Hume.
  In *American Responses*: selection from pp. 322–324.
- Craik, George L. (1798–1866). *The pictorial history of England: being a history of the people as well as a history of the kingdom to the reign of George III.* London, C. Knight, 1838–1841, 4 v.
  Notes: praises Hume's *History*.
  In *History Responses*: selections included in "Miscellaneous Comments on Hume's History."
  Reviews: [Herman Merivale], *Edinburgh Review*, Vol. 74, January 1842, pp.

430–473 (selection in *History Responses* in "Miscellaneous Comments on Hume's *History*").

● [Simpson, George]. *Refutation of the argument a priori for the being and attributes of God; showing the fallacious reasoning of Dr. Samuel Clarke and others, especially of Mr. Gillespie. By Antitheos.* Glasgow, 1838.

Notes: criticism of Gillesie's *Argument* (1833), to which Gillesie responded; discusses Hume's *Dialogues*.

Editions: 1842.

&1839&

● [Adam, William (1751–1839)]. *Sequel to the Gift of a Grandfather*, [Edinburgh], 1839, 64 p.

Notes: stories about Hume based on personal acquaintance.

In *Life Responses*: selections; from 1839 edition.

Editions: selections from section on Hume in Burton's *Life* (1846), Vol. 2, pp. 439–440; no further editions.

● [De Quincey, Thomas (1785–1859)]. "On Hume's Argument Against Miracles." *Blackwood's Edinburgh Magazine*, July 1839, Vol. 46, pp. 91–99.

Editions: in De Quincey's *Works*, Vol. 8.

In *Hume on Miracles*: complete article; from *Blackwood's Edinburgh Magazine*.

● [Everett, Alexander Hill (1790–1847)]. Review of 1838 translation of Kant's *Critick of Pure Reason*, in *The North American Review*, 1839, Vol. 49, pp. 44–68.

Notes: connects Hume's scepticism with Kant's transcendental philosophy.

In *American Responses*: selection from pp. 54–55.

&1840&

● Lindsay, Alexander Crawford (1812–1880), ed. *Lives of the Lindsays; or, A memoir of the houses of Crawford and Balcarres.* Wigan [England], Printed by C. S. Simms, 1840, 4 v.

Notes: letter from Anne Lindsay-Barnard to her sister Margaret Lindsay (c. 1770) describing Hume at her family's house.

In *Life Responses*: complete letter fragment; from *Lives of The Lindsays*, London, Murray, 1858, Vol. 2, pp. 321–322.

Editions: 1749, 1758; included in Burton's *Life* (1846), Vol. 2, pp. 445–446; included in Mossner's *Life* (1980), p. 569.

Reviews: [J.G. Lockhart], *Quarterly Review*, March 1846, Vol. 77, pp. 465–496 (positive).

● Smyth, William (1765–1849). *Lectures on modern history: from the irruption of the northern nations to the close of the American Revolution.* London: William Pickering; J. and J.J. Deighton, 1840, 2 v.

Notes: criticizes Hume's Tory view of royal prerogative.

In *History Responses*: selections from Lectures 5, 10, 14 and 18; from 1840 edition.

Editions: several 19th century editions, 1955 (abridged).

Discussions: Francis Palgrave, "Hume and his Influence upon History" (1826).

&1841&

● Murray, Thomas (1792–1872). *Letters of David Hume and extracts from letters referring to him.* Edinburgh, Adam and Charles Black, 1841, 80 p.

Notes: Preface describes origin and value of the letters.

In *Life Responses*: complete Preface; from 1841 edition.

Editions: 1841 (second edition), 1842.

Microform: Goldsmiths'-Kress library of economic literature, no. 31947.

- Warburton, William (1698–1779). Paper on "Of Miracles" (1749?), from Francis Kilvert, *A selection from unpublished papers of ... William Warburton*. London, J.B. Nichols and Son, 1841, xx, 449 p., pp. 311–315.
  Notes: criticizes Hume's "Of Miracles."
  In *Religion Responses*: complete essay.

ঌ1843ঙ

- Anonymous. "Hume: 1711-1776," *The New Englander*, January 1843, Vol. 1, pp. 169–176.
  Notes: biographical sketch, discussion of religious views.
- Anonymous. "Hume, Voltaire, and Rousseau, A concise, impartial, and authentic account of their lives and their assaults upon Christianity," in *New Englander*, April 1843, Vol. 1, pp. 169–183.

ঌ1844ঙ

- Chambers, Robert (1802–1871). "David Hume," in *Cyclopædia of English literature; a history, critical and biographical, of British authors, from the earliest to the present times*. Edinburgh, W. and R. Chambers, 1844, 2 v.
  Notes: criticizes Hume for inaccuracy and partiality.
  In *History Responses*: selections; from 1867 Philadelphia edition, Vol. 2, pp. 169–170.
  Editions: several editions.
- [Palgrave, Francis (1788–1861)]. "Hume and his influence upon history," in *Quarterly Review*, March 1844, Vol. 73, pp. 536–592.
  Notes: criticizes Hume for inaccuracy and religious bias.
  In *History Responses*: complete article.
  In *Life Responses*: brief anecdote about Hume's writing habits included in "Miscellaneous Hume Anecdotes."
  Editions: *Palgrave's Collected Historical Works*, (Cambridge, 1922, Vol. 9, pp. 535–592).
  Discussions: Discussions: H.E. Maldin, editor's introduction to Palgrave's *Works*, 1922, (relevant quotations included in editors introduction to Palgrave's "Anglo-Saxon History" in *History Responses*).

ঌ1845ঙ

- Brougham, Henry (1778–1868). *Lives of men of letters & science, who flourished in the time of George III*. London, Knight, 1845, Vol. 1, 516 p.
  Notes: chapter titled "Hume" contains a biographical sketch of Hume with an appendix of unpublished letters.
  In *Life Responses*: brief anecdote of Hume's views of religion included in "Miscellaneous Hume Anecdotes."
  Editions: several editions and in *Works*.
  Reviews: [James Roche], *Dublin Review*, June 1845, Vol. 18, pp. 518–555, *Dublin University Magazine*, June 1845, Vol. 25, pp. 690–709, *Fraser's Magazine*, June 1845, Vol. 31, pp. 647–659, [John Hill Burton], *Tate's Edinburgh Magazine*, June 1845, Vol. 16 (12 n.s.), pp. 341–358, [John Gibson Lockhart], *Quarterly Review*, June 1845, Vol. 76, pp. 62–98; [William Bourn Oliver Peabody], *North American Review*, 1845, Vol. 61, pp. 383–421.
- [Peabody, William Bourn Oliver (1799–1847)]. Review of Brougham's *Lives of Men of Letters and Science*, in *The North American Review*, 1845, Vol. 61, pp. 383–421.
  Notes: adaptation of Brougham's chapter on Hume.
  In *American Responses*: selection from pp. 399–405.
- Lawrence, Alexander Hamilton (1812–1857). *An examination of Hume's argument on the subject of miracles*. Washington, J. and G.S. Gideon, 1845, 20 p.

Notes: criticizes Hume's "Of Miracles."

In *American Responses*: criticizes Starkie's refutation of Hume's "Of Miracles" and offers a refutation of his own.

Reviews: *North American Review*, 1846, Vol. 62, pp. 263–264 (positive; in *American Responses*).

• Morehead, Robert (1777–1842). *Philosophical dialogues*. London: Simpkin, Marshall, and Company, 1845, v, 163 p.

Notes: continuation of Morehead's *Dialogues* (1830); a critique of Hume's account of the intellectual powers.

☙1846❧

• Anonymous. Review of Alexander Hamilton Lawrence's *Examination of Hume's Argument on the Subject of Miracles*, in *The North American Review*, 1846, Vol. 62, pp. 263–264.

Notes: favourable review.

In *American Responses*: complete article.

• Burton, John Hill (1809–1881). *Life and correspondence of David Hume: from the papers bequeathed by his nephew to the Royal Society of Edinburgh, and other original sources*. Edinburgh: W. Tait, 1846, 2 v.

Notes: biography based on material that was in the possession of Hume's family after his death; includes previously unpublished Hume anecdotes gathered by Burton.

In *Life Responses*: complete Advertisement and selected anecdotes from Chapters 16 and 17; from 1846.

Editions: no further editions.

Facsimiles: 1967 (Franklin of 1846), 1969 (Scientia of 1846), 1983 (Garland of 1846), Microform: Goldsmiths'-Kress library of economic literature, no. 34504.

Reviews: [William Jerdan], *Tait's Edinburgh Magazine*, March and April 1846, Vol. 17 (n.s. 13), pp. 137–145; 205–215; *Dublin University Magazine*, March and May 1846 Vol. 27, pp. 356–571, 576–591 (also in *Eclectic Magazine*, Vol. 8, pp. 80 ff., 258 ff.); [Taylor, William Cooke]; "The philosophy of David Hume," *Bentley's Miscellany*, May 1846, Vol. 19, pp. 494–502; [R.N.] *Westminster Review*, October 1846, Vol. 46, pp. 144–174; [William Charles Lake], *Quarterly Review*, June 1846, Vol. 78, pp. 75–113; [William Empson], *Edinburgh Review*, January 1847, Vol. 85, pp. 1–72; [James Moncreiff?] *North British Review*, August 1847, Vol. 7, pp. 539–560; *Athenaeum*, 1846 261 ff., 289 ff.; *Christian Rem*, Vol. 13, p. 62.

• Hopkins, Mark (1802–1887). *Lectures on the evidences of Christianity before the Lowell Institute, January, 1844*. Boston: T. R. Marvin, 1846, 383 p.

Notes: discusses "Of Miracles."

Editions: several 19th century editions.

Reviews: [Noah Porter]. *The New-Englander*, 1846, Vol. 4, pp. 401–410 (in *American Responses*, listed separately in this bibliography).

• [Porter, Noah (1811–1892)]. Review of Mark Hopkins, *Lectures on the Evidences of Christianity*, in *The New-Englander*, 1846, Vol. 4, pp. 401–410.

Notes: Porter discusses "Of Miracles," criticising both Hume and Hopkins.

In *American Responses*: selection from pp. 405–409.

• Walker, Alexander (1779–1852). *Beauty; illustrated chiefly by an analysis and classification of beauty in woman, preceded by a critical view of the general hypotheses respecting beauty, by Hume, Hogarth, Burke, Knight, Alison, &c. and followed by a similar view of the hypotheses of beauty in sculpture and painting, by Leonardo da Vinci, Winckelmann, Mengs, Bossi*. London, H.G. Bohn, 1846 vi, [7]–225 p.

Notes: discusses Hume's view of beauty.

Editions: several editions.

Microform: History of women, reel 232, no. 1547 (of 1846 second edition).
- Young, John Radford (1799–1885). *Three lectures addressed to the students of Belfast college on some of the advantages of mathematical study; to which is added an examination of Hume's argument against miracles.* London, Souter and Law, 1846, vi, 88, p.
  Notes: discusses Hume's "Of Miracles."

❧1847❧

- [Peabody, William Bourn Oliver (1799–1847)]. Review of Brougham's *Lives of Men of Letters and Science*, in *The North American Review*, 1847, Vol. 64, pp. 59–97;
  Notes: criticizes Adam Smith's "Letter... to William Strahan."
  In *American Responses*: selection from p. 72.

❧1849❧

- Anonymous. Review of 1849 edition of Hume's *History*, in *The Knickerbocker, or New-York Monthly Magazine*, 1849, Vol. 34, p. 257.
  Notes: presents a biographical sketch based "My Own Life."
  In *American Responses*: complete article.
- Anonymous. Review of 1849 edition of Hume's *History*, Vols 1–4, in *Graham's American Magazine*, 1849, Vol. 35, p. 379.
  Notes: positive review noting that Hume's history "ranks with the greatest historical works ever written in this world."
  In *American Responses*: complete article.
- [Bowen, Francis (1811–1890)]. Review of 1849 edition of Hume's *History*, in *The North American Review*, 1849, Vol. 69, pp. 527–528.
  Notes: positive review stating that "the book is immortal."
  In *American Responses*: complete article.
- Burton, John Hill (1809–1881). *Letters of eminent persons addressed to David Hume. From the papers bequeathed by his nephew to the Royal Society of Edinburgh*, Edinburgh, 1849, xxxi, 334 p.
  Notes: transcription of 147 from the approximately 525 letters to Hume that were among Hume's personal collection of manuscripts, which in Burton's time were in possession of the Royal Society of Edinburgh. The letters are presented complete, with little annotation, and the table of contents summarizes each letter. Many letters reveal the contents of letters written by Hume which are now lost.
  In *History Responses*: Owen Ruffhead, letter to Hume, March 1, 1763, Complete letter, opposes Hume's view of the powerlessness of the Saxon Commons.
  In *Life Responses*: Introductory Notice, describes value of the letters.
  Editions: no further editions.
  Facsimiles: 1989 (Thoemmes Press of 1849).
  Microform: British culture series, Group I, no. 7.

❧1850❧

- Anonymous. Review of 1849 edition of Hume's *History*, Vol. 5, in *Graham's American Magazine*, 1850, Vol. 36, p. 223.
  Notes: short paragraph, positive review.
  In *American Responses*: complete article.
- Anonymous. Review of 1850 edition of Hume's *History*, in *The New Englander*, 1850, Vol. 8 , pp. 322–323.
  Notes: mixed review stating that Hume "distorts the transactions which he records."
  In *American Responses*: complete article.
- Burgess, George (1809–1966). *The Last Enemy; Conquering and Conquered,*

Philadelphia: H. Hooker, 1850, iv, 330 p.

Notes: "The Mind in Death," p. 163, criticizes Adam Smith's praise of Hume in "Letter ... to William Strahan."

In *Life Responses*: short quote only; from 1850 edition, p. 163.

Editions: 1861.

• Tucker, George (1775–1861). *An essay on cause and effect; being an examination of Hume's doctrine, that we can perceive no necessary connexion between them.* Philadelphia, Lea & Blanchard, 1850, 1 p. l., [2], [9]–52 p.

Notes: criticizes Hume's view of causality.

In *Metaphysical Responses*: complete pamphlet; from 1850 edition.

Editions: contained in Tucker's *Essays, Moral and Metaphysical* (1860).

☙1852❧

• Haldane, Alexander (1800–1882). *Memoirs of the lives of Robert Haldane of Airthrey, and of his brother, James Alexander Haldane,* London: Hamilton, Adams, and co., 1852 xvi, 676 p.

Notes: discusses Robert Haldane's anecdote on Hume's deathbed anguish.

In *Life Responses*: selections from Chapter 24; from 1852 edition.

Editions: no further editions.

• Wardlaw, Ralph (1779–1853). *On miracles.* Edinburgh: A. Fullarton, 1852, xvi, 317 p.

Notes: Chapter 3 titled "Mr. Hume's Argument."

Editions: 1853, 1857, 1861.

Microform: ATLA fiche 1989–1465.

☙1853❧

• Ballantyne, John (1778–1830). "On the Being of a God," in John Brown, *Theological tracts, selected and original.* Edinburgh: A. Fullarton, 1853–1854, 3 v.

Notes: Volume 2, pp. 37–53 includes Ballantyne's posthumous "On the Being of a God," which argues that Paley's defence of the design argument needs to be strengthened if it is to avoid Hume's criticism.

☙1854❧

• Mure, William (1799–1860). ed., *Selections from the Family papers preserved at Caldwell,* Glasgow, [Maitland Club Publications], 1854, 2 pt. in 3 v.

Notes: stories about Hume in correspondence from acquaintances. Includes a letter from James Oswald of Dunnikier (1715–1769) criticizing Hume's economic essay "Of the Balance of Trade" prior to its publication in *Political Discourses*.

In *Essays Responses*: Oswald's letter, complete; from 1854 edition, Part 2, Vol. 1, pp. 93-107.

In *Life Responses*: selections from Part 2, Volumes 1 and 2; from 1854 edition.

Editions: 1883 (second edition).

Selections from Oswald's Letter: Eugene Rotwein, ed., *David Hume: Writings on Economics,* Madison: University of Wisconsin, 1970, pp. 190–196 (taken from Mure's *Selctions*).

Reviews: *Quarterly Review,* September 1855, Vol. 97, pp. 378–407 (positive).

☙1855❧

• Lawrence, Eugene (1823–1894). *The lives of British historians.* New York, C. Scribner, 1855, 2 v.

Notes: Hume is discussed in Vol. 2.

• Mathews, James McFarlane (1785–1870). *The Bible and men of learning; in a course of lectures*, New York, Fanshaw, 1855, 392 p., p. 176.

Notes: brief criticism of Smith's account of Hume's death.

In *Life Responses*: relevant selections in "Miscellaneous Comments on Adam Smith's 'Letter'"; as appears in John Reid's *Voices* (1865).

● Potter, Alonzo (1800–1865). Introduction, in *Lectures on the evidences of Christianity, delivered in Philadelphia, by clergymen of the Protestant Episcopal church.* Philadelphia, E.H. Butler & co., 1855, 408 p.

Notes: criticizes Adam Smith's praise of Hume in "Letter ... to William Strahan."

In *Life Responses*: short quote only; from 1873 edition, p. 37.

Editions: 1873.

● Stewart, Dugald (1753–1828). *Lectures on political economy now first published.* Edinburgh: Thomas Constable and Co. Hamilton, Adams, and Co., London, 1855, 2 Vol.

Notes: criticizes Hume's views in "Of Money", "Of Interest", "Of Public Credit", "Of the Idea of a Perfect Commonwealth", and "Of the Independency of Parliament."

In *Essays Responses*: 1.2.2.3, pp. 371–380; 1.2.2.5, pp. 396–408; 1.2.4.1, pp. 217–220; 2.1.2.1, pp. 373–376; 2.2.2, pp. 444–452; from Vol. 8 and 9 in *Collected Works* (1855).

Editions: several editions; see *Common Sense Bibliography* for a complete list.

● Tagart, Edward (1804–1858). *Locke's writings and philosophy historically considered, and vindicated from the charge of contributing to the scepticism of Hume.* London: Longman, Brown, Green and Longmans, 1855, xi, 504 p.

Editions: 1900.

Facsimiles: 1984 (Garland of 1855).

☜1856☞

● Anonymous. Comment on Hume. *Notes and Queries*, January 26, 1856, Vol. 1 (second series), p. 72.

Notes: discusses whether Hume squinted.

In *Life Responses*: included in "Miscellaneous Hume Anecdotes."

● Cockburn, Henry (1779–1854). *Memorials of his time*, Edinburgh: Adam and Charles Black, 1856, viii, 470 p.

Notes: discusses John Leslie controversy.

In *Life Responses*: selections from Chapter 3; from *Memorials of his Time*, New York, D. Appleton & company, 1859.

Editions: 1859, 1909, 1946, and 1974.

● Rogers, Samuel (1763–1855). In Alexander Dyce, *Recollections of the table-talk of Samuel Rogers.* London, E. Moxon, 1856, [v]–viii, 355 p.

Notes: stories about Hume related by Hume's friends.

In *Life Responses*: selections; from *Recollections*, New York: D. Appleton, 1856.

Editions: 1856 (two additional editions), 1887.

● Vincent, George Giles. *The science of moral nature... and an introductory discourse on two essays of Mr. David Hume.* London, 1856, xxix, 249.

Notes: Introduction to 1856 edition discusses Hume's "Of a Particular Providence" in the *Enquiry*.

In *Hume on Natural Religion*: complete introduction.

☜1857☞

● Anonymous (pseud. "Mathus"). *Exposure of the real nature and sophisms of David Hume's argument against miracles: showing that the replies given to that celebrated argument by Drs. Campbell, Paley, Chalmers, Wardlaw, Buchanan, and others, have failed to exhibit it in its true light, by Mathus.* Glasgow: Thomas Murray and Son, 1857, 48 p.

Notes: criticizes Hume's "Of Miracles."

Editions: no further editions.

- Boswell, James (1740–1795). *Letters of James Boswell, addressed to the Rev. W.J. Temple. Now first published from the original mss. with an introduction and notes.* Andrew Erskine, ed. London: Richard Bentley, publisher in ordinary to Her Majesty, 1857, xlvii, 407 p.

    Notes: letters to temple relate Boswell's conversations with Hume.

    In *Life Responses*: selections; from Letters of James Boswell to the Rev. W.J. Temple, London: Sidgwick, 1908.

    Editions: 1908, 1924 (newly transcribed), 1997 (newly transcribed).

    Microform: Library of English literature, LEL 11536 (of 1857).

❧1859❧

- Powell, Baden (1796–1860). *The order of nature: considered in reference to the claims of revelation, a third series of essays.* London: Longman, Brown, Green, Longmans & Roberts, 1859, xviii, 495 p.

    Notes: Powell denies that miracles, such as the resurrection, can be proven, and recommends modifying such interpretations. He admires and discusses Hume's *Dialogues*.

    Microform: Literature of theology and church history, 253.

    Reviews: [William Fitzgerald and others], Quarterly Review, October 1959, Vol. 106, pp. 420–454.

❧1860❧

- Carlyle, Alexander (1722–1805). *The autobiography of Alexander Carlyle of Inveresk; containing memorials of the men, and events of his times,* ed. John Hill Burton, Edinburgh, London, W. Blackwood, 1860, x, 576 p.

    Notes: vivid account of Carlyle's life and friends from 1722 until 1770; includes stories about Hume based on personal acquaintance. Written by Carlyle about 1800.

    In *Life Responses*: selections; from 1910 edition, pp. 55, 285–293, 297–298, 345–346, 426–427.

    Editions: 1861, 1910, 1972.

    Facsimiles: 1990 (Thoemmes Press of 1910).

    Reviews: [James Lorimer], *Edinburgh Review*, January 1861, Vol. 113, pp. 144–181 (positive); [James Moncreiff], *North British Review*, February 1861, Vol. 34, pp. 239–254; [James White], *Blackwood's Edinburgh Magazine* Dec 1860, Vol. 88, pp Page 734–757.

- Tucker, George (1775–1861). *Essays, moral and metaphysical.* Philadelphia: sold by all the booksellers, 1860, 288 p.

    Notes: 12 essays on philosophical, psychological and economic topics; Hume is discussed in several. This work contains Tucker's *Essay on Cause and Effect* (1850).

    Editions: no further editions.

- Webb, Thomas Ebenezer (1821–1903). "The metaphysician: a retrospect." *Fraser's Magazine for Town and Country*, April 1860, Vol. 61, pp. 503–517.

    Notes: discusses theories from Hume to Hamilton.

    Editions: *The Veil of Isis; a Series of Essays on Idealism*, 1885.

❧1862❧

- Frothingham, Washington (b. 1822). *Atheos; or, The tragedies of unbelief.* New York, Sheldon, 1862, 408 p.

    Notes: final chapter titled "The Philosopher" is on Hume.

• Napier, Joseph (1804–1882). *Butler's argument on miracles, explained and defended: with observations on Hume, Baden Powell and J.S. Mill. To which is added a critical dissertation by... H.L. Mansel.* Dublin, Hodges, 1863, ii, 53 p.
  In *Hume on Miracles*: pages 31–34 only.

• Reid, John (fl. 1865–1891). *Voices of the soul answered in God.* New York: R. Carter & brothers, 1865, xvi p., 374 p.
  Notes: criticizes Adam Smith's praise of Hume in "Letter ... to William Strahan."
  In *Life Responses*: short quote only; from 1866 edition, pp. 334–335.
  Editions: 1866, 1871.

• Laurie, Simon Somerville (1829–1909). *Notes expository and critical on certain British theories of morals.* Edinburgh, Edmonston and Douglas, 1868, 156 p.
  Notes: Chapter 5, pp. 72–76 summarises Hume's moral theory.
  In *Moral Responses*: relevant selections from 1868 edition.
  Editions: no further editions.
  Facsimiles: 1990 (Thoemmes Press of 1868).

• Lowrie, John Marshall (1817–1867). *The life of David*, Philadelphia: Presbyterian Board of Pub. 1869, 448 p.
  Notes: criticizes Adam Smith's praise of Hume in "Letter ... to William Strahan."
  In *Life Responses*: short quote only; pp. 418–419.
  Editions: only edition.
• [Oliphant, Margaret (1828–1897)]. "The Sceptic," *Blackwood's Edinburgh Magazine,* June 1869, Vol. 105, pp. 665–691.
  Notes: Number 11 in her series of "Historical Sketches of the Reign of George II." Sympathetic biographical sketch, relying heavily on Burton.
• Hunt, John (1827–c.1908). "David Hume," *The Contemporary Review*, May 1869, Vol. 11, pp. 79–100.
  Notes: discussion of Hume's life and religious writings.
  In *Hume on Natural Religion*: complete article.

• Smith, Thomas Frederick. *The metaphysical miracles of the New Testament collected and considered mainly with reference to the doctrine of Hume that no amount of testimony can be credited against the fixity of nature's laws.* London: William Skeffington, 1871, 79 p.
  Notes: criticizes Hume's "Of Miracles."
  Editions: no further editions.
• Wallace, Alfred Russel (1823–1913). *An answer to the arguments of Hume, Lecky, and others, against miracles.* [London]: Printed for private circulation by James Beveridge, Fullwood's Rents, High Holborn, 1871, 24 p.

• Anonymous. "Hume's Philosophy," in *Southern Review*, 1872, Vol. 11, pp. 92–120, 309–336.
  Notes: critical evaluation of Hume's metaphysical and religious views.

- Stanley, Arthur (1815–1881). *Lectures on the history of the Church of Scotland, delivered in Edinburgh in 1872.* London: J. Murray, 1872, xiv, 180 p.

  Notes: short defence Adam Smith's praise of Hume in "Letter … to William Strahan"; also contains new version of Patrick Boyle's story about Hume's reaction to his mother's death.

  In *Life Responses*: short quotes only in "Miscellaneous Responses to Adam Smith's 'Letter'" and "Miscellaneous Hume Anecdotes"; from 1872 New York edition, Lecture 3, pp. 147–148.

  Editions: 1872 (New York), 1877.

๛1873๛

- Thornton, William Thomas (1813–1880). *Old-fashioned ethics and common-sense metaphysics, with some of their applications.* London, Macmillan and co., 1873, vii, 298 p.

  Notes: pages 113–157 discuss Hume's metaphysical views.

  Editions: no further editions.

๛1874๛

- Green, Thomas Hill (1836–1882), Grose, Thomas Hodge (1845–1905). *The philosophical works of David Hume in four volumes.* London, Longmans, Green, and Co., 1874, 4 v.

  Notes: Volume 1 contains a several hundred page discussion of Hume and Locke's philosophy by Green. Volume 3, pp. 15–84, contains Grose's "History of the Editions."

  Editions of *Philosophical Works*: 1875, 1878, 1882, 1886, 1890, 1898, 1907, 1909.

  Facsimiles *Philosophical Works*: 1964 (Scientia Verlag of 1886).

  Other Editions of Green's introduction: in Green's *Works*, 1885, Vol. 1; *Hume and Locke* (New York, Crowell, 1968).

- Sidgwick, Henry (1838–1900). *The methods of ethics.* London: Macmillan, 1874, xxiii, 473 p.

  Notes: discusses Hume's view of utility.

  In *Moral Responses*: Book 4, Ch. 3, Sect. 1, selections; from seventh edition of 1907.

  Editions: several editions.

๛1875๛

- Anonymous. Preface and Postscript, *Dialogues concerning natural religion, A new edition, with a preface and notes, which bring the subject down to the present time.* London, T. Scott, 1875, 125 p.

  Notes: anonymous Preface and Postscript gives background on Hume's religious writings.

  In *Hume on Natural Religion*: complete Preface and Postscript.

- Jackson, William (1817?–1891?). *The philosophy of natural theology. As essay, in confutation of the scepticism of the present day,* New York, A.D.F. Randolph & co., 1875, xviii, 398 p.

  Notes: brief criticism of Smith's account of Hume's death.

  In *Life Responses*: relevant selections in "Miscellaneous Comments on Adam Smith's 'Letter'."

- McCosh, James (1811–1894). *The Scottish philosophy.* London: Macmillan, 1875, vii, 481 p.

  Notes: summarizes and criticizes *Treatise* Books 1, 2 and 3, based on earlier published essays by McCosh .

  In *Metaphysical Responses*: Section 19, selections, pp. 133–149, 153–161; from 1875 edition.

In *Moral Responses*: Section 19, selections, pp. 149–153; from 1875 edition.
Editions: 1875, 1880, 1890.
Facsimiles: 1966 (Georg Olms); 1980 (AMS Press); 1990 (Thoemmes Press).
Microform: American Theological Library Association, ATLA fiche 1989–2258; American culture series, reel 255.2; Religion in America: early books and manuscripts, reel 26, no. 8.

• Wallace, Alfred Russel (1823–1913). *On miracles and modern spiritualism. Three essays.* London, J. Burns, 1875, viii, 236 p.
Notes: discusses Hume's "Of Miracles."
Editions: several editions.
Facsimiles: 1975 (Arno of 1896), 2000 (Thoemmes Press of 1875).

❧1876❧

• Stephen, Leslie (1832–1904). *History of English thought in the eighteenth century.* London: Smith, Elder, 1876, 2 v.
Notes: Chapter 6 criticizes key points of Hume's moral theory; Chapter 4 criticizes Hume's political theory mainly from *Essays* Part I.
In *Moral Responses*: Moral Philosophy, Ch. 6, Sects. 92–113, complete sections; from 1876 edition.
Essay responses: Political Theories, Ch. 4, Sects. 55–59, complete sections; from 1876 edition.
Editions: several editions.
Reviews: [Henry Craik], *Quarterly Review*, January 1877, Vol. 143, p. 404–423 (mixed).

• Watson, John (1847–1939). "Kant's reply to Hume," *Journal of Speculative Philosophy*, 1876, Vol. 10, pp. 113–134.
Notes: discusses Hume's view of causality.

❧1878❧

• Wilson, Daniel (1816–1892). *Reminiscences of Old Edinburgh*, Edinburgh: David Douglas, 1878, Vol. 2, pp. 261–262.
Notes: includes a brief anecdote about Hume at St. David's Street.
In *Life Responses*: story included in "Miscellaneous Hume Anecdotes."
Microform: CIHM/ICMH collection de microfiches, no. 25995.

❧1879❧

• Huxley, Thomas Henry (1825–1895). *Hume.* London, 1879, vi, 208 p.
Notes: survey of Hume's life and writings.
In *Hume on Natural Religion*: Chapter 9 complete; from 1881 edition.
In *Hume on Miracles*: Chapter 7 complete; from 1881 edition.
Editions: several editions.
Reviews: G. C. Robertson, *Mind*, 1879, Vol. 4, pp. 270–274; Noah Porter, *Princeton Review*, November 1879, Vol. 55, pp. 421–450; Granville G. Greenwood, *Westminster Review*, July 1895, Vol. 144, pp. 1–10.

• Thompson, Joseph Parrish (1819–1879). *Final cause a critique of the failure of Paley and the fallacy of Hume ... with an appendix on Professor Huxley's "Hume."* London, Hardwicke, 1879, 22 p.
Notes: discusses Hume's views on religion.
Editions: 1884 (second edition), American Comments on European Questions, 1884, pp. 300–330.

હ્1880હ્

● [Maitland, Brownlow (1816–1902)]. "David Hume," *The Quarterly Review*, Vol. 149, April 1880, pp. 287–330.
Notes: critical evaluation of Hume's philosophical writings.

● Morris, George Sylvester (1840–1889). *British thought and thinkers; introductory studies, critical, biographical and philosophical.* Chicago, S.C. Griggs, 1880, 388 p.
Notes: Hume is discussed on pages 234–264.
Editions: no further editions.

● Latimer, James Fair (1845–1892). *Immediate perception as held by Reid and Hamilton considered as a refutation of the skepticism of Hume.* Leipzig, Metzger and Wittig, 1880, 49 p.
Editions: no further editions.

હ્1882હ્

● Wheeler, Joseph Mazzini (1850–1898). Introduction to David Hume's *An essay on miracles*, London: Freethought Pub. Co., 1882, 24 p.
Notes: Wheeler's introduction criticizes Hume's "Of Miracles."
In *Hume on Miracles*: complete introduction.

હ્1883હ્

● Grimthorpe, Edmund Beckett (1816–1905). *A review of Hume and Huxley on miracles.* London: Society for Promoting Christian Knowledge; New York: Young, 1883, 55 p.
Notes: discusses "Of Miracles."
Editions: 1884.

● Sidgwick, Henry (1838–1900). *The principles of political economy, by Henry Sidgwick.* London, Macmillan, 1883, xx, 591 p.
Notes: section 1.4.5. discusses "Of Commerce."
In *Essays Responses*: selections included in "Miscellaneous Comments on Hume's Essays."

હ્1884હ્

● Boswell, James (1740–1795). *Boswelliana: the common place book of James Boswell*, ed. Charles Rogers. London, Grampian Club, 1874, xxiii, 343 p.
Notes: posthumously published manuscript of anecdotes includes several about Hume.
In *Life Responses*: selections; from 1876 edition.
Editions: 1876; no further editions.

● Botta, Anne Charlotte Lynch (1815–1891). *Memoirs of Anne C.L. Botta*, New York, J. Selwin Tait, 1894, 459 p.
Notes: p. 359 criticizes Smollett's continuation of Hume.
In *History Responses*: selections included in "Miscellaneous Comments on Hume's History;" from 1984 edition.

● McCosh, James (1811–1894). *Agnosticism of Hume and Huxley with a notice of the Scottish school.* New York: Scribner, 1884, iv, 70 p.
Editions: 1884 (New York, Robert Carter), 1886.

હ્1885હ્

● Cain, J.A. "Hume's theory of cause and effect the basis of his skeptical philosophy," in *American Catholic Quarterly Review*, Vol. 10, October 1885, pp. 616–634.
Notes: criticizes Hume's view of causality.
In *Metaphysical Responses*: complete article.

● Pringle-Pattison, Andrew Seth (1856–1931). *Scottish philosophy. A comparison of the*

Scottish and German answers to Hume. Edinburgh & London, xii, 1885, 218 p.
Editions: 1890, 1899, 1907.
Facsimiles: 1971 (Franklin of 1890), 1983 Garland facsimile of 1890.
- Webb, Thomas Ebenezer (1821–1903). *The veil of Isis: a series of essays on idealism.* Dublin, Hodges, Figgis, & Co., 1885, xiii, 365 p.
  Notes: pages 67–124 discuss Hume.
  Editions: no further editions.
  Facsimiles: 1972 (Books for Libraries Press Of 1885), 1990 (Thoemmes Press of 1885).

❧1886❧

- Knight, William Angus (1836–1916). *Hume.* Edinburgh and London, W. Blackwood and sons, 1886, x, 239 p.
  Notes: survey of Hume's life and writings.
  Editions: 1895, 1901, 1902, 1905, 1909, 1914.
  Facsimiles: 1970, Kennikat Press (of 1886).
- Sidgwick, Henry (1838–1900). *Outlines of the history of ethics for English readers.* London, New York: Macmillan, 1886, xxiv, 276 p.
  Notes: Chapter 4, section 9 summarises Hume's moral theory.
  In *Moral Responses*: selections from section 9, from 1902 fifth edition, 1902, pp. 204–213.
  Editions: several editions.

❧1887❧

- Robert Munro, "The Scottish Sceptic," in *British and Foreign Evangelical Review*, 1887, Vol. 36, pp. 667–678.

❧1888❧

- Case, Thomas (1844–1925). *Physical realism, being an analytical philosophy from the physical objects of science to the physical data of sense.* London, New York, Longmans, Green, and co., 1888, 387 p.
  Notes: pages 256–318 discuss Hume.
  Editions: no further editions.
- Hill, George Birkbeck Norman (1835–1903). *Letters of David Hume to William Strahan, now first edited, with notes, index, etc. by G. Birkbeck Hill, D.C.L. Pembrook College.* Oxford, Clarendon Press, 1888, xlvi, 386 p.
  Notes: collection of letters from Hume to Strahan. Extensive annotations by Hill comprise three quarters of the book. The Preface discusses the value of the letters.
  In *Life Responses*: selections from Preface; from 1888 edition.
  Editions: no further editions.
- Ingram, John Kells (1823–1907). *A history of political economy*, Edinburgh: Black, 1888, ix, 250 p.
  Notes: summarises Hume's contribution to economic theory.
  In *Essays Responses*: Chapter 5, selections; from 1888 edition.
  Editions: 1893, 1897, 1907, 1909, 1915, 1923.
  Facsimiles: 1967 (Kelley of 1915).

❧1893❧

- Hyslop, James H. (1854–1920). *Hume's Treatise of Morals and Selections from the Treatise of Passions.* Boston, Ginn & Co., 1893, 275 pp.
  Notes: contains an introduction of 66 pages on Hume's moral theory and a lengthy bibliography.

諮1895豀

● Fraser, Alexander Campbell (1819–1914). *Philosophy of theism: being the Gifford lectures delivered before the University of Edinburgh in 1894-95, 1895-96.* Edinburgh: Blackwood, 1895–1896, 2 v.

Notes: Contains a lecture on Hume, reinterpreting Hume's notion of custom.

Reviews: [Andrew Seth Pringle-Pattison], *Quarterly Review*, January 1898, Volume 187, pp. 61–85 (positive).

● Greenwood, Granville G. (1830–1909). "Professor Huxley on Hume and Berkeley," *Westminster Review*, Vol. 144, July 1895, pp. 1–10.

諮1896豀

● Carlile, William W. "The Humist doctrine of causation," in *Philosophical Review*, Boston, March 1896, Vol. 5, pp. 113–134.

Notes: criticizes Hume's and Mill's views of causality.

In *Metaphysical Responses*: complete article.

諮1897豀

● Albee, Ernest (1865–1927). "Hume's Ethical System," in *Philosophical Review*, 1797. Vol. 6, pp. 337–355.

Notes: criticizes Hume's view of utility.

In *Moral Responses*: Chapter 5, complete; from 1902 edition.

Editions: reprinted in Chapter 5 of his *A history of English utilitarianism*. London: Allen and Unwin; New York: Macmillan, 1901, xx, 427 p.

諮1898豀

● Calderwood, Henry (1830–1897). *David Hume*. Edinburgh: Oliphant, Anderson & Ferrier, 1898, 158 p.

Notes: survey of Hume's life and writings.

Facsimiles: 1977 (Folcroft Library Editions of 1898), 1989 (Thoemmes Press, of 1898).

諮1899豀

● Caird, John (1820–1898); Caird, Edward (1835–1908). *University addresses: being addresses on subjects of academic study, delivered to the University of Glasgow.* Glasgow, J. MacLehose, 1899, x, 383 p.

Notes: chapter 6 is on Hume.

諮1900豀

● Knight, William Angus (1836–1916). *Lord Monboddo and some of his contemporaries.* London, J. Murray, 1900, xv, 314 p.

Notes: letter to James Harris, June 18, 1769 contains a brief anecdote about Hume's view of Berkeley.

In *Life Responses*: story included in "Miscellaneous Hume Anecdotes."

Editions: 1900 (New York).

Facsimiles: 1993 (Thoemmes Press).

諮1901豀

● Albee, Ernest (1865–1927). *A history of English utilitarianism.* London: Allen and Unwin; New York: Macmillan, 1901, xx, 427 p.

Notes: criticizes Hume's view of utility.

In *Moral Responses*: Chapter 5, complete; from 1902 edition.

● Graham, Henry Grey (1842–1906). *Scottish men of letters in the eighteenth century.*

London: A. and C. Black, 1901, xii, 441 p.

Notes: contains a chapter on Hume relating anecdotes.

Editions: 1908.

Facsimiles: 1983 (Garland of 1908).

Microform: Library of English literature, LEL 11078 (of 1901)

&1907&

- M'Ewen, Bruce (1876?–1923), ed., David Hume, *Dialogues concerning natural religion.* Edinburgh: William Blackwood, 1907, cviii, 191 p.

  Notes: lengthy Introduction by M'Ewen discusses the *Dialogues.*

  In *Hume on Natural Religion*: complete Introduction.

&1927&

- Mackenzie, Henry (1745–1831). *The anecdotes and egotisms of Henry Mackenzie, 1745-1831, now first published, edited with an introduction by Harold William Thompson.* London: Oxford University Press, 1927, xxxiv, 303 p.

  Notes: contains a section of anecdotes about Hume, similar to Mackenzie's discussion of Hume in his *Account* (1822). This previous unpublished manuscript was written by Mackenzie around 1830.

  In *Life Responses*: selections; from 1927 edition.

  Facsimiles: 1996 (Thoemmes Press of 1927).

&1928&

- Boswell, James (1740–1795). *The Private papers of James Boswell,* ed. Geoffrey Scott and Frederick A. Pottle, Mount Vernon, N.Y., W.E. Rudge, 1928–1934, 18 v.

  Manuscript location: Yale University.

  Notes: transcription of Boswell's journals discovered at Malahide Castle. Boswell discusses Hume throughout, but includes two detailed interviews with Hume. First, "Journal of my Jaunt," November 4, 1762, in Vol. 1, pp. 126–131. Second, "An Account of my Last Interview with David Hume, Esq.," July 7, 1776, Vol. 12, pp. 227–232. An alternative copy of Boswell's journals was discovered at Fettercairn House; this does not contain the 1762 interview, but does contain that of 1776 with additional material. This was published in *Boswell in Extremes* (1970).

  Editions of 1762 interview: "Journal of My Jaunt" is included in *London journal, 1762-1763, together with Journal of my jaunt, harvest, 1762,* ed. Frederick Albert Pottle, London, Heineman, 1951.

  Editions of 1776 interview: in *Hume's Dialogues Concerning Natural Religion,* Norman Kemp Smith, ed., (1935), as appears in *Private Papers.* The Fettercairn House copy of interview contained in *Boswell in Extremes 1776–1778,* ed. Charles McC. Weis and Frederick A. Pottle, New York, McGraw-Hill, 1970, pp. 11–15.

&1938&

- Diderot, Denis (1713–1784). *Lettres à Sophie Volland; textes publiés d'après les manuscrits originaux,* ed. André Babelon, Paris, Gallimard, Éditions de la Nouvelle revue française, 1938, 2 v.

  Notes: Vol. 2, p. 77 contains a brief anecdote about Hume's view of religion.

  In *Life Responses*: story included in "Miscellaneous Hume Anecdotes"; from translation in Mossner's *Life,* p. 483.

&-1948-&

- Rush, Benjamin (1745–1813). *Autobiography of Benjamin Rush*, ed., George Washington Corner, Princeton: Philadelphia: American Philosophical Society, 1948, 399 p.

  Notes: brief comment on Hume's personal character on page 49.

  In *Life Responses*: comment included in "Miscellaneous Hume Anecdotes."

&-1950-&

- Neville, Sylas (1741–1840). *The Diary of Sylas Neville 1767-1788*, ed. Basil Conzens-Hardy, London: Oxford University Press, 1950, xvi, 357 p.

  Notes: 1772–1776 diary entries describe Neville's visit to Hume.

  In *Life Responses*: story included in "Miscellaneous Hume Anecdotes"; from 1950 edition, pp. 192, 202, 247.

&-1995-&

- Stewart, M.A. (b. 1937). *The kirk and the infidel: an inaugural lecture delivered ay Lancaster University on 9 November 1994*. Lancaster: Lancaster University Publications, 1995, 29 p.

  Editions: 2001 (corrected).

  Notes: pp. 25–29 contains "Appendix: The Wishart Speedhand," which is a new transcription by Stewart of William Wishart's "Copy of Letter, or Speech, Intended: and Letter to John Forrest. June 5, 1745." The manuscript document in shorthand details Wishart's motives in blocking Hume's chances of academic appointment in 1745.

&-2004-&

- Beattie, James (1735–1803). *The Correspondence of James Beattie*, Roger J. Robinson, ed., Bristol: Thoemmes Press, 2004.

  Notes: edition of Beattie's letters, newly transcribed. Most of these letters do not appear in Forbes's *The Life and Writings of James Beattie* (1806). Many contain discussions of Hume.

  In *Life Responses*: selections from Letter 140, Beattie to Thomas Blacklock, October 11, 1769; selections from Letter 490, Beattie to Frances Mayne, January 2, 1774.

- Stewart, M.A. (b. 1937) "Rational Religion and Common Sense," in J. Houston, ed., *Thomas Reid: Context, Influence and Significance*. Edinburgh: Dunedin Academic Press, 2004.

  Notes: includes transcription by Stewart of "Mr Humes notion of Causes ..." (c. 1764), an undated manuscript relating to Reid's logic lectures at Aberdeen in the early 1760s, probably written after the *Inquiry*. Reid criticizes Hume's view of causality and necessity. "Appendix: Reid's Critique of Hume's *Enquiry*" is a transcription of a segment of a student's copy of Reid's Logic lectures at King's College, Aberdeen in 1763, as these bear on "Of Miracles" and "Of a Particular Providence" in Hume's first Enquiry.

INDEX OF AUTHORS

Below is an alphabetical index of authors and anonymously published titles of works listed in the Bibliography of *Early Responses to Hume*. The date of each publication is listed as appears in the Bibliography, where the item may be referenced. Entries below contain brief content descriptions. Some entries contain a list of items elsewhere in this bibliography that discuss the work in question. An "Index of Topics" follows this.

Holy Scriptures (1830); criticizes "Of Miracles."

Allen, John (1771–1843). *Illustrations of Mr. Hume's essay concerning liberty and necessity* (1795); defends Hume's view of necessity against Gregory. Review of John Lingard's *A history of England*, in *Edinburgh Review* (1825); analyses Hume views of civil liberty and partiality for kings.

Anderson, George (1676–1756). *An estimate of the profit and loss of religion* (1753); criticizes Kames's and Hume's moral theories; also discusses Hume's "Of a Particular Providence," and "Of the Protestant Succession". Discussions: *Address to the Synod* (1757).

Anderson, Walter (1723–1800). *The philosophy of ancient Greece investigated* (1791); criticizes Hume's view of causality.

"Anecdote of David Hume," *European Magazine and London Review* (1794); anecdote about Hume's knowledge of British history.

Anecdote of Hume, in *Atheneum; or, Spirit of the English Magazines* (1824); anecdote about Hume at dinners.

Anecdotes about James Balfour, *European Magazine and London Review*, Vol. 3, January, 1783, pp. 39–40; anecdotes about Balfour and Hume.

Annet, Peter (1693–1769). *Social bliss considered* (1749); critiques "Of Polygamy and Divorces."

"Answer to an Extract from a Letter from Dr. Beattie," *London Review* 1780); criticizes Beattie's attack on Hume.

Answer to David Hume, and others (1785); criticism of Hume's determinism.

Arthur, Archibald (1744–1797). *Discourses on theological and literary subjects* (1803); criticizes the *Dialogues* and "Of a Particular Providence."

Austen, Jane (1775–1817). *Northanger abbey: and persuasion* (1818); character in novel praises Hume's *History*.

Balfour, James (1705–1795). *A delineation of the nature and obligation of morality* (1753); criticizes Hume's moral theory. *Philosophical dissertations* (1782); criticizes Hume's broad catalogue of the virtues. *Philosophical essays* (1768); Essays 1 and 2 criticize "Of the Academical or Sceptical Philosophy" and

"Of the Idea of Necessary Connection." Discussions: Thomas Hepburn, *Specimen* (1774).

Ballantyne, John (1778–1830). *An examination of the human mind* (1828); discusses Hume's view of association. "On the Being of a God" (1853); discusses Hume's critique of the design argument.

Beasley, Frederick (1777–1845). *A Search of Truth in the Science of the Human Mind* (1822); several discussions of Hume's philosophy.

Beattie, James (1735–1803). "The Castle of Scepticism: A Vision" (1767); fictitious dream that satirically criticizes Hume and other sceptics. Letter to Thomas Blacklock (October 11, 1769), in James Beattie, *Correspondence of James Beattie* (2004); discusses Blacklock's resentment of Hume. *Essay on the nature and immutability of truth* (1770); criticizes Hume's views of personal identity, causality, scepticism, necessity, theistic proofs, the virtues, and Black inferiority. Letter to Frances Mayne, January 2, 1774 in James Beattie, *Correspondence of James Beattie* (2004); discusses attacks on Beattie by Hume's friends. Letter to Elizabeth Montagu (June 25, 1779), in William Forbes, *The Life and Writings of James Beattie* (1806); anecdote about Hume's views of scepticism. *Dissertations moral and critical* (1783); brief comment on Hume at dinners. See topical index for discussions of Beattie's *Essay*.

Beattie, James Hay (1768–1790). *Essays and fragments in prose and verse* (1794); "The Modern Tippling Philosophers" and Dialogue between "Socrates, Mercury, and a Modern Philosopher" satirize Hume's philosophy.

Beauties of Hume and Bolingbroke (1782); editor's introduction discusses similarities between Hume and Bolingbroke.

Beddoes, Thomas (1760–1808). *Observations on the nature of demonstrative evidence* (1793); passing discussions of Hume's philosophy. "Belief and Unbelief," *Christian Examiner* (1830); defends Hume's scepticism.

Belsham, Thomas (1750–1829). *Elements of the philosophy of the mind, and of moral philosophy* (1801); defends Hume's view of utility.

Belsham, William (1752–1827). *Essays, philosophical, historical, and literary* (1789–1791); critique Hume's view that virtue, utility, Tory view of royal prerogative, Elizabeth's tyrannical reign.

Bentham, Jeremy (1748–1832). *A fragment on government* (1776); discusses Hume's view of utility. *An introduction to the principles of morals and legislation.* (1789); theory of utility influenced by Book 3 of Hume's *Treatise. Supply without burthen* (1795); criticizes Hume's account of moveable property in the *History. A plea for the Constitution* (1803); discusses Hume's view of the British Constitution in the *History. Chrestomathia* (1816); discusses Hume's is/ought distinction and Hume's impact on Bentham.

Bethune, John (1725–1774). *Essays and dissertations on various subjects* (1771); criticizes Hume's skepticism and praises Beattie.

Birch, Thomas (1705–1766). *An inquiry into the share* (1756); criticizes Hume's account of the Irish Rebellion in the *History*. Discussions: Francis Jeffrey, review of Brodie in *Edinburgh Reivew* (1824).

Bisset, Robert (1759–1805). *The life of Edmund Burke* (1798); discussing dispute with Hume over Irish rebellion of 1641.

Blackburne, Francis (1705–1787). *A short historical view of the controversy* (1765); supports Hume's view in the *History* regarding superstition in the age of Thomas Becket.

Blacklock, Thomas (1721–1791) and others. *Poems on several occasions* (1754); 1754 edition contains a poem that mentions Hume as a sceptic. Six letters in *Weekly Magazine or Edinburgh Amusement* (July–September 1771); six letter exchange regarding the propriety of the harsh attack on Hume by James Beattie in his *Essay* (1770). Review of Priestley's *Examination* (1774) in *Edinburgh Magazine and Review* (1774); critiques Hume's scepticism and view of impressions.

Blair, Hugh (1718–1800). *Observations upon a pamphlet, intitled, An analysis* (1755); defends Home and Hume against John Bonar's *Analysis* (1755). *Lectures on rhetoric and belles lettres* (1783); criti-

cizes Hume's "Of Eloquence". Discussions of *Observations*: Thomas Walker, "Letter on Sopho's Doctrine" (1755); Thomas Walker, *Infidelity* (1756); *Address to the Synod* (1757); James Bonar, "Memoir" (1815–1817).

Blakey, Robert (1795–1878). *The history of moral science* (1833); defends Hume's view of utility.

Böhm von Bawerk, Eugen (1851–1914). *Capital and interest* (1890); discusses "Of Interest."

Bonar, James (1757–1821). "Memoir of the Rev. Archibald Bonar, minister of Cramond," in Archibald Bonar, *Sermons chiefly on devotional subjects* (1815–1817); discusses John Bonar's *Analysis* (1755) and Hugh Blair's *Observations* (1755).

Bonar, John (1722–1761). *An analysis of the moral and religious sentiments* (1755); attacks Home's and Hume's theories. Discussions: Hugh Blair, *Observations* (1755); *Address to the Synod* (1757); Alexander Fraser Tytler, *Memoirs* (1808); James Bonar, "Memoir" (1815–1817).

Boswell, James (1740–1795). Letters to William Temple, 1758–1775, in *Letters of James Boswell* (1857); letters to Temple relate Boswell's conversations with Hume. "Journal of my Jaunt," November 4, 1762, in *The Private papers of James Boswell* (1928–1934); relates detailed conversation at Hume's apartment in 1762. "Boswelliana" (c. 1772–1785) in *Boswelliana* (1884); posthumously published manuscript of anecdotes includes several about Hume. "An Account of my Last Interview with David Hume, Esq." (July 7, 1776), in *Private papers of James Boswell* (1928–1934); conversation between Boswell and Hume about life after death. *The journal of a tour to the Hebrides* (1785); criticizes Smith's account of Hume's death. *The life of Samuel Johnson,* (1791); includes stories about Hume. *The Private papers of James Boswell* (1928–1934); Boswell's journals discovered at Malahide Castle, includes a 1762 and 1776 interview with Hume.

Botta, Anne Charlotte Lynch (1815–1891). *Memoirs of Anne C.L. Botta* (1894); criticizes Smollett's continuation of Hume.

Briggs, John (1728/9–1804). letter to the editor, *London Review* (1775); criticizes review of Priestley's *Examination* and defends Beattie's right to ridicule Hume. *The nature of religious zeal* (1775); attack on infidels, with a criticism of "Of Miracles."

Brodie, George (1786?–1867). *A history of the British Empire* (1822); criticizes Hume's Tory view of royal prerogative, especially during Elizabeth's reign.

Brooks, Edward (1784–1850). Review of Clarendon's *History* in *North American Review* (1828); criticizes Hume's *History* for sophistry and misrepresentation. Review of John Lingard's *Constitutional History* in *North American Review* (1829); criticizes Hume's *History*.

Brougham, Henry (1778–1868). *A discourse of natural theology* (1835); discusses "Of Miracles" and Hume's critique of the design argument. *Lives of men of letters & science, who flourished in the time of George III* (1845); biographical sketch of Hume with an appendix of unpublished letters.

Brown, John (1715–1766). *Essays on the Characteristics* (1751); critique of Hume's view of disinterested pleasure in "Of the Dignity or Meanness of Human Nature." *An estimate of the manners and principles of the times.* (1757–1758); critices Hume's view of the clergy in "Whether the British Government."

Brown, Thomas (1778–1820). *Observations on the nature and tendency of the doctrine of Mr. Hume* (1805); defends Hume's view of causality. *Lectures on the philosophy of the human mind* (1820); critique Hume's principles of association and utility. Discussions of Brown's *Observations*: Mary Shepherd, *Essay upon the Relation of Cause and Effect* (1824); George Tucker, *Essay on Cause and Effect* (1850).

Bruce, John (1745–1826). *Elements of the science of ethics* (1786); summarises Hume's moral theory.

Bruce, William (1757–1841). *A treatise on the being and attributes of God* (1818); criticizes Hume's *Dialogues* and religious views.

Buffier, Claude (1661–1737). Translator's Preface to *First truths* (1780); translator

criticizes Hume for the bad effects of his writings.

Burdy, Samuel (1760–1820). *The life of the late Rev. Philip Skelton* (1792); anecdote of Hume proofing Skelton's book.

Burgess, George (1809–1966). *The Last Enemy; Conquering and Conquered* (1850); criticizes Smith's account of Hume's death.

Burgh, William (1741–1808). *An inquiry into the belief of the Christians* (1778); critiques Hume's defense of the Stuarts in his *History*. Discussions: Henry Edwards Davis, *A reply to Mr. Gibbon's vindication* (1779).

Burke, Edmund (1729–1797). Possible reviewer of *History of England* in *Annual Register for the year 1761* (1761); *Reflections on the revolution in France* (1790); includes brief Hume anecdote.

Burnett, James, Lord Monboddo (1714–1799). Letter to James Harris (June 18, 1769), in William Knight, *Lord Monboddo* (1900); anecdote regarding of Hume's view of Berkeley. *Of the origin and progress of language* (1773–1794); criticizes Hume's view of ideas and impressions. *Ancient metaphysics* (1779–1799); criticizes Hume's views of necessity, the external world, causality, and ideas.

Burton, John Hill (1809–1881). *Life and correspondence of David Hume* (1846); biography based material that was in the possession of Hume's family after his death. *Letters of eminent persons addressed to David Hume* (1849); transcription of 147 letters to Hume.

Cain, J.A. "Hume's theory of cause and effect the basis of his skeptical philosophy," in *American Catholic Quarterly Review* (1885); criticizes Hume's view of causality.

Caird, John (1820–1898); Caird, Edward (1835–1908). *University addresses* (1899); contains chapter on Hume.

Calderwood, Henry (1830–1897). *David Hume* (1898); survey of Hume's life and writings.

Campbell, George (1719–1796). *A dissertation on miracles* (1762); criticizes "Of Miracles." *The philosophy of rhetoric* (1776); criticizes of Hume's "Of Tragedy." Discussions: Thomas Hepburn, *Specimen* (1774); William

Smellie, *Encyclopaedia Britannica* (1768–1771).

Capital. A satyrical admonition (1758); attack in verse on politics and other subjects, with a stanza on Hume.

Carlile, William W. "The Humist doctrine of causation," in *Philosophical Review* (1896); criticizes Hume's and Mill's views of causality.

Carlyle, Alexander (1722–1805). Recollections about Hume (c. 1800) in Alexander Carlyle *The autobiography of Alexander Carlyle* (1860); stories about Hume based on personal acquaintance.

Carlyle, Thomas (1795–1881). "Burns," *Edinburgh Review* (1828); brief comment on Hume's cosmopolitan writings. "Characteristics," *Edinburgh Review* (1831); compares Hume's and Johnson's lives and deaths.

Carr, William Windle. *Poems on various subjects* (1791); attacks Voltaire, Rousseau, and Hume in verse.

Carroll, Charles (1737–1832); Dulany Daniel (1722–1797). Letters in the *Maryland Gazette*, March–July, 1773; eight pseudonymous letters rely on discussions in Hume's *History*.

Carter, James G. (1795–1849). Review of *Hume and Smollet Abridged*, in *The United States Literary Gazette*, (1824); criticizes Hume's account of the Commonwealth.

Case, Thomas (1844–1925). *Physical realism* (1888).

Caulfeild, James (1728–1799). *Memoirs of the political and private life of James Caulfeild* (1810); contains stories about Hume based on personal acquaintance.

Caulfield (fl. 1778). *An essay on the immateriality and immortality of the soul* (1778); attack on Priestley contains a defense of Beattie's critique of Hume.

Chalmers, Thomas (1780–1847). *On Natural Theology* (1836); discusses Hume's criticisms of theistic proofs.

Chambers, Robert (1802–1871). *Traditions of Edinburgh* (1825); describes Hume's Edinburgh dwellings and a dinner at Alison Cockburn's house. "David Hume," in *Cyclopædia of English literature* (1844); criticizes Hume's *History*. *Scottish jests and anecdotes* (1832); relates anecdotes about Hume. *Walks in Edinburgh* (1825); anecdote about Hume

at St. David's Street.

Channing, Edward Tyrrel (1790–1856). Review of James Ogilvie's "*Philosophical Essays*," in *The North American Review* (1817); discusses Ogilvie's Humean account of causality.

Channing, William Ellery (1780–1842). *A discourse on the evidences of revealed religion* (1821); criticizes "Of Miracles."

Chapone, Hester (1727–1801). *Letters on the improvement of the mind* (1773); praises Hume's *History*.

"Character of the Works of David Hume Esq," in *The Weekly Magazine or Edinburgh Amusement* (1773); critical appraisal of Hume's *History* and moral theory.

Chastellux, François Jean, Marquis de (1734–1788). *De la félicité publique* (1772). English: *An essay on public happiness* (1774); defends "Of the Populousness of Ancient Nations".

Chelsum, James (ca. 1740–1801). *Remarks on the two last chapters of Mr. Gibbon's History* (1776); critiques Hume's view of polytheism in the "Natural History of Religion." Discussions: Henry Edwards Davis, *A reply to Mr. Gibbon's Vindication* (1779); Edward Gibbon, *A Vindication of some Passages* (1779).

Christianity older than the religion of nature (1761); criticism of Hume's religious views.

Church of Scotland, Summary of Committee of Overtures Debate, *Scots Magazine* (1756); vote tally regarding Church censuring of Hume.

Clarke, Thomas Brooke, *A survey of the strength and opulence of Great Britain* (1801); discusses Hume's view of the British mercantile economy.

Clayton, Robert (1695–1758). *Some thoughts on self-love* (1753); criticizes Hume's views of self-interest and free will.

Cockburn, Henry (1779–1854). *Memorials of his time* (1856); discusses John Leslie controversy.

Cogan, Eliezer (1762–1855). "Examination of Mr. Hume's Objection to the Argument for the Being of God," in *Monthly Repository* (1822); criticizes the *Dialogues*.

Cogan, Eliezer (1762–1855), and three

Essays on suicide, and the immortality of the soul ... With remarks (1783); 10 anonymous notes criticizing "Of Suicide" and "Of the Immortality of the Soul."

Essays, poetical, moral, and critical (1769); contains a poem criticising Hume's religious infidelity.

Everett, Alexander Hill (1790–1847). Review of 1838 translation of Kant's *Critick*, in *The North American Review* (1839); connects Hume's scepticism with Kant's transcendental philosophy.

Everett, Edward (1794–1865). Review of de Sismondi's *Prospect*, in *The North American Review* (1831); discusses "Whether the British Government."

Ewell, Thomas (1785–1826). *Philosophical Essays on Morals, Literature, and Politics, By David Hume* (1817); discusses attitudes about Hume's writings in the early 19th century.

"Examination of Mr. Hume's Objection to Miracles," *Monthly Repository* (1817); criticizes "Of Miracles."

Exposure of the real nature and sophisms of David Hume's argument against miracles (1857); criticizes "Of Miracles."

Feder, Johann Georg Heinrich (1740–1821). Review of "Essays on Suicide" in *Göttingische Anzeigen* (1784), No. 210, pp. 2100–2103.

Ferguson, Adam (1723–1816). *An essay on the history of civil society* (1767); discusses "Of the Populousness of Ancient Nations." *Principles of moral and political science* (1792); discusses Hume's view of external objects and utility.

Fleming, Caleb (1689–1779). *Three questions resolved.* (1757); criticizes "The Natural History of Religion".

Flexman, Roger (1708–1795). Review of *The History of Great Britain. Vol. 1. Containing the Reigns of James I and Charles I*, in *Monthly Review*, March 1754, Vol. 12, pp. 206–229.

Forbes, William (1739–1806). *An account of the life and writings of James Beattie* (1806); biography and letters of Beattie, many of which discuss his opposition to Hume and the composition of the *Essay* (1770).

Foster, John (1770–1843). Review of Ritchie's *Account* in *Eclectic Review* (1808); criticizes Smith's account of

Hume's death. Discussions: "Death of Hume," *Panoplist* (1810).

Fraser, Alexander Campbell (1819–1914). *Philosophy of theism* (1895–1896); discusses Hume's notion of custom.

Frothingham, Washington (b. 1822). *Atheos; or, The tragedies of unbelief* (1862); chapter titled "The Philosopher" on Hume.

Fulton, Robert (1765–1815). "Mr. Fulton's Communication," in Albert Gallatin, *Report of the Secretary of the Treasury* (1808); draws on Hume's political and economic views.

Garden, Francis, Lord Gardenstone (1721–1793). *Miscellanies in Prose and Verse* (1791); criticizes Hume's limited historical research and Tory ideology.

"Genius and Passion," and related articles, in *The Portico* (1817); four letters discuss "Of the Delicacy of Taste and Passion."

Gerard, Alexander (1728–1795). *An essay on taste* (1759); discusses theory of superior admiration in the *Treatise* and "Of the Standard of Taste." *The influence of the pastoral office* (1760); criticizes Hume's attack on the clergy in "Of National Characters." *Dissertations on subjects relating to the genius and the evidences of Christianity* (1766); discusses Hume's "Of Miracles." Discussions of *Influence*: Thomas Hepburn, *Specimen* (1774). Discussions of *Essay on Taste*: Dugald Stewart, *Philosophical Essays* (1810).

Gibbon, Edward (1737–1794). *A vindication of some passages* (1779); praises Hume's discussion of religion. *Miscellaneous works of Edward Gibbon* (1796); occasional references to Hume. "Gibbon, Voltaire, Hume," *The Gospel Trumpet* (1823); comment on Hume's house on St. David's Street.

Gillies, John (1747–1836). *Aristotle's Ethics and Politics* (1797); criticizes Hume's principles of association and theory of money. *The history of the world* (1807); critiques "Of the Populousness of Ancient Nations."

Gillespie, William Honyman (1808–1875). *An argument, a priori, for the being and attributes of God* (1833); criticizes Hume's *Dialogues*. Discussions: George Simpson, *Refutation of the Argument* (1838).

grandmother.

Lowrie, John Marshall (1817–1867). *The life of David* (1869); criticizes Smith's account of Hume's death.

Ludlam, Thomas (1727–1811). *Logical tracts* (1805); criticizes Hume's view of knowledge.

M'Ewen, Bruce (1876?–1923), ed., David Hume, *Dialogues concerning natural religion* (1907); Introduction discusses the *Dialogues*.

Mably, Abbé de (1709–1785). *De la maniere d'écrire l'histoire* (1783); criticizes Hume's writing style in the *History*.

Macaulay, Catharine (1731–1791). *The history of England* (1763–1783); contains various criticisms of Hume's *History*. *A treatise on the immutability of moral truth* (1783); discusses Hume's view of utility. *Letters on education* (1790); material adapted from Macaulay's *Treatise* (1783); critiques Hume's view of utility.

Mackenzie, Henry (1745–1831). "The Story of La Roche," *The Mirror* (1779); fictitious story of Hume's good natured relation with a French man and his daughter. *An account of the life and writings of John Home* (1822); stories about Hume based on personal acquaintance. Anecdotes of David Hume (c. 1830) in Henry Mackenzie, *The anecdotes and egotisms of Henry Mackenzie* (1927); contains a section of anecdotes about Hume. Discussions of "Story of La Roche": *An Interesting Anecdote of a well known English Philosopher* (1811); Henry Mackenzie, *An Account of the Life and Writings of John Home* (1822); Henry Mackenzie, *Anecdotes and Egotisims* (1927).

Mackintosh, James (1765–1832). *A general view of the progress of ethical philosophy* (1832); opposes Coleridge's claim that Hume plagiarized his principles of association from Aquinas.

Maclaine, Archibald (1722–1804). *An ecclesiastical history, antient and modern* (1765); criticizes Hume's view of the Protestant Reformation and fanaticism. Discussions: Joseph Towers, *Observations* (1778).

MacLaurin, John (1734–1796). *The philosopher's opera*. (1757); satirical opera with Hume as a character. *Apology for the writers against the tragedy of*

Douglas (1757); criticizes Hume and his friends for puffing Home's *Douglas*. Discussions of *Philosopher's Opera*: "Account" in *The works of the late John MacLaurin* (1798).

MacQueen, Daniel (d. 1777). *Letters on Mr. Hume's History of Great Britain.* (1756); criticizes Hume's account of the Protestant Reformation and religious fanaticism. Discussions: Thomas Hepburn, *Specimen* (1774); Gilbert Stuart, review of Whitaker's *History* (1771–1775) in *Edinburgh Magazine and Review* (1774); Joseph Towers, *Observations* (1778).

Mahon's *The Life of Belisarius*, review of in *Christian Examiner* (1829); praises Hume's *History*.

Maitland, Brownlow (1816–1902). "David Hume," *The Quarterly Review* (1880); critical evaluation of Hume's philosophical writings.

Malkin, Benjamin Heath (1769–1842). *Essays on subjects connected with civilization* (1795); criticizes "Of Miracles."

Malthus, Thomas (1766–1834). *An Essay on the principle of population* (1798); criticizes "Of the Populousness of Ancient Nations." *The grounds of an opinion* (1815); discusses Hume's "Of the Balance of Trade." Discussions: David Ricardo *An Essay on the influence* (1815).

Manning, Owen (1721–1801). *An inquiry into the grounds and nature of the several species of ratiocination*. (1754); criticizes "Of Miracles."

Mason, John Mitchell (1770–1829). "Remarks on the accounts of the death of David Hume, Esqr. and Samuel Finley, D.D.," *Christian's Magazine* (1806); criticizes Smith's account of Hume's death. Discussions: "The Contrast" in *The Ordeal* (1809); "Considerations" in *The Ordeal* (1809); "More of the 'Contrast'" (1809).

Mason, William (1725–1797). *An heroic epistle to Sir William Chambers* (1773); satirical poem ridicules Hume.

Mathews, James McFarlane (1785–1870). *The Bible and men of learning; in a course of lectures* (1855); criticizes Smith's account of Hume's death.

McCosh, James (1811–1894). *The Scottish philosophy* (1875); summarizes and criticizes *Treatise* Books 1, 2 and 3. *Agnosticism of Hume and Huxley with a notice of the Scottish school* (1884); discusses Hume's religious views.

McIlvaine, Charles Pettit (1799–1873). *The evidences of Christianity* (1832); criticizes Smith's account of Hume's death.

Mecom, Benjamin (1732–1776). "The famous Oliver Cromwel's private Life" in *New-England Magazine of Knowledge and Pleasure* (1758); criticizes Hume's account of Cromwell in the *History*.

Meiners, Christoph (1740–1810). Review of *Dialogues*, in *Zugabe zu den Göttingischen gelehrten Anzeigen* (1779).

Melvill, Thomas (1726–1753). "Observations on Light and Colours", in *Essays and Observations, Physical and Literary* (1756); criticizes Hume's view of indivisible space in *Treatise* 1.2. "Memorandums for an Essay against Luxury" in *The National Register* (1817); defends "Of Refinement in the Arts."

Michell, Charles (1756–1841). *Principles of legislation* (1796); criticizes "Of Commerce."

Mickle, William Julius (1735–1788). *Voltaire in the shades* (1770); fictitious dialogues on natural and revealed religion in which Hume is a speaker. *The poetical works of William Mickle* (1799); contains a poem on the death of Hume.

Mill, James (1773–1836). *Elements of political economy* (1821); criticizes "Of Money."

Mill, John Stuart (1806–1873). Review of George Brodie's *History of the British Empire* in *Westminster Review*, (1824); discusses Hume's dishonest artifices in creating a Tory history.

Millar, John (1735–1801). *Observations concerning the distinction of ranks in Society* (1771); criticizes "Of the Populousness of Ancient Nations." *An historical view of the English government* (1787); criticizes Hume's Tory view of the Witenagemot and Elizabeth's tyranny. Discussions of *Historical view*: Francis Jeffrey, review of Brodie in *Edinburgh Review* (1824).

Millot, Claude Francois Xavier (1726–1785). *Élémens de l'histoire d'Angleterre* (1769). English: *Elements of the history of England* (1771); praises

Hume's *History*.

Milner, Joseph (1744–1797). *Gibbon's account of Christianity considered* (1781); criticizes Hume's *Dialogues*.

Moore, Charles (1743–1811). *A full inquiry into the subject of suicide.* (1790); criticizes "Of Suicide."

"More of the 'Contrast.'," *The Ordeal* (1809); criticizes Mason's attack on Smith's "Letter... to William Strahan."

More, Hannah (1745–1833). *Hints towards forming the character of a young princess* (1805); criticizes Hume's *History*. *Practical Piety* (1811); criticizes Smith's account of Hume's death.

More, Hannah (1745–1833); Roberts, William (1767–1849). *Memoirs of the life and correspondence of Mrs. Hannah More* (1834); anecdote about Hume's stay in Bristol, letter from More regarding Hume's death.

Morehead, Robert (1777–1842). *Dialogues on natural and revealed religion* (1830); criticizes Hume's *Dialogues* and philosophy. *Philosophical dialogues* (1845); criticizes Hume's account of the intellectual powers.

Morgan, William (1750–1833). *Memoirs of the life of the Rev. Richard Price* (1815); discusses Price's friendly relationship with Hume.

Morris, George Sylvester (1840–1889). *British thought and thinkers* (1880); a section discusses Hume's philosophy.

"Mr. Hume's Objection to Miracles Considered," *Monthly Repository* (1809); criticizes "Of Miracles."

Mure, of Caldwell, William (1764–1775), letters to, in William Mure (1799–1860), ed., *Selections from the Family papers preserved at Caldwell* (1824); stories about Hume in correspondence from acquaintances.

Murray, Thomas (1792–1872). *Letters of David Hume and extracts from letters referring to him* (1841); Preface describes origin and value of the letters.

Napier, Joseph (1804–1882). *Butler's argument on miracles, explained and defended* (1863); criticizes "Of Miracles."

Neville, Sylas (1741–1840). Diary entries of 1772–1776 in *The Diary of Sylas Neville* (1950); posthumously published diary includes a brief account of Neville's visit to Hume.

on industry.

Richter, Henry James (1772–1857). "On Mr. Hume's Account of the Origin of the Idea of Necessary Connection," in *Monthly Magazine, and British Register* (1797); criticizes Hume's view of the idea of causal power.

Rider, William (1723–1785). *An historical and critical account* (1762); short biographical sketch of Hume.

Riqueti, Marquis de Mirabeau, Victor (1715–1789). *L'ami des Hommes, ou Trait de la Population* (1755); Criticises Hume's "Of the Populousness of Ancient Nations."

Ritchie, Thomas Edward (fl. 1800). *An account of the life and writings of David Hume* (1807); discusses Ritchie's methodology and Hume's character.

Robert Munro, "The Scottish Sceptic," in *British and Foreign Evangelical Review* (1887); discusses Hume's scepticism.

Rogers, Samuel (1763–1855). In Alexander Dyce, *Recollections of the table-talk of Samuel Rogers* (1856); stories about Hume related by Hume's friends.

Rose, William (1719–1786). Review of *Enquiry Concerning the Principles of Morals* (1752). Review of *Political discourses* (1752). Review of *Four Dissertations* (1757). Review of *The History of Great Britain. Vol. 2.* (1757). Review of *Concise and Genuine Account* (1766). Review of *Dialogues* (1779). Review of *Essays on Suicide* (1784). Discussions of review of *Essays on Suicide*: William Cowper, *Memoir* (1816).

Rousseau, Jean-Jacques (1712–1778). *Les confessions de J.J. Rousseau* (1782). English: *The Confessions*; discussion of Rousseau's first acquaintance with Hume.

Ruffhead, Owen (1723–1769). Review of *The History of England*, Tudor (1759). Review of *The History of England*, early periods (1761). Letter to Hume, (March 1, 1763); opposes Hume's view of the powerlessness of the Saxon Commons.

Rush, Benjamin (1745–1813), "Contrast between the Death of a Deist and a Christian" (1779); implied criticism of Hume's death. *Essays, literary, moral and philosophical* (1798), "Thoughts on Common Sense" rejects Hume and

adopts Reid. *Autobiography of Benjamin Rush* (1948); comment on Hume's personal character.

Rutherforth, Thomas (1712–1771). *The credibility of miracles defended* (1751); criticizes "Of Miracles."

Scott, Thomas (1747–1821), *The rights of God* (1793); criticizes "Of Miracles."

Select parts of the introduction to Doctor Gregory's Philosophical and literary essays (1792); attacks Gregory's criticism of Hume's determinism.

Shaw, Duncan (1725–1795). *A comparative view of the several methods of promoting religious instruction* (1776); criticizes "Of Superstition and Enthusiasm" and "The Natural History of Religion." *The history and philosophy of Judaism* (1787); criticizes "The Natural History of Religion."

Shepherd, Mary (1777–1847). *Enquiry respecting the relation of cause and effect* (1819); criticism of Hume's view of causality. *An essay upon the relation of cause and effect* (1824); criticism of Hume's view of causality. *Essays on the perception of an external universe* (1827); criticism of Berkeley's denial of an external physical world with criticisms of Hume's view.

Sidgwick, Henry (1838–1900). *The methods of ethics* (1874); discusses Hume's view of utility. *The principles of political economy* (1883); discusses "Of Commerce." *Outlines of the history of ethics for English readers* (1886); summarises Hume's moral theory.

Silliman, Benjamin (1779–1864). *A journal of travels in England, Holland, and Scotland* (1810); contains an anecdote about Hume's reaction to his mother's death and another regarding Hume's deathbed anguish. Discussions: Editor's Note on Silliman and Baron Hume, *Quarterly Review* (1816).

Simpson, George. *Refutation of the argument a priori* (1838); criticizes Hume's *Dialogues*.

Skelton, Philip (1707–1787). *Ophiomaches: or, Deism revealed* (1749); criticizes "Of Miracles." "Some Thoughts on Common Sense," in *An appeal to common sense* (1784); argues that Hume's scepticism is its own refutation. Discussions: Samuel Burdy *Life* (1792).

"Skepticism," *The Christian Examiner and*

Theological Review (1824); discusses the mournful consequences of Hume's philosophy.

Smellie, William (1740–1795). *Encyclopaedia Britannica* (1768–1771); The entry on "Abridgement" summarizes "Of Miracles," entry on "Academics" discusses Berkeley and Hume as modern sceptics. *Literary and characteristical lives of John Gregory* (1800); chapter on Hume contains biographical sketch and anecdotes.

Smith, Adam (1723–1790). *The theory of moral sentiments* (1759); critiques Hume's view of pleasure and utility. *An inquiry into the nature and causes of the wealth of nations* (1776); criticizes "Of the Balance of Trade" and Hume's endorsement of state-sponsored religion in the *History*. "Letter from Adam Smith, LL.D. to William Strahan" in *The life of David Hume* (1777); describes Hume's final days and death. Discussions of *The theory of moral sentiments*: John Bruce, *Elements* (1786); Thomas Brown, *Lectures* (1820); Dugald Stewart, *Philosophy of the Active and Moral Powers* (1828); Henry Sidgwick, *Methods of Ethics* (1874); Henry Sidgwick, *Outlines* (1886). Discussions of "Letter": See "Hume's Deathbed tranquility."

Smith, Samuel Stanhope (1751–1819). "The Celebrated Objection of Mr. Hume to the Miracles of the Gospel," in *The Assembly's Missionary Magazine* (1805); criticizes "Of Miracles." *A Comprehensive View of the Leading and Most Important Principles of Natural and Revealed Religion* (1815); criticizes "Of Miracles."

Smith, Thomas Frederick. *The metaphysical miracles of the New Testament* (1871); criticizes "Of Miracles."

Smith, William (1727–1803)?. "Dispute about the Tragedy of Douglas," from *The American Magazine and Monthly Chronicle for the British Colonies*, (February 1758), Vol. 1, pp. 203–209; comments on reviews of John Home's *Douglas*.

Smollett, Tobias (1721–1771). Review of *The History of Great Britain*, Charles II (1756). Review of *The History of England*, Tudors (1759).

Smyth, William (1765–1849). *Lectures on modern history* (1840); criticizes Hume's Tory view of royal prerogative.

Some late opinions concerning the foundations of morality examined (1753); criticizes Kames's *Essays* and Hume's moral *Enquiry*.

Somerville, James. *Remarks on an article in the Edinburgh Review: in which the doctrines of Hume on Miracles is maintained* (1815); criticizes "Of Miracles."

Sparks, Jared (1789–1866). Review of Edward Everett's *Oration*, in *The North American Review* (1825); discusses "Of the Rise and Progress of the Arts and Sciences."

Spence, Joseph (1699–1768). *An account of the life, character, and poems of Mr. Blacklock* (1754); Praises Thomas Blacklock's Poems (1754), citing Hume's letter to Spence.

Stanley, Arthur Penrhyn (1815–1881). *Lectures on the history of the Church of Scotland* (1872); defends Smith's "Letter... to William Strahan" and discusses Hume's reaction to his mother's death.

Starkie, Thomas (1782–1849). *A practical treatise of the law of evidence* (1824); discusses Hume's notion of experience in "Of Miracles."

Stephen, Leslie (1832–1904). *History of English thought in the eighteenth century* (1876); criticizes Hume's moral and political theory.

Steuart, James (1712–1780). *An inquiry into the principles of political economy* (1767); criticizes "Of Money" and "Of the Balance of Trade." Discussions: John Wheatley, *An Essay* (1807); Dugald Stewart, *Lectures on Political Economy* (1855).

Stewart, Dugald (1753–1828). *Elements of the philosophy of the human mind* (1792); criticizes Hume's account of the association of ideas. *Outlines of moral philosophy* (1793); discusses artificial justice and other topics in Hume's moral theory. "Account of the life and writings of Adam Smith" (1794); anecdote about Hume's composition of the *History*. *Account of the life and writings of William Robertson* (1801); comment on Hume's personal character. *A short statement of some important facts* (1805); discusses John Leslie controversy and Hume's view of causality. Letter to William Forbes on Beattie (c. 1806); defends Reid and Beattie's notions of common sense, making mention of Hume. *Philosophical essays* (1810); criticizes "Of Tragedy." *Dissertation on the Progress of Philosophy* (1821); discusses Hume's scepticism and place in philosophy and presents Gilbert Elliot's letter on Hume's *Dialogues*. *The philosophy of the active and moral powers of man* (1828); criticizes Hume's views of utility and artificial justice. *Lectures on political economy* (1855); criticizes Hume's views in "Of Money", "Of Interest", "Of Public Credit", "Of the Idea of a Perfect Commonwealth", and "Of the Independency of Parliament."

Stewart, John (d. 1766). "Some Remarks on the Laws of Motion, and the Inertia of Matter." in *Essays and observations, physical and literary* (1754); critique of Hume's views of causality and personal identity.

Stona, Thomas (1727/8–1792). *Remarks upon The natural history of religion by Mr. Hume* (1758); criticizes Hume's "Of Miracles" and "The Natural History of Religion".

Strange, Robert (1721–1792). Untitled Character Sketch of David Hume (1742); criticizes his womanizing and *Essays*.

"Strictures on the 'Account of The Life and Writings of the Late David Hume, Esq.'" *Weekly Magazine, or Edinburgh Amusement* (1777); criticizes Pratt's *Apology* (1777) and John Home's "Account of the Life" (1776), and defends Beattie.

"Strictures on the Life of David Hume," in *Gentleman's Magazine* (1777); criticizes Smith's account of Hume's death.

"Striking Evidences of the Divinity of the Scriptures" *The Moral and Religious Cabinet* (1808); criticizes Smith's account of Hume's death.

Stuart, Gilbert (1742–1786). Review of Cristof Hermann Manstein's *Memoirs of Russia*, in *Monthly Review* (1770); comments on Hume's "Advertisement" to the *Memoirs*. Reviews in *Edinburgh Magazine and Review* (1774); defends

Hume's principles of association. *A view of society in Europe* (1778); criticizes Hume's Tory view of royal prerogative, especially in early British history. *Observations concerning the public law* (1779); criticizes Hume's account of the burgess and royal prerogative in the *History*.

Sulivan, Richard Joseph (1752–1806). *A view of nature* (1794); critiques "Of Miracles."

Swediaur, François Xavier (1748–1824). *Philosophical dictionary* (1786); criticizes Hume's view of Black inferiority in "Of National Characters."

Tagart, Edward (1804–1858). *Locke's writings and philosophy historically considered* (1855); discusses Hume's scepticism.

"Tear to Hume," in *Medley; or Monthly Miscellany* (1803); short poem honouring Hume.

Tennemann, Wilhelm Gottlieb (1761–1819). *Grundriss der Geschichte der Philosophie* (1812). English: *A manual of the history of philosophy* (1832); discusses how Hume's philosophy grew from Locke, and led to scepticism.

Thomas, Daniel (b. 1748). *An answer, on their own principles to direct and consequential atheists* (1791); criticizes Hume's scepticism and harshly attacks Beattie.

Thompson, Joseph Parrish (1819–1879). *Final cause a critique of the failure of Paley and the fallacy of Hume* (1879); discusses Hume's views on religion.

Thornton, William Thomas (1813–1880). *Old-fashioned ethics and common-sense metaphysics* (1873); discuss Hume's metaphysical views.

Towers, Joseph (1737–1799). *Observations on Mr. Hume's History of England* (1778); criticizes Hume's Tory view of royal prerogative. *An essay on the life, character, and writings, of Dr. Samuel Johnson* (1786); criticizes Smith's account of Hume's death.

Tragedy of Douglas analysed (1757); defends Hume's assessment of Home's *Douglas*. Discussions: John Hawkesworth's *A Letter to Mr. David Hume* (1757); review of *Douglas* in *Literary Magazine* (1757).

Traill, Robert (1720–1775). *The qualifica-*

INDEX OF TOPICS

The topics listed here are largely restricted to those surrounding discussions of Hume's theories, publications, and key events in his life. Discussions of Hume's critics are listed in the "Index of Authors," within the entries of the author in question.

"Advertisement" (by DH) to Manstein's *Memoirs of Russia* (1770), reviews of. *Critical Review* (1770); Gilbert Stuart, *Monthly Review* (1770).

Anedcotes of DH, major collections of. John Home, Diary of a Journey (1776); William Cullen, Letter to John Hunter (1776); Adam Smith, "Letter from Adam Smith" (1777); Samuel Jackson Pratt, *Supplement* (1777); James Boswell, *The journal of a tour to the Hebrides* (1785); George Norvell, letter to Alexander Stenhouse (1788); James Boswell, *The life of Samuel Johnson,* (1791); William Smellie, *Literary and Characteristical Lives* (1800); George Norvell, "Anecdotes of David Hume" (1802); James Caulfeild, *Memoirs* (1810); Isaac Disraeli, *Calamities of Authors* (1812); William Morgan, *Memoirs* (1815); Henry Mackenzie, *An Account* (1822); Robert Chambers, *Traditions of Edinburgh* (1825); Henry Mackenzie, *The Anecdotes* (1927); Robert Chambers, *Scottish Jests* (c.1832); William Adam, *Two Short Essays* (1736); William Adam, *Sequel* (1839); Anne Lindsay Barnard, in Alexander Crawford Lindsay, *Lives of the Lindsays* (1840); John Hill Burton, *Life* (1846); Letters to William Mure of Caldwell, in *Selections from the Family Papers Preserved at Caldwell* (1854); Samuel Rogers, *Recollections* (1856); James Boswell, *Letters of James Boswell* (1857); Alexander Carlyle, *Autobiography* (1860); James Boswell, *Boswelliana* (1884); Henry Grey Graham, *Scottish men of letters* (1901); James Boswell, *The Private papers of*

James Boswell (1928–1934).

Association, DH's principles of. Gilbert Stuart, reviews in *Edinburgh Magazine and Review* (1774); Thomas Reid, *Essays on the intellectual powers* (1785); Dugald Stewart, *Elements of the philosophy of the human mind* (1792); John Gillies, *Aristotle's Ethics and Politics* (1797); Samuel Taylor Coleridge, *Biographia literaria,* (1817); "David Hume Charged by Mr Coleridge" (1818); Thomas Brown, *Lectures* (1820); John Ballantyne, *An examination of the human mind* (1828); James Mackintosh, *A General View* (1834).

Beattie's *Essay*, discussions of. John Bethune, *Essays* (1771); letters by "Orthodoxus," "Democritus," and "Eumenes" (i.e., Thomas Blacklock) in *Weekly Magazine,* (1771); James Boswell, *Boswelliana* (1772); Joseph Priestley, *Institutes* (1772–1774); *The Essay … Shewn to be Sophistical* (1773); Letter to the editors, *Weekly Magazine* (1773); Joseph Priestley *Examination* (1774); Thomas Hepburn, *Specimen* (1774); John Briggs, letter to *London Review* (1777); Thomas Gray, *Poems* (1775); John Home, "Account" (1777); Postilion, "Observations" (1777); Tobias Simple, "Strictures" (1777); Samuel Jackson Pratt, *Supplement* (1777); George Horne, *Letter* (1777); Laicus, "Observations" (1777); Caulfield (fl. 1778), *An essay* (1778); James Boswell, *Journal of a Tour* (1785); William Jones, *Memoirs* (1795); Daniel Thomas, *An Answer* (1791); James Steuart, "Observations" (1805); Dugald Stewart,

Garden, Lord Gardenstone, *Miscellanies* (1791); "On Mr. Hume's Political Inconsistencies" (1821); George Brodie, *A history of the British Empire* (1822); Francis Jeffrey, review of George Brodie's *History* (1822); John Stuart Mill, review of George Brodie's *History* (1822); John Allen, review of John Lingard's *History* (1825); Francis Palgrave, "Anglo-Saxon History" (1826); William Smyth, *Lectures on modern history* (1840); Francis Palgrave, "Hume and his Influence upon History" (1844).